A First Book of Visual C++®

Gary J. Bronson
Fairleigh Dickinson University

Australia • Canada • Mexico • Singapore • Spain • United Kingdom • United States

Dedicated to Rochelle, David, Matthew, and Jeremy Bronson

Sponsoring Editor: *Kallie Swanson*
Marketing Team: *Nathan Wilbur, Samantha Cabaluna*
Developmental Editor: *Suzanne Jeans*
Marketing Assistant: *Christina DeVeto*
Editorial Assistant: *Grace Fujimoto*
Production Coordinator: *Keith Faivre*
Production Service: *Professional Book Center*
Manuscript Editor: *Professional Book Center*
Permissions Editor: *Mary Kay Hancharick*
Cover Design Coordinator: *Roy R. Neuhaus*
Cover Design: *Denise Davidson*
Cover Photo: *PhotoDisc®*
Interior Design: *Professional Book Center*
Interior Illustration: *Professional Book Center*
Print Buyer: *Vena Dyer*
Typesetting: *Professional Book Center*
Cover Printing: *Phoenix Color Corporation*
Printing and Binding: *R.R. Donnelley & Sons, Crawfordsville*

For more information, contact:
BROOKS/COLE
511 Forest Lodge Road
Pacific Grove, CA 93950 USA
www.brookscole.com

Printed in United States of America

10 9 8 7 6 5 4 3

Library of Congress Cataloging-in-Publication Data

Bronson, Gary J.
A first book of Visual C++ / by Gary Bronson.
p. cm.
Includes bibliographical references and index.
ISBN 0-534-95313-1
1. C++ (Computer program language) 2. Microsoft Visual C++. I. Title.

QA76.73.C153 B765 1999
005.26'8--dc21 99-056139

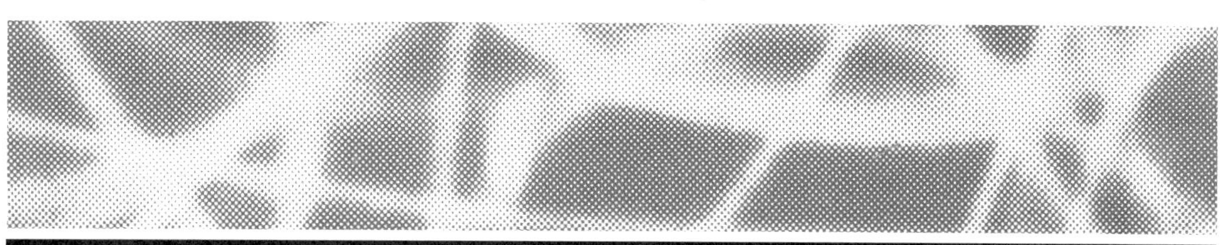

Contents

5 Repetition Structures 221

6 Modularity Using Functions 277

7 Visual Programming Basics 343

Preface

Learning Visual C++® requires familiarity with three elements, only one of which is common to traditional procedural programming languages such as Pascal and C. These are:

- The integrated development environment, which is used in creating traditional character-based C++ console programs to sophisticated Windows®-based applications
- The concept of event-based programming, by which the user, using visual objects such as Command buttons and Check boxes and so forth, determines the sequence of operations that will be executed
- The traditional concept of procedural program code

The major objective of this textbook is to introduce each of these elements, within the context of sound programming principles, in a manner that is accessible to the beginning programmer and provides a firm foundation for more advanced work.

Distinctive Features

Writing Style. I firmly believe that ultimately college-level textbooks do not teach students—professors teach students. For a textbook to be useful it must provide a clearly defined supporting role to the leading role of the professor. Once the professor sets the stage, however, the textbook must encourage, nurture, and assist the student in acquiring and owning the material presented in class. To do this the text must be written in a manner that makes sense to the student. Thus, first and foremost, the writing style used to convey the concepts presented is the most important and distinctive aspect of the text.

Flexibility. To be an effective teaching resource, this text is meant to provide a flexible tool that each professor can use in a variety of ways, depending on *how many* programming concepts and programming techniques are to be introduced in a single course, and *when* it is to be introduced. This is accomplished by partitioning the text into three parts and providing a number of enrichment sections within each chapter.

Part I of the text presents the basic features of the integrated development environment and the procedural syntax, flow control, and modularity topics that are needed for an effective presentation of C++'s object features. Once Part I is completed, Parts II and III on object-oriented programming and data structures, respectively, are *interchangeable.* Thus, if you want to present object-oriented programming early, you would follow a Part I→Part II→Part III progression. On the other hand, if you want to continue with additional procedural programming reinforcement and present object-oriented programming toward the end of the course, you would use the sequence Part I→Part III→Part II. In either case, the material on files presented in Chapter 8 can be introduced at any time after Part I, either as an introduction to object-oriented programming or at the end of the course. Similarly, the material on arrays presented in Chapter 12 can also be covered immediately after Part I. Thus, depending on time, interest, and proficiency constraints, the text can be used for a basic single-semester introductory course as well as a more in-depth two-semester course that uses visual objects, such as Command buttons, Check boxes, and so on. The text makes use of the Microsoft Foundation Classes (MFC) library for constructing more sophisticated Windows applications. The flexibility of topic presentation is illustrated by the following topic dependency chart:

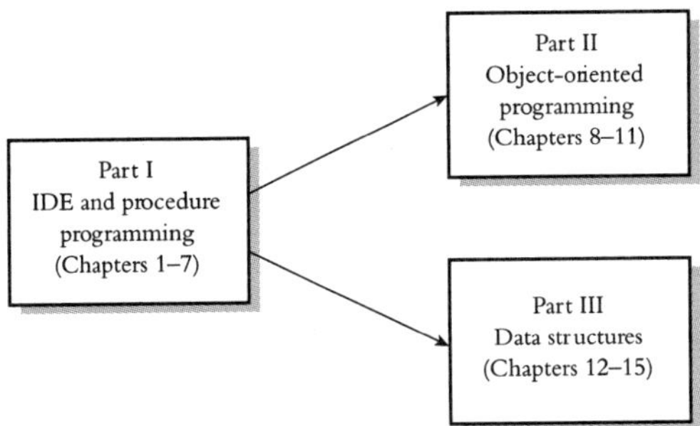

As the topics shown in the dependency chart indicate, this text is designed for a CS1 course, with an introduction to CS2, and follows the guideline of the Association of Computing Machinery (ACM-IEEE-CS) Joint Curriculum Task Force for this first course. The topics recommended by the ACM for a CS1 course form the central content of the text.

Software Engineering. Although this is primarily an introduction to Visual C++ text, as opposed to a CS1 introduction-to-programming book, the text is meant to familiarize students with the fundamentals of software engineering from both a procedural and object-oriented viewpoint. This introduction begins in Section 1.4 and is a thread that is maintained throughout the text. In some instances this concept material can be skipped. For example, in a strictly language-oriented course, the introductory section on repetition statements (Section 5.1), which presents the concepts of both pre- and posttest loops, might be omitted. In most cases, however, the more general programming aspects are interwoven within the text's main language component, precisely because the text is meant to introduce and strengthen the *why* as well as the *how*.

Program Testing. Every single Visual C++ program in this text has been successfully entered and executed using Microsoft Visual C++, version 6.0. Source code for all console-based programs is available on the Internet. This will permit students to experiment as well as extend the existing programs and more easily modify them as required by a number of end-of-section exercises.

Pedagogical Features

To facilitate the goal of making Visual C++ accessible as a first-level course, the following pedagogical features have been incorporated into the text.

End of Section Exercises. Almost every section in the book contains numerous and diverse skill-builder and programming exercises. Additionally, solutions to selected odd-numbered exercises.

Pseudocode Descriptions. Pseudocode is stressed throughout the text. Flowchart symbols are presented, but are used only in visually presenting flow-of-control constructs.

Common Programming Errors and Chapter Summary. Each chapter ends with a section on common programming errors or problems and a review of the main topics covered in the chapter.

Enrichment Sections. Given the many different emphases that can be applied in teaching Visual C++, a number of C++ and enrichment topics have been included. These sections vary and may include material such as using the Help facility, additional topics such as defining error types and using the wizards, or basic material such as an introduction to MFC. The purpose of these sections is to provide flexibility in the choice of which topics to present and the timing of when to present them.

Programmer's Notes. A set of shaded boxes are primarily meant as a reference for commonly used tasks, such as creating a new project, saving a project, or successfully navigating through the integrated development environment (IDE). They are also used to highlight programming techniques and provide additional concept material.

Appendices

An expanded set of appendices is provided. These include appendices on operator precedence, ASCII character codes, namespaces, the Standard Template Library, and solutions to selected odd-numbered exercises.

Acknowledgments

This book began as an idea. It became a reality only due to the encouragement, skills, and efforts supplied by many people. First and foremost, these include my developmental editor, Suzanne Jeans, and editor, Kallie Swanson, both of whom have become what all authors wish for—truly skilled editors who become working partners. Additionally, I am very grateful and wish to thank Grace Fujimoto for handling numerous scheduling and review details that permitted me to concentrate on the actual writing of the text.

I also wish to express my gratitude to the individual reviewers who supplied extremely detailed and constructive reviews of the original manuscript as well as a number of revisions. Their suggestions, attention to detail, and comments were extraordinarily helpful as the manuscript evolved and matured through the editorial process.

David C. Platt, Mesa Community College; Marty Kaliski, California Polytechnic State University, San Luis Obispo; Vernon Blackledge, Arizona State University; Ka-Wing Wong, Eastern Kentucky University; George Whitson, The University of Texas at Tyler; Bob Blucher, Chemekata College; Charlotte Turner, CMT Enterprises; and Catherine Wyman, DeVry Institute of Technology–Phoenix.

The task of turning the final manuscript into a textbook required a dedicated production staff. For this I especially want to thank Keith Faivre, the production editor; and the staff and freelancers of Professional Book Center who provided copyediting, figure rendering, composition, proofreading, and indexing. The dedication of these individuals, their attention to detail, and their high standards, have helped immensely to improve the quality of this edition. Almost from the moment the book moved to the production stage, these individuals seemed to take personal ownership of the text, and I am very grateful to them.

Special thanks also go to Janie Schwark, academic product manager of developer tools, at Microsoft for providing invaluable support and product information.

I gratefully acknowledge the direct encouragement and support provided by my dean, Dr. Paul Lerman; my associate dean, Dr. Ron Heim; and my chair, Dr. Joel Harmon. Without their support, this text could not have been written.

Finally, I deeply appreciate the patience, understanding, and love provided by my wife, friend, and partner, Rochelle.

Gary Bronson
2000

PART ONE

FUNDAMENTALS

1 Introduction to Visual C++®

2 Procedural Programming Basics

3 Completing the Basics

4 Selection Structures

5 Repetition Structures

6 Modularity Using Functions

7 Visual Programming Basics

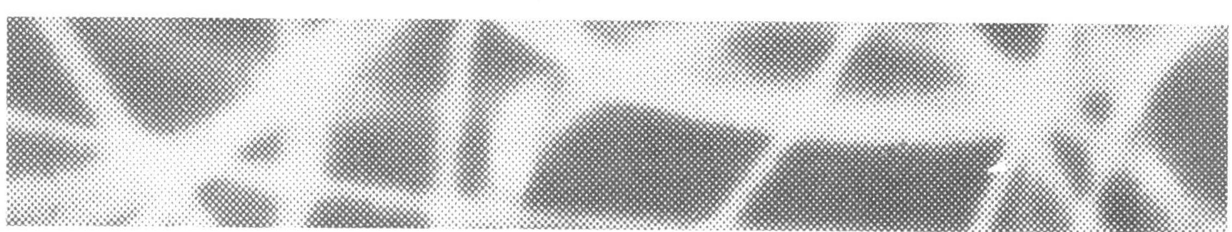

1 Introduction to Visual C++

1.1 Introduction

Visual C++ provides a graphics-based development system for creating two types of C++ programs. The first type, which is referred to as a **console application,** is a traditional character-based program. This type of program, an example of which is shown in Figure 1.1, receives all of its interactive user input from characters typed at the keyboard and displays the entered data and any other information on the console screen as character data. For example, the name Rochelle shown on the screen in Figure 1.1 was entered at the keyboard when the program was run. After the user pressed the Enter key, the next line, "Hello Rochelle," was displayed by the program. Typically, this type of program is executed under either a non–windows-based operating system, such as DOS or UNIX, or within a DOS window. Console applications can also access data from files and produce output on a printer. In each case, however, the data are in the form of a series of

FIGURE 1.1

Sample console application

characters, identical to that obtained from the keyboard and displayed on the console screen.

In addition to being a character-based program, a second distinguishing feature of a console application is that all processing is controlled from within the program itself. Thus, all inputs to the program are made in response to specific program instructions, and all output is similarly controlled from within the program. This is quite different from a typical windows-based program, such as that shown in Figure 1.2. Here, the program presents a number of graphical objects, which include labels, two Edit boxes, and two Command buttons, shown on the figure, as well as a host of additional graphical items that can be placed within the window. Each of these graphical elements is referred to as a **control.** As a group, such controls are used to display data, make the window easier to read, or to perform some action. When selected by the user, a control that performs some action can activate either additional graphical screens or initiate a processing task. In this type of application, once the window is displayed the program effectively waits until the user activates a control, and then responds based on the selected control. Programs that react in this way are referred to as **event-driven** programs, and such programs require visual controls that can be user activated.

The change in programming types from Visual C++ console to event-driven programs was a consequence of, and mirrors, the current change in operating system programs. Thus, as the predominant operating system environment has evolved from the keyboard-centered approach of DOS and UNIX to the graphical, mouse-driven approach of Windows, so have C++ programs. This is not unexpected, as major parts of each of these operating systems have been written either in C, the immediate predecessor of C++, or C++ itself. We take a moment now to describe this evolution, and in so doing, we shed light on the development of modern programming practices from procedural, to object-oriented, to event-driven applications.

Formally, a **computer program** is defined as a structured combination of data and instructions that is used to operate a computer. The set of instructions, data, and rules that can be used to construct a program is called a **programming language.**

Programming languages are usefully classified by level and orientation. Languages that use instructions resembling written languages, such as English, are referred to as **high-level languages.** Visual C++ is an example of a high-level language. Programs written in Visual C++ languages can ultimately be run on a variety of computer types. In

FIGURE 1.2

Sample windows-based program

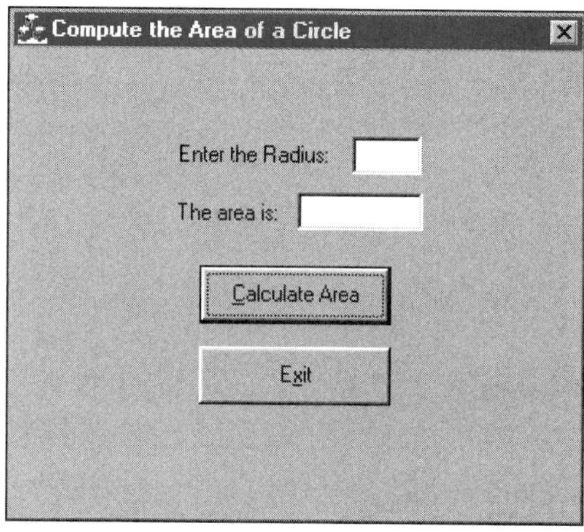

contrast, **low-level languages** use instructions that are directly tied to one type of computer, such as IBM®, Apple®, or DEC.[1] Although programs written in low-level languages are limited in that they can be run only on the type of computer for which they were written, they do permit using special features of the computer that are different from other machines. Low-level language programs also can be written to execute faster than programs written in high-level languages. In addition to being a high-level language, Visual C++ also can be used to take advantage of a variety of features associated with low-level languages.

Procedure-Oriented Languages

High-level languages, which began with the commercial introduction of FORTRAN in 1957, grew rapidly to include COBOL, BASIC, Pascal, and C. All of these languages are procedure-oriented languages. The term **procedure-oriented** reflects the fact that the available instructions allowed programmers to concentrate on the procedures they were using to solve a problem without regard for the specific hardware that would ultimately run the program. Unlike low-level languages that permitted only one mathematical operation per instruction, a single procedural-language instruction permitted many such operations to be performed. For example, an instruction in a procedure-oriented high-level language to add two numbers and multiply the result by a third number could appear as:

```
answer = (first + second) * third
```

---

1 In actuality, the low-level language is defined for the processor around which the computer is constructed. These processors include the Intel microprocessor for IBM-type personal computers, Motorola chips for Apple-based computers, and alpha chips for many DEC computers.

FIGURE 1.3

Traditional procedural programming steps to create a program

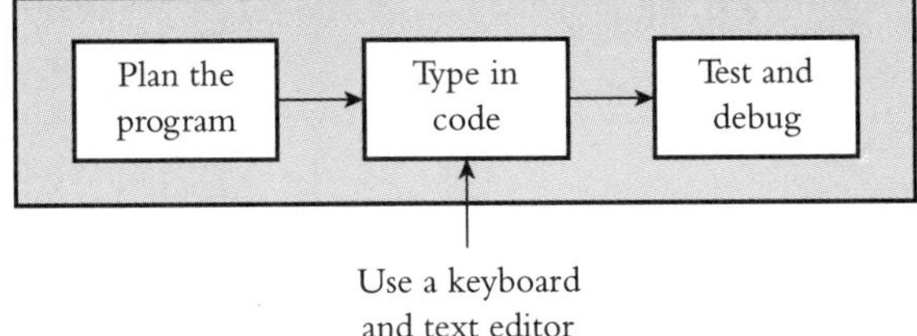

Typically, a group of such statements are combined together to create a logically consistent set of instructions, called a **procedure,** that is used to produce one specific result. A complete program would then be composed of multiple procedures that together fulfill the desired programming objective.

Until the early 1980s, all new programming languages were predominately high-level procedure-oriented languages. Programs written in these languages are produced following the steps shown in Figure 1.3. Here the programmer first plans what the program will do. The required instructions are then entered into the computer using a text-editing program and stored together as a file, which is referred to as the **source program** or **source file.** The source program is then translated into machine language by a translator program, linked together with any necessary library or other existing routines, and subsequently run on a computer. The final machine-language program is referred to as an **executable program,** or **executable,** for short.

Translation into a machine language program is accomplished in two ways. When each statement in a high-level language source program is translated individually and executed immediately, the programming language is referred to as an **interpreted language,** and the program doing the translation is called an **interpreter.**

When all of the statements in a source program are translated before any one statement is executed, the programming language used is called a **compiled language.** In this case, the program doing the translation is called a **compiler.** Both compiled and interpreted versions of a language can exist, although one usually predominates. For example, although some interpreted versions of C do exist, this language as well as C++ and Visual C++ are predominately compiled languages.

Although all high-level source programs must still be translated into machine code to run on a computer, the development steps shown in Figure 1.3 have changed dramatically over the last few years with the introduction of two new types of high-level languages, called **object-oriented** and **event-driven languages,** respectively.

Object-Oriented Languages

Although high-level languages represented a major advancement over their low-level counterparts, the procedural aspect of high-level languages began to reveal some problems. One of these was the difficulty of reusing procedural programs for new or similar

FIGURE 1.4

A multiwindowed screen

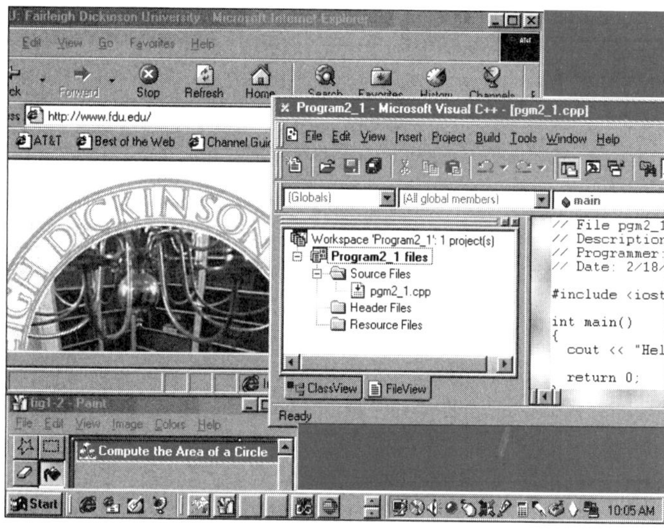

applications without extensive revision, retesting, and revalidation. The second and more fundamental reason for disenchantment with procedural-based programming was the emergence of graphical screens and the subsequent interest in window applications.

Programming multiple windows on the same graphical screen is virtually impossible using standard procedural programming techniques. The reason for this is that the major procedural languages were developed before the advent of graphical screens. Because the standard input and output devices prior to the 1980s were all character-based text, such as that produced by a keyboard and printer, procedural languages were geared to the input, processing, and output of text characters, and not to the creation of graphical images such as shown in Figure 1.4. Clearly, at a minimum, a new way of constructing and then interacting with such images was required.

The solution to producing programs that efficiently manipulate graphical screens and provide reusable windowing code was found in artificial intelligence-based and simulation programming techniques. The former area, artificial intelligence, contained extensive research on geometrical object specification and recognition. The latter area, simulation, contained considerable background on simulating items as objects, with well-defined interactions between them. This object-based paradigm[2] fitted well in a graphical windows environment, where each window could be constructed as a self-contained object.

An object is also well suited to a programming representation because it can be specified by two basic characteristics: a current **state,** which defines how the object appears at the moment, and a **behavior,** which defines how the object reacts to external inputs. To make this fact more concrete, consider the screen image shown in Figure 1.5.

Figure 1.5 is a very simple windows-based program—one, in fact, that we will write in the next chapter. Formally, the screen shown in the figure is an example of a graphical

---

2 A *paradigm* is a way of thinking about or doing something.

FIGURE 1.5

Screen image of an executing Visual C++ program

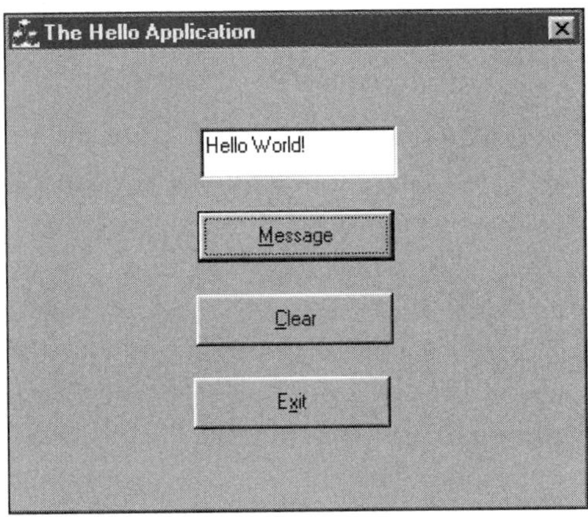

user interface (GUI, pronounced "goo-eey"), because it provides a graphical way for the user to interact with the program. Figure 1.5 contains a number of objects; the user can directly interact with each at will. The first object is the window itself, which contains the caption, "The Hello Application," and a Close button containing an X in the top right corner.

Within the window illustrated in Figure 1.5 are four basic objects, which consist of three Command buttons and one Edit box. Each of the Command buttons has its own caption, which are Message, Clear, and Exit, respectively. Additionally, there is an Edit box that currently contains the text `Hello World!`. In object-oriented terms, the three Command buttons and the single Edit box are objects that have been placed on a Dialog control when the program was being designed and developed. When the program is run, producing the image shown in Figure 1.5, the Dialog control becomes a Dialog box, which is a window. Each object in the Dialog box is defined by a set of properties that determine where and how the object appears. The most obvious properties of the Command buttons are their position within the window and their captions; each of these properties was set by the programmer.

Events

The most noticeable difference between console-based and windows-based programs is the manner in which the user interacts with a running program. Take another look at Figure 1.5 and notice the number of options. The user can choose to click any of the internal Command buttons, in any sequence, or the Close button on the top line of the window itself. For the moment, let us only concern ourselves with the three Command buttons labeled Message, Clear, and Exit. The selection of any one of these buttons constitutes an **event.** As a practical matter, a user-initiated event is triggered in one of the following three ways:

- by placing the mouse pointer over a Command button and clicking the left mouse button (clicking means pushing and releasing the left mouse button)
- by simultaneously holding down the Alt key and pressing one of the underlined letters (this is called "activating an accelerator key")
- by using the tab key until the desired button is highlighted with a dotted line and then pressing the Enter key.

The control that is highlighted with the dotted line is said to "have the focus." (As shown in Figure 1.5, the Message button has the focus, so pressing Enter will activate this control.) Once an event is triggered by a user, which in this case is done by simply selecting and activating one of the two button controls in the window, program instructions take over. If the programmer has written instructions for the user-activated event, some processing will take place; otherwise, no processing occurs. For the program shown on Figure 1.5, there are three events for which code was written. If the user activates the Message Command button, the message `Hello World!` is displayed in the Edit box. Pushing the Clear Command button clears the text area of the Edit box, and pushing the Exit command button results in a beep and termination of the program.

Notice that the sequence of events—that is, which action is to be taken—*is controlled by the user.* This is typical of an event-based Windows® program. This user-determination of which event will take place next, as the program is running, is quite a different approach than the traditional procedure-based programming approach. In a conventional procedure-based program, the decisions as to which actions can be taken, and in what order, are controlled by the programmer when the program is being developed.

Notice that an event-based graphical user interface such as that illustrated in Figure 1.5 does not eliminate the need for all procedural code. Rather, the programmer must still provide the code to appropriately process the events triggered by the user. From a design standpoint, then, the construction of a Window-based program proceeds using the steps shown in Figure 1.6.

The evolutionary aspect of programming languages such as Visual C++ is that they provide a basic set of objects that can be placed within a window while a program is being

FIGURE 1.6

Steps in developing a Windows-based program

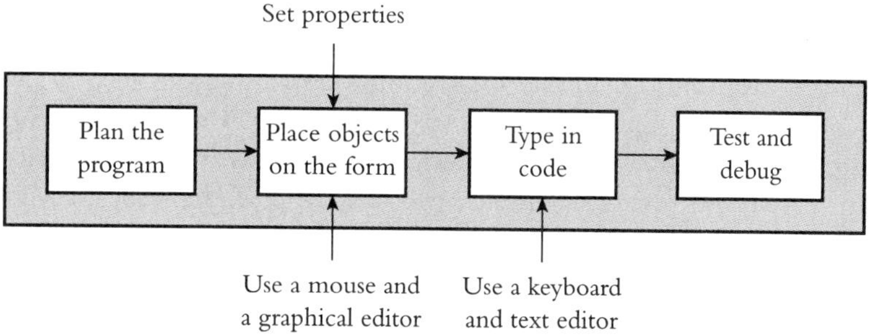

developed. This is done within an integrated design environment that makes creating the graphical interface quite easy. Thus, in using Visual C++ to create Windows-based programs, the programmer does not have to be concerned with writing the code for either producing the graphical objects or for recognizing when certain events, such as "mouse was clicked," actually occur. Once the desired objects are selected and placed within the window, Visual C++ takes care of creating the object and recognizing appropriate object events, such as clicking on a Command button. Programming languages that permit the programmer to manipulate graphical objects directly, with the programming language subsequently providing the necessary code to support the selected objects and their interface, are sometimes referred to as visual languages. Visual C++ is an example of a visual language. Using such a language, however, still requires programmer responsibility for

1. initially selecting and placing objects within a window when the program is being developed,
2. writing and including procedural code to correctly processes events that can be triggered by a user's interaction with the program's objects when the program is run.

To use the existing integrated development environment (IDE; pronounced as both I-D-E and "eye-dee") provided by Visual C++ to create Windows-based programs you will need to know how to use the language's visual resources to construct a GUI containing objects such as Dialog boxes, Command buttons, and Edit box controls. You will also need to be proficient in traditional C++ procedural code to process the various events that can be initiated using these visual controls. These topics are covered in Part I of the text.

To actually understand the "behind the scenes" structure of Windows programs you will need to understand Visual C++'s object-oriented features. Additionally, you will have to understand the Microsoft Foundation Classes (MFC), which is a library of prewritten object-oriented code that underlies the capability to quickly create Windows-based C++ programs. Object-oriented programming, including an introduction to MFC, is provided in Part II.

Finally, to continue your journey into mastering MFC and Windows programming requires that you be very familiar with the concepts of pointers, strings, and data structures, which are presented in Part III of this text. The reason for this is that code for the Microsoft Foundation Classes was initially developed from procedural-based C language routines, called the Application Programming Interface (API), which relied heavily on the use of pointers and data structures. Thus, to fully understand MFC you need to be familiar with these programming features. Realize, however, that to create and run a Windows-based program, a full or even partial understanding of MFC is not required. Fully functional Visual C++ programs can be quickly created using the integrated development environment described in the next section and the visual techniques presented in Chapter 7.

EXERCISES 1.1

1. Define the following terms:
  a. console application
  b. event-driven
  c. computer program
  d. programming language
  e. high-level language
  f. low-level language
  g. interpreter
  h. compiler
  i. procedure
  j. procedure-oriented language
  k. object-oriented language
  l. graphical user interface
  m. MFC

2. Describe the similarities and differences between procedure- and object-oriented languages.

3. What capabilities does the MFC provide to a Visual C++ program?

1.2 Developer Studio

To successfully create C++ programs using Visual C++, you must first understand the development environment provided by a product known as Developer Studio®. Developer Studio is the coordinating program under which many of Microsoft's programming languages, such as Visual C++ and Java are developed, compiled, and executed.[3] This is analogous to Microsoft's Office product, which effectively provides an "umbrella" under which a spreadsheet program, a database program, and a word processing program can be executed. Alternatively, each of these programs can be purchased separately as Excel, Access, and Word, and executed as a "stand-alone" product with no connection to Office.

When you purchase and install Visual C++ version 6.0, the integrated development environment known as Developer Studio is installed. It is within this environment that

3 Developer Studio currently supports the following development products: Visual C++, Visual J++®, Visual Basic®, Visual InterDev®, Visual SourceSafe®, and Microsoft Development Network (MSDN)™ Library.

you create your Visual C++ programs.[4] For example, if you have installed the professional edition of Visual C++, the graphical interface presented when a new project is started provides you with the choices shown in Figure 1.7. The listed project types explicitly relate to some aspect of creating a Visual C++ project. In the next section we begin to differentiate between these project choices. Formally, a **project** consists of a group of files that can produce an executable program, which includes all configuration settings necessary for creating the executable program. Individual descriptions of the files that collectively constitute a project are presented in the next section.

The number of project types displayed in Figure 1.7 depends on the number of installed Developer Studio products. For example, if you have also installed Visual J++ (Microsoft's Java product), the options appropriate to this second language would also appear within the dialog shown in Figure 1.7. What happens is that one copy of Developer Studio is installed with your first programming language, and the second programming language simply provides additional options within the single Developer Studio graphical interface. Thus, a second advantage of using the Developer Studio interface is that, in addition to providing a central location for controlling development of a project written in a language such as Visual C++, it provides a common set of development tools and windows that can be used for both other languages and projects consisting of a combination of programming languages. So once you have learned how to develop a Visual C++ project, you have also learned the basic techniques required for developing projects in all of the languages supported by Developer Studio. Therefore, as a prelude to our journey into specifically creating Visual C++ programs, we need to become familiar with the graphical interface provided by Developer Studio.

From a programming standpoint, all of the tools and features needed to create, debug, compile, link, and execute a Visual C++ program are accessed from Developer Studio's central graphical interface. A sample of this interface is shown in Figure 1.8; this is the initial working screen provided by Developer Studio when Visual C++ is started and is the screen that is used to activate the screen previously shown in Figure 1.7. This interface is an IDE (integrated development environment), which simply means that all program development tools, from editing source code and visual elements to compilation and production of an executable program, are accessible from the same window.[5]

The IDE as a Windows Workspace

As seen in Figure 1.8, the IDE consists of a standard Microsoft window, where the conventional window components, such as the Title bar, Menu bar, and various toolbars have

---

4 Earlier versions presented an option that permitted you to omit installation of Developer Studio and use the original C++ development environment.

---

5 Historically, the concept of an IDE was introduced with Borland's Turbo Pascal product.

FIGURE 1.7

Visual C++ project types presented by Developer Studio (professional edition)

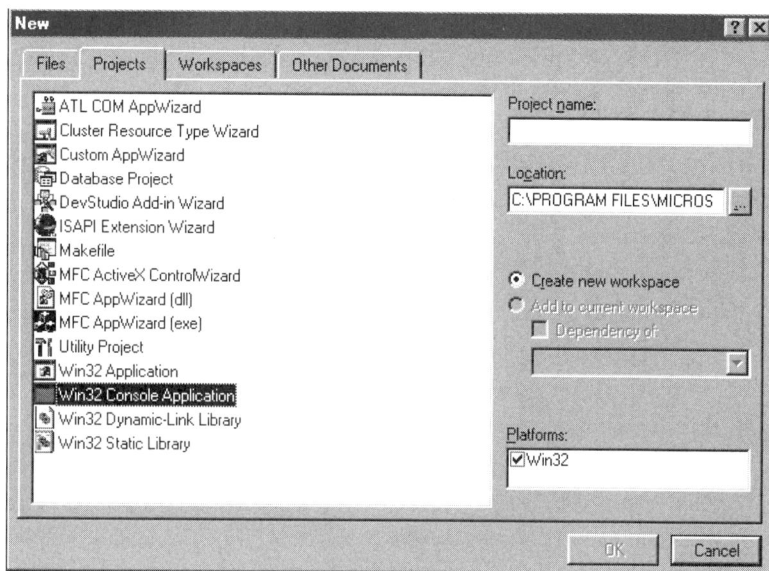

been labeled around the window's outside border. Table 1.1 lists the purpose of each of these components.

The toolbars shown in Figure 1.8 are just three of ten possible toolbars that can be displayed as part of the IDE. The simplest method for both displaying and hiding a specific toolbar is to click the right mouse button within either the Menu bar or any individually visible toolbar. Doing this will bring up the menu shown in Figure 1.9. Menus that are displayed using the right mouse button are referred to as both **context menus** and **context-sensitive menus,** because what is displayed by the menu depends on (i.e., is sensitive to) the context in which the menu is activated. Practically, this means that the displayed menu depends on where in the window the right mouse is clicked.[6] For example, the context menu shown in Figure 1.9 is displayed only when the right mouse button is clicked within a toolbar or the Menu Bar, whereas other context menus are displayed if the right mouse button is clicked in other areas of the IDE. Any individual toolbar listed in the context menu shown in Figure 1.9 can be selected or deselected by clicking on the desired menu item. As seen in the figure, the Output window is currently chosen (it is highlighted). By clicking on this item an Output window would be selected and added to the development screen shown in Figure 1.8. Similarly, for the context menu illustrated, the Workspace, Standard toolbar, Build Minibar, and WizardBar items have all been selected, which is indicated by the check marks to the left of each item. In general, a con-

6 More correctly, context-sensitive menus are activated by the *secondary mouse button,* which is usually the right button. The *primary mouse button,* which is typically the left button, is the button configured for Windows click and double-click operations.

FIGURE 1.8

Developer Studio's integrated development environment

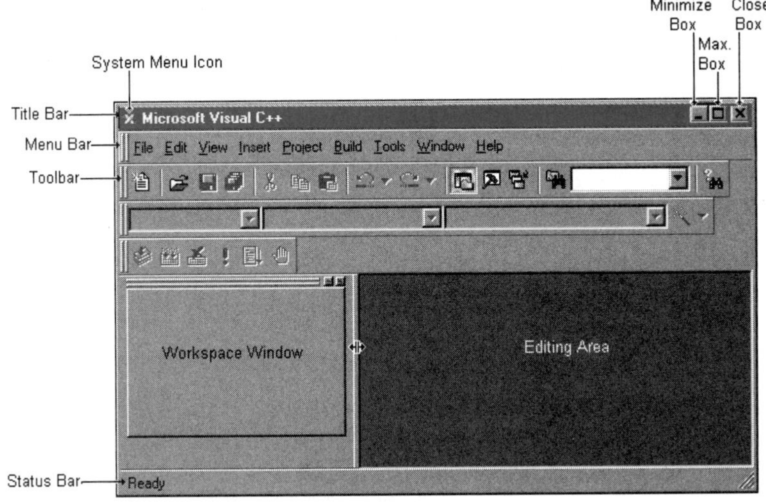

TABLE 1.1 IDE window components

Component	Description
Title bar	The colored bar at the top edge of a window that contains the window's name.
Menu bar	Contains the names of the menus that can be used with the currently active window. The Menu bar can be modified but cannot be deleted from the window.
Toolbars	The IDE contains ten toolbars, all of which can be visible at the same time. A toolbar contains icons, also referred to as buttons, that provide quick access to commonly used Menu bar commands. Clicking a toolbar button initiates the designated action represented by the button.
Status bar	The Status bar consists of individual "panes" that provide indicators about the window and its current status.
System Menu icon	Clicking on the System Menu icon causes a pop-up menu to appear. The pop-up menu contains options to set the window's size, position, or to close the window.
Minimize box	Clicking on the Minimize icon causes the Windows operating system to reduce the window to the size of an icon.
Resize box	Clicking on the Resize icon causes the Windows operating system to reduce the size of the window and replaces the Resize box with a Maximize box.
Maximize box	Clicking on the Maximize icon causes the Windows operating system to enlarge the window to the size of the screen and replaces the Maximize box with a Resize box.
Close box	Clicking on the Close icon causes the Windows operating to close the window.

FIGURE 1.9

Context-sensitive menu

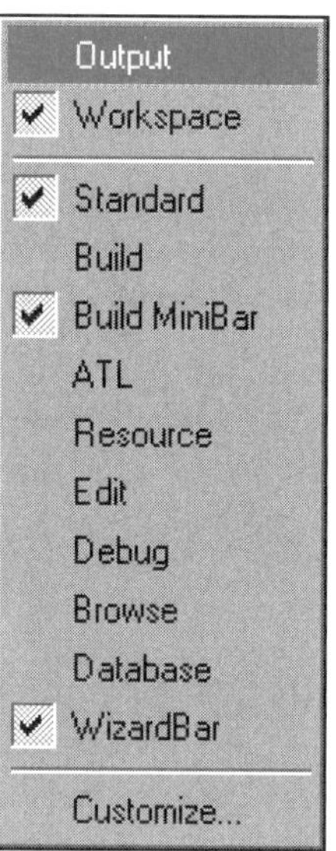

text menu simply provides shortcuts to frequently performed actions for the designated portion of a window in which the menu is activated. As always, grayed items within a menu are deactivated and cannot be selected. Alternatively, you can use the Toolbars tab within the Tools menu Customize option to select or deselect specific toolbars.

Pay particular attention to the two areas labeled internally as the Workspace Window and Editing Area within the IDE shown in Figure 1.8. We use these two areas extensively in the normal course of developing a Visual C++ program.

MDI Windows As a complete entity, the IDE shown in Figure 1.8 is an example of a typical Windows 95 and 98 MDI window. The term MDI is an acronym for **Multiple Document Interface,** which means the window consists of a single "parent" or main window that can contain multiple "child" windows. This is the same type of interface presented by both Excel and Access, each of which is an example of an MDI application.

As a Windows-based application, each child window within the overall parent window, as well as the parent window itself, can be resized and closed in the same manner as all Windows 95 and 98 windows. Thus, to close the Workspace window, for example, you can double click on the X in its upper right-hand corner. Similarly, each window can be resized by first moving the mouse pointer to a window's border. Then, when the pointer changes to a double-headed arrow, click and drag the border in the desired direction. With one exception, each internal window component, be it another window, Menu bar, or toolbar, can be moved by simply clicking the mouse within a window's Title bar, or within a Menu bar or toolbar, and then dragging the selected component to the desired position on the screen. The one exception is when a component is docked with another component, as is the case for the components contained within the windows shown in Figure 1.8.

FIGURE 1.10

Context-sensitive menu illustrating the dockable property

Docking In Developer Studio, internal window components can be aligned and attached to other components, which ensures that each such component remains visible and accessible. This alignment and attachment of two or more components is referred to as **docking.** It is extremely useful because components that are docked together always remain visible and are never hidden behind any other window, tool, or Menu bar.

If you need to see more of a particular docked window, simply resize one of its borders. If you resize a side border that is common to all of the docked windows, the complete set of windows will be resized; otherwise, if you resize a border separating two windows, the increase in size of one of the docked windows will be made at the expense of its immediately attached neighbor, leaving the overall size of the complete set of docked windows the same. When dealing with a docked window border, the cursor will appear as the double arrow shown between the Workspace window and Editing area in Figure 1.8.

Windows may by docked and undocked in a variety of ways. One method is to click the right mouse button within a selected window, which will bring up a context-sensitive menu similar to the one shown in Figure 1.10. This particular context menu was obtained by clicking the right mouse button within the Workspace window. As shown in this figure, the Docking View item has been checked, indicating that the window is in a dockable state. Simply clicking on this item will deselect it and permit the window to be moved about the screen independent of any other window.

Another method for undocking components is to use the two **gripper bars,** which are located within a docked component's left or top edge. Figure 1.11 illustrates a number of gripper bars within the IDEs. Here you can see the gripper bars located at the left of

FIGURE 1.11

Docked component's gripper bars

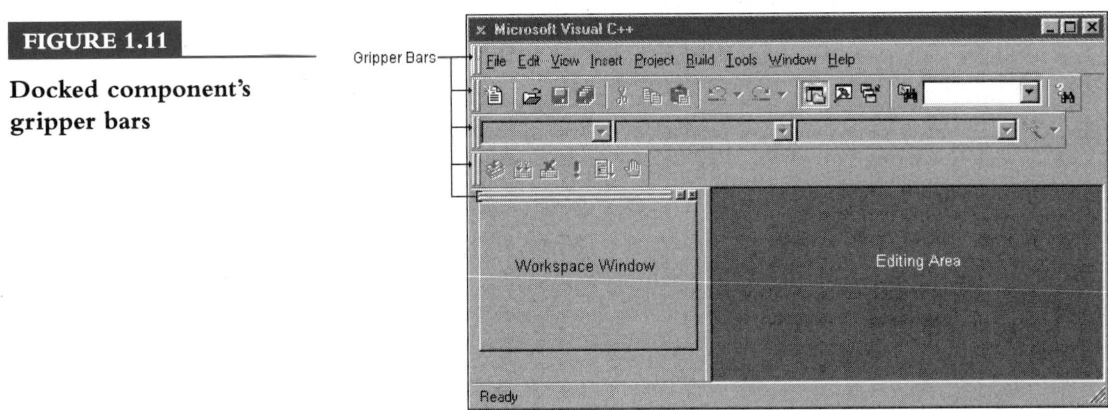

each menu and toolbar and at the top of the Workspace window. Double-clicking on these bars will undock the component and cause it to free-float, whereas double-clicking an undocked window's title bar or within an undocked menu or toolbar will cause it to return to its original docked position.

Docked components can always be dragged to a new position by selecting a component and holding down the left mouse button and then moving the component to its new position (this is Windows' standard drag-and-drop feature). Pressing the Ctrl key while a docked component is being dragged temporarily suppresses its docking state. While a component is being dragged it will appear as a fuzzy gray outlined region. Whenever the dragged component comes into contact with the edge of another component the outline is enclosed by a thin black line; this is your notification that the component will be docked to the nearest edge if it is dropped. Toolbar and Menu bars are automatically docked in a horizontal position against the top or bottom edges and in a vertical position against the side edges.

Dockable components, whether in their docked or undocked (free-floating) states, will always be displayed over a nondockable window. This is sometimes frustrating when a dockable component overlays the editing area, and code you are working on within the editing area becomes hidden. If this happens, either hide the offending dockable component using a right mouse-activated context menu or drag the dockable component out of the way.

Finally, a dockable component that is in its free-floating state will exhibit a Title bar and a free-floating window will exhibit standard Minimize, Maximize, and Close buttons. Interestingly, the Close button works whether the window is in a docked or undocked state, whereas the Close command from within the Menu bar's Window item works only when a window is in an undocked state.

The Menu Bar A more comprehensive manner of both selecting and determining the set of dockable windows is to use the Menu bar (see Figure 1.12). Initially, in fact, the Menu bar is the most important item on the screen, because you can use it to tailor the IDE to your particular needs. This includes bringing up any of the windows that may be missing from the screen, adding additional toolbars, or making specific windows dockable and undockable. For example, you can determine which windows are dockable and then make your modifications by using the Options item from within the Menu bar's Tools submenu (see Figure 1.13). This will bring up the Options dialog (shown in Figure 1.14). By selecting the Workspace tab, as shown in Figure 1.14, you can easily check all of the

FIGURE 1.12

Developer Studio's Menu bar

File Edit View Insert Project Build Tools Window Help

FIGURE 1.13

The Tools submenu

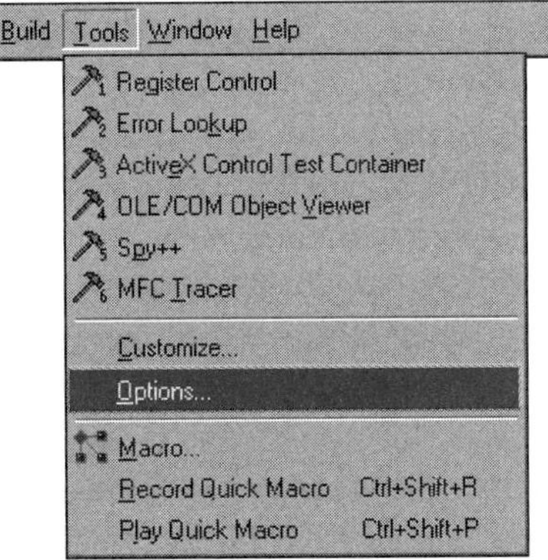

windows that you want to be docked, as well as set other options for the displayed workspace. One of the most important of these settings is the option "Reload last workspace at startup", which is the fourth option from the top on the right side of the display. If this box is checked, the last project on which you were working when you shut down the Studio will automatically be reloaded at startup. If this option is not selected, you will always begin with the initial IDE window previously shown in Figure 1.8, from which you can either start a new project or reload an existing project using the File menu.

Projects

One of the first uses of the Menu bar is to begin a new project. In Visual C++ terminology, a **project** refers to the complete set of files needed to build an executable program, including all user-entered source code files and all graphical elements.

FIGURE 1.14

The Options dialog

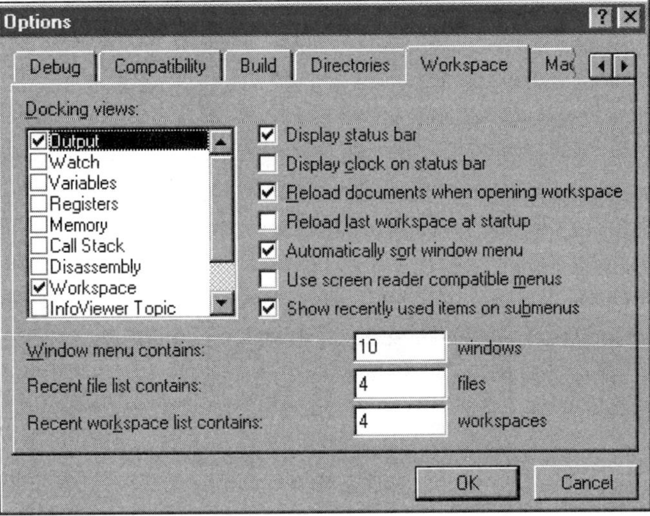

FIGURE 1.15

The New Project dialog box

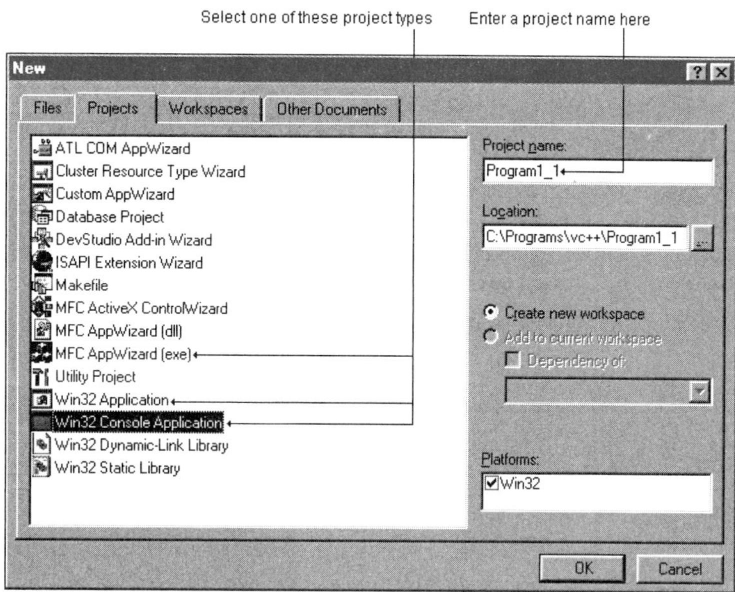

Another term used in relation to all Windows operating systems is **application.** This term is frequently used in preference to the word *program* for two reasons: (1) it is the term selected by Microsoft to designate any program that can be run under a Windows operating system, and (2) it can be used to avoid confusion with older procedural programs that had no graphical capabilities. In common practice, however, the terms *program* and *application* are frequently used interchangeably. Formally, however, it is more correct to say that each Visual C++ application is developed and stored as a project.

For each Visual C++ application that you create, Developer Studio uses a project workspace to store all of the files needed for a project. A **project workspace,** or **workspace** for short, is simply a folder under which additional subfolders and files related to a specific project are stored.[7] Prior to version 5.0, each individual project required its own workspace, so that the terms *project* and *workspace* were used as synonyms. With both versions 5.0 and 6.0, a single workspace (that is, a folder) can contain multiple projects, so the correspondence between a single project and a single workspace no longer holds.

As shown in Figure 1.15, the Visual C++ Professional Edition provides a choice of 15 project types; those most commonly used are listed in Table 1.2. In this text we will always use one of the three project types pointed to in Figure 1.15.

---

7 The files need not all reside in the same workspace folder, although for convenience they typically do.

TABLE 1.2 The Professional Edition's available project types

Project Type	Description
ATL COM AppWizard	Use an applications wizard to develop a COM object.
Custom AppWizard	Use an applications wizard to develop a complete customized application.
ISAPI Extension Wizard	Use an applications wizard to create modules that extend Internet web servers.
Makefile	Create your own Makefile that automatically compiles source code and create an executable application.
MFC ActiveX ControlWizard	Use an applications wizard to create an ActiveX control.
MFC AppWizard (dll)	Use an applications wizard to create a dynamic link library MFC-based module.
MFC AppWizard (exe)	Use an applications wizard to create an executable MFC-based application.
Win32 Application	Create a windows-based application that does not have to use the Microsoft Foundation Classes (the MFC can also be used in these applications).
Win32® Console Application	Create an empty project file with options correctly set to build a character-mode application.
Win32 Dynamic-Link Library	Create an empty project file with options correctly set to build a dynamic-link library (DLL).
Win32 Static Library	Create a static library file

For learning C++'s procedural and object-oriented features, we will always select a Win32 Console Application project type from the New Project dialog box shown in Figure 1.15. For creating hand-coded windows-based applications you would use the Win32 Application project type, and for creating Windows-based applications that make use of precoded graphical elements and provide a skeleton program structure into which you add your own code, you would start with the MFC AppWizard (exe) project type. The skeleton program structure provided by this latter type is referred to as an **Application Framework.** Table 1.3 summarizes the uses of these three project types for creating specific types of applications. In reviewing the entries in this table, note that full-featured windows programs can be constructed using both the Win 32 Application and MFC AppWizard (exe) project types. Also notice that a Win 32 Application project need not use the MFC for producing windows-based applications.

TABLE 1.3 Project types used in this text

Project Type	Uses MFC	Application Type	Comments
Win32 Console Application	No	Character-based	Used for traditional C and C++ programs. Input and output is character-based (nongraphical) and the complete program is user-entered (hand-coded). The final program runs in a DOS window under the Windows operating system.
Win32 Application	No	Windows-based	Visual elements and program structure are user-entered. Uses C-style functions (API) for graphical effects and window control.
	Yes	Windows-based	Visual elements and program structure are user-entered. Uses MFC for graphical effects and window control.
MFC AppWizard (exe)	Yes	Windows-based	The application's structure, initial visual elements and window control is constructed by the Application Wizard program.

EXERCISES 1.2

1. Define the terms:
   a. IDE
   b. context-sensitive menu
   c. MDI
   d. docking
   e. application
   f. project
   g. project workspace
2. a. Start execution of Developer Studio and produce the IDE shown in Figure 1.8.
   b. Use the Menu bar's View item to close and open the Workspace.
   c. Use the Menu bar's View item to open an Output window.

3. For what type of applications would you choose the following application types?
   a. Win32 Console Application
   b. Win32 Application
   c. MFC AppWizard (exe)

4. With Developer Studio's IDE displayed on your monitor, use a context-sensitive menu to display the following toolbars:
   a. Build toolbar
   b. Debug toolbar
   c. Edit toolbar
   d. Browse toolbar

5. a. With Developer Studio's IDE displayed on your monitor undock each displayed toolbar using the gripper bars.
   b. Redock each toolbar by double-clicking within the bar.
   c. What appeared and disappeared when you undocked and docked each toolbar?

1.3 Creating a Console Application

From a programming viewpoint Visual C++[8] is an object-oriented programming language that consists of two fundamental parts, a visual part and a language part. The visual part of the language consists of a set of objects that can be used to construct the visual elements of a graphical user interface, whereas the language part consists of a high-level procedural and object-oriented programming language.

The two elements of the language, the visual part and the programming language part, can be used together to create Windows-based applications (in a much more complicated manner, a complete Windows-based application can also be created using only the programming part). For our purposes, then, we can express the elements of a Visual C++ Windows-based application this way:

Visual C++ application = Visual part + Programming language part

Thus, to create a Windows-based application, the programmer must become very familiar with both elements, visual and language. In this section we show how to construct applications that use just the language part.

To concentrate on just the programming language part, console-based applications can be used. These types of applications are character based in that they do not use any internal visual components (except that they are automatically executed within a separate

8 Except where noted, the term Visual C++ is used in the text to describe the features common to the three version 6.0 editions: Learning, Professional, and Enterprise.

FIGURE 1.16

The Visual C++ icon within the Visual C++ group

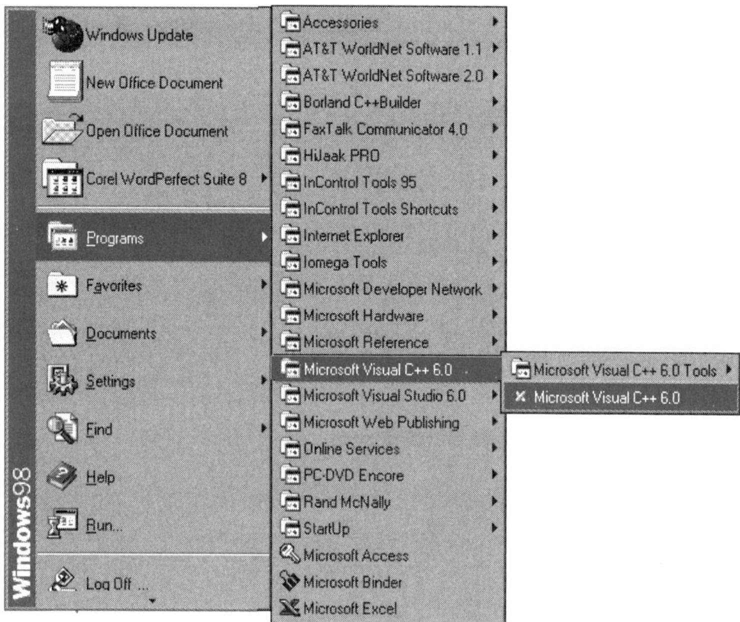

window) provided by Visual C++; as such, they permit concentration on the basic syntax of the C++ language.

To bring up the opening Developer Studio screen, double-click on the Visual C++ icon (see Figure 1.16), which will either be located within its own Visual C++ group or within the Visual Studio group. Alternatively, if you have a shortcut to Visual C++ on the desktop, double-click this icon. When this is done, Developer Studio's IDE, shown in Figure 1.17, will be visible on your screen.[9]

The first step in creating a new Visual C++ console application is to choose the File item from the Menu bar, which will bring up the File submenu illustrated in Figure 1.18. As seen in this figure, the File submenu provides a number of file options, which we will use for creating a new application, as well as saving and recalling existing applications. For now, select the New option from within this submenu, which will bring up the New dialog box shown in Figure 1.19 (see page 25).

To create a console application, always select a Win32 Console Application project type from the New dialog box shown in Figure 1.19 (if you inadvertently select another project type, press the Cancel button on the next screen that appears). As shown in Figure 1.19, when starting a new project, first make sure that the Projects tab is active. From within the Projects tab, you must actively designate three items. The first item to select is

---

9 Because Visual C++ runs as an application under the Windows operating system, before launching Visual C++ you should be familiar with the fundamental window elements and operations, including how to use a mouse and how to select menu options.

FIGURE 1.17

Developer Studio's IDE

the project type. The second item that must be provided is the name of the project. This project name must be entered in the Project name Text box shown in Figure 1.19. In this book, each individual application will be constructed in its own project workspace, using project names such as Program1_1. Specifically, what this does for new projects is to create a new folder, which in this case is named Program1_1. As shown in Figure 1.19, the location of this folder is within the path listed in the Location drop-down list box, which is the third item that must be provided. Typically, the initial path for all project workspaces

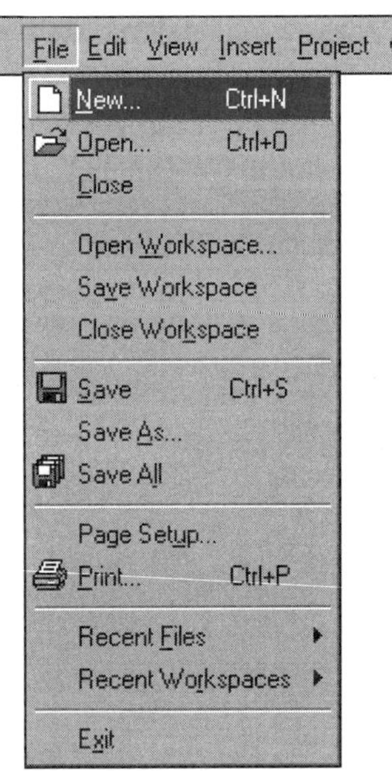

FIGURE 1.18

The File submenu

FIGURE 1.19

The New dialog box

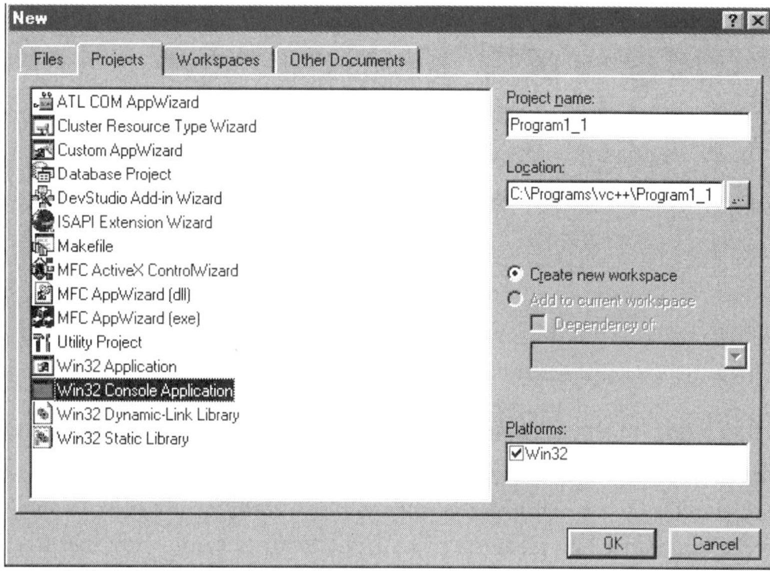

(again, this means folders) that you create is a default selectable from within the Options submenu of Developer Studio's Tools menu.

Once you have provided the information required by the dialog shown in Figure 1.19, and have selected the OK Command button, the dialog shown in Figure 1.20 will appear. From this dialog, select the first Radio button option labeled "An empty project" and press the Finish button. This selection will bring up the information dialog shown in Figure 1.21.

FIGURE 1.20

Selecting the type of console application

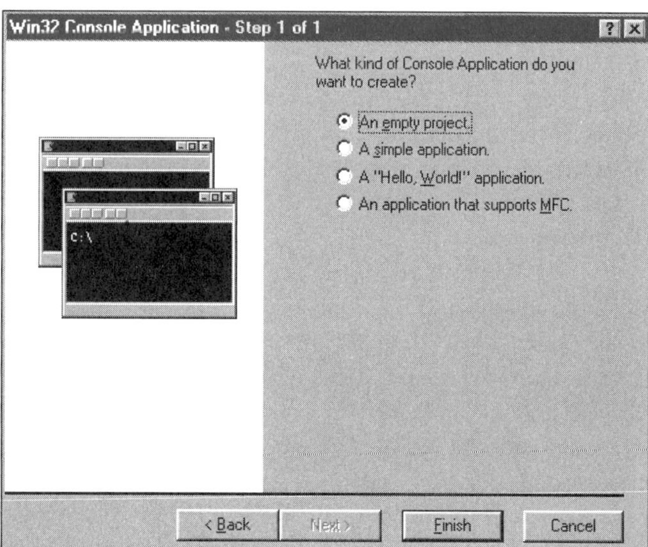

PROGRAMMER'S NOTES

Creating a Console Application

To create a console application:

1. Select the File Menu and select New (or use the accelerator key sequence Ctrl+N), which will bring up a New dialog box.
2. Click on the Projects tab.
3. Select Win32 Console Application as the project type.
4. Enter a Project name, which becomes the name of the workspace folder for the project.
5. Modify, if necessary, the workspace folder's path.
6. Click the OK Command button.

Pressing the Finish button on the dialog box shown in Figure 1.20 causes two things to happen. The first is that a number of files are automatically created and placed in the workspace folder for the new project. A list of the file types that are created is provided in Table 1.4. Next, Developer Studio's IDE will appear as shown in Figure 1.22. In this figure, pay particular attention to the Workspace window (the window toward the middle of the screen on the left side, with two tabs showing). This window, which is also referred to as the Project Workspace window, displays a hierarchical list of projects in the current workspace, and shows all of the items contained within each project.

FIGURE 1.21

The application's Information dialog

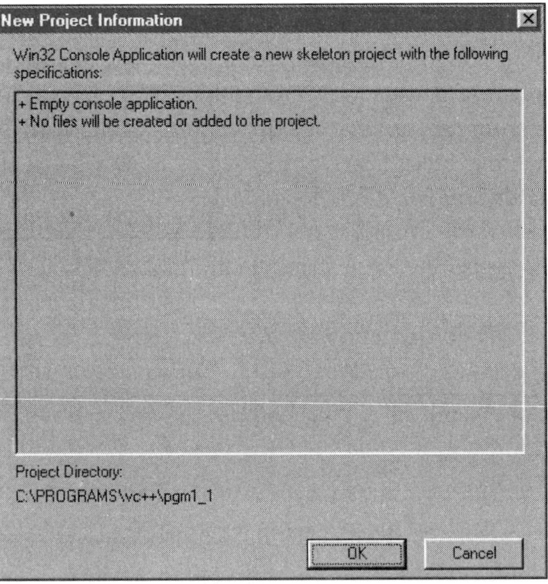
New Project Information
Win32 Console Application will create a new skeleton project with the following specifications:
+ Empty console application.
+ No files will be created or added to the project.
Project Directory:
C:\PROGRAMS\vc++\pgm1_1
OK
Cancel

TABLE 1.4 File types provided within a workspace folder

File Extension	Description
.dsw	A project workspace file used to store global project information.
.dsp	A project file that contains information about how the executable version of a single project is to be built. This is equivalent to the Makefile used in earlier versions of Visual C++ that had the extension .mak.
.opt	The workspace options file, which is used to store project workspace settings. This file contains local settings, such as the appearance of the project workspace using your hardware configuration. A new options file is created automatically whenever a workspace is opened and no workspace options file is found.

Although only one workspace can be open at a time, a single workspace can contain multiple projects. Also notice that two additional tabs have been added to the Workspace window, the ClassView and FileView tabs. As files are now added or removed from a project, Visual C++ will reflect all of these changes within the displayed hierarchical tree. The hierarchical tree used in both the ClassView and FileView tabs is a standard Windows' folder tree structure, which means that you can expand and contract tree sections by clicking on plus (+) and minus (-) symbols, respectively. As always, sections of the tree that are hidden from view due to the size of the window can be displayed using the attached scroll bars.

FIGURE 1.22

The IDE containing an active workspace

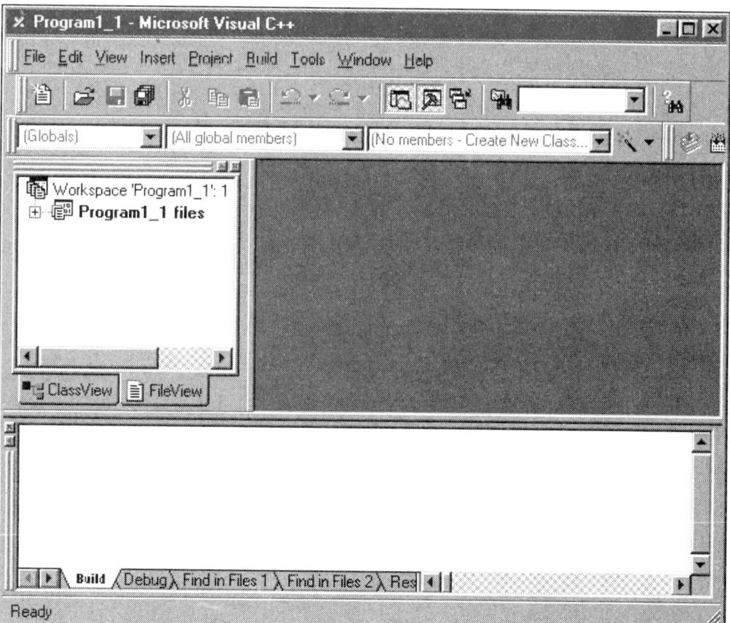

Adding Source Code

The procedure for adding C++ source code into a project is almost identical to the one used in creating the project itself. To create the source code file, select the New option from within the Menu bar's File menu. This will bring up the New dialog, which we previously used in creating a new project (see Figure 1.19). In this case, however, activate the Files tab, as illustrated in Figure 1.23. Within this dialog you will see that the Check box to add a file to the existing project has been checked, and the active project workspace name has been inserted within the first drop-down List box. Additionally, the drive and path for this current project workspace folder will automatically be provided in the file Location Text box. Your responsibility is now to select a file type and provide the file with a name.

From the list of file types provided in the New dialog box shown in Figure 1.23, select the `C++ Source File` choice, and then provide a name for the file. In Figure 1.23, the name we have given to the source file is pgm1_1. When you have provided this information and pressed the dialog's OK Command button, Developer Studio will create a file named pgm1_1.cpp within the Program 1_1 folder. Notice that the cpp extension to the file name is automatically appended by Developer Studio because Visual C++ requires that all source code files have this extension. After this is done, the IDE will appear as shown in Figure 1.24.

In reviewing Figure 1.24 pay particular attention to the Workspace window. Activating the FileView tab and then expanding the tree, as shown in Figure 1.25, will reveal that a file named pgm1_1.cpp has been added to the hierarchy tree. The arrow that is displayed within the icon indicates that this file is an active part of the project (for example, it is not part of some other project that is being stored in the current workspace folder) and will

FIGURE 1.23

Creating a C++ source code file

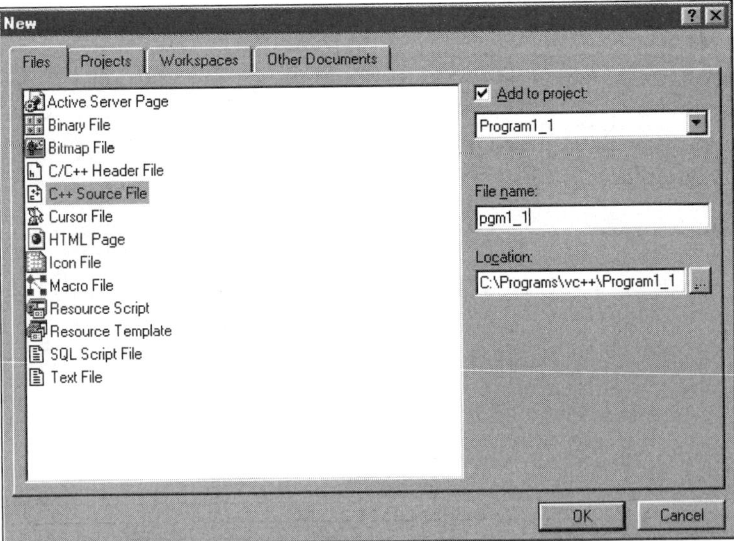

FIGURE 1.24

The IDE with an active project

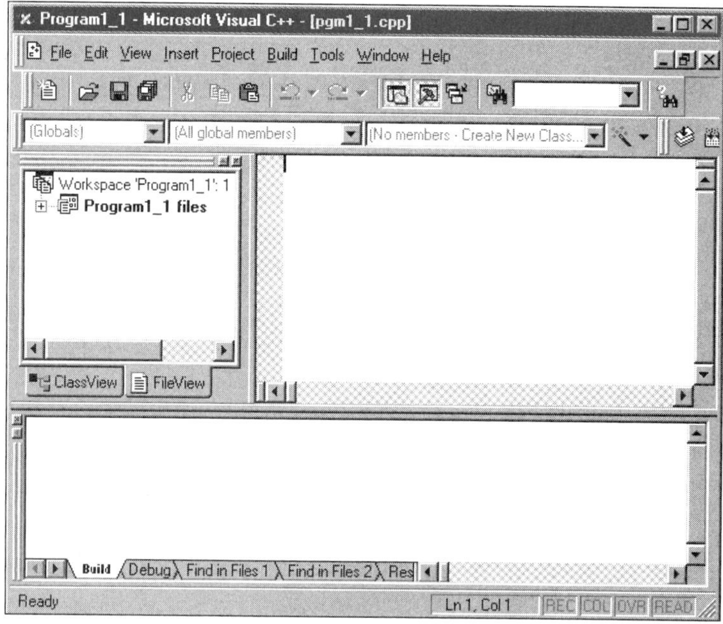

be used when an executable file is ultimately built. At this stage the Visual C++ text editor has been loaded and C++ source code now entered in the Editing area will be stored as the file pgm1_1.cpp.

An alternative to creating a new source file, as we have done using the New dialog box (see Figure 1.23), is to select either of the middle two options previously shown in

FIGURE 1.25

Activating a source code file

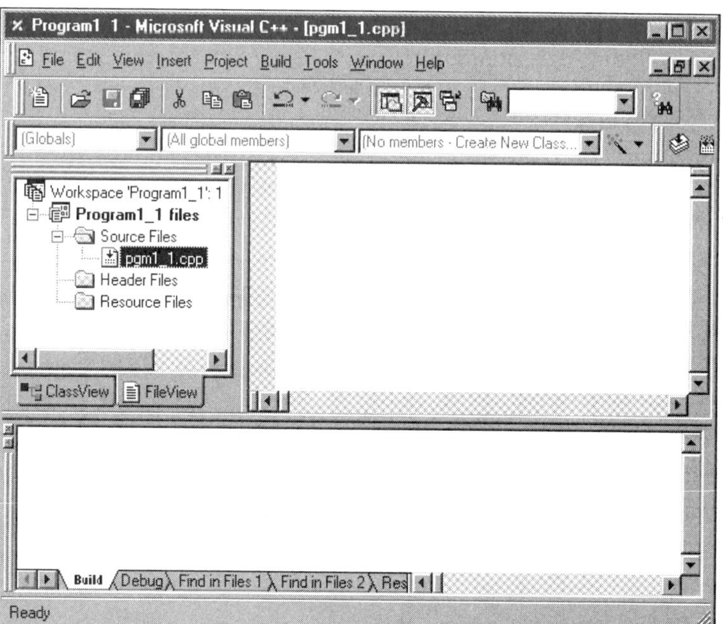

PROGRAMMER'S NOTES

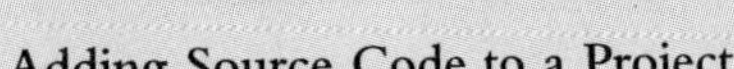

Adding Source Code to a Project

To add a new source code file to a currently active project:

1. Select the File menu and select New (or use the accelerator key sequence Ctrl+N), which will bring up a New dialog box.
2. Click on the Files tab.
3. Select C++ Source File as the file type.
4. Enter a File name.
5. Modify, if necessary, the file's folder path.
6. Click the OK Command button.

Figure 1.20. Both of these choices will automatically create a source code file and display the Editor window shown in Figure 1.25, with a number of code lines already added. All of the provided code is not needed, so you can delete it and type in the desired code, starting with the line `#include <iostream.h>`. The source code entered in the Editing area will be saved as the file pgm1_1.cpp.

A second alternative to entering source code manually is to insert an existing source code file into the current project. For example, if you wanted to run one of the console applications contained in this text, you could insert the desired source code directly from the source code supplied on the Web pages associated with this text. To do this, you would first select the File As Text option from the Insert menu, as shown in Figure 1.26, and then provide the correct path and file name in the next displayed dialog. For now, however, we will leave this as an empty file and wait until the next chapter before actually entering in a valid C++ program. We will simply save the existing project, including the empty file named pgm1_1, and show how to recall this project for further additions and modifications.

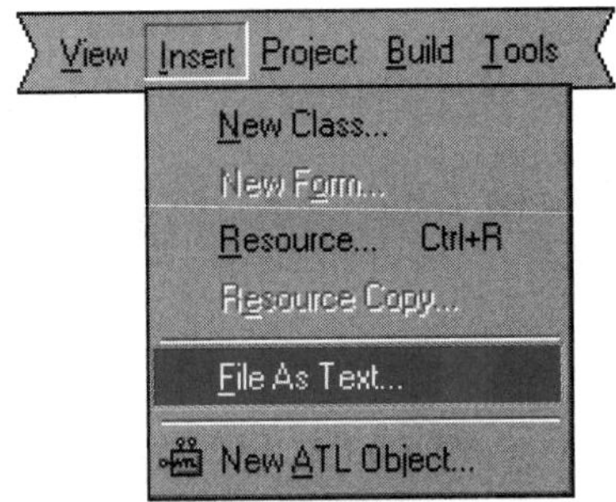

FIGURE 1.26

Inserting a source code file

Saving and Recalling a Project

To save a project, first select the File menu and then select either the Save Workspace or the Save All option, as shown on Figure 1.27. Doing so will save all of the files in the current workspace. It should be noted that even the smallest console application requires its own separate workspace, and that all workspaces must be closed (use the File menu's Close Workspace option) before starting a new application.

To retrieve a project, either select the Open Workspace option from the File submenu, or select the Recent Workspaces option from this same submenu, as shown in Figure 1.28. If you select the Open Workspace option, you will be presented with a standard Windows Open dialog, which requires that you select a disk, folder, and file name. By using the Recent Workspace option you will be presented with a number of recently used workspaces from which you can select the desired workspace. The maximum number of recently used workspaces that is displayed can be set using the Workspace tab under the Options selection of the Tools submenu, as previously shown in Figure 1.14. Also note on Figure 1.14, and as mentioned in the last section, if "Reload last workspace at startup"

FIGURE 1.27

Saving a project

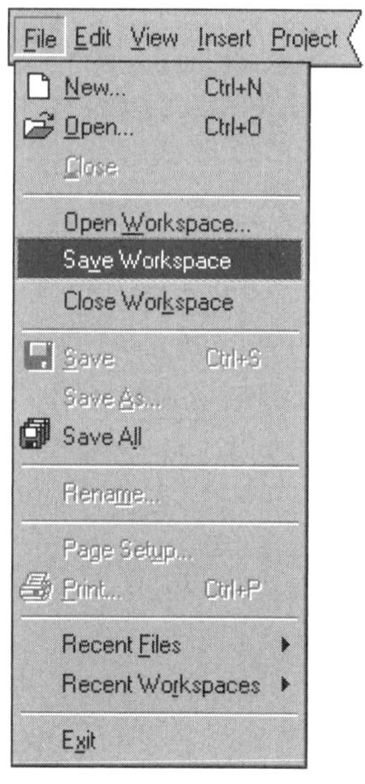

FIGURE 1.28

Retrieving a recently used workspace

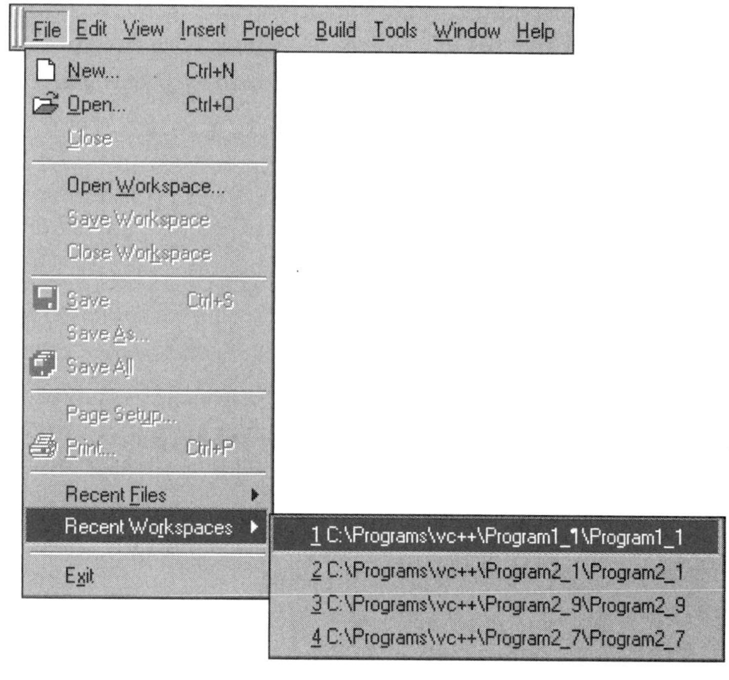

is checked, the last project that you were working on when you shut down the Studio will automatically be reloaded at startup.

Using the Toolbar

Once you have become comfortable with the Menu bar items and see how they operate and interconnect, you should take a closer look at the standard toolbar. For the most commonly used features of Visual C++, a click on the appropriate toolbar icon performs the desired operation. To make sure the standard toolbar is visible, simply right-click the mouse on the Menu bar and make sure that a check mark (✓) appears to the left of the Standard item. For your immediate use, the most useful standard toolbar button is the Save All icon, which is the fourth icon from the left. It is the icon that appears as a stacked set of three diskettes.

EXERCISES 1.3

1. What additional tabs are displayed in the Project Workspace window when a new project is created?

2. a. What tab must be active in the New dialog to create a new project?
   a. List the two items that a programmer must explicitly provide in the New dialog when a new project is created.
   b. What additional item must be checked by the programmer to ensure that the newly created project workspace folder is correctly located in the desired folder path?

3. a. What tab must be active in the New dialog to create a new source file?
   b. List the two items that a programmer must provide in the New dialog when a new source code file is created.

4. What steps would you need to take to set the most recently used workspace list size to ten items?

5. Do you think you could remove a complete project workspace folder by deleting it from Explorer's tree structure?

1.4 Procedures and Algorithms

Before any source code is actually written, a programmer must clearly understand what data are to be used, the desired result, and the steps to be used to produce this result. The procedure, or solution, selected to produce the result is referred to as an algorithm. More precisely, an **algorithm** is defined as a step-by-step sequence of instructions that describes how the data are to be processed to produce the desired output.

Only after we clearly understand the data that we will be using and select an algorithm can any coding begin. Seen in this light, writing an event procedure is simply translating a selected algorithm into a language that the computer can use.

To illustrate an algorithm, we shall consider a simple problem. Assume that a procedure must calculate the sum of all whole numbers from 1 through 100. Figure 1.29 illustrates three methods we could use to find the required sum. Each method constitutes an algorithm.

Clearly, most people would not bother to list the possible alternatives in a detailed step-by-step manner, as we have done here, and then select one of the algorithms to solve the problem. But then, most people do not think algorithmically; they tend to think intuitively. For example, if you had to change a flat tire on your car, you would not think of

FIGURE 1.29

Summing the numbers 1 through 100

Method 1 – Columns: Arrange the numbers from 1 to 100 in a column and add them.

$$\begin{array}{r} 1 \\ 2 \\ 3 \\ 4 \\ \bullet \\ \bullet \\ \bullet \\ 98 \\ 99 \\ +\ 100 \\ \hline 5050 \end{array}$$

Method 2 – Groups: Arrange the numbers in groups that sum to 101 and multiply the number of groups by 101.

$$\left.\begin{array}{l} 1 + 100 = 101 \\ 2 + \ \ 99 = 101 \\ 3 + \ \ 98 = 101 \\ 4 + \ \ 97 = 101 \\ \bullet \qquad\ \ \bullet \\ \bullet \qquad\ \ \bullet \\ \bullet \qquad\ \ \bullet \\ 49 + \ \ 52 = 101 \\ 50 + \ \ 51 = 101 \end{array}\right\} \text{50 groups} \rightarrow (50 \times 101) = 5050$$

Method 3 – Formula: Use the formula

$$Sum = \frac{n(a + b)}{2}$$

Where n = number of terms to be added (100)
a = first number to be added (1)
b = last number to be added (100)

$$Sum = \frac{100(1 + 100)}{2} = 5050$$

FIGURE 1.30

Flowchart symbols

Symbol	Name	Meaning
	Terminal	Indicates the beginning or end of a program
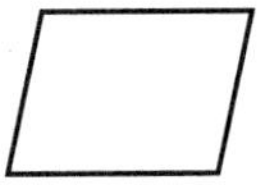	Input/Output	Indicates an input or output operation
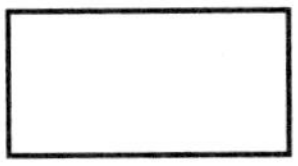	Process	Indicates computation or data manipulation
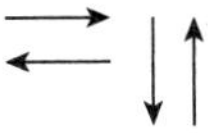	Flow Lines	Used to connect the other flowchart symbols and indicate the logic flow
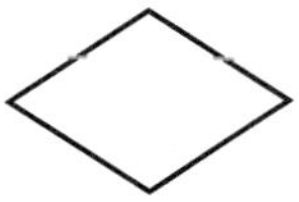	Decision	Indicates a program branch point
	Loop	Indicates the initial limit and increment values of a loop
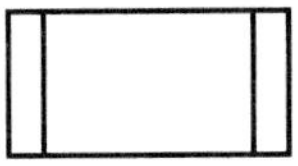	Predefined Process	Indicates a predefined process, as in calling a function
	Connector	Indicates an entry to, or exit from, another part of the flowchart or a connection point
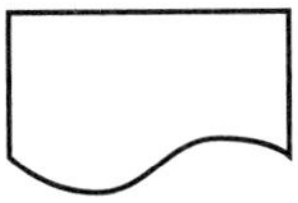	Report	Indicates a written output report

all the steps required—you would simply change the tire or call someone else to do the job. This is an example of intuitive thinking.

Unfortunately, computers do not respond to intuitive commands. A general statement such as "add the numbers from 1 to 100" means nothing to a computer, because the computer only can respond to algorithmic commands written in an acceptable language such as Visual C++. To program a computer successfully, you must clearly understand this difference between algorithmic and intuitive commands. A computer is an "algorithm-responding" machine; it is not an "intuitive-responding" machine. You cannot tell a computer to change a tire or to add the numbers from 1 through 100. Instead, you must give the computer a detailed step-by-step set of instructions that, collectively, forms an algorithm. For example, the set of instructions:

Set n equal to 100
Set $a = 1$
Set b equal to 100
Calculate sum $= \dfrac{n(a+b)}{2}$
Print the sum

form a detailed method, or algorithm, for determining the sum of the numbers from 1 through 100. Notice that these instructions are not a Visual C++ procedure. Unlike a procedure, which must be written in a language to which the computer can respond, an algorithm can be written or described in various ways. When English-like phrases are used to describe the algorithm (the processing steps), as in this example, the description is called **pseudocode.** When mathematical equations are used, the description is called a **formula.** When diagrams that employ the symbols shown in Figure 1.30 are used, the description is referred to as a **flowchart.** Figure 1.31 illustrates the use of these symbols in depicting an algorithm for determining the average of three numbers.

Because flowcharts are cumbersome to revise and can easily support unstructured programming practices, they have fallen out of favor with professional programmers; instead, the use of pseudocode to express the logic of algorithms has gained increasing acceptance. In describing an algorithm using pseudocode, short English phrases are used. An example of pseudocode for describing the steps needed to compute the average of three numbers is:

Input the three numbers into the computer's memory.
Calculate the average by adding the numbers and dividing the sum by three.
Display the average.

FIGURE 1.31

Flowchart for calculating the average of three numbers

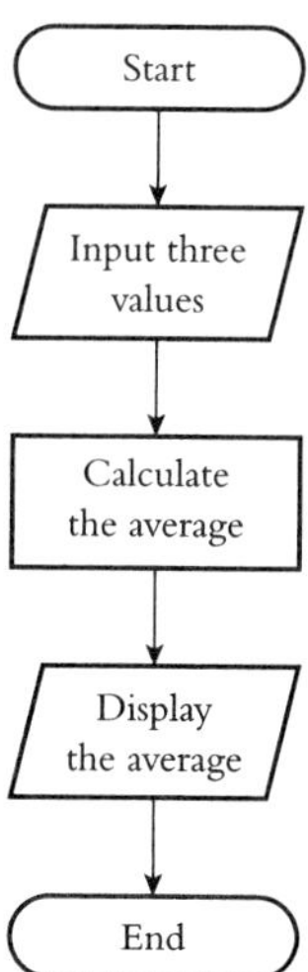

FIGURE 1.32

Coding an algorithm

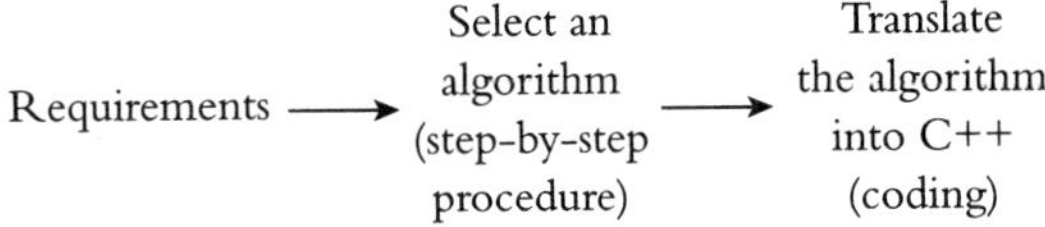

Only after an algorithm has been selected and the programmer understands the steps required can the algorithm be written using computer-language statements. The writing of an algorithm using computer-language statements is called **coding** the algorithm, which is the third step in our program development procedure (see Figure 1.32).

EXERCISES 1.4

1. Determine a step-by-step procedure (list the steps) to do these tasks: (*Note:* There is no one single correct answer for each of these tasks. The exercise is designed to give you practice in converting intuitive-type commands into equivalent algorithms and making the shift between the thought processes involved in the two types of thinking.)

a. Fix a flat tire.

b. Make a telephone call.

c. Go to the store and purchase a loaf of bread.

d. Roast a turkey.

2. a. Determine the six possible step-by-step procedures (list the steps) to paint the flower shown in Figure 1.33, with the restriction that each color must be completed before a new color can be started. (*Hint:* One of the algorithms is Use yellow first, green second, black last.)

FIGURE 1.33

A simple paint-by-number figure

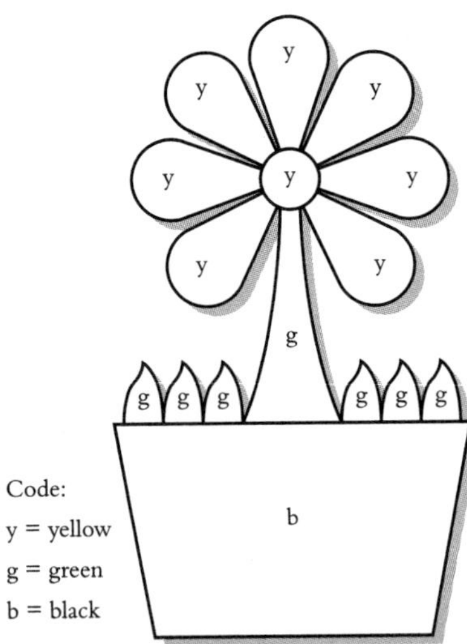

b. Which of the six painting algorithms (series of steps) is best if we are limited to using one paintbrush and we know there is no way to clean the brush?

3. Determine and write an algorithm (list the steps) to interchange the contents of two cups of liquid. Assume that a third cup is available to hold the contents of either cup temporarily. Each cup should be rinsed before any new liquid is poured into it.

4. Write a detailed set of instructions, in English, to calculate the dollar amount of money in a piggybank that contains h half-dollars, q quarters, n nickels, d dimes, and p pennies.

5. Write a set of detailed, step-by-step instructions, in English, to find the smallest number in a group of three integer numbers.

6. a. Write a set of detailed, step-by-step instructions, in English, to calculate the change remaining from a dollar after a purchase is made. Assume that the cost of the goods purchased is less than a dollar. The change received should consist of the smallest number of coins possible.

b. Repeat Exercise 6a, but assume the change is to be given only in pennies.

7. a. Write an algorithm to locate the first occurrence of the name Swanson in a list of names arranged in random order.

b. Discuss how you could improve your algorithm for Exercise 7a if the list of names was arranged in alphabetical order.

8. Write an algorithm to determine the total occurrences of the letter e in any sentence.

9. Determine and write an algorithm to sort four numbers into ascending (from lowest to highest) order.

Project Structuring Exercises

Most projects, both programming and nonprogramming, can usually be structured into smaller subtasks or units of activity. These smaller subtasks can often be delegated to different people so that when all the tasks are finished and integrated, the project or program is completed. For Exercises 10 through 15, determine a set of subtasks that, taken together, complete the project. Be aware that there are many possible solutions for each exercise. The only requirement is that the set of subtasks selected, when taken together, complete the required task.

Note: The purpose of these exercises is to have you consider the different ways that complex tasks can be structured. Although there is no one correct solution to these exercises, there are incorrect solutions and solutions that are better than others. An incorrect solution is one that does not fully specify the task. One solution is better than another if it more clearly or easily identifies what must be done.

10. You are given the task of wiring and installing lights in the attic of your house. Determine a set of subtasks that, taken together, will accomplish this. (*Hint:* The first subtask would be to determine the placement of the light fixtures.)

11. You are given the job of preparing a complete meal for five people next weekend. Determine a set of subtasks, that taken together, accomplish this. (*Hint:* One subtask, not necessarily the first one, would be to buy the food.)

12. You are a sophomore in college and are planning to go to law school after you graduate. List a set of major objectives that you must fulfill to meet this goal. (*Hint:* One objective is "Take the right courses.")

13. You are given the job of planting a vegetable garden. Determine a set of subtasks that accomplish this. (*Hint:* One such subtask would be to plan the layout of the garden.)

14. You are responsible for planning and arranging the family camping trip this summer. List a set of subtasks that, taken together, accomplish this objective successfully. (*Hint:* One subtask would be to select the camp site.)

15. a. A national medical testing laboratory desires a new computer system to analyze its test results. The system must be capable of processing each day's results. Additionally, the laboratory wants the capability to retrieve and output a printed report of all results that meet certain criteria—for example, all results obtained for a particular doctor, or all results obtained for hospitals in a particular state. Determine three or four major program units into which this system could be separated. (*Hint:* One possible program unit is "Prepare daily results" to create each day's reports.)

b. Suppose someone enters incorrect data for a particular test result, and this is discovered after the data have been entered and stored by the system. What program unit is needed to take care of correcting this problem? Discuss why such a program unit might or might not be required by most systems.

c. Assume a program unit exists that allows a user to alter or change data that have been incorrectly entered and stored. Discuss the need for including an "audit trail" that would allow for a later reconstruction of the changes made, when they were made, and who made them.

1.5 Common Programming Errors

The most common errors associated with the material presented in this chapter are:

1. A major programming error made by most beginning programmers is the rush to create and run an application before fully understanding what is required, including the algorithms that will be used to produce the desired result. A symptom of this haste to get a program entered into the computer is the lack of any documentation or even a program outline. Many problems can be caught just by checking the selected algorithm written in pseudocode.

2. A second error made is not correctly choosing either a `Win32 Console Application` or `MFC AppWizard (exe)` project type when starting a new console project.

3. A third major error is not correctly saving all files associated with a project.

4. The fourth error made by many new programmers is not understanding that computers respond only to explicitly defined algorithms. Telling a computer to add a group of numbers is quite different than telling a friend to add the numbers. The computer must be given, in a programming language, the precise instructions for doing the addition.

1.6 Chapter Summary

1. A Visual C++ Console Application is a character-based program that receives all user-interactive input from the keyboard and can display only characters on the monitor. Such programs are run under a Windows operating system within a DOS window.

2. A Visual C++ Windows-based application can make full use of all of Windows' graphics features. Such applications are constructed either as Win32 Applications, in which case they do not have to use the Microsoft Foundation Classes, or MFC AppWizard (exe) applications, in which case they require the use of the Microsoft Foundation Classes.

3. Visual C++ provides a graphics-based development system for creating both console and true windows-based applications.

4. A **computer program** is a structured combination of data and instructions that is used to operate a computer. The set of instructions, data, and rules that can be used to construct a program is called a **programming language.**

5. **High-level languages** are programming languages that are written using instructions that resemble a written language, such as English, and can be run on a variety of computer types. Compiler languages require a compiler to translate the program into machine code, whereas interpreter languages require an interpreter to do the translation.

6. **Procedure-oriented** languages consist of a series of procedures that direct the operation of a computer.

7. **Object-oriented** languages permit the use of objects within a program. Each object is defined by a **state,** which defines how the object appears at the moment and includes such properties as its size and color, and a **behavior,** which defines how the object reacts to external inputs.

8. Event-based programs execute program code depending on what events occur, which in turn depends on what the user does.

9. Developer Studio is the development environment under which Visual C++ applications are created. The main development interface provided by Developer Studio is a graphical-based integrated development environment (IDE).

10. Visual C++ applications are developed as projects; a **project** consists of all of the files needed by Developer Studio to create an executable application.

11. Project files are stored in project workspaces; a **project workspace** is simply a folder.

12. The IDE provided by Developer Studio is a standard window that contains a single Menu bar, multiple toolbars, and three internal windows: the Project Workspace window, the Output window, and the Editing area.

13. The Project Workspace window provides a number of tabs that present different views of a project. The ClassView tab displays a hierarchical tree of the classes used by project. The FileView tab provides a hierarchical tree structure of all of the folders and files within a project. Double-clicking on a resource or file icon opens the designated resource or text file and activates an editor within the Editing area appropriate to the selected item.

14. A Visual C++ program consists of a visual part and a language part. The visual part is provided by the objects used in the design of the graphical user interface and the language part consists of procedural code.

15. A console-based Visual C++ program is a character-based program that executes within a DOS window.

16. An **algorithm** is a step-by-step sequence of instructions that describes how a computation is to be performed.

1.7 Knowing About: Computer Hardware

All computers, from large super computers costing millions of dollars to smaller desktop personal computers must perform a minimum set of functions and provide the capability to

1. accept input
2. display output
3. store information in a logically consistent format (traditionally binary)

FIGURE 1.34

Basic hardware units of a computer

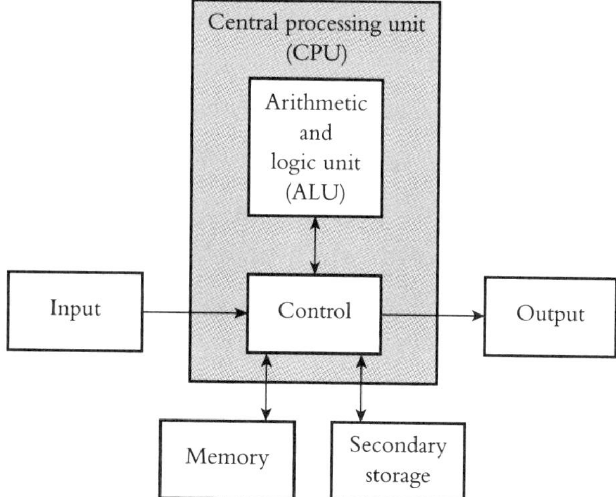

4. perform arithmetic and logic operations on either the input or stored data
5. monitor, control, and direct the overall operation and sequencing of the system

Figure 1.34 illustrates the computer hardware components that support these capabilities. These physical components are collectively referred to as **hardware.**

Memory Unit This unit stores information in a logically consistent format. Typically, both instructions and data are stored in memory, usually in separate and distinct areas.

Each computer contains memory of two fundamental types: RAM and ROM. **RAM,** which is an acronym for *random access memory,* is usually volatile, which means that whatever is stored there is lost when the computer's power is turned off. Your programs and data are stored in RAM while you are using the computer. The size of a computer's RAM memory is usually specified in terms of how many bytes of RAM are available to the user. Personal computer (PC) memories currently consist of from 32 to 128 million bytes. A million bytes is denoted as a megabyte (MB).

ROM, which is an acronym for *read-only memory,* contains fundamental instructions that cannot be lost or changed by the casual computer user. These instructions include those necessary for loading anything else into the machine when it is first turned on and any other instructions the manufacturer requires to be permanently accessible when the computer is turned on. ROM is *nonvolatile;* its contents are not lost when the power goes off.

Control Unit The control unit directs and monitors the overall operation of the computer. It keeps track of where in memory the next instruction resides, issues the signals needed to both read data from and write data to other units in the system, and executes all instructions.

Arithmetic and Logic Unit (ALU) The ALU performs all the arithmetic and logic functions, such as addition, subtraction, and comparison, provided by the system.

Input/Output (I/O) Unit This unit provides access to and from the computer. It is the interface to which peripheral devices such as keyboards, cathode ray screens, and printers are attached.

Secondary Storage Because RAM memory in large quantities is still relatively expensive and volatile, it is not practical as a permanent storage area for programs and data. Secondary or auxiliary storage devices are used for this purpose. Although data have been stored on punched cards, paper tape, and other media in the past, virtually all secondary storage is now done on magnetic tape, magnetic disks, and optical storage media.

The surfaces of magnetic tapes and disks are coated with a material that can be magnetized by a write head, and the stored magnetic field can be detected by a read head. Current tapes are capable of storing thousands of characters per inch of tape, and a single tape may store up to hundreds of megabytes. Tapes, by nature, are sequential storage media, which means that they allow data to be written or read in one sequential stream from beginning to end. Should you desire access to a block of data in the middle of the tape, you must scan all preceding data on the tape to find the block you want. Because of this, tapes are primarily used for mass backup of the data stored on large-capacity disk drives.

A more convenient method of rapidly accessing stored data is provided by a **direct access storage device** (DASD), where any one file or program can be written or read independent of its position on the storage medium. The most popular DASD in recent years has been the magnetic disk. A **magnetic hard disk** consists of either a single rigid platter or several platters that spin together on a common spindle. A movable access arm positions the read/write heads over, but not quite touching, the recordable surfaces.

Another common magnetic disk storage device is the removable **floppy diskette.** Currently, the most popular size for these is 3-1/2 inches in diameter, with a capacity of 1.44 megabytes.

In optical media, data are stored by using laser light to change the reflective surface properties of a single removable diskette, identical to an audio compact disk. The disk is called a **CD ROM** and is capable of storing several thousand megabytes.[10] Although the majority of CD ROMs are currently read-only devices, erasable methods are coming into use that permit the user to record, erase, and reuse optical disks in the same manner as a very high capacity magnetic disk.

---

10 A thousand megabytes is referred to as a gigabyte.

FIGURE 1.35

VLSI chip connections for a desktop computer

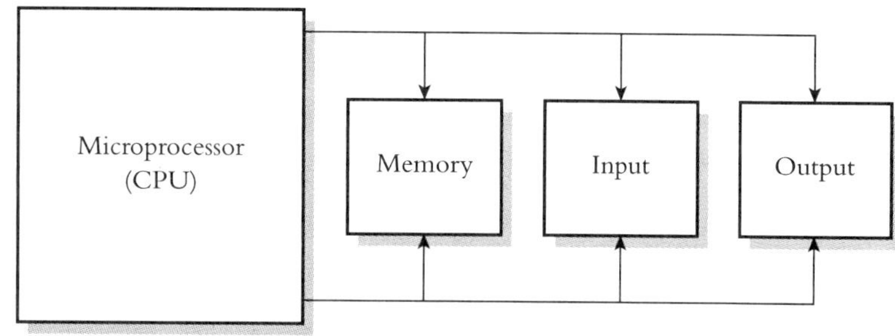

Hardware Evolution

In the first commercially available computers of the 1950s, all hardware units were built using relays and vacuum tubes. The resulting computers were extremely large pieces of equipment. They were capable of making thousands of calculations per second, and they cost millions of dollars. With the introduction of transistors in the 1960s, both the size and cost of computer hardware were reduced. The transistor was approximately one-twentieth the size of its vacuum tube counterpart. The transistor's small size allowed manufacturers to combine the arithmetic and logic unit with the control unit into a single new unit. This combined unit is called the **central processing unit** (CPU). The combination of the ALU and control units into one CPU made sense because a majority of control signals generated by a program are directed to the ALU in response to arithmetic and logic instructions within the program. Combining the ALU with the control unit simplified the interface between these two units and provided improved processing speed.

The mid-1960s saw the introduction of integrated circuits (ICs), which resulted in still another significant reduction in the space required to produce a CPU. Initially, integrated circuits were manufactured with up to 100 transistors on a single 1-cm^2 chip of silicon. Such devices are referred to as small-scale integrated (SSI) circuits.

Current versions of these chips contain from hundreds of thousands to more than a million transistors and are referred to as very large scale integrated (VLSI) chips. VLSI chip technology has provided the means of transforming the giant computers of the 1950s into today's desktop personal computers. The individual units required to form a computer (CPU, memory, and I/O) are now all manufactured on individual VLSI chips, respectively, and the single-chip CPU is referred to as a **microprocessor.** Figure 1.35 illustrates how these chips are connected internally within current personal computers, such as the IBM PCs.

Concurrent with the remarkable reduction in computer hardware size has been an equally dramatic decrease in cost and increase in processing speeds. Equivalent computer hardware that cost more than a million dollars in 1950 can now be purchased for less than a hundred dollars. If the same reductions occurred in the automobile industry, for example, a Rolls-Royce could now be purchased for ten dollars! The processing speeds of current computers have also increased by a factor of a thousand over their 1950s predecessors, with the computational speeds of current machines being measured in both millions of instructions per second (MIPS) and billions of instructions per second (BIPS).

Bits and Bytes

It would have been very convenient if a computer stored numbers and letters inside its memory and arithmetic and logic units the way that people do. The number 126, for example, would then be stored as 126, and the letter A stored as the letter A. Unfortunately, due to the physical components used in building a computer, this is not the case.

The smallest and most basic data item in a computer is called a **bit.** Physically, a bit is really a switch that can be either open or closed. By convention, the open and closed positions of each switch are represented as a 0 and a 1, respectively.

A single bit that can represent the values 0 and 1, by itself, has limited usefulness. All computers, therefore, group a set number of bits together, both for storage and transmission. The grouping of eight bits to form a larger unit is an almost universal computer standard. Such groups are commonly referred to as **bytes.** A single byte consisting of eight bits, where each bit is either a 0 or 1, can represent any one of 256 distinct patterns. These consist of the pattern 00000000 (all eight switches open) to the pattern 11111111 (all eight switches closed), and all possible combinations of 0s and 1s in between. Each of these patterns can be used to represent either a letter of the alphabet, other single characters, such as a dollar sign, comma, or other symbol, a single digit, or numbers containing more than one digit. The patterns of 0s and 1s used to represent letters, single digits, and other single characters are called **character codes** (one such code, called the ANSI code, is presented in Section 2.3). The patterns used to store numbers are called **number codes,** one of which is presented below.

Two's Complement Numbers

The most common number code for storing integer values inside a computer is called the **two's complement** representation. Using this code, the integer equivalent of any bit pattern, such as 10001101, is easy to determine and can be found for either positive or negative integers, with no change in the conversion method. For convenience we will assume byte-sized bit patterns consisting of a set of eight bits each, although the procedure carries directly over to larger size bit patterns.

The easiest way to determine the integer represented by each bit pattern is to first construct a simple device called a value box. Figure 1.36 illustrates such a box for a single byte. Mathematically, each value in the box illustrated in Figure 1.36 represents an

FIGURE 1.36

An eight-bit value box

-128	64	32	16	8	4	2	1

FIGURE 1.37

Converting 10001101 to a base 10 number

−128	64	32	16	8	4	2	1
1	0	0	0	1	1	0	1

−128 + 0 + 0 + 0 + 8 + 4 + 0 + 1 = −115

increasing power of two. Because two's complement numbers must be capable of representing both positive and negative integers, the leftmost position, in addition to having the largest absolute magnitude, also has a negative sign.

Conversion of any binary number, for example 10001101, simply requires inserting the bit pattern in the value box and adding the values having ones under them. Thus, as illustrated in Figure 1.37, the bit pattern 10001101 represents the integer number -115.

The value box can also be used in reverse, to convert a base 10 integer number into its equivalent binary bit pattern. Some conversions, in fact, can be made by inspection. For example, the base 10 number -125 is obtained by adding 3 to -128. Thus, the binary representation of -125 is 10000011, which equals -128 + 2 + 1. Similarly, the two's complement representation of the number 40 is 00101000, which is 32 plus 8.

Although the value box conversion method is deceptively simple, the method is directly related to the underlying mathematical basis of two's complement binary numbers. The original name of the two's complement code was the weighted-sign code, which correlates directly to the value box. As the name **weighted-sign** implies, each bit position has a weight, or value, of two raised to a power and a sign. The signs of all bits except the leftmost bit are positive, and the sign of the leftmost bit is negative.

In reviewing the value box, it is evident that any two's complement binary number with a leading 1 represents a negative number, and any bit pattern with a leading 0 represents a positive number. By using the value box, you can easily determine the most positive and negative values capable of being stored. The most negative value that can be stored in a single byte is the decimal number -128, which has the bit pattern 10000000. Any other nonzero bit will simply add a positive amount to the number. Additionally, it is clear that a positive number must have a 0 as its leftmost bit. From this you can see that the largest positive 8-bit two's complement number is 01111111 or 127.

Words

One or more bytes may themselves be grouped into larger units, called **words,** which facilitate faster and more extensive data access. For example, retrieving a word consisting of four bytes from a computer's memory results in more information than that obtained by retrieving a word consisting of a single byte. Such a retrieval is also considerably faster than four individual byte retrievals. This increase in speed and capacity, however, is accompanied by an increase in the computer's cost and complexity.

TABLE 1.5 Integer values and word size

Word Size	Minimum Integer Value	Maximum Integer Value
1 Byte	-128	127
2 Bytes	-32768	32767
4 Bytes	-2147483648	2147483647

Early personal computers, such as the Apple IIe and Commodore machines, internally stored and transmitted words consisting of single bytes. The first IBM PCs used word sizes consisting of two bytes, whereas more current Pentium-based PCs store and process words consisting of four bytes each.

The number of bytes in a word determines the maximum and minimum values that can be represented by the word. Table 1.5 lists these values for 1-, 2-, and 4-byte words (each of the values listed can be derived using 8-, 16-, and 32-bit value boxes, respectively).

In addition to representing integer values, computers must also store and transmit numbers containing decimal points, which are mathematically referred to as real numbers. The codes used for real numbers are more complex than those used for integers, but still depend on a two's complement type of representation.

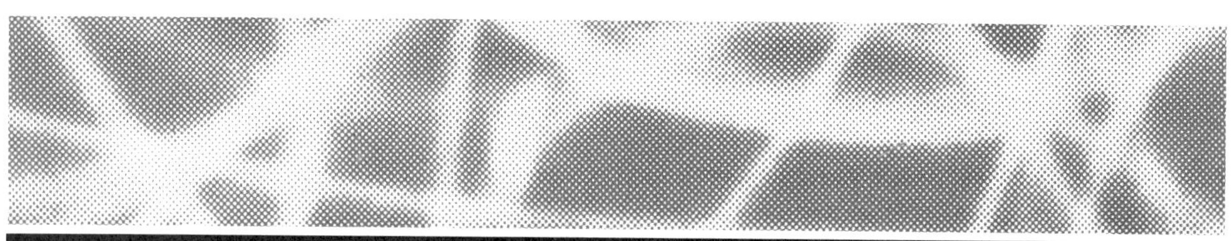

2 Procedural Programming Basics

2.1 Functions and Classes

A well-designed program is constructed using a design philosophy similar to that used in constructing a well-designed building; it doesn't just happen, but depends on careful planning and execution for the final design to accomplish its intended purpose. Just as the structure is an integral part of the design of a building, it is for a program as well.

Programs whose structure consists of interrelated segments, arranged in a logical and easily understandable order to form an integrated and complete unit, are referred to as **modular programs** (Figure 2.1). Modular programs are noticeably easier to develop,

FIGURE 2.1

A well-designed program is built using modules

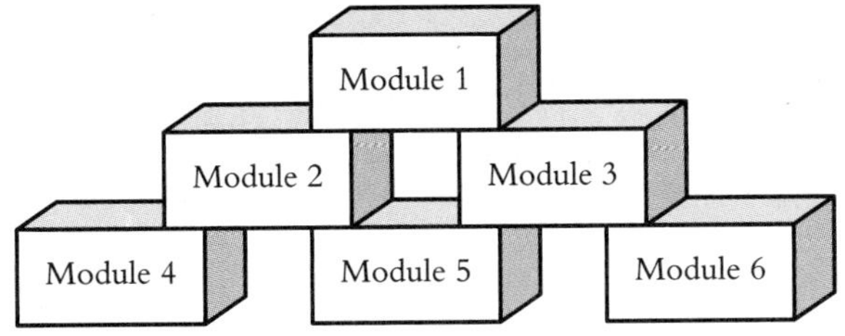

correct, and modify than programs constructed otherwise. In programming terminology, the smaller segments used to construct a modular program are referred to as **modules.**

Each module is designed and developed to perform a specific task and is really a small subprogram all by itself. A complete Visual C++ console application is constructed by combining as many modules as necessary to produce the desired result. The advantage of modular construction is that the overall design of the program can be developed before any single module is written. Once the requirements for each module are finalized, it can be programmed and integrated within the overall program as the module is completed.

In Visual C++, modules can be either classes or functions. It helps to think of a **function** as a small machine that transforms the data it receives into a finished product. For example, Figure 2.2 illustrates a function that accepts two numbers as inputs and multiplies the two numbers to produce one output. As shown, the interface to the function is its inputs and results. How the inputs are converted to results are both encapsulated and hidden within the function. In this regard the function can be thought of as a single unit providing a special purpose operation. A similar analogy is appropriate for a class.

A **class** is a more complicated unit than a function because it contains both a data structure, which is described in Chapter 12, and specific functions appropriate for manipulating the data structure. Thus, unlike a function, which is used to encapsulate a set of operations, a class encapsulates both data and one or more sets of operations. As such, each class contains all of the elements required for the input, output, and processing of its objects and can be thought of as a small dedicated computer. Initially, we will be predominantly concerned with the more basic function module.

FIGURE 2.2

A multiplying function

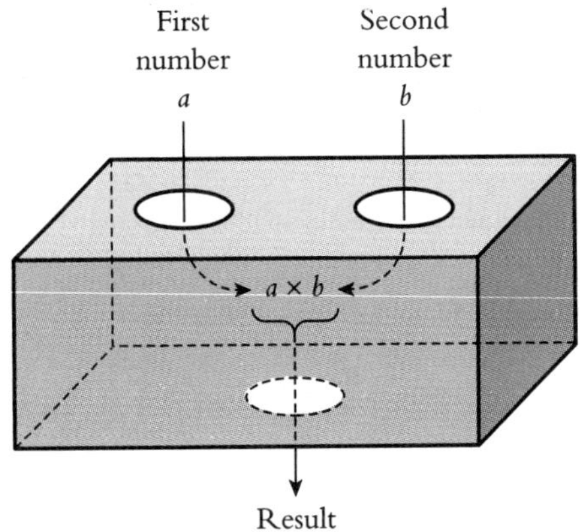

One important requirement for designing a good function or class is to give it a name that conveys to the reader some idea about what the function or class does. The names permissible for functions and classes are also used to name other elements of the Visual C++ language, and are collectively referred to as **identifiers.** Identifiers can be made up of any combination of letters, digits, or underscores (_) selected according to the following rules.

1. The first character of the name must be a letter or underscore (_).
2. Only letters, digits, or underscores may follow the initial letter. Blank spaces are not allowed; use capital letters or underscores to separate words in a name consisting of multiple words.
3. A function name cannot be one of the keywords listed in Table 2.1. (A **keyword** is a word that is set aside by the language for a special purpose and can be used only in a specified manner.[1])
4. The maximum number of characters in a function name is 255 characters (this is compiler dependent).

Examples of valid Visual C++ identifiers are:

```
DegToRad   intersect   addNums   slope
bessel     multTtwo    FindMax   density
```

TABLE 2.1 Keywords

asm1	default	for	public	true
auto	delete	friend	register	try
bad_cast	do	goto	reinterpret_cast	type_info
bad_typeid	double	if	return	typeid
bool	dynamic_cast	inline	short	typename
break	else	int	signed	union
case	enum	long	sizeof	unsigned
catch	except	mutable	static_cast	using
char	explicit	namespace	struct	virtual
class	extern	new	switch	void
const	false	operator	template	volatile
const_cast	finally	private	this	while
continue	float	protected	throw	xalloc

1 Keywords in C are also reserved words, which means they must be used only for their specified purpose. Attempting to use them for any other purpose will generate an error message.

Examples of invalid identifiers are:

```
?AB3     (begins with a number, which violates rule 1)
E*6      (contains a special character, which violates rule 2)
while    (this is a keyword, which violates rule 3)
```

In addition to conforming to Visual C++'s identifier rules, a Visual C++ function name must always be followed by parentheses (the reason for these will be seen shortly). Also, a good function name should be a **mnemonic**—a word or name designed as a memory aid. For example, the function name `DegToRad()` (note that we have included the required parentheses after the identifier, which clearly marks this as a function name) is a mnemonic if it is the name of a function that converts degrees to radians. Here, the name itself helps to identify what the function does.

Examples of valid function names that are not mnemonics are:

```
easy()     c3po()     r2d2()     TheForce()     mike()
```

Nonmnemonic function names should not be used because they convey no information about what the function does. Notice that function names can be typed in mixed upper and lowercase letters. This is becoming increasingly common in Visual C++, although it is not absolutely necessary, as is the use of capital letters to separate words in multiword identifiers. All uppercase identifiers are usually reserved for symbolic constants, a topic covered in Chapter 3.

Note that Visual C++ is a **case-sensitive** language, which means that the compiler distinguishes between uppercase and lowercase letters. Thus, in Visual C++, the names `TOTAL`, `total`, and `TotaL` represent three distinct and different names.

The `main()` Function

A distinct advantage of using functions and classes in Visual C++ is that the overall structure of the program in general, and individual modules in particular, can be planned in advance, including provision for testing and verifying each module's operation. Each function and class can then be written to meet its intended objective.

To provide for the orderly placement and execution of modules, each Visual C++ console application must have one and only one function named `main()`. The `main()` function is referred to as a driver function, because it drives, or tells the other modules the sequence in which they are to execute (Figure 2.3).[2]

Figure 2.4 illustrates a structure for the `main()` function. The first line of the function, in this case `int main()`, is referred to as a **function header line.** A function

---

2 Modules executed from `main()` may, in turn, execute other modules. Each module, however, always returns to the module that initiated its execution. This is true even for `main()`, which returns control to the operating system in effect when `main()` was initiated.

FIGURE 2.3

The `main()` function directs all other functions

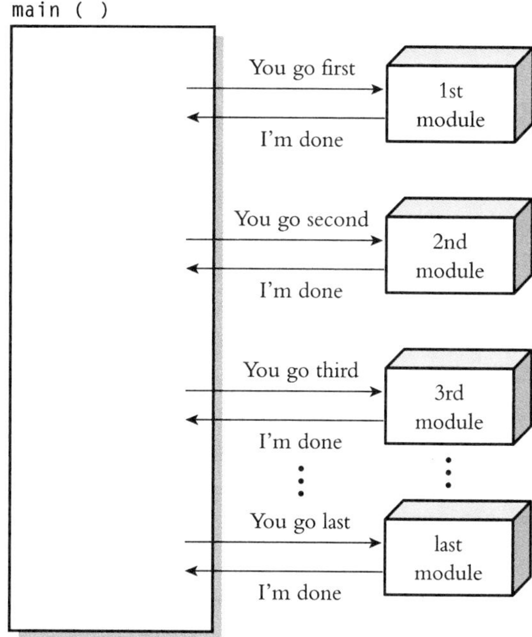

header line, which is always the first line of a function, contains three pieces of information:[3]

1. what type of data, if any, is returned from the function
2. the name of the function
3. what type of data, if any, is sent into the function

The keyword before the function name defines the type of value the function returns when it has completed operating. When placed before the function's name, the keyword `int` (see Table 2.1) designates that the function will return an integer value. Similarly, empty parentheses following the function name signify that no data will be transmitted into the function when it is run. (Data transmitted into a function at run time are referred to as **arguments** of the function.) Braces, { and }, determine the beginning and end, respectively, of the function body and enclose the statements making up the function. The statements inside the braces determine what the function does. Each statement inside the function must end with a semicolon (;).

You will be naming and writing many of your own Visual C++ functions. In fact, the rest of this book is primarily about the statements required to construct useful functions and how to combine functions and data into useful classes and programs. Each console

3 A class method must also begin with a header line that adheres to these same rules.

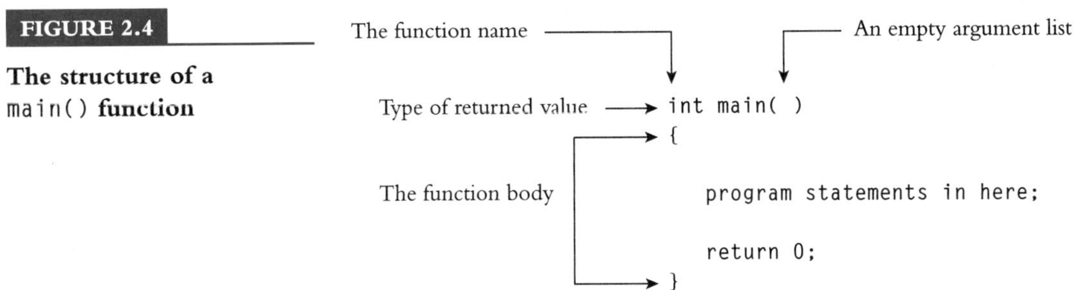

FIGURE 2.4

The structure of a `main()` function

program, however, must have one and only one `main()` function. Until we learn how to pass data into a function and return data from a function (the topics of chapter 6), the header line illustrated in Figure 2.4 will serve us for all the programs we need to write. For simple programs the first two lines

```
int main()
{
```

designate that "the console program begins here," and the last two lines

```
  return 0;
}
```

designate the end of the program.[4] Fortunately, however, many useful functions and classes have already been written for us. We will now see how to use an object created from one of these classes to create our first working Visual C++ console application.

The `cout` Object

One of the most versatile and commonly used objects provided in Visual C++ is named `cout` (pronounced "see out"). This object, whose name was derived from Console OUTput, is an output object that sends data given to it to the standard output display device.[5] For most systems this display device is a video screen. The `cout` object displays on the monitor whatever is transmitted to it. For example, if the message `Hello world!` is transmitted to `cout`, this is printed (or displayed) on your terminal screen. The message `Hello`

---

4 Note: The header line for the `main()` function can also be written as `void main()`, in which case no return statement is required. By having `main()` explicitly return a value, we can, if necessary, have the operating system check the return value when `main()` has finished executing.

---

5 The `cout` object is formally created from the `ostream` class, which is described in detail in Chapter 8.

`world!` is transmitted to the `cout` object by simply putting the insertion ("put to") symbol, `<<`, before the message and after the object's name as follows (the reason for including the `\n` is explained shortly).

```
cout << "Hello world!\n";
```

It is useful to think of this statement as "the `cout` object *gets* the string `Hello world!\n` and then displays it." The `\n`, which consists of the two separate characters, `\` and `n`, tells `cout` to output a new line after the characters `Hello world!` have been displayed.

Now let's put all this together into valid Visual C++ source code that can be incorporated into a project and run on your computer. Consider Program 2.1.

PROGRAM 2.1

```
// File: Pgm2_1.cpp
// Description: Displays Hello World!
// Programmer: G. Bronson
// Date: 2/18/99

#include <iostream.h>

int main()
{
  cout << "Hello world!\n";

  return 0;
}
```

The first four lines of program code, each of which begins with two slash symbols, `//`, are comments. We will have much more to say about comments in the next section, but for now it is important to understand that each source code program should begin with comments similar to those used here. These initial comment lines, at a minimum, should provide the file name under which the source code is saved, a short program description, the name of the programmer, and the date that the program was last modified.

For all of the programs contained in this text, the file name refers to the name of the file as it exists on the source code provided with this text.

The sixth line (counting blank lines) in the source code

```
#include <iostream.h>
```

is a **preprocessor** command. Preprocessor commands begin with a pound sign, (#), and perform some action before the compiler translates the source code into object code. Specifically, the `#include` preprocessor command causes the contents of the named file, in this case `iostream.h`, to be inserted where the `#include` command appears.[6] The file `iostream.h` is referred to as a **header file** because it is placed at the top, or head, of a Visual C++ console application using the `#include` command. In particular, the `iostream.h` file provides descriptions of two classes, `istream` and `ostream`. These two classes contain the actual data definitions and operations used for data input and output.[7] This header file must be included in all programs that use `cout`. As also indicated in Program 2.1, preprocessor commands *do not* end with a semicolon.

Following the preprocessor command is the start of the program's `main()` function. The `main()` function begins with the header line developed in the previous section and the body of the function, enclosed in braces, consists of only two statements. Remember that all statements within a function end with a semicolon (`;`). The statement in `main()` passes one message to the `cout` object. The message is the string `Hello world!\n`.

Because `cout` is an object of a prewritten class, we do not have to write it; it is available for use just by activating it correctly. Like all Visual C++ objects, `cout` can perform only certain well-defined actions. For `cout`, the action is to assemble data for output display. When a string of characters is provided to `cout`, the object sees to it that the string is correctly displayed on the monitor. Formally, a string in Visual C++ is any combination of letters, numbers, and special characters enclosed in double quotes ("string in here"). The double quotes are used to delimit (mark) the beginning and ending of the string and are not considered part of the string. Thus, the string of characters making up the message sent to `cout` must be enclosed in double quotes, as we have done in Program 2.1.

Entering Program 2.1

To create an executable version of the source code listed as Program 2.1, first create a new project named `Program2_1`. To do this, use Developer Studio and the procedures previously given in Section 1.3 for constructing a new project. After creating this project, add a new source file named `pgm2_1` to it, again using the procedures given in Section 1.3.

---

6 Two other alternatives that use the `iostream` designation without the `.h` suffix are explained in Appendix C.

---

7 Formally, `cout` is an object of the class `ostream`.

FIGURE 2.5

Developer Studio's IDE before entering Program 2.1

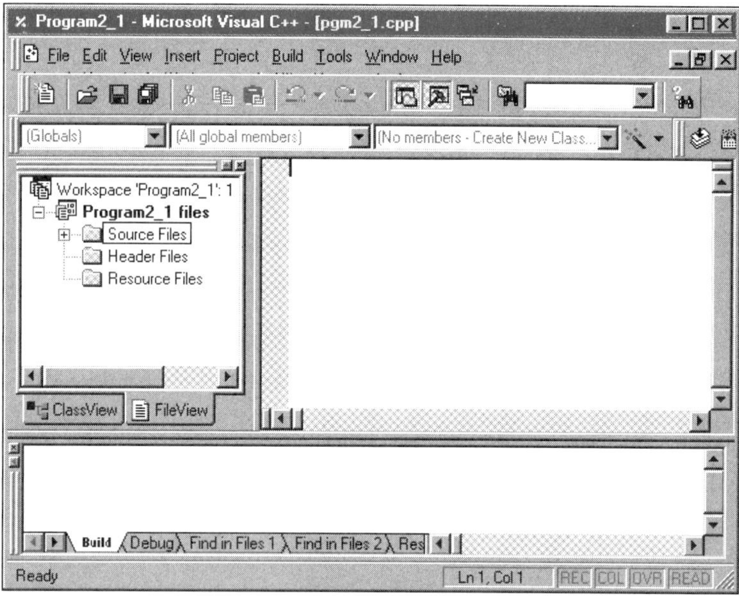

When you have completed this, Developer's Studio IDE should appear as shown in Figure 2.5.

Once your IDE appears as shown in Figure 2.5, click in the Editing area and enter Program 2.1's source code. When this is done, your screen should appear as shown in Figure 2.6. In entering your code make sure to terminate each of the two lines between the brace pair, { }, with a semicolon. Notice that as you enter this code all comment lines

FIGURE 2.6

Developer Studio's IDE after entering Program 2.1

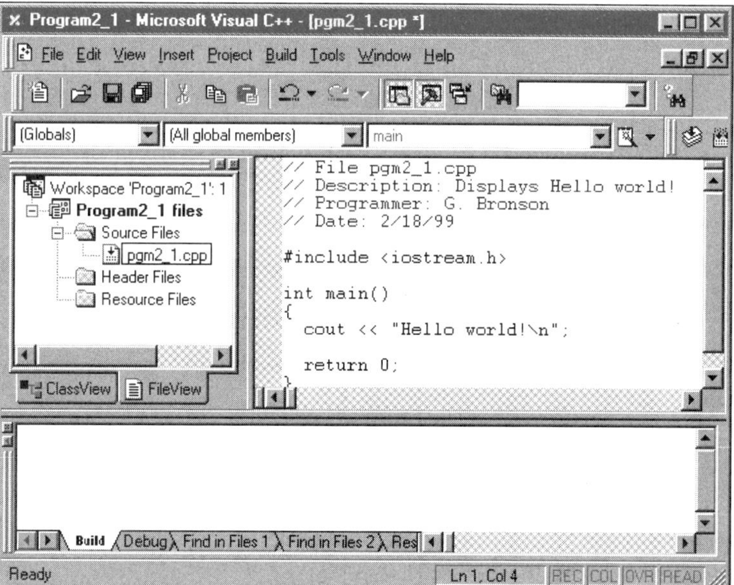

(those beginning with a double slash, //) will appear in green, all keywords will appear in blue, and all of the other text in black. This default coloring, which can be adjusted as a user-option (see Programmer's Notes box on page 57), provides a visual clue about the structure and state of your code.

Building a Console Application

Once you have completed entering Program 2.1 and your screen looks like that shown in Figure 2.6, you are ready to construct an executable version of the program. To do this, you use the build options provided in Visual C++. Figure 2.7 illustrates the build alternatives provided by the Menu bar's Build option. Prior to using the appropriate options shown in Figure 2.7 to actually construct an executable application, there is one setting that you should check; this setting is accessed through the Set Active Configuration... option highlighted in the figure. Selecting this option brings up the dialog box shown in Figure 2.8.

For all of the programs in this text, we assume that the Debug version option is active when the executable application is actually built. This option creates an executable debugging version that can be processed using the interactive debugging facilities provided with Developer Studio. These facilities help significantly in testing a program and locating and correcting errors. We will see how to use these facilities starting in Chapter 5. Programs built as release versions contain no debugging information, but are optimized for maximum execution speed. Thus, in practice, a Release version would be built once all program testing has been completed.

FIGURE 2.7

The Build submenu options

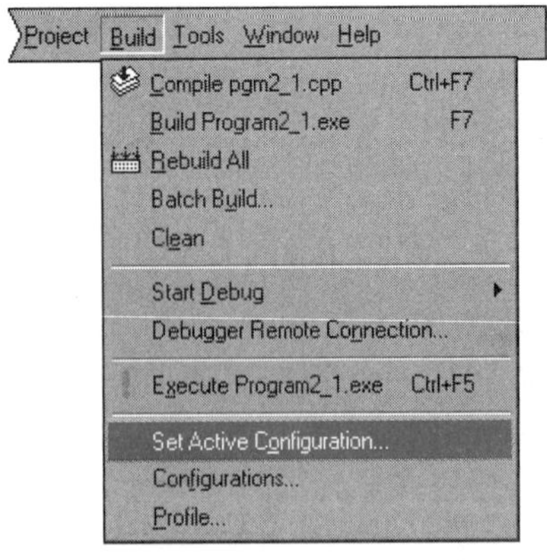

FIGURE 2.8

Selecting the Debug release configuration

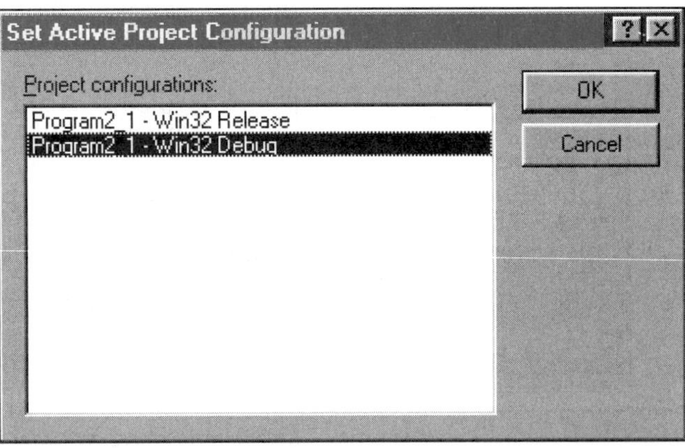

PROGRAMMER'S NOTES

Text Editor Options

The text editor provided with Visual C++ 6.0 provides a number of options that are very useful when you are entering code into Editing area. These include:

Color Coded Instructions

The editor displays procedural code in a variety of user-selected colors. By default, the following color selections are used:

- Keywords—Blue
- Comment—Green
- Other Text—Black

Font Style

The default font style is Courier.

Font Size

The default font size is 10 pt.

All of these options can be changed from within the Format tab in the Tools menu Options dialog box. To affect only the text editor make sure that the category selected within the Format tab is selected as Source Windows. Additionally, the tab and indent settings can be adjusted from within the Options dialog Tabs tab, and the editor being used can be set from within the Compatibility tab.

To actually build an executable application, regardless of its type (Debug or Release), you would use either the Build .exe option highlighted in Figure 2.9, one of the equivalent toolbar buttons shown in Figure 2.10, or the equivalent F7 accelerator key. All of these options cause all source code files that have been added or modified since the last build to be compiled and then linked with any additionally necessary object files to pro-

FIGURE 2.9

Building an executable application

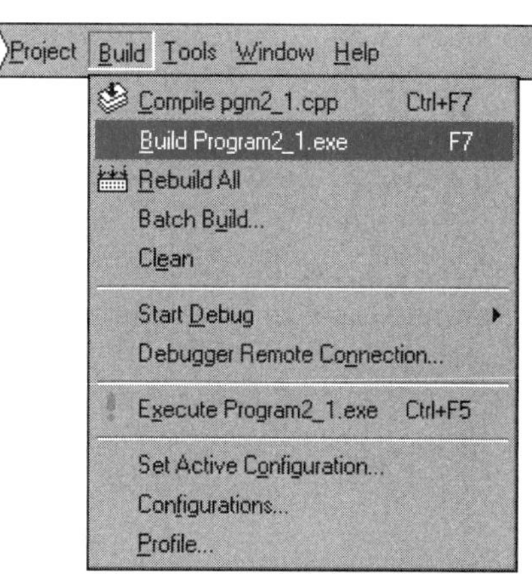

PROGRAMMER'S NOTES

Building an Executable Application

To build an executable version of an application, use one of the following methods:

1. From the Menu bar select the Build menu and then select the Build Project .exe option.
2. From the Menu bar select the Build menu and then select the Rebuild All option.
3. Press the accelerator key F7.
4. Press the Build button on either the Build or Build MiniBar toolbar. (If the desired toolbar is not visible, select it by clicking the right mouse button on either the Menu bar or any visible toolbar.)

Prior to building the executable version, you should set the active configuration to Debug version, which produces a version with full debugging information. The Release version provides no debugging information, but is optimized for maximum execution speed. The choice between version types is made using the Build menu's Set Active Configuration... option.

duce an executable file. In contrast to this, the Rebuild All option shown in Figure 2.9 does not check whether a source file has been added or modified, and simply recompiles all source files in a project. For large projects a Build is generally the faster and preferred method of creating an executable program. Also notice that if you simply want to compile your source code without creating an executable version you can do so using either the Compile option, Compile toolbar button, or the accelerator key sequence Ctrl+F7.

If your source code has no errors, a successful build will produce the output shown in the Output window in Figure 2.11. When this message occurs you are ready to execute the application.

FIGURE 2.10

(a) The Build MiniBar toolbar

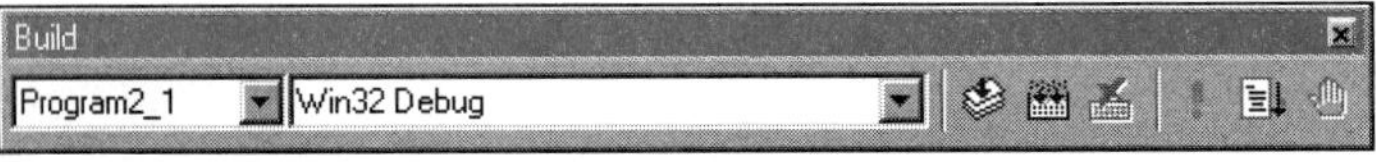

(b) The Build toolbar

PROGRAMMER'S NOTES

What Is Syntax?

A programming language's syntax is the set of rules for formulating grammatically correct language statements. In practice, this means that a Visual C++ statement with correct syntax has the proper form specified for the compiler. As such, the compiler will accept the statement and not generate an error message.

It should be noted that an individual statement can be syntactically correct and still be logically incorrect. Such a statement would be correctly structured but produce an incorrect result. This is similar to an English statement that is grammatically correct but makes no sense. For example, although the statement "The tree is a ragged cat" is grammatically correct, it makes no sense.

If you incorrectly entered the program—for example, by omitting the closing semicolon in the statement containing the `cout` object—you will be notified of the error in the Output window, as shown in Figure 2.12. If you now double-click on the error in the Output window, the error message will be highlighted and a bullet-like arrow will be placed to the left of the line at which the error was detected. In this case, as shown in Figure 2.12, the arrow is placed to the left of the `return 0;` line. The complete error message highlighted in the Output window, which can be viewed using the bottom scroll bar, is

```
Pgm2_1.cpp(12) : error C2143 : syntax error : missing ';' before 'return'
```

FIGURE 2.11

The Output window indicating a successful build

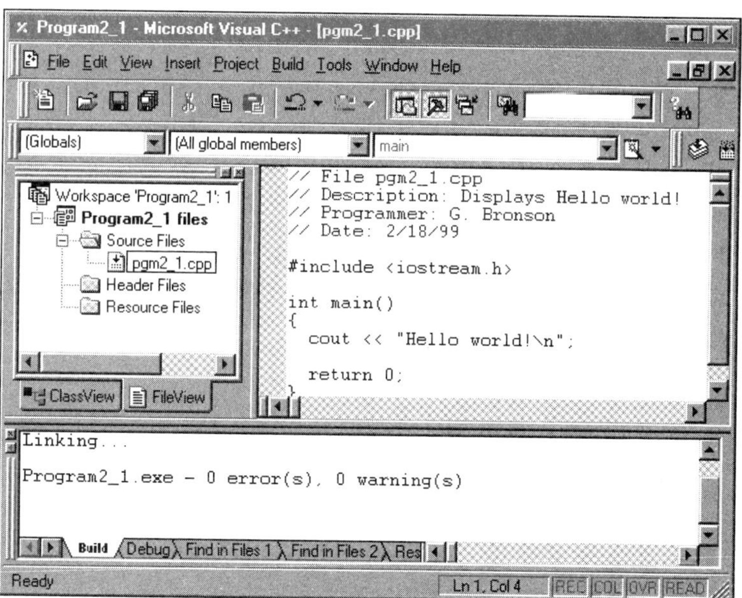

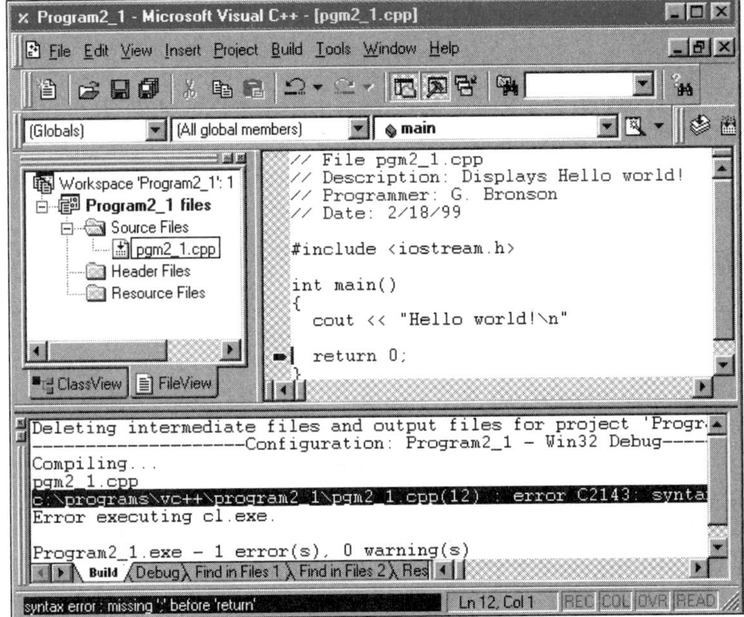

FIGURE 2.12

A build with a compiler error

The `(12)` in this line indicates that the error was detected on the 12th line down from the top of the source code, which is where the bullet-like arrow is placed. As indicated, there is no semicolon in the code, which should appear before the `return` keyword. In this case, you would correct the error by placing a semicolon at the end of line 11 in the code, and rebuild the application.

In addition to double-clicking on the error line in the Output window, another useful feature is to select the error line using a single click and then press the F1 key. Doing this will automatically invoke the online help feature and display a more detailed description of the compiler error code in the Editing area. This feature can also be invoked by pressing the F1 key when the error line is highlighted, as it is in Figure 2.12.

Executing an Application

Once you have successfully built an executable application, it can be executed by using one of the following three methods:

1. Select the Build menu and then select the Run .exe option.
2. Use the accelerator key sequence Ctrl+F5.
3. Click the Run button (!) on either the Build or Build MiniBar toolbar.

If you do this now for Program 2.1, the program will appear as shown in Figure 2.13.

FIGURE 2.13

Output produced by Program 2.1

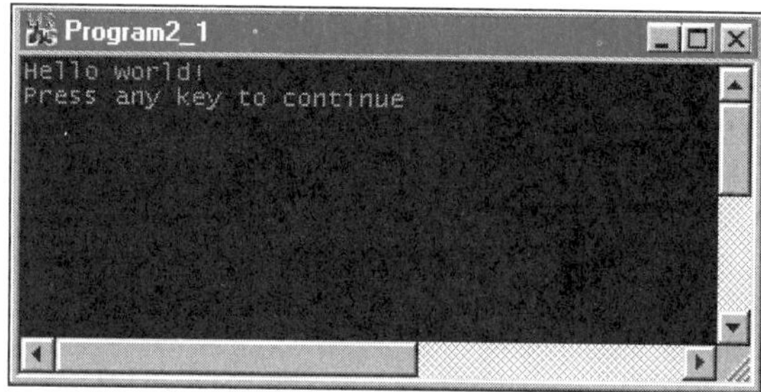

Notice that because this project was constructed as a console application, when the application is run under Windows, it is run within a DOS window. This window can be manipulated using standard window techniques. As such, you can click on the maximize or minimize buttons, move or resize the window, and close the application by double clicking on the Close (X) button. The output within the window, however, except for the line `Press any key`, is controlled by the Visual C++ code within the source code file `Pgm2_1`.

Notice that the `\n` after the exclamation point did not appear in the output shown in Figure 2.13. The two characters `\` and `n`, when used together, are called a **newline escape sequence.** They tell `cout` to send instructions to the display device to move to a new line. It is this escape sequence that causes the second line in the output display to be placed on a new line. Without the `\n`, the two lines would appear together on a single line. In Visual C++, the backslash (`\`) character provides an "escape" from the normal interpretation of the character following it by altering the meaning of the next character.

Let us write another program to illustrate `cout`'s versatility. Read Program 2.2 to determine what it does.

PROGRAM 2.2

```
// File: Pgm2_2.cpp
// Description: Test program
// Programmer: G. Bronson
// Date: 2/18/99
#include <iostream.h>

int main()
{
  cout << "Computers, computers everywhere\n";
  cout << "   as far as I can C\n";

  return 0;
}
```

PROGRAMMER'S NOTES

Running an Application

While creating a Visual C++ console application, you can run the application at any time by using any of the following procedures:

1. Select the Build menu and then select the Run .exe option.
2. Use the accelerator key sequence Ctrl+F5.
3. Click the Run button (!) on either the Build or Build MiniBar toolbar. (If the desired toolbar is not visible, select it by clicking the right mouse button on either the Menu bar or any visible toolbar.)

When Program 2.2 is run, the output shown in Figure 2.14 is displayed. If the backslash was omitted from the second `cout` statement in Program 2.2, the `n` would be printed as the letter *n* and the program would print out:

```
Computers, computers everywheren   as far as I can C
```

FIGURE 2.14

Program 2.2's output

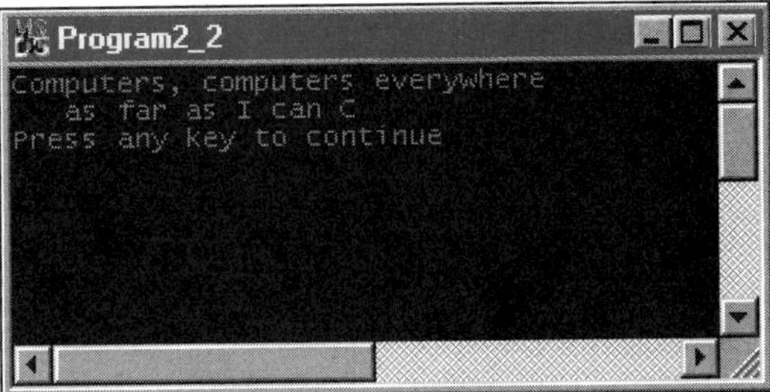

Newline escape sequences can be placed anywhere within the message passed to `cout`. See if you can determine the display produced by Program 2.3.

PROGRAM 2.3

```
// File: Pgm2_3.cpp
// Description: Test program
// Programmer: G. Bronson
// Date: 2/18/99
#include <iostream.h>

int main()
{
  cout << "Computers everywhere\n as far as\n\nI can see\n";

  return 0;
}
```

FIGURE 2.15

Program 2.3's output

The output produced by Program 2.3 is displayed in Figure 2.15.

EXERCISES 2.1

1. State whether the following are valid function names. If they are valid, state whether they are mnemonic names (recall that a mnemonic function name conveys some idea about the function's purpose). If they are invalid names, state why.

```
m1234()         newBal()      abcd()        A12345()      1A2345()
power()         absVal()      mass()        do()          while()
add_5()         taxes()       netPay()      12345()       int()
cosine()        a2b3c4d5()    net$Pay()     amount()      $sine()
oldBalance()    newValue()    salestax()    1stApprox()   float()
```

2. Assume that the following functions have been written:

   `inputPrice(), calcSalestax(), calcTotal()`

   a. From the functions' names, what do you think each function might do?

   b. In what order do you think a `main()` function might execute these functions (based on their names)?

3. Assume that the following functions have been written:

   `getLength(), getWidth(), calcArea(), displayArea()`

   a. From the functions' names, what do you think each function might do?

   b. In what order do you think a `main()` function might execute these functions (based on their names)?

4. Determine names for functions that do the following:

   a. Find the average of a set of numbers.

   b. Find the area of a rectangle.

   c. Find the minimum value in a set of numbers.

d. Convert a lowercase letter to an uppercase letter.

e. Convert an uppercase letter to a lowercase letter.

f. Sort a set of numbers from lowest to highest.

g. Alphabetize a set of names.

5. Just as the keyword `int` can be used to signify that a function will return an integer value, the keywords `void`, `char`, `float`, and `double` can be used to signify that a function will return an integer, a character, floating point number, and double precision number, respectively. Using this information, write header lines for a `main()` function that will receive no arguments but will return:

a. no value

b. a character

c. a floating point number

d. a double precision number

6. Using `cout`, write and execute a Visual C++ console application that displays your name on one line; your street address on a second line; and your city, state, and zip code on the third line.

7. Write and execute a Visual C++ console application to display the following verse:

```
Computers, computers everywhere
   as far as I can see
I really, really like these things,
   Oh joy, Oh joy for me!
```

8. a. How many `cout` statements would you use to display the following:

```
PART NO.              PRICE
T1267                 $6.34
T1300                 $8.92
T2401                $65.40
T4482                $36.99
```

b. What is the minimum number of `cout` statements that could be used to print the table in Exercise 8a?

c. Write and execute a Visual C++ console application to produce the output illustrated in Exercise 8a.

9. In response to a newline escape sequence, `cout` positions the next displayed character at the beginning of a new line. This positioning of the next character actually represents two distinct operations. What are they?

10. a. Assuming a case-insensitive compiler, determine which of these program unit names are equivalent:

```
AVERAG    averag   MODE    BESSEL    Mode
Total     besseL   TeMp    Density   TEMP
density   MEAN     total   mean      moDE
```

b. Redo Exercise 10a assuming a case-sensitive compiler.

2.2 Programming Style

Visual C++ console applications start execution at the beginning of the `main()` function. Because a program can have only one starting point, every Visual C++ language program must contain one and only one `main()` function. As we have seen, all of the statements that make up the `main()` function are then included within the braces `{ }` following the function name. Although the `main()` function must be present in every Visual C++ console application, Visual C++ does not require that the word `main`, the parentheses `()`, or the braces `{ }` be placed in any particular form. The form used in the last section

```
int main()
{
  program statements in here;

  return 0;
}
```

was chosen strictly for clarity and ease in reading the program.[8] For example, the following general form of a `main()` function would also work:

```
int main
(
) { first statement;second statement;
          third statement;fourth
statement;
return 0;}
```

Notice that more than one statement can be put on a line, or one statement can be written across lines. Except for strings, double quotes, identifiers, and keywords, Visual C++ ignores all white space (white space refers to any combination of one or more blank spaces, tabs, or new lines). For example, changing the white space in Program 2.1 and

8 If one of the program statements uses `cout`, the `#include <iostream.h>` preprocessor command is also required.

making sure not to split the string `Hello world!\n` across two lines results in the following valid program:

```
#include <iostream.h>

int main
(
){
cout <<
"Hello world!\n";
 return 0;
}
```

Although this version of `main()` does work, it is an example of extremely poor programming style. It is difficult to read and understand. For readability, the `main()` function should always be written in standard form as:[9]

```
int main()
{
   program statements in here;

   return 0;
}
```

In this standard form the function name starts in column 1 and is placed with the required parentheses on a line by itself. The opening brace of the function body follows on the next line and is placed under the first letter of the line containing the function name. Similarly, the closing function brace is placed by itself in column 1 as the last line of the function. This structure serves to highlight the function as a single unit.

Within the function itself, all program statements are indented at least two spaces. Indentation is another sign of good programming practice, especially if the same indentation is used for similar groups of statements. Review Program 2.2 to see that the same indentation was used for both `cout` statements.

As you progress in your understanding and mastery of Visual C++, you will develop your own indentation standards. Just keep in mind that the final form of your programs should be consistent and should always serve as an aid to its readability and understandability.

---

9 If the `main()` function did not return an integer value to the operating system, the appropriate first line would be `void main()`.

Comments

Comments are explanatory remarks made within a program. When used carefully, comments can be very helpful in clarifying what the complete program is about, what a specific group of statements is meant to accomplish, or what one line is intended to do. Visual C++ supports two types of comments: line and block. Both types of comments can be placed anywhere within a program and have no effect on program execution. The computer ignores all comments—they are there strictly for the convenience of anyone reading the program.

A line comment begins with two slashes (//) and continues to the end of the line. For example, the following lines are all line comments:

```
// this is a comment
// this program prints out a message
// this program calculates a square root
```

The symbols //, with no white space between them, designate the start of the line comment. The end of the line on which the comment is written designates the end of the comment.

A line comment can be written either on a line by itself or at the end of the same line containing a program statement. Program 2.4 illustrates the use of line comments within a program.

PROGRAM 2.4

```
// this program displays a message
#include <iostream.h>

int main()
{
   cout << "Hello world!\n";    // this displays a message

   return 0;
}
```

The first comment appears on a line by itself at the top of the program and describes what the program does. This is generally a good location to include a short comment describing the program's purpose. If more comments are required, they can be added, one per line. Thus, when a comment is too long to be contained on one line, it can be separated into two or more line comments, with each separate comment preceded by the double slash symbol set //. The comment

```
// this comment is invalid because it
   extends over two lines
```

will result in a Visual C++ error message on your computer. This comment is correct when written as:

```
// this comment is used to illustrate a
// comment that extends across two lines
```

Comments that span across two or more lines are, however, more conveniently written as block comments rather than as multiple line comments. Such comments begin with the symbols /* and end with the symbols */. For example,

```
/* This is a block comment that
    spans
    across three lines */
```

In Visual C++, a program's structure is intended to make the program readable and understandable, making the use of extensive comments unnecessary. This is reinforced if function, class, and variable names, described in the next chapter, are carefully selected to convey their meaning to anyone reading the program. However, if the purpose of a function, class, or statement is still not clear from its structure, name, or context, include comments where clarification is needed. Obscure code with no comments is a sure sign of bad programming. Excessive comments are also a sign of bad programming, because they imply that insufficient thought was given to having the code itself be self-explanatory. Typically, any program that you write should begin with a set of initial program comments that include a short program description, your name, and the date that the program was last modified. For space considerations, and because all programs in this text were written by the author, initial comments will be used only for short program descriptions when they are not provided as part of the accompanying descriptive text.

EXERCISES 2.2

1. a. Will the following program work?

```
#include <iostream.h>
int main(){cout << "Hello there world!"; return 0;}
```

b. Why is the program given in Exercise 1a not a good program?

2. Rewrite the following programs to conform to good programming practice.

a.
```
#include <iostream.h>
  int main(
  ){
  cout          <<
  "The time has come"
  ; return 0;}
```

b.
```
#include <iostream.h>
  int main
  (    ){cout << "Newark is a city\n";cout <<
  "In New Jersey\n"; cout <<
  "It is also a city\n"
  ; cout << "In Delaware\n"
  ; return 0;}
```

c.
```
#include <iostream.h>
 int main(){cout << Reading a program\n";cout <<
 "is much easier\n"
 ;cout << "if a standard form for main is used\n")
 ;cout
 <<"and each statement is written\n";cout
 <<            "on a line by itself\n")
 ; return 0;}
```

d.
```
#include <iostream.h>
 int main
 (    ){cout << "Every Visual C++ console application"
 ;cout
 <<"\nmust have one and only one"
 ;
 cout << "main function"
 ;
 cout <<
 "\n the escape sequence of characters")
 ;cout <<
  "\nfor a newline can be placed anywhere"
 ;cout
 <<"\n within the message passed to cout"
 ; return 0;}
```

3. **a.** When used in a message, the backslash character alters the meaning of the character immediately following it. If we wanted to print the backslash character, we would have to tell cout to escape from the way it normally interprets the backslash. What character do you think is used to alter the way a single backslash character is interpreted?

b. Using your answer to Exercise 3a, write the escape sequence for printing a backslash.

4. a. A token of a computer language is any sequence of characters that, as a unit, with no intervening characters or white space, has a unique meaning. Using this definition of a token, determine whether escape sequences, function names, and the keywords listed in Table 2.1 are tokens of the Visual C++ language.

b. Discuss whether adding white space to a message alters the message. Discuss whether messages can be considered tokens of Visual C++.

c. Using the definition of a token given in Exercise 4a, determine whether the following statement is true: "Except for tokens of the language, Visual C++ ignores all white space."

2.3 Data Values and Arithmetic Operations

Visual C++ console applications can process different types of data in different ways. For example, calculating the bacteria growth in a polluted pond requires mathematical operations on numerical data, and sorting a list of names requires comparison operations using alphabetical data. In this section we introduce Visual C++'s elementary data types and the operations that can be performed on them. Additionally, we show how to use the `cout` object to display the results of these operations.

Traditionally, there were three basic data values used in Visual C++; integers, floating point numbers, and character values. A fourth type, Boolean, was introduced by the ANSI/ISO standard for C++.[10] Each of these data values is described in the following subsections.

Integer Values

An **integer value** is zero, or any positive or negative number without a decimal point. Examples of valid integer values are:

0 5 –10 +25 1000 253 –26351 +36

As these examples illustrate, integers may be signed (have a leading + or – sign) or unsigned (no leading + or – sign). No commas, decimal points, or special symbols, such as the dollar sign, are allowed. Examples of invalid integer values are:

$255.62 2,523 3. 6,243,892 1,492.89 +6.0

10 ANSI is an acronym for American National Standards Institute. ISO stands for International Standards Organization.

Different computer types have their own internal limit on the largest (most positive) and smallest (most negative) integer values that can be used in a program. These limits depend on the amount of storage each computer sets aside for an integer; as such, they are said to be implementation dependent. The more commonly used storage allocations are listed in Table 2.2. It is interesting to note that in all cases the magnitude of the most negative integer allowed is always one more than the magnitude of the most positive integer. This is due to the method most commonly used to represent integers, called two's complement representation. For an explanation of two's complement representation, see Section 1.7.

By referring to your computer's reference manual or using the `sizeof` operator introduced in Section 2.5, you can determine the actual number of bytes allocated by your computer for each integer value. (Review Section 1.7 if you are unfamiliar with the concept of a byte.[11]) To store integer values greater than those supported by the memory allocation shown in Table 2.2 requires using integer qualifiers. These qualifiers are described in Section 2.5.

TABLE 2.2 **Integer values and word size**

Word Size	Minimum Integer Value	Maximum Integer Value
1 Byte	–128	127
2 Bytes	–32768	32767
4 Bytes	–2147483648	2147483647

Floating Point Values

A **floating point value,** which is also called a **real number,** is any signed or unsigned number having a decimal point. Examples of floating point numbers are:

+10.625   5.   –6.2   3251.92   0.0   0.33   –6.67   +2.

Notice that the numbers 5., 0.0, and +2. are classified as floating point values, whereas the same numbers written without a decimal point (5, 0, +2) would be integer values. As with integer values, special symbols, such as the dollar sign and the comma, are not permitted in real numbers. Examples of invalid real numbers are:

5,326.25   24   123   6,459 $10.29

Visual C++ supports three different categories of floating point values: float, double, and long double. The differences among these numbers relate to the amount of storage that a computer uses for each type. Most computers use twice the amount of storage for

---

11 The limits imposed by the compiler can also be found in the `limits.h` header file. The values listed are in hexadecimal notation and are defined as the constants `INI_MAX` and `INI_MIN`.

doubles as for floats, which allows a double to have approximately twice the precision of a float (for this reason floats are sometimes referred to as **single precision** numbers and doubles as **double precision** numbers). Similarly, long double numbers typically use twice the storage used for doubles, with a consequent increase in precision. The actual storage allocation for each data type, however, depends on the particular computer. In computers that use the same amount of storage for double and single precision numbers, these two data types become identical. The same is true for long doubles. The `sizeof` operator introduced in Section 2.5 will allow you to determine the amount of storage reserved by your computer for each of these data types. A float number is indicated to the computer by appending either an `F` or `f` after the number, and a long double is created by appending either an `L` or `l` to the number. In the absence of these suffixes, a floating point number is considered as a double. For example:

`9.234`	indicates a double
`9.234f`	indicates a float
`9.234L`	indicates a long double

The only difference in these numbers is the amount of storage the computer may use to store them. The only requirement made by Visual C++ is that a long double must provide at least the same precision as a double and that a double must provide at least the same precision as a float.

Exponential Notation

Floating point numbers can be written in exponential notation, which is similar to scientific notation and is commonly used to express both very large and very small numbers in a compact form. The following examples illustrate how numbers with decimals can be expressed in exponential and scientific notation.

Decimal Notation	Exponential Notation	Scientific Notation
1625.	1.625e3	1.625×10^{3}
63421.	6.3421e4	6.3421×10^{4}
.00731	7.31e–3	7.31×10^{-3}
.000625	6.25e–4	6.25×10^{-4}

In exponential notation the letter e stands for exponent. The number following the e represents a power of 10 and indicates the number of places the decimal point should be moved to obtain the standard decimal value. The decimal point is moved to the right if the number after the e is positive, or moved to the left if the number after the e is negative. For example, the e3 in the number 1.625e3 means move the decimal place three

PROGRAMMER'S NOTES

What Is Precision?

In number theory a statement such as "this computation is precise to the fifth decimal place" is used to mean that the fifth digit after the decimal point has been rounded and that the number is accurate to within $\pm 0.5 \times 10^{-5}$.

In computer programming, precision refers to the number of significant digits in the number, where significant digits mean the number of clearly correct digits plus one. For example, if the number 12.6874 has been rounded to the fourth decimal place, it is correct to say that this number is precise to the fourth decimal place. This statement means that all of the digits in the number are accurate except for the fourth digit, which has been rounded. Similarly, it can be said that the number has a precision of six digits, which means that the first five digits are correct and the sixth digit has been rounded. Another way of saying this is that the number 12.6874 has six significant digits.

Notice that the significant digits in a number need not have any relation to the number of displayed digits. For example, if the number 687.45678921 has five significant digits, it is precise only to the value 687.46, where the last digit is assumed to be rounded. In a similar manner, dollar values in many very large financial applications are frequently rounded to the nearest hundred thousand dollars. In such applications a displayed dollar value of $12,400,000, for example, is not precise to the closest dollar. Because this value has only three significant digits it is precise only to the 10^5th, or hundred thousandth digit. In Visual C++ the digits displayed to the left of the decimal point are assumed to be significant.

places to the right, so that the number becomes 1625. The e–3 in the number 7.31e–3 means move the decimal point three places to the left, so that 7.31e–3 becomes .00731.

Character Values

The third basic type of data recognized by Visual C++ is character data. Characters include the letters of the alphabet (both uppercase and lowercase), the ten digits 0 through 9, and special symbols such as + $. , – !. A single **character value** is any one letter, digit, or special symbol enclosed by single quotes. Examples of valid character values are:

```
'A'   '$'   'b'   '7'   'y'   '!'   'M'   'q'
```

Character values are typically stored in a computer using either the ASCII or ANSI codes. **ASCII,** pronounced AS-KEY, is an acronym for American Standard Code for Information Interchange, and consists of 128 codes. **ANSI,** pronounced ANN-SEE, is an acronym for American National Standards Institute, and is an extended set of 256 codes, the first 128 of which are the same as the ASCII codes. Each of these codes assigns individual characters to a specific pattern of 0s and 1s. Table 2.3 lists the correspondence between bit patterns and the uppercase and lowercase letters of the alphabet used by both the ASCII and ANSI codes.

TABLE 2.3 **The ASCII and ANSI letter codes**

Letter	Code	Letter	Code	Letter	Code	Letter	Code
a	01100001	n	01101110	A	01000001	N	01001110
b	01100010	o	01101111	B	01000010	O	01001111
c	01100011	p	01110000	C	01000011	P	01010000
d	01100100	q	01110001	D	01000100	Q	01010001
e	01100101	r	01110010	E	01000101	R	01010010
f	01100110	s	01110011	F	01000110	S	01010011
g	01100111	t	01110100	G	01000111	T	01010100
h	01101000	u	01110101	H	01001000	U	01010101
i	01101001	v	01110110	I	01001001	V	01010110
j	01101010	w	01110111	J	01001010	W	01010111
k	01101011	x	01111000	K	01001011	X	01011000
l	01101100	y	01111001	L	01001100	Y	01011001
m	01101101	z	01111010	M	01001101	Z	01011010

Using Table 2.3, we can determine how the characters `'J'`, `'E'`, `'A'`, `'N'`, and `'S'`, for example, are stored inside a computer that uses the ASCII character code. Using the ASCII code, this sequence of characters requires five bytes of storage (one byte for each letter) and would be stored as illustrated in Figure 2.16.

Escape Sequences

When a backslash (\) is used directly in front of a select group of characters, the backslash tells the computer to escape from the way these characters would normally be interpreted. For this reason, the combination of a backslash and these specific characters are called **escape sequences.** We have already encountered an example of this in the newline escape sequence, `\n`. Table 2.4 lists Visual C++'s most commonly used escape sequences.

Although each escape sequence listed in Table 2.4 is made up of two distinct characters, the combination of the two characters with no intervening white space causes the computer to store one character code. Table 2.5 lists the ASCII code byte patterns for the escape sequences listed in Table 2.4.

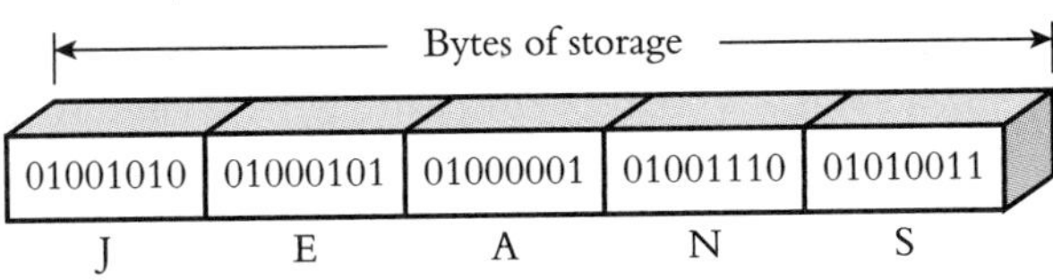

FIGURE 2.16

The letters `JEANS` stored inside a computer

TABLE 2.4 Escape sequences

Escape Sequence	Meaning
\b	move back one space
\f	move to next page
\n	move to next line
\r	carriage return
\t	move to next tab setting
\\	backslash character
\'	single quote
\"	double quote
\nnn	treat nnn as an octal number

TABLE 2.5 The ASCII escape sequence codes

C++ Escape Sequence	Computer Code
\b	00001000
\f	00001100
\n	00001010
\r	00001101
\t	00001001
\\	01011100
\'	00100111
\"	00100010

Arithmetic Operations

Integers and real numbers can be added, subtracted, multiplied, and divided. Although it is usually better not to mix integers and real numbers when performing arithmetic operations, predictable results are obtained when different data types are used in the same arithmetic expression. Somewhat surprising is the fact that character data can also be added and subtracted with both character and integer data to produce useful results.

The operators used for arithmetic operations, called **arithmetic operators,** are listed next:

Operation	Operator
Addition	+
Subtraction	-
Multiplication	*
Division	/
Modulus division	%

A **simple arithmetic expression** consists of an arithmetic operator connecting two operands in the form:[12]

operand *operator* operand

---

12 Formally, an operand is either a constant, a variable, which is described in the next section, or valid combinations of constants and variables.

PROGRAMMER'S NOTES

Boolean Data

Boolean data are restricted to one of two values, either **true** or **false.** Traditionally, both C and C++ did not support built-in Boolean data.

As specified by the ANSI/ISO C++ standard, C++ now incorporates a Boolean data type and permits using the two Boolean values, **true** and **false.** In C++ compilers currently implementing a Boolean data type, the actual values represented by the two boolean values, **true** and **false,** have been the integer values 1 and 0, respectively.

In actual practice, Boolean data are most useful when examining a specific condition, and as a result of the condition being **true** or **false,** taking a prescribed course of action. The examination of conditions is considered in Chapter 4, and we encounter Boolean data once again in that chapter.

Examples of arithmetic expressions are:

```
3 + 7
18 - 3
12.62 + 9.8
.08 * 12.2
12.6 / 2.
```

The spaces around the arithmetic operators in these examples are inserted strictly for clarity and can be omitted without affecting the value of the expression.

The value of any arithmetic expression can be displayed on the standard output device using `cout`. To do this we must pass the desired value to this object. For example, the statement

```
cout << (6 + 15);
```

yields the display `21`. Strictly speaking, the parentheses surrounding the expression `6 + 15` are not required to indicate that it is the value of the expression, which is `21`, that is being placed on the output stream.[13]

In addition to displaying a numerical value, a string identifying the output can also be displayed by passing the string to `cout` as we did in Section 2.1. For example, the statement:

```
cout << "The sum of 6 and 15 is " <<  (6 + 15);
```

---

13 This is because the + operator has a higher precedence than the << operator, as explained later in this section.

causes two pieces of data to be sent to cout, a string and a value. Individually, each set of data is sent to cout preceded by its own insertion operator symbol (<<). Here, the first data sent to the stream is the string "The sum of 6 and 15 is ", and the second item sent to the stream is the value of the expression 6 + 15. The display produced by this statement is:

```
The sum of 6 and 15 is 21
```

Notice that the space between the word is and the number 21 is caused by the space placed within the string passed to cout. As far as cout is concerned, its input is simply a set of characters that are then sent on to be displayed in the order they are received. Characters from the input are queued, one behind the other, and sent to an output stream for display. Placing a space in the input causes this space to be part of the output stream that is ultimately displayed. For example, the statement

```
cout << "The sum of 12.2 and 15.754 is " << (12.2 + 15.754);
```

yields the display

```
The sum of 12.2 and 15.754 is 27.954
```

We should mention that insertion of data into the output stream can be made over multiple lines and is only terminated by a semicolon. Thus, the prior display is also produced by the statement

```
cout << "The sum of 12.2 and 15.754 is "
     << (12.2 + 15.754);
```

The restrictions in using multiple lines are that a string contained within double quotes cannot be split across lines and that the terminating semicolon must appear only on the last line. Within a line, multiple insertion symbols can be used.

As the last display indicates, floating point numbers are displayed with sufficient decimal places to the right of the decimal place to accommodate the fractional part of the number. This is true if the number has six or fewer decimal digits. If the number has more than six decimal digits, the fractional part is rounded to six decimal digits, and if the number has no decimal digits, neither a decimal point nor any decimal digits are displayed.[14]

---

14 It should be noted that none of this output is defined as part of the C++ language. Rather, it is defined by a set of classes and routines provided with each C++ compiler.

Character data can also be displayed using `cout`. For example, the statement

```
cout << "The first letter of the alphabet is an " << 'a';
```

causes the display

```
The first letter of the alphabet is an a
```

Program 2.5 illustrates using `cout` to display the results of an expression within the statements of a complete program. Note that the escape sequence `'\n'` inserted into the output stream simply causes a new line to be started after each expression is displayed.

PROGRAM 2.5

```
#include <iostream.h>

int main()
{
  cout << "15.0 plus 2.0 equals "        << (15.0 + 2.0) << '\n'
       << "15.0 minus 2.0 equals "       << (15.0 - 2.0) << '\n'
       << "15.0 times 2.0 equals "       << (15.0 * 2.0) << '\n'
       << "15.0 divided by 2.0 equals " << (15.0 / 2.0) << '\n';

  return 0;
}
```

The output produced by Program 2.5 is shown in Figure 2.17.

FIGURE 2.17

Program 2.5's output

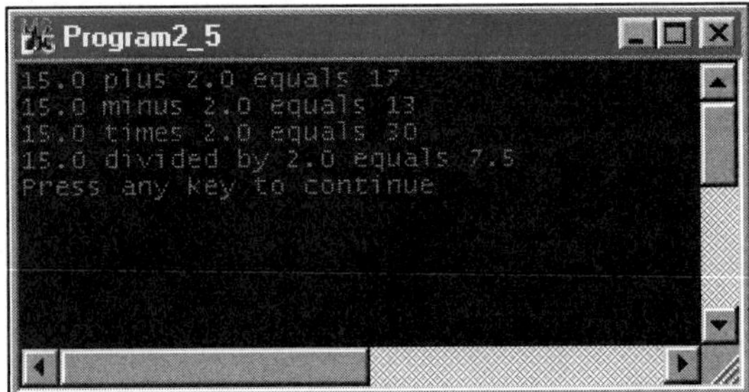

Expression Types An **expression** that contains only integer operands is called an **integer expression,** and the result of the expression is an integer value. Similarly, an expression containing only floating point operands (single and double precision) is called a **floating point** expression, and the result of such an expression is a floating point value. An expression containing both integer and floating point operands is called a **mixed-mode** expression. Although it is usually better not to mix integer and floating point operands in arithmetic operations, the data type of each operation is determined by the following rules:

1. If both operands are integers, the result of the operation is an integer.
2. If one operand is a floating point value, the result of the operation is a double precision value.

Note that the result of an arithmetic expression is never a single precision (float) number. This is because the computer temporarily converts all floats to double precision numbers when arithmetic is being done.

Integer Division

The division of two integers can produce rather strange results for the unwary. For example, dividing the integer 15 by the integer 2 yields an integer result. But because integers cannot contain a fractional part, the expected result, 7.5, is not obtained. In Visual C++, the fractional part of the result obtained when dividing two integers is dropped (truncated). Thus, the value of 15/2 is 7, the value of 9/4 is 2, and the value of 19/5 is 3.

Often, however, we would like to retain the remainder of an integer division. To do this, Visual C++ provides an arithmetic operator that captures the remainder when two integers are divided. This operator, called the modulus operator, has the symbol `%`. The modulus operator can be used only with integers. For example,

`9 % 4` is 1
`17 % 3` is 2
`14 % 2` is 0

A Unary Operator (Negation)

Besides the binary operators for addition, subtraction, multiplication, and division, Visual C++ also provides unary operators. One of these unary operators uses the same symbol that is used for binary subtraction (-). The minus sign used in front of a single numerical operand negates (reverses the sign of) the number.

Table 2.6 summarizes the six arithmetic operations we have described so far and lists the data type of the result produced by each operator based on the data type of the operands involved.

TABLE 2.6 Summary of arithmetic operators

Operation	Operator	Type	Operand	Result
Addition	+	Binary	Both integers One operand not an integer	Integer Double precision
Subtraction	-	Binary	Both integers One operand not an integer	Integer Double precision
Multiplication	*	Binary	Both integers One operand not an integer	Integer Double precision
Division	/	Binary	Both integers One operand not an integer	Integer Double precision
Modulus	%	Binary	Both integers One integer	Integer Integer
Negation	-	Unary	One floating point or double precision operand	Double precision

Operator Precedence and Associativity

Besides simple expressions such as `5 + 12` and `.08 * 26.2`, we frequently need to create more complex arithmetic expressions. Visual C++, like most other programming languages, requires that certain rules be followed when writing expressions containing more than one arithmetic operator. These rules are:

1. Two binary arithmetic operator symbols must never be placed side by side. For example, `5 * %6` is invalid because the two operators `*` and `%` are placed next to each other.

2. Parentheses should be used to form groupings, and all expressions enclosed within parentheses are evaluated first. For example, in the expression `(6 + 4) / (2 + 3)`, the `6 + 4` and `2 + 3` are evaluated first to yield `10 / 5`. The `10 / 5` is then evaluated to yield `2`.

3. Sets of parentheses may also be enclosed by other parentheses. For example, the expression `(2 * (3 + 7) ) / 5` is valid. When parentheses are used within parentheses, the expressions in the innermost parentheses are always evaluated first. The evaluation continues from innermost to outermost parentheses until the expressions in all parentheses have been evaluated. The number of right-facing parentheses, `(`, must always equal the number of left-facing parentheses, `)`, so that there are no unpaired sets.

4. Parentheses cannot be used to indicate multiplication. The multiplication operator, `*`, must be used. For example, the expression `(3 + 4) (5 + 1)` is invalid. The correct expression is `(3 + 4) * (5 + 1)`.

TABLE 2.7 Operator precedence and associativity

Precedence	Associativity
`unary -`	right to left
`* / %`	left to right
`+ -`	left to right

Parentheses should be used to specify logical groupings of operands and to indicate clearly to both the computer and programmers the intended order of arithmetic operations. In the absence of parentheses, expressions containing multiple operators are evaluated by the priority, or precedence, of the operators. Table 2.7 lists both the precedence and associativity of the operators considered in this section.

The precedence of an operator establishes its priority relative to all other operators. Operators at the top of Table 2.7 have a higher priority than operators at the bottom of the table. In expressions with multiple operators, the operator with the higher precedence is used before an operator with a lower precedence. For example, in the expression `6 + 4 / 2 + 3`, the division is done before the addition, yielding an intermediate result of `6 + 2 + 3`. The additions are then performed to yield a final result of `11`.

Expressions containing operators with the same precedence are evaluated according to their associativity. This means that evaluation is either from left to right or from right to left as each operator is encountered. For example, in the expression `8 + 5 * 7 % 2 * 4`, the multiplication and modulus operator are of higher precedence than the addition operator and are evaluated first. Both of these operators, however, are of equal precedence. Therefore, these operators are evaluated according to their left-to-right associativity, yielding

```
8 +  5 * 7 % 2 * 4  =
    8 + 35 % 2 * 4  =
         8 + 1 * 4  =
             8 + 4  =  12
```

EXERCISES 2.3

1. Determine data types appropriate for the following data:

a. the average of four grades

b. the number of days in a month

c. the length of the Golden Gate Bridge

d. the part numbers in a state lottery

e. the distance from Brooklyn, N.Y., to Newark, N.J.

f. the names in a mailing list

2. Convert the following numbers into standard decimal form:

`6.34e5`   `1.95162e2`   `8.395e1`   `2.95e-3`   `4.623e-4`

3. Write the following decimal numbers using exponential notation:

126.   656.23   3426.95   4893.2   .321   .0123   .006789

4. Listed below are correct algebraic expressions and incorrect Visual C++ expressions corresponding to them. Find the errors and write corrected Visual C++ expressions.

Algebra	*Visual C++ Expression*
a. (2)(3) + (4)(5)	`(2)(3) + (4)(5)`
b. $\frac{6+8}{2}$	`6 + 18 / 2`
c. $\frac{4.5}{12.2-3.1}$	`4.5 / 12.2 - 3.1`
d. 4.6(3.0 + 14.9)	`4.6(3.0 + 14.9)`
e. (12.1 + 18.9)(15.3 - 3.8)	`(12.1 + 18.9)(15.3 - 3.8)`

5. Determine the values of the following integer expressions:

a. `3 + 4 * 6`

b. `3 * 4 / 6 + 6`

c. `2 * 3 / 12 * 8 / 4`

d. `10 * (1 + 7 * 3)`

e. `20 - 2 / 6 + 3`

f. `20 - 2 / (6 + 3)`

g. `(20 - 2) / 6 + 3`

h. `(20 - 2) / (6 + 3)`

i. `50 % 20`

j. `(10 + 3) % 4`

6. Determine the values of the following floating point expressions:

a. `3.0 + 4.0 * 6.0`

b. `3.0 * 4.0 / 6.0 + 6.0`

c. `2.0 * 3.0 / 12.0 * 8.0 / 4.0`

d. `10.0 * (1.0 + 7.0 * 3.0)`

e. `20.0 - 2.0 / 6.0 + 3.0`

f. `20.0 - 2.0 / (6.0 + 3.0)`

g. `(20.0 - 2.0) / 6.0 + 3.0`
h. `(20.0 - 2.0) / (6.0 + 3.0)`

7. Evaluate the following mixed mode expressions and list the data type of the result. In evaluating the expressions be aware of the data types of all intermediate calculations.

a. `10.0 + 15 / 2 + 4.3`
b. `10.0 + 15.0 / 2 + 4.3`
c. `3.0 * 4 / 6 + 6`
d. `3 * 4.0 / 6 + 6`
e. `20.0 - 2 / 6 + 3`
f. `10 + 17 * 3 + 4`
g. `10 + 17 / 3.0 + 4`
h. `3.0 * 4 % 6 + 6`
i. `10 + 17 % 3 + 4.`

8. Assuming that `distance` has the integer value 1, `v` has the integer value 50, `n` has the integer value 10, and `t` has the integer value 5, evaluate the following expressions:

a. `n / t + 3`
b. `v / t + n - 10 * distance`
c. `v - 3 * n + 4 * distance`
d. `distance / 5`
e. `18 / t`
f. `-t * n`
g. `-v / 20`
h. `(v + n) / (t + distance)`
i. `v + n / t + distance`

9. Repeat Exercise 8 assuming that `distance` has the value 1.0, `v` has the value 50.0, `n` has the value 10.0, and `t` has the value 5.0.

10. Using the system reference manuals for your computer, determine the character code used by your computer.

11. Determine the output of the following program:

```
#include <iostream.h>

int main()  // a program illustrating integer truncation
{
  cout << "answer1 is the integer " << 9/4 << '\n';
  cout << "answer2 is the integer" << 17/3 << '\n';

  return 0;
}
```

12. Determine the output of the following program:

```
#include <iostream.h>

int main()  // a program illustrating the % operator
{
  cout << "The remainder of 9 divided by 4 is " << 9 % 4 << '\n';
  cout << "The remainder of 17 divided by 3 is " << 17 % 3 << '\n';

  return 0;
}
```

13. Write a Visual C++ console application that displays the results of the expressions `3.0 * 5.0`, `7.1 * 8.3 - 2.2`, and `3.2 / (6.1 * 5)`. Calculate the value of these expressions manually to verify that the displayed values are correct.

14. Write a Visual C++ console application that displays the results of the expressions `15 / 4`, `15 % 4`, and `5 * 3 - (6 * 4)`. Calculate the value of these expressions manually to verify that the displayed values are correct.

15. Show how the name `KINGSLEY` would be stored inside a computer that uses the ASCII code. That is, draw a figure similar to Figure 2.16 for the letters `KINGSLEY`.

16. Repeat Exercise 15 using the letters of your own last name.

17. Enter, compile, and run Program 2.5 on your computer system.

18. Because computers use different representations for storing integer, floating point, double precision, and character values, discuss how a program might alert the compiler to the data types of the various values it will be using.

19. Although we have concentrated on operations involving integers, and floating point numbers, Visual C++ allows characters and integers to be added or subtracted. This can be done because Visual C++ always converts a character to an equivalent integer value whenever a character is used in an arithmetic expression. Thus, characters and integers can be freely mixed in such expressions. For example, if your computer uses the ASCII code, the expression `'a' + 1` equals `'b'`, and `'z' - 1` equals `'y'`. Similarly, `'A' + 1` is `'B'`, and `'Z' - 1` is `'Y'`. With this as background, determine the character results of the following expressions (assume that all characters are stored using the ASCII code).

a. `'m' - 5`

b. `'m' + 5`

c. `'G' + 6`

d. `'G' - 6`

e. `'b' - 'a'`

f. `'g' - 'a' + 1`

g. `'G' - 'A' + 1`

Note: for the following exercise the reader should have an understanding of basic computer storage concepts. Specifically, if you are unfamiliar with the concept of a byte, refer to Section 1.7 before doing the next exercise.

20. Although the total number of bytes varies from computer to computer, memory sizes of 65,536 to more than several million bytes have been used. In computer language, the letter K is used to represent the number 1024, which is 2 raised to the 10th power, and M is used to represent the number 1,048,576, which is 2 raised to the 20th power. Thus, a memory size of 640 K bytes is really 640 times 1024, or 655,360 bytes, and a memory size of 4 M bytes is really 4 times 1,048,576, or 4,194,304 bytes. Using this information, calculate the actual number of bytes in:

a. a memory containing 512 K bytes
b. a memory containing 32 M bytes
c. a memory containing 64 M bytes
d. a memory containing 128 M bytes
e. a memory consisting of 64 M words, where each word consists of 2 bytes
f. a memory consisting of 64 M words, where each word consists of 4 bytes
g. a floppy diskette that can store 1.44 M bytes

2.4 Variables and Declaration Statements

All integer, floating point, and other values used in a computer program are stored and retrieved from the computer's memory unit. Conceptually, individual memory locations in the memory unit are arranged like the rooms in a large hotel. Like hotel rooms, each memory location has a unique address ("room number"). Before high-level languages such as C++ existed, memory locations were referenced by their addresses. For example, to store the integer values 45 and 12 in the memory locations 1652 and 2548 (see Figure 2.18), respectively, required instructions equivalent to

put a 45 in location 1652
put a 12 in location 2548

FIGURE 2.18

Enough storage for two integers

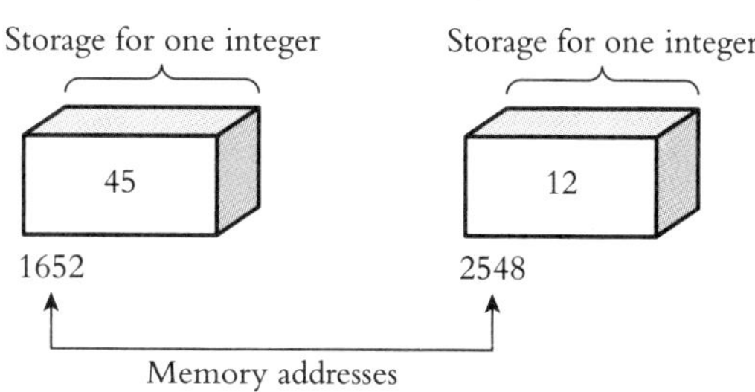

To add the two numbers just stored and save the result in another memory location, for example at location 3000, we would need a statement comparable to

Add the contents of location 1652
to the contents of location 2548
and store the result into location 3000.

Clearly this method of storage and retrieval is a cumbersome process. In high-level languages such as Visual C++, symbolic names are used in place of actual memory addresses. These symbolic names are called **variables.** A variable is simply a name, given by the programmer, that is used to refer to computer storage locations. The term *variable* is used because the value stored in the variable can change, or vary. For each name that the programmer uses, the computer keeps track of the actual memory address corresponding to that name. In our hotel room analogy, this is equivalent to putting a name on the door of a room and referring to the room by this name, such as the "blue" room, rather than using the actual room number.

In Visual C++ the selection of variable names is left to the programmer, as long as the following rules are observed:

1. The variable name must begin with a letter or underscore (_), and may contain only letters, underscores, or digits. It cannot contain any blanks, commas, or special symbols, such as ( ) & , $ # . ! \ ?

2. A variable name cannot be a keyword (see Table 2.1). Use capital letters to separate names consisting of multiple words.

3. The variable name cannot consist of more than 255 characters (this is compiler dependent).

These rules are similar to those used for selecting function names. As with function names, variable names should be mnemonics that give some indication of the variable's use. For example, a good name for a variable used to store a value that is the total of some other values would be `sum` or `total`. Variable names that give no indication of the value stored, such as `r2d2`, `linda`, `bill`, and `getum` should not be selected. As with function names, variable names can be typed in uppercase and lowercase letters.

Now assume that the first memory location illustrated in Figure 2.18, which has address 1652, is given the name `num1`. Also assume that memory location 2548 is given the variable name `num2`, and memory location 3000 is given the variable name `total`, as illustrated in Figure 2.19.

Using these variable names, the operation of storing 45 in location 1652, storing 12 in location 2548, and adding the contents of these two locations is accomplished by the Visual C++ statements

```
num1  = 45;
num2  = 12;
total  = num1 + num2;
```

FIGURE 2.19

Naming storage locations

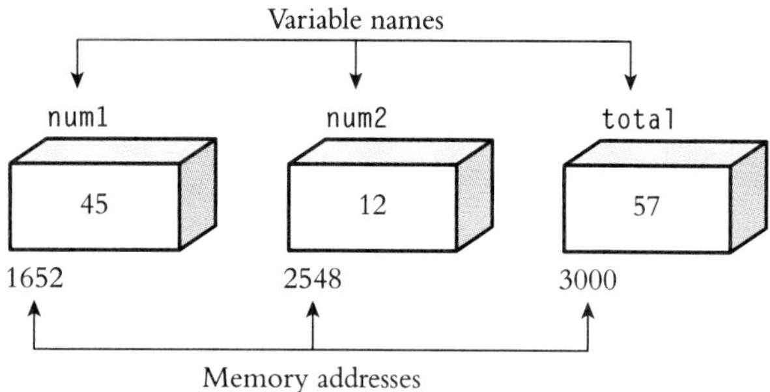

Each of these three statements is called an **assignment statement** because it tells the computer to assign (store) a value into a variable. Assignment statements always have an equal (=) sign and one variable name immediately to the left of this sign. The value on the right of the equal sign is determined first and this value is assigned to the variable on the left of the equal sign. The blank spaces in the assignment statements are inserted for readability. We have much more to say about assignment statements in Chapter 3, but for now we can use them to store values in variables.

A variable name is useful because it frees the programmer from concern over where data are physically stored inside the computer. We simply use the variable name and let the compiler worry about where in memory the data are actually stored. Before storing a value into a variable, however, Visual C++ requires that we clearly declare the type of data that is to be stored in it. We must tell the compiler, in advance, the names of the variables that will be used for characters, the names that will be used for integers, and the names that will be used to store the other Visual C++ data types.

Declaration Statements

Naming a variable and specifying the data type that can be stored in it are accomplished using **declaration statements.** A declaration statement has the general form:

data-type variable-name;

where data-type designates a valid Visual C++ data type and variable-name is a user-selected variable name. For example, variables used to hold integer values are declared using the keyword **int** to specify the data type and have the form:

`int` variable-name;

Thus, the declaration statement

```
int sum;
```

declares sum as the name of a variable capable of storing an integer value.

PROGRAMMER'S NOTES

Atomic Data

The variables we have declared have all been used to store atomic data values. An atomic data value is a value that is considered a complete entity by itself and is not decomposable into a smaller data type supported by the language. For example, although an integer can be decomposed into individual digits, Visual C++ does not have a numerical digit type. Rather, each integer is regarded as a complete value by itself and, as such, is considered atomic data. Similarly, since the integer data type supports only atomic data values, it is said to be an atomic data type. As you might expect, floating-point, character, and Boolean data types are atomic data types also.

In addition to the reserved word `int` used to specify an integer, the reserved word `long`, which is considered a data type qualifier, is used to specify a long integer.[15] For example, the statement

```
long int datenum;
```

declares `datenum` as a variable that will be used to store a long integer. When using the long qualifier the keyword `int` can omitted. Thus, the previous declaration can be written as:

```
long datenum;
```

Variables used to hold single precision floating point values are declared using the keyword `float`, whereas variables that will be used to hold double precision values are declared using the keyword `double`. For example, the statement

```
float firstnum;
```

declares `firstnum` as a variable that will be used to store a floating point number. Similarly, the statement

```
double secnum;
```

declares that the variable `secnum` will be used to store a double precision number.

Although declaration statements may be placed anywhere within a function, most declarations are typically grouped together and placed immediately after the function's opening brace. In all cases, however, a variable must be declared before it can be used, and like all Visual C++ statements, declaration statements must end with a semicolon. If the

---

15 Additionally, the reserved words `unsigned int` are used to specify an integer that can store only nonnegative numbers and the reserved words `short int` are used to specify a short integer.

declaration statements are placed after the opening function brace, a simple `main()` function containing declaration statements would have the general form

```
#include <iostream.h>

int main()
{
 declaration statements;

 other statements;

 return 0;
}
```

Program 2.6 illustrates this form in declaring and using four floating point variables, with the `cout` object used to display the contents of one of the variables.

PROGRAM 2.6

```
#include <iostream.h>

int main()
{
  float grade1;  // declare grade1 as a float variable
  float grade2;  // declare grade2 as a float variable
  float total;   // declare total as a float variable
  float average; // declare average as a float variable

  grade1 = 85.5;
  grade2 = 97.0;
  total = grade1 + grade2;
  average = total/2.0;  // divide the total by 2.0
  cout << "The average grade is " << average << endl;

  return 0;
}
```

The placement of the declaration statements in Program 2.6 is straightforward, although we will shortly see that the four individual declarations can be combined into a single declaration. When Program 2.6 is run, the following output is displayed:

```
The average grade is 91.25
```

Notice that when a variable name is sent to `cout`, the value stored in the variable is placed on the output stream and displayed. Also notice the use of the term `endl` as the last item to be inserted into the output stream. endl is an example of a Visual C++ **manipulator,** which is an item used to manipulate how the output stream of characters is displayed. In particular, the endl manipulator first causes a newline character ('\n') to be added to the output stream and then forces an immediate flushing of the output stream. When used with the cout object this has the effect of ensuring an immediate display of the stream on the terminal. (Section 3.2 contains a list of the more commonly used manipulators.) On most systems, the endl manipulator, which is never enclosed in quotes, and the \n escape sequence, which must always be enclosed in quotes, are processed the same and produce the same effect. The one exception is on those systems where the output is accumulated internally until there are sufficient characters to make it advantageous to display them all, in one burst, on the screen. In such systems, which are referred to as "buffered," the endl manipulator forces all accumulated output to be displayed immediately, without waiting for any additional characters to fill the buffer area before being printed. As a practical matter, you would not notice a difference in the final display. Thus, as a general rule, you should use the \n escape sequence whenever it can be included within an existing string, and use the endl manipulator whenever a \n would appear by itself or to formally signify the end of a specific group of output display.

Just as integer and real (floating point, double precision, and long double) variables must be declared before they can be used, a variable used to store a single character must also be declared. Character variables are declared using the reserved word char. For example, the declaration

```
char ch;
```

declares ch to be a character variable. Program 2.7 illustrates this declaration and the use of cout to display the value stored in a character variable.

PROGRAM 2.7

```
#include <iostream.h>

int main()
{
  char ch;      // this declares a character variable
  ch = 'a';     // store the letter a into ch
  cout << "The character stored in ch is " << ch << endl;
  ch = 'm';     // now store the letter m into ch
  cout << "The character now stored in ch is "<< ch << endl;

  return 0;
}
```

When Program 2.7 is run, the output shown in Figure 2.20 is produced.

FIGURE 2.20

Program 2.7's output

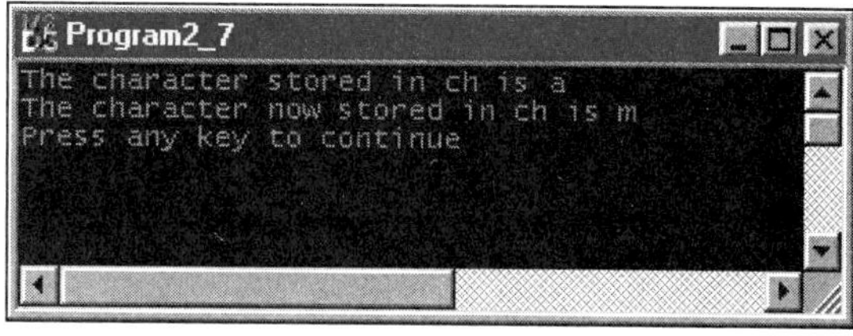

Notice in Program 2.7 that the first letter stored in the variable `ch` is `a` and the second letter stored is `m`. Because a variable can be used to store only one value at a time, the assignment of `m` to the variable automatically causes `a` to be overwritten.

Multiple Declarations

Variables having the same data type can always be grouped together and declared using a single declaration statement. The common form of such a declaration is:

data-type variable list;

For example, the four separate declarations used in Program 2.6,

```
float grade1;
float grade2;
float total;
float average;
```

can be replaced by the single declaration statement

```
float grade1, grade2, total, average;
```

Similarly, the two character declarations,

```
char ch;
char key;
```

can be replaced with the single declaration statement

```
char ch, key;
```

Note that declaring multiple variables in a single declaration requires that the data type of the variables be given only once, that all the variable names be separated by commas, and that only one semicolon be used to terminate the declaration. The space after each comma is inserted for readability and is not required.

Declaration statements can also be used to store an initial value into declared variables. For example, the declaration statement

```
int num1 = 15;
```

both declares the variable `num1` as an integer variable and sets the value of `15` into the variable. When a declaration statement is used to store a value into a variable, the variable is said to be **initialized.** Thus, in this example it is correct to say that the variable `num1` has been initialized to `15`. Similarly, the declaration statements

```
float grade1 = 87.0;
float grade2 = 93.5;
float total;
```

declare three floating point variables and initialize two of them. When initializations are used, good programming practice dictates that each initialized variable be declared on a line by itself. Constants, expressions using only constants (such as `87.0 + 12 - 2`), and expressions using constants and previously initialized variables can all be used as initializers within a function. For example, Program 2.6 with declaration initialization becomes Program 2.6a.

PROGRAM 2.6A

```
#include <iostream.h>

int main()
{
  float grade1 = 85.5;
  float grade2 = 97.0;
  float total, average;

  total = grade1 + grade2;
  average = total/2.0;  // divide the total by 2.0
  cout << "The average grade is " << average << endl;

  return 0;
}
```

Notice the blank line after the last declaration statement. Inserting a blank line after the variable declarations placed at the top of a function body is good programming practice. It improves a program's appearance as well as its readability.

An interesting feature of Visual C++ is that variable declarations may be freely intermixed and even contained with other statements; the only requirement is that a variable must be declared prior to its use. For example, the variable `total` in Program 2.6a could be declared when it is first used using the statement `float total = grade1 + grade2`. In very restricted situations (such as debugging, as described in Section 4.7, or in a `for` loop, described in Section 5.4), declaring a variable at its point of use can be helpful. In general, it is preferable not to disperse declarations but rather to group them, in as concise and clear a manner as possible, at the top of each function.

Memory Allocation

The declaration statements we have introduced have performed both software and hardware tasks. From a software perspective, declaration statements always provide a list of all variables and their data types. In this software role, variable declarations also help to control an otherwise common and troublesome error caused by the misspelling of a variable's name within a program. For example, assume that a variable named `distance` is declared and initialized using the statement

```
int distance = 26;
```

Now assume that this variable is inadvertently misspelled in the statement

```
mpg = distnce / gallons;
```

In languages that do not require variable declarations, the program would treat `distnce` as a new variable and either assign an initial value of zero to the variable or use whatever value happened to be in the variable's storage area. In either case a value would be calculated and assigned to `mpg`, and finding the error or even knowing that an error occurred could be extremely troublesome. Such errors are impossible in Visual C++ because the compiler will flag `distnce` as an undeclared variable. The compiler cannot, of course, detect when one declared variable is typed in place of another declared variable.

In addition to their software role, declaration statements can also perform a distinct hardware task. Because each data type has its own storage requirements, the computer can allocate sufficient storage for a variable only after knowing the variable's data type. Because variable declarations provide this information, they can be used to force the compiler to reserve sufficient physical memory storage for each variable. Declaration statements used for this hardware purpose are also called **definition statements,** because they define or tell the compiler how much memory is needed for data storage.

All the declaration statements we have encountered so far have also been definition statements. Later, we will see cases of declaration statements that do not cause any new storage to be allocated and are used simply to declare or alert the program to the data types of variables that are created elsewhere in the program.

Figure 2.21 illustrates the series of operations set in motion by declaration statements that also perform a definition role. The figure shows that definition statements (or, if you prefer, declaration statements that also cause memory to be allocated) "tag" the first byte of each set of reserved bytes with a name. This name is, of course, the variable's name and is used by the computer to correctly locate the starting point of each variable's reserved memory area.

FIGURE 2.21

(a) **Defining the integer variable named** `total`

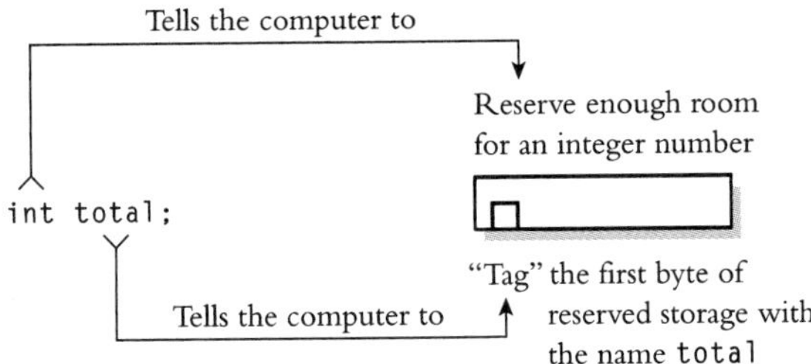

(b) **Defining the floating point variable named** `firstnum`

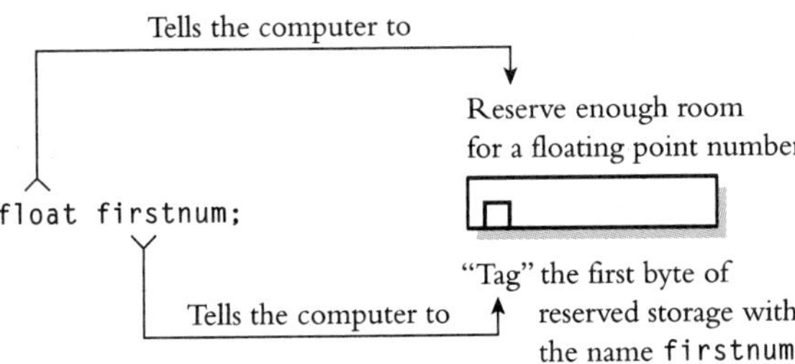

(c) **Defining the double precision variable named** `secnum`

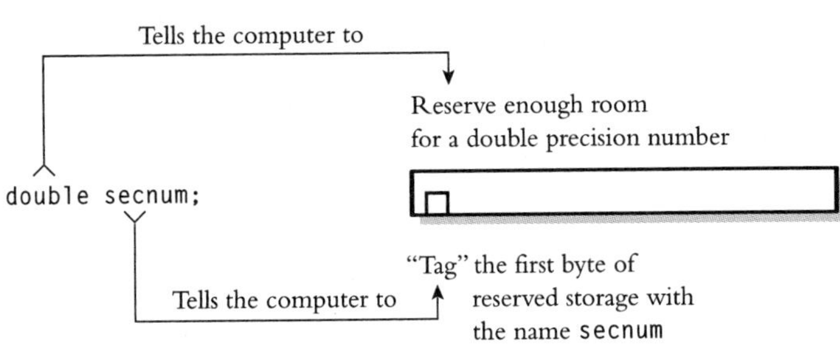

(d) **Defining the character variable named** `key`

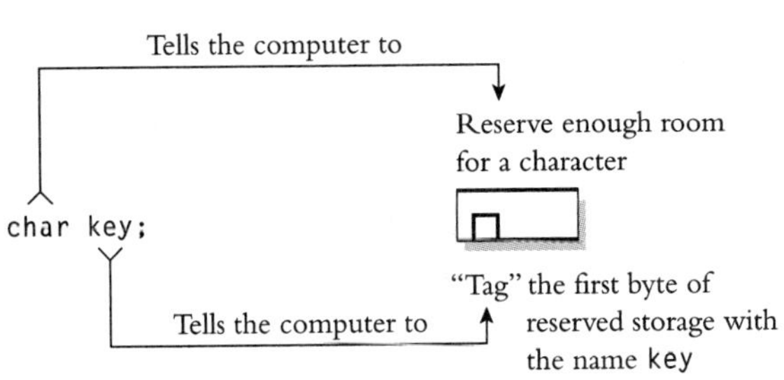

Within a program, after a variable has been declared, it is typically used by a programmer to refer to the contents of the variable (that is, the variable's value). Where in memory this value is stored is generally of little concern to the programmer. The compiler, however, must be concerned with where each value is stored and with correctly locating each variable. In this task the computer uses the variable name to locate the first byte of storage previously allocated to the variable. Knowing the variable's data type then allows the compiler to store or retrieve the correct number of bytes.

FIGURE 2.22

A typical variable

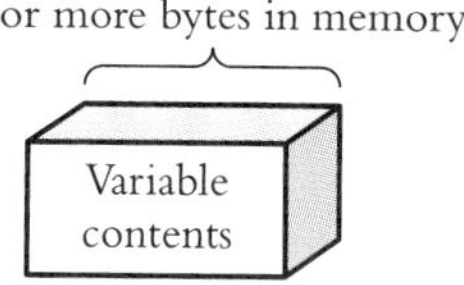

Displaying a Variable's Address[16]

Every variable has three major items associated with it: its data type, the actual value stored in the variable, and the address of the variable. The value stored in the variable is referred to as the variable's contents, and the address of the first memory location used for the variable constitutes its address. How many locations are actually used for the variable, as we have just seen, depends on the variable's data type. The relationships among these three items (type, contents, location) is illustrated in Figure 2.22.

Programmers are usually concerned only with the value assigned to a variable (its contents) and give little attention to where the value is stored (its address). For example, consider Program 2.8.

PROGRAM 2.8

```
#include <iostream.h>

int main()
{
  int num;

  num = 22;
  cout << "The value stored in num is " << num << endl;

  return 0;
}
```

The output displayed when Program 2.8 is run is:

```
The value stored in num is 22
```

Program 2.8 merely prints the value `22`, which is the contents of the variable `num`. We can go further, however, and ask, "Where is the number 22 actually stored?" Although the answer is "in `num`," this is only half of the answer. The variable name `num` is simply a convenient symbol for real, physical locations in memory, as illustrated in Figure 2.23.

---

16 This section may be omitted on first reading without loss of subject continuity.

FIGURE 2.23

Somewhere in memory

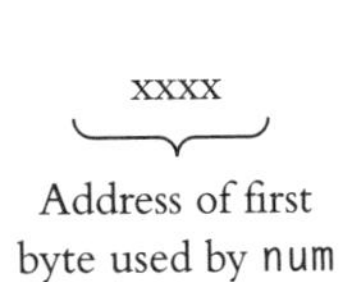

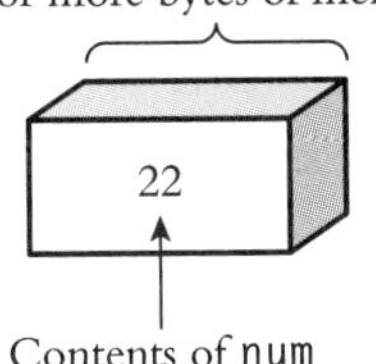

To determine the address of `num`, we can use Visual C++'s address operator, `&`, which means "the address of." Except when used in a declaration statement, the address operator placed in front of a variable's name refers to the address of the variable.[17] For example, `&num` means *the address of* `num`, `&total` means *the address of* `total`, and `&price` means *the address of* `price`. Program 2.9 uses the address operator to display the address of the variable `num`.

PROGRAM 2.9

```
#include <iostream.h>

int main()
{
  int num;

  num = 22;
  cout << "The value stored in num is " << num << endl;
  cout << "The address of num = " << &num << endl;

  return 0;
}
```

The output produced by Program 2.9 is shown in Figure 2.24.

FIGURE 2.24

Program 2.9's output

17 When used in declaring reference variables and arguments, as presented in Chapter 6, the ampersand refers to the data type *preceding* it. Thus, the declaration `float &num` is read as "`num` is the address of a `float`", or more commonly as "`num` is a reference to a `float`".

FIGURE 2.25

A more complete picture of the variable `num`

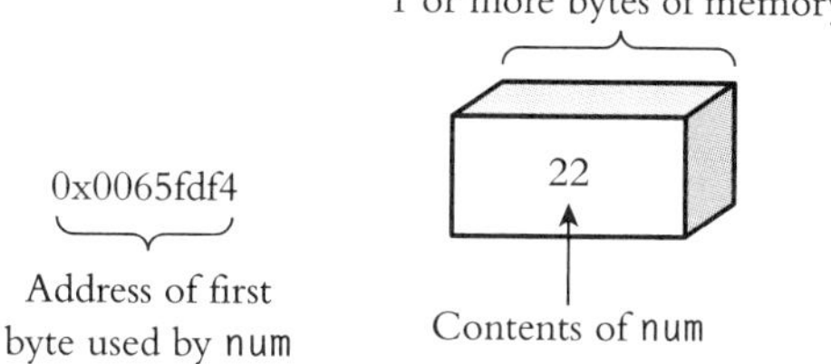

Figure 2.25 illustrates the additional address information provided by the output of Program 2.9.

Clearly, the address output by Program 2.9 depends on the computer used to run the program. Every time Program 2.9 is executed, however, it displays the address of the first memory location used to store the variable `num`. As illustrated by the output of Program 2.9, the display of addresses is in hexadecimal notation. This display has no effect on how addresses are used internal to the program; it merely provides us with a means of displaying addresses that is helpful in understanding them. As we see in Chapters 6 and 13, using addresses as opposed to only displaying them is an extremely important and powerful programming tool.

EXERCISES 2.4

1. State whether the following variable names are valid or invalid. If they are invalid, state the reason.

```
productA    c1234     abcd       _c3      12345
newamp      watts     $total     new$al   a1b2c3d4
9ab6        sum.of    average    volts1   finvolt
```

2. State whether the following variable names are valid or invalid. If they are invalid, state the reason. Also indicate which of the valid variable names should not be used because they convey no information about the variable.

```
current    a243    r2d2     first_num    cc_al
harry      sue     c3p0     total        sum
maximum    okay    a        awesome      goforit
3sum       for     tot.al   c$five       netpower
```

3. a. Write a declaration statement to declare that the variable `count` will be used to store an integer.

b. Write a declaration statement to declare that the variable `volt` will be used to store a floating point number.

c. Write a declaration statement to declare that the variable `power` will be used to store a double precision number.

d. Write a declaration statement to declare that the variable `keychar` will be used to store a character.

4. Write declaration statements for the following variables.
   a. `num1`, `num2`, and `num3` used to store integer numbers
   b. `grade1`, `grade2`, `grade3`, and `grade4` used to store floating point numbers
   c. `temp1`, `temp2`, and `temp3` used to store double precision numbers
   d. `ch`, `let1`, `let2`, `let3`, and `let4` used to store character types

5. Write declaration statements for the following variables.
   a. `firstnum` and `secnum` used to store integers
   b. `speed`, `acceleration`, and `distance` used to store floating point numbers
   c. `maturity` used to store a double precision number

6. Rewrite each of these declaration statements as three individual declarations.
   a. `int month, day = 30, year;`
   b. `double hours, rate, otime = 15.62;`
   c. `float price, amount, taxes;`
   d. `char inKey, ch, choice = 'f';`

7. a. Determine what each statement causes to happen in the following program.

```
#include <iostream.h>

int main()
{
  int num1, num2, total;
  num1 = 25;
  num2 = 30;
  total = num1 + num2;
  cout << "The total of" << num1 << " and "
       << num2 << " is " << total << endl;

 return 0;
}
```

   b. What is the output that will be printed when the program listed in Exercise 7a is run?

8. Every variable has at least two items associated with it. What are these two items?

Note for Exercises 9 through 11: Assume that a character requires one byte of storage, an integer two bytes, a floating point number four bytes, a double precision number eight bytes, and that variables are assigned storage in the order they are declared. (Review Section 1.7 if you are unfamiliar with the concept of a byte.)

FIGURE 2.26

Memory bytes for Exercises 9, 10, and 11

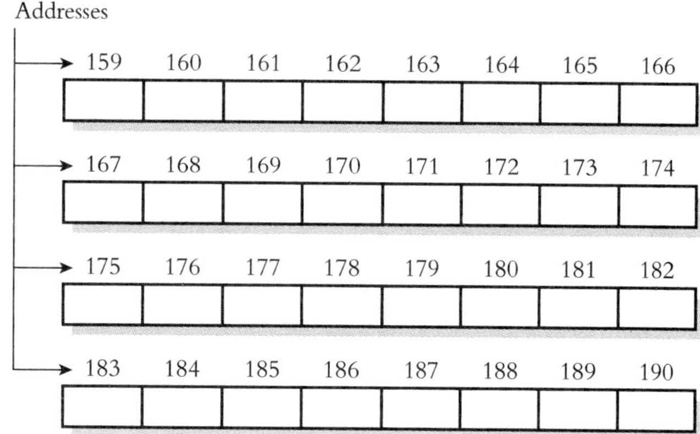

9. a. Using Figure 2.26 and assuming that the variable name `rate` is assigned to the byte having memory address 159, determine the addresses corresponding to each variable declared in the following statements. Also fill in the appropriate bytes with the initialization data included in the declaration statements (use letters for the characters, not the computer codes that would actually be stored).

```
float rate;
char ch1 = 'w', ch2 = 'o', ch3 = 'w', ch4 = '!';
double taxes;
int num, count = 0;
```

b. Repeat Exercise 9a, but substitute the actual byte patterns that a computer using the ASCII code would use to store the characters in the variables `ch1`, `ch2`, `ch3`, and `ch4`. (*Hint:* Use Table 2.3.)

10. a. Using Figure 2.26 and assuming that the variable named `cn1` is assigned to the byte at memory address 159, determine the addresses corresponding to each variable declared in the following statements. Also fill in the appropriate bytes with the initialization data included in the declaration statements (use letters for the characters and not the computer codes that would actually be stored).

```
char cn1 = 'a', cn2 = ' ', cn3 = 'b', cn4 = 'u', cn5 = 'n';
char cn6 = 'c', cn7 = 'h', key = '\\', sch = '\'', inc = 'o';
char inc1 = 'f';
```

b. Repeat Exercise 10a, but substitute the actual byte patterns that a computer using the ASCII code would use to store the characters in each of the declared variables. (*Hint:* Use Table 2.3.)

11. Using Figure 2.26 and assuming that the variable name `miles` is assigned to the byte at memory address 159, determine the addresses corresponding to each variable declared in the following statements.

```
float miles;
int count, num;
double dist, temp;
```

2.5 Qualifiers and Determining Storage Allocation

Integer numbers are generally used in programs as counters to keep track of the number of times that something has occurred. For most applications, the counts needed are less than 32,767, which is the maximum signed integer value that can be stored in two bytes. Most compilers allocate at least two bytes for integers, so there is usually no problem.

Cases do arise, however, in which larger integer numbers are needed. In financial applications, for example, dates such as 7/12/1989 can be converted to the number of days from the turn of the last century (1/1/1900). This conversion makes it possible to store and sort dates using a single number for each date. Unfortunately, for dates after 1987, the number of days from the turn of the century is larger than the maximum value of 32,767 allowed when only two bytes are allocated for each integer variable. For financial programs dealing with mortgages and bonds maturing after 1987 that are run on computers allocating only two bytes per integer, the limitation on the maximum integer value must be overcome.

To accommodate real application requirements such as this, Visual C++ provides long integer, short integer, and unsigned integer data types. These three additional integer data types are obtained by adding the qualifiers `long`, `short`, or `unsigned`, respectively, to the normal integer declaration statements. For example, the declaration statement

```
long int days;
```

declares the variable `days` to be a long integer. The word `int` in a long integer declaration statement is optional, so the previous declaration statement can also be written as `long days;`. The amount of storage allocated for a long integer depends on the compiler being used. Although you would expect that a long integer variable would be allocated more space than a standard integer, this may not be the case. About all that can be said is that long integers will provide no less space than regular integers. The actual amount of storage allocated by your computer should be checked using the `sizeof` operator described at the end of this section.

Once a variable is declared as a long integer, integer values may be assigned as usual for standard integers, or an optional letter `L` (either uppercase or lowercase, with no space between the number and letter) may be appended to the integer. For example, the declaration statement

```
long days = 38276L;
```

declares days to be of type long integer and assigns the long integer constant 38276 to the variable `days`.

In addition to the long qualifier, Visual C++ also provides for a short qualifier. Although you would expect a short integer to conserve computer storage by reserving fewer bytes than used for an integer, this is not always the case. Some compilers use the same amount of storage for both integers and short integers. Again, the amount of memory space allocated for a short integer data type depends on your compiler, and can be checked using the `sizeof` operator (described at the end of this section). As with long integers, short integers may be declared using the terms `short` or `short int` in a declaration statement. Once a variable is declared as a short integer, values are assigned as normally done with integers.

The final integer data type is the unsigned integer. This data type is obtained by prefixing the reserved word `int` with the qualifier `unsigned`. For example, the declaration statement

```
unsigned int days;
```

declares the variable `days` to be of type unsigned. Unsigned integers are generally used only for positive integers and effectively double the positive value that can be stored without increasing the number of bytes allocated to an integer. This is accomplished by treating all unsigned integers as positive numbers, as illustrated in Figure 2.27.

Figure 2.28 illustrates all of Visual C++'s fundamental data types and their relationship to each other.

FIGURE 2.27

Unsigned integers storage using two bytes

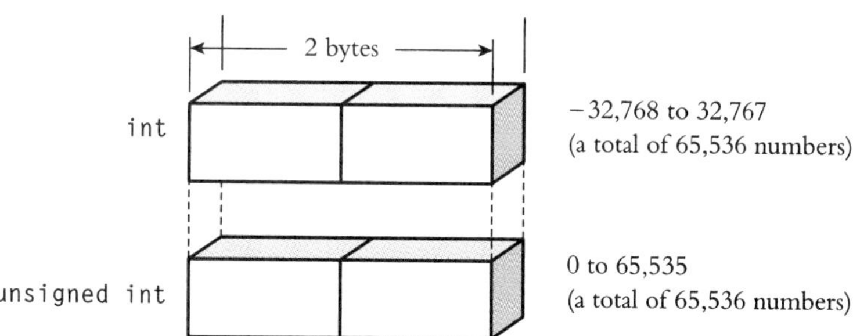

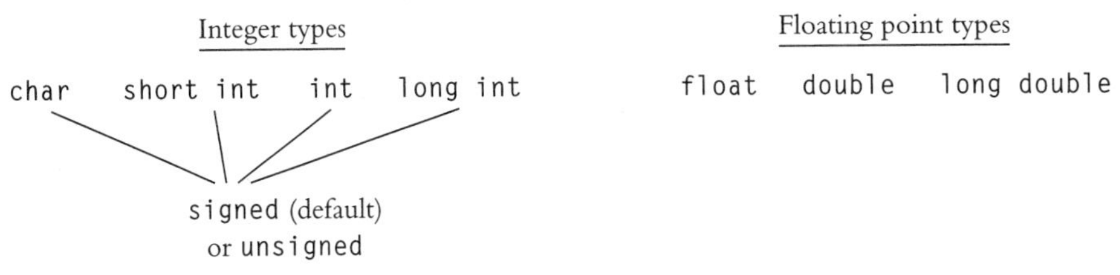

FIGURE 2.28

Visual C++'s fundamental numerical data types

Data Type Conversions

The general rules for converting integer and floating point operands in mixed-mode arithmetic expressions were presented in the Section 2.4. A more complete set of conversion rules for arithmetic operators, which includes character, short, and long integer operands, is provided in Table 2.8, in which the rules are applied in order.

TABLE 2.8 Conversion rules for arithmetic operators

1. If both operands are either character or integer operands:
   a. When both operands are character, short, or integer data types the result of the expression is an integer value.
   b. When one of operands is a long integer the result is a long integer, unless one of the operands is an unsigned integer. In this latter case the other operand is converted to an unsigned integer value and the resulting value of the expression is an unsigned value.
2. If any one operand is a floating point value:
   a. When one or both operands are floats the result of the operation is a floating point value.
   b. When one or both operands are doubles the result of the operation is a double value.
   c. When one or both operands are long doubles the result is a long double value.

Note that these rules apply to each individual arithmetic operation in their correct order of evaluation. For example, in the expression `14.78F - 4 * 3L`, the multiplication, which has a higher precedence than the subtraction, is performed first. For this multiplication of two integer operands, the integer `4` is converted to a long integer value, and the result of the expression is `12L` (rule 1b). The result of the next operation, `14.78F - 12L`, is the single precision (float) value `2.78` (rule 2a).

Determining Storage Size[18]

Visual C++ provides an operator for determining the amount of storage your compiler allocates for each data type. This operator, called the `sizeof()` operator, returns the number of bytes of the variable or data type included in the parentheses. Unlike a function, which itself is made of Visual C++ statements, the `sizeof()` operator is an integral part of the Visual C++ language itself. Examples using the `sizeof` operator are:

```
sizeof(num1)    sizeof(int)    sizeof(float)
```

If the item in parentheses is a variable, as in the example `sizeof(num1)`, `sizeof()` returns the number of bytes of storage that the compiler reserved for the variable. If the item in parentheses is a data type, such as `int` or `char`, `sizeof` will return the number of bytes of storage that the compiler uses for the given data type. Using either approach, we can use `sizeof` to determine the amount of storage used by different data types. Consider Program 2.10.

PROGRAM 2.10

```
#include <iostream.h>

int main()
{
  char ch;
  int num1;
  cout << "Bytes of storage used by a character: "
       << sizeof(ch) << endl;
  cout << "Bytes of storage used by an integer: "
       << sizeof(num1) << endl;

  return 0;
}
```

Program 2.10 declares that the variable `ch` is used to store a character and that the variable `num1` is used to store an integer. From our discussion in the last section, we know that each of these declaration statements is also a definition statement. As such, the first declaration statement instructs the compiler to reserve enough storage for a character, and

18 This section assumes a basic understanding of computer storage concepts and terms. If you are unfamiliar with these concepts, please review Section 1.7.

the second declaration statement instructs the compiler to reserve enough storage for an integer. The `sizeof()` operator is then used to tell us how much room the computer really set aside for these two variables. The `sizeof()` operator itself is used as an argument to the `cout` object. When Program 2.10 is run on an IBM personal computer, the following output is obtained:

```
Bytes of storage used by a character: 1
Bytes of storage used by an integer: 2
```

EXERCISES 2.5

1. **a.** Run Program 2.10 to determine how many bytes your computer uses to store character and integer data types.

   b. Expand Program 2.10 to determine how many bytes your computer uses for short integers, long integers, and unsigned integers.

2. After running the program written for Exercise 1b, use Table 2.2 to determine the maximum and minimum numbers that can be stored in integer, short integer, and long integer variables for your computer.

3. Program 2.10 did not actually store any values into the variables `ch` and `num1`. Why was this not necessary?

4. **a.** Expand Program 2.10 to determine how many bytes your computer uses to store floating point and double precision numbers.

   b. Although there is no long float data class, double precision numbers are sometimes considered as the equivalent long form for floating point numbers. Why is this so? Does the output of the program written for Exercise 4a support this statement?

2.6 Common Programming Errors

Part of learning any programming language is making the elementary mistakes commonly encountered as you begin to use the language. These mistakes tend to be quite frustrating; each language seems to have its own set of common programming errors waiting for the unwary. The more common errors made when initially programming in Visual C++ are:

1. Omitting the parentheses after main.

2. Omitting or incorrectly typing the opening brace { that signifies the start of a function body.

3. Omitting or incorrectly typing the closing brace } that signifies the end of a function.

4. Misspelling the name of an object or function; for example, typing `cot` instead of `cout`.

5. Forgetting to close a string sent to `cout` with a double quote symbol.

6. Forgetting to separate individual data streams passed to `cout` with an insertion ("put-to") symbol, <<.

7. Omitting the semicolon at the end of each Visual C++ statement.

8. Adding a semicolon at the end of the `#include` preprocessor command.

9. Forgetting the `\n` to indicate a new line.

10. Incorrectly typing the letter `O` for the number zero (`0`), or vice versa. Incorrectly typing the letter `l`, for the number `1`, or vice versa.

11. Forgetting to declare all the variables used in a program. This error is detected by the compiler and an error message is generated for all undeclared variables.

12. Misspelling a variable's name or forgetting about the precise case sensitivity of Visual C++.

13. Storing an inappropriate data type in a declared variable. This error is detected by the compiler and the assigned value is converted to the data type of the variable to which it is assigned.

14. Using a variable in an expression before a value has been assigned to the variable. Here, whatever value happens to be in the variable will be used when the expression is evaluated, and the result will be meaningless.

15. Dividing integer values incorrectly. This error is usually disguised within a larger expression and can be a very troublesome error to detect. For example, the expression

```
3.425 + 2/3 + 7.9
```

yields the same result as the expression

```
3.425 + 7.9
```

because the integer division of 2/3 is 0.

16. Mixing data types in the same expression without clearly understanding the effect produced. Because Visual C++ allows expressions with "mixed" data types, it is important to understand the order of evaluation and the data type of all intermediate calculations. As a general rule, it is better never to mix data types in an expression unless a specific effect is desired.

Errors 3, 5, 7, 8, and 9 in this list are initially the most common, and even experienced programmers occasionally make error 10. It is worthwhile for you to write a program and specifically introduce each of these errors, one at a time, to see what error messages are produced by your compiler. Then, when these error messages appear due to inadvertent errors, you will have had experience in understanding the messages and correcting the errors.

On a more fundamental level, a major programming error made by all beginning programmers is the rush to code and run a program before the programmer fully understands what is required and the algorithms and procedures that will be used to produce the desired result. A symptom of this haste to get a program entered into the computer is the lack of either an outline of the proposed program or a written program itself. Many problems can be caught just by checking a copy of the program, either handwritten or listed from the computer, before it is ever compiled.

2.7 Chapter Summary

1. A Visual C++ console application consists of one or more modules called functions. One of these functions must be called `main()`. The `main()` function identifies the starting point of a Visual C++ console application.

2. The simplest Visual C++ console application consists of the single function `main()`.

3. Following the function name, the body of a function has the general form:

```
{
   All Visual C++ statements in here;
}
```

4. All Visual C++ statements must be terminated by a semicolon.

5. Three types of data were introduced in this chapter: integer, floating point, and character data. Each of these types of data is typically stored in a computer using different amounts of memory. Visual C++ recognizes each of these data types in addition to other types yet to be presented.

6. The `cout` object can be used to display all of Visual C++'s data types.

7. When the `cout` object is used within a program, the preprocessor command `#include <iostream.h>` must be placed at the top of the program. Preprocessor commands do not end with a semicolon.

8. Every variable in a Visual C++ console application must be declared as to the type of value it can store. Declarations within a function may be placed anywhere within a function, although a variable can be used only after it is declared. Variables may also be initialized when they are declared. Additionally, variables of the same type may be de-

clared using a single declaration statement. Variable declaration statements have the general form:

data-type variable-name(s);

9. A simple Visual C++ console application containing declaration statements has the typical form:

```
#include <iostream.h>

int main()
{
  declaration statements;

  other statements;

  return 0;
}
```

Although declaration statements may be placed anywhere within the function's body, a variable may be used only after it is declared.

10. Declaration statements always play a software role of informing the compiler of a function's valid variable names. When a variable declaration also causes the computer to set aside memory locations for the variable, the declaration statement is also called a definition statement. (All the declarations we have used in this chapter have also been definition statements.)

11. The `sizeof()` operator can be used to determine the amount of storage reserved for variables.

12. An expression is any combination of constants and/or variables that can be evaluated to yield a value.

13. Expressions are evaluated according to the precedence and associativity of the operators used in the expression.

2.8 Knowing About: The Help Facility

No matter how experienced you become using Visual C++, there will be times when you'll need some help in either performing a particular task, looking up the exact syntax of a statement, or finding the parameters required by a built-in function. For these tasks, as well as locating numerous technical articles, you can use Visual C++'s online Help facility. With version 6.0 the online Help consists of the complete MSDN (Microsoft Developer

FIGURE 2.29

Help menu options

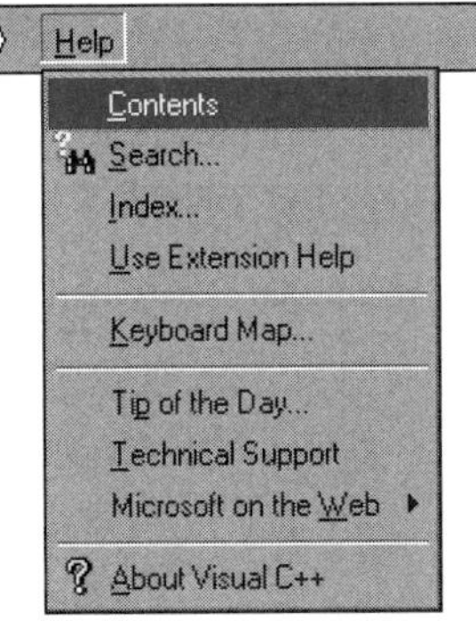

Network) Library, which is supplied on two CD ROMs. Prior to version 6.0, the MSDN Library came only with a paid subscription to the Microsoft Developer Network, which is a service targeted at sophisticated applications developers. The complete MSDN Library now doubles as the online Help facility. It is an extremely powerful programming aid that contains a treasure trove of documentation, reference material, technical articles, and sample code.

To access the online Help, select either the Contents, Search, or Index options from the Help menu, as shown in Figure 2.29. When any of these options is selected, one of the screens shown as Figure 2.30, 2.31, or 2.32 will be displayed. If the screen shown in Figure 2.30 is displayed, you do not have access to the online help and must install the MSDN Library before proceeding. The screen shown in Figure 2.31 simply requires you to locate and insert the second MSDN CD ROM disk into the CD ROM drive, at which point the main online Help window shown in Figure 2.32 will appear. Notice that this main online Help window is divided into two panes.

The left pane, which is referred to as the Navigation pane, contains the four tabs labeled Contents, Index, Search, and Favorites. Each of these tabs provides a different way of accessing information from the online Help, as summarized in Table 2.9. The right section, which is the Documentation pane, displays all information retrieved from the MSDN Library.

FIGURE 2.30

Online Help is not installed

FIGURE 2.31

Second CD ROM is required

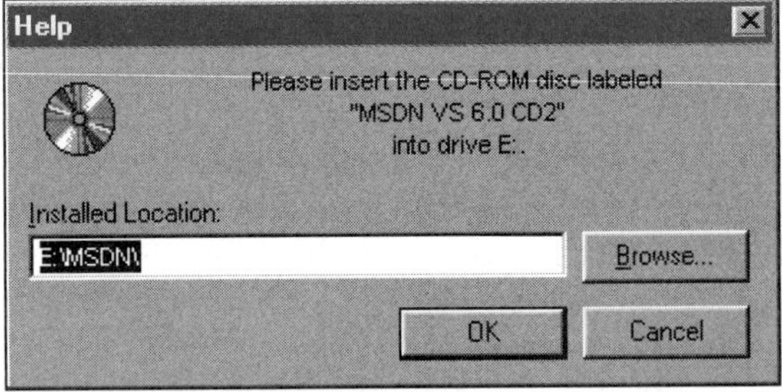

FIGURE 2.32

Main online Help window

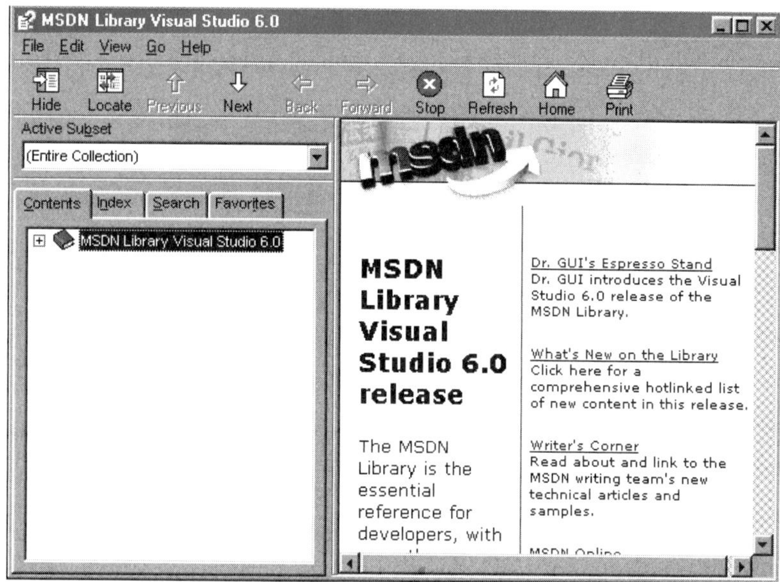

As shown in Figure 2.32, the Contents tab, because it is on top of the other tabs, is the currently active tab. This arrangement occurred because the Contents option was selected from the Help menu (see Figure 2.29). If either the Index or Search options had been selected, the same main online Help window would appear, except that the respective Index or Search tab would be active. No matter which tab is currently active, however, you can switch from one tab to another by clicking on the desired tab.

TABLE 2.9 The online Help tabs

Tab	Description
Contents	Displays a table of contents for the online documentation. This table can be expanded to display individual topic titles; double-clicking a title displays the associated documentation in the Documentation pane.
Index	Provides both a general index of topics and a Text box for user entry of a specific topic. Entry of a topic causes focus to shift to the closest matching topic within the general index. Double clicking on an index topic displays the associated documentation in the Documentation pane.
Search	Provides a means of entering a search word or phrase. All topics matching the entered word(s) are displayed in a List box. Clicking on a topic displays the corresponding documentation in the Documentation pane.
Favorites	Provides a means of storing the name and location of a Documentation topic that can then be directly accessed by clicking on the saved topic name.

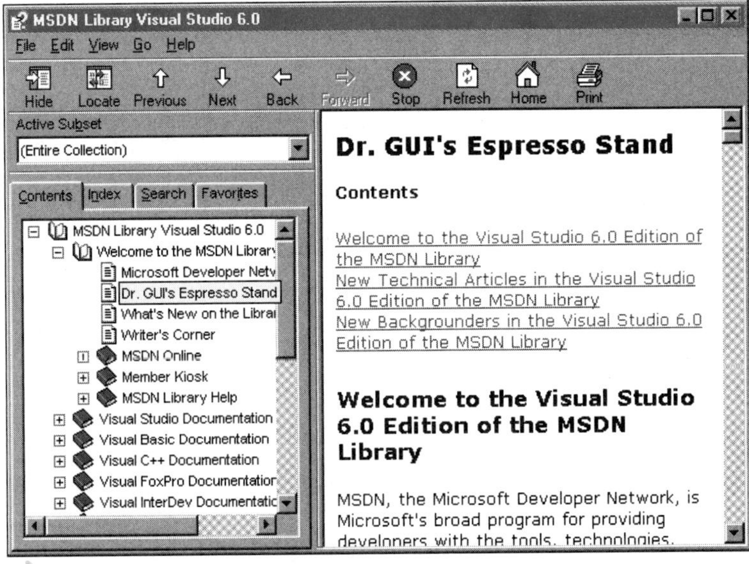

FIGURE 2.33

Using the Contents tab

The Contents Tab

The Contents tab provides a means of browsing through all of the available reference materials and technical articles contained within the MSDN Library. Essentially, this tab provides a table of contents for all of the material in the library, and displays the topics using the using the same folder tree structure found in Windows 95 and 98. For example, if you expand the single topic shown in Figure 2.32 by clicking on the plus sign box [+], and then expand the Visual C++ Documentation topic, you will see the tree shown in Figure 2.33. The information provided in the documentation pane was displayed by double-clicking on the page highlighted in the Navigation pane. A hard copy of the displayed page is easily obtained by either selecting the Print option from the File menu or right-clicking the mouse in the Documentation pane and selecting the Print option.

A very useful feature of the online documentation are the hyperlinks embedded within the displayed documentation text. By positioning the mouse on underlined text and clicking, the referenced text will be displayed. This permits you to rapidly jump from topic to topic, all while staying within the Documentation pane.

The Index Tab

For actual online help, as opposed to locating reference material or browsing for technical articles, the most useful of the tabs shown in Figure 2.32 is the Index tab. When you select this tab, the main online window illustrated in Figure 2.34 is displayed. As shown in Figure 2.34, the Index tab is on top of the other tabs, which makes it the active tab. This tab operates much like an index in a book, with one major improvement. In a book, after

FIGURE 2.34

Activated Index tab

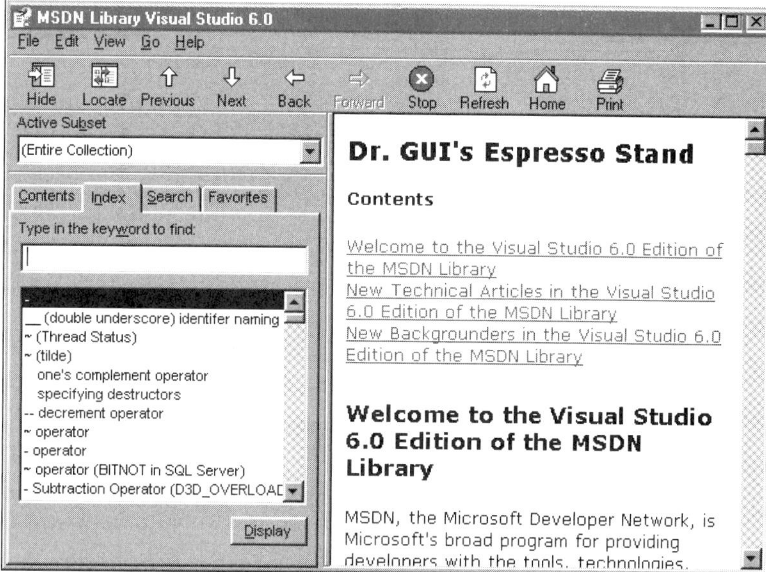

looking up the desired topic, you must manually turn to the referenced page or pages. In the online Help facility this look up and display is automatic, once you indicate the desired topic. Selection of the topic is accomplished by double-clicking on an item within the list of topics contained in the List box (this is the box located at the bottom of the tab). To locate a topic, you can either type the topic's name within the tab's keyword Text box, which causes the item to be highlighted in the List box, or use the scroll bar at the right of the List box and manually move to the desired item.

For example, in Figure 2.35, the topic `iostream` has been typed in the keyword Text box, and the List box entry for this topic has been selected. As each letter is typed in the

FIGURE 2.35

Index tab with a typed entry

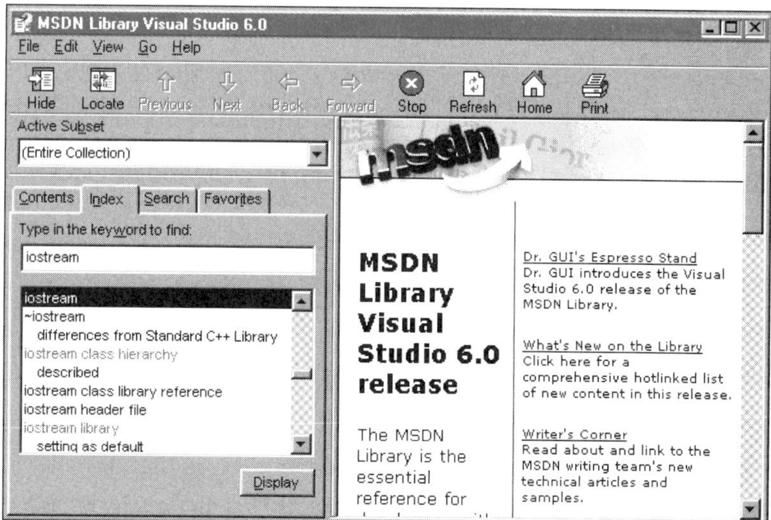

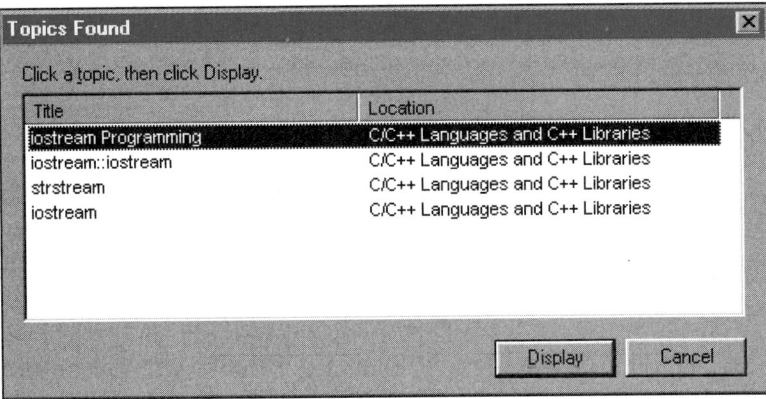

FIGURE 2.36

Multiple topics dialog box

Text box, the selected entry in the List box changes to match the input letters as closely as possible. In this case, because there are multiple library entries for the highlighted topic, if you double-click on the highlighted topic or press the Display Command button, the Multiple Topics dialog box shown in Figure 2.36 appears. Either by highlighting a desired topic in the Multiple Topics dialog box and clicking the Display button, or by double-clicking on the desired item directly in the List box, the documentation for the selected topic is displayed in the Documentation area. Figure 2.37 illustrates the documentation for the item highlighted in Figure 2.36.

A handy feature of the online Help facility is that once you have selected and displayed the desired topic you can easily generate a hard copy of the information. This is accomplished by either selecting the Print item from the File menu button at the top of the MSDN Library window, or by using the context menu provided by clicking the right-mouse button from within the displayed information.

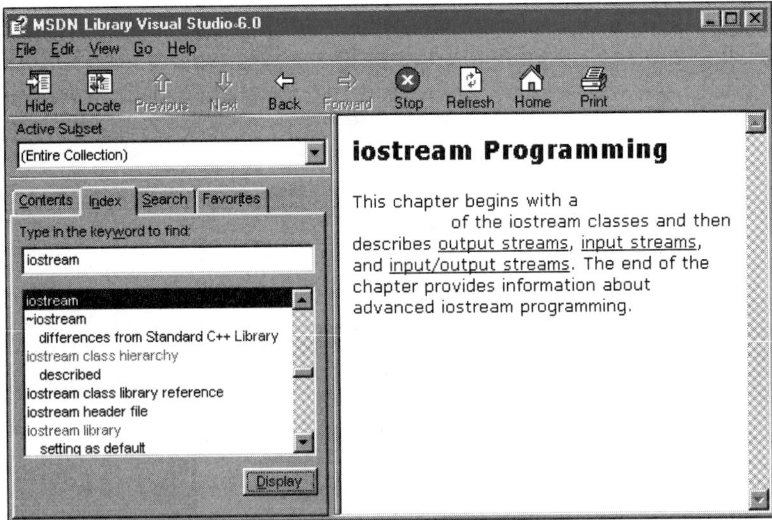

FIGURE 2.37

Documentation display

FIGURE 2.38

Using the Search tab

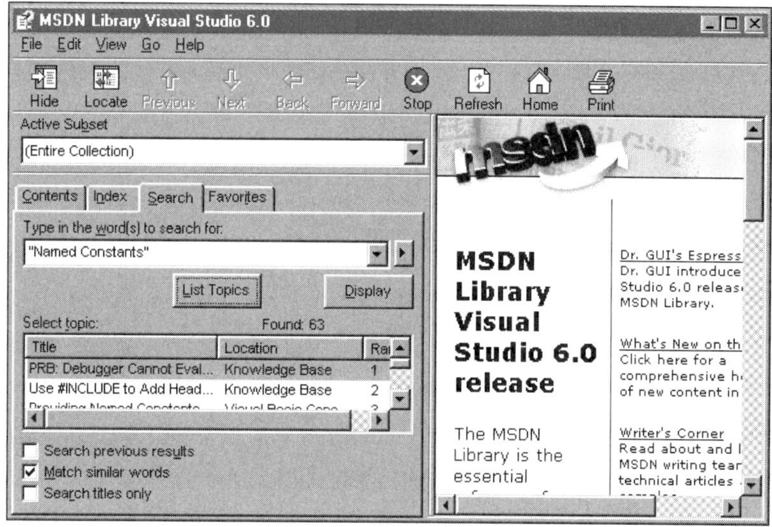

The Search Tab

The Search tab, which is shown as the active tab in Figure 2.38, permits searching either the complete MSDN Library, or sections of it, for the words entered into the tab's text box. In creating a search phrase, you should enclose a phrase within double quotes and make use of Boolean operators to limit the search. For example, by using the current MSDN Library at the time when this book was written, a list of 63 topics was generated for the phrase `"Named Constants"` when the List Topics command button shown in Figure 2.38 was pressed. The double quotes tells the search to look for the words `Named Constants` together. If the double quotes are omitted, the search finds all occurrences of either the word `Named` or `Constants`, and turns up 500 matches.

The Favorites Tab

Frequently, while navigating through the online Help, you will locate one or more references and articles that you would like to explore in more detail at some later time. Many times the article will have been located by following a circuitous route through hyperlinks contained within the documentation itself. To mark such a topic for later retrieval, first click the Favorites tab. When this tab is active, the currently displayed topic is automatically entered in the Current topic Text box, as illustrated in Figure 2.39.

To add the current topic to the favorites list, press the Add button. If you want to rename the displayed topic, you can enter a new name in the Current topic text box before clicking the Add button; the new name will still refer to the displayed topic in the documentation pane. You then can retrieve the article at any future time by opening the Favorites tab and clicking on the desired entry.

FIGURE 2.39

The Favorites tab

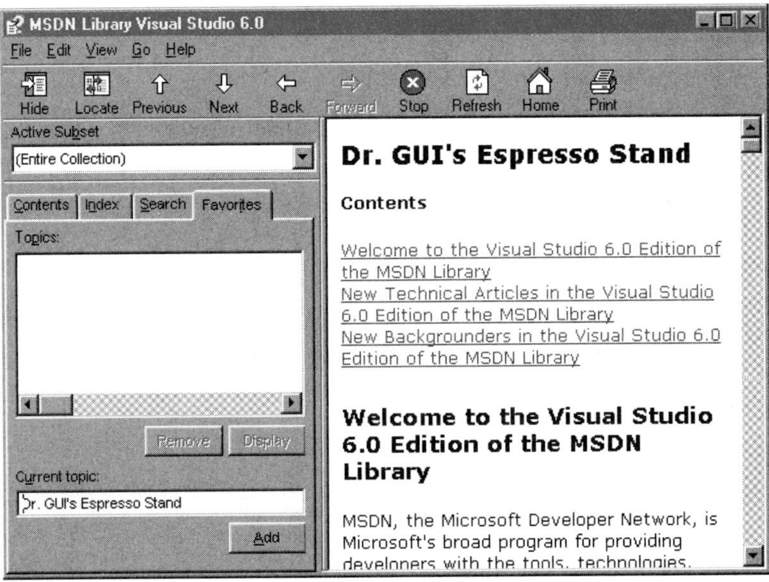

EXERCISES 2.8

1. Using the online Help facility's Contents tab, and expanding the documentation folder tree to look like that shown in Figure 2.40, display the illustrated documentation page.

FIGURE 2.40

Figure for Exercise 1

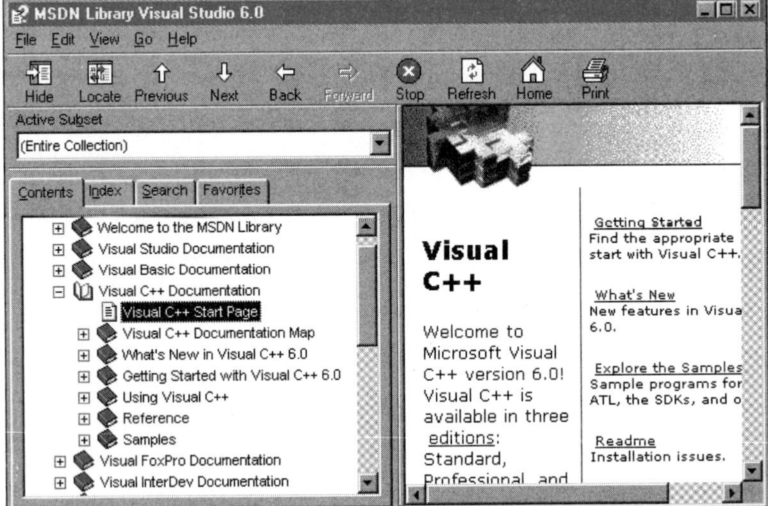

FIGURE 2.41

Figure for Exercise 2

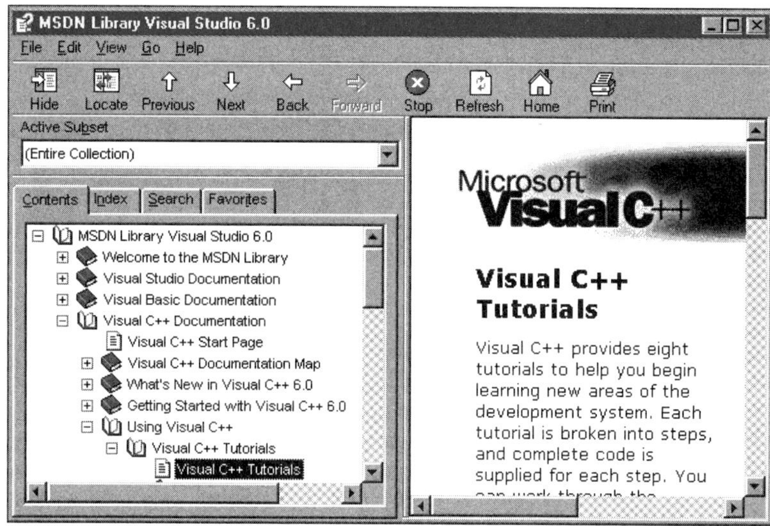

2. Using the online Help facility's Contents tab, and expanding the documentation folder tree to look like that shown in Figure 2.41, display the illustrated documentation page.

3. a. Using the online Help facility's Contents tab, and expanding the documentation folder tree to look like that shown in Figure 2.42, display the illustrated documentation page.

b. Obtain a hard copy printout of each documentation page displayed for Exercise 3a.

FIGURE 2.42

Figure for Exercise 3a

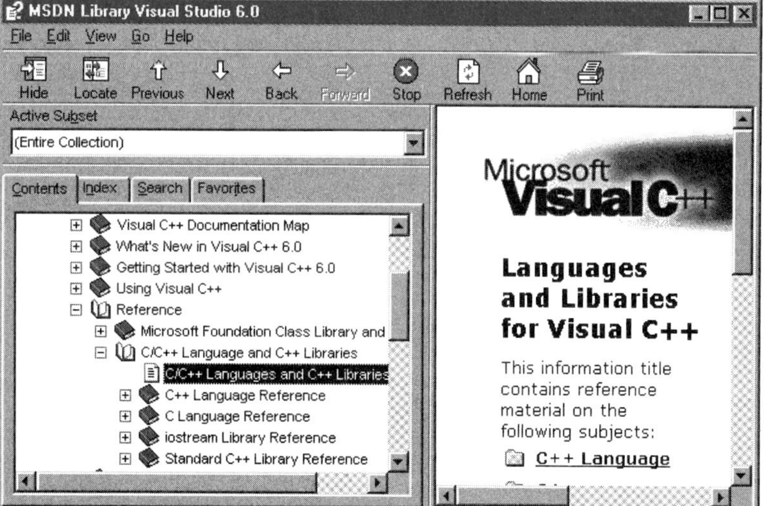

FIGURE 2.43

Figure for Exercise 4a

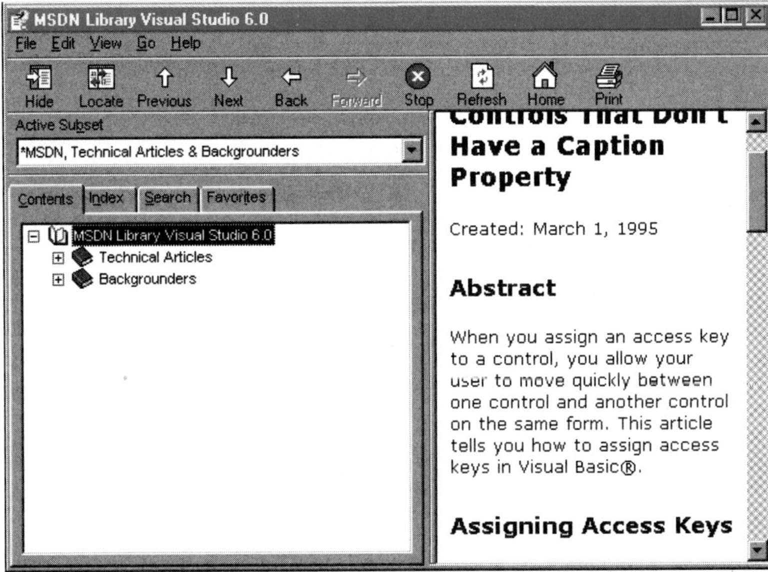

4. a. By starting with screen shown in Figure 2.43, and expanding the Technical Articles topic, locate a technical article of your choosing. (*Note:* To obtain this screen you will have to alter the text in the Active Subset text box to that shown in the figure.) Add the selected article to the Favorites list and close the Help facility.

b. Reopen the Help facility and by using the Favorites tab, locate the article that you saved in Exercise 4a. Obtain a hard copy printout of the article.

3 Completing the Basics

In the last chapter we explored how results are displayed using C++'s `cout` object and how numerical data are stored and processed using variables and assignment statements. In this chapter we complete our introduction to C++ by presenting additional processing and input capabilities.

3.1 Assignment Operations

We have already encountered simple assignment statements in Chapter 2. Assignment statements are the most basic C++ statements for both assigning values to variables and performing computations. This statement has the syntax:

variable = expression;

The simplest expression in C++ is a single constant. In each of the following assignment statements, the operand to the right of the equal sign is a constant:

```
length = 25;
width = 17.5;
```

In each of these assignment statements the value of the constant to the right of the equal sign is assigned to the variable on the left of the equal sign. It is important to note that the equal sign in C++ does not have the same meaning as an equal sign in algebra. The equal sign in an assignment statement tells the computer first to determine the value of the operand to the right of the equal sign and then to store (or assign) that value in the locations associated with the variable to the left of the equal sign. In this regard, the C++ statement `length = 25;` is read "length is assigned the value 25." The blank spaces in the assignment statement are inserted for readability only.

Recall that a variable can be initialized when it is declared. If an initialization is not done within the declaration statement, the variable should be assigned a value with an assignment statement or input operation before it is used in any computation. Subsequent assignment statements can, of course, be used to change the value assigned to a variable. For example, assume the following statements are executed one after another and that `total` was not initialized when it was declared:

```
total = 3.7;
total = 6.28;
```

The first assignment statement assigns the value of 3.7 to the variable named `total`.[1] The next assignment statement causes the computer to assign a value of `6.28` to `total`. The `3.7` that was in `total` is overwritten with the new value of `6.28` because a variable can store only one value at a time. It is sometimes useful to think of the variable to the left of the equal sign as a temporary parking spot in a huge parking lot. Just as an individual parking spot can be used by only one car at a time, each variable can store only one value at a time. The "parking" of a new value in a variable automatically causes the program to remove any value previously parked there.

In addition to being a constant, the operand to the right of the equal sign in an assignment statement can be a variable or any other valid C++ expression. An **expression** is any combination of constants, variables, and function calls that can be evaluated to yield a result. Thus, the expression in an assignment statement can be used to perform calculations

1 This is the first time a value is explicitly assigned to this variable, so it is frequently referred to as an initialization. This stems from historical usage in which a variable was initialized the first time a value was assigned to it. Under this usage it is correct to say that "total is initialized to 3.7." From an implementation viewpoint, however, this later statement is incorrect. This is because the assignment operation is handled differently by the C++ compiler than an initialization performed when a variable is created by a declaration statement. This difference is important only when using C++'s class features and is explained in detail in Section 9.1.

using the arithmetic operators introduced in Section 2.3. Examples of assignment statements using expressions containing these operators are:

```
sum = 3 + 7;
diff = 15 -6;
product = .05 * 14.6;
tally = count + 1;
newtotal = 18.3 + total;
taxes = .06 * amount;
totalWeight = factor * weight;
average = sum / items;
total = (y2 - y1) / (x2 - x1);
```

As always in an assignment statement, the computer first calculates the value of the expression to the right of the equal sign and then stores this value in the variable to the left of the equal sign. For example, in the assignment statement `totalWeight = factor * weight;` the arithmetic expression `factor * weight` is first evaluated to yield a result. This result, which is a number, is then stored in the variable `totalWeight`.

In writing assignment expressions, you must be aware of two important considerations. First, because the expression to the right of the equal sign is evaluated first, all variables used in the expression must previously have been given valid values if the result is to make sense. For example, the assignment statement `totalWeight = factor * weight;` causes a valid number to be stored in `totalWeight` only if the programmer first takes care to assign valid numbers to `factor` and `weight`. Thus the sequence of statements:

```
factor = 1.06;
weight = 155.0;
totalWeight = factor * weight;
```

tells us the values being used to obtain the result that will be stored in `totalWeight`. Figure 3.1 illustrates the values stored in the variables `factor`, `weight`, and `totalWeight`.

The second consideration to keep in mind is that because the value of an expression is stored in the variable to the left of the equal sign, only one variable can be listed in this position. For example, the assignment statement

```
amount + 1892 = 1000 + 10 * 5;
```

is invalid. The expression on the right-hand side of the equal sign evaluates to the integer 1050, which can be stored only in a variable. But because `amount + 1892` is not a valid

FIGURE 3.1

Values stored in the variables

factor

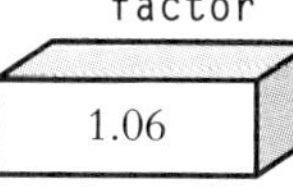

weight

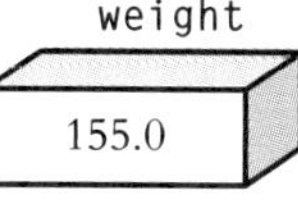

totalWeight

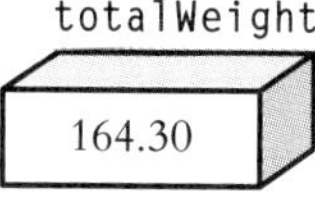

variable name, the computer does not know where to store the calculated value. Program 3.1 illustrates the use of assignment statements in calculating the area of a rectangle.

PROGRAM 3.1

```
#include <iostream.h>
int main()
{
  float length, width, area;

  length = 27.2;
  width = 13.6;
  area = length * width;
  cout << "The length of the rectangle is " << length << endl;
  cout << "The width of the rectangle is " << width << endl;
  cout << "The area of the rectangle is " << area << endl;

  return 0;
}
```

The output displayed when Program 3.1 is run is shown in Figure 3.2.

Consider the flow of control that the computer uses in executing Program 3.1. Program execution begins with the first statement within the body of the `main()` function and continues sequentially, statement by statement, until the closing brace of `main` is encountered. This flow of control is true for all programs. The computer works on one statement at a time, executing that statement with no knowledge of what the next statement will be. This explains why all operands used in an expression must have values assigned to them before the expression is evaluated. When the computer executes the statement `area = length * width;` in Program 3.1, it uses whatever value is stored in the variables `length` and `width` at the time the assignment statement is executed. If no values

FIGURE 3.2

Output displayed by Program 3.1

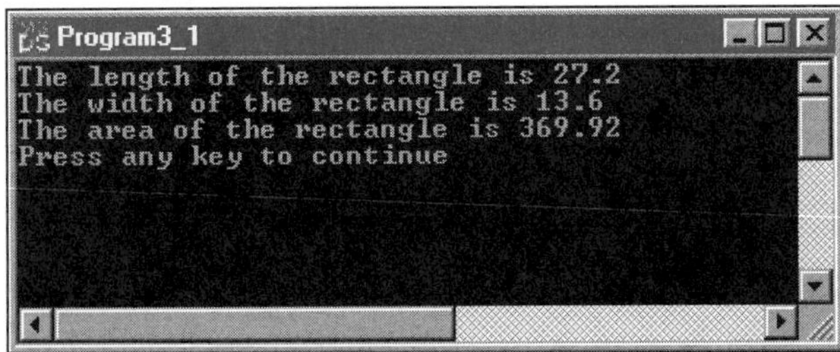

have been specifically assigned to these variables before they are used in the assignment statement, the computer uses whatever values happen to occupy these variables when they are referenced (most C++ compilers automatically initialize all variables to zero). The computer does not "look ahead" to see if you assign values to these variables later in the program.

It is important to realize that in C++, the equal sign, =, used in assignment statements is itself an operator, which differs from the way most other high-level languages process this symbol. In C++ (as in C), the = symbol is called the **assignment operator,** and an expression using this operator, such as `interest = principal * rate`, is an assignment expression. Because the assignment operator has a lower precedence than any other arithmetic operator, the value of any expression to the right of the equal sign will be evaluated first, prior to assignment.

Like all expressions, assignment expressions themselves have a value. The value of the complete assignment expression is the value assigned to the variable on the left of the assignment operator. For example, the expression `a = 5` both assigns a value of `5` to the variable `a` and results in the expression itself having a value of 5. The value of the expression can always be verified using a statement such as

```
cout << "The value of the expression is " << (a = 5);
```

Here, the value of the expression itself is displayed and not the contents of the variable `a`. Although both the contents of the variable and the expression have the same value, it is worthwhile realizing that we are dealing with two distinct entities.

From a programming perspective, it is the actual assignment of a value to a variable that is significant in an assignment expression; the final value of the assignment expression itself is of little consequence. However, the fact that assignment expressions have a value has implications that must be considered when C++'s relational operators are presented.

Any expression that is terminated by a semicolon becomes a C++ statement. The most common example of this is the assignment statement, which is simply an assignment expression terminated with a semicolon. For example, terminating the assignment expression `a = 33` with a semicolon results in the assignment statement `a = 33;`, which can be used in a program on a line by itself.

Because the equal sign is an operator in C++, multiple assignments are possible in the same expression or its equivalent statement. For example, in the expression `a = b = c = 25` all the assignment operators have the same precedence. The assignment operator has a right-to-left associativity, so the final evaluation proceeds in the sequence

```
c = 25
b = c
a = b
```

PROGRAMMER'S NOTES

lvalue and rvalue

The terms lvalue and rvalue are frequently used terms in programming technology. Both of these terms are language independent and mean the following: An lvalue can have a value assigned to it whereas an rvalue cannot.

In both C and C++ this means that an lvalue can appear on the left side of an assignment operator and an rvalue can appear on the right side of an assignment operator. For example, each variable we have encountered can be either an lvalue or an rvalue, but a number can only be an rvalue. Not all variables, however, can be an lvalue and an rvalue. For example, an array type, which is introduced in Chapter 12, cannot be an lvalue or an rvalue, but individual array elements can be both.

In this case, this has the effect of assigning the number 25 to each of the variables individually, and can be represented as

```
a = (b = (c = 25))
```

Appending a semicolon to the original expression results in the multiple assignment statement

```
a = b = c = 25;
```

This latter statement assigns the value 25 to the three individual variables equivalent to the following order:

```
c = 25;
b = 25;
a = 25;
```

Note that data type conversions can take place across assignment operators: that is, the value of the expression on the right side of the assignment operator is converted to the data type of the variable to the left of the assignment operator. Thus, assigning an integer value to a real variable causes the integer to be converted to a real value. Similarly, assigning a real value to an integer variable forces conversion of the real value to an integer, which always results in the loss of the fractional part of the number due to truncation. For example, if temp is an integer variable, the assignment temp = 25.89 causes the integer value 25 to be stored in the integer variable temp.[2]

A more complete example of data type conversions, which includes both mixed-mode and assignment conversion, is the evaluation of the expression

```
a = b * d
```

---

2 The correct integer portion, clearly, is retained only when it is within the range of integers allowed by the compiler.

where a and b are integer variables and d is a floating point variable. When the mixed-mode expression b * d is evaluated,[3] the value of d used in the expression is converted to a double precision number for purposes of computation (it is important to note that the value stored in d remains a floating point number). Because one of the operands is a double precision variable, the value of the integer variable b is converted to a double precision number for the computation (again, the value stored in b remains an integer), and the resulting value of the expression b * d is a double precision number. Finally, data type conversion across the assignment operator comes into play. Because the left side of the assignment operator is an integer variable, the double precision value of the expression (b * d) is truncated to an integer value and stored in the variable a.

Assignment Variations

Although only one variable is allowed immediately to the left of the equal sign in an assignment expression, the variable on the left of the equal sign can also be used on the right of the equal sign. For example, the assignment expression sum = sum + 10 is valid. Clearly, as an algebra equation, sum could never be equal to itself plus 10. But in C++, the expression sum = sum + 10 is not an equation—it is an expression that is evaluated in two major steps. The first step is to calculate the value of sum + 10. The second step is to store the computed value in sum. See if you can determine the output of Program 3.2.

PROGRAM 3.2

```
#include <iostream.h>
int main()
{
  int sum;

  sum = 25;
  cout << "The number stored in sum is " << sum << endl;
  sum = sum + 10;
  cout << "The number now stored in sum is " << sum << endl;

  return 0;
}
```

The assignment statement sum = 25; tells the computer to store the number 25 in sum, as shown in Figure 3.3.

The first cout statement causes the value stored in sum to be displayed by the message The number stored in sum is 25. The second assignment statement in Program

3 Review the rules in Table 2.8 in Section 2.5 for the evaluation of mixed-mode expressions, if necessary.

FIGURE 3.3

The integer `25` **is stored in** `sum`

sum

25

3.2, `sum = sum + 10;`, causes the computer to retrieve the `25` stored in `sum` and add `10` to this number, yielding the number `35`. The number `35` is then stored in the variable on the left side of the equal sign, which is the variable `sum`. The `25` that was in `sum` is simply overwritten with the new value of `35`, as shown in Figure 3.4.

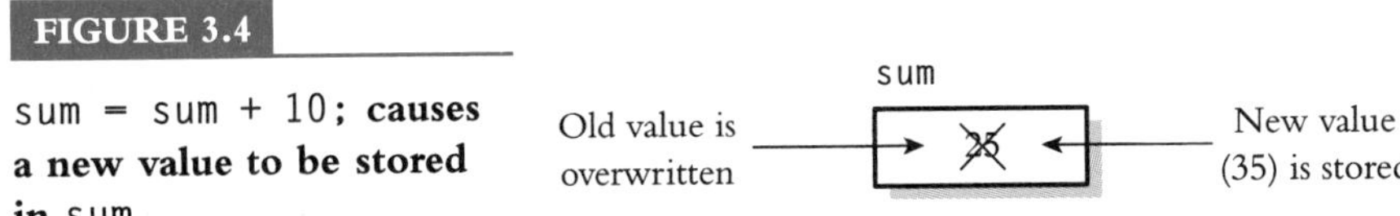

FIGURE 3.4

`sum = sum + 10;` **causes a new value to be stored in** `sum`

Assignment expressions such as `sum = sum + 25`, which use the same variable on both sides of the assignment operator, can be written using the following shortcut **assignment operators:**

`+=` `-=` `*=` `/=` `%=`

For example, the expression `sum = sum + 10` can be written as `sum += 10`. Similarly, the expression `price *= rate` is equivalent to the expression `price = price * rate`.

When you use these new assignment operators it is important to note that the variable to the left of the assignment operator is applied to the complete expression on the right. For example, the expression `price *= rate + 1` is equivalent to the expression `price = price * (rate + 1)`, not `price = price * rate + 1`.

Accumulating

Assignment expressions such as `sum += 10` or its equivalent, `sum = sum + 10`, are very common in programming. These expressions are required in accumulating subtotals when data are entered one number at a time. For example, if we want to add the numbers 96, 70, 85, and 60 in calculator fashion, the following statements could be used:

Statement	Value in sum
`sum = 0;`	0
`sum = sum + 96;`	96
`sum = sum + 70;`	166
`sum = sum + 85;`	251
`sum = sum + 60;`	311

The first statement initializes `sum` to `0`. This removes any number ("garbage value") stored in `sum` that would invalidate the final total. As each number is added, the value stored in `sum` is increased accordingly. After completion of the last statement, `sum` contains the total of all the added numbers. Program 3.3 illustrates the effect of these statements by displaying `sum`'s contents after each addition is made.

PROGRAM 3.3

```
#include <iostream.h>
int main()
{
  int sum;

  sum = 0;
  cout << "The value of sum is initially set to " << sum << endl;
  sum = sum + 96;
  cout << "  sum is now " << sum << endl;
  sum = sum + 70;
  cout << "  sum is now " << sum << endl;
  sum = sum + 85;
  cout << "  sum is now " << sum  << endl;
  sum = sum + 60;
  cout << "  The final sum is " << sum << endl;

  return 0;
}
```

The output displayed by Program 3.3 is shown in Figure 3.5.

Although Program 3.3 is not a practical program (it is easier to add the numbers by hand), it does illustrate the subtotaling effect of repeated use of statements having the form

variable = variable + newValue;

FIGURE 3.5

Output displayed by Program 3.3

```
Program3_3
The value of sum is initially set to 0
  sum is now 96
  sum is now 166
  sum is now 251
  The final sum is 311
Press any key to continue
```

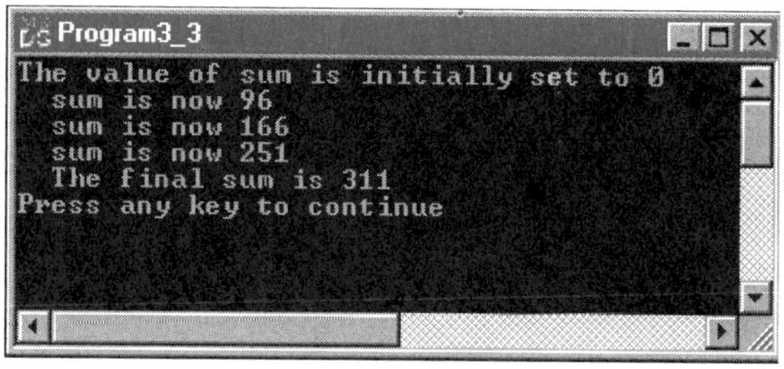

We will find many uses for this type of statement when we become more familiar with the repetition statements introduced in Chapter 5.

Counting

An assignment statement that is very similar to the accumulating statement is the counting statement. Counting statements have the form:

variable = variable + fixedNumber;

Examples of counting statements are:

```
i = i + 1;
n = n + 1;
count = count + 1;
j = j + 2;
m = m + 2;
kk = kk + 3;
```

In each of these examples the same variable is used on both sides of the equal sign. After the statement is executed the value of the respective variable is increased by a fixed amount. In the first three examples the variables `i`, `n`, and `count` have all been increased by one. In the next two examples the respective variables have been increased by two, and in the final example the variable `kk` has been increased by three.

For the special case in which a variable is either increased or decreased by one, C++ provides two unary operators. Using the increment operator,[4] ++, the expression `variable = variable + 1` can be replaced by either the expression `variable++` or `++variable`. Examples of the increment operator are:

Expression	Alternative
`i = i + 1`	`i++` or `++i`
`n = n + 1`	`n++` or `++n`
`count = count + 1`	`count++` or `++count`

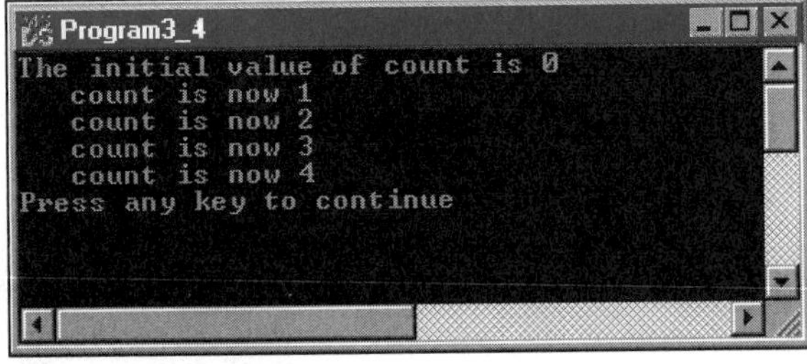

FIGURE 3.6

Output displayed by Program 3.4

4 As a historical note, the "++" in C++ was inspired from the increment operator symbol. It was used to indicate that C++ was the next increment to the C language.

Program 3.4 illustrates the use of the increment operator.

PROGRAM 3.4

```
#include <iostream.h>
int main()
{
  int count;

  count = 0;
  cout << "The initial value of count is " << count << endl;
  count++;
  cout << "   count is now " << count << endl;
  count++;
  cout << "   count is now " << count << endl;
  count++;
  cout << "   count is now " << count << endl;
  count++;
  cout << "   count is now " << count << endl;

  return 0;
}
```

The output displayed by Program 3.4 is shown in Figure 3.6.

When the ++ operator appears before a variable it is called a **prefix increment operator;** when it appears after a variable it is called a **postfix increment operator.** The distinction between a prefix and postfix increment operator is important when the variable being incremented is used in an assignment expression. For example, the expression `k = ++n` does two things in one expression. Initially the value of `n` is incremented by one and then the new value of `n` is assigned to the variable `k`. Thus, the statement `k = ++n;` is equivalent to the following two statements

```
n = n + 1;    // increment n first
k = n;        // assign n's value to k
```

The assignment expression `k = n++`, which uses a postfix increment operator, reverses this procedure. A postfix increment operates after the assignment is completed. Thus, the statement `k = n++;` first assigns the current value of `n` to `k` and then increments the value of `n` by one. This is equivalent to the two statements

```
k = n;        // assign n's value to k
n = n + 1;    // and then increment n
```

In addition to the increment operator, C++ also provides a decrement operator, `--`. As you might expect, the expressions `variable--` and `--variable` are both equivalent to the expression `variable = variable - 1`. Examples of the decrement operator are:

Expression	Alternative
`i = i - 1`	`i--` or `--i`
`n = n - 1`	`n--` or `--n`
`count = count - 1`	`count--` or `--count`

When the `--` operator appears before a variable it is called a **prefix decrement operator.** When the decrement appears after a variable it is called a **postfix decrement operator.** For example, both of the expressions `n--` and `--n` reduce the value of `n` by one. These expressions are equivalent to the longer expression `n = n - 1`. As with the increment operator, however, the prefix and postfix decrement operators produce different results when used in assignment expressions. For example, the expression `k = --n` first decrements the value of `n` by one before assigning the value of `n` to `k`, whereas the expression `k = n--` first assigns the current value of `n` to `k` and then reduces the value of `n` by one.

EXERCISES 3.1

1. **a.** Write an assignment statement to calculate the circumference of a circle having a radius of 3.3 inches. The equation for determining the circumference, c, of a circle is $c = 2\pi r$, where r is the radius and $\pi = 3.1416$.

   b. Write an assignment statement to calculate the area of a circle. The equation for determining the area, a, of a circle is $a = \pi r^2$, where r is the radius and $\pi = 3.1416$.

2. Write an assignment statement to convert temperature in degrees Fahrenheit to degrees Celsius. The equation for this conversion is $Celsius = (5/9)\ (Fahrenheit - 32)$.

3. Determine and correct the errors in the following programs.

   a.
```
#include <iostream.h>
int main()
{
  width = 15
  area = length * width;
  cout << "The area is " << area
}
```

b.
```
#include <iostream.h>
int main()
{
  int length, width, area;
  area = length * width;
  length = 20;
  width = 15;
  cout << "The area is   \n" << area
```

c.
```
#include <iostream.h>
int main()
{
  int length = 20; width = 15, area;
  length * width = area;
  cout << "The area is   \n" << area

 }
```

4. By mistake a student reordered the statements in Program 3.3 as follows:

```
#include <iostream.h>
int main()
{
  int sum;
  sum = 0;
  sum = sum + 96;
  sum = sum + 70;
  sum = sum + 85;
  sum = sum + 60;
  cout << "The value of sum is initially set to " << sum << endl;
  cout << "  sum is now " << sum << endl;
  cout << "  sum is now " << sum << endl;
  cout << "  sum is now " << sum << endl;
  cout << "  The final sum is " << sum << endl;

  return 0;
}
```

Determine the output that this program produces.

5. Using Program 3.1, determine the area of rectangles having the following lengths and widths:

Length (in.)	Width (in.)
1.62	6.23
2.86	7.52
4.26	8.95
8.52	10.86
12.29	15.35

6. **a.** Write a C++ program to calculate and display the average of the numbers 32.6, 55.2, 67.9, and 48.6.
   b. Run the program written for Exercise 6a on a computer.
7. **a.** Write a C++ program to calculate the circumference of a circle. The equation for determining the circumference of a circle is *circumference* = 2 ★ 3.1416 ★ *radius*. Assume that the circle has a radius of 3.3 inches.
   b. Run the program written for Exercise 7a on a computer.
8. **a.** Write a C++ program to calculate the area of a circle. The equation for determining the area of a circle is *area* = 3.1416 ★ *radius* ★ *radius*. Assume that the circle has a radius of 5 inches.
   b. Run the program written for Exercise 8a on a computer.
9. **a.** Write a C++ program to calculate the volume of a pool. The equation for determining the volume is *volume* = *length* ★ *width* ★ *depth*. Assume that the pool has a length of 25 feet, a width of 10 feet, and a depth of 6 feet.
   b. Run the program written for Exercise 9a on a computer.
10. **a.** Write a C++ program to convert temperature in degrees Fahrenheit to degrees Celsius. The equation for this conversion is *Celsius* = (5.0/9.0) ★ (*Fahrenheit* – 32.0). Have your program convert and display the Celsius temperature corresponding to 98.6 degrees Fahrenheit.
    b. Run the program written for Exercise 10a on a computer.
11. **a.** Write a C++ program to calculate the dollar amount contained in a piggy bank. The bank currently contains 12 half-dollars, 20 quarters, 32 dimes, 45 nickels, and 27 pennies.
    b. Run the program written for Exercise 11a on a computer.
12. **a.** Write a C++ program to calculate the distance, in feet, of a trip that is 2.36 miles long. One mile is equal to 5,280 feet.
    b. Run the program written for Exercise 12a on a computer.

13. a. Write a C++ program to calculate the elapsed time it took to make a 183.67-mile trip. The equation for computing elapsed time is *elapsed time = total distance / average speed*. Assume that the average speed during the trip was 58 miles per hour.

b. Run the program written for Exercise 13a on a computer.

14. a. Write a C++ program to calculate the sum of the numbers from 1 to 100. The formula for calculating this sum is $sum = (n/2) \star (2\star a + (n - 1)\star d)$, where n = number of terms to be added, a = the first number, and d = the difference between the successive numbers.

b. Run the program written for Exercise 14a on a computer.

15. Determine why the expression `a - b = 25` is invalid but the expression `a - (b = 25)` is valid.

3.2 Numerical Output Using `cout`

Besides displaying correct results, it is extremely important that a program present its results attractively. Most programs are judged, in fact, on the perceived ease of data entry and the style and presentation of their output. For example, displaying a monetary result as 1.897000 is not in keeping with accepted report conventions. The display should be either $1.90 or $1.89, depending on whether rounding or truncation is used.

The format of numbers displayed by `cout` can be controlled by field width manipulators included in each output stream. Table 3.1 lists the most commonly used manipulators available for this purpose.[5] For example, the statement

```
cout << "The sum of 6 and 15 is" << setw(3) <<  21;
```

causes the printout

```
The sum of 6 and 15 is 21
```

The `setw(3)` field width manipulator included in the stream of data passed to `cout` is used to set the displayed field width. The 3 in this manipulator sets the default field width for the next number in the stream to be three spaces wide. This field width setting causes `21` to be printed in a field of three spaces, which includes one blank and the number 21. As illustrated, integers are right-justified within the specified field.

Field width manipulators are useful in printing columns of numbers so that the numbers in each column align correctly. For example, Program 3.5 illustrates how a column of integers would align in the absence of field width manipulators.

---

5 As was noted in Chapter 2, the `endl` manipulator inserts a `newline` and then flushes the stream.

TABLE 3.1 Commonly used stream manipulators

Manipulator	Action
`setw(n)`	Set the field width to n
`setprecision(n)`	Set the floating-point precision to n places. If the display format is exponential or fixed, then the precision indicates the number of digits after the decimal point; otherwise, the precision indicates the total number of displayed digits.
`setiosflags(flags)`	Set the format flags (see Table 3.3 for flag settings)
`dec`	Set output for decimal display
`hex`	Set output for hexadecimal display
`oct`	Set output for octal display

PROGRAM 3.5

```
#include <iostream.h>
int main()
{
  cout << 6 << endl
       << 18 << endl
       << 124 << endl
       << "---\n"
       << (6+18+124) << endl;

  return 0;
}
```

Note in Program 3.5 that we have kept with the general rule concerning the use of the `endl` manipulator and the `\n newline` escape sequence presented in Section 2.4; that is, we have used the `\n` escape sequence when it could be included within an output string, which in this case is `"---\n"`, and have used the `endl` manipulator in all of the other lines where a `\n` would have to appear by itself. The output display produced by Program 3.5 appears as shown in Figure 3.7.

Because no field width manipulators are given, the `cout` object allocates enough space for each number as it is received. To force the numbers to align on the units digit requires a field width wide enough for the largest displayed number. For Program 3.5, a width of three suffices. The use of this field width is illustrated in Program 3.6.

FIGURE 3.7

Output displayed by Program 3.5

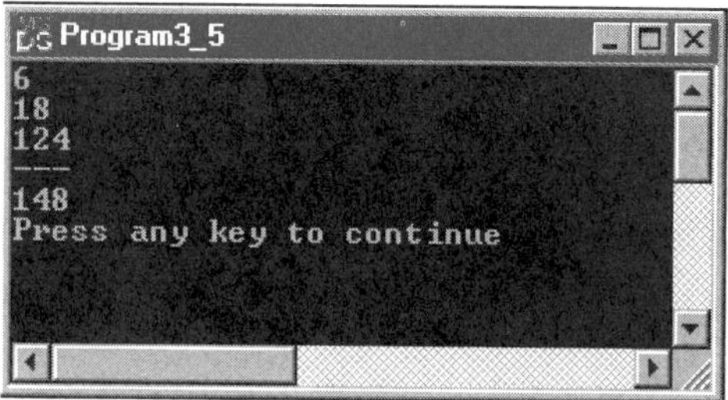

PROGRAM 3.6

```
#include <iostream.h>
#include <iomanip.h>
int main()
{
  cout << setw(3) << 6 << endl
       << setw(3) << 18 << endl
       << setw(3) << 124 << endl
       << "---\n"
       << (6+18+124) << endl;

  return 0;
}
```

The output produced by Program 3.6 appears as shown in Figure 3.8.

Notice that the field width manipulator must be included for each occurrence of a number inserted onto the data stream sent to `cout`, and that the manipulator applies only to the next insertion of data immediately following it. Also notice that if manipulators are to be included within an output display, the `iomanip.h` header file must be included as

FIGURE 3.8

Output displayed by Program 3.6

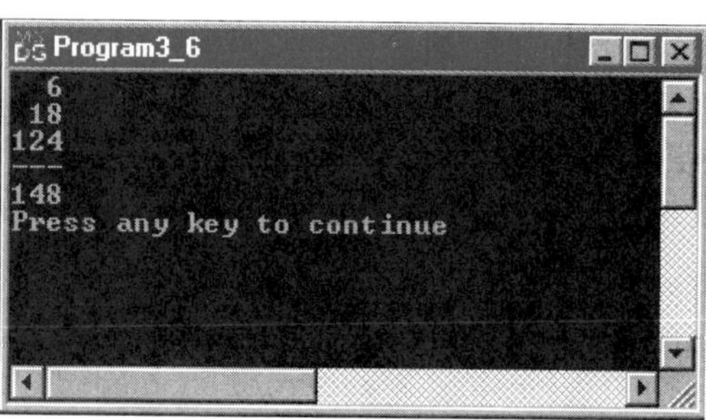

part of the program. This is accomplished by the preprocessor command #include `<iomanip.h>`.[6]

Formatted floating point numbers require the use of two field width manipulators. The first manipulator sets the total width of the display, including the decimal point; the second manipulator determines how many digits can be printed to the right of the decimal point. For example, the statement

```
cout << "|" << setw(10) << setiosflags(ios::fixed)
     << setprecision(3) << 25.67 << "|";
```

causes the printout

```
|    25.670|
```

the bar symbol, |, in the example is used to delimit (mark) the beginning and end of the display field. The `setw` manipulator tells `cout` to display the number in a total field of 10, and the `setprecision` manipulator tells `cout` to display three digits to the right of the decimal point. The `setiosflags` manipulator using the `ios::fixed` flag ensures that the output is displayed in conventional decimal format; that is, as a fixed-point rather than an exponential number.

For all numbers (integers, floating point, and double precision), `cout` ignores the `setw` manipulator specification if the total specified field width is too small, and allocates enough space for the integer part of the number to be printed. The fractional part of both floating point and double precision numbers is displayed up to the precision set with the `setprecision` manipulator (in the absence of a `setprecision` manipulator, the default precision is set to six decimal places). If the fractional part of the number to be displayed contains more digits than called for in the `setprecision` manipulator, the number is rounded to the indicated number of decimal places; if the fractional part contains fewer digits than specified, the number is displayed with the fewer digits. Table 3.2 illustrates the effect of various format manipulator combinations. Again, for clarity, the bar symbol, |, is used to clearly delineate the beginning and end of the output fields.

In addition to the `setw` and `setprecision` manipulators, a field justification manipulator is also available. As we have seen, numbers sent to `cout` are normally displayed right-justified in the display field, whereas strings are displayed left-justified. To alter the default justification for a stream of data, the `setiosflags` manipulator can be used. For example, the statement

```
cout << "|" << setw(10) << setiosflags(ios::left) << 142 << "|";
```

6 The `iomanip.h` header file will include the `iostream.h` header file if it has not already been included, so the `#include` statement for `iostream.h` can be omitted.

causes the following left-justified display

```
|142       |
```

As we have previously seen, because data passed to `cout` may be continued across multiple lines, the previous display would also be produced by the statement

```
cout << "|" << setw(10)
     << setiosflags(ios::left)
     << 142 << "|";
```

As always, the field width manipulator is in effect only for the next single set of data passed to `cout`. Right-justification for strings in a stream is obtained by the manipulator `setiosflags(ios::right)`. The symbols `ios` in both the function name and the `ios::right` argument comes from the first letters of the words *input output stream.*

TABLE 3.2 Effect of format manipulators

Manipulators	Number	Display	Comments
`setw(2)`	3	`| 3|`	Number fits in field
`setw(2)`	43	`|43|`	Number fits in field
`setw(2)`	143	`|143|`	Field width ignored
`setw(2)`	2.3	`|2.3|`	Field width ignored

`setw(5)`
`setiosflags (ios::fixed)`
`setprecision(2)`
	2.366	`| 2.37|`	Field width of 5 with 2 decimal digits

`setw(5)`
`setiosflags(ios::fixed)`
`setprecision(2)`
	42.3	`| 42.3|`	Number fits in field

`setw(5)`
`setiosflags(ios::fixed)`
`setprecision(2)`
	142.364	`|142.36|`	Field width ignored but precision specification is used

`setw(5)`
`setiosflags(ios::fixed)`
`setprecision(2)`
	142.366	`|142.37|`	Field width ignored but precision specification is used

`setw(5)`
`setiosflags(ios::fixed)`
`setprecision(2)`
	142	`|   142|`	Field width used precision irrelevant

Note: If either the manipulator flags `ios::fixed` or `ios::scientific` are not in effect, the `setprecision` value indicates the total number of significant digits displayed rather than the number of digits after the decimal point.

PROGRAMMER'S NOTES

What Is a Flag?

In current programming usage, the term **flag** refers to an item, such as a variable or argument, that sets a condition usually considered as either active or nonactive. Although the exact origin of this term in programming is not known, it probably originates from the use of real flags to signal a condition, such as the Stop, Go, Caution, and Winner flags commonly used at car races.

In a similar manner, each flag argument to the `setiosflags()` manipulator function activates a specific condition. For example, the `ios::dec` flag sets the display format to decimal, whereas the flag `ios::oct` activates the octal display format. Because these conditions are mutually exclusive, which means that only one condition can be active at a time, activating one such flag automatically deactivates the other flags.

Flags that are not mutually exclusive, such as `ios::dec, ios::showpoint`, and `ios::fixed` can all be set at the same time. This can be done using three individual `setiosflag()` calls or combining all arguments into one call as follows:

```
cout << setiosflags(ios::dec || ios::showpoint || ios::fixed);
```

In addition to the left and right flags that can be used with the `setiosflags()` manipulator, other flags may also be used to affect the output. The most commonly used flags for this manipulator are listed in Table 3.3.

TABLE 3.3 Format Flags for use with `setiosflags()`

Flag	Meaning
`ios::showpoint`	always display a decimal point. In the absence of the `ios::fixed` flag, a numerical value with a decimal point is displayed with a default of 6 significant digits. If the integer part of the number requires more than 6 digits the display will be in exponential notation, unless the `ios::fixed` flag is in effect. For example, the value 1234567. is displayed as 1.23457e6 unless the `ios::fixed` flag is in effect. This flag has no effect on integer values.
`ios::showpos`	display a leading + sign when the number is positive
`ios::fixed`	display the number in conventional fixed-point decimal notation (that is, with an integer and fractional part separated by a decimal point), and not in exponential notation.
`ios::scientific`	use exponential notation on output
`ios::dec`	display as a decimal number (this is the default)
`ios::oct`	display as an octal number
`ios::hex`	display as a hexadecimal number
`ios::left`	left-justify output
`ios::right`	right-justify output

Notice that all of the flags in Table 3.3 are used as arguments to the `setiosflags()` manipulator function. Because the terms **argument** and **parameter** are synonymous, another name for a manipulator function that uses arguments is a parameterized manipulator. As an example of using parameterized manipulator functions, consider the statement:

```
cout << setiosflags(ios::fixed)
     << setiosflags(ios::showpoint)
     << setprecision(4);
```

This forces all subsequent floating point numbers sent to the output stream to be displayed with a decimal point and four decimal digits. If the number has fewer than four decimal digits it will be padded with trailing zeros.

In addition to outputting integers in decimal notation, the `ios::oct` and `ios:hex` flags permit conversions to octal and hexadecimal, respectively. Program 3.7 illustrates the use of these flags. Because decimal is the default display, an `ios::dec` flag is not required in the first output stream.

PROGRAM 3.7

```
// a program to illustrate output conversions
#include <iostream.h>
#include <iomanip.h>
int main()
{
  cout << "The decimal (base 10) value of 15 is " << 15 << endl
       << "The octal (base 8) value of 15 is "
       << setiosflags(ios::oct) << 15 << endl
       << "The hexadecimal (base 16) value of 15 is "
       << setiosflags(ios::hex) << 15 << endl;

  return 0;
}
```

The output produced by Program 3.7 is shown in Figure 3.9.

FIGURE 3.9

Output displayed by Program 3.7

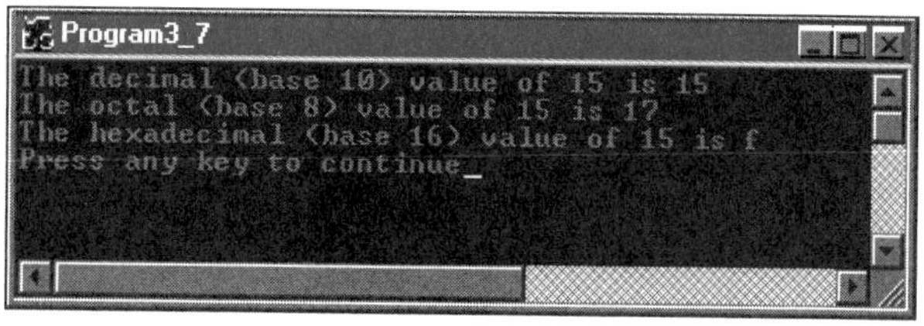

```
Program3_7
The decimal (base 10) value of 15 is 15
The octal (base 8) value of 15 is 17
The hexadecimal (base 16) value of 15 is f
Press any key to continue_
```

PROGRAMMER'S NOTES

Formatting `cout` Stream Data

The data in a `cout` output stream can be formatted in precise ways. One of the most common format requirements is to display numbers in a monetary format by always displaying two digits after the decimal point, such as 123.45. This can be done with the following statement:

```
cout << setiosflags(ios::fixed)
     << setiosflags(ios::showpoint)
     << setprecision(2);
```

The first manipulator flag, `ios::fixed`, forces all numbers placed on the `cout` stream to be placed in conventional decimal notation, and not in exponential form. The next flag, `ios::showpoint`, tells the stream to always display a decimal point. Thus, a value such as 1.0 will appear as `1.0`, and not as a 1 with no displayed decimal value. Finally, the `setprecision` manipulator tells the stream to always display 2 decimal values after the decimal point. Thus, the number 1.0, for example, will appear as `1.00`.

Instead of using manipulators, you can also use the `cout` stream functions `setf()` and `precision()`. For example, the previous formatting can also be accomplished using the code:

```
cout.setf(ios::fixed);
cout.setf(ios::showpoint);
cout.precision(2);
```

Note the syntax here: the name of the object, `cout`, is separated from the function with a period. As we shall see in Chapter 9, this is the standard way of specifying a function and connecting it to a specific object.

Which style you select is a matter of preference. In both cases the formats need only be specified once, and they remain in effect for every number subsequently inserted into the `cout` stream.

In place of the conversion flags `ios::dec`, `ios::oct`, and `ios::hex`, three simpler manipulators, `dec`, `oct`, and `hex`, are provided in `<iostream.h>`. These simpler manipulators, unlike their longer counterparts, leave the conversion base set for all subsequent output streams. Using these simpler manipulators, Program 3.7 can be rewritten as:

```
#include <iostream.h>
int main()  // a program to illustrate output conversions
{
  cout << "The decimal (base 10) value of 15 is " << 15 << endl
       << "The octal (base 8) value of 15 is " << oct << 15 << endl
       << "The hexadecimal (base 16) value of 15 is " << hex << 15 << endl;

  return 0;
}
```

The display of integer values in one of the three possible number systems (decimal, octal, and hexadecimal) does not affect how the number is actually stored inside a computer. All numbers are stored using the computer's own internal codes. The manipulators sent to cout simply tell the object how to convert the internal code for output display purposes.

Besides integers being displayed in octal or hexadecimal form, integer constants can also be written in a program in these forms. To designate an octal integer constant, the number must have a leading zero. The number 02, for example, is an octal number in C++. Hexadecimal numbers are denoted using a leading 0x. The use of octal and hexadecimal integer constants is illustrated in Program 3.8.

PROGRAM 3.8

```
#include <iostream.h>
int main()
{
  cout << "The decimal value of 025 is " << 025 << endl
       << "The decimal value of 0x37 is "<< 0x37 << endl;

  return 0;
}
```

When Program 3.8 is run, the output shown in Figure 3.10 is obtained.

The relationship between the input, storage, and display of integers is illustrated in Figure 3.11.

FIGURE 3.10

Output displayed by Program 3.8

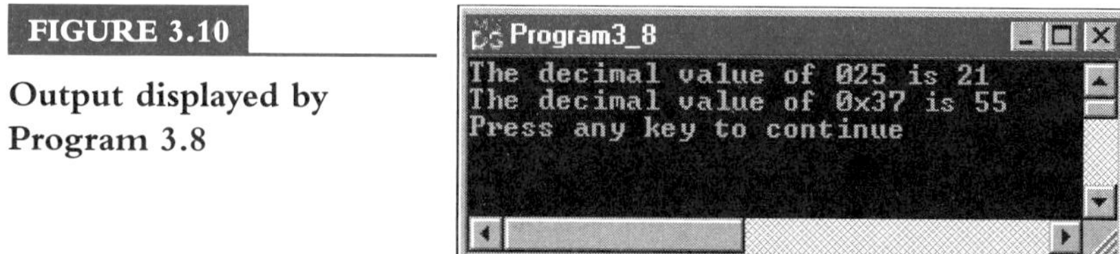

Program3_8
The decimal value of 025 is 21
The decimal value of 0x37 is 55
Press any key to continue

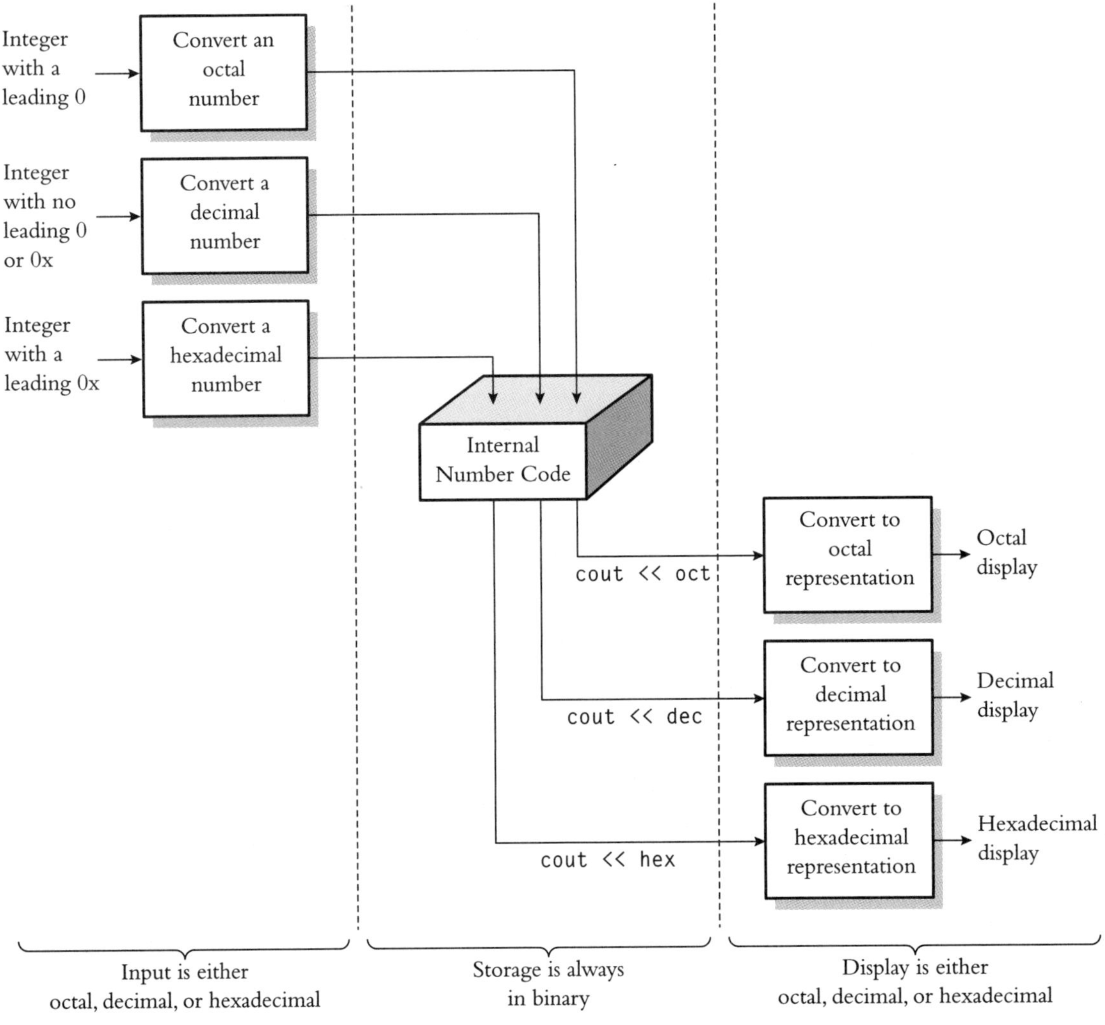

FIGURE 3.11

Input, storage, and display of integers

EXERCISES 3.2

1. Determine the output of the following program:

```
#include <iostream.h>
int main()  // a program illustrating integer truncation
{
```

```
  cout << "answer1 is the integer " <<  27/5
       << "\nanswer2 is the integer " <<  16/6 << endl;

  return 0;
}
```

2. Determine the output of the following program:

```
#include <iostream.h>
int main()  // a program illustrating the % operator
{
  cout << "The remainder of 9 divided by 4 is " <<  9 % 4
       << "\nThe remainder of 17 divided by 3 is " <<  17 % 3
       << endl;

  return 0;
}
```

3. Determine the errors in each of the following statements:

a. `cout << "\n << " 15)`

b. `cout << "setw(4)" << 33;`

c. `cout << "setprecision(5)" << 526.768;`

d. `"Hello World!" >> cout;`

e. `cout << 47 << setw(6);`

f. `cout << set(10) << 526.768 << setprecision(2);`

4. Determine and write out the display produced by the following statements:

a. `cout << "|" << 5 <<"|";`

b. `cout << "|" << setw(4) << 5 << "|";`

c. `cout << "|" << setw(4) << 56829 << "|";`

d.
```
cout << "|" << setw(5) << setiosflags(ios::fixed)
     << setprecision(2) << 5.26 << "|";
```

e.
```
cout << "|" << setw(5) << setiosflags(ios::fixed)
     << setprecision(2) << 5.267 << "|";
```

f.
```
cout << "|" << setw(5) << setiosflags(ios::fixed)
     << setprecision(2) << 53.264 << "|";
```

g.
```
cout << "|" << setw(5) << setiosflags(ios::fixed)
     << setprecision(2) << 534.264 << "|";
```

h.
```
cout << "|" << setw(5) << setiosflags(ios::fixed)
     << setprecision(2) << 534. << "|";
```

5. Write out the display produced by the following statements.

a.
```
cout << "The number is " << setw(6) << setiosflags(ios::fixed)
     << setprecision(2) << 26.27 << endl;
cout << "The number is " << setw(6) << setiosflags(ios::fixed)
     << setprecision(2) << 682.3 << endl;
cout << "The number is " << setw(6) << setiosflags(ios::fixed)
     << setprecision(2) << 1.968 << endl;
```

b.
```
cout << setw(6) << setiosflags(ios::fixed)
     << setprecision(2) << 26.27 << endl;
cout << setw(6) << setiosflags(ios::fixed)
     << setprecision(2) << 682.3 << endl;
cout << setw(6) << setiosflags(ios::fixed)
     << setprecision(2) << 1.968 << endl;
cout << "------\n";
cout << setw(6) << setiosflags(ios::fixed)
     << setprecision(2) << 26.27 + 682.3 + 1.968 << endl;
```

c.
```
cout << setw(5) << setiosflags(ios::fixed)
     << setprecision(2) << 26.27 << endl;
cout << setw(5) << setiosflags(ios::fixed)
     << setprecision(2) << 682.3 << endl;
cout << setw(5) << setiosflags(ios::fixed)
     << setprecision(2) << 1.968 << endl;
cout << "-----\n";
cout << setw(5) << setiosflags(ios::fixed)
     << setprecision(2) << 26.27 + 682.3 + 1.968 << endl;
```

d.
```
cout << setw(5) << setiosflags(ios::fixed)
     << setprecision(2) << 36.164 << endl;
cout << setw(5) << setiosflags(ios::fixed)
     << setprecision(2) << 10.003 << endl;
cout << "-----" << endl;
```

6. The following table lists the correspondence between the decimal numbers 1 through 15 and their octal and hexadecimal representation.

```
    Decimal:  1 2 3 4 5 6 7  8  9 10 11 12 13 14 15
      Octal:  1 2 3 4 5 6 7 10 11 12 13 14 15 16 17
Hexadecimal:  1 2 3 4 5 6 7  8  9  a  b  c  d  e  f
```

Using the above table, determine the output of the following program.

```
#include <iostream.h>
#include <iomanip.h>
```

```
int main()
{
  cout << "\nThe value of 14 in octal is " << oct << 14 <<
       << "\nThe value of 14 in hexadecimal is " << hex << 14
       << "\nThe value of 0xA in decimal is " << dec << 0xA
       << "\nThe value of 0xA in octal is " << oct << 0xA
       << endl;

  return 0;
}
```

3.3 Using Mathematical Library Functions

As we have seen, assignment statements can be used to perform arithmetic computations. For example, the assignment statement

```
totalPrice = unitPrice * amount;
```

multiplies the value in `unitPrice` times the value in `amount` and assigns the resulting value to `totalPrice`. Although addition, subtraction, multiplication, and division are easily accomplished using C++'s arithmetic operators, no such operators exist for raising a number to a power, finding the square root of a number, or determining trigonometric values. To facilitate such calculations, C++ provides standard preprogrammed functions that can be included in a program.

Before using one of C++'s mathematical functions, you need to know:

- the name of the desired mathematical function
- what the mathematical function does
- the type of data required by the mathematical function
- the data type of the result returned by the mathematical function
- how to include the library

To illustrate the use of C++'s mathematical functions, consider the mathematical function named `sqrt()`, which calculates the square root of a number. The square root of a number is computed using the expression

```
sqrt(number)
```

FIGURE 3.12

Passing data to the `sqrt()` function

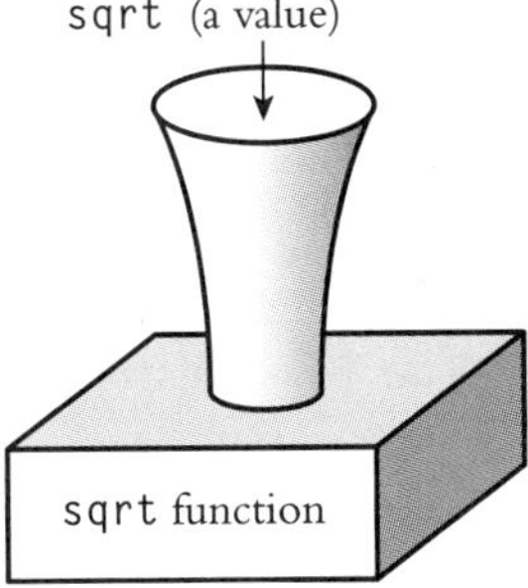

where the function's name, in this case `sqrt`, is followed by parentheses containing the number for which the square root is desired. The purpose of the parentheses following the function name is to provide a funnel through which data can be passed to the function (see Figure 3.12). The items that are passed to the function through the parentheses are called arguments of the function and constitute its input data. For example, the following expressions are used to compute the square root of the arguments 4, 17.0, 25, 1043.29, and 6.4516, respectively:

```
sqrt(4)
sqrt(17.0)
sqrt(25)
sqrt(1043.29)
sqrt(6.4516)
```

Notice that the argument to the `sqrt()` function can be either an integer or real value. This is an example of C++'s function overloading capabilities. Function overloading permits the same function name to be defined for different argument data types. In this case there are really five square root functions named `sqrt()`—defined for integer, long integer, float, double, and long double arguments. The correct `sqrt()` function is called depending on the type of value given it. The `sqrt()` function determines the square root of its argument and returns the result as a double. The values returned by the previous expressions are:

Expression	Value Returned
sqrt(4)	2.0
sqrt(17.0)	4.123106
sqrt(25)	5.0
sqrt(1043.29)	32.3
sqrt(6.4516)	2.54

TABLE 3.4 Common C++ functions

Function Name	Description	Returned Value
`abs(a)`	absolute value	same data type as argument
`pow(a1,a2)`	a1 raised to the a2 power	data type of argument a1
`sqrt(a)`	square root of a	same data type as argument
`sin(a)`	sine of a (a in radians)	double
`cos(a)`	cosine of a (a in radians)	double
`tan(a)`	tangent of a (a in radians)	double
`log(a)`	natural logarithm of a	double
`log10(a)`	common log (base 10) of a	double
`exp(a)`	e raised to the a power	double

Table 3.4 lists the more commonly used mathematical functions provided in C++, including the `sqrt()` function. To access these functions in a program requires that the header file name `math.h`, which contains appropriate declarations for the mathematical function, be included with the function. This is done by placing the following preprocessor statement at the top of any program using a mathematical function

```
#include <math.h>  <---- no semicolon
```

Although some of the mathematical functions listed require more than one argument, all functions, by definition, can directly return at most one value. Additionally, all of the functions listed are overloaded; this means the same function name can be used with integer and real arguments. Table 3.5 illustrates the value returned by selected functions using example arguments.

In each case that a mathematical function is used it is called into action by giving the name of the function and passing any data to it within the parentheses following the function's name (see Figure 3.13).

TABLE 3.5 Selected function examples

Example	Returned Value
`abs(-7.362)`	7.362000
`abs(-3)`	3
`pow(2.0,5.0)`	32.00000
`pow(10,3)`	1000
`log(18.697)`	2.928363
`log10(18.697)`	1.271772
`exp(-3.2)`	0.040762

FIGURE 3.13

Using and passing data to a function

function name(data passed to the function);

This identifies the called function — This passes data to the function

The arguments that are passed to a function need not be single constants. Expressions can also be arguments provided that the expression can be computed to yield a value of the required data type. For example, the following arguments are valid for the given functions:

```
sqrt(4.0 + 5.3 * 4.0)          abs(2.3 * 4.6)
sqrt(16.0 * 2.0 - 6.7)         sin(theta - phi)
sqrt(x * y - z/3.2)            cos(2.0 * omega)
```

The expressions in parentheses are first evaluated to yield a specific value. Thus, values would have to be assigned to the variables `theta`, `phi`, `x`, `y`, `z`, and `omega` before their use in the above expressions. After the value of the argument is calculated, it is passed to the function.

Functions may be included as part of larger expressions. For example:

```
  4 * sqrt(4.5 * 10.0 - 9.0) - 2.0
= 4 * sqrt(36.0) - 2.0
= 4 * 6.0 - 2.0
= 24.0 - 2.0
= 22.0
```

The step-by-step evaluation of an expression such as

```
3.0 * sqrt(5 * 33 - 13.71) / 5
```

is:

```
Step                                      Result
-----------------------------------------------------------------------
1. Perform multiplication in argument     3.0 * sqrt(165 - 13.71) / 5
2. Complete argument calculation          3.0 * sqrt(151.29) / 5
3. Return a function value                3.0 * 12.3 / 5
4. Perform the multiplication             36.9 / 5
5. Perform the division                   7.38
```

Program 3.9 illustrates the use of the `sqrt` function to determine the time it takes a ball to hit the ground after it has been dropped from an 800-foot tower. The mathematical formula used to calculate the time, in seconds, that it takes to fall a given distance, in feet, is:

```
time = sqrt(2 * distance / g)
```

where `g` is the gravitational constant equal to 32.2 ft/sec^2.

PROGRAM 3.9

```
#include <iostream.h>  // this line may be placed second instead of first
#include <math.h>      // this line may be placed first instead of second
int main()
{
  int height;
  double time;

  height = 800;
  time = sqrt(2 * height / 32.2);
  cout << "It will take " << time << " seconds to fall "
       << height << " feet." << endl;

  return 0;
}
```

The output produced by Program 3.9 is shown in Figure 3.14.

As used in Program 3.9, the value returned by the `sqrt()` function is assigned to the variable `time`. In addition to assigning a function's returned value to a variable, the

FIGURE 3.14

Output displayed by Program 3.9

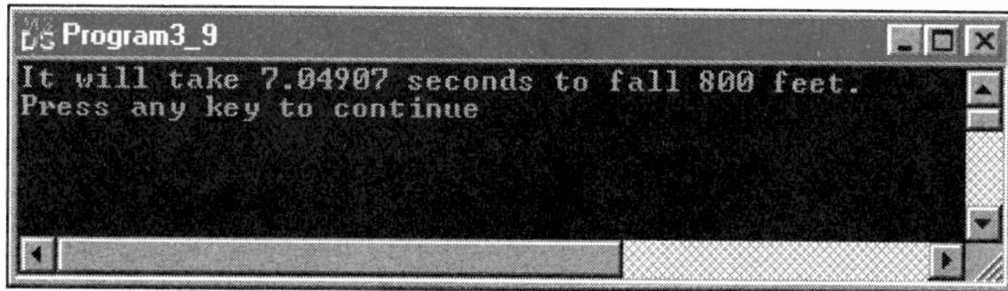
Program3_9
It will take 7.04907 seconds to fall 800 feet.
Press any key to continue

returned value may be included within a larger expression, or even used as an argument to another function. For example, the expression

```
sqrt( pow( abs(num1),num2 ) )
```

is valid. The computation proceeds from the inner to the outer pairs of parentheses. Thus, the absolute value of num1 is computed first and used as an argument to the pow() function. The value returned by the pow() function is then used as an argument to the sqrt function.

Casts

We have already seen the conversion of an operand's data type within mixed-mode arithmetic expressions (Section 2.3) and across assignment operators (Section 3.1). In addition to these implicit data type conversions that are automatically made within mixed-mode arithmetic and assignment expressions, C++ also provides for explicit user-specified type conversions. The operators that are used to force the conversion of a value to another type are the cast operators. C++ provides both compile-time and run-time cast operators.

The compile-time cast is a unary operator having the syntax data-type (expression), where data-type is the desired data type that the expression within parentheses will be converted to. For example, the expression

```
int (a * b)
```

ensures that the value of the expression a * b is converted to an integer value.[7]

With the introduction of the new C++ standard, run-time casts were introduced. In this type of cast, the requested type conversion is checked at run time and is applied only if the conversion results in a valid value. Although four different types of run-time casts are available, the most commonly used cast and the one corresponding to the compile-time cast has the syntax static-cast<data-type>(expression). For example, the run-time cast static-cast<int>(a*b) is equivalent to the compile-time cast (int) (a * b).

EXERCISES 3.3

1. Write function calls to determine:
   a. The square root of 6.37.
   b. The square root of $x - y$.
   c. The sine of 30 degrees.

---

7 The C type cast syntax, in this case (int) (a * b), where the parentheses are placed around int, also works in C++.

d. The sine of 60 degrees.

f. The absolute value of $a^2 - b^2$.

h. The value of e raised to the 3rd power.

2. For $a = 10.6, b = 13.9, c = -3.42$, determine the value of:

a. `int (a)`

b. `int (b)`

c. `int (c)`

d. `int (a + b)`

e. `int (a) + b + c`

f. `int (a + b) + c`

g. `int (a + b + c)`

h. `float (int (a)) + b`

i. `float (int (a + b))`

j. `abs(a) + abs(b)`

k. `sqrt(abs(a - b))`

3. Write C statements for the following:

a. $c = \sqrt{a^2 + b^2}$

b. $p = \sqrt{|\ m - n\ |}$

c. $sum = \dfrac{a(r^n - 1)}{r - 1}$

4. Write, compile, and execute a C++ program that calculates and returns the 4th root of the number 81, which is 3. When you have verified that your program works correctly, use it to determine the fourth root of 1,728.896400. Your program should make use of the `sqrt` function.

5. Write, compile, and execute a C++ program that calculates the distance between two points whose coordinates are (7,12) and (3,9). Use the fact that the distance between two points having coordinates $(x1,y1)$ and $(x2,y2)$ is

$$\text{distance} = \sqrt{[x1 - x2]^2 + [y1 - y2]^2}.$$

When you have verified that your program works correctly, by calculating the distance between the two points manually, use your program to determine the distance between the points (-12,-15) and (22,5).

6. A model of worldwide population, in billions of people, after 1995 is given by the equation

$$\text{Population} = 6.0e^{.02[Year - 1995]}$$

Using this formula, write, compile, and execute a C++ program to estimate the worldwide population in the year 2005. Verify the result displayed by your program by calculating the answer manually. After you have verified your program is working correctly, use it to estimate the world's population in the year 2012.

7. Although we have been concentrating on integer and real arithmetic, C++ allows characters and integers to be added or subtracted. This can be done because C++ always converts a character to an equivalent integer value whenever a character is used in an arithmetic expression (the decimal value of each character can be found in Appendix B). Thus, characters and integers can be freely mixed in arithmetic expressions. For example, if your computer uses the ASCII code, the expression `'a' + 1` equals 98, and `'z' - 1` equals 121. These values can be converted back into characters using the cast operator. Thus, `char ('a' + 1) = 'b'` and `char ('z' - 1) = 'y'`. Similarly, `char('A' + 1)` is `'B'`, and `char('Z' - 1)` is `'Y'`. With this as background, determine the character results of the following expressions (assume that all characters are stored using the ASCII code).

a. `char ('m' - 5)`

b. `char ('m' + 5)`

c. `char ('G' + 6)`

d. `char ('G' - 6)`

8. a. The table in Appendix B lists the integer values corresponding to each letter stored using the ASCII code. Using this table, notice that the uppercase letters consist of contiguous codes starting with an integer value of 65 for *A* and ending with 90 for the letter *Z*. Similarly, the lowercase letters begin with the integer value of 97 for the letter *a* and end with 122 for the letter *z*. With this as background, determine the character value of the expressions `char ('A' + 32)` and `char ('Z' + 32)`.

b. Using Appendix B, determine the integer value of the expression `'a' - 'A'`.

c. Using the results of Exercises 8a and 8b, determine the character value of the following expression, where *uppercase letter* can be any uppercase letter from A to Z:

`char (`uppercase letter `+ 'a' - 'A')`

3.4 Program Input Using the `cin` Object

Data for programs that are going to be executed only once may be included directly in the program. For example, if we wanted to multiply the numbers 30.0 and 0.05, we could use Program 3.10.

PROGRAM 3.10

```
#include <iostream.h>
int main()
{
  float num1, num2, product;

  num1 = 30.0;
  num2 = 0.05;
  product = num1 * num2;
  cout << "30.0 times 0.05 is " << product << endl;

  return 0;
}
```

The output line displayed by Program 3.10 is:

```
30.0 times 0.05 is 1.5
```

Program 3.10 can be shortened, as illustrated in Program 3.11. Both programs, however, suffer from the same basic problem that they must be rewritten in order to multiply different numbers. Both programs lack the facility for entering different numbers on which to operate.

PROGRAM 3.11

```
#include <iostream.h>
int main()
{
  cout << "30.0 times 0.05 is " << 30.0 * 0.05 << endl;

  return 0;
}
```

Except for the practice provided to the programmer of writing, entering, and running the program, programs that do the same calculation only once, on the same set of numbers, are clearly not very useful. After all, it is simpler to use a calculator to multiply two numbers than to enter and run either Program 3.10 or 3.11.

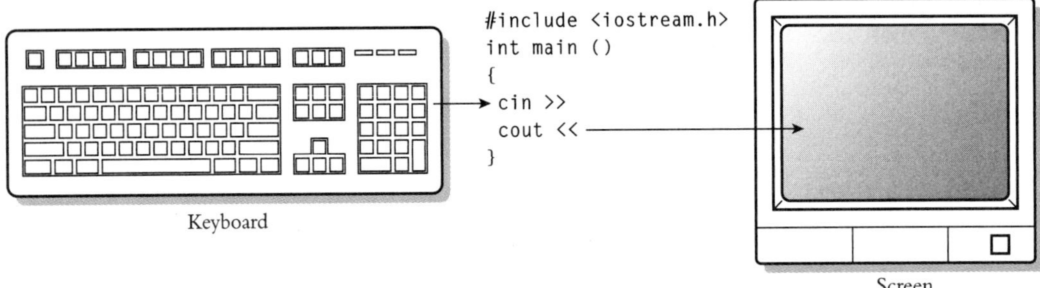

FIGURE 3.15

`cin` **is used to enter data;** `cout` **is used to display data**

This section presents the `cin` object, which is used to enter data into a program while it is executing. Just as the `cout` object displays a copy of the value stored inside a variable, the `cin` object allows the user to enter a value at the terminal (see Figure 3.15). The value is then stored directly in a variable.

When a statement such as `cin >> num1;` is encountered, the computer stops program execution and accepts data from the keyboard. When a data item is typed, the `cin` object stores the item into the variable listed after the extraction ("get from") operator, `>>`. The program then continues execution with the next statement after the call to `cin`. To see this, consider Program 3.12.

PROGRAM 3.12

```
#include <iostream.h>
int main()
{
  float num1, num2, product;

  cout << "Please type in a number: ";
  cin  >> num1;
  cout << "Please type in another number: ";
  cin  >> num2;
  product = num1 * num2;
  cout << num1 << " times " << num2 << " is " << product << endl;

  return 0;
}
```

FIGURE 3.16

Sample run using Program 3.12

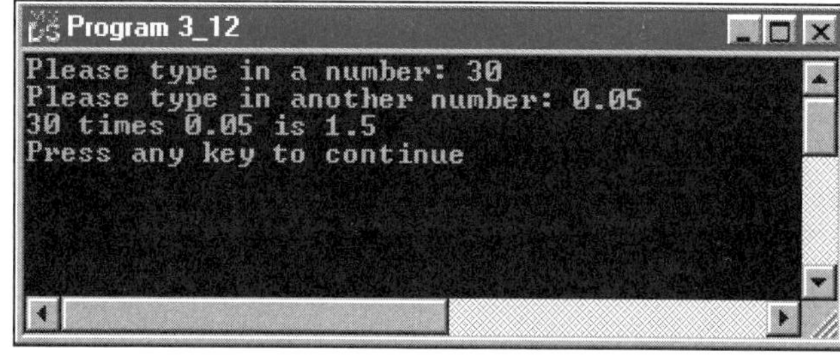
Program 3_12
Please type in a number: 30
Please type in another number: 0.05
30 times 0.05 is 1.5
Press any key to continue

The first `cout` statement in Program 3.12 prints a string that tells the person at the terminal what should be typed. When an output string is used in this manner it is called a **prompt.** In this case the prompt tells the user to type a number. The computer then executes the next statement, which uses a `cin` object. The `cin` object puts the computer into a temporary pause (or wait) state for as long as it takes the user to type a value. Then the user signals the `cin` object that the data entry is finished by pressing the return key after the value has been typed. The entered value is stored in the variable to the right of the extraction symbol (`num1` here), and the computer is taken out of its paused state. Program execution then proceeds with the next statement, which in Program 3.12 is another statement using `cout`. This statement causes the next message to be displayed. The following statement then uses `cin` to again put the program into a temporary wait state while the user types a second value. This second number is stored in the variable `num2`. Figure 3.16 illustrates a sample run that was made using Program 3.12.

In Program 3.12, each time `cin` is encountered it is used to store one value into a variable. The `cin` object, however, can be used to enter and store as many values as there are extraction symbols, >>, and variables to hold the entered data. For example, the statement

```
cin >> num1 >> num2;
```

results in two values being read from the terminal and assigned to the variables `num1` and `num2`. If the data entered at the terminal was

```
0.052 245.79
```

the variables `num1` and `num2` would contain the values `0.052` and `245.79`, respectively. Notice that when actually entering numbers such as `0.052` and `245.79`, there must be at least one space between the numbers. The space between the entered numbers clearly indicates where one number ends and the next begins. Inserting more than one space between numbers has no effect on `cin`.

The same spacing also is applicable to entering character data; that is, the extraction operator, >>, will skip blank spaces and store the next nonblank character in a character variable. For example, in response to the statements

```
char ch1, ch2, ch3;  // declare three character variables
cin >> ch1 >> ch2 >> ch3;  // accept three characters
```

The input

```
a  b  c
```

causes the letter a to be stored in the variable ch1, the letter b to be stored in the variable ch2, and the letter c to be stored in the variable ch3. Because a character variable can be used to store only one character, the input

```
abc
```

can also be used.

Any number of statements using the cin object may be made in a program, and any number of values may be input using a single cin statement. Program 3.13 illustrates using the cin object to input three numbers from the keyboard. The program then calculates and displays the average of the numbers entered.

PROGRAM 3.13

```
#include <iostream.h>
int main()
{
  int num1, num2, num3;
  float average;

  cout << "Enter three integer numbers: ";
  cin  >> num1 >> num2 >> num3;
  average =  (num1 + num2 + num3) / 3.0;
  cout << "The average of the numbers is " << average << endl;

  return 0;
}
```

A sample run using Program 3.13 is shown in Figure 3.17.

FIGURE 3.17

Sample run using Program 3.13

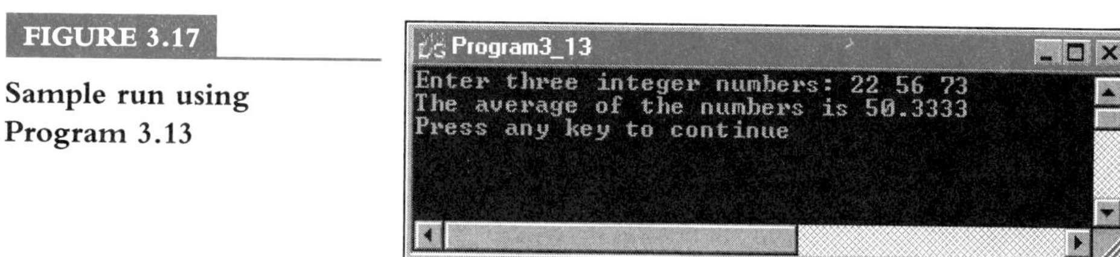

Note that the data typed at the keyboard for this sample run consists of the input:

```
22 56 73
```

In response to this stream of input, Program 3.13 stores the value `22` in the variable `num1`, the value `56` in the variable `num2`, and the value `73` in the variable `num3` (see Figure 3.18). Because the average of three integer numbers can be a floating point number, the variable `average`, which is used to store the average, is declared as a floating point variable. Note also that the parentheses are needed in the assignment statement `average = (num1 + num2 + num3) / 3.0;`. Without these parentheses, the only value that would be divided by 3.0 would be the integer in `num3` (because division has a higher precedence than addition).

The extraction operation used with the `cin` object, like its `cout` insertion operation counterpart, is "clever" enough to make a few data type conversions. For example, if an integer is entered in place of a floating point or double precision number, the integer will be converted to the correct data type.[8] Similarly, if a floating point or double precision number is entered when an integer is expected, only the integer part of the number will be used. For example, assume the following numbers are typed in response to the state-

FIGURE 3.18

Inputting data into the variables `num1`, `num2`, **and** `num3`

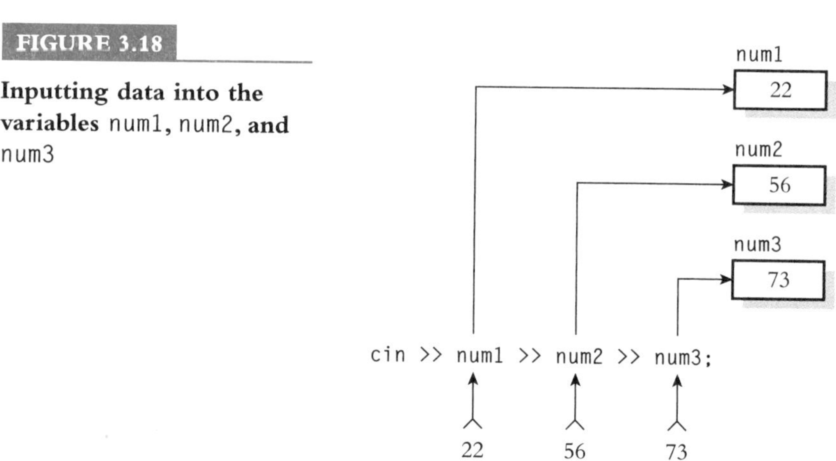

8 Strictly speaking, what comes in from the keyboard is not any data type, such as an `int` or `float`, but is simply a sequence of characters. The extraction operation handles the conversion from the character sequence to a defined data type.

ment `cin >> num1 >> num2 >> num3;`, where `num1` and `num3` have been declared as floating point variables and `num2` is an integer variable

```
56  22.879  33.923
```

The `56` will be converted to `56.0` and stored in the variable `num1`. The extraction operation continues extracting data from the input stream sent to it, expecting an integer value. As far as `cin` is concerned, the decimal point after the `22` in the number `22.879` indicates the end of an integer and the start of a decimal number. Thus, the number `22` is assigned to `num2`. Continuing to process its input stream, `cin` takes the `.879` as the next floating point number and assigns it to in `num3`. As far as `cin` is concerned, `33.923` is extra input and is ignored. If, though, you do not initially type enough data, the `cin` object will continue to make the computer pause until sufficient data have been entered.

EXERCISES 3.4

1. For the following declaration statements, write a statement using the `cin` object that will cause the computer to pause while the appropriate data are typed by the user.

a. `int firstnum;`

b. `float grade;`

c. `double secnum;`

d. `char keyval;`

e.
```
int month, years;
float average;
```

f.
```
char ch;
int num1,num2;
double grade1,grade2;
```

g.
```
float interest, principal, capital;
double price, yield;
```

h.
```
char ch,letter1,letter2;
int num1,num2,num3;
```

i.
```
float temp1,temp2,temp3;
double volts1,volts2;
```

2. a. Write a C++ program that first displays the following prompt:

```
Enter the temperature in degrees Celsius:
```

Have your program accept a value entered from the keyboard and convert the temperature entered to degrees Fahrenheit, using the formula *Fahrenheit* = (9.0/5.0) ★ *Celsius* + 32.0. Your program should then display the temperature in degrees Celsius, using an appropriate output message.

b. Compile and execute the program written for Exercise 2a. Verify your program by calculating by hand, and then using your program, the Fahrenheit equivalent of the following test data:

Test data set 1: 0 degrees Celsius.
Test data set 2: 50 degrees Celsius.
Test data set 3: 100 degrees Celsius.

When you are sure your program is working correctly, use it to complete the following table:

Celsius	Fahrenheit
45	
50	
55	
60	
65	
70	

3. Write, compile, and execute a C++ program that displays the following prompt:

```
Enter the radius of a circle:
```

After accepting a value for the radius, your program should calculate and display the circumference of the circle. (*Hint: circumference* = 2.0 ★ 3.1416 ★ *radius.*) For testing purposes, verify your program using a test input radius of 3 inches. After manually determining that the result produced by your program is correct, use your program to complete the following table:

Radius (in.)	Circumference (in.)
1.0	
1.5	
2.0	
2.5	
3.0	
3.5	

4. a. Write, compile, and execute a C++ program that displays the following prompts:

```
Enter the miles driven:
Enter the gallons of gas used:
```

After each prompt is displayed, your program should use an input statement to accept data from the keyboard for the displayed prompt. After the gallons of gas used number has been entered, your program should calculate and display miles per gallon obtained. This value should be included in an appropriate message and calculated using the equation *miles per gallon = miles/gallons used*. Verify your program using the following test data:

Test data set 1: Miles = 276, Gas = 10 gallons.
Test data set 2: Miles = 200, Gas = 15.5 gallons.

When you have completed your verification, use your program to complete the following table:

Miles Driven	Gallons Used	MPG
250	16.00	
275	18.00	
312	19.54	
296	17.39	

b. For the program written for Exercise 4a, determine how many verification runs are required to ensure the program is working correctly and give a reason supporting your answer.

5. a. Write, compile, and execute a C++ program that displays the following prompts:

```
Enter a number:
Enter a second number:
Enter a third number:
Enter a fourth number:
```

After each prompt is displayed, your program should use an input statement to accept a number from the keyboard for the displayed prompt. After the fourth number has been entered, your program should calculate and display the average of the numbers. The average should be included in an appropriate message. Check the average displayed by your program using the following test data:

Test data set 1: 100, 100, 100, 100
Test data set 2: 100, 0, 100, 0

When you have completed your verification, use your program to complete the following table:

Numbers	Average
92, 98, 79, 85	
86, 84, 75, 86	
63, 85, 74, 82	

b. Repeat Exercise 5a, making sure that you use the same variable name, number, for each number input. Also use the variable sum for the sum of the numbers. (*Hint:* To do this, you may use the statement `sum = sum + number` after each number is accepted. Review the material on accumulating presented in Section 2.3.)

6. Write a C++ program that prompts the user to type in a number. Have your program accept the number as an integer and immediately display the integer using a `cout` object call. Run your program three times. The first time you run the program enter a valid integer number, the second time enter a floating point number, and the third time enter a character. Using the output display, see what number your program actually accepted from the data you entered.

7. Repeat Exercise 6 but have your program declare the variable used to store the number as a floating point variable. Run the program four times. The first time enter an integer, the second time enter a decimal number with less than six decimal places, the third time enter a number having more than six decimal places, and the fourth time enter a character. Using the output display, keep track of what number your program actually accepted from the data you typed in. What happened, if anything, and why?

8. Repeat Exercise 6 but have your program declare the variable used to store the number as a double precision variable. Run the program four times. The first time enter an integer, the second time enter a decimal number with less than six decimal places, the third time enter a number having more than six decimal places, and the fourth time enter a character. Using the output display, keep track of what number your program actually accepted from the data you typed in. What happened, if anything, and why?

3.5 The `const` Qualifier

Quite frequently, literal data used within a program have a more general meaning that is recognized outside the context of the program. Examples of these types of constants include the number 3.1416, which is π accurate to four decimal places; 32.2 ft/sec^2, which is the gravitational constant; and the number 2.71828, which is Euler's number accurate to five decimal places.

The meaning of certain other constants appearing in a program are defined strictly within the context of the application being programmed. For example, in a program used to determine bank interest charges, the interest rate would typically appear in a number of different places throughout the program. Similarly, in determining the weight of various sized objects, the density of the material being used takes on a special significance. Numbers such as these are sometimes referred to by programmers as **magic numbers.** By themselves the numbers are quite ordinary, but in the context of a particular application they have a special ("magical") meaning. Frequently, the same magic number appears repeatedly within the same program. This recurrence of the same constant throughout a program is a potential source of error should the constant have to be changed. For example, if either the interest rate or sales tax rate changes, as rates are prone to do, the programmer would have the cumbersome task of changing the value everywhere it appears in the program. Multiple changes, however, are subject to error—if just one rate value is overlooked and not changed, the result obtained when the program is run will be incorrect and the source of the error difficult to locate.

To avoid the problem of having a magic number spread throughout a program in many places and to permit clear identification of more universal constants, such as π, C++ allows the programmer to give these constants their own symbolic name. Then, instead of using the number throughout the program, the symbolic name is used instead. If the number ever has to be changed, the change need only be made once at the point where the symbolic name is equated to the actual number value. Equating numbers to symbolic names is accomplished using a `const` declaration qualifier. The `const` qualifier specifies that the declared identifier can be read only after it is initialized; it cannot be changed. Three examples using this qualifier are:

```
const float SALESTAX = 0.05;
const double PI = 3.1416;
const int MAXNUM = 100;
```

The first declaration statement creates a floating point symbolic constant named `SALESTAX` and initializes it with the value `0.05`. The second declaration statement creates the double precision symbolic constant named `PI` and initializes it to `3.1416`. Finally, the third declaration creates an integer symbolic constant named `MAXNUM` and initializes it with the value `100`.

Once a symbolic constant is created and initialized, the value stored in the identifier cannot be changed. Thus, for all practical purposes, the name of the constant and its value are linked together for the duration of the program that declares them.

Although we have typed the symbolic constants in uppercase letters, lowercase letters could have been used. It is common in C++, however, to use uppercase letters for symbolic constants to easily identify them as such. Then, whenever a programmer sees all uppercase letters in a program, he or she will know that the identifier is not a variable whose value can be changed within the program.

Once declared, a `const` variable can be used in any C++ statement in place of the number it represents. For example, the assignment statements

```
circum = 2 * PI * radius;
tax = SALESTAX * purchase;
```

are both valid. These statements must, of course, appear after the declarations for all their variables. Because a `const` declaration effectively equates a constant value to a variable, and the variable name can be used as a direct replacement for its initializing constant, such variables are commonly referred to as **symbolic constants** or **named constants.** We shall use these terms interchangeably.

Placement of Statements

At this stage we have introduced a variety of statement types. The general rule in C+ for statement placement is simply that a variable or named constant must be declared before it can be used. Although this rule permits both preprocessor directives and declaration statements to be placed throughout a program, doing so results in a very poor program structure. As a matter of good programming form, the following statement ordering should be used:

```
preprocessor directives

int main()
{
  named constants
  variable declarations

  other executable statements

  return value
}
```

As new statement types are introduced we will expand this placement structure to accommodate them. Notice that comment statements can be freely intermixed anywhere within this basic structure. Program 3.14 illustrates the use of a symbolic constant.

Figure 3.19 illustrates a sample run that was made using Program 3.14.

FIGURE 3.19

Sample run using Program 3.14

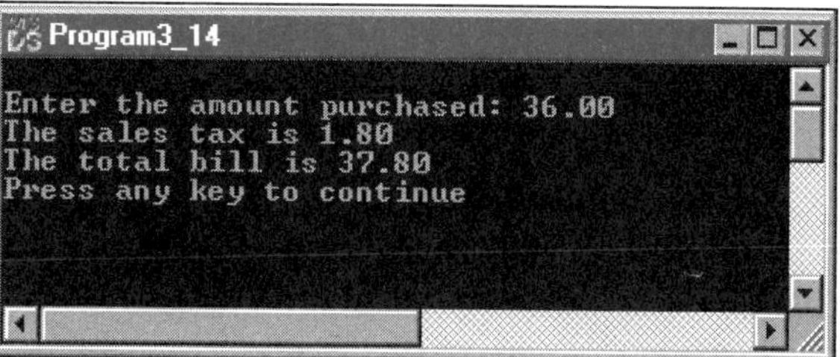

PROGRAM 3.14

```
#include <iostream.h>
#include <iomanip.h>
int main()
{
  const float SALESTAX = 0.05;
  float amount, taxes, total;

  cout << "\nEnter the amount purchased: ";
  cin  >> amount;
  taxes = SALESTAX * amount;
  total = amount + taxes;
  cout << "The sales tax is "
       << setiosflags(ios::fixed)
       << setiosflags(ios::showpoint)
       << setprecision(2) << taxes << endl;
  cout << "The total bill is " << total << endl;

  return 0;
}
```

Notice that the manipulator settings stay in effect until they are changed, so the desired settings need be made only once, in the first `cout` stream.

The advantage of using the named constant `SALESTAX` in Program 3.14 is that it permits a programmer to change the value of the sales tax without having to search through the program to see where the sales tax is used. It should be understood that a named constant represents a constant value that must not be altered after it is defined. Whenever a named constant appears in an instruction it has the same effect as the constant it represents. Thus, `SALESTAX` in Program 3.14 is simply another way of representing the number `0.05`. Because `SALESTAX` and the number `0.05` are equivalent, the value of `SALESTAX` may not be subsequently changed within the program. Once `SALESTAX` has been defined as a constant, an assignment statement such as:

```
SALESTAX = 0.06;
```

is meaningless and will result in an error message because `SALESTAX` is not a variable. `SALESTAX` is only a stand-in for the value `0.05`, so this statement is equivalent to writing the invalid statement `0.05 = 0.06`.

Although we have used the const qualifier to construct symbolic constants, we will encounter this data type once again in Chapter 6, where we will show that they are useful as function arguments in ensuring that the argument is not modified within the function.

EXERCISES 3.5

1. Modify Program 3.9 to use the named constant GRAV in place of the value 32.2 used in the program. Compile and execute your program to verify it produces the same result as shown in the text.

2. Rewrite the following program to use the named constant FACTOR in place of the expression (5.0/9.0) contained within the program.

```
#include <iostream.h>
int main()
{
  float fahren, celsius;
  cout << "Enter a temperature in degrees Fahrenheit: ";
  cin  >> fahren;
  celsius = (5.0/9.0) * (fahren - 32.0);
  cout << "The equivalent Celsius temperature is "
       << celsius << endl;

  return 0;
}
```

3. Rewrite the following program to use the named constant PRIME_RATE in place of the value 0.08 contained within the program.

```
#include <iostream.h>
int main()
{
  float prime, amount, interest;
  prime = 0.08;      // prime interest rate
  cout << <Enter the amount: ";
  cin  >> amount;
  interest = prime * amount;
  cout << "The interest earned is "
       << interest << " dollars" << endl;

  return 0;
}
```

3.6 Common Programming Errors

In using the material presented in this chapter, be aware of the following possible errors:

1. Forgetting to assign or initialize values for all variables before the variables are used in an expression. Such values can be assigned by assignment statements, initialized within a declaration statement, or assigned interactively by entering values using the `cin` object.

2. Using a mathematical library function without including the preprocessor statement `#include <math.h>` (and on a UNIX-based system forgetting to include the `-lm` argument to the `cc` command).

3. Using a library function without providing the correct number or arguments having the proper data type.

4. Applying either the increment or decrement operator to an expression. For example, the expression

```
(count + n)++
```

is incorrect. The increment and decrement operators can be applied only to individual variables.

5. Forgetting to separate all variables passed to `cin` with an extraction symbol, >>.

6. Being unwilling to test a program in depth. After all, you wrote the program, so you assume it is correct or you would have changed it before it was compiled. It is extremely difficult to back away and honestly test your own software. As a programmer, you must constantly remind yourself that just because you think your program is correct does not make it so. Finding errors in your own program is a sobering experience, but one that will help you become a master programmer.

7. A more exotic and less common error occurs when the increment and decrement operators are used with variables that appear more than once in the same expression. This error basically occurs because C++ does not specify the order in which operands are accessed within an expression. For example, the value assigned to result in the statement

```
result = i + i++;
```

is compiler dependent. If your compiler accesses the first operand, `i`, first, the above statement is equivalent to

```
result = 2 * i;
i++;
```

However, if your compiler accesses the second operand, `i++`, first, the value of the first operand will be altered before it is used the second time and the value `2i + 1` is assigned to `result`. As a general rule, therefore, do not use either the increment or decrement operator in an expression when the variable it operates on appears more than once in the expression.

3.7 Chapter Summary

1. An **expression** is a sequence of one or more operands separated by operators. An operand is a constant, a variable, or another expression. A value is associated with an expression.

2. Expressions are evaluated according to the precedence and associativity of the operators used in the expression.

3. The assignment symbol, =, is an operator. Expressions using this operator assign a value to a variable; additionally, the expression itself takes on a value. Because assignment is an operation in C++, multiple uses of the assignment operator are possible in the same expression.

4. The increment operator, ++, adds one to a variable, and the decrement operator, `--`, subtracts one from a variable. Both of these operators can be used as prefixes or postfixes. In prefix operation the variable is incremented (or decremented) before its value is used. In postfix operation the variable is incremented (or decremented) after its value is used.

5. C++ provides library functions for calculating square root, logarithmic, and other mathematical computations. Each program using one of these mathematical functions must either include the statement `#include <math.h>` or have a function declaration for the mathematical function before it is called.

6. Every mathematical library function operates on its arguments to calculate a single value. To use a library function effectively, you must know what the function does, the name of the function, the number and data types of the arguments expected by the function, and the data type of the returned value.

7. Data passed to a function are called **arguments** of the function. Arguments are passed to a library function by including each argument, separated by commas, within the parentheses following the function's name. Each function has its own requirements for the number and data types of the arguments that must be provided.

8. Functions may be included within larger expressions.

9. The `cin` object is used for data input. This object accepts a stream of data from the keyboard and assigns the data to variables. The general form of a statement using `cin` is:

```
cin >> var1 >> var2 . . . >> varn;
```

The extraction symbol, >>, must be used to separate the variable names.

10. When a `cin` statement is encountered, the computer temporarily suspends further statement execution until sufficient data have been entered for the number of variables contained in the `cin` function.

11. It is good programming practice to display a message, prior to a `cin` statement, that alerts the user as to the type and number of data items to be entered. Such a message is called a **prompt.**

12. Values can be equated to a single variable, using the `const` variable qualifier when the variable is declared. This makes the variable read-only after it is initialized within the declaration statement. This declaration has the syntax

`const` data-type identifier = initial value;

and permits the identifier to be used instead of the initial value anywhere in the program after the command. Generally, such declarations are placed before the variable declarations within a C++ program.

4 Selection Structures

Many advances have occurred in the theoretical foundations of programming since the inception of high-level languages in the late 1950s. One of the most important of these advances was the recognition in the late 1960s that any algorithm, no matter how complex, could be constructed using combinations of four standardized **flow of control** structures: sequential, selection, repetition, and invocation.

The term **flow of control** refers to the order in which a program's statements are executed. Unless directed otherwise, the normal flow of control for all programs is **sequential.** This means that statements are executed in sequence, one after another, in the order in which they are placed within the program.

Selection, repetition, and invocation structures permit the sequential flow of control to be altered in precisely defined ways. As you might have guessed, the selection structure is used to select which statements are to be performed next, and the repetition structure is used to repeat a set of statements. This chapter presents C++'s selection statements. Repetition and invocation techniques are presented in Chapters 5 and 6.

4.1 Selection Criteria

In the solution of many problems, different actions must be taken depending upon the value of the data. Examples of simple situations include calculating an area *only if* the measurements are positive, performing a division *only if* the divisor is not zero, printing different messages *depending upon* the value of a grade received, and so on.

The `if-else` statement in C++ is used to implement such a decision structure in its simplest form—that of choosing between two alternatives. The most commonly used pseudocode syntax of this statement is:

```
if (condition)
  statement executed if condition is true;
else
  statement executed if condition is false;
```

When an executing program encounters the `if` statement, the condition is evaluated to determine its numerical value, which is then interpreted as either true or false. If the condition evaluates to any positive or negative nonzero numerical value, the condition is considered as a "true" condition and the statement following the `if` is executed. If the condition evaluates to a zero numerical value, the condition is considered as a "false" condition and the statement following the `else` is executed. The `else` part of the statement is optional and may be omitted.

The condition used in an `if` statement can be any valid C++ expression (including, as we will see, even an assignment expression). The most commonly used expressions, however, are called **relational expressions.** A **simple relational expression** consists of a relational operator that compares two operands, as shown in Figure 4.1.

FIGURE 4.1

Anatomy of a simple relational expression

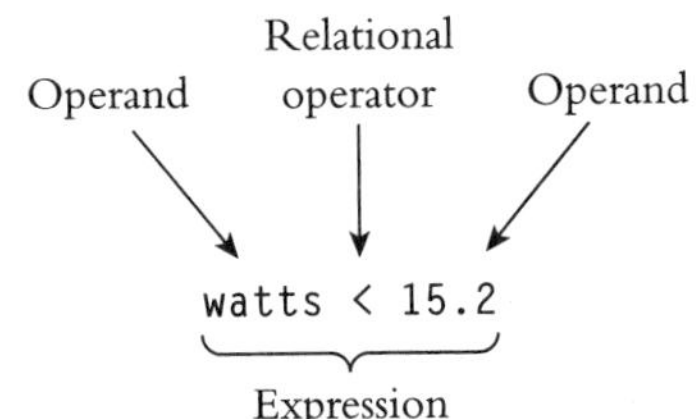

Whereas each operand in a relational expression can be either a variable or constant, the relational operators must be one of those listed in Table 4.1. These relational operators may be used with integer, float, double, or character operands, but must be typed exactly as given in Table 4.1. Thus, even though the following examples are all valid:

```
age > 40        length <= 50      temp > 98.6
  3 < 4         flag == done      idNum == 682
day != 5        2.0 > 3.3         hours > 40
```

TABLE 4.1 Relational operators

Relational Operator	Meaning	Example
`<`	less than	`age < 30`
`>`	greater than	`height > 6.2`
`<=`	less than or equal to	`taxable <= 20000`
`>=`	greater than or equal to	`temp >= 98.6`
`==`	equal to	`grade == 100`
`!=`	not equal to	`number != 250`

the following are invalid:

```
length =< 50        // operator out of order
2.0 >> 3.3          // invalid operator
flag = = done       // spaces are not allowed
```

Relational expressions are sometimes called **conditions,** and we use both terms to refer to these expressions. Like all C++ expressions, relational expressions are evaluated to yield a numerical result.[1] In the case of a relational expression, the value of the expression can be only the integer value of 1 or 0, which is interpreted as true and false, respectively. *A relational expression that we would interpret as true evaluates to an integer value of 1, and a false relational expression results in an integer value of 0.* For example, because the relationship 3 < 4 is always true, this expression has a value of 1, and because the relationship 2.0 > 3.3 is always false, the value of the expression itself is 0. This can be verified using the statements

```
cout << "The value of 3 < 4 is " << (3 < 4) << endl;
cout << "The value of 2.0 > 3.0 is " << (2.0 > 3.3) << endl;
```

which result in the display

```
The value of 3 < 4 is 1
The value of 2.0 > 3.0 is 0
```

1 In this regard, C++ differs from other high-level computer languages that yield a Boolean (true, false) result.

The value of a relational expression such as `hours > 40` depends on the value stored in the variable `hours`.

In a C++ program, a relational expression's value is not as important as the interpretation C++ places on the value when the expression is used as part of a selection statement. In these statements, which are presented in the next section, we will see that *a zero value is used by C++ to represent a false condition and any nonzero value is used to represent a true condition.* The selection of which statement to execute next is then based on the value obtained.

In addition to numerical operands, character data can also be compared using relational operators. For example, in the ASCII code the letter `'A'` is stored using a code having a lower numerical value than the letter `'B'`, the code for a `'B'` is lower in value than the code for a `'C'`, and so on. For character sets coded in this manner, the following conditions are evaluated as shown.

Expression	Value	Interpretation
`'A' > 'C'`	0	False
`'D' <= 'Z'`	1	True
`'E' == 'F'`	0	False
`'G' >= 'M'`	0	False
`'B' != 'C'`	1	True

Comparing letters is essential in alphabetizing names or using characters to select a particular choice in decision-making situations.

Logical Operators

In addition to using simple relational expressions as conditions, more complex conditions can be created using the logical operations `AND`, `OR`, and `NOT`. These operations are represented by the symbols `&&`, `||`, and `!`, respectively.

When the `AND` operator, `&&`, is used with two simple expressions, the condition is true only if both individual expressions are true by themselves. Thus, the logical condition:

```
(age > 48) && (term < 10)
```

is true only if `age` is greater than `48` and `term` is less than `10`. Because relational operators have a higher precedence than logical operators, the parentheses in this logical expression could have been omitted.

The logical OR operator, `||`, is also applied between two expressions. When using the OR operator, the condition is satisfied if either one or both of the two expressions is true. Thus, the condition

```
(age > 48) || (term < 10)
```

is true if either `age` is greater than `48`, `term` is less than `10`, or if both conditions are true. Again, the parentheses surrounding the relational expressions are included to make the expression easier to read. Because of the higher precedence of relational operators with respect to logical operators the same evaluation would be made even if the parentheses were omitted.

For the declarations

```
int i, j;
float a, b, complete;
```

the following represent valid conditions:

```
a > b
(i == j) || (a < b) || complete
(a/b > 5) && (i <= 20)
```

Before these conditions can be evaluated, the values of `a`, `b`, `i`, `j`, and `complete` must be known. Assuming `a = 12.0`, `b = 2.0`, `i = 15`, `j = 30`, and `complete = 0.0`, the previous expressions yield the following results:

Expression	Value	Interpretation
`a > b`	1	True
`(i == j) || (a < b) || complete`	0	False
`(a/b > 5) && (i <= 20)`	1	True

The NOT operator is used to change an expression to its opposite state; that is, if the expression has any nonzero value (true), `!expression` produces a zero value (false). If an expression is false to begin with (has a zero value), `!expression` is true and evaluates to 1. For example, assuming the number `26` is stored in the variable `age`, the expression `age > 40` has a value of zero (it is false), whereas the expression `!(age > 40)` has a value of 1. Because the NOT operator is used with only one expression, it is a unary operator.

TABLE 4.2 Operator precedence

<table>
<tr><th>Operator</th><th>Associativity</th></tr>
<tr><td>! unary - ++ --</td><td>right to left</td></tr>
<tr><td>* / %</td><td>left to right</td></tr>
<tr><td>+ -</td><td>left to right</td></tr>
<tr><td>< <= > >=</td><td>left to right</td></tr>
<tr><td>== !=</td><td>left to right</td></tr>
<tr><td>&&</td><td>left to right</td></tr>
<tr><td>||</td><td>left to right</td></tr>
<tr><td>= += -= /=</td><td>right to left</td></tr>
</table>

The relational and logical operators have a hierarchy of execution similar to the arithmetic operators. Table 4.2 lists the precedence of these operators in relation to the other operators we have used.

The following example illustrates the use of an operator's precedence and associativity to evaluate relational expressions, assuming the following declarations:

```
char key = 'm';
int i = 5, j = 7, k = 12;
double x = 22.5;
```

Expression	Equivalent Expression	Value	Interpretation
i + 2 == k - 1	(i + 2) == (k - 1)	0	False
3 * i - j < 22	(3 * i) - j < 22	1	True
i + 2 * j > k	(i + (2 * j)) > k	1	True
k + 3 <= -j + 3 * i	(k + 3) <= ((-j) + (3*i))	0	False
'a' + 1 == 'b'	('a' + 1) == 'b'	1	True
key - 1 > 'p'	(key - 1) > 'p'	0	False
key + 1 == 'n'	(key + 1) == 'n'	1	True
25 >= x + 1.0	25 >= (x + 1.0)	1	True

As with all expressions, parentheses can be used to alter the assigned operator priority and improve the readability of relational expressions. By evaluating the expressions within parentheses first, the following compound condition is evaluated as:

```
(6 * 3 == 36 / 2) || (13 < 3 * 3 + 4) && !(6 - 2 < 5)
       (18 == 18) ||    (13 < 9 + 4)   && !(4 < 5)
                1 ||    (13 < 13)      && !1
                1 ||        0          &&  0
                1 ||        0
                  1
```

A Numerical Accuracy Problem

A problem that can occur with C++'s relational expressions is a subtle numerical accuracy problem relating to floating point and double precision numbers. Due to the way computers store these numbers, tests for equality of floating point and double precision values and variables using the relational operator == should be avoided.

The reason for this is that many decimal numbers, such as 0.1, for example, cannot be represented exactly in binary using a finite number of bits. Thus, testing for exact equality for such numbers can fail. When equality of noninteger values is desired it is better to require that the absolute value of the difference between operands be less than some extremely small value. Thus, for floating point and double precision operands the general expression:

```
operand-1 == operand-2
```

should be replaced by the condition

```
fabs(operand-1 - operand-2) < 0.000001
```

where the value 0.000001 can be altered to any other acceptably small value. Thus, if the difference between the two operands is less than 0.000001 (or any other user-selected amount), the two operands are considered essentially equal. For example, if `x` and `y` are floating point variables, a condition such as

```
x/y == 0.35
```

should be programmed as

```
fabs(x/y - 0.35) < EPSILON
```

where `EPSILON` can be a named constant set to any acceptably small value, such as 0.000001.[2] This latter condition ensures that slight inaccuracies in representing noninteger numbers in binary do not affect evaluation of the tested condition. All computers have an exact binary representation of zero, so comparisons for exact equality to zero don't encounter this numerical accuracy problem.

---

2 Using the `fabs()` function requires inclusion of the `math.h` header file. This is done by placing the preprocessor statement `#include <math.h>` either immediately before or after the `#include <iostream.h>` preprocessor statement. It may also require specific inclusion of the math library at compile time with a `-lm` command line argument.

EXERCISES 4.1

1. Determine the value of the following expressions. Assume `a = 5`, `b = 2`, `c = 4`, `d = 6`, and `e = 3`.
   a. `a > b`
   b. `a != b`
   c. `d % b == c % b`
   d. `a * c != d * b`
   e. `d * b == c * e`
   f. `!(a * b)`
   g. `!(a % b * c)`
   h. `!(c % b * a)`
   i. `b % c * a`

2. Using parentheses, rewrite the following expressions to correctly indicate their order of evaluation. Then evaluate each expression assuming `a = 5`, `b = 2`, and `c = 4`.
   a. `a % b * c && c % b * a`
   b. `a % b * c || c % b * a`
   c. `b % c * a && a % c * b`
   d. `b % c * a || a % c * b`

3. Write relational expressions to express the following conditions (use variable names of your own choosing):
   a. a person's age is equal to 30
   b. a person's temperature is greater than 98.6
   c. a person's height is less than 6 feet
   d. the current month is 12 (December)
   e. the letter input is m
   f. a person's age is equal to 30 and the person is taller than 6 feet
   g. the current day is the 15th day of the 1st month
   h. a person is older than 50 or has been employed at the company for at least 5 years
   i. a person's identification number is less than 500 and the person is older than 55
   j. a length is greater than 2 feet and less than 3 feet

4. Determine the value of the following expressions, assuming `a = 5`, `b = 2`, `c = 4`, and `d = 5`.
   a. `a == 5`
   b. `b * d == c * c`
   c. `d % b * c > 5 || c % b * d < 7`

4.2 The if-else Statement

The if-else structure directs the program to select a sequence of one or more instructions based on the result of a comparison. For example, suppose we are to calculate the area of a circle given the radius as an input value. If the input is a negative number we are to print a message that the radius cannot be a negative value, otherwise we are to calculate and print the circle's area. The if-else structure can be used in this situation to select the correct operation based on whether the radius is negative. The general syntax of the if-else statement is:

```
if (expression) statement1;
else statement2;
```

The expression is evaluated first. If the value of the expression is nonzero, *statement1* is executed. If the value is zero, the statement after the keyword else is executed. Thus, one of the two statements (either *statement1* or *statement2*, but not both) is always executed depending on the value of the expression. Notice that the tested expression must be put in parentheses and a semicolon is placed after each statement.

For clarity, the if-else statement should be written on four lines using the form:

```
if (expression)   <-------- no semicolon here
  statement1;
else  <-------------------- no semicolon here
  statement2;
```

The form of the if-else statement that is selected generally depends on the length of statements 1 and 2. However, when using the second form, do not put a semicolon after the parentheses or the keyword else. The semicolons go only after the ends of the statements.

The flowchart for the if-else statement is shown in Figure 4.2.

As a specific example of an if-else structure, we will construct a C++ program for determining the area of a circle by first examining the value of the radius. The condition to be tested is whether the radius is less than zero. An appropriate if-else structure for this situation is:[3]

```
if (radius < 0.0)
  cout << "A negative radius is invalid" << endl;
else
  cout << "The area of this circle is " << 3.1416 * pow(radius,2) << endl;
```

3 Note that in actual practice the value of π in this statement would be defined as a named constant.

FIGURE 4.2

The `if-else` flowchart

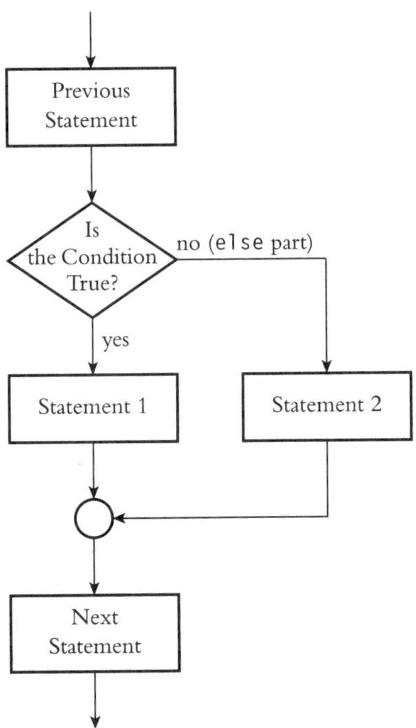

Here we have used the relational operator `<` to represent the relation "less than." If the value of `radius` is less than 0, the condition is true (has a value of 1) and the statement `cout << "A negative radius is invalid";` is executed. If the condition is not true, the value of the expression is 0, and the statement after the keyword `else` is executed. Program 4.1 illustrates the use of this statement in a complete program. A blank line was inserted before and after the `if-else` statement to highlight it in the complete program. We will continue to do this throughout the text to emphasize the statement being presented.

To illustrate selection in action, Program 4.1 was run twice with different input data. Figures 4.3 and 4.4 illustrate the program for two different values input for the radius. In reviewing this output observe that the radius in the first run of the program was less than

FIGURE 4.3

Entering a negative radius value

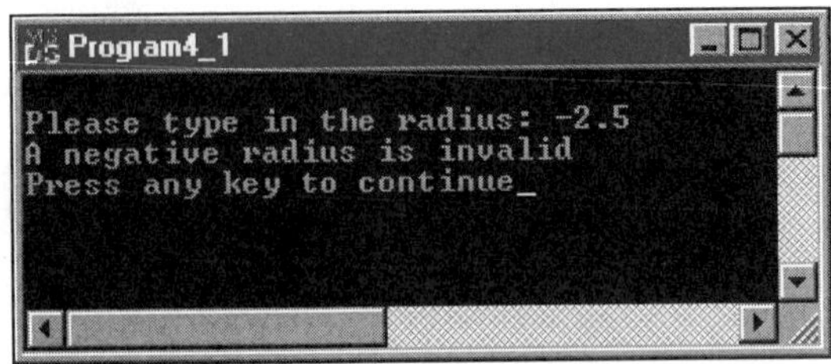

FIGURE 4.4

Entering a positive radius value

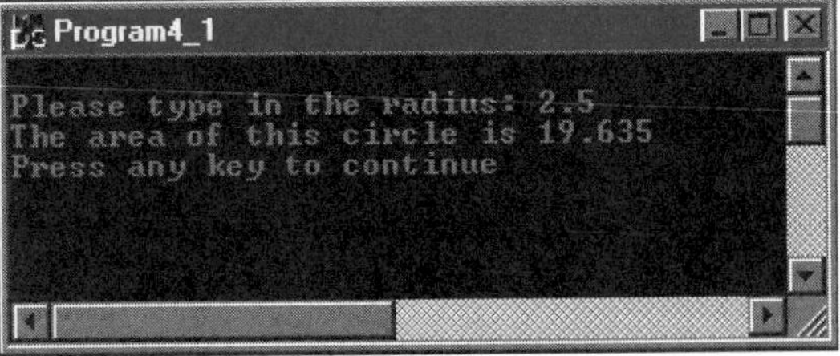

PROGRAM 4.1

```
#include <iostream.h>
#include <iomanip.h>
#include <math.h>

int main()
{
  float radius;

  cout << "\nPlease type in the radius: ";
  cin  >> radius;

  if (radius < 0.0)
    cout << "A negative radius is invalid" << endl;
  else
    cout << "The area of this circle is " << 3.1416 * pow(radius,2) << endl;

  return 0;
}
```

0 and the `if` part of the `if-else` structure correctly executed the `cout` statement telling the user that a negative radius is invalid. In the second run, the radius is not negative and the `else` part of the `if-else` structure was used to yield a correct area computation of

$$3.1416 * (2.5)^2 = 19.635$$

Although any expression can be tested by an `if-else` statement, relational expressions are predominately used. However, statements such as:

```
if (num)
   cout << "Bingo!";
else
   cout << "You lose!";
```

are valid. Because `num`, by itself, is a valid expression, the message `Bingo!` is displayed if `num` has any nonzero value, and the message `You lose!` is displayed if `num` has a value of zero.

Compound Statements

Although only a single statement is permitted in both the `if` and `else` parts of the `if-else` statement, this statement can be a single compound statement. A compound statement is a sequence of single statements contained between braces, as shown in Figure 4.5.

FIGURE 4.5

A compound statement consists of individual statements enclosed within braces.

```
{
  statement1;
  statement2;
  statement3;
       .
       .
       .
  last statement;
}
```

The use of braces to enclose a set of individual statements creates a single block of statements, which may be used anywhere in a C++ program in place of a single statement. The next example illustrates the use of a compound statement within the general form of an `if-else` statement.

```
if (expression)
 {
   statement1;     // as many statements as necessary
   statement2;     // can be put within the braces
   statement3;     // each statement must end with a ;
 }
 else
{
  statement4;
  statement5;
       .
       .
  statementn;
}
```

Program 4.2 illustrates the use of a compound statement in an actual program.

PROGRAM 4.2

```
#include <iostream.h>
#include <iomanip.h>
// a temperature conversion program
int main()
{
  char tempType;
  float temp, fahren, celsius;

  cout << "\nEnter the temperature to be converted: ";
  cin  >> temp;
  cout << "Enter an f if the temperature is in Fahrenheit";
  cout << "\n or a c if the temperature is in Celsius: ";
  cin  >> tempType;

    // set output formats
  cout << setiosflags(ios::fixed)
       << setiosflags(ios::showpoint)
       << setprecision(2);

  if (tempType == 'f')
  {
    celsius = (5.0 / 9.0) * (temp - 32.0);
    cout << "\nThe equivalent Celsius temperature is "
         << celsius << endl;
  }
  else
  {
    fahren =  (9.0 / 5.0) * temp + 32.0;
    cout << "\nThe equivalent Fahrenheit temperature is "
         << fahren << endl;
  }

  return 0;
}
```

Program 4.2 checks whether the value in `tempType` is `f`. If the value is `f`, the compound statement corresponding to the `if` part of the `if-else` statement is executed. Any other letter results in execution of the compound statement corresponding to the `else` part. A sample run of Program 4.2 is shown in Figure 4.6.

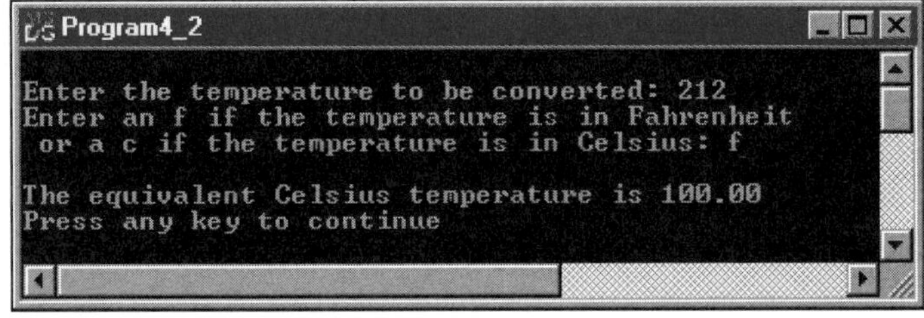

FIGURE 4.6

Sample run using Program 4.2

Block Scope

All statements contained within a compound statement constitute a single block of code and any variable declared within such a block has meaning only between its declaration and the closing braces defining the block. For example, consider the following section of code, which consists of two blocks of code:

```
{   // start of outer block
   int a = 25;
   int b = 17;

   cout << "The value of a is " << a
        <<" and b is " << b << endl;

   {     // start of inner block
     float a = 46.25;
     int c = 10;

     cout << "a is now " << a
          << " b is now " << b
          << " and c is " << c << endl;
   }   // end of inner block

   cout << "a is now " << a
        << " and b is " << b << endl;

}   // end of outer block
```

The output that is produced by this section of code is:

```
The value of a is 25 and b is 17
a is now 46.25 b is now 17 and c is 10
a is now 25 and b is 17
```

PROGRAMMER'S NOTES

Placement of Braces in a Compound Statement

A common practice for some C++ programmers is to place the opening brace of a compound statement on the same line as the if and else statements. By this convention, the if statement in Program 4.2 would appear as shown below. (This placement is a matter of style only—both styles are used and both are acceptable.)

```
if (tempType == 'f') {
    celsius = (5.0 / 9.0) * (temp - 32.0);
    cout << setiosflags(ios::showpoint)
      << setprecision(2)
      << "\nThe equivalent Celsius temperature is "
      << celsius << endl;
}
else {
  fahren = (9.0 / 5.0) * temp + 32.0;
  cout << "\nThe equivalent Fahrenheit temperature is "
       << fahren << endl;
}
```

This output is produced as follows: The first block of code defines two variables named a and b, which may be used anywhere within this block after their declaration, including any block contained inside of it. Within the inner block, two new variables have been declared, named a and c. At this stage, then, we have created four different variables, two of which have the same name. Any referenced variable first results in an attempt to access a variable declared within the block containing the reference. If no variable is defined within the block, an attempt is made to access a variable in the next immediate outside block until a valid access results.

Thus, the values of the variables a and c referenced within the inner block use the values of the variables a and c declared in that block. No variable named b was declared inside the inner block, so the value of b displayed from within the inner block is obtained from the outer block. Finally, the last cout object, which is outside of the inner block, displays the value of the variable a declared in the outer block. If an attempt was made to display the value of c anywhere in the outer block, the compiler would issue an error message stating that c is an undefined symbol.

The location within a program where a variable can be used is formally referred to as the **scope of the variable,** and we will have much more to say on this subject in Chapter 6.

One-Way Selection

A useful modification of the `if-else` statement involves omitting the `else` part of the statement altogether. In this case, the `if` statement takes the shortened and frequently useful form:

```
if (expression)
  statement;
```

The statement following `if` (expression) is executed only if the expression has a nonzero value (a true condition). As before, the statement may be a compound statement. The flowchart for this statement is illustrated on Figure 4.7.

This modified form of the `if` statement is called a one-way `if` statement. Program 4.3 uses this statement to selectively display a message for cars that have been driven more than 3000 miles.

As an illustration of its one-way selection criteria in action, Program 4.3 was run twice, each time with different input data. Figure 4.8 illustrates the case for which the input data cause the statement within the `if` part to be displayed, whereas in Figure 4.9 the input data are below the limit so that the over-the-limit message is not displayed.

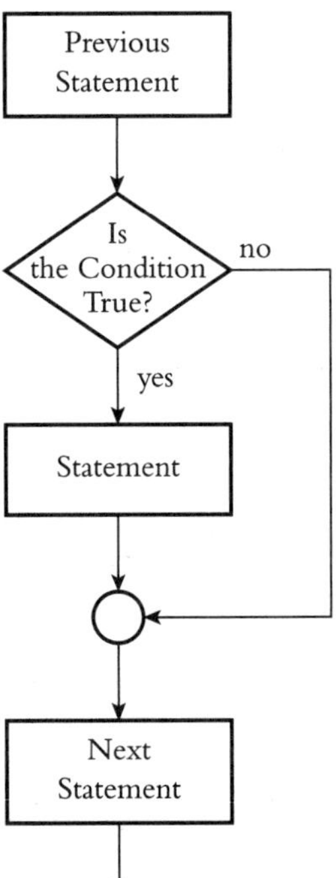

FIGURE 4.7

Flowchart for the one-way `if` statement

PROGRAM 4.3

```
#include <iostream.h>
int main()
{

  const float LIMIT = 3000.0;
  int idNum;
  float miles;

  cout << "\nPlease type in car number and mileage: ";
  cin  >> idNum >> miles;

  if(miles > LIMIT)
    cout << "  Car " << idNum << " is over the limit." << endl;
  cout << "End of program output." << endl;

  return 0;
}
```

FIGURE 4.8

Input data over the limit

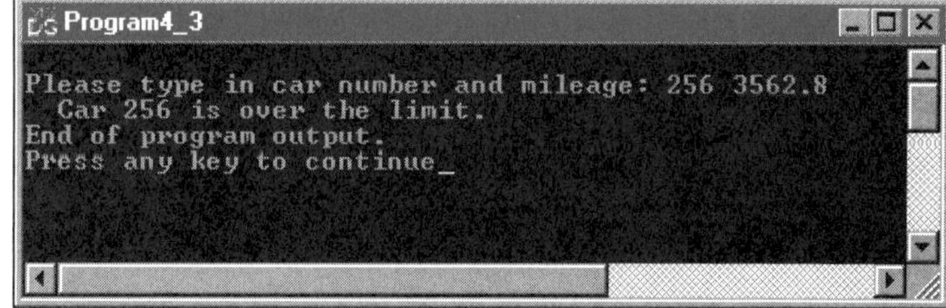

FIGURE 4.9

Input data not over the limit

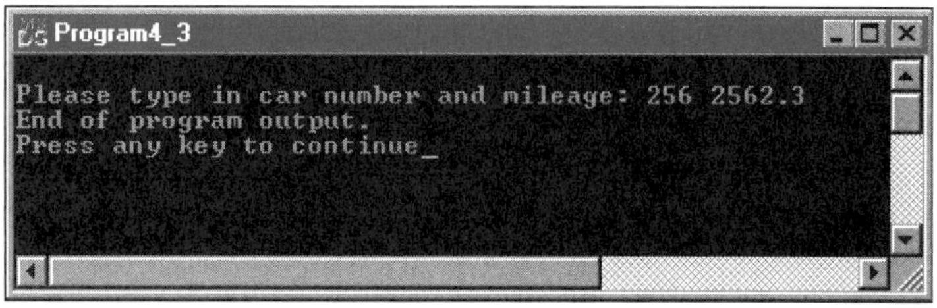

```
Program4_3
Please type in car number and mileage: 256 2562.3
End of program output.
Press any key to continue_
```

Problems Associated with the `if-else` Statement

Two of the most common problems encountered in initially using C++'s `if-else` statement are:

1. Misunderstanding the full implications of what an expression is
2. Using the assignment operator, =, in place of the relational operator ==

Recall that an expression is any combination of operands and operators that yields a result. This definition is extremely broad and more encompassing than is initially apparent. For example, all of the following are valid C++ expressions:

```
age + 5
age = 30
age == 40
```

Assuming that the variables are suitably declared, each of the above expressions yields a result. Program 4.4 uses the `cout` object to display the value of these expressions when `age = 18`.

PROGRAM 4.4

```
#include <iostream.h>
int main()
{
  int age = 18;

  cout << "\nThe value of the first expression is " << (age + 5) << endl;
  cout << "The value of the second expression is " << (age = 30) << endl;
  cout << "The value of the third expression is " << (age == 40) << endl;

  return 0;
}
```

The display produced by Program 4.4 is shown in Figure 4.10. As the output in Program 4.4 illustrates, each expression, by itself, has a value associated with it. The value of the first expression is the sum of the variable `age` plus 5, which is 23. The value of the

FIGURE 4.10

Output displayed by Program 4.4

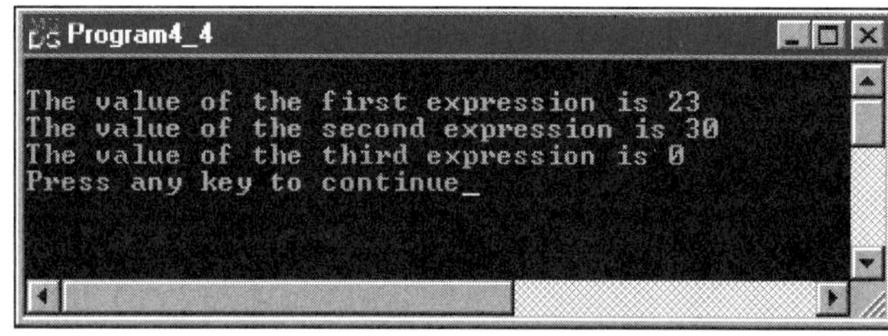

second expression is 30, which is also assigned to the variable `age`. The value of the third expression is zero, because `age` is not equal to 40, and a false condition is represented in C++, with a value of zero. If the value in `age` had been 40, the relational expression `a == 40` would be true and would have a value of 1.

Now assume that the relational expression `age == 40` was intended to be used in the `if` statement

```
if (age == 40)
  cout << "Happy Birthday!";
```

but was mistyped as `age = 40`, resulting in

```
if (age = 40)
  cout << "Happy Birthday!";
```

Because the mistake results in a valid C++ expression, and any C++ expression can be tested by an `if` statement, the resulting `if` statement is valid and will cause the message `Happy Birthday!` to be printed regardless of what value was previously assigned to `age`. Can you see why?

The condition tested by the `if` statement does not compare the value in `age` to the number `40`, but assigns the number `40` to `age`. That is, the expression `age = 40` is not a relational expression at all, but an assignment expression. At the completion of the assignment the expression itself has a value of `40`. Because C++ treats any nonzero value as true, the call to `cout` is made. Another way of looking at this is to realize that the `if` statement is equivalent to the following two statements:

```
age = 40;      // assign 40 to age
if (age)       // test the value of age
  cout << "Happy Birthday!";
```

Because a C++ compiler has no means of knowing that the expression being tested is not the desired one, you must be especially careful when writing conditions.

PROGRAMMER'S NOTES

The Boolean Data Type

Traditionally, both C and C++ did not have a built-in Boolean data type with its two Boolean values, **true** and **false.** Because this data type was not originally a part of the language, a tested expression could not evaluate to a Boolean value. Thus, the syntax

```
if(boolean expression is true)
   execute this statement;
```

was also not built-in to either C or C++. Rather, both C and C++ use the more encompassing syntax:

```
if(expression)
   execute this statement;
```

where *expression* is any expression that evaluates to a numeric value. If the value of the tested expression is a nonzero value it is considered as true, and only a zero value is considered as false.

As specified by the ANSI/ISO C++ standard, C++ will have a new Boolean data type containing the two values, **true** and **false.** Boolean variables will be declared using the keyword **bool.** As currently implemented, the actual values represented by the two Boolean values, **true** and **false,** are the integer values 1 and 0, respectively. For example, consider the following program, which declares two Boolean variables.

```
#include <iostream.h>
int main()
{
  bool t1, t2;

  t1 = true;
  t2 = false;

  cout <<"The value of t1 is " << t1
       << "\n and the value of t2 is " << t2 << endl;
   return 0;
}
```

The output produced by this program is:

```
The value of t1 is 1
 and the value of t2 is 0
```

As seen by this output, the Boolean values **true** and **false** are represented by the integer values 1 and 0, respectively. The Boolean values **true** and **false** have the following relationships:

```
!true = false
!false = true
```

(continued next page)

PROGRAMMER'S NOTES

Additionally, applying either a postfix or prefix ++ operator to a variable of type **bool** will set the Boolean value to **true.** The postfix and prefix -- operators cannot be applied to a Boolean variable.

Boolean values can also be compared, as illustrated by the following code:

```
if (t1 == t2)
  cout << "The values are equal" << endl;
else
  cout << "The values are not equal" << endl;
```

Lastly, assigning any nonzero value to a Boolean variable results in the variable being set to **true;** that is, a value of 1, and assigning a zero value to a Boolean variable results in the variable being set to **false;** that is, a value of 0.

EXERCISES 4.2

1. Write appropriate `if` statements for each of the following conditions:

a. If angle is equal to 90 degrees, print the message "The angle is a right angle," else print the message "The angle is not a right angle."

b. If the temperature is above 100 degrees, display the message "above the boiling point of water," else display the message "below the boiling point of water."

c. If the number is positive add the number to `possum`, else add the number to `negsum`.

d. If the slope is less than .5 set the variable `flag` to zero, else set `flag` to one.

e. If the difference between `num1` and `num2` is less than .001, set the variable `approx` to zero, else calculate `approx` as the quantity `(num1 - num2) / 2.0`.

f. If the difference between `temp1` and `temp2` exceeds 2.3 degrees, calculate `error` as `(temp1 - temp2) * factor`.

g. If x is greater than y and z is less than 20, read in a value for p.

h. If the distance is greater than 20 and it is less than 35, read in a value for the time.

2. Write `if` statements corresponding to the conditions illustrated by each of the following flow charts.

a.

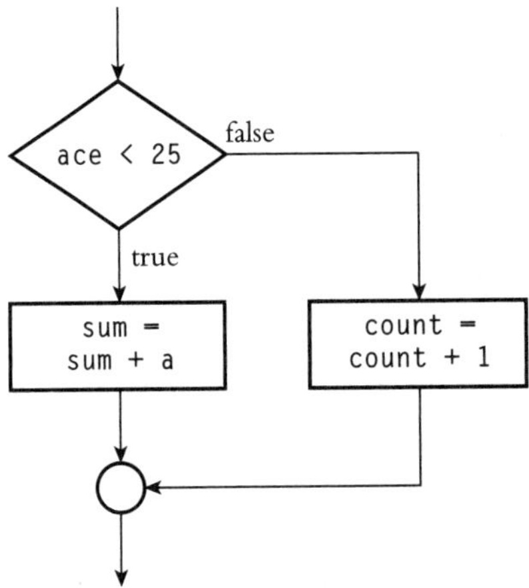

b.

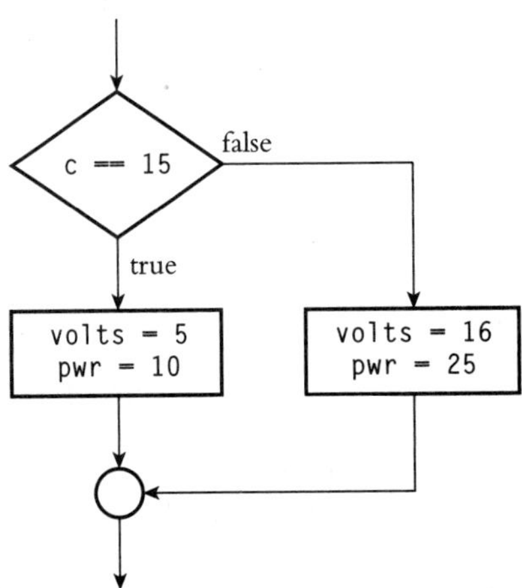

c.

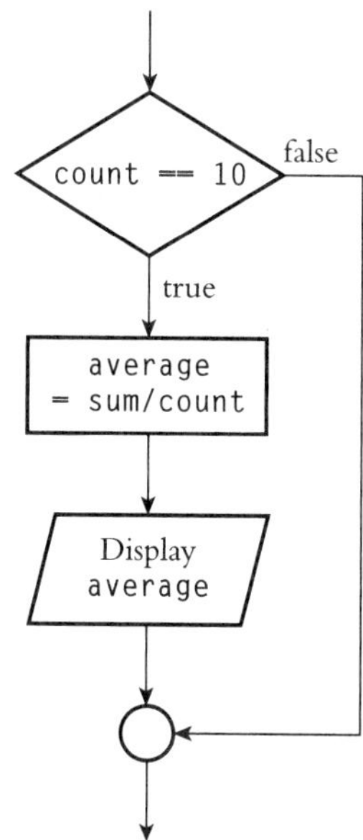

d.

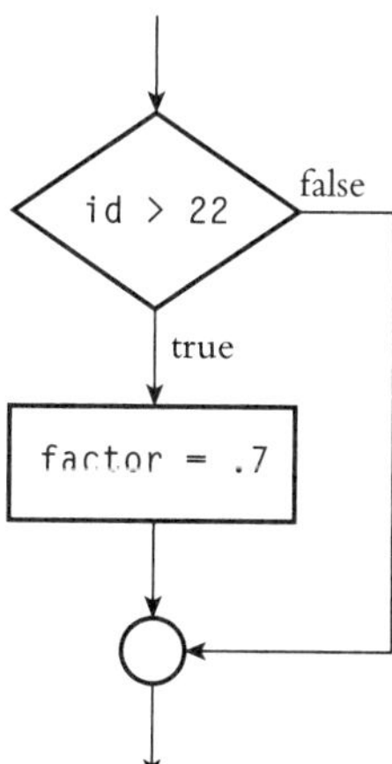

3. In the state of New Jersey, state income taxes are assessed at 2 percent of income for incomes less than or equal to $20,000. For incomes greater than $20,000, state taxes are 2.5 percent of the income that exceeds $20,000 plus a fixed amount of $400. Thus, an appropriate `if-else` statement for computing state income taxes is

```
if(income <= 20,000.0)
  taxes = 0.02 * taxable;
else
  taxes = 0.025 * (taxable - 20,000) + 400.0;
```

Using this information, write a C++ program that calculates the state income tax for a user-entered income value. In writing your program, include the following symbolic constants:

```
const float LIMIT = 20000.0;
const float REGRATE = 0.02;
const float HIGHRATE = 0.025;
const float FIXED = 400.0;
```

(If necessary, review Section 3.5 for the use of symbolic constants.)

4. a. If money is left in a particular bank for more than 5 years, the interest rate given by the bank is 9.5 percent, else the interest rate is 5.4 percent. Write a C++ program that uses the `cin` object to accept the number of years into the variable `numYrs` and display the appropriate interest rate depending on the value input into `numYrs`.

b. How many runs should you make for the program written in Exercise 4a to verify that it is operating correctly? What data should you input in each of the program runs?

5. a. In a pass/fail course, a student passes if the grade is greater than or equal to 70 and fails if the grade is lower. Write a C++ program that accepts a grade and prints the message `A passing grade` or `A failing grade`, as appropriate.

b. How many runs should you make for the program written in Exercise 5a to verify that it is operating correctly? What data should you input in each of the program runs?

6. a. Write a C++ program to compute and display a person's weekly salary as determined by the following expressions:

If the hours worked are less than or equal to 40, the person receives $8.00 per hour, otherwise the person receives $320.00 plus $12.00 for each hour worked over 40 hours.

The program should request the hours worked as input and should display the salary as output.

b. How many runs should you make for the program written in Exercise 6a to verify that it is operating correctly? What data should you input in each of the program runs?

7. a. Write a C++ program that displays either the message `I feel great today!` or `I feel down today!` depending on the input. If the character *u* is entered in the variable `ch`, the first message should be displayed, else the second message should be displayed.

b. How many runs should you make for the program written in Exercise 7a to verify that it is operating correctly? What data should you input in each of the program runs?

8. a. Write a program to display the following two prompts:

Enter a month (use a 1 for Jan, etc.):
Enter a day of the month:

Have your program accept and store a number in the variable `month` in response to the first prompt, and accept and store a number in the variable `day` in response to the second prompt. If the month entered is not between 1 and 12 inclusive, print a message informing the user that an invalid month has been entered. If the day entered is not between 1 and 31, print a message informing the user that an invalid day has been entered.

b. What will your program do if the user types a number with a decimal point for the month? How can you insure that your `if` statements check for an integer number?

9. Write a C++ program that accepts a character and determines if the character is a lowercase letter. A lowercase letter is any character that is greater than or equal to `'a'` and less than or equal to `'z'`. If the entered character is a lowercase letter, display the message `The character just entered is a lowercase letter.` If the entered letter is not lowercase, display the message `The character just entered is not a lowercase letter.`

10. Write a C++ program that first determines if an entered character is a lowercase letter (see Exercise 9). If the letter is lowercase, determine and print out its position in the alphabet. For example, if the entered letter is *c*, the program should print out 3, because *c* is the third letter in the alphabet. (*Hint:* If the entered character is in lowercase, its position can be determined by subtracting `'a'` from the letter and adding 1.)

11. Repeat Exercise 8 to determine if the character entered is an uppercase letter. An uppercase letter is any character greater than or equal to `'A'` and less than or equal to `'Z'`.

12. Write a C++ program that first determines if an entered character is an uppercase letter (see Exercise 11). If the letter is uppercase, determine and print its position in the alphabet. For example, if the entered letter is G, the program should print out 7, because G is the seventh letter in the alphabet. (*Hint:* If the entered character is in uppercase, its position can be determined by subtracting `'A'` from the letter and adding 1.)

13. Write a C++ program that accepts a character. If the character is a lowercase letter (see Exercise 9), convert the letter to uppercase and display the letter in its uppercase form. (*Hint:* Subtracting the integer value 32 from a lowercase letter yields the code for the equivalent uppercase letter. Thus, `'A' = char ('a' - 32)`.)

14. The following program displays the message `Hello there!` regardless of the letter input. Determine where the error is and, if possible, why the program always causes the message to be displayed.

```
#include <iostream.h>
int main()
{
  char letter;

  cout << "Enter a letter: ";
  cin  >> letter;
  if (letter = 'm')
    cout << "Hello there!";

  return 0;
}
```

15. Write a C++ program that asks the user to input two numbers. After your program accepts these numbers have your program check the numbers. If the first number entered is greater than the second number, print the message `The first number is greater.`, else print the message `The first number is not greater.` Test your program by entering the numbers 5 and 8 and then using the numbers 11 and 2. What will your program display if the two numbers entered are equal?

4.3 Nested `if` Statements

As we have seen, an `if-else` statement can contain simple or compound statements. Any valid C++ statement can be used, including another `if-else` statement. Thus, one or more `if-else` statements can be included within either part of an `if-else` statement. The inclusion of one or more `if` statements within an existing `if` statement is called a **nested** `if` statement. For example, substituting the one-way `if` statement

```
if (distance > 500)
  cout << "snap";
```

for `statement1` in the following `if` statement

```
if (hours < 9)
  statement1;
else
  cout << "pop";
```

results in the nested `if` statement

```
if (hours < 9)
{
  if (distance > 500)
    cout << "snap";
}
else
  cout << "pop";
```

The braces around the inner one-way `if` are essential, because in their absence C++ associates an `else` with the closest unpaired `if`. Thus, without the braces, the above statement is equivalent to

```
if (hours < 9)
  if (distance > 500)
    cout << "snap";
  else
    cout << "pop";
```

Here the `else` is paired with the inner `if`, which destroys the meaning of the original `if-else` statement. Notice also that the indentation is irrelevant as far as the compiler is concerned. Whether the indentation exists or not, *the statement is compiled by associating the last* `else` *with the closest unpaired* `if`*, unless braces are used to alter the default pairing.*

The process of nesting `if` statements can be extended indefinitely, so that the `cout << "snap";` statement could itself be replaced by either a complete `if-else` statement or another one-way `if` statement.

Figure 4.11 illustrates the general form of a nested `if-else` statement when an `if-else` statement is nested (a) within the `if` part of an `if-else` statement and (b) within the `else` part of an `if-else` statement.

The `if-else` Chain

In general, the nesting illustrated in Figure 4.11(a) tends to be confusing and is best avoided in practice. However, an extremely useful construction occurs for the nesting illustrated in Figure 4.11 (b), which has the form:

```
if (expression-1)
  statement1;
else
  if (expression-2)
    statement2;
else
  statement3;
```

FIGURE 4.11(a)

(a) Nesting within the `if` part of an `if-else` statement

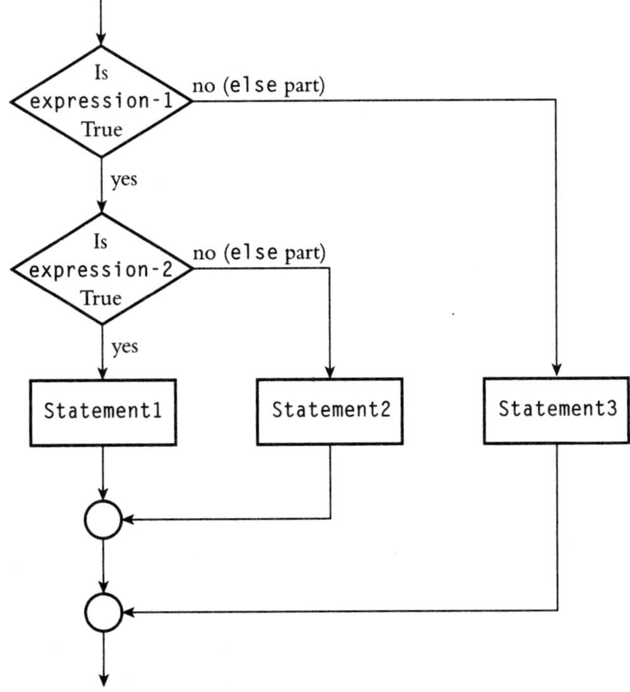

(b) Nesting within the `else` part of an `if-else` statement

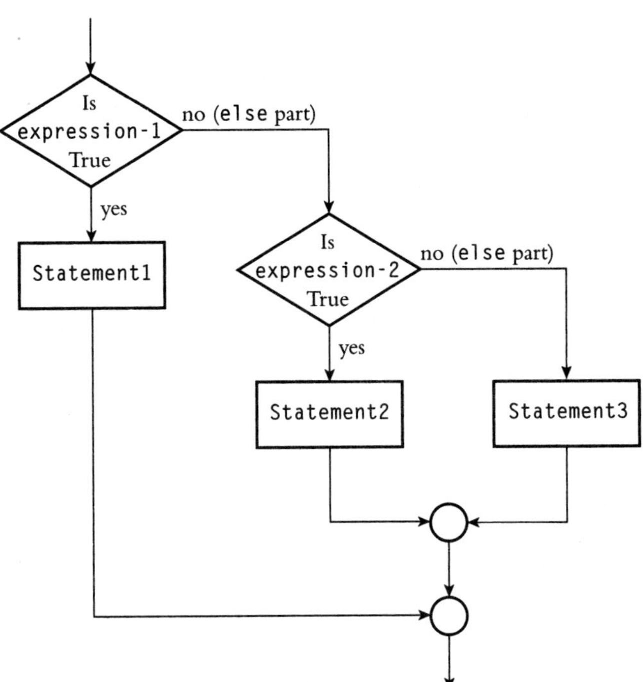

As with all C++ programs, white space is ignored, so the indentation shown is not required. More typically, the preceding construction is written using the following arrangement:

```
if (expression-1)
  statement1;
else if (expression-2)
  statement2;
else
  statement3;
```

This form of a nested `if` statement is extremely useful in practice, and is formally referred to as an `if-else` chain. Each condition is evaluated in order, and if any condition is true the corresponding statement is executed and the remainder of the chain is terminated. The statement associated with the final `else` is executed only if none of the previous conditions is satisfied. This serves as a default or catch-all case that is useful for detecting an impossible or error condition.

The chain can be continued indefinitely by repeatedly making the last statement another `if-else` statement. Thus, the general form of an `if-else` chain is:

```
if (expression-1)
  statement1;
else if (expression-2)
  statement2;
else if (expression-3)
  statement3;
        .
        .
        .
else if (expression-n)
  statement-n;
else
  last-statement;
```

Each condition is evaluated in the order it appears in the statement. For the first condition that is true, the corresponding statement is executed, and the remainder of the statements in the chain are not executed. Thus, if `expression-1` is true, only `statement1` is executed; otherwise `expression-2` is tested. If `expression-2` is then true, only `statement2` is executed; otherwise `expression-3` is tested, and so on. The final `else` in the chain is optional, and `last-statement` is executed only if none of the previous expressions was true. To illustrate the `if-else` chain, Program 4.5 displays a person's marital status corresponding to a letter input. The following letter codes are used:

Marital Status	Input Code
Married	M
Single	S
Divorced	D
Widowed	W

PROGRAM 4.5

```
#include <iostream.h>
int main()
{
  char marcode;

  cout << "\nEnter a marital code: ";
  cin  >> marcode;

  if (marcode == 'M')
    cout << "\nIndividual is married." << endl;
  else if (marcode == 'S')
    cout << "\nIndividual is single." << endl;
  else if (marcode == 'D')
    cout << "\nIndividual is divorced." << endl;
  else if (marcode == 'W')
    cout << "\nIndividual is widowed." << endl;
  else
    cout << "\nAn invalid code was entered." << endl;

  return 0;
}
```

As a final example illustrating the if-else chain, let us calculate the monthly income of a salesperson using the following commission schedule:

Monthly Sales	Income
greater than or equal to \$50,000	\$375 plus 16% of sales
less than \$50,000 but greater than or equal to \$40,000	\$350 plus 14% of sales
less than \$40,000 but greater than or equal to \$30,000	\$325 plus 12% of sales
less than \$30,000 but greater than or equal to \$20,000	\$300 plus 9% of sales
less than \$20,000 but greater than or equal to \$10,000	\$250 plus 5% of sales
less than \$10,000	\$200 plus 3% of sales

The following if-else chain can be used to determine the correct monthly income, where the variable monthlySales is used to store the salesperson's current monthly sales:

```
if (monthlySales >= 50000.00)
  income = 375.00 + .16 * monthlySales;
else if (monthlySales >= 40000.00)
  income = 350.00 + .14 * monthlySales;
else if (monthlySales >= 30000.00)
  income = 325.00 + .12 * monthlySales;
else if (monthlySales >= 20000.00)
  income = 300.00 + .09 * monthlySales;
else if (monthlySales >= 10000.00)
  income = 250.00 + .05 * monthlySales;
else
  income = 200.000 + .03 * monthlySales;
```

Notice that this example makes use of the fact that the chain is stopped once a true condition is found. This is accomplished by checking for the highest monthly sales first. If the salesperson's monthly sales are less than \$50,000, the if-else chain continues checking for the next highest sales amount until the correct category is obtained.

Program 4.6 uses this if-else chain to calculate and display the income corresponding to the value of monthly sales input to the program. A sample run using Program 4.6 is illustrated in Figure 4.12.

PROGRAM 4.6

```
#include <iostream.h>
#include <iomanip.h>
int main()
{
  float monthlySales, income;

  cout << "\nEnter the value of monthly sales: ";
  cin  >> monthlySales;

  if (monthlySales >= 50000.00)
    income = 375.00 + .16 * monthlySales;
  else if (monthlySales >= 40000.00)
    income = 350.00 + .14 * monthlySales;
  else if (monthlySales >= 30000.00)
    income = 325.00 + .12 * monthlySales;
  else if (monthlySales >= 20000.00)
    income = 300.00 + .09 * monthlySales;
  else if (monthlySales >= 10000.00)
    income = 250.00 + .05 * monthlySales;
  else
    income = 200.00 + .03 * monthlySales;

   cout << setiosflags(ios::fixed)
        << setiosflags(ios::showpoint)
        << setprecision(2)
        << "The income is $" << income << endl;

  return 0;
}
```

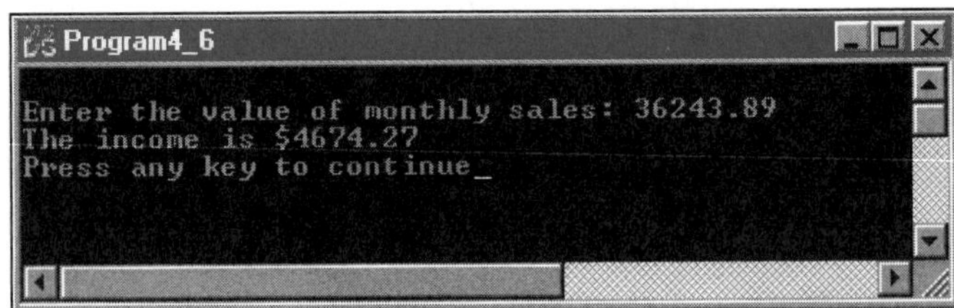

FIGURE 4.12

Sample run using Program 4.6

EXERCISES 4.3

1. Modify Program 4.5 to accept both lower and uppercase letters as marriage codes. For example, if a user enters either an m or an M, the program should display the message `Individual is married.` End the screen display with `Thanks for participating in the survey.`

2. Write nested `if` statements corresponding to the conditions illustrated in each of the following flowcharts.

a.

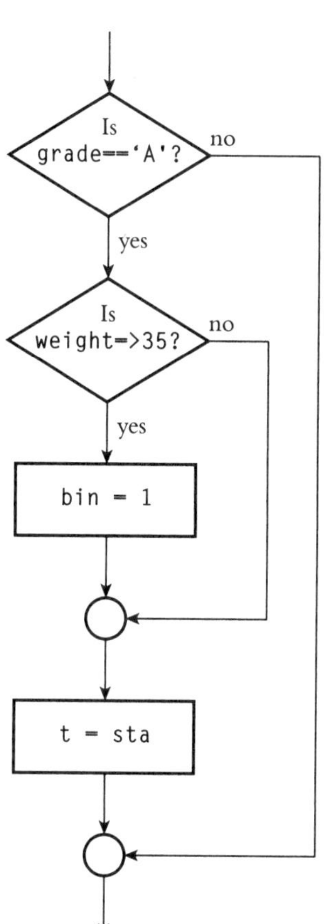

b.

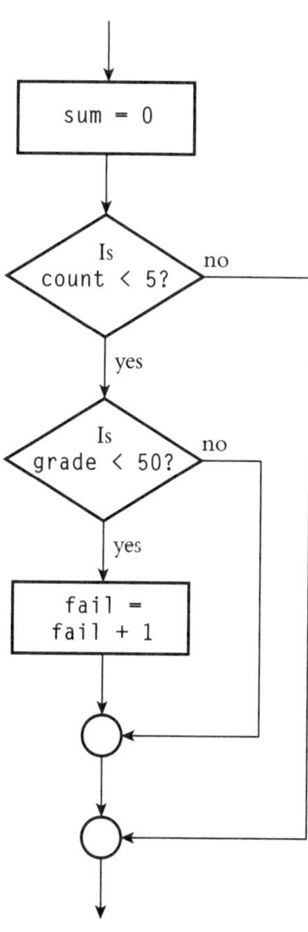

3. An angle is considered acute if it is less than 90 degrees, obtuse if it is greater than 90 degrees, and a right angle if it is equal to 90 degrees. Using this information, write a C++ program that accepts an angle, in degrees, and displays the type of angle corresponding to the degrees entered.

4. The grade level of undergraduate college students is typically determined according to the following schedule:

Number of Credits Completed	Grade Level
less than 32	Freshman
32 to 63	Sophomore
64 to 95	Junior
96 or more	Senior

Using this information, write a C++ program that accepts the number of credits a student has completed, determines the student's grade level, and displays the grade level.

5. A student's letter grade is calculated according to the following schedule:

Numerical Grade	Letter Grade
greater than or equal to 90	A
less than 90 but greater than or equal to 80	B
less than 80 but greater than or equal to 70	C
less than 70 but greater than or equal to 60	D
less than 60	F

Write a C++ program that accepts a student's numerical grade, converts the numerical grade to an equivalent letter grade, and displays the letter grade.

6. The interest rate used on funds deposited in a bank is determined by the amount of time the money is left on deposit. For a particular bank, the following schedule is used:

Time on Deposit	Interest Rate
greater than or equal to 5 years	.095
less than 5 years but greater than or equal to 4 years	.09
less than 4 years but greater than or equal to 3 years	.085
less than 3 years but greater than or equal to 2 years	.075
less than 2 years but greater than or equal to 1 year	.065
less than 1 year	.058

Write a C++ program that accepts the time that funds are left on deposit and displays the interest rate corresponding to the time entered.

7. Write a C++ program that accepts a number followed by one space and then a letter. If the letter following the number is `f`, the program is to treat the number entered as a temperature in degrees Fahrenheit, convert the number to the equivalent degrees Celsius, and print a suitable display message. If the letter following the number is `c`, the program is to consider the number entered as a Celsius temperature, convert the number to the equivalent degrees Fahrenheit, and print a suitable display message. If the letter is neither `f` nor `c` the program is to print a message that the data entered is invalid and terminate. Use an `if-else` chain in your program and make use of the conversion formulas:

$$Celsius = (5.0 / 9.0) \star (Fahrenheit - 32.0)$$
$$Fahrenheit = (9.0 / 5.0) \star Celsius + 32.0$$

8. Using the commission schedule from Program 4.6, the following program calculates monthly income:

```
#include <iostream.h>
#include <iomanip.h>
int main()
{
  float monthlySales, income;

  cout << "Enter the value of monthly sales: ";
  cin  >> monthlySales;

  if (monthlySales >= 50000.00)
    income = 375.00 + .16 * monthlySales;
  if (monthlySales >= 40000.00 && monthlySales < 50000.00)
    income = 350.00 + .14 * monthlySales;
  if (monthlySales >= 30000.00 && monthlySales < 40000.00)
    income = 325.00 + .12 * monthlySales;
```

(continued next page)

```
  if (monthlySales >= 20000.00 && monthlySales < 30000.00)
    income = 300.00 + .09 * monthlySales;
  if (monthlySales >= 10000.00 && monthlySales < 20000.00)
    income = 250.00 + .05 * monthlySales;
  if (monthlySales < 10000.00)
    income = 200.00 + .03 * monthlySales;

  cout << setiosflags(ios::showpoint)
       << setiosflags(ios:: fixed)
       << setprecision(2)
       << "\n\nThe income is $" << income << endl;

  return 0;
}
```

a. Will this program produce the same output as Program 4.6?

b. Which program is better and why?

9. The following program was written to produce the same result as Program 4.6:

```
#include <iostream.h>
#include <iomanip.h>
int main()
{
  float monthlySales, income;

  cout << "Enter the value of monthly sales: ";
  cin  >> monthlySales;

  if (monthlySales < 10000.00)
    income = 200.00 + .03 * monthlySales;
  else if (monthlySales >= 10000.00)
    income = 250.00 + .05 * monthlySales;
  else if (monthlySales >= 20000.00)
    income = 300.00 + .09 * monthlySales;
  else if (monthlySales >= 30000.00)
    income = 325.00 + .12 * monthlySales;
  else if (monthlySales >= 40000.00)
    income = 350.00 + .14 * monthlySales;
  else if (monthlySales >= 50000.00)
    income = 375.00 + .16 * monthlySales;

  cout << setiosflags(ios::fixed)
       << setiosflags(ios::showpoint)
       << setprecision(2)
       << "\n\nThe income is $" << income << endl;

       return 0;
  }
```

a. Will this program run?

b. What does this program do?

c. For what values of monthly sales does this program calculate the correct income?

4.4 The switch Statement

The `if-else` chain is used in programming applications for which one set of instructions must be selected from many possible alternatives. The `switch` statement provides an alternative to the `if-else` chain for cases that compare the value of an integer expression to a specific value. The general form of a switch statement is:

```
switch (expression)
{    // start of compound statement
  case value-1:  <-----------------  terminated with a colon
    statement1;
    statement2;
         .
         .
    break;
  case value-2:  <-----------------  terminated with a colon
    statementm;
    statementn;
         .
         .
    break;
         .
         .
  case value-n:  <-----------------  terminated with a colon
    statementw;
    statementx;
         .
         .
    break;
  default:       <-----------------  terminated with a colon
    statementaa;
    statementbb;
         .
         .
}    // end of switch and compound statement
```

The `switch` statement uses four new keywords: `switch`, `case`, `default`, and `break`. Let's see what each of these words does.

The keyword `switch` identifies the start of the `switch` statement. The expression in parentheses following this word is evaluated and the result of the expression compared to various alternative values contained within the compound statement. The expression in the `switch` statement must evaluate to an integer result or a compilation error results.

Internal to the `switch` statement, the keyword `case` is used to identify or label individual values that are compared to the value of the `switch` expression. The `switch` expression's value is compared to each of these `case` values in the order in which these values are listed until a match is found. When a match occurs, execution begins with the statement immediately following the match. Thus, as illustrated in Figure 4.13, the value of the expression determines where in the `switch` statement execution actually begins.

FIGURE 4.13

The expression determines an entry point.

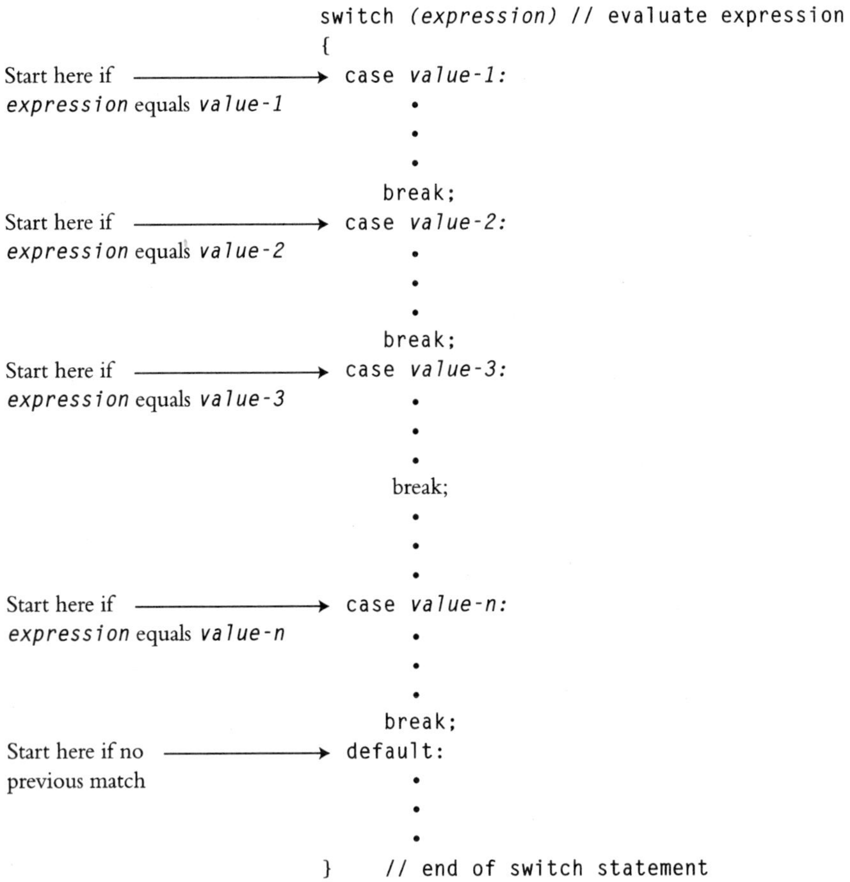

```
                                switch (expression) // evaluate expression
                                {
Start here if           ------>   case value-1:
expression equals value-1               •
                                        •
                                        •
                                      break;
Start here if           ------>   case value-2:
expression equals value-2               •
                                        •
                                        •
                                      break;
Start here if           ------>   case value-3:
expression equals value-3               •
                                        •
                                        •
                                      break;
                                        •
                                        •
                                        •
Start here if           ------>   case value-n:
expression equals value-n               •
                                        •
                                        •
                                      break;
Start here if no        ------>   default:
previous match                          •
                                        •
                                        •
                                }    // end of switch statement
```

Any number of case labels may be contained within a switch statement, in any order. If the value of the expression does not match any of the case values, however, no statement is executed unless the keyword default is encountered. The word default is optional and operates the same as the last else in an if-else chain. If the value of the expression does not match any of the case values, program execution begins with the statement following the word default.

Once an entry point has been located by the switch statement, all further case evaluations are ignored and execution continues through the end of the compound statement unless a break statement is encountered. This is the reason for the break statement, which identifies the end of a particular case and causes an immediate exit from the switch statement. Thus, just as the word case identifies possible starting points in the compound statement, the break statement determines terminating points. If the break statements are omitted, all cases following the matching case value, including the default case, are executed.

When writing a switch statement, we can use multiple case values to refer to the same set of statements; the default label is optional. For example, consider the following:

```
switch (number)
{
  case 1:
    cout << "Have a Good Morning" << endl;
    break;
  case 2:
    cout << "Have a Happy Day" << endl;
    break;
  case 3:
  case 4:
  case 5:
    cout << "Have a Nice Evening" << endl;
}
```

If the value stored in the variable number is 1, the message Have a Good Morning is displayed. Similarly, if the value of number is 2, the second message is displayed. Finally, if the value of number is 3 or 4 or 5, the last message is displayed. Because the statement to be executed for these last three cases is the same, the cases for these values can be "stacked together" as shown in the example. Also, because there is no default, no message is printed if the value of number is not one of the listed case values. Although it is good programming practice to list case values in increasing order, this is not required by the switch statement. A switch statement may have any number of case values, in any order; only the values being used for testing need be listed.

Program 4.7 uses a `switch` statement to select the arithmetic operation (addition, multiplication, or division) to be performed on two numbers depending on the value of the variable `opselect`.

PROGRAM 4.7

```
#include <iostream.h>
int main()
{
  int opselect;
  double fnum, snum;

  cout << "\nPlease type in two numbers: ";
  cin  >> fnum >> snum;
  cout << "Enter a select code: ";
  cout << "\n         1 for addition";
  cout << "\n         2 for multiplication";
  cout << "\n         3 for division : ";
  cin  >> opselect;

  switch (opselect)
  {
    case 1:
      cout << "The sum of the numbers entered is " << fnum+snum;
      break;
    case 2:
      cout << "The product of the numbers entered is " << fnum*snum;
      break;
    case 3:
      cout << "The first number divided by the second is " << fnum/snum;
      break;
  }     // end of switch

  cout << endl;

  return 0;
}
```

Program 4.7 was run twice, each time with different input data for the selection code. The resulting displays shown in Figures 4.14 and 4.15 clearly identify the case selected.

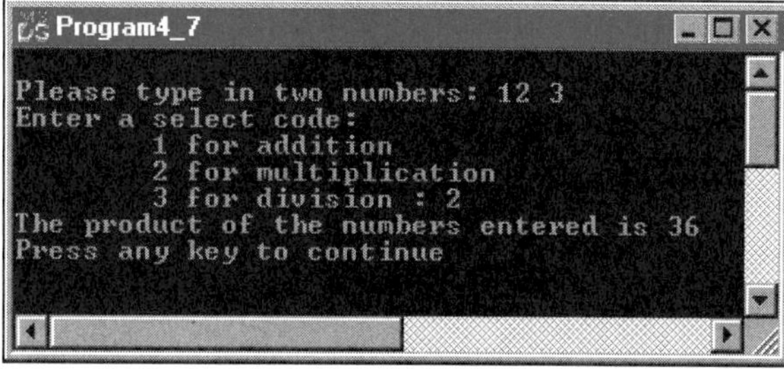

FIGURE 4.14

Sample run for multiplication using Program 4.7

```
Please type in two numbers: 12 3
Enter a select code:
        1 for addition
        2 for multiplication
        3 for division : 3
The first number divided by the second is 4
Press any key to continue_
```

FIGURE 4.15

Sample run for division using Program 4.7

In reviewing Program 4.7, notice the `break` statement in the last `case`. Although this `break` is not necessary, it is a good practice to terminate the last `case` in a `switch` statement with a `break`. This prevents a possible program error later, if an additional `case` is subsequently added to the `switch` statement. With the addition of a new `case`, the `break` between `cases` becomes necessary; having the `break` in place ensures you will not forget to include it at the time of a later modification.

Because character data types are always converted to integers in an expression, a `switch` statement can also be used to "switch" based on the value of a character expression. For example, assuming that `choice` is a character variable, the following `switch` statement is valid:

```
switch(choice)
{
  case 'a':
  case 'e':
  case 'i':
  case 'o':
  case 'u':
    cout << "The character in choice is a vowel" << endl;
    break;
  default:
    cout << "The character in choice is not a vowel" << endl;
    break;    // this break is optional
}    // end of switch statement
```

EXERCISES 4.4

1. Rewrite the following `if-else` chain using a `switch` statement:

```
if (letterGrade == 'A')
  cout << "The numerical grade is between 90 and 100\n";
else if (letterGrade == 'B')
  cout << "The numerical grade is between 80 and 89.9\n";
else if (letterGrade == 'C')
  cout << "The numerical grade is between 70 and 79.9\n";
else if (letterGrade == 'D';
  cout << "How are you going to explain this one\n";
else
{
  cout << "Of course I had nothing to do with the grade.\n";
  cout << "It must have been the professor's fault.\n";
}
```

2. Rewrite the following `if-else` chain using a `switch` statement:

```
if (factor == 1)
  pressure = 25.0
else if (factor == 2)
  pressure = 36.0
else if (factor == 3)
 pressure = 45.0
else if (factor == 4) || (factor == 5) || (factor == 6)
  pressure = 49.0
```

3. Each disk drive in a shipment of these devices is stamped with a code from 1 through 4, which indicates a drive manufacturer as follows:

Code	Disk Drive Manufacturer
1	3M Corporation
2	Maxell Corporation
3	Sony Corporation
4	Verbatim Corporation

Write a C++ program that accepts the code number as an input, and based on the value entered, displays the correct disk drive manufacturer.

4. Rewrite Program 4.5 using a `switch` statement.

5. Determine why the `if-else` chain in Program 4.6 cannot be replaced with a `switch` statement.

6. Rewrite Program 4.7 using a character variable for the select code. (*Hint:* Review Section 3.4 if your program does not operate as you think it should.)

4.5 Common Programming Errors

Three programming errors are common to C++'s selection statements:

1. Using the assignment operator, =, in place of the relational operator, ==. This can cause an enormous amount of frustration because any expression can be tested by an `if-else` statement. For example, the statement:

```
if (opselect = 2)
   cout << "Happy Birthday";
else
   cout << "Good Day";
```

always results in the message `Happy Birthday` being printed, regardless of the initial value in the variable `opselect`. The reason for this is that the assignment expression `opselect = 2` has a value of 2, which is considered a true value in C++. The correct expression to determine the value in `opselect` is `opselect == 2`.

2. Letting the `if-else` statement appear to select an incorrect choice. In this typical debugging problem, the programmer mistakenly concentrates on the tested condition as the source of the problem. For example, assume that the following `if-else` statement is part of your program:

```
if (key == 'F')
{
  contemp = (5.0/9.0) * (intemp - 32.0);
  cout << "Conversion to Celsius was done";
}
else
{
  contemp = (9.0/5.0) * intemp + 32.0;
  cout << "Conversion to Fahrenheit was done";
}
```

This statement will always display `Conversion to Celsius was done` when the variable `key` contains `F`. Therefore, if this message is displayed when you believe `key` does not contain `F`, investigation of `key`'s value is called for. As a general rule, whenever a selection statement does not act as you think it should, test your assumptions about the values assigned to the tested variables by displaying their values. If an unanticipated value is displayed, you have at least isolated the source of the problem to the variables themselves, rather than the structure of the `if-else` statement. From there you will have to determine where and how the incorrect value was obtained.

3. Using nested `if` statements without including braces to indicate the desired structure. Without braces the compiler defaults to pairing `else`s with the closest unpaired `if`s, which sometimes destroys the original intent of the selection statement. To avoid this problem and to create code that is readily adaptable to change, it is useful to write all `if-else` statements as compound statements in the form:

```
if (expression)
{
  one or more statements in here
}
else
{
  one or more statements in here
}
```

By using this form, no matter how many statements are added later, the original integrity and intent of the `if` statement is maintained.

4.6 Chapter Summary

1. Relational expressions, which are also called **simple conditions,** are used to compare operands. If a relational expression is true, the value of the expression is the integer 1. If the relational expression is false, it has an integer value of 0. Relational expressions are created using the following relational operators:

Relational Operator	Meaning	Example
<	Less than	`age < 30`
>	Greater than	`height > 6.2`
<=	Less than or equal to	`taxable <= 20000`
>=	Greater than or equal to	`temp >= 98.6`
==	Equal to	`grade == 100`
!=	Not equal to	`number != 250`

2. More complex conditions can be constructed from relational expressions using C++'s logical operators, `&&` (AND), `||` (OR), and `!` (NOT).

3. An `if-else` statement is used to select between two alternative statements based on the value of an expression. Although relational expressions are usually used for the tested expression, any valid expression can be used. In testing an expression, `if-else` statements interpret a nonzero value as true and a zero value as false. The general form of an `if-else` statement is:

```
if (expression)
  statement1;
else
  statement2;
```

This is a two-way selection statement. If the expression has a nonzero value it is considered as true, and `statement1` is executed; otherwise `statement2` is executed.

4. An `if-else` statement can contain other `if-else` statements. In the absence of braces, each `else` is associated with the closest preceding unpaired `if`.

5. The `if-else` chain is a multiway selection statement having the general form:

```
if (expression-1)
  statement-1;
else if (expression-2)
  statement-2;
else if (expression-3)
  statement-3;
      .
      .
      .
else if (expression-m)
  statement-m;
else
  statement-n;
```

Each expression is evaluated in the order in which it appears in the chain. Once an expression is true (has a nonzero value), only the statement between that expression and the next `else-if` or `else` is executed, and no further expressions are tested. The final `else` is optional, and the statement corresponding to the final `else` is executed only if none of the previous expressions is true.

6. A compound statement consists of any number of individual statements enclosed within the brace pair, { and }. Compound statements are treated as a single unit and can be used anywhere a single statement is used.

7. The `switch` statement is a multiway selection statement. The general form of a `switch` statement is:

```
switch (expression)
{    // start of compound statement
  case value-1:          <---------------  terminated with a colon
    statement1;
    statement2;
        .
        .
    break;
  case value-2:          <---------------  terminated with a colon
    statementm;
    statementn;
        .
        .
    break;
        .
        .
  case value-n:          <---------------  terminated with a colon
    statementw;
    statementx;
        .
        .
    break;
  default:               <---------------  terminated with a colon
    statementaa;
    statementbb;
        .
        .
}    // end of switch and compound statement
```

For this statement the value of an integer expression is compared to a number of integer or character constants or constant expressions. Program execution is transferred to the first matching `case` and continues through the end of the `switch` statement unless an optional `break` statement is encountered. The `case`s in a `switch` statement can appear in any order and an optional `default` case can be included. The `default` case is executed if none of the other `case`s is matched.

4.7 Knowing About: Errors, Testing, and Debugging

The ideal in programming is to produce readable, error-free programs that work correctly and can be modified or changed with a minimum of testing required for reverification. In this regard it is useful to know the different types of errors that can occur, when they are detected, and how to correct them.

Compile-Time and Run-Time Errors

A program error can be detected at a variety of times:

1. Before a program is compiled
2. While the program is being compiled
3. While the program is being run
4. After the program has been executed and the output is being examined
5. Not at all

Errors detected by the compiler are formally referred to as **compile-time errors,** and errors that occur while the program is being run are formally referred to as **run-time errors.**

Methods are available for detecting errors before a program is compiled and after it has been executed. The method for detecting errors after a program has been executed is called **program verification and testing.** The method for detecting errors before a program is compiled is called **desk checking.** Desk checking refers to the procedure of checking a program, by hand, at a desk or table for syntax and logic errors, which are described next.

Syntax and Logic Errors

Computer literature distinguishes between two primary types of errors, called syntax and logic errors. A **syntax error** is an error in the structure or spelling of a statement. For example, the statements

```
cout << "There are four syntax errors here\n
cot " Can you find tem";
```

contain four syntax errors. These errors are:

1. A closing quote is missing in line 1.
2. A terminating semicolon (;) is missing in line 1.
3. The keyword `cout` is misspelled in line 2.
4. The insertion symbol is missing in line 2.

All of these errors will be detected by the compiler when the program is compiled. This is true of all syntax errors—because they violate the basic rules of C++, if they are not discovered by desk checking, the compiler will detect them and display an error message indicating that a syntax error exists.[4] In some cases the error message is extremely clear and the error is obvious; in other cases it takes a little detective work to understand the error message displayed by the compiler. Because all syntax errors are detected at compile time, the terms **compile-time errors** and **syntax errors** are frequently used interchangeably. Strictly speaking, however, compile-time refers to when the error was detected and syntax refers to the type of error detected. Note that the misspelling of the word **tem** in the second `cout` statement is not a syntax error. Although this spelling error will result in an undesirable output line being displayed, it is not a violation of C++'s syntactical rules. It is a simple case of a **typographical error,** commonly referred to as a "typo."

Logic errors are characterized by erroneous, unexpected, or unintentional errors that are a direct result of some flaw in the program's logic. These errors, which are never caught by the compiler, may be detected by desk-checking, by program testing, by accident when a user obtains an obviously erroneous output, while the program is executing, or not at all. If the error is detected while the program is executing, a run-time error occurs that results in an error message being generated and/or abnormal and premature program termination.

Because logic errors may not be detected by the computer, they are always more difficult to detect than syntax errors. If not detected by desk checking, a logic error will reveal itself in two predominant ways. In one instance, the program terminates; in the other instance, the program executes to completion but produces incorrect results. Logic errors of this latter type include:

No output: This is either caused by an omission of a `cout` statement or a sequence of statements that inadvertently bypasses a `cout` statement.

Unappealing or misaligned output: This is caused by an error in a `cout` statement.

---

4 They may not, however, all be detected at the same time. Frequently, one syntax error "masks" another error and the second error is detected only after the first error is corrected.

Incorrect numerical results: This is caused by either incorrect values assigned to the variables used in an expression, the use of an incorrect arithmetic expression, an omission of a statement, roundoff error, or the use of an improper sequence of statements.

See if you can detect the logic error in Program 4.8.

PROGRAM 4.8

```
#include <iostream.h>
#include <iomanip.h>
#include <math.h>

int main()    // a compound interest program
{
  float capital, amount, rate, nyrs;

  cout << "\nThis program calculates the amount of money\n"
       << "in a bank account for an initial deposit\n"
       << "invested for n years at an interest rate r.\n\n"
       << "Enter the initial amount in the account: ";
  cin  >> amount;
  cout << "Enter the number of years: ";
  cin  >> nyrs;
  capital = amount * pow((1 + rate/100.0), nyrs);

    // set output formats
  cout << setiosflags(ios::fixed)
       << setiosflags(ios::showpoint)
       << setprecision(2);

  cout << "\nThe final amount of money is "
       << '$' << capital << endl;

  return 0;
}
```

Figure 4.16 illustrates a sample run using Program 4.8.

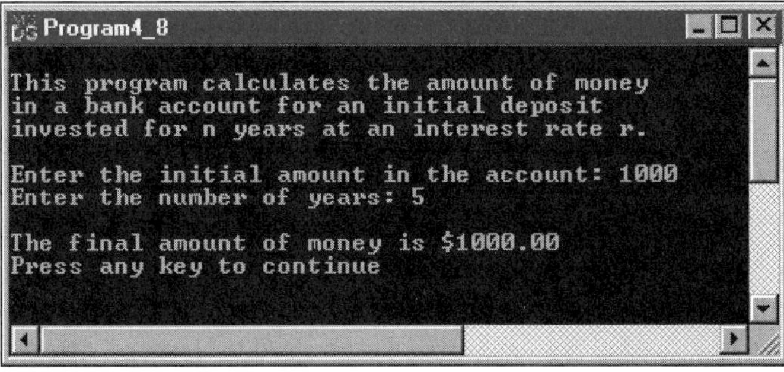
Program4_8
This program calculates the amount of money
in a bank account for an initial deposit
invested for n years at an interest rate r.
Enter the initial amount in the account: 1000
Enter the number of years: 5
The final amount of money is $1000.00
Press any key to continue

FIGURE 4.16

Sample run using Program 4.8

As indicated in the output shown in Figure 4.16, the final amount of money is identical to the initial amount input. Did you spot the error in Program 4.8 that produced this apparently erroneous output?

Unlike a misspelled output message, the error in Program 4.8 causes a mistake in a computation. Here the error is that the program does not initialize the variable `rate` before this variable is used in the calculation of `capital`. When the assignment statement that calculates `capital` is executed the program uses whatever value is stored in `rate`. On those systems that initialize all variables to zero, the value zero will be used for `rate`. However, on those systems that do not initialize all variables to zero, the program will use whatever "garbage" value happens to occupy the storage locations corresponding to the variable `rate`. (The manuals supplied with your compiler will indicate which of these two actions your compiler takes.) In either case an error is produced.

Although the logic error in this example program did not cause premature program termination, faulty or incomplete program logic can cause this type of run-time error. Attempts to divide by zero or to take the square root of a negative number are examples of logic errors that will cause premature run-time program terminations.

Any program testing that is done should be well thought out to maximize the possibility of locating errors. An important programming realization is that although a single test can reveal the presence of an error, it does not verify the absence of one. The fact that one error is revealed by a particular verification run does not indicate that another error is not lurking somewhere else in the program; the fact that one test revealed no errors does not indicate that there are no errors.

Once an error is discovered, however, the programmer must locate where the error occurs and then fix it. In computer jargon, a program error is referred to as a **bug,** and the process of isolating, correcting, and verifying the correction is called **debugging.**[5]

---

5 The derivation of this term is rather interesting. When a program stopped running on the MARK I computer at Harvard University in September 1945, the malfunction was traced to a dead moth that had gotten into the electrical circuits. The programmer, Grace Hopper, recorded the incident in her log book as "First actual case of bug being found."

Although there are no hard-and-fast rules for isolating the cause of an error, some useful techniques can be applied. The first of these is preventive. Many errors are simply introduced by the programmer in the rush to code and run a program before fully understanding what is required and how the result is to be achieved. A symptom of this haste to get a program entered into the computer is the lack of an outline of the proposed program (pseudocode or flowcharts) or a handwritten program itself. Many errors can be eliminated simply by checking a copy of the program before it is ever entered or compiled by desk checking the program.

A second useful technique is to mimic the computer and execute each statement, by hand, as the computer would. This means writing down each variable as it is encountered in the program and listing the value that should be stored in the variable as each input and assignment statement is encountered. Doing this also sharpens your programming skills because it requires that you fully understand what result comes from each statement in your program. Such a check is called **program tracing.**

A third and very powerful debugging technique is to use one or more diagnostic `cout` statements to display the values of selected variables. In this same manner, another use of `cout` statements in debugging is to immediately display the values of all input data. This technique is referred to as **echo printing,** and is useful in establishing that the program is correctly receiving and interpreting the input data.

The fourth and most powerful debugging technique is to use the debugger that comes with Visual C++.

Finally, no discussion of program verification is complete without mentioning the primary ingredient needed for successful isolation and correction of errors. This is the attitude and spirit you bring to the task. You wrote the program, and your natural assumption is that it is correct or you would have changed it before it was compiled. It is extremely difficult to honestly test and find errors in your own software. As a programmer, you must constantly remind yourself that just because you *think* your program is correct does not make it so. Finding errors in your own programs is a sobering experience, but one that will help you become a master programmer. It can also be exciting and fun if approached as a detection problem with you as the master detective.

Testing and Debugging

In theory, a comprehensive set of test runs would reveal all possible program errors and ensure that a program will work correctly for any and all combinations of input and computed data. In practice, this requires checking all possible combinations of statement execution. Due to the time and effort required, this is an impossible goal except for extremely simple programs. Let us see why this is so. Consider Program 4.9.

PROGRAM 4.9

```
#include <iostream.h>

int main()
{
  int num;

  cout << "Enter a number: ";
  cin  >> num;
  if (num == 5)
    cout << "Bingo!" << endl;
  else
    cout << "Bongo!" << endl;

    return 0;
}
```

Program 4.9 has two paths that can be traversed from when the program is run to when the program reaches its closing brace. The first path, which is executed when the input number is 5, is the sequence:

```
cout << "Enter a number";
cin  >> num;
cout << "Bingo!\n";
```

The second path, which is executed whenever any number except 5 is input, includes the sequence of instructions:

```
cout << "Enter a number";
cin  >> num;
cout << "Bongo!\n";
```

To test each possible path through Program 4.9 requires two runs of the program, with a judicious selection of test input data to ensure that both paths of the `if` statement are exercised. The addition of one more `if` statement in the program increases the number of possible execution paths by a factor of two and requires four (2^2) runs of the program for complete testing. Similarly, two additional `if` statements increase the number of paths by a factor of four and requires eight (2^3) runs for complete testing, and three additional `if` statements would produce a program that required sixteen (2^4) test runs.

Now consider a modestly sized program consisting of only ten modules, each module containing five `if` statements. Assuming the modules are always called in the same sequence, there are 32 possible paths through each module (2 raised to the fifth power) and more than 1,000,000,000,000,000 (2 raised to the 50th power) possible paths through the complete program (all modules executed in sequence). The time needed to create individual test data to exercise each path and the actual computer run time required to check each path make the complete testing of such a program almost impossible.

The inability to fully test all combinations of statement execution sequences has led to the programming saying, "There is no error-free program." It has also led to the realization that any testing that is done should be well thought out to maximize the possibility of locating errors. At a minimum, test data should include appropriate values for input values, illegal input values that the program should reject, and limiting values that are checked by selection statements within the program.

5 Repetition Structures

The programs examined so far have illustrated the programming concepts involved in input, output, assignment, and selection capabilities. By this time you should have gained enough experience to be comfortable with these concepts and the mechanics of implementing them using C++. Many problems, however, require a repetition capability, in which the same calculation or sequence of instructions is repeated, over and over, using different sets of data. Examples of such repetition include continual checking of user data entries until an acceptable entry, such as a valid password, is entered, counting and accumulating running totals, and constant acceptance of input data and recalculation of output values that stops only upon entry of a prespecified value.

This chapter explores the different methods that programmers use in constructing repeating sections of code and how they can be implemented in C++. More commonly, a section of code that is repeated is referred to as a **loop,** because after the last statement in the code is executed the program branches, or loops back to the first statement and starts another repetition through the code. Each repetition is also referred to as an **iteration** or **pass through the loop.**

5.1 Introduction

The real power of a program is realized when the same type of operation must be made over and over, each time using different data, without the necessity of rerunning the program for each new set of data values. This is accomplished using repetitive sections of code.

Constructing a repetitive section of code requires that four elements be present. The first necessary element is a repetition statement. This **repetition statement** both defines the boundaries containing the repeating section of code and controls whether the code will be executed. In general, there are three different forms of repetition structures, all of which are provided in C++:

1. `while` structure
2. `for` structure
3. `do while` structure

Each of these structures requires a condition that must be evaluated, which is the second required element for constructing repeating sections of code. Valid conditions are identical to those used in selection statements. If the condition is true, the code is executed; otherwise, it is not.

The third required element is a statement that initially sets the condition. This statement must always be placed before the condition is first evaluated to ensure correct loop execution the first time the condition is evaluated.

Finally, there must be a statement within the repeating section of code that allows the condition to become false. This is necessary to ensure that, at some point, the repetitions stop.

Pretest and Posttest Loops

The condition being tested can be evaluated at either the beginning or the end of the repeating section of code. Figure 5.1 illustrates the case for which the test occurs at the beginning of the loop. This type of loop is referred to as a **pretest loop** because the condition is tested before any statements within the loop are executed. If the condition is true, the executable statements within the loop are executed. If the initial value of the condition is false, the executable statements within the loop are never executed at all and control transfers to the first statement after the loop. To avoid infinite repetitions, the

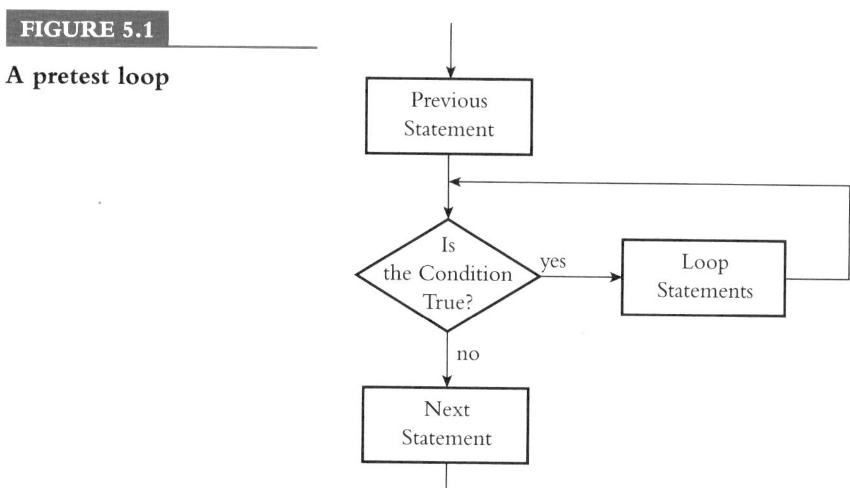

FIGURE 5.1

A pretest loop

condition must be updated within the loop. Pretest loops are also referred to as **entrance-controlled loops.** The `while` and `for` loop structures are examples of such loops.

A loop that evaluates a condition at end of the repeating section of code, as illustrated in Figure 5.2, is referred to as **posttest** or **exit-controlled loop.** Such loops always execute the loop statements at least once before the condition is tested. Because the executable statements within the loop are continually executed until the condition becomes

FIGURE 5.2

A posttest loop

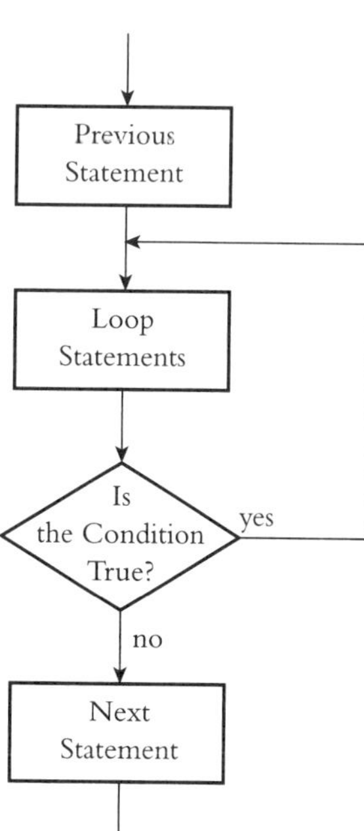

false, there always must be a statement within the loop that updates the condition and permits it to become false. The `do while` construct is an example of a posttest loop.

Fixed Count versus Variable Condition Loops

In addition to the point at which the condition is tested (pretest or posttest), repeating sections of code are also classified as to the type of condition being tested. In a **fixed count loop,** the condition is used to keep track of how many repetitions have occurred. For example, we might want to produce a table of 10 numbers, including their squares and cubes, or a fixed design such as:

```
*************************
*************************
*************************
```

In each of these cases, a fixed number of calculations is performed or a fixed number of lines is printed, at which point the repeating section of code is exited. All of C++'s repetition statements can be used to produce fixed count loops.

In many situations the exact number of repetitions is not known in advance or the items are too numerous to count beforehand. For example, when entering a large amount of market research data we might not want to take the time to count the number of actual data items that are to be entered. In cases such as this, a variable condition loop is used. In a **variable condition loop** the tested condition does not depend on a count being achieved, but rather on a variable that can change interactively with each pass through the loop. When a specified value is encountered, regardless of how many iterations have occurred, repetition stops. All of C++'s repetition statements can be used to create variable condition loops.[1] In this chapter we encounter examples of both fixed count and variable condition loops.

5.2 `while` Loops

In C++, a `while` **loop** is constructed using a `while` statement. The syntax of this statement is:

```
while (expression)
  statement;
```

---

1 In this, C++ differs from most other languages such as BASIC, FORTRAN, and Pascal. In each of these languages the `for` structure (which is implemented using a DO statement in FORTRAN) can only be used to produce fixed count loops. C++'s `for` structure, as we will see shortly, is virtually interchangeable with its `while` structure.

The expression contained within parentheses is the condition tested to determine if the statement following the parentheses is executed. The expression is evaluated in exactly the same manner as that contained in an `if-else` statement; the difference is in how the expression is used. As we have seen, when the expression is true (has a nonzero value) in an `if-else` statement, the statement following the expression is executed once. In a `while` statement the statement following the expression is executed repeatedly as long as the expression evaluates to a nonzero value. Considering just the expression and the statement following the parentheses, the process used by the computer in evaluating a `while` statement is:

1. Test the expression
2. If the expression has a nonzero (true) value
  a. execute the statement following the parentheses
  b. go back to step 1
 else
  exit the `while` statement and execute the next executable statement following the `while` statement

Notice that step 2b forces program control to be transferred back to step 1. This transfer of control back to the start of a `while` statement to reevaluate the expression is what forms the program loop. The `while` statement literally loops back on itself to recheck the expression until it evaluates to zero (becomes false). This naturally means that, somewhere in the loop, provision must be made that permits the value of the tested expression to be altered. As we will see, this is indeed the case.

This looping process produced by a `while` statement is illustrated in Figure 5.3. A diamond shape is used to show the entry and exit points required in the decision part of the `while` statement.

To make this a little more tangible, consider the relational expression `count <= 10` and the statement `cout << count;`. Using these, we can write the following valid `while` statement:

```
while (count <= 10)
  cout << count;
```

Although this statement is valid, the alert reader will realize that we have created a situation in which the `cout` object either is called forever (or until we stop the program) or is not called at all. Let us see why this happens.

If `count` has a value less than or equal to 10 when the expression is first evaluated, the `cout` statement is executed. The `while` statement then automatically loops back on itself and retests the expression. Because we have not changed the value stored in `count`, the expression is still true and another call to `cout` is made. This process continues forever, or until the program containing this statement is prematurely stopped by the user. However, if `count` starts with a value greater than 10, the expression is false to begin with and the `cout` statement is executed.

FIGURE 5.3

Anatomy of a `while` loop

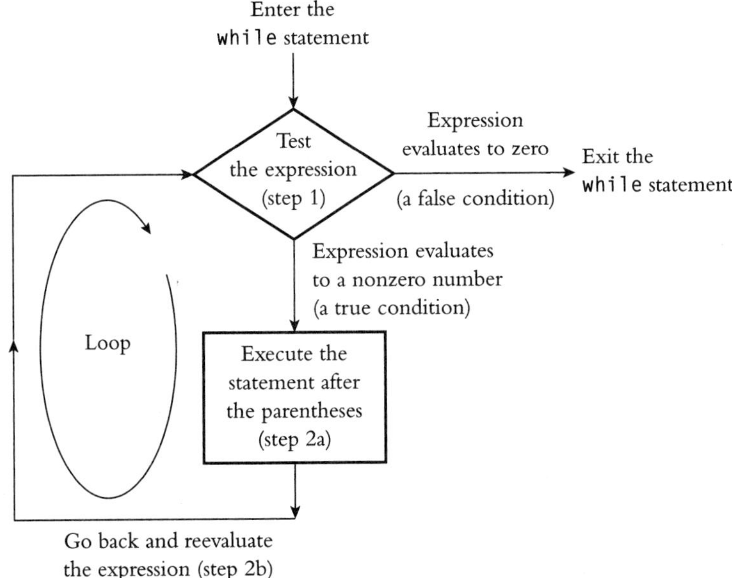

How do we set an initial value in `count` to control what the `while` statement does the first time the expression is evaluated? The answer, of course, is to assign values to each variable in the tested expression before the `while` statement is encountered. For example, the following sequence of instructions is valid:

```
count = 1;
while (count <= 10)
  cout << count;
```

Using this sequence of instructions, we have ensured that `count` starts with a value of 1. We could assign any value to `count` in the assignment statement—the important thing is to assign some value. In practice, the assigned value depends on the application.

We must still change the value of `count` so that we can finally exit the `while` statement. To do this requires an expression such as `count++` to increment the value of `count` each time the `while` statement is executed. The fact that a `while` statement provides for the repetition of a single statement does not prevent us from including an additional statement to change the value of `count`. All we have to do is replace the single statement with a compound statement. For example:

```
count = 1;               // initialize count
while (count <= 10)
{
  cout << count;
  count++;               // increment count
}
```

Note that, for clarity, we have placed each statement in the compound statement on a different line. This is consistent with the convention adopted for compound statements in the last chapter. Let us now analyze the above sequence of instructions.

The first assignment statement sets count equal to 1. The while statement is then entered and the expression is evaluated for the first time. The value of count is less than or equal to 10, so the expression is true and the compound statement is executed. The first statement in the compound statement causes cout to display the value of count. The next statement adds 1 to the value currently stored in count, making this value equal to 2. The while statement now loops back to retest the expression. The value of count is still less than or equal to 10, so the compound statement is again executed. This process continues until the value of count reaches 11. Program 5.1 illustrates these statements in an actual program.

PROGRAM 5.1

```
#include <iostream.h>
int main()
{
  int count;

  count = 1;                    // initialize count
  while (count <= 10)
  {
    cout << count << "  ";
    count++;                   // increment count
  }

  return 0;
}
```

The following output will be displayed on the screen when Program 5.1 is executed:

```
1  2  3  4  5  6  7  8  9  10
```

There is nothing special about the name count used in Program 5.1. Any valid integer variable could have been used.

Before we consider other examples of the while statement two comments concerning Program 5.1 are in order. First, the statement count++ can be replaced with any statement that changes the value of `count`. A statement such as `count = count + 2`, for example, would cause every second integer to be displayed. Second, it is the programmer's responsibility to ensure that `count` is changed in a way that ultimately leads to a normal exit from the `while`. For example, if we replace the expression `count++` with the expression `count--`, the value of `count` will never exceed 10 and an **infinite loop** will be created. An infinite loop is a loop that never ends; the program just keeps displaying numbers until you realize that the program is not working as you expected.

Now that you have some familiarity with the `while` statement, see if you can read and determine the output of Program 5.2.

PROGRAM 5.2

```
#include <iostream.h>
int main()
{
  int i;

  i = 10;
  while (i >= 1)
  {
    cout << i << "  ";
    i--;                   // subtract 1 from i
  }

  return 0;
}
```

The assignment statement in Program 5.2 initially sets the `int` variable `i` to 10. The `while` statement then checks to see if the value of `i` is greater than or equal to 1. If the expression is true, the value of `i` is displayed by the `cout` object and the value of `i` is decremented by 1. When `i` finally reaches zero, the expression is false and the program exits the `while` statement. Thus, the following display is obtained when Program 5.2 is run:

```
10  9  8  7  6  5  4  3  2  1
```

To illustrate the power of the `while` statement, consider the task of printing a table of numbers from 1 to 10 with their squares and cubes. This can be done with a simple `while` statement as illustrated by Program 5.3.

PROGRAM 5.3

```
#include <iostream.h>
#include <iomanip.h>
int main()
{
  int num;

  cout << endl; // print a blank line
  cout << "NUMBER    SQUARE    CUBE\n"
       << "------    ------    ----" << endl;

  num = 1;
  while (num < 11)
  {
    cout << setw(3) << num << "        "
         << setw(3) << num * num      << "      "
         << setw(4) << num * num * num << endl;
    num++;         // increment num
  }

  return 0;
}
```

When Program 5.3 is run, the display shown in Figure 5.4 is produced.

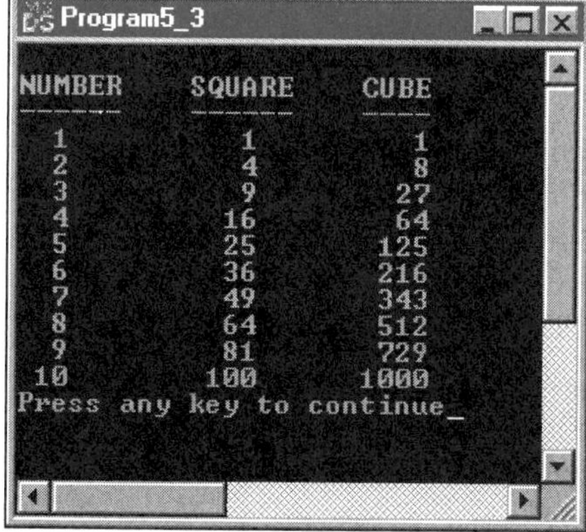

FIGURE 5.4

Output displayed by Program 5.3

Note that the expression used in Program 5.3 is `num < 11`. For the integer variable `num`, this expression is exactly equivalent to the expression `num <= 10`. The choice of which to use is entirely up to you.

If we want to use Program 5.3 to produce a table of 1000 numbers, all we do is change the expression in the `while` statement from `i < 11` to `i < 1001`. Changing the 11 to 1001 produces a table of 1000 lines—not bad for a simple seven-line `while` statement.

All the program examples illustrating the `while` statement are examples of fixed-count loops, because the tested condition is a counter that checks for a fixed number of repetitions. A variation on the fixed-count loop can be made by which the counter is incremented each time through the loop not by one but by some other value. For example, consider the task of producing a Celsius to Fahrenheit temperature conversion table. Assume that Fahrenheit temperatures corresponding to Celsius temperatures ranging from 5 to 50 degrees are to be displayed in increments of five degrees. The desired display can be obtained with the series of statements:

```
celsius = 5;      // starting Celsius value
while (celsius <= 50)
{
  fahren = (9.0/5.0) * celsius + 32.0;
  cout << celsius
       << fahren;
  celsius = celsius + 5;
}
```

As before, the `while` statement consists of everything from the word `while` through the closing brace of the compound statement. Prior to entering the `while` loop we have made sure to assign a value to the counter being evaluated, and there is a statement to alter the value of the counter within the loop (in increments of 5 Celsius) to ensure an exit from the `while` loop. Program 5.4 illustrates the use of this code in a complete program.

The display obtained when Program 5.4 is executed is shown in Figure 5.5.

FIGURE 5.5

Output displayed by Program 5.4

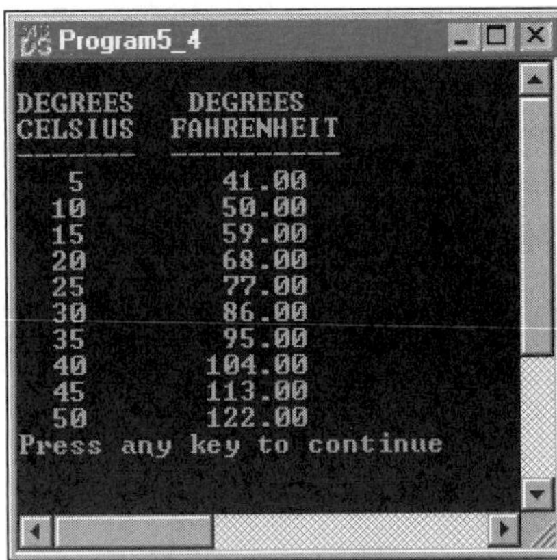

Program5_4
DEGREES   DEGREES
CELSIUS   FAHRENHEIT
5   41.00
10   50.00
15   59.00
20   68.00
25   77.00
30   86.00
35   95.00
40   104.00
45   113.00
50   122.00
Press any key to continue

PROGRAM 5.4

```
#include <iostream.h>
#include <iomanip.h>
// a program to convert Celsius to Fahrenheit
int main()
{
  const int MAXCELSIUS = 50;
  const int STARTVAL = 5;
  const int STEPSIZE = 5;
  int celsius;
  float fahren;

  cout << endl; // print a blank line
  cout << "DEGREES   DEGREES\n"
       << "CELSIUS  FAHRENHEIT\n"
       << "-------  ----------" << endl;

  celsius = STARTVAL;

  // set output formats for floating point numbers
  cout << setiosflags(ios::fixed)
       << setiosflags(ios::showpoint)
       << setprecision(2);

  while (celsius <= MAXCELSIUS)
  {
    fahren = (9.0/5.0) * celsius + 32.0;
    cout << setw(4)  << celsius
                     << setw(13) << fahren << endl;
    celsius = celsius + STEPSIZE;
  }

  return 0;
}
```

EXERCISES 5.2

1. Rewrite Program 5.1 to print the numbers 2 to 10 in increments of two. The output of your program should be:

```
2  4  6  8  10
```

2. Rewrite Program 5.3 to produce a table that starts at a Celsius value of –10 and ends with a Celsius value of 60, in increments of ten degrees.

3. **a.** For the following program, determine the total number of items displayed. Also determine the first and last numbers printed.

```
#include <iostream.h>
int main()
{
  int num = 0;
  while (num <= 20)
  {
    num++;
    cout << num << " ";
  }

  return 0;
}
```

b. Enter and run the program from Exercise 3a on a computer to verify your answers to the exercise.

c. How would the output be affected if the two statements within the compound statement were reversed (that is, if the `cout` statement was placed before the `num++` statement)?

4. Write a C++ program that converts gallons to liters. The program should display gallons from 10 to 20 in one-gallon increments and the corresponding liter equivalents. Use the relationship that 1 gallon contains 3.785 liters.

5. Write a C++ program that converts feet to meters. The program should display feet from 3 to 30 in three-foot increments and the corresponding meter equivalents. Use the relationship that there are 3.28 feet in a meter.

6. A machine purchased for $28,000 is depreciated at a rate of $4,000 a year for seven years. Write and run a C++ program that computes and displays a depreciation table for seven years. The table should have the form:

Year	Depreciation	End-of-Year Value	Accumulated Depreciation
----	------------	-----------------	------------
1	4000	24000	4000
2	4000	20000	8000
3	4000	16000	12000
4	4000	12000	16000
5	4000	8000	20000
6	4000	4000	24000
7	4000	0	28000

7. An automobile travels at an average speed of 55 miles per hour for four hours. Write a C++ program that displays the distance driven, in miles, that the car has traveled after 0.5, 1, 1.5, 2, etc., hours until the end of the trip.

5.3 Interactive `while` Loops

Combining interactive data entry with the repetition capabilities of the `while` statement produces very adaptable and powerful programs. To understand the concept involved, consider Program 5.5, in which a `while` statement is used to accept and then display four user-entered numbers, one at a time. Although it uses very simple idea, the program highlights the flow of control concepts needed to produce more useful programs.

Figure 5.6 illustrates a sample run of Program 5.5 after four numbers have been entered.

FIGURE 5.6

Sample run of Program 5.5

```
Program5_5

This program will ask you to enter 4 numbers.

Enter a number: 26.2
The number entered is 26.2
Enter a number: 5
The number entered is 5
Enter a number: 103.456
The number entered is 103.456
Enter a number: 1267.89
The number entered is 1267.89
Press any key to continue_
```

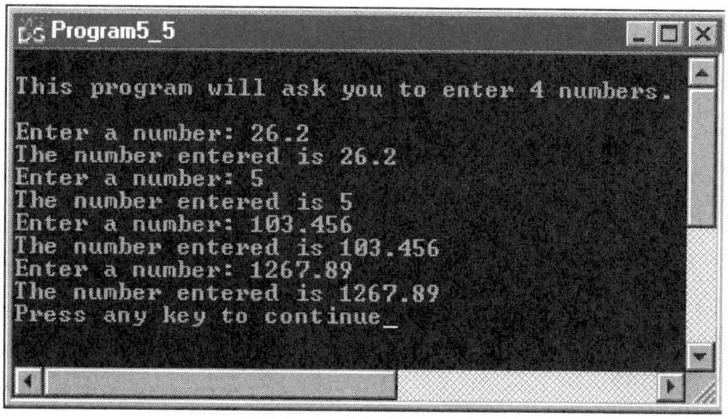

PROGRAM 5.5

```
#include <iostream.h>
int main()
{
  const int MAXNUMS = 4;
  int count;
  float num;

  cout << "\nThis program will ask you to enter "
       << MAXNUMS << " numbers." << endl;
  count = 1;

  while (count <= MAXNUMS)
  {
    cout << "\nEnter a number: ";
    cin  >> num;
    cout << "The number entered is " << num;
    count++;
  }
  cout << endl;

  return 0;
}
```

Let us review the program so we clearly understand how the output illustrated in Figure 5.6 was produced. The first message displayed is caused by execution of the first `cout` statement. This statement is outside and before the `while` statement, so it is executed once before any statement in the `while` loop.

Once the `while` loop is entered, the statements within the compound statement are executed while the tested condition is true. The first time through the compound statement, the message `Enter a number:` is displayed. The program then uses `cin`, which forces the computer to wait for a number to be entered at the keyboard. Once a number is typed and the Return or Enter key is pressed, the `cout` object displays the number. The variable `count` is then incremented by one. This process continues until four passes through the loop have been made and the value of `count` is 5. Each pass causes the message `Enter a number:` to be displayed, causes one `cin` statement to be executed, and causes the message `The number entered is` to be displayed. Figure 5.7 illustrates this flow of control.

Rather than simply displaying the entered numbers, Program 5.5 can be modified to use the entered data. For example, let us add the numbers entered and display the total. To do this, we must be very careful about how we add the numbers because the same

FIGURE 5.7

Flow of control diagram for Program 5.5

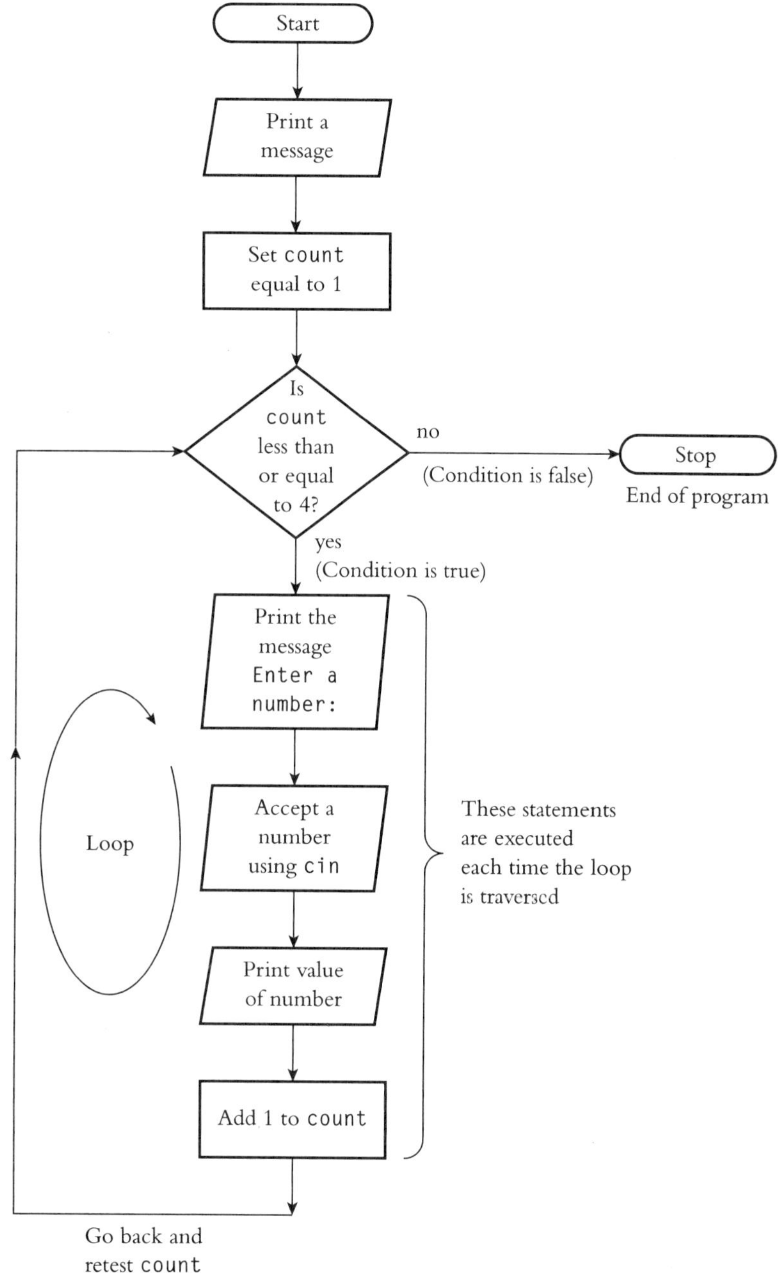

variable, num, is used for each number entered. Because of this the entry of a new number in Program 5.5 automatically causes the previous number stored in num to be lost. Thus, each number entered must be added to the total before another number is entered. The required sequence is:

Enter a number
Add the number to the total

How do we add a single number to a total? A statement such as `total = total + num` does the job perfectly. This is the accumulating statement introduced in Section 3.1. After each number is entered, the accumulating statement adds the number into the total, as illustrated in Figure 5.8. The complete flow of control required for adding the numbers is illustrated in Figure 5.9.

In reviewing Figure 5.9, observe that we have made a provision for initially setting the total to zero before the `while` loop is entered. If we were to clear the `total` inside

FIGURE 5.8

Accepting and adding a number to a total

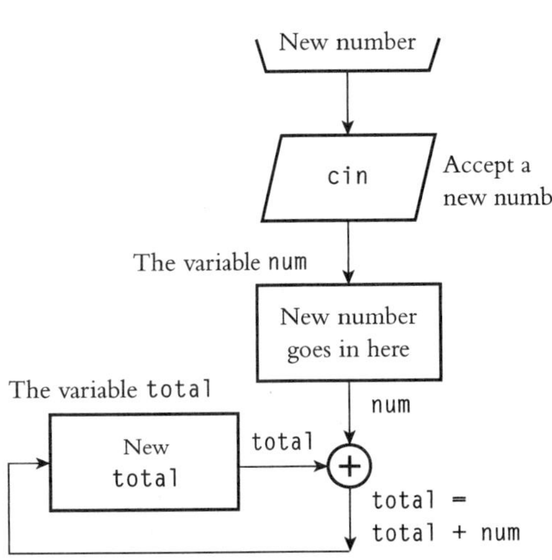

FIGURE 5.9

Accumulation flow of control

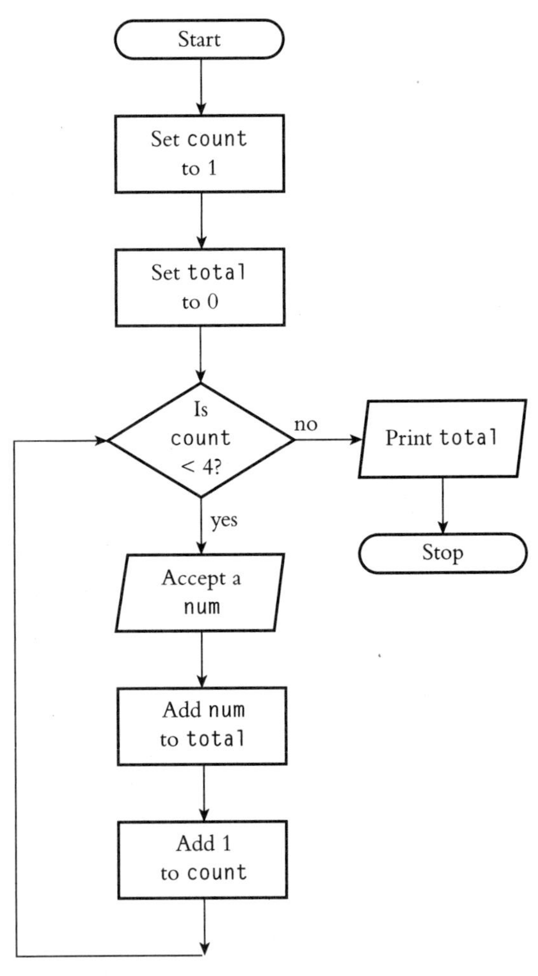

the while loop, it would be set to zero each time the loop was executed and any value previously stored would be erased.

Program 5.6 incorporates the necessary modifications to Program 5.5 to total the numbers entered. As indicated in the flow diagram shown in Figure 5.9, the statement total = total + num; is placed immediately after the cin statement. Putting the accumulating statement at this point in the program ensures that the entered number is immediately "captured" into the total.

PROGRAM 5.6

```
#include <iostream.h>
int main()
{
  const int MAXNUMS = 4;
  int count;
  float num, total;

  cout << "\nThis program will ask you to enter "
       << MAXNUMS << " numbers." << endl;
  count = 1;
  total = 0;

  while (count <= MAXNUMS)
  {
    cout << "\nEnter a number: ";
    cin  >> num;
    total = total + num;
    cout << "The total is now " << total;
    count++;
  }

  cout << "\n\nThe final total is " << total << endl;

  return 0;
}
```

Let us review Program 5.6. The variable total was created to store the total of the numbers entered. Prior to entering the while statement the value of total is set to zero. This ensures that any previous value present in the storage location(s) assigned to the

FIGURE 5.10

Sample run of Program 5.6

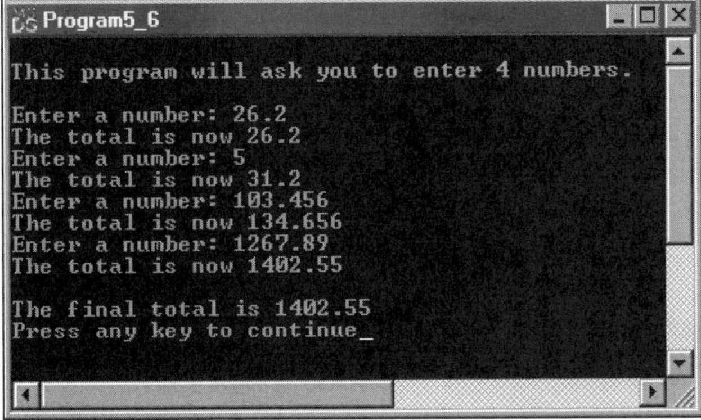

variable `total` is erased. Within the `while` loop the statement `total = total + num;` is used to add the value of the entered number into `total`. As each value is entered, it is added into the existing `total` to create a new `total`. Thus, `total` becomes a running subtotal of all the values entered. Only when all numbers are entered does `total` contain the final sum of all the numbers. After the `while` loop is finished, the last `cout` statement is used to display this sum.

Program5_6
This program will ask you to enter 4 numbers.
Enter a number: 26.2
The total is now 26.2
Enter a number: 5
The total is now 31.2
Enter a number: 103.456
The total is now 134.656
Enter a number: 1267.89
The total is now 1402.55
The final total is 1402.55
Press any key to continue_

The result of a sample run of Program 5.6, using the same data we entered in the sample run for Program 5.5, is illustrated in Figure 5.10.

Having used an accumulating assignment statement to add the numbers entered, we can now go further and calculate the average of the numbers. Where do we calculate the average—within the `while` loop or outside of it?

In the case at hand, calculating an average requires that both a final sum and the number of items in that sum be available. The average is then computed by dividing the final sum by the number of items. At this point, we must ask, "At what point in the program is the correct sum available, and at what point is the number of items available?" In reviewing Program 5.6, we see that the correct sum needed for calculating the average is available after the `while` loop is finished. In fact, the whole purpose of the `while` loop is to ensure that the numbers are entered and added correctly to produce a correct sum. After the loop is finished, we also have a count of the number of items used in the sum. However, due to the way the `while` loop was constructed, the number in `count` (5) when the loop is finished is 1 more than the number of items (4) used to obtain `total`. Knowing this, we simply subtract one from `count` before using it to determine the average. With this as background, let us look at Program 5.7.

Program 5.7 is almost identical to Program 5.6, except for the calculation of the average. We have also removed the constant display of the `total` within and after the `while` loop. The loop in Program 5.7 is used to enter and add four numbers. Immediately after the loop is exited, the average is computed and displayed.

A sample run of Program 5.7 is illustrated in Figure 5.11.

PROGRAM 5.7

```
#include <iostream.h>
int main()
{
  const int MAXNUMS = 4;
  int count;
  float num, total, average;

  cout << "\nThis program will ask you to enter "
       << MAXNUMS << " numbers." << endl;
  count = 1;
  total = 0;

  while (count <= MAXNUMS)
  {
    cout << "Enter a number: ";
    cin  >> num;
    total = total + num;
    count++;
  }

  count--;
  average = total / count;
  cout << "\nThe average of the numbers is " << average << endl;

  return 0;
}
```

FIGURE 5.11

Sample run of Program 5.7

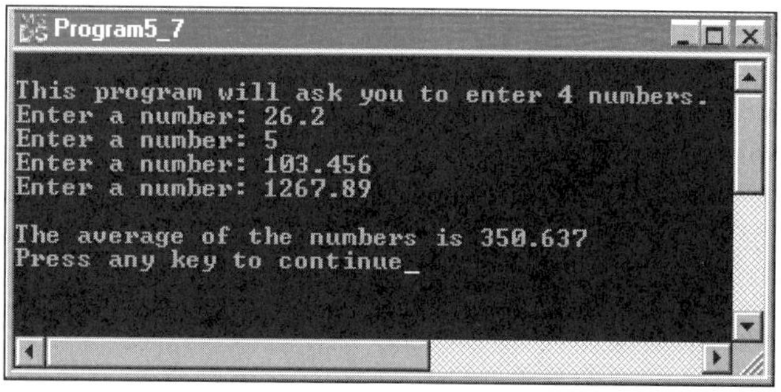

Program5_7

```
This program will ask you to enter 4 numbers.
Enter a number: 26.2
Enter a number: 5
Enter a number: 103.456
Enter a number: 1267.89

The average of the numbers is 350.637
Press any key to continue_
```

Sentinels

All of the loops we have created thus far have been examples of fixed `count` loops, in which a counter has been used to control the number of loop iterations. By means of a `while` statement, variable condition loops may also be constructed. For example, when entering grades we may not want to count the number of grades that will be entered, but would prefer to enter the grades continuously and, at the end, type in a special data value to signal the end of data input.

In computer programming, data values used to signal either the start or end of a data series are called **sentinels.** The sentinel values must, of course, be selected so as not to conflict with legitimate data values. For example, if we were constructing a program to process a student's grades, assuming that no extra credit is given that could produce a grade higher than 100, we could use any grade higher than 100 as a sentinel value. Program 5.8 illustrates this concept. In Program 5.8 data are continuously requested and accepted until a number larger than 100 is entered. Entry of a number higher than 100 alerts the program to exit the `while` loop and display the sum of the numbers entered.

PROGRAM 5.8

```
#include <iostream.h>
int main()
{
  const int HIGHGRADE = 100;
  float grade, total;

  grade = 0;
  total = 0;
  cout << "\nTo stop entering grades, type in any number"
       << " greater than 100.\n" << endl;
  cout << "Enter a grade: ";
  cin  >> grade;

  while (grade <= HIGHGRADE)
  {
    total = total + grade;
    cout << "Enter a grade: ";
    cin  >> grade;
  }

  cout << "\nThe total of the grades is " << total << endl;

  return 0;
}
```

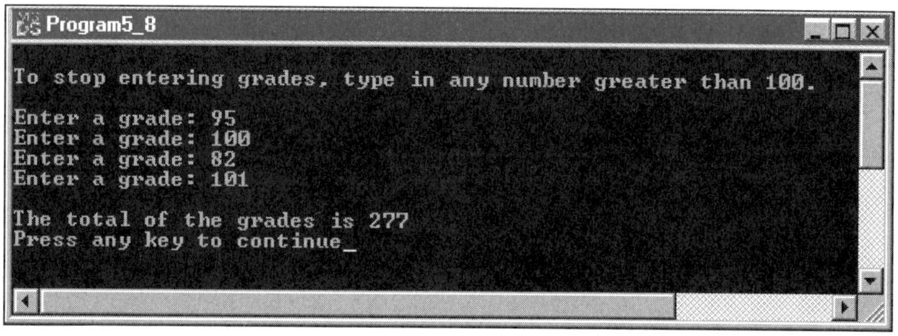

```
To stop entering grades, type in any number greater than 100.

Enter a grade: 95
Enter a grade: 100
Enter a grade: 82
Enter a grade: 101

The total of the grades is 277
Press any key to continue_
```

FIGURE 5.12

Sample run using Program 5.8

A sample run using Program 5.8 is illustrated in Figure 5.12. As long as a grade less than or equal to 100 is entered, the program continues to request and accept additional data. When a number less than or equal to 100 is entered, the program adds this number to the total. When a number greater than 100 is entered, the `while` loop is exited and the sum of the grades that were entered is displayed.

`break` and `continue` Statements

Two useful statements in connection with repetition statements are the `break` and `continue` statements. We have encountered the `break` statement in relation to the `switch` statement. The syntax of this statement is:

```
break;
```

A `break` statement, as its name implies, forces an immediate break, or exit, from `switch`, `while`, and the `for` and `do-while` statements presented in the next sections.

For example, execution of the following `while` loop is immediately terminated if a number greater than 76 is entered.

```
while(count <= 10)
{
  cout << "Enter a number: ";
  cin  >> num;
  if (num > 76)
  {
    cout << "You lose!\n";
    break;       // break out of the loop
  }
```

(continued next page)

```
  else
    cout << "Keep on trucking!\n";
  count++;
}
// break jumps to here
```

The `break` statement violates pure structured programming principles because it provides a second, nonstandard exit from a loop. Nevertheless, the `break` statement is extremely useful and valuable for breaking out of loops when an unusual condition is detected. The `break` statement is also used to exit from a `switch` statement, but this is because the desired case has been detected and processed.

The `continue` statement is similar to the `break` statement but applies only to loops created with `while`, `do while`, and `for` statements. The general format of a `continue` statement is:

continue;

When a `continue` is encountered in a loop, the next iteration of the loop is immediately begun. For `while` loops this means that execution is automatically transferred to the top of the loop and reevaluation of the tested expression is initiated. Although the `continue` statement has no direct effect on a `switch` statement, it can be included within a `switch` statement that itself is contained in a loop. Here the effect of `continue` is the same: the next loop iteration is begun.

As a general rule, the `continue` statement is less useful than the `break` statement, but it is convenient for skipping over data that should not be processed while remaining in a loop. For example, invalid grades are simply ignored in the following section of code and only valid grades are added to the total:[2]

```
while (count < 30)
{
  cout << "Enter a grade: ";
  cin  >> grade;
  if(grade < 0 || grade > 100)
    continue;
  total = total + grade;
  count++;
}
```

---

2 The `continue` is not essential, however, and the selection could have been written as:

```
If (grade >= 0 && grade <= 100)
{
  total = total + grade;
  count++;
}
```

The Null Statement

All statements must be terminated by a semicolon. A semicolon with nothing preceding it is also a valid statement, called the **null statement.** Thus, the statement

```
;
```

is a null statement. This is a do-nothing statement that is used where a statement is syntactically required, but no action is called for. Null statements typically are used with either `while` or `for` statements. An example of a `for` statement using a null statement is found in Program 5.10c in the next section.

EXERCISES 5.3

1. Rewrite Program 5.6 to compute the total of eight numbers.

2. Rewrite Program 5.6 to display the prompt:

```
Please type in the total number of data values to be added:
```

In response to this prompt, the program should accept a user-entered number and then use this number to control the number of times the `while` loop is executed. Thus, if the user enters 5 in response to the prompt, the program should request the input of five numbers and display the total after five numbers have been entered.

3. a. Write a C++ program to convert Celsius degrees to Fahrenheit. The program should request the starting Celsius value, the number of conversions to be made, and the increment between Celsius values. The display should have appropriate headings and list the Celsius value and the corresponding Fahrenheit value. Use the relationship

$$Fahrenheit = (9.0 / 5.0) \star Celsius + 32.0.$$

b. Run the program written in Exercise 3a on a computer. Verify that your program starts at the correct starting Celsius value and contains the exact number of conversions specified in your input data.

4. a. Modify the program written in Exercise 3 to request the starting Celsius value, the ending Celsius value, and the increment. Thus, instead of the condition checking for a fixed count, the condition will check for the ending Celsius value.

b. Run the program written in Exercise 4a on a computer. Verify that your output starts at the correct beginning value and ends at the correct ending value.

5. Rewrite Program 5.7 to compute the average of ten numbers.

6. Rewrite Program 5.7 to display the prompt:

```
Please type in the total number of data values to be averaged:
```

In response to this prompt, the program should accept a user-entered number and then use this number to control the number of times the `while` loop is executed. Thus, if the user enters 6 in response to the prompt, the program should request the input of six numbers and display the average of the next six numbers entered.

7. By mistake, a programmer put the statement `average = total / count;` within the `while` loop immediately after the statement `total = total + num;` in Program 5.7. Thus, the `while` loop becomes:

```
while (count <= MAXNUMS)
{
  cout << "Enter a number: ";
  cin  >> num;
  total = total + num;
  average = total / count;
  count++;
}
```

Will the program yield the correct result with this `while` loop? From a programming perspective, which `while` loop is better to use, and why?

8. a. Modify Program 5.8 to compute the average of the grades entered.

b. Run the program written in Exercise 8a on a computer and verify the results.

9. a. A bookstore summarizes its monthly transactions by keeping the following information for each book in stock:

Book identification number
Inventory balance at the beginning of the month
Number of copies received during the month
Number of copies sold during the month

Write a C++ program that accepts these data for each book and then displays the book identification number and an updated book inventory balance using the relationship:

New Balance = *Inventory balance at the beginning of the month*
+ *Number of copies received during the month*
– *Number of copies sold during the month*

Your program should use a `while` statement with a fixed `count` condition so that information on only three books is requested.

b. Run the program written in Exercise 9a on a computer. Review the display produced by your program and verify that the output produced is correct.

10. Modify the program you wrote for Exercise 9 to keep requesting and displaying results until a sentinel identification value of 999 is entered. Run the program on a computer.

5.4 `for` Loops

In C++, a **for loop** is constructed using a `for` statement. This statement performs the same functions as the `while` statement, but uses a different form. In many situations, especially those that use a fixed `count` condition, the `for` statement format is easier to use than its `while` statement equivalent.

The syntax of the `for` statement is:

```
for (initializing list; expression; altering list)
  statement;
```

Although the `for` statement looks a little complicated, it is really quite simple if we consider each of its parts separately.

Within the parentheses of the `for` statement are three items, separated by semicolons. Each of these items is optional and can be described individually, but the semicolons must be present.

In its most common form, the initializing list consists of a single statement used to set the starting (initial value) of a counter, the expression contains the maximum or minimum value the counter can have and determines when the loop is finished, and the altering list provides the increment value that is added to or subtracted from the counter each time the loop is executed. Examples of simple `for` statements having this form are:

```
for (count = 1; count < 10; count = count + 1)
  cout << count;
```

and

```
for (i = 5; i <= 15; i = i + 2)
  cout << i;
```

In the first `for` statement, the counter variable is named `count`, the initial value assigned to `count` is 1, the loop continues as long as the value in `count` is less than 10, and the value of `count` is incremented by one each time through the loop. In the next `for` statement, the counter variable is named `i`, the initial value assigned to `i` is 5, the loop continues as long as `i`'s value is less than or equal to 15, and the value of `i` is incremented by two each time through the loop. In both cases a `cout` statement is used to display the value of the counter. Another example of a `for` loop is given in Program 5.9.

PROGRAM 5.9

```
#include <iostream.h>
#include <iomanip.h>
#include <math.h>

int main()
{
  const int MAXCOUNT = 5;
  int count;

  cout << "NUMBER    SQUARE ROOT\n"
       << "------    -----------" << endl;

  cout << setiosflags(ios::showpoint);
  for (count = 1; count <= MAXCOUNT; count++)
    cout << setw(4) << count
         << setw(15) << sqrt(count) << endl;

  return 0;
}
```

When Program 5.9 is executed, the following display is produced:

```
Number    Square Root
-----     -----------
1         1.00000
2         1.41421
3         1.73205
4         2.00000
5         2.23607
```

The first two lines displayed by the program are produced by the two `cout` statements placed before the `for` statement. The remaining output is produced by the `for` loop. This loop begins with the `for` statement and is executed as follows: The initial value assigned to the counter variable `count` is 1. Because the value in `count` does not exceed the final value of 5, the execution of the `cout` statement within the loop produces the display

```
1         1.00000
```

Control is then transferred back to the `for` statement, which then increments the value in `count` to 2, and the loop is repeated, producing the display

```
2         1.41421
```

This process continues until the value in `count` exceeds the final value of 5, producing the complete output table.

For comparison purposes, a `while` loop equivalent to the `for` loop contained in Program 5.9 is:

```
count = 1
while (count <= MAXCOUNT)
{
  cout << setw(4) << count
       << setw(15) << setiosflags(ios::showpoint)
       << sqrt(count) << endl;
  count++;
}
```

As seen in this example, the difference between the `for` and `while` loops is the placement of the initialization, condition test, and incrementing items. The grouping of these items in the `for` statement is very convenient when fixed-count loops must be constructed. See if you can determine the output produced by Program 5.10.

PROGRAM 5.10

```
#include <iostream.h>
int main()
{
  int count;

  for (count = 2; count <= 20; count = count + 2)
    cout << count << "  ";

  return 0;
}
```

Did you figure it out? The loop starts with a `count` initialized to 2, stops when `count` exceeds 20, and increments `count` in steps of 2. The output produced by Program 5.10 is

```
2  4  6  8  10  12  14  16  18  20
```

The `for` statement does not require that any of the items in parentheses be present or that they be used for initializing or altering the values in the expression statements. However, the two semicolons must be present within the `for`'s parentheses. For example, the construction `for ( ; count <= 20 ;)` is valid.

If the initializing list is missing, the initialization step is omitted when the `for` statement is executed. This, of course, means that the programmer must provide the required initializations before the `for` statement is encountered. Similarly, if the altering list is missing, any expressions needed to alter the evaluation of the tested expression must be included directly within the statement part of the loop. The `for` statement ensures that all expressions in the initializing list are executed only once, before the first evaluation of the tested expression, and that all expressions in the altering list are executed at the end of each loop iteration before the tested expression is rechecked. Thus, Program 5.10 can be rewritten in any of the three ways shown in Programs 5.10a, 5.10b, and 5.10c.

PROGRAM 5.10A

```
#include <iostream.h>
int main()
{
  int count;

  count = 2;     // initializer outside for statement
  for ( ; count <= 20; count = count + 2)
    cout << count << "  ";

  return 0;
}
```

PROGRAM 5.10B

```
#include <iostream.h>
int main()
{
  int count;

  count = 2;     // initializer outside for loop
  for( ; count <= 20; )
  {
    cout << count << "  ";
    count = count + 2;     // alteration statement
  }

  return 0;
}
```

PROGRAM 5.10C

```
#include <iostream.h>
int main()   // all expressions within the for's parentheses
{
  int count;

  for (count = 2; count <= 20; cout << count << "  ", count = count + 2);

  return 0;
}
```

In Program 5.10a, `count` is initialized outside the `for` statement and the first list inside the parentheses is left blank. In Program 5.10b, both the initializing list and the altering list are removed from within the parentheses. Program 5.10b also uses a compound statement within the `for` loop, with the expression-altering statement included in the compound statement. Finally, Program 5.10c has included all items within the parentheses, so there is no need for any useful statement following the parentheses. Here the null statement satisfies the syntactical requirement of one statement to follow the `for`'s parentheses.

Observe also in Program 5.10c that the altering list (last set of items in parentheses) consists of two items, and that a comma has been used to separate these items. The use of commas to separate items in both the initializing and altering lists is required if either of these two lists contains more than one item. Last, note the fact that Programs 5.10a, 5.10b, and 5.10c are all inferior to Program 5.10, and although you may encounter them in your programming career, you should not use them. Adding items other than loop control variables and their updating conditions within the `for` statement tends to confuse its readability and can introduce unwanted effects. Keeping the loop control structure "clean," as is done in Program 5.10, is important and a good programming practice.

Although the initializing and altering lists can be omitted from a `for` statement, omitting the tested expression results in an infinite loop. For example, such a loop is created by the statement

```
for (count = 2; ; count = count + 1)
  cout << count;
```

As with the `while` statement, both `break` and `continue` statements can be used within a `for` loop. The `break` forces an immediate exit from the `for` loop, as it does in the `while` loop. The `continue`, however, forces control to be passed to the altering list in a `for` statement, after which the tested expression is reevaluated. This differs from the action of `continue` in a `while` statement, where control is passed directly to the reevaluation of the tested expression.

PROGRAMMER'S NOTES

Where to Place the Opening Braces

There are two styles of writing `for` loops that are used by professional C++ programmers. These styles come into play only when the `for` loop contains a compound statement.The style illustrated and used in the text takes the form:

```
for (expression)
{
  compound statement in here
}
```

An equally acceptable style that is used by many programmers places the initial brace of the compound statement on the first line. Using this style, a `for` loop appears as:

```
for (expression) {
  compound statement in here
}
```

The advantage of the first style is that the braces line up under one another, making it easier to locate brace pairs. The advantage of the second style is that it makes the code more compact and saves a display line, permitting more code to be viewed in the same display area. Both styles are used but are almost never intermixed. Select whichever style appeals to you and be consistent in its use. As always, the indentation you use within the compound statement (two or four spaces, or a tab) should also be consistent throughout all of your programs. The combination of styles that you select becomes a "signature" for your programming work.

Figure 5.13 illustrates the internal workings of a `for` loop. As shown, when the `for` loop is completed, control is transferred to the first executable statement following the loop. To avoid the necessity of always illustrating these steps, a simplified set of flowchart symbols is available for describing `for` loops. Using the fact that a `for` statement can be represented by the flowchart symbol

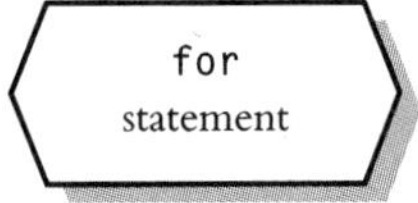

complete `for` loops can alternatively be illustrated as shown on Figure 5.14.

FIGURE 5.13

`for` **loop flowchart**

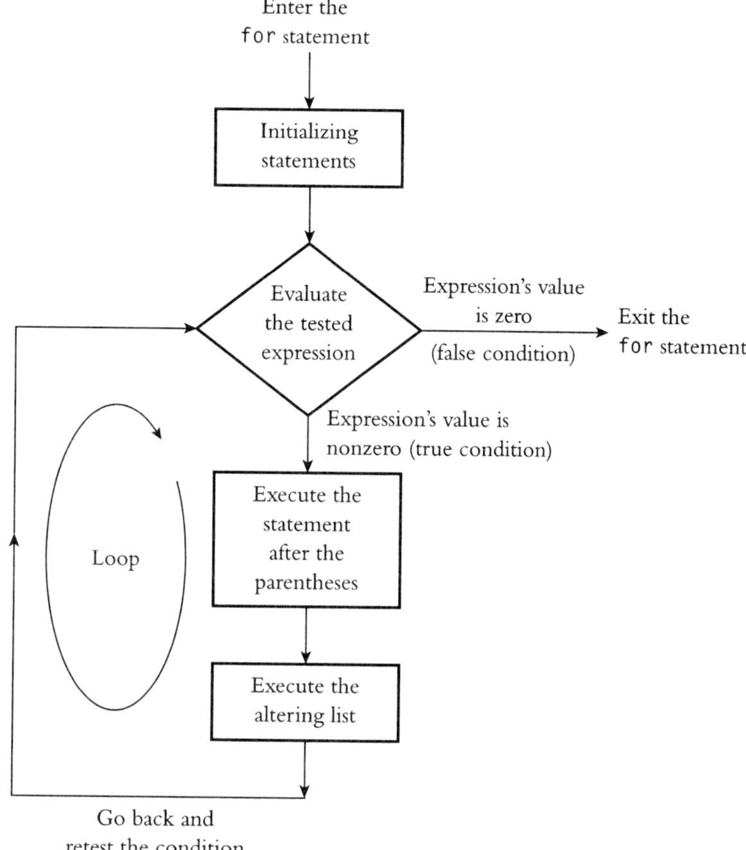

FIGURE 5.14

Simplified `for` **loop flowchart**

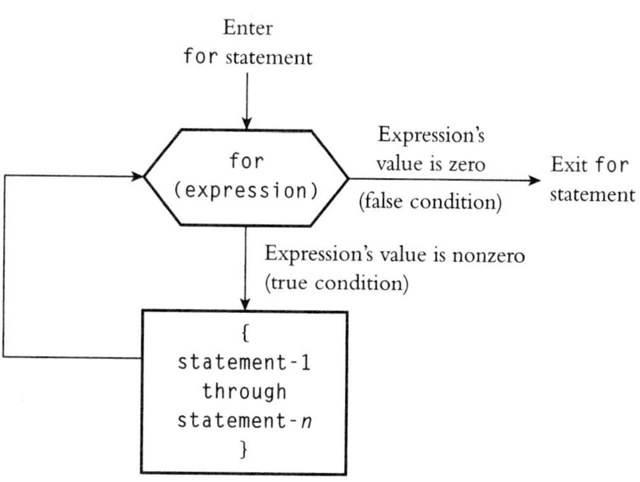

To understand the enormous power of `for` loops, consider the task of printing a table of numbers from 1 to 10, including their squares and cubes, using this statement. Such a table was previously produced using a `while` loop in Program 5.3. You may wish to review Program 5.3 and compare it to Program 5.11 to get a further sense of the equivalence between `for` and `while` loops.

PROGRAM 5.11

```
#include <iostream.h>
#include <iomanip.h>
int main()
{
  const int MAXNUMS = 10;
  int num;

  cout << endl; // print a blank line
  cout << "NUMBER    SQUARE    CUBE\n"
       << "------    ------    ----" << endl;

  for (num = 1; num <= MAXNUMS; num++)
    cout << setw(3) << num << "        "
         << setw(3) << num * num << "       "
         << setw(4) << num * num * num << endl;

  return 0;
}
```

When Program 5.11 is run, the display shown in Figure 5.15 is produced.

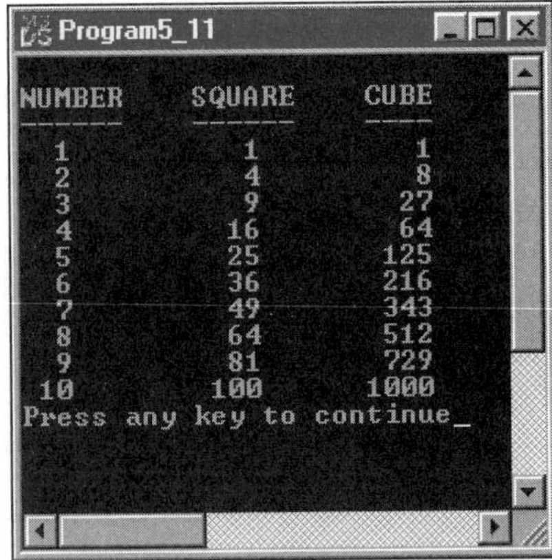

FIGURE 5.15

Output displayed by Program 5.11

PROGRAMMER'S NOTES

Should You Use a `for` or `while` Loop?

A question commonly asked by beginning programmers is which loop structure should be used—a `for` loop or `while` loop? This is a good question because both of these loop structures are pretest loops that, in C++, can be used to construct both fixed count and variable condition loops.

In almost all other computer languages, including Visual Basic and Pascal, the answer is relatively straightforward, because the `for` statement can be used only to construct fixed count loops. Thus, in these languages, `for` statements are used to construct fixed count loops and `while` statements are generally used only when constructing variable condition loops.

In C++, this easy distinction does not hold because each statement can be used to create each type of loop. The answer in C++, then, is really a matter of style. Because `for` and `while` loops are interchangeable in C++, either loop is appropriate. Some professional programmers always use a `for` statement for every pretest loop they create and almost never use a `while` statement; others always use a `while` statement and rarely use a `for` statement. Still a third group tends to retain the convention used in other languages—a `for` loop is generally used to create fixed count loops and a `while` loop is used to create variable condition loops. In C++ it is all a matter of style, and you will encounter all three styles in your programming career.

Simply changing the number 10 in the `for` statement of Program 5.11 to a 1000 creates a loop that is executed 1000 times and produces a table of numbers from 1 to 1000. As with the `while` statement this small change produces an immense increase in the processing and output provided by the program. Notice also that the expression `num++` was used in the altering list in place of the usual `num = num + 1`.

EXERCISES 5.4

1. Write individual `for` statements for the following cases:
   a. Use a counter named `i` that has an initial value of 1, a final value of 20, and an increment of 1.
   b. Use a counter named `icount` that has an initial value of 1, a final value of 20, and an increment of 2.
   c. Use a counter named `j` that has an initial value of 1, a final value of 100, and in increment of 5.
   d. Use a counter named `icount` that has an initial value of 20, a final value of 1, and an increment of –1.
   e. Use a counter named `icount` that has an initial value of 20, a final value of 1, and an increment of –2.

f. Use a counter named `count` that has an initial value of 1.0, a final value of 16.2, and an increment of 0.2.

g. Use a counter named `xcnt` that has an initial value of 20.0, a final value of 10.0, and an increment of -0.5.

2. Determine the number of times that each `for` loop is executed for the `for` statements written for Exercise 1.

3. Determine the value in `total` after each of the following loops is executed.

a.
```
total = 0;
for (i = 1; i <= 10; i = i + 1)
  total = total + 1;
```

b.
```
total = 1;
for (count = 1; count <= 10; count = count + 1)
  total = total * 2;
```

c.
```
total = 0
for ( i = 10; i <= 15; i = i + 1)
  total = total + i;
```

d.
```
total = 50
for (i = 1; i <= 10; i = i + 1)
  total = total - i;
```

e.
```
total = 1
for (icnt = 1; icnt <= 8; icnt++)
  total = total * icnt;
```

f.
```
total = 1.0
for (j = 1; j <= 5; j++)
  total = total / 2.0;
```

4. Determine the output of the following program.

```
#include <iostream.h>
int main()
{
  int i;

  for (i = 20; i >= 0; i = i - 4)
    cout << i << " ";

  return 0;
}
```

5. Modify Program 5.11 to produce a table of the numbers zero through 20 in increments of 2, with their squares and cubes.

6. Modify Program 5.11 to produce a table of numbers from 10 to 1, instead of 1 to 10 as it currently does.

7. Write and run a C++ program that displays a table of 20 temperature conversions from Fahrenheit to Celsius. The table should start with a Fahrenheit value of 20 degrees and be incremented in values of 4 degrees. Recall that *Celsius* = (5 – 0/9.0) ★ (*Fahrenheit* – 32).

8. Modify the program written for Exercise 7 to initially request the number of conversions to be made.

9. Write a C++ program that converts Fahrenheit to Celsius temperature where the initial value of Fahrenheit temperature, the increments, and the total conversions to be made are to be requested as user input during program execution. Recall that *Celsius* = (5.0/9.0) ★ (*Fahrenheit* – 32.0).

10. Write and run a C++ program that accepts six Fahrenheit temperatures, one at a time, and converts each value entered to its Celsius equivalent before the next value is requested. Use a `for` loop in your program. The conversion required is *Celsius* = (5.0/9.0) ★ (*Fahrenheit* – 32).

11. Write and run a C++ program that accepts ten individual values of gallons, one at a time, and converts each value entered to its liter equivalent before the next value is requested. Use a `for` loop in your program. There are 3.785 liters in one gallon of liquid.

12. Modify the program written for Exercise 11 to initially request the number of data items that will be entered and converted.

13. Is the following program correct? If it is, determine its output. If it is not, determine and correct the error so the program will run.

```
#include <iostream.h>
int main()
{

  for(int i = 1; i < 5; i++)
   cout << i << endl;

  for (int i = 1; i < 3; i++)
   cout << i << endl;

  return 0;
}
```

14. Write and run a C++ program that calculates and displays the amount of money available in a bank account that initially has $1,000 deposited in it and that earns 8 percent interest a year. Your program should display the amount available at the end of each year for a period of ten years. Use the relationship that the money available at the end of each year equals the amount of money in the account at the start of the year plus .08 times the amount available at the start of the year.

15. **a.** Modify the program written for Exercise 14 to initially prompt the user for the amount of money initially deposited in the account.
    b. Modify the program written for Exercise 14 to initially prompt the user for both the amount of money initially deposited and the number of years that should be displayed.
    c. Modify the program written for Exercise 14 to initially prompt for the amount of money initially deposited, the interest rate to be used, and the number of years to be displayed.

16. A machine purchased for $28,000 is depreciated at a rate of $4,000 a year for seven years. Write and run a C++ program that computes and displays a depreciation table for seven years. The table should have the form:

```
                     Depreciation Schedule
                     ---------------------
                                 End-of-Year     Accumulated
  Year      Depreciation            Value        Depreciation
  ----      ------------         -----------     ------------
   1            4000               24000              4000
   2            4000               20000              8000
   3            4000               16000             12000
   4            4000               12000             16000
   5            4000                8000             20000
   6            4000                4000             24000
   7            4000                   0             28000
```

5.5 Nested Loops

In many situations it is convenient to use a loop contained within another loop. Such loops are called **nested loops.** A simple example of a nested loop is:

```
for(i = 1; i <= 5; i++)               // start of outer loop   <------+
{                                     //                              |
  cout << "\ni is now " << i << endl;  //                             |
                                      //                              |
  for(j = 1; j <= 4; j++)             // start of inner loop          |
    cout << "  j = " << j;            // end of inner loop            |
}                                     // end of outer loop    <-------+
```

The first loop, controlled by the value of i, is called the **outer loop.** The second loop, controlled by the value of j, is called the **inner loop.** Notice that all statements in the inner loop are contained within the boundaries of the outer loop and that we have used a different variable to control each loop. For each single trip through the outer loop,

FIGURE 5.16

For each value of `i`, a `j` loop occurs

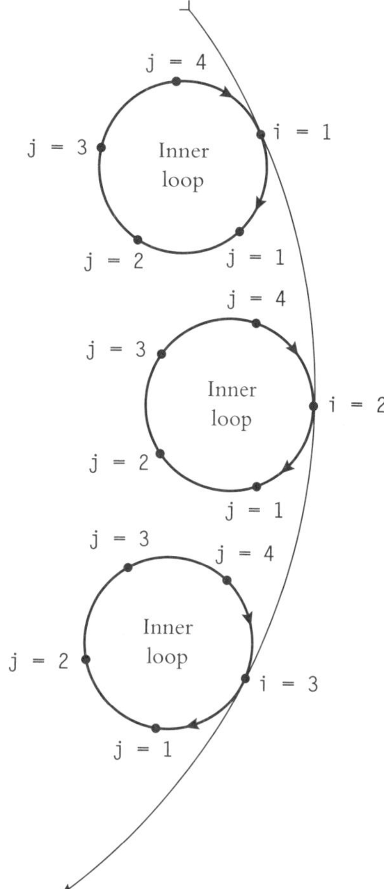

the inner loop runs through its entire sequence. Thus, each time the `i` counter increases by 1, the inner `for` loop executes completely. This situation is illustrated in Figure 5.16.

Program 5.12 includes the preceding code in a working program. Figure 5.17 illustrates the display produced when Program 5.12 is executed.

FIGURE 5.17

Display produced by Program 5.12

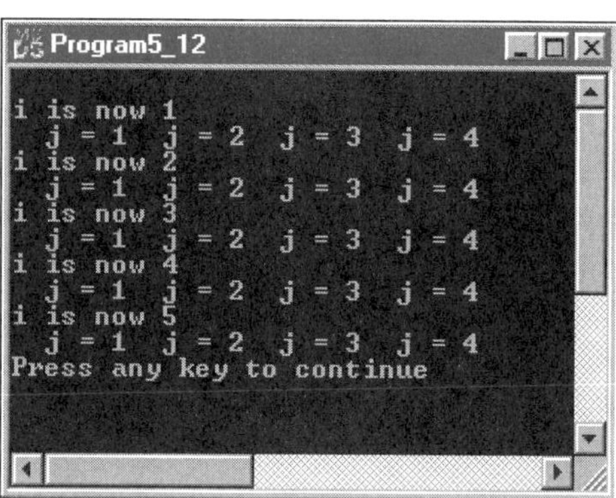

PROGRAM 5.12

```
#include <iostream.h>
int main()
{
  const int MAXI = 5;
  const int MAXJ = 4;
  int i, j;

  for(i = 1; i <= MAXI; i++)     // start of outer loop <------+
  {                                       //                |
    cout << "\ni is now " << i << endl;   //                |
                                          //                |
    for(j = 1; j <= MAXJ; j++)   // start of inner loop     |
      cout << "  j = " << j;     // end of inner loop       |
  }                              // end of outer loop <------+

  cout << endl;

  return 0;
}
```

To illustrate the usefulness of a nested loop, we use one here to compute the average grade for each student in a class of 20 students. Each student has taken four exams during the course of the semester. The final grade is calculated as the average of these examination grades. The pseudocode describing how this computation can be done is:

For 20 times
  Set the student grade total to zero
  For 4 times
    Input a grade
    Add the grade to the total
  EndFor // end of inner for loop
  Calculate student's average grade
    Print the student's average grade
EndFor // end of outer for loop

As described by the pseudocode, an outer loop consisting of 20 passes will be used to compute the average grade for each student. The inner loop will consist of 4 passes. One examination grade is entered in each inner loop pass. As each grade is entered it is added to the total for the student, and at the end of the loop the average is calculated and displayed. Because both outer and inner loops are fixed count loops of 20 and 4, respectively, we use `for` statements to create these loops. Program 5.13 provides the C++ code corresponding to the pseudocode.

PROGRAM 5.13

```
#include <iostream.h>
int main()
{
  const int NUMGRADES = 4;
  const int NUMSTUDENTS = 20;
  int i, j;
  float grade, total, average;

  for (i = 1; i <= NUMSTUDENTS; i++) // start of outer loop
  {
    total = 0;                       // clear the total for this student
    for (j = 1; j <= NUMGRADES; j++) // start of inner loop
    {
      cout << "Enter an examination grade for this student: ";
      cin  >> grade;
      total = total + grade;         // add the grade into the total
    }                                // end of the inner for loop
    average = total / NUMGRADES;     // calculate the average
    cout << "\nThe average for student " << i
         << " is " << average << "\n\n";
  }                                  // end of the outer for loop

  return 0;
}
```

In reviewing Program 5.13, pay particular attention to the initialization of `total` within the outer loop, before the inner loop is entered. The variable `total` is initialized 20 times, once for each student. Also notice that the average is calculated and displayed immediately after the inner loop is finished. Because the statements that compute and print the average are also contained within the outer loop, 20 averages are calculated and displayed. The entry and addition of each grade within the inner loop use techniques we have seen before, which should now be familiar to you.

EXERCISES 5.5

1. Four experiments are performed, each experiment consisting of six test results. The results for each experiment are given below. Write a program using a nested loop to compute and display the average of the test results for each experiment.

1st experiment results: 23.2 31 16.9 27 25.4 28.6
2nd experiment results: 34.8 45.2 27.9 36.8 33.4 39.4
3rd experiment results: 19.4 16.8 10.2 20.8 18.9 13.4
4th experiment results: 36.9 39 49.2 45.1 42.7 50.6

2. Modify the program written for Exercise 1 so that the number of test results for each experiment is entered by the user. Write your program so that a different number of test results can be entered for each experiment.

3. a. A bowling team consists of five players. Each player bowls three games. Write a C++ program that uses a nested loop to enter each player's individual scores and then computes and displays the average score for each bowler. Assume that each bowler has the following scores:

1st bowler: 286 252 265
2nd bowler: 212 186 215
3rd bowler: 252 232 216
4th bowler: 192 201 235
5th bowler: 186 236 272

b. Modify the program written for Exercise 3a to calculate and display the average team score. (*Hint:* Use a second variable to store the total of all the players' scores.)

4. Rewrite the program written for Exercise 3a to eliminate the inner loop. To do this, you will have to input three scores for each bowler rather than one at a time.

5. Write a program that calculates and displays values for y when

$$y = xz/(x - z)$$

Your program should calculate y for values of x ranging between 1 and 5 and values of z ranging between 2 and 6. x should control the outer loop and be incremented in steps of 1 and z should be incremented in steps of 1. Your program should also display the message `Function Undefined` when the x and z values are equal.

6. Write a program that calculates and displays the yearly amount available if $1000 is invested in a bank account for 10 years. Your program should display the amounts available for interest rates from 6% to 12% inclusively, in 1% increments. Use a nested loop, with the outer loop controlling the interest rate and the inner loop controlling the years. Use the relationship that the money available at the end of each year equals the amount of money in the account at the start of the year, plus the interest rate times the amount available at the start of the year.

7. In the Duchy of Upenchuck, the fundamental unit of currency is the Upenchuck Dragon (UD). Income tax deductions are base on salary in units of 10,000 UD and on the number of dependents the employee has. The formula, designed to favor low-income families, is

$$\textit{deduction}\ (\text{UD}) = \textit{dependents} \star 500 + 0.05 \star (50{,}000 - \textit{salary})$$

Beyond 5 dependents and beyond 50,000 UD, the Deduction does not change. There is no tax, hence no deduction, on incomes of less than 10,000 UD. Based on this information, create a table of Upenchuck income tax deductions, with dependents 0 to 5 as the column headings and salary 10000, 20000, 30000, 40000, and 50000 as the rows.

5.6 `do while` Loops

Both the `while` and `for` statements evaluate an expression at the start of the repetition loop; as such they are always used to create pretest loops. Posttest loops, which are also referred to as exit-controlled loops, can also be constructed in C++. The basic structure of such a loop, which is referred to as a `do while` loop, is illustrated in Figure 5.18. Notice that a `do while` loop continues iterations through the loop while the condition is true and exits the loop when the condition is false.

FIGURE 5.18

`do while` **loop structure**

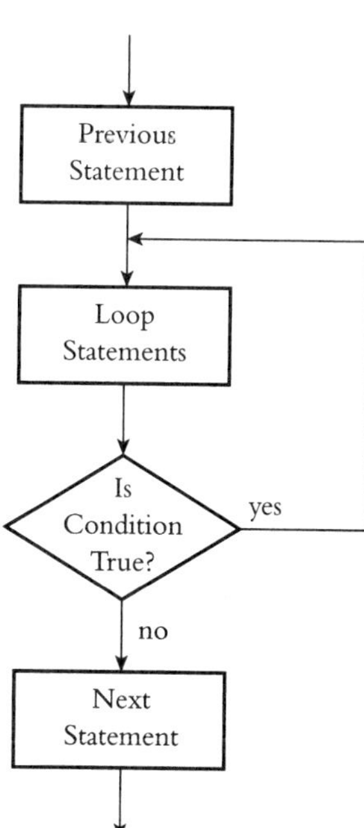

FIGURE 5.19

The `do` statement's flow of control

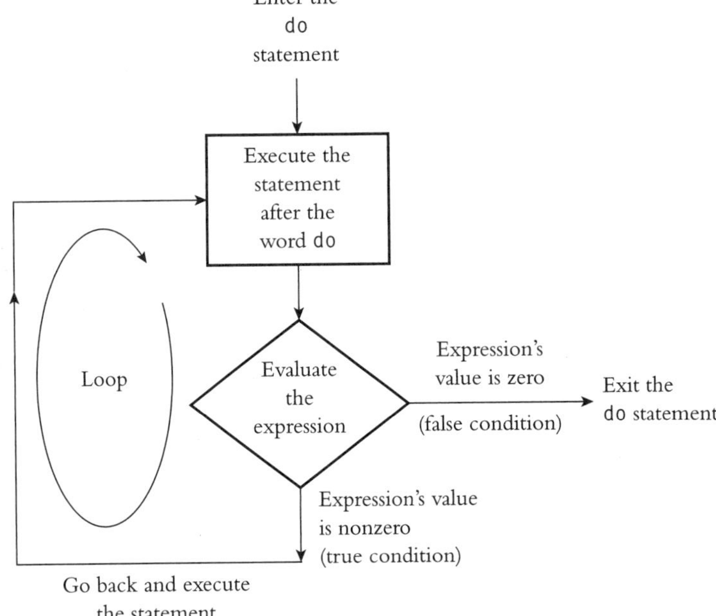

In C++, a posttest loop is created using a `do` statement. As its name implies, this statement allows us to do some statements before an expression is evaluated at the end of the loop. The general form of C++'s do statement is:

```
do
  statement;
while (expression);  ←—— don't forget the final ;
```

As with all C++ programs, the single statement in the `do` may be replaced with a compound statement. A flow-control diagram illustrating the operation of the `do` statement is shown in Figure 5.19.

As illustrated, all statements within the `do` statement are executed at least once before the expression is evaluated. Then, if the expression has a nonzero value, the statements are executed again. This process continues until the expression evaluates to zero (becomes false). For example, consider the following `do` statement:

```
do
{
  cout << "\nEnter a price: ";
  cin  >> price;
  if (abs(price - SENTINEL) < 0.0001)
    break;
    salestax = RATE * price;
```

```
    cout << setiosflags(ios::showpoint)
         << setprecision(2)
          << "The sales tax is $ " << salestax;
}
while (price != SENTINEL);
```

Observe that only one prompt and `cin` statement are used here because the tested expression is evaluated at the end of the loop.

As with all repetition statements, the `do` statement can always replace or be replaced by an equivalent `while` or `for` statement. The choice of which statement to use depends on the application and the style preferred by the programmer. In general, the `while` and `for` statements are preferred because they clearly let anyone reading the program know what is being tested "right up front" at the top of the program loop.

Validity Checks

The `do` statement is particularly useful in filtering user-entered input and providing data validation checks. For example, assume that an operator is required to enter a valid customer identification number between the numbers 1000 and 1999. A number outside this range is to be rejected, and a new request for a valid number made. The following section of code provides the necessary data filter to verify the entry of a valid identification number:

```
do
{
  cout << "\nEnter an identification number: ";
  cin  >> idNum;
}
while (idNum < 1000 || idNum > 1999);
```

Here, a request for an identification number is repeated until a valid number is entered. This section of code is "bare bones" in that it neither alerts the user to the cause of the new request for data nor allows premature exit from the loop if a valid identification number cannot be found. An alternative removing the first drawback is:

```
do
{
  cout << "\nEnter an identification number: ";
  cin  >> idNum;
  if (idNum < 1000 || idNum > 1999)
  {
    cout << "An invalid number was just entered\n";
    cout << "Please check the ID number and re-enter\n";
  }
```

```
    else
      break;    // break if a valid id num was entered
  } while(1);   // this expression is always true
```

Here we have used a break statement to exit from the loop. Because the expression being evaluated by the do statement is always 1 (true), an infinite loop has been created that is exited only when the break statement is encountered.

EXERCISES 5.6

1. **a.** Using a do statement, write a program to accept a grade. The program should request a grade continuously as long as an invalid grade is entered. An invalid grade is any grade less than 0 or greater than 100. After a valid grade has been entered, your program should display the value of the grade entered.
   b. Modify the program written for Exercise 1a so that the user is alerted when an invalid grade has been entered.
   c. Modify the program written for Exercise 1b so that it allows the user to exit the program by entering the number 999.
   d. Modify the program written for Exercise 1b so that it automatically terminates after five invalid grades are entered.
2. **a.** Write a program that continuously requests a grade to be entered. If the grade is less than 0 or greater than 100, your program should print an appropriate message informing the user that an invalid grade has been entered, else the grade should be added to a total. When a grade of 999 is entered, the program should exit the repetition loop and compute and display the average of the valid grades entered.
   b. Run the program written in Exercise 2a on a computer and verify the program using appropriate test data.
3. **a.** Write a program to reverse the digits of a positive integer number. For example, if the number 8735 is entered, the number displayed should be 5378. (*Hint:* Use a do statement and continuously strip off and display the units digit of the number. If the variable num initially contains the number entered, the units digit is obtained as (num % 10). After a units digit is displayed, dividing the number by 10 sets up the number for the next iteration. Thus, (8735 % 10) is 5 and (8735 / 10) is 873. The do statement should continue as long as the remaining number is not zero).
   b. Run the program written in Exercise 3a on a computer and verify the program using appropriate test data.
4. Repeat any of the exercises in Section 5.4 using a do statement rather than a for statement.

5.7 Common Programming Errors

Six errors are commonly made by beginning C++ programmers when using repetition statements. The most troublesome of these for new programmers is the "off by one" error, where the loop executes either one too many or one too few times than was intended. For example, the loop created by the statement `for(i = 1; i < 11; i++)` executes ten times, not eleven, even though the number 11 is used in the statement. Thus, an equivalent loop can be constructed using the statement `for(i = 1; i <= 10; i++)`. However, if the loop is started with an initial value of i = 0, using the statement `for(i = 0; i < 11; i++)`, the loop will be traversed 11 times, as will a loop constructed with the statement `for(i = 0; i <=10; i++)`. Thus, in constructing loops, you must pay particular attention to both initial and final conditions used to control the loop to ensure that number of loop traversals is not off by one too many or one too few executions.

The next two errors pertain to the tested expression, and have already been encountered with the `if` and `switch` statements. The first is the inadvertent use of the assignment operator, =, for the equality operator, ==, in the tested expression. An example of this error is typing the assignment expression `a = 5` instead of the desired relational expression `a == 5`. Because the tested expression can be any valid C++ expression, including arithmetic and assignment expressions, this error is not detected by the compiler.

As with the `if` statement, repetition statements should not use the equality operator, ==, when testing floating point or double precision operands. For example, the expression `fnum == 0.01` should be replaced by a test requiring that the absolute value of `fnum - 0.01` be less than an acceptable amount. The reason for this is that all numbers are stored in binary form. Using a finite number of bits, decimal numbers such as .01 have no exact binary equivalent, so that tests requiring equality with such numbers can fail.

The next two errors are particular to the `for` statement. The most common is to place a semicolon at the end of the `for`'s parentheses, which frequently produces a do-nothing loop. For example, consider the statements

```
for(count = 0; count < 10; count++);
  total = total + num;
```

Here the semicolon at the end of the first line of code is a null statement. This has the effect of creating a loop that is executed 10 times with nothing done except the incrementing and testing of `count`. This error tends to occur because C++ programmers are used to ending most lines with a semicolon.

The next error occurs when commas are used to separate the items in a `for` statement instead of the required semicolons. An example of this is the statement

```
for (count = 1, count < 10, count++)
```

Commas must be used to separate items within the initializing and altering lists, and semicolons must be used to separate these lists from the tested expression.

The last error occurs when the final semicolon is omitted from the `do` statement. This error is usually made by programmers who have learned to omit the semicolon after the parentheses of a `while` statement and carry over this habit when the reserved word `while` is encountered at the end of a `do` statement.

5.8 Chapter Summary

1. A section of repeating code is referred to as a **loop.** The loop is controlled by a repetition statement that tests a condition to determine whether the code will be executed. Each pass through the loop is referred to as a **repetition** or **iteration.** The tested condition must always be explicitly set prior to its first evaluation by the repetition statement. Within the loop there must always be a statement that permits altering of the condition so that the loop, once entered, can be exited.

2. There are three basic type of loops:

   a. `while`
   b. `for`
   c. `do while`

The `while` and `for` loops are **pretest** or **entrance-controlled loops.** In this type of loop the tested condition is evaluated at the beginning of the loop, which requires that the tested condition be explicitly set prior to loop entry. If the condition is true, loop repetitions begin; otherwise, the loop is not entered. Iterations continue as long as the condition remains true. In C++, `while` and `for` loops are constructed using `while` and `for` statements, respectively.

The `do while` loop is a **posttest** or **exit-controlled loop,** where the tested condition is evaluated at the end of the loop. This type of loop is always executed at least once. The `do while` loops continue to execute as long as the tested condition remains true.

3. Loops are also classified as to the type of tested condition. In a **fixed count loop,** the condition is used to keep track of how many repetitions have occurred. In a **variable condition loop,** the tested condition is based on a variable that can change interactively with each pass through the loop.

4. In C++, a `while` loop is constructed using a `while` statement. The most commonly used form of this statement is:

```
while (expression)
{
  statements;
}
```

The expression contained within parentheses is the condition tested to determine if the statement following the parentheses, which is generally a compound statement, is executed. The expression is evaluated in exactly the same manner as that contained in an `if-else` statement; the difference is how the expression is used. In a `while` statement the statement following the expression is executed repeatedly as long as the expression retains a nonzero value, rather than just once, as in an `if-else` statement. An example of a `while` loop is:

```
count = 1;                  // initialize count
while (count <= 10)
{
  cout << count << "  ";
  count++;                    // increment count
}
```

The first assignment statement sets `count` equal to 1. The `while` statement is then entered and the expression is evaluated for the first time. As the value of `count` is less than or equal to 10, so the expression is true and the compound statement is executed. The first statement in the compound statement uses the `cout` object to display the value of `count`. The next statement adds 1 to the value currently stored in `count`, making this value equal to 2. The `while` statement now loops back to retest the expression. Because `count` is still less than or equal to 10, the compound statement is again executed. This process continues until the value of `count` reaches 11.

The `while` statement always checks its expression at the top of the loop. This requires that any variables in the tested expression must have values assigned before the `while` is encountered. Within the `while` loop there must be a statement that alters the tested expression's value.

5. In C++, a `for` loop is constructed using a `for` statement. This statement performs the same functions as the `while` statement, but uses a different form. In many situations, especially those that use a fixed count condition, the `for` statement format is easier to use than its `while` statement equivalent. The most commonly used form of the `for` statement is:

```
for (initializing list; expression; altering list)
{
  statements;
}
```

Within the parentheses of the `for` statement are three items, separated by semicolons. Each of these items is optional but the semicolons must be present.

The initializing list is used to set any initial values before the loop is entered; generally it is used to initialize a counter. Statements within the initializing list are executed only once. The expression in the `for` statement is the condition being tested: It is tested at the start of the loop and prior to each iteration. The altering list contains loop statements that are not contained within the compound statement; generally, it is used to increment or decrement a counter each time the loop is executed. Multiple statements within a list are separated by commas. An example of a `for` loop is:

```
for (total = 0, count = 1; count < 10; count++)
{
  cout << "Enter a grade: ";
  cin  >> grade;
  total = total + grade;
}
```

In this `for` statement, the initializing list is used to initialize both `total` and `count`. The expression determines that the loop will execute as long as the value in `count` is less than 10, and the value of `count` is incremented by one each time through the loop.

6. The `for` statement is extremely useful in creating fixed count loops. This is because the initializing statements, the tested expression, and statements affecting the tested expression can all be included in parentheses at the top of a `for` loop for easy inspection and modification.

7. The `do` statement is used to create posttest loops because it checks its expression at the end of the loop. This ensures that the body of a `do` loop is executed at least once. Within a `do` loop there must be at least one statement that alters the tested expression's value.

5.9 Knowing About: Random Numbers and Simulation

There are many scientific and engineering simulation problems in which probability must be considered or statistical sampling techniques must be used. For example, in simulating automobile traffic flow or telephone usage patterns, statistical models are required. Additionally, applications such as simple computer games and more involved simulation scenarios can be described only statistically. All of these statistical models require the generation of **random numbers;** that is, a series of numbers whose order cannot be predicted.

In practice, there are no truly random numbers. Dice never are perfect, cards are never shuffled completely randomly, the supposedly random motions of molecules are influenced by the environment, and digital computers can handle numbers only within a finite range and with limited precision. The best one can do is to generate **pseudorandom numbers,** which are sufficiently random for the task at hand.

Some computer languages contain a library function that produces random numbers; others do not. The functions provided by C++ are named `rand()` for generating random numbers and `srand()` for setting initial random "seed" values. We present these two functions and then use them in an application that simulates the tossing of a coin to determine the number of resulting heads and tails.

Generating Pseudorandom Numbers

Two functions are provided by C++ compilers for creating random numbers: `rand()` and `srand()`. The `rand()` function produces a series of random numbers in the range 0 ≤ `rand()` ≤ `RAND_MAX`, where the constant `RAND_MAX` is defined in the `stdlib.h` header file. The `srand()` function provides a starting "seed" value for `rand()`. If `srand()` or some other equivalent "seeding" technique is not used, `rand()` will always produce the same series of random numbers.

The general procedure for creating a series of N random numbers using C++'s library functions is illustrated by the following code:

```
srand(time(NULL));  // this generates the first "seed" value

for (int i = 1; i <= N; i++)  // this generates N random numbers
{
  rvalue = rand();
  cout << rvalue << endl;
}
```

Here, the argument to the `srand()` function is a call to the `time()` function with a `NULL` argument. With this argument the `time()` function reads the computer's internal clock time, in seconds. The `srand()` function then uses this time, converted to an unsigned `int`, to initialize the random number generator function `rand()`.[3] Program 5.14 uses this code to generate a series of ten random numbers.

The following is the output produced by one run of Program 5.14:

```
20203
21400
15265
26935
 8369
10907
31299
15400
 5074
20663
```

3 Alternatively, many C++ compilers have a `randomize()` routine that is defined using the `srand()` function. If this routine is available, the call `randomize()` can be used in place of the call `srand(time(NULL))`. In either case, the initializing "seed" routine is called only once, after which the `rand()` function is used to generate a series of numbers.

PROGRAM 5.14

```
#include <iostream.h>
#include <iomanip.h>
#include <stdlib.h>
#include <time.h>

// this program generates ten pseudo-random numbers
// using C++'s rand() function

int main()
{
  const int NUMBERS = 10;

  float randvalue;
  int i;

  srand(time(NULL));
  for (i = 1; i <= NUMBERS; i++)
  {
    randvalue = rand();
    cout << setw(20) << randvalue << endl;
  }

  return 0;
}
```

Because of the `srand()` function call in Program 5.14, the series of ten random numbers will differ each time the program is executed. Without the randomizing "seeding" effect of this function the same series of random numbers would be always be produced. Note also the inclusion of the `stdlib.h` and `time.h` header files. The `stdlib.h` file contains the function prototypes for the `srand()` and `rand()` functions, and the `time.h` header file contains the function prototype for the `time()` function.

Scaling

One modification to the random number produced by the `rand()` function typically must be made in practice. In most applications either the random numbers are required as floating point values within the range 0.0 to 1.0 or as integers within a specified range, such as 1 to 100. The method for adjusting the random numbers produced by a random number generator to reside within such ranges is called **scaling.**

Scaling random numbers to reside within the range 0.0 to 1.0 is easily accomplished by dividing the returned value of `rand()` by `RAND_MAX`. Thus, the expression `float(rand())/RAND_MAX` produces a floating point random number between 0.0 and 1.0.

Scaling a random number as an integer value between 0 and N is accomplished using either of the expressions `rand() % (N+1)` or `int((rand()/RAND_MAX) * N)`. For example, the expression `int(rand()/RAND_MAX * 100)` produces a random integer between 0 and 100.[4]

To produce an integer random number between 1 and N the expression `1 + rand() % N` can be used. For example, in simulating the roll of a die, the expression `1 + rand() % 6` produces a random integer between 1 and 6. The more general scaling expression `a + rand() % (b + 1 - a)` can be used to produce a random integer between the numbers `a` and `b`.

Simulation

A common use of random numbers is to simulate events using a program, rather than going through the time and expense of constructing a real-life experiment. For example, statistical theory tells us that the probability of having a single tossed coin turn up heads is 0.5. Similarly, there is a 50 percent probability of having a single tossed coin turn up tails.

Using these probabilities we would expect a single coin that is tossed 1000 times to turn up heads 500 times and tails 500 times. In practice, however, this is never exactly realized for a single experiment consisting of 1000 tosses. Instead of actually tossing a coin 1000 times we can use a random number generator to simulate these tosses.

For this problem two outputs are required: the percentage of heads and the percentage of tails that result when a simulated coin is tossed 1000 times.

The percentage of heads and tails are determined as:

$$\textit{Percentage of heads} = \frac{\textit{Number of heads}}{1000} \times 100\%$$

$$\textit{Percentage of tails} = \frac{\textit{Number of tails}}{1000} \times 100\%$$

To determine the number of heads and tails, we will have to simulate 1000 random numbers in such a manner that we can define a result of "heads" or "tails" from each generated number. There are a number of ways to do this.

4 Many C++ compilers have a routine named `random()` that can be used to produce the same result. For example, if your compiler has the `random()` function, the call `random(100)` will produce a random integer between 0 and 100.

One way is to use the `rand()` function to generate integers between 0 and `RAND_MAX`. Knowing that any single toss has a 50% chance of being either a head or a tail, we could designate a "head" as an even random number and a "tail" as an odd random number. A second method would be to scale the return value from `rand()` to reside between 0.0 and 1.0 as described above. Then we could define a "head" as any number greater than 0.5 and any other result as a "tail." This is the algorithm we adopt here.

Having defined how we will create a single toss that has a 50% chance of turning up heads or tails, the generation of 1000 tosses is rather simple: we use a fixed count loop that generates 1000 random numbers. For each generation we identify the result as either a head or tail, and accumulate the results in a heads and tails counter. Thus, the complete simulation algorithm is given by the pseudocode:

```
Initialize a heads count to zero
Initialize a tails count to zero
For 1000 times
   Generate a random number between 0 and 1
   If the random number is greater than .5
      consider this as a head and
      add one to the heads count
   Else
      Consider this as a tail and
       add one to the tails count
   End If
End For
Calculate the percentage of heads as
   the number of heads divided by 1000 x 100%
Calculate the percentage of tails as
   the number of tails divided by 1000 x 100%
Print the percentage of heads and tails obtained
```

Program 5.15 codes this algorithm in C++.

Following are two output displays obtained using Program 5.15.

```
Heads came up 51.599998 percent of the time
Tails came up 48.400002 percent of the time
```

and

```
Heads came up 47.299999 percent of the time
Tails came up 52.700001 percent of the time
```

PROGRAM 5.15

```
#include <iostream.h>
#include <iomanip.h>
#include <stdlib.h>
#include <time.h>

// a program to simulate the tossing of a coin NUM TOSSES times

int main()
{
  const int NUMTOSSES = 1000;

  int heads = 0;  // initialize heads count
  int tails = 0;  // initialize tails count
  int i;
  float flip, perheads, pertails;

    // simulate NUMTOSSES tosses of a coin
  srand(time(NULL));
  for (i = 1; i <= NUMTOSSES; i++)
  {
    flip = float(rand())/RAND_MAX;    // scale the number between 0 and 1
    if (flip > 0.5)
      heads = heads + 1;
    else
      tails = tails + 1;
  }
  perheads = (heads / float (NUMTOSSES)) * 100.0;  // calculate heads percentage
  pertails = (tails / float (NUMTOSSES)) * 100.0;  // calculate tails percentage
  cout << "\nHeads came up " << perheads << " percent of the time";
  cout << "\nTails came up " << pertails << " percent of the time"
       << endl;

  return 0;
}
```

Writing and executing Program 5.15 is certainly easier than manually tossing a coin 1000 times. It should be noted that the validity of the results produced by the program depends on how random the numbers produced by `rand()` actually are. For our purposes, we have used a previously written library function and accept the "randomness" of the generator (see Exercise 3 for a method of verifying the function's randomness).

EXERCISES 5.9

1. Modify Program 5.15 so that it requests the number of tosses from the user. (*Hint:* Make sure to have the program correctly determine the percentages of heads and tails obtained.)

2. Many algorithms have been developed for generating pseudorandom numbers. Some of these algorithms utilize a counting scheme, such as counting bits beginning at some arbitrary location in a changing memory. Another scheme, which creates pseudorandom numbers by performing a calculation, is the *power residue method.*

The power residue method begins with an odd n-digit integer, which is referred to as the "seed" number. The seed is multiplied by the value $(10^{n/2} - 3)$. Using the lowest n digits of the result (the "residue") produces a new seed. Continuing this procedure produces a series of random numbers, with each new number used as the seed for the next number. If the original seed has four or more digits (n equal to or greater than 4) and is not divisible by either two or five, this procedure yields $5 \times 10^{(n-2)}$ random numbers before a sequence of numbers repeats itself. For example, starting with a 6-digit seed ($n = 6$), such as 654321, a series of $5 \times 10^4 = 50{,}000$ random numbers can be generated.

As an algorithm, the specific steps in generating pseudorandom numbers using a power residue procedure consist of the following:

Step 1: Have a user enter a six-digit integer seed that is not divisible by 2 or 5. This means the number should be an odd number not ending in 5.

Step 2: Multiply the seed number by 997, which is $10^3 - 3$.

Step 3: Extract the lower 6 digits of the result produced by step 2. Use this random number as the next seed.

Step 4: Repeat Steps 2 and 3 for as many random numbers as needed.

Thus, if the user-entered seed number is 654321 (Step 1), the first random number generated is calculated as follows:

Step 2: 654321 * 997 = 652358037

Step 3: Extract the lower 6 digits of the number obtained in Step 2. This is accomplished using a standard programming "trick."

The trick involves:

Step 3a: Divide the number by $10^6 = 1000000$.
For example, 652358037 / 1000000 = 652.358037

Step 3b: Take the integer part of the result of Step 3a.
For example, the integer part of 652.358037 = 652

Step 3c: Multiply the previous result by 10^6
For example, $652 \times 10^6 = 652000000$

Step 3d: Subtract this result from the original number.
For example, $652358037 - 652000000 = 358037$

The integer part of a floating point number can either be taken by assigning the floating point number to an integer variable, or by a C++ cast (see Section 3.3). In our procedure we use the cast mechanism. Thus, the algorithm for producing a random number can be accomplished using the following code:

```
i = int(997.0 * x / 1.e6);    // take the integer part
x = 997.0 * x - i * 1.e6;
```

Using this information:

a. Create a function named `randnum()` that accepts a floating point "seed" as a parameter and returns a floating point random number between 0 and 1.e6.

b. Incorporate the `randnum()` function created in Exercise 2a into a working C++ program that produces ten random numbers between 0 and 1.e6.

c. Test the randomness of the `randnum()` function created in Exercise 2a using the method described in Exercise 3. Try some even seed values and some odd seed values that end in 5 to determine whether these affect the randomness of the numbers.

3. Write a program that tests the effectiveness of the `rand()` library function. Start by initializing 10 counters, such as `zerocount`, `onecount`, `twocount`, . . . , `ninecount` to 0. Then generate a large number of pseudorandom integers between 0 and 9. Each time a 0 occurs, increment `zerocount`; when a 1 occurs, increment `onecount`, etc. Finally, display the percentage of the number of times the 0s, 1s, 2s, etc. occurred. For a truly random function, each number should occur 10 percent of the time.

6 Modularity Using Functions

6.1 Function and Parameter Declarations
6.2 Returning a Single Value
6.3 Returning Multiple Values
6.4 Variable Scope
6.5 Variable Storage Class
6.6 Common Programming Errors
6.7 Chapter Summary

Professional programs are designed, coded, and tested very much like hardware, as a set of modules that are integrated to perform a completed whole. A good analogy of this is an automobile, for which one major module is the engine, another is the transmission, a third the braking system, and so on. Each of these modules is linked together and ultimately placed under the control of the driver, who can be compared to a supervisor or main program module. The whole now operates as a complete unit, able to do useful work, such as driving to the store. During the assembly process, each module is individually constructed, tested, and found to be free of defects (bugs) before it is installed in the final product.

Now think of what you might do if you wanted to improve your car's performance. You might have the existing engine altered or removed altogether and replaced with a new engine. Similarly, you might change the transmission or tires or shock absorbers, making each modification individually as your interest and budget allowed. In each case the majority of the other modules can stay the same, but the car now operates differently.

In this analogy, each of the major components of a car can be compared to a function. For example, the driver calls on the engine when the gas pedal is pressed. The engine accepts inputs of fuel, air, and electricity to turn the driver's request into a useful product—power—and then sends this output to the transmission for further processing. The transmission receives the output of the engine and converts it to a form that can be used by the drive axle. An additional input to the transmission is the driver's selection of gears (drive, reverse, neutral, etc.).

In each case, the engine, transmission, and other modules "know" only the universe bounded by their inputs and outputs. The driver need know nothing of the internal operation of the engine, transmission, air conditioning, and other modules that are being controlled. All that is required is an understanding of what each unit does and how to use it. The driver simply "calls" on a module, such as the engine, brakes, air conditioning, and steering, when that module's output is required. Communication among modules is restricted to passing needed inputs to each module as it is called upon to perform its task, and each module operates internally in a relatively independent manner. This same modular approach is used by programmers to create and maintain reliable C++ programs using functions.

As we have seen, each C++ program must contain a `main()` function. In addition to this required function, C++ programs may also contain any number of additional functions. In this chapter we learn how to write these functions, pass data to them, process the passed data, and return a result.

6.1 Function and Parameter Declarations

In creating C++ functions we must be concerned with both the function itself and how it interacts with other functions, such as `main()`. This includes correctly passing data into a function when it is called and returning values from a function. In this section we describe the first part of the interface, passing data to a function and having the function correctly receive, store, and process the transmitted data.

As we have already seen with mathematical functions, a function is called, or used, by giving the function's name and passing any data to it, as arguments, within the parentheses following the function name (see Figure 6.1).

FIGURE 6.1

Calling and passing data to a function

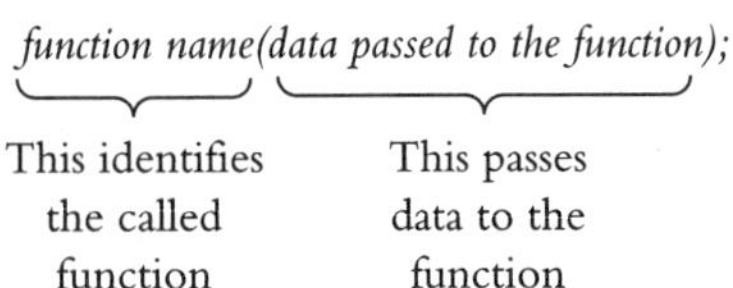
function name(data passed to the function);
This identifies the called function
This passes data to the function

The called function must be able to accept the data passed to it by the function doing the calling. Only after the called function successfully receives the data can the data be manipulated to produce a useful result.

To clarify the process of sending and receiving data, consider Program 6.1, which calls a function named `FindMax()`. The program, as shown, is not yet complete. Once the function `FindMax()` is written and included in Program 6.1, the completed program, consisting of the functions `main()` and `FindMax()`, can be compiled and executed.

PROGRAM 6.1

```
#include <iostream.h>

void FindMax(int, int);  // the function declaration (prototype)

int main()
{
  int firstnum, secnum;

  cout << "\nEnter a number: ";
  cin  >> firstnum;
  cout << "Great! Please enter a second number: ";
  cin  >> secnum;

  FindMax(firstnum, secnum); // the function is called here

  return 0;
}
```

Let us examine the declaration and calling of the function `FindMax()` from `main()`. We will then write `FindMax()` to accept the data passed to it and determine the largest or maximum value of the two passed values.

The function `FindMax()` is referred to as the **called function,** because it is called or summoned into action by its reference in `main()`. The function that does the calling, in this case `main()`, is referred to as the **calling function.** The terms *called* and *calling* come from standard telephone usage, where one party calls the other on a telephone. The party initiating the call is referred to as the calling party, and the party receiving the call is referred to as the called party. The same terms describe function calls. The called function, in this case FindMax(), is declared as a function that expects to receive two integer numbers and to return no value (a void) to main(). This declaration is formally referred to as a function prototype. The function is then called by the last statement in the program.

Function Prototypes

Before a function can be called, it must be declared to the function that will do the calling. The declaration statement for a function is referred to as a **function prototype.** The function prototype tells the calling function the type of value that will be formally returned, if any, and the data type and order of the values that the calling function should transmit to the called function. For example, the function prototype previously used in Program 6.1:

```
void FindMax(int, int);
```

declares that the function FindMax() expects two integer values to be sent to it, and that this particular function formally returns no value (void). Function prototypes may be placed with the variable declaration statements of the calling function, above the calling function name, or in a separate header file that will be included using a #include preprocessor statement. Thus, the function prototype for FindMax() could have been placed either before or after the statement #include <iostream.h>, prior to main(), or within main(). Placing the prototype before main() permits the FindMax() function to be called by any and all functions in the file; placing the prototype within main() restricts the call to within main(), unless the FindMax() function is placed physically in front of main() as further described in Section 6.2. The general form of function prototype statements is:

return-data-type function-name(list of argument data types);

where "data-type" refers to the data type of the value that will be formally returned by the function. An "argument" is a value that is passed into a function when the function is actually called. Examples of function prototypes are:

```
int fmax(int, int);
float swap(int, char, char, double);
void display(double, double);
```

In the first example, the function prototype for fmax() declares that this function expects to receive two integer arguments and will formally return an integer value. The function prototype for swap() declares that this function requires four arguments consisting of an integer, two characters, and a double precision argument, in this order, and will formally return a floating point number. Finally, the function prototype for display()

declares that this function requires two double precision arguments and does not return any value. Such a function might be used to display the results of a computation directly, without returning any value to the called function.

The use of function prototypes permits error checking of data types by the compiler. If the function prototype does not agree with the data types defined when the function is written, an error message (typically *Undefined symbol*) will occur. The prototype also serves another task; it ensures conversion of all arguments passed to the function to the declared argument data type when the function is called.

Calling a Function

Calling a function is a rather easy operation. The only requirements are that the name of the function be used and that any data passed to the function be enclosed within the parentheses following the function name using the same order and type as declared in the function prototype. The items enclosed within the parentheses in the call statement are called **arguments** of the called function (see Figure 6.2). Other terms used as synonyms for arguments are **actual arguments** and **actual parameters.** All of these terms to the data values supplied to a function when a call is made.

If a variable is one of the arguments in a function call, the called function receives a copy of the value stored in the variable. For example, the statement `FindMax(firstnum, secnum);` calls the function `FindMax()` and causes the values currently residing in the variables `firstnum` and `secnum` to be passed to `FindMax()`. The variable names in parentheses are arguments that provide values to the called function. After the values are passed, control is transferred to the called function.

As illustrated in Figure 6.3, the function `FindMax()` *does not receive the variables named* `firstnum` *and* `secnum` *and has no knowledge of these variable names.*[1] The function simply receives the values in these variables and must itself determine where to store these values before it does anything else. Although this procedure for passing data to a function may seem surprising, it is really a safety procedure for ensuring that a called function does not

FIGURE 6.2

Calling and passing two values to `FindMax()`

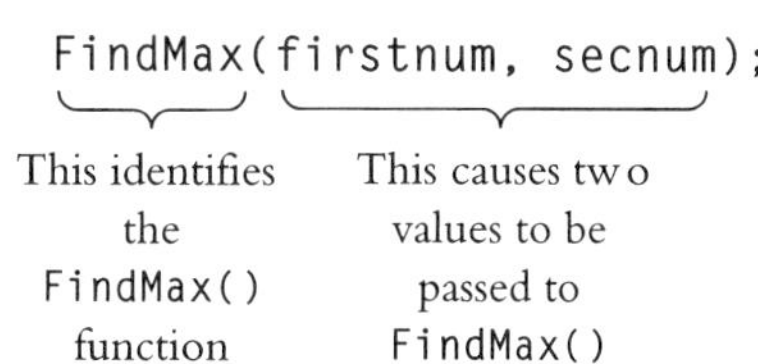
FindMax(firstnum, secnum);
This identifies the FindMax() function
This causes two values to be passed to FindMax()

1 This is significantly different from computer languages such as FORTRAN, where functions and subroutines receive access to the variable and can pass data back through them. In Section 6.3 we see, using reference parameters, that C++ can also directly access a calling function's variables.

FIGURE 6.3

`FindMax()` **receives actual values**

The variable `firstnum`

A value

The variable `secnum`

A value

`firstnum`

Get the value stored in

stored in `secnum`

Get the value

```
FindMax(firstnum, secnum) ;
```

Send the value to `FindMax()`

Send the value to `FindMax()`

inadvertently change data stored in a variable. The function gets a copy of the data to use. It may change its copy and, of course, change any variables declared inside itself. However, unless specific steps are taken to do so, a function is not allowed to change the contents of variables declared in other functions.

Now we will begin writing the function FindMax() to process the values passed to it.

Defining a Function

A function is defined when it is written. Each function is defined once (that is, written once) in a program and can then be used by any other function in the program that suitably declares it.

Like the `main()` function, every C++ function consists of two parts, a **function header** and a **function body,** as illustrated in Figure 6.4. The purpose of the function header is to identify the data type of the value returned by the function; provide the func-

FIGURE 6.4

General format of a function

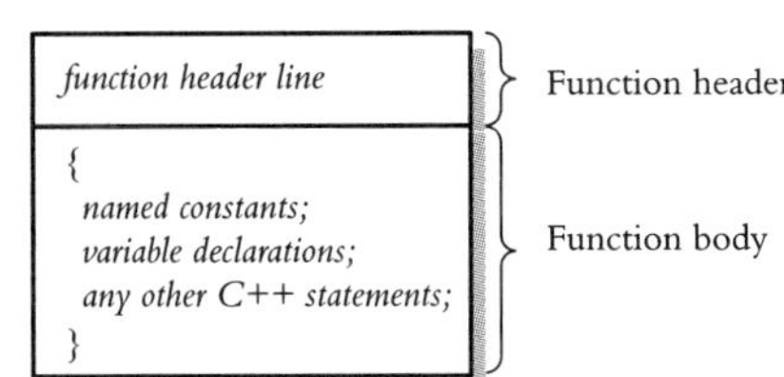
function header line
{
named constants;
variable declarations;
any other C++ statements;
}
Function header
Function body

tion with a name; and specify the number, order, and type of arguments expected by the function. The purpose of the function body is to operate on the passed data and directly return, at most, one value back to the calling function. (We see in Section 6.3 how a function can be made to return multiple values through the argument list.)

The function header is always the first line of a function and contains the function's returned value type, its name, and the names and data types of its arguments. Because `FindMax()` will not formally return any value and is to receive two integer arguments, the following header line can be used:

```
void FindMax(int x, int y) <—— no semicolon
```

The identifer names in the header are referred to as **formal parameters, formal arguments,** and **parameters** of the function; we will use these terms interchangeably.[2] Thus, the parameter x will be used to store the first value passed to `FindMax()` and the parameter y will be used to store the second value passed at the time of the function call. The function does not know where the values come from when the call is made from `main()`. The first part of the call procedure executed by the computer involves going to the variables `firstnum` and `secnum` and retrieving the stored values. These values are then passed to `FindMax()` and ultimately stored in the parameters `x` and `y` (see Figure 6.5).

The function name and all parameter names in the header, in this case `FindMax`, `x`, and `y`, are chosen by the programmer. Any names selected according to the rules for choosing variable names can be used. All parameters listed in the function header line must be separated by commas and must have their individual data types declared separately.

FIGURE 6.5

Storing values into parameters

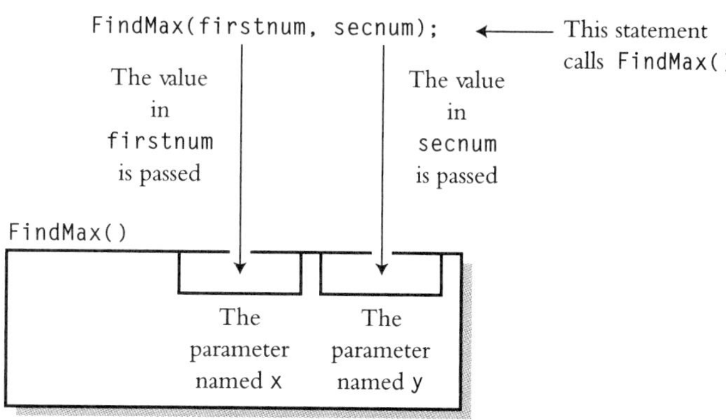

2 The portion of the function header that contains the function name and parameters is formally referred to as a *function declarator.*

FIGURE 6.6

Structure of a function body

```
{
  named constants
  variable declarations

  other C++ statements
}
```

Now that we have written the function header for the `FindMax()` function, we can construct its body. Let us assume that the `FindMax()` function selects and displays the larger of the two numbers passed to it.

As illustrated in Figure 6.6, a function body begins with an opening brace, {, contains any necessary named constants, variable declarations, and other C++ statements, and ends with a closing brace, }. This structure should be familiar to you because it is the same as that used in all the `main()` functions we have written. This fact should not be a surprise, because `main()` is itself a function and must adhere to the rules for constructing all legitimate functions.

In the body of the function `FindMax()`, we declare one variable to store the maximum of the two numbers passed to it. We then use an `if-else` statement to find the maximum of the two numbers. Finally, a `cout` object stream is used to display the maximum. The complete function definition for the `FindMax()` function therefore is:

```
void FindMax(int x, int y)
{                         // start of function body
  int maxnum;             // variable declaration

  if (x >= y)             // find the maximum number
    maxnum = x;
  else
    maxnum = y;

  cout << "\nThe maximum of the two numbers is "
       << maxnum << endl;

}  // end of function body and end of function
```

Notice that the parameter declarations are made within the header line and the variable declaration is made immediately after the opening brace of the function's body. This is in keeping with the concept that parameter values are passed to a function from outside the function, and that variables are declared and assigned values from within the function body.

PROGRAMMER'S NOTES

Function Definitions and Function Prototypes

A **function definition** defines a function. Thus, when you write a function, you are really writing a function definition. Each definition begins with a header line that includes a parameter list, if any, enclosed in parentheses and ends with the closing brace that terminates the function's body. The parentheses are required whether or not the function uses any parameters. A commonly used syntax for a function definition is:

```
return-data-type function-name(parameter list)
{
  constant declarations
  variable declarations

  other C++ statements

  return value
}
```

A **function prototype** declares a function. The syntax for a function prototype, which provides the return data type of the function, the function's name, and the function's argument list, is:

```
return-data-type function-name(list of argument data types);
```

As such, the prototype along with the pre- and postcondition comments (see Programmer's Notes on page 287) should provide a user with all the programming information needed to successfully call the function.

Generally, all function prototypes are placed at the top of the program, and all definitions are placed after the `main()` function. However, this placement can be changed. The only requirement in C++ is that a function cannot be called before it has been either declared or defined.

Program 6.2 includes the `FindMax()` function within the program code previously listed in Program 6.1. Program 6.2 can be used to select and print the maximum of any two integer numbers entered by the user. A sample run using Program 6.2 is shown in Figure 6.7.

FIGURE 6.7

Sample run using Program 6.2

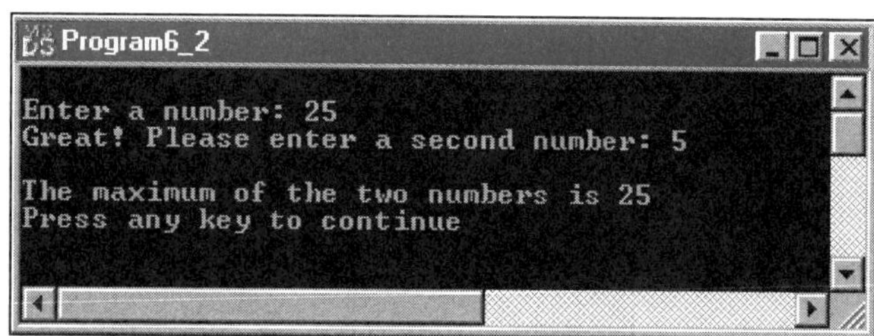
Program6_2
Enter a number: 25
Great! Please enter a second number: 5
The maximum of the two numbers is 25
Press any key to continue

PROGRAM 6.2

```
#include <iostream.h>

void FindMax(int, int);  // the function prototype

int main()
{
  int firstnum, secnum;

  cout << "\nEnter a number: ";
  cin  >> firstnum;
  cout << "Great! Please enter a second number: ";
  cin  >> secnum;

  FindMax(firstnum, secnum); // the function is called here

  return 0;
}

// following is the function FindMax()

void FindMax(int x, int y)
{                       // start of function body
  int maxnum;           // variable declaration

  if (x >= y)           // find the maximum number
    maxnum = x;
  else
    maxnum = y;

  cout << "\nThe maximum of the two numbers is "
       << maxnum << endl;

  return;
} // end of function body and end of function
```

The placement of the `FindMax()` function after the `main()` function in Program 6.2 is a matter of choice. We will always list `main()` first because it is the driver function that should give anyone reading the program an idea of what the complete program is about before encountering the details of each function. In no case, however, can the definition

PROGRAMMER'S NOTES

Preconditions and Postconditions

Preconditions are any set of conditions required by a function to be true if it is to operate correctly. For example, if a function uses the named constant MAXCHARS, which must have a positive value, a precondition is that MAXCHARS be declared with a positive value before the function is called.

Similarly, a postcondition is a condition that will be true after the function is executed, assuming that the preconditions are met.

Pre- and postconditions are typically written as user comments. For example, consider the following declaration and statements:

```
int leapyr(int)
// Preconditions: the integer parameter must represent a year in a four
//              : digit form, such as 1999
// Postcondition: a 1 is returned if the year is a leap year;
//              : otherwise a 0 will be returned
```

Pre- and postcondition comments should be included with both function prototypes and function definitions whenever clarification is needed.

of FindMax() be placed inside main(). This is true for all C++ functions, which must be defined by themselves outside any other function. Each C++ function is a separate and independent entity with its own parameters and variables; nesting of functions is never permitted.

Placement of Statements

C++ does not impose a rigid statement-ordering structure on the programmer. The general rule for placing statements in a C++ program is simply that all preprocessor directives, variables, named constants, and function calls must be either declared or defined before they can be used. As noted previously, although this rule permits both preprocessor directives and declaration statements to be placed throughout a program, doing so results in a very poor program structure.

As a matter of good programming form, the following statement ordering should form the basic structure around which C++ programs are constructed.

```
preprocessor directives

function prototypes

int main()
{
  named constants
  variable declarations
```

```
  other executable statements
  return value
}

function definitions
```

As always, comment statements can be freely intermixed anywhere within this basic structure.

Function Stubs

An alternative to completing each function required in a program is to write the `main()` function first and to add the functions later as they are developed. The problem that arises with this approach, however, is the same problem that occurred with Program 6.1; that is, the program cannot be run until all of the functions are included. For convenience, we have reproduced the code for Program 6.1 below.

```
#include <iostream.h>

void FindMax(int, int);  // the function declaration (prototype)

int main()
{
  int firstnum, secnum;

  cout << "\nEnter a number: ";
  cin  >> firstnum;
  cout << "Great! Please enter a second number: ";
  cin  >> secnum;

  FindMax(firstnum, secnum); // the function is called here

  return 0;
}
```

This program would be complete if there were a function definition for `FindMax`. But we really don't need a *correct* FindMax function to test and run what has been written, we just need a function that *acts* like it is correct: a "fake" `FindMax` that accepts the proper number and types of parameters and returns values of the proper form for the function call is all we need to allow initial testing. This fake function is called a *stub*. A

PROGRAMMER'S NOTES

Isolation Testing

One of the most successful software testing methods known is to always embed the code being tested within an environment of working code. For example, assume you have two untested functions that are called in the order shown below, and the result returned by the second function is incorrect.

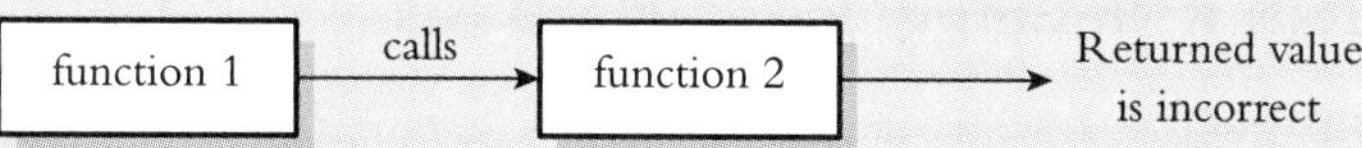

From the information shown in this figure, one or possibly both of the functions could be operating incorrectly. The first order of business is to isolate the problem to a specific function.

One of the most powerful methods of performing this code isolation is to decouple the functions. This is done by either testing each function individually or by testing one function first, and only when you know it is operating correctly, reconnecting it to the second function. Then if an error occurs you have isolated the error to either the transfer of data between functions or the internal operation of the second function.

This specific procedure is an example of the *basic rule of testing,* which states that each function should be tested only in a program in which all other functions are known to be correct. This means that one function must first be tested by itself, using stubs if necessary for any called functions, then a second function should be tested either by itself or with a previously tested function, and so on. This ensures that each new function is isolated within a test bed of correct functions, with the final program effectively built up of tested function code.

stub is the beginning of a final function that can be used as a placeholder for the final unit until the final unit is completed. A stub for `FindMax` is is as follows:

```
void FindMax(int x, int y)
{
  cout << "In FindMax()\n"
       << "\nThe value of x is " << x
       << "\nThe value of x is " << y << endl;
}
```

This stub function can now be compiled and linked with the previously completed code to obtain an executable program. The code for the function can then be further developed, with the "real" code, when it is completed, replacing the stub portion. The minimum requirement of a stub function is that it compile and link with its calling module. In practice, it is a good idea to have a stub display both a message that it has been entered successfully and the value(s) of its received parameters, as in the stub for `FindMax()`. As the function is refined, you let it do more and more, perhaps allowing it to return intermediate or incomplete results. This incremental, or stepwise, refinement is an important concept in efficient program development that provides you with the means to run a program that does not yet meet all of its final requirements.

Functions with Empty Parameter Lists

Although useful functions having an empty parameter list are extremely limited (one such function is provided in Exercise 9), they can occur. The function prototype for such a function requires either writing the keyword `void` or nothing at all between the parentheses following the function's name. For example, both prototypes

```
int display();
```

and

```
int display(void);
```

indicate that the `display()` function takes no parameters and returns an integer. A function with an empty parameter list is called by its name with nothing written within the required parentheses following the function's name. For example, the statement `display();` correctly calls the `display()` function whose prototype was given above.

Default Arguments[3]

A convenient feature of C++ is its flexibility of providing default arguments in a function call. The primary use of default arguments is to extend the parameter list of existing functions without requiring any change in the calling argument lists already in place within a program.

Default argument values are listed in the function prototype and are automatically transmitted to the called function when the corresponding arguments are omitted from the function call. For example, the function prototype

```
void example(int, int = 5, float = 6.78);
```

---

3 This topic may be omitted on first reading with no loss of subject continuity.

provides default values for the last two arguments. If any of these arguments is omitted when the function is actually called, the C++ compiler will supply these default values. Thus, all of the following function calls are valid:

```
example(7, 2, 9.3)  // no defaults used
example(7, 2)       // same as example(7, 2, 6.78)
example(7)          // same as example(7, 5, 6.78)
```

Four rules must be followed when using default parameters. The first is that default values can be assigned only in the function prototype. The second is that if any parameter is given a default value in the function prototype, all parameters following it must also be supplied with default values. The third rule is that if one argument is omitted in the actual function call, then all arguments to its right must also be omitted. These two rules make it clear to the C++ compiler which arguments are being omitted and permits the compiler to supply correct default values for the missing arguments, starting with the rightmost argument and working in toward the left. The last rule specifies that the default value used in the function prototype may be an expression consisting of constants as well as previously declared variables. If such an expression is used, it must pass the compiler's check for validly declared variables, even though the actual value of the expression is evaluated and assigned at run time.

Default arguments are extremely useful when extending an existing function to include more features that require additional parameters. Adding new arguments to the right of the existing arguments and providing each new argument with a default value permits all existing function calls to remain as they are. Thus, the effects of the new changes are conveniently isolated from existing code in the program.

Function Templates[4]

In most high-level languages, including C++'s immediate predecessor, C, each function requires its own unique name. In theory this makes sense, but in practice it can lead to a profusion of function names, even for functions that perform essentially the same operations. For example, consider determining and displaying the absolute value of a number. If the number passed into the function can be either an integer, a floating-point, or a double precision value, three distinct functions would be written to correctly handle each case. Certainly, we could give each of these functions a unique name, such as `abs()`, `fabs()`, and `dabs()`, respectively, having the function prototypes:

```
void abs(int);
void fabs(long);
void dabs(double);
```

4 This topic may be omitted on first reading with no loss of subject continuity.

Clearly, each of these three functions performs essentially the same operation, but on different parameter data types. A much cleaner and more elegant solution is to write a general function that handles all cases, but whose parameters, variables, and even return type can be set by the compiler based on the actual function call. This is possible in C++ using function templates.

A **function template** is a single, complete function that serves as a model for a family of functions. Which function from the family that is actually created depends on subsequent function calls. To make this more concrete, consider a function template that computes and displays the absolute value of a passed argument. An appropriate function template is:

```
template <class T>
void showabs(T number)
{
  if (number < 0)
    number = -number;
  cout << "The absolute value of the number "
       << " is " << number << endl;

  return
}
```

For the moment, ignore the first line, `template <class T>`, and look at the second line, which consists of the function header `void showabs(T number)`. Notice that this header line has the same syntax that we have been using for all of our function definitions, except for the `T` where a data type is usually placed. For example, if the header line were `void showabs(int number)`, you should recognize this as a function named `showabs` that expects one integer argument to be passed to it and that returns no value. Similarly, if the header line were `void showabs(float number)`, you should recognize it as a function that expects one floating point argument to be passed when the function is called.

The advantage in using the `T` within the function template header line is that it represents a general data type that is replaced by an actual data type, such as `int`, `float`, `double`, etc., when the compiler encounters an actual function call. For example, if a function call with an integer argument is encountered, the compiler will use the function template to construct the code for a function that expects an integer parameter. Similarly, if a call is made with a floating point argument, the compiler will construct a function that expects a floating point parameter. As a specific example of this, consider Program 6.3.

PROGRAM 6.3

```
#include <iostream.h>

template <class T>
void showabs(T number)
{

  if (number < 0)
    number = -number;
  cout << "The absolute value of the number is "
       << number << endl;

  return;
}

int main()
{
  int num1 = -4;
  float num2 = -4.23;
  double num3 = -4.23456;

  cout << endl;    // display a blank line
  showabs(num1);
  showabs(num2);
  showabs(num3);

 return 0;
}
```

First notice the three function calls made in the `main()` function shown in Program 6.3, which call the function `showabs()` with an integer, float, and double value, respectively. Now review the function template for `showabs()` and let us consider the first line `template <class T>`. This line, called a **template prefix,** is used to inform the compiler that the function immediately following is a template that uses a data type named `T`. Within the function template the `T` is used in the same manner as any other data type, such as `int`, `float`, `double`, etc. Then, when the compiler encounters an actual function call for `showabs`, the data type of the argument passed in the call is substituted for `T`

FIGURE 6.8

Output produced by Program 6.3

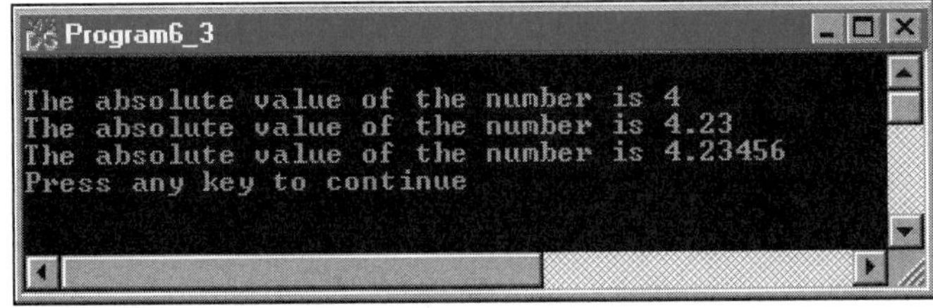
Program6_3
The absolute value of the number is 4
The absolute value of the number is 4.23
The absolute value of the number is 4.23456
Press any key to continue

throughout the function. In effect, the compiler creates a specific function, using the template, that expects the argument type in the call. Program 6.3 makes three calls to `showabs`, each with a different argument data type, so the compiler will create three separate `showabs()` functions. The compiler knows which function to use based on the arguments passed at the time of the call. The output displayed when Program 6.3 is executed is shown in Figure 6.8.

The letter `T` used in the template prefix `template <class T>` is simply a placeholder for a data type that is defined when the function is actually invoked. As such, any letter or nonkeyword identifier can be used instead. Thus, the `showabs()` function template could just as well have been defined as:

```
template <class DTYPE>
void showabs(DTYPE number)
{

  if (number < 0)
    number = -number;
  cout << "The absolute value of the number is "
              << number << endl;

  return;
}
```

In this regard, it is sometimes simpler and clearer to read the word *class* in the function prefix as the words *data type*. Thus, the function prefix `template <class T>` can be read as "we are defining a function template that has a data type named T." Then, within both the header line and body of the defined function the data type `T` (or any other letter or identifier defined in the prefix) is used in the same manner as any built-in data type, such as `int`, `float`, `double`, etc.

Now, suppose we would like to create a function template to include both a return type and an internally declared variable. For example, consider the following function template:

```
template <class T> // template prefix
T abs(T number)     // header line
{
  T absnum;  // variable declaration

  if (number < 0)
    absnum = -number;
  else
    absnum = number;

  return (absnum);
}
```

In this template definition, we have used the data type `T` to declare three items: the return type of the function, the data type of a single function parameter named `number`, and one variable declared within the function. Program 6.4 illustrates how this function template could be used within the context of a complete program.

PROGRAM 6.4

```
#include <iostream.h>

template <class T> // template prefix
T abs(T number)     // header line
{
  T absnum;  // variable declaration

  if (number < 0)
    absnum = -number;
  else
    absnum = number;

  return (absnum);
}

int main()
{
  int num1 = -4;
  float num2 = -4.23;
  double num3 = -4.23456;
```

(continued next page)

(*continued from previous page*)

```
  cout << endl;  // display a blank line
  cout << "The absolute value of " << num1
       << " is " << abs(num1) << endl;
  cout << "The absolute value of " << num2
       << " is " << abs(num2) << endl;
  cout << "The absolute value of " << num3
       << " is " << abs(num3) << endl;

  return 0;
}
```

In the first call to `abs()` made within `main()`, an integer value is passed as an argument. In this case, the compiler substitutes an `int` data type for the `T` data type in the function template and creates the following function:

```
int abs(int number) // header line
{
  int absnum;  // variable declaration

  if (number < 0)
    absnum = -number;
  else
    absnum = number;

  return (absnum);
}
```

Similarly, in the second and third function calls, the compiler creates two more functions, one in which the data type `T` is replaced by the keyword `float`, and one in which the data type `T` is replaced by the keyword `double`. The output produced by Program 6.4 is shown in Figure 6.9.

FIGURE 6.9

Output produced by Program 6.4

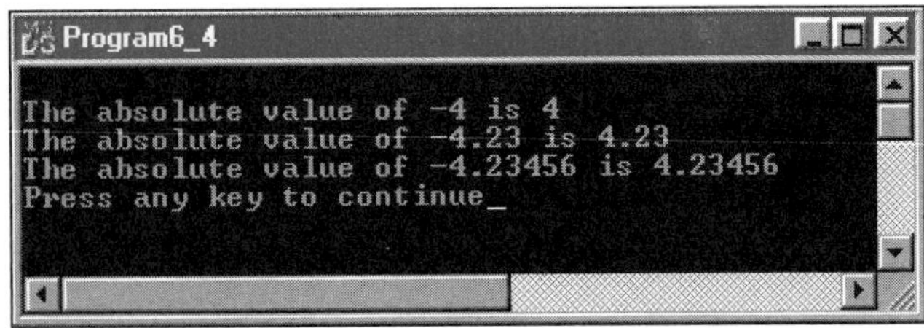

Program6_4
The absolute value of -4 is 4
The absolute value of -4.23 is 4.23
The absolute value of -4.23456 is 4.23456
Press any key to continue_

The value of using the function template is that one function definition has been used to create three different functions, each of which uses the same logic and operations but operates on different data types.

Finally, although both Programs 6.3 and 6.4 define a function template that uses a single placeholder data type, function templates with more than one data type can be defined. For example, the template prefix

```
template <class DTYPE1, class DTYPE2, class DTYPE3>
```

can be used to create a function template that requires three different data types. As before, within the header and body of the function template, the data types `DTYPE1`, `DTYPE2`, and `DTYPE3` would be used in the same manner as any built-in data type, such as an `int`, `float`, `double`, etc. Additionally, as noted previously, the names `DTYPE1`, `DTYPE2`, and `DTYPE3` can be any nonkeyword identifier. Conventionally, only the letter `T` followed by zero or more digits is used, such as `T`, `T1`, `T2`, `T3`, etc.

Reusing Function Names (Overloading)[5]

C++ provides the capability of using the same function name for more than one function, which is referred to as **function overloading.** The only requirement in creating more than one function with the same name is that the compiler must be able to determine which function to use based on the data types of the parameters (not the data type of the return value, if any). For example, consider the following three functions, all named `cdabs()`.

```
void cdabs(int x)  // compute and display the absolute value of an integer
{
  if ( x < 0 )
    x = -x;
  cout << "The absolute value of the integer is  " << x << endl;
}

void cdabs(float x)  // compute and display the absolute value of a float
{
  if ( x < 0 )
    x = -x;
  cout << "The absolute value of the float is  " << x << endl;
}
```

5 This topic may be omitted on first reading with no loss of subject continuity.

```
void cdabs(double x)  // compute and display the absolute value of a double
{
  if ( x < 0 )
    x = -x;
  cout << "The absolute value of the double is  " << x << endl;
}
```

Which of the three functions named `cdabs()` is actually called depends on the argument types supplied at the time of the call. Thus, the function call `cdabs(10);` would cause the compiler to use the function named `cdabs();` that expects an integer argument, and the function call `cdabs(6.28f);` would cause the compiler to use the function named `cdabs()` that expects a floating-point argument.[6]

Notice that overloading a function's name simply means using the same name for more than one function. Each function that uses the name must still be written and exists as a separate entity. The use of the same function name does not require that the code within the functions be similar, although good programming practice dictates that functions with the same name should perform essentially the same operations. All that is formally required in using the same function name is that the compiler can distinguish which function to select based on the data types of the arguments when the function is called. Clearly, however, if all that is different about the overloaded functions is the argument types, a better programming solution is simply to create a function template. Overloaded functions, however, are extremely useful with constructor functions, a topic that is presented in Section 9.3.

EXERCISES 6.1

1. For the following function headers, determine the number, type, and order (sequence) of the values that must be passed to the function:

a. `void factorial(int n)`

b. `void price(int type, double yield, double maturity)`

c. `void yield(int type, double price, double maturity)`

d. `void interest(char flag, float price, float time)`

e. `void total(float amount, float rate)`

f. `void roi(int a, int b, char c, char d, float e, float f)`

g. `void getval(int item, int iter, char decflag, char delim)`

---

6 This is accomplished by a process referred to as *name mangling.* Using this process, the function name actually generated by the C++ compiler differs from the function name used in the source code. The compiler appends information to the source code function name depending on the type of data being passed, and the resulting name is said to be a mangled version of the source code name.

2. **a.** Write a function named `check()` that has three parameters as follows. The first parameter should accept an integer number, the second parameter a floating point number, and the third parameter a double precision number. The body of the function should just display the values of the data passed to the function when it is called.

   Note: When tracing errors in functions, it is very helpful to have the function display the values it has been passed. Quite frequently, the error is not in what the body of the function does with the data, but in the data received and stored.

   b. Include the function written in Exercise 2a in a working program. Make sure your function is called from `main()`. Test the function by passing various data to it.

3. **a.** Write a function named `FindAbs()` that accepts a double precision number passed to it, computes its absolute value, and displays the absolute value. The absolute value of a number is the number itself if the number is positive, and the negative of the number if the number is negative.

   b. Include the function written in Exercise 3a in a working program. Make sure your function is called from `main()`. Test the function by passing various data to it.

4. **a.** Write a function called `mult()` that accepts two floating point numbers as parameters, multiplies these two numbers, and displays the result.

   b. Include the function written in Exercise 4a in a working program. Make sure your function is called from `main()`. Test the function by passing various data to it.

5. **a.** Write a function named `squareIt()` that computes the square of the value passed to it and displays the result. The function should be capable of squaring numbers with decimal points.

   b. Include the function written in Exercise 5a in a working program. Make sure your function is called from `main()`. Test the function by passing various data to it.

6. **a.** Write a function named `powfun()` that raises an integer number passed to it to a positive integer power and displays the result. The positive integer power should be the second value passed to the function. Declare the variable used to store the result as a long integer data type to ensure sufficient storage for the result.

   b. Include the function written in Exercise 6a in a working program. Make sure your function is called from `main()`. Test the function by passing various data to it.

7. **a.** Write a function that produces a table of the numbers from 1 to 10, their squares, and cubes. The function should produce the same display as that produced by Program 5.11.

   b. Include the function written in Exercise 7a in a working program. Make sure your function is called from `main()`. Test the function by passing various data to it.

8. **a.** Modify the function written for Exercise 7 to accept the starting value of the table, the number of values to be displayed, and the increment between values. If the increment is not explicitly sent, the function should use a default value of 1. Name your

function `selTab()`. A call to `selTab(6,5,2);` should produce a table of five lines, the first line starting with the number 6 and each succeeding number increasing by 2.

b. Include the function written in Exercise 8a in a working program. Make sure your function is called from `main()`. Test the function by passing various data to it.

9. A useful function that uses no parameters can be constructed to return a value π that is accurate to the maximum number of decimal places allowed by your computer. This value is obtained by taking the arcsine of 1.0, which is $\pi/2$, and multiplying the result by 2. In C++, the required expression is 2.0 * *asin*(1.0), where the `asin()` function is provided in the standard C++ mathematics library (remember to include `math.h`). Using this expression, write a C++ function named `Pi()` that calculates and displays the value of π.

10. a. Write a function template named `display()` that displays the value of the single argument that is passed to it when the function is called.

b. Include the function template created in Exercise 10a within a complete C++ program that calls the function four times: once with a character argument, once with an integer argument, once with a floating point argument, and once with a double precision argument.

11. a. Write a function template named `whole()` that returns the integer value of any argument that is passed to it when the function is called.

b. Include the function template created in Exercise 11a within a complete C++ program that calls the function four times: once with a character argument, once with an integer argument, once with a floating point argument, and once with a double precision argument.

12. a. Write a function template named `maximum()` that returns the maximum value of three arguments that are passed to the function when it is called. Assume that all three arguments will be of the same data type.

b. Include the function template created for Exercise 12a within a complete C++ program that calls the function with three integers and then with three floating point numbers.

13. a. Write the function template named `square()` that squares then computes and returns the square of the single argument passed to the function when it is called.

b. Include the function template created for Exercise 13a within a complete C++ program.

6.2 Returning a Single Value

By using the method of passing data into a function presented in the previous section, the called function receives only copies of the values contained in the arguments at the time of the call (review Figure 6.3 if this is unclear to you). When a value is passed to a called

FIGURE 6.10

A function directly returns at most one value when it is called by value

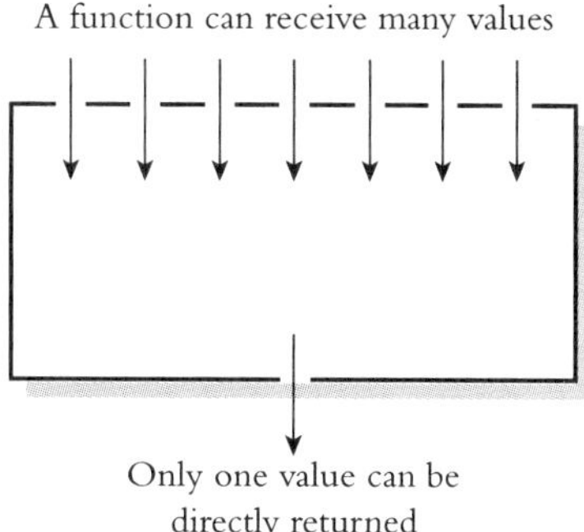
A function can receive many values
Only one value can be directly returned

function in this manner, the passed argument is referred to as **passed by value** and is a distinct advantage of C++.[7] Because the called function does not have direct access to the variables used as arguments by the calling function, it cannot inadvertently alter the value stored in one of these variables.

The function receiving the passed by value arguments may process the values sent to it in any fashion desired and directly return at most one, and only one, "legitimate" value to the calling function (see Figure 6.10). In this section we see how such a value is returned to the calling function. As you might expect, given C++'s flexibility, there is a way of returning more than a single value; that is the topic of the next section, Returning Multiple Values.

As with calling a function, directly returning a value requires that the interface between the called and calling functions be handled correctly. From its side of the return transaction, the called function must provide the following items:

- the data type of the returned value
- the actual value being returned

A function returning a value must specify, in its header line, the data type of the value that will be returned. Recall that the function header line is the first line of the function, which includes both the function's name and a list of parameter names. As an example, consider the `FindMax()` function written in the last section. It determined the maximum value of two numbers passed to the function. For convenience, the `FindMax()` code is listed here again.

7 This is also referred to as a **call by value.** This term, however, does not refer to the function call as a whole, but to how an individual argument is passed when the call to a function is made.

```
void FindMax(int x, int y)
{                        // start of function body
  int maxnum;            // variable declaration

  if (x >= y)            // find the maximum number
    maxnum = x;
  else
    maxnum = y;

  cout << "\nThe maximum of the two numbers is "
       << maxnum << endl;

} // end of function body and end of function
```

As written, the function's header line is

```
void FindMax(int x, int y)
```

where `x` and `y` are the names chosen for the function's parameters.

If `FindMax()` is now to return a value, the function's header line must be amended to include the data type of the value being returned. For example, if an integer value is to be returned, the proper function header line is

```
int FindMax(int x, int y)
```

Similarly, if the function is to receive two floating point values and return a floating point value the correct function header line is

```
float FindMax(float x, float y)
```

and if the function is to receive two double precision values and return a double precision value the header line would be[8]

```
double FindMax(double x, double y)
```

Let us now modify the function `FindMax()` to return the maximum value of the two numbers passed to it. To do this, we must first determine the data type of the value that is to be returned and include this data type in the function's header line.

---

8 The return data type is related only to the parameter data types inasmuch as the returned value is computed from parameter values. In this case, because the function is used to return the maximum value of its parameters, it would make little sense to return a data type that did not match the function's parameter types.

The maximum value determined by `FindMax()` is stored in the integer variable `maxnum`, so it is the value of this variable that the function should return. Returning an integer value from `FindMax()` requires that the function declaration be

```
int FindMax(int x, int y)
```

Observe that this is the same as the original function header line for `FindMax()` with the substitution of the keyword `int` for the keyword `void`.

Having declared the data type that `FindMax()` will return, all that remains is to include a statement within the function to cause the return of the correct value. To return a value, a function must use a `return` statement, which has the form:[9]

return expression;

When the return statement is encountered, the expression is evaluated first. The value of the expression is then automatically converted to the data type declared in the function header before being sent back to the calling function. After the value is returned, program control reverts to the calling function. Thus, to return the value stored in `maxnum`, all we need to do is add the statement `return maxnum;` before the closing brace of the `FindMax()` function. The complete function code is:

These should be the same data type

```
int FindMax(int x, int y)   // function header line
{                           // start of function body
 int maxnum;                // variable declaration

  if (x >= y)
    maxnum = x;
  else
    maxnum = y;

  return maxnum;         // return statement
}
```

In this new code for the function `FindMax()`, note that the data type of the expression contained within the parentheses of the `return` statement correctly matches the data type in the function's header line. It is up to the programmer to ensure that this is so for every function returning a value. Failure to exactly match the `return` value with the function's declared data type may not result in an error when your program is compiled, but it may lead to undesired results because the `return` value is always converted to the data type declared in the function declaration. Usually this is a problem only when the

---

9 Many programmers place the expression within parentheses, yielding the statement `return (expression);`. Although either form can be used, for consistency only one should be adopted.

fractional part of a returned floating point or double precision number is truncated because the function was declared to return an integer value.

Having taken care of the sending side of the `return` transaction, we must now prepare the calling function to receive the value sent by the called function. On the calling (receiving) side, the calling function must:

- be alerted to the type of value to expect
- properly use the returned value

Alerting the calling function as to the type of return value to expect is properly taken care of by the function prototype. For example, including the function prototype

```
int FindMax(int, int);
```

before the `main()` function is sufficient to alert `main()` that `FindMax()` is a function that will return an integer value.

To actually use a returned value we must either provide a variable to store the value or use the value directly in an expression. Storing the returned value in a variable is accomplished using a standard assignment statement. For example, the assignment statement

```
max = FindMax(firstnum, secnum);
```

can be used to store the value returned by `FindMax()` in the variable named `max`. This assignment statement does two things. First the right-hand side of the assignment statement calls `FindMax()`, then the result returned by `FindMax()` is stored in the variable `max`. Because the value returned by `FindMax()` is an integer, the variable `max` must also be declared as an integer variable within the calling function's variable declarations.

The value returned by a function need not be stored directly in a variable, but can be used wherever an expression is valid. For example, the expression `2 * FindMax(firstnum, secnum)` multiplies the value returned by `FindMax()` by two, and the statement

```
cout << FindMax(firstnum, secnum);
```

displays the returned value.

Program 6.5 illustrates the inclusion of both prototype and assignment statements for `main()` to correctly call and store a returned value from `FindMax()`. As before, and in keeping with our convention of placing the `main()` function first, we have placed the `FindMax()` function after `main()`.

PROGRAM 6.5

```
#include <iostream.h>

int FindMax(int, int);  // the function prototype

int main()
{
  int firstnum, secnum, max;

  cout << "\nEnter a number: ";
  cin  >> firstnum;
  cout << "Great! Please enter a second number: ";
  cin  >> secnum;

  max = FindMax(firstnum, secnum); // the function is called here

  cout << "\nThe maximum of the two numbers is " << max << endl;

  return 0;
}

int FindMax(int x, int y)
{                         // start of function body
  int maxnum;             // variable declaration

  if (x >= y)             // find the maximum number
    maxnum = x;
  else
    maxnum = y;

  return maxnum;          // return statement
}
```

In Program 6.5 it is important to note the four items we have introduced in this section. The first item is the prototype for `FindMax()`. This statement, which ends with a semicolon, as all declaration statements do, alerts `main()` to the data type that `FindMax()` will be returning. The second item to notice in `main()` is the use of an assignment statement to store the returned value from the `FindMax()` call into the variable `max`. We have also made sure to correctly declare `max` as an integer within `main()`'s variable declarations so that it matches the data type of the returned value.

The last two items of note concern the coding of the `FindMax()` function. The first line of `FindMax()` declares that the function will return an integer value, and the expression in the `return` statement evaluates to a matching data type. Thus, `FindMax()` is internally consistent in sending an integer value back to `main()`, and `main()` has been correctly alerted to receive and use the returned integer.

In writing your own functions, you must always keep these four items in mind. For another example, see if you can identify these four items in Program 6.6.

PROGRAM 6.6

```
#include <iostream.h>

double tempvert(double);  // function prototype

int main()
{
  const CONVERTS = 4;  // number of conversions to be made
  int count;           // start of declarations
  double fahren;

  for(count = 1; count <= CONVERTS; count++)
  {
    cout << "\nEnter a Fahrenheit temperature: ";
    cin  >> fahren;
    cout << "The Celsius equivalent is "
         << tempvert(fahren) << endl;
  }

  return 0;
}

// convert fahrenheit to celsius
double tempvert(double inTemp)
{
  return (5.0/9.0) * (inTemp - 32.0);
}
```

In Program 6.6, let us first analyze the `tempvert()` function. The complete definition of the function begins with the function's header line and ends with the closing brace after the `return` statement. The function is declared as a double; this means the expression in the function's `return` statement must evaluate to a double precision number, which it does. Because a function header line is not a statement but the start of the code defining the function, the function header line does not end with a semicolon.

For the receiving side, there is a prototype for the function `tempvert()` that agrees with `tempvert()`'s function definition. No variable is declared in `main()` to store the returned value from `tempvert()` because the returned value is immediately passed to `cout` for display.

One further point is worth mentioning here. One of the purposes of declarations, as we learned in Chapter 2, is to alert the computer to the amount of internal storage reserved for the data. The prototype for `tempvert()` performs this task and tells the compiler how much storage area must be accessed when the returned value is retrieved. Had we placed the `tempvert()` function before `main()`, however, the function header line for `tempvert()` would suffice to alert the compiler to the type of storage needed for the returned value. In this case, the function prototype for `tempvert()` could be eliminated. Because we have chosen always to list `main()` as the first function in a file, we must include function prototypes for all functions called by `main()`.

Inline Functions

Calling a function places a certain amount of overhead on a computer.[10] This consists of placing argument values in a reserved memory region to which the function has access (this memory region is referred to as the *stack*), passing control to the function, providing a reserved memory location for any returned value (again, the stack region of memory is used for this purpose), and finally returning to the proper point in the calling program. Paying this overhead is well justified when a function is called many times because it can significantly reduce the size of a program. Rather than repeating the same code each time it is needed, the code is written once, as a function, and then called whenever it is needed.

For small functions that are not called many times, however, paying the overhead for passing and returning values may not be warranted. It still would be convenient, though, to group repeating lines of code together under a common function name and have the compiler place this code directly into the program wherever the function is called. This capability is provided by inline functions.

Telling the C+ compiler that a function is *inline* causes a copy of the function code to be placed in the program at the point the function is called. For example, consider the function `tempvert()` defined in Program 6.6. This is a relatively short function, so it is an ideal candidate to be an inline function. To make this, or any other function, an inline one

---

10 This section is optional and may be omitted on first reading without loss of subject continuity.

simply requires placing the reserved word `inline` before the function name, and defining the function before any calls are made to it. This is done for the `tempvert()` function in Program 6.7.

PROGRAM 6.7

```
#include <iostream.h>

inline double tempvert(double inTemp)  // an inline function
{
  return (5.0/9.0) * (inTemp - 32.0);
}

int main()
{
  const CONVERTS = 4;    // number of conversions to be made
  int count;             // start of declarations
  double fahren;

  for(count = 1; count <= CONVERTS; count++)
  {
    cout << "\nEnter a Fahrenheit temperature: ";
    cin  >> fahren;
    cout << "The Celsius equivalent is "
         << tempvert(fahren) << endl;
  }

  return 0;
}
```

Observe in Program 6.7 that the inline function is placed ahead of any calls to it. This is a requirement of all inline functions and obviates the need for a function prototype. Because the function is now an inline one, its code will be expanded directly into the program wherever it is called.

The advantage of using an inline function is an increase in execution speed. Because the inline function is directly expanded and included in every expression or statement calling it, there is no execution time loss due to the call and return overhead required by a noninline function. The disadvantage is the increase in program size when an inline function is called repeatedly. Each time an inline function is referenced the complete function code is reproduced and stored as an integral part of the program. A noninline function, however, is stored in memory only once. No matter how many times the function is called, the same code is used. Therefore, inline functions should be used only for small functions that are not extensively called in the program.

EXERCISES 6.2

1. Write function headers for the following:
   a. a function named `check()`, which has three parameters. The first parameter should accept an integer number, the second argument a floating point number, and the third parameter a double precision number. The function returns no value.
   b. a function named `FindAbs()` that accepts a double-precision number passed to it and returns its absolute value.
   c. a function named `Mult()` that accepts two floating point numbers as parameters, multiplies these two numbers, and returns the result.
   d. a function named `squareIt()` that computes and returns the square of the integer value passed to it.
   e. a function named `powfun()` that raises an integer number passed to it to a positive integer power (also passed as an argument) and returns the result.
   f. a function that produces a table of the numbers from 1 to 10, their squares, and cubes. No arguments are to be passed to the function and the function returns no value.
2. a. Write a C++ function named `FindAbs()` that accepts a double precision number passed to it, computes its absolute value, and returns the absolute value to the calling function. The absolute value of a number is the number itself if the number is positive, and the negative of the number if the number is negative.
   b. Include the function written in Exercise 4a in a working program. Make sure your function is called from `main()` and correctly returns a value to `main()`. Have `main()` use `cout` to display the value returned. Test the function by passing various data to it.
3. a. Write a C++ function called `Mult()` that uses two double precision numbers as parameters, multiplies these two numbers, and returns the result to the calling function.
   b. Include the function written in Exercise 5a in a working program. Make sure your function is called from `main()` and correctly returns a value to `main()`. Have `main()` display the value returned. Test the function by passing various data to it.
4. a. Write a C++ function named `powfun()` that raises an integer number passed to it to a positive integer power (also passed as an argument) and returns the result to the calling function. Declare the variable used to return the result as a long integer data type to ensure sufficient storage for the result.

b. Include the function written in Exercise 6a in a working program. Make sure your function is called from `main()` and correctly returns a value to `main()`. Have `main()` display the value returned. Test the function by passing various data to it.

5. Write a function named `Hypotenuse()` that accepts the lengths of two sides of a right triangle as the parameters `a`, `b`, respectively. The subroutine should determine and return the hypotenuse, `c`, of the triangle. (*Hint:* Use Pythagoras' theorem that $c^2 = a^2 + b^2$.)

6. a. The volume, v, of a cylinder is determined using the formula

$$v = \pi r^2 l$$

where r is the cylinder's radius and l is its length. Use this formula to write a C++ function named `cylvol()` that accepts the radius and length of a cylinder and returns its volume.

b. Include the function written in Exercise 8a in a working program. Make sure your function is called from `main()` and correctly returns a value to `main()`. Have `main()` display the value returned. Test the function by passing various data to it.

7. A second-degree polynomial in x is given by the expression $ax^2 + bx + c$, where a, b, and c are known numbers, and a is not equal to zero. Write a C++ function named `PolyTwo(a,b,c,x)` that computes and returns the value of a second-degree polynomial for any passed values of `a`, `b`, `c`, and `x`.

8. a. Rewrite the function `tempvert()` in Program 6.6 to accept a temperature and a character as parameters. If the character passed to the function is the letter `f`, the function should convert the passed temperature from Fahrenheit to Celsius, else the function should convert the passed temperature from Celsius to Fahrenheit.

b. Modify the `main()` function in Program 6.6 to call the function written for Exercise 8a. Your `main()` function should ask the user for the type of temperature being entered and pass the type (`f` or `c`) into `tempvert()`.

9. a. An extremely useful programming algorithm for rounding a real number to n decimal places is:

Step 1: multiply the number by 10^n
Step 2: add .5
Step 3: delete the fractional part of the result
Step 4: divide by 10^n

For example, using this algorithm to round the number 78.374625 to three decimal places yields:

Step 1: $78.374625 \times 10^3 = 78374.625$
Step 2: $78374.625 + .5 = 78375.125$

Step 3: Retaining the integer part = 78375
Step 4: 78375 divided by 10^3 = 78.375

Use this information to write a C++ function named `Round()` that rounds the value of its first argument to the number of decimal places specified by its second argument. Incorporate the `Round()` function into a program that accepts a user-entered value of money, multiplies the entered amount by an 8.675% interest rate, and displays the result rounded to two decimal places.

b. Enter, compile, and execute the program written for Exercise 9a.

10. a. Write a C++ function named `whole()` that returns the integer part of any number passed to the function. (*Hint:* Assign the passed argument to an integer variable.)

b. Include the function written in Exercise 10a in a working program. Make sure your function is called from `main()` and correctly returns a value to `main()`. Have `main()` display the value returned. Test the function by passing various data to it.

11. a. Write a C++ function named `fracpart()` that returns the fractional part of any number passed to the function. For example, if the number 256.879 is passed to `fracpart()`, the number .879 should be returned. Have the function `fracpart()` call the function `whole()` that you wrote in Exercise 10. The number returned can then be determined as the number passed to `fracpart()` less the returned value when the same argument is passed to `whole()`. The completed program should consist of `main()` followed by `fracpart()` followed by `whole()`.

b. Include the function written in Exercise 11a in a working program. Make sure your function is called from `main()` and correctly returns a value to `main()`. Have `main()` display the value returned. Test the function by passing various data to it.

6.3 Returning Multiple Values

In a typical function invocation the called function receives values from its calling function, stores and manipulates the passed values, and directly returns at most one single value. The method of passing data in this manner is referred to as a **pass by value.**

Calling a function and passing arguments by value is a distinct advantage of C++. It allows functions to be written as independent entities that can use any variable or parameter name without concern that other functions may also be using the same name. It also alleviates any concern that altering a parameter or variable in one function may inadvertently alter the value of a variable in another function. Under this approach, parameters can be considered as either initialized variables or variables that will be assigned values when the function is executed. At no time, however, does the called function have direct access to any variable defined in the calling function, even if the variable is used as an argument in the function call.

There are times, however, when it is necessary to alter this approach by giving a called function direct access to the variables of its calling function. This allows one function, which is the called function, to use and change the value of variables that have been defined in the calling function. To do this requires that the address of the variable be passed to the called function. Once the called function has the variable's address, it "knows where the variable lives," so to speak, and can access and change the value stored there directly.

Passing addresses is referred to as a function **pass by reference,**[11] because the called function can reference, or access, the variable whose address has been passed. C++ provides two types of address parameters, references and pointers. In this section we describe the method that uses reference parameters.

Passing and Using Reference Parameters

As always in exchanging data between two functions, we must be concerned with both the sending and receiving sides of the data exchange. From the sending side, however, calling a function and passing an address as an argument that will be accepted as a reference parameter on the receiving side is exactly the same as calling a function and passing a value: the called function is summoned into action by giving its name and a list of arguments. For example, the statement `newval(firstnum, secnum);` both calls the function named `newval()` and passes two arguments to it. Whether a value or an address is actually passed depends on the parameter types declared for `newval()`. Let us now write the `newval` function and prototype so that it receives the addresses of the variables `firstnum` and `secnum`, which we assume to be floating point variables, rather than their values.

One of the first requirements in writing `newval()` is to declare two reference parameters for accepting passed addresses. In C++ a reference parameter is declared using the syntax

    data-type& reference-name

For example, the reference declaration

```
float& num1;
```

declares that `num1` is a reference parameter that will be used to store the address of a floating point value. Similarly, `int& secnum` declares that `secnum` is a reference to an integer, and `char& key` declares that `key` is a reference to a character.

---

11 It is also referred to as a **call by reference,** where, again, the term applies only to the arguments whose address has been passed.

Recall from Section 2.4 that the ampersand symbol, `&`, in C++ means "the address of." Additionally, when the `&` symbol is used within a declaration it refers to "the address of" the preceding data type. Using this information, declarations such as `float& num1` and `int& secnum` are sometimes more clearly understood if they are read backwards. Reading the declaration `float& num1` in this manner yields the information that "`num1` is the address of a floating point value."

Because we need to accept two addresses in the parameter list for `newval()`, the declarations `float& num1` and `float& num2` can be used. By including these declarations within the parameter list for `newval()`, and assuming that the function returns no value (`void`), we obtain the function header for `newval()`:

```
void newval(float& num1, float& num2)
```

For this function header line, an appropriate function prototype is:

```
void newval(float&, float&);
```

This prototype and header line are included in Program 6.8, which includes a completed `newval()` function body that both displays and directly alters the values stored in these reference arguments from within the called function.

PROGRAM 6.8

```
#include <iostream.h>

void newval(float&, float&);  // prototype with two references

int main()
{
  float firstnum, secnum;

  cout << "\nEnter two numbers: ";
  cin  >> firstnum >> secnum;
  cout << "\nThe value in firstnum is: " << firstnum << endl;
  cout << "The value in secnum is: " << secnum << "\n\n";

  newval(firstnum, secnum);   // call the function
```

(continued next page)

(continued from previous page)

```
  cout << "The value in firstnum is now: " << firstnum << endl;
  cout << "The value in secnum is now: " << secnum << endl;

  return 0;
}

void newval(float& xnum, float& ynum)
{
   cout << "The value in xnum is: " << xnum << endl;
   cout << "The value in ynum is: " << ynum << "\n\n";
   xnum = 89.5;
   ynum = 99.5;

  return;
}
```

In calling the `newval()` function within Program 6.8 it is important to understand the connection between the arguments, `firstnum` and `secnum`, used in the function call and the parameters, `xnum` and `ynum`, used in the function header. *Both refer to the same data items.* The significance of this fact is that the values in the arguments (`firstnum` and `secnum`) can now be altered from within `newval()` by using the parameter names (`xnum` and `ynum`). Thus, the parameters `xnum` and `ynum` do not store copies of the values in `firstnum` and `secnum`, but directly access the locations in memory set aside for these two arguments. The equivalence of argument and parameter names in Program 6.8, which is the essence of a pass by reference, is illustrated in Figure 6.11. As illustrated in this figure, the

FIGURE 6.11

The equivalence of arguments and parameters in Program 6.8

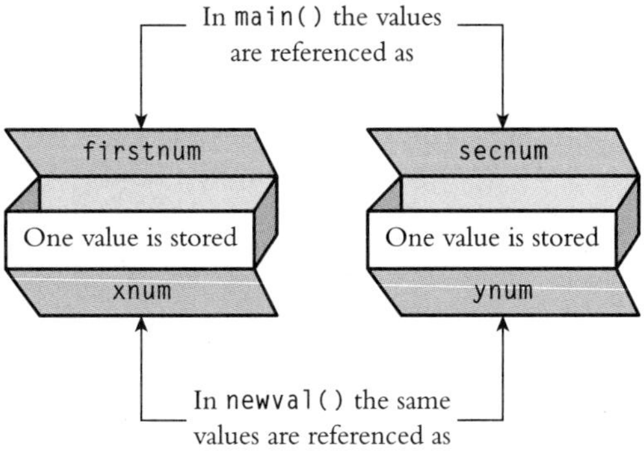

FIGURE 6.12

Sample run using Program 6.8

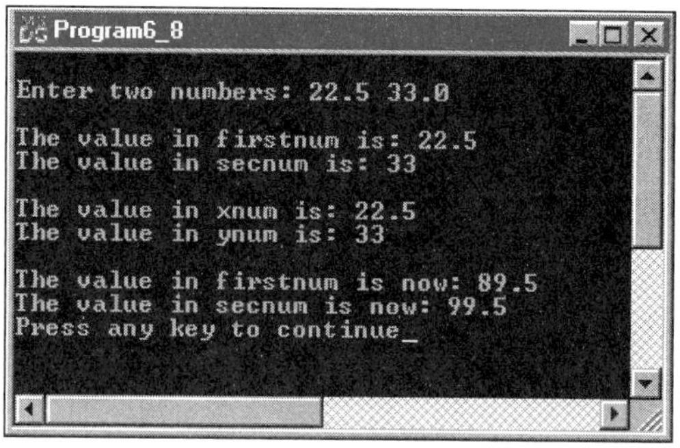

```
Program6_8

Enter two numbers: 22.5 33.0

The value in firstnum is: 22.5
The value in secnum is: 33

The value in xnum is: 22.5
The value in ynum is: 33

The value in firstnum is now: 89.5
The value in secnum is now: 99.5
Press any key to continue_
```

argument names and their matching parameter names are simply different names referring to the same memory storage areas. In `main()` these memory locations are referenced by the names `firstnum` and `secnum`, respectively, whereas in `newval()` the same locations are referenced by the parameter names `xnum` and `ynum`, respectively.

Figure 6.12 illustrates a sample run obtained using Program 6.8. In reviewing this output, notice that the values initially displayed for the parameters `xnum` and `ynum` are the same as those displayed for the arguments `firstnum` and `secnum`. Because `xnum` and `ynum` are reference parameters, however, `newval()` now has direct access to the arguments `firstnum` and `secnum`. Thus, any change to `xnum` within `newval()` directly alters the value of `firstnum` in `main()`, and any change to `ynum` directly changes `secnum`'s value. As illustrated by the final displayed values, the assignment of values to `xnum` and `ynum` within `newval()` is reflected in `main()` as the altering of `firstnum`'s and `secnum`'s values.

The equivalence between actual calling arguments and function parameters illustrated in Program 6.8 provides the basis for returning multiple values from within a function. For example, assume that a function is required to accept three values, compute the sum and product of these values, and return these computed results to the calling routine. By naming the function `calc()` and providing five parameters (three for the input data and two references for the returned values), we can use the following function.

```
void calc(float num1, float num2, float num3, float& total, float& product)
{
  total = num1 + num2 + num3;
  product = num1 * num2 * num3;
  return;
}
```

This function has five parameters, named `num1`, `num2`, `num3`, `total`, and `product`, of which only the last two are declared as references. Thus, the first three parameters are passed by value and the last two parameters are passed by reference. Within the function, only the last two parameters are altered. The value of the fourth parameter, total, is calculated as the sum of the first three parameters, and the last parameter, `product`, is computed as the product of the parameters `num1`, `num2`, and `num3`. Program 6.9 includes this function in a complete program.

PROGRAM 6.9

```
#include <iostream.h>

void calc(float, float, float, float&, float&);  // prototype

int main()
{
  float firstnum, secnum, thirdnum, sum, product;

  cout << "\nEnter three numbers: ";
  cin  >> firstnum >> secnum >> thirdnum;

  calc(firstnum, secnum, thirdnum, sum, product);  // function call

  cout << "\nThe sum of the numbers is: " << sum << endl;
  cout << "The product of the numbers is: " << product << endl;

  return 0;
}

void calc(float num1, float num2, float num3, float& total, float& product)
{
  total = num1 + num2 + num3;
  product = num1 * num2 * num3;
  return;
}
```

Within `main()`, the function `calc()` is called using the five arguments `firstnum`, `secnum`, `thirdnum`, `sum`, and `product`. As required, these arguments agree in number and data type with the parameters declared by `calc()`. Of the five arguments passed, only `firstnum`, `secnum`, and `thirdnum` have been assigned values when the call to `calc()` is made. The remaining two arguments have not been initialized and will be used to receive values back from `calc()`. Depending on the compiler used in compiling the program, these arguments will initially contain either zeros or "garbage" values. Figure 6.13

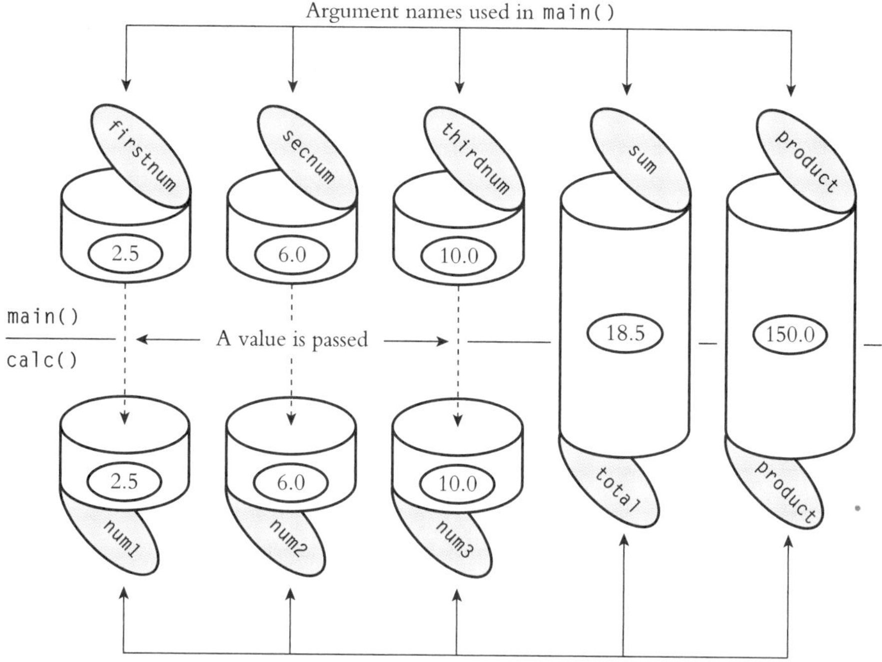

FIGURE 6.13

Relationship between argument and parameter names

illustrates the relationship between actual and parameter names and the values they contain after the return from `calc()`.

Once `calc()` is called, it uses its first three parameters to calculate values for `total` and `product` and then returns control to `main()`. Because of the order of its actual calling arguments, `main()` knows the values calculated by `calc()` as `sum` and `product`, which are then displayed. Figure 6.14 illustrates a sample run using Program 6.9.

As a final example to illustrate the usefulness of passing references to a called function, we construct a function named `swap()` that exchanges the values of two of `main()`'s floating point variables. Such a function is useful when sorting a list of numbers.

FIGURE 6.14

Sample run using Program 6.9

```
Program6_9

Enter three numbers: 2.5 6.0 10.0

The sum of the numbers is: 18.5
The product of the numbers is: 150
Press any key to continue
```

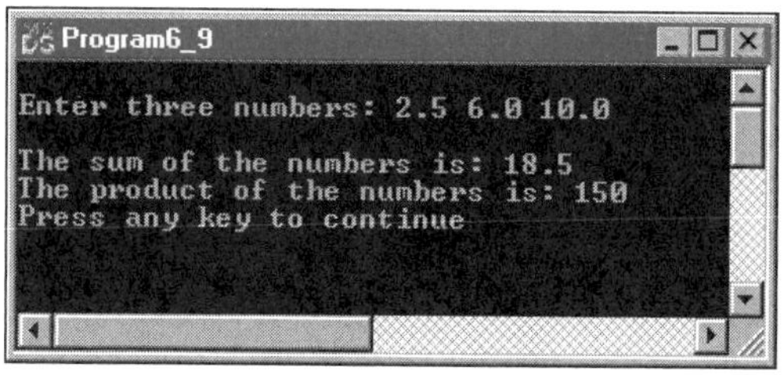

Because the values of more than a single variable are affected, `swap()` cannot be written as a pass by value function that returns a single value. The desired exchange of `main()`'s variables by `swap()` can be obtained only by giving `swap()` access to `main()`'s variables. One way of doing this is by using reference parameters.

We have already seen how to pass references in Program 6.8. We now construct a function to exchange the values in the passed reference parameters. Exchanging values in two parameters is accomplished using the three-step exchange algorithm:

1. Save the first parameter's value in a temporary location (see Figure 6.15a).
2. Store the second parameter's value in the first parameter (see Figure 6.15b).
3. Store the temporary value in the second parameter (see Figure 6.15c).

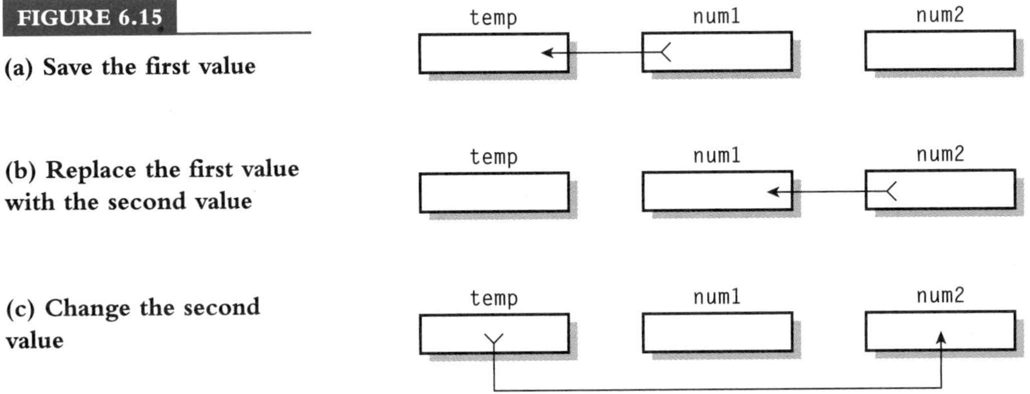

FIGURE 6.15

(a) Save the first value

(b) Replace the first value with the second value

(c) Change the second value

Following is the function `swap` written according to these specifications:

```
void swap(float& num1, float& num2)
{
  float temp;

  temp = num1;     // save num1's value
  num1 = num2;     // store num2's value in num1
  num2 = temp;     // change num2's value

  return;
}
```

Notice that the use of references in `swap()`'s header line gives `swap()` access to the equivalent arguments in the calling function. Thus, any change to the two reference parameters in swap() automatically changes the values in the calling function's arguments. Program 6.10 contains swap() in a complete program.

PROGRAM 6.10

```
#include <iostream.h>

void swap(float&, float&);   // function receives 2 references

int main()
{
  float firstnum = 20.5, secnum = 6.25;

  cout << "\nThe value stored in firstnum is: " << firstnum
       << "\nThe value stored in secnum is: "<< secnum << endl;

  swap(firstnum, secnum);   // call the function with references

  cout << "\nAfter calling swap()"
       << "\nThe value stored in firstnum is now: " << firstnum
       << "\nThe value stored in secnum is now: " << secnum << endl;

  return 0;
}

void swap(float& num1, float& num2)
{
  float temp;

  temp = num1;      // save num1's value
  num1 = num2;      // store num2's value in num1
  num2 = temp;      // change num2's value

  return;
}
```

Figure 6.16 illustrates the output produced by Program 6.10.

FIGURE 6.16

Output produced by Program 6.10

```
The value stored in firstnum is: 20.5
The value stored in secnum is: 6.25

After calling swap()
The value stored in firstnum is now: 6.25
The value stored in secnum is now: 20.5
Press any key to continue_
```

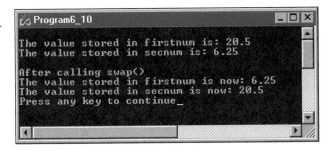

As illustrated by this output, the values stored in `main()`'s variables have been modified from within `swap()`, which was made possible by the use of reference parameters. If a pass by value had been used instead, the exchange within `swap()` would affect only `swap()`'s parameters and would accomplish nothing with respect to `main()`'s variables. Thus, a function such as `swap()` can be written only by using references or some other means that provides access to `main()`'s variables (this "other means" is by pointers, the topic of Chapter 13).

In using reference parameters, two cautions must be mentioned. The first is that reference parameters *cannot* be used to change constants. For example, calling `swap()` with two constants, such as in the call `swap(20.5, 6.5)` passes two constants to the function. Although `swap()` may execute, it will not change the values of these constants.[12]

The second caution to note is that a function call itself gives no indication that the called function will be using reference parameters. The default in C++ is to make passes by value rather than passes by reference, precisely to limit a called function's ability to alter variables in the calling function. This calling procedure should be adhered to whenever possible, which means that reference parameters should be used only in very restricted situations that actually require multiple return values, such as in the `swap()` function illustrated in Program 6.10. The `calc()` function included in Program 6.9, although useful for illustrative purposes, could also be written as two separate functions, each returning a single value.

EXERCISES 6.3

1. Write parameter declarations for
   a. a parameter named amount that will be a reference to a floating point value
   b. a parameter named price that will be a reference to a double precision number
   c. a parameter named minutes that will be a reference to an integer number
   d. a parameter named key that will be a reference to a character
   e. a parameter named yield that will be a reference to a double precision number

12 Most compilers will catch this error.

2. Three integer arguments are to be used in a call to a function named `time()`. Write a suitable function header for `time()`, assuming that `time()` accepts these arguments as the reference parameters: `sec`, `min`, and `hours`; and returns no value to its calling function.

3. Rewrite the `FindMax()` function in Program 6.5 so that the variable `max`, declared in `main()`, is used to store the maximum value of the two passed numbers. The value of `max` should be set directly from within `FindMax()`. (*Hint:* A reference to `max` will have to be accepted by `FindMax()`.)

4. Write a function named `change()` that has a floating point parameter and four integer reference parameters named `quarters`, `dimes`, `nickels`, and `pennies`, respectively. The function is to consider the floating point passed value as a dollar amount and convert the value into an equivalent number quarters, dimes, nickels, and pennies. Using the references the function should directly alter the respective arguments in the calling function.

5. Write a function named `time()` that has an integer parameter named `totSecs` and three integer reference parameters named `hours`, `mins`, and `secs`. The function is to convert the passed number of seconds into an equivalent number of `hours`, `minutes`, and `seconds`. By using the references, the function should directly alter the respective actual arguments in the calling function.

6. Write a function named `YearCalc()` that has a long integer parameter representing the total number of days from the date 1/1/1900 and reference parameters named `year`, `month`, and `day`. The function is to calculate the current year, month, and day for the given number of days passed to it. By using the references, the function should directly alter the respective arguments in the calling function. For this problem assume that each year has 360 days and each month has 30 days.

7. Write a function named `liquid()` that has an integer number parameter named `totCups` and reference parameters named `gallons`, `quarts`, `pints`, and `cups`. The passed integer represents the total number of cups and the function is to determine the number of gallons, quarts, pints, and cups in the passed value. By using the references, the function should directly alter the respective arguments in the calling function. Use the relationships of two cups to a pint, four cups to a quart, and 16 cups to a gallon.

8. The following program uses the same argument and parameter names in both the calling and called function. Determine if this causes any problem for the compiler.

```
#include <iostream.h>
void time(int &, int &);  // function prototype
int main()
{
  int min, hour;

  cout << "Enter two numbers :";
  cin  >> min >> hour;
  time(min, hour);
```

```
  return 0;
}

void time(int &min, int &hour)    // accept two references
{
  int sec;

  sec = (hour * 60 + min) * 60;
  cout << "The total number of seconds is " << sec << endl;

  return;
}
```

6.4 Variable Scope

Now that we have begun to write programs containing more than one function, we can look more closely at the variables declared within each function and their relationships to variables in other functions.

By their very nature, C++ functions are constructed to be independent modules. As we have seen, values are passed to a function using the function's parameter list and a value is returned from a function using a `return` statement. Seen in this light, a function can be thought of as a closed box, with slots at the top to receive values and a single slot at the bottom of the box to return a value (see Figure 6.17).

The metaphor of a closed box is useful because it emphasizes the fact that what goes on inside the function, including all variable declarations within the function's body, are hidden from the view of all other functions. The variables created inside a function are conventionally available only to the function itself, so they are said to be local to the function, or **local variables.** This term refers to the **scope** of an identifier, where *scope* is defined as the section of the program where the identifier, such as a variable, is valid or

FIGURE 6.17

A function can be considered a closed box

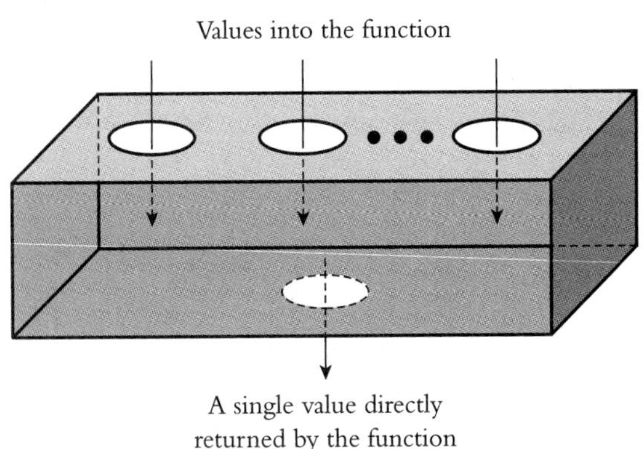

"known." This section of the program is also referred to as where the variable is visible. A variable can have either a local scope or a global scope. A variable with a local scope is simply one that has had storage locations set aside for it by a declaration statement made within a function body. Local variables are meaningful only when used in expressions or statements inside the function that declared them. This means that the same variable name can be declared and used in more than one function. For each function that declares the variable, a separate and distinct variable is created.

All the variables we have used until now have been local variables. This is a direct result of placing our declaration statements inside functions and using them as definition statements that cause the compiler to reserve storage for the declared variable. As we shall see, declaration statements can be placed outside functions and need not act as definitions that cause new storage areas to be reserved for the declared variable.

A variable with **global scope,** more commonly termed a **global variable,** is one whose storage has been created for it by a declaration statement located outside any function. These variables can be used by all functions that are physically placed after the global variable declaration. This is shown in Program 6.11, where we have purposely used the same variable name inside both functions contained in the program.

PROGRAM 6.11

```
#include <iostream.h>

int firstnum;     // create a global variable named firstnum

void valfun(void);   // function prototype (declaration)

int main()
{
  int secnum;     // create a local variable named secnum

  firstnum = 10; // store a value into the global variable
  secnum = 20;   // store a value into the local variable

  cout << "\nFrom main(): firstnum = " << firstnum
       << "\nFrom main(): secnum =  " << secnum << endl;

  valfun();       // call the function valfun

  cout << "\nFrom main() again: firstnum = " << firstnum
       << "\nFrom main() again: secnum = " << secnum << endl;
```

(continued next page)

(continued from previous page)

```
  return 0;
}

void valfun(void)   // no values are passed to this function
{
  int secnum;  // create a second local variable named secnum

  secnum = 30; // this only affects this local variable's value

  cout << "\nFrom valfun(): firstnum = " << firstnum
       << "\nFrom valfun(): secnum = " << secnum << endl;

  firstnum = 40;    // this changes firstnum for both functions

  return;
}
```

The variable `firstnum` in Program 6.11 is a global variable because its storage is created by a definition statement located outside a function. Because both functions, `main()` and `valfun()`, follow the definition of `firstnum`, both of these functions can use this global variable with no further declaration needed.

Program 6.11 also contains two separate local variables, both named `secnum`. Storage for the `secnum` variable named in `main()` is created by the definition statement located in `main()`. A different storage area for the `secnum` variable in `valfun()` is created by the definition statement located in the `valfun()` function. Figure 6.18 illustrates the three distinct storage areas reserved by the three definition statements found in Program 6.11.

Each of the variables named `secnum` is local to the function in which their storage is created, and each of these variables can be used only from within the appropriate function. Thus, when `secnum` is used in `main()`, the storage area reserved by `main()` for its `secnum` variable is accessed, and when `secnum` is used in `valfun()`, the storage area reserved by `valfun()` for its `secnum` variable is accessed. Figure 6.19 illustrates the output produced when Program 6.11 is run.

Let's analyze this output. Because `firstnum` is a global variable, both the `main()` and `valfun()` functions can use and change its value. Initially, both functions print the value of 10 that `main()` stored in `firstnum`. Before returning, `valfun()` changes the value of `firstnum` to 40, which is the value displayed when the variable `firstnum` is next displayed from within `main()`.

Because each function "knows" only its own local variables, `main()` can send only the value of its `secnum` to the `cout` object, and `valfun()` can send only the value of its

FIGURE 6.18

The three storage areas created by Program 6.11

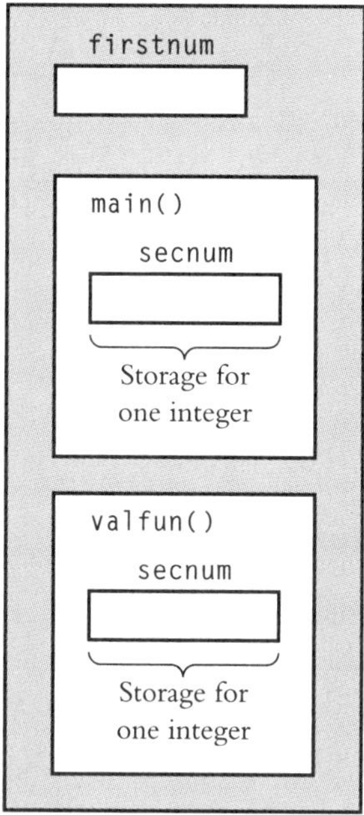

secnum to the cout object. Thus, whenever secnum is obtained from main() the value of 20 is displayed, and whenever secnum is obtained from valfun() the value 30 is displayed.

C++ does not confuse the two secnum variables because only one function can execute at a given moment. While a function is executing, only those variables and parameters that are "in scope" for that function (global and local) can be accessed.

The scope of a variable in no way influences or restricts the data type of the variable. Just as a local variable can be a character, integer, float, double, or any of the other data types (long/short) we have introduced, so can global variables be of these data types, as illustrated in Figure 6.20. The scope of a variable is determined by the placement of the definition statement that reserves storage for it and optionally by a declaration statement that makes it visible, whereas the data type of the variable is determined by using the

FIGURE 6.19

Output produced using Program 6.11

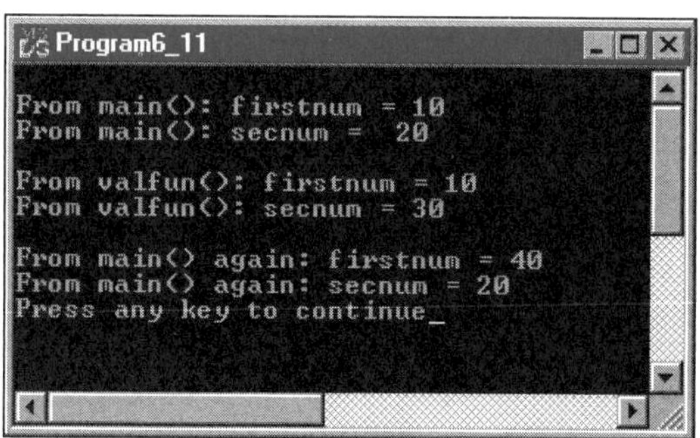

FIGURE 6.20

Relating the scope and type of a variable

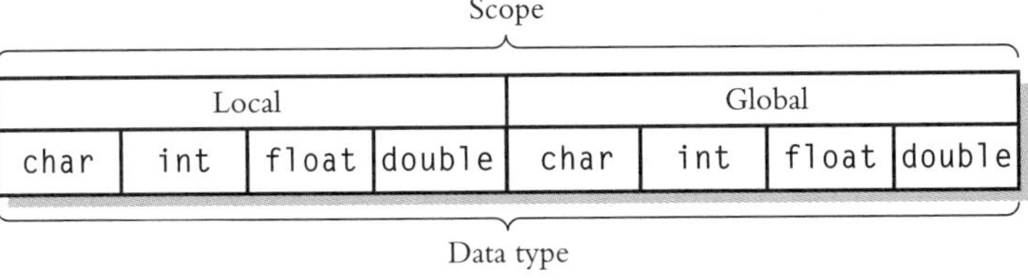

appropriate keyword (`char`, `int`, `float`, `double`, etc.) before the variable's name in a declaration statement.

Scope Resolution Operator

When a local variable has the same name as a global variable, all uses of the variable's name made within the scope of the local variable refers to the local variable. This situation in illustrated in Program 6.12, in which the variable name `number` is defined as both a global and local variable.

PROGRAM 6.12

```
#include <iostream.h>

float number = 42.8;        // a global variable named number

int main()
{
  float number = 26.4;      // a local variable named number

  cout << "The value of number is " << number << endl;

  return 0;
}
```

When Program 6.12 is executed, the following output line is displayed.

```
The value of number is 26.4
```

As shown by this output, the local variable name takes precedence over the global variable. In such cases, we can still access the global variable by using C++'s scope resolution operator. This operator, which has the symbol `::`, must be placed immediately before the variable name, as in `::number`. When used in this manner the `::` tells the compiler to use the global variable. As an example, the global resolution operator is used in Program 6.12a.

PROGRAM 6.12a

```
#include <iostream.h>

float number = 42.5;        // a global variable named number

int main()
{
  float number = 26.4;      // a local variable named number

  cout << "The value of number is " << ::number << endl;

  return 0;
}
```

The output line produced by Program 6.12a is:

```
The value of number is 42.5
```

As indicated by this output, the global resolution operator causes the global, rather than the local variable to be accessed.

Misuse of Globals

Global variables allow the programmer to "jump around" the normal safeguards provided by functions. Rather than passing variables to a function, it is possible to make all variables global ones. **Do not do this.** By indiscriminately making all variables global, you instantly destroy the safeguards C++ provides to make functions independent and insulated from each other, including the necessity of carefully designating the type of parameters needed by a function, the variables used in the function, and the value returned.

Using only global variables can be especially disastrous in larger programs that have many user-created functions. Because all variables in a function must be declared, creating functions that use global variables requires that you remember to write the appropriate global declarations at the top of each program using the function—they no longer come along with the function. More devastating than this, however, is the horror of trying to track down an error in a large program using global variables. Because a global variable can be accessed and changed by any function following the global declaration, locating the origin of an erroneous value is a time-consuming and frustrating task

Global variables are sometimes useful, however, in creating variables and named constants that must be shared among many functions. Rather than passing the same value to each function, it is easier to define a variable or constant once as a global. Doing so also alerts anyone reading the program that many functions use the variable. Most large programs make use of a few global variables. Smaller programs containing a few functions, however, should almost never contain globals.

EXERCISES 6.4

1. a. For the following section of code, determine the data type and scope of all declared variables. To do this use a separate sheet of paper and list the three column headings that follow (we have filled in the entries for the first variable):

Variable Name	Data Type	Scope
`price`	integer	global to `main()`, `roi()`, and `step()`

```
#include <iostream.h>

int price;
long int years;
double yield;

int main()
{
  int bondtype;
  double interest, coupon;
     .
     .
  return 0;
}

double roi(int mat1, int mat2)
{
  int count;
  double effectiveInt;
     .
     .
```

```
   return effectiveInt;
}

int step(float first, float last)
{
   int numofyrs;
   float fracpart;
       .
       .
   return 10*numofyrs;
}
```

b. Draw boxes around the appropriate section of the above code to enclose the scope of each variable.

c. Determine the data type of the parameters for the functions `roi()` and `step()`, and the data type of the value returned by these functions.

2. a. For the following section of code, determine the data type and scope of all declared variables. To do this use a separate sheet of paper and list the three column headings that follow (we have filled in the entries for the first variable):

Variable Name	**Data Type**	**Scope**
`key`	character	global to `main()`, `func1()`, and `func2()`

```
#include <iostream.h>

char key;
long int number;

int main()
{
  int a,b,c;
  double x,y;
      .
      .
  return 0;
}

double secnum;
```

```
int func1(int num1, int num2)
{
  int o,p;
  float q;
      .
      .
  return p;
}

double func2(float first, float last)
{
  int a,b,c,o,p;
  float r;
  double s,t,x;
      .
      .
  return s * t;
}
```

b. Draw a box around the appropriate section of the above code to enclose the scope of the variables `key`, `secnum`, `y`, and `r`.

c. Determine the data type of the parameters for the functions `func1()` and `func2()`, and the data type of the value returned by these functions.

3. Besides speaking about the scope of a variable, we can also apply the term to a function's parameters. What do you think is the scope of all function parameters?

4. Determine the values displayed by the following program:

```
#include <iostream.h>

int firstnum = 10;  // declare and initialize a global variable
void display(void);  // function prototype

int main()
{
  int firstnum = 20;    // declare and initialize a local variable
  cout << "\nThe value of firstnum is " << firstnum;
  display();

  return 0;
}
```

```
void display(void)
{
  cout << "\nThe value of firstnum is now " << firstnum;

  return;
}
```

6.5 Variable Storage Class

The scope of a variable defines the location within a program where that variable can be used. Given a program, you could take a pencil and draw a box around the section of the program where each variable is valid. The space inside the box would represent the scope of a variable. From this viewpoint, the scope of a variable can be thought of as the space within the program where the variable is valid.

In addition to the space dimension represented by its scope, a variable also has a time dimension. The time dimension refers to the length of time that storage locations are reserved for a variable. This time dimension is referred to as the variable's "lifetime." For example, all variable storage locations are released back to the operating system when a program is finished running. However, while a program is still executing, interim variable storage areas are also reserved and subsequently released back to the operating system. Where and how long a variable's storage locations are kept before they are released can be determined by the **storage class** of the variable.

Besides having a data type and scope, every variable also has a storage class. The four available storage classes are called `auto`, `static`, `extern`, and `register`. If one of these class names is used, it must be placed before the variable's data type in a declaration statement. Examples of declaration statements that include a storage class designation are:

```
auto int num;       // auto storage class and int data type
static int miles;   // static storage class and int data type
register int dist;  // register storage class and int data type
extern int volts;   // extern storage class and int data type
auto float coupon;  // auto storage class and float data type
static double yrs;  // static storage class and double data type
extern float yld;   // extern storage class and float data type
auto char in_key;   // auto storage class and char variable
```

To understand what the storage class of a variable means, we first consider local variables (those variables created inside a function) and then global variables (those variables created outside a function).

Local Variable Storage Classes

Local variables can be members only of the auto, static, or register storage classes. If no class description is included in the declaration statement, the variable is automatically assigned to the auto class. Thus, auto is the default storage used by C++. All the local variables we have used so far, without a the storage class designation, have been auto variables.

The term *auto* is short for **automatic.** Storage for automatic local variables is automatically reserved (that is, created) each time a function declaring automatic variables is called. As long as the function has not returned control to its calling function, all automatic variables local to the function are "alive"—that is, storage for the variables is available. When the function returns control to its calling function, its local automatic variables "die"—that is, the storage for the variables is released back to the operating system. This process repeats itself each time a function is called. For example, consider Program 6.13, in which the function testauto() is called three times from main().

PROGRAM 6.13

```
#include <iostream.h>

void testauto(void);    // function prototype

int main()
{
  int count;                // count is a local auto variable

  cout << endl;   // display a blank line
  for(count = 1; count <= 3; count++)
    testauto();

  return 0;
}

void testauto(void)
{
  int num = 0;       // num is a local auto variable
                     // that is initialized to zero
  cout << "The value of the automatic variable num is "
       << num << endl;
  num++;

  return;
}
```

FIGURE 6.21

Output produced using Program 6.13

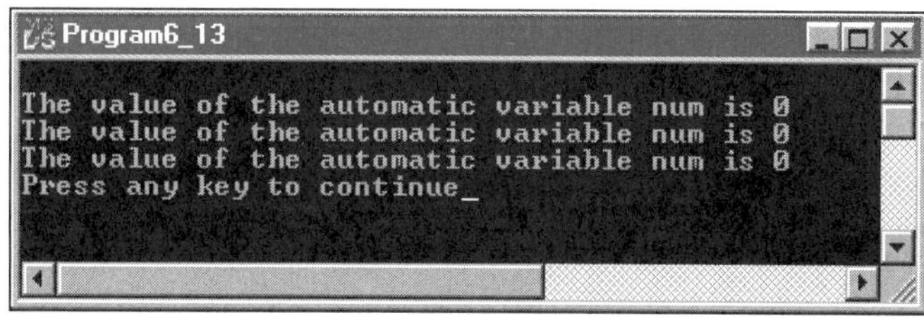
Program6_13
The value of the automatic variable num is 0
The value of the automatic variable num is 0
The value of the automatic variable num is 0
Press any key to continue_

The output produced by Program 6.13 is shown in Figure 6.21.

Each time `testauto()` is called, the automatic variable `num` is created and initialized to zero. When the function returns control to `main()`, the variable `num` is destroyed along with any value stored in `num`. Thus, the effect of incrementing `num` in `testauto()`, before the function's `return` statement, is lost when control is returned to `main()`.

For most applications, the use of automatic variables works just fine. There are cases, however, where we would like a function to remember values between function calls. This is the purpose of the `static` storage class. A local variable that is declared as `static` causes the program to keep the variable and its latest value even when the function that declared it is through executing. Examples of `static` variable declarations are:

```
static int rate;
static float taxes;
static double amount;
static char inKey;
static long resistance;
```

A local static variable is not created and destroyed each time the function declaring the static variable is called. Once created, local static variables remain in existence for the life of the program. This means that the last value stored in the variable when the function is finished executing is available to the function the next time it is called.

Because local static variables retain their values, they are not initialized within a declaration statement in the same way as `auto` variables. To understand why, consider the `auto` declaration `int num = 0;`, which causes the automatic variable `num` to be created and set to zero each time the declaration is encountered. This is called a **run-time initialization** because initialization occurs each time the declaration statement is encountered when the program is running. This type of initialization would be disastrous for a static variable, because resetting the variable's value to zero each time the function is called would destroy the very value we are trying to save.

The initialization of `static` variables (both local and global) is done only once, when the program is first compiled. At compilation time the variable is created and any initialization value is placed in it.[13] Thereafter, the value in the variable is kept without further initialization each time the function is called. To see how this works, consider Program 6.14.

PROGRAM 6.14

```
#include <iostream.h>

void teststat(void);     // function prototype

int main()
{
  int count;      // count is a local auto variable

  cout << endl;   // display a blank line
  for(count = 1; count <= 3; count++)
    teststat();

  return 0;
}

void teststat(void)
{
  static int num = 0;     // num is a local static variable
  cout << "The value of the static variable num is now "
       << num << endl;
  num++;

  return;
}
```

The output produced by Program 6.14 is shown in Figure 6.22.

As illustrated in Figure 6.22, the static variable `num` is set to zero only once. The function `teststat()` then increments this variable just before returning control to `main()`. The value that `num` has when leaving the function `teststat()` is retained and displayed when the function is next called.

---

13 Some compilers initialize `static` local variables the first time the definition statement is executed rather than when the program is compiled.

FIGURE 6.22

Output produced using Program 6.14

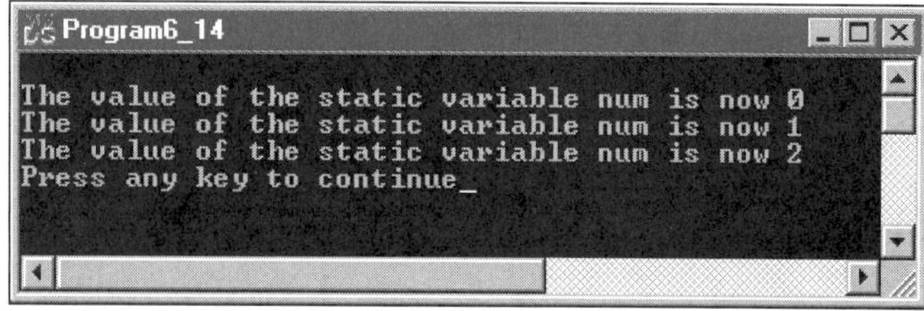

Unlike automatic variables, which can be initialized by either constants or expressions using both constants and previously initialized variables, static variables can be initialized only using constants or constant expressions, such as 3.2 + 8.0. Also, unlike automatic variables, all static variables are set to zero when no explicit initialization is given. Thus, the specific initialization of `num` to zero in Program 6.13 is not required.

The remaining storage class available to local variables, the `register` class, is not used as extensively as either automatic or static variables. Examples of register variable declarations are:

```
register int time;
register double diffren;
register float coupon;
```

Register variables have the same time duration as automatic variables; that is, a local register variable is created when the function declaring it is entered, and is destroyed when the function completes execution. The only difference between register and automatic variables is where the storage for the variable is located.

Storage for all variables (local and global), except register variables, is reserved in the computer's memory area. Most computers have a few additional high-speed storage areas located directly in the computer's processing unit that can also be used for variable storage. These special high-speed storage areas are called *registers.* Since registers are physically located in the computer's processing unit, they can be accessed faster than the normal memory storage areas located in the computer's memory unit. Also, computer instructions that access registers typically require less space than instructions that access memory locations because there are fewer registers that can be accessed than there are memory locations. When the compiler substitutes the location of a register for a variable during program compilation, less space in the instruction is needed than is required to address a memory having millions of locations.

Besides decreasing the size of a compiled C++ program, using register variables can also increase the execution speed of a C++ program, if the compiler supports this data type. Variables declared with the `register` storage class are automatically switched to the `auto` storage class if the compiler does not support register variables or if the declared register variables exceed the computer's register capacity.

The only restriction in using the `register` storage class is that the address of a register variable, using the address operator `&`, cannot be taken. This is easily understood when you realize that registers do not have standard memory addresses.

Global Variable Storage Classes

Global variables are created by definition statements external to a function. By their nature, these externally defined variables do not come and go with the calling of any function. Once a global variable is created, it exists until the program in which it is declared is finished executing. Thus, global variables cannot be declared as either `auto` or `register` variables that are created and destroyed as the program is executing. Global variables may additionally be declared as members of the `static` or `extern` storage classes (but not both). Examples of declaration statements including these two class descriptions are:

```
extern int sum;
extern double volts;
static double current;
```

The `static` and `extern` classes affect only the scope, not the time duration, of global variables. As with static local variables, all global variables are initialized to zero at compile time.

The purpose of the `extern` storage class is to extend the scope of a global variable beyond its normal boundaries. To understand this, we must first note that the programs we have written so far have always been contained together in one file. Thus, when you have saved or retrieved programs you have given the computer only a single name for your program. This is not required by C++.

Larger programs can consist of many functions stored in multiple files. An example of this is shown in Figure 6.23, where the three functions `main()`, `func1()`, and `func2()` are stored in one file and the two functions `func3()` and `func4()` are stored in a second file.

For the files illustrated in Figure 6.23, the global variables `volts`, `current`, and `power` declared in `file1` can be used only by the functions `main()`, `func1()`, and `func2()` in this file. The single global variable, `factor`, declared in `file2` can be used only by the functions `func3()` and `func4()` in `file2`.

Although the variable `volts` has been created in `file1`, we may want to use it in `file2`. Placing the declaration statement `extern int volts;` in `file2`, as shown in Figure 6.24, allows us to do this. Putting this statement at the top of `file2` extends the scope of the variable `volts` into `file2` so that it may be used by both `func3()` and `func4()`. Thus, the `extern` designation simply declares a global variable that is defined in another file. So placing the statement `extern float current;` in `func4()` extends the scope of this global variable, created in `file1`, into `func4()`, and the scope of the global variable `factor`, created in `file2`, is extended into `func1()` and `func2()` by the declaration

FIGURE 6.23

A program may extend beyond one file

```
file1                          file2

int volts;                     double factor;
float current;                 int func3()
static double power;           {
     .                              .
     .                              .
     .                              .
int main()                     }
{                              int func4()
    func1();                        .
    func2();                        .
    func3();                        .
    func4();                   }
}
int func1()
{
     .
     .
     .
}
int func2()
{
     .
     .
     .
}
```

statement `extern double factor;` placed before `func1()`. Notice that `factor` is not available to `main()`.

A declaration statement that specifically contains the word `extern` is different from every other declaration statement in that it does not cause the creation of a new variable by reserving new storage for the variable. An `extern` declaration statement simply informs the compiler that a global variable already exists and can now be used. The actual storage for the variable must be created somewhere else in the program using one, and only one, global declaration statement in which the word `extern` has not been used. Initialization of the global variable can, of course, be made with the original declaration of the global variable. Initialization within an `extern` declaration statement is not allowed and will cause a compilation error.

The existence of the `extern` storage class is the reason we have been so careful to distinguish between the creation and declaration of a variable. Declaration statements containing the word `extern` do not create new storage areas; they only extend the scope of existing global variables.

The last global class, `static` global variables, is used to prevent the extension of a global variable into a second file. Global `static` variables are declared in the same way as local static variables, except that the declaration statement is placed outside any function.

PROGRAMMER'S NOTES

Storage Classes

- Variables of the type `auto` and `register` are always local variables.
- Only nonstatic global variables may be `extern`ed, which extends the variable's scope into another file or function.
- Making a global variable `static` makes the variable private to the file in which it is declared. Thus, `static` variables cannot be `extern`ed. Except for `static` variables, all variables are initialized each time they come into scope.

The scope of a `static` global variable cannot be extended beyond the file in which it is declared. This provides a degree of privacy for static global variables. Because they are "known" and can be used only in the file in which they are declared, other files cannot access or change their values. Thus, static global variables cannot be subsequently extended to a second file using an `extern` declaration statement. Trying to do so will result in a compilation error.

FIGURE 6.24

Extending the scope of a global variable

```
file1

int volts;
float current;
static double power;
    .
    .
    .
int main()
{
    func1();
    func2();
    func3();
    func4();
}
extern double factor;
int func1()
{
    .
    .
    .
}
int func2()
{
    .
    .
    .
}
```

```
file2

double factor;

extern int volts;

int func3()
{
    .
    .
    .
}
int func4()
{
   extern float current;
    .
    .
    .
}
```

EXERCISES 6.5

1. **a.** List the storage classes available to local variables.
   b. List the storage classes available to global variables.

2. Describe the difference between a local `auto` variable and a local `static` variable.

3. What is the difference between the following functions:

```
void init1(void)
{
  static int yrs = 1;
  cout << "\nThe value of yrs is " << yrs;
  yrs = yrs + 2;

  return;
}

void init2(void)
{
  static int yrs;
  yrs = 1;
  cout << "\nThe value of yrs is " << yrs;
  yrs = yrs + 2;

  return;
}
```

4. **a.** Describe the difference between a `static` global variable and an `extern` global variable.
   b. If a variable is declared with an `extern` storage class, what other declaration statement must be present somewhere in the program?

5. The declaration statement `static double years;` can be used to create either a local or global static variable. What determines the scope of the variable `years`?

6. For the function and variable declarations illustrated in Figure 6.25, place an `extern` declaration to individually accomplish the following:
   a. Extend the scope of the global variable `choice` into all of file2.
   b. Extend the scope of the global variable `flag` into function `pduction()` only.
   c. Extend the scope of the global variable `date` into `pduction()` and `bid()`.
   d. Extend the scope of the global variable `date` into `roi()` only.
   e. Extend the scope of the global variable `coupon` into `roi()` only.

FIGURE 6.25

Files for Exercise 6

```
file1                         file2

char choice;                  char bondtype;
int flag;                     double maturity;
long date, time;              double roi()
int main()                    {
{                               .
  .                             .
  .                             .
  .                           }
}                             double pduction()
double coupon;                {
doube price()                   .
{                               .
  .                             .
  .                           }
  .                           double bid
}                             {
double yield()                  .
{                               .
  .                             .
  .                           }
  .
}
```

f. Extend the scope of the global variable `bondtype` into all of `file1`.

g. Extend the scope of the global variable `maturity` into both `price()` and `yield()`.

6.6 Common Programming Errors

An extremely common programming error related to functions is passing incorrect data types. The values passed to a function must correspond to the data types of the parameters declared for the function. One way to verify that correct values have been received is to display all passed values within a function's body before any calculations are made. Once this verification has taken place, the display can be deleted.[14]

Another common error occurs when the same variable is declared locally within both the calling and called functions. Even though the variable name is the same, a change to one local variable does not alter the value in the other local variable.

Related to this error is the error caused when a local variable has the same name as a global variable. Within the function declaring it, the use of the local variable name affects only the local variable's contents unless the global resolution operator, `::`, is used.

14 In practice, a debugger program should be used.

Another common error is omitting the called function's prototype. The called function must be alerted to the type of value that will be returned, and this information is provided by the function prototype. The prototype can be omitted if the called function is physically placed in a program before its calling function. Although it is also permissible to omit the prototype and return type for functions returning an integer, it is poor documenting practice to do so. The actual value returned by a function can be verified by displaying it both before and after it is returned.

The last two common errors are terminating a function's header line with a semicolon and forgetting to include the data type of a function's parameters.

6.7 Chapter Summary

1. A function is called by giving its name and passing any data to it in the parentheses following the name. If a variable is one of the arguments in a function call, the called function receives a copy of the variable's value.

2. The commonly used form of a user-written function is:

```
return-type   function-name(parameter list)
{
  named constants;
  variable declarations
  other C++ statements;
  return expression;
}
```

The first line of the function is called the **function header.** The opening and closing braces of the function and all statements in between these braces constitute the function's **body.** The parameter list is a comma-separated list of parameter declarations.

3. A function's return type is the data type of the value returned by the function. If no type is declared, the function is assumed to return an integer value. If the function does not return a value it should be declared as a `void` type.

4. Functions can directly return at most a single data type value to their calling functions. This value is the value of the expression in the `return` statement.

5. Using reference parameters a function can be passed the address of a variable. If a called function is passed an address, it has the capacity of directly accessing the respective calling function's variable. Using passed addresses permits a called function to effectively return multiple values.

6. Functions can be declared to all calling functions by means of a **function prototype.** The prototype provides a declaration for a function that specifies the data type returned by the function, its name, and the data types of the parameters expected by the function. As with all declarations, a function prototype is terminated with a semicolon and may be included within local variable declarations or as a global declaration. The most common form of a function prototype is:

data-type function-name(argument data types);

If the called function is placed physically above the calling function, a prototype is not required, because the function's definition serves as a global declaration to all following functions.

7. Every variable used in a program has a **scope,** which determines where in the program the variable can be used. The scope of a variable is either local or global and is determined by where the variable's definition statement is placed. A local variable is defined within a function and can be used only within its defining function or block. A global variable is defined outside a function and can be used in any function following the variable's definition. All global variables that are not specifically initialized by the user are initialized to zero by the compiler and can be shared between files using the keyword `extern`.

8. Every variable has a **class.** The class of a variable determines how long the value in the variable will be retained. `auto` variables are local variables that exist only while their defining function is executing. `register` variables are similar to `auto` variables but are stored in a computer's internal registers rather than in memory. `static` variables can be either global or local and retain their values for the duration of a program's execution. `static` variables are also set to zero when they are defined, if they are not explicitly initialized by the user.

7 Visual Programming Basics

7.1 Creating a Windows-based Application

Recall from Chapter 1 that we used the following characterization of a Visual C++ application:

Visual C++ Application = Visual Part + Programming Language Part

Although console programs are extremely efficient for learning the programming basics of Visual C++, the integrated development environment allows you to easily create event-driven Windows-based applications that make full use of the visual elements. From

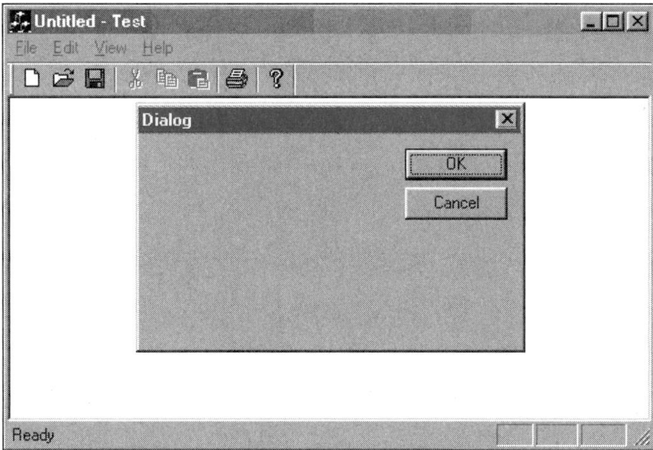

FIGURE 7.1

A user's view of an application

a user's standpoint, these visual elements form the basis of a graphical user interface (GUI); this permits the user to see the inputs and outputs provided by the application within the context of a true window. For example, consider Figure 7.1, which shows how a particular Windows-based application looks to a user.

From a programmer's perspective the graphical user interface shown in Figure 7.1 is constructed from a set of visual objects provided as resources when the program is being developed. Let's take a moment to see what these visual resources can be. A closer look at the elements shown in Figure 7.1 reveals that the application's **main window** is defined by its border, which contains the Title Bar and the Minimize, Resize, and Close buttons. Additionally, although they are not shown, scroll bars could also be present. The scroll bars are considered as part of the main window and would be located within the main window's inside bottom and right-side borders. The main window and all of its components are the same for all Windows-based applications; as such, they can be automatically generated using features of Developer Studio that are presented later in this section.

The area within the main window is referred to as the **client area,** and it is within this area that each application must be individually constructed. For example, inside the client area shown in Figure 7.1 is a dialog box, which itself contains a number of controls. Although dialog boxes and controls are usually considered together, a control is more formally defined as an object, such as a Command button, that provides a unique capability to display data, perform an action, or make the GUI easier to read.[1] A dialog box is a special type of control that has the ability to contain one or more additional controls. These controls provide a user with the capability to enter text, choose options, and generally direct the actions of the program.

---

1 More specifically, a dialog is a *parent window,* and the individual controls placed on it function as *child windows.*

FIGURE 7.2

Standard Visual C++ toolbox

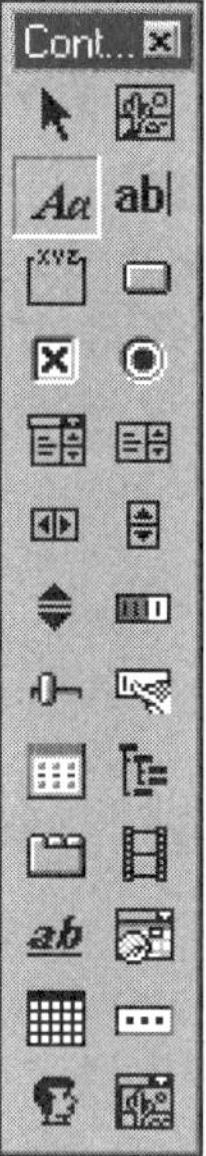

Dialog boxes, which are also referred to as dialogs, for short, consist of two general types. The **modal** type must be closed before any other part of the program using the dialog can be accessed.[2] **Nonmodal** dialogs, on the other hand, can remain open while other elements in the same program containing the dialog are activated.

Let's take a moment to look at the visual objects provided in Visual C++ that we will have at our disposal to create our own graphical user interfaces. When Visual C++'s resource editor is activated, one of the windows that is used with it is the Controls window, which is also referred to as the **toolbox.** This toolbox window, illustrated in Figure 7.2, provides the visual objects we will use in constructing each graphical user interface. Each of these objects is a control in that it permits a user to input information or receive output from an executing application.

Surprisingly, a majority of applications can be constructed using a minimal set of the controls provided in the toolbox window. This minimal set consists of the Label, Edit box, and Command button objects. The next set of objects that are more frequently found in applications include the Check box, Radio button, Group box, List box, and Combo box controls. Table 7.1 lists these object types and describes each object's use. In the remaining sections of the chapter we show you how to use selected objects in the toolbox, with special emphasis on the Command button, Edit box, and Label controls that you will use in almost every Windows-based application that you develop.

Don't be overwhelmed by all of the available controls. Each control is placed on a dialog in the same simple manner, which is described in the next section. Another charac-

---

2 Control can be transferred, however, to other programs.

TABLE 7.1 Fundamental object types and their uses

Object Type	Use
Check Box	Select one option from two mutually exclusive options
Command Button (also called a push button)	Initiate an action, such as a display or calculation
Edit Box	Enter and display data
Group Box	A rectangular area within a dialog box in which logically related controls can be grouped together
Label	Create text that a user cannot directly change.
Radio Button (also called an option button)	Select one option from a group of mutually exclusive options
List Box	Display a list of items from which one can be selected
Combo Box	Display a list of items from which one can be selected plus permit users to type the value of the desired item

teristic that is common to all controls is that they are really valid C++ objects. As objects, they are ultimately defined by two features, referred to as *properties* and *methods.*

An object's **properties** define its state, which for controls is simply how the object appears on the screen. For example, the properties of an Edit box include the location of the Edit box within a dialog, the color of the box (the background color), the color that text will be displayed in the box (the foreground color), and whether it is read-only or can also be written to by the user. **Methods,** as they apply to controls, are predefined procedures that are supplied with the object for performing specific tasks. For example, you can use a method to move an object to a different location or change its size. In general, a method is used to alter an object's properties.

Additionally, each object recognizes certain actions. For example, a Command button recognizes when the mouse pointer is pointing to it and the left mouse button is clicked. These types of actions, as we have seen, are referred to as **events.** In our example we would say that the Command button recognizes a mouse-click event. Once an event is activated, however, the programmer must still write a procedure to do something in response to the event. This is done using Visual C++'s language element. Figure 7.3 illustrates the interaction between an event and program code.

As illustrated in Figure 7.3, an event, such as clicking the mouse on a Command button, sets in motion a sequence of occurrences. If code has been written for the event, the code is executed, otherwise the event is ignored. This is, of course, the essence of graphical user interfaces and event-driven applications—the selection of which code is executed

FIGURE 7.3

An event "triggers" the initiation of a procedure

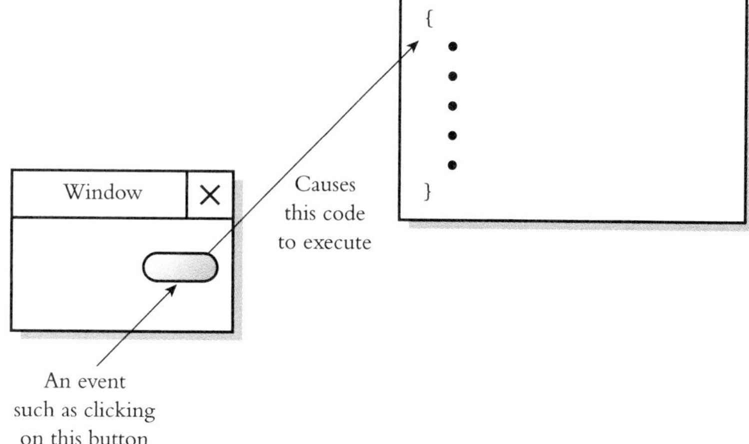

depends on what events occur, which ultimately depends on what the user does. The code, however, must still be written by the programmer.

With these basics in mind, it is now time to create our first Visual C++ Windows-based application. For this we create an application that uses only a single object, a dialog itself. In the next section we add other objects and code to create a more complete Windows-based application.

Dialog-based Applications

Although a full-featured Windows-based application can be developed using code only, you would need extensive and advanced knowledge of the Microsoft Foundation Class (MFC) library to produce such a program. Fortunately, even advanced programmers no longer create applications using only code. This is because Visual C++ provides a number of features that permit rapid development of the GUI required for a Windows-based program. To use these features, launch Visual C++ and make sure that you have the IDE shown in Figure 7.4 on your screen.

Once you have the IDE active, creating a Visual C++ Windows-based application requires the following three steps:

1. Create the graphical user interface.
2. Set the properties of each object on the interface.
3. Write the code.

PROGRAMMER'S NOTES

Dialogs and Controls

When designing an application, a **dialog** is a container upon which other controls are placed. When an application is executed, the dialog becomes a dialog box. It can either be contained within the client area of an SDI or MDI window or be displayed by itself as a stand-alone window. The acronym SDI stands for Single Document Interface, which means that only one main window at a time can be displayed by an application. SDI applications can have multiple windows, but only one window at a time can be viewed by a user. The acronym MDI refers to Multiple Document Interface, which means the application consists of a single "parent" or main window that can contain multiple "child" or internal windows. For example, the Notepad application supplied with the Windows operating system is an SDI application, whereas Excel and Access are both MDI applications. A stand-alone dialog is essentially an SDI application without a main window surrounding the dialog.

A **control** is an object that can be placed on a dialog and has its own set of recognized properties, methods, and events. Controls are used to receive user input, display output, and trigger event procedures. Formally, a control is considered as a child window.

To begin creating the GUI (step 1) choose the `File` menu from the Menu bar shown in Figure 7.4, which will bring up the `File` submenu illustrated in Figure 7.5. Then, to bring up the New dialog box shown in Figure 7.6, select the `New` option.

To continue the process of creating a GUI that makes use of precoded graphical elements and provides a skeleton program structure into which we can add visual elements and code, select the `MFC AppWizard (exe)` project type. When you have completed this part of the process you will have a fully functioning skeleton program, referred to as an **application framework,** that can then be modified to meet your specific requirements. Selecting the `MFC AppWizard (exe)` project type will bring up the AppWizard window

FIGURE 7.4

Visual Studio's IDE

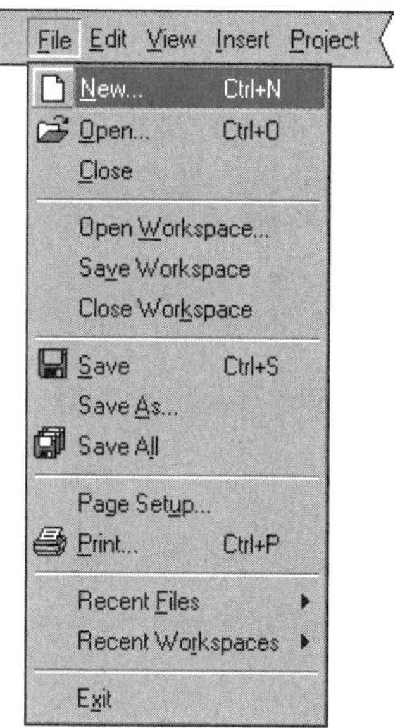

FIGURE 7.5

The File submenu

shown in Figure 7.7. The AppWizard is an application program that will construct a working Windows program.

Once you have the window shown in Figure 7.7 displayed on your screen, select a `Dialog based` type of application. This application type will produce a dialog like the one shown in the client area of Figure 7.1, without the surrounding main window. For most applications this initial dialog is more than sufficient. In Section 10.6, we will see how to create both SDI and MDI applications. However, at this stage we cannot use these other two types because we do not yet have the necessary background to add in visual

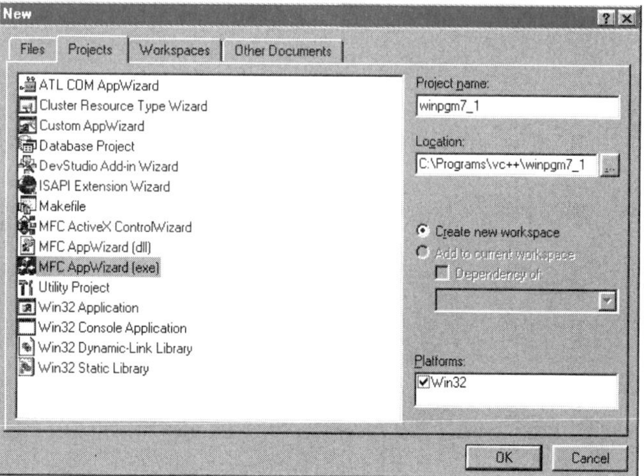

FIGURE 7.6

The New dialog box

FIGURE 7.7

The first AppWizard window

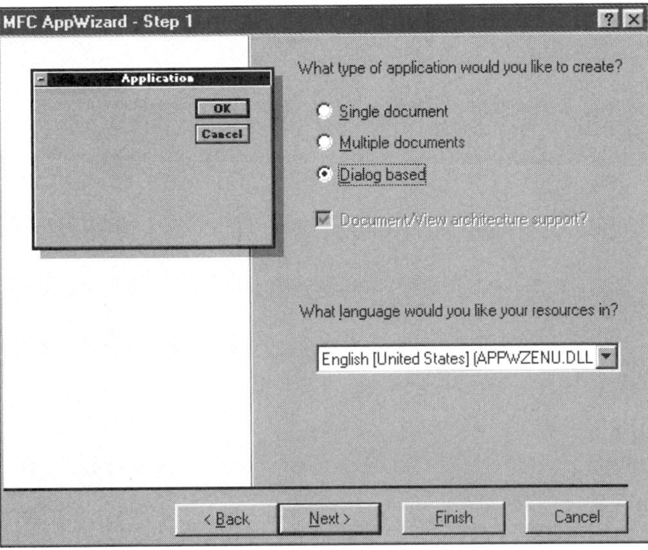

elements within the application's client area. So if you inadvertently find yourself in either an SDI or MDI application type, simply press either the `<Back` or `Cancel` button on the next screen that appears. Once you have selected a `Dialog based` type, press either the `Next>` or `Finish` button. Pressing the `Finish` button will jump you to the end of the AppWizard process (see Figure 7.11), whereas pressing the `Next>` button will display the window shown in Figure 7.8.

FIGURE 7.8

The second AppWizard window

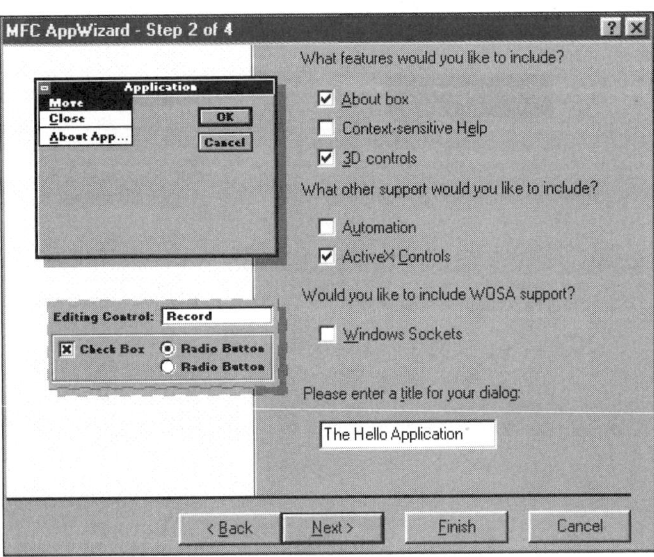

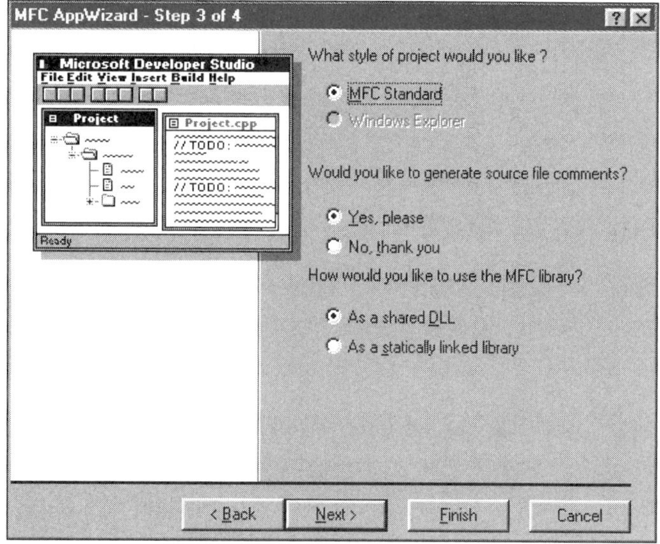

FIGURE 7.9

The third AppWizard window

When the window shown in Figure 7.8 is displayed, accept all of the checked defaults and enter a title for the dialog. As shown in the figure, the title we have entered is `The Hello Application`. Pressing the `Next>` button (again, you can press the `Finish` button to jump over all intervening steps) will produce the window shown in Figure 7.9. For this window, accept all of the defaults, and then press the `Next>` button. Doing so will cause the window shown in Figure 7.10 to appear.

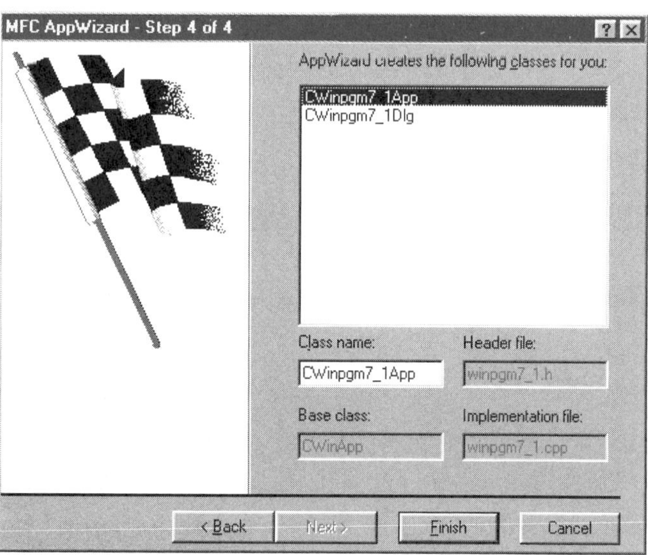

FIGURE 7.10

The fourth AppWizard window

The interesting information to note in Figure 7.10 is that AppWizard is now set to create the two classes listed in the top List box. Note that the Base class name for the highlighted class is CWinApp, which is a class that is provided by MFC. If you click on the second class listed, you would see that its Base class is CDialog, which is also an MFC class name. What a Base class is, and the significance of the CDialog and CWinApp classes, are topics presented in Part 2 of this text. Finally, note that a Header file and Implementation file, named winpgm7_1.h and winpgm7_1.cpp, respectively, are now present. The names of these two files are automatically derived from the selected project name (see Figure 7.6). Once you have reviewed the fourth AppWizard window, press the `Finish` button. Doing so will bring up the New Project Information dialog shown in Figure 7.11. Accept this dialog by pressing either the `OK` button or `Enter` key. At this stage the window shown in Figure 7.12 will be displayed.

What we have asked AppWizard to produce is a skeleton Dialog application. This type of application consists of a Dialog box, which is reflected in Figure 7.12. Notice that in this figure the IDE's Editing Area now contains the Visual C++ resource editor, and the resource displayed within the editor's work area is a Dialog box, which is a visual element. Just as the text editor is used for editing C++ source code, the resource editor is used to edit all visual elements. Also note the Test Switch, which is the first icon within the Dialog toolbar. If this toolbar is not visible on your screen either right-click the

FIGURE 7.11

The New project information dialog

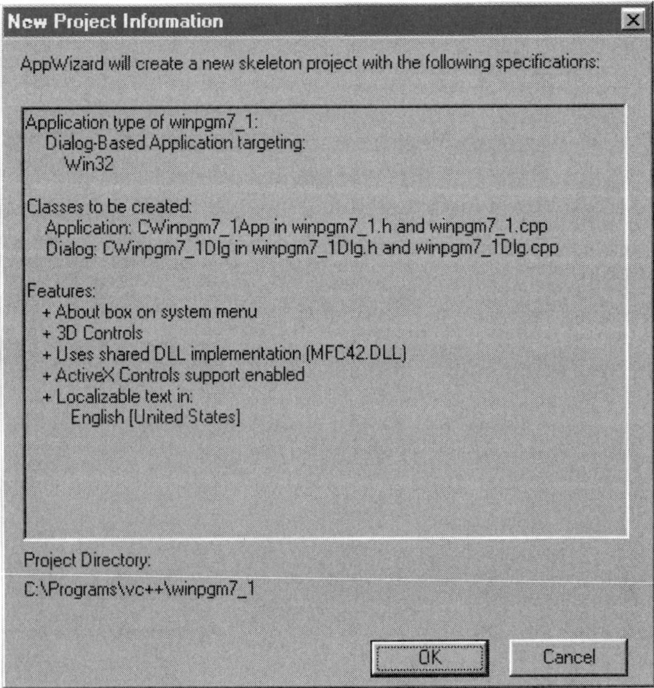

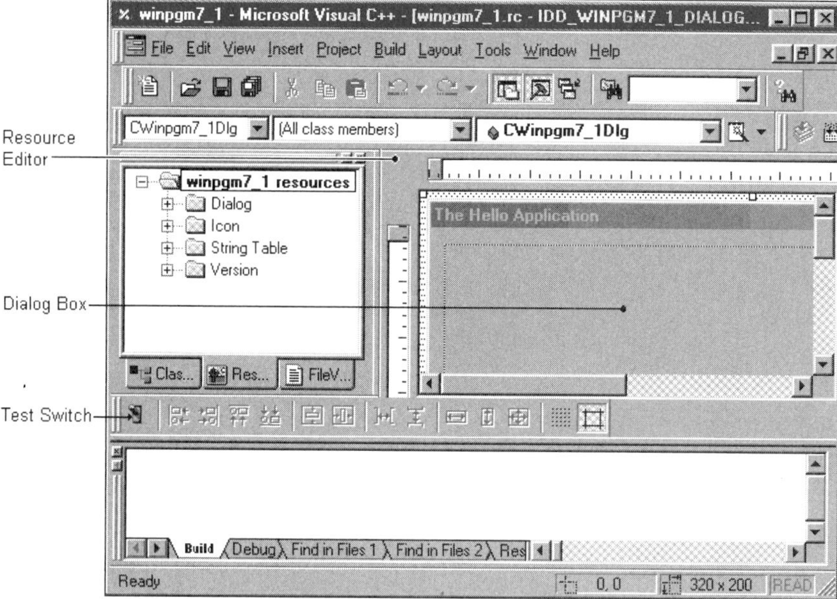

FIGURE 7.12

The IDE window containing a Dialog resource

mouse on one of the other toolbars and select the Dialog toolbar, or select it from the Toolbars tab within the `Tools` menu `Customize` option. We will use this Test Switch shortly to see how the currently edited resource, which in this case is a dialog, looks when the program containing it is executed.

The dialog currently in the resource editor is the one created for us by AppWizard, and is the one that will be initially displayed when our application is compiled and executed. To see the name of this dialog, first make sure that the Resource view tab is activated in the Workspace window. Then, expand the Dialog folder in the hierarchy tree, as shown in Figure 7.13. As seen in this figure, the name of the dialog resource supplied by AppWizard for our application is IDD_WINPGM7_1_DIALOG. As you develop your expertise in Visual C++ you will rely more and more on the Workspace window to rapidly move you around within each application. For example, if you inadvertently find yourself in unfamiliar areas of the current program, you can always get back to the main dialog shown in Figure 7.13 by double-clicking on its icon within the Workspace window's ResourceView hierarchy tree.

We can now place various controls on the dialog shown in Figures 7.12 and 7.13 to produce the interface that we want our users to see when the program is executed. When the program is run, this dialog becomes a window and the controls that we placed on it become the visual controls that are used to input data, display output, and activate events.

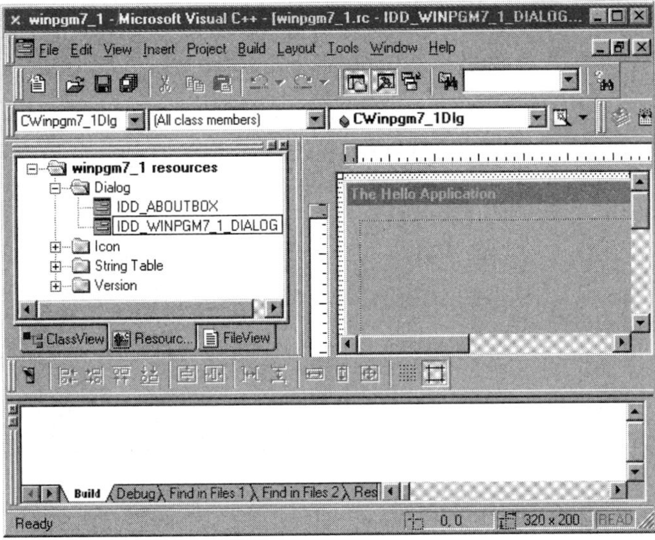

FIGURE 7.13

The expanded Dialog folder tree

The controls that can be placed on the dialog are contained within the toolbox previously shown in Figure 7.2.

To better view the dialog within the Resource editor, select the `View` menu's `Full Screen` option, as illustrated in Figure 7.14. This will produce the full screen display shown in Figure 7.15.

When the resource editor is in full screen view, both the complete dialog and the toolbox become visible. In Section 7.3 we see how to use the toolbox to add additional controls into the dialog. For now, however, there are three important points you need to know. First, whenever you find yourself in full screen editing mode (either with the source code or Resource editor), you can always return to the IDE window by either

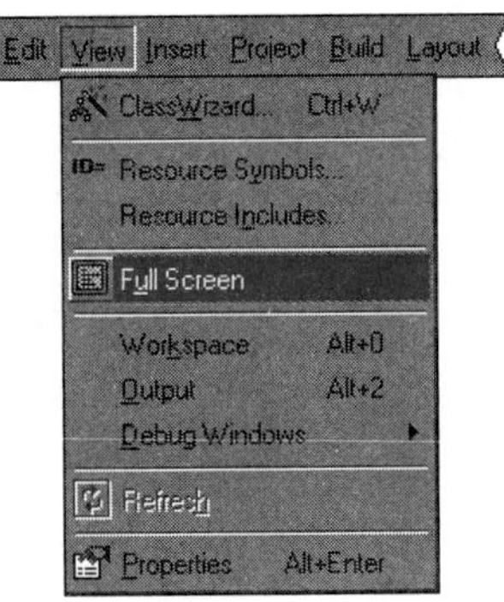

FIGURE 7.14

Selecting `Full Screen` view

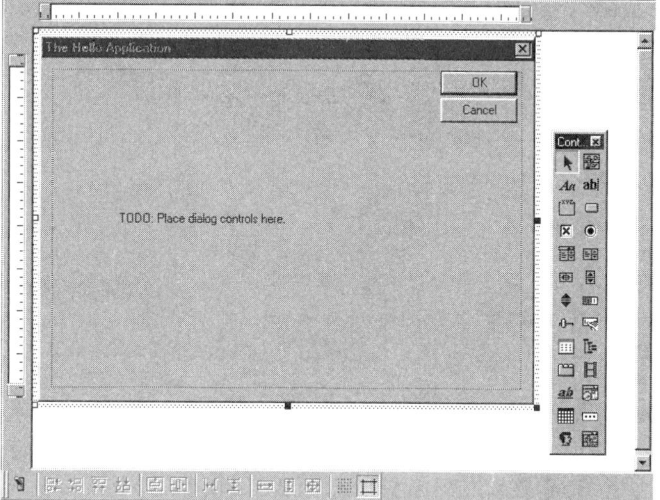

FIGURE 7.15

The resource editor in full screen view

pressing the ESC key or activating the Menu bar's View option using the keyboard accelerator key sequence Alt + V, and then selecting the Full Screen option (that is, the Menu bar is available in full screen mode and can be activated using the keyboard keys, and the Full Screen option is really a toggle that permits you to switch back and forth from IDE to Full screen mode). Second, notice that the Dialog toolbar is visible at the bottom of the figure. This toolbar's Test Switch can be pressed at any time to see how the current resource will appear when the program containing it is executed. Pressing this icon now will produce the display shown in Figure 7.16. Once you have activated the Test Switch, to return to the development window shown in Figure 7.12, either press one of

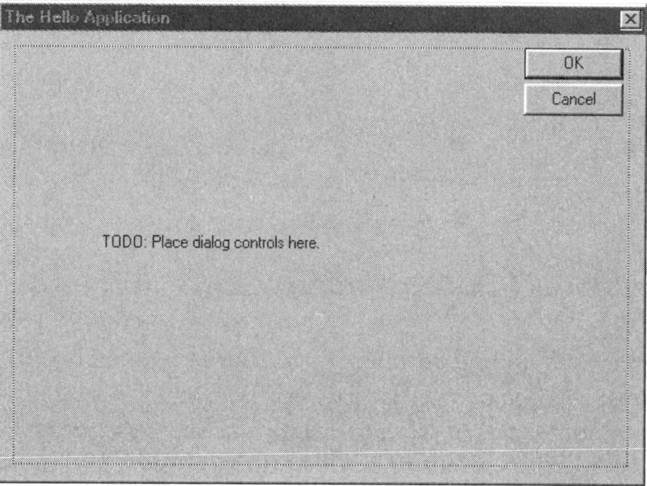

FIGURE 7.16

The Dialog box as it appears at run time

the dialog's displayed buttons, click the Close (X) button, or press the ESC key. Finally, you can always activate the Controls window (i.e., the toolbox) when the Resource editor is in non-Full screen mode by right clicking the mouse on the main menu bar and checking the Controls option from the displayed context menu.

The Resource File

All graphical resources used in an application are stored in individual files, with their names and locations recorded in a single resource file (one resource file per project). This resource file has an extension of rc, and is a text file that can be examined and modified using Visual C++'s text editor. The resource file provides the source code for a separate resource compiler, which compiles the program's graphics and text resources before they are linked with the object-oriented and procedure code into a final executable program.

Defining the visual element of a program in a single resource text file permits a clean separation between the visual part of the GUI and the traditional source code. Doing so makes it possible to use the Test Switch to see what the visual elements of a resource will look like at run time without having to compile and execute the complete application.

The individual resources provided by MFC for use in Visual C++ are listed in Table 7.2, along with the prefixes used to identify them. Note that each prefix consists of the letters ID followed by a third letter, which is used to distinguish between resource types, followed by an underscore. Thus the prefix IDD_, for example, is the prefix used for all Dialog resources, and the prefix IDC_ is the prefix used for all controls placed on a dialog.

TABLE 7.2 Resource type prefixes

Prefix	Resource Type
IDB_	Bitmap
IDC_	Control
IDD_	Dialog
IDR_	Accelerator Table, Menu, and Toolbar
IDS_	String

Setting an Object's Properties

As we have already discovered, all objects have properties. These define the object's position within its defining window, its color, size, and various other attributes. To gain an understanding of these properties, we first examine the most common Visual C++ object, the dialog itself, and then see how push-button properties can be set.

FIGURE 7.17

The View submenu

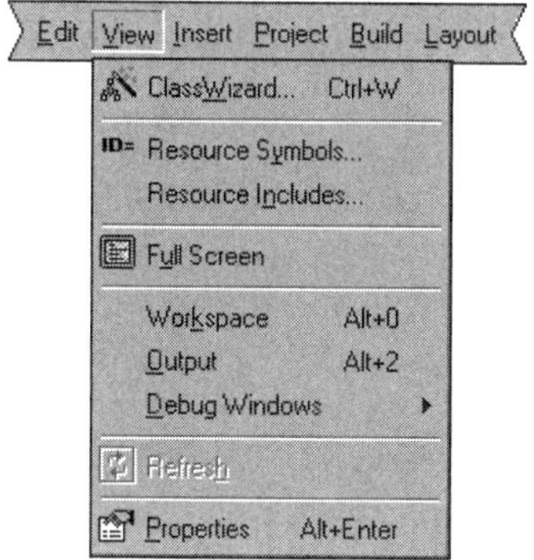

FIGURE 7.18

Using a Context menu

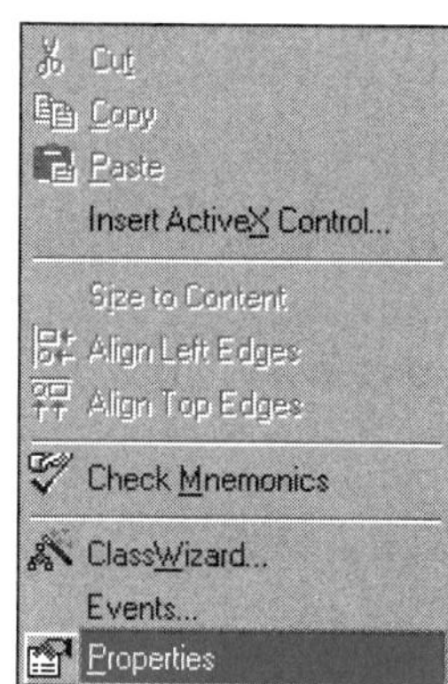

Like any other visual object, a dialog has properties that define how it will appear as a window when the program is run. As an introduction to the ease with which properties are set, we first explore these dialog properties. To do this make sure you have the IDE window shown in Figure 7.13 displayed on your computer.

Now activate the Properties window by selecting the `Properties` option from the `View` menu, which is the last option shown in Figure 7.17. Alternatively, this same option can be obtained by right-clicking the mouse when the dialog shown in Figure 7.15 has been selected. The context-sensitive menu displayed using this approach is shown in Figure 7.18. Using either of these methods, the Properties dialog, shown in Figure 7.19, will be displayed. It is this dialog that is used for setting and viewing an object's properties.

As seen in Figure 7.19, the Properties dialog contains a number of tabs. For now, we will be concerned only with the information contained in the General tab. We will use this tab to modify a control's ID name, Caption, and Font properties. Notice in Figure 7.19 the drop-down List box to the right of the label `ID:`. The ID designation in this List box, which is currently IDD_WINPGM7_1_DIALOG, provides the object's name (identification). Clicking the arrowhead at the right side of this box provides a drop-down list of all available object identifications for this project. Now notice the caption `The Hello Application` in the `Caption` List box. This is the caption we previously entered in step 2 (see Figure 7.8) when the AppWizard was constructing the project.

With the Properties Dialog box shown in Figure 7.19 open, we could now change both the ID and Caption settings for the Dialog box by simply typing in new values. For now, however, we will leave the property value settings as shown in this figure.

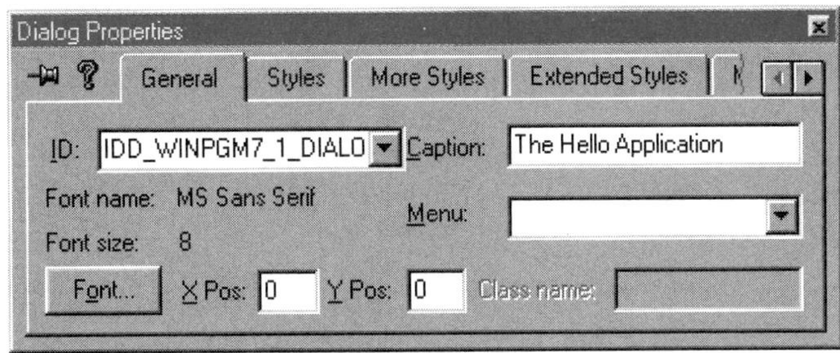

FIGURE 7.19

The Properties dialog

Unlike ID and Caption properties, other properties have a more restricted set of available values. For example, the Font property, which determines the type of font used for an object's displayed text, such as its caption, can be selected only from a pre-defined list of available fonts. Likewise, the BackColor and ForeColor properties, which determine the background color and the color of text displayed in the foreground, can be selected only from a predefined pallet of colors. When one of these properties is selected, either a down-facing arrowhead property button (▼) or an ellipsis (...) property button will appear to the right of the selected setting. Clicking on this button will show you the available settings. A selection is then made by clicking on the desired value. In the case of colors, a palette of available colors is displayed, and clicking on a color sets the numerical code for the chosen color as the property's value. For example, Figure 7.20 shows the dialog that is displayed when the Properties dialog `Font...` Command button (see Figure 7.19) is pressed. Now let's take a look at the individual controls on the dialog.

There is nothing inherently wrong with keeping the default name that Visual C++ provides for each control placed on a dialog. Good programming practice, however, dictates that all control ID names be more descriptive and convey some idea about the use of these controls. The names permissible for all controls are the same used to name other

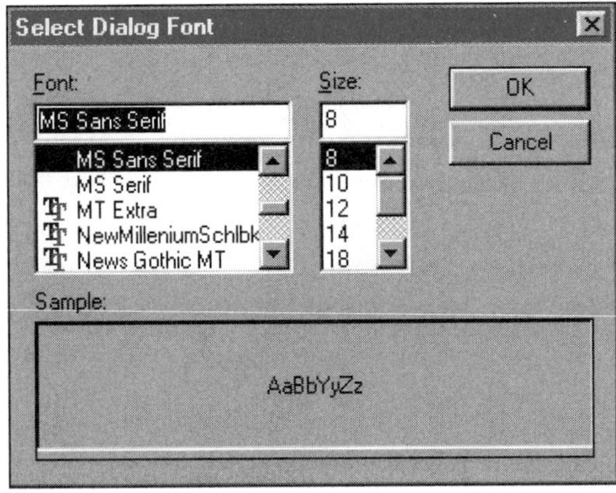

FIGURE 7.20

The Font selection dialog

elements in the Visual C++ programming language, which means that control ID names must be valid C++ identifiers and conform to the following rules for selecting identifiers:

1. The control's ID name must begin with a letter or underscore (_), and may contain only letters, underscores, or digits. It cannot contain any blanks, commas, or special symbols, such as ( ) &, $ # . ! \ ?.
2. A control's ID name cannot be a keyword.
3. The control's ID name cannot consist of more than 255 characters (this is compiler dependent).

Unlike variable names, underscores, (_), are conventionally used to separate control names consisting of multiple words.

By using these rules, we follow the convention that provides each control with a name beginning with the standard three letter prefix to identify the control type (see Table 7.2), followed by a descriptive name for the specific control, followed by a suffix describing the control's type. The standard control suffixes used for all controls are listed in Table 7.3.

Whereas a control's name property is important to the programmer when developing an application, for those controls that have a caption property, it is the control's caption that is important to the user when a program is run. This is because it is the caption that the user sees when the application is executing. For example, as previously shown in Figure 7.16, the caption on the dialog itself is `The Hello Application`, whereas the captions on the two command buttons are `OK` and `Cancel`, respectively. A user will use these captions to refer to these items, and will generally have no knowledge of the control's actual name as it is known by the program.

To change both the name and caption for any control, the procedure is to activate the control's Property dialog, using any of the techniques described in the Programmer's

TABLE 7.3 Standard control object prefixes

Control	Suffix	Example
Check Box	CHECK	IDC_REVERSE_CHECK
Command Button	BUTTON	IDC_MESSAGE_BUTTON
Edit Box	EDIT	IDC_TEMP_EDIT
Group Box	BOX	IDC_STATUS_BOX
Label	LABEL	IDC_TEMP_LABEL
Line	LINE	IDC_BREAK_LINE
Radio Button	RADIO	IDC_STATUS_BUTTON

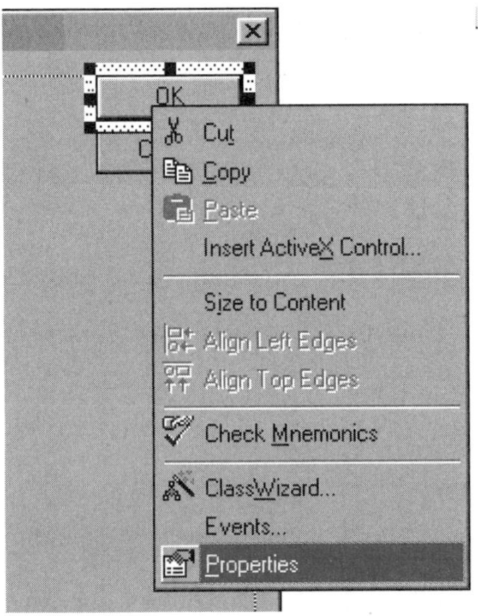

FIGURE 7.21

Selecting the `OK` button's `Properties` option

Notes box (see page 361), and then make the desired changes. For example, to change the ID name and Caption for the current application's two Command buttons (again, see Figure 7.16), first right-click the mouse when it is positioned over the button with the `OK` caption. Doing this will produce the display shown in Figure 7.21. As shown in this figure, select the Properties option, which will cause the `Properties` dialog illustrated in Figure 7.22 to appear.

To change the name and caption properties, simply type in the new values in place of the provided default. For example, Figure 7.23 shows the Properties dialog after we entered both a new ID name and caption. Notice that as you type the caption, it automatically appears on the designated control. If either name or caption is larger than the space available in the List boxes, the characters will scroll as you type them in.

Before we set the properties for the second Command button, one comment is in order concerning the ampersand (`&`) symbol included in the caption shown in Figure 7.23. This symbol should be typed exactly as shown. Its visual effect is to cause the character

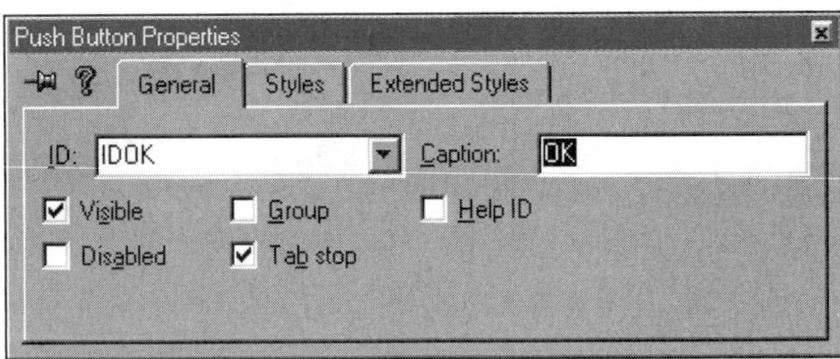

FIGURE 7.22

The `OK` button's Properties dialog

PROGRAMMER'S NOTES

The Properties Dialog

The Properties window is where you set an object's initial properties—the properties that the object will exhibit when the application is first run. These properties can be altered later, using procedural code.

To Activate the Dialog

To activate a particular object's Properties window, make sure the object is visible in the resource editor and select it. Then, either

right click on the object and select the `Properties` option, or

select the `Properties` option from the View menu, or

press the `Alt` and `Enter` keys at the same time.

immediately following it to be underlined. Its operational effect is to create an accelerator key. An **accelerator key,** which is also referred to as a **shortcut key,** is simply a keyboard short cut for a user to initiate an action.[3] When used with a Command button it permits the user to activate the button by simultaneously pressing the Alt key with the underlined letter key, rather than either clicking the mouse or first selecting the Command button and then pressing the Enter key.

Having now changed both the ID name and Caption properties for one of our Command buttons, we rapidly repeat the same procedure for the second button. To do so, right-click the mouse on the second Command button to obtain the context-sensitive menu shown in Figure 7.24. When this menu is displayed, select the Properties option to obtain the Properties dialog shown in Figure 7.25.

FIGURE 7.23

The Properties dialog after the name and caption changes

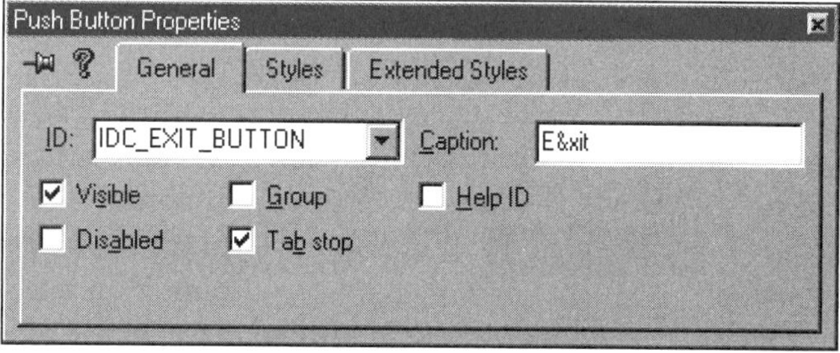

3 If the action can be initiated only with a keystroke sequence, it is referred to as a *hot key* sequence. Additionally, any key sequence that permits a user to make a menu selection is referred to as an *access key* sequence. All of these terms are used rather loosely, frequently as synonyms.

FIGURE 7.24

Selecting the `Cancel` button's `Properties` option

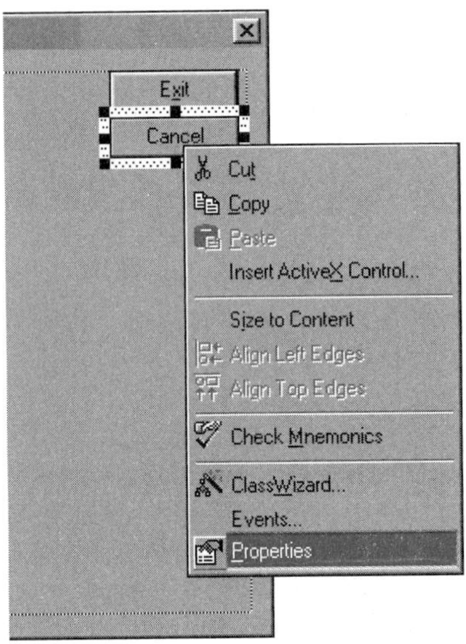

FIGURE 7.25

The `Cancel` button's Properties dialog

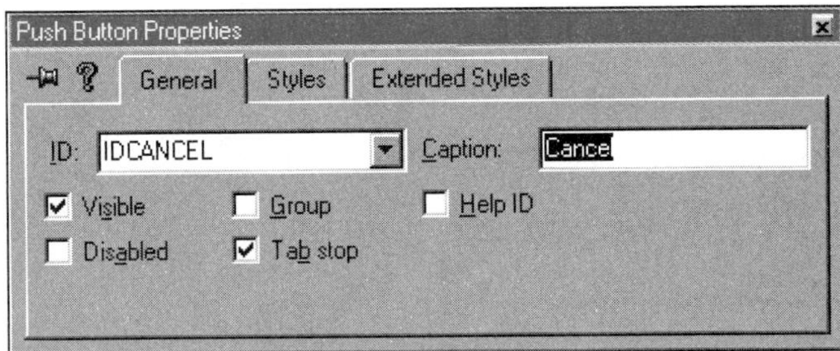

Once you have the window shown in Figure 7.25 displayed, change the name (ID) and caption settings to those shown in Figure 7.26.

In the next section we add program code to the two existing Command buttons. Then, in the following sections we show you how to add more controls to a dialog directly from the toolbox, and how to provide each control with its own set of event-handling code. For now, using the same techniques that you have been using to save all of your console applications, save the project, close the workspace, and exit from Visual C++.

FIGURE 7.26

The Properties dialog after the name and caption changes

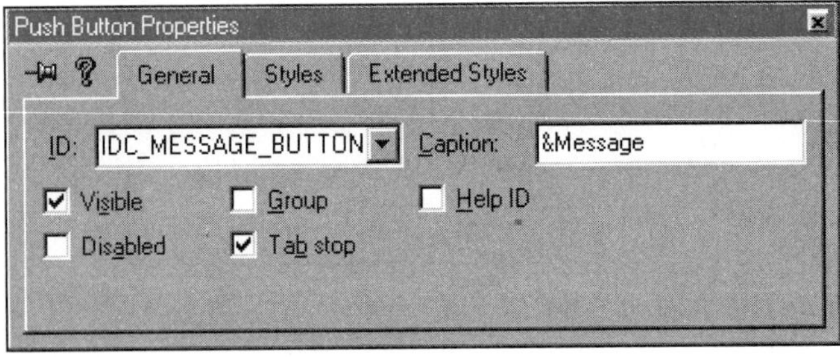

EXERCISES 7.1

1. List the three types of Windows-based applications that can be created in Visual C++.
2. What is the purpose of a GUI and what elements does a user see in a GUI?
3. What does the Visual C++ Controls window provide?
4. Name and describe the use of the four most commonly used toolbox objects.
5. When an application is run, what does a dialog become?
6. What gets executed when an event occurs?
7. a. What are the two windows that should be visible during an application's design?
   b. What are the steps for bringing up each of the windows listed in your answer to Exercise 7a?
8. What is one dialog property that should be changed for every application?
9. List the steps for creating a Visual C++ Dialog-based application.
10. What is the three letter prefix that should be used in every dialog's name?
11. a. Design a Visual C++ application that consists of a single dialog with the caption `Test Dialog`.
    b. Test the GUI you designed in Exercise 11a.

7.2 Adding an Event Handler

In the previous section we completed the first two steps required in constructing a Visual C++ Windows-based application, which are:

1. Create the graphical user interface.
2. Set initial object properties.

Specifically, Figure 7.27 shows how Windows Program 7.1 (winpgm7_1) appears when it is executed. In this section we finish this application by completing the third step required in constructing Windows applications:

3. Add the procedural code.

In a well-designed Visual C++ application, the procedural code contained within an individual function consists of a set of instructions necessary to complete a well-defined task. The specific functions that are executed when an event occurs, such as the clicking

FIGURE 7.27

Windows Program 7.1 GUI at run time

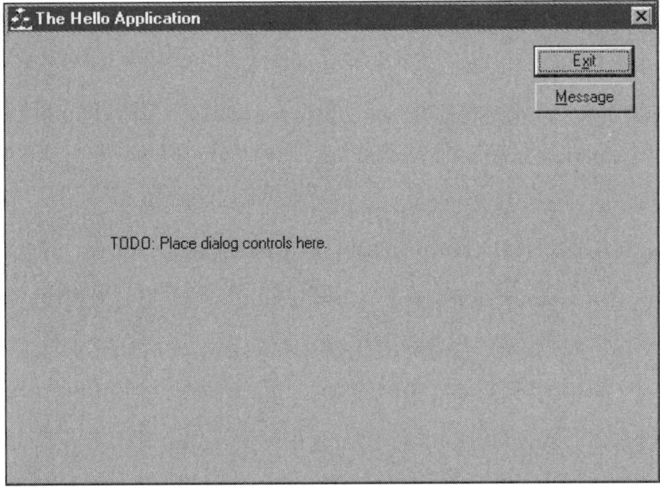

of a Command button, are referred to as **event handlers.** In this section we are concerned only with writing this specific type of function. However, because all C++ functions must adhere to the standard format presented in the last chapter, our work will actually be more concerned with locating the exact spots within an application to insert the required code.

It is worthwhile to understand that each control can have a number of event handlers, but that there can only be one event handler for each unique event. For example, the two events associated with a Command button are the click and double-click events. Thus, we could write one event handler that will be executed when a user clicks on a specific Command button and another event handler that will be executed when the user double-clicks the same button. Notice that each of these handlers are button specific; it is a function's header line that will designate both the control and the event for which the event handler is executed. Figure 7.28 illustrates the general format used for all event handlers. Except for the class name and double colons separating the class name from the

FIGURE 7.28

The structure of an event handler

```
Return-type Class-name::Function-name(parameter list) // function header line
{  // start of function body

   // procedural statements in here

}  // end of function body
```

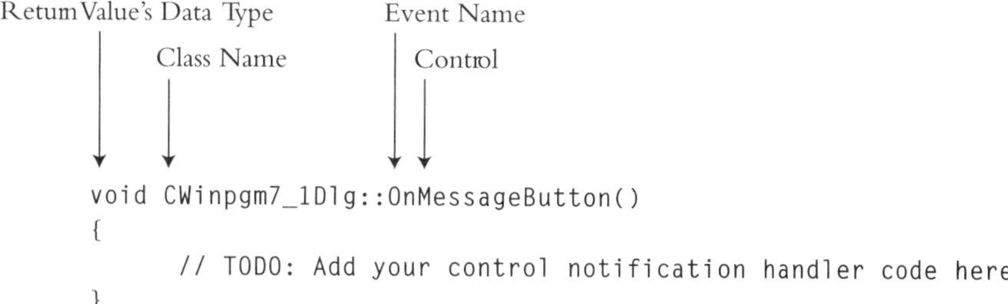

FIGURE 7.29

An `On` click event handler

function's name, event handlers use the same format as all C++ functions. For now, do not worry about the class name. This name is always provided to you by Visual C++, and will make more sense after you have completed Chapters 8 through 11.

As a specific example of an event handler, consider Figure 7.29, which illustrates the function provided by Visual C++ for the click event associated with the IDC_MESSAGE_BUTTON button shown in Figure 7.27 (the button with the `Message` caption). First notice that this event handler does follow the form shown in Figure 7.28, and except for the class name and the double colons, `::`, this function structure should look very familiar to you. Here, the function's name is `OnMessageButton()`.

Because the parentheses in the header line shown in Figure 7.29 are empty, this particular function expects no arguments. Also, due to the leading keyword `void`, no value will be returned from the function. The `On` keyword at the start of the function's name immediately after the double colons, `::`, designates the event that will trigger this function, where `On` represents the event "On button clicked." If this function were meant to handle the double-click event, the words `OnDoubleclicked` would appear in place of the word `On`. The words `MessageButton` in the header line designates the control for which this event is associated. Finally, notice that the braces defining the function's body and a comment are also present. This complete structure is automatically provided by Visual C++ upon request of the programmer. Once this structure has been provided, it is the programmer's responsibility to replace the comment with appropriate code. It is important to understand that you do not have to write event handler code for every possible event. *If an event handler does not exist, or no code is inserted into the skeleton form provided by Visual C++ for a specific event handler, no action will take place when a user triggers the event.* Thus, you write code only for those specific events for which you want the application to respond.

Before activating the Code window, we need to decide what Visual C++ statements will be included in the body of our event procedure. First we look at ways to display an output message.

The `MessageBox()` Function

Visual C++ provides more than 1,000 different class methods and intrinsic functions that can be used in constructing event handlers. The first function we use here is the `MessageBox()` function. The purpose of this function is to display a programmer-defined message and title, plus combinations of predefined icons and push buttons. For example, the boxes illustrated in Figure 7.30 were all created using the MessageBox function. The general syntax for a MessageBox function call is:

```
MessageBox("message", "title", type);
```

Although numerous types of predefined message boxes are available, for now we limit ourselves to the four types listed in Table 7.4.

For example, the function call

```
MessageBox("Hello World!", "Sample", MB_ICONEXCLAMATION);
```

produced the message box shown in Figure 7.30a. Notice that the message `Hello World!` is included within the box, and the title at the top of the box is `Sample`. The exclamation icon included within the box is produced by the **MB_ICONEXCLAMATION** type used in the statement (MB_ICONEXCLAMATION is a named constant provided by Visual C++). The icons shown in Figures 7.30b through 7.30d were produced using the **MB_ICONQUESTION, MB_ICONINFORMATION,** and **MB_ICONSTOP** types, respectively. That is, Figure 7.30b was produced by the function call

```
MessageBox("Hello World!", "Sample", MB_ICONQUESTION);
```

The message boxes shown in Figure 7.30 are all special cases of a modal dialog box that requires the user to supply additional information to complete a task. In the case of the message boxes illustrated in Figure 7.30, the required additional information is simply that the user must either click the `OK` box or push the Enter key to permit the application to continue.

TABLE 7.4 MessageBox types

Type	Icon	Example
MB_ICONEXCLAMATION	Exclamation Point	Figure 7.30a
MB_ICONQUESTION	Question Mark	Figure 7.30b
MB_ICONINFORMATION	The Letter I	Figure 7.30c
MB_ICONSTOP	The Letter X	Figure 7.30d

(a) MB_ICONEXCLAMATION

(b) MB_ICONQUESTION

(c) MB_ICONINFORMATION

(d) MB_ICONSTOP

FIGURE 7.30

Message Boxes

As always, blank spaces may be freely inserted between arguments in the function call to improve its appearance. For example, both of the following calls produce the same result

```
MessageBox ("Hello World!","Sample",MB_ICONEXCLAMATION);
MessageBox ("Hello World!", "Sample",   MB_ICONEXCLAMATION);
```

Just be sure to capitalize the M and B in MessageBox and the icon type in the named constant, or you will get a compiler error message.

Now let's include a MessageBox into the event handler for the Message push-button previously shown in Figure 7.27. When we are done, the completed procedure will be:

```
void CWinpgm7_1Dlg::OnMessageButton()
{
  MessageBox("Hello World", "Sample", MB_ICONEXCLAMATION);
}
```

To enter this code, first make sure that you have the workspace containing Windows Program 7.1 open and that either the IDE looks like that shown in Figure 7.31, or that the resource dialog shown in the figure is also on your screen (in either Full or non-Full

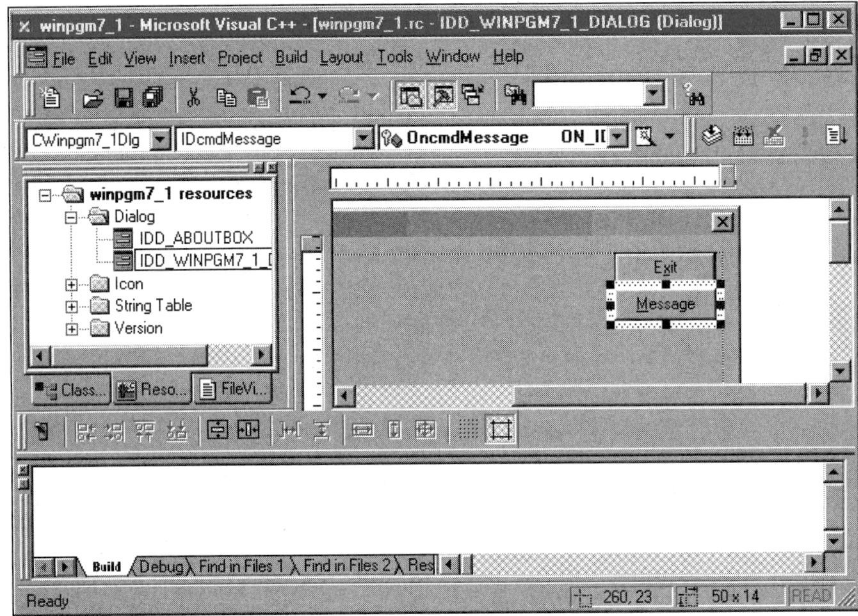

FIGURE 7.31

Windows Program 7.1's IDE

screen mode). Then, right click on the `Message` push-button to produce the context menu shown in Figure 7.32.

From the menu shown in Figure 7.32, select the `Events...` option, which will cause the New Message and Event Handler Dialog shown in Figure 7.33 to be displayed. When this dialog appears, make sure that the BN_CLICKED event is highlighted in the left-

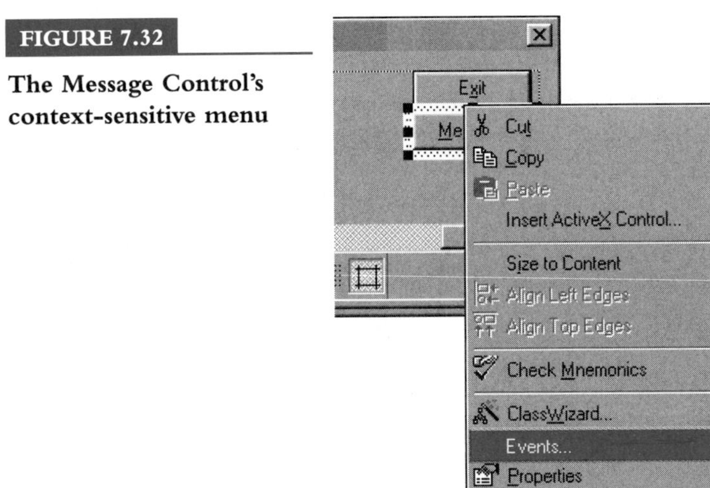

FIGURE 7.32

The Message Control's context-sensitive menu

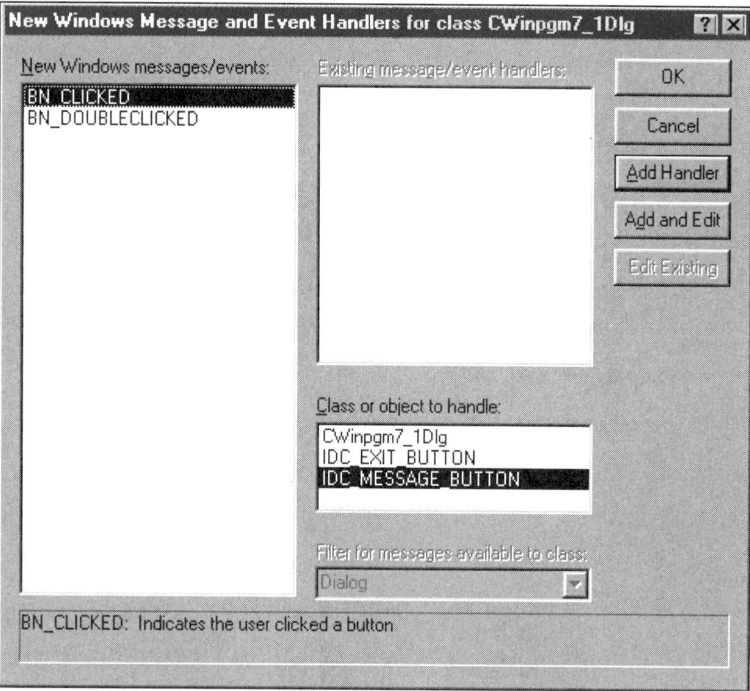

FIGURE 7.33

The New Message and Event Handler dialog

most List box and that the IDC_MESSAGE_BUTTON object is also highlighted in the lower right List box. Then press either the `Add Handler` or the `Add and Edit` push buttons. Either action will cause the Add Member Function dialog, shown in Figure 7.34 to appear.

When the Add Member Function dialog is displayed, check that it looks like the one shown in Figure 7.34, where the function being added is named `OnMessageButton`. The `Message` type and `Object` identification, listed at the bottom of the dialog, tell us that this function will respond to the BN_CLICKED message for the control object named IDC_MESSAGE_BUTTON. When you have verified this information, press the `OK` button. Doing so will create an event handler named `OnMessageButton()` that will be called whenever the primary mouse button is clicked on your `Message` Command button.

What happens next depends on the push button you previously selected for the dialog shown in Figure 7.33. If you pressed the `Add Handler` button, the dialog shown in Figure 7.35 is displayed. Notice that this is the same dialog shown in Figure 7.33, except

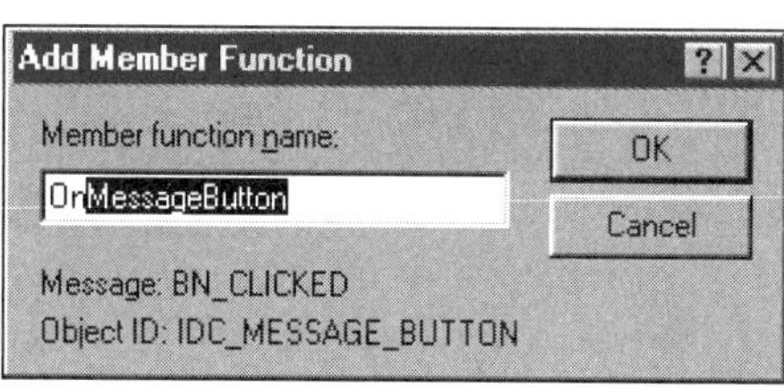

FIGURE 7.34

The Add Member Function dialog

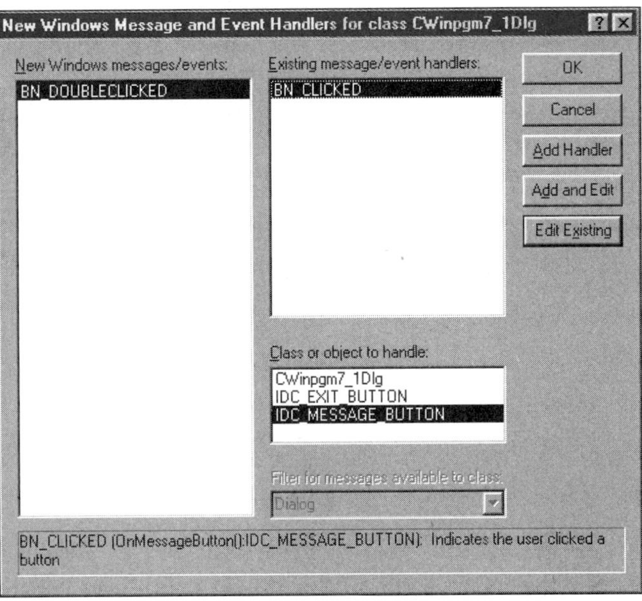

FIGURE 7.35

The Message and Event Handler dialog with an existing event handler

that the BN_CLICKED message has been moved from the New to the Existing List box. If this dialog is displayed, press the `Edit Existing` push button, which will bring up the IDE shown in Figure 7.36. The IDE in this figure is, however, automatically displayed if you had selected the `Add and Edit` push button in the dialog previously shown in Figure 7.33.

FIGURE 7.36

The IDE with the Code window in the Editing Area

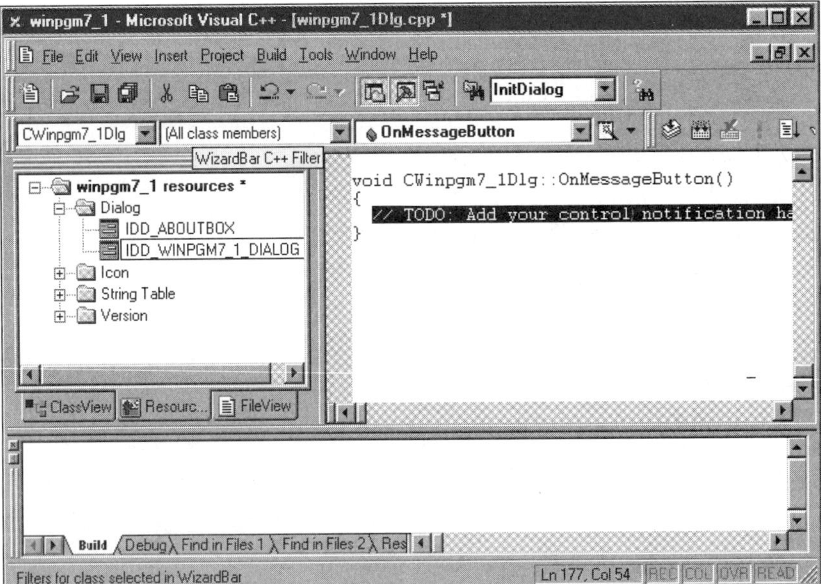

PROGRAMMER'S NOTES

Full Screen Mode

To place the currently active Text editor or Resource editor into Full Screen mode use one of the following procedures:

1. Select the Full Screen option from the View menu, or
2. Use the accessor keyboard key combination `Alt + V/ u`

To contract an existing Full Screen presentation into the IDE's Editing Area

1. Press the `Esc` key, or
2. Use the accessor keyboard key combination `Alt + V/ u`

When you have the Code window shown in Figure 7.36 visible, delete the highlighted line and enter the statement

```
MessageBox("Hello World", "Sample", MB_ICONEXCLAMATION);
```

Once this is done, the Code window should look like that shown in Figure 7.37. Notice that we have indented the single Visual C++ statement using two spaces. Although this is not required, as we have stressed throughout the text, indentation is a sign of good

FIGURE 7.37

The completed event handler

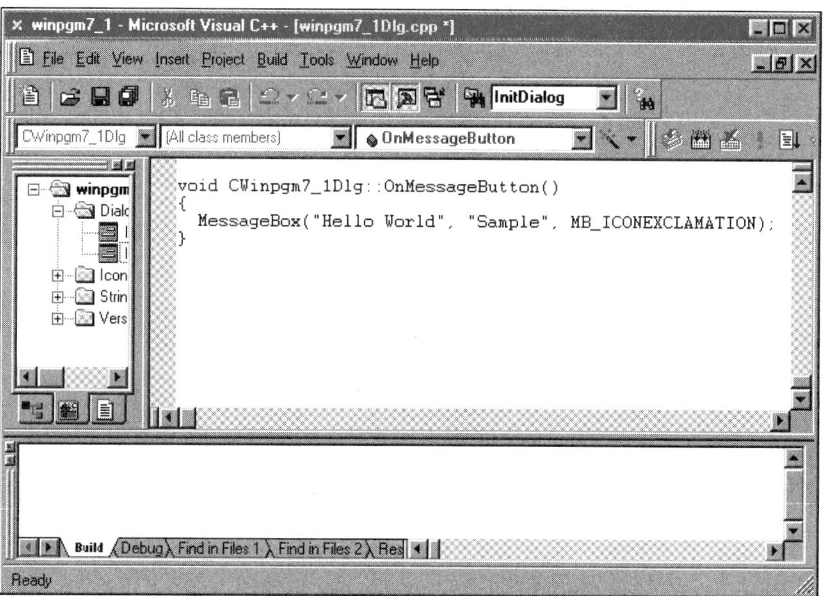

FIGURE 7.38

Initial run-time application window

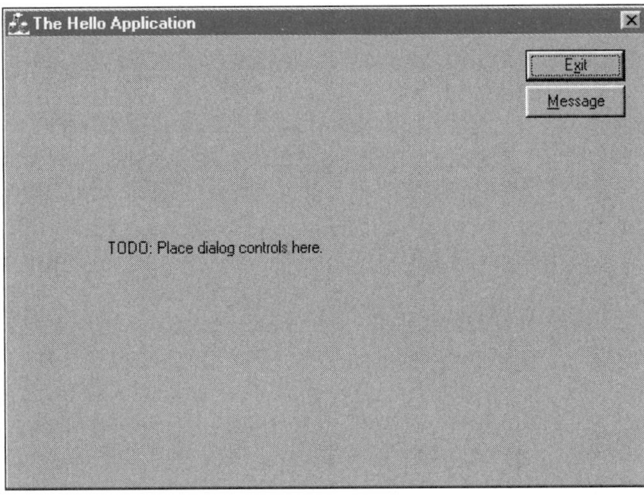

programming practice. Here it permits the statement within the event handler to be easily identified. You should also be aware that the Code window could have been expanded into Full Screen mode and contracted in the same manner as the Resource window.

Our event handler is now complete. When you run the program, using the Build menu in the same manner as you did for console applications, the application should appear as shown in Figure 7.38. Clicking the `Message` push button will create the window shown in Figure 7.39. To remove the message box either press the Escape (`Esc`) or Enter key, or click the `OK` button.

FIGURE 7.39

Effect of the mouse click event

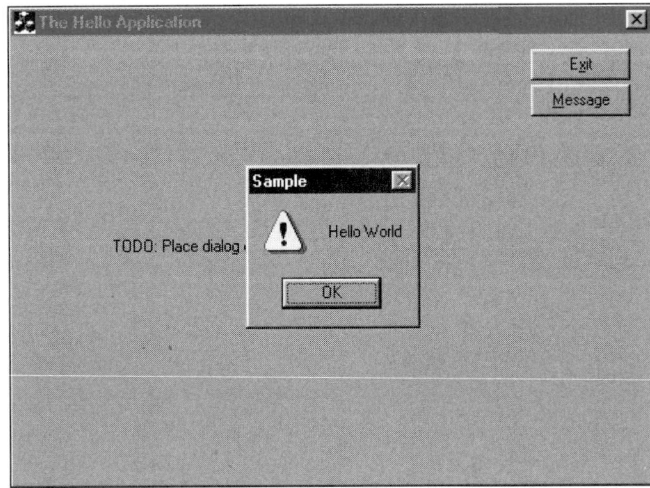

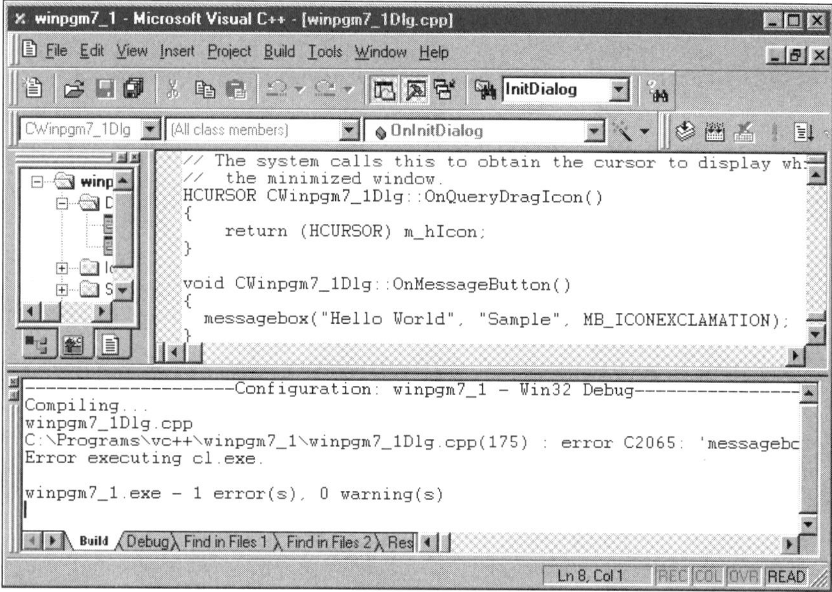

FIGURE 7.40

Notification of an error

Correcting Errors If you incorrectly typed the message box statement in your procedure, the code box with this procedure will automatically be displayed with the highlight placed on the incorrect statement when the program is compiled. For example, if you inadvertently entered **MessageBox** as `messagebox`, the window shown in Figure 7.40 will appear when you attempt to compile and run the program. By double clicking on the line containing the error code in the Output window, the invalid line of code is both highlighted and pointed to by an arrow in the left margin of the Code window, as shown in Figure 7.41. Once the error is understood and the correction is made you can recompile and execute the program.

Completing the Application

Two tasks remain to complete our application. These are to delete the default label placed on the dialog by the AppWizard, and add an event handler to the Exit button.

Deleting any control from a dialog is extremely simple. This is done by selecting the control and then

- pressing the `Del` key, or
- pressing the `Ctrl+X` keys, or
- activating the control's context-sensitive menu and selecting the `Cut` option.

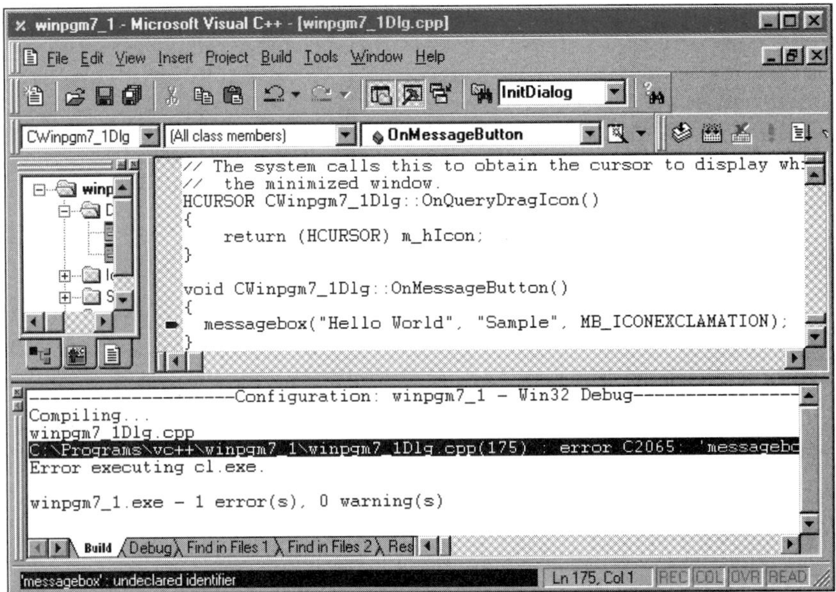

FIGURE 7.41

Identification of the invalid statement and its procedure

Figure 7.42 shows the context-sensitive menu activated for the label that we want to delete. Selecting the `Cut` option from this menu deletes the label.

We now present two different event handlers that can be used for the `Exit` button Click event. This is done to introduce you to a new set of C++ functions. The simplest of these two event handlers is

```
void CWinpgm7_1Dlg::OnExitButton()
{

    MessageBeep(0xFFFFFFFF);
    SendMessage(WM_CLOSE);
  }
```

In reviewing this code, pay attention to the two statements within the function's body because the function's header will automatically be provided by Visual C++. The first statement

```
MessageBeep(0xFFFFFFFF);
```

calls Visual C++'s `MessageBeep()` function, which tells the computer to issue a beep through its internal speaker. Other sounds that can be activated by the `MessageBeep()`

PROGRAMMER'S NOTES

Code Editor Options

The text editor provided with Visual C++ 6.0 provides a number of options that are very useful when you are entering procedural code. All of these options can be accessed by first selecting the `Options...` item from the `Tools` menu.

Color Coded Instructions

The Visual C++ editor displays procedural code in a variety of user-selected colors. By default, the following color selections are used:

Keywords—Blue

Comments—Green

Other Text—Black

These default colors can be changed from within the Options dialog's Format tab (remember to first select the `Options...` item from the Tools menu). The Format tab is the last tab to the right, so you may have to scroll to see this tab. Once the Format tab is active, use the `Colors List` box to first select the item whose color you want to change, such as Keyword or Comment, and then use the drop-down List boxes to set the desired foreground and background colors.

Tab Settings

Change the default tab setting of 4 spaces and Auto indent features from within the Option dialog's Tabs tab.

Miscellaneous Options

Change the editor's Window settings, Save options, and Statement completion options using the Option dialog's Editor tab.

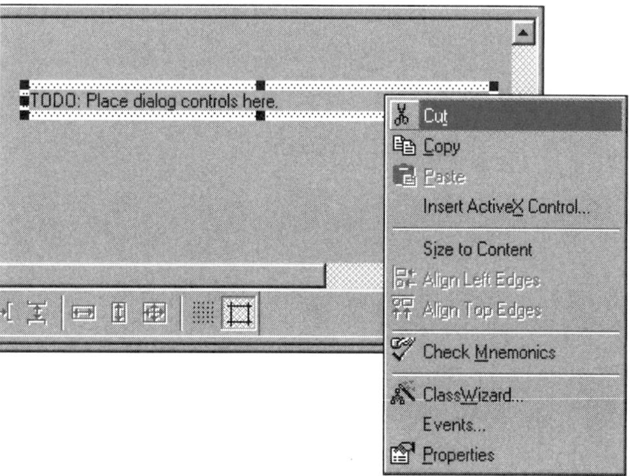

FIGURE 7.42

Deleting the dialog's Default label

TABLE 7.5 Acceptable `MessageBeep()` arguments

Argument	Sound
0xFFFFFFFF	Standard beep using the computer's speaker
MB_ICONASTERISK	SystemAsterisk
MB_ICONEXCLAMATION	SystemExclamation
MB_ICONHAND	SystemHand
MB_ICONQUESTION	SystemQuestion
MB_OK	SystemDefault

function are listed in Table 7.5. The actual sound produced by each of the named constant arguments depends on the settings for each sound type that are set for your system.[4] Each of these sounds, except for the first argument listed, also requires that your system have an installed sound card, whereas the first argument requires that you do not have a sound card. The reason for this is that if a sound card is installed, the computer's speaker will have been deactivated, and the first argument will have no effect.

The event handler's second statement

```
SendMessage(WM_CLOSE);
```

sends a message to the dialog to perform all necessary shutdown operations and then stop program execution.

To include this event handler into the application, you would perform the same set of steps that we used for the `Message` button. That is, right click on the `Exit` button to display this control's context-sensitive menu, as shown in Figure 7.43, and select the

FIGURE 7.43

The Exit Control's context-sensitive menu

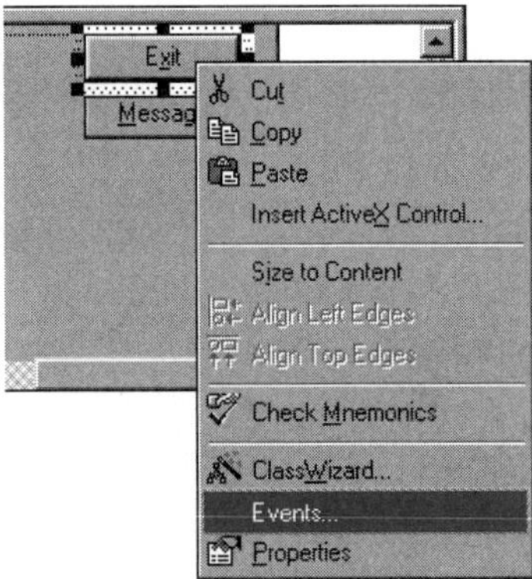

4 The sound settings can be accessed and modified using the Control Panel option of the Settings menu, which is activated using Windows' Start button.

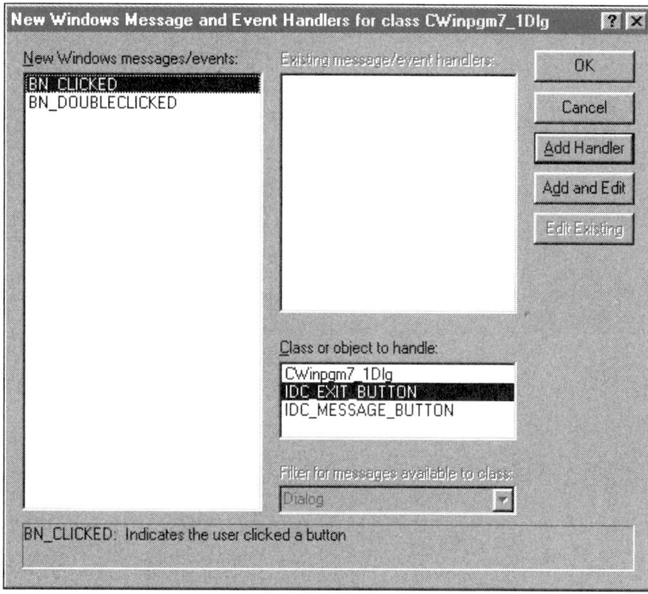

FIGURE 7.44

The New Message and Event Handler dialog

`Events...` option. This will cause the New Message and Event Handler dialog, shown in Figure 7.44, to be displayed.

When the dialog shown in Figure 7.44 appears, make sure that the BN_CLICKED event is highlighted in the leftmost List box and that the IDD_EXIT_BUTTON object is also highlighted in the lower right List box. Then press the `Add and Edit` push button. Doing this will cause the Add Member Function dialog, shown in Figure 7.45, to appear.

When the Add Member Function dialog is displayed, check that it contains the information displayed in Figure 7.45. When you have verified this information, press the `OK` button. Doing so will create an event handler named IDD_EXIT_BUTTON that will be called whenever the primary mouse button is clicked on our `Exit` command button, and cause the IDE shown in Figure 7.46 to be displayed. When you have this screen on your monitor, delete the line beginning with `// TODO:` and type in the two lines of code:

```
MessageBeep(0xFFFFFFFF);
SendMessage(WM_CLOSE);
```

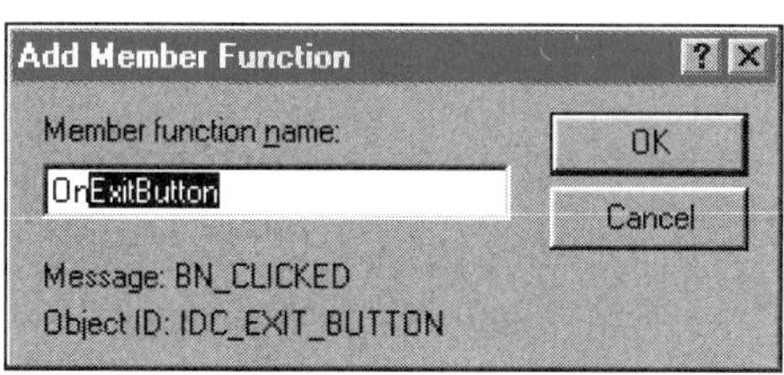

FIGURE 7.45

The Add Member Function dialog

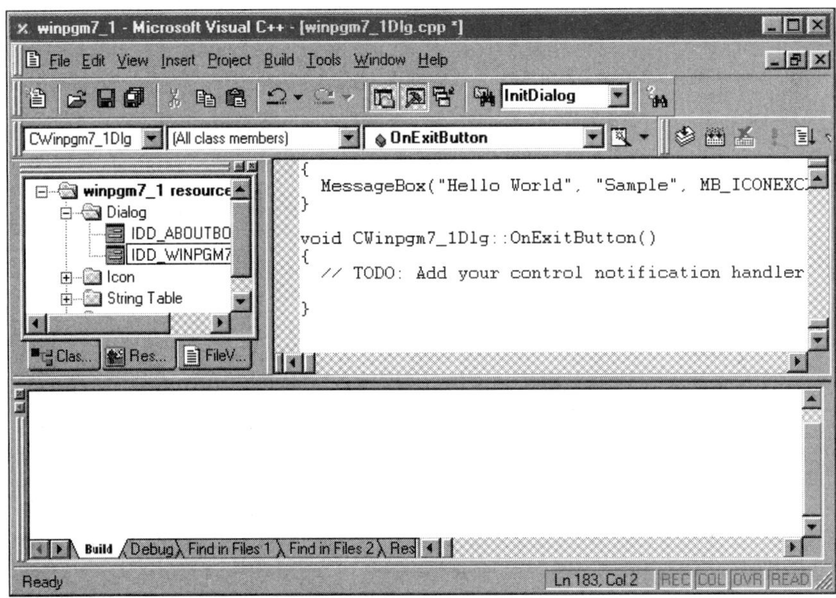

FIGURE 7.46

The Exit button's event handler

At this point you can execute the application and see that pressing the `Exit` button does indeed close down the application. Before continuing, however, we present a slightly more detailed event handler that provides the user with a chance to verify the termination choice before the application is closed. This version of the event handler is instructive because it shows how to provide a message box with additional buttons and how to respond to the user's actual selection.

An Alternative Exit Event Handler[5] Besides the default single button provided by the `MessageBox()` function, the actual number, types, and default button can be explicitly set when the function is called. For example, Figure 7.47 shows a message box containing three buttons—`Yes`, `No`, and `Cancel` buttons—and Figures 7.48a and b illustrate a message box containing `OK` and `Cancel` buttons. The difference between these two figures is the button that has been designated as having the default focus. This is the button with the dotted line in it, and is the button that can be selected by pressing the Enter key. In Figure 7.48a the default button is the `OK` button, whereas in Figure 7.48b it is the `Cancel` button. Table 7.6 presents the complete set of buttons that can be included in a message box.

---

5 This topic can be omitted on first reading with no loss of subject continuity.

FIGURE 7.47

Alternative `MessageBox()` **buttons**

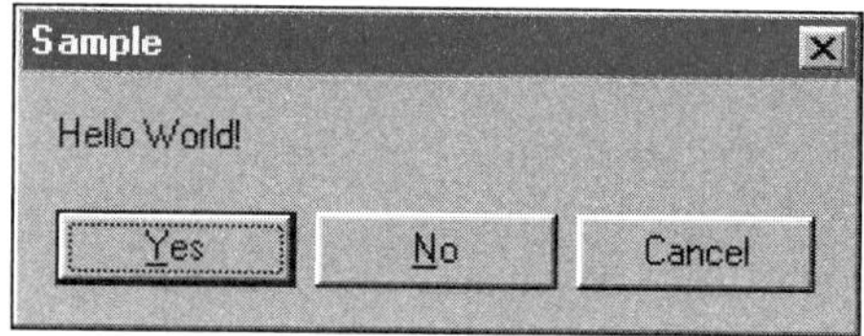

For example, the message box previously displayed as Figure 7.47 was produced by the statement

```
MessageBox("Hello World", "Sample", MB_YESNOCANCEL);
```

Notice that Figure 7.47 does not contain an icon. To include an icon value, you can combine the icon and button type named constants with an OR symbol, which is the | keyboard key. For example, the statement

```
MessageBox("Hello World", "Sample", MB_ICONEXCLAMATION | MB_YESNOCANCEL);
```

would create the message box shown in Figure 7.47, but with an exclamation icon included in the box.

In addition to specifying the icon type and button combinations, the `MessageBox()` function also permits explicit specification of the default button. This is accomplished using the named constants listed in Table 7.7. For example, the default button shown in Figure 7.48b was created using the statement

```
MessageBox("Hello World", "Sample", MB_ICONEXCLAMATION | MB_OKCANCEL | MB_DEFBUTTON2);
```

Again, notice that multiple combinations of icon, number of buttons, and default button are specified by separating each named constant with the | symbol.

In addition to specifying the types of buttons that a message box can contain, it is also possible to detect which button was actually pressed, and then select the code to execute based on the detection. This can be done because the MessageBox function returns a

FIGURE 7.48

(a) First button as default

(b) Second button as default

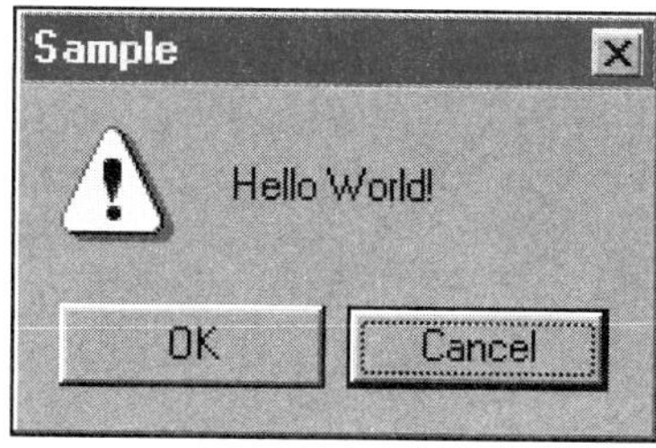

TABLE 7.6 Available message box buttons

Named Constant	Effect
MB_OK	The message box will contain one push button: OK. This is the default unless another named constant is specified.
MB_OKCANCEL	The message box will contain two push buttons: OK and Cancel
MB_YESNO	The message box will contain two push buttons: Yes and No
MB_YESNOCANCEL	The message box will contain three push buttons: Yes, No, and Cancel
MB_RETRYCANCEL	The message box will contain two push buttons: Retry and Cancel
MB_ABORTRETRYIGNORE	The message box will contain three push buttons: Abort, Retry, and Ignore

value based on the selected button. These return values, all of which are integer numbers, are listed in Table 7.8.

Using the return values listed in Table 7.8, we can now modify the `Exit` button's event handler to query the user and confirm that they really do want to exit the application. The modified event handler follows:

```
void CWinpgm7_1Dlg::OnExitButton()
{
  int answer;

  answer = MessageBox("Exit the Application?","Exit", MB_YESNO);
  if (answer == IDYES)
  {
    MessageBeep(0xFFFFFFFF);
    SendMessage(WM_CLOSE);
  }
}
```

TABLE 7.7 Specifying the default button

Named Constant	Effect
MB_DEFBUTTON1	The first button is the default. This is the default unless another default button is explicitly specified.
MB_DEFBUTTON2	The second button is the default. This has no effect if the message box has only one button.
MB_DEFBUTTON3	The third button is the default. This has no effect if the message box has only one or two buttons.

TABLE 7.8 `MessageBox()` **return values**

Selected Button	Returned Value
OK	IDOK
Yes	IDYES
No	IDNO
Cancel	IDCANCEL (Also returned if a Cancel button is available and the Esc key is pressed)
Abort	IDABORT
Retry	IDRETRY
Ignore	IDIGNORE

In reviewing this event handler, notice that the Return code provided by the `MessageBox()` function is first assigned to an integer variable, which we have named `answer`. This name is not required, and any programmer-selected variable name can be used in its place. The value assigned to this variable is then compared to the named constant IDYES. Only if the value in `answer` is IDYES, which can be obtained only by the user pressing the message box's `Yes` button, will the application be closed. The termination of the application is provided by the same two lines of code previously included in our original `Exit` button's event handler.

Introduction to ClassWizard

In completing Windows Program 7.1, we used a context-sensitive menu (see Figure 7.32) to create event handlers for both of the program's Command buttons. Another, actually more powerful, means of accessing or adding code to an application is to use the ClassWizard. This wizard provides a centralized means of locating and navigating through all of a project's procedural code, and can be activated in one of the following three ways.

- Select the `ClassWizard` option from the View menu (see Figure 7.49).
- Select the `ClassWizard` option from any control's context-sensitive menu (see Figure 7.50).
- Activate the ClassWizard using the accelerator key sequence `Ctrl+W`.

Once the ClassWizard has been activated, the ClassWizard dialog shown in Figure 7.51 is displayed. Within this dialog you can select the project, class, and object you wish to use. To see how to access the event handler that we developed for our project's `Message` button, click on the IDC_MESSAGE_BUTTON object displayed within the Ob-

FIGURE 7.49

Activating the ClassWizard from the View menu

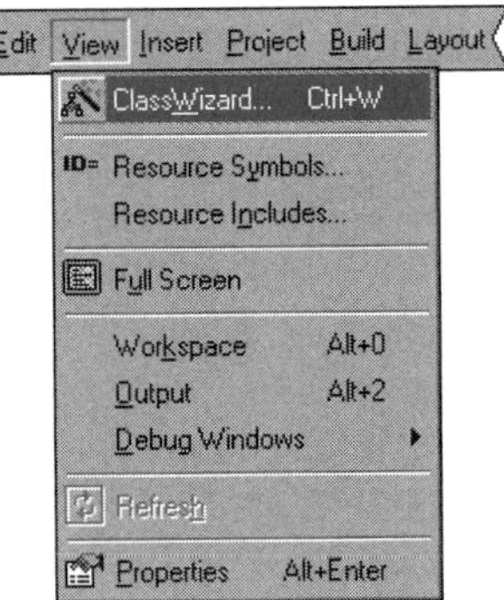

ject ID List box. As shown in Figure 7.52, this provides a list of the messages that can be used for this control.

Figure 7.52 should look somewhat familiar, in that it provides the same information as previously shown in Figure 7.33. Notice that in Figure 7.52 the BN_CLICKED message is boldfaced and the BN_DOUBLECLICKED is not. This means a message handler has already been created for the first message, but not for the second. If we now clicked on the BN_CLICKED message, the `Add Command` button would be grayed, and we would have the choice of using either the `Delete Function` or `Edit Code` buttons. Pressing the latter button would activate the IDE, and place the appropriate event handler function in the Code window, as was previously shown in Figure 7.37. If, however, we clicked on the BN_DOUBLECLICKED message, the `Delete Function` button would be grayed and we would have access to the `Add Function` button. Pressing this button would take you to the Add Member Function dialog, a sample of which was previously shown in Figure 7.34. At this stage you would be back into creating a new event handler function in the same manner with which you are already familiar.

FIGURE 7.50

Activating the ClassWizard from a context-sensitive menu

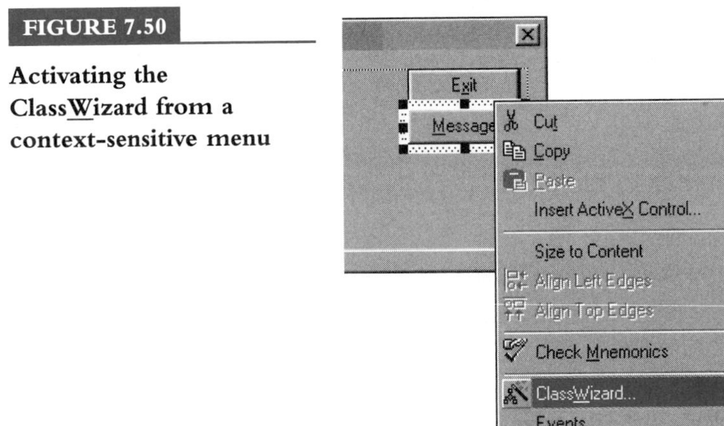

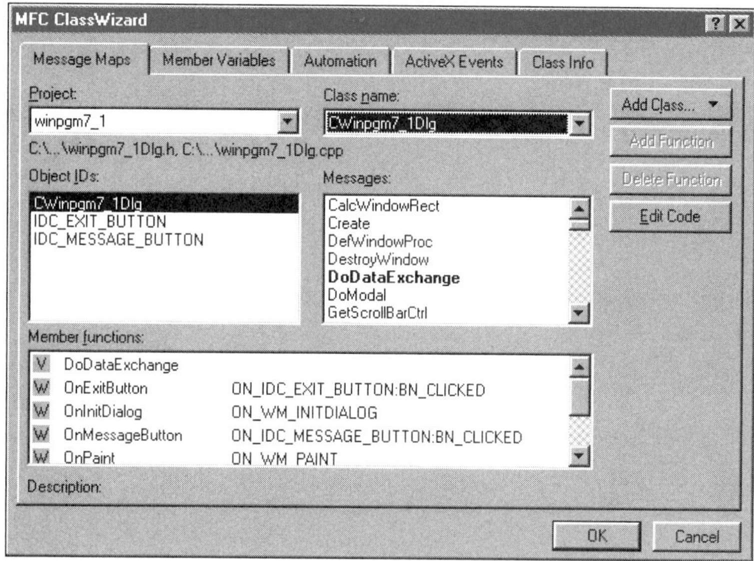

FIGURE 7.51

The MFC ClassWizard dialog

As you begin to create more Windows-based applications, you will come to rely on the ClassWizard to quickly move you into the project's procedural code and provide you with easy access to specific locations within the code.

Comparing Console and Windows Applications

Now that you have constructed a working Windows application, complete with event handler code, it is instructive to compare the structure of this application with the console

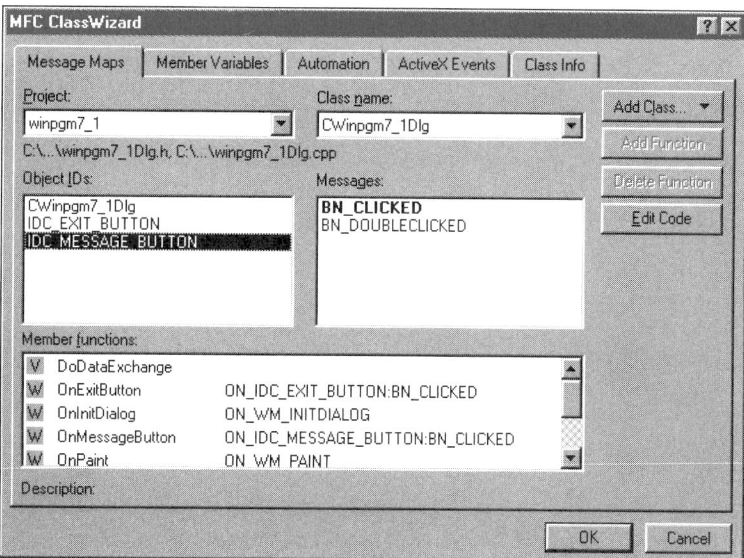

FIGURE 7.52

Selecting the IDC_MESSAGE_BUTTON Object

FIGURE 7.53

Program control under DOS

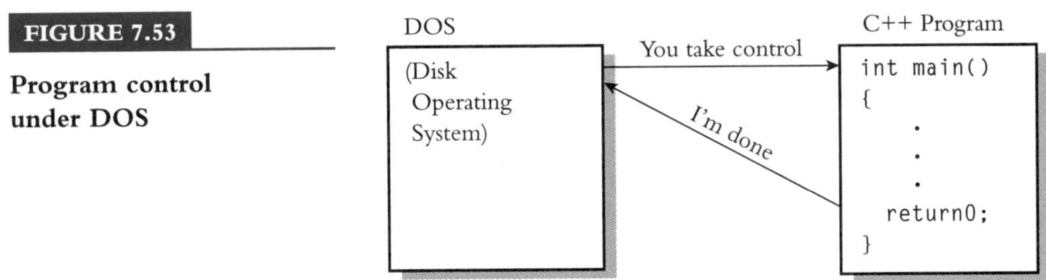

programs with which you are familiar.[6] As we shall see, the structures of these two types of programs are quite different. For example, if you search the Windows application for a `main()` function, which constitutes the heart of a console program, you won't find one. Let's see why.

A console program is a carryover from earlier times when the predominant operating system was DOS (Disk Operating System). DOS was a single-tasking operating system, in which only a single program would execute at one time. Once DOS gave control to a program—one written in C++, for example—the executing program took control of the computer. This situation is illustrated in Figure 7.53. Notice in this figure that DOS effectively relinquishes control over the computer's operation to the executing C++ program. Specifically, control is transferred to the start of the C++ program, which is designated by the `main` keyword. Any operating system resources that the C++ program needs, such as accessing data from a file, are initiated from within the C++ program itself. Only after the C++ program has finished executing, either by reaching the closing brace in the `main` function's body or by an explicit `return` statement, does control pass from the program back to the operating system.

The situation is quite different under a multitasking operating system such as Windows. Because multiple programs can be executing, it is essential that the operating system retain primary control, at all times, in the management of the computer's resources. This control prevents any one program from effectively taking control and inhibiting other programs from running. It also is necessary to ensure that information destined for one application does not become lost or inadvertently accepted by another application. To see why this is so, consider the following case.

Assume that two different programs are executing and have open windows on the screen. In this situation a user could click on controls in either application. If one of the applications were in total control of the computer, it would be responsible for determining on what object, and in which program the user clicked the mouse. Clearly, the programmer who developed one of the executing programs would not be concerned or even be expected to know how to intercept and correctly route an event used by any of the other myriad programs that the operating system might also be executing. So if a

6 This topic can be omitted on first reading with no loss of subject continuity.

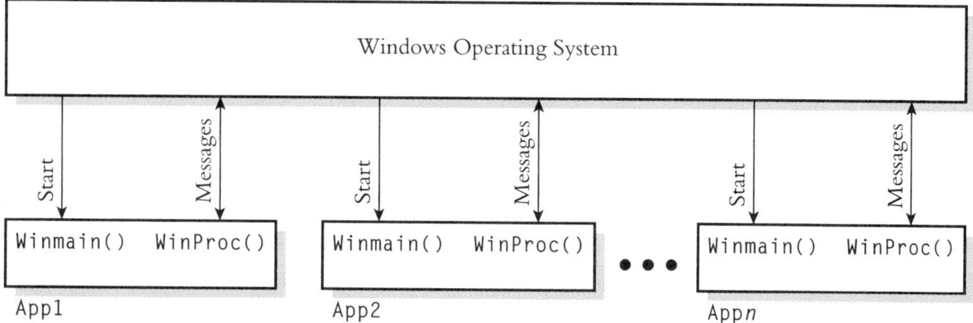

FIGURE 7.54

Program control under Windows

mouse click in another program occurred, it would most likely be lost while any one of the other programs had control of the computer's resources.

The solution to this problem is to allow only the operating system, which is Windows, to have total control of the computer, and to never relinquish this control to any executing programs. Essentially, all executing programs spend most of their time in a sleep-type of mode. When Windows, which is always running, detects an event, such as a mouse click, it determines what the event was and in which application window the event occurred. This type of operation is shown in Figure 7.54. Once the correct determination is made as to event and application, Windows passes the event, in the form of a specific message, to the appropriate application, and only then permits the application to take action. The action, however, may be interrupted at any time if Windows detects another event taking place.

A sample of the most common messages passed by the operating system to an application are listed in Table 7.9. The two-letter prefix, WM, used for all of these messages identifies each one as a Window Message. Essentially these are messages that Windows sends to an application, but they can also be sent from an application to Windows. In fact, you should notice the WM_CLOSE message, which is one we used in Windows Program 7.1 to terminate the application. In that application, the message was generated by the `Exit` button's click event handler and is sent to the Windows operating system to close down the application.

If you wanted to respond directly to the messages listed in Table 7.9, you would have to create prototypes for each message-handling function, and include these function prototypes within what is defined as the Message Map section of the Visual C++ code. This section of code provides a listing of the prototypes for all event handlers that will be used to process Windows messages, as opposed to the conventional procedural functions that are called from within an application for internal use and processing. You would then have to write the event-handler functions, as we have done in this section, to respond to the

TABLE 7.9 A sampling of Windows messages

Message	Meaning
WM_LBUTTONDOWN	The left mouse button has been pressed
WM_LBUTTONUP	The left mouse button has been released
WM_RBUTTONDOWN	The right mouse button has been pressed
WM_RBUTTONUP	The right mouse button has been released
WM_CHAR	A key has been pressed
WM_PAINT	Repaint your window
WM_CLOSE	Terminate the application

messages in a useful or required manner. By using either ClassWizard or a control's context-sensitive menu's `Events...` option, the required entries in the Message Map are made for you, and the header lines for each corresponding event handler are constructed. As you might have noticed, the name of each event handler begins with the word On, and includes the name of the Window's message it is meant to handle. If you want, you can verify the entries in the Message Map for the Windows program completed in this section by scrolling through the program's code window and locating the Message Map section.

In addition to Windows messages that begin with the prefix WM, there are other message types used by Windows. Examples of these other types include Button Notification messages that use a BN prefix and indicate messages sent from buttons to an application, Edit Notification messages that use an EN prefix and indicate messages sent from Edit boxes to an application, and the equivalent BM and EM messages that indicate notifications from an application to buttons and Edit boxes, respectively.

The situation previously shown in Figure 7.54 effectively standardizes the user interface provided by Windows because the operating system determines how events will be recognized and how information can be displayed. Your application needs to know only how to accept and act on the received message and how to display information using standardized Windows procedures. In particular, for Visual C++ programs, it also eliminates the need for a `main()` function. In its place, a true Windows application expects all Visual C++ programs to have a procedure named `WinMain()` and a message processing procedure. The `WinMain()` procedure is used to initialize and start the application, and the message processing procedure, which is usually, but not required to be, named `WndProc()`, is responsible for receiving and acting on the messages sent by Windows to the application.

If you were writing a Windows application by hand, you would be responsible for providing your application with these two procedures. When you use MFC to build your applications, these two procedures are constructed for you automatically and are buried deep within the classes, so that you won't see either one of them explicitly listed in the generated code.

EXERCISES 7.2

1. Define the following terms:
   a. event handler
   b. dialog box
   c. method
   d. property
2. a. What window do you use to enter the code for an event procedure?
   b. List two ways of activating the window you listed as the answer for Exercise 2a.
3. Assume that you have created a dialog-based project with a dialog named frmMain that contains two command buttons named IDC_FIRST_BUTTON and IDC_SECOND_BUTTON. Write the header line that would be used for each button's click and double-click event procedures. Assume a class name of CWinpgm7_1Dlg.
4. Using either ClassWizard or a Command button's context sensitive menu, determine how many event procedures are associated with each Command button.
5. Design and run the application completed in this section.
6. Design and run a Visual C++ application that displays your name and address in a message box when you click on a Command button.
7. Design and run a Visual C++ application that prints the following verse in a message box when a user clicks the mouse on a Command button.

```
Computers, computers everywhere
   as far as I can see
I really, really like these things,
   Oh joy, Oh joy for me!
```

7.3 Adding Command Button, Edit Box, and Static Text Controls

The application presented in the previous section used two Command buttons that were provided by AppWizard. In this and the next two sections, we see how to add our own controls from the toolbox and add event procedures to these controls. In this section, we add our own Command button and Edit box controls, whereas in the next section we provide these controls with member variables and event handlers.

FIGURE 7.55

Program 7.2's Interface

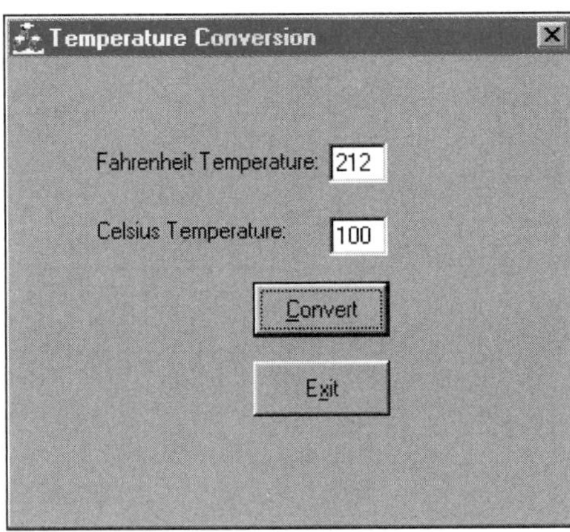

Placing a control on a dialog is quite simple, and the same techniques can be used for all controls. Thus, after placing one control on the dialog you have effectively learned how to place all toolbox controls on a dialog. In all cases, after you have placed a control on a dialog, you can always reposition or resize the control, or delete it altogether.

The simplest procedure for placing a control on a dialog is to first select the control by clicking on it in the toolbox (this is done by pressing and releasing the primary mouse button on the desired control[7]). Then, move the cursor into the Dialog box, at which point the cursor will change to a crosshair, and click the mouse within the Dialog box. The selected control will appear centered at the clicked location. Once the control is located within the dialog you can change its size, position, and set any additional properties, such as its ID name, Caption, or color. These later properties are modified from within the control's Properties dialog in the same manner as we modified the properties for AppWizard-provided controls in Section 7.1.

By far the most commonly used toolbox controls are the Command button, Edit box, Static Text (Labels), Radio buttons, and Check boxes. For our second application we use the first three of these control types, the Command button, Edit box, and Label controls to create the interface shown in Figure 7.55.

To start this new project, either select the `New` option from the `File` menu, or use the accelerator key sequence `Alt+F` keys followed by the `N` key (`Alt+F/N`), or use the shortcut key sequence `Ctrl+N`. Then select the MFC `AppWizard(exe)` project type from within the Projects tab, name the project `winpgm7_2`, and use the AppWizard to construct a `Dialog based` application, as shown in Figure 7.56.

When AppWizard finishes its work, expand the ResourceView's hierarchy tree to produce the screen shown in Figure 7.57. From the view shown in Figure 7.57, with the Resource editor active and containing the project's initial Dialog, use the `View` menu's

7 Conventionally, the primary mouse button is configured as the left button, but can be configured as the right button. Subsequently, when we specify the left button we are assuming that this has been configured as the primary, or "click" button.

FIGURE 7.56

Starting a new dialog-based AppWizard-generated project

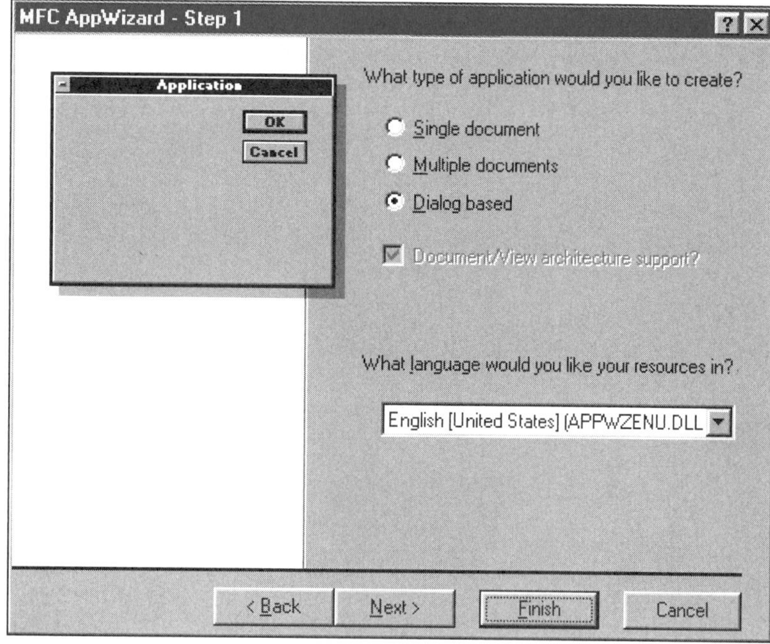

FIGURE 7.57

The IDE with the Resource editor active

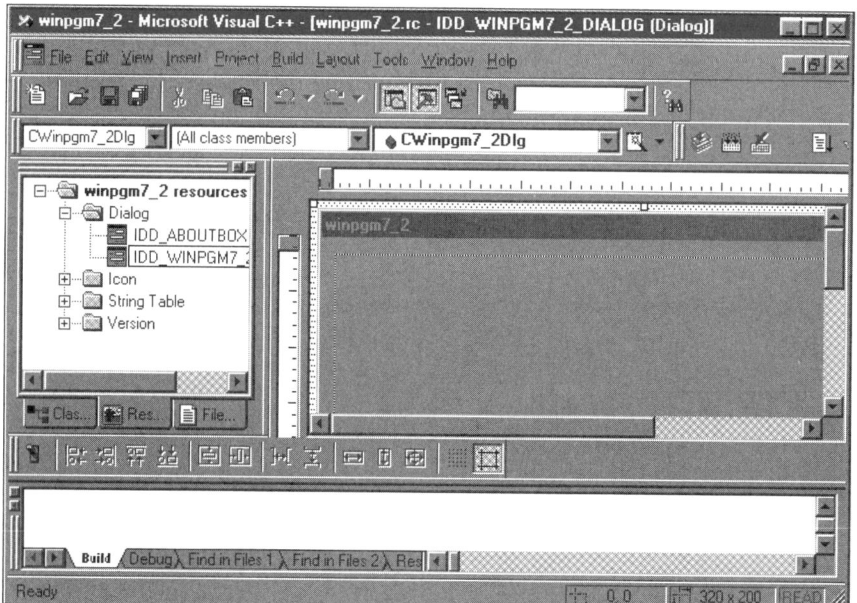

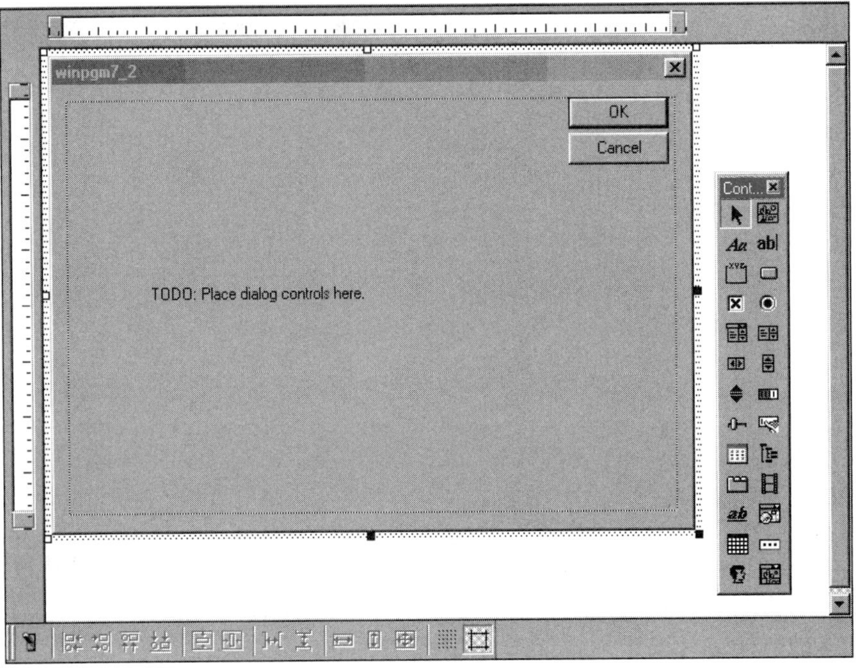

FIGURE 7.58

The dialog in Full screen mode

`Full Screen` option to expand to Full screen mode, so that you have the display shown in Figure 7.58.

With the dialog in Full screen mode, as shown in Figure 7.58, position the cursor on the label `TODO: Place dialog controls here` and press the right mouse button to bring up the context menu shown in Figure 7.59 (this selection can also be done when the Resource editor is not in Full screen mode). From the displayed context menu select

FIGURE 7.59

Deleting the Label (Static text control)

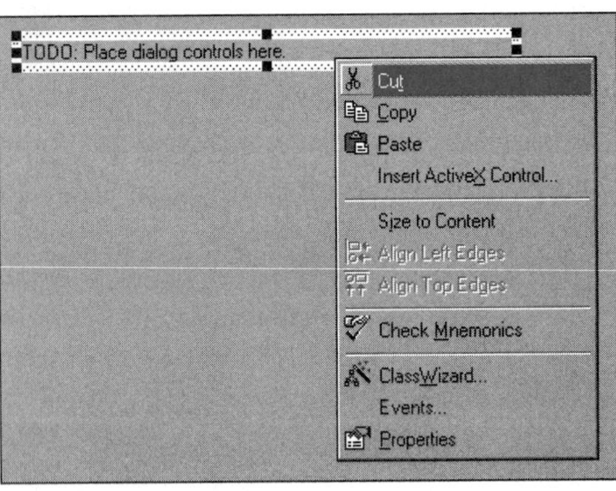

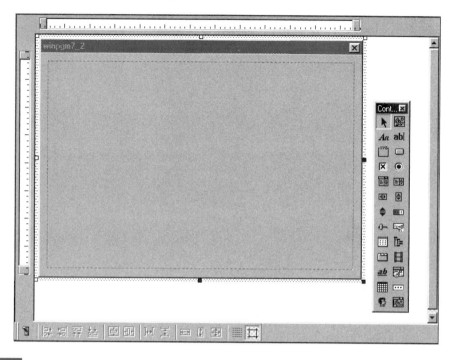

FIGURE 7.60

Dialog box with all controls deleted

the `Cut` option, as highlighted in the figure, to delete the Label. Repeat this process to delete the dialog's two Command buttons. When you have completed deleting all three controls, the Full screen Resource editor should appear as shown in Figure 7.60. It is on this blank Dialog box that we will explicitly place our new controls.

Adding a Command Button

To place a Command button on the Dialog, click on the Command button icon. This icon is the third icon in the toolbox's right column and consists of a rectangle with rounded corners. Now move the mouse cursor anywhere into the Dialog box and click the mouse again. Doing this will cause a Command button control to be centered at the point where you clicked the mouse.

Figure 7.61 shows how the newly placed Command button will look. By default, this button will have the caption Button1 and be named IDC_BUTTON1. Additionally, you will notice that the button is surrounded by eight small squares, which are referred to as **sizing handles.** The fact that the sizing handles are showing indicates that the control is *active,* which means that it can be moved, resized, and have its other properties changed. Only one control can be active at a time. To deactivate the currently active control, use

FIGURE 7.61

The first command button placed on the Dialog box

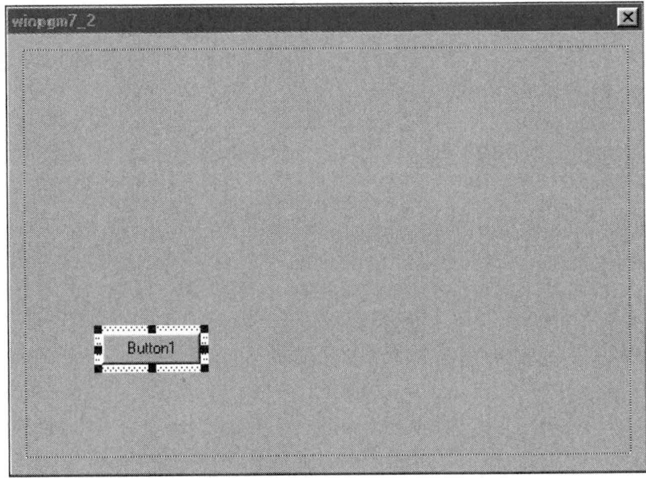

the mouse to click anywhere outside of it. Clicking on another control will activate this other control (there are no other controls here yet), whereas clicking on an area of the Dialog box where no control is located activates the Dialog box itself.

The active control, which should now be the Command button just placed on the Dialog box, can be moved by placing the mouse pointer anywhere inside the control (but not on the sizing handles), holding down the mouse's left button, and dragging the control to its desired new position. Do this now and place this first Command button in roughly the position of the button shown in Figure 7.62. Also resize the Dialog box itself, so that when you are done your Dialog box and Command control should look like the one shown in Figure 7.62.

FIGURE 7.62

The final placement of the first Command button

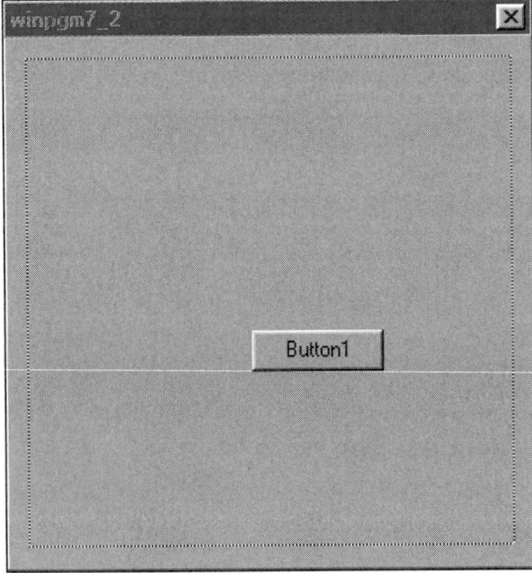

PROGRAMMER'S NOTES

Creating and Deleting Controls

To Add a Control

Select the desired control by clicking on it in the toolbox. Then, move the cursor into the Dialog box, at which point the cursor will change to a crosshair, and click the mouse within the dialog. The selected control will appear centered at the clicked location.

Or, drag and drop the selected control from the toolbox into the Dialog. This is done by clicking on the desired toolbox control, but not releasing the clicked mouse button. With the primary mouse button (which is conventionally the left button) still in its down position, move the mouse until the cursor is at the desired position within the Dialog. As you do this, a dotted rectangle will appear in the Dialog and outline the dragged control. When you release the primary mouse button, the selected control will drop and be centered about the position you released the mouse button.

Or, click on the desired control in the toolbox and then move the mouse pointer onto the Dialog. When the mouse pointer moves onto the Dialog, the cursor will change to a crosshair. Press and hold the left mouse button down when the crosshairs are correctly positioned for any corner of the control and drag the mouse diagonally away from this corner, in any direction, to generate the opposite corner. When the control is the desired size, release the left mouse button.

To Resize a Control

Activate the control by clicking inside of it. Place the mouse pointer on one of the sizing handles, which will cause the mouse pointer to change to a double sided arrow, <=>. Hold the left mouse button down and move the mouse in the direction of either arrowhead. Release the mouse button when the desired size is reached.

To Move a Control

Whether the control is active or not, place the mouse pointer inside of the control and hold down the left mouse button. Drag the control to the desired position and then release the mouse button.

To Delete a Control

Activate the control by clicking inside of it, and then press the `Del` key.

Once you have successfully placed the first Command button on the dialog, either use the same procedure to place one more Command button in the position shown in Figure 7.63, or use one of the alternative procedures given above in the Programmer's Notes box on Creating and Deleting Controls. Included in this box are also the procedures for resizing, moving, and deleting a control.

With a control placed on the Dialog we could immediately proceed to modify its properties and add event handler code, as we did in the last section. We will, however, continue to add the additional controls that we want our application to have before we modify each control's properties and add event handlers. The choice as to when you explicitly set a control's properties and event handlers, however, is really up to you.

FIGURE 7.63

Placement of two Command buttons on the Dialog

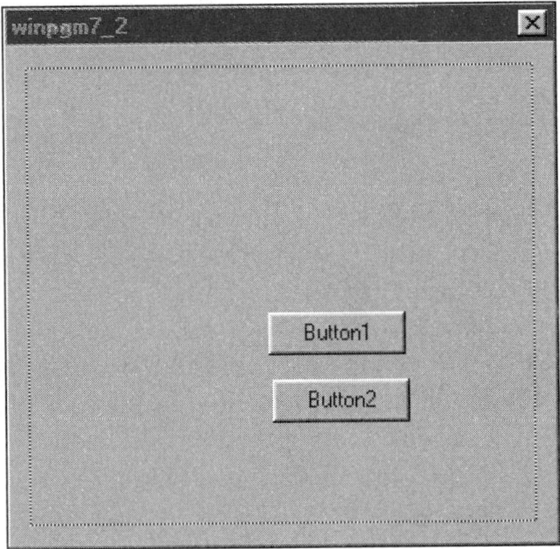

Adding an Edit Box

Edit boxes can be used for both entering data and displaying results. In our current application we will add one Edit box for inputting a Fahrenheit temperature and a second Edit box for displaying the equivalent Celsius temperature when one of the Dialog's Command buttons is clicked.

The Edit box icon is the second icon in the toolbox's second column. Placing an Edit box control on a Dialog is done in the same way as we placed the two Command button controls: that is, by simply clicking on the Edit box icon in the toolbox, and then clicking again within the Dialog. If you happen to click the wrong icon, simply go back and click on the desired one. If you notice the error after you have placed the control on the Dialog, activate the control and delete it using its context sensitive menu. Now place two Edit boxes on the Dialog and resize them so that they appear as shown in Figure 7.64.

FIGURE 7.64

Placement of the Edit boxes

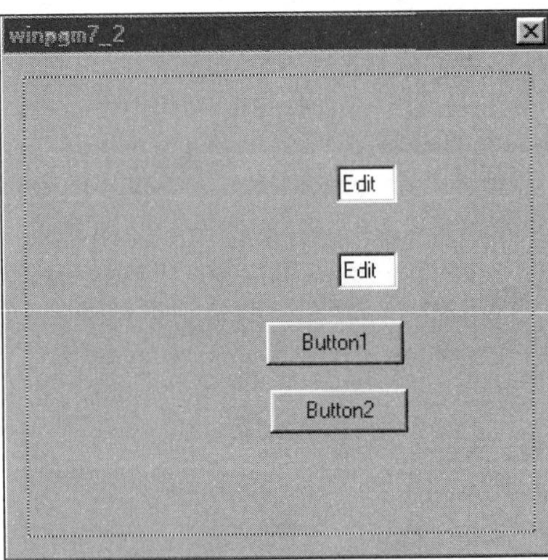

The Label Control

Labels, which are constructed as Static Text controls in Visual C++, are used to provide the user with information. As such, they appear either as headings within a Dialog box or next to a control to let user know the control's purpose. As a Command button's Caption property typically identifies its usage, Command buttons rarely have labels associated with them.

Creating a label is very simple; all that is required is to select the Static Text icon from the toolbox (it is the icon to the left of the Edit box icon), place the control on the Dialog, and resize it to accept the desired text. By definition, a Static Text control is a read-only control that has no active event associated with it; hence the name of the control as static.

When you have finished putting the two labels on the Dialog, you should have the design screen shown in Figure 7.65. Within the context of a complete program development we have achieved the first step in our three-step process, which is

1. Create the graphical user interface.
2. Set the properties of each control on the interface.
3. Write the code.

We complete the second and third steps for each control in the next section. At this stage of development, however, you can preview how the GUI will look at run time by either pressing the Dialog toolbar's Test Switch or actually building and running the application by pressing the `Ctrl+F5` keys. Although clicking on any of the controls produces no effect (precisely because we have not yet attached any code to these buttons), we can use the application to introduce two important concepts connected with any application: *focus* and *tab* sequence.

FIGURE 7.65

Placement of Static Text controls

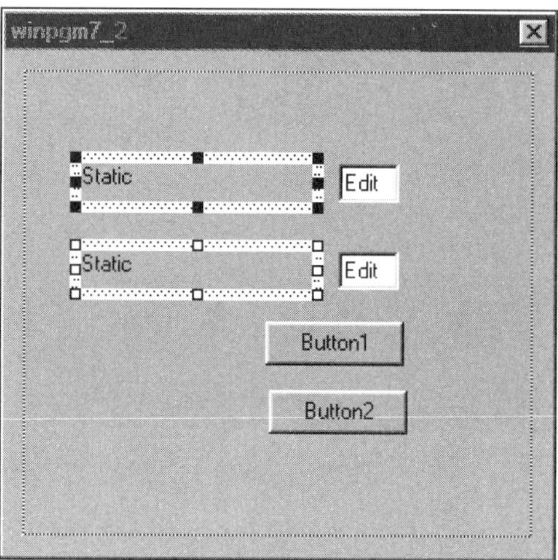

Focus and Tab Sequence

When an application is executed, only one dialog control can have **input focus,** or **focus,** for short. The control with focus is the control that will be affected by pressing a key or clicking the mouse. For example, when a Command button has the focus, its caption will be surrounded by a dotted rectangle, as shown in Figure 7.66. Similarly, when an Edit box has the focus, a solid cursor appears, indicating that the user can type in data.

A control can receive focus only if it is capable of responding to user input through either the keyboard or mouse. Thus, controls such as Label and Line controls can never receive the focus. In order to actually get the focus, a control must have its `Visible` and `Tab stop` properties checked, and its `Disabled` property not checked. If the control is disabled it becomes incapable of responding to user-generated events, such as tabbing to it or clicking a mouse. The `Visible` property determines whether a control will actually be visible on the window during run time (it is always available for view during design time). A checked `Tab Stop` setting forces a tab stop for the control, whereas an unchecked `Tab Stop` property value causes the control to be skipped over in the tab stop sequence. Because the default settings for all three properties are correct for tab stop behavior, they do not usually have to be checked for normal tab operation. A control capable of receiving focus, such as a Command button, can get the focus in one of three ways:

1. A user clicks the mouse directly on the control.
2. A user presses the tab key until the control gets the focus.
3. The code activates the focus.

To see how the first method operates, either click on the Dialog toolbar's Test Switch (shown in Figure 7.67) or select the `Test` Switch option from the `Layout` menu for the currently active Windows Program 7.2. Once the run time GUI is active, click on any of the Edit boxes or Command buttons. As you do, notice how the focus shifts. If any control does not respond, close the Dialog box by clicking on its Close button. This will bring you back to the design stage. Now make sure that the nonresponding control's

FIGURE 7.66

Command button with and without focus

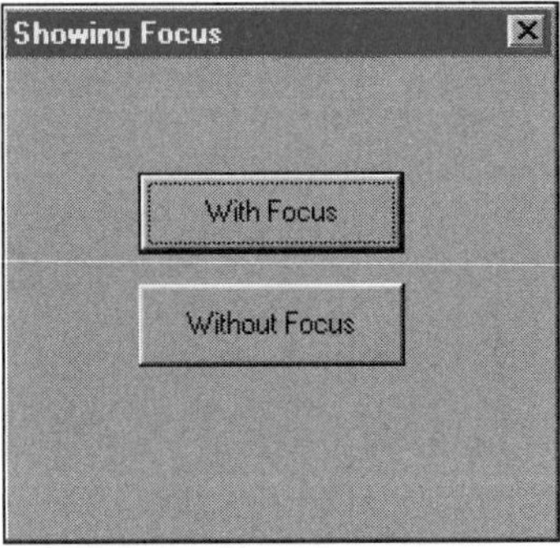

FIGURE 7.67

Locating the Dialog toolbar's Test Switch

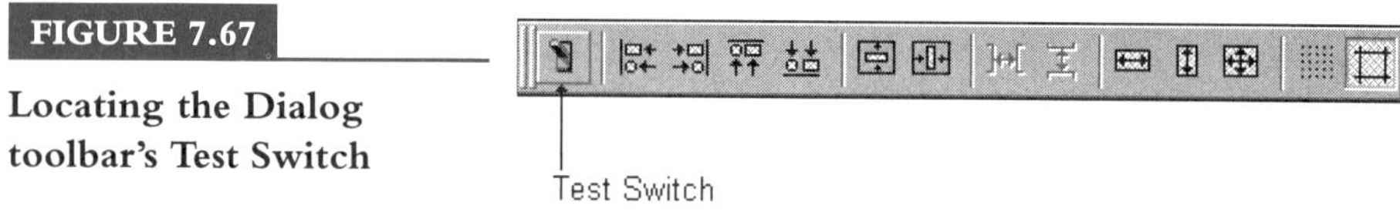

Di<u>s</u>abled property has not been checked and that its Vi<u>s</u>ible and Ta<u>b</u> stop properties are checked. Now go back into test mode and press the tab key a few times to see how the focus shifts from control to control. The sequence in which the focus shifts from control to control as the tab key is pressed is called the **tab sequence.** This sequence is initially determined by the order in which controls are placed on the Dialog. For example, assume you first placed two Command buttons named Button1 and Button2 on the Dialog, followed by two Edit boxes named Edit1 and Edit2. When the application is run, Button1 will have the focus. As you press the tab key, focus will shift to Button2, then to the Edit1 box, and finally to the Edit2 box. Thus, the tab sequence is Button1 to Button2 to Edit1 to Edit2 (this assumes that each control has its Vi<u>s</u>ible, Ta<u>b</u> stop, and Dis<u>a</u>bled properties set correctly to receive focus).

The default tab order obtained as a result of placing controls on the Dialog can be altered by modifying the control's tab order value. Initially, the first control placed on a Dialog is assigned a tab order value of 1, the second control is assigned a tab order value of 2, and so on. To see the current tab order values, either select the <u>L</u>ayout menu's Tab <u>O</u>rder option, as shown in Figure 7.68, or use the Ctrl+0 shortcut key sequence. When you do this for Windows Program 7.2, you will see the tab order shown in Figure 7.69.

To change the tab order, simply click each control in the desired sequence, starting with the control that should have input focus when the application is initially executed. Alternatively, you can change the existing tab order starting at the point that it differs from the order you want. To do this, press the Ctrl key while clicking on the control hav-

FIGURE 7.68

Activating the Tab <u>O</u>rder **sequence**

FIGURE 7.69

Windows Program 7.2's initial tab order

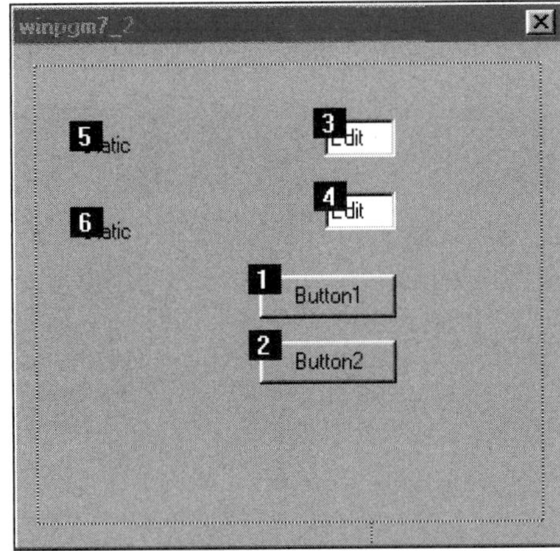

ing the highest correct tab order value, release the `Ctrl` key, and continue clicking controls in the desired order. No matter how you select the tab order, Visual C++ will renumber the remaining controls in a logical order. For example, if you have six controls on the dialog with tab order values from 1 to 6, and change the control with value 4 to a value of 1, the controls with initial values of 1, 2, and 3 will have their values automatically changed to 2, 3, and 4, respectively. Thus, the sequence from one control to another is always uniquely specified. If, however, you ever get confused, simply reset the complete sequence in the desired order by manually starting with a tab order value of 1, and then assigning values in the desired order. A control whose `Tab stop` property has not been checked maintains its tab order value, but is simply skipped over for the next control in the tab sequence.

The Layout Menu[8]

The `Layout` menu option provides the ability to align and move selected controls as a unit, as well as making selected controls the same size. This is a great help in constructing a consistent look on a Dialog box that contains numerous controls.

As a specific example using the `Layout` menu, consider Figure 7.70, which shows two Command buttons on a Dialog. To align and make both controls the same size, the first operation that you must perform is to select the desired controls. This can be done by clicking on the Dialog box and dragging the resulting dotted line to enclose all of the controls that you wish to format, as is illustrated in Figure 7.70, or by holding the Shift key down and clicking on the desired controls.

---

8 This topic may be omitted on first reading with no loss of subject continuity.

FIGURE 7.70

Preparing two controls for formatting

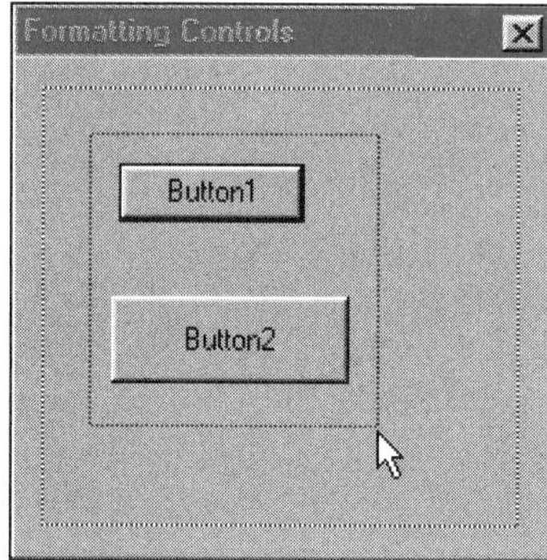

FIGURE 7.71

Locating the defining control

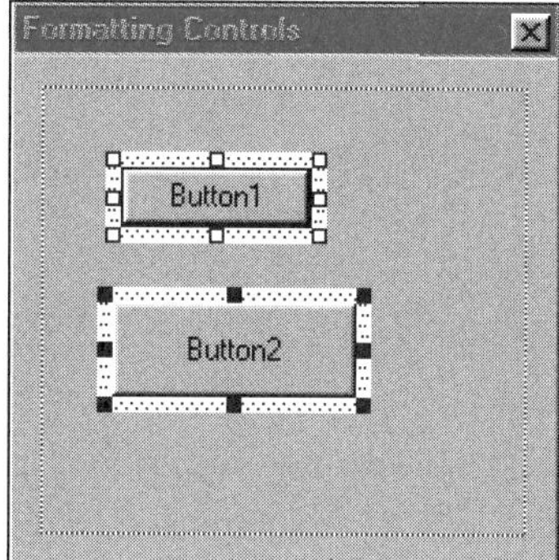

Once you have selected the desired controls for formatting, the last selected control will appear with solid sizing handles. For example, in Figure 7.71 this is the lower command control. The solid sizing handles designate the control that is the **defining control.** This control sets the pattern for both sizing and aligning the other selected controls. If this control is not the defining control that you want, simply select another by clicking on it.

Having selected the desired defining control, click on the `Layout` menu item and then select the desired layout option. For example, Figure 7.72 illustrates selection for making all controls within the dotted lines the same size. Within this submenu, you have the further choice of making either the width, height, or both dimensions of all controls equal to the defining control's respective dimensions.

In addition to sizing controls, you may also want to align a group of controls within a Dialog box. Figure 7.73 illustrates the options that are provided for the `Align` submenu. As shown, controls may be aligned in six different ways, all of which are aligned relative to

FIGURE 7.72

Making controls the same size

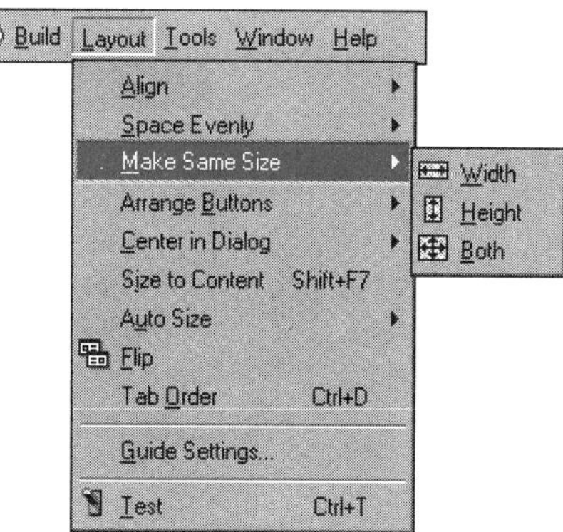

FIGURE 7.73

Aligning controls to the defining control

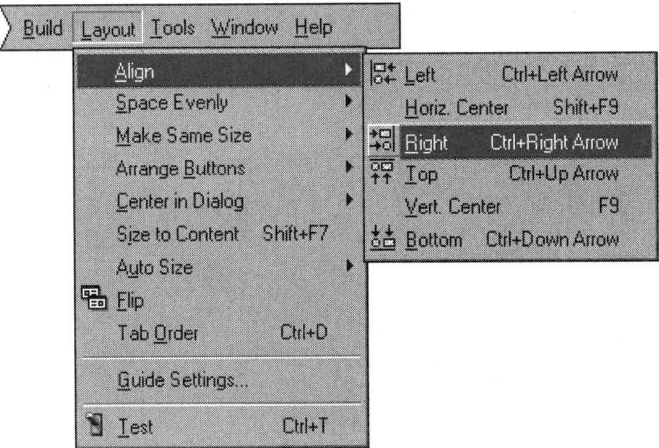

the position of the defining control. Choosing any one of these options will move all other formatted controls in relation to the defining control; the position of the defining control is *not* altered.

An additional and very useful feature of the layout selection process is that all selected controls can be moved as a unit. This is accomplished by clicking within one of the selected controls and dragging the control. As the control is dragged, all other selected controls will move, as a group, while maintaining their positions relative to each other. Finally, all of the layout options can also be selected from the Dialog toolbar, a copy of which was previously illustrated in Figure 7.67. The last two icons on the Dialog toolbar are for the grid and ruler toggle buttons. Pressing the grid button places a series of evenly spaced grid dots within the Dialog, or turns the grid marks off if they are on. The ruler button toggles a ruler line along the side and top of the displayed dialog.

EXERCISES 7.3

1. Create the GUI shown in Figure 7.55.
2. Create the GUI shown in Figure 7.74.

FIGURE 7.74

Dialog for Exercise 2

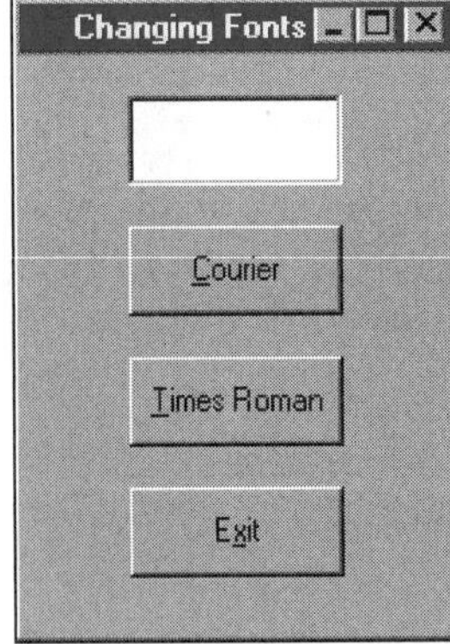

3. Create the GUI shown in Figure 7.75

FIGURE 7.75

Dialog for Exercise 3

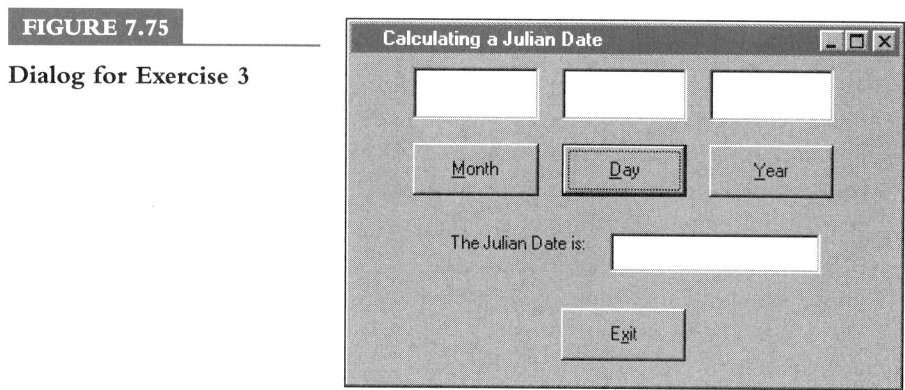

4. Create the GUI shown in Figure 7.76.

FIGURE 7.76

Dialog for Exercise 4

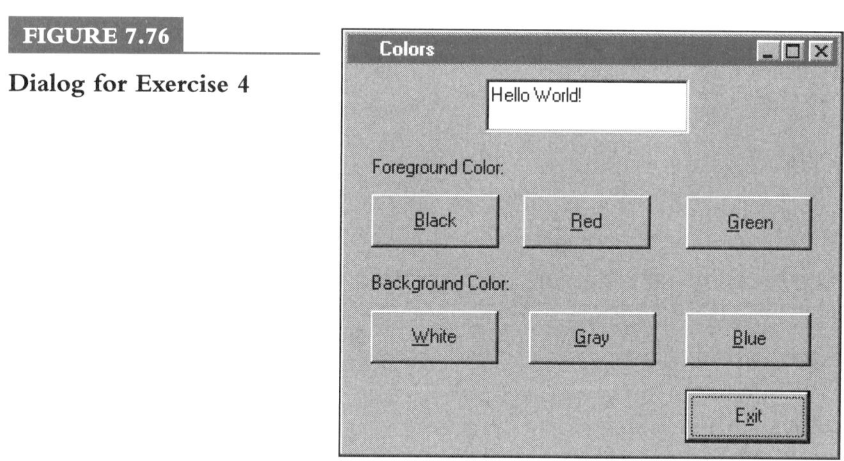

5. Create the GUI shown in Figure 7.77.

FIGURE 7.77

Dialog for Exercise 5

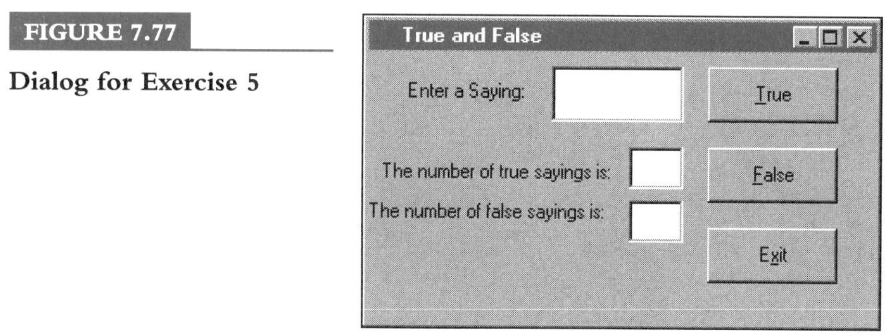

6. What are the three ways that a control can receive focus?

7. To receive focus in the tab sequence, what three properties must be set, and what are the correct settings?

8. a. Create a graphical user interface that contains two Command buttons and two Edit boxes. Set the tab sequence so that tab control goes from the first Edit box to the second Edit box and then through the two Command buttons.

   b. For the tab sequence established in Exercise 8a, deselect the `Tab stop` property of one of the Command buttons (keep all other selections the same as in Exercise 8a), and determine how the tab sequence is affected. What was the effect on the controls' tab sequence values?

   c. For the tab sequence established in Exercise 8a, deselect the `Visible` property of one of the Command buttons (keep all other selections the same as in Exercise 8a), and determine how the tab sequence is affected. What was the effect on the controls' tab sequence values?

   d. For the tab sequence established in Exercise 8a, select the `Disabled` property of one of the Command buttons (keep all other selections the same as in Exercise 8a), and determine how the tab sequence is affected. What was the effect on the controls' tab sequence values?

   e. Change the tab sequence so that focus starts on an Edit box, then goes to one of the Command buttons, then to the other Command button, and finally to the second Edit box.

7.4 Completing Windows Program 7.2

In the previous section we assembled all of the dialog controls required for Windows Program 7.2's graphical user interface. Thus, at this stage of development the application's GUI should appear as shown in Figure 7.78.

FIGURE 7.78

Windows Program 7.2's GUI

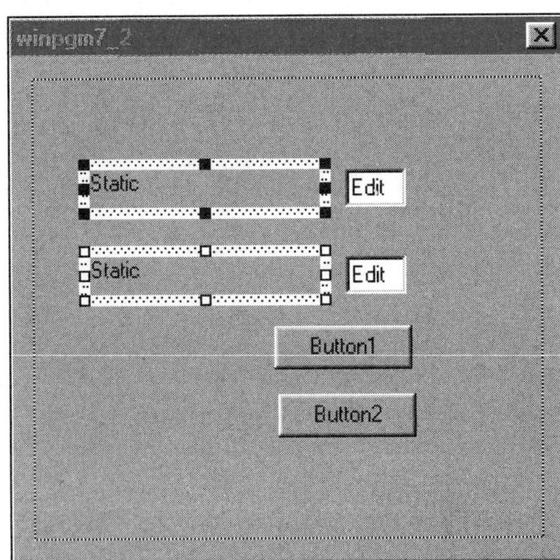

In this section we complete this application by explicitly modifying a number of each control's initial properties, and then writing the application's procedural code, which includes all necessary event handlers. These will be rather easy tasks, because setting control properties and adding event code for a programmer-placed control is the same as setting properties and adding event code for a control created by AppWizard. Thus, we will use the same techniques that were used in Sections 7.1 and 7.2 for the AppWizard-created dialog controls.

Changing a Control's Properties

Table 7.10 is an example of a program Properties table. In general, this type of table provides the initial property settings that must be made for a dialog and each of its child controls that are different than the default settings provided for the control. In particular, Table 7.10 lists the initial property settings for Windows Program 7.2 that must be explicitly set by the programmer. Any property not included in a Properties table is assumed to have the default value set for it when the control is placed on a dialog. While all of the settings in Table 7.10 happen to deal with ID and Caption properties, they also could include any other properties, such as the Tab stop, Visible, and Disabled properties.

Figure 7.79 shows how the Windows Program 7.2's GUI should appear within Visual C++'s IDE at the present time.

Recall from Section 7.1 that a control's properties are set from its Properties dialog. This dialog, which is control specific, can be activated by first selecting a control and then either selecting the `Properties` option from the `View` menu, as illustrated in Figure 7.80,

TABLE 7.10 Program 7.2's initial Properties table

Control	Property	Setting
Dialog	Caption	Temperature Conversion Program
Button1	ID	IDC_CONVERT_BUTTON
	Caption	&Convert to Celsius
Button2	ID	IDC_EXIT_BUTTON
	Caption	E&xit
Static1	ID	IDC_FAHREN_LABEL
	Caption	Fahrenheit Temperature:
Static1	ID	IDC_CELSIUS_LABEL
	Caption	Celsius Temperature:
Edit1	ID	IDC_FAHREN_EDIT
Edit2	ID	IDC_CELSIUS_EDIT

PROGRAMMER'S NOTES

To Activate a Control's Properties Dialog:

1. Select the desired control by clicking on it and then use any of the following :
   a. Press the right mouse button, and select the `Properties` option from the context-sensitive menu.
   b. Select the `View` menu's `Properties` option.
   c. Press the `Alt+Enter` access key sequence.

or by selecting the `Properties` option from the control's context-sensitive menu, a sample of which is shown in Figure 7.81.

Using either of these two methods, you should now set the ID and Caption property values for each of the control objects listed in Table 7.10. Figure 7.82 illustrates how the main Dialog's Properties dialog appears while its caption is being changed. Notice that as you enter the new caption, the text will scroll to accommodate a longer string than can fit in the List box's visible area. Figure 7.83 illustrates how an Edit box's Properties dialog appears. Notice in this figure that we have changed the control's ID, but that the dialog does not contain a Caption property.

In setting each Command button's caption, again notice the effect of the ampersand (&) symbol that is included in each caption. Its visual effect is to cause the character immediately following it to be underlined. Its operational effect is to create an accelerator

FIGURE 7.79

The IDE containing Windows Program 7.2

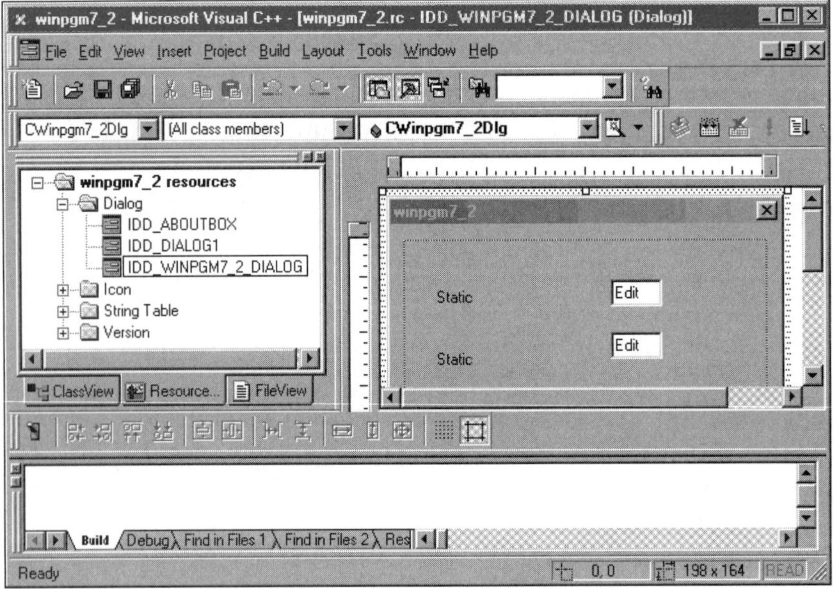

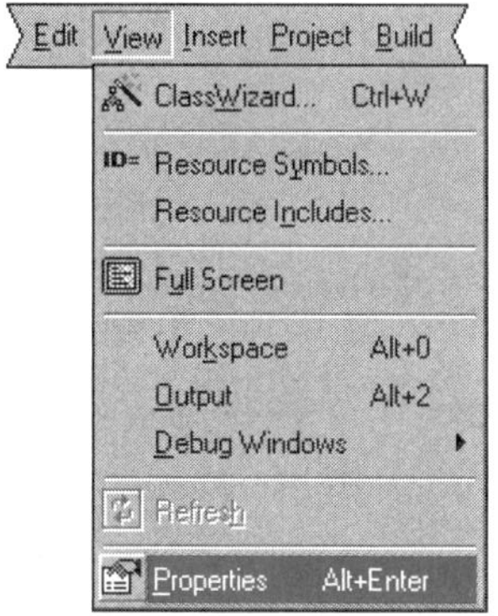

FIGURE 7.80

Selecting the `Properties` option from the `View` menu

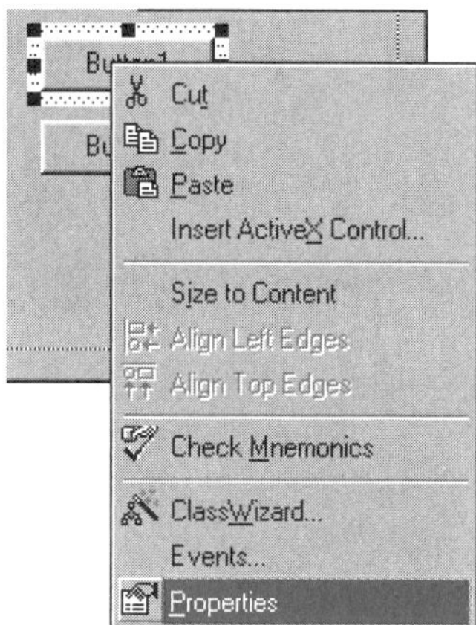

FIGURE 7.81

Selecting the `Properties` option from a context menu

key. Recall from Section 7.1 that an accelerator key, which is also referred to as a shortcut key sequence, is simply a keyboard shortcut for a user to initiate an action. When used with a Command button it permits the user to activate the button by simultaneously pressing the `Alt` key with the underlined letter key, rather than either clicking with the mouse or activating the Command button by first selecting it and then pressing the `Enter` key.

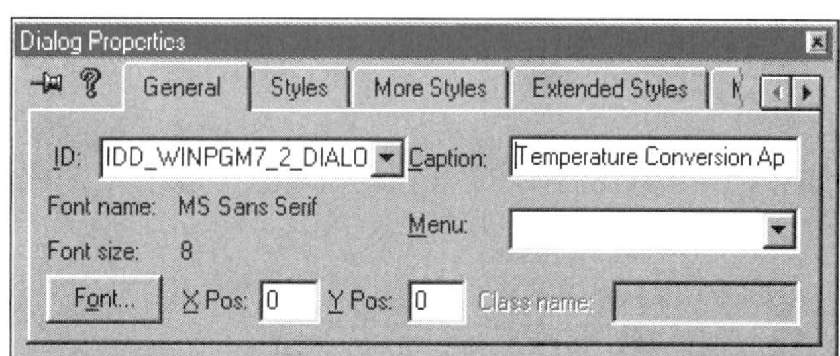

FIGURE 7.82

Changing the Dialog's Caption property value

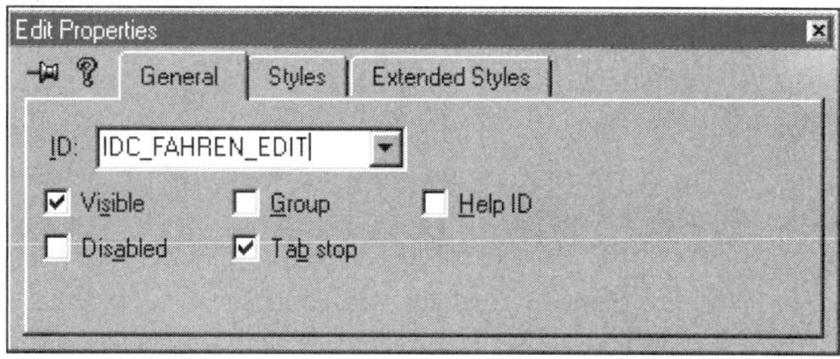

FIGURE 7.83

An Edit box's Properties dialog

FIGURE 7.84

The GUI with its final captions

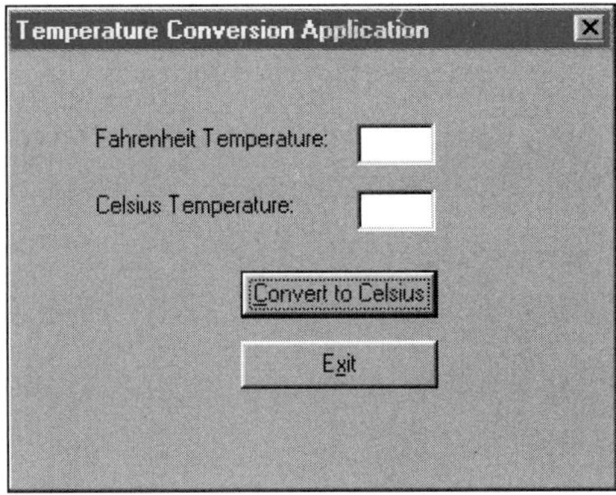

At this stage you should have completed setting all of the property values in Table 7.10, and the GUI should appear as shown in Figure 7.84. Notice that although we have set the initial properties for all of the controls at the same time, this was not necessary. We did so here to centralize the various settings in one place. In practice, many programmers prefer to set each control's properties individually, immediately after the control has been placed on a dialog.

Member Variables

Just as a procedure can have its own set of declared variables, each control can also have its own set of declared variables. Variables declared for a control are referred to as a control's **member variables.** Member variables are extremely useful in providing a link between data contained within a control, such as an Edit box, and procedural code that can then be used to both read the data and change the data in the control. Before seeing how to use a member variable to accomplish this, we first declare a member variable for each of Windows Program 7.2's Edit boxes.

Member variables are declared for each control using the ClassWizard. Since this name may be a bit intimidating (because we have not yet even defined what a class is), it is more useful to think of this wizard as your personal code wizard. As such, this wizard is one of the most useful tools provided in Visual C++ for locating, accessing, and entering procedural code. As you advance in your Visual C++ programming abilities, you will rely more and more on this wizard's capabilities.[9]

To add a member variable, activate the ClassWizard using any of the procedures listed in the Programmer's Notes box (see page 408). When this is done, you will have the screen shown in Figure 7.85. Notice that the highlighted Object ID name is CWinpgm7_2Dlg. Since this is the dialog's ID, it means that the dialog was selected when the wizard was activated. Also notice that the Message Maps tab is currently active. For our immediate purpose in declaring a member variable, we will have to click on the sec-

9 You may want to review the information on the ClassWizard provided in Section 7.2.

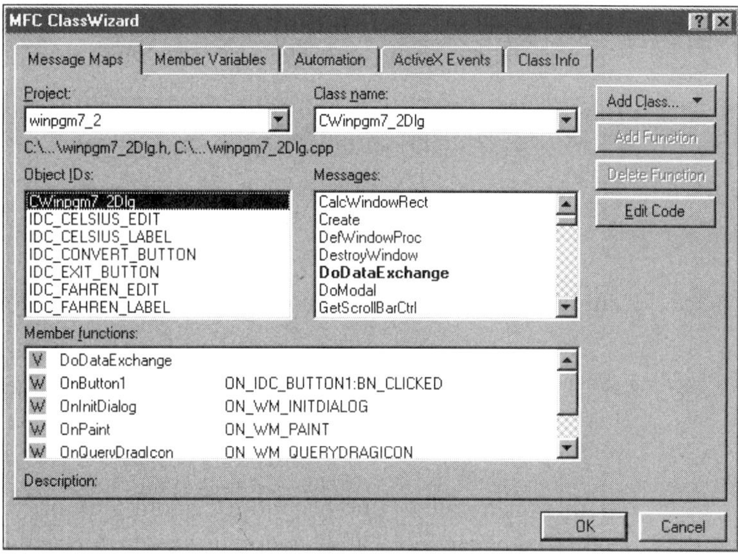

FIGURE 7.85

The ClassWizard's dialog

ond tab, which is labeled Member Variables. The window shown in Figure 7.86 will be displayed when this second tab is clicked.

When you have the dialog box shown in Figure 7.86, select the IDC_FAHREN_EDIT object, as shown, and then press the `Add Variable` Command button. Doing this will cause the Add Member Variable Dialog box shown in Figure 7.87 to appear. Notice that this dialog requires that a name and data type be entered for the variable that we are about to declare. Exactly where in the code this declaration is placed is correctly handled by the ClassWizard. After the declaration is completed, you can search the code to see where it has been placed, and after you have completed the object-oriented chapters of

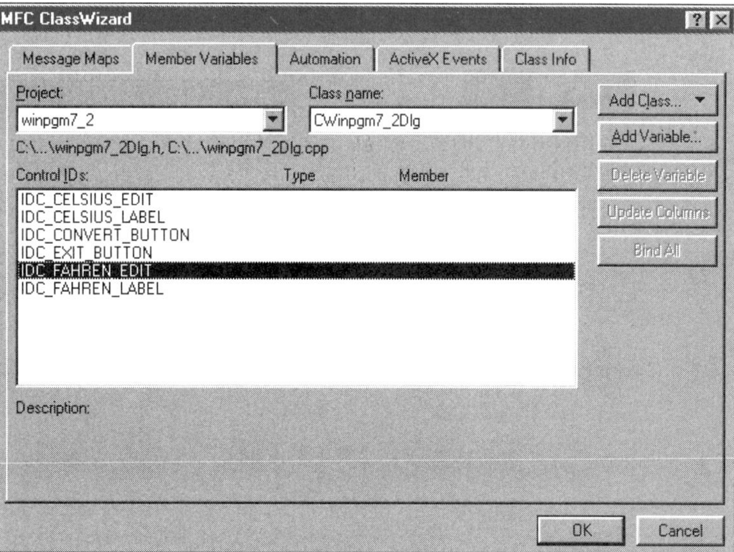

FIGURE 7.86

The Member Variables tab is now active

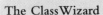

PROGRAMMER'S NOTES

The ClassWizard

The ClassWizard is the predominate tool you will use to locate and access procedural and object-oriented code. For practical purposes you should regard it as your personal code wizard.

To Activate the ClassWizard

1. Select any control by clicking on it, activate the control's context menu, and select the `ClassWizard` option.
2. Select the `View` menu's `ClassWizard` option.
3. Press the `Ctrl+W` access key sequence.

To Add a Member Variable

1. Make sure that the Member Variables tab is active.
2. Highlight the desired control to which the variable will be attached.
3. Press the `Add Variable` button.
4. Enter the variable's Name, Category, and Data Type on the displayed Add Member Variable dialog.

To Add an Event Handler

1. Make sure that the Message Maps tab is active.
2. Highlight the desired control's ID and the Message that will be processed by the event handler.
3. Press the `Add Function` button to have the function's prototype and a stub definition function added to the program's code.
4. Press the `Edit Code` button to access the event handler's stub function and complete the event code.

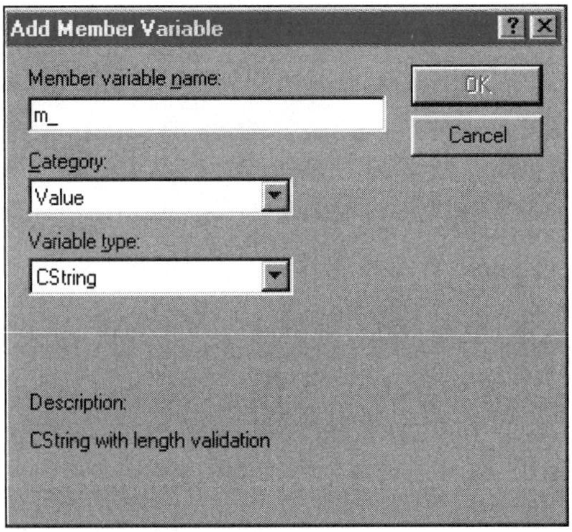

FIGURE 7.87

The Add Member Variable Dialog box

FIGURE 7.88

A completed member variable declaration

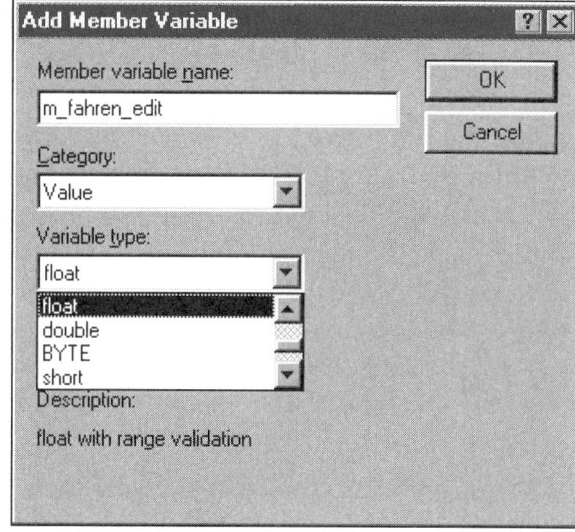

this text, you will understand why this placement was selected. For now, however, let's just complete the declaration.

Figure 7.88 shows how the Add Member Variable dialog should be filled in for the new member variable that we are attaching to the IDC_FAHREN_EDIT box. By convention, all member variable names begin with the characters m_, so this part of the variable's name has been filled in by the ClassWizard. Notice that a drop-down box permits selection of the variable's data type, which we have selected as a `float`. Additionally, the Category type has been left with its default of `Value`. When this information has been completed, and the `OK` button pressed, the MFC ClassWizard dialog is redisplayed, as shown on Figure 7.89.

FIGURE 7.89

The ClassWizard dialog showing a declared member variable

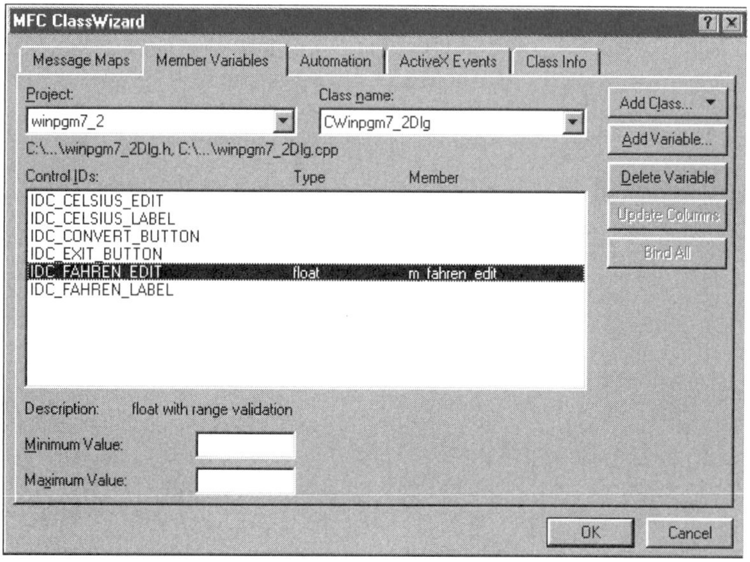

Observe that, on the dialog shown in Figure 7.89, the new member variable's data type and member name are displayed on the same line as the IDC_FAHREN_EDIT Control ID. Also notice that, at the bottom of the dialog, you can now enter both a minimum and maximum value for the member variable. If you enter any values in these boxes, the application will automatically display a dialog box with an error message in it whenever a user attempts to enter an invalid number in the Edit box while the application is executing. The error message will inform the user of the valid range of values and that the currently entered value is not a permissible value.

Member variables are important in a Windows application for the following two reasons:

1. In conjunction with the `UpdateData()` function, member variables whose Category has been set to `Value` permits a control, such as an Edit box, to exchange its data with the rest of the application. This is done using the member variable within the context of procedural code, in the same manner that a function's local variables are used.

2. In conjunction with member functions that are a part of the MFC's `CWnd` class, such as the `EnableWindow()` and `SetFocus()` functions, member variables whose Category has been set to `Control` permit these MFC functions to modify the properties of the control, at run time, to which the member variable is attached.

We will provide examples of both types of usage when we attach event handlers to Windows Program 7.2. For now, using the same procedure that we used to create the m_fahren_edit member variable, add the remaining member variables listed in Table 7.11. (To do this, simply highlight the selected control in the ClassWizard dialog, press the `Add Variable` button, and then make the required declarations.) When you are finished adding the remaining member variables, the ClassWizard dialog should appear as shown in Figure 7.90. If you discover you have made a mistake after adding a member variable, you can always highlight the offending variable and then press the `Delete Variable` button to delete it.

TABLE 7.11 **Windows Program 7.2 member variables**

Control ID	Variable Name	Variable Category	Variable Data Type
IDC_FAHREN_EDIT	m_fahren_edit	Value	float
IDC_FAHREN_EDIT	m_fahren_control	Control	CEdit
IDC_CELSIUS_EDIT	m_celsius_edit	Value	float
IDC_CELSIUS_EDIT	m_celsius_control	Control	CEdit

FIGURE 7.90

The ClassWizard dialog showing Windows Program 7.2's member variables

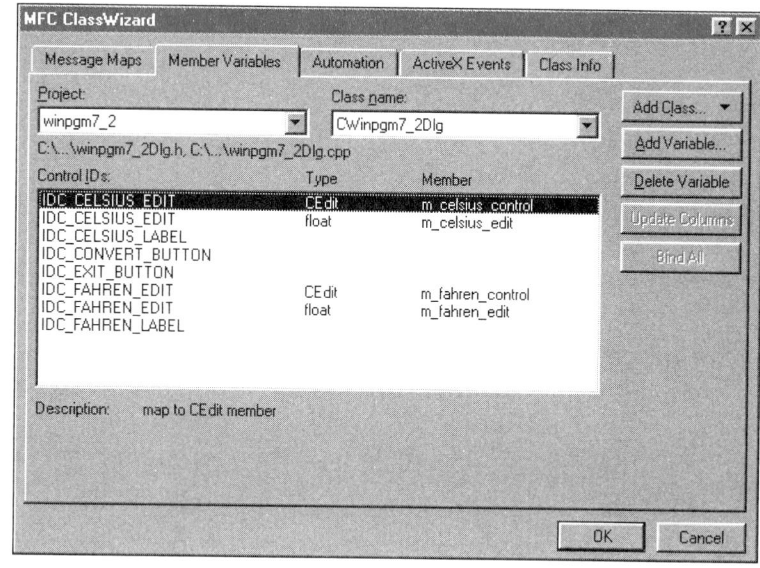

Defining the Event Handlers

Now that we have added two member variables—whose specific purpose will become clear shortly—to each Edit box, we can add the event handlers to make our application respond in a "reasonable" manner. To understand what reasonable means for this application, consider Figure 7.91, which shows Windows Program 7.2's graphical user interface. This figure, in conjunction with Properties Table 7.10, defines the state of each control object when Windows Program 7.2 is executed.

The purpose of Program 7.2 is to permit a user to enter a Fahrenheit temperature, and then, by pressing the `Convert` button, have the program calculate and display the corresponding Celsius temperature. Due to the event-driven nature of the program, however, a user might attempt to enter a Celsius temperature inadvertently. Similarly, after having one Fahrenheit temperature converted, the user could then enter a second such

FIGURE 7.91

Windows Program 7.2's run time interface

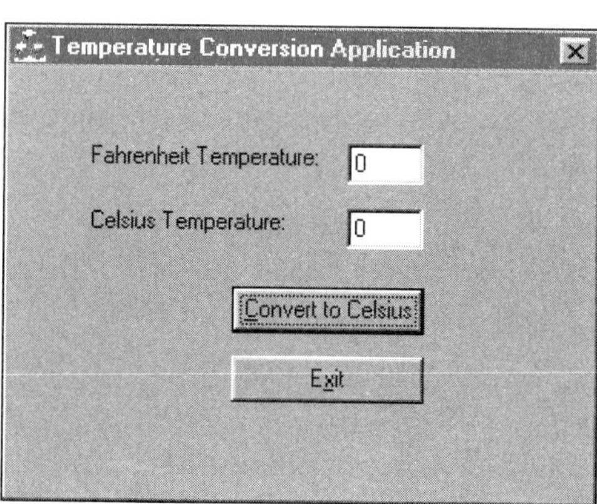

temperature, which would overwrite the first temperature that was correctly converted. At that point the interface would show the new Fahrenheit temperature alongside the Celsius temperature that corresponded to the previously entered value.

To forestall such program operation, the required event handlers and a commentary on why we have chosen these actions follow:

Event Handler Requirements for the Fahrenheit Edit Box

When this box gets the focus:

Set the Celsius box to a disabled (shadowed) state.

Reset the value in the Celsius Edit box to 0.

Commentary on this event handler:

Putting a blank string in the Celsius box would be better, but since the Celsius box is set to display a value, and not a string, some value must be displayed. The box's disabled (shadowed) state should alert the user that the value is not valid.

Event Handler for the Celsius Edit Box

When this box gets the focus:

Set the focus to the Fahrenheit edit box.

Commentary on this event handler:

This will prevent a user from entering a value into the Celsius Edit box because this box can get the focus from a user only if the user tabs to it or clicks on it. Under these conditions, our event handler will automatically set the focus on the Fahrenheit box, which is where the user should be when trying to enter a value. Once the focus gets shifted to the Fahrenheit box, that box's event handler (see above) will disable the Celsius box.

Event Handler for the Convert Command Button

When this button is clicked:

Enable the Celsius Edit box.

Retrieve the Fahrenheit Edit box's data value.

Convert the Fahrenheit data to a Celsius value using the formula

$$Celsius = 5.0/9.0 \star (Fahrenheit - 32.0)$$

Display the calculated Celsius value.

Commentary on this event handler:

This is a straightforward task of converting the input value to an output value, and enabling the box so that the displayed value is not shadowed.

Event Handler for the Exit Command Button

When this button is clicked:

Beep the sound card.

Close down the application.

Commentary on this event handler:

This is the standard closing event handler that we previously used in Windows Program 7.1.

Although the actions taken by our event handler functions are straightforward and typical of the types of actions that a reasonably simple Windows program must take, we will need some help from the Microsoft Foundation Class (MFC) Library to perform them. Table 7.12 lists the three available MFC functions that we will need. (A more complete list of functions can be obtained from the Help facility under the title `CWnd Class Members`. The CWnd Class, which is MFC's primary class for controlling a window, is described in more detail in Section 11.1.)

The required event handlers described above can now be written using the functions listed in Table 7.12. The actual code that we use is listed as Windows Program 7.2's Event Handler Code. In reviewing this code pay particular attention to the notation used with the `EnableWindow()` and `SetFocus()` functions. To use these two functions to change a control's property while a program is running, a function call having the form `ControlMemberVariableName.FunctionName()` is used. The period between the object's member variable's name and the function name is required. The member variable name, which must be a `Control` Category variable, effectively defines the object on which the function will operate. For example, the statement

```
m_celsius_control.EnableWindow(FALSE);
```

calls the `EnableWindow()` function, passes it the argument value `FALSE`, and tells it to operate on the Celsius Edit box, which is the box associated with the `m_celsius_control` variable.

TABLE 7.12 Useful MFCWnd Class Member Functions

Function	Description
`UpdateData()`	`UpdateData(TRUE)` retrieves the data value in each control by copying each data value into the control's associated `Value` Category member variable. `UpdateData(FALSE)` copies the values currently assigned to `Value` category member variables into their respective controls, which force their display in the control.
`EnableWindow()`	`EnableWindow(TRUE)` enables the designated control. The control is designated by prefixing a `Control` Category member variable's name to the function. `EnableWindow(FALSE)` disables the designated control. The control is designated by prefixing a `Control` Category member variable's name to the function.
`SetFocus()`	`SetFocus(TRUE)` enables the designated control. The control is designated by prefixing a `Control` Category member variable's name to the function. `SetFocus(FALSE)` disables the designated control. The control is designated by prefixing a `Control` Category member variable's name to the function.

Windows Program 7.2's Event Handler Code

```
void CWinpgm7_2Dlg::OnSetfocusFahrenEdit()
{
  m_celsius_edit = 0; // assign a value
  m_celsius_control.EnableWindow(FALSE);
  UpdateData(FALSE); // display the value
}

void CWinpgm7_2Dlg::OnSetfocusCelsiusEdit()
{
  m_fahren_control.SetFocus();   // set focus on the Fahrenheit edit box
}

void CWinpgm7_2Dlg::OnConvertButton()
{
  UpdateData(TRUE);  // retrieve edit box values
  m_celsius_edit = 5.0/9.0 * (m_fahren_edit - 32.0);
  m_celsius_control.EnableWindow(TRUE);   // enable the Celsius edit box
  UpdateData(FALSE);   // display the calculated Celsius value
}

void CWinpgm7_2Dlg::OnExitButton()
{
  MessageBeep(MB_OK);
  SendMessage(WM_CLOSE);
}
```

Having defined the required event handlers, all that remains is to get them entered as part of the application. We do this next.

Entering the Event Handlers

Recall from Section 7.2 that a control's events are set by first adding a member function for the desired handler. This can be done by either highlighting a control and then selecting the `Events...` option from the control's context-sensitive menu, a sample of which is shown in Figure 7.92, or by invoking the ClassWizard, which will bring up the dialog shown in Figure 7.93. We use the ClassWizard here because it can be invoked directly from the Text editor by pressing the `Ctrl+W` buttons and does not require us to reinvoke the Resource editor to activate a new context menu for each control's event handler.

Once you have the MFC ClassWizard dialog active, as shown in Figure 7.93, highlight both the IDC_CONVERT_BUTTON and the BN_CLICKED Message (note this message is in a normal, *not* a bold, style), and then press the `Add Function` button. These actions will cause the Add Member Function dialog shown in Figure 7.94 to appear. Press this dialog's `OK` button, and the dialog shown in Figure 7.93 will reappear, but this time

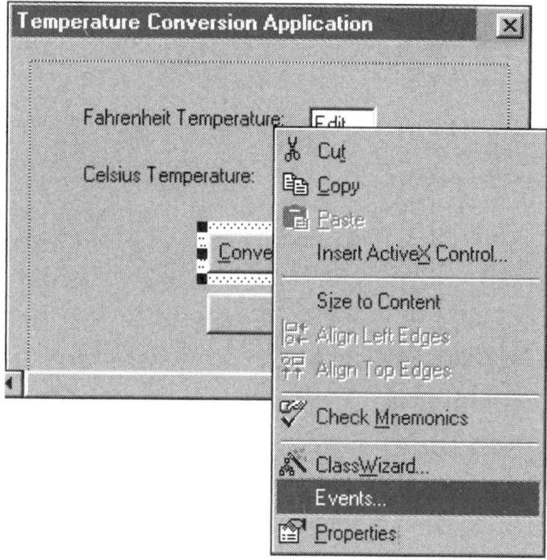

FIGURE 7.92

Selecting the `Events` **option from a context menu**

the BN_CLICKED Message will be listed in bold to indicate that the event handler for this function (which, from Figure 7.94, we know is named OnConvertButton) has been added to the application. To access this event handler, simply press the `Edit Code` button. Doing so will activate the IDE shown in Figure 7.95. As is seen on this figure, the applications procedural code has been entered into the Text editor and the editor is currently centered within the body of the newly created `OnConvertButton()` event handler. When you have this window active, enter the `OnConvertButton()` code from the code listed previously under Windows Program 7.2's Event Handler Code. After you have completed this, the IDE will appear as shown in Figure 7.96.

Once you have added this first event handler, redo all of the steps necessary to add and enter the remaining three event handlers. When this is done, you can build and execute Windows Program 7.2.

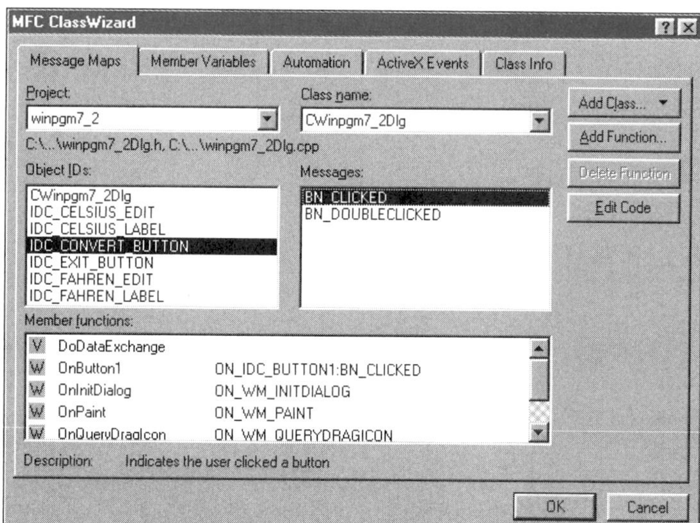

FIGURE 7.93

Adding an event handler using the ClassWizard

FIGURE 7.94

Naming the event handler

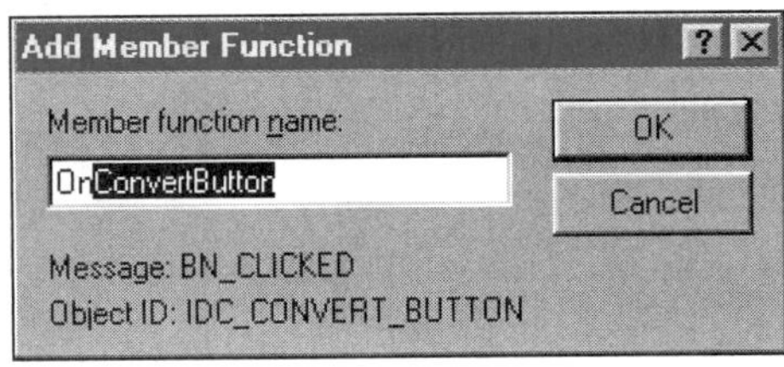

Before leaving this application, one additional comment is worth noting. In addition to creating skeleton event handlers to which you can add your own code, the ClassWizard silently performs an additional task for each new handler function it is asked to create; this is to add the function's prototype within the Message Map area of the code (review Section 7.2 for a description of the Message Map's purpose). You can easily scroll through the code to locate this area and verify that each added event handler does indeed have its function prototype listed. If you do, the code that you will see is

```
BEGIN_MESSAGE_MAP(CWinpgm7_2Dlg, CDialog)
        //{{AFX_MSG_MAP(CWinpgm7_2Dlg)
        ON_WM_SYSCOMMAND()
        ON_WM_PAINT()
        ON_WM_QUERYDRAGICON()
        ON_EN_SETFOCUS(IDC_CELSIUS_EDIT, OnSetfocusCelsiusEdit)
        ON_EN_SETFOCUS(IDC_FAHREN_EDIT, OnSetfocusFahrenEdit)
        ON_BN_CLICKED(IDC_EXIT_BUTTON, OnExitButton)
        ON_BN_CLICKED(IDC_CONVERT_BUTTON, OnConvertButton)
        //}}AFX_MSG_MAP
END_MESSAGE_MAP()
```

FIGURE 7.95

The newly added event handler

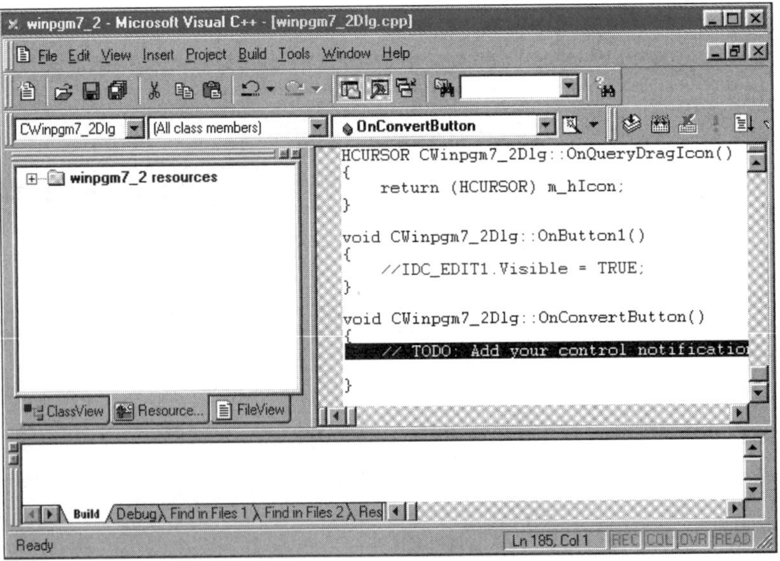

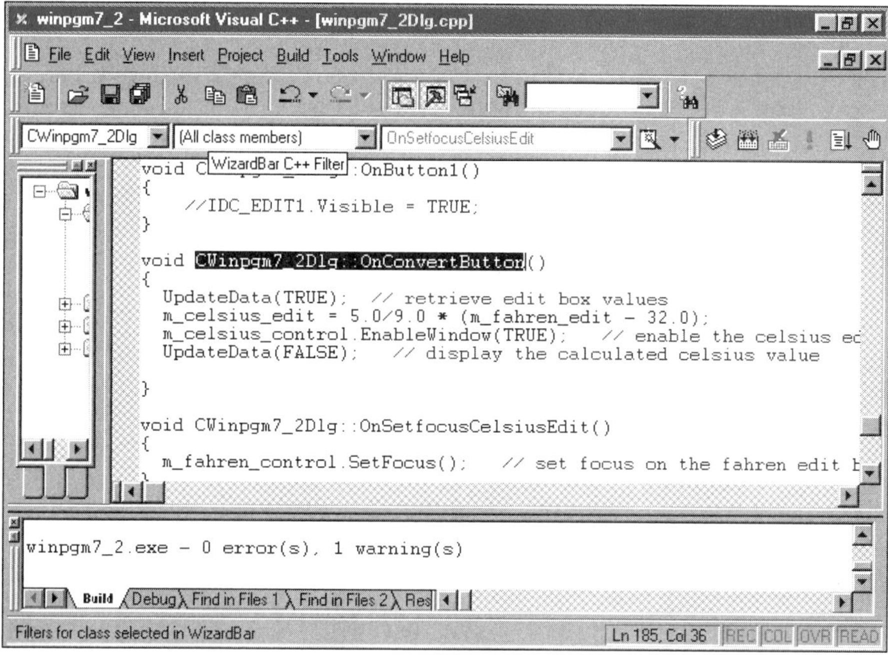

FIGURE 7.96

The completed event handler

Notice that the four event handlers that we have added have indeed been appended to the end of the Message Map area.

EXERCISES 7.4

1. Enter and execute Windows Program 7.2 on your computer.

2. a. Write a Visual C++ program that can be used to convert Celsius temperatures to their equivalent Fahrenheit values. Use a label to display the following prompt:

```
Enter the temperature in degrees Celsius:
```

After accepting a value entered from the keyboard into an Edit box, the program should convert the entered temperature to degrees Fahrenheit, using the equation *Fahrenheit* = (9.0 / 5.0) * *Celsius* + 32.0. The program should then display the temperature in degrees Fahrenheit in a clearly labeled Edit box. A Command button should be provided to terminate the application.

b. Verify your program by first calculating the Fahrenheit equivalent of the following test data by hand and then using your program to see it produces the correct results.

```
Test data set 1: 0 degrees Celsius.
Test data set 2: 50 degrees Celsius.
Test data set 3: 100 degrees Celsius.
```

When you are sure your procedure is working correctly, use it to complete the following table:

```
Celsius      Fahrenheit
  45
  50
  55
  60
  65
  70
```

3. Write and execute a Visual C++ program that displays the following prompts, using two label controls:

```
Enter the length of the office:
Enter the width of the office:
```

Have your program accept the user input in two Edit boxes. When a Command button is clicked, your program should calculate the area of the office and display the area in an Edit box. This display should be cleared whenever any of the input Edit boxes receive the focus. A second Command button should be provided to terminate the application. Verify your procedure using the following test data:

```
Test data set 1: length = 12.5, width = 10
Test data set 2: length = 12.4, width = 0
Test data set 3: length = 0, width = 10
```

4. **a.** Write and execute a Visual C++ program that displays the following prompts and uses two Edit boxes to receive the input data.

```
Enter the miles driven:
Enter the gallons of gas used:
```

The program should calculate and display the miles per gallon in an Edit box when a Command button is clicked. Use the equation *miles per gallon = miles / gallons used.* The display should be cleared whenever any of the Edit boxes gets the focus. A second Command button should be provided to terminate the application. Verify your procedure using the following test data:

```
Test data set 1: miles = 276, gallons used = 10
Test data set 2: miles = 200, gallons used = 15.5
```

When you have completed your verification, use your procedure to complete the following table:

```
miles          gallons used     miles per gallon
 250              16.00
 275              18.00
 312              19.54
 296              17.39
```

b. For the procedure written for Exercise 4a, determine how many verification runs are required to ensure the procedure is working correctly, and give a reason to support your answer.

5. Write a Visual C++ program that displays the following prompts:

```
Enter the length of the swimming pool:
Enter the width of the swimming pool:
Enter the average depth of the swimming pool:
```

Have your program accept the user input in three Edit boxes. When a Command button is clicked your program should calculate the volume of the swimming pool and display the volume in an Edit box. This display should be cleared whenever the input Edit boxes receive the focus. A second Command button should be provided to terminate the application. In calculating the volume use the equation *volume* = *length* * *width* * *average depth.*

6. Write and execute a Visual C++ program that provides three Edit boxes for the input of three user input numbers. There should be a single label prompt that tells the user to enter three numbers in the boxes. When the user clicks a Command button the program should calculate the average of the numbers and then display the average in a clearly labeled Edit box. The displayed value should be cleared whenever one of the Edit boxes receives the focus. A second Command button should be provided to terminate the application. Verify your procedure using the following test data:

```
Test data set 1: 100, 100, 100
Test data set 2: 100, 50, 0
```

When you have completed your verification, use your program to complete the following table:

```
   Numbers              Average
92, 98, 79, 85
86, 84, 75, 86
63, 85, 74, 82
```

7. Write a Visual C++ program that prompts the user to input two numbers, each accepted by an Edit box, and that has a Command button with the caption `Swap`. When this Command button is pressed the values in the two Edit boxes should be switched.

8. Write a Visual C++ program that prompts the user to type in an integer number. Have your procedure accept the number as an integer and immediately display the integer. Run your procedure three times. The first time you run the procedure enter a valid integer number, the second time enter a floating point number, and the third time enter the string `"Help"`. Using the output display, see what numbers your procedure actually accepted from the data you entered.

9. Repeat Exercise 8, but have your procedure declare the variable used to store the number as a single precision floating point variable. Run the procedure four times. The first time enter an integer, the second time enter a decimal number with less than fourteen decimal places, the third time enter a number having more than fourteen decimal places, and the fourth time enter the string `"Oops"`. Using the output display, keep track of what number your procedure actually accepted from the data you typed in. What happened, if anything, and why?

10. a. Why do you think that most successful applications procedures contain extensive data input validity checks? (*Hint:* Review Exercises 8 and 9.)

b. What do you think is the difference between a data type check and a data reasonableness check?

c. Assume that a procedure requests that the velocity and acceleration of a car be entered by the user. What are some checks that could be made on the entered data?

7.5 Adding Check Box, Radio Button, and Group Box Controls

The Radio button and Check box controls are extremely useful in presenting users with a set of defined choices. The difference between these two types of controls is in the nature of the choice that must be made. In a Radio button group, the user can select only one choice from a mutually exclusive set of choices; for example, selecting a category of either being single, married, divorced, or widowed. Here the user is presented a list of choices, from which one and only one selection can be made. In a Check box control the user is also presented with a list of one or more choices, but each choice can be selected or not, independent of any other selection. An example of this is a list of style choices for displaying text, such as bold and italic. The user can select one, both, or neither choice. Because these two types of controls are closely related, we present both of them together in this section.

FIGURE 7.97

An interface containing a check box

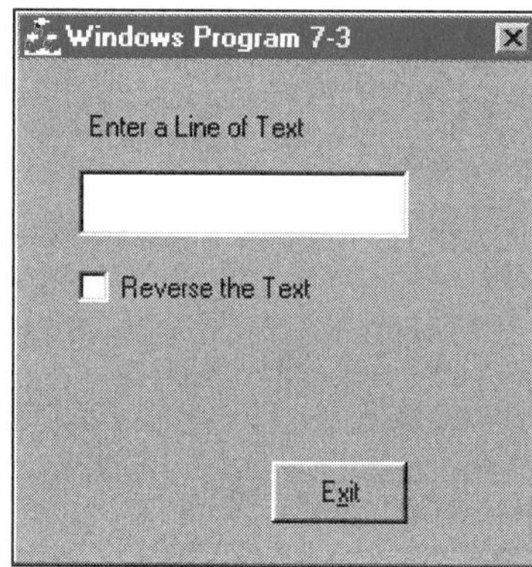

The Check Box Control

The Check box control provides a user with a simple Yes or No type of option. For example, in the interface shown in Figure 7.97 there is a single Check box. The properties for this interface are listed in Table 7.13.

TABLE 7.13 The Properties Table for Figure 7.97

Control	Property	Setting
Dialog	Caption	Windows Program 7.3
Static1	ID	IDC_TEXT_LABEL
	Caption	Enter a Line of Text
Edit1	ID	IDC_TEXT_EDIT
Check1	ID	IDC_REVERSE_CHECK
Button1	ID	IDC_EXIT_BUTTON
	Caption	E&xit

Using the information provided in Table 7.13, you should construct the GUI shown in Figure 7.97. The Check box control is the control with a Check Mark (`X`) contained within a box. Once you have the GUI assembled, add the two member variables listed in Table 7.14. Figures 7.98 and 7.99 show how the Add Member Variable dialog boxes will appear when you add these two member variables.

TABLE 7.14 Windows Program 7.3's member variables

Control ID	Variable Name	Variable Category	Variable Data Type
IDC_TEXT_EDIT	`m_edittext`	Value	CString
IDC_REVERSE_CHECK	`m_revcheck`	Value	BOOL

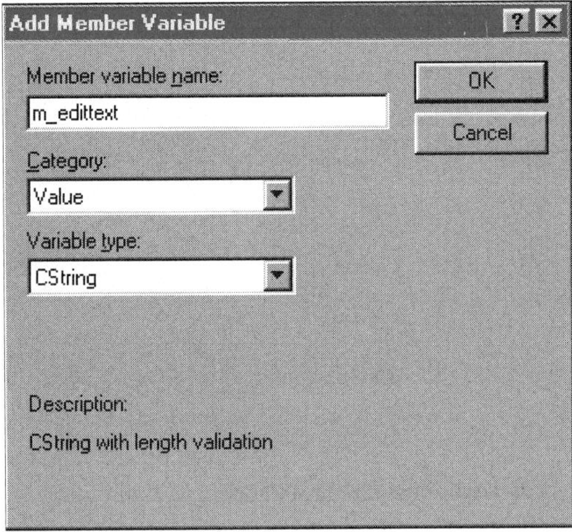

FIGURE 7.98

Adding the `m_edittext` **member variable**

The data type of the first member variable listed in Table 7.14 needs a bit of explanation. The CString data type is a non-MFC class that is provided in Visual C++ and is described in detail in Section 14.5. For now we can use it by observing that a CString variable stores a string of characters, and that the CString class comes with a number of useful member functions. Three of these supplied functions are listed in Table 7.15.

Once the control's member variables have been declared, all that remains to be done is add an event handler to correctly process the data when the Check box has been checked. Using the ClassWizard, we can add this function easily by selecting the Message

FIGURE 7.99

Adding the `m_revcheck` **member variable**

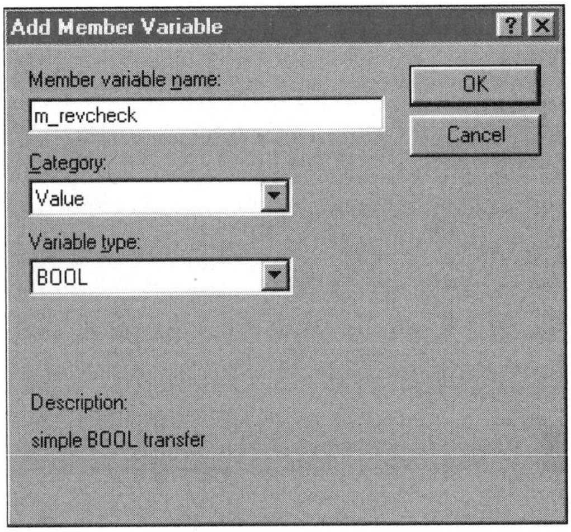

Add Member Variable
Member variable name:
m_revcheck
OK
Cancel
Category:
Value
Variable type:
BOOL
Description:
simple BOOL transfer

TABLE 7.15 CString supplied text processing functions

Function	Description
`MakeReverse()`	Reverse the characters in a CString variable
`MakeUpper()`	Convert all characters in a CString to uppercase
`MakeLower()`	Convert all characters in a CString to lowercase

Map tab and adding a function for the Check box's click event. Once you have added this function, supply it with the following code:

```
void CWinpgm7_3Dlg::OnReverseCheck()
{
  UpdateData(TRUE);  //retrieve the box's state
  if (m_revcheck)
  {
    m_edittext.MakeReverse();
    UpdateData(FALSE); // set the data
  }
}
```

Notice that the first thing this code does is to call the `UpdateData()` function to retrieve the state of all member variables. It then checks the Check box's member variable to see if this Boolean data variable has a value of `TRUE`, which indicates that the box has been checked. If the box is checked, the `MakeReverse()` function is applied to the `m_edittext` variable. The effect of this CString function is to reverse the letters in the string. Figure 7.100 shows how text appears in the application before the Check box has been checked, and Figure 7.101 shows how the text looks after the box has been checked.

FIGURE 7.100

The application without the Check box being checked

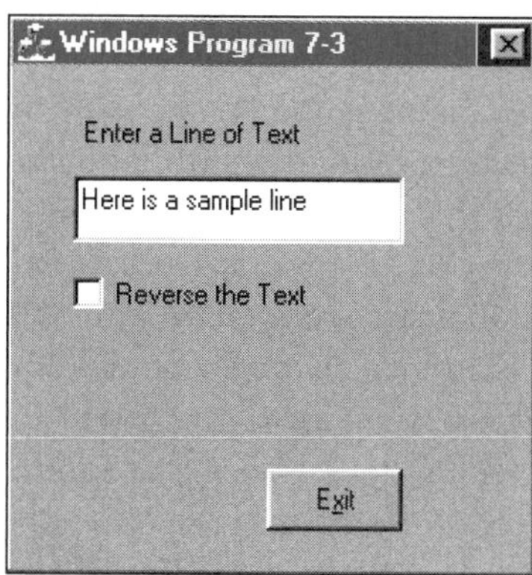

FIGURE 7.101

After the Check box has been checked

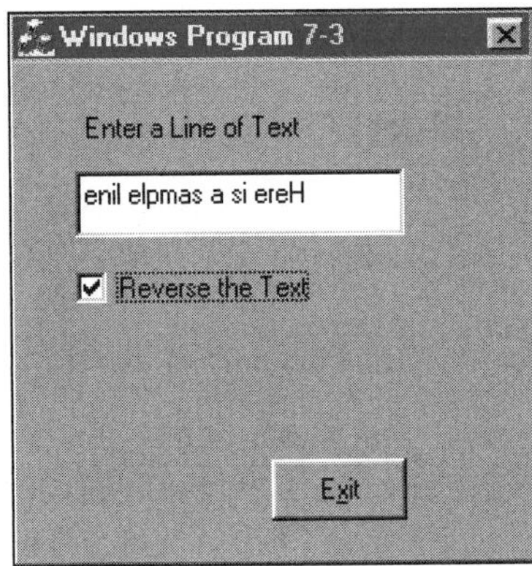

It is important to understand that each Check box in an application is independent of any other Check box. This means that the choice made in one box has no effect on, and does not depend on, the choice made in another box. As such, Check boxes are useful for providing a set of one or more options that can be in effect at the same time, provided that each option is individually of the yes/no, on/off, or true/false type. In Windows Program 7.3, there is only one Check box, and the box is checked only to see if it has effectively been turned on. So to rereverse the string shown in Figure 7.101 the Check box would have to be unchecked, which causes no action to be taken by the event handler (although the handler could be expanded to include the unchecked case), and then checked again.

The Radio Button and Group Box Controls

The Radio button control, which is also referred to as an Option button control, provides a user with a set of one or more choices, only one of which can be selected. Radio buttons always operate as a group, and selecting one Radio button immediately deselects and clears all of the other buttons in the group. Thus, the choices in a Radio button group are mutually exclusive. Radio buttons get their name because they operate in the same manner as the channel selector buttons provided on many radios, in which selecting one channel automatically deselects all other channels.

As an example using Radio buttons, consider a dialog that requires information on the marital status of an employee. As the employee can be either single, married, divorced, or widowed, selection of one category automatically means the other categories are not selected. This type of choice is ideal for a Radio button group, as shown in Figure 7.102, where the group consists of four individual Radio buttons.

Individual Radio buttons operate in terms of groups, where a group consists of at least one Radio button and usually consists of two or more buttons. For example, all of the buttons shown in Figure 7.102 belong to the same group. Within a group a user can move from one Radio button to another using the keyboard arrow keys, and

FIGURE 7.102

A Radio button group

when one button in the group is selected, all other buttons in the group will be automatically deselected.

The first button defining a group is determined by checking the button's Group property, which sets this property to TRUE. Thereafter, all buttons in the tab sequence following the button whose Group property was checked will be members of the same group, as long as these additional buttons do not have their Group property checked (that is, the remaining buttons in the group all have their Group properties set to FALSE). The next radio button whose Group property is checked becomes the first button in a new group, and so on. This permits you to have as many separate groups of Radio buttons as you need. Typically, each group of Radio buttons is enclosed within a Group box control, one of which is shown in Figure 7.103. The Group box control, like a Label control, is a static control. Although a Group box should logically enclose Radio buttons belonging to the same button group, the placement of a Group box does not define the button group; it is merely a passive control that can be used anywhere on a dialog to visually improve the dialog's appearance.

Windows Program 7.4 uses a Radio button group to capture the marital status of the user. This program's interface is shown in Figure 7.103, and its control properties are listed in Table 7.16. Using the information in the figure and table, you should construct the program's GUI, as it is shown in Figure 7.103.

Notice in Properties Table 7.16 that only one of the Radio button Group properties has been checked. Setting any other Radio button's Group property would automatically start a new button group.

FIGURE 7.103

Windows Program 7.4's GUI

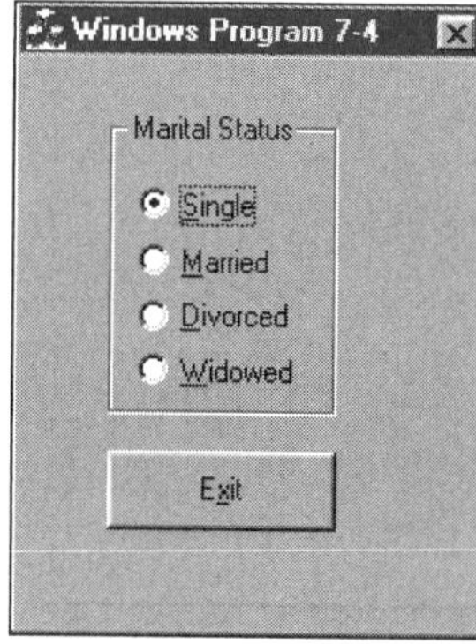

TABLE 7.16 Windows Program 7.4's Properties Table

Control	Property	Setting
Dialog	Caption	Windows Program 7.4
Static1	ID	IDC_GROUP_BOX
	Caption	Marital Status
Radio1	ID	IDC_SING_RADIO
	Caption	Single
	Visible	Checked
	Group	Checked
	Tab stop	Checked
Radio2	ID	IDC_MAR_RADIO
	Caption	Married
	Visible	Checked
	Group	Not Checked
	Tab stop	Checked
Radio3	ID	IDC_DIV_RADIO
	Caption	Divorced
	Visible	Checked
	Group	Not Checked
	Tab stop	Checked
Radio4	ID	IDC_WID_RADIO
	Caption	Widowed
	Visible	Checked
	Group	Not Checked
	Tab stop	Checked
Button1	ID	IDC_EXIT_BUTTON
	Caption	E&xit

All that now remains is to add a member variable to the button group (one variable serves the complete group), add event handlers for each button, and initialize one button in the group to be in a selected state when the program is initially executed. Except for the initialization procedure, adding a member variable and event handlers should, by now, be familiar to you. Nevertheless, we quickly review each of these steps here, as they apply to Windows Program 7.4.

Adding a Member Variable Figure 7.104 shows how the ClassWizard Member Variables tab will initially appear before any member variables are declared (invoke ClassWizard using the shortcut key sequence `Ctrl+W`). As is seen, only one Control ID is shown, which is always the group's starting button (the one whose Group property was checked). For this button, add the member variable whose properties are shown in Figure 7.105.

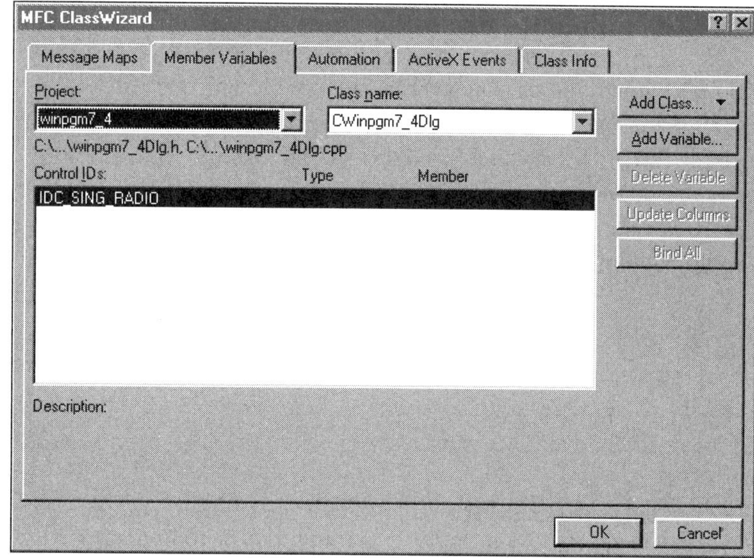

FIGURE 7.104

Adding a member variable

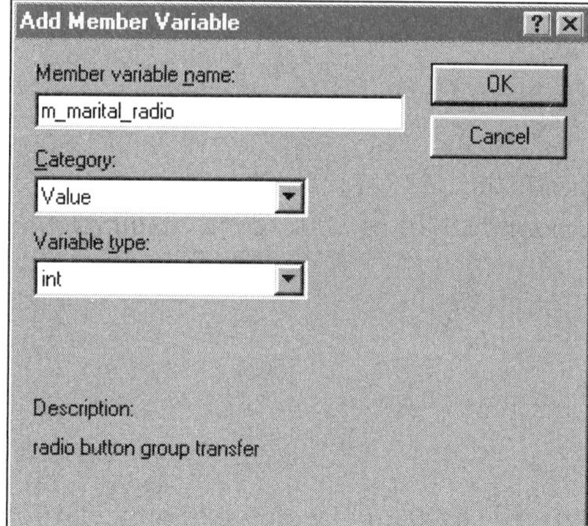

FIGURE 7.105

Declaring the member variable

Adding Event Handlers For Windows Program 7.4 we add five event handlers; the code for all of these is listed here:

Windows Program 7.4's Event Handler Code

```
void CWinpgm7_4Dlg::OnSingRadio()
{
  if (m_marital_radio == 0)
     MessageBox("User Checked Single", "Test", MB_OK);
}
```

```
void CWinpgm7_4Dlg::OnMarRadio()
{
  if (m_marital_radio == 0)
     MessageBox("User Checked Married", "Test", MB_OK);
}


void CWinpgm7_4Dlg::OnDivRadio()
{
  if (m_marital_radio == 0)
     MessageBox("User Checked Divorced", "Test", MB_OK);

}

void CWinpgm7_4Dlg::OnWidRadio()
{
  if (m_marital_radio == 0)
     MessageBox("User Checked Widowed", "Test", MB_OK);
}

void CWinpgm7_4Dlg::OnExitButton()
{
  MessageBeep(MB_OK);
  SendMessage(WM_CLOSE);
}
```

This code should be entered using ClassWizard's Message Map tab. Figure 7.106 shows how this tab will look when you add an event handler function for the `Single` button's click event, and Figure 7.107 shows the Add Member Function dialog for the added function. You will have to repeat each of the steps used to add the OnSingRadio event handlers for the remaining four event handlers. As each handler is added to the project, you should edit the provided skeleton function and add the appropriate code listed above.

Initializing the Radio Button Group All that remains to complete Windows Program 7.4 is to initialize the Radio button group so that the first button in the group is shown as selected when the program is first executed. This initialization is most easily accomplished using the program's own initialization procedure, which is automatically executed when the program is first loaded into memory. The required procedure is named `OnInitDialog()`, and will have the form shown in Figure 7.108.

FIGURE 7.106

Adding an event handler

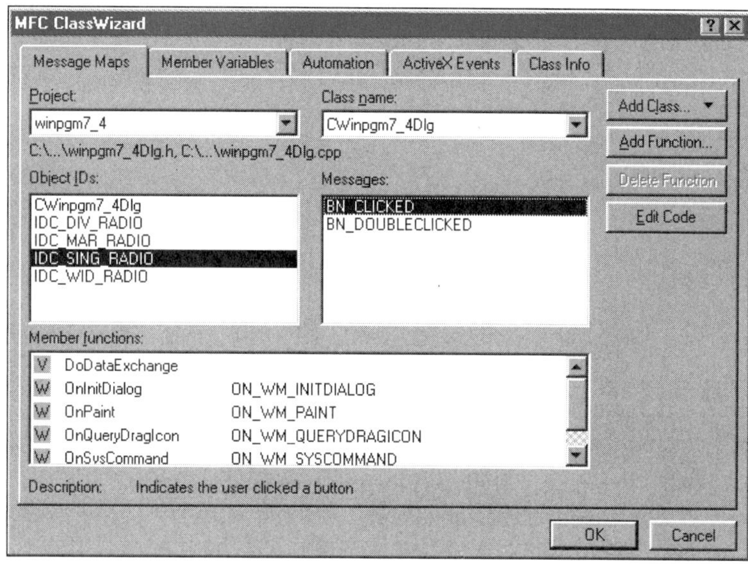


```
BOOL CWinpgm7_4Dlg::OnInitDialog()
{
            .
            .
            .
  // TODO: Add extra initialization here
            .
            .
}
```

You can locate this procedure either manually, by searching through the code or by using the Edit menu's `Find...` command, or by using our old friend and master code locator, the ClassWizard (`Ctrl+W`). Figure 7.109 shows the required selections in the ClassWizard's Message Maps tab to locate the `OnInitDialog()` function.

FIGURE 7.107

The Add Member Function dialog

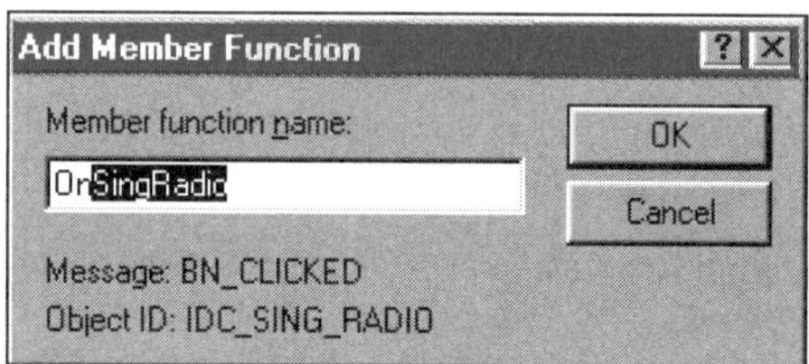

Once you have the function in the Text editor, locate the line

```
// TODO: Add extra initialization here
```

FIGURE 7.108

Windows Program 7.4's initialization function

```
BOOL CWinpgm7_4Dlg::OnInitDialog()
{
              •
              •
              •
   // TODO: Add extra initialization here
              •
              •
}
```

Immediately below this line enter the following two lines of code:

```
m_marital_radio = 0;
UpdateData(FALSE); // set the data
```

Once this is done, the Single button will automatically be selected when the program is initially executed. A user can then change this selection at run time in one of the following three ways:

- Clicking the mouse on the desired button
- Tabbing to the button group and using the arrow keys
- Using the accelerator (shortcut) keys

FIGURE 7.109

Using the ClassWizard to locate the initialization function

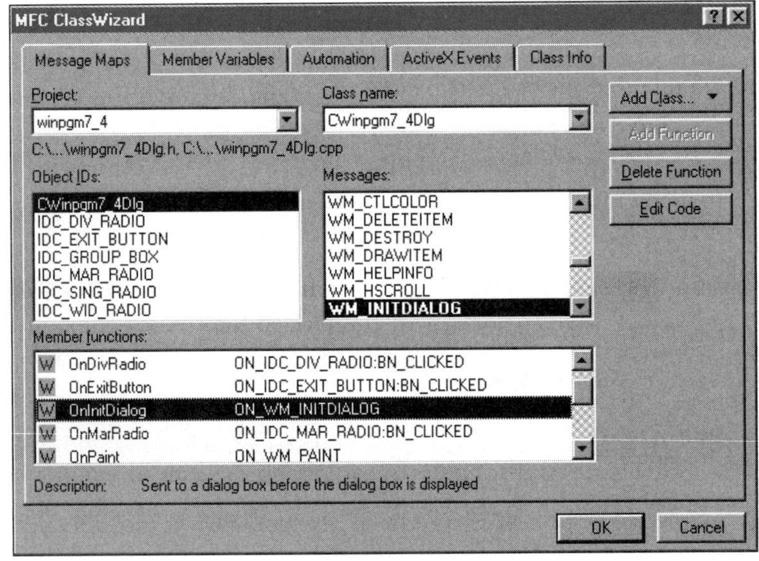

EXERCISES 7.5

1. Determine whether the following choices should be presented on a GUI using Check boxes or Radio buttons:
   a. The choice of air conditioning or not on a new automobile order form.
   b. The choice of automatic or manual transmission on a new automobile order form.
   c. The choice of AM/FM, AM/FM Tape, or AM/FM CD Radio on a new automobile order form.
   d. The choice of tape backup system or no tape backup system on a new computer order form.
   e. The choice of a 14-, 15-, or 17-inch color monitor on a new computer order form.
   f. The choice of zip drive or not on a new computer order form.
   g. The choice of a 16-, 24-, or 32-speed CD-ROM drive on a new computer order form.
   h. The choice of a 200, 300, or 400 MHz Pentium processor on a new computer order form.
2. Enter and run Windows Program 7.3 on your computer.
3. a. Modify Windows Program 7.3 so that the choices presented by the Check box are replaced by two Command buttons.
   b. Based on your experience with Exercise 3a, determine what type of input choice is best presented using a Check box rather than Command buttons.
4. a. Modify Windows Program 7.3 so that the choices presented by the Check boxes are replaced by Radio buttons.
   b. Based on your experience with Exercise 4a, determine what type of input choice is best presented using a Check box rather than a Radio button.
5. Enter and run Windows Program 7.4 on your computer.
6. Modify Windows Program 7.3 so that a user can select whether to make the displayed text uppercase or lowercase using a Radio button group consisting of two buttons. (*Hint:* Use the `MakeUpper()` and `MakeLower()` functions listed in Table 7.15.)

7.6 Common Programming Errors and Problems

One of the most frustrating problems when creating Windows-based programs in Visual C++ is not being able to locate all of the elements needed to create an application. This means not having either the Resource editor or Toolbox visible, or not knowing how to get out of Full screen editing mode. To bring up the Resource editor, activate the IDE's ResourceView tab, expand the hierarchy tree, and double click on the desired resource name. To bring up the Toolbox window, when the Resource editor is active, right click the mouse on the Main Menu bar and check the Controls option from the displayed context menu. To get out of Full screen editing mode, press the `Esc` key.

A second common error made by beginning programmers is forgetting to save a project at periodic intervals while an application is being developed. Although you can usually get away without periodic saves, every experienced programmer knows the agony of losing work due to a variety of mistakes or an unexpected power outage. To avoid this, you should develop the habit of periodically saving your work.

A third common error is not being able to locate an existing project. The easiest way to retrieve a saved project is to use the `File` menu's `Recent Workspaces` option. If the desired project is not in the `Recent Workspaces` list, use the `File` menu's `Open Workspace...` option, and then open the file that has the .dsw extension. This is the file that contains all of the information needed by Visual C++ to locate all of the header, source code, and resource files used in a project.

Finally, the most consistently troublesome error occurs when the programmer does not change a dialog or object's ID name immediately when beginning to work with it. *Changing a name after you have added Event Code detaches the object from the code.* This occurs because the Event Code procedure name is based on the object's name at the time the code is defined. The Event Code doesn't become lost, it just becomes another function that can be accessed using the Control Wizard.

7.7 Chapter Summary

1. A Windows-based Visual C++ program is a full-featured program that consists of a visual part and a language part. The visual part is provided by the objects used in the design of the graphical user interface, and the language part consists of procedural code.

2. A graphical user interface (GUI) provides the user with control objects that recognize events, such as clicking a mouse.

3. The basic steps in developing a Visual C++ program are:

1. Create the graphical user interface.
2. Set the properties of each object on the interface.
3. Write procedural code.

4. A Single Document Interface (SDI) application is one that permits only one main window to be displayed at a time. SDI applications can have multiple main windows, but only one window can be viewed at a time by a user. The Notepad application supplied with the Windows operating system is an SDI application,

5. A Multiple Document Interface (MDI) application consists of a single "parent" or main window that can contain multiple "child" or internal windows. The Excel and Access applications are both MDI applications.

6. A Dialog based application is an application that uses a single dialog box as a Main window. Dialog boxes always permit the display of controls within the dialog area.

7. Visual C++ provides an applications wizard (AppWizard) that can be used to construct a skeleton Windows application. The application can be a SDI, MDI, or Dialog based application.

8. The most commonly placed objects on a dialog are Command buttons, Edit boxes, and Labels.

9. Each control placed on a dialog has an ID name property that is used to identify the control. Additionally, many controls also have a Caption property that is visible to a user when an application is executing.

10. A member variable is a variable that is attached to a control. Like function variables, member variables must be declared as to name and data type. Additionally, a member variable can be either a Value or Control variable.

11. Value member variables are used to transfer values to and from controls.

12. Control member variables are used to identify a control and affect its operation, generally by using MFC supplied functions.

13. Event handlers are functions attached to controls that are invoked by events, such as pressing a button.

14. The ClassWizard is the primary tool for creating and accessing both member variables and event handler functions. This wizard also takes care of the requirement of creating each event handler's prototype and placing the prototype in a class's Message Map section.

15. A Check box is a control that appears as a square box with an attached label, and provides the user with a Yes or No type of selection. If multiple Check boxes are used, the choice supplied by each box can be selected or not, independent of any other selection. Thus, a user can select one, all, or no boxes.

16. In a Radio button group, the user can select only one choice from a mutually exclusive set of choices. Here the user is presented a list of choices, from which one and only one selection can be made.

PART TWO

OBJECT-ORIENTED PROGRAMMING

8 I/O File Streams and Data Files

The data for the programs we have seen so far have either been assigned internally within the programs or entered interactively during program execution. This type of data entry is fine for small amounts of data.

In this chapter we learn how to store data outside of a program using C++'s object-oriented capabilities.[1] This external data storage permits a program to use the data without the user having to interactively recreate it each time the program is executed. This provides the basis for sharing data between programs, so that the data output by one program can be input directly to another program. Additionally, it serves as an introduction

---

1 This stand-alone chapter on file usage can be used as an introduction to object-oriented programming, or can be omitted on first reading with no loss of subject continuity.

to the stream objects used in delivering data to and from a program. As such, this provides an early presentation to the more general topic of object-oriented programming.

8.1 I/O File Stream Objects and Methods

To store and retrieve data on a file in C++ three items are required:

- A file
- A file stream object
- A mode

Files

Any collection of data that is stored together under a common name on a storage medium other than the computer's main memory is called a **data file.** Data files typically are stored on a disk, magnetic tape, or CD-ROM. For example, the C++ programs that you store on disk are examples of files. The stored data in this particular form of a file is referred to as a **program file** and consists of the program code that becomes input data to the C++ compiler.

A file is physically stored on an external medium such as a disk by using a unique file name referred to as the **external file name.** This external name is the name of the file as it is known by the operating system. It is the external name that is displayed when you use an operating system command or icon for displaying the contents of a folder.

Each computer operating system has its own specification as to the maximum number of characters permitted for an external file name. Table 8.1 lists these specifications for the more commonly used operating systems.

To ensure that the examples presented in this text are compatible with all of the operating systems listed in Table 8.1 we adhere to the more restrictive DOS and VMX specifications. If you are using one of the other operating systems, however, you should take advantage of the increased length specification to create descriptive file names within the context of a manageable length (generally considered to be no more that 12 to 14 characters). Very long file names should be avoided. Although such names can be extremely descriptive, they do take more time to type and are prone to typing errors.

Using the more restrictive DOS convention, then, the following are all valid computer data file names:

```
bessel.dat       records      info.txt
exper1.dat       volts.dat    math.mem
```

TABLE 8.1 Maximum allowable file name characters

Operating System	Maximum Length
DOS	8 characters plus an optional period and 3 character extension
VMX	8 characters plus an optional period and 3 character extension
Windows 3.1*	8 characters plus an optional period and 3 character extension
Windows 95	255 characters
Windows 98	255 Characters
UNIX	
Early Versions	14 characters
Current Versions	255 characters

*Because Windows 3.1 runs under DOS, it has the same restrictions as DOS. Technically, Windows 3.1 is not an operating system at all, but an application that runs under DOS. It should more properly be referred to as a dynamic linker and file managing application.

Computer file names should be chosen to indicate both the type of data in the file and the application for which it is used. Frequently, the first eight characters are used to describe the data and an extension (the three characters after the decimal point) is used to describe the application. For example, the Lotus 123 spreadsheet program automatically applies an extension of `wk3` to all spreadsheet files; the Microsoft Word and WordPerfect word processing programs use the extensions `doc` and `wpx` (where `x` refers to the version number), respectively; and most C++ compilers require a program file to have the extension `cpp`. When creating your own file names you should adhere to this practice. For example, the name `exper1.dat` is appropriate in describing a file of data corresponding to experiment number 1.

File Stream Objects and Modes

A **file stream** is a one-way transmission path that is used to connect a file stored on a physical device, such as a disk or CD-ROM, to a program. Associated with every file stream is a **mode,** which determines the direction of data on the transmission path; that is, whether the path will be used for moving data from a file into a program, or whether the path will be used for moving data from a program to a file. A file stream with a mode designated as **input** is referred to as an **input file stream** and is used to receive or read data from a file. A file stream with an **output** mode designation is referred to as an **output file stream** and is used to send or write data to a file. Figure 8.1 illustrates the data flow from and to a file using input and output streams.

FIGURE 8.1

Input and output file streams

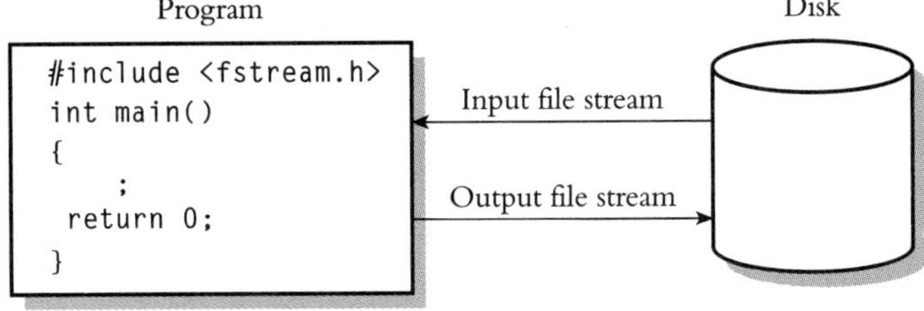

For each file that your program uses, a distinct file stream object must be created. If you are going to both read and write to a file, input and output file stream objects are both required. Input file stream objects are declared to be of type `ifstream`, and output file streams are declared to be of type `ofstream`. For example, the declaration

```
ifstream inStream;
```

declares an input file stream object named `inStream` that is of type `ifstream`. Similarly, the declaration

```
ofstream outStream;
```

declares an output file stream object named `outStream` that is of type `ofstream`. Within a C++ program a file stream is always accessed by its appropriate stream object name, one name for reading the file and one name for writing to the file. Object names, such as `inStream` and `outStream`, can be any programmer-chosen names that conform to C++'s identifier rules.

File Stream Methods

Each file stream object has access to prewritten functions defined for its respective `ifstream` or `ofstream` class. These functions include connecting a stream to an external file name (called *opening a file*), determining if a successful connection has been made, closing a connection (called *closing a file*), getting the next data item into the program from an input stream, putting a new data item from the program onto an output stream, and detecting when the end of a file has been reached.

Opening a file connects each file stream object to a specific external file name. This is accomplished using a file stream's `open()` function, which is a "cookbook" procedure that accomplishes two purposes. First, opening a file establishes the physical connecting link between a program and a file. Details of this link are handled by the computer's oper-

PROGRAMMER'S NOTES

Input and Output Streams

A *stream* is a one-way transmission path between a source and a destination. What gets sent down this transmission path is a stream of bytes. A good analogy to this "stream of bytes" is a stream of water that provides a one-way transmission path of water from a source to a destination.

Two stream objects that we have already used extensively are the input stream object named `cin` and the output stream object named `cout`. The `cin` object provides a transmission path from keyboard to program, and the `cout` object provides a transmission path from program to terminal screen. These two objects are created from the stream classes named `istream` and `ostream`, respectively. When the `iostream.h` header file is included in a program using the `#include<iostream.h>` directive, the `cin` and `cout` stream objects are automatically declared as belonging to these streams, and are opened by the C++ compiler for use by the compiled program.

File stream objects provide the same capabilities as the `cin` and `cout` objects, except they connect a program to a file rather than the keyboard or terminal screen. Also, file stream objects must be explicitly declared. File stream objects that will be used for input must be declared as type `ifstream`, whereas file stream objects that will be used for output must be declared as type `ofstream`. These two classes, as well as the capability for automatically constructing the `cin` and `cout` objects, are made available to a program by inclusion of the `fstream.h` header file using the directive `#include<fstream.h>`.

ating system and are transparent to the program, so the programmer normally need not consider them.

From a coding perspective, the second purpose of opening a file is more relevant. Besides establishing the actual physical connection between a program and a data file, opening a file equates the file's external computer name to the stream object name used internally by the program. The function that performs this task is named `open()` and is provided by both the `ifstream` and `ofstream` classes.

In using the `open()` function to connect the file's external name to its internal object stream name, only one argument is required—the external file name. For example, the statement

```
inFile.open("test.dat");
```

connects the external file named `test.dat` to the internal program file stream object named `inFile`. This assumes, of course, that `inFile` has been declared as either an `ifstream` or `ofstream` object. Although this statement may look a little strange for a function call, there is a good reason for it. The part of the name to the left of the required period identifies a specific object, and the part of the name to the right of the period identifies the function being called. This notation is used because, when dealing with objects such as a file stream, more than one function with the same name can exist. For example, there is more than one `open()` function.

Specifically, there is a function named `open()` that is used for opening input streams and a differenct function, also named `open()`, that is used for opening output streams. Although both functions clearly perform a similar "opening" task, one effectively opens a file for input, whereas the other one is used to open a file for output. The compiler correctly determines which `open()` function to use by the name that appears to the left of the period. Functions, such as `open()`, that are associated with objects are referred to as both **member functions** and **methods** (the terms are used interchangeably), and using such functions requires that the function name be preceded by a period and an object name.

Once an input stream has been opened with the previous statement, the program accesses the file using the internal object name `inFile`, and the computer saves the file under the external name `test.dat`. Notice that the external file name argument passed to `open()` is a string contained between double quotes.

When an existing file is connecting to an input file stream, the file's data are made available for input, starting at the first data item in the file. Similarly, a file connected to an output file stream creates a new file and make the file available for output. If a file exists with the same name as a file opened in output mode, the old file is erased and all its data are lost.

When opening a file, for input or output, good programming practice requires that you check that the connection has been established before attempting to use the file in any way. The check can be made using the `fail()` method. This method will return a true value, which is a 1, if the open was successful, or a false value, which is a 0, if the open failed. To correctly use the `fail()` method for a file that will be used for input, however, you must open the file in `ios::nocreate` mode, as is shown below.[2] Doing this sets a `fail` bit when the file is not found, which is the bit used by `fail()` to determine if a successful open occurred. (See Programmer's Notes on pages 444 and 446.) The `fail()` method is used in code similar to the following, which attempts to open a file named `test.dat`, checks that a valid connection was made, and reports an error message if the file was not successfully opened for input:

```
ifstream inFile;  // any object name can be used here

inFile.open("test.dat", ios::nocreate);  // open the file

// check that the connection was successfully opened
if (inFile.fail())
```

---

2 Opening a file using the `ios::nocreate` mode prevents a new file from being created if the named file does not exist, and the `fail()` method will correctly report that the file was not opened.

```
{
  cout << "\nThe file was not successfully opened"
       << "\n Please check that the file currently exists."
       << endl;
  exit(1);
}
```

If the `fail()` method returns a true, which indicates that the open failed, a message is displayed by this code, and the `exit()` function, which is a request to the operating system to end program execution immediately, is called. The `exit()` function requires inclusion of the `stdlib.h` header function in any program that uses this function, and `exit()`'s single integer argument is passed directly to the operating system for possible further operating system program action or user inspection. Throughout the remainder of the text, we include this type of error checking whenever a file is opened.

Program 8.1 illustrates the statements required to open a file in input mode, including an error-checking routine to ensure that a successful open was obtained.

PROGRAM 8.1

```
#include <fstream.h>
#include <stdlib.h>   // needed for exit()

int main()
{
  ifstream inFile;

  inFile.open("test.dat",ios::nocreate);  // open the file with the
                                          // external name test.dat
  if (inFile.fail())  // check for a successful open
  {
    cout << "\nThe file was not successfully opened"
         << "\n Please check that the file currently exists."
         << endl;
    exit(1);
  }

  cout << "\nThe file has been successfully opened for reading"
       << endl;

  return 0;
}
```

PROGRAMMER'S NOTES

Checking for a Successful Connection

It is important to check that the `open()` method successfuly established a connection between a file stream and an external file. This is because the `open()` call is really a request to the operating system that can fail for a variety of reasons. (Chief among these reasons is a request to open an existing file for reading that the operating system cannot locate.) If the operating system cannot satisfy the open request, you need to know about it and gracefully terminate your program. Failure to do so almost always results in some abnormal program behavior or a subsequent program crash.

There are two styles of coding for checking the return value. The most common method for checking that a fail did not occur is the one coded in Program 8.1. It is used to clearly distinguish the `open()` request from the check made via the `fail()` call, and is repeated below for convenience:

```
inFile.open("test.dat",ios::nocreate);  // request to open the file

if (inFile.fail())  // check for a failed connection
{
  cout << "\nThe file was not successfully opened"
         << "\n Please check that the file currently exists."
        << endl;
  exit(1);
}
```

Alternatively, you may encounter programs that use `fstream` objects in place of both `ifstream` and `ofstream` objects. When using `fstream`'s `open()` method, two arguments are required: a file's external name and an explicit mode indication. If the `open()` function is not successful, the `fstream` stream object is assigned the named constant `NULL`. Using this named constant, the open request and check would appear as follows:

```
fstream inFile;

infile.open("external file name", ios::in | ios::nocreate;
if (inFile == NULL)
{
  cout << "\nThe file was not successfully opened"
        << "\n Please check that the file currently exists."
        << endl;
  exit(1);
}
```

Notice that the `ios::nocreate` mode is `OR`ed with the `ios::in` mode. The definitions for these modes are presented in the next Programmer's Notes box on page 446. Many times the conditional expression `inFile == NULL` is replaced by the equivalent expression `!inFile`. Although we will always use `ifstream` and `ofstream` objects, be prepared to encounter the styles that use `fstream` objects.

Assuming that a file named `test.dat` is available on the current directory, a sample run using Program 8.1 will display the following output line:

```
The file has been successfully opened for reading.
```

Although Program 8.1 can be used to open an existing file in input mode, it lacks statements to either read the file's data or close the file. These topics are discussed shortly. Before leaving Program 8.1, however, two items should be noted. First, the `iostream.h` header file did not have to be included in the program to use the `cout` object because its definition is incorporated within the `fstream.h` header file. Next, it is possible to combine the declaration of an `fstream` object and its associated open statement into one statement. For example, the two statements in Program 8.1:

```
ifstream inFile;
inFile.open("test.dat", ios::nocreate);    // open the file
```

can be combined into the single statement

```
ifstream inFile("test.dat", ios::nocreate);
```

In this text we continue to declare all `ifstream` and `ofstream` objects at the top of the program and explicitly call the `open()` method in a separate statement. You may, however, choose to use the alternative single statement form.

Embedded and Interactive File Names

Two practical problems with Program 8.1 are:

1. The external file name is embedded within the program code.
2. There is no provision for a user to enter the desired file name while the program is executing.

As Program 8.1 is written, to change the file name, a programmer must modify the external file name in the call to `open()` and recompile the program. Both of these problems can be alleviated by assigning the file name to a string variable.

A **string variable** is a variable that can hold a string value, which is any sequence of zero or more characters enclosed within double quotes. For example, `"Hello World"`, `"test.dat"`, and `""` are all strings. Notice that strings are always written with double quotes that delimit the beginning and end of a string but are not stored as part of the string.

PROGRAMMER'S NOTES

Using `fstream` Objects

In using both `ifstream` and `ofstream` objects, the mode—input or output—is implied by the object. Thus, `ifstream` objects can be used only for input, whereas `ofstream` objects can be used only for output.

Another means of creating file streams is to use `fstream` objects that can be used for input or output, but require an explicit mode assignment. An `fstream` object is declared using the syntax

```
fstream object-name;
```

When using the `fstream` class's `open()` member function, two arguments are required: a file's external name and a mode indicator. Permissible mode indicators are:

Indicator	*Description*
`ios::in`	Open in input mode
`ios::out`	Open in output mode
`ios::app`	Open in append mode
`ios::ate`	Go to the end of the opened file
`ios::binary`	Open in binary mode (default is text)
`ios::trunc`	Delete file contents if it exists
`ios::nocreate`	If file does not exist, open fails
`ios::noreplace`	If file exists, open for output fails

As with `ofstream` objects, an `fstream` object in output mode creates a new file and makes the file available for writing. If a file exists with the same name as a file opened for output, the old file is erased. For example, assuming that `file1` has been declared as an object of type `fstream` using the statement

```
fstream file1;
```

then the statement

```
file1.open("test.dat",ios::out);
```

attempts to open the file named `test.dat` for output. Once this file has been opened, the program accesses the file using the internal object name `file1`, and the computer saves the file under the external name `test.dat`.

An `fstream` file object opened in `append` mode means that an existing file is available for data to be added to the end of the file. If the file opened for appending does not exist, a new file with the designated name is created and made available to receive output from the program. For example, again assuming that `file1` has been delcared to be of type `fstream`, the statement

```
file1.open("test.dat",ios::app);
```

attempts to open a file named `test.dat` and makes it available for data to be appended to the end of the file.

Finally, an `fstream` object opened in input mode means that an existing external file has been connected and its data are available as input. For example, assuming that `file1` has been declared to be of type `fstream`, the statement

```
file1.open("test.dat",ios::in);
```

attempts to open a file named `test.dat` for input.

PROGRAMMER'S NOTES

Character and String Variables

The primary difference between character and string variables is that a character variable can store only a single character value whereas a string variable can store a string value of zero or more characters. The stored value, however, always contains an additional end-of-string symbolic constant named `NULL`. For example, consider the declarations

```
char nameOne = 'x';
char nameTwo[2] = "x";
```

First, notice that the initializing character value is enclosed within single quotes, whereas the initializing string value is enclosed in double quotes. In the first case only one character, an `x`, is stored in the character variable `nameOne`. In the second case, two characters are stored. These consist of the `x` character plus an end-of-string termination character supplied by the compiler. For all string variables, this character is the named constant `NULL`, which has the value `'\0'`. As we will see in Chapter 14, this end-of-string `NULL` constant is extremely useful in processing strings. This is because it provides a relatively easy method of always determining where a string ends without knowing, beforehand, the actual string length.

Because of this terminating `NULL`, a string variable such as "" is not stored as an empty string, but consists of the single `NULL` terminating character.

One other very important difference between character and string variables is that assignment to a string variable is always invalid except within a declaration statement. Assignment in nondeclarative statements is accomplished using the `strcopy()` function, which is described in Chapter 14.

The concepts, storage, and manipulation of strings and string variables are discussed in detail in Chapter 14; however, the declaration of a string variable, discussed here, is extremely simple. For example, whereas the declaration

```
char filename = 'a';
```

declares a character variable named `filename` and initializes this character variable to the single letter `a`, the declaration

```
char filename[21] = "test.dat";
```

declares a string variable capable of holding 21 characters in total and initializes the string variable with the string value `"test.dat"`.

In declaring and initializing a string variable, three items must be considered. First, the maximum length of the string must be specified within brackets immediately after the variable's name. This is the function of the `[21]` in the above declaration. Second, *the number in brackets always represents one more than* the maximum number of characters that you can assign to the variable. This is because the compiler always adds a final end-of-string character to terminate the string. Thus the string value "test.dat", which consists of 8 characters is actually stored as 9 characters, where the extra character is an end-of-string marker supplied by the compiler. Finally, each initializing string value can be any sequence of characters from zero to one less than the maximum length specified in brackets. Thus the maximum string value assignable to the string variable filename declared by the declaration filename[21] is a string value consisting of 20 characters.

Once a string variable is declared to store a filename, it can be used in one of two ways. First, as shown in Program 8.1a, it can placed at the top of a program to identify a file's external name, rather than embedded within an open() method call.

PROGRAM 8.1a

```
#include <fstream.h>
#include <stdlib.h>

int main()
{
  const int MAXLENGTH = 21;  // maximum file name length
  char file1[MAXLENGTH] = "test.dat";   // place the file name up front
  ifstream inFile;

  inFile.open(file1, ios::nocreate);  // open the file

  if (inFile.fail())  // check for successful open
  {
    cout << "\nThe file named " << file1 << " was not successfully opened"
         << "\n Please check that the file currently exists." << endl;
    exit(1);
  }

  cout << "\nThe file has been successfully opened for reading.\n";

  return 0;
}
```

In reviewing Program 8.1a, notice that we have used a symbolic constant named MAXLENGTH to define the length of the string variable file1 and that we have declared and initialized this string variable at the top of the program for easy file identification. Next, notice that when a string variable is used, as opposed to a string value, the variable name *is not* enclosed within double quotes in the open() method call. Finally, notice that in the fail() method code we can display the file's external name by inserting the string variable name in the cout standard output stream. For all of these reasons we will continue to identify the external names of files in this manner.

The second, extremely useful role played by string variables is to permit the user to enter the file name as the program is executing. For example, the code

```
const int MAXLENGTH = 21;
char file1[MAXLENGTH];

cout << "Please enter the name of the file you wish to open: ";
cin  >> file1;
```

allows a user to enter a file's external name at run time. The only restriction in this code is that the user *must not* enclose the entered string value in double quotes, which is an advantage, and that the entered string value cannot contain any blanks. The reason for this is that the compiler will terminate the string when it encounters a blank.

Program 8.1b uses this code in the context of a complete program.

PROGRAM 8.1b

```
#include <fstream.h>
#include <stdlib.h>

int main()
{
  const int MAXLENGTH = 21;    // maximum file name length
  char file1[MAXLENGTH];
  ifstream inFile;

  cout << "Please enter the name of the file you wish to open: ";
  cin  >> file1;

  inFile.open(file1, ios::nocreate);  // open the file

  if (inFile.fail())  // check for successful open
  {
    cout << "\nThe file named " << file1 << " was not successfully opened"
         << "\n Please check that the file currently exists." << endl;
    exit(1);
  }
  cout << "\nThe file has been successfully opened for reading.\n";

  return 0;
}
```

Figure 8.2 illustrates a sample run using Program 8.1b.

FIGURE 8.2

Sample run using Program 8.1b

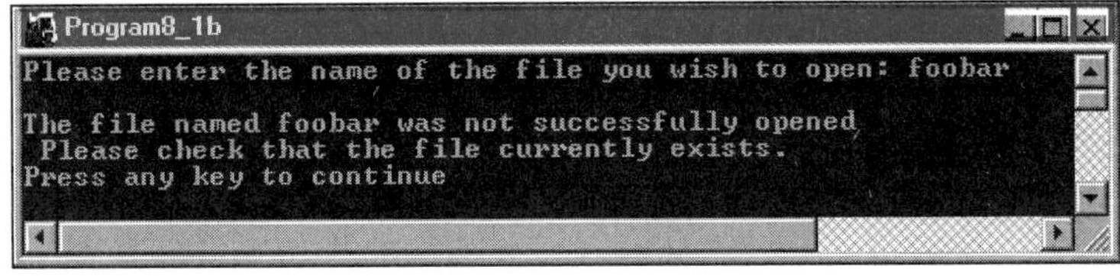
Program8_1b
Please enter the name of the file you wish to open: foobar
The file named foobar was not successfully opened
Please check that the file currently exists.
Press any key to continue

Closing a File

A file is closed using the `close()` method. This method breaks the connection between the file's external name and the file stream object, which can then be used for another file. For example, the statement

```
inFile.close();
```

closes the `inFile` stream's connection to its current file. As indicated, the `close()` method takes no argument.

All computers have a limit on the maximum number of files that can be open at one time, so closing files that are no longer needed makes good sense. Any open files existing at the end of normal program execution will be automatically closed by the operating system.

EXERCISES 8.1

1. **a.** Enter and execute Program 8.1 on your computer.
   b. Add a `close()` method to Program 8.1 and then execute the program.
2. **a.** Enter and execute Program 8.1a on your computer.
   b. Add a `close()` method to Program 8.1a and then execute the program.
3. **a.** Enter and execute Program 8.1b on your computer.
   b. Add a `close()` method to Program 8.1b and then execute the program.
4. Using the reference manuals provided with your computer's operating system, determine:
   a. the maximum number of characters that can be used to name a file for storage by the computer system.
   b. the maximum number of data files that can be open at the same time.

5. Would it be appropriate to call a saved C++ source program a file? Why or why not?

6. a. Write a suitable declaration statement for each of the following `ifstream` objects: `inData`, `prices`, `coupons`, and `file1`.

   b. Write a suitable declaration statement for each of the following `ofstream` objects; `outDate`, `rates`, `distance`, and `file2`.

7. Write individual declaration and open statements to link the following external data file names to their corresponding internal object names:

External Name	Object Name	Mode
`coba.mem`	`memo`	output
`book.let`	`letter`	output
`coupons.bnd`	`coups`	output
`yield.bnd`	`ptYield`	input
`test.dat`	`priFile`	input
`rates.dat`	`rates`	input

8. Write close statements for each of the files opened in Exercise 7.

8.2 Reading and Writing Files

Reading or writing to a file involves almost the identical operations for reading input from a terminal and writing data to a display screen. For writing to a file, the `cout` object is replaced by the `ofstream` object declared in the program. For example, if `outFile` is declared as an object of type `ofstream`, the following output statements are valid.

```
outFile << 'a';
outFile << "Hello World!";
outFile << descrip << ' ' << price;
```

The file name in each of these statements, in place of `cout`, simply directs the output stream to a specific file instead of to the screen. Program 8.2 illustrates the use of a file write function to write a list of descriptions and prices to a file.

PROGRAM 8.2

```
#include <fstream.h>
#include <stdlib.h>
#include <iomanip.h>

int main()
{
  const int MAXLENGTH = 21;  // maximum file name length
  char filename[MAXLENGTH] = "test.dat";  // put the filename up front
  ofstream outFile;

  outFile.open(filename);

  if (outFile.fail())
  {
    cout << "The file was not successfully opened" << endl;
    exit(1);
  }

     // set the output file stream formats
   outFile << setiosflags(ios::fixed)
           << setiosflags(ios::showpoint)
           << setprecision(2);

     // send data to the file
   outFile << "Batteries " << 39.95 << endl
           << "Bulbs "  << 3.22 << endl
           << "Fuses " << 1.00;
   outFile.close();
   return 0;
}
```

Notice that in Program 8.2 we have not used the `ios::nocreate` mode in the `open()` function call. The reason for this is that we want to create the file for writing even if it does not currently exist. Here, we want to know only that a fail has occurred for any reason except that the file doesn't already exist. Thus, when Program 8.2 is executed, a file named `test.dat` will be created and saved by the computer. The file is a sequential file that, after it is opened, is written with the following data:

```
Batteries 39.95
Bulbs 3.22
Fuses 1.00
```

The actual storage of characters in the file depends on the character codes used by the computer. Although only 35 characters appear to be stored in the file, corresponding to the descriptions, blanks, and prices written to the file, the file actually contains 38 characters. The extra characters consist of the newline escape sequence at the end of the first two lines and the special end-of-file marker placed as the last item in the file when the file is closed. Assuming characters are stored using the ASCII code, the `test.dat` file is physically stored as illustrated in Figure 8.3. For convenience, the character corresponding to each hexadecimal code is listed below the code. A code of 20 represents the blank character. Although the actual code used for the end-of-file marker depends on the system you are using, the hexadecimal code 26, corresponding to `Control-Z`, is common for the DOS operating system.

Reading data from a file is almost identical to reading data from a standard keyboard, except that the `cin` object is replaced by the `ifstream` object declared in the program. For example, if `inFile` is declared as an object of type `ifstream` that is opened for input, the input statement

```
inFile >> descrip >> price;
```

will read the next two items in the file and store them in the variables `descrip` and `price`. The file stream name in this statement, in place of `cin`, simply directs the input to come from the file stream rather than the standard input device stream, `cin`. Other methods that can be used for stream I/O are listed in Table 8.2. Each of these methods must, of course, be preceded by a stream object name.

Reading data from a file requires that the programmer know how the data appear in the file. This is necessary for correct "stripping" of the data from the file into appropriate variables for storage. All files are read sequentially, so that once an item is read, the next item in the file becomes available for reading.

FIGURE 8.3

The `test.dat` file as stored by the computer

```
42 61 74 74 65 72 69 65 73 20 33 39 2e 32 35 0A 42 75 6c 62 73
 B  a  t  t  e  r  i  e  s     3  9  .  2  5 \n  B  u  l  b  s

20 33 2e 32 32 0A 46 75 73 65 73 20 31 2e 30 32 26
    3  .  2  2 \n  F  u  s  e  s     1  .  0  0 ^Z
```

PROGRAMMER'S NOTES

Formatting Output File Stream Data

Output file streams can be formatted in the same manner as the `cout` standard output stream. For example, if an output stream `fileOut` has been delcared, the statement

```
fileOut << setiosflags(ios::fixed)
        << setiosflags(ios::showpoint)
        << setprecision(2);
```

formats all data inserted in the `fileOut` stream in the same way that these parameterized manipulators work for the `cout` stream. The first manipulator parameter, `ios::fixed`, causes the stream to output all numbers in conventional fixed-point notation (not exponential). The next parameter, `ios::showpoint`, tells the stream to always provide a decimal point. Thus, a value such as 1.0 will appear as 1.0, and not 1. Finally, the `setprecision` manipulator tells the stream to always display 2 decimal values after the decimal point. Thus, the number 1.0, for example, will appear as 1.00.

Instead of using manipulators, you can also use the stream methods `setf()` and `precision()`. For example, the previous formatting can also be accomplished using the code:

```
fileOut.setf(ios::fixed);
fileOut.setf(ios::showpoint);
fileOut.precision(2)
```

Which style you select is a matter of preference. In both cases, the formats need be specified only once and will remain in effect for every number subsequently inserted into the file stream.

TABLE 8.2 `fstream` **methods**

Method Name	Description
`get(character-variable)`	Extract the next character from the input stream.
`getline(string var,int n,'\n')`	Extract characters from the input stream until either n-1 characters are read or a newline is encountered (terminates the input with a `'\0'`).
`peek(character-variable)`	Return the next character in the input stream without extracting it from the stream.
`put(character-expression)`	Put a character on the output stream.
`putback(character-expression)`	Push back a character onto the input stream. Does not alter the data in the file.
`eof(void)`	Returns a True if a read has been attempted past the `EOF` (end-of-file).
`ignore(int n)`	Skip over the next *n* characters; If *n* is omitted, the default is to skip over the next single character.

PROGRAMMER'S NOTES

The istream get() and putback() Methods

All input streams have a `get()` method that permits character-by-character input from the stream. This method works in a manner similar to character extraction using the >> operator with two important differences: if a newline character `'\n'`, or a blank character, `' '`, are encountered, these characters are read in the same manner as any other alphanumeric character. The syntax of this method call is

istream-name.get(*character-variable*);

For example, the following code can be used to read the next character from the standard input stream and store the character into the variable `ch`:

```
char ch:
cin.get(ch);
```

In a similar manner, if `inFile` is an `ifstream` object that has been opened to a file, the following code reads the next character in the stream and assigns it to the character keycode:

```
char keycode;
inFile.get(keycode);
```

In addition to the `get()` method, all input streams have a `putback()` method that can be used to put the last character from an input stream back on the stream. This method has the syntax

istream-name.putback(*character-expression*);

where *character-expression* can be any character variable or character value.

The `putback()` method provides an output capability to an input stream. It should be noted that the putback character need not be the last character read; rather, it can be any character. All putback characters, however, have no effect on the data file but only on the open input stream. Thus, the data file characters remain unchanged, although the characters subsequently read from the input stream can change. For this reason `putback()` is typically used to permit prescanning a character from an input stream using `get()` followed by an immedate return of the same character to the stream.

Program 8.3 illustrates reading the `test.dat` file that was created in Program 8.2. The program also illustrates how the `EOF` marker, which is the `NULL` character, can be detected by the `peek()` function. As long as the `EOF` has not been detected, the program will continue to read characters from the file.

PROGRAM 8.3

```
#include <fstream.h>
#include <stdlib.h>
#include <iomanip.h>
```

(continued next page)

(continued from previous page)

```
int main()
{
  const int MAXLENGTH = 21;   // maximum file name length
  const int MAXCHARS = 31;    // maximum description length

  char filename[MAXLENGTH] = "test.dat";
  char descrip[MAXCHARS];
  int ch;
  float price;
  ifstream inFile;

  inFile.open(filename, ios::create);

  if (inFile.fail())  // check for successful open
  {
    cout << "\nThe file was not successfully opened"
      << "\n Please check that the file currently exists."
      << endl;
    exit(1);
  }

    // set the format for the standard output stream
  cout << setiosflags(ios::fixed)
       << setiosflags(ios::showpoint)
       << setprecision(2);

  cout << endl;  // start on a new line

    // read and display the file's contents
  while ( (ch = inFile.peek()) != EOF ) // check next character
  {
    inFile >> descrip >> price;  // input the data
    cout   << descrip << ' ' << price << endl;
  }

  inFile.close();
  cout << endl;

  return 0;
}
```

PROGRAMMER'S NOTES

The `iostream` `put()` Method

All output streams have a `put()` method that permits character-by-character output to a stream. This method works in the same manner as the character insertion operator, <<. The syntax of this method call is

***ostream-name* put (*character-expression*);**

where the *character-expression* can be either a character variable or character value.

For example, the following code can be used to output an `'a'` to the standard output stream:

```
cin.put('a');
```

In a similar manner, if `outFile` is an `ofstream` object that has been opened to a file, the following code outputs the character value in the character variable named `keycode` to this output.

```
char keycode;
      .
      .
outFile.put(keycode);
```

Program 8.3 continues to read the file until the `EOF` marker has been detected. Each time the file is read, a string and a floating point number are input to the program. The display produced is illustrated in Figure 8.4.

In place of the `inFile` extraction, >>, used in Program 8.3, a `getline()` method call can be used. The `getline()` requires three arguments: a string variable where the characters read from the file will be stored, the maximum number of characters to be input in a single read, and a terminating character. For example, the function call

```
inFile.getline(line,80,'\n');
```

causes a maximum of 79 characters (one less than the specified number) to be read from the file named `inFile` and stored in the string variable named `line`, and continues reading characters until 79 characters have been read or a newline character has been encoun-

FIGURE 8.4

Output displayed by Program 8.3

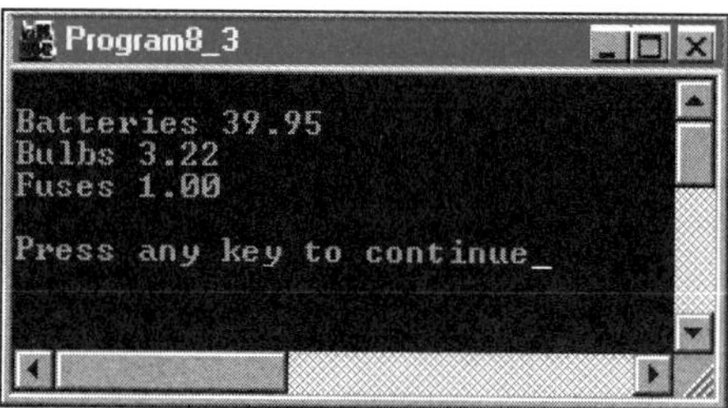

tered. If a newline character is encountered, it is included with the other entered characters before the string is terminated with the end-of-string `NULL` marker, `\0`. Program 8.4 illustrates the use of `getline()` in a working program.

PROGRAM 8.4

```
#include <fstream.h>
#include <stdlib.h>
#include <iomanip.h>

int main()
{
  const int MAXLENGTH = 21;  // maximum file name length
  const int MAXCHARS = 80;   // maximum line length
  char file1[MAXLENGTH] = "test.dat";
  char line[MAXCHARS];
  int ch;
  ifstream inFile;

  inFile.open(file1, ios::nocreate);
  if (inFile.fail())   // check for successful open
  {
    cout << "\nThe file was not successfully opened"
         << "\n Please check that the file currently exists."
         << endl;
    exit(1);
  }

  cout << endl;   // start on a new line

    // now read the file
  while( (ch = inFile.peek()) != EOF )
  {
    inFile.getline(line,MAXCHARS,'\n');
    cout << line << endl;
  }

  inFile.close();
  cout << endl;

  return 0;
}
```

Program 8.4 is really a line-by-line text-copying program, reading a line of text from the file and then displaying it on the terminal. The display produced by Program 8.4 is the same as that produced by Program 8.3 (see Figure 8.4).

If it were necessary to obtain the description and price as individual variables, either Program 8.3 should be used or the string returned by `getline()` in Program 8.4 must be processed further to extract the individual data items.

Standard Device Files

The file stream objects we have used have all been logical file objects. A **logical file object** is a stream that connects a file of logically related data such as a data file to a program. In addition to logical file objects, C++ also supports **physical file objects.** A physical file object is a stream that connects to a hardware device, such as a keyboard, screen, or printer.

The actual physical device assigned to your program for data entry is formally called the **standard input file.** Usually this is the keyboard. When a `cin` object is encountered in a C++ program, a request goes to the operating system to this standard input file for the expected input. Similarly, when a `cout` object method call is encountered, the output is automatically displayed or "written to" a device that has been assigned as the **standard output file.** For most systems this is a terminal screen, although it can be a printer.

When a program is executed, the standard input stream `cin` is automatically connected to the standard input device. Similarly, the standard output stream `cout` is automatically connected to the standard output device. These two object streams are always available for programmer use.

Other Devices

The keyboard, display, and error-reporting devices are automatically connected to the internal stream objects named `cin`, `cout`, and `cerr`, respectively, by a C++ program using either the `iostream.h` or `fstream.h` header files. Additionally, other devices can be used for input or output if the name assigned by the system is known. For example, most IBM or IBM-compatible personal computers assign the name `prn` to the printer connected to the computer. For these computers a statement such as `outFile.open("prn")` connects the printer to the `ofstream` object named `outFile`. A subsequent statement, such as `outFile << "Hello World!";` would then cause the string `Hello World!` to be printed directly on the printer. Notice that as the name of an actual file, `prn` must be enclosed in double quotes in the `open()` function call.

EXERCISES 8.2

1. a. Write a C++ program that accepts lines of text from the keyboard and writes each line to a file named `text.dat` until an empty line is entered. An empty line is a line with no text—just a new line caused by pressing the Enter (or Return) key.

   b. Modify Program 8.4 to read and display the data stored in the `text.dat` file created in Exercise 1a.

2. Determine the operating system procedure or command provided by your computer to display the contents of a saved file. Compare its operation with the program developed for Exercise 1b.

3. Write, compile, and run a C++ program that writes the four real numbers 92.65, 88.72, 77.46, and 82.93 to a text file named `result`. After writing the data to the file, your program should read the data from the file, determine the average of the four numbers read, and display the average. Verify the output produced by your program by manually calculating the average of the four input numbers.

4. a. Write, compile, and execute a C++ program that creates a text file named `points` and writes the following numbers to the file:

6.3	8.2	18.25	24.32
4.0	4.0	10.0	-5.0
-2.0	5.0	4.0	5.0

   b. Using the data in the `points` file created in Exercise 4a, write, compile, and run a C++ program that reads each line and interprets the first and second numbers in each line as the coordinates of one point and the third and fourth numbers as the coordinates of a second point. Have your program compute and display the slope and midpoint of the line connecting the two points entered.

5. a. Write, compile, and run a C++ program that creates a text file named `volts` and writes the following five records to the file:

120.3	122.7	90.3	99.8
95.3	120.5	127.3	120.8
123.2	118.4	123.8	115.6
122.4	95.6	118.2	120.0
123.5	130.2	123.9	124.4

   b. Using the data in the `volts` file created in Exercise 5a, write, compile, and run a C++ program that reads each line in the file, computes the average for each line, and displays the average.

6. a. Create a file containing the following car numbers, number of miles driven, and number of gallons of gas used by each car:

Car No.	Miles Driven	Gallons Used
54	250	19
62	525	38
71	123	6
85	1,322	86
97	235	14

b. Write a C++ program that reads the data in the file created in Exercise 6a and displays the car number, miles driven, gallons used, and the miles per gallon for each car. The output should additionally contain the total miles driven, total gallons used, and average miles per gallon for all the cars. These totals should be displayed at the end of the output report.

7. a. A file named `polar.dat` contains the polar coordinates needed in a graphics program. Currently, this file contains the following data:

```
DISTANCE        ANGLE
(INCHES)      (DEGREES)
--------     ----------
  2.0           45.0
  6.0           30.0
 10.0           45.0
  4.0           60.0
 12.0           55.0
  8.0           15.0
```

Write a C++ program to create this file on your computer system.

b. Using the `polar.dat` file created in Exercise 7a, write a C++ program that reads this file and creates a second file named `xycord.dat`. The entries in the new file should contain the rectangular coordinates corresponding to the polar coordinates in the `polar.dat` file. Polar coordinates are converted to rectangular coordinates using the equations

$$x = r \cos\theta$$

$$y = r \sin\theta$$

where r is the distance coordinate and θ is the radian equivalent of the angle coordinate in the `polar.dat` file.

8. a. Store the following data in a file:

```
5 96 87 78 93 21 4 92 82 85 87 6 72 69 85 75 81 73
```

b. Write a C++ program to calculate and display the average of each group of numbers in the file created in Exercise 9.a. The data are arranged in the file so that each group of numbers is preceded by the number of data items in the group. Thus, the first number in the file, 5, indicates that the next five numbers should be grouped together. The number 4 indicates that the following four numbers are a group, and the 6 indicates that the last six numbers are a group.

8.3 Random File Access

File organization refers to the way data are stored in a file. All the files we have used have **sequential organization.** This means that the characters in the file are stored in a sequential manner, one after another. Additionally, we have read the files in a sequential manner. The way data are retrieved from the file is called **file access.** The fact that the characters in the file are stored sequentially, however, does not force us to access the file sequentially.

In **random access** any character in the file can be read directly, without first having to read all the characters stored ahead of it. To provide random access to files, each `ifstream` object establishes a file position marker. This marker is a long integer that represents an offset from the beginning of each file and keeps track of where the next character is to be read from or written to. The functions that are used to access and change the file position marker are listed in Table 8.3.

The `seek()` functions allow the programmer to move to any position in the file. In order to understand this function, you must first understand how data are referenced in the file using the file position marker.

Each character in a data file is located by its position in the file. The first character in the file is located at position 0, the next character at position 1, and so on. A character's position is also referred to as its offset from the start of the file. Thus, the first character has a 0 offset, the second character has an **offset** of 1, and so on for each character in the file.

The `seek()` functions require two arguments: the offset, as a long integer, into the file; and where the offset is to be calculated from, as determined by the mode. The three possible alternatives for the mode are `ios::beg`, `ios::cur`, and `ios::end`, which denote

TABLE 8.3 File position marker functions

Name*	Description
`seekg(offset, mode)`	For input files, move to the offset position as indicated by the mode
`seekp(offset, mode)`	For output files, move to the offset position as indicated by the mode
`tellg(void)`	For input files, return the current value of the file position marker
`tellp(void)`	For output files, return the current value of the file position marker

*The suffixes `g` and `p` denote get and put, respectively, where get refers to an input (get from) stream and put refers to an output (put to) stream.

PROGRAMMER'S NOTES

A Way to Clearly Identify a File's Name and Location

During program development test files are usually placed in the same directory as the program.Therefore, a method call such as `inFile.open("exper.dat")` causes no problems to the operating system. In production systems, however, it is not uncommon for data files to reside in one directory while program files reside in another. For this reason, it is always a good idea to include the full path name of any file opened.

For example, if the `exper.dat file` resides in the directory `/test/files, the open()` call should include the full path name: `inFile.open("/test/files/exper.dat")`. Then, no matter from where the program is run, the operating system will know where to locate the file.

Another important convention is to list all file names at the top of a program instead of embedding the names deep within the code. This can easily be accomplished by string variables to store each file name.

For example, if the statements

```
const int MAXLENGTH=31;

char file1[MAXLENGTH] = "\test\files\exper.dat";
```

are placed at the top of a program file, the declaration statement clearly lists both the name of the desired file and its location. Then, if some other file is to be tested, all that is required is a simple one-line change at the top of the program.

Using a string variable for the file's name is also useful for the `fail()` method check. For example, consider the following code:

```
ifstream inFile;

inFile.open(file1)

if(inFile.fail())
{
  cout << "\nThe file named "<<file1<<was not successfully opened"
       <<\n Please check that this file currently exists."
     exit(1);
}
```

In this code the name of the file that failed to open is directly displayed within the error message without the name being embedded as a string value.

the beginning, current position, and the end of the file, respectively. Thus, a mode of `ios::beg` means the offset is the true offset from the start of the file. A mode of `ios::cur` means that the offset is relative to the current position in the file, and an `ios::end` mode means the offset is relative to the end of the file. A positive offset means to move forward in the file and a negative offset means to move backward. Examples of `seek()` function calls are shown below. In these examples, assume that `inFile` has been opened as an input file and `outFile` as an output file:

```
inFile.seekg(4L,ios::beg);     // go to the fifth character in the input file
outFile.seekp(4L,ios::beg);    // go to the fifth character in the output file
inFile.seekg(4L,ios::cur);     // move ahead five characters in the input file
outFile.seekp(4L,ios::cur);    // move ahead five characters in the output file
inFile.seekg(-4L,ios::cur);    // move back five characters in the input file
outFile.seekp(-4L,ios::cur);   // move back five characters in the output file
inFile.seekg(0L,ios::beg);     // go to start of the input file
outFile.seekp(0L,ios::beg);    // go to start of the output file
inFile.seekg(0L,ios::end);     // go to end of the input file
outFile.seekp(0L,ios::end);    // go to end of the output file
inFile.seekg(-10L,ios::end);   // go to 10 characters before the input file's end
outFile.seekp(-10L,ios::end); // go to 10 characters before the output file's end
```

Notice, in these examples, that the offset passed to `seekg()` and `seekp()` must be a long integer.

As opposed to the `seek()` functions that move the file position marker, the `tell()` functions simply return the offset value of the file position marker. For example, if ten characters have already been read from an input file named `inFile`, the function call

```
inFile.tellg();
```

returns the long integer 10. This means that the next character to be read is offset ten byte positions from the start of the file, and is the eleventh character in the file.

Program 8.5 illustrates the use of `seekg()` and `tellg()` to read a file in reverse order, from last character to first. As each character is read it is also displayed.

PROGRAM 8.5

```
#include <fstream.h>
#include <stdlib.h>

int main()
{
  const int MAXLENGTH = 21;
  char filename[MAXLENGTH] = "test.dat";
  char ch;
  long offset, last;
  ifstream inFile;
  inFile.open(filename,ios::nocreate);
```

(continued next page)

(continued from previous page)

```
  if (inFile.fail())    // check for successful open
  {
    cout << "\nThe file was not successfully opened"
         << "\n Please check that the file currently exists"
         << endl;
    exit(1);
  }

  inFile.seekg(0L,ios::end);    // move to the end of the file
  last = inFile.tellg();        // save the offset of the last character
  for(offset = 1L; offset <= last; offset++)
  {
    inFile.seekg(-offset, ios::end);
    ch = inFile.get();
    cout << ch << " : ";
  }

  inFile.close();
  return 0;
}
```

Assuming the file `test.dat` contains the following data,

```
The grade was 92.5
```

the output line displayed by Program 8.5 is:

```
5 : . : 2 : 9 :   : s : a : w :   : e : d : a : r : g :   : e : h : T :
```

Program 8.5 initially goes to the last character in the file. The offset of this character, which is the end-of-file character, is saved in the variable last. Because `tellg()` returns a long integer, `last` has been declared as a long integer.

Starting from the end of the file, `seekg()` is used to position the next character to be read, referenced from the end of the file. As each character is read, the character is displayed and the offset adjusted in order to access the next character. It should be noted that the first offset used is –1, which represents the character immediately preceding the `EOF` marker.

It is worth noting that the two lines of code in the program:

```
ifstream inFile;

inFile.open(filename,ios::nocreate);
```

can be replaced by the single statement:

```
ifstream inFile(filename,ios::nocreate);
```

In this latter statement the `open()` method is automatically called.

EXERCISES 8.3

1. **a.** Either by using a Text editor or by copying the file `test.dat` provided with this book, create a file named `test.dat` on the directory that contains your program files.
   b. Enter and execute Program 8.5 on your computer.

2. Rewrite Program 8.5 so that the origin for the `seekg()` function used in the `for` loop is the start of the file rather than the end.

3. The `seek()` functions return 0 if the position specified has been reached, or 1 if the position specified was beyond the file's boundaries. Modify Program 8.5 to display an error message if `seekg()` returns 1.

4. Write a program that will read and display every second character in a file named `test.dat`.

8.4 File Streams as Function Arguments

A file stream object can be a function argument. The only requirement is that the function's formal parameter be a reference to an appropriate stream, either as `ifstream&` or `ofstream&`. For example, in Program 8.6 an `ofstream` object named `outFile` is opened in `main()` and this stream object is passed to the function `inOut()`. Notice that both the function prototype and header line for `inOut()` declare the formal parameter as a reference to an `ostream` object type. The `inOut()` function is then used to write five lines of user-entered text to the file.

PROGRAM 8.6

```
#include <fstream.h>
#include <stdlib.h>

void inOut(ofstream&);    // function prototype
```

(continued next page)

(continued from previous page)

```
int main()
{
  const int MAXCHARS = 21;
  char fname[MAXCHARS] = "list.dat"; // here is the file we are working with
  ofstream outFile;

  outFile.open(fname);
  if (outFile.fail())    // check for a successful open
  {
    cout << "\nThe output file " << fname << " was not successfully opened"
         << endl;
    exit(1);
   }
  inOut(outFile);  // call the function

  return 0;
}

void inOut(ofstream& fileOut)
{
  const int LINELEN = 80;  // longest length of a line of text
  const int NUMLINES = 5;  // number of lines of text
  int count;
  char line[LINELEN];  // enough storage for one line of text

  cout << "Please enter five lines of text:" << endl;
  for (count = 0; count < NUMLINES; count++)
  {
    cin.getline(line,LINELEN,'\n');
    fileOut << line << endl;
  }

  return;
}
```

Within `main()` the file is an `ostream` object named `outFile`. This object is passed to the `inOut()` function and is accepted as the formal parameter named `fileOut`, which is declared to be a reference to an `ostream` object type. The function `inOut()` then uses its reference parameter `fileOut` as an output file stream name in a manner identical to how `main()` would use the `fileOut` stream object. Notice also that Program 8.6 uses the `getline()` method introduced in Section 8.2 (see Table 8.2). Although we have explicitly included the newline character as the third argument passed to `getline()`, this argument can be omitted. This is because the `'\n'` is a default value for this argument.

In Program 8.7 we have expanded on Program 8.6 by adding a `getOpen()` function to perform the open. Notice that `getOpen()`, like `inOut()`, accepts a reference argument to an `ofstream` object. After the `getOpen()` function completes execution, this reference is passed to `inOut()`, as it was in Program 8.6. Although you might be tempted to write `getOpen()` to return a reference to an `ofstream`, this will not work because it ultimately results in an attempt to assign a returned reference to an existing one.

PROGRAM 8.7

```
#include <fstream.h>
#include <stdlib.h>

int getOpen(ofstream&);  // pass a reference to an fstream
void inOut(ofstream&);   // pass a reference to an fstream

int main()
{
  ofstream outFile;     // file1 is an fstream object

  getOpen(outFile);     // open the file
  inOut(outFile);       // write to it
}

int getOpen(ofstream& fileOut)
{
  const int MAXCHARS = 21;
  char name[MAXCHARS];

  cout << "\nEnter a file name: " << endl;
  cin.getline(name,MAXCHARS,'\n');

  fileOut.open(name);       // open the file

  if (fileOut.fail())       // check for successful open
  {
    cout << "Cannot open the file" << endl;
    exit(1);
  }
```

(continued next page)

(continued from previous page)

```
  else
    return 0;
}

void inOut(ofstream& fileOut)
{
  const int NUMLINES = 5;  // number of lines
  const int LINELEN = 80;  // maximum line length
  int count;
  char line[LINELEN];   // enough storage for one line of text

  cout << "Please enter five lines of text:" << endl;
  for (count = 0; count < NUMLINES; count++)
  {
    cin.getline(line,LINELEN,'\n');
    fileOut << line << endl;
  }

  return;
}
```

Program 8.7 is simply a modified version of Program 8.6 that now allows the user to enter a file name from the standard input device and then opens the `ofstream` connection to the external file. If the name of an existing data file is entered, the file will be destroyed when it is opened for output. A useful "trick" that you may encounter to prevent this type of mishap is to open the entered file using an input file stream. Then, if the file exists, the `fail()` method will indicate a successful open (i.e., the open does not fail), which indicates that the file is available for input. This can be used to alert the user that a file with the entered name currently exists in the system and to request confirmation that the data in the file can be destroyed and the file reopened for output. Before the file is reopened for output, the input file stream should be closed. The implementation of this algorithm is left as an exercise.

EXERCISES 8.4

1. A function named `pFile()` is to receive a file name as a reference to an `ifstream` object. What declarations are required to pass a file name to `pFile()`?

2. Write a function named `fcheck()` that checks whether a file exists. The function should accept an `ifstream` object as a formal reference parameter. If the file exists, the function should return a value of 1; otherwise the function should return a value of zero.

3. Rewrite the function `getOpen()` used in Program 8.7 to incorporate the file-checking procedures described at the end of this section. Specifically, if the entered file name exists, an appropriate message should be displayed. The user should then be presented with the option of entering a new file name or allowing the program to overwrite the existing file. Use the function written for Exercise 2 in your program.

4. Assume that a data file consisting of a group of individual lines has been created. Write a function named `printLine()` that will read and display any desired line of the file. For example, the function call `printLine(fstream& fName,5);` should display the fifth line of the passed object stream.

5. Using the `seek()` and `tell()` functions, write a function named `countChars()` that returns the total number of characters in a file.

6. Write a function named `readChars()` that reads and displays *n* characters starting from any position in a file. The function should accept three arguments: a file object name, the offset of the first character to be read, and the number of characters to be read. (*Note:* the prototype for `readChars()` should be `void readChars(fstream&, long, long)`).

8.5 Common Programming Errors

Three programming errors are common when using files. The most common error is to use the file's external name in place of the internal file stream object name when accessing the file. The only stream method that uses the data file's external name is the `open()` function. As always, all stream methods presented in this chapter must be preceded by a stream object name and a period.

A second error occurs when using the `EOF` marker to detect the end of a file. Any variable used to accept the `EOF` must be declared as an integer variable. For example, if `ch` is declared as a character variable, the expression

```
while ( (ch = inFile.peek()) != EOF )
```

produces an infinite loop.[3] This occurs because a character variable can never take on an `EOF` code. `EOF` is an integer value (usually –1) that has no character representation. This ensures that the `EOF` code can never be confused with any legitimate character encountered as normal data in the file. To terminate the loop created by the above expression, the variable `ch` must be declared as an integer variable.

3 This will not occur on UNIX systems, in which characters are stored as signed integers.

The last error concerns the offset argument sent to the `seekg()` and `seekp()` functions. This offset must be a long integer constant or variable. Any other value passed to these functions can result in an unpredictable effect.

8.6 Chapter Summary

1. A **data file** is any collection of data stored together in an external storage medium under a common name.

2. A data file is connected to a file stream using an `open()` function. This function connects a file's external name with an internal object name. After the file is opened, all subsequent accesses to the file require the internal object name.

3. A file can be opened in input or output mode. An opened output file stream either creates a new data file or erases the data in an existing opened file. An opened input file stream makes an existing file's data available for input. An error condition results if the file does not exist; this can be detected using the `fail()` method.

4. All file streams must be declared as objects of either the `ifstream` or `ofstream` classes. This means that a declaration similar to either

```
ifstream inFile;
```

or

```
ofstream outFile;
```

must be included with the declarations in which the file is opened. The stream object names `inFile` and `outFile` can be replaced with any user-selected object name.

5. In addition to any files opened within a function, the standard stream objects `cin`, `cout`, and `cerr` are automatically declared and opened when a program is run. `cin` is the object name of an input file stream used for data entry (usually from the keyboard), `cout` is the object name of an output file stream used for default data display (usually the terminal screen), and `cerr` is the object name of an output file stream used for displaying system error messages (usually the terminal screen).

6. Data files can be accessed randomly using the `seekg()`, `seekp()`, `tellg()`, and `tellp()` methods. The `g` versions of these functions are used to alter and query the file position marker for input file streams, whereas the `p` versions do the same for output file streams.

7. Table 8.4 lists the methods supplied by the `fstream` class for file manipulation.

TABLE 8.4 `fstream` **methods**

Method Name	Description
`get(character-variable)`	Extract the next character from the input stream.
`getline(string var,int n,'\n')`	Extract characters from the input stream until either n-1 characters are read or a newline is encountered (terminates the input with a `'\0'`).
`peek(character-variable)`	Return the next character in the input stream without extracting it from the stream.
`put(character-expression)`	Put a character on the output stream.
`putback(character-expression)`	Push back a character onto the input stream. Does not alter the data in the file.
`eof(void)`	Returns a True if a read has been attempted past the `EOF` (end-of-file).
`ignore(int n)`	Skip over the next *n* characters; If *n* is omitted, the default is to skip over the next single character.

8.7 Knowing About: The `iostream` Class Library

The `iostream` class library provided as part of each C++ compiler is not part of the C++ language.[4] By convention, each C++ compiler provides an Input/Output library, named `iostream`, that contains a number of classes that adhere to a common ANSI specification.

As we have already seen, the classes contained within the `iostream` class library access files using entities called streams. For most systems the data bytes transferred on a stream represent either ASCII characters or binary numbers.

When the data transfer between a computer and an external data file modifies the data, so that the data stored in the file *are not* an exact representation of the data as they are stored internally within the computer, the file is referred to as a **formatted file.** Examples of this are files that store their data using ASCII codes. Such files are also referred to as **text files,** and the terms *text* and *formatted* are sometimes used interchangeably.

When the data transfer between a computer and an external data file is done without modification, so that the data stored in the file *are* an exact representation of the data as they are stored internally within the computer, the file is referred to as a **binary** or **unformatted file.**

---

4 This section contains enrichment material that can be omitted on first reading with no loss of subject continuity.

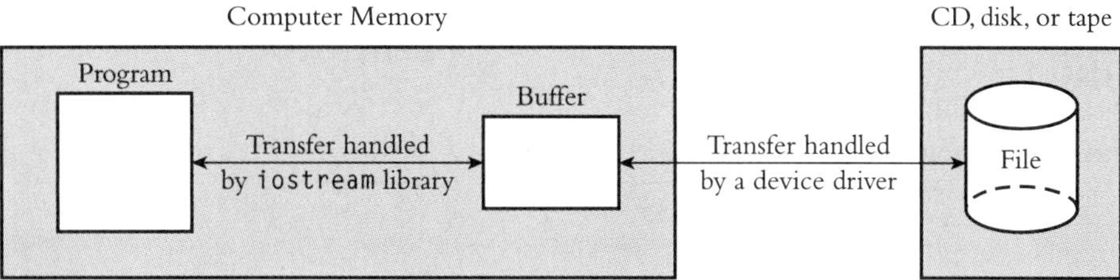

FIGURE 8.5

The data transfer mechanism

The mechanism for reading a byte stream from a file or writing a byte stream to a file, with or without formatting, is always hidden when using a high-level language such as C++. Nevertheless, it is useful to understand this mechanism so that we can place the services provided by the iostream class library in their appropriate context.

File Stream Transfer Mechanism

The mechanism for transferring data between a program and a data file is illustrated in Figure 8.5.

As illustrated in Figure 8.5, transferring data between a program and a file involves an intermediate file buffer contained in the computer's memory. Each opened file is assigned its own file buffer, which is simply a storage area that is used by the data as it is transferred between the program and the file.

From its side, the program either writes a set of data bytes to the file buffer or reads a set of data bytes from the file buffer using a stream object.

On the other side of the buffer the transfer of data between the device storing the actual data file (usually a tape, disk, or CD-ROM) and the file buffer is handled by special operating system programs that are referred to as **device drivers.**[5] Typically a disk device driver will transfer data between the disk and file buffer only in fixed sizes, such as 1024 bytes at a time. Thus, the file buffer provides a convenient means of permitting a device driver to transfer data in blocks of one size while the program can access them using a different size (usually as individual characters or as a fixed number of characters per line).

5 Device drivers are not stand-alone programs but are an integral part of the operating system. Essentially the device driver is a section of operating system code that accesses a hardware device, such as a disk unit, and handles the data transfer between the device and the computer's memory. As such it must correctly synchronize the speed of the data transferred between the computer and the device sending or receiving the data. This is because the computer's internal data transfer rate is generally much faster than any device connected to it.

FIGURE 8.6

The base class `ios` and its derived classes (not all derived classes are shown)

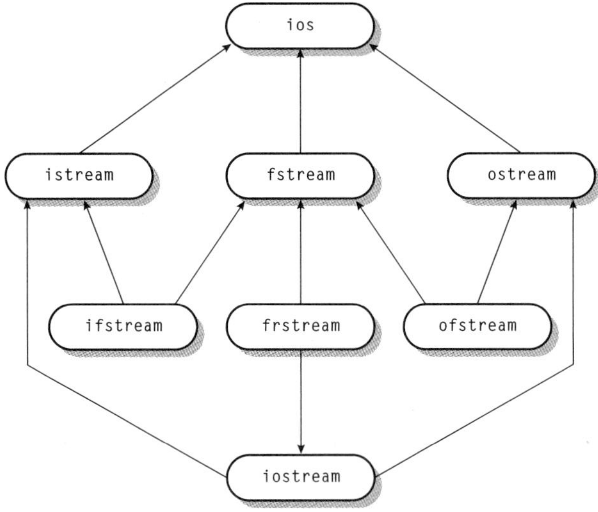

Components of the `iostream` Class Library

The `iostream` class library consists of two primary base classes, the `streambuf` class and the `ios` class.[6] The `streambuf` class provides the file buffer illustrated in Figure 8.5 and a number of general routines for transferring data when little or no formatting is required. The `ios` class contains a pointer to the file buffers provided by the `streambuf` class and a number of general routines for transferring data with formatting. From these two base classes a number of other classes are derived and included in the `iostream` class library.

Figure 8.6 illustrates an inheritance diagram for the `ios` family of classes as it relates to the `ifstream`, `ofstream`, and `fstream` classes. The inheritance diagram for the `streambuf` family of classes is shown in Figure 8.7. As described in Chapter 11, the conven-

FIGURE 8.7

The base class `streambuf` and its derived classes (not all derived classes are shown)

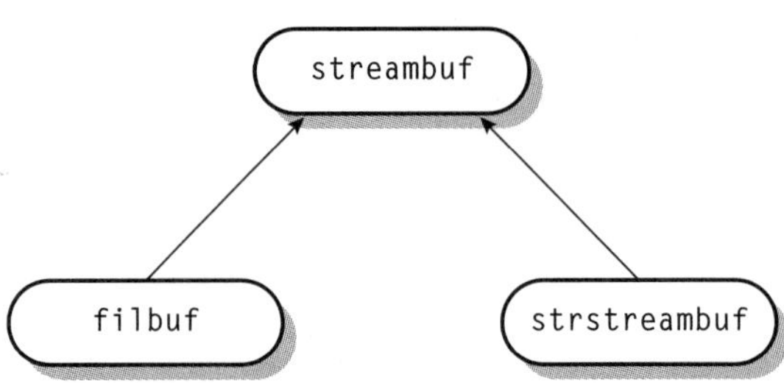

6 Although this section contains material directly relating to file streams, an understanding of it requires the material presented in Chapter 11. As such, this section should not be read until Chapter 11 has been completed.

TABLE 8.5 Correspondence between ios and streambuf

ios Class	streambuf Class	Header File
istream ostream iostream	streambuf	iostream.h or fstream.h
ifstream ofstream fstream	filebuf	fstream.h

tion adopted for inheritance diagrams is that the arrows point from a derived class to a base class.

The correspondence between the classes illustrated in Figures 8.6 and 8.7, including the header files that define these classes, is listed in Table 8.5.

Thus, the ifstream, ofstream, and fstream classes that we have used for file access all use a buffer provided by the filebuf class that is defined in the fstream.h header file. Similarly, the cin, cout, and cerr iostream objects that we have been using throughout the text use a buffer provided by the streambuf class and defined in both the iostream.h and fstream.h header files.

In-Memory Formatting

In addition to the classes illustrated in Figure 8.6, a class named strstream is also derived from the ios class. This class uses the ststreambuf class illustrated in Figure 8.7, requires the ststream.h header file, and provides capabilities for writing and reading strings to and from in-memory defined streams.

As an output stream, such streams are typically used to "assemble" a string from smaller pieces until a complete line of characters is ready to be written, either to cout or to a file. Attaching a strstream object to a buffer for this purpose is done in a manner similar to attaching an fstream object to an output file. For example, the statement

```
strstream inmem(buf, 72, ios::out);
```

attaches a strstream object to an existing buffer of 72 bytes in output mode. Program 8.8 illustrates using this statement within the context of a complete program.

PROGRAM 8.8

```
#include <strstream.h>
#include <iomanip.h>

int main()
{
  const int MAXCHARS = 81;  // one more than the maximum characters in a line
  char buf[MAXCHARS];
  int units = 10;
  float price = 36.85;

  strstream inmem(buf, MAXCHARS, ios::out);  // open an in-memory stream

    // write to the buffer through the stream
  inmem << "No. of units = "
        << setw(3) << units
        << "  Price per unit = $"
        << setw(8) << setprecision(2) << price << '\0';

  cout << '|' << buf << '|';

  return 0;
}
```

The output line displayed by Program 8.8 is:

```
|No. of units =  10  Price per unit = $   36.85|
```

As illustrated by this output, the character buffer has been correctly filled in by insertions to the `inmem` stream (note that the end-of-string `NULL`, `\0`, which is the last insertion to the stream, is required to correctly close off the string). Once the `buf` string variable has been filled, it would be written out to a file as a single string.

In a similar manner, a `strstream` object can be opened in input mode. Such a stream would be used as a working storage area, or buffer, for storing a complete line of text from either a file or standard input. Once the buffer has been filled, the extraction operator would be used to "disassemble" the string into component parts and convert each data item into its designated data type. Doing this permits inputting data from a file on a line-by-line basis prior to assigning individual data items to their respective variables.

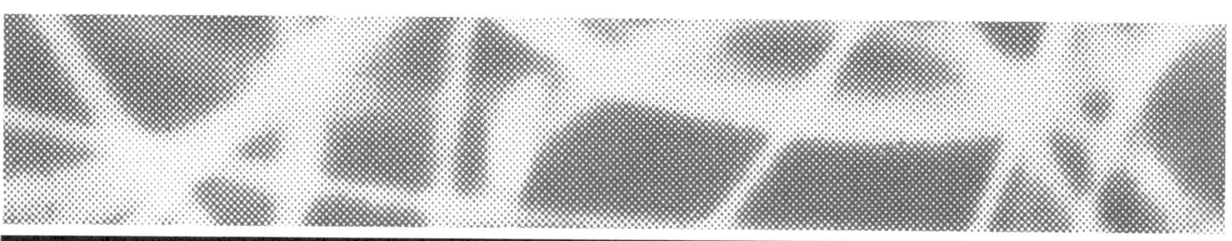

9 Introduction to Classes

Besides being an improved version of C, the distinguishing characteristic of C++ is its support of object-oriented programming. Central to this object orientation is the concept of an **abstract data type,** which is a programmer-defined data type. In this chapter we explore the implications of permitting programmers to define their own data types and then present C++'s mechanism for constructing abstract data types. As we will see, the construction of a data type is based on both variables and functions; variables provide the means for creating new data configurations and functions provide the means for preforming operations on these structures. What C++ provides is a unique way of combining variables and functions together in a self-contained, cohesive unit from which objects can be created.

PROGRAMMER'S NOTES

Procedural, Hybrid, and Pure Object-Oriented Languages

Most high-level programming languages can be categorized into one of three main categories: *procedural, hybrid,* or *object-oriented.* FORTRAN, which was the first commercially available high-level programming language, is procedural. This makes sense because FORTRAN was designed to perform mathematical calculations that used standard algebraic formulas. Formally, these formulas were described as algorithms and then the algorithms were coded using function and subroutine procedures. Other procedural languages that followed FORTRAN included BASIC, COBOL, and Pascal.

Currently there are only two pure object-oriented languages; Smalltalk and Eiffel. The first requirement of a pure object-oriented language is that it contain three specific features: classes, inheritance, and polymorphism (these features are described in this and the next two chapters). In addition to providing these features, however, a "pure" object-oriented language must, as a minimum, always use classes. In a pure object-oriented language all data types are constructed as classes, all data values are objects, all operators can be overloaded, and every data operation can only be executed using a class member function. *It is impossible in a pure object-oriented language not to use object-oriented features* throughout a program. This is not the case in a hybrid language.

In a hybrid language, such as C++, *it is impossible not to use elements of a procedural program.* This is because the use of any built-in data type or operation effectively violates the pure object-oriented paradigm. Although a hybrid language must have the ability to define classes, the distinguishing feature of a hybrid language is that it is possible to write a complete program using only procedural code. Additionally, hybrid languages need not even provide inheritance and polymorphic features—but they must provide classes. Languages that use classes but do not provide inheritance and polymorphic features are referred to as *object-based* languages rather than *object-oriented.* All versions of Visual Basic prior to Version 4 are examples of object-based hybrid languages.

9.1 Abstract Data Types in C++ (Classes)

We live in a world full of objects—planes, trains, cars, telephones, books, computers, and so forth. Until quite recently, however, programming techniques had not reflected this at all. The primary programming paradigm[1] had been procedural, defining a program as an algorithm written in a machine-readable language. The reasons for this emphasis on procedural programming are primarily historical.

When computers were developed in the 1940s they were used by mathematicians for military purposes—computing bomb trajectories, decoding enemy orders, and diplomatic transmissions. After World War II computers were still primarily used by mathematicians for computations. This reality was reflected in the name of the first commercially available high-level language introduced in 1957. The language's name was FORTRAN,

---

1 A *paradigm* is a standard way of thinking about or doing something.

FIGURE 9.1

Cost of most computer projects

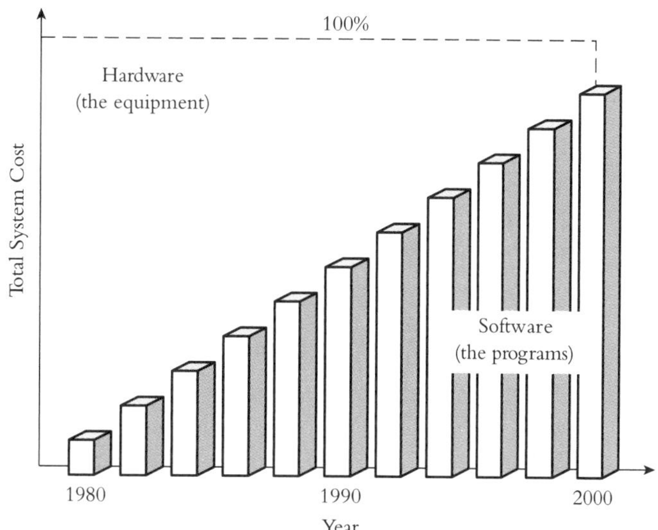

which was an acronym for FORmula TRANslation. Further reflecting this predominant use was the fact that in the 1980s almost all computer courses were taught in either engineering or mathematics departments. The term *computer science* was not yet in common use, and computer science departments were just being formed.

This situation has changed dramatically, primarily for two reasons. One of the reasons for disenchantment with procedural-oriented programs has been the failure of traditional procedural languages to provide an adequate means of containing software costs. Software costs include all costs associated with initial program development and subsequent program maintenance. As illustrated in Figure 9.1, the major cost of most computer projects today, whether technical or commercial, is for software.

Software costs contribute so heavily to total project costs because they are directly related to human productivity (they are labor intensive), whereas the equipment associated with hardware costs is related to manufacturing technologies. For example, microchips that cost more than $500 only ten years ago can now be purchased for less than $1.

It is far easier, however, to dramatically increase manufacturing productivity a thousandfold, with the consequent decrease in hardware costs, than it is for programmers to double either the quantity or quality of the code they produce. So as hardware costs have plummeted, software productivity and its associated costs have remained relatively constant. Thus, the ratio of software costs to total system costs (hardware plus software) has increased dramatically.

One way to significantly increase programmer productivity is to create code that can be reused without extensive revision, retesting, and revalidation. The inability of procedurally structured code to provide this type of reusability has led to the search for other software approaches.

The second reason for disenchantment with procedural-based programming has been the emergence of graphical screens and the subsequent interest in window applications. Providing a graphical user interface (GUI) by which a user can easily move around in even a single window is a challenge using procedural code. Programming multiple and possibly overlapping windows on the same graphical screen simply increases the complexity enormously when procedural code is used.

Unlike a procedural approach, however, an object-oriented approach fits well to graphical windowed environments, where each window can be specified as a self-contained rectangular object that can be moved and resized in relation to other objects on the screen. Additionally, within each window other graphical objects, such as check boxes, option buttons, labels, and text boxes, can easily be placed and moved.

To provide this object creation capability, extensions to the procedural language C were developed. This extension became the new language named C++, which permits a programmer to both use and create new objects.

Central to the creation of objects is the concept of an abstract data type, which is simply a user-defined data type, as opposed to the built-in data types provided by all languages (such as integer and floating point types). Permitting a programmer to define new data types, such as a rectangular type, out of which specific rectangular objects can be created and displayed on a screen, forms the basis of C++'s object orientation.

Abstract Data Types

To gain a clear understanding of what an abstract data type is, consider the following three built-in data types supplied in C++: integers, floats, and characters. In using these data types we would declare one or more variables of the desired type, use them in their accepted ways, and avoid using them in ways that are not specified. Thus, for example, we would not use the modulus operator on two floating point numbers. Because this operation makes no sense for floating point numbers it is never defined, in any programming language, for such numbers. Thus, although we usually don't consider it, each data type consists of *both* a type of data, such as integer or float, *and* specific operational capabilities provided for each type.

In computer terminology, the combination of data and their associated operations is defined as a **data type.** That is, a data type defines *both* the types of data and the types of operations that can be performed on the data. Seen in this light, the integer data type, the floating point data type, and the character data type provided in C++ are all examples of *built-in* data types that are defined by a type of data and specific operational capabilities provided for initializing and manipulating the type. In a simplified form this relationship can be described as

Data Type = Allowable Data + Operational Capabilities

TABLE 9.1 C++'s data type capabilities

Capability	Example
Define one or more variables of the data type	`int a, b;`
Initialize a variable at definition	`int a = 5;`
Assign a value to a variable	`a = 10;`
Assign one variable's value to another variable	`a = b;`
Perform mathematical operations	`a + b`
Perform relational operations	`a > b`
Convert from one data type to another	`a = int (7.2);`

Thus, the operations that we have been using in C++ are an inherent part of each data type we have used. For each of these data types the designers of C++ had to carefully consider, and then implement, specific operations.

To understand the importance of the operational capabilities provided by a programming language, let's take a moment to list some of those supplied with C++'s built-in data types (`ints`, `floats`, and `chars`). The minimum set of the capabilities provided by C++'s built-in data types is listed in Table 9.1.[2]

Now let's see how all of this relates to abstract data types (ADTs). By definition an **abstract data type** is simply a user-defined type that defines both a type of data and the operations that can be performed on the data. Such user-defined data types are required when we wish to create objects that are more complex than simple integers and characters. If we are to create our own data types we must be aware of both the type of data we are creating and the capabilities that we will provide to initialize and manipulate the data.

As a specific example, assume that we are programming an application that uses dates extensively. From a data processing standpoint, a date must be capable of accessing and storing a month, day, and year designation. Although from an implementation standpoint there are a number of means of storing a date, from a user viewpoint the actual implementation is not relevant. For example, a date can be stored as three integers, one each for the month, day, and year, respectively. Alternatively, a single long integer in the form *yyyymmdd* can be used. Using the long integer implementation, the date 5/16/02 would be stored as the integer 20020516. The long integer format is very attractive for sorting dates, because the numerical sequence of the dates corresponds to their calendar sequence.

---

2 You might notice the absence of reading and writing operations. In both C and C++, except for very primitive operations, input and output are provided by standard library routines and class functions.

Unfortunately, the method of internally structuring the date supplies only a partial answer to our programming effort. We must still supply a set of operations that can be used with dates. Clearly, such operations could include assigning values to a date, subtracting two dates to determine the number of days between them, comparing two dates to determine which is earlier and which is later, and displaying a date in a form such as 12/03/01.

Notice that the details of how each operation works are dependent on how we choose to store a date (formally referred to as its *data structure*) and are of interest to us only as we develop each operation. For example, the implementation of comparing two dates will differ if we store a date using a single long integer as opposed to using separate integers for the month, day, and year, respectively.

The combination of the storage structure used for dates with a set of available operations appropriate to dates would then define an abstract date data type. Once this date type is developed, programmers who want to use it need never be concerned with *how* dates are stored or *how* the operations are performed. All that they need to know is *what* each operation does and how to invoke it, much as they use C++'s built-in operations. For example, we don't really care how the addition of two integers is performed but only that it is done correctly.

In C++ an abstract data type is referred to as a **class.** Construction of a class is inherently easy, and we already have all the necessary tools in variables and functions. What C++ provides is a mechanism for packaging these two items together in a self-contained unit. Let's see how this is done.

Class Construction

A class defines both data and functions. This is usually accomplished by constructing a class in two parts, a declaration section and an implementation section. As illustrated in Figure 9.2, the declaration section declares both the data types and functions of the class. The implementation section is then used to define the functions whose prototypes have been declared in the declaration section.[3]

The variables and functions listed in the class declaration section are collectively referred to as **class members.** Individually, the variables are referred to as both **data members** and **instance variables** (the terms are synonymous), and the functions are referred to as **member functions.** A member function name may not be the same as a data member name.

---

3 This separation into two parts is not mandatory, because the implementation can be included within the declaration section if inline functions are used.

FIGURE 9.2

Format of a class definition

```
// class declaration section
class ClassName
{
 data members
  (instance and variables)
 function members
  (inline or prototypes)
};
// class implementation section
function definitions
```

As a specific example of a class, consider the following definition of a `class` named `Date`.

```
//--- class declaration section

class Date
{
  private:
    int month;
    int day;
    int year;
  public:
    Date(int = 7, int = 4, int = 2001); // constructor with defaults
    void setdate(int, int, int);        // member function to copy a date
    void showdate();                    // member function to display a date
};

//--- class implementation section

Date::Date(int mm, int dd, int yyyy)
{
  month = mm;
  day = dd;
  year = yyyy;
}

void Date::setdate(int mm, int dd, int yyyy)
{
  month = mm;
  day = dd;
  year = yyyy;
```

```
  return;
}

void Date::showdate()
{
  cout << "The date is ";
  cout << setfill('0')
       << setw(2) << month << '/'
       << setw(2) << day << '/'
       << setw(2) << year % 100; // extract the last 2 year digits
  cout << endl;
  return;
}
```

This definition may initially look overwhelming, but first simply notice that it does consist of two sections—a declaration section and an implementation section. Now consider each of these sections individually.

The class declaration section begins with the keyword `class` followed by a class name. Following the class name are the class's variable declarations and function prototypes, enclosed in a brace pair that is terminated with a semicolon. Thus, the general structure of the form that we have used is[4]

```
class Name
{
  private:
    a list of variable declarations
  public:
    a list of function prototypes
};
```

Notice that this format is followed by our `Date` class, which for convenience we have listed below with no internal comments:

```
//--- class declaration section

class Date
{
```

4 Other forms are possible. Because this form is one of the most commonly used and easily understood, it serves as our standard model throughout the text.

```
  private:
    int month;
    int day;
    int year;
  public:
    Date(int = 7, int = 4, int = 2001);
    void setdate(int, int, int);
    void showdate();
};  // this is a declaration - don't forget the semi-colon
```

The name of this class is `Date`. Although the initial capital letter is not required, it is conventionally used to designate a class. The body of the declaration section, which is enclosed within braces, consists of variable and function declarations. In this case the data members `month`, `day`, and `year` are declared as integers and three functions named `Date()`, `setdate()`, and `showdate()` are declared via prototypes. The keywords `private` and `public` are access specifiers that define access rights. The `private` keyword specifies that the class members following, in this case the data members `month`, `day`, and `year`, may be accessed only by using the class functions (or friend functions, as will be discussed in Section 10.2).[5] The purpose of the private designation is specifically meant to enforce data security by requiring all access to private data members through the provided member functions. This type of access, which restricts a user from seeing how the data are actually stored, is referred to as **data hiding.** Once a class category such as `private` is designated it remains in force until a new category is listed.

Specifically, we have chosen to store a date using three integers: one for the month, day, and year, respectively. We will also always store the year as a four-digit number. Thus, for example, we will store the year 1998 as 1998 and not as 98. Making sure to store all years with their correct century designation will eliminate a multitude of problems that can crop up if only the last two digits, such as 98, are stored. For example, the number of years between 2002 and 1999 can be quickly calculated as 2002 – 1999 = 3 years, whereas this same answer is not so easily obtained if only the year values 02 and 99 are used. Additionally, we are sure of what the year 2000 means, whereas a two-digit value such as 00 could refer to either 1900 or 2000.[6]

Following the private class data members, the function prototypes listed in the `Date` class have been declared as `public`. This means that these class functions *can* be called by any objects and functions not in the class (outside). In general, all class functions should be public; as such they furnish capabilities to manipulate the class variables from outside of

---

5 Note that the default membership category in a class is private, which means that this keyword can be omitted. In this text we explicitly use the private designation to reinforce the idea of access restrictions inherent in class membership.

---

6 These problems are all included under the designation "The year 2000 (or Y2K) problem."

FIGURE 9.3

Format of a member function

```
return-type class-name::function-name(parameter list)
{
  function body
}
```

the class. For our `Date` class we have initially provided three functions, named `Date()`, `setdate()`, and `showdate()`. Notice that one of these member functions has the same name, `Date`, as the class name. This particular function is referred to as a **constructor** function, and it has a specially defined purpose: it can be used to initialize class data members with values. The default values that are used for the `Date` function are the numbers 7, 4, and 2001, which, as we will shortly see, are used as the default `month`, `day`, and `year` values, respectively. The only point to notice at this point is that the default year is correctly represented as a four-digit integer that retains the century designation. Also notice that the constructor function has no return type, which is a requirement for this special function. The two remaining functions declared in our declaration example are `setdate()` and `showdate()`, both of which have been declared as returning no value (`void`). In the implementation section of the class these three member functions will be written to permit initialization, assignment, and display capabilities, respectively.

The **implementation section** of a class is where the member functions declared in the declaration section are written.[7] Figure 9.3 illustrates the general form of functions included in the implementation section. This format is correct for all functions except the constructor, which, as we have stated, has no return type.

As shown in Figure 9.3, member functions defined in the implementation section have the same format as all user-written C++ functions with the addition of the class name and scope resolution operator, `::`, that identifies the function as a member of a particular class. Let us now reconsider the implementation section of our `Date` class, which is repeated below for convenience:

```
//--- class implementation section

Date::Date(int mm, int dd, int yyyy)
{
  month = mm;
  day = dd;
  year = yyyy;
}
```

7 It is also possible to define these functions within the declaration section by declaring and writing them as inline functions. Examples of inline member functions are presented in Section 9.2.

```
void Date::setdate(int mm, int dd, int yyyy)
{
  month = mm;
  day = dd;
  year = yyyy;

  return;
}

void Date::showdate()
{
  cout << "The date is ";
  cout << setfill('0')
       << setw(2) << month << '/'
       << setw(2) << day << '/'
       << setw(2) << year  % 100;  // extract the last 2 year digits
  cout << endl;
  return;
}
```

Notice that the first function in this implementation section has the same name as the class, which makes it a constructor function. As such, it has no return type. The `Date::` included at the beginning of the function header line identifies this function as a member of the `Date` class. The rest of the header line,

```
Date(int mm, int dd, int yyyy)
```

defines the function as having three integer parameters. The body of this function simply assigns the data members `month`, `day`, and `year` with the values of the parameters `mm`, `dd`, and `yyyy`, respectively.

The next function header line

```
void Date::setdate(int mm, int dd, int yyyy)
```

defines this as the `setdate()` function belonging to the `Date` class (`Date::`). This function returns no value (`void`) and expects three integer parameters, `mm`, `dd`, and `yyyy`. In a manner similar to the `Date()` function, the body of this function assigns the data members `month`, `day`, and `year` with the values of its parameters. In a moment we will see the difference between `Date()` and `setdate()`.

Finally, the last function header line in the implementation section defines a function named `showdate()`. This function has no parameters, returns no value, and is a member of the `Date` class. The body of this function, however, needs a little more explanation.

Although we have chosen to internally store all years as four-digit values that retain century information, users are accustomed to seeing dates where the year is represented as a two-digit value, such as 12/15/99. To display the last two digits of the year value, the expression `year % 100` can be used. For example, if the year is 1999, the expression `1999 % 100` yields the value 99, and if the year is 2001, the expression `2001 % 100` yields the value 1. Notice that if we had used an assignment such as `year = year % 100;` we would actually be altering the stored value of `year` to correspond to the last two digits of the year. Because we want to retain the year as a four-digit number, we must be careful to manipulate only the displayed value using the expression `year % 100` within the `cout` stream. The `setfill` and `setw` manipulators are used to ensure that the displayed values correspond to conventionally accepted dates. For example, the date March 9, 2002, could appear as either 3/9/02 or 03/09/02. The `setw` manipulator forces each value to be displayed in a field width of 2. Because this manipulator remains in effect only for the next insertion, we have included it before the display of each date value. The `setfill` manipulator, however, remains in effect until the fill character is changed, so we have to include it only once.[8] We have used the `setfill` manipulator here to change the fill character from its default of a blank space to the character 0. Doing this ensures that a date such as December 9, 2002, will appear as 12/09/02 and not 12/ 9/ 2.

To see how our `Date` class can be used within the context of a complete program, consider Program 9.1. To make the program easier to read, it has been shaded in lighter and darker areas. The lighter area contains the class declaration and implementation sections that we have already considered. The darker area contains the header and `main()` function. For convenience we will retain this shading convention for all programs using classes.[9]

PROGRAM 9.1

```
#include <iostream.h>
#include <iomanip.h>

// class declaration

class Date
{
```

(continued next page)

8 This type of information is easily obtained using the on-line Help facility, as described in Section 2.6.

9 This shading is not accidental. In practice the lighter shaded region containing the class definition would be placed in a separate file. A single `#include` statement would then be used to include this class declaration in the program. Thus, the final program would consist of the two darker shaded regions illustrated in Program 9.1 with the addition of one more `#include` statement in the first region.

(continued from previous page)

```
  private:
    int month;
    int day;
    int year;
  public:
    Date(int = 7, int = 4, int = 2001); // constructor with defaults
    void setdate(int, int, int);        // member function to copy a date
    void showdate();                    // member function to display a date
};

// implementation section

Date::Date(int mm, int dd, int yyyy)
{
  month = mm;
  day = dd;
  year = yyyy;
}

void Date::setdate(int mm, int dd, int yyyy)
{
  month = mm;
  day = dd;
  year = yyyy;

  return;
}

void Date::showdate()
{
  cout << "The date is ";
  cout << setfill('0')
       << setw(2) << month << '/'
       << setw(2) << day << '/'
       << setw(2) << year % 100; // extract the last 2 year digits
  cout << endl;
  return;
}
```

(continued next page)

(*continued from previous page*)

```
int main()
{
  Date a, b, c(4,1,1998);  // declare 3 objects and initialize
                           // 1 of them

  b.setdate(12,25,2002);  // assign values to b's data members
  cout << endl;

  a.showdate();  // display object a's values
  b.showdate();  // display object b's values
  c.showdate();  // display object c's values

  cout << endl;

  return 0;
}
```

The declaration and implementation sections contained in the lighter shaded region of Program 9.1 should look familiar to you, because they contain the class declaration and implementation sections that we have already discussed. Notice, however, that this region declares only the class, it does not create any variables of this class type. This is true of all C++ types, including the built-in types such as integers and floats. Just as a variable of an integer type must be defined, variables of a user-declared class must also be defined. Variables defined to be of a user-declared class are referred to as **objects.**

Using this new terminology, the first statement in Program 9.1's `main()` function, contained in the darker area, defines three objects, named `a`, `b`, and `c`, to be of class type `Date`. In C++ whenever a new object is defined, memory is allocated for the object and its data members are automatically initialized. This is done by an automatic call to the class constructor function. For example, consider the definition `Date a, b, c(4,1,1998);` contained in `main()`. When the object named `a` is defined, the constructor function `Date` is automatically called. No parameters have been assigned to `a`, so the default values of the constructor function are used, resulting in the initialization:

```
a.month = 7
a.day = 4
a.year = 2001
```

Notice the notation that we have used here. It consists of an object name and an attribute name separated by a period. This is the standard syntax for referring to an object's attribute, namely:

object-name.attribute-name

where *object-name* is the name of a specific object and *attribute-name* is the name of a data member defined for the object's class

Thus, the notation `a.month = 7` refers to the fact that object `a`'s `month` data member has been set to the value 7. Similarly, the notation `a.day = 4` and `a.year =2001` refer to the facts that `a`'s `day` and `year` data members have been set to the values 4 and 2001, respectively. In the same manner, when the object named `b` is defined, the same default parameters are used, resulting in the initialization of `b`'s data members as:

```
b.month = 7
b.day = 4
b.year = 2001
```

The object named `c`, however, is defined with the arguments 4, 1, and 1998. These three arguments are passed into the constructor function when the object is defined, resulting in the initialization of `c`'s data members as:

```
c.month = 4
c.day = 1
c.year = 1998
```

The next statement in `main()`, `b.setdate(12,25,2002)`, calls `b`'s `setdate` function, which assigns the argument values 12, 25, 2002 to `b`'s data members, resulting in the assignment:

```
b.month = 12
b.day = 25
b.year = 2002
```

Notice the syntax for referring to an object's method. This syntax is

object-name.method-name(arguments)

where *object-name* is the name of a specific object and *method-name* is the name of one of the functions defined for the object's class. Because we have defined all class functions as public, a statement such as `b.setdate(12,25,2002)` is valid inside the `main()` function and is a call to the class' `setdate()` function. This statement tells the `setdate()` function to operate on the `b` object with the arguments 12, 25, and 2002. It is important to understand that because all class data members were specified as private, a statement such as

PROGRAMMER'S NOTES

Interfaces, Implementations, and Information Hiding

The terms *interface* and *implementation* are used extensively in object-oriented programming literature. Each of these terms can be equated to specific parts of a class's declaration and implementation sections.

An **interface** consists of a class's public member function declarations and any supporting comments. As such, the interface should be all that is required to tell a programmer how to use the class.

The **implementation** consists of both the class's implementation section, which consists of both private and public member function definitions *and* the class's private data members, which is contained in a class's declaration section.

The implementation is the essential means of providing information hiding. In its most general context, **information hiding** refers to the principle that *how* a class is internally constructed is not relevant to any programmer who wishes to use the class. That is, the implementation can and should be hidden from all class users precisely to ensure that the class is not altered or compromised in any way. All that a programmer need know to correctly use class should be provided by the interface.

`b.month = 12` would be invalid from within `main()`. We are therefore forced to rely on member functions to access data member values.

The last three statements in `main()` call the `showdate()` function to operate on the `a`, `b`, and `c` objects. The first call results in the display of `a`'s data values, the second call in the display of `b`'s data values, and the third call in the display of `c`'s data values. Thus, the output displayed by Program 9.1 is as shown in Figure 9.4.

FIGURE 9.4

Output displayed by Program 9.1

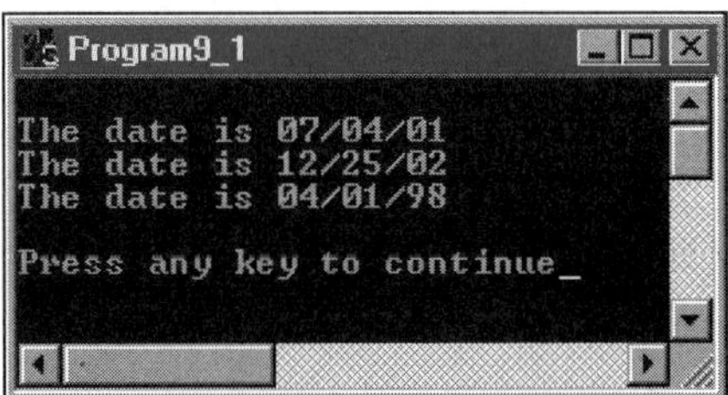

Notice that a statement such as `cout << a;` is invalid within `main()` because `cout` does not know how to handle an object of class `Date`. Thus, we have supplied our class with a function that can be used to access and display an object's internal values.

Terminology

There is sometimes confusion about the terms *classes, objects,* and other terminology associated with object-oriented programming, so let us take a moment to clarify and review the terminology.

A **class** is a programmer-defined data type from which objects can be created. **Objects** are created from classes; they have the same relationship to classes as variables do to C++'s built-in data types. For example, in the declaration

```
int a;
```

`a` is said to be a variable, whereas in Program 9.1's declaration

```
Date a;
```

`a` is said to be an object. If it initially helps you to think of an object as a variable, do so.

Objects are also referred to as **instances** of a class and the process of creating a new object is frequently referred to as an **instantiation** of the object. Each time a new object is instantiated (created), a new set of data members belonging to the object is created.[10] The particular values contained in these data members determines the object's **state.**

Seen in this way, a class can be thought of as a blueprint out of which particular instances (objects) can be created. Each instance (object) of a class will have its own set of particular values for the set of data members specified in the class declaration section.

In addition to the data types allowed for an object, a class also defines **behavior**—that is, the operations that are permitted to be performed on an object's data members. Users of the object need to know *what* these functions can do and how to activate them through function calls, but unless run time or space implications are relevant, they do not need to know *how* the operation is done. The actual implementation details of an object's operations are contained in the class implementation, which can be hidden from the user. Other names for the operations defined in a class implementation section are procedures, functions, services, and methods. We use these terms interchangeably throughout the remainder of the text.

EXERCISES 9.1

1. Define the following terms:
   a. class
   b. object
   c. declaration section
   d. implementation section
   e. instance variable
   f. member function
   g. data member

---

10 Note that only one set of class functions is created. These functions are shared between objects.

h. constructor

i. class instance

j. services

k. methods

l. interface

m. state

n. behavior

2. a. In place of specifying a rectangle's location by listing the position of two diagonal corner points, what other attributes could be used?

b. What other attributes, besides length and width, might be used to describe a rectangle if the rectangle is to be drawn on a color monitor?

c. Describe a set of attributes that could be used to define circles that are to be drawn on a black-and-white monitor.

d. What additional attributes would you add to those selected in response to Exercise 2c if the circles were to be drawn on a color monitor?

3. a. The attributes of a class represent how objects of the class appear to the outside world. The behavior represents how an object of a class reacts to an external stimulus. Given this, what do you think is the mechanism by which one object "triggers" the designated behavior in another object?

b. If behavior in C++ is constructed by defining an appropriate function, how do you think the behavior is activated in C++?

4. Write a class declaration section for each of the following specifications. In each case include a prototype for a constructor and a member function named `showdata()` that can be used to display member values.

a. A class named `Time` that has integer data members named `secs`, `mins`, and `hours`.

b. A class named `Complex` that has floating point data members named `real` and `imaginary`.

c. A class named `Circle` that has integer data members named `xcenter` and `ycenter` and a floating point data member named `radius`.

5. a. Construct a class implementation section for the constructor and `showdata()` function members corresponding to the class declaration created for Exercise 4a.

b. Construct a class implementation section for the constructor and `showdata()` function members corresponding to the class declaration created for Exercise 4b.

c. Construct a class implementation section for the constructor and `showdata()` function members corresponding to the class declaration created for Exercise 4c.

6. a. Include the class declaration and implementation sections prepared for Exercises 4a and 5a in a complete working program.

b. Include the class declaration and implementation sections prepared for Exercises 4b and 5b in a complete working program.

c. Include the class declaration and implementation sections prepared for Exercises 4c and 5c in a complete working program.

7. Determine the errors in the following class declaration section:

```
class employee
{
public:
  int empnum;
  char code;
private:
  class(int = 0);
  void showemp(int, char);
};
```

8. a. Construct a class named `Rectangle` that has floating point data members named `length` and `width`. The class should have member functions named `perimeter()` and `area()` to calculate the perimeter and area of a rectangle, a member function named `setdata()` to set a rectangle's `length` and `width`, and a member function named `showdata()` to display a rectangle's `length`, `width`, `perimeter`, and `area`.

b. Include the `Rectangle` class constructed in Exercise 8a within a working C++ program.

9. a. Modify the `Date` class defined in Program 9.1 to include a `nextDay()` function that increments a date by one day. Test your function to ensure that it correctly increments days into a new month and into a new year.

b. Modify the `Date` class defined in Program 9.1 to include a `priorDay()` function that decrements a date by one day. Test your function to ensure that it correctly decrements days into a prior month and into a prior year.

10. Modify the `Date` class in Program 9.1 to contain a method that compares two `Date` objects and returns the larger of the two. The method should be written according to the following algorithm:

Comparison function
Accept two Date values as parameters
Determine the later date using the following procedure:
Convert each date into a long integer value having the form yyyymmdd.
(This can be accomplished using the formula year * 10000 + month * 100 + day.)
Compare the corresponding integers for each date.
The larger integer corresponds to the later date.
Return the later date

11. **a.** Add a member function to Program 9.1's class definition named `dayOfWeek()` that determines the day of the week for any `Date` object after the date October 15, 1582. An algorithm for determining the day of the week can be found using Zeller's algorithm. This algorithm assumes a date of the form *mm/dd/ccyy*, where *mm* is the month, *dd* is the day, *cc* is the century, and *yy* is the year in the century (for example, for the date 12/28/1997, *mm* = 12, *dd* = 28, *cc* = 19, and *yy* = 97).

If the month is less than 3
  Set *mm* = *mm* + 12 and *ccyy* = *ccyy* – 1
EndIf
Set the variable T = *dd* + int(26 * (month – 1) / 10) + *yy* + int(*yy*/4) + int(*cc*/4) - 2 * *cc*
dayOfWeek = T % 7
If dayOfWeek is less than 0
  dayOfWeek = dayOfWeek + 7
EndIf

Using this algorithm the variable `dayOfWeek` will have a value of 0 if the date is a Saturday, 1 if a Sunday, etc.

b. Include the class definition constructed for Exercise 11a in a complete C++ program. The `main()` function should display the name of the day (Sun, Mon, Tue, etc.) for the `Date` object being tested.

9.2 Constructors

A **constructor** function is any function that has the same name as its class. Multiple constructors can be defined for each class as long as they are distinguishable by the number and types of their parameters.

The intended purpose of a constructor is to initialize a new object's data members. As such, depending on the number and types of supplied arguments, one constructor function is automatically called each time an object is created. If no constructor function is written, the compiler supplies a do-nothing default constructor. In addition to its initialization role, a constructor function may also perform other tasks when it is called and can be written in a variety of ways. In this section we present the possible variations of constructor functions and introduce another function, the destructor, which is automatically called whenever an object goes out of existence.

Figure 9.5 illustrates the general format of a constructor. As shown in this figure, a constructor:

- must have the same name as the class to which it belongs
- must have no return type (not even `void`)

FIGURE 9.5

Constructor format

```
class-name::class-name(parameter list)
{
  function body
}
```

If you do not include a constructor in your class definition, the compiler supplies a do-nothing default one for you. For example, consider the following class declaration:

```
class Date
{
  private:
    int month, day, year;
  public:
    void setdate(int, int, int);
    void showdate()
};
```

Because no user-defined constructor has been declared here, the compiler creates a default constructor. For our `Date` class this default constructor is equivalent to the implementation `Date(void){}`—that is, the compiler-supplied default constructor expects no parameters and has an empty body. Clearly, this default constructor is not very useful, but it does exist if no other constructor is declared.

The term **default constructor** is used quite frequently in C++. It refers to any constructor that does not require any arguments when it is called. This can be because no parameters are declared, which is the case for the compiler-supplied default, or because all parameters have been given default values. For example, the constructor `Date(int = 7, int = 4, int = 2001)` is a valid prototype for a default constructor. Here, each argument has been given a default value, and an object can be declared as type `Date` without supplying any further arguments. Using such a constructor, the declaration `Date a;` initializes the `a` object with the default values 7, 4, and 2001.

To verify that a constructor function is automatically called whenever a new object is created, consider Program 9.2. Notice that in the implementation section the constructor function uses `cout` to display the message `Created a new data object with data values.` Thus, whenever the constructor is called, this message is displayed. Because the `main()` function creates three objects, the constructor is called three times and the message is displayed three times. The output displayed by Program 9.2 is shown in Figure 9.6.

PROGRAM 9.2

```
#include <iostream.h>
#include <iomanip.h>

// class declaration section

class Date
{
  private:
    int month;
    int day;
    int year;
  public:
    Date(int = 7, int = 4, int = 2001); // constructor with defaults
};

// implementation section

Date(int mm, int dd, int yyyy)
{
  month = mm;
  day = dd;
  year = yyyy;
  cout << "Created a new data object with data values "
       << month << ", " << day << ", " << year << endl;
}

int main()
{
  Date a;             // declare an object
  Date b;             // declare an object
  Date c(4,1,2002);   // declare an object

  return 0;
}
```

Although any legitimate C++ statement can be used within a constructor function, such as the `cout` statement used in Program 9.2, it is best to keep constructors simple and use them only for initializing purposes. One further point needs to be made with respect

FIGURE 9.6

Output displayed by Program 9.2

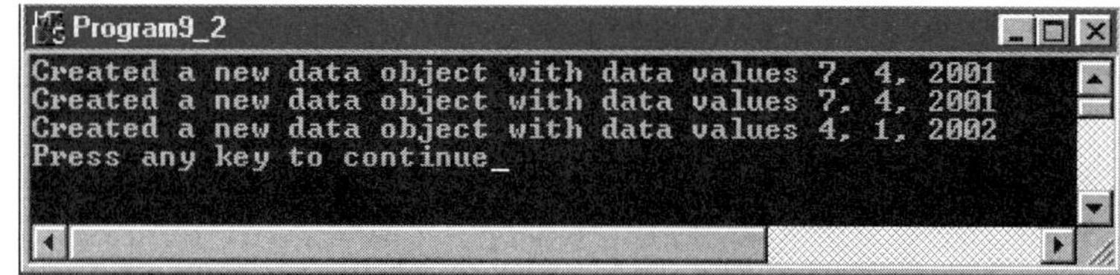

to the constructor function contained in Program 9.2. According to the rules of C++, object members are initialized in the order they are declared in the class declaration section and *not* in the order they may appear in the function's definition within the implementation section. Usually this will not be an issue, unless one member is initialized using another data member's value.

Calling Constructors

As we have seen, constructors are called whenever an object is created. The actual declaration, however, can be made in a variety of ways. For example, the declaration

```
Date c(4,1,2002);
```

used in Program 9.2 could also have been written as

```
Date c = Date(4,1,2002);
```

This second form declares `c` as being of type `Date` and then makes a direct call to the constructor function with the arguments 4, 1, and 2002. This second form can be simplified when only one argument is passed to the constructor. For example, if only the `month` data member of the `c` object needed to be initialized with the value 8, and the day and year members can use the default values, the object can be created using the declaration

```
Date c = 8;
```

Because this style resembles declarations in C, it and its more complete form using the equal sign are referred to as the *C style of initialization*. The form of declaration used in Program 9.2 is referred to as the *C++ style of initialization,* and is the form we use predominantly throughout the remainder of the text.

Regardless of which initialization form you use, in no case should an object be declared with empty parentheses. For example, the declaration `Date a();` is not the same as the declaration `Date a;`. The latter declaration uses the default constructor values, whereas the former declaration results in no object being created.

Overloaded and Inline Constructors

The primary difference between a constructor and other user-written functions is how the constructor is called: Constructors are called automatically each time an object is created, whereas other functions must be explicitly called by name.[11] As a function, however, a constructor must still follow all of the rules applicable to user-written functions that were presented in Chapter 6. This means that constructors may have default arguments, as was illustrated in Programs 9.1 and 9.2, may be overloaded, and may be written as inline functions.

Recall from Section 6.1 that function overloading permits the same function name to be used with different parameter lists. Based on the supplied argument types, the compiler determines which function to use when the call is encountered. Let's see how this can be applied to our `Date` class. For convenience the appropriate class declaration is repeated below:

```
// class declaration section
class Date
{
  private:
    int month;
    int day;
    int year;
  public:
    Date(int = 7, int = 4, int = 2001);      // constructor
};
```

Here, the constructor prototype specifies three integer parameters, which are used to initialize the `month`, `day`, and `year` data members.

An alternate method of specifying a date is to use a long integer in the form *year* ⋆ 10000 + *month* ⋆ 100 + *day*. For example, the date 12/24/1998 using this form is 19981224 and the date 2/5/2002 is 20020205.[12] A suitable prototype for a constructor that uses dates of this form is:

```
Date(long);    // an overloaded constructor
```

Here, the constructor is declared as receiving one long integer argument. The code for this new `Date` function must, of course, correctly convert its single argument into a

11 This is true for all functions except destructors, which are described later in this section. A destructor function is automatically called each time an object is destroyed.

12 The reason for specifying dates in this manner is that only one number needs to be used per date and sorting the numbers automatically puts the corresponding dates into chronological order.

month, day, and year, and would be included within the class implementation section. The actual code for such a constructor is:

```
Date::Date(long yyyymmdd)   // a second constructor
{
  year = int(yyyymmdd/10000.0);    // extract the year
  month = int( (yyyymmdd - year * 10000.0) / 100.00 ); // extract the month
  day = int(yyyymmdd - year * 10000.0 - month * 100.0); // extract the day
}
```

Do not be overly concerned with the actual conversion code used within the function's body. The important point here is the concept of overloading the `Date()` function to provide two constructors. Program 9.3 contains the complete class definition within the context of a working program.

PROGRAM 9.3

```
#include <iostream.h>
#include <iomanip.h>

// class declaration

class Date
{
  private:
    int month;
    int day;
    int year;
  public:
    Date(int = 7, int = 4, int = 2001);// constructor with defaults
    Date(long);                  // another constructor
    void showdate();             // member function to display a date
};

// implementation section

Date::Date(int mm, int dd, int yyyy)
{
  month = mm;
  day = dd;
  year = yyyy;
}
```

(continued next page)

(continued from previous page)

```
Date::Date(long yyyymmdd)
{
  year = int(yyyymmdd/10000.0);     // extract the year
  month = int( (yyyymmdd - year * 10000.0)/100.00 ); // extract the month
  day = int(yyyymmdd - year * 10000.0 - month * 100.0); // extract the day
}

void Date::showdate()
{
   cout << "The date is " << setfill('0')
        << setw(2) << month << '/'
        << setw(2) << day << '/'
        << setw(2) << year % 100; // extract the last 2 year digits

  return;
}
```

```
int main()
{
  Date a, b(4,1,1998), c(20020515L); // declare three objects

  cout << endl;

  a.showdate();          // display object a's values
  cout << endl;

  b.showdate();          // display object b's values
  cout << endl;

  c.showdate();          // display object c's values
  cout << endl << endl;

  return 0;
}
```

The output displayed by Program 9.3 is shown in Figure 9.7.

Three objects are created in Program 9.3's `main()` function. The first object, a, is initialized with the default constructor using its default arguments. Object `b` is also initial-

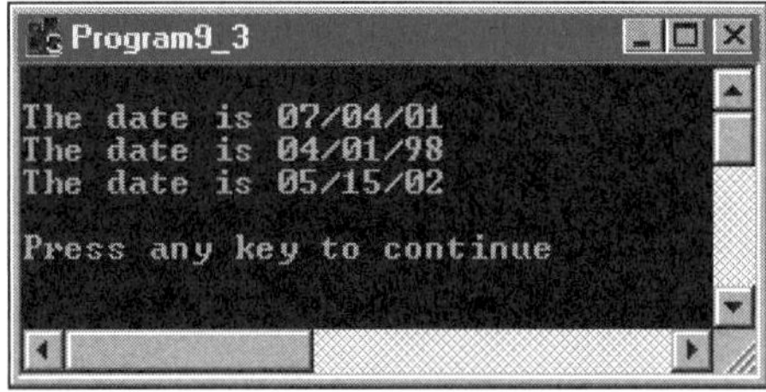
Program9_3
The date is 07/04/01
The date is 04/01/98
The date is 05/15/02
Press any key to continue

FIGURE 9.7

Output displayed by Program 9.3

ized with the default constructor but uses the arguments 4, 1, and 1998. Finally, object c, which is initialized with a long integer, uses the second constructor in the class implementation section. The compiler knows to use this second constructor because the argument specified, 20020515L, is designated as a long integer. It is worthwhile pointing out that a compiler error would occur if both Date constructors had default values. In such a case a declaration such as `Date d;` would be ambiguous to the compiler because it would not be able to determine which constructor to use. Thus, in each implementation section only one constructor can be written as the default.

Just as constructors may be overloaded, they may also be written as **inline member functions.** Doing so simply means defining the function in the class declaration section. For example, making both of the constructors contained in Program 9.3 inline is accomplished by the declaration section:

```
/ class declaration
class Date
{
  private:
    int month;
    int day;
    int year;
  public:
    Date(int mm = 7, int dd = 4, int yyyy = 2001)
    {
      month = mm;
      day = dd;
      year = yyyy;
    }
    Date(long yyyymmdd)    // here is the overloaded constructor
    {
      year = int(yyyymmdd/10000.0);     // extract the year
      month = int( (yyyymmdd - year * 10000.0)/100.00 );  // extract the month
      day = int(yyyymmdd - year * 10000.0 - month * 100.0); // extract the day
    }
    void showdate();
};
```

PROGRAMMER'S NOTES

Constructors

A *constructor* is any function that has the same name as its class. The primary purpose of a constructor is to initialize an object's member variables when an object is created. As such, a constructor is automatically called when an object is declared.

A class can have multiple constructors provided that each constructor is distinguishable by having a different formal parameter list. A compiler error results when unique identification of a constructor is not possible. If no constructor is provided, the compiler will supply a do-nothing default constructor.

Every constructor function must be declared *with no return type* (not even `void`). Because they are functions, constructors may also be explicitly called in nondeclarative statements. When used in this manner, the function call requires parentheses following the constructor name, even if no parameters are used. However, when used in a declaration, parentheses *must not* be included for a zero parameter constructor. For example, the declaration `Date a();` is incorrect. The correct declaration is `Date a;`. When parameters are used, however, they must be enclosed within parentheses in both declarative and nondeclarative statements. Default parameter values should be included within the constructor's prototype.

The keyword `inline` is not required in this declaration because member functions defined inside the class declaration are inline by default.

Generally, only functions that can be coded on a single line are good candidates for inline functions. This reinforces the convention that inline functions should be small. Thus, the first constructor is more conventionally written as

```
Date(int mm = 7, int dd = 4, int yyyy = 2001)
      { month = mm; day = dd; year = yyyy; }
```

The second constructor, which extends over three lines, should not be written as an inline function.

Destructors

The counterpart to constructor functions are destructor functions. Destructors are functions having the same class name as constructors, but preceded with a tilde (~). Thus, for our `Date` class, the destructor name is `~Date()`. Like constructors, a default do-nothing destructor is provided by the C++ compiler in the absence of an explicit destructor. Unlike constructors, however, there can only be one destructor function per class. This is because destructors take no parameters—they also return no values.

Destructors are automatically called whenever an object goes out of existence, and are meant to "clean up" any undesirable effects that might be left by the object. Generally such effects occur only when an object contains a pointer member.

PROGRAMMER'S NOTES

Accessor Functions

An *accessor function* is any nonconstructor member function that accesses a class's private data members. For example, the function `showdate()` in the `Date` class is an accessor function. Such functions are extremely important because they provide a means of displaying private data member's stored values.

When you construct a class make sure to provide a complete set of accessor functions. Each accessor function does not have to return a data member's exact value, but it should return a useful representation of the value. For example, assume that a date such as 12/25/2002 is stored as a long integer member in the form 20022512. Although an accessor function could display this value, a more useful representation would typically be either 12/25/02, or December 25, 2002.

Besides being used for output, accessor functions can also provide a means of data input. For example, the `setdate()` function in the `Date` class is an example of an input accessor function. As we will see in Section 10.4, both the extraction and insertion operators can be overloaded to provide another means of object data input and output. Constructor functions, whose primary purpose is to initialize an object's member variables, are not considered as accessor functions.

EXERCISES 9.2

1. Determine whether the following statements are true or false:

a. A constructor function must have the same name as its class.

b. A class can have only one constructor function.

c. A class can have only one default constructor function.

d. A default constructor can be supplied only by the compiler.

e. A default constructor can have no parameters or all parameters must have default values.

f. A constructor must be declared for each class.

g. A constructor must be declared with a return type.

h. A constructor is automatically called each time an object is created.

i. A class can have only one destructor function.

j. A destructor must have the same name as its class, preceded by a tilde (~).

k. A destructor can have default arguments.

l. A destructor must be declared for each class.

m. A destructor must be declared with a return type.

n. A destructor is automatically called each time an object goes out of existence.

o. Destructors are not useful when the class contains a pointer data member.

2. For Program 9.3, what date would be initialized for object `c` if the declaration `Date c(15);` was used in place of the declaration `Date c(20020515L);` ?

3. Modify Program 9.3 so that the only data member of the class is a long integer named `yyyymmdd`. Do this by substituting the declaration

```
long yyyymmdd;
```

for the existing declarations

```
int month;
int day;
int year;
```

Then, using the same constructor function prototypes currently declared in the class declaration section, rewrite them so that the `Date(long)` function becomes the default constructor and the `Date(int, int, int)` function converts a month, day, and year into the proper form for the class data member.

4. **a.** Construct a `Time class` containing integer data members `seconds`, `minutes`, and `hours`. Have the class contain two constructors: the first should be a default constructor having the prototype `time(int, int, int)`, which uses default values of 0 for each data member. The second constructor should accept a long integer representing a total number of seconds and disassemble the long integer into `hours`, `minutes`, and `seconds`. The final member function should display the class data members.

   b. Include the class written for Exercise 4a within the context of a complete program.

5. **a.** Construct a class named `Student` consisting of an integer student identification number, an array of five floating point grades, and an integer representing the total number of grades entered. The constructor for this class should initialize all `Student` data members to zero. Included in the class should be member functions to (1) enter a student ID number, (2) enter a single test grade and update the total number of grades entered, and (3) compute an average grade and display the student ID followed by the average grade.

   b. Include the class constructed in Exercise 5a within the context of a complete program. Your program should declare two objects of type `Student` and accept and display data for the two objects to verify operation of the member functions.

6. **a.** In Exercise 4 you were asked to construct a `Time` class. For such a class include a `tick()` function that increments the time by one second. Test your function to ensure that it correctly increments into a new minute and a new hour.

   b. Modify the `Time` class written for Exercise 6a to include a `detick()` function that decrements the time by one second. Test your function to ensure that it correctly decrements time into a prior hour and into a prior minute.

9.3 Examples

Now that you have an understanding of how classes are constructed and the terminology used in describing them, let us apply this knowledge to construct two new examples using an object-oriented programming approach. In the first example we construct a single elevator object. We assume that the elevator can travel between the 1st and 15th floors of a building and that the location of the elevator must be known at all times. In the second example we simulate the operation of a gas pump.

Example 1: Constructing an Elevator Object

In this example we will simulate the operation of an elevator. What is required is an output that describes the current floor at which the elevator is either stationed, or is passing by and an internal elevator request button that is pushed as a request to move to another floor. The elevator can travel between the 1st and 15th floor of the building in which it is situated.

Solution: For this application we have one object, which is an elevator. The only attribute of interest is the location of the elevator. The single requested service is the ability to request a change in the elevator's position (state). Additionally, we must be able to establish the initial floor position when a new elevator is put in service.

The location of the elevator, which corresponds to its current floor position, can be represented by an integer member variable. The value of this variable, which we will name `currentFloor`, effectively represents the current state of the elevator. The services that we will provide for changing the state of the elevator will be an initialization function to set the initial floor position when a new elevator is put in service, and a request function to change the elevator's position (state) to a new floor. Putting an elevator in service is accomplished by declaring a single class instance (declaring an object of type `Elevator`), while requesting a new floor position is equivalent to pushing an elevator button. To accomplish this, a suitable class declaration is:

```
// class declaration section
class Elevator
{
  private:
    int currentFloor;
  public:
    Elevator(int = 1);        // constructor
    void request(int);
};
```

Notice that we have declared one data member, `currentFloor`, and two class functions. The data member, `currentFloor`, is used to store the current floor position of the elevator. As a private member it can be accessed only through member functions. The two declared public member functions, `Elevator()` and `request()`, will be used to define the external services provided by each `Elevator` object. The `Elevator()` function, which has the same name as its class, becomes a constructor function that is automatically called when an object of type `Elevator` is created. We will use this function to initialize the starting floor position of the elevator. The `request()` function is used to alter the position of the elevator. To accomplish these services, a suitable class implementation section is:

```
// class implementation section

Elevator::Elevator(int cfloor)   // constructor
{
  currentFloor = cfloor;
}

void Elevator::request(int newFloor)  // access function
{
  if (newFloor < 1 || newFloor > MAXFLOOR || newFloor == currentFloor)
    ; // do nothing
  else if ( newFloor > currentFloor)  // move elevator up
  {
    cout << "\nStarting at floor " << currentFloor << endl;
    while (newFloor > currentFloor)
    {
      currentFloor++;    // add one to current floor
      cout << "   Going Up - now at floor " << currentFloor << endl;
    }
    cout << "Stopping at floor " << currentFloor << endl;
  }
  else  // move elevator down
  {
    cout << "\nStarting at floor " << currentFloor << endl;
    while (newFloor < currentFloor)
    {
      currentFloor--;   // subtract one from current floor
      cout << "   Going Down - now at floor " << currentFloor << endl;
    }
    cout << "Stopping at floor " << currentFloor << endl;
  }

  return;
}
```

The constructor function is straightforward. When an `Elevator` object is declared it is initialized to the floor specified; if no floor is explicitly given, the default value of 1 will be used. For example, the declaration

```
Elevator a(7);
```

initializes the variable `a.currentFloor` to 7, whereas the declaration

```
Elevator a;
```

uses the default argument value and initializes the variable `a.currentFloor` to 1.

The `request()` function defined in the implementation section is more complicated and provides the class's primary service. Essentially this function consists of an `if-else` statement having three parts: (1) if an incorrect service is requested, no action is taken; (2) if a floor above the current position is selected, the elevator is moved up; and (3) if a floor below the current position is selected, the elevator is moved down. For movement up or down the function uses a `while` loop to increment the position one floor at a time, and reports the elevator's movement using a `cout` object stream. Program 9.4 includes this class in a working program.

PROGRAM 9.4

```
#include <iostream.h>

const int MAXFLOOR = 15;
// class declaration

class Elevator
{
  private:
    int currentFloor;
  public:
    Elevator(int = 1);       // constructor
    void request(int);
};

// implementation section

Elevator::Elevator(int cfloor)
{
  currentFloor = cfloor;
}
```

(continued next page)

(continued from previous page)

```
void Elevator::request(int newFloor)
{
  if (newFloor < 1 || newFloor > MAXFLOOR || newFloor == currentFloor)
    ;  // do nothing
  else if ( newFloor > currentFloor)  // move elevator up
  {
    cout << "\nStarting at floor " << currentFloor << endl;
    while (newFloor > currentFloor)
    {
      currentFloor++;    // add one to current floor
      cout << "   Going Up - now at floor " << currentFloor << endl;
    }
    cout << "Stopping at floor " << currentFloor << endl;
  }
  else  // move elevator down
  {
    cout << "\nStarting at floor " << currentFloor << endl;
    while (newFloor < currentFloor)
    {
      currentFloor--;   // subtract one from current floor
      cout << "   Going Down - now at floor " << currentFloor << endl;
    }
    cout << "Stopping at floor " << currentFloor << endl;
  }

  return;
}
```

```
int main()
{
  Elevator a;   // declare 1 object of type Elevator

  a.request(6);
  a.request(3);

  return 0;
}
```

FIGURE 9.8

Output displayed by Program 9.4

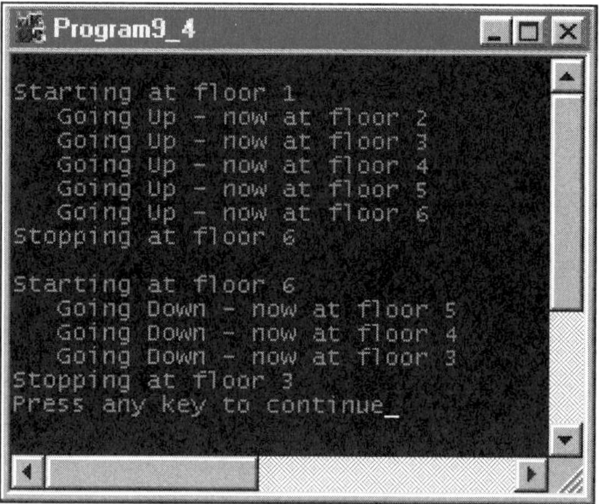

Testing the `Elevator` class entails testing each class operation. To do this we first include the `Elevator` class within the context of a working program, which is listed as Program 9.4.

The lightly shaded portion of Program 9.4 contains the class construction that we have already described. To see how this class is used, concentrate on the darker shaded section of the program. At the top of the program we have included the `iostream.h` header file and declared a named constant `MAXFLOOR`, which corresponds to the highest floor that can be requested.

Within the `main()` function three statements are included. The first statement creates an object named `a` of type `Elevator`. Because no explicit floor has been given, this elevator will begin at floor 1, which is the default constructor argument.

A request is then made to move the elevator to floor 6, which is followed by a request to move to floor 3. The output produced by Program 9.4 is illustrated in Figure 9.8.

The basic requirements of object-oriented programming are evident in even as simple a program as Program 9.4. Before the `main()` function can be written a useful class must be constructed. This is typical of programs that use objects. For such programs the design process is front-loaded with the requirement that careful consideration of the class—its declaration and implementation—be given. Code contained in the implementation section effectively removes code that would otherwise be part of `main()`'s responsibility. Thus, any program that uses the object does not have to repeat the implementation details within its `main()` function. Rather, the `main()` function and any function called by `main()` is concerned only with sending messages to its objects to activate them appropriately. How the object responds to the messages and how the state of the object is retained is not `main()`'s concern—these details are hidden within the class construction.

One further point should be made concerning Program 9.4, which is the control provided by the `main()` function. Notice that this control is sequential, with two calls made to the same object operation using different argument values. This control is perfectly correct for testing purposes. However, by incorporating calls to `request()` within a `while` loop and using the random number function `rand()` to generate random floor requests, a continuous simulation of the elevator's operation is possible (see Exercise 3).

Example 2: A Single Object Gas Pump Simulation

Assume that we have been requested to write a program that simulates the operation of a gas pump. At any time during the simulation we should be able to determine, from the pump, the price-per-gallon of gas and the amount remaining in the supply tank from which the gas is being pumped. If a request for gas, in gallons, is less than the amount of gas in the tank, the request should be filled; otherwise only the available amount in the supply tank should be used. Each time the gas is pumped, the total price of the gallons pumped should be displayed and the amount of gas, in gallons, that was pumped should be subtracted from the amount in the supply tank.

For the simulation assume that the pump is randomly idle for 1 to 15 minutes between customers and that a customer randomly requests between 3 and 20 gallons of gas. Although the tank capacity is 500 gallons, assume that the initial amount of gas in the tank is only 300 gallons. Initially, the program should simulate a half-hour time frame.

Additionally, for each arrival and request for gas we want to know the idle time before the customer arrived, how many gallons of gas were pumped, and the total price of the transaction. The pump itself must keep track of the price per gallon of gas and the amount of gas remaining in the tank. Although the price per gallon is usually $1.00, the specific price for this simulation is $1.25.

For this part of the simulation, we construct a gas-pump class that can be used in the final simulation, which is completed in Section 10.4.

Solution This problem involves two distinct object types. The first is a person who can arrive randomly between 1 and 15 minutes and can randomly request between 3 and 20 gallons of gas. The second object type is the gas pump. For this part of the problem, our goal is to create a suitable gas pump class.

The model for constructing a gas pump class that meets the requirements of the simulation are easily described in pseudocode as:

Put pump in service
Initialize the amount of gas in the tank
Initialize the price per gallon of gas

Display values
Display the amount of gas in the tank
Display the price per gallon

Pump an amount of gas
If the amount in the tank greater than or equal to the amount to be pumped
Set pumped amount equal to the amount to be pumped
Else
Set pumped amount equal to the amount in the tank
EndIf
Subtract the pumped amount from the amount in the tank
Calculate the total price as (price per gallon * pumped amount)
Display the pumped amount
Display the amount remaining in the tank
Display the total price

From this pseudocode description, the implementation of a `Pump` class is rather straightforward. The attributes of interest for the pump are the amount of gallons in the tank and the price per gallon. The required operations include supplying initial values for the pump attributes, interrogating the pump for its attribute values, and satisfying a request for gas.

Because the two attributes, the amount in the tank and the price per gallon, can have fractional values, it is appropriate to make them floating point values. Additionally, three services need to be provided. The first consists of initializing a pump's attributes, which consists of setting values for the amount in the supply tank and the price per gallon. The second consists of satisfying a request for gas, and the third service simply provides a reading of the pump's current attribute values. To accomplish this, a suitable class declaration is:

```
// class declaration

class Pump
{
  private:
    float amtInTank;
    float price;
  public:
    Pump(float = 500.0, float = 1.00);    // constructor
    void values(void);
    void request(float);
};
```

Notice that we have declared two data members and three member functions. As private members, the two data attributes can be accessed only through the class's declared member functions: `Pump()`, `values()`, and `request()`. It is these functions that provide the external services available to each `Pump` object.

The `Pump()` function, which has the same name as its class, is the constructor function that is automatically called when an object of type `Pump` is created. The `values()`

function simply provides a readout of the current attribute values, and the `request()` function handles the logic for fulfilling a customer's request for gas. To accomplish these services, a suitable class implementation section is:

```
// implementation section

Pump::Pump(float start, float todaysPrice)
{
  amtInTank = start;
  price = todaysPrice;
}

void Pump::values(void)
{
  cout << setiosflags(ios::fixed) << setiosflags(ios::showpoint)
       << setprecision(2);
  cout << "The gas tank has " << amtInTank << " gallons of gas." << endl;
  cout << "The price per gallon of gas is $" << price << endl;

  return;
}

void Pump::request(float pumpAmt)
{
  float pumped;

  if (amtInTank >= pumpAmt)
     pumped = pumpAmt;
  else
     pumped = amtInTank;

  amtInTank -= pumped;

  cout << setiosflags(ios::fixed) << setiosflags(ios::showpoint)
       << setprecision(2);
  cout << "    Gallons requested: " << pumpAmt << endl;
  cout << "    Gallons pumped: " << pumped << endl;
  cout << "    Gallons remaining in tank: " << amtInTank << endl;
  cout << "    The price of the sale is $" << (pumped * price) << endl;

  return;
}
```

The constructor function is straightforward. When a `Pump` object is declared it will be initialized to a given amount of gas in the supply tank and a given price per gallon. If no values are given, the defaults of 500 gallons and $1 per gallon will be used.

The `values()` function defined in the implementation section simply provides a readout of the current attribute values. It is the `request()` function that is the most complicated because it provides the primary `Pump` service. The code follows the requirements of the pump as captured by the functional model; that is, it provides all of the gas required unless the amount remaining in the supply tank is less the requested amount. Finally, it subtracts the amount pumped from the amount in the tank and calculates the total dollar value of the transaction.

Testing the `Pump` class entails testing each `class` operation. To do this we first include the `Pump` class within the context of a working program, which is listed as Program 9.5.

PROGRAM 9.5

```
#include <iostream.h>
#include <iomanip.h>
const float AMT_IN_TANK = 300;  // initial gallons in the tank
const float TODAYS_PRICE = 1.25;  // price-per-gallon

// class declaration

class Pump
{
  private:
    float amtInTank;
    float price;
  public:
    Pump(float = 500.0, float = 1.00);   // constructor
    void values(void);
    void request(float);
};

// implementation section

Pump::Pump(float start, float todaysPrice)
{
  amtInTank = start;
  price = todaysPrice;
}

void Pump::values(void)
{
  cout << setiosflags(ios::fixed) << setiosflags(ios::showpoint)
       << setprecision(2);
```

(continued next page)

(continued from previous page)

```
  cout << "The gas tank has " << amtInTank << " gallons of gas." << endl;
  cout << "The price per gallon of gas is $" << price << endl;

  return;
}

void Pump::request(float pumpAmt)
{
  float pumped;

  if (amtInTank >= pumpAmt)
     pumped = pumpAmt;
  else
     pumped = amtInTank;

  amtInTank -= pumped;

  cout << setiosflags(ios::fixed) << setiosflags(ios::showpoint)
       << setprecision(2);
  cout << "    Gallons requested: " << pumpAmt << endl;
  cout << "    Gallons pumped: " << pumped << endl;
  cout << "    Gallons remaining in tank: " << amtInTank << endl;
  cout << "    The price of the sale is $" << (pumped * price) << endl;

  return;
}
```

```
int main()
{
  Pump a(AMT_IN_TANK, TODAYS_PRICE);   // declare 1 object of type Pump

  a.values();
  cout << endl;
  a.request(30.0);
  cout << endl;
  a.request(280.0);

  return 0;
}
```

FIGURE 9.9

Output displayed by Program 9.5

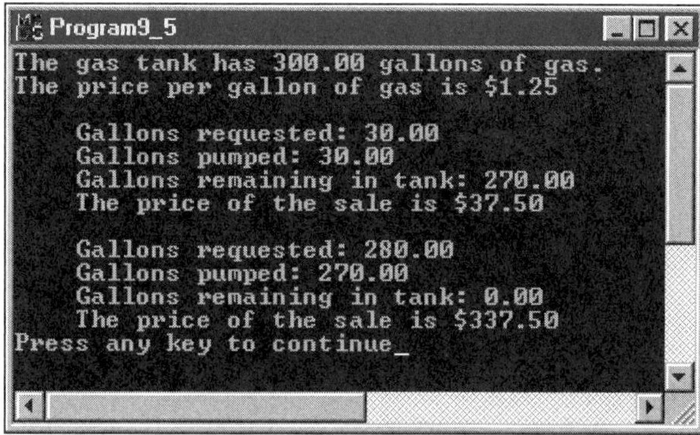

The lightly shaded portion of Program 9.5 contains the class construction that we have already described. To see how this class is used, concentrate on the darker shaded section of the program. At the top of the program we have included the required `#include` files and two constants `AMT_IN_TANK` and `TODAYS_PRICE`, which corresponds to the data that are to be used in the simulation.

Within the `main()` function six statements are included. The first statement creates an object named `a` of type `Pump`. The supply tank for this pump contains `AMT_IN_TANK` gallons and the price per gallon is set to `TODAYS_PRICE`.

A request is then made to `values()` to display the pump's attribute values, which are correctly set at 300 gallons and $1.25 per gallon. The next `cout` statement simply provides a blank line.

The first request for gas is for 30 gallons, followed by a `cout` statement to again provide a blank line. Finally, the last statement is a request for 280 gallons, which exceeds the available gas in the supply tank. The output produced by Program 9.5 is shown in Figure 9.9.

EXERCISES 9.3

1. Enter Program 9.4 in your computer and execute it.

2. a. Modify the `main()` function in Program 9.4 to put a second elevator in service starting at the 5th floor. Have this second elevator move to the 1st floor and then move to the 12th floor.

b. Verify that the constructor function is called by adding a message within the constructor that is displayed each time a new object is created. Run your program to ensure its operation.

3. Modify the `main()` function in Program 9.4 to use a `while` loop that calls the `Elevator`'s request function with a random number between 1 and 15. If the random number is the same as the elevator's current floor, generate another request. The `while` loop should terminate after five valid requests have been made and satisfied by movement of the elevator. (*Hint:* Review Section 5.9 for the use of random numbers.)

4. a. Modify the `main()` function in Program 9.5 to use a `while` loop that calls the `Pump`'s request function with a random number between 3 and 20. The `while` loop should terminate after five requests have been made.

b. Modify the `main()` function written for Exercise 4a to provide a 30-minute simulation of the gas pump's operation. To do this you will have to modify the `while` loop to select a random number between 1 and 15 that represents the idle time between customer requests. Have the simulation stop once the idle time exceeds 30 minutes. (*Hint:* Review Section 5.9 for the use of random numbers.)

5. a. Construct a class definition of a `Person` object type. The class is to have no attributes, a single constructor function, and two additional member functions named `arrive()` and `gallons()`.The constructor function should simply call `srand()` with the argument `time(NULL)` to initialize the `rand()` function. The `arrive()` function should provide a random number between 1 and 15 as a return value, and the `gallons()` function should provide a random number between 3 and 20. (*Hint:* Review Section 5.9 for the use of random numbers.)

b. Test the `Person` class functions written for Exercise 5a in a complete working program.

c. Use the `Person` class function to simulate a random arrival of a person and a random request for gallons of gas within the program written for Exercise 4b.

6. Modify Program 9.5 so that the `Pump` class definition resides in a file named `PUMP.H`. Then have Program 9.5 use an `#include` statement to include the class definition within the program. Make sure to use a full path name in the `#include` statement. For example, if `PUMP.H` resides in the directory named `FOO` on the C drive, the `#include` statement should be `#include <C:\FOO\PUMP.C>`.

7. Construct a class named `Light` that simulates a traffic light. The color attribute of the class should change from `Green` to `Yellow` to `Red` and then back to `Green` by the class's `change()` function. When a new `Light` object is created its initial color should be `Red`.

8. a. Construct a class definition that can be used to represent an employee of a company. Each employee is defined by an integer ID number, a floating point pay rate, and the maximum number of hours the employee should work each week. The services provided by the class should be the ability to enter data for a new employee, the ability to change data for a new employee, and the ability to display the existing data for a new employee.

b. Include the class definition created for Exercise 8a in a working C+ program that asks the user to enter data for three employees and displays the entered data.

PROGRAMMER'S NOTES

Encapsulation

The term *encapsulation* refers to the packaging of a number of items into a single unit. For example, a function is used to encapsulate the details of an algorithm. Similarly, a class encapsulates both a data structure and functions together in a single package.

Although the term encapsulation is sometimes used to refer to the process of information hiding, this usage is technically not accurate. The correct relationship between terms is that information hiding refers to the encapsulation *and* hiding of all implementation details.

9.4 Common Programming Errors

The more common programming errors initially associated with the construction of classes are:

1. Failing to terminate the class declaration section with a semicolon.

2. Including a return type with the constructor's prototype or failing to include a return type with the other functions' prototypes.

3. Using the same name for a data member as for a member function.

4. Defining more than one default constructor for a class.

5. Forgetting to include the class name and scope operator, `::`, in the header line of all member functions defined in the class implementation section.

All of these errors will result in a compiler error message.

9.5 Chapter Summary

1. A **class** is a programmer-defined data type. **Objects** of a class may be defined and have the same relationship to their class as variables do to C++'s built-in data types.

2. A class definition consists of a declaration and implementation section. The most common form of a class definition is:

```
// class declaration section
class name
{
  private:
   a list of variable declarations;
```

```
    public:
      a list of function prototypes;
  };

  // class implementation section
  class function definitions
```

The variables and functions declared in the class declaration section are collectively referred to as **class members.** The variables are individually referred to as class data members and the functions as class member functions. The terms *private* and *public* are access specifiers. Once an access specifier is listed it remains in force until another access specifier is given. The `private` keyword specifies that the class members following it are private to the class and can be accessed only by member functions. The `public` keyword specifies that the class members following may be accessed from outside the class. Generally all data members should be specified as private and all member functions as public.

3. `Class` functions listed in the declaration section may either be written inline or their definitions included in the class implementation section. Except for constructor and destructor functions, all class functions defined in the class implementation section have the header line form:

return-type class-name::function-name(parameter list);

Except for the addition of the class name and scope operator, `::`, which are required to identify the function name with the class, this header line is identical to the header line used for any user-written function.

4. A **constructor function** is a special function that is automatically called each time an object is declared. It must have the same name as its class and cannot have any return type. Its purpose is to initialize each declared object.

5. If no constructor is declared for a class the compiler will supply a default constructor. This is a do-nothing function having the definition

```
class-name::class-name(void){}
```

6. The term **default constructor** refers to any constructor that does not require any arguments when it is called. This can be because no parameters are declared (as is the case for the compiler-supplied default constructor) or because all parameters have been given default values.

7. Each class may only have one default constructor. If a user-defined constructor is defined, the compiler will not create its default constructor. Thus if any constructor is defined for a class, a user-defined default constructor should be written because the compiler will not supply it.

8. Objects are created using either a C++ or C style of declaration. The C++ style of declaration has the form:

class-name list of object names(list of initializers);

where the list of initializers is optional. An example of this style of declaration, including initializers, for a class named `Date` is:

```
Date a, b, c(12,25,2002);
```

Here the objects `a` and `b` are declared to be of type `Date` and are initialized using the default constructor, and the object `c` is initialized with the values 12, 25, and 2002.

The equivalent C style of declaration, including the optional list of initializers, has the form:

class-name object-name = class-name(list of initializers);

An example of this style of declaration for a class named `Date` is:

```
Date c = Date(12,25,2002)
```

Here the object `c` is created and initialized with the values 12, 25, and 2002.

9. Constructors may be overloaded in the same manner as any other user-written C++ function.

10. A destructor function is called each time an object goes out of scope. Destructors must have the same name as their class, but preceded with a tilde (~). There can be only one destructor per class.

11. A **destructor function** takes no arguments and returns no value. If a user-defined destructor is not included in a class the compiler will provide a do-nothing destructor.

9.6 Knowing About: Insides and Outsides

Just as the concept of an algorithm is central to procedures, the concept of encapsulation is central to objects. In this section we present this encapsulation concept using an inside-outside analogy, which should help in your understanding of what object-oriented programming is all about.[13]

In programming terms, an object's attributes are described by data, such as the length and width of a rectangle, and the operations that can be applied to the attributes are described by procedures and functions.

---

13 This section contains enrichment material that can be omitted on first reading with no loss of subject continuity.

FIGURE 9.10

The boiled egg object model

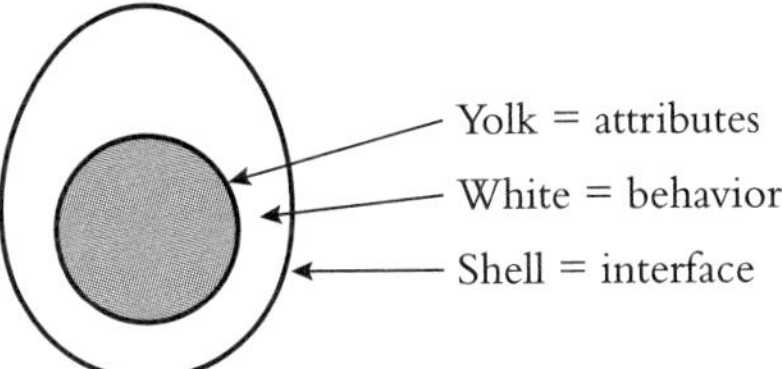

As a practical example of this, assume that we will be writing a program that can deal a hand of cards. From an object-oriented approach, one of the objects that we must model is, clearly, a deck of cards. For our purposes, the attribute of interest for the card deck is that it contains 52 cards, consisting of four suits (hearts, diamonds, spades, and clubs), with each suit consisting of thirteen pip values (ace to ten, jack, queen, and king).

Now consider the behavior of our deck of cards, which consists of the operations that can be applied to the deck. At a minimum we will want the ability to shuffle the deck and be able to deal single cards. Let's now see how this simple example relates to encapsulation using an inside-outside concept.

A useful visualization of the inside-outside concept is to consider an object as a boiled egg, such as shown in Figure 9.10. Notice that the egg consists of three parts: a very inside yolk, a less inside white surrounding the yolk, and an outside shell, which is the only part of the egg visible to the outside world.

In terms of our boiled egg model, the attributes and behavior of an object correspond to the yolk and white, respectively, which are inside the egg. That is, the innermost protected area of an object, its data attributes, can be compared to the egg yolk. Surrounding the data attributes, in a similar manner as an egg's white surrounds its yolk, are the operations that we choose to incorporate within an object. Finally, in this analogy, the interface to the outside world, which is represented by the shell, represents how a user gets to invoke the object's internal procedures.

The egg model, with its egg shell interface separating the inside of the egg from the outside, is useful precisely because it so clearly depicts the separation between what should be contained inside an object and what should be seen from the outside. This separation forms an essential element in object-oriented programming. Let's see why this is so.

From an inside-outside perspective, an object's data attributes, the selected algorithms for the object's operations, and how these algorithms are actually implemented are always inside issues that are hidden from the view of an object user. The remaining concept of how a user or another object can actually activate an inside procedure is an outside issue.

Now let's apply this concept to our card deck example. First, consider how we might represent cards in the deck. Any of the following attributes (there are others) could be used to represent a card:

1. Two integer variables, one representing a suit (a number from 1 to 4) and one representing a value (a number from 1 to 13).

2. One character value and one integer value. The character represents a card's suit, and the integer represents a card's value.

3. One integer variable having a value from 0 to 51. The expression `int (number / 13 + 1)` provides a number from 1 to 4, which represents the suit, and the expression `(number % 13 + 1)` represents a card value from 1 to 13.

Whichever one we choose, however, is not relevant to the outside. The specific way we choose to represent a card is an inside issue to be decided by the designer of the deck object. From the outside, all that is of concern is that we have access to a deck consisting of 52 cards having the necessary suits and pip values.

The same is true for the operations we decide to provide as part of our card deck object. Consider just the shuffling for now.

There are a number of algorithms for producing a shuffled deck. For example, we could use C++'s random number function, `rand()`, or create our own random number generator. Again, the selected algorithm is an inside issue to be determined by the designer of the deck. The specifics of which algorithm is selected and how it is applied to the attributes we have chosen for each card in the deck are not relevant from the object's outside. For purposes of illustration, assume that we decide to use C++'s `rand()` function to produce a randomly shuffled deck.

If we use the first attribute set previously given, each card in a shuffled deck is produced using `rand()` at least twice; once to create a random number from 1 to 4 for the suit, and then again to create a random number from 1 to 13 for the card's pip value. This sequence must be done to construct 52 different attribute sets, with no duplicates allowed.

If, on the other hand, we use the second attribute set previously given, a shuffled deck can be produced in exactly the same fashion as above, with one modification: the first random number (from 1 to 4) must be changed into a character to represent the suit.

Finally, if we use the third representation for a card, we need to use `rand()` once for each card, to produce 52 random numbers from 0 to 51, with no duplicates allowed.

The important point here is that the selection of an algorithm and how it will be applied to an object's attributes are implementation issues *and implementation issues are always inside issues.* A user of the card deck, who is outside, does not need to know how the shuffling is done. All the user of the deck must know is how to produce a shuffled deck. In practice, this means that the user is supplied with sufficient information to correctly invoke the shuffle function. This corresponds to the interface, or outer shell of the egg.

Abstraction and Encapsulation

The distinction between insides and outsides relates directly to the concepts of abstraction and encapsulation. Abstraction means concentrating on what an object is and does, before making any decisions about how the object will be implemented. Thus, abstractly, we define a deck and the operations we want to provide. (If our abstraction is to be useful, it had better capture the attributes and operations of a real-world deck.) Once we have decided on the attributes and operations, we can actually implement them.

Encapsulation means separating (and, by convention, hiding) the implementation details of the chosen abstract attributes and behavior from outside users of the object. The external side of an object should provide only the necessary interface to users of the object for activating internal procedures. Imposing a strict inside-outside discipline when creating objects is really another way of saying that the object successfully encapsulates and hides all implementation details. In our deck-of-cards example, this means that users need never know how we have internally modeled the deck or how an operation, such as shuffling, is performed; the user needs to know only how to activate the given operations.

Code Reuse and Extensibility

A direct advantage of an inside-outside object approach is that it encourages both code reuse and extensibility. This is a direct result of having all interactions between objects centered on the outside interface and hiding all implementation details inside the object.

For example, consider the object shown in Figure 9.11. Here, imagine that any of the two object's operations can be activated by correctly stimulating either the circle or square on the outside. In practice, the stimulation is simply a method call. We have used a circle and square to emphasize that two different methods are provided for outside use. In our card deck example, activation of one method might produce a shuffled deck, whereas activation of another method might result in a card suit and pip value being returned from the object.

Now assume that we want to alter the implementation of an existing operation or add more functionality to our object. *As long as the existing outside interface is maintained, the internal implementation of any and all operations can be changed without the user ever being aware that a change took place.* This is a direct result of encapsulating the attribute data and operations within an object.

Additionally, as long as the interface to existing operations is not changed, new operations can be added as they are needed. Essentially, from the outside world, all that is being added is another function call that accesses the inside attributes and modifies them in a new way.

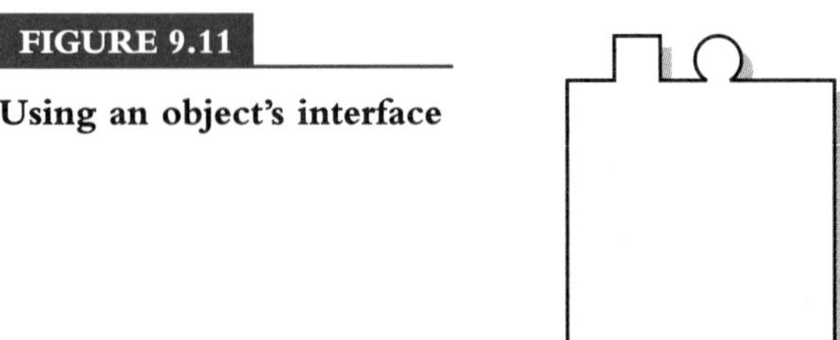

FIGURE 9.11

Using an object's interface

10 Class Functions and Conversions

The creation of a class requires that we provide the capability to declare, initialize, assign, manipulate, and display data members. In the previous chapter the declaration, initialization, and display of objects was presented. In this chapter we continue our construction of classes by providing the ability to create operator and conversion capabilities similar to those inherent in C++'s built-in types. With these additions our user-defined types will have all of the functionality of built-in types.

10.1 Assignment

In Chapter 3 we saw how C++'s assignment operator, =, performs assignment between variables. In this section we see how assignment works when it is applied to objects and how to define our own assignment operator to override the default provided for user-defined classes.

For a specific assignment example, consider the `main()` function of Program 10.1.

Notice that the implementation section of the `Date` class in Program 10.1 contains no assignment function. Nevertheless, we would expect the assignment statement `a = b;` in `main()` to assign `b`'s data member values to their counterparts in `a`. This is, in fact, the case, and it is verified by the output shown in Figure 10.1, which is produced when Program 10.1 is executed.

The type of assignment illustrated in Program 10.1 is referred to as **memberwise assignment.** In the absence of any specific instructions to the contrary, the C++ compiler builds this type of default assignment operator for each class. If the class *does not* contain any pointer data members this default assignment operator is adequate and can be used without further consideration. Before considering the problems that can occur with pointer data members, let's see how to construct our own explicit assignment operators.

Assignment operators, like all class members, are declared in the class declaration section and defined in the class implementation section. For the declaration of operators, however, the keyword `operator` must be included in the declaration. Using this keyword, a simple assignment operator declaration has the form:

```
void operator=(class-name&);
```

Here the keyword `void` indicates that the assignment returns no value, the `operator=` indicates that we are overloading the assignment operator with our own version, and the class name and ampersand within the parentheses indicates that the argument to the operator is a class reference. For example, to declare a simple assignment operator for our `Date` class, the declaration:

```
void operator=(Date&);
```

can be used.

Program10_1
The date stored in a is originally 04/01/99
After assignment the date stored in a is 12/18/01
Press any key to continue_

FIGURE 10.1

Output displayed by Program 10.1

PROGRAM 10.1

```
#include <iostream.h>
#include <iomanip.h>

// class declaration

class Date
{
  private:
     int month;
     int day;
     int year;
   public:
     Date(int = 7, int = 4, int = 2001);  // constructor prototype with defaults
     void showdate();      // member function to display a Date
};

// implementation section

Date::Date(int mm, int dd, int yyyy)
{
  month = mm;
  day = dd;
  year = yyyy;
}

void Date::showdate()
{
  cout << setfill('0')
       << setw(2) << month << '/'
       << setw(2) << day << '/'
       << setw(2) << year % 100;
  return;
}

int main()
{
  Date a(4,1,1999), b(12,18,2001); // declare two objects
```

(continued next page)

(continued from previous page)

```
  cout << "\nThe date stored in a is originally ";
  a.showdate();  // display the original date
  a = b;         // assign b's value to a
  cout << "\nAfter assignment the date stored in a is ";
  a.showdate();  // display a's values
  cout << endl;

  return 0;
}
```

The actual implementation of the assignment operator is defined in the implementation section. For our declaration, a suitable implementation is:

```
void Date::operator=(Date& newdate)
{
  day = newdate.day;       // assign the day
  month = newdate.month;   // assign the month
  year = newdate.year;     // assign the year
}
```

The use of the reference parameter in the definition of this operation is not accidental. In fact, one of the primary reasons for adding reference variables to C++ was to facilitate the construction of overloaded operators and make the notation more natural. In this definition `newdate` is defined as a reference to a `Date` class. Within the body of the definition the `day` member of the object referenced by `newdate` is assigned to the `day` member of the current object, which is then repeated for the `month` and `year` members. Assignments such as `a.operator=(b);` can then be used to call the overloaded assignment operator and assign `b`'s member values to `a`. For convenience, the expression `a.operator=(b)` can be replaced with `a = b;`. Program 10.2 contains our new assignment operator within the context of a complete program.

Except for the addition of the overloaded assignment operator declaration and definition, Program 10.2 is identical to Program 10.1 and produces the same output. Its usefulness to us is that it illustrates how we can explicitly construct our own assignment definitions. In the next section, when we introduce pointer data members, we will see how C++'s default assignment can cause troublesome errors that are circumvented by constructing our own assignment operators. Before moving on, however, two simple modifications to our assignment operator need to be made.

PROGRAM 10.2

```
#include <iostream.h>
#include <iomanip.h>
```

```
// class declaration

class Date
{
  private:
     int month;
     int day;
     int year;
   public:
     Date(int = 7, int = 4, int = 2001); // constructor prototype with defaults
     void operator=(Date&);    // define assignment of a date
     void showdate();          // member function to display a date
};

// implementation section

Date::Date(int mm, int dd, int yyyy)
{
  month = mm;
  day = dd;
  year = yyyy;
}

void Date::operator=(Date& newdate)
{

  day = newdate.day;        // assign the day
  month = newdate.month;    // assign the month
  year = newdate.year;      // assign the year

  return;
}
```

(continued next page)

(continued from previous page)

```
void Date::showdate()
{
  cout << setfill('0')
       << setw(2) << month << '/'
       << setw(2) << day << '/'
       << setw(2) << year % 100;

  return;
}
```

```
int main()
{
  Date a(4,1,1999), b(12,18,2001); // declare two objects

  cout << "\nThe date stored in a is originally ";
  a.showdate();  // display the original date
  a = b;         // assign b's value to a
  cout << "\nAfter assignment the date stored in a is ";
  a.showdate();  // display a's values
  cout << endl;

  return 0;
}
```

First, to preclude any inadvertent alteration to the object used on the right hand side of the assignment a constant reference parameter should be used. For our `Date` class, this takes the form:

```
void Date::operator=(const Date& secdate);
```

The final modification concerns the operation's return value. As constructed, our simple assignment operator returns no value, which precludes us from using it in multiple assignments such as `a = b = c`. The reason for this is that overloaded operators retain the same precedence and associativity as their equivalent built-in versions. Thus, an expression such as `a = b = c` is evaluated in the order `a = (b = c)`. As we have defined assignment, unfortunately, the expression `b = c` returns no value, making subsequent assignment to

FIGURE 10.2

Initialization and Assignment

```
                    c = a;      <------ Assignment
Type definition --> Date c = a; <------ Initialization
```

the a object an error. To provide for multiple assignments a more complete assignment operation would return a reference to its class type. Because the implementation of such an assignment requires a special class pointer, the presentation of this more complete assignment operator is deferred until the material presented in Section 11.5 is introduced. Until then, our simple assignment operator will be more than adequate for our needs.

Copy Constructors

Although assignment looks similar to initialization, it is worthwhile to note that they are two entirely different operations. In C++ an initialization occurs every time a new object is created. In an assignment no new object is created—the value of an existing object is simply changed. Figure 10.2 illustrates this difference.

One type of initialization that closely resembles assignment occurs in C++ when one object is initialized using another object of the same class. For example, in the declaration

```
Date b = a;
```

or its entirely equivalent form

```
Date b(a);
```

the b object is initialized to a previously declared a object. The constructor that performs this type of initialization is called a **copy constructor,** and if you do not declare one, the compiler will construct one for you. The compiler's **default copy constructor** performs in a manner similar to the default assignment operator by doing a memberwise copy between objects. Thus, for the declaration `Date b = a;` the default copy constructor sets b's month, day, and year values to their respective counterparts in a. As with default assignment operators, default copy constructors work just fine unless the class contains pointer data members. Before considering the complications that can occur with pointer data members and how to handle them, it will be helpful to see how to construct our own copy constructors.

Copy constructors, like all class functions, are declared in the class declaration section and defined in the class implementation section. The declaration of a copy constructor has the general form:

class-name(const class-name&);

As with all constructors, the function name must be the class name. As further illustrated by the declaration, the parameter is a reference to the class, which is a characteristic of all copy constructors.[1] To ensure that the parameter is not inadvertently altered, it is always specified as a constant. Applying this general form to our `Date` class, a copy constructor can be explicitly declared as:

```
Date(const Date&);
```

The actual implementation of this constructor, if it were to perform the same memberwise initialization as the default copy constructor, would take the form:

```
Date:: Date(const Date& olddate)
{
  month = olddate.month;
  day = olddate.day;
  year = olddate.year;
}
```

As with the assignment operator, the use of a reference parameter for the copy constructor is no accident: The reference parameter again facilitates a simple notation within the body of the function. Program 10.3 contains this copy constructor within the context of a complete program.

The output produced by Program 10.3 is illustrated in Figure 10.3.

FIGURE 10.3

Output displayed by Program 10.3

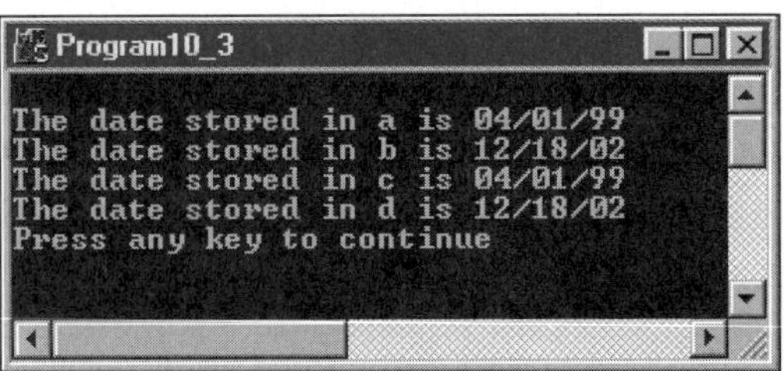

Program10_3
The date stored in a is 04/01/99
The date stored in b is 12/18/02
The date stored in c is 04/01/99
The date stored in d is 12/18/02
Press any key to continue

---

1 A copy constructor is frequently defined as a constructor whose first parameter is a reference to its class type, with any additional parameters being defaults.

PROGRAM 10.3

```
#include <iostream.h>
#include <iomanip.h>
```

```
// class declaration

class Date
{
  private:
     int month;
     int day;
     int year;
   public:
     Date(int = 7, int = 4, int = 2001); // constructor with defaults
     Date(const Date&);      // copy constructor
     void showdate();         // member function to display a date
};

// implementation section

Date::Date(int mm, int dd, int yyyy)
{
  month = mm;
  day = dd;
  year = yyyy;
}

Date::Date(const Date& olddate)
{
  month = olddate.month;
  day = olddate.day;
  year = olddate.year;
}

void Date::showdate()
{

  cout << setfill('0')
       << setw(2) << month << '/'
```

(continued next page)

(continued from previous page)

```
        << setw(2) << day << '/'
        << setw(2) << year % 100;

  return;
}
```

```
int main()
{
  Date a(4,1,1999), b(12,18,2002); // use the constructor
  Date c(a);    // use the copy constructor
  Date d = b;   // use the copy constructor

  cout << "\nThe date stored in a is ";
  a.showdate();
  cout << "\nThe date stored in b is ";
  b.showdate();
  cout << "\nThe date stored in c is ";
  c.showdate();
  cout << "\nThe date stored in d is ";
  d.showdate();

  return 0;
}
```

As illustrated by this output, c's and d's data members have been initialized by the copy constructor to a's and b's values, respectively. Although the copy constructor defined in Program 10.3 adds nothing to the functionality provided by the compiler's default copy constructor, it does provide us with the fundamentals of defining copy constructors. In the next subsection we will see how to modify this basic copy constructor to handle cases that are not adequately taken care of by the compiler's default.

Base/Member Initialization

Except for the reference names `olddate` and `secdate`, a comparison of Program 10.3's copy constructor to Program 10.2's assignment operator shows them to be essentially the same function.[2] The difference in these functions is that the copy constructor first creates

---

2 The material in this section is presented for completeness only, and may be omitted without loss of subject continuity.

PROGRAMMER'S NOTES

Values and Identities

Apart from any behavior that an object is given, a characteristic feature of objects—one they share with variables—is that they always have a unique identity. It is an object's identity that permits us to distinguish one object from another. This is not true of a value, such as the number 5, because all occurrences of 5 are indistinguishable from one another. As such, values are not considered as objects in object-oriented programming languages such as C++.

Another distinguishing feature between an object and a value is that a value can never be a container whose value can change, whereas an object clearly can. A value is simply an entity that stands for itself.

Now consider a string such as `"Chicago"`. As a string this is a value. However, since `Chicago` could also be a specific and identifiable object of type `City`, the context in which the name is used is important. Notice that if the string `"Chicago"` were assigned to an object's name attribute, it reverts to being a value.

an object's data members before the body of the constructor uses assignment to specify member values. Thus, the copy constructor does not perform a true initialization, but rather a creation followed by assignment.

A true initialization would have no reliance on assignment whatsoever and is possible in C++ using a *base/member initialization list.* Such a list can be applied only to constructor functions and may be written in two ways.

The first way to construct a base/member initialization list is within a class' declaration section using the form:

class-name(parameter list) : list of data members(initializing values) {}

For example, using this form a default constructor that performs a true initialization is:

```
// class declaration section

public:
  Date(int mo = 7, int da = 4, int yr = 2001) : month(mo), day(da), year(yr) {}
```

The second way is to declare a prototype in the class' declaration section followed by the initialization list in the implementation section. For our `Date` constructor this takes the form:

```
// class declaration section

public:
  Date(int = 7, int = 4, int = 2001);  // prototype with defaults

// class implementation section

Date::Date(int mo, int da, int yr) : month(mo), day(da), year(yr) {}
```

Notice that in both forms the body of the constructor function is empty. This is not a requirement, and the body can include any subsequent operations that you would like the constructor to perform. The interesting feature of this type of constructor is that it clearly differentiates between the initialization tasks performed in the member initialization list contained between the colon and the braces and any subsequent assignments that might be contained within the function's body. Although we will not be using this type of initialization subsequently, it is required whenever there is a `const` class instance variable.

EXERCISES 10.1

1. Describe the difference between assignment and initialization.

2. **a.** Construct a class named `Time` that contains three integer data members named `hrs`, `mins`, and `secs`, which will be used to store hours, minutes, and seconds. The function members should include a constructor that provides default values of 0 for each data member, a display function that prints an object's data values, and an assignment operator that performs a memberwise assignment between two time objects.

   b. Include the `Time` class developed in Exercise 2a in a working C++ program that creates and displays two time objects, the second of which is assigned the values of the first object.

3. **a.** Construct a class named `Complex` that contains two floating point data members named `real` and `imag`, which will be used to store the real and imaginary parts of a complex number. The function members should include a constructor that provides default values of 0 for each data member, a display function that prints an object's data values, and an assignment operator that performs a memberwise assignment between two complex number objects.

   b. Include the class written for Exercise 3a in a working C++ program that creates and displays the values of two complex objects, the second of which is assigned the values of the first object.

4. **a.** Construct a class named `Cartesian` that contains two floating point data members named `x` and `y`, which will be used to store the `x` and `y` values of a point in rectangular coordinates. The function members should include a constructor that initializes the `x` and `y` values of an object to 0, and functions to input and display an object's `x` and `y` values. Additionally, there should be an assignment function that performs a memberwise assignment between two `Cartesian` objects.

   b. Include the class written for Exercise 4a in a working C++ program that creates and displays the values of two `Cartesian` objects, the second of which is assigned the values of the first object.

5. **a.** Construct a class named `Car` that contains the following three data members: a floating point variable named `engineSize`, a character variable named `bodyStyle`, and an integer variable named `colorCode`. The function members should include a constructor that provides default values of 0 for each numeric data member and an `'X'` for each character variable; a display function that prints the engine size, body style, and color code; and an assignment operator that performs a memberwise assignment between two car objects for each instance variable.

   b. Include the class written for Exercise 5a in a working C++ program that creates and displays two car objects, the second of which is assigned the values of the first object, except for the pointer data member.

6. **a.** Construct a class named `Savings` that contains three floating point data members named `balance`, `rate`, and `interest`, and a constructor that initializes each of these members to 0. Additionally, there should be a member function that inputs a balance and rate and then calculates an interest. The rate should be stored as a percent, such as 6.5 for 6.5%, and the interest computed as $interest = balance \times rate/100$. Additionally, there should be a member function to display all member values.

   b. Include the class written for Exercise 6a in a working C++ program that tests each member function.

10.2 Class Scope and Friend Functions

This section presents additional features pertaining to classes. These include the scope of a class, creating static class members, and granting access privileges to nonmember functions. Each of these topics may be read independently of the others.

Class Scope

We have already encountered local and global scope in Sections 6.4 and 6.5. As we saw, the scope of a variable defines the portion of a program in which the variable can be accessed.

For local variables this scope is defined by any block contained within a brace pair, `{ }`. This includes both the complete function body and any internal subblocks. Additionally, all parameters of a function are considered as local function variables.

Global variables are accessible from their point of declaration throughout the remaining portion of the file containing them, with three exceptions:

1. If a local variable has the same name as a global variable, the global variable can be accessed only within the scope of the local variable by using the global resolution operator, `::`.

2. The scope of a global variable can be extended into another file by using the keyword `extern`.

3. Static global variables are unknown outside their immediate file and cannot be `externed`.

In addition to local and global scopes, each class also defines an associated **class scope.** That is, the names of the data and function members are local to the scope of their class. Thus, if a global variable name is reused within a class, the global variable is hidden by the class data member in the same manner as a local function variable hides a global variable of the same name. Similarly, member function names are local to the class in which they are declared, and can be used only by objects declared for the class. Additionally, local function variables also hide the names of class data members having the same name. Figure 10.4 illustrates the scope of the variables and functions for the following declarations:

```
float rate;    // global
// class declaration
class Test
{
  private:
    float amount, price, total;  // class scope
  public:
    float extend(float, float);  // class scope
};
```

Static Class Members

As each class object is created, it gets its own block of memory for its data members. In some cases, however, it is convenient for every instantiation of a class to share the *same* memory location for a specific variable. For example, consider a class consisting of employee records, where each employee is subject to the same state sales tax. Clearly, we could make the sales tax a global variable, but this is not very safe. Such data could be modified anywhere in the program, could conflict with an identical variable name within a function, and certainly violates C++'s principle of data hiding.

This type of situation is handled in C++ by declaring a class variable to be `static`. Static data members share the same storage space for all objects of the class; as such, they act as global variables for the class and provide a means of communication between objects.

FIGURE 10.4

Example of scopes

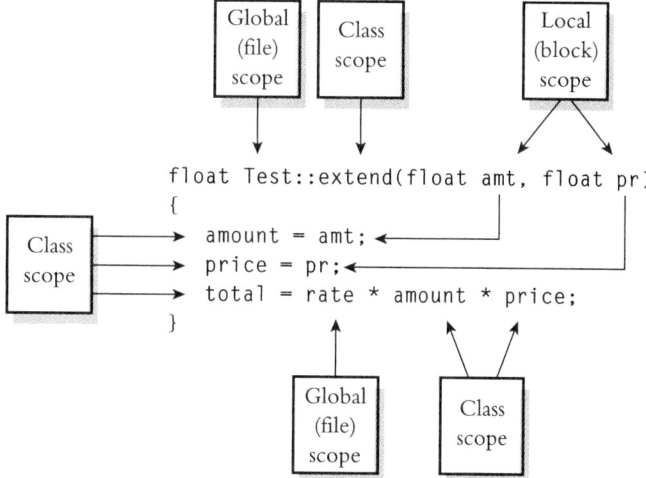

C++ requires that static variables be declared as such within the class' declaration section. Since a static data member requires only a single storage area, regardless of the number of class instantiations, it is defined in a single place outside of the class definition. This is typically done in the global part of the program where the class implementation section is provided. For example, assuming the class declaration

```
//class declaration

class Employee
{
  private:
    static float taxRate;
    int idNum;
  public:
    Employee(int);    //constructor
    void display();
};
```

the definition and initialization of the static variable `taxRate` is accomplished using a statement such as

```
float Employee::taxRate = 0.0025;
```

Here the scope resolution operator, `::`, is used to identify `taxRate` as a member of the class `Employee`, and the keyword `static` is not included. Program 10.4 uses this definition within the context of a complete program.

PROGRAM 10.4

```
#include <iostream.h>

// class declaration

class Employee
{
  private:
    static float taxRate;
    int idNum;
  public:
    Employee(int = 0);     // constructor
    void display();   // access function
};

// static member definition
float Employee::taxRate = 0.0025;

// implementation section

Employee::Employee(int num)
{
  idNum = num;
}

void Employee::display()
{
  cout << "\nEmployee number " << idNum
       << " has a tax rate of " << taxRate << endl;

  return;
}

int main()
{
  Employee emp1(11122), emp2(11133);

  emp1.display();
  emp2.display();

  return 0;
}
```

FIGURE 10.5

Output displayed by Program 10.4

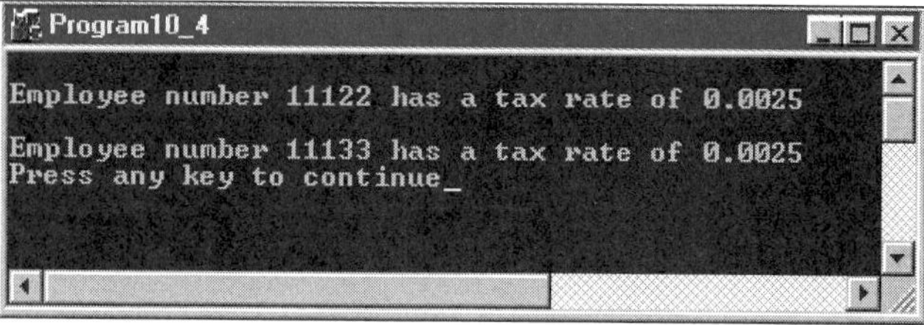

The output produced by Program 10.4 is shown in Figure 10.5.

Although it might appear that the initialization of `taxRate` is global, it is not. Once the definition is made, any other definition will result in an error. Thus, the actual definition of a static member remains the responsibility of the class creator. The storage sharing produced by the static data member and the objects created in Program 10.4 is illustrated in Figure 10.6.

FIGURE 10.6

Sharing the static data member `taxRate`

emp1 — (Local to object) `idNum`

emp2 — `idNum` (Local to object)

`taxRate` (Global to class)

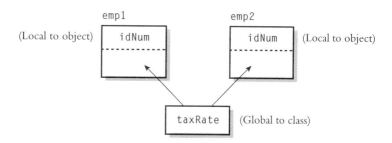

In addition to static data members, static member functions can also be created. Such functions apply to a class as a whole rather than for individual class objects and can access only static data members and other static member functions of the class.[3] An example of such a function is provided by Program 10.5.

The output produced by Program 10.5 is shown in Figure 10.7.

FIGURE 10.7

Output displayed by Program 10.5

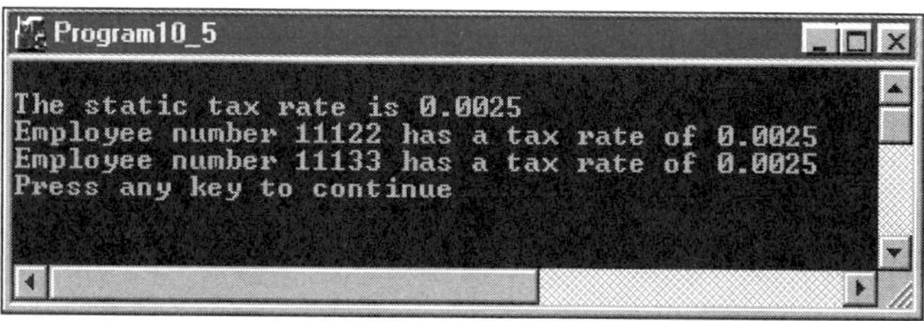

---

3 The reason for this is that the `this` pointer, discussed next, is not passed to static member functions.

PROGRAM 10.5

```
#include <iostream.h>

// class declaration

class Employee
{
  private:
    static float taxRate;
    int idNum;
  public:
    Employee(int = 0);    // constructor
    void display();      // access function
    static void disp();  // static function
};

// static member definition
float Employee::taxRate = 0.0025;

// implementation section

Employee::Employee(int num)
{
  idNum = num;
}

void Employee::display()
{
  cout << "Employee number " << idNum
       << " has a tax rate of " << taxRate << endl;

  return;
}

void Employee::disp()
{
  cout << "\nThe static tax rate is " << taxRate << endl;

  return;
}
```

(continued next page)

(*continued from previous page*)

```
int main()
{
  Employee::disp();    // call the static functions
  Employee emp1(11122), emp2(11133);

  emp1.display();
  emp2.display();

  return 0;
}
```

In reviewing Program 10.5 notice that the keyword `static` is used only when static data and function members are declared: it is not included in the definition of these members. Also notice that the static member function is called using the resolution operator with the function's class name. Finally, because static functions access only static variables that are not contained within a specific object, static functions may be called before any instantiations are declared.

Friend Functions

The only method we currently have for accessing and manipulating private class data members is through the class's member functions. Conceptually, this arrangement can be viewed as illustrated in Figure 10.8a. There are times, however, when it is useful to provide such access to selected nonmember functions.

The procedure for providing this external access is rather simple—the class maintains its own approved list of nonmember functions that are granted the same privileges as

FIGURE 10.8a

Direct access provided to member functions

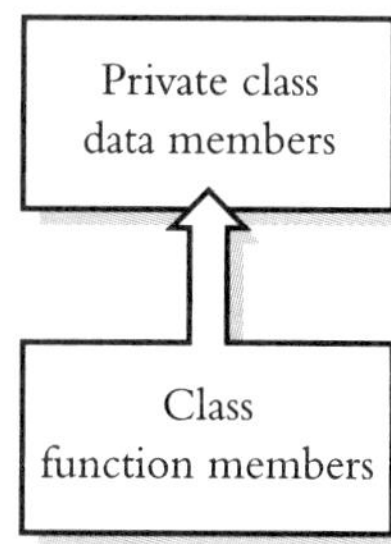

FIGURE 10.8b

Access provided to nonmember functions

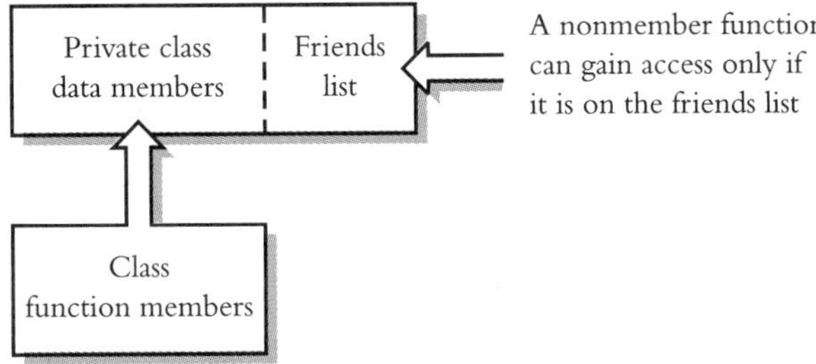

member functions. The nonmember functions on the list are called **friend functions,** and the list is referred to as a **friends list.**

Figure 10.8b conceptually illustrates the use of such a list for nonmember access. Any such function attempting access to an object's private data members is first checked against the friends list: if the function is on the list, access is approved; otherwise access is denied.

From a coding standpoint the friends list is simply a series of function prototype declarations that are preceded with the word `friend` and included in the class's declaration section. For example, if the functions named `addreal()` and `addimag()` are to be allowed access to the private members of a class named `Complex`, the following prototypes would be included within `Complex`'s declaration section.

```
friend float addreal(Complex&, Complex&);
friend float addimag(Complex&, Complex&);
```

Here the friends list consists of two declarations. The prototypes indicate that each function returns a floating point number and expects two references to objects of type `Complex` as arguments. Program 10.6 includes these two friend declarations in a complete program.

The output produced by Program 10.6 is shown in Figure 10.9

FIGURE 10.9

Output displayed by Program 10.6

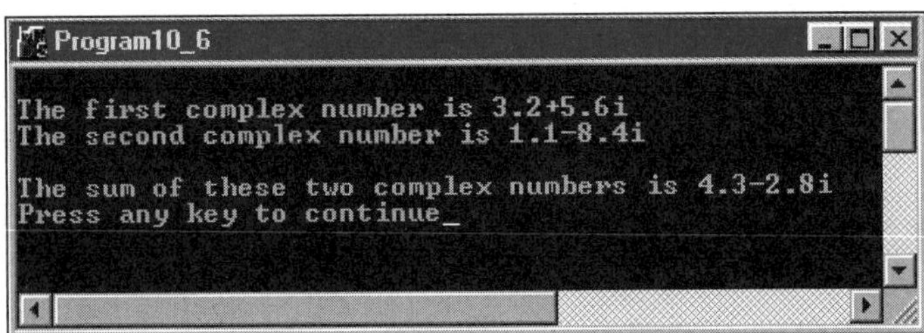

PROGRAM 10.6

```
#include <iostream.h>
#include <math.h>
```

```
// class declaration

class Complex
{
  // friends list
  friend float addreal(Complex&, Complex&);
  friend float addimag(Complex&, Complex&);
  private:
    float real;
    float imag;
  public:
    Complex(float = 0, float = 0);  // constructor
    void display();

};

// implementation section

Complex::Complex(float rl, float im)
{
  real = rl;
  imag = im;
}

void Complex::display()
{
  char sign = '+';

  if(imag < 0) sign = '-';
  cout << real << sign << fabs(imag) << 'i';

  return;
}

// friend implementations
```

(continued next page)

(continued from previous page)

```
float addreal(Complex &a, Complex &b)
{
  return(a.real + b.real);
}

float addimag(Complex &a, Complex &b)
{
  return(a.imag + b.imag);
}
```

```
int main()
{
  Complex a(3.2, 5.6), b(1.1, -8.4);
  float re, im;

  cout << "\nThe first complex number is ";
  a.display();
  cout << "\nThe second complex number is ";
  b.display();

  re = addreal(a,b);
  im = addimag(a,b);
  Complex c(re,im);  // create a new Complex object
  cout << "\n\nThe sum of these two complex numbers is ";
  c.display();
  cout << endl;

  return 0;
}
```

In reviewing Program 10.6, notice four items. The first is that because friends are not class members, they are unaffected by the access section in which they are declared—*they may be declared anywhere within the declaration section.* The convention we have followed is to include all friend declarations immediately following the class header. The second item to notice is that the keyword `friend` (like the keyword `static`) is used only within the class declaration and not in the actual function definition. Third, because a friend function is intended to have access to an object's private data members, at least one of the friend's arguments should be a reference to an object of the class that has made it a friend. Finally, as illustrated by Program 10.6, it is the class that grants friend status to a function, and not the other way around. The function can never confer friend status on itself, because to do so would violate the concepts of data hiding and access provided by a class.

EXERCISES 10.2

1. a. Rewrite Program 10.5 to include an integer static data member named `numemps`. This variable should act as a counter that is initialized to zero and is incremented by the class constructor each time a new object is declared. Rewrite the static function `disp()` to display the value of this counter.
   b. Test the class written for Exercise 1a. Have the `main()` function call `disp()` after each `Employee` object is created.

2. a. Construct a class named `Circle` that contains two integer data members named `xCenter` and `yCenter`, and a floating point data member named `radius`. Additionally, the class should contain a static data member named `scaleFactor`. Here the `xCenter` and `yCenter` values represent the center point of a circle, `radius` represents the circle's actual radius, and `scaleFactor` represents a scale factor that will be used to scale the circle to fit on a variety of display devices.
   b. Include the class written for Exercise 2a in a working C++ program.

3. a. Could the following three statements in Program 10.6

```
re = addreal(a,b);
im = addimag(a,b);
Complex c(re,im);   // create a new complex object
```

   be replaced by the single statement

```
Complex(addread(a,b), addimag(a,b)); ?
```

   b. Verify your answer to Exercise 3a by running Program 10.6 with the suggested replacement statement.

4. a. Rewrite the program written for Exercise 2a, but include a friend function that multiples an object's radius by a static scale factor and then displays the actual radius value and the scaled value. b. Include the program written for Exercise 4a in a working C++ program.

5. Rewrite Program 10.6 to have only one friend function named `addcomplex()`. This function should accept two complex objects and return a complex object. The real and imaginary parts of the returned object should be the sum of the real and imaginary parts, respectively, of the two objects passed to `Complex()`.

6. a. Construct a class named `Coord` that contains two floating point data members named `xval` and `yval`, which will be used to store the `x` and `y` values of a point in rectangular coordinates. The function members should include appropriate constructor and display functions and a friend function named `convPol()`. The `convPol()` function should accept two floating point numbers that represent a point in polar coordinates and convert them into rectangular coordinates. For conversion from polar to rectangular coordinates, use the formulas:

$$x = r \cos \theta$$

$$y = r \sin \theta$$

b. Include the program written for Exercise 6a in a working C++ program.

7. a. Construct two classes named `RecCoord` and `PolCoord`. The class named `RecCoord` should contain two floating point data members named `xval` and `yval`, which will be used to store the `x` and `y` values of a point in rectangular coordinates. The function members should include appropriate constructor and display functions and a friend function named `convPol()`.

The class named `PolCoord` should contain two floating point data members named `dist` and `theta`, which will be used to store the distance and angle values of a point represented in polar coordinates. The function members should include appropriate constructor and display functions and a friend function named `convPol()`.

The friend function should accept an integer argument named `dir`; two floating point arguments named `val1` and `val2`; and two reference arguments named `recref` and `polref`, the first of which should be a reference to an object of type `recCoord`, and the second to an object of type `polCoord`. If the value of `dir` is 1, `val1` and `val2` are to be considered as `x` and `y` rectangular coordinates that are to be converted to polar coordinates; if the value of `dir` is any other value, `val1` and `val2` are to be considered as distance and angle values that are to be converted to rectangular coordinates. For conversion from rectangular to polar coordinates, use the formulas:

$$r = \sqrt{x^2 + y^2}$$

$$\theta = \tan^{-1}(y/x)$$

For conversion from polar to rectangular coordinates, use the formulas:

$$x = r \cos \theta$$

$$y = r \sin \theta$$

b. Include the class written for Exercise 7a in a working C++ program.

10.3 Operator Functions

A simple assignment operator was constructed in Section 10.1. In this section we extend this capability and show how to broaden C++'s built-in operators to work with class objects. As we will discover, class operators are themselves either member or friend functions.

The only symbols permitted for user-defined purposes are the subset of C++'s built-in symbols listed in Table 10.1. Each of these symbols may be adopted for class use with no limitation as to its meaning.[4] This is done by making each operation a function that can be overloaded like any other function.

The operation of the symbols listed in Table 10.1 can be redefined as we see fit for our classes, subject to the following restrictions:

- Symbols not in Table 10.1 cannot be redefined. For example, the `.`, `::`, and `?:` symbols cannot be redefined.
- New operator symbols cannot be created. For example, because `%%` is not an operator in C++, it cannot be defined as a class operator.
- Neither the precedence nor the associativity of C++'s operators can be modified. Thus, you cannot give the addition operator a higher precedence than the multiplication operator.
- Operators cannot be redefined for C++'s built-in types.
- A C++ operator that is unary cannot be changed to a binary operator and a binary operator cannot be changed to a unary operator.
- The operator must either be a member of a class or be defined to take at least one class member as an operand.

The first step in providing a class with operators from Table 10.1 is to decide which operations make sense for the class and how they should be defined. As a specific example, we continue to build on the `Date` class introduced previously. For this class a small, meaningful set of class operations is defined.

Clearly, the addition of two dates is not meaningful. The addition of a date with an integer, however, does make sense if the integer is taken as the number of days to be added to the date. Likewise, the subtraction of an integer from a date makes sense. Also, the subtraction of two dates is meaningful if we define the difference to mean the

---

4 The only limitation is that the syntax of the operator cannot be changed. Thus, a binary operator must remain binary and a unary operator must remain unary. Within this syntax restriction, an operator symbol can be used to produce any operation, whether or not the operation is consistent with the symbol's accepted usage. For example, we could redefine the addition symbol to provide multiplication. Clearly this violates the intent and spirit of making these symbols available to us. We shall be very careful to redefine each symbol in a manner consistent with its accepted usage.

TABLE 10.1 Operators available for class use

<table>
<tr><th>Operator</th><th>Description</th></tr>
<tr><td>()</td><td>Function call</td></tr>
<tr><td>[]</td><td>Array element</td></tr>
<tr><td>-></td><td>Structure member pointer reference</td></tr>
<tr><td>new</td><td>dynamically allocate memory</td></tr>
<tr><td>delete</td><td>dynamically deallocate memory</td></tr>
<tr><td>+</td><td>Increment</td></tr>
<tr><td>--</td><td>Decrement</td></tr>
<tr><td>-</td><td>Unary minus</td></tr>
<tr><td>!</td><td>Logical negation</td></tr>
<tr><td>~</td><td>One's complement</td></tr>
<tr><td>*</td><td>Indirection</td></tr>
<tr><td>*</td><td>Multiplication</td></tr>
<tr><td>/</td><td>Division</td></tr>
<tr><td>%</td><td>Modulus (remainder)</td></tr>
<tr><td>+</td><td>Addition</td></tr>
<tr><td>-</td><td>Subtraction</td></tr>
<tr><td><<</td><td>Left shift</td></tr>
<tr><td>>></td><td>Right shift</td></tr>
<tr><td><</td><td>Less than</td></tr>
<tr><td><=</td><td>Less than or equal to</td></tr>
<tr><td>></td><td>Greater than</td></tr>
<tr><td>>=</td><td>Greater than or equal to</td></tr>
<tr><td>==</td><td>Equal to</td></tr>
<tr><td>!=</td><td>Not equal to</td></tr>
<tr><td>&&</td><td>Logical AND</td></tr>
<tr><td>||</td><td>Logical OR</td></tr>
<tr><td>&</td><td>Bitwise AND</td></tr>
<tr><td>^</td><td>Bitwise exclusive OR</td></tr>
<tr><td>|</td><td>Bitwise inclusive OR</td></tr>
<tr><td>=</td><td>Assignment</td></tr>
<tr><td>+= -= *=</td><td>Assignment</td></tr>
<tr><td>/= %= &=</td><td>Assignment</td></tr>
<tr><td>^= |=</td><td>Assignment</td></tr>
<tr><td><<= >>=</td><td>Assignment</td></tr>
<tr><td>,</td><td>Comma</td></tr>
</table>

number of days between the two dates. Similarly, it makes sense to compare two dates and determine if the dates are equal or one date occurs before or after another date. Let's now see how these operations can be implemented using C++'s operator symbols.

A user-defined operation is created as a function that redefines C++'s built-in operator symbols for class use. Functions that define operations on class objects and use C++'s built-in operator symbols are referred to as **operator functions.**

Operator functions are declared and implemented in the same manner as all member functions with one exception: It is the function's name that connects the appropriate operator symbol to the operation defined by the function. An operator function's name is always of the form operator<symbol> where <symbol> is one of the operators listed in Table 10.1. For example, the function name `operator+` is the name of the addition function, and the function name `operator==` is the name of the equal-to comparison function.

Once the appropriate function name is selected, the process of writing the function simply amounts to having it accept the desired inputs and produce the correct returned value.[5] For example, in comparing two `Date` objects for equality we would select C++'s equality operator. Thus, the name of our function becomes `operator==`. We would want our comparison operation to accept two `Date` objects, internally compare them, and return an integer value indicating the result of the comparison: for example, 1 for equality and 0 for inequality. As a member function a suitable prototype that could be included in the class declaration section is:

```
int operator==(Date&);
```

This prototype indicates that the function is named `operator==`, that it returns an integer, and that it accepts a reference to a `Date` object.[6] Only one `Date` object is required here because the second `Date` object will be the object that calls the function. Let's now write the function definition to be included in the class implementation section. Assuming our class is named `Date`, a suitable definition is:

```
int Date::operator==(Date& Date2)
{
  if( day == date2.day && month == date2.month && year == date2.year)
    return 1;
  else
    return 0;
}
```

---

5 As previously noted, this implies that the specified operator can be redefined to perform any operation. Good programming practice, however, dictates against such redefinitions.

---

6 The prototype `int operator==(Date)` also works. Passing a reference, however, is preferable to passing an object because it reduces the function call's overhead. This is because passing an object means that a copy of the object must be made for the called function, whereas passing a reference gives the function direct access to the object whose address is passed.

Once this function has been defined, it may be called using the same syntax as for C++'s built-in types. For example, if `a` and `b` are objects of type `Date`, the expression `if (a == b)` is valid. Program 10.7 includes the call as well as the declaration and definition of this operator function within the context of a complete program.

PROGRAM 10.7

```
#include <iostream.h>

// class declaration

class Date
{
  private:
    int month;
    int day;
    int year;
  public:
    Date(int = 7, int = 4, int = 2001);      // constructor
    int operator==(Date &);  // declare the operator== function
};

// implementation section

Date::Date(int mm, int dd, int yyyy)
{
  month = mm;
  day = dd;
  year = yyyy;
}

int Date::operator==(Date& date2)
{
  if(day == date2.day && month == date2.month && year == date2.year)
    return 1;
  else
    return 0;
}
```

(continued next page)

(*continued from previous page*)

```
int main()
{
  Date a(4,1,1999), b(12,18,2001), c(4,1,1999); // declare 3 objects

  if (a == b)
    cout << "\nDates a and b are the same." << endl;
  else
    cout << "\nDates a and b are not the same." << endl;

  if (a == c)
    cout << "Dates a and c are the same.\n" << endl;
  else
    cout << "Dates a and c are not the same.\n" << endl;

  return 0;
}
```

The output produced by Program 10.7 is shown in Figure 10.10.

The first new feature to be illustrated in Program 10.7 is the declaration and implementation of the function named `operator==()`. Except for its name, this operator function is constructed in the same manner as any other member function: it is declared in the declaration section and defined in the implementation section. The second new feature is how the function is called. Operator functions may be called using their associated symbols rather than in the way other functions are called. Because operator functions are true functions, however, the traditional method of calling them can also be used—by specifying the name and including appropriate arguments. Thus, in addition to being called using the expression `a == b` in Program 10.7, the call `a.operator==(b)` could also have been used.

FIGURE 10.10

Output displayed by Program 10.7

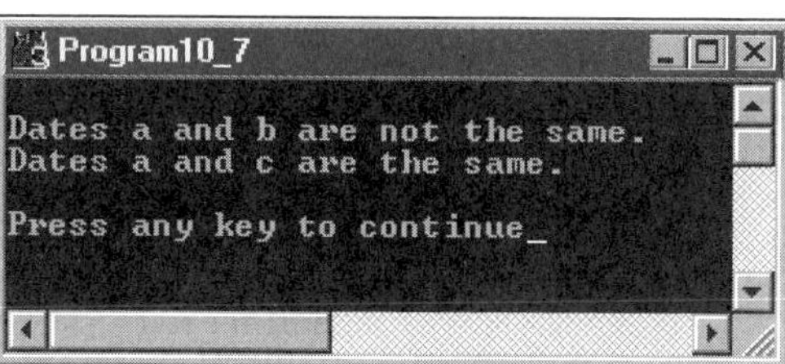

Program10_7
Dates a and b are not the same.
Dates a and c are the same.
Press any key to continue_

Let's now create another operator for our `Date` class—an addition operator. As before, creating this operator requires that we specify three items:

1. The name of the operator function
2. The processing that the function is to perform
3. The data type, if any, that the function is to return

For addition, the correct choice is to use the operator function named `operator+`. Having selected the function's name we must now determine what we want this function to do, as it specifically relates to `Date` objects. As we noted previously, the sum of two dates makes no sense. Adding an integer to a date is meaningful, however, when the integer represents the number of days either before or after the given date. Here the sum of an integer to a `Date` object is simply another `Date` object, which should be returned by the addition operation. Thus, a suitable prototype for our addition function is:

```
Date operator+(int);
```

This prototype would be included in the class declaration section. It specifies that an integer is to be added to a class object and the operation returns a `Date` object. Thus, if `a` is a `Date` object, the function call `a.operator+(284)`, or its more commonly used alternative, `a + 284`, should cause the number 284 to be correctly added to `a`'s date value. We must now construct the function to accomplish this.

Constructing the function requires that we first select a specific date convention. For simplicity, we will adopt the financial date convention that considers each month to consist of 30 days and each year to consist of 360 days. Using this convention our function will first add the integer number of days to the `Date` object's `day` value and then adjust the resulting `day` value to lie within the range 1 to 30 and the `month` value to lie within the range 1 to 12. A function that accomplishes this is:

```
Date Date::operator+(int days)
{
  Date temp;  // a temporary Date to store the result

  temp.day = day + days;  // add the days
  temp.month = month;
  temp.year = year;
  while (temp.day > 30)    // now adjust the months
  {
    temp.month++;
    temp.day -= 30;
  }
```

```
  while (temp.month > 12)  // adjust the years
  {
    temp.year++;
    temp.month -= 12;
  }
  return temp;     // the values in temp are returned
}
```

The important feature to notice here is the use of the `temp` object. The purpose of this object is to ensure that none of the function's parameters, which become the operator's operands, is altered. To understand this, consider a statement such as `b = a + 284;` that uses this operator function, where `a` and `b` are `Date` objects. This statement should never modify `a`'s value. Rather, the expression `a + 284` should yield a `Date` value that is then assigned to `b`. The result of the expression is, of course, the `temp Date` object returned by the `operator+()` function. Program 10.8 uses this function within the context of a complete program.

PROGRAM 10.8

```
#include <iostream.h>
#include <iomanip.h>

// class declaration

class Date
{
  private:
    int month;
    int day;
    int year;
  public:
    Date(int = 7, int = 4, int = 2001);     // constructor
    Date operator+(int);  // overload the + operator
    void showdate();      // member function to display a date
};

// implementation section
```

(continued next page)

(continued from previous page)

```
Date::Date(int mm, int dd, int yyyy)
{
  month = mm;
  day = dd;
  year = yyyy;
}

Date Date::operator+(int days)
{
  Date temp;  // a temporary date to store the result

  temp.day = day + days;  // add the days
  temp.month = month;
  temp.year = year;
  while (temp.day > 30)    // now adjust the months
  {
    temp.month++;
    temp.day -= 30;
  }
  while (temp.month > 12)  // adjust the years
  {
    temp.year++;
    temp.month -= 12;
  }
  return temp;     // the values in temp are returned
}

void Date::showdate()
{
  cout << setfill('0')
       << setw(2) << month << '/'
       << setw(2) << day << '/'
       << setw(2) << year % 100;

  return;
}
```

(continued next page)

(*continued from previous page*)

```
int main()
{
  Date a(4,1,1999), b; // declare two objects

  cout << "\nThe initial date is ";
  a.showdate();
  b = a + 284;    // add in 284 days = 9 months and 14 days
  cout << "\nThe new date is ";
  b.showdate();
  cout << endl;

  return 0;
}
```

The output produced by Program 10.8 is shown in Figure 10.11.

FIGURE 10.11

Output displayed by Program 10.8

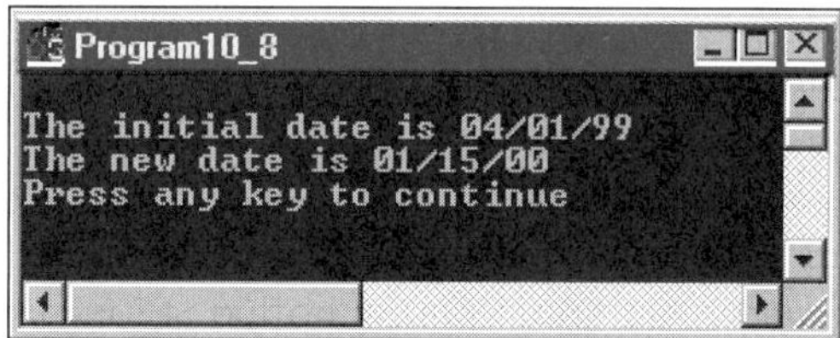
Program10_8
The initial date is 04/01/99
The new date is 01/15/00
Press any key to continue

Operator Functions as Friends

The operator functions in both Programs 10.7 and 10.8 have been constructed as class members. An interesting feature of operator functions is that, except for the operator functions =, ( ), [ ], and ->, they may also be written as friend functions. For example, if the `operator+()` function used in Program 10.8 were written as a friend, a suitable declaration section prototype is:

```
friend Date operator+(Date& , int);
```

Notice that the friend version contains a reference to a `Date` object that is not contained in the member function version. In all cases the equivalent friend version of a member operator function *must* contain an additional class reference that is not required by the member function.[7] This equivalence is listed in Table 10.2 for both unary and binary operators.

7 This extra parameter is necessary to identify the correct object. This parameter is not needed when using a member function because the member function "knows" which object it is operating on. The mechanism of this "knowing" is supplied by an implied member function parameter named `this`, which is explained in detail in Section 11.3.

TABLE 10.2 Operator function argument requirements

	Member Function	Friend Function
Unary operator	1 implicit	1 explicit
Binary operator	1 implicit and 1 explicit	2 explicit

Program 10.8's `operator+()` function written as a friend function is:

```
Date Date::operator+(Date& op1, int days)
{
  Date temp;  // a temporary Date to store the result

  temp.day = op1.day + days;  // add the days
  temp.month = op1.month;
  temp.year = op1.year;
  while (temp.day > 30)    // now adjust the months
  {
    temp.month++;
    temp.day -= 30;
  }
  while (temp.month > 12)  // adjust the years
  {
    temp.year++;
    temp.month -= 12;
  }
  return temp;      // the values in temp are returned
}
```

The only difference between this version and the member version is the explicit use of a `Date` argument named `op1` (the choice of this name is entirely arbitrary) in the friend version. This means that within the body of the friend function the first three assignment statements explicitly reference `op1`'s data members as `op1.day`, `op1.month`, and `op1.year`, whereas the member function simply refers to its arguments as `day`, `month`, and `year`.

In making the determination to overload a binary operator as either a friend or member operator function, the following convention can be applied: *friend functions are more appropriate for binary functions that modify neither of their operands, such as ==, +, -, etc., whereas member functions are more appropriate for binary functions, such as =, +=, -= etc., that are used to modify one of their operands.*

EXERCISES 10.3

1. a. Define a *greater than* relational operator function named `operator>()` that can be used with the `Date` class declared in Program 10.7.
   b. Define a *less than* operator function named `operator<()` that can be used with the `Date` class declared in Program 10.7.
   c. Include the operator functions written for Exercises 1a and 2b in a working C++ program.

2. a. Define a subtraction operator function named `operator-()` that can be used with the `Date` class defined in Program 10.7. The subtraction should accept an integer argument that represents the number of days to be subtracted from an object's date and return a `Date`. In doing the subtraction, use the financial assumption that all months consist of 30 days and all years of 360 days. Additionally, an end-of-month adjustment should be made, if necessary that converts any resulting day of 31 to a day of 30, except if the month is February. If the resulting month is February and the day is either 29, 30, or 31, it should be changed to 28.
   b. Define another subtraction operator function named `operator-()` that can be used with the `Date` class defined in Program 10.7. The subtraction should yield an integer that represents the difference in days between two dates. In calculating the day difference, use the financial day count basis that assumes that all months have 30 days and all years have 360 days.

3. a. Determine if the following addition operator function provides the same result as the function used in Program 10.8.

```
Date Date::operator+(int days)    // return a Date object
{
  Date temp;
  temp.day = day + days;    // add the days in
  temp.month = month + int(day/30);  // determine total months
  temp.day = temp.day % 30;           // determine actual day
  temp.year = year + int(temp.month/12);  // determine total years
  temp.month = temp.month % 12;        // determine actual month
  return temp;
}
```

   b. Verify your answer to Exercise 3a by including the function in a working C++ program.

4. Rewrite the equality relational operator function in Program 10.7 as a friend function.
   b. Verify the operation of the friend operator function written for Exercise 4a by including it within a working C++ program.

5. a. Rewrite the addition operator function in Program 10.8 to account for the actual days in a month, neglecting leap years.

   b. Verify the operation of the operator function written for Exercise 5a by including it within a working C++ program.

6. a. Construct an addition operator for the Complex class declared in Program 10.6. This should be a member function that adds two complex numbers and returns a complex number.

   b. Add a member multiplication operator function to the program written for Exercise 6a that multiplies two complex numbers and returns a complex number.

   c. Verify the operation of the operator functions written for Exercises 6a and 6b by including them within a working C++ program.

7. Create a class named `Fractions` having two integer data members named for a fraction's numerator and denominator. The class's default constructor should provide both data members with default values of 1 if no explicit user initialization is provided. The constructor must also prohibit a 0 denominator value. Additionally, provide member functions for displaying an object's data values. Also provide the class with overloaded operators that are capable of adding, subtracting, multiplying, and dividing two `Fraction` objects according to the following formulas:

$$\text{Sum of two fractions: } \frac{a}{b} + \frac{c}{d} = \frac{ad + cb}{bd}$$

$$\text{Difference of two fractions: } \frac{a}{b} - \frac{c}{d} = \frac{ad - cb}{bd}$$

$$\text{Product of two fractions: } \frac{a}{b} \times \frac{c}{d} = \frac{ac}{bd}$$

$$\text{Division of two fractions: } \frac{a}{b} \div \frac{c}{d} = \frac{ad}{cb}$$

   b. Include the class written for Exercise 7a within a working C++ program that tests each of the class's member functions.

8. a. Include a member function named `gcd()` in the Fractions class constructed in Exercise 7 that returns a fraction's greatest common denominator. This value is the largest common divisor of the fraction's numerator and denominator. A famous mathematician, Euclid, discovered an efficient method to do this over 2,000 years ago. Right now, however, we'll settle for a stub function. Thus, write the integer function stub `gcd(n1, n2)`, where `n1` is the value of a fraction's numerator and `n2` the value of the fraction's denominator. Simply have the stub function return a value that suggests it received its arguments correctly. (*Hint:* `n1 + n2` is a good choice of return values. Why isn't `n1/n2` a good choice?).

b. Euclid's method for finding the greatest common divisor (GCD) of two positive integers consists of the following steps:

Step 1: Divide the larger number by the smaller and retain the remainder.
Step 2: Divide the smaller number by the remainder, again retaining the remainder.
Step 3: Continue dividing the prior remainder by the current remainder until the remainder is zero, at which point the last nonzero remainder is the greatest common divisor.

For example, assume the two positive integers are 84 and 49, we have:

Step 1: 84/49 yields a remainder of 35.
Step 2: 49/35 yields a remainder of 14.
Step 3: 35/14 yields a remainder of 7.
14/7 yields a remainder of 0.

Thus, the last nonzero remainder, which is 7, is the greatest common divisor of 84 and 49.

Using Euclid's algorithm, replace the stub function written for Exercise 8a with an actual function that determines and returns the GCD of its two integer arguments.

c. Modify the constructor written for Exercise 7 to include a call to `gcd()` so that every initialized fraction is in lowest common terms. Thus, a fraction such as 2/4 would be reduced to 1/2. Also make sure that each overloaded operator function also uses `gcd()` to return a fraction in lowest common terms.

d. Replace the display function with an overloaded insertion operator so that a `Fractions` object can be inserted directly into the `cout` stream. Also include an overloaded extraction operator that will use the `cin` stream with a `Fractions` object.

10.4 Examples

The first example presented in this section completes the gas pump simulation begun in Section 9.3. Because this example uses random numbers provided by C++'s standard library `rand()` function, you may wish to review the more detailed information on this function presented in Section 5.9 before beginning this first example. The second example shows how to overload both the extraction, >>, and the insertion, <<, operators for `Date` objects. Doing so permits us to input and output `Date` types as complete entities using `cout` and `cin` in the same manner as built-in data types use these two objects. Once you understand how the overloading is done, you will be able to provide standard input and output using the `cin` and `cout` stream objects for any class that you construct.

Example 1: A Multiobject Gas Pump Simulation

In Section 9.3 (Example 2) we presented a requirement to construct a C++ program that simulated a gas pump's operation over the course of one-half hour. For convenience we repeat this requirement below.

We have been requested to write a program that simulates the operation of a gas pump. At any time during the simulation we should be able to determine, from the pump, the price-per-gallon of gas and the amount remaining in the supply tank from which the gas is being pumped. If a request for gas, in gallons, is less than the amount of gas in the tank, the request should be filled; otherwise only the available amount in the supply tank should be used. Each time the gas is pumped, the total price of the gallons pumped should be displayed and the amount of gas, in gallons, that was pumped should be subtracted from the amount in the supply tank.

For the simulation assume that the pump is randomly idle for 1 to 15 minutes between customers and that a customer randomly requests between 3 and 20 gallons of gas. Although the tank capacity is 500 gallons, assume that the initial amount of gas in the tank is only 300 gallons. Initially, the program should simulate a half-hour time frame.

Additionally, for each arrival and request for gas we want to know the idle time before the customer arrived, how many gallons of gas were pumped, and the total price of the transaction. The pump itself must keep track of the price per gallon of gas and the amount of gas remaining in the tank. Typically, the price per gallon is $1.00, but the price used for the simulation should be $1.25.

In Section 9.3 we constructed a `Pump` object type that can be used for this simulation. In this problem we complete the simulation by providing a `Customer` object type and the controlling code within a `main()` function to create an actual multiobject simulation program.

Solution As specified, the problem entails two types of objects: a gas pump and a customer. Let's consider these object types separately.

The Pump A `Pump` class was designed and implemented in Section 9.3 and is repeated below for convenience.

```
// class declaration

class Pump
{
  private:
    float amtInTank;
    float price;
  public:
    Pump(float = 500.0, float = 1.00);    // constructor
    void values(void);
    void request(float);
};
```

```
// implementation section

Pump::Pump(float start, float todaysPrice)
{
  amtInTank = start;
  price = todaysPrice;
}

void Pump::values(void)
{
  cout << setiosflags(ios::fixed) << setiosflags(ios::showpoint)
       << setprecision(2);
  cout << "The gas tank has " << amtInTank << " gallons of gas." << endl;
  cout << "The price per gallon of gas is $" << price << endl;

  return;
}

void Pump::request(float pumpAmt)
{
  float pumped;

  if (amtInTank >= pumpAmt)
     pumped = pumpAmt;
  else
     pumped = amtInTank;

  amtInTank -= pumped;

  cout << setiosflags(ios::fixed) << setiosflags(ios::showpoint)
       << setprecision(2);
  cout << "    Gallons requested: " << pumpAmt << endl;
  cout << "    Gallons pumped: " << pumped << endl;
  cout << "    Gallons remaining in tank: " << amtInTank << endl;
  cout << "    The price of the sale is $" << (pumped * price) << endl;

  return;
}
```

You should review Example 2 in Section 9.3 if either the data or function members of this Pump class are not clear. For later convenience in writing the required simulation program, assume that the code for the Pump class has been stored in a file named PUMP.H within a folder named CLASSES on the C drive. Once this is done, including the Pump class definition within a program simply requires the single line preprocessor directive #include <C:\CLASSES\PUMP.H>.[8]

The Customer For this problem there are multiple instances of customers arriving randomly between 1 and 15 minutes apart and requesting gas in amounts that vary randomly between 3 and 20 gallons. From an object viewpoint, however, we are not interested in storing the arrival and number of gallons requested by each customer. We simply need a customer object to present us with an arrival time and a request for gas in gallons. As such, a Customer object consists of no attributes and two operations. The first operation, which we call arrival(), is used to provide a random arrival time between 1 and 15 minutes. The second operation, called gallons(), is used to provide a random request of between 3 and 20 gallons of gas. This class is relatively simple and can be implemented by the following code:

```
#include <stdlib.h>
#include <time.h>

//class declaration and implementation
class Customer
{
  public:
    Customer(void) {srand(time(NULL));};
    int arrive(void) {return(1 + rand() % 16);};
    int gallons(void) {return(3 + rand() % 21);};
};
```

In reviewing this code, notice that the class constructor is used to randomize the rand() function, which is a standard library function that provides random numbers between 0 and 1 (review Section 5.7 if you are unfamiliar with either the srand() or rand() functions). The arrive() function simply scales the random number returned by rand() to be a random integer between 1 and 15, and the gallons() function scales the random number returned by rand() to be a random integer between 3 and 20 (we leave it as an exercise for you to rewrite the gallons() function to return a floating point value). Because all of the functions are single line, we have included their definitions within the declaration section as inline functions.

---

8 The reason for using a full path name in the #include statement is to ensure that the preprocessor accesses the PUMP.H class that we have placed in the named folder. We do not want the preprocessor to either search its default folder and possibly locate some other PUMP.H that we do not know about or be unable to locate the PUMP.H file at all.

Again, for later convenience in writing the complete simulation program, assume that the code for the `Customer` class is placed in a file named `CUSTOMER.H` within a folder named `CLASSES` on the C drive. Once this is done, including the `Customer` class definition within a program requires the single line preprocessor directive `#include <C:\CLASSES\CUSTOMER.H>`.

Having defined the two classes that we will be using, we still need to analyze and define the logic to correctly control the interaction between these two objects for a valid simulation. In this particular case, the only interaction between a `Customer` object and the single `Pump` object is that a customer's arrival, followed by a request, determines when the pump is activated and how much gas it delivers. Thus, each interaction between a `Customer` and the `Pump` can be expressed by the following pseudocode:

```
Obtain a Customer arrival time
Obtain a Customer request for gas
Activate the Pump with the request
```

Although this repetition of events takes place continuously over the course of a day, we are interested only in a half-hour period. Therefore, we must place these three events in a loop that is executed until the required simulation time has elapsed. We have already developed and coded the two required classes, `Pump` and `Customer`, for the simulation. What remains to be developed is the control logic within the `main()` function for correctly activating individual class events. Essentially, this logic will consist of two initializations when a `Pump` and `Customer` object are instantiated, followed by a loop that is controlled by elapsed time. A suitable control structure for the `main()` function is described by the following pseudocode:

```
Create a Pump object with the required initial gallons of gas
Display the values in the initialized Pump
Set the elapsed time to 0

Obtain a Customer arrival time   // first arrival
Add the arrival time to the elapsed time

While the elapsed time does not exceed the simulation time
  Display the elapsed time
  Obtain a Customer request for gas
  Activate the Pump with the request
  Obtain a Customer arrival time  // next arrival
  Add the arrival time to the elapsed time
EndWhile

Display a message that the simulation is over
```

The C++ code corresponding to this algorithm is illustrated in Program 10.9.

PROGRAM 10.9

```
#include <iostream.h>
#include <iomanip.h>

#include <C:\CLASSES\PUMP.H>      // note use of full path name here
#include <C:\CLASSES\CUSTOMER.H>  // again - a full path name is used

const float SIMTIME = .5;         // simulation time in hours
const int MINUTES = 60;           // number of minutes in an hour
const float AMT_IN_TANK = 300;    // initial gallons in the tank
const float TODAYS_PRICE = 1.25;  // price-per-gallon

int main()
{
  Pump a(AMT_IN_TANK, TODAYS_PRICE);   // declare 1 object of type Pump
  Customer b;                          // declare 1 object of type Customer
  int elapsedTime = 0;
  int idleTime;
  int amtRequest;
  int SimMinutes;  // simulation time in minutes

  SimMinutes = SIMTIME * MINUTES;
  cout << "\nStarting a new simulation - simulation time is "
       << SimMinutes << " minutes" << endl;
  a.values();

  // get the first arrival
  idleTime = b.arrive();
  elapsedTime += idleTime;

  while (elapsedTime <= SimMinutes)
  {
    cout << "\nThe idle time is " << idleTime << " minutes"
         << " and we are " << elapsedTime
         << " minutes into the simulation." << endl;
    amtRequest = b.gallons();
    a.request(float(amtRequest));
```

(continued next page)

(continued from previous page)

```
        // get the next arrival
        idleTime = b.arrive();
        elapsedTime += idleTime;
    }
    cout << "\nThe idle time is " << idleTime << " minutes."
         << " As the elapsed time now exceeds the\n"
         << " simulation time, this simulation run is over." << endl;

    return 0;
}
```

Prewritten classes, such as `Pump` and `Customer`, would be fully tested and then incorporated into a **class library,** just as library functions are included in a function library. This isolation of classes is precisely one of the advantages of using an object-oriented approach. By using previously written and tested class definitions in a program, we can focus our attention on the remaining code that controls the flow of events between objects.

In this case, then, assuming that the `Pump` and `Customer` classes correctly meet their respective specifications, we concentrate on Program 10.9's `main()` function, which controls the use and interaction of `Pump` and `Customer` objects. By itself, the `main()` function consists of a straightforward `while` loop where the pump's idle time corresponds to the time between customer arrivals. The output of a sample run, shown in Figure 10.12, verifies that the loop is operating correctly.

FIGURE 10.12

Sample output produced by Program 10.9

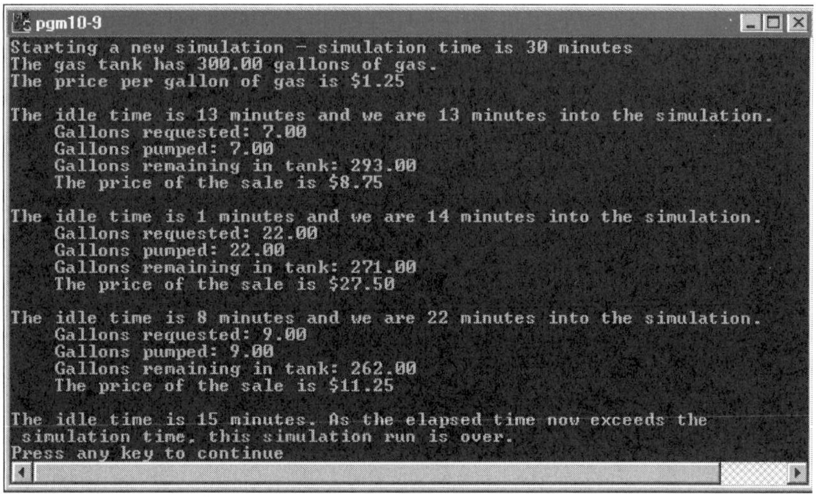

```
pgm10-9
Starting a new simulation - simulation time is 30 minutes
The gas tank has 300.00 gallons of gas.
The price per gallon of gas is $1.25

The idle time is 13 minutes and we are 13 minutes into the simulation.
    Gallons requested: 7.00
    Gallons pumped: 7.00
    Gallons remaining in tank: 293.00
    The price of the sale is $8.75

The idle time is 1 minutes and we are 14 minutes into the simulation.
    Gallons requested: 22.00
    Gallons pumped: 22.00
    Gallons remaining in tank: 271.00
    The price of the sale is $27.50

The idle time is 8 minutes and we are 22 minutes into the simulation.
    Gallons requested: 9.00
    Gallons pumped: 9.00
    Gallons remaining in tank: 262.00
    The price of the sale is $11.25

The idle time is 15 minutes. As the elapsed time now exceeds the
 simulation time, this simulation run is over.
Press any key to continue
```

PROGRAMMER'S NOTES

Program and Class Libraries

The concept of a program library began with FORTRAN, which was the first commercial high-level language, introduced in 1954. The FORTRAN library consisted of a group of completely tested and debugged mathematical routines that were provided with the compiler. Since that time every programming language has provided its own library of functions. In both C and C++, this library is referred to as the standard program library. It includes more than 100 functions declared in 15 different header files. Examples of standard library functions include `sqrt()`, `pow()`, `abs()`, `rand()`, `srand()`, and `time()`. The advantage of library functions is that they significantly enhance program development and design by providing code that is known to work correctly without the need for additional testing and debugging.

With the introduction of object-oriented languages, the concept of a program library has been extended to include class libraries. A *class library* is a library of tested and debugged classes that includes both interfaces and implementations. Generally, the interface portion is placed in a header file and the implementation in a separate implementation file.

One of the key practical features of class libraries is that they help realize the goal of code reuse in a significant way. By providing tested and debugged code consisting of both data and function members, class libraries furnish large sections of prewritten and reusable code ready for incorporation within new applications. This shifts the focus of writing application programs from the creation of new code to understanding how to use predefined objects and stitching them together in a cohesive and useful way. A prime example of this is the visual object classes consisting of check boxes, list boxes, dialogs, command buttons, and option buttons provided in Visual C++.

In reviewing the operation of Program 10.9 it should be realized that we have used the same `Customer` object for each arrival and request. In Section 11.4 we will see how to dynamically create a new `Customer` object for each arrival and destroy the created object when it has completed its designated task.

Example 2: Overloading the Insertion, <<, and Extraction, >>, Operators

For all of the class examples seen so far, a display function has been used to output an object's attribute values. A user-defined type should provide all of the functionality of a built-in type, so we should be able to input and output object values using `cin` and `cout`, respectively. This, in fact, is the case.

Every C++ compiler provides a class library that includes a number of predefined classes. Three of these classes are named `ostream`, `istream`, and `iostream`. The relationships among these classes is shown in Figure 10.13 and explained in detail in Section 8.7. As you might have guessed, the `istream` name is derived from *in*stream, the `ostream` name from *out*stream, and the `iostream` name from *input/output* stream. In this context, a **stream** is simply a one-way path between a source and a destination down which a

FIGURE 10.13

Relationships among classes

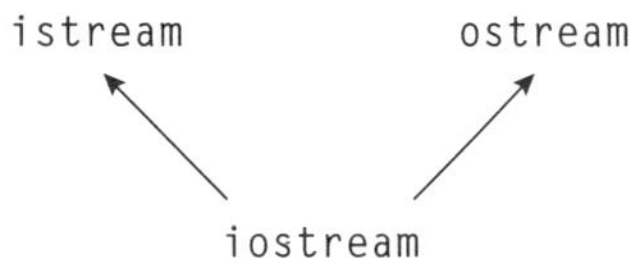

sequence of bytes can be sent. A very good analogy to a stream of bytes is a stream of water that provides a one-way path for the water from a source to a destination. Specifically, `cin` is the name of an input stream object of the class `istream` that connects data sent from the standard input device, which is the keyboard, to a program. Similarly, `cout` is an output stream object of class `ostream` that connects output from the program to the standard output device, which is the screen.[9]

For our current purposes, all that we need to know is that the insertion, or "put to," operator << is both defined and overloaded in the `ostream` class to handle the output of built-in types, and the extraction, or "get from," operator >> is both defined and overloaded in the `istream` class to handle input of built-in types. The capabilities of both the `ostream` and `istream` classes are available to the `iostream` class (through the process of inheritance, explained in the next chapter). Thus, we have access to the `cin` and `cout` streams, and the insertion and extraction operators through the `iostream` class that we have been including in all of our programs. This access permits us to create our own overloaded versions of the << and >> operator functions to specifically handle user-defined object types.

Specifically, the process of making `cin` extractions and `cout` insertions available to a user-defined class consists of:

1. Making each overloaded operator function a friend of the user-defined class (this ensures that these overloaded functions will have access to a class's private data members).
2. Constructing an overloaded version for each operator function that is appropriate to the user-defined class.

What makes overloading the insertion and extraction operators so easy is that the function prototypes and header lines for each overloaded function are essentially "cook book." To understand how this is accomplished in practice, consider Program 10.10, which overloads the insertion and extraction operators to handle objects of type `Date`.

9 A third object, `cerr`, is an output stream of class `ostream` from the program to the standard error device, which is usually the screen. The major difference between `cerr` and `cout` is that the `cout` stream object is buffered, whereas the `cerr` stream object is not.

PROGRAM 10.10

```
#include <iostream.h>

// class declaration

class Date
{
  friend ostream& operator<<(ostream&, const Date&); // overload inserion operator
  friend istream& operator>>(istream&, Date&); // overload extraction operator
  private:
     int month;
     int day;
     int year;
   public:
     Date(int = 7, int = 4, int = 2001); // constructor with defaults
};

// implementation section

// overloaded insertion operator function
ostream& operator<<(ostream& out, const Date& adate)
{
   out << setfill('0')
      << setw(2) << adate.month << '/'
      << setw(2) << adate.day << '/'
      << setw(2) << adate.year % 100; // only display the last 2 year digits

  return out;
}

// overloaded extraction operator function
istream& operator>>(istream& in, Date& somedate)
{
  const int CUTOFF = 50; // years below this are assigned to 2000

  in >> somedate.month;    // accept the month part
  in.ignore(1);            // ignore 1 character, the /
  in >> somedate.day;      // get the day part
  in.ignore(1);            // ignore 1 character, the /
  in >> somedate.year;     // get the year part
```

(continued next page)

(continued from previous page)

```
    if (somedate.year < CUTOFF)
      somedate.year += 2000;
    else if (somedate.year < 100)
      somedate.year += 1900;

    return in;
}

Date::Date(int mm, int dd, int yyyy)   // constructor
{
    month = mm;
    day = dd;
    year = yyyy;
}
```

```
int main()
{
    Date a;

    cout << "\nEnter a date: ";
    cin  >> a;       // accept the date using cin
    cout << "The date just entered is " << a << "\n\n";

    return 0;
}
```

A sample run using Program 10.10 is illustrated in Figure 10.14.

FIGURE 10.14

Sample run using Program 10.10

```
Program10_10

Enter a date: 1/15/2005
The date just entered is 01/15/05

Press any key to continue
```

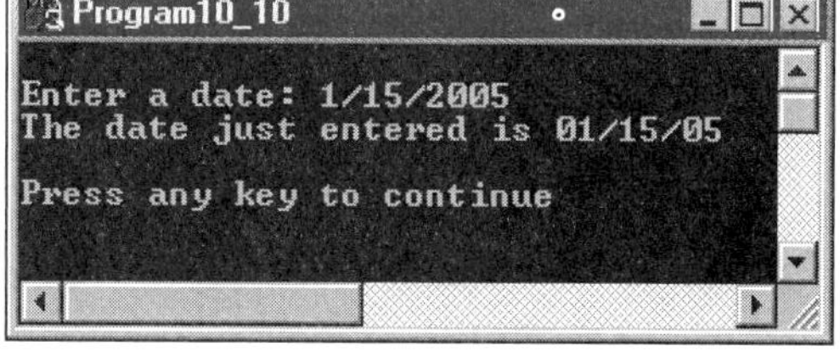

In reviewing Program 10.10, first notice that within the `main()` function a `Date` object is entered using `cin` and is output using `cout`. Now take a look at the class declaration for `Date` and notice that two friend functions have been included in the friend's list using the function prototype declarations

```
friend ostream& operator<<(ostream&, const Date&);
friend istream& operator>>(istream&, Date&);
```

The first declaration makes the overloaded insertion operator function, <<, a friend of the `Date` class, and the second statement does the same for the overloaded extraction operator function, >>. In the first declaration, the << operator has been declared to return a reference to the `ostream` object and to have two formal parameters, a reference to an `ostream` object and a reference to a `Date` class, which is a constant. Similarly, in the second declaration, the >> operator has been declared to return a reference to an `istream` object and to have two formal parameters, a reference to an `istream` object and a reference to a `Date` object. By simply changing the class name `Date` to the name of any other class and including these declarations within the class's declaration section, these two prototypes can be used for any user-defined class. Thus, the general syntax of these declarations, applicable to any class are:

```
friend ostream& operator<<(ostream&, const class-name&);
friend istream& operator>>(istream&, class-name&);
```

Now consider the implementations of these overloaded functions. Consider first the overloaded insertion operator function, which for convenience we repeat below:

```
ostream& operator<<(ostream& out, const Date& adate)
{
  out << setfill('0')
      << setw(2) << adate.month << '/'
      << setw(2) << adate.day << '/'
      << setw(2) << adate.year % 100; // only display the last 2 year digits
  return out;
}
```

Although the name of the reference to a `Date` object has been named `adate`, any user-selected name would do. Similarly, the parameter named `out`, which is a reference to an `ostream` object, can be any user-selected name. Within the body of the function we insert the `month`, `day`, and `year` members of the `Date` object to the `out` object, which is then returned from the function. As required in the header line, `out` is a reference to an `ostream` object. Also notice the notation used in inserting the `month`, `day`, and `year` to `out`, viz:

```
adate.month
adate.day
adate.year
```

This notation follows the notation introduced in Section 9.1 that includes both the object name and attribute name with the names separated by a period. This was the reason for making the overloaded operator function a friend of the Date class. By so doing, the overloaded insertion operator has direct access to a Date object's month, day, and year data members.

Now consider the implementations of the overloaded extraction operator function, which for convenience is written below:

```
// overloaded extraction operator function
istream& operator>>(istream& in, Date& somedate)
{
  const int CUTOFF = 50; // years below this are assigned to 2000

  in >> somedate.month;    // accept the month part
  in.ignore(1);            // ignore 1 character, the /
  in >> somedate.day;      // get the day part
  in.ignore(1);            // ignore 1 character, the /
  in >> somedate.year;     // get the year part

  if (somedate.year < CUTOFF)
    somedate.year += 2000;
  else if (somedate.year < 100)
    somedate.year += 1900;

  return in;
}
```

The header line for this function declares that it will return a reference to an istream object and has two reference parameters: a reference to an istream object and a reference to a Date object. The parameter names, in and somedate, can be replaced by any other user-selected names.

The body of the function first extracts a value for the month member of the Date, then uses the ignore member function of istream to ignore the next input character, which is usually a slash, /. The value for the day member is then extracted, the next character is ignored, and finally the value of the year member is extracted. Thus, if the user typed in the date 1/15/2005 or the date 1-15-2005, the overloaded extractor function would extract 1, 15, and 2005 as the month, day, and year values, respectively. Although, this same effect is produced by the single line

```
in >> somedate.month >> '/' >> somedate.day >> '/' >> somedate.year;
```

the coding used in Program 10.10 makes it clear that we are ignoring the delimiting character.

A real problem with users entering dates is that a typical user will not be used to inputting a four-digit year. By convention, users would expect to input the date 1/15/2005 as 1/15/05, and a date such as 12/25/1999 as 12/25/99. We certainly could include data checking within the overloaded insertion operator function to force all years to be entered as four-digit numbers. Doing so, however, would probably antagonize a majority of users and severely color their perception of the software. A better solution is to make the software respond in as close a manner as possible to normal user expectations. This would mean that a user input of 12/25/99 would correspond to the year 1999, whereas a user input of 1/15/05 would correspond to the year 2005.

To achieve this effect, we have assumed that any two-digit year less than a symbolic constant named `CUTOFF` corresponds to the 21st century, whereas any two-digit value greater than `CUTOFF` corresponds to the 20th century. The assignment of the value 50 as `CUTOFF`'s value is reasonable, but rather arbitrary. In actual practice, this value would be set depending on the application's use of dates. For program maintenance purposes, however, this feature would have to be clearly documented.

EXERCISES 10.4

1. Enter Program 10.9 on your computer and execute it.

2. a. Remove the `inline` functions in the `Customer` class declaration and implementation section by constructing individual declaration and implementation sections. Discuss which form of the `Customer` class you prefer and why.

b. Rewrite the `gallons()` function in the `Customer` class so that it returns a floating point number between 3.0 and 20.0 gallons.

3. In place of the `main()` function used in Program 10.9, a student proposed the following:

```
int main()
{
  Pump a(AMT_IN_TANK, TODAYS_PRICE);    // declare 1 object of type Pump
  Customer b;                          // declare 1 object of type Customer
  int totalTime = 0;
  int idleTime;
  int amtRequest;
  int SimMinutes;  // simulation time in minutes

  SimMinutes = SIMTIME * MINUTES;
  cout << "\nStarting a new simulation - simulation time is "
       << SimMinutes << " minutes" << endl;
  a.values();
```

```
  do
  {
    idleTime = b.arrive();
    totalTime += idleTime;
    if (totalTime > (SIMTIME * MINUTES))
    {
      cout << "\nThe idle time is " << idleTime << " minutes." << endl
         << "As the total time now exceeds the simulation time, " << endl
         << "   this simulation run is over." << endl;
      break;
    }
    else
    {
      cout << "\nThe idle time is " << idleTime << " minutes" << endl
           << "   and we are " << totalTime
           << " minutes into the simulation." << endl;
      amtRequest = b.gallons();
      a.request(float(amtRequest));
    }
  } while (1);  // always true

  return 0;
}
```

Determine if this `main()` function produces a valid simulation. If it does not, discuss why not. If it does, discuss which version you prefer and why.

4. Enter Program 10.10 on your computer and execute it.

5. Using the `Elevator` class defined in Section 9.3 and defining a new class named `Person`, construct a simulation whereby a `Person` randomly arrives at any time from 1 to 10 minutes on any floor and calls the elevator. If the elevator is not on the same floor as the person, it must move to the floor where the person is. Once inside the elevator the person can select any floor except the current one. Run the simulation for three randomly arriving people and have the simulation display the movement of the elevator.

6. a. Modify the overloaded insertion operator function in Program 10.10 so that it displays dates in the form day-month-year, which is the European standard.

b. Modify the overloaded insertion operator function in Program 10.10 to accept a third character argument. If the actual argument is an `E`, the displayed date should be in European format of day-month-year; otherwise, it should be in the American standard form of month/day/year.

7. For the `Time` class constructed in Exercise 2 of Section 10.1, remove the display function and include overloaded extraction and insertion extraction operator functions for the input and output of `Time` objects using `cin` and `cout`, respectively. Times should be displayed in the form hrs:min:sec.

8. For the `Complex` class constructed in Exercise 3 of Section 10.1, remove the display function and include overloaded extraction and insertion extraction operator functions for the input and output of `Complex` objects using `cin` and `cout`, respectively.

10.5 Data Type Conversions

The conversion from one built-in data type to another was previously described in Section 3.2. With the introduction of user-defined data types, the possibilities for conversion between data types expands to the following cases:

- Conversion from built-in type to built-in type
- Conversion from built-in type to user-defined type
- Conversion from user-defined type to built-in type
- Conversion from user-defined type to user-defined type

The first conversion is handled either by C++'s built-in implicit conversion rules or its explicit cast operator. The second conversion type is made using a *type conversion constructor.* The third and fourth conversion types are made using a *conversion operator function.* This section presents the specific means of performing each of these conversions.

Built-In to Built-In Conversion

The conversion from one built-in data type to another has already been presented in Section 3.2. To review this case briefly, this type of conversion is either implicit or explicit.

An implicit conversion occurs in the context of one of C++'s operations. For example, when a floating point value is assigned to an integer variable only the integer portion of the value is stored. The conversion is implied by the operation and is performed automatically by the compiler.

An explicit conversion occurs whenever a cast is used. In C++ two cast notations exist. Using the older C notation, a cast has the form *(data-type) expression,* whereas the newer C++ notation has the function-like form *data-type(expression).* For example, both of the expressions `(int)24.32` and `int(24.32)` cause the floating point value 24.32 to be truncated to the integer value 24.

Built-In to Class Conversion

User-defined casts for converting a built-in to a user-defined data type are created using constructor functions. A constructor whose first argument is not a member of its class and whose remaining arguments, if any, have default values is a **type conversion constructor.** If the first argument of a type conversion constructor is a built-in data type, the constructor can be used to cast the built-in data type to a class object. Clearly, one restriction of such functions is that, as constructors, they must be member functions.

Although this type of cast occurs when the constructor is invoked to initialize an object, it is actually a more general cast than might be evident at first glance. This is because a constructor function can be explicitly invoked after all objects have been declared, whether or not it was invoked previously as part of an object's declaration. Before exploring this further, let's first construct a type conversion constructor. We can then see how to use it as a cast independent of its initialization purpose.

The cast we will construct converts a long integer into a `Date` object. Our `Date` object consists of dates in the form month/day/year and uses our by now familiar `Date` class. The long integer will be used to represent dates in the form `year * 10000 + month * 100 + day`. For example, by using this representation, the date 12/31/2000 becomes the long integer 20001231. Dates represented in this fashion are very useful for two reasons: (1) it permits a date to be to stored as a single integer, and (2) such dates are in numerically increasing date order, making sorting extremely easy. For example, the date 01/03/2002, which occurs after 12/31/2001 becomes the integer 20020103, which is larger than 20011231. Because the integers representing dates can exceed the size of a normal integer, the integers are always declared as longs.

A suitable constructor function for converting from a long integer date to a date stored as a month, day, and year is:

```
// type conversion constructor from long to Date

Date::Date(long findate)
{
  year = int(findate/10000.0);
  month = int((findate - year * 10000.0)/100.0);
  day = int(findate - year * 10000.0 - month * 100.0);
}
```

Program 10.11 uses this type conversion constructor both as an initialization function at declaration time and as an explicit cast later on in the program.

PROGRAM 10.11

```
#include <iostream.h>
#include <iomanip.h>

// class declaration

class Date
{
  private:
    int month, day, year;
  public:
    Date(int = 7, int = 4, int = 2001);  // constructor
    Date(long);            // type conversion constructor
    void showdate();
};

// implementation section

// constructor
Date::Date(int mm, int dd, int yyyy)
{
  month = mm;
  day = dd;
  year = yyyy;
}

// type conversion constructor from long to date
Date::Date(long findate)
{
  year = int(findate/10000.0);
  month = int((findate - year * 10000.0)/100.0);
  day = int(findate - year * 10000.0 - month * 100.0);
}

// member function to display a date
void Date::showdate()
{
  cout << setfill('0')
       << setw(2) << month << '/'
       << setw(2) << day << '/'
       << setw(2) << year % 100;
```

(continued next page)

(continued from previous page)

```
  return;
}
```

```
int main()
{
  Date a, b(20011225L), c(4,1,1999);  // declare 3 objects - initialize 2 of them

  cout << "\nDates a, b, and c are \n   ";
  a.showdate();
  cout << ", ";
  b.showdate();
  cout << ", and ";
  c.showdate();
  cout << ".\n";

  a = Date(20020101L);  // cast a long to a date

  cout << "Date a is now ";
  a.showdate();
  cout << ".\n\n";

  return 0;
}
```

The output produced by Program 10.11 is shown in Figure 10.15.

FIGURE 10.15

Output displayed by Program 10.11

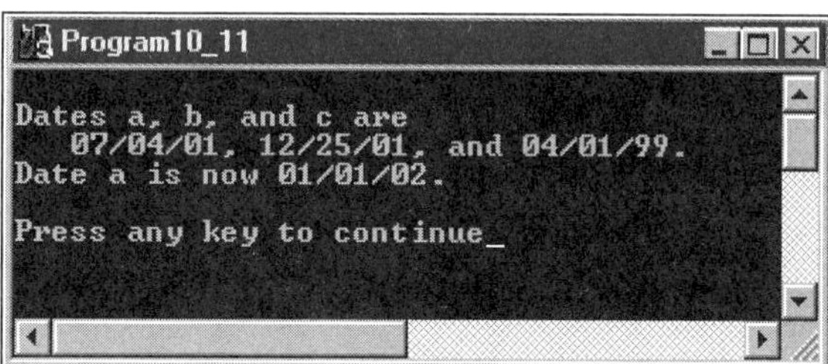

The change in a's date value illustrated by this output is produced by the assignment expression `a = Date(20020101L)`, which uses a type conversion constructor to perform the cast from `long` to `Date`.

Class to Built-In Conversion

Conversion from a user-defined data type to a built-in data type is accomplished using a conversion operator function. A **conversion operator function** is a member operator function having the name of a built-in data type or class. When the operator function has a built-in data type name, it is used to convert from a class to a built-in data type. For example, a conversion operator function for casting a class object to a long integer would have the name `operator long()`. Here the name of the operator function indicates that a conversion to a long integer will take place. If this function were part of a `Date` class it would be used to cast a `Date` object into a long integer. This usage is illustrated by Program 10.12.

PROGRAM 10.12

```
#include <iostream.h>
#include <iomanip.h>

// class declaration

class Date
{
  private:
    int month, day, year;
  public:
    Date(int = 7, int = 4, int = 2001);    // constructor
    operator long();        // conversion operator function
    void showdate();
};

// implementation section

// constructor
Date::Date(int mm, int dd, int yyyy)
{
  month = mm;
  day = dd;
  year = yyyy;
}

// conversion operator function converting from Date to long
Date::operator long()   // must return a long
{
  long yyyymmdd;
```

(continued next page)

(continued from previous page)

```
  yyyymmdd = year * 10000.0 + month * 100.0 + day;

  return(yyyymmdd);
}

// member function to display a date
void Date::showdate()
{
   cout << setfill('0')
        << setw(2) << month << '/'
        << setw(2) << day << '/'
        << setw(2) << year % 100;

  return;
}
```

```
int main()
{
  Date a(4,1,1999);  // declare and initialize one object of type date
  long b;            // declare an object of type long

  b = a;             // a conversion takes place here

  cout << "\n a's date is ";
  a.showdate();
  cout << "\n This date, as a long integer, is "
       << b << "\n\n";

  return 0;
}
```

The output produced by Program 10.12 is shown in Figure 10.16.

FIGURE 10.16

Output displayed by Program 10.12

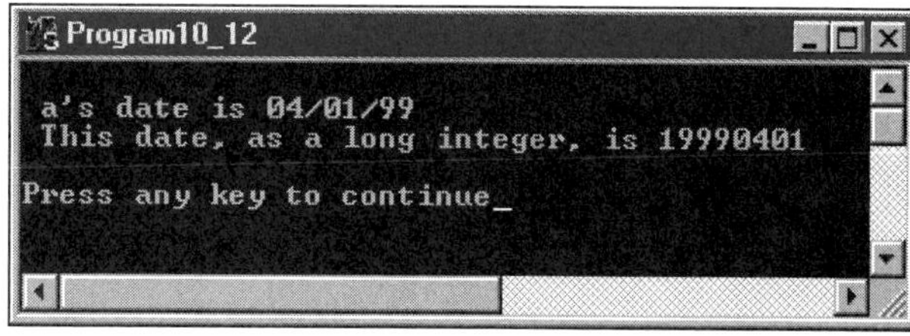

Program10_12
a's date is 04/01/99
This date, as a long integer, is 19990401
Press any key to continue_

The change in a's date value to a long integer illustrated by this output is produced by the assignment expression `b = a`. This assignment, which also could have been written as `b = long(a)`, calls the conversion operator function `long()` to perform the cast from `Date` to a long integer. In general, because explicit conversion more clearly documents what is happening, its use is preferred to implicit conversion.

Notice that the conversion operator has no explicit argument and has no explicit return type. This is true of all conversion operators: Its implicit argument will always be an object of the class being cast from, and the return type is implied by the name of the function. Additionally, as previously indicated, a conversion operator function *must be* a member function.

Class to Class Conversion

Converting from a user-defined data type to a user-defined data type is performed in the same manner as a cast from a user-defined to a built-in data type—it is done using a member **conversion operator function.** In this case, however, the operator function uses the class name being converted to rather than a built-in data name. For example, if two classes named `Date` and `Intdate` exist, the operator function named `operator Intdate()` could be placed in the `Date` class to convert from a `Date` object to an `Intdate` object. Similarly, the operator function named `Date()` could be placed in the `Intdate` class to convert from an `Intdate` to a `Date`.

Notice that, as before, in converting from a user-defined data type to a built-in data type, *the operator function's name determines the result of the conversion;* the class containing the operator function determines the data type being converted from.

Before providing a specific example of a class to class conversion, one additional point must be noted. Converting between classes implies that we have two classes, one of which is always defined first and one of which is defined second. Having, within the second class, a conversion operator function with the name of the first class poses no problem because the compiler knows of the first class's existence. However, including a conversion operator function with the second class's name in the first class does pose a problem because the second class has not yet been defined. This is remedied by including a declaration for the second class prior to the first class's definition. This declaration, which is formally referred to as a **forward declaration,** is illustrated in Program 10.13, which also includes conversion operators between the two defined classes.

PROGRAM 10.13

```
#include <iostream.h>
#include <iomanip.h>
```

(continued next page)

(continued from previous page)

```
// forward declaration of class Intdate
class Intdate;

// class declaration for Date
class Date
{
  private:
    int month, day, year;
  public:
    Date(int = 7, int = 4, int = 2001);  // constructor
    operator Intdate();  // conversion operator Date to Intdate
    void showdate();
};
// class declaration for Intdate
class Intdate
{
  private:
    long yyyymmdd;
  public:
    Intdate(long = 0);    // constructor
    operator Date();  // conversion operator intdate to date
    void showint();
};

// implementation section for Date
Date::Date(int mm, int dd, int yyyy)  // constructor
{
  month = mm;
  day = dd;
  year = yyyy;
}
// conversion operator function converting from Date to Intdate class
Date::operator Intdate()   // must return an Intdate object
{
  long temp;

  temp = year * 10000.0 + month * 100.0 + day;
  return(Intdate(temp));
}
```

(continued next page)

(continued from previous page)

```
// member function to display a Date
void Date::showdate()
{

  cout << setfill('0')
       << setw(2) << month << '/'
       << setw(2) << day << '/'
       << setw(2) << year % 100;
  return;
}

// implementation section for Intdate
Intdate::Intdate(long ymd)  // constructor
{
  yyyymmdd = ymd;
}
// conversion operator function converting from Intdate to Date class
Intdate::operator Date()    // must return a Date object
{
  int mo, da, yr;
```

```
  yr = int(yyyymmdd/10000.0);
  mo = int((yyyymmdd - yr * 10000.0)/100.0);
  da = int(yyyymmdd - yr * 10000.0 - mo * 100.0);
  return(Date(mo,da,yr));
}
// member function to display an Intdate
void Intdate::showint()
{
  cout << yyyymmdd;
  return;
}
```

```
int main()
{
  Date a(4,1,1999), b;      // declare two Date objects
  Intdate c(20011215L), d;  // declare two Intdate objects

  b = Date(c);        // cast c into a Date object
  d = Intdate(a);     // cast a into an Intdate object
```

(continued next page)

(*continued from previous page*)

```
    cout << "\n a's date is ";
    a.showdate();
    cout << "\n   as an Intdate object this date is ";
    d.showint();

    cout << "\n c's date is ";
    c.showint();
    cout << "\n   as a Date object this date is ";
    b.showdate();
    cout << "\n\n";

    return 0;
}
```

The output produced by Program 10.13 is shown in Figure 10.17.

FIGURE 10.17

Output displayed by Program 10.13

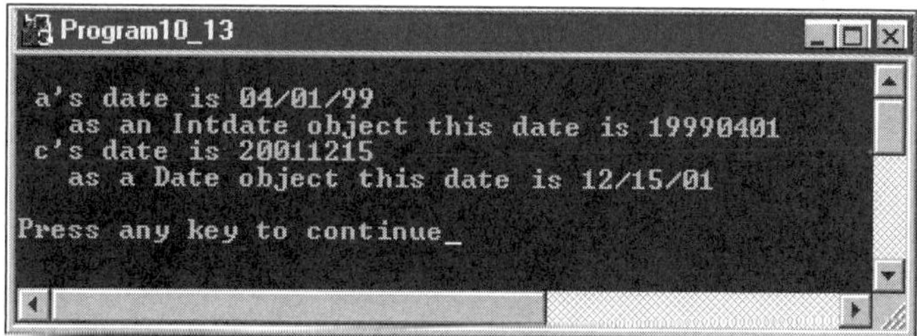

As illustrated by Program 10.13, the cast from `Date` to `Intdate` is produced by the assignment `b = Date(c)` and the cast from `Intdate` to `Date` is produced by the assignment `d = Intdate(a)`. Alternatively, the assignments `b = c` and `d = a` would produce the same results. Notice also the forward declaration of the `Intdate` class prior to the `Date` class's declaration. This is required so that the `Date` class can reference `Intdate` in its operator conversion function.

EXERCISES 10.5

1. **a.** Define the four data type conversions available in C++ and the method of accomplishing each conversion.
   b. Define the terms *type conversion constructor* and *conversion operator function* and describe how they are used in user-defined conversions.

2. Write a C++ program that declares a class named `Time` having integer data members named `hours`, `minutes`, and `seconds`. Include in the program a type conversion constructor that converts a long integer, representing the elapsed seconds from midnight, into an equivalent representation as hours:minutes:seconds. For example, the long integer 30336L should convert to the time 8:25:36. Use a military representation of time so that 2:30 pm is represented as 14:30:00. The relationship between time representations is

$$elapsed\ seconds = hours \star 3600 + minutes \star 60 + seconds.$$

3. A Julian date is a date represented as the number of days from a known base date. Although there are many Julian algorithms, one algorithm for converting from a Gregorian date, in the form month/day/year, to a Julian date with a base date of 00/00/0000 is given below. All of the calculations in this algorithm use integer arithmetic, which means that the fractional part of all divisions must be discarded. In this algorithm *mm* = month, *dd* = day, and *yyyy* = 4-digit year.

> **If *mm* is less than or equal to 2**
> **set the variable *MP* = 0 and *YP* = *yyyy* – 1**
> **Else**
> **set *MP* = int(0.4 * *mm* + 2.3) and *YP* = *yyyy***
> ***T* = int(*YP*/4) – int(*YP*/100) + int(*YP*/400)**
> **Julian date = 365 * *yyyy* + 31 * (*mm* – 1) + *dd* + *T* – *MP***

Using this algorithm, modify Program 10.12 to cast from a Gregorian date object to its corresponding Julian representation as a long integer. Test your program using the Gregorian dates 1/31/1985 and 3/16/1986, which correspond to the Julian dates 725037 and 725446, respectively.

4. Modify the program written for Exercise 2 to include a member conversion operator function that converts an object of type `Time` into a long integer representing the number of seconds from 12 midnight.

5. Write a C++ program that has a `Date` class and a `Julian` class. The `Date` class should be the same `Date` class as that used in Program 10.13, whereas the Julian class should represent a date as a long integer. For this program include a member conversion operator function within the `Date` class that converts a `Date` object to a `Julian` object, using the algorithm presented in Exercise 3. Test your program by converting the dates 1/31/1995 and 3/16/1998, which correspond to the Julian dates 728689 and 729099, respectively.

6. Write a C++ program that has a `Time` class and an `Ltime` class. The `Time` class should have integer data members named `hours`, `minutes`, and `seconds`, and the `Ltime` class should have a long data member named `elsecs`, which represents the number of elapsed seconds since midnight. For the `Time` class include a member conversion operator function named `Ltime()` that converts a `Time` object to an `Ltime` object. For the `Ltime` class include a member conversion operator function named `Time()` that converts an `Ltime` object to a `Time` object.

10.6 Common Programming Errors

1. Using a user-defined assignment operator in a multiple-assignment expression when the operator has not been defined to return an object.

2. Using the keyword `static` when defining either a static data or function member. Here, the `static` keyword should be used only within the class declaration section.

3. Using the keyword `friend` when defining a friend function. The `friend` keyword should be used only within the class declaration section.

4. Failing to instantiate static data members before creating class objects that must access these data members.

5. Attempting to redefine an operator's meaning as it applies to C++'s built-in data types.

6. Redefining an overloaded operator to perform a function not indicated by its conventional meaning. Although this will work, it is an example of extremely bad programming practice.

7. Attempting to make a conversion operator function a friend, rather than a member function.

8. Attempting to specify a return type for a member conversion operator function.

10.7 Chapter Summary

1. An **assignment operator** may be declared for a class with the function prototype:

```
void operator=(class-name& );
```

Here, the argument is a reference to the class name. The return type of void precludes using this operator in multiple assignment expressions such as `a = b = c`.

2. A type of initialization that closely resembles assignment occurs in C++ when one object is initialized using another object of the same class. The constructor that performs this type of initialization is called a **copy constructor** and has the function prototype:

```
class-name(const class-name& );
```

This is frequently represented using the notation *`X(X&)`*.

3. Each class has an associated class scope, which is defined by the brace pair, `{}`, containing the class declaration. Data and function members are local to the scope of their class and can be used only by objects declared for the class. If a global variable name is reused within a class, the global variable is hidden by the class variable. Within the scope of the class variable the global variable may be accessed using the scope resolution operator, `::`.

4. For each class object a separate set of memory locations is reserved for all data members, except those declared as static. A `static` data member is a shared by all class objects and provides a means of communication between objects. Static data members must be declared as such within the class declaration section and are defined outside of the declaration section.

6. Static function members apply to the class as a whole, rather than individual objects. As such, a static function member can access only static data members and other static function members. Static function members must be declared as such within the class declaration section and are defined outside of the declaration section.

7. A nonmember function may access a class's private data members if it is granted friend status by the class. This is accomplished by declaring the function as a friend within the class's declaration section. Thus, it is always the class that determines which nonmember functions are friends; a function can never confer friend status on itself.

8. User-defined operators can be constructed for classes using member operator functions. An operator function has the form `operator<symbol>`, where `<symbol>` is one of the following:

```
()  []  ->  new  delete  ++  --  !  ~  *  /  %  +  -
<<  >>  <  <=  >  >=  ++ !=  &&  ||  &  ^  |  =  +=
-=  *=  /=  %=  &=  ^=  |=  <<=  >>=  ,
```

For example, the function prototype `Date operator+(int);` declares that the addition operator will be defined to accept an integer and return a `Date` object.

9. User-defined operators may be called in either of two ways—as a conventional function with arguments or as an operator expression. For example, for an operator having the header line

```
Date Date::operator+(int)
```

if `dte` is an object of type `Date`, the following two calls produce the same effect:

```
dte.operator+(284)
dte + 284
```

10. Operator functions may also be written as friend functions. The equivalent friend version of a member operator function will always contain an additional class reference that is not required by the member function.

11. There are four categories of data type conversions. They are conversions from

- built-in types to built-in types
- built-in types to user-defined (class) types
- user-defined (class) types to built-in types
- user-defined (class) types to user-defined (class) types

Built-in to built-in type conversions are done using C++'s implicit conversion rules or explicitly using casts. Built-in to user-defined type conversions are done using type conversion constructors. Conversions from user-defined types to either built-in or other user-defined types are done using conversion operator functions.

12. A **type conversion constructor** is a constructor whose first argument is not a member of its class and whose remaining arguments, if any, have default values.

13. A conversion operator function must be a member function. It has no explicit arguments or return type; rather, the return type is the name of the function.

14. The `cout` insertion operator, <<, and the `cin` extraction operator, >>, can be overloaded to work with any class objects using the process of:

1. Making each overloaded operator function a friend of the user-defined class (this ensures that these overloaded functions will have access to a class's private data members).
2. Constructing an overloaded version for each operator function that is appropriate to the user-defined class.

The general function prototype syntax for providing these operator functions with friend status is:

```
friend ostream& operator<<(ostream&, const class-name&);
friend istream& operator>>(istream&, class-name&);
```

These prototypes should be placed in the declaration section of the desired class and the class name in each declaration changed to the actual class name.

10.8 Knowing About: The Application Framework

In practice, a fully functioning Windows application is created from the set of classes provided in the Microsoft Foundation Class (MFC) Library. Additionally, the basic structure of all such applications is the same, and is referred to as an **application framework.** By using an application framework you are assured that standard Windows operations and features, such as resizing, Menu bar options, and Toolbar buttons are provided and work as expected. This is because the framework provides an enormous amount of standard code to handle the processing tasks associated with each of the standard Windows features. Once the framework is constructed you can then provide additional functionality to it in

FIGURE 10.18

The File menu's `New` option

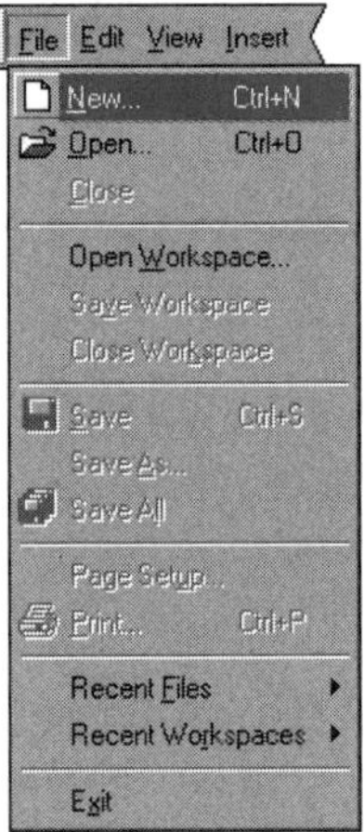

the form of resources (Dialog boxes, Command buttons, Edit boxes, and so forth) and processing code to tailor the framework to your particular application.

To construct a basic application framework, or framework for short, you use the AppWizard. This is the same wizard we used in Chapter 7 to construct a Dialog-based application. In this section we expand our use of the AppWizard to provide a Single Document Interface (SDI) application framework and use it to introduce the fundamental MFC classes that underlie all Windows programs. In the next chapter we expand on this introduction to see how the classes within the MFC are organized and then provide additional resources and code to an application framework.

To begin the process of creating an application framework, which is simply a working skeleton program, select the File menu's `New` option, as shown in Figure 10.18. This will cause the `New` dialog to appear. From this dialog, activate the `Projects` tab, as shown in Figure 10.19, and invoke the `MFC AppWizard`, as shown in Figure 10.19. For purposes of illustration, we have named our project `Wbpgm10_1`, for Windows-based Program 10.1.

FIGURE 10.19

Invoking the `AppWizard`

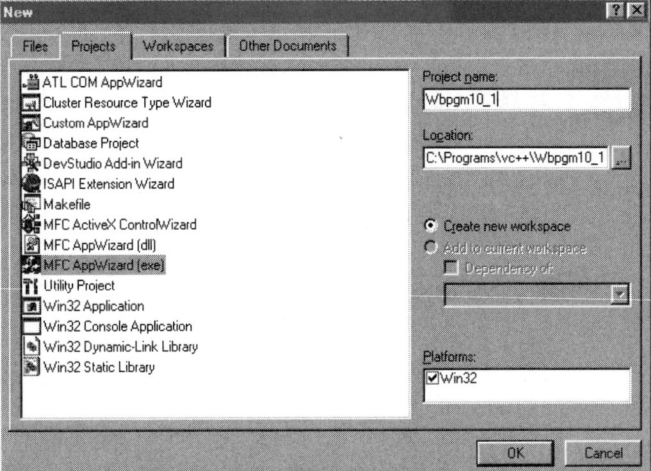

FIGURE 10.20

The `Step 1` dialog

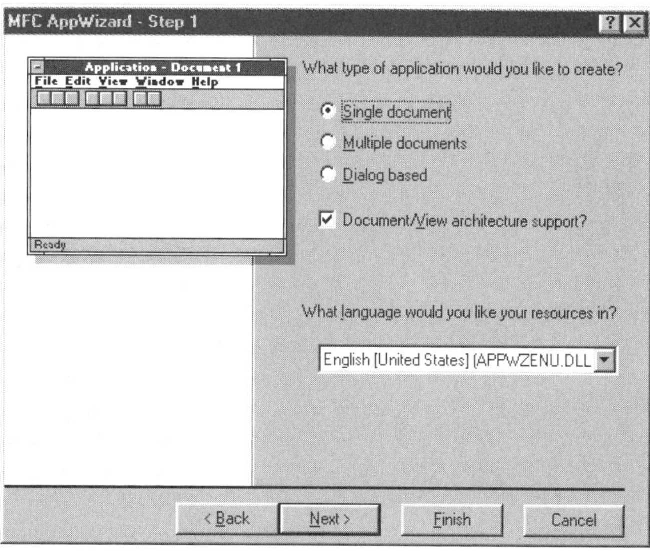

After you have named your project on the dialog shown in Figure 10.19, press the `OK` button. Doing so will bring up the `Step 1` dialog shown in Figure 10.20. As shown in this figure, you can always return to the previous window by pressing the `Back` button. Thus, for example, if you wanted to rename your project with a different name than the one shown in Figure 10.19, you could use the `Back` button to redisplay the `New` dialog, rename your project, and then press the `OK` button to return to the `Step 1` dialog.

Once you have the `Step 1` dialog displayed, select the `Single document` type of application, as shown on Figure 10.20, and press the `Next>` button. Doing so will bring up the `Step 2` dialog, which is shown in Figure 10.21.

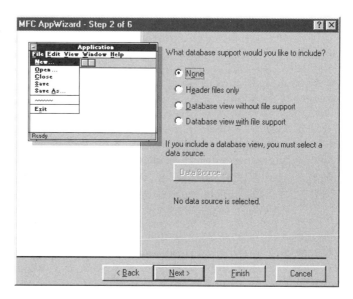

FIGURE 10.21

The `Step 2` dialog

MFC AppWizard - Step 2 of 6

Application

File Edit View Window Help

New...

Open...

Close

Save

Save As...

Exit

Ready

What database support would you like to include?

None

Header files only

Database view without file support

Database view with file support

If you include a database view, you must select a data source.

Data Source...

No data source is selected.

< Back

Next >

Finish

Cancel

FIGURE 10.22

The `Step 3` dialog

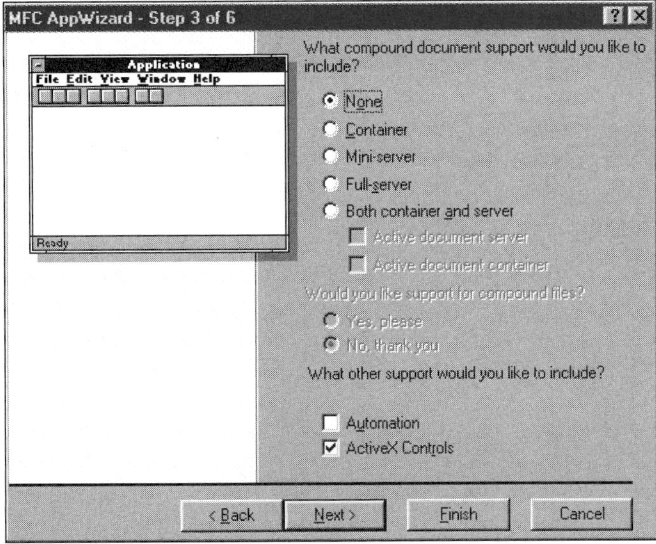

Accept the defaults provided by the `Step 2` dialog, which means that our framework application will not provide any database support. Thus, when the `Step 2` dialog is displayed, simply click on the `Next>` button, which will cause the `Step 3` dialog, shown in Figure 10.22, to be displayed.

When the `Step 3` dialog is displayed, accept the provided defaults and press the `Next>` button. Doing so provides the application with code that can be used to support `ActiveX` components. At its most basic level, an `ActiveX` component is either a control or unit of executable code that can be created or purchased and then incorporated into a Windows application, in the same manner as a standard Visual C++ resource such as a Check box, for example. At this stage, by clicking on the `Next>` button , the `Step 4` dialog, shown in Figure 10.23, will be displayed.

The `Step 4` dialog provides a number of options that can be included in the application framework (that is, the skeleton application) that we are developing. Table 10.3 lists the functionality provided by each of the available options provided in the `Step 4` dialog. For our immediate purposes we will accept all of the defaults provided for the standard options, but will change one of the advanced defaults. To make this change, click on the `Advanced` button provided toward the bottom of the dialog. Doing so will cause the `Advanced Options` dialog, shown in Figure 10.24, to be displayed.

The only advanced option that we will modify in the `Advanced Options` dialog is the `Main frame caption`. In the edit box for this option, enter `A Text Editor`, so that

FIGURE 10.23

The `Step 4` **dialog**

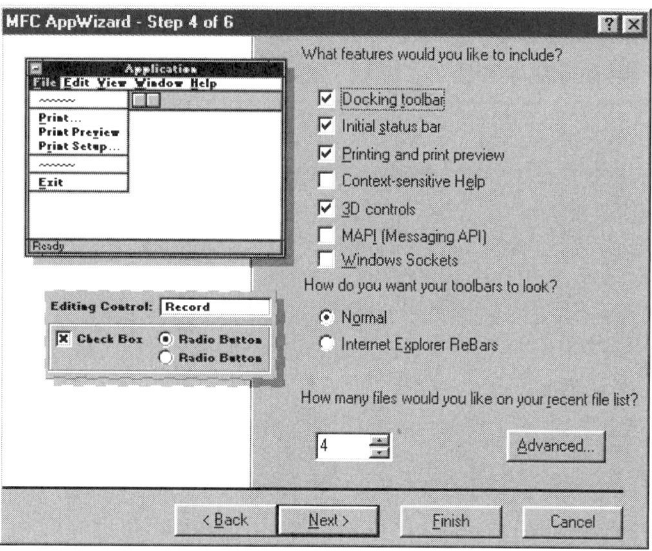

it appears as shown in Figure 10.24. Doing this will change the default caption option, which is the project's name, to the entered text. Once you have made this change, press the `Close` button, which will cause the `Step 4` dialog to be redisplayed, and then press this dialog's `Next>` button. This will cause the `Step 5` dialog to be displayed, which is

FIGURE 10.24

The `Advanced Options` **dialog**

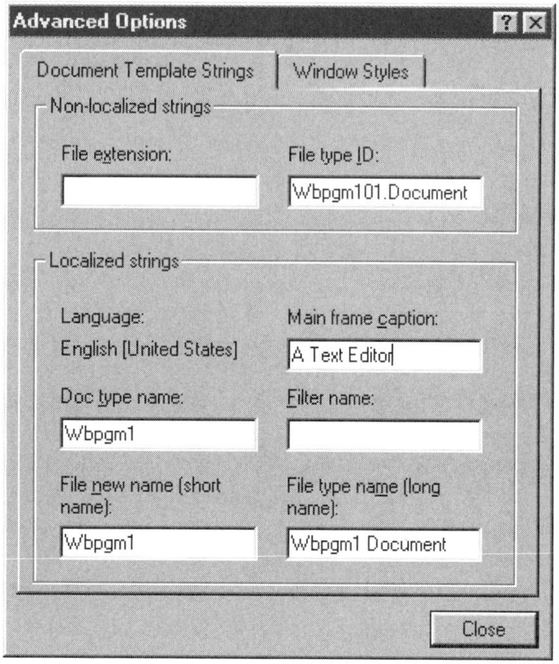

Advanced Options
Document Template Strings
Window Styles
Non-localized strings
File extension:
File type ID:
Wbpgm101.Document
Localized strings
Language:
English [United States]
Main frame caption:
A Text Editor
Doc type name:
Wbpgm1
Filter name:
File new name (short name):
Wbpgm1
File type name (long name):
Wbpgm1 Document
Close

TABLE 10.3 The Standard Features (Step 4) Options*

Feature	Description
Toolbar	Select this option to add a toolbar to your program. The toolbar contains buttons for creating a new document; opening and saving document files; cutting copying, pasting, or printing text; displaying the About box; and entering Help mode. Enabling this option also adds menu commands to display or hide the toolbar. By default, programs have a docking toolbar.
Initial status bar	Select this option to add a status bar to your program. The status bar contains automatic indicators for the keyboard's `CAPS LOCK`, `NUM LOCK`, and `SCROLL LOCK` keys and a message line that displays help strings for menu commands and toolbar buttons. Enabling this option also adds menu commands to display or hide the status bar. By default, programs have a status bar.
Printing and print preview	Select this option if you want AppWizard to generate the code to handle the print, print setup, and print preview commands by calling member functions in the `CView` class from the MFC library. (Available only for programs with the Doc View architecture; see Step 1 of the Wizard.) AppWizard also adds commands for these functions to the program's menu. By default, programs have printing support.
Context-sensitive Help	Select this option if you want AppWizard to generate a set of Help files for context-sensitive Help. Help support requires the Help compiler. If you do not have the Help compiler, you can install it by re-running Setup.
3D controls	Select this option if you want the program's interface to have three-dimensional shading. By default, programs have three-dimensional shading.
MAPI (Messaging API)	Select this option if you want a program that creates, manipulates, transfers, and stores mail messages.
Windows sockets	Select this option if you want your program to support Windows sockets. Windows sockets allow you to write programs that communicate over TCP/IP networks.

*The description for each feature was obtained in Visual C++ by selecting the feature on the dialog and then pressing the F1 button. Doing so invokes the context-sensitive Help provided by Microsoft for each feature. This same context-sensitive Help can be invoked for all of the options provided in each dialog.

FIGURE 10.25

The `Step 5` dialog

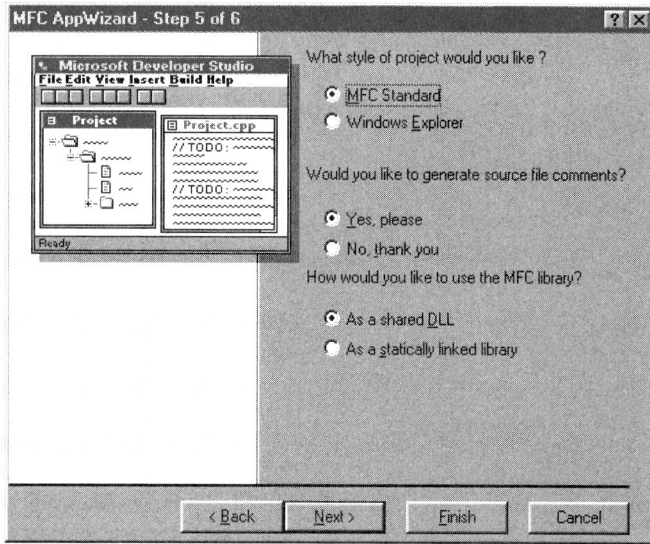

shown as Figure 10.25. Accept all of the defaults on this dialog, and press its `Next>` button, which will cause the `Step 6` dialog, shown in Figure 10.26, to be displayed.[10]

The `Step 6` dialog lists the classes that AppWizard will create as the foundation for the application framework that it is developing. As seen in Figure 10.26, four classes will be created. Notice that each class begins with a capital `C`, which is the convention used for

FIGURE 10.26

The `Step 6` dialog

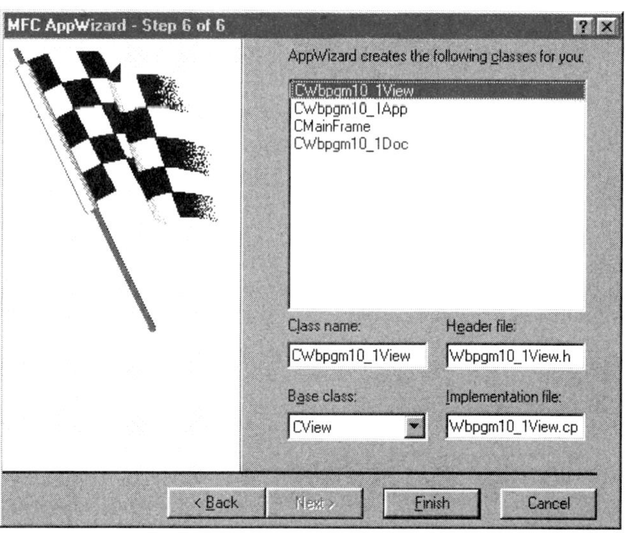

10 Again, if you want a description of any of the options provided on this (or any other) dialog, simply click on the desired option and press the F1 key. Doing so will invoke the context-sensitive Help descriptions for the selected item.

all MFC classes or any class derived from an MFC class. Also notice the suffixes `View`, `App`, `Frame`, and `Doc` used, respectively, for each class name listed in the top List box. These tell us that AppWizard has created a view, application, frame, and document class for our application. Although a working Windows application can be constructed using only an application (App) and frame class, the overwhelming majority of Windows applications use all four classes. The specifics of each of these four classes are presented in the next chapter, after we have introduced Visual C++'s inheritance capabilities. For now, with one exception, it is enough to notice that four classes are being used.

The exception concerns the one change we will make to AppWizard's construction of the View class. To make the change, notice that the first class listed in Figure 10.26 is named `CWbpgm10_1View`, and that this class name is highlighted. The highlight was obtained by clicking on this class name. For the selected class name, AppWizard provides four items of information at the bottom of the dialog, which includes the class name, the header file and implementation (source code) file that will be created, and a base class name. This base class name is the name of an existing MFC class from which the new class for our application is being derived. It is here that we will make our change.

By clicking on the down-facing arrowhead (▼), the drop-down list shown in Figure 10.27 will be displayed. From this list we will select the `CEditView` class as the base class. The `CEditView` class is the name of another MFC supplied class that provides basic text editing capabilities not available in the default CView class. Once you have made this change, click the `Step 6` dialog's `Next>` button to bring up the `New Project Information` dialog shown in Figure 10.28, and then click this dialog's `OK` button to complete the construction of the application framework. Doing so will bring up the IDE window shown in Figure 10.29.

FIGURE 10.27

Selecting a different view `Base class`

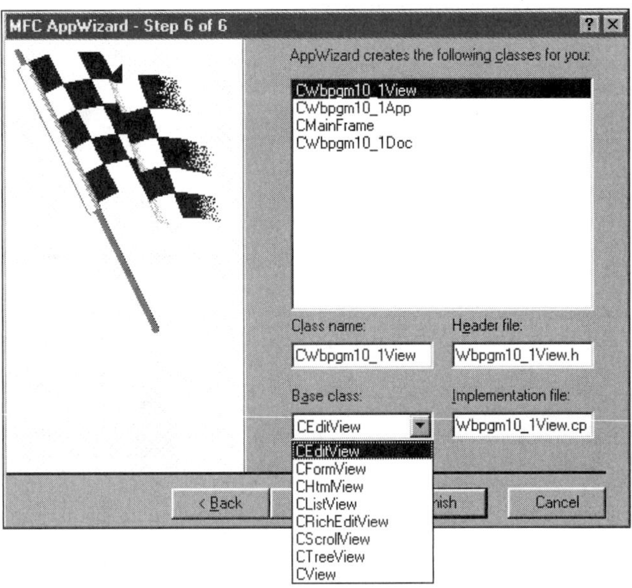

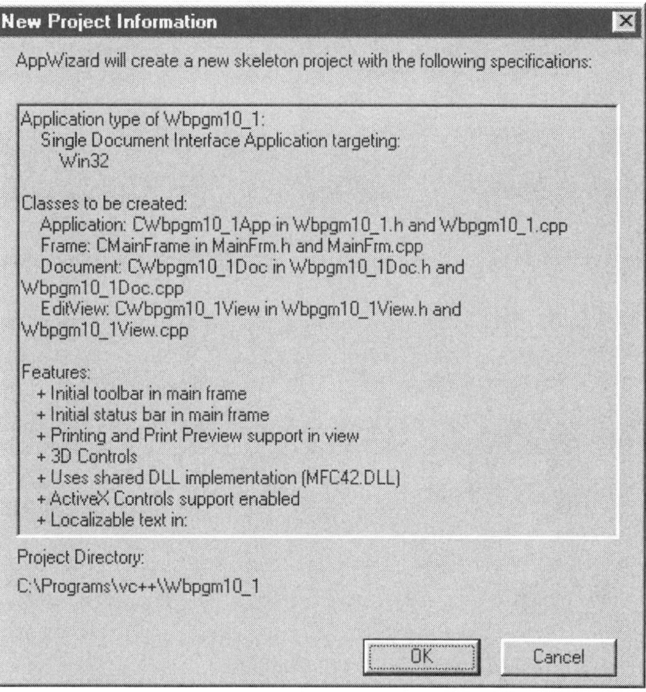

FIGURE 10.28

The `New Project Information` **dialog**

Once you have the window shown in Figure 10.29 on your screen, you can expand the `ClassView` hierarchy tree (see Figure 10.30), activate the `ResourceView` tab and expand the ResourceView hierarchy tree (see Figure 10.31), or activate the `FileView` tab and activate its hierarchy tree to both see and access all of the code files, header files, and resources provided by AppWizard for the developed application (see Figure 10.32). This

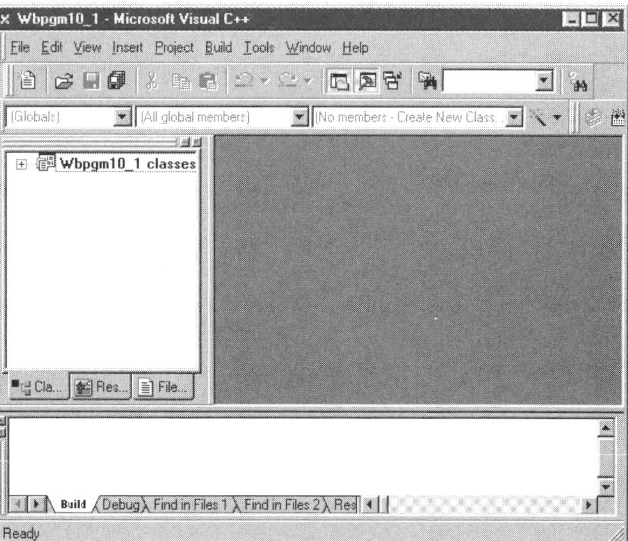

FIGURE 10.29

The IDE containing the developed application

FIGURE 10.30

The application framework's ClassView hierarchy tree

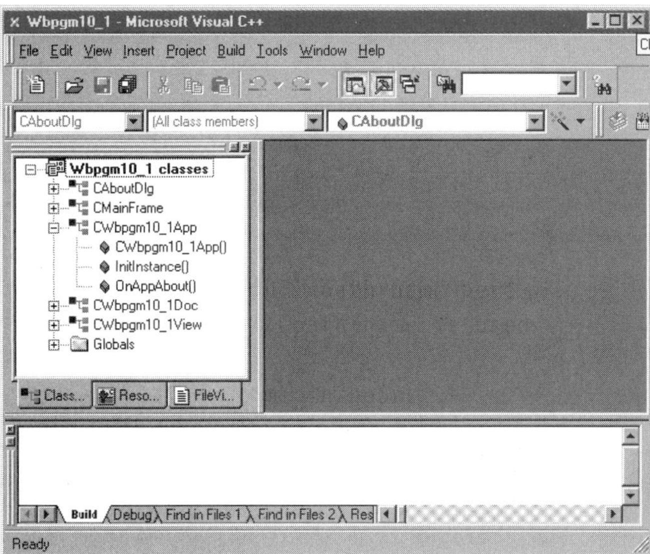

set of classes, code, and resources, provides a rather strong framework upon which you can now add any additional functionality that your particular application requires. Although we will show you how to add additional resources in Chapter 11's Knowing About section, you can actually run the application that we have just developed. As it now stands, this application provides a Text editor very similar to Microsoft's NotePad application.

FIGURE 10.31

The application framework's ResourceView hierarchy tree

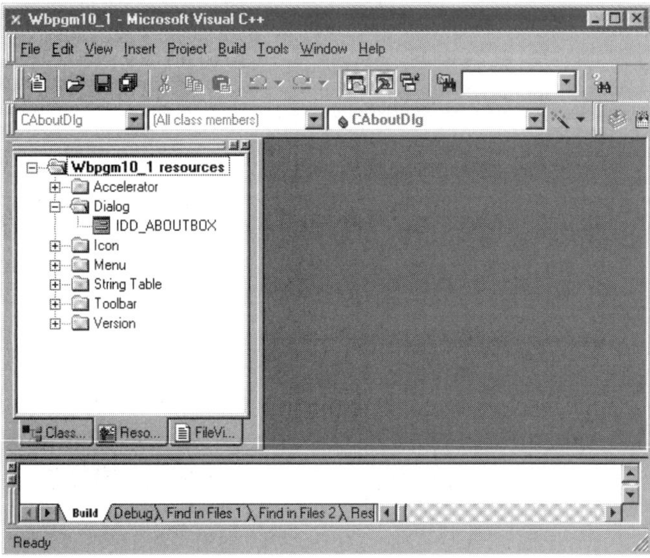

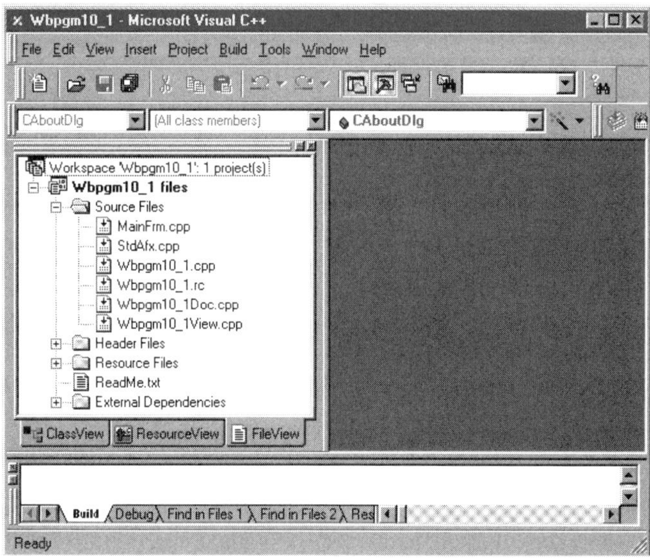

FIGURE 10.32

The application framework's FileView hierarchy tree

To execute our newly developed application framework, select the `Execute` option from the Menu bar's `Build` item, as shown in Figure 10.33, and then permit Visual C++ to build and compile the application. When the process is complete, the window shown in Figure 10.34 will be displayed.

Because we used the CEditView class as our base view class (see Figure 10.27), our new application can be used as a Text editor. This means that we can enter text into the

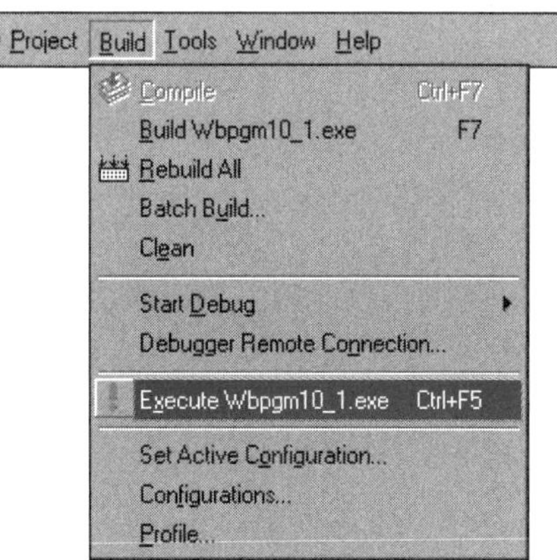

FIGURE 10.33

Building the application

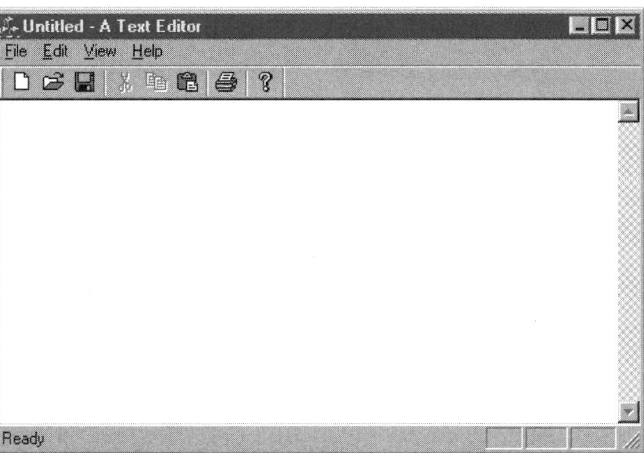

FIGURE 10.34

The completed application

application window's client area, as shown in Figure 10.35, and use the Menu bar's options to edit, save, retrieve, and print the text. Additionally, all of the standard Window's features, such as resizing and closing the application, are also available. That is an extraordinary amount of functionality provided by the application framework. In the next chapter's Knowing About section we will see how we can modify this framework by adding our own controls and code.

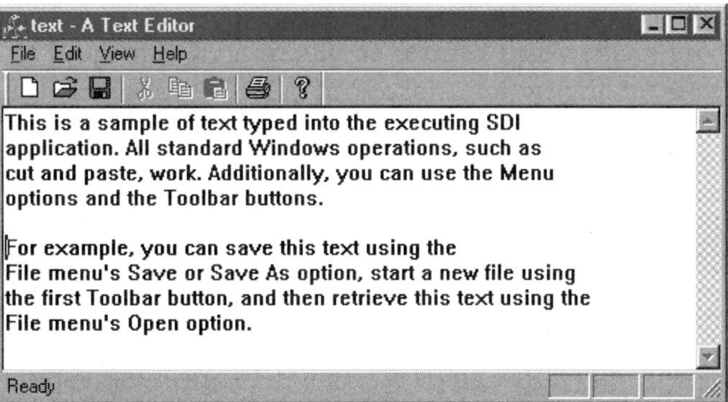

FIGURE 10.35

Entering text into the client area

11 Inheritance and Dynamic Memory Allocation

This chapter shows how a class designed by one programmer can be altered by another in a way that retains the integrity and design of the original class. This is accomplished using inheritance, which is a new feature that is central to object-oriented programming. Inheritance permits reusing and extending existing code in a way that ensures the new code does not adversely affect what has already been written.

In addition to class construction and inheritance, the third required feature of all object-oriented languages is the ability to produce polymorphic behavior. This feature permits the same method name to invoke different responses in inherited class objects.

Finally, the topic of dynamic creation and allocation of objects, as a program is executing, is presented.

11.1 Class Inheritance

The ability to create new classes from existing ones is the underlying motivation and power behind class and object-oriented programming techniques. Doing so facilitates reusing existing code in new ways without the need for retesting and validation. It permits the designers of a class to make it available to others for additions and extensions without relinquishing control over the existing class features.

Constructing one class from another is accomplished using a capability called **inheritance.** Related to this capability is an equally important feature named **polymorphism.** Polymorphism provides the ability to redefine how member functions of related classes operate based on the class object being referenced. In fact, for a programming language to be classified as an object-oriented language it must provide the features of classes, inheritance, and polymorphism. In this section we describe the inheritance and polymorphism features provided in C++.

Inheritance

Inheritance is the capability of deriving one class from another class. The initial class used as the basis for the derived class is referred to as either the **base, parent,** or **superclass.** The derived class is referred to as either the **derived, child,** or **subclass.**

A derived class is a completely new class that incorporates all of the data and member functions of its base class. It can, and usually does, however, add its own additional new data and function members and can override any base class function.

As an example of inheritance, consider three geometric shapes, consisting of a circle, cylinder, and sphere. All of these shapes share a common characteristic, a radius. Thus, for these shapes we can make the circle a base type for the other two shapes, as illustrated in Figure 11.1. Reformulating these shapes as class types, we would make the circle the base class and derive the cylinder and sphere classes from it.

FIGURE 11.1

Relating object types

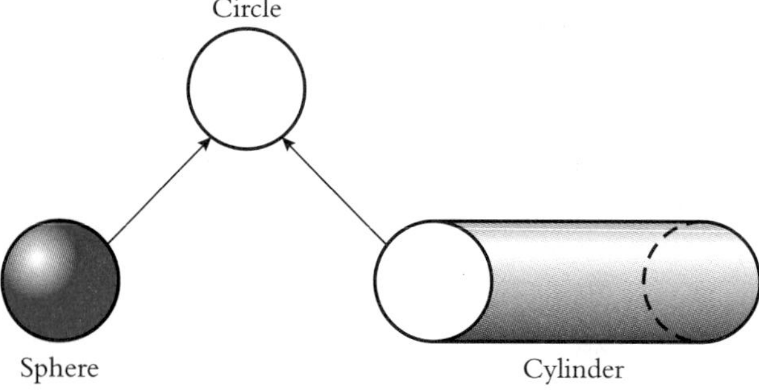

PROGRAMMER'S NOTES

Object-Based versus Object-Oriented Languages

An *object-based* language is one in which data and operations can be incorporated together in such a way that data values can be isolated and accessed through the specified class functions. The ability to bind the data members with operations in a single unit is referred to as *encapsulation*. In C++, encapsulation is provided by its class capability.

For a language to be classified as *object-oriented* it must also provide inheritance and polymorphism. *Inheritance* is the capability to derive one class from another. A derived class is a completely new data type that incorporates all of the data members and member functions of the original class with any new data and function members unique to itself. The class used as the basis for the derived type is referred to as the *base* or *parent* class and the derived data type is referred to as the *derived* or *child* class.

Polymorphism permits the same method name to invoke one operation in objects of a parent class and a different operation in objects of a derived class.

C++, which provides encapsulation, inheritance, and polymorphism, is an object-oriented language. Because C, which is C++'s predecessor, does not provide these features, it is neither an object-based nor an object-oriented language.

The relationships illustrated in Figure 11.1 are examples of simple inheritance. In **simple inheritance,** each derived type has only one immediate base type. The complement to simple inheritance is multiple inheritance. In **multiple inheritance** a derived type has two or more base types. Figure 11.2 illustrates an example of multiple inheritance. In this text we consider only simple inheritance.

The class derivations illustrated in Figures 11.1 and 11.2 are formally referred to as **class hierarchies** because they illustrate the hierarchy, or order, in which one class is derived from another. Let's now see how to derive one class from another.

A derived class has the same form as any other class in that it consists of both a declaration and an implementation. The only difference is in the first line of the declaration section. For a derived class this line is extended to include an access specification and a base class name and has the form:

```
class DerivedClassName : class-access baseClassName
```

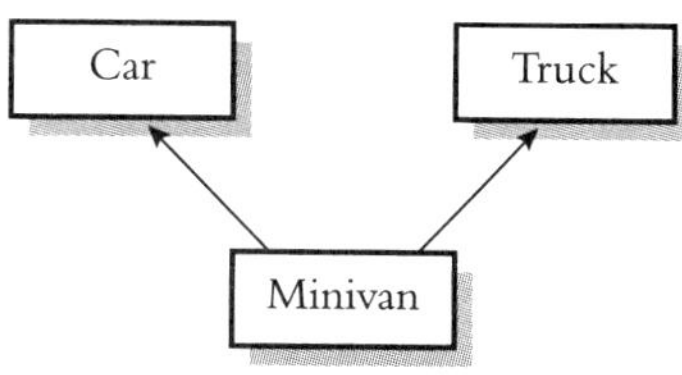

FIGURE 11.2

An example of multiple inheritance

For example, if `Circle` is the name of an existing class, a new class named `Cylinder` can be derived as follows:

```
class Cylinder : public Circle
{
    // add any additional data and
    // function members in here
};  // end of Cylinder class declaration
```

Except for the class-access specifier after the colon and the BaseClassName, there is nothing inherently new or complicated about the construction of the `Cylinder` class. Before providing a description of the `Circle` class and adding data and function members to the derived `Cylinder` class, we will need to reexamine access specifiers and how they relate to derived classes.

Access Specifications

Until now we have used only private and public access specifiers within a class. Giving all data members private status ensured that they could only be accessed by either class member functions or friends. This restricted access prevents access by any nonclass functions (except friends), *which also precludes access by any derived class functions.* This is a sensible restriction because if it did not exist anyone could "jump around" the private restriction by simply deriving a class.

To retain a restricted type of access across derived classes, C++ provides a third specification—protected access. Protected access behaves identically to private access in that it permits only member or friend function access, but it permits this restriction to be inherited by any derived class. The derived class then defines the type of inheritance it is willing to take on, subject to the base class's access restrictions. This is done by the class-access specifier, which is listed after the colon at the start of its declaration section. Table 11.1 lists the resulting derived class member access based on the base class member specifications and the derived class-access specifier.

Table 11.1 shows (shaded region) that if the base class member has a protected access and the derived class specifier is public, then the derived class member will be protected to its class. Similarly, if the base class has a public access and the derived class specifier is public, the derived class member will be public. This is the most commonly used type of specification for base class data and function members; therefore, it is the one we will use. This means that for all classes intended for use as a base class we use a protected data member access in place of a private designation.

An Example

To illustrate the process of deriving one class from another, we will derive a `Cylinder` class from a base `Circle` class. The definition of the `Circle` class is:

```
// class declaration

class Circle
{
  protected:
    double radius;
  public:
    Circle(double);  // constructor
    double calcval();
};

// class implementation

// constructor
Circle::Circle(double r = 1.0)  // constructor
{
  radius = r;
}

// calculate the area of a circle
double Circle::calcval(void)
{
  return(PI * radius * radius);
}
```

TABLE 11.1 Inherited access restrictions

Base Class Member	Derived Class Access	Derived Class Member
private -------------->	: private ---------------->	inaccessible
protected ------------>	: private ---------------->	private
public --------------->	: private ---------------->	private
private -------------->	: public ----------------->	inaccessible
protected ------------>	: public ----------------->	protected
public --------------->	: public ----------------->	public
private -------------->	: protected -------------->	inaccessible
protected ------------>	: protected -------------->	protected
public --------------->	: protected -------------->	protected

Except for the substitution of the access specifier `protected` in place of the usual `private` specifier for the data member, this is a standard class definition. The only identifier not defined is `PI`, which is used in the `calcval()` function. We define this as:

```
const double PI = 2.0 * asin(1.0);
```

This is simply a "trick" that forces the computer to return the value of pi accurate to as many decimal places as allowed by your computer. This value is obtained by taking the arcsin of 1.0, which is $\pi/2$, and multiplying the result by 2.

Having defined our base class, we can now extend it to a derived class. The definition of the derived class is:

```
// class declaration where
// Cylinder is derived from Circle

class Cylinder : public Circle
{
  protected:
    double length;  // add one additional data member and
  public:           // two additional function members
    Cylinder(double r = 1.0, double l = 1.0) : Circle(r), length(l) {}
    double calcval();
};

// class implementation

double Cylinder::calcval(void)    // this calculates a volume
{
  return (length * Circle::calcval()); // note the base function call
}
```

This definition encompasses several important concepts relating to derived classes. First, as a derived class, `Cylinder` contains all of the data and function members of its base class, `Circle`, plus any additional members that it may add. In this particular case the `Cylinder` class consists of a `radius` data member, inherited from the `Circle` class, plus an additional `length` member. Thus, each `Cylinder` object contains *two* data members, as is illustrated in Figure 11.3.

In addition to having two data members, the `Cylinder` class also inherits `Circle`'s function members. This is illustrated in the `Cylinder` constructor, which uses a base member initialization list (see Section 10.1) that specifically calls the `Circle` constructor. It is also illustrated in `Cylinder`'s `calcval()` function, which makes a call to `Circle::calcval()`.

FIGURE 11.3

Relationship between `Circle` and `Cylinder` data members

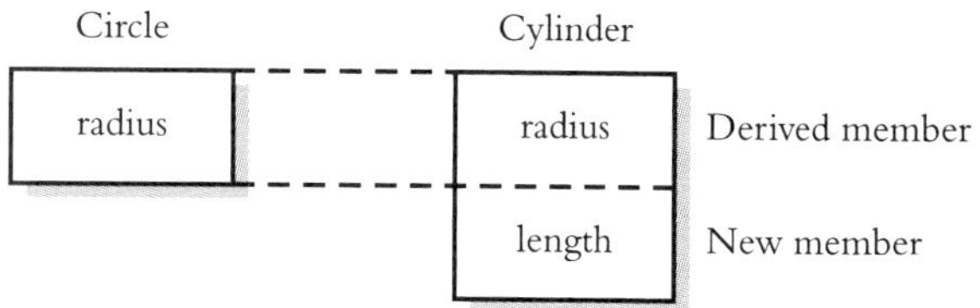

In both classes the same function name, `calcval()`, has been specifically used to illustrate the overriding of a base function by a derived function. When a `Cylinder` object calls `calcval()` it is a request to use the `Cylinder` version of the function, whereas a `Circle` object call to `calcval()` is a request to use the `Circle` version. In this case the `Cylinder` class can access only the `Circle` class version of `calcval()` using the scope resolution operator, as is done in the call `Circle::calcval()`. Program 11.1 uses these two classes within the context of a complete program.

PROGRAM 11.1

```
#include <iostream.h>
#include <math.h>

const double PI = 2.0 * asin(1.0);

// class declaration

class Circle
{
  protected:
    double radius;
  public:
    Circle(double r = 1);  // constructor
    double calcval();
};

// implementation section for Circle

// constructor
Circle::Circle(double r)
{
  radius = r;
}
```

(continued next page)

(continued from previous page)

```
// calculate the area of a circle
double Circle::calcval()
{
  return(PI * radius * radius);
}

// class declaration for the derived class
// Cylinder which is derived from Circle
class Cylinder : public Circle
{
  protected:
    double length;  // add one additional data member and
  public:           // two additional function members
    Cylinder(double r = 1.0, double l = 1.0) : Circle(r), length(l) {}
    double calcval();
};

// implementation section for Cylinder

double Cylinder::calcval()    // this calculates a volume
{
  return length * Circle::calcval(); // note the base function call
}
```

```
int main()
{
  Circle circle_1, circle_2(2);  // create two Circle objects
  Cylinder cylinder_1(3,4);      // create one Cylinder object

  cout << "\nThe area of circle_1 is " << circle_1.calcval() << endl;
  cout << "The area of circle_2 is " << circle_2.calcval() << endl;
  cout << "The volume of cylinder_1 is " << cylinder_1.calcval() << endl;

  circle_1 = cylinder_1;  // assign a cylinder to a Circle

  cout << "\nThe area of circle_1 is now "
       << circle_1.calcval() << endl;

  return 0;
}
```

FIGURE 11.4

Output displayed by Program 11.1

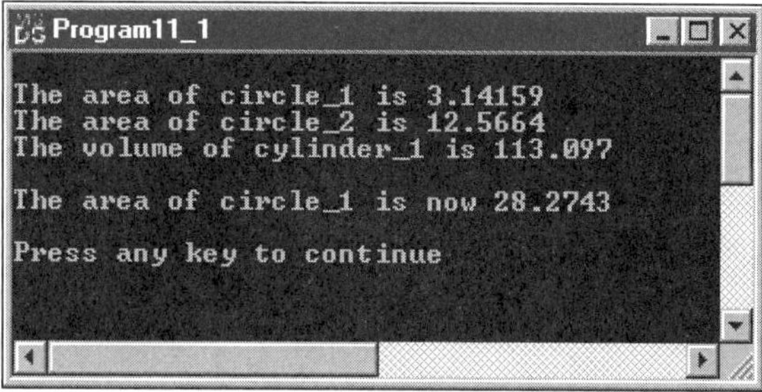

The output produced by Program 11.1 is shown in Figure 11.4.

The first three output lines are all straightforward and are produced by the first three `cout` statements in the program. As the output shows, a call to `calcval()` using a `Circle` object activates the `Circle` version of this function, whereas a call to `calcval()` using a `Cylinder` object activates the `Cylinder` version.

The assignment statement `circle_1 = cylinder_1;` introduces another important relationship between a base and derived class: *A derived class object can be assigned to a base class object.* This should not be surprising because both base and derived classes share a common set of data member types. In this type of assignment it is only this set of data members, which consist of all the base class data members, that are assigned. Thus, as illustrated in Figure 11.5, our `Cylinder` to `Circle` assignment results in the following memberwise assignment:

```
circle_1.radius = cylinder_1.radius;
```

The `length` member of the `Cylinder` object is not used in the assignment because it has no equivalent variable in the `Circle` class. The reverse cast, from base to derived class, is not as simple and requires a constructor to correctly initialize the additional derived class members not in the base class.

Before leaving Program 11.1, one additional point should be made. Although the `Circle` constructor was explicitly called using a base/member initialization list for the `Cylinder` constructor, an implicit call could also have been made. In the absence of an explicitly derived class constructor, the compiler will automatically call the default base class constructor first, before the derived class constructor is called. This works because

FIGURE 11.5

Assignment from derived to base class

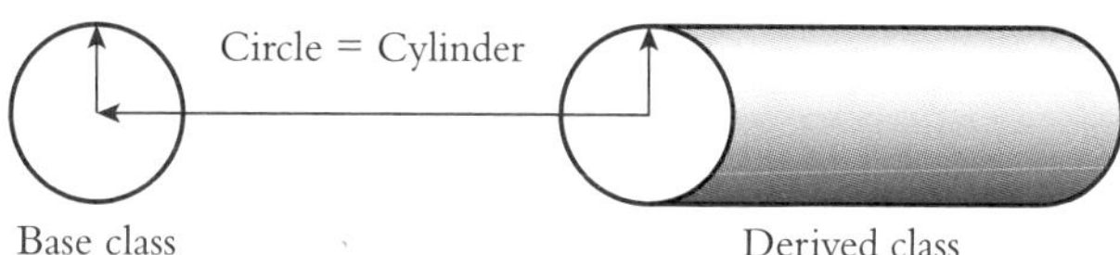

the derived class contains all of the base class data members. In a similar fashion the destructor functions are called in the reverse order—first derived class and then base class.

The MFC Hierarchy

The MFC Library[1] consists of more than 200 individual classes, of which 187 are derived, either directly or indirectly, from the base class `CObject`. Of all of the classes within MFC there is a subset of 11 classes that are used in almost every Windows application. Figure 11.6 shows the class hierarchy chart for these 11 basic classes.[2] The arrows in this figure point from a base class to a derived class. Table 11.2 describes the purpose of each of these classes.

At a minimum, a Windows-based application must contain a main window class that is derived from `CFrameWnd` and an application class that is derived for `CWinApp`. Windows Program 11.1 illustrates a fully functioning Windows-based program that is based on these two classes only. This program was not generated by the AppWizard; rather, it was hand-coded and constructed as a `Win32 Application` project type.

FIGURE 11.6

Simplified MFC hierarchy chart

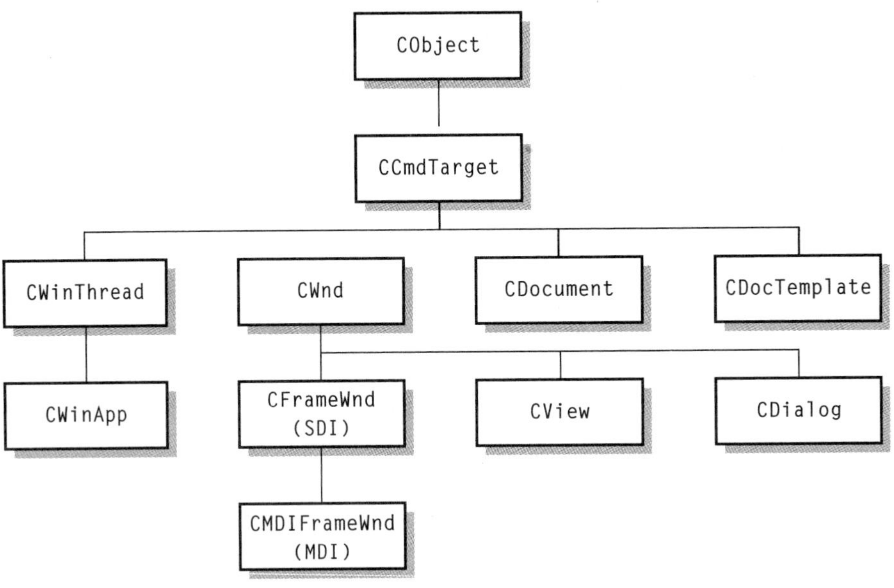

1 This topic may be omitted with no loss of subject continuity.

2 Note that MFC does not support multiple inheritance between its classes.

TABLE 11.2 MFC Class Descriptions

Class	Description
CObject	This is the primary base class for most of the MFC classes.
CCmdTarget	Derived directly from CObject. This is the base class for routing commands and messages to the member functions you write to handle them, which is referred to as the MFC Library message-map architecture. (A command is considered as a message from a menu item, command button, or accelerator key.)
CWinThread	Derived directly from CCmdTarget and used as the base class for CWinApp.
CWinApp	The main application class in MFC that encapsulates the initialization, running, and termination of an application for Windows. A framework application must have one and only one object of a class derived from CWinApp. This object, which is the main application object for an application, must be constructed before any windows are created. The CWinApp class is derived from the CWinThread class.
CWnd	This class and its derived classes provide the constructors, destructors, and member functions to initialize and create all Windows structures, and then access them. An application can have only one object of type CWnd. Once this object is created, the application begins its execution.
CFrameWnd	This class is a child of the CWnd class, and is the base class for the main frame window object used in every MFC application. An SDI application uses a single main frame window that is instantiated from this class.
CMDIFrameWnd	This class is a child of the CFrameWnd class. An MDI application's main frame window is instantiated from this class.
CView	This class provides the basic functionality for programmer-defined view classes. A view is the image of the document that is seen within a window, and is the interface that accepts and interprets user operations on the part of the document that is being displayed (the complete document might also be displayed).
CDialog	The CDialog class provides an interface for managing Dialog boxes, which typically is the way an application communicates with a user. The Visual C++ dialog editor can be used to design Dialog boxes and create their resources. The Class Wizard can be used to initialize and validate controls placed in a Dialog box, and for creating the variables to capture values entered by a user.
CDocument	This class provides the basic functionality for programmer-defined document classes. A document represents the unit of data that a user typically opens with the Open command on the File menu and saves with the Save command on the File menu.
CDocTemplate	This class defines the basic functionality for document templates. A document template defines the relationships among a document class, a view class, and a frame window class that contains the view.

WINDOWS PROGRAM 11.1

```
// This is a hand-coded (non-AppWizard created) windows application that uses the MFC
// The project type should be specified as a Win32 Application empty project
//  and then add a New File of type C++ Source File and enter the code below
//  as the source code
// Make sure to set the Project Settings General tab option to use MFC, either as a
// static or dll library. If this is setting is not made you will get the link error
//....unresolved external symbol __endthreadex....
//....unresolved external symbol __beginthreadex....
//
// Also, make sure to close the executing application window before
// attempting a rebuild

#include <afxwin.h>

// The Window class derived from CFrameWnd
// Declaration Section
class CMainWin : public CFrameWnd
{
  public:
    CMainWin();
};

// Implementation Section
CMainWin::CMainWin()  // constructor
{
  Create(NULL,"WinProgram11_1");
}

// The Application class derived from CWinApp
// Declaration section
class CApp : public CWinApp
{
  public:
    BOOL InitInstance();
};

// Implementation section
BOOL CApp::InitInstance()
```

(continued next page)

(*continued from previous page*)

```
{
  m_pMainWnd = new CMainWin;
  m_pMainWnd->ShowWindow(m_nCmdShow);
  m_pMainWnd->UpdateWindow();
  return TRUE;
}

CApp App; // create an object of type CApp
```

In reviewing the program's code, notice that the CMainWin class, which is the programmer-selected name given to this particular program's window class, has been derived from the MFC CFrameWnd using the statement

```
classCMainWin : public CFrameWnd
```

and that the CApp class, which is the programmer-selected name given to this particular program's application class, has been derived from the MFC CWinApp class using the statement

```
class CApp : public CWinApp
```

Figure 11.7 shows the run-time interface produced by Windows Program 11.1 after it has been compiled and executed. The interface consists of a main window with a central icon, title, and minimize, resize, and close buttons.

To gain an appreciation of the functionality provided by the MFC, Windows Program 11.2 illustrates the same Windows-based program written without using any MFC functions. (*Note:* If you are going to execute either Windows Program 11.1 or 11.2, pay attention to the project settings documented in the comments preceding each program.)

FIGURE 11.7

Windows Program 11.1's run-time GUI

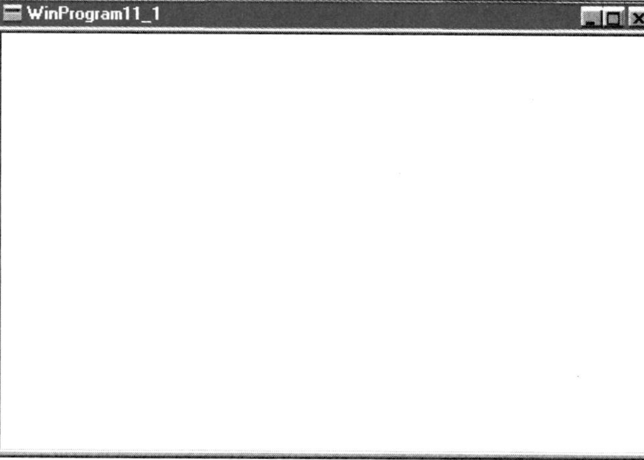

WINDOWS PROGRAM 11.2

```
// This is a windows application that does not use the MFC
// The project type should be specified as a Win32 Application empty project
//  and then add a New File of type C++ Source File and enter the code below
//  as the source code
// Make sure to set the Project Settings General tab option to Not Use MFC.
// If this is not done you will get a variety of link error of the type
// ....unresolved external symbol __imp__DispatchMessageA@@4....
// If you construct this project as a Console App you will get the link error
// ....unresolved external symbol _main....
//
// Also, make sure to close the executing application window before
// attempting a rebuild

#include <windows.h>

LRESULT CALLBACK WndProc(HWND,UINT,UINT,LONG);   // function prototype


int WINAPI WinMain(HANDLE hInstance, HANDLE hPrevInstance,
    LPSTR lpszCmdLine, int nCmdShow)
{
    static char szAppName[] = "HelloApp";
    HWND        hwnd;
    MSG         msg; // message structure
    WNDCLASS    wndclass;   // define a structure of type WNDCLASS

       // Populate the structure - this defines the window's characteristics

    wndclass.style          = CS_HREDRAW | CS_VREDRAW;
    wndclass.lpfnWndProc    = WndProc; // name of window procedure function
                                       // that will handle messages
    wndclass.cbClsExtra     = 0;
    wndclass.cbWndExtra     = 0;
    wndclass.hInstance      = hInstance; // this becomes a function parameter
    wndclass.hIcon          = LoadIcon(NULL, IDI_APPLICATION);
    wndclass.hCursor        = LoadCursor(NULL, IDC_ARROW);
    wndclass.hbrBackground = GetStockObject(GRAY_BRUSH);
    wndclass.lpszMenuName  = NULL;
    wndclass.lpszClassName = szAppName;  // window class name

    RegisterClass(&wndclass);
```

(continued next page)

(continued from previous page)

```
    hwnd = CreateWindow(szAppName,  // window class name
        "WinProgram11_1",           // window caption
        WS_OVERLAPPEDWINDOW,        // window style
        CW_USEDEFAULT,              // initial x position
        CW_USEDEFAULT,              // initial y position
        CW_USEDEFAULT,              // initial x size
        CW_USEDEFAULT,              // initial y size
        NULL,                       // parent window handle - None
        NULL,                       // window menu handle - None
        hInstance,                  // program instance handle
        NULL);                      // creation parameters

   ShowWindow(hwnd, nCmdShow);
   UpdateWindow(hwnd);

   while (GetMessage(&msg, NULL, 0, 0))
   {
       TranslateMessage(&msg);
       DispatchMessage(&msg);
   }
   return msg.wParam;
}

LRESULT CALLBACK WndProc(HWND hwnd,UINT message, UINT wParam, LONG lParam)
{
    HDC         hdc;
    HPEN        hpen, hpenOld;
    PAINTSTRUCT ps;
    RECT        rect;

    switch (message)
       {
        case WM_PAINT:
            hdc = BeginPaint(hwnd, &ps);
            GetClientRect(hwnd, &rect);

                 SetBkColor(hdc, RGB(0,0,255));
                    SetTextColor(hdc, RGB(255,255,255));
                    DrawText(hdc, "Hello World!", -1, &rect,
                    DT_SINGLELINE | DT_CENTER | DT_VCENTER);
```

(continued next page)

(continued from previous page)

```
            SelectObject(hdc, hpenOld);
            DeleteObject(hpen);
            EndPaint(hwnd, &ps);
            return 0;
        case WM_DESTROY:
            PostQuitMessage(0);
            return 0;
    }
    return DefWindowProc(hwnd, message, wParam, lParam);
}
```

Although Windows Program 11.1 is obviously simpler to code than Windows Program 11.2, even this former program would become tedious to modify if even minimal Windows capabilities to access and view a file were needed. This is the reason for the other MFC classes shown in Figure 11.6.

EXERCISES 11.1

1. Define the following terms:
   a. inheritance
   b. base class
   c. derived class
   d. simple inheritance
   e. multiple inheritance
   f. class hierarchy

2. Describe the difference between a private and a protected class member.

3. What three features must a programming language provide for it to be classified as an object-oriented language?

4. a. Modify Program 11.1 to include a derived class named `Sphere` from the base `Circle` class. The only additional class members of `Sphere` should be a constructor and a `calcval()` function that returns the volume of the sphere.

(Note: volume $= \frac{4}{3}\pi$ *radius*^{3}*.)*

b. Include the class constructed for Exercise 4a in a working C++ program. Have your program call all of the member functions in the `Sphere` class.

5. a. Create a base class named `Point` that consists of an `x` and `y` coordinate. From this class derive a class named `Circle` having an additional data member named `radius`. For this derived class the `x` and `y` data members represent the center coordinates of a circle. The function members of the first class should consist of a constructor, an `area` function named area that returns zero, and a `distance()` function that returns the distance between two points, where

$$distance = \sqrt{(x2 - x1)^2 + (y2 - y1)^2}$$

Additionally, the derived class should have a constructor and an override function named `area()` that returns the area of a circle.

b. Include the classes constructed for Exercise 5a in a working C++ program. Have your program call all of the member functions in each class. In addition, call the base class `distance` function with two `Circle` objects and explain the result returned by the function.

6. a. Using the classes constructed for Exercise 5a, derive a class named `Cylinder` from the derived `Circle` class. The `Cylinder` class should have a constructor and a member function named `area()` that determines the surface area of the cylinder. For this function use the algorithm *surface area* $= 2\pi r\ (l + r)$, where r is the radius of the cylinder and l is the length.

b. Include the classes constructed for Exercise 6a in a working C++ program. Have your program call all of the member functions in the `Cylinder` class.

c. What do you think might be the result if the base class `distance()` function was called with two `Cylinder` objects?

7. a. Create a base class named `Rectangle` that contains `length` and `width` data members. From this class derive a class named `Box` having an additional data member named `depth`. The function members of the base `Rectangle` class should consist of a constructor and an `area()` function. The derived `Box` class should have a constructor, an override function named `area()`, which returns the surface area of the box, and a `volume()` function.

b. Include the classes constructed for Exercise 7a in a working C++ program. Have your program call all of the member functions in each class and explain the result when the `distance()` function is called using a `Box` object.

11.2 Polymorphism

The overriding of a base member function using an overloaded derived member function, as was illustrated by the `calcval()` function in Program 11.1, is an example of polymorphism. **Polymorphism** permits the same function name to invoke one response in objects of a base class and another response in objects of a derived class. In some cases, however, this method of overriding does not work as one might desire. To understand why this is so, consider Program 11.2.

PROGRAM 11.2

```
#include <iostream.h>
#include <math.h>

// class declaration for the base class

class One
{
  protected:
    float a;
  public:
    One(float = 2);    // constructor
    float f1(float);    // a member function
    float f2(float);    // another member function
};

// class implementation for One

One::One(float val)   // constructor
{
  a = val;
}

float One::f1(float num)  // a member function
{
  return num/2;
}
float One::f2(float num)  // another member function
{
  return pow(f1(num),2);  // square the result of f1()
}

// class declaration for the derived class

class Two : public One
{
  public:
    float f1(float);    // this overrides class One's f1()
};
```

(continued next page)

(*continued from previous page*)

```
// class implementation for Two

float Two::f1(float num)
{
  return num/3;
}
```

```
int main()
{
  One object_1;  // object_1 is an object of the base class
  Two object_2;  // object_2 is an object of the derived class

     // call f2() using a base class object call
  cout << "The computed value using a base class object call is "
       << object_1.f2(12) << endl;

    // call f2() using a derived class object call
  cout << "The computed value using a derived class object call is "
       << object_2.f2(12) << endl;

  return 0;
}
```

The output display that is produced by this program is:

```
The computed value using a base class object call is 36
The computed value using a derived class object call is 36
```

As this output shows, the same result is obtained no matter which object type calls the `f2()` function. This result is produced because the derived class does not have an override to the base class `f2()` function. Thus, both calls to `f2()` result in the base class `f2()` function being called.

Once invoked, the base class `f2()` function will always call the base class version of `f1()` rather than the derived class override version. This behavior is due to a process referred to as **function binding.** In normal function calls static binding is used. In **static binding** the determination of which function is called is made at compile time. Thus, when the compiler first encounters the `f1()` function in the base class it makes the determination that whenever `f2()` is called, either from a base or derived class object, it will subsequently call the base class `f1()` function.

In place of static binding we would like a binding method that is capable of determining which function should be invoked at run time based on the object type making the call. This type of binding is referred to as **dynamic binding.** To achieve dynamic binding C++ provides virtual functions.

A **virtual function** specification tells the compiler to create a pointer to a function, but not fill in the value of the pointer until the function is actually called. Then, at run time, *and based on the object making the call,* the appropriate function address is used. Creating a virtual function is extremely easy—all that is required is that the keyword `virtual` be placed before the function's return type in the declaration section. For example, consider Program 11.3, which is identical to Program 11.2 except for the virtual declaration of the `f1()` function.

The output produced by Program 11.3 is:

```
The computed value using a base class object call is 36
The computed value using a derived class object call is 16
```

As illustrated by this output, the `f2()` function now calls different versions of the overloaded `f1()` function based on the object type making the call. This selection, based on the object making the call, is the classic definition of polymorphic function behavior and is caused by the dynamic binding imposed on `f1()` by virtue of its being a virtual function.

Once a function is declared as virtual *it remains virtual for the next derived class with or without a virtual declaration in the derived class.* Thus, the second `virtual` declaration in the derived class is not strictly needed, but should be included both for clarity and to ensure that any subsequently derived classes correctly inherit the function. To understand why, consider the inheritance diagram illustrated in Figure 11.8, where class C is derived from class B and class B is derived from class A. In this situation, if function `f1()` is virtual in class A, but is not declared in class B, it will not be virtual in class C. The only other requirement is that once a function has been declared as virtual the return type and parameter list of all subsequent derived class override versions *must be* the same.

FIGURE 11.8

Inheritance diagram

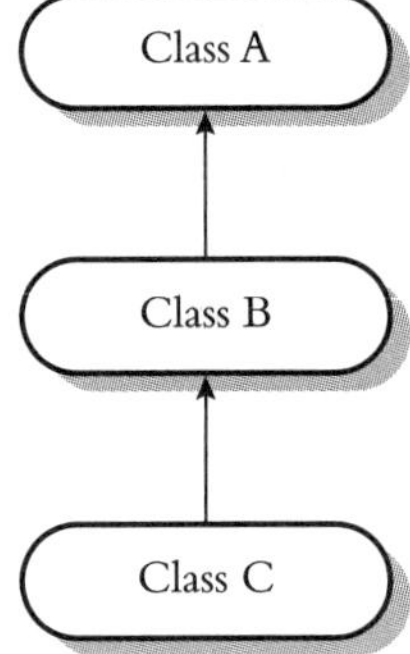

PROGRAM 11.3

```
#include <iostream.h>
#include <math.h>
```

```
// class declaration for the base class

class One
{
  protected:
    float a;
  public:
    One(float = 2);   // constructor
    virtual float f1(float);   // a member function
    float f2(float);   // another member function
};

// class implementation for One

One::One(float val)   // constructor
{
  a = val;
}

float One::f1(float num)  // a member function
{
  return num/2;
}

float One::f2(float num)  // another member function
{
  return pow(f1(num),2);  // square the result of f1()
}

// class declaration for the derived class

class Two : public One
{
  public:
    virtual float f1(float);    // this overrides class One's f1()
};
```

(continued next page)

(continued from previous page)

```
// class implementation for Two

float Two::f1(float num)
{
  return num/3;
}
```

```
int main()
{
  One object_1;  // object_1 is an object of the base class
  Two object_2;  // object_2 is an object of the derived class

      // call f2() using a base class object call
  cout << "The computed value using a base class object call is "
       << object_1.f2(12) << endl;

     // call f2() using a derived class object call
  cout << "The computed value using a derived class object call is "
       << object_2.f2(12) << endl;

  return 0;
}
```

EXERCISES 11.2

1. Enter and execute Programs 11.2 and 11.3 on your computer so that you understand the relationship between function calls in each program.

2. Describe the two methods C++ provides for implementing polymorphism.

3. Describe the difference between static binding and dynamic binding.

4. Describe the difference between a virtual function and a nonvirtual function.

5. Describe what polymorphism is and provide an example of polymorphic behavior.

6. Discuss, with reasons, whether the multiplication operator provided for both the integer and float built-in types is an example of polymorphism.

11.3 The this Pointer

Except for static data members, which are shared by all class objects, each object maintains its own set of member variables. This permits each object to have its own clearly defined state as determined by the values stored in its member variables.

For example, consider the Date class previously defined in Program 9.1 and repeated below for convenience:

```
#include <iostream.h>

// class declaration

class Date
{
  private:
     int month;
     int day;
     int year;
   public:
     Date(int, int, int); // constructor
     void showdate(); // member function to display a Date
};

// implementation section

Date::Date(int mm = 7, int dd = 4, int yyyy = 2001)
{
  month = mm;
  day = dd;
  year = yyyy;
}

void Date::showdate()
{
  cout << "The date is ";
  cout << setfill('0')
      << setw(2) << month << '/'
      << setw(2) << day << '/'
      << setw(2) << year % 100;
  cout << endl;
  return;
}
```

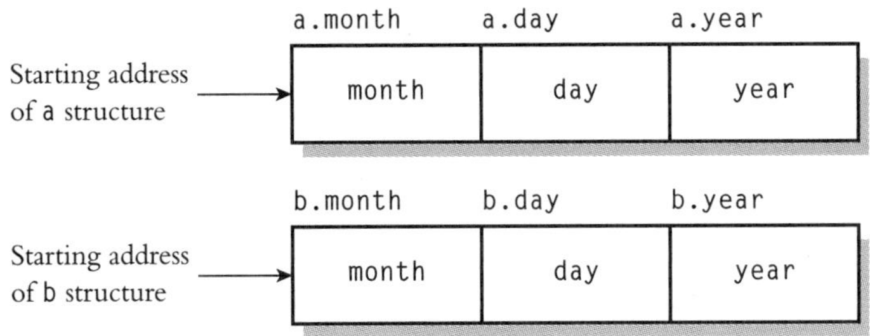

FIGURE 11.9

The storage of two `Date` objects in memory

Each time an object is created from this class, a distinct area of memory is set aside for its data members. For example, if two objects named `a` and `b` are created from this class, the memory storage for these objects would be as illustrated in Figure 11.9. Notice that each set of data members has its own starting address in memory, which corresponds to the address of the first data member for the object.

This replication of data storage is not implemented for member functions. In fact, for each class *only one copy of the member functions is retained in memory,* and each object uses these same functions.

Sharing member functions requires providing a means of identifying on which specific data structure a member function should be operating. This is accomplished by providing address information to the function indicating where in memory the particular data structure, corresponding to a specific object, is located. This address is provided by the name of the object, which is in fact, a reference name. For example, again using our `Date` class and assuming `a` is an object of this class, the statement `a.showdate()` passes the address of the `a` object into the `showdate()` member function. (Review Section 2.4 for information on memory addresses.)

An obvious question at this point is how this address is passed to `showdate()` and where it is stored. The answer is that the address is stored in a special parameter named `this`, which is automatically supplied as a hidden argument to each nonstatic member function when the function is called.

Unlike a reference parameter, the `this` parameter is a pointer parameter. Although pointer parameters, explained in detail in Chapter 13, provide much more flexibility in using addresses than reference parameters, for our current purposes all that we need to know is that to gain access to the object whose address is provided by the `this` pointer we must apply C++'s dereference operator, `*`, to `this`.

Before proceeding to use the `this` pointer in a "cookbook" manner, let's take a moment to compare the differences between a pointer's address and a reference address. Recall from Section 6.3 that whenever a reference parameter is encountered, it is always *the contents of the reference address* that is accessed. This type of access is referred to as automatic or implicit dereferencing of the address and effectively hides the fact that a reference parameter is fundamentally a named constant for an address. In using a pointer parameter, dereferencing is not automatic. To access the contents of the address provided by the this pointer, the notation *this, or its equivalent this-> must be used, which formally provides what is known as explicit dereferencing.

Returning now to our Date class, which has three member functions, the actual parameter list of the constructor Date() function is equivalent to

```
Date(Date *this, int mm = 7, int dd = 4, int yyyy = 2001)
```

where the declaration Date *this means that the this pointer contains the address of a specific Date object in a manner similar to the declaration Date& refarg meaning that the refarg reference argument is the address of a Date object. Similarly, the parameter list of showdate() is equivalent to

```
showdate(Date *this)
```

The important point here is to understand that when a member function is called, it actually receives an extra, hidden parameter that is the address of a Date object. Although it is usually not necessary to do so, this pointer data member can be explicitly used within all member functions. For example, consider Program 11.4, which uses the hidden argument this within the body of each member function to access the appropriate data member variables.

PROGRAM 11.4

```
#include <iostream.h>
#include <iomanip.h>

// class declaration

class Date
{
  private:
     int month;
     int day;
     int year;
   public:
     Date(int, int, int);      // constructor
     void showdate();          // member function to display a Date
};

// implementation section
```

(continued next page)

(*continued from previous page*)

```
Date::Date(int mm = 7, int dd = 4, int yyyy = 2001)
{
  (*this).month = mm;
  (*this).day = dd;
  (*this).year = yyyy;
}

void Date::showdate()
{
   cout << setfill('0')
        << setw(2) << (*this).month << '/'
        << setw(2) << (*this).day << '/'
        << setw(2) << (*this).year % 100;
   return;
}
```

```
int main()
{
  Date a(4,1,1999), b(12,18,2001); // declare two objects

  cout << "\nThe date stored in a is originally ";
  a.showdate();  // display the original date
  a = b;         // assign b's value to a
  cout << "\nAfter assignment the date stored in a is ";
  a.showdate();  // display a's values
  cout << endl;

  return 0;
}
```

The output produced by Program 11.4 is illustrated in Figure 11.10.

FIGURE 11.10

Output displayed by Program 11.4

```
Program11_4

The date stored in a is originally 04/01/99
After assignment the date stored in a is 12/18/01
Press any key to continue_
```

This is the same output produced by Program 10.1, which omits using the this pointer to access the data members. Clearly, using the this pointer in Program 11.4 is unnecessary and simply clutters the member function code. There are times, however, when an object must pass its address on to other functions. In these situations, one of which we now consider, the address stored in the this pointer must explicitly be used.

The Assignment Operator Revisited

A simple assignment operator function was defined in Program 10.2 and is repeated below for convenience:

```
void Date::operator=(Date& newdate)
{
  day = newdate.day;       // assign the day
  month = newdate.month;   // assign the month
  year = newdate.year;     // assign the year
}
```

The drawback of this function is that it returns no value, making multiple assignments such as a = b = c impossible. Now that we have the this pointer at our disposal, we can fix our simple assignment operator function to provide an appropriate return type. In this case the return value should be a Date rather than a void. Making this change in the function's prototype for our assignment operator yields:

```
Date operator=(const Date&);
```

Notice also that we have declared the function's argument to be a const, which ensures that this operand cannot be altered by the function. A suitable function definition for this prototype is:

```
Date Date::operator=(const Date& newdate)
{
  day = newdate.day;        // assign the day
  month = newdate.month;    // assign the month
  year = newdate.year;      // assign the year
  return *this;
}
```

In the case of an assignment such as b = c, or its equivalent form b.operator=(c), the function first alters b's member values from within the function and then returns the value of this object, which may be used in a subsequent assignment. Thus, a multiple assignment expression such as a = b = c is possible, as illustrated in Program 11.5.

PROGRAM 11.5

```
#include <iostream.h>
#include <iomanip.h>

// class declaration

class Date
{
  private:
    int month;
    int day;
    int year;
  public:
    Date(int = 7, int = 4, int = 2001);  // constructor
    Date operator=(const Date&);  // define assignment of a date
    void showdate();            // member function to display a date
};

// implementation section
Date::Date(int mm, int dd, int yyyy)
{
  month = mm;
  day = dd;
  year = yyyy;
}

Date Date::operator=(const Date& newdate)
{
  day = newdate.day;        // assign the day
  month = newdate.month;    // assign the month
  year = newdate.year;      // assign the year
  return *this;
}

void Date::showdate()
{
  cout << setfill('0')
      << setw(2) << month << '/'
      << setw(2) << day << '/'
      << setw(2) << year % 100;
  return;
}
```

(continued next page)

(continued from previous page)

```
int main()
{
  Date a(4,1,1999), b(12,18,2001), c(1,1,2002); // declare three objects

  cout << "\nBefore assignment a's date value is ";
  a.showdate();
  cout << "\nBefore assignment b's date value is ";
  b.showdate();
  cout << "\nBefore assignment c's date value is ";
  c.showdate();
  cout << endl;

  a = b = c;  // multiple assignment

  cout << "\nAfter assignment a's date value is ";
  a.showdate();
  cout << "\nAfter assignment b's date value is ";
  b.showdate();
  cout << "\nAfter assignment c's date value is ";
  c.showdate();
  cout << endl;

  return 0;
}
```

The output produced by Program 11.5 is shown in Figure 11.11.

FIGURE 11.11

Output displayed by Program 11.5

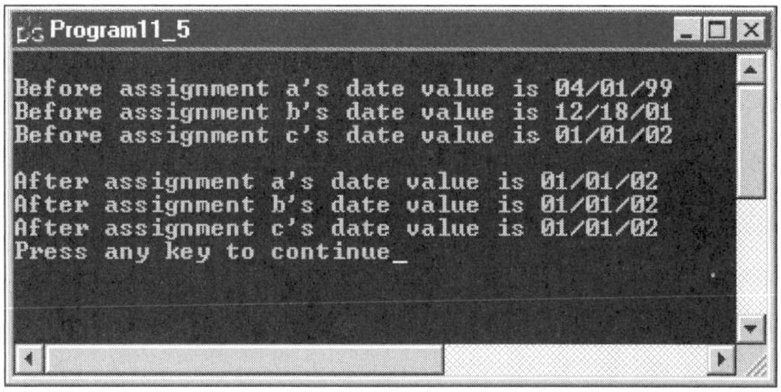

```
Program11_5

Before assignment a's date value is 04/01/99
Before assignment b's date value is 12/18/01
Before assignment c's date value is 01/01/02

After assignment a's date value is 01/01/02
After assignment b's date value is 01/01/02
After assignment c's date value is 01/01/02
Press any key to continue_
```

As noted previously in Section 10.3, the only restriction on the assignment operator function is that it can be overloaded only as a member function. It cannot be overloaded as a friend function.

EXERCISES 11.3

1. Discuss the difference between the automatic dereferencing that occurs when a reference parameter is used and the explicit dereferencing required by the `this` argument.

2. Modify Program 11.4 so that the notation `this->` is used in place of the notation `*this` within the body of both the constructor and `showdate()` functions. In doing so, notice that the `->` symbol is constructed using a minus sign, `-`, followed by a right facing arrowhead, `>`.

3. Rewrite the `Date()`, `setdate()`, and `showdate()` member functions in Program 10.2 to explicitly use the `this` pointer when referencing all data members. Run your program and verify that the same output as produced by Program 10.2 is achieved.

4. A problem with the assignment operator defined in this section is that it does not return a suitable `lvalue` (recall from Section 3.1 that an `lvalue` is a value that can be used on the left side of an assignment statement). Although Program 11.5 defines a return type for the `Date` assignment operator, the return type is not used as an `lvalue` because the expression `a = b = c` is evaluated as `a = (b = c)`. Thus, in both the initial assignment `b = c` and the subsequent assignment `a = b`, the return value of the assignment operator is used as an `rvalue` (i.e., it is used on the right-hand side of an assignment). Modify the assignment operator so that the expression returns a correct `lvalue`. This means that in the evaluation of the expression `(a = b) = c`, the initial `lvalue` returned should be `a`.

11.4 Examples

A multiobject simulation was presented in Section 10.4. In that simulation the same customer object was reused to simulate multiple customer arrivals. In the problem presented in this chapter, different customer objects are dynamically created as they are needed and deleted once their task has been completed.

To understand how the dynamic creation and deletion is accomplished, we first present an example that shows how the dynamic allocation of memory storage can be achieved in practice. This information is then incorporated into the second example, which presents a complete multiobject simulation with dynamically created customer objects.

Example 1: Dynamic Object Creation and Deletion

As each variable or object is defined in a program, sufficient storage for it is designated by the compiler and assigned from a pool of computer memory locations before the program is executed. Once specific memory locations have been assigned, they remain fixed for the lifetime of the variable and object or until the program has finished executing. For example, if a function requests storage for three nonstatic integers and five objects of a user-defined class, the storage for these integers and objects remains fixed from the point of their definition until the function finishes executing.

An alternative to this fixed allocation of memory is a dynamic allocation. Under **dynamic allocation,** the amount of allocated storage is determined and assigned as the function is executing, rather than being fixed prior to execution.

Although dynamic allocation of memory is most useful when dealing with lists because it allows the list to expand as new items are added and to contract as items are deleted, it can also be useful in simulation programs. For example, in simulating the arrival and departure of customers, it is helpful to have a mechanism whereby a new customer can be randomly created and then removed after being serviced. Two C++ operators, `new` and `delete`, provide this capability, as described in Table 11.3.

From an operational viewpoint, dynamically allocated variables and objects created using the `new` operator are accessible only using the address returned by `new`. This means that, like the `this` pointer, the address of the newly created variable or object must be stored in a pointer variable. The mechanism for doing this is rather simple. For example, the statement `int *num = new int;` both reserves a memory area sufficient to hold one integer and places the address of this storage area into a pointer variable named `num`. This same dynamic allocation can also be made in two steps; the first step is to declare a pointer variable using a declaration statement and the second uses a subsequent statement requesting dynamic allocation. Using this two-step process, the single statement `int *num = new int;` can be replaced by the sequence of statements

```
int *num;        // this declares a pointer variable that can
                 // store the address of an integer
num = new int;   // this reserves memory for an integer and
                 // puts the address of the memory area into num
```

TABLE 11.3 Descriptions of `new` and `delete`

Operator Name	Description
`new`	Reserves the correct number of bytes for the variable or object type requested by the declaration. Returns the address of the first reserved location or a `NULL` address if sufficient memory is not available.
`delete`	Releases previously reserved memory.

PROGRAMMER'S NOTES

Using a `typedef` Statement

Among other uses, a `typedef` statement can be used to create a new and shorter name for pointer definitions. The syntax for a `typedef` statement is:

```
typedef data-type new-type-name;
```

For example, to make the name `PtrToInt` a synonym for the terms `int *`, the following statement can be used:

```
typedef int * PtrToInt;
```

Such a statement would normally be placed at the top of a program file immediately after all `#include`s. Now, whenever a variable is to be declared as a pointer to an `int`, the term `PtrToInt` can be used in place of the `int *`. Thus, for example, the declaration

```
int *pointer1;
```

can be replaced by the statement

```
PtrToInt pointer1;
```

By convention, all `typedef` names are written in either initial capital or all uppercase letters, but this is not mandatory. The names used in a `typedef` statement can be any name that conforms to C++'s identifier naming rules.

In either case the allocated storage area comes from the computer's free storage area.[3] In a similar manner and of more usefulness is the dynamic allocation of a user-defined object. For example, the declaration

```
Customer *anotherCust;
```

declares `anotherCust` as a pointer variable that can be used to store the address of a `Customer` object. The actual creation of a new `Customer` object is completed by the statement

```
anotherCust = new Customer;
```

This statement both creates a new `Customer` object and stores the address of the first reserved memory location into the pointer variable `anotherCust`. Program 11.6 illustrates this sequence of code within the context of a complete program.

---

3 The free storage area of a computer is formally referred to as the *heap.* The heap consists of unallocated memory that can be allocated to a program, as requested, while the program is running.

PROGRAMMER'S NOTES

Pointers versus References

The distinguishing characteristic of a pointer, either as a formal parameter or variable, is that *every pointer contains a value that is an address.* Whereas a pointer is a variable or parameter *whose contents is an address,* a reference is *an address.* As such, a reference can be thought of as a named constant, where the constant is a value that happens to be a valid memory address.

From an operational viewpoint, pointers are much more flexible than references. This is because a pointer's contents can be manipulated in much the same manner as any other variable's value. For example, if `foo` is a pointer variable, the statement `cout << foo;` displays the value stored in the pointer variable. This is identical to the operation of displaying the value of an integer or floating point variable. That the value stored in a pointer happens to be an address is irrelevant as far as `cout` is concerned.

The disadvantage of pointers is that their very flexibility makes them more complicated to understand and use than reference parameters or variables. Because references can be used only as named addresses, they are easier to use. Thus, when the compiler encounters a reference it automatically dereferences the address to obtain the contents of the address. This is not the case with pointers. If you use a pointer's name, as we have noted, you access the pointer's contents. To correctly dereference the address stored in a pointer you must explicitly use C++'s dereference operator, *, in front of the pointer name. This informs the compiler that what you want is the item *whose address is in the pointer variable.*

PROGRAM 11.6

```
#include <iostream.h>
#include <iomanip.h>
#include <time.h>
```

```
// Customer class declaration
// precondition: srand() must be called once before any function methods
// postcondition: arrive(void) returns a random integer between 1 and 15
//              : gallons(void) returns a random integer between 3 and 20

#include <stdlib.h>
class Customer
{
  public:
    Customer(void) {cout << "\n**** A new customer has been created ****" << endl;};
    ~Customer(void) {cout << "!!!! This customer object has been deleted !!!!" << endl;};
    int arrive(void) {return(1 + rand() % 16);};
    int gallons(void) {return(3 + rand() % 21);};
};
```

(continued next page)

(continued from previous page)

```
int main()
{
  Customer *anotherCust;   // declare 1 pointer to an object of type Customer
  int i, howMany;
  int interval, request;

  cout << "Enter the number of customers to be created: ";
  cin  >> howMany;
  srand(time(NULL));
  for(i = 1; i <= howMany; i++)
  {
    // create a new object of type Customer
    anotherCust = new Customer;

    // use the pointer to access the member functions
    interval = anotherCust->arrive();
    request = anotherCust->gallons();
    cout << "The arrival interval is " << interval << " minutes" << endl;
    cout << "The new customer requests " << request << " gallons" << endl;
    cout << "The memory address of this object is: "<< anotherCust << endl;

      // delete anotherCust; (see page 636 for an explanation)
  }

  return 0;
}
```

Before looking at a sample output produced by Program 11.6 and analyzing how this output was produced by the `main()` function, consider the declaration of the `Customer` class. Notice that we have included an inline constructor function to display the message

```
**** A new customer has been created ****
```

whenever an object is created and an inline destructor function to display the message

```
!!!! This customer object has been deleted !!!!
```

whenever an object is deleted. These messages are used only to help you monitor the creation and deletion of an object when the program is executed. Also notice that we have not included the `srand()` function call within the constructor as we did in our

FIGURE 11.12

Sample output produced using Program 11.6

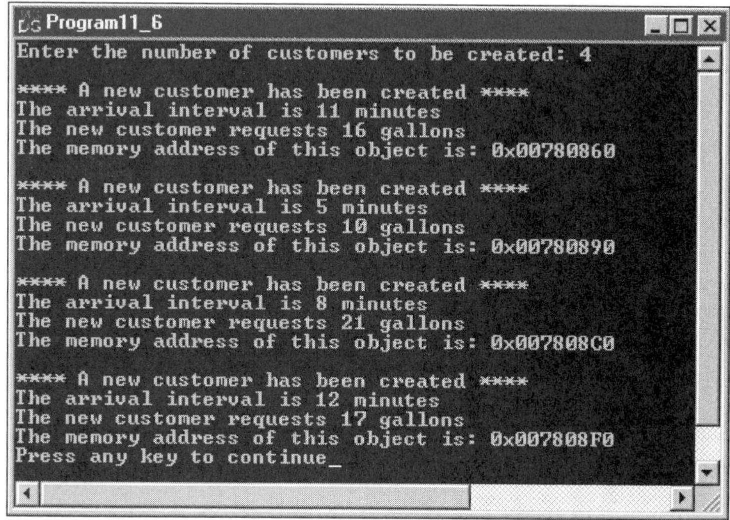

original `Customer` class implementation presented in Section 10.4. Rather, we have made the calling of `srand()` a precondition to using any member function.

Program11_6
Enter the number of customers to be created: 4
**** A new customer has been created ****
The arrival interval is 11 minutes
The new customer requests 16 gallons
The memory address of this object is: 0x00780860
**** A new customer has been created ****
The arrival interval is 5 minutes
The new customer requests 10 gallons
The memory address of this object is: 0x00780890
**** A new customer has been created ****
The arrival interval is 8 minutes
The new customer requests 21 gallons
The memory address of this object is: 0x007808C0
**** A new customer has been created ****
The arrival interval is 12 minutes
The new customer requests 17 gallons
The memory address of this object is: 0x007808F0
Press any key to continue_

The primary reason for not including an `srand()` call in the `Customer` class constructor is that inclusion of this function would mean that it is called each time an object is created, when a single initial call to `srand()` is really all that is necessary for any single program execution. For large simulation runs in which hundreds or even thousands of `Customer` objects can be created and deleted, execution times can be excessive, and the savings in run times by careful placement of both function calls and calculations within repetitive loops can be dramatic.

Figure 11.12 shows a sample output produced by Program 11.6.

As illustrated by this output, we can make the decision as to how many objects are to be created by Program 11.6 while the program is executing. Figure 11.13 illustrates the allocation of memory space corresponding to this sample output just before the program completes execution.

FIGURE 11.13

Memory allocation produced by the sample execution of Program 11.6

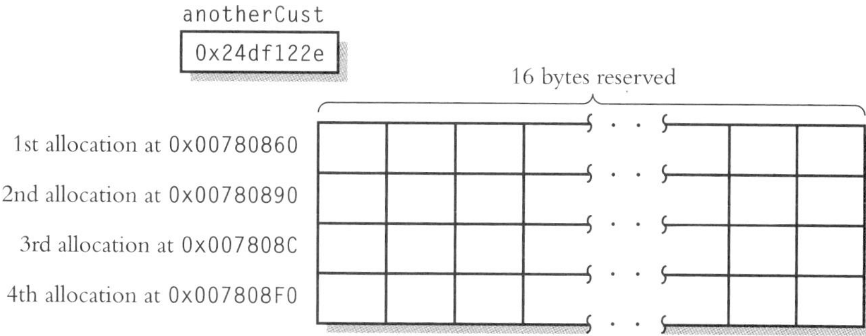

Now look at the `main()` function to see how this output was produced. First notice that new `Customer` objects are created using the statements:

```
Customer *anotherCust;
anotherCust = new Customer;
```

The first statement defines a single pointer variable named `anotherCust`. Each time the second statement is executed, a new object is created and its address is stored in the `anotherCust` variable (the old address is lost).[4] Notice also that this stored address can be displayed by inserting the pointer variable name in the `cout` stream as we have done in the last executable statement contained within `main()`'s body. Because the contents of a pointer variable is a value, this value, even though it happens to be an address, can be displayed using the `cout` stream. Each time the value is displayed, it simply represents the current address stored in the variable. Notice also that the last line in `main()`'s body comments out the statement `delete anotherCust;`. This was done intentionally to force each newly created object into a new memory area. If a `delete` had been used to release the previously allocated block of storage, the operating system would simply provide the same locations right back for the next allocation. In this case you would not see the assigned address change while the programming is executing.[5] In practice, however, it is very important to delete dynamically created objects when their usefulness ends. As you can see by the sample output, if you don't, the computer system starts to effectively "eat up" available memory space.

Finally, notice the notation used to access the member functions of each dynamically created object. For example, the notation `anotherCust->arrival()` calls the `arrival()` function of the object whose address resides in the pointer variable `anotherCust`. Because dynamically created objects do not have symbolic names, they can be accessed only using the address information contained within the pointer variable. This can be done either by using the notation `pointerName->functionName()` shown in Program 11.6 or by using the equivalent notation `(*pointerName).functionName()`.

Example 2: Dynamic Gas Pump Simulation

In the multiobject simulation presented in Section 10.4, the same customer object was used repeatedly to simulate multiple customer arrivals. The current example shows how to write a simulation that dynamically creates new and different customer objects as

---

4 In practice, the object whose address is currently in the pointer variable would have been deleted prior to reusing the pointer variable, so that the address being overwritten would be of no use anyway.

---

5 The allocated storage would automatically be returned to the heap when the program has completed execution. It is, however, good practice to formally restore the allocated storage back to the heap using `delete` when the memory is no longer needed. This is especially true for larger programs that make numerous requests for additional storage areas.

they are needed and then deletes each object once its task is completed. To accomplish this you will need the information presented on dynamic memory allocation in the previous example.

Solution All dynamic allocations require that at least one pointer variable be made available to store the starting address of the newly allocated object. The `new` operator is used to actually reserve the memory space and then returns the starting address, which should be assigned to the pointer variable. For example, the declaration

```
Customer *anotherCust;
```

declares a pointer variable named `anotherCust` that can be used to store an address of a `Customer` object.[6] Once a pointer has been defined, the pointer name can be used in an assignment statement such as `anotherCust = new Customer;` that both allocates new storage and stores the starting address of the allocated area into the pointer variable.

For our simulation we will require both a `Pump` class and a `Customer` class. The `Customer` class, which is identical to that used in Program 11.6 except for the message displayed by the constructor, is:

```
#include <stdlib.h>

// Customer class declaration
// precondition: srand() must be called once before any function methods
// postcondition: arrive(void) returns a random integer between 1 and 15
//               : gallons(void) returns a random integer between 3 and 20

class Customer
{
  public:
     Customer(void) {cout << "\n**** A new customer has arrived ****" << endl;};
    ~Customer(void) {cout << "!!!! The customer has departed !!!!" << endl;};
    int arrive(void) {return(1 + rand() % 16);};
    int gallons(void) {return(3 + rand() % 21);};
};
```

For convenience we assume that this class declaration is stored as `CUSTOM_ 1.H` in the `CLASSES` directory of a `C` drive.

---

6 It should be noted that the width of all addresses is the same, be they addresses of `Customer` objects, `Pump` objects, or `integer` variables. Typically an address is either 16 or 32 bits wide. The reason for specifying the type of object is to inform the compiler of how many bytes must be accessed when the address is dereferenced. The actual allocation of memory for the object depends on how many data members it has, plus a fixed minimum size, which is typically 8 or 16 bytes.

The Pump class is exactly the same as that developed in Section 10.4 for Program 10.9 and is repeated below for convenience.

```
// class declaration

class Pump
{
  private:
    float amtInTank;
    float price;
  public:
    Pump(float = 500.0, float = 1.00);   // constructor
    void values(void);
    void request(float);
};

// implementation section

Pump::Pump(float start, float todaysPrice)
{
  amtInTank = start;
  price = todaysPrice;
}

void Pump::values(void)
{
     cout << setiosflags(ios::fixed) << setiosflags(ios::showpoint)
          << setprecision(2);
  cout << "The gas tank has " << amtInTank << " gallons of gas." << endl;
  cout << "The price per gallon of gas is $" << price << endl;

  return;
}

void Pump::request(float pumpAmt)
{
  float pumped;

  if (amtInTank >= pumpAmt)
     pumped = pumpAmt;
```

```
  else
     pumped = amtInTank;

  amtInTank -= pumped;

  cout << setiosflags(ios::fixed) << setiosflags(ios::showpoint)
       << setprecision(2);
  cout << "    Gallons requested: " << pumpAmt << endl;
  cout << "    Gallons pumped: " << pumped << endl;
  cout << "    Gallons remaining in tank: " << amtInTank << endl;
  cout << "    The price of the sale is $" << (pumped * price) << endl;

  return;
}
```

We assume that this class has been thoroughly tested and has been stored on a `C` drive in the `CLASSES` directory as `PUMP.H`. By using the preexisting classes, `Pump` and `Customer`, all that remains to be developed is the control logic within the `main()` function for correctly creating `Pump` and `Customer` objects, and controlling the interaction between objects by appropriately activating class methods. A suitable control structure for `main()` is described by the algorithm

Create a Pump object with the required initial gallons of gas
Display the values in the initialized Pump
Set the elapsed time to 0

Create the first Customer object
Obtain the Customer's interval arrival time
Add the arrival time to the elapsed time

While the elapsed time does not exceed the simulation time
    Display the total time
    Obtain a Customer request for gas
    Activate the Pump with the request
    Delete this Customer object

    Create a new Customer // next arrival
    Obtain the Customer's interval arrival time
    Add the arrival time to the elapsed time

EndWhile

Display a message that the simulation is over

The C++ code corresponding to our design is illustrated in Program 11.7.

PROGRAM 11.7

```
#include <iostream.h>
#include <iomanip.h>
#include <time.h>
```

```
// precondition: srand() must be called once before any CUSTOMER methods are used
// postcondition: arrive(void) returns a random integer between 1 and 15
//               : gallons(void) returns a random integer between 3 and 20
#include <C:\CLASSES\PUMP.H>      // note use of full path name here
#include <C:\CLASSES\CUSTOM_1.H>  // again - a full path name is used

const float SIMTIME = .5;         // simulation time in hours
const int MINUTES = 60;           // number of minutes in an hour
const float AMT_IN_TANK = 300;    // initial gallons in the tank
const float TODAYS_PRICE = 1.25;  // price-per-gallon
```

```
int main()
{
  Pump a(AMT_IN_TANK, TODAYS_PRICE);   // declare 1 object of type Pump
  Customer *anotherCust;  // declare 1 pointer to an object of type Customer
  int totalTime = 0;
  int idleTime;
  int amtRequest;
  int SimMinutes;  // simulation time in minutes

  SimMinutes = SIMTIME * MINUTES;
  cout << "\nStarting a new simulation - simulation time is "
       << SimMinutes << " minutes" << endl;
  a.values();

  srand(time(NULL));

  // create a new object of type Customer
  anotherCust = new Customer;

  // get the customer's arrival time
  idleTime = anotherCust->arrive();
  totalTime += idleTime;

  while (totalTime <= SimMinutes)
  {
```

(continued next page)

(continued from previous page)

```
    cout << "The idle time is " << idleTime << " minutes" << endl
         << "   and we are " << totalTime
         << " minutes into the simulation." << endl;
    amtRequest = anotherCust->gallons();
    a.request(float(amtRequest));

    // delete this Customer
    delete anotherCust;

    // create the next Customer
    anotherCust = new Customer;
    // get the next arrival
    idleTime = anotherCust->arrive();
    totalTime += idleTime;
  }
  cout << "The idle time is " << idleTime << " minutes." << endl
       << "\nAs the total time now exceeds the simulation time, " << endl
       << "   this simulation run is over." << endl;

  return 0;
}
```

By itself, the `main()` function in Program 11.7 uses a straightforward `while` loop that creates and deletes `Customer` objects within a simulated time span of `SIMTIME` hours. Within the program the `Pump` idle time corresponds to the time between customer arrivals. Notice that the notation used to dereference the address in the pointer variable `anotherCust` and activate the `arrival()` method is `anotherCust->arrival()`. As an alternative to this notation, the notation `(*anotherCust).arrival()` could have been used. The output of a sample run is shown below.[7]

```
Starting a new simulation - simulation time is 30 minutes
The gas tank has 300.00 gallons of gas.
The price per gallon of gas is $1.25
```

---

7 Because the output produced by the simulation can exceed the size allocated to a standard console window, an alternative is to call the executable program from a DOS window and redirect the output to a file; for example using the DOS command `pgm11.7 > t1`. This assumes that the executable file name is `pgm11.7.cpp` and that the output will be placed in a file named `t1`.

```
**** A new customer has arrived ****
The idle time is 11 min. and we are 11 min. into the simulation.
    Gallons requested: 5.00
    Gallons pumped: 5.00
    Gallons remaining in tank: 295.00
    The price of the sale is $6.25
!!!! The customer has departed !!!!

**** A new customer has arrived ****
The idle time is 13 min. and we are 24 min. into the simulation.
    Gallons requested: 8.00
    Gallons pumped: 8.00
    Gallons remaining in tank: 287.00
    The price of the sale is $10.00
!!!! The customer has departed !!!!

**** A new customer has arrived ****
The idle time is 11 min.
As the total time now exceeds the simulation time,
   this simulation run is over.
```

EXERCISES 11.4

1. a. Describe what a pointer is.

   b. For each of the following pointer declarations, identify the name of the pointer variable and the type of object that will be accessed when the address in the pointer variable is dereferenced.

   ```
   Customer *a;
   Pump *pointer1;
   Pump *addrOfaPump;
   int *addrOfanInt;
   float *b;
   ```

   c. If the asterisks, *, were removed from the declarations in Exercise 1b, what would the names immediately preceding the semicolon represent?

2. a. Describe what dynamic allocation of memory is.

   b. Describe the process of creating a dynamically allocated object. Specifically, discuss the roles of a pointer variable and the `new` operator in creating a dynamically allocated object.

   c. Discuss the importance of deleting dynamically allocated objects and what can happen if deletion is not used.

3. Programs 9.5 and 11.7 both produce a valid simulation. The type of simulation produced by each program is essentially the same. Discuss the advantages and disadvantages of using multiple `Customer` objects in Program 11.7 as opposed to using a single `Customer` object in Program 9.5.

4. **a.** Modify Program 11.7 to use the `Customer` class defined in Program 9.5 (i.e., put the `srand()` function call back into the constructor function). Now run the program and notice that the same arrival times are obtained for each newly created customer object. What do you think is occurring to produce this effect?

   b. To correct for the problem noticed in Exercise 4a, place the following loop in the constructor function. (*Note:* Due to the loop, the constructor can no longer be written as an inline function.)

```
for(int i = 0; i < 500000; i++);
```

   What does this loop accomplish? Run the program and notice that the randomness of customer arrivals has been restored. What do you notice about the time it takes to execute a complete simulation. Comment about the efficiency of your modified program as compared to Program 11.7.

11.5 Pointers as Class Members

As we saw in Section 9.1, a class can contain any C++ data type.[8] Thus, the inclusion of a pointer variable in a class should not seem surprising. For example, the class declaration:

```
// class declaration

class Test
{
  private:
    int idNum;
    double *ptPay;
  public:
    Test(int = 0, double * = NULL); // constructor
    void setvals(int, double *);    // access function
    void display();                 // access function
};
```

8 The material in this section requires a good grounding in pointer fundamentals. As such, it should be read after the material in Section 13.1 is covered.

declares a class consisting of two member variables and three member functions. The first member variable is an integer variable named idNum, and the second instance variable is a pointer named ptPay, which is a pointer variable to a double precision number. We will use the setvals() member function to store values into the private member variables and the display() function for output purposes. The implementation of these two functions along with the constructor function Test() is contained in the class implementation section:

```
// implementation section

Test::Test(int id, double *pt)
{
  idNum = id;
  ptPay = pt;
}

void Test::setvals(int a, double *b)
{
  idNum = a;
  ptPay = b;

  return;
}

void Test::display()
{
  cout << "\nEmployee number " << idNum
       << " was paid $"
       << setiosflags(ios::fixed)
       << setiosflags(ios::showpoint)
       << setw(6) << setprecision(2)
       << *ptPay << endl;

  return;
}
```

In this implementation, the Test() constructor initializes its idNum data member to its first parameter and its pointer member to its second parameter; if no arguments are provided when the function is called, these variables are initialized to a 0 and NULL, respectively. The display function simply outputs the value pointed to by its pointer member. As defined in this implementation, the setvals() function is very similar to the constructor and is used to alter member values after the object has been declared: the function's first parameter (an integer) is assigned to idNum and its second parameter (an address) is assigned to ptPay.

The main() function in Program 11.8 illustrates the use of the Test class by first creating one object, named emp, which is initialized using the constructor's default arguments. The setvals() function is then used to assign the value 12345 and the address of the variable pay to the data members of this emp object. Finally, the display() function is used to display the value whose address is stored in emp.ptPay. As illustrated by the program, the pointer member of an object is used like any other pointer variable.

PROGRAM 11.8

```
#include <iostream.h>
#include <iomanip.h>

// class declaration

class Test
{
  private:
    int idNum;
    double *ptPay;
  public:
    Test(int = 0, double * = NULL); // constructor
    void setvals(int, double *);    // access function
    void display();                 // access function
};

// implementation section

Test::Test(int id, double *pt)
{
  idNum = id;
  ptPay = pt;
}

void Test::setvals(int a, double *b)
{
  idNum = a;
  ptPay = b;

  return;
}
```

(continued next page)

(continued from previous page)

```
void Test::display()
{
  cout << "\nEmployee number " << idNum
       << " was paid $"
       << setiosflags(ios::fixed)
       << setiosflags(ios::showpoint)
       << setw(6) << setprecision(2)
       << *ptPay << endl;

  return;
}
```

```
int main()
{
  Test emp;
  double pay = 456.20;

  emp.setvals(12345, &pay);
  emp.display();

  return 0;
}
```

The output produced by executing Program 11.8 is shown in Figure 11.14.

Figure 11.15 illustrates the relationship between the data members of the `emp` object defined in Program 11.8 and the variable named `pay`. The value assigned to `emp.idNum` is the number 12345 and the value assigned to pay is 456.20. The address of the `pay` variable is assigned to the object member `emp.ptPay`. Because this member has been defined as a pointer to a double precision number, placing the address of the double precision variable

FIGURE 11.14

Output displayed by Program 11.8

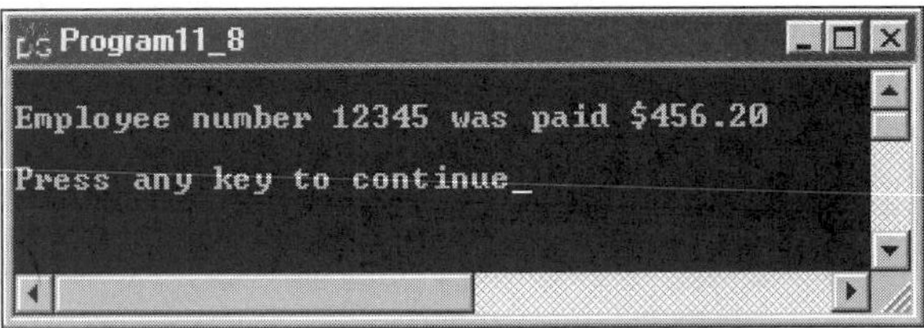

FIGURE 11.15

Storing an address in a data member

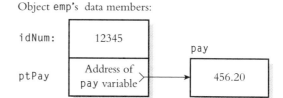

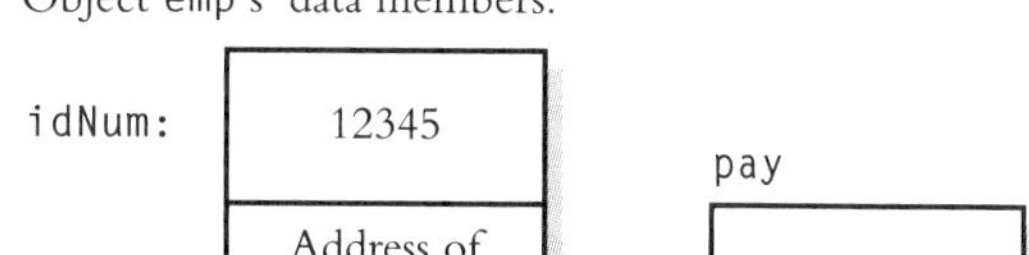

pay in it is a correct use of this data member. Although the pointer defined in Program 11.8 has been used in a rather trivial manner, the program does illustrate the concept of including a pointer in a class.

Clearly it would be more efficient to include the pay variable directly as a data member of the Test class rather than using a pointer to it. In some cases, however, pointers are very advantageous. For example, assume we need to store a list of book titles. Rather than use a fixed length character array as a data member to hold each title, we could include a pointer member to a character array, and then allocate the correct size array for each book title as it is needed. This arrangement is illustrated in Figure 11.16, which shows two objects, a and b, each of which consists of a single pointer data member. As depicted, object a's pointer contains the address of ("points to") a character array containing the characters DOS Primer, and object b's pointer contains the address of a character array containing the characters A Brief History of Western Civilization.

FIGURE 11.16

Two objects containing pointer data members

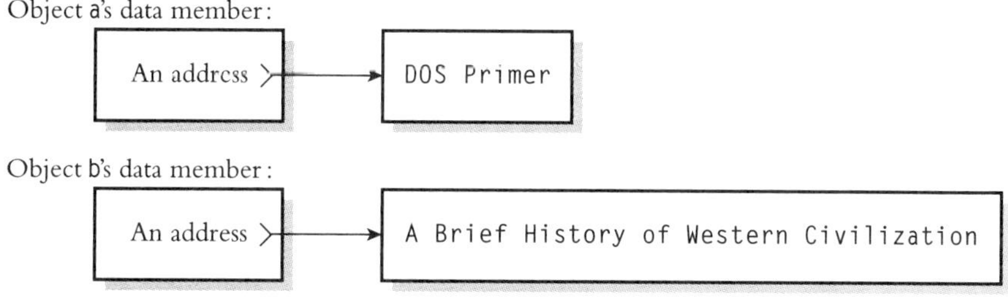

A suitable class declaration section for a list of book titles that is to be accessed as illustrated in Figure 11.16 follows.

```
// class declaration
class Book
{
  private:
    char *title;   // a pointer to a book title
```

(continued next page)

(*continued from previous page*)

```
  public:
    Book(char * = '\0');  // constructor
    void showtitle(void); // display the title
};
```

The definition of the constructor function, `Book()`, and the display function, `showtitle()`, are defined in the implementation section as:

```
// class implementation

Book::Book(char *name)
{
  title = new char[strlen(name)+1];  // allocate memory
  strcpy(title,name);                // store the string
}

void Book::showtitle(void)
{
  cout << title << endl;
}
```

The body of the `Book()` constructor contains two statements. The first statement, `title = new char[strlen(name)+1];`, performs two tasks: first, the right-hand side of the statement allocates enough storage for the length of the name argument plus one, to accommodate the end of string null character, `'\0'`. Next, the address of the first allocated character position is assigned to the pointer variable title. These operations are illustrated in Figure 11.17. The second statement in the constructor copies the characters in the name argument to the newly created memory allocation. If no argument is passed to the constructor, then `title` is the empty string; that is, `title` is set to `NULL`. Program 11.9 uses this class definition within the context of a complete program.

FIGURE 11.17

Allocating memory for `title = new char[strlen(name)+1]`

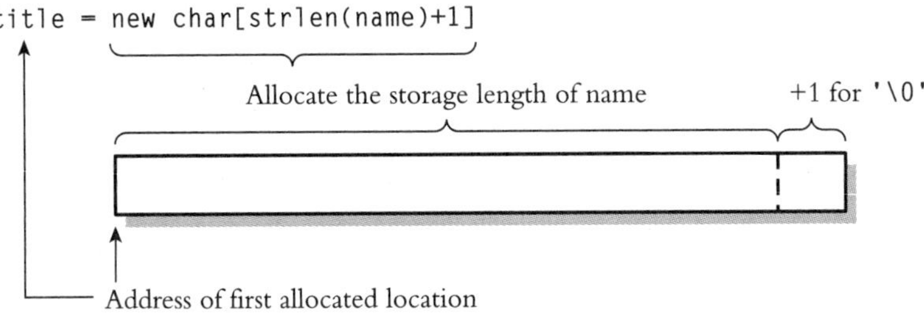

PROGRAM 11.9

```
#include <iostream.h>
#include <string.h>

// class declaration

class Book
{
  private:
    char *title;   // a pointer to a book title
  public:
    Book(char * = '\0');   // constructor
    void showtitle(void);  // display the title
};

// class implementation

Book::Book(char *strng)
{
  title = new char[strlen(strng)+1];  // allocate memory
  strcpy(title,strng);                // store the string
}

void Book::showtitle(void)
{
  cout << title << endl;

  return;
}

int main()
{
  Book  book1("DOS Primer");   // create 1st title
  Book  book2("A Brief History of Western Civilization");  // 2nd title

  book1.showtitle();   // display book1's title
  book2.showtitle();   // display book2's title

  return 0;
}
```

The output produced by Program 11.9 is shown in Figure 11.18.

FIGURE 11.18

Output display produced by Program 11.9

Assignment Operators and Copy Constructors Reconsidered[9]

When a class contains no pointer data members, the compiler-provided defaults for the assignment operator and copy constructor adequately perform their intended tasks. Both of these defaults provide a member-by-member operation that produces no adverse side effects. This is not the case when a pointer member is included in the class declaration. Let's see why this is so.

Figure 11.19a illustrates the arrangement of pointers and allocated memory produced by Program 11.9 just before it completes execution. Let's now assume that we insert the assignment statement `book2 = book1;` before the closing brace of the `main()` function. Because we have not defined an assignment operation, the compiler's default assignment is used. As we know, this assignment produces a memberwise copy (that is, `book2.title = book1.title`) and means that the address in `book1`'s pointer is copied into `book2`'s pointer. Thus, both pointers now "point to" the character array containing the characters `DOS Primer`, and the address of `A Brief History of Western Civilization` has been lost. This situation is illustrated in Figure 11.19b.

The memberwise assignment illustrated in Figure 11.19b results in the loss of the address of `A Brief History of Western Civilization`, but there is no way for the program to release this memory storage (it will be cleaned up by the operating system when the program terminates). Worse, however, is the case where a destructor attempts to release the memory. Once the memory pointed to by `book2` is released (again, referring to Figure 11.19b), `book1` points to an undefined memory location. If this memory area is subsequently reallocated before `book1` is deleted, the deletion will release memory that another other object is using. The results of this can wreak havoc on a program.

What is usually desired is that the book titles themselves be copied, and their pointers left alone, as shown in Figure 11.19c. This situation also removes all of the side effects of a subsequent deletion of any `Book` object. To achieve the desired assignment, we must explicitly write our own assignment operator. A suitable definition for this operator is:

---

9 The material in this section pertains to the problems that occur when using the default assignment, copy constructor, and destructor functions with classes containing pointer members, and how to overcome these problems. On first reading, this section can be omitted without loss of subject continuity.

```
void Book::operator=(Book& oldbook)
{
  if(oldbook.title != NULL)  // check that it exists
    delete(title);           // release existing memory
  title = new char[strlen(oldbook.title) + 1];  // allocate new memory
  strcpy(title, oldbook.title);  // copy the title
}
```

FIGURE 11.19a

Before the assignment `book2 = book1;`

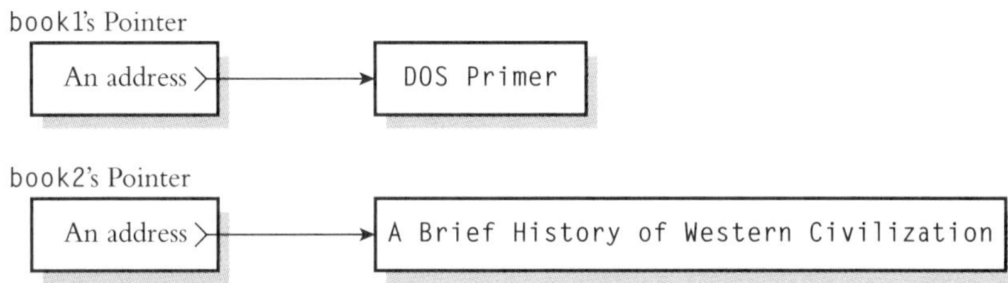

FIGURE 11.19b

Effect produced by default assignment

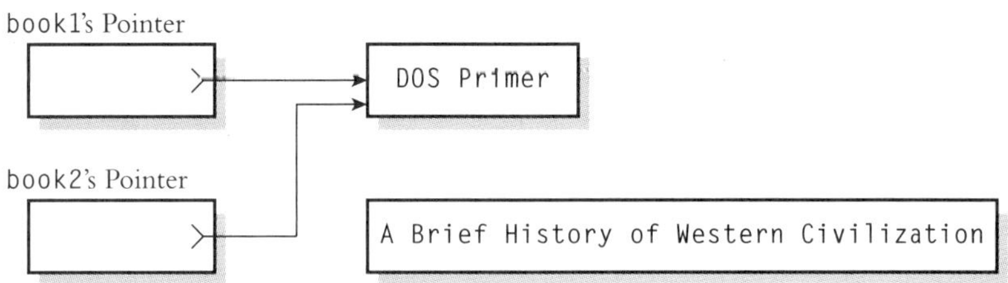

FIGURE 11.19c

Desired effect

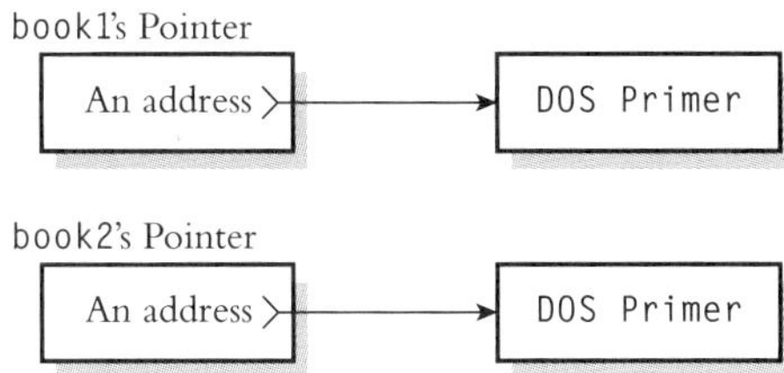

This definition cleanly releases the memory previously allocated for the object and then allocates sufficient memory to store the copied title.

The problems associated with the default assignment operator also exist with the default copy constructor, because it also performs a memberwise copy. As with assignment, these problems are avoided by writing our own copy constructor. For our Book class such a constructor is:

```
Book::Book(Book& oldbook)
{
  title = new char[strlen(oldbook.title) + 1];  // allocate new memory
  strcpy(title, oldbook.title);  // copy the title
}
```

Comparing the body of this copy constructor to the assignment operator's function body reveals they are identical except for the deallocation of memory performed by the assignment operator. This is because the copy constructor does not have to release the existing array prior to allocating a new one because none exists when the constructor is called.

EXERCISES 11.5

1. Include the copy constructor and assignment operator presented in this section in Program 11.9 and run the program to verify their operation.

2. Write a suitable destructor function for Program 11.9.

3. a. Construct a class named `Car` that contains the following four data members: a floating point variable named `engineSize`, a character variable named `bodyStyle`, an integer variable named `colorCode`, and a character pointer named `vinPtr` to a vehicle identification code. The function members should include a constructor that provides default values of 0 for each numeric data member, an `'X'` for each character variable, and a `NULL` for each pointer; a display function that prints the engine size, body style, color code, and vehicle identification number; and an assignment operator that performs a memberwise assignment between two `Car` objects that correctly handles the pointer member.

b. Include the program written for Exercise 5a in a working C++ program that creates two car objects, the second of which is assigned the values of the first object.

4. Modify Program 11.9 to include the assignment statement `b = a`, then run the modified program to assess the error messages, if any, that occur.

5. Using Program 11.9 as a start, write a program that creates five `Book` objects. The program should allow the user to enter the five book titles interactively and then display the titles entered.

6. Modify the program written in Exercise 5 so that the program sorts the entered book titles in alphabetical order before it displays them. (*Hint:* You will have to define a sort routine for the titles.)

11.6 Common Programming Errors

The common programming errors associated with inheritance, pointers, and dynamic memory allocation are the following:

1. Attempting to override a virtual function without using the same type and number of arguments as the original function.

2. Using the keyword `virtual` in the class implementation section. Functions are declared only as virtual in the class declaration section.

3. Using the default copy constructor and default assignment operators with classes containing pointer members. Because these default functions do a memberwise copy, the address in the source pointer is copied to the destination pointer. Usually this is not what is wanted, because both pointers end up pointing to the same memory area.

4. Forgetting that `this` is a pointer that must be dereferenced using either `*this` or `this->`.

11.7 Chapter Summary

1. **Inheritance** is the capability of deriving one class from another class. The initial class used as the basis for the derived class is referred to as the base, parent, or superclass. The derived class is referred to as either the derived, child, or subclass.

2. Base member functions can be overridden by derived member functions with the same name. The override function is simply an overloaded version of the base member function defined in the derived class.

3. **Polymorphism** is the capability of having the same function name invoke different responses based on the object making the function call. It can be accomplished using either override functions or virtual functions.

4. In **static binding** the determination of which function actually is invoked is made at compile time. In **dynamic binding** the determination is made at run time.

5. A **virtual function** specification designates that dynamic binding should take place. The specification is made in the function's prototype by placing the keyword `virtual` before the function's return type. Once a function has been declared as virtual it remains so for all derived classes as long as there is a continuous trail of function declarations through the derived chain of classes.

6. For each class only one copy of the member functions is retained in memory, and each object uses the same function. The address of the object's data members is provided to the member function by passing a hidden parameter, corresponding to the memory address of the selected object, to the member function. The address is passed in a special pointer parameter named `this`. The `this` pointer may be used explicitly by a member function to access a data member.

7. Pointers may be included as class data members. A pointer member adheres to the same rules as a pointer variable.

8. The default copy constructor and default assignment operators are typically not useful with classes containing pointer members. This is because these default functions do a memberwise copy in which the address in the source pointer is copied to the destination pointer, resulting in both pointers "pointing to" the same memory area. For these situations you must define your own copy constructor and assignment operator.

11.8 Knowing About: Modifying the Application Framework

In Section 10.8 we used the AppWizard to create a basic framework application. The skeleton application built by the wizard is always constructed using the classes and member functions provided by the MFC Library. Once the wizard has finished its work, it is up to you to customize the generated application framework by providing it with the specific functionality required by your specific application.[10]

Figure 11.20 shows the run-time GUI of the application framework program that was constructed as an SDI program. This particular SDI application, unlike the one produced in Section 10.8, was produced by the AppWizard by accepting all of the wizard's default options. We will now provide a general procedure for adding a dialog resource to this framework application. Once you have added the dialog, you can then add individual controls into the dialog using the information provided in Chapter 7.

---

10 We are using the terms *application framework* and *framework application* as synonyms for the skeleton application provided by the AppWizard. Although Microsoft uses the terminology "application framework," it is sometimes easier for beginning programmers to realize that what is being referred to is a no-frills, basic application that can be used as the starting point for a more complete application.

FIGURE 11.20

The executable GUI provided for an AppWizard SDI application framework

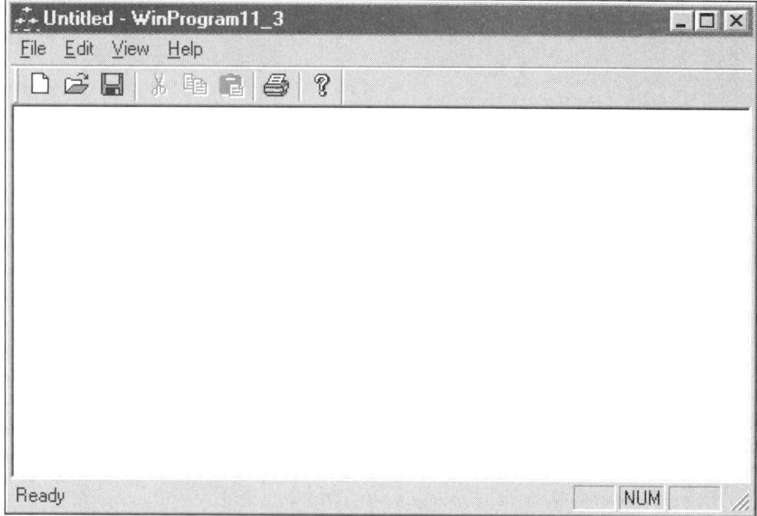

Figure 11.21 shows the design-time IDE for the GUI illustrated in Figure 11.20. Notice in Figure 11.21 that we have activated the `ResourceView` tab, expanded the resource hierarchy tree, and selected the `Dialog` folder. With this folder selected, pressing the right-mouse button will cause the context-sensitive menu shown in Figure 11.22 to be displayed.

FIGURE 11.21

The framework application's IDE

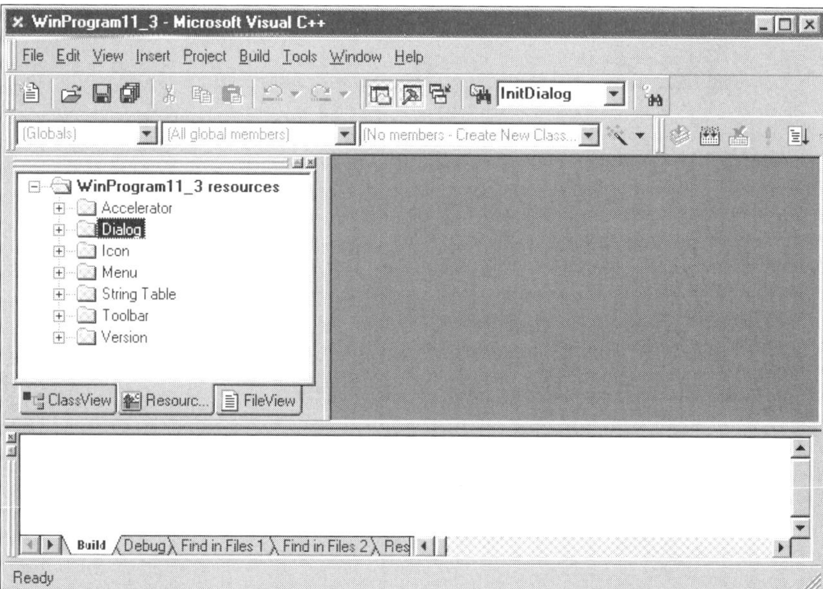

FIGURE 11.22

The context-sensitive dialog resource menu

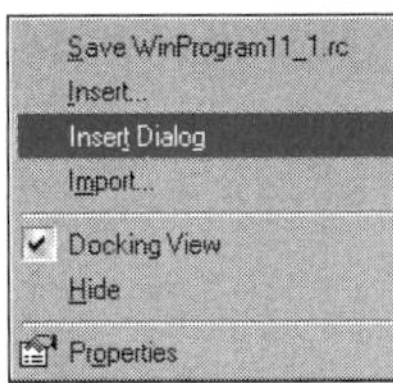

Clicking on the context-menu's `Insert Dialog` option (see Figure 11.22) will activate the resource editor with the new dialog, producing the IDE shown in Figure 11.23. Once this new dialog is visible, all that is necessary is to create a class to which we can attach the dialog, and then provide procedural code to activate the dialog's display at run time.

To create the required class, press the `Ctrl+W` keys to activate the Class Wizard (alternatively, you can use any of the other procedures described in Chapter 7 to activate this wizard). When you have done so, the `Adding a Class` dialog shown in Figure 11.24 will be displayed.

When the dialog box shown in Figure 11.24 is displayed, accept the default Radio button selection and press the `OK` button; doing so will cause the `New Class` Dialog box, shown in Figure 11.25 to appear. The only choice you should make with this dialog is the name of your new class. Since the base class for this dialog is an MFC class (which in this

FIGURE 11.23

The added dialog resource

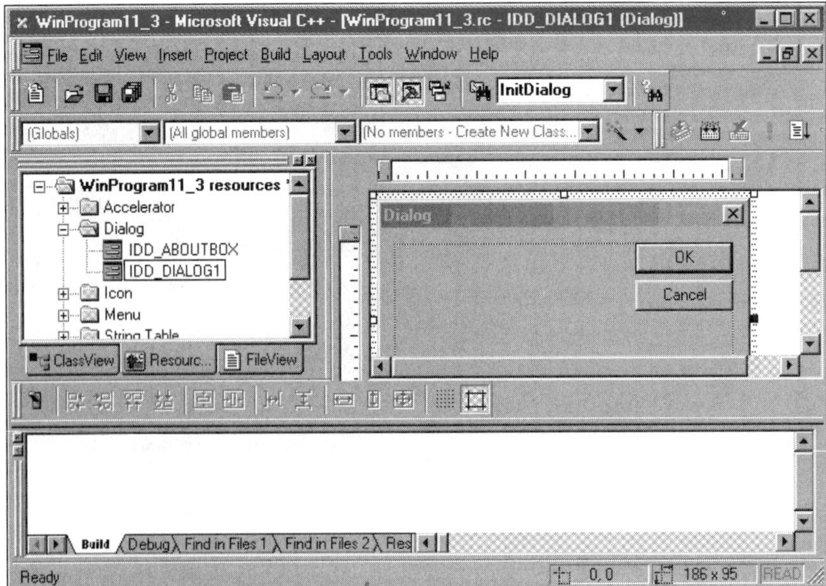

FIGURE 11.24

The Adding a Class dialog

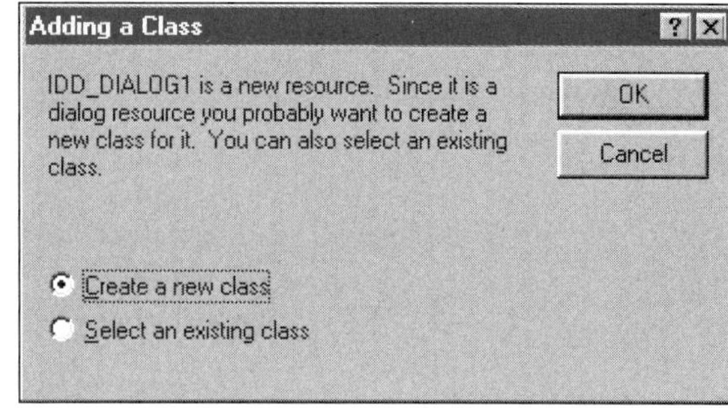

case is the CDialog class), the convention is to have the first letter of the derived class's name also begin with a capital C. We will honor this convention and name our new class `CFoo`. Here, the `C` is required by the convention, and the `Foo` can be replaced by any valid class name you wish to use.

Once you have named the new class and pressed the `OK` button for the dialog shown in Figure 11.25, a number of "behind the scenes" operations will take place. For our immediate purposes, however, only two of these operations are of importance. The first is that the Class Wizard will create a source file named `Foo.cpp`, into which a number of functions are created, and where we can add additional procedural code to the class. The second item that is automatically created is a header file, which is named `Foo.h`. In each case the name of the source file and the header file match our class name, without the leading capital C. Figure 11.26 shows the class hierarchy chart for the newly created class. Notice that the `CFoo` class is derived from the `CDialog` class, which itself is a subclass of `CWnd`.

FIGURE 11.25

Creating the `CFoo` class

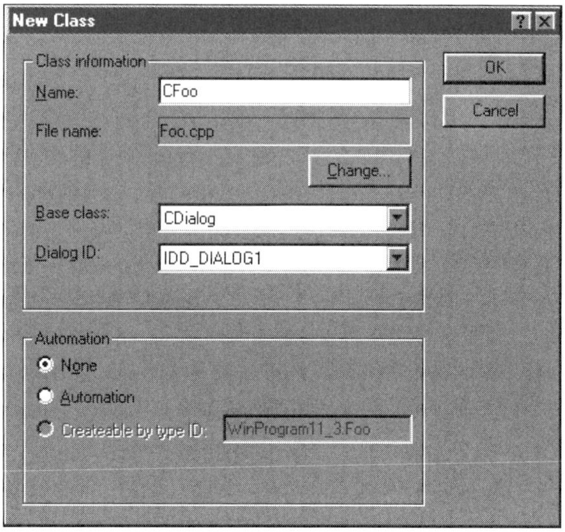

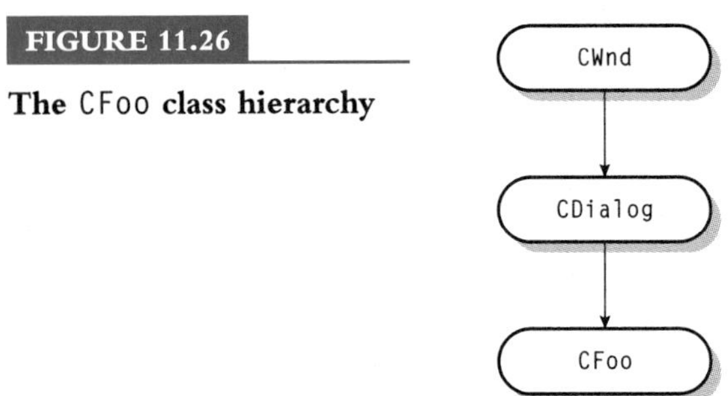

FIGURE 11.26

The CFoo class hierarchy

Once the new CFoo class is created, the Class Wizard dialog shown in Figure 11.27 will be displayed. At this point either press the Esc key or press the dialog's Edit Code button. Either of these actions will close the Class Wizard dialog and redisplay the IDE. When the IDE is visible, click on the ClassView tab and expand the file hierarchy tree to that shown in Figure 11.28.

Once you have located the InitInstance() method on the expanded ClassView hierarchy tree, double click on it, which will cause the code for this function to be loaded in the code editor and displayed in the editing area, as shown in Figure 11.28.

All that remains now is to add three lines of code to the InitInstance() function; one line before the function's header line and two lines immediately before its return statement, as shown on the next page.

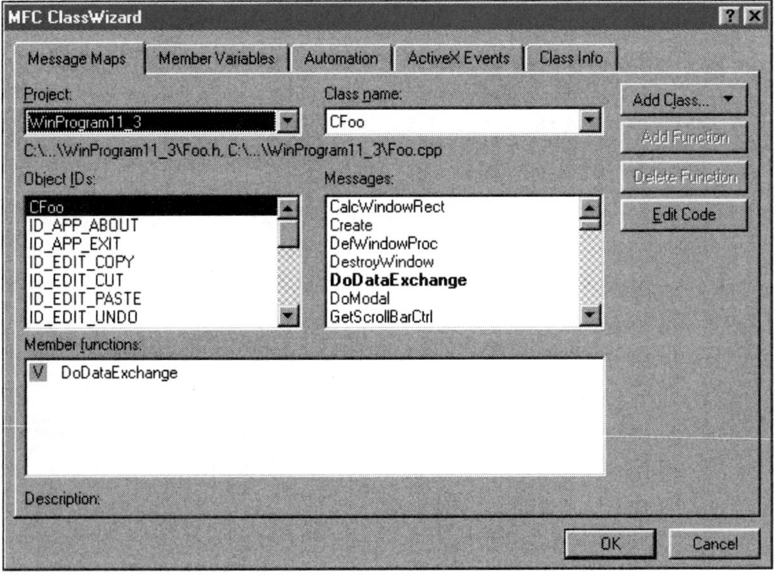

FIGURE 11.27

The Class Wizard dialog

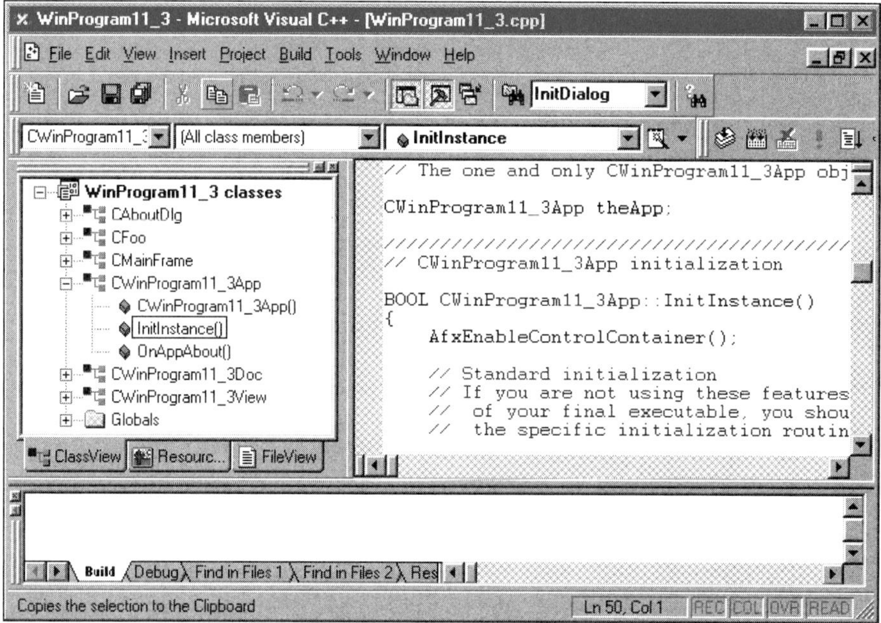

FIGURE 11.28

The IDE in ClassView

```
// CWinProgram11_3App initialization

#include "Foo.h"  // <--- This is the 1st line to add
BOOL CWinProgram11_1App::InitInstance()
{
      AfxEnableControlContainer();

      // Standard initialization
      // If you are not using these features and wish to reduce the size
      //  of your final executable, you should remove from the following
      //  the specific initialization routines you do not need.
            .
            .
            .
            .
            .
      CFoo *test = new CFoo;    // <--- This is the 2nd line to add
      test->DoModal();          // <--- This is the 3rd line to add
      return TRUE;
}
```

FIGURE 11.29

The executing application with the new Dialog box

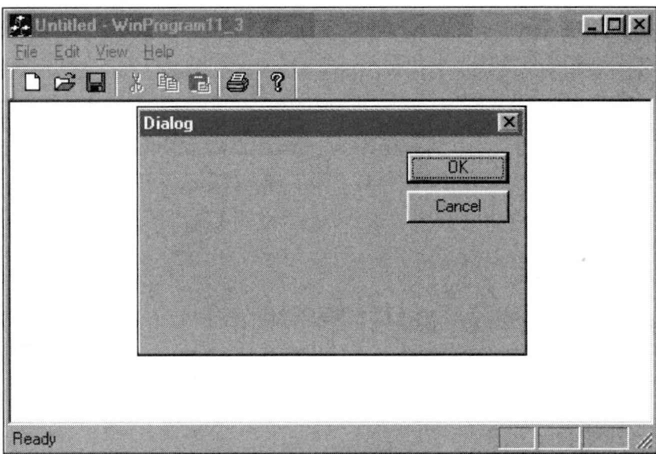

The first added line makes the `Foo.h` header file available to the `InitInstance()` function. The second line creates an object of type `CFoo`, which is our added dialog box, and defines a pointer to this new object. Finally, the third line causes the Dialog box to be displayed. If you now build and execute the program, the run-time window shown in Figure 11.29 is displayed. This is the same GUI previously produced by the application framework (see Figure 11.20), customized to include our new Dialog box.

PART THREE

DATA STRUCTURES

12 Arrays

The variables that we have used so far have all had a common characteristic: each variable could be used to store only a single value at a time. For example, although the variables `key`, `count`, and `grade` declared in the statements

```
char key;
int count;
float grade;
```

are of different data types, each variable can store only one value of the declared data type. These types of variables are called atomic variables. An **atomic variable,** which is also referred to as a **scalar variable,** is a variable whose value cannot be further subdivided or separated into a legitimate data type.

Frequently we have a set of values all of the same data type that form a logical group. For example, Figure 12.1 illustrates three groups of items. The first group is a list of five integer grades, the second group is a list of four character codes, and the last group is a list of six floating point prices.

FIGURE 12.1

Three lists of items

Grades	Codes	Prices
98	Z	10.96
87	C	6.43
92	K	2.58
79	L	.86
85		12.27
		6.39

A simple list containing individual items of the same data type is called a **one-dimensional array.** In this chapter we describe how one-dimensional arrays are declared, initialized, stored inside a computer, and used. Additionally, we explore the use of one-dimensional arrays with example programs, and then present the procedures for declaring and using multidimensional arrays.

12.1 One-Dimensional Arrays

A **one-dimensional array**, which is also referred to as either a **single-dimensional array** or a vector, is a list of related values with the same data type that is stored using a single group name.[1] In C++, as in other computer languages, the group name is referred to as the array name. For example, consider the list of grades illustrated in Figure 12.2.

All the grades in the list are integer numbers and must be declared as such. However, the individual items in the list do not have to be declared separately. The items in the list can be declared as a single unit and stored under a common variable name called the **array name.** For convenience, we will choose `grade` as the name for the list shown in Figure 12.2. To specify that `grade` is to store five individual integer values requires the declaration statement `int grade[5]`. Notice that this declaration statement gives the array (or list) name, the data type of the items in the array, and the number of items in the array. It is a specific example of the general array declaration statement having the syntax:

data-type array-name[number-of-items]

Good programming practice requires defining the number of items in the array as a constant before declaring the array. Thus, the previous array declaration for `grade` would, in practice, be declared using two statements, such as:

```
const int NUMELS = 5; // define a constant for the number of items
float grade[NUMELS];   // declare the array
```

1 Note that lists can be implemented in a variety of ways. An array is simply one implementation of a list in which all of the list elements are of the same type and each element is stored consecutively in a set of contiguous memory locations.

FIGURE 12.2

List of grades

Grades
98
87
92
79
85

Further examples of array declarations using this two-line syntax are:

```
const int NUMELS = 5;
int temp[NUMELS];

const int ARRAYSIZE = 4;
char code[ARRAYSIZE];

const int SIZE = 100;
float amount[SIZE];
```

In these declaration statements, each array is allocated sufficient memory to hold the number of data items given in the declaration statement. Thus, the array named `temp` has storage reserved for five integers, the array named `code` has storage reserved for four characters, and the array named `amount` has storage reserved for 100 floating point numbers. The constant identifiers, `NUMELS`, `ARRAYSIZE`, and `SIZE` are programmer-selected names.

Figure 12.3 illustrates the storage reserved for the `grade` and `code` arrays.

Each item in an array is called an **element** or **component** of the array. The individual elements stored in the arrays illustrated in Figure 12.3 are stored sequentially, with the

FIGURE 12.3

The `grade` and `code` arrays in memory

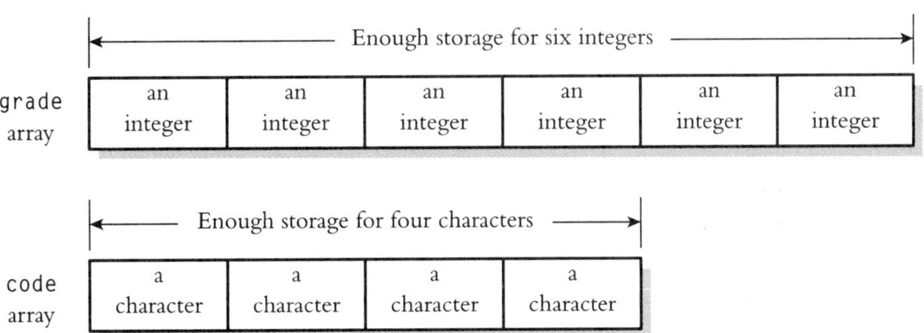

first array element stored in the first reserved location, the second element stored in the second reserved location, and so on until the last element is stored in the last reserved location. This contiguous storage allocation for the list is a key feature of arrays because it provides a simple mechanism for easily locating any single element in the list.

Because elements in the array are stored sequentially, any individual element can be accessed by giving the name of the array and the element's position. This position is called the element's **index** or **subscript** value (the two terms are synonymous). For a single-dimensional array, the first element has an index of 0, the second element has an index of 1, and so on. In C++, the array name and index of the desired element are combined by listing the index in braces after the array name. For example, given the declaration `int grade[5]`,

grade[0] refers to the first grade stored in the grade array
grade[1] refers to the second grade stored in the grade array
grade[2] refers to the third grade stored in the grade array
grade[3] refers to the fourth grade stored in the grade array
grade[4] refers to the fifth grade stored in the grade array

Figure 12.4 illustrates the grade array in memory with the correct designation for each array element. Each individual element is referred to as an **indexed variable** or a **subscripted variable** because both a variable name and an index or subscript value must be used to reference the element. Remember that the index or subscript value gives the *position* of the element in the array.

The subscripted variable `grade[0]` is read as "grade sub zero." This is a shortened way of saying "the grade array subscripted by zero," and distinguishes the first element in an array from an atomic variable that could be declared as `grade0`. Similarly, `grade[1]` is read as "grade sub one," `grade[2]` as "grade sub two," and so on.

Although it may seem unusual to reference the first element with an index of zero, doing so increases the computer's speed when it accesses array elements. Internally, unseen by the programmer, the computer uses the index as an offset from the array's starting position. As illustrated in Figure 12.5, the index tells the computer how many elements to skip, starting from the beginning of the array, to get to the desired element.

FIGURE 12.4

Identifying individual array elements

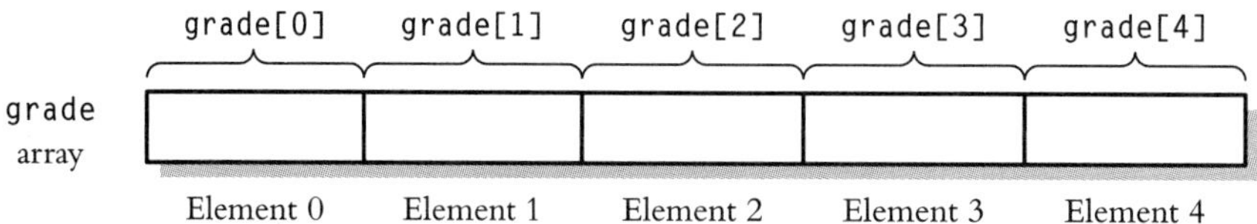

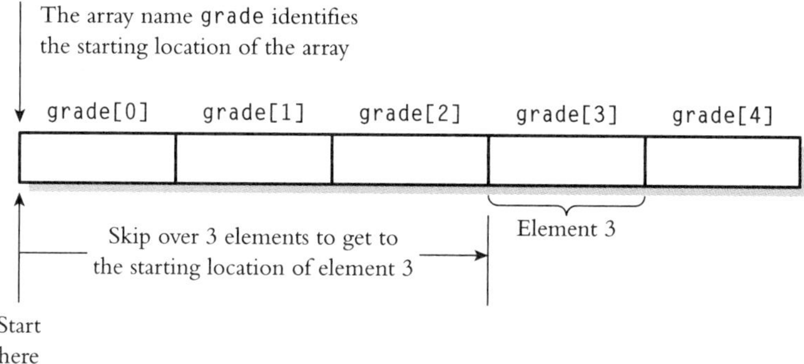

FIGURE 12.5

Accessing an individual array element—element 3

Subscripted variables can be used anywhere that scalar variables are valid. Examples using the elements of the grade array are:

```
grade[0] = 98;
grade[1] = grade[0] - 11;
grade[2] = 5 * grade[0];
grade[3] = 79;
grade[4] = (grade[1] + grade[2] - 3) / 2;
sum = grade[0] + grade[1] + grade[2] + grade[3] + grade[4];
```

The subscript contained within brackets need not be an integer constant; any expression that evaluates to an integer may be used as a subscript.[2] In each case, of course, the value of the expression must be within the valid subscript range defined when the array is declared. For example, assuming that i and j are int variables, the following subscripted variables are valid:

```
grade[i]
grade[2*i]
grade[j-i]
```

One extremely important advantage of using integer expressions as subscripts is that it allows sequencing through an array by using a loop. This makes statements such as

```
sum = grade[0] + grade[1] + grade[2] + grade[3] + grade[4];
```

2 Some compilers permit floating point variables as subscripts; in these cases, the floating point value is truncated to an integer value.

unnecessary. The subscript values in this statement can be replaced by a `for` loop counter to access each element in the array sequentially. For example, the code

```
sum = 0;                      // initialize the sum to zero
for (i = 0; i < 5; i++)
  sum = sum + grade[i];        // add in a grade
```

sequentially retrieves each array element and adds the element to `sum`. Here the variable `i` is used both as the counter in the `for` loop and as a subscript. As `i` increases by one each time through the loop, the next element in the array is referenced. The procedure for adding the array elements within the `for` loop is similar to the accumulation procedure we have used many times before.

The advantage of using a `for` loop to sequence through an array becomes apparent when working with larger arrays. For example, if the `grade` array contained 100 values rather than just 5, simply changing the number 5 to 100 in the `for` statement is sufficient to sequence through the 100 elements and add each grade to the sum.

As another example of using a `for` loop to sequence through an array, assume that we want to locate the maximum value in an array of 1,000 elements named `prices`. The procedure we will use to locate the maximum value is to assume initially that the first element in the array is the largest number. Then, as we sequence through the array, the maximum is compared to each element. When an element with a higher value is located, that element becomes the new maximum. The following code does the job.

```
const int NUMELS = 1000;

maximum = prices[0];            // set the maximum to element zero
for (i = 1; i < NUMELS; i++)    // cycle through the rest of the array
  if (prices[i] > maximum)      // compare each element to the maximum
    maximum = prices[i];        // capture the new high value
```

In this code the `for` statement consists of one `if` statement. The search for a new maximum value starts with element 1 of the array and continues through the last element. Each element is compared to the current maximum, and when a higher value is encountered it becomes the new maximum.

Input and Output of Array Values

Individual array elements can be assigned values interactively using the `cin` object. Examples of individual data entry statements are:

```
cin >> grade[0];
cin >> grade[1] >> grade[2] >> grade[3];
cin >> grade[4] >> grade[5];
```

In the first statement, a single value will be read and stored in the variable named `grade[0]`. The second statement will cause three values to be read and stored in the variables `grade[1]`, `grade[2]`, and `grade[3]`, respectively. Finally, the last `cin` statement can be used to read values into the variables `grade[4]` and `grade[5]`.

Alternatively, a `for` loop can be used to cycle through the array for interactive data input. For example, the code

```
const int NUMELS = 5;

for (i = 0; i < NUMELS; i++)
{
  cout << "Enter a grade: ";
  cin  >> grade[i];
}
```

prompts the user for five grades. The first grade entered is stored in `grade[0]`, the second grade entered in `grade[1]`, and so on until five grades have been input.

One caution should be mentioned about storing data in an array. C++ does not check the value of the index being used (called a **bounds check**). If an array has been declared as consisting of ten elements, for example, and you use an index of 12, which is outside the bounds of the array, C++ will not notify you of the error when the program is compiled. The program will attempt to access element 12 by skipping over the appropriate number of bytes from the start of the array. Usually this results in a program crash—but not always. If the referenced location itself contains a value of the correct data type, the new value will simply overwrite the value in the referenced memory locations. This leads to more errors, which are particularly troublesome to locate when the variable legitimately assigned to the storage location is used at a different point in the program. Using named constants, as we have done, helps to eliminate this problem.

During output, individual array elements can be displayed using a `cout` statement or complete sections of the array can be displayed by including a `cout` statement within a `for` loop. Examples of this are:

```
cout << prices[6];
```

and

```
cout << "The value of element " << i << " is " << grade[i];
```

and

```
const int NUMELS = 20;

for (k = 5; k < NUMELS; k++)
 cout <<  k << "  " << amount[k] << endl;
```

The first statement displays the value of the subscripted variable `prices[6]`. The second statement displays the value of the subscript `i` and the value of `grade[i]`. Before this statement can be executed, `i` would have to have an assigned value. Finally, the last example includes a `cout` statement within a `for` loop. Both the value of the index and the value of the elements from 5 to 19 are displayed.

Program 12.1 illustrates these input and output techniques using an array named `grade` that is defined to store five integer numbers. Included in the program are two `for` loops. The first `for` loop is used to cycle through each array element and allows the user to input individual array values. After five values have been entered, the second `for` loop is used to display the stored values.

PROGRAM 12.1

```
#include <iostream.h>

int main()
{
  const int MAXGRADES = 5;

  int i, grade[MAXGRADES];

  cout << endl;
  for (i = 0; i < MAXGRADES; i++)      // Enter the grades
  {
    cout << "Enter a grade: ";
    cin  >> grade[i];
  }

  cout << endl;

  for (i = 0; i < MAXGRADES; i++)      // Print the grades
    cout << "grade " << i << " is " << grade[i] << endl;

  return 0;
}
```

PROGRAMMER'S NOTES

Aggregate Data Types

In contrast to atomic types, such as integer and floating point data, there are aggregate types. An aggregate type, which is also referred to as both a *structured type* and a *data structure,* is any type whose values can be decomposed into simpler types and are related by some defined structure. Additionally, operations must be available for retrieving and updating individual values in the data structure.

Single-dimensional arrays are examples of a structured type. In a single-dimensional array, such as an array of integers, the array is composed of individual integer values, and the integers are related by their position in the list. Indexed variables provide the means of accessing and modifying values in the array.

A sample run of Program 12.1 is illustrated in Figure 12.6. In reviewing the output produced by Program 12.1, pay particular attention to the difference between the index value displayed and the numerical value stored in the corresponding array element. The index value refers to the location of the element in the array, whereas the subscripted variable refers to the value stored in the designated location.

In addition to simply displaying the values stored in each array element, the elements can also be processed by appropriately accessing the desired element. For example, in Program 12.2, the value of each element is accumulated in a total. This total is then used to compute an average grade, which is displayed upon completion of the individual display of each array element.

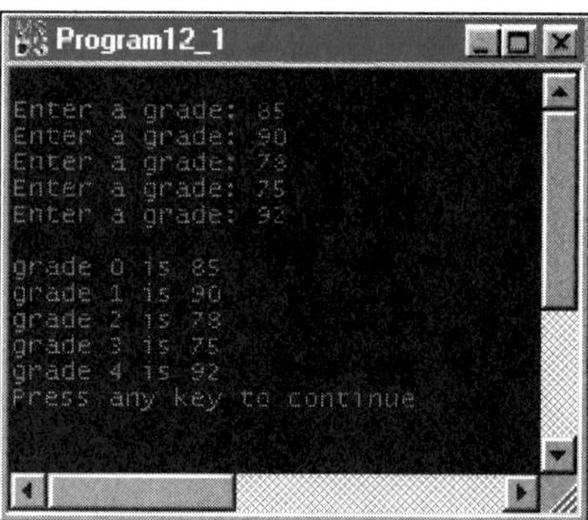

FIGURE 12.6

Sample run produced using Program 12.1

PROGRAM 12.2

```
#include <iostream.h>

int main()
{
  const int MAXGRADES = 5;

  int i, grade[MAXGRADES], total = 0;

  cout << endl;
  for (i = 0; i < MAXGRADES; i++)      // Enter the grades
  {
    cout << "Enter a grade: ";
    cin  >> grade[i];
  }

  cout << "\nThe average of the grades";

  for (i = 0; i < MAXGRADES; i++)      // Display and total the grades
  {
     cout << "  " << grade[i];
     total =  total + grade[i];
  }

  cout << " is " << total/MAXGRADES << endl;

  return 0;
}
```

A sample run using Program 12.2 is shown in Figure 12.7. Notice that in Program 12.2, unlike Program 12.1, only the values stored in each array element are displayed and not their index numbers. Although the second `for` loop was used to accumulate the total of each element, the accumulation could also have been accomplished in the first loop by placing the statement `total = total + grade[i];` after the `cin` statement used to enter a value. Also notice that the `cout` statement used to display the total is made outside of the second `for` loop, so that the total is displayed only once, after all values have been added to the total. If this `cout` statement were placed inside of the `for` loop, five totals would be displayed, with only the last displayed `total` containing the sum of all of the array values.

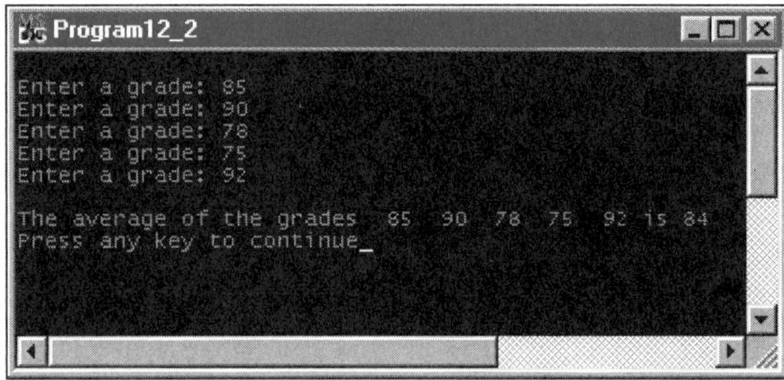

FIGURE 12.7

Sample run produced using Program 12.2

EXERCISES 12.1

1. Write array declarations for the following:

   a. a list of 100 integer grades

   b. a list of 50 floating point temperatures

   c. a list of 30 integers, each representing a code

   d. a list of 100 integer years

   e. a list of 32 floating point velocities

   f. a list of 1000 floating point distances

   g. a list of 6 integer code numbers

2. Write appropriate notation for the first, third, and seventh elements of the following arrays:

   a. `int grades[20]`

   b. `float prices[10]`

   c. `float amps[16]`

   d. `int dist[15]`

   e. `float velocity[25]`

   f. `float time[100]`

3. a. Using the `cin` object, write individual statements that can be used to enter values into the first, third, and seventh elements of each of the arrays declared in Exercises 2a through 2f.

   b. Write a `for` loop that can be used to enter values for the complete array declared in Exercise 2a.

4. a. Write individual statements that can be used to display the values from the first, third, and seventh elements of each of the arrays declared in Exercises 2a through 2f.

   b. Write a `for` loop that can be used to display values for the complete array declared in Exercise 2a.

5. List the elements that will be displayed by the following sections of code:

a.
```
for (m = 1; m <= 5; m++)
    cout << a[m] << " ";
```

b.
```
for (k = 1; k <= 5; k = k + 2)
    cout << a[k] << " ";
```

c.
```
for (j = 3; j <= 10; j++)
    cout << b[j] << " ";
```

d.
```
for (k = 3; k <= 12; k = k + 3)
    cout << b[k] << " ";
```

e.
```
for (i = 2; i < 11; i = i + 2)
    cout << c[i] << " ";
```

6. **a.** Write a program to input the following values into an array named `prices`: 10.95, 16.32, 12.15, 8.22, 15.98, 26.22, 13.54, 6.45, 17.59. After the data have been entered, have your program output the values.

   b. Repeat Exercise 6a, but after the data have been entered, have your program display them in the following form:

```
10.95  16.32  12.15
 8.22  15.98  26.22
13.54   6.45  17.59
```

7. Write a C++ program to input eight integer numbers into an array named `grade`. As each number is input, add the numbers into a total. After all numbers are input, display the numbers and their average.

8. **a.** Write a C++ program to input ten integer numbers into an array named `fmax` and determine the maximum value entered. Your program should contain only one loop and the maximum should be determined as array element values are being input. (*Hint:* Set the maximum equal to the first array element, which should be input before the loop used to input the remaining array values.)

   b. Repeat Exercise 8a, keeping track of both the maximum element in the array and the index number for the maximum. After displaying the numbers, display theses two messages:

```
The maximum value is: ___
This is element number ___ in the list of numbers
```

   Have your program display the correct values in place of the underlines in the messages.

   c. Repeat Exercise 8b, but have your program locate the minimum of the data entered.

9. **a.** Write a C++ program to input the following integer numbers into an array named `grades`: 89, 95, 72, 83, 99, 54, 86, 75, 92, 73, 79, 75, 82, 73. As each number is input, add the numbers to a total. After all numbers are input and the total is obtained, cal-

culate the average of the numbers and use the average to determine the deviation of each value from the average. Store each deviation in an array named `deviation`. Each deviation is obtained as the element value less the average of all the data. Have your program display each deviation alongside its corresponding element from the `grades` array.

b. Calculate the variance of the data used in Exercise 9a. The variance is obtained by squaring each individual deviation and dividing the sum of the squared deviations by the number of deviations.

10. Write a C++ program that specifies three one-dimensional arrays named `price`, `amount`, and `total`. Each array should be capable of holding ten integer elements. Using a `for` loop, input values for the `price` and `amount` arrays. The entries in the `total` array should be the product of the corresponding values in the `price` and `amount` arrays (thus, `total[i] = price[i] * amount[I]`). After all the data have been entered, display the following output:

```
total          price          amount
-----          -----          ------
```

Under each column heading display the appropriate value.

11. a. Write a program that inputs ten floating point numbers into an array named `raw`. After ten user-input numbers are entered into the array, your program should cycle through `raw` ten times. During each pass through the array, your program should select the lowest value in `raw` and place the selected value in the next available slot in an array named `sorted`. Thus, when your program is complete, the `sorted` array should contain the numbers in `raw` in sorted order from lowest to highest. (*Hint:* Make sure to reset the lowest value selected during each pass to a very high number so that it is not selected again. You will need a second `for` loop within the first `for` loop to locate the minimum value for each pass.)

b. The method used in Exercise 11a to sort the values in the array is very inefficient. Can you determine why? What might be a better method of sorting the numbers in an array?

12.2 Array Initialization

Array elements can be initialized within their declaration statements in the same manner as for scalar variables, except that the initializing elements must be included in braces. Examples of such initializations are:

```
int grade[5] = {98, 87, 92, 79, 85};
char codes[6] = {'s', 'a', 'm', 'p', 'l', 'e'};
double width[7] = {10.96, 6.43, 2.58, .86, 5.89, 7.56, 8.22};
```

Initializers are applied in the order they are written, with the first value used to initialize element 0, the second value used to initialize element 1, and so on, until all values have been used. Thus, in the declaration

```
int grade[5] = {98, 87, 92, 79, 85};
```

`grade[0]` is initialized to 98, `grade[1]` is initialized to 87, `grade[2]` is initialized to 92, `grade[3]` is initialized to 79, and `grade[4]` is initialized to 85.

Because white space is ignored in C++, initializations may be continued across multiple lines. For example, in the declarations

```
const int NUMGALS = 20;
int gallons[NUMGALS] = {19, 16, 14, 19, 20, 18,  // initializing values
                        12, 10, 22, 15, 18, 17,  // may extend across
                        16, 14, 23, 19, 15, 18,  // multiple lines
                        21, 5};
```

four lines are used to initialize all of the array elements.

If the number of initializers is less than the declared number of elements listed in square brackets, the initializers are applied starting with array element zero. Thus, in the declarations

```
const int ARRAYSIZE = 7;
float length[ARRAYSIZE] = {7.8, 6.4, 4.9, 11.2};
```

only `length[0]`, `length[1]`, `length[2]`, and `length[3]` are initialized with the listed values. The other array elements will be initialized to zero.

Unfortunately, there is no method of either indicating repetition of an initialization value or initializing later array elements without first specifying values for earlier elements.

A unique feature of initializers is that the size of an array may be omitted when initializing values are included in the declaration statement. For example, the declaration

```
int gallons[] = {16, 12, 10, 14, 11};
```

reserves enough storage room for five elements. Similarly, the following declarations are equivalent:

```
const int NUMCODES = 6;
char codes[NUMCODES] = {'s', 'a', 'm', 'p', 'l', 'e'};
```

and

```
char codes[] = {'s', 'a', 'm', 'p', 'l', 'e'};
```

Both of these declarations set aside six character locations for an array named `codes`. An interesting and useful simplification can also be used when initializing character arrays. For example, the declaration

```
char codes[] = "sample";    // no braces or commas
```

uses the string `"sample"` to initialize the `codes` array. Recall that a string is any sequence of characters enclosed in double quotes. This last declaration creates an array named `codes` having seven elements and fills the array with the seven characters illustrated in Figure 12.8. The first six characters, as expected, consist of the letters `s`, `a`, `m`, `p`, `l`, and `e`. The last character, which is the escape sequence `\0`, is called the **null character.** The null character is automatically appended to all strings by the C++ compiler. This character has an internal storage code that is numerically equal to zero (the storage code for the zero character has a numerical value of decimal 48, so the two cannot be confused by the computer), and is used as a marker, or sentinel, to mark the end of a string.

FIGURE 12.8

String terminated with a special sentinel

codes[0]	codes[1]	codes[2]	codes[3]	codes[4]	codes[5]	codes[6]
s	a	m	p	l	e	\0

Once values have been assigned to array elements, either through initialization within the declaration statement or using interactive input, the array elements can be processed as described in the previous section. For example, Program 12.3 illustrates the initialization of array elements within the declaration of the array and then uses a `for` loop to locate the maximum value stored in the array.

PROGRAM 12.3

```
#include <iostream.h>

int main()
{
  const int MAXELS = 5;

  int i, max, nums[MAXELS] = {2, 18, 1, 27, 16};
```

(continued next page)

(continued from previous page)

```
  max = nums[0];

  for (i = 1; i < MAXELS; i++)
    if (max < nums[i])
      max = nums[i];

  cout << "\nThe maximum value of the array elements is " << max << endl;

  return 0;
}
```

The output line displayed by Program 12.3 is:

```
The maximum value of the array elements is 27
```

EXERCISES 12.2

1. Write array declarations, including initializers, for the following:
   a. a list of ten integer grades: 89, 75, 82, 93, 78, 95, 81, 88, 77, 82
   b. a list of five double precision amounts: 10.62, 13.98, 18.45, 12.68, 14.76
   c. a list of 100 double precision interest rates; the first six rates are 6.29, 6.95, 7.25, 7.35, 7.40, 7.42
   d. a list of 64 floating point temperatures; the first ten temperatures are 78.2, 69.6, 68.5, 83.9, 55.4, 67.0, 49.8, 58.3, 62.5, 71.6
   e. a list of 15 character codes; the first seven codes are f, j, m, q, t, w, z

2. Write an array declaration statement that stores the following values in an array named `prices`: 16.24, 18.98, 23.75, 16.29, 19.54, 14.22, 11.13, 15.39. Include these statements in a program that displays the values in the array.

3. Write a program that uses an array declaration statement to initialize the following numbers in an array named `slopes`: 17.24, 25.63, 5.94, 33.92, 3.71, 32.84, 35.93, 18.24; 6.92. Your program should locate and display both the maximum and minimum values in the array.

4. Write a program that stores the following grades in an array named `prices`: 9.92, 6.32, 12.63, 5.95, 10.29. Your program should also create two arrays named `units` and `amounts`, each capable of storing five double precision numbers. Using a `for` loop and a `cin` statement, have your program accept five user-input numbers into the `units` array when the

program is run. Your program should store the product of the corresponding values in the `prices` and `units` arrays in the `amounts` array (for example, `amounts[1] = prices[1] * units[1]`) and display the following output (fill in the table appropriately):

```
Price       Units       Amount
-----       -----       ------
 9.92         .           .
 6.32         .           .
12.63         .           .
 5.95         .           .
10.29         .           .
                        ------
Total:                    .
```

5. The string of characters `"Good Morning"` is to be stored in a character array named `goodstr1`. Write the declaration for this array in three different ways.

6. a. Write declaration statements to store the string of characters `"Input the Following Data"` in a character array named `message1`, the string `"-----------------------"` in the array named `message2`, the string `"Enter the Date: "` in the array named `message3`, and the string `"Enter the Account Number: "` in the array named `message4`.

b. Include the array declarations written in Exercise 6a in a program that uses `cout` statements to display the messages. For example, the statement `cout << message1;` causes the string stored in the `message1` array to be displayed. Your program will require four such statements to display the four individual messages. (*Hint:* Using a `cout` statement to display a string requires that the end of string marker `\0` is present in the character array used to store the string.)

7. a. Write a declaration to store the string `"This is a test"` into an array named `strtest`. Include the declaration in a program to display the message using the following loop:

```
for (int i = 0; i <= 14; i++)
  cout << strtest[i];
```

b. Modify the `for` statement in Exercise 7a to display only the array characters `t`, `e`, `s`, and `t`.

c. Include the array declaration written in Exercise 7a in a program that uses the `cout` object to display characters in the array. For example, the statement `cout << strtest;` will cause the string stored in the `strtest` array to be displayed. Using this statement requires that the last character in the array is the end-of-string marker `\0`.

d. Repeat Exercise 7a using a `while` loop. (*Hint:* Stop the loop when the `\0` escape sequence is detected. The expression `while (strtest[i] != '\0')` can be used.)

12.3 Arrays as Arguments

Individual array elements are passed to a called function in the same manner as are individual scalar variables; they are simply included as subscripted variables when the function call is made. For example, the function call

```
FindMax(grade[2], grade[6]);
```

passes the values of the elements `grade[2]` and `grade[6]` to the function `FindMax()`.

Passing a complete array of values to a function is in many respects an easier operation than passing individual elements. The called function receives access to the actual array, rather than a copy of the values in the array. For example, if `grade` is an array, the function call `FindMax(grade);` makes the complete `grade` array available to the `FindMax()` function. This is different from passing a single variable to a function.

Recall that when a single scalar argument is passed to a function, the called function receives only a copy of the passed value, which is stored in one of the function's parameters. If arrays were passed in this manner, a copy of the complete array would have to be created. For large arrays, making duplicate copies of the array for each function call would be wasteful of computer storage and would frustrate the effort to return multiple element changes made by the called program (recall that a function returns at most one value). To avoid these problems, the called function is given direct access to the original array.[3] Thus, any changes made by the called function are made directly to the array itself. For the following specific examples of function calls, assume that the arrays `nums`, `keys`, `units`, and `prices` are declared as:

```
int nums[5];                      // an array of five integers
char keys[256];                   // an array of 256 characters
double units[500], prices[500];   // two arrays of 500 doubles
```

For these arrays, the following function calls can be made:

```
FindMax(nums);
FindChar(keys);
calcTotal(nums, units, prices);
```

In each case, the called function receives direct access to the named array.

---

3 This is accomplished because the starting address of the array is actually passed as an argument. The parameter receiving this address argument is a pointer. The intimate relationship between array names and pointers is presented in Chapter 13.

On the receiving side, the called function must be alerted that an array is being made available. For example, suitable function header lines for the previous functions are:

```
int FindMax(int vals[5])
char FindChar(char inKeys[256])
void calcTotal(int arr1[5], double arr2[500], double arr3[500])
```

In each of these function header lines, the names in the parameter list are chosen by the programmer. However, the parameter names used by the functions still refer to the original array created outside the function. This is made clear in Program 12.4.

PROGRAM 12.4

```
#include <iostream.h>

const int MAXELS = 5;

int FindMax(int [MAXELS]);       // function prototype

int main()
{
  int nums[MAXELS] = {2, 18, 1, 27, 16};

  cout << "\nThe maximum value in the array is "
       << FindMax(nums) << endl;

  return 0;
}

// find the maximum value
int FindMax(int vals[MAXELS])
{
  int i, max = vals[0];
  for (i = 1; i < MAXELS; i++)
    if (max < vals[i])
      max = vals[i];

  return max;
}
```

Notice that the function prototype for `FindMax()` declares that `FindMax()` will return an integer and expects an array of five integers as an argument. It is also important to know that only one array is created in Program 12.4. In `main()` this array is known as `nums`, and in `FindMax()` the array is known as `vals`. As illustrated in Figure 12.9, both names refer to the same array. Thus, in Figure 12.9 `vals[3]` is the same element as `nums[3]`.

Both the `FindMax()` prototype and the function header line in Program 12.4 actually contains extra information that is not required by the function. All that `FindMax()` must know is that the parameter `vals` is an array of integers. Because the array has been created in `main()` and no additional storage space is needed in `FindMax()`, the declaration for `vals` can omit the size of the array. Thus, an alternative function header line is:

```
int FindMax(int vals[])
```

This form of the function header makes more sense when you realize that only one item is actually passed to `FindMax` when the function is called, which is the starting address of the `nums` array. This is illustrated in Figure 12.10.

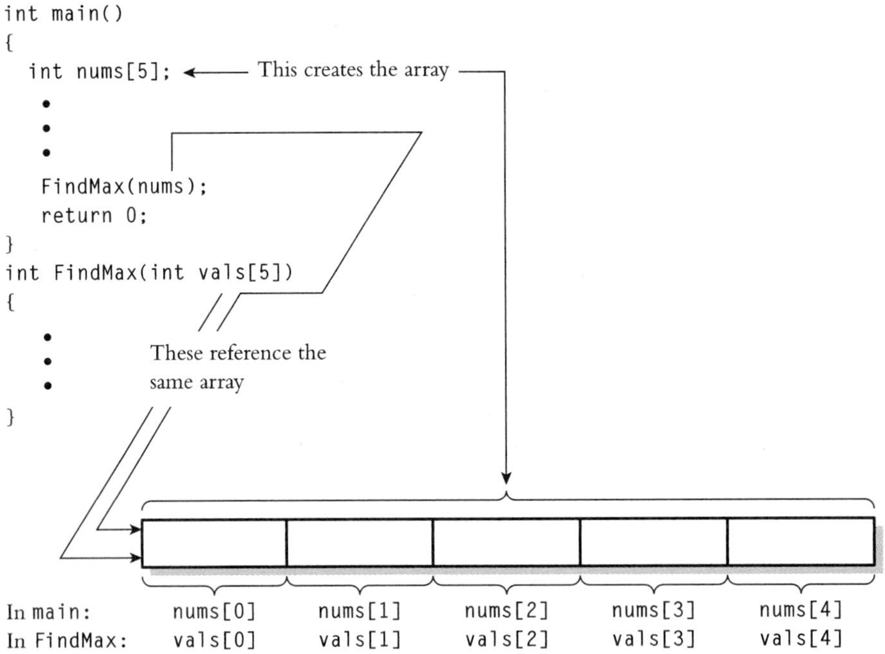

FIGURE 12.9

Only one array is created

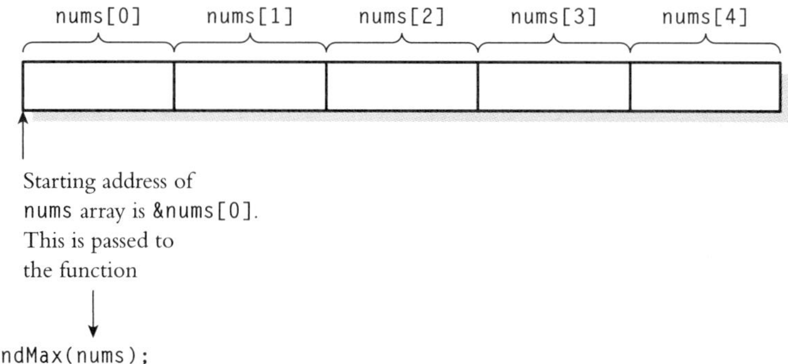

FIGURE 12.10

The starting address of the array is passed

Only the starting address of `vals` is passed to `FindMax()`, so the number of elements in the array need not be included in the declaration for `vals`.[4] In fact, it is generally advisable to omit the size of the array in the function header line. For example, consider the more general form of `FindMax()`, which can be used to find the maximum value of an integer array of arbitrary size:

```
int FindMax(int vals[], int numEls)    // find the maximum value
{
  int i, max = vals[0];

  for (i = 1; i < numEls; i++)
   if (max < vals[i])
     max = vals[i];

  return(max);
}
```

The more general form of `FindMax()` declares that the function returns an integer value. The function expects the starting address of an integer array and the number of elements in the array as arguments. Then, using the number of elements as the boundary for its search, the function's `for` loop causes each array element to be examined in sequential

---

4 An important consequence of this is that `FindMax()` has direct access to the passed array. This means that any change to an element of the `vals` array actually is a change to the `nums` array. This is significantly different than the situation with scalar variables, where the called function does not receive direct access to the passed variable.

order to locate the maximum value. Program 12.5 illustrates the use of `FindMax()` in a complete program.

PROGRAM 12.5

```
#include <iostream.h>

int FindMax(int [], int);    // function prototype

int main()
{
  const int MAXELS = 5;
  int nums[MAXELS] = {2, 18, 1, 27, 16};


  cout << "\nThe maximum value in the array is "
       << FindMax(nums, MAXELS) << endl;

  return 0;
}

// find the maximum value
int FindMax(int vals[], int numEls)
{
  int i, max = vals[0];

  for (i = 1; i < numEls; i++)
    if (max < vals[i])
      max = vals[i];

  return max;
}
```

The output line displayed by both Programs 12.4 and 12.5 is:

```
The maximum value in the array is 27
```

EXERCISES 12.3

1. The following declarations were used to create the `grades` array:

```
const int NUMGRADES = 500;
double grades[NUMGRADES];
```

Write two different function header lines for a function named `sortArray()` that accepts the `grades` array as an argument named `inArray` and returns no value.

2. The following declarations were used to create the `keys` array:

```
const int NUMKEYS = 256;
char keys[NUMKEYS];
```

Write two different function header lines for a function named `findKey()` that accepts the `keys` array as an argument named `select` and returns a character.

3. The following declarations were used to create the `rates` array:

```
const int NUMRATES = 256;
float rates[NUMRATES];
```

Write two different function header lines for a function named `prime()` that accepts the `rates` array as an argument named `rates` and returns a floating point number.

4. **a.** Modify the `FindMax()` function in Program 12.4 to locate the minimum value of the passed array.
   b. Include the function written in Exercise 4a in a complete program and run the program on a computer.

5. Write a program that has a declaration in `main()` to store the following numbers into an array named `rates`: 6.5, 7.2, 7.5, 8.3, 8.6, 9.4, 9.6, 9.8, 10.0. There should be a function call to `show()` that accepts the `rates` array as a parameter named `rates` and then displays the numbers in the array.

6. **a.** Write a program that has a declaration in `main()` to store the string `"Vacation is near"` into an array named `message`. There should be a function call to a function named `display()` that accepts `message` in a parameter named `strng` and then displays the message.
   b. Modify the `display()` function written in Exercise 6a to display the first eight elements of the `message` array.

7. Write a program that declares three single-dimensional arrays named `price`, `quantity`, and `amount`. Each array should be declared in `main()` and should be capable of holding

ten double precision numbers. The numbers that should be stored in `price` are 10.62, 14.89, 13.21, 16.55, 18.62, 9.47, 6.58, 18.32, 12.15, 3.98. The numbers that should be stored in `quantity` are 4, 8.5, 6, 7.35, 9, 15.3, 3, 5.4, 2.9, 4.8. Your program should pass the three arrays to a function called `extend()`, which should calculate the elements in the `amount` array as the product of the corresponding elements in the `price` and `quantity` arrays (for example, `amount[1] = price[1] * quantity[1]`). After `extend()` has put values into the `amount` array, the values in the array should be displayed from within `main()`.

8. Write a program that includes two functions named `calcAverage()` and `variance()`. The `calcAverage()` function should calculate and return the average of the values stored in an array named `testvals`. The array should be declared in `main()` and include the values 89, 95, 72, 83, 99, 54, 86, 75, 92, 73, 79, 75, 82, 73. The `variance()` function should calculate and return the variance of the data. The variance is obtained by subtracting the average from each value in `testvals`, squaring the differences obtained, adding these squares, and dividing by the number of elements in `testvals`. The values returned from `calcAverage()` and `variance()` should be displayed using `cout` statements from within `main()`.

12.4 Two-Dimensional Arrays

A **two-dimensional array,** which is sometimes referred to as a **table,** consists of both rows and columns of elements. For example, the array of numbers

```
 8  16   9  52
 3  15  27   6
14  25   2  10
```

is called a two-dimensional array of integers. This array consists of three rows and four columns. To reserve storage for this array, both the number of rows and the number of columns must be included in the array's declaration. Calling the array `val`, the correct specification for this two-dimensional array is

```
int val [3][4];
```

Similarly, the declarations

```
float grade [10][5];
char code [6][26];
```

declare that the array `grade` consists of 10 rows and 5 columns of floating point numbers and that the array `code` consists of 6 rows and 26 columns, with each element capable of holding one character.

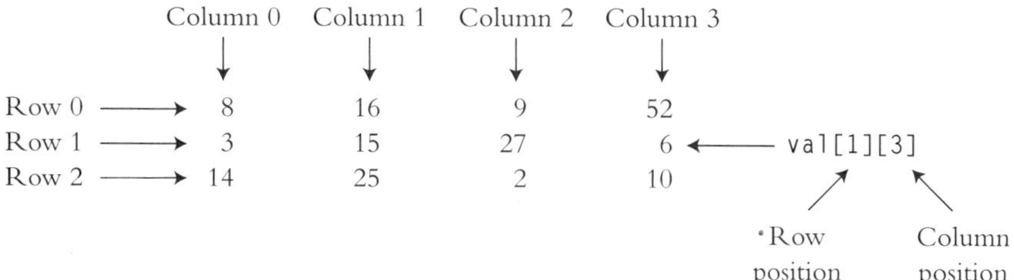

FIGURE 12.11

Each array element is identified by its row and column position

To locate each element in a two-dimensional array, an element is identified by its position in the array. As illustrated in Figure 12.11, the term `val[1][3]` uniquely identifies the element in row 1, column 3. As with single-dimensional array variables, double-dimensional array variables can be used anywhere that scalar variables are valid. Examples that use elements of the `val` array are:

```
watts = val[2][3];
val[0][0] = 62;
newnum = 4 * (val[1][0] - 5);
sumRow0 = val[0][0] + val[0][1] + val[0][2] + val[0][3];
```

The last statement causes the values of the four elements in row 0 to be added and the sum to be stored in the scalar variable `sumRow0`.

As with single-dimensional arrays, two-dimensional arrays can be initialized from within their declaration statements. This is done by listing the initial values within braces and separating them by commas. Additionally, braces can be used to separate individual rows. For example, the declaration

```
int val[3][4] = { {8,16,9,52},
                  {3,15,27,6},
                  {14,25,2,10} };
```

declares `val` to be an array of integers with three rows and four columns, with the initial values given in the declaration. The first set of internal braces contains the values for row 0 of the array, the second set of internal braces contains the values for row 1, and the third set of braces the values for row 2.

Although the commas in the initialization braces are always required, the inner braces can be omitted. Thus, the initialization for `val` may be written as

```
int val[3][4] = {8,16,9,52,
                  3,15,27,6,
                 14,25,2,10};
```

The separation of initial values into rows in the declaration statement is not necessary because the compiler assigns values beginning with the [0][0] element and proceeds row by row to fill in the remaining values. Thus, the initialization

```
int val[3][4] = {8,16,9,52,3,15,27,6,14,25,2,10};
```

is equally valid but does not clearly illustrate to another programmer where one row ends and another begins.

As illustrated in Figure 12.12, the initialization of a two-dimensional array is done in row order. First, the elements of the first row are initialized, then the elements of the second row are initialized, and so on, until the initializations are completed. This row ordering is also the same ordering used to store two-dimensional arrays. That is, array element [0][0] is stored first, followed by element [0][1], followed by element [0][2], and so on. Following the first row's elements are the second row's elements and so on, for all the rows in the array.

As with single-dimensional arrays, two-dimensional arrays may be displayed by individual element notation or by using loops (either while or for). This is illustrated in Program 12.6, which displays all of the elements of a three by four two-dimensional array using two different techniques. Notice in Program 12.6 that we have used named constants to define the array's rows and columns.

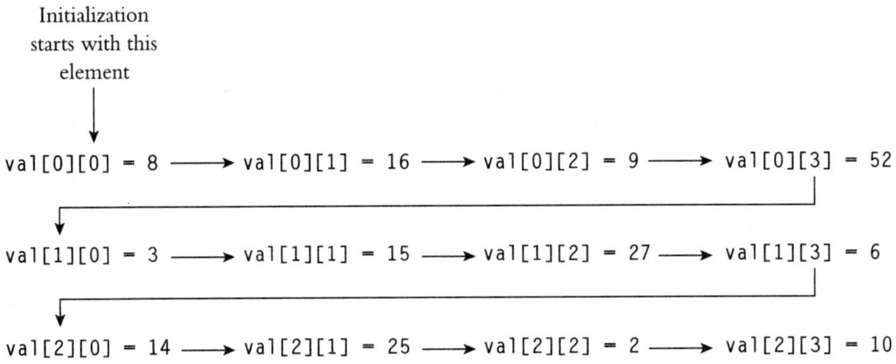

FIGURE 12.12

Storage and initialization of the val[] array

PROGRAM 12.6

```
#include <iostream.h>
#include <iomanip.h>

int main()
{

  const int NUMROWS = 3;
  const int NUMCOLS = 4;

  int i, j;
  int val[NUMROWS][NUMCOLS] = {8,16,9,52,3,15,27,6,14,25,2,10};

  cout << "\nDisplay of val array by explicit element"
       << endl << setw(4) << val[0][0] << setw(4) << val[0][1]
       << setw(4) << val[0][2] << setw(4) << val[0][3]
       << endl << setw(4) << val[1][0] << setw(4) << val[1][1]
       << setw(4) << val[1][2] << setw(4) << val[1][3]
       << endl << setw(4) << val[2][0] << setw(4) << val[2][1]
       << setw(4) << val[2][2] << setw(4) << val[2][3];

  cout << "\n\nDisplay of val array using a nested for loop";

  for (i = 0; i < NUMROWS; i++)
  {
    cout << endl;      // print a new line for each row
    for (j = 0; j < NUMCOLS; j++)
      cout << setw(4) <<  val[i][j];
  }

  cout << endl;

  return 0;
}
```

The display produced by Program 12.6 is shown in Figure 12.13.

FIGURE 12.13

Output displayed by Program 12.6

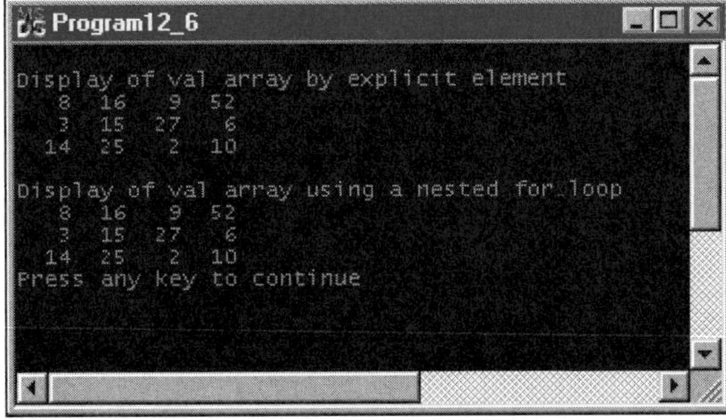

The first display of the `val` array produced by Program 12.6 is constructed by explicitly designating each array element. The second display of array element values, which is identical to the first, is produced using a nested `for` loop. Nested loops are especially useful when dealing with two-dimensional arrays because they allow the programmer to designate and cycle through each element easily. In Program 12.6, the variable `i` controls the outer loop, and the variable `j` controls the inner loop. Each pass through the outer loop corresponds to a single row, with the inner loop supplying the appropriate column elements. After a complete row is printed, a new line is started for the next row. The effect is a display of the array in a row-by-row fashion.

Once two-dimensional array elements have been assigned, array processing can begin. Typically, `for` loops are used to process two-dimensional arrays because, as was previously noted, they allow the programmer to designate and cycle through each array element easily. For example, the nested `for` loop illustrated in Program 12.7 is used to multiply each element in the `val` array by the scalar number 10 and display the resulting value.

PROGRAM 12.7

```
#include <iostream.h>
#include <iomanip.h>

int main()
{
  const int NUMROWS = 3;
  const int NUMCOLS = 4;

  int i, j;
  int val[NUMROWS][NUMCOLS] = {8,16,9,52,
                               3,15,27,6,
                              14,25,2,10};
```

(continued next page)

(continued from previous page)

```
// multiply each element by 10 and display it
  cout << "\nDisplay of multiplied elements";
  for (i = 0; i < NUMROWS; i++)
  {
    cout << endl;   // start each row on a new line
    for (j = 0; j < NUMCOLS; j++)
    {
      val[i][j] = val[i][j] * 10;
      cout << setw(5) << val[i][j];
    }  // end of inner loop
  }    // end of outer loop
  cout << endl;

  return 0;
}
```

The output produced by Program 12.7 is illustrated in Figure 12.14.

Passing two-dimensional arrays into a function is a process identical to passing single-dimensional arrays. The called function receives access to the entire array. For example, the function call `display(val);` makes the complete `val` array available to the function named `display()`. Thus, any changes made by `display()` will be made directly to the `val` array. Assuming that the following two-dimensional arrays named `test`, `code`, and `stocks` are declared as:

```
int test[7][9];
char code[26][10];
double stocks256][52];
```

the following function calls are valid:

```
FindMax(test);
obtain(code);
price(stocks);
```

FIGURE 12.14

Output displayed by Program 12.7

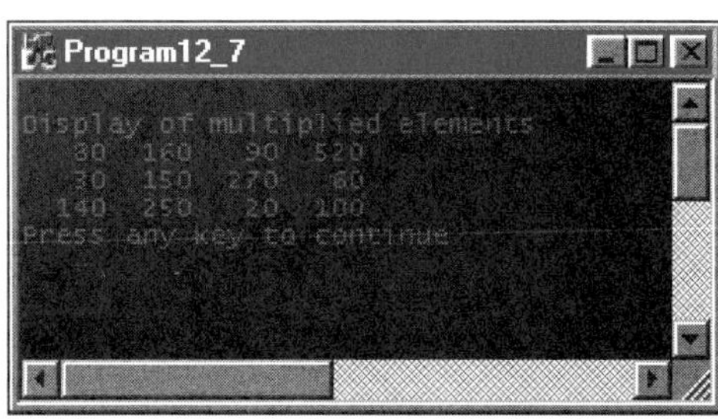

On the receiving side, the called function must be alerted that a two-dimensional array is being made available. For example, assuming that each of the previous functions returns an integer, suitable function header lines for the functions are:

```
int FindMax(int nums[7][9])
int obtain(char key[26][10])
int double prices(double vals[256][52])
```

In each of these function header lines, the parameter names chosen will be used internal to the function's body. However, these parameter names still refer to the original array created outside the function. Program 12.8 illustrates passing a two-dimensional array into a function that displays the array's values.

PROGRAM 12.8

```
#include <iostream.h>
#include <iomanip.h>

const int ROWS = 3;
const int COLS = 4;

void display(int [ROWS][COLS]);    // function prototype

int main()
{
  int val[ROWS][COLS] = {8,16,9,52,
                          3,15,27,6,
                         14,25,2,10};

  display(val);

  return 0;
}

void display(int nums[ROWS][COLS])
{
  int rowNum, colNum;
  for (rowNum = 0; rowNum < ROWS; rowNum++)
  {
    for(colNum = 0; colNum < COLS; colNum++)
      cout << setw(4) <<nums[rowNum][colNum];
    cout << endl;
  }

  return;
}
```

Only one array is created in Program 12.8. This array is known as `val` in `main()` and as `nums` in `display()`. Thus, `val[0][2]` refers to the same element as `nums[0][2]`.

Notice the use of the nested `for` loop in Program 12.8 for cycling through each array element. In Program 12.8, the variable `rowNum` controls the outer loop and the variable `colNum` controls the inner loop. For each pass through the outer loop, which corresponds to a row, the inner loop makes one pass through the column elements. After a complete row is printed, the `\n` escape sequence causes a new line to be started for the next row. The effect is a display of the array in a row-by-row fashion:

```
 8  16   9  52
 3  15  27   6
14  25   2  10
```

The prototype and header line for `nums` in `display()` contains extra information that is not required by the function. The declaration for `nums` can omit the row size of the array. Thus, an alternative function header line is:

```
void display(int nums[][4])
```

The reason the column size must be included whereas the row size is optional becomes obvious when you consider how the array elements are stored in memory. Starting with element `val[0][0]`, each succeeding element is stored consecutively, row by row, as `val[0][0]`, `val[0][1]`, `val[0][2]`, `val[0][3]`, `val[1][0]`, `val[1][1]`, etc., as illustrated in Figure 12.15.

FIGURE 12.15

Storage of the `val` array

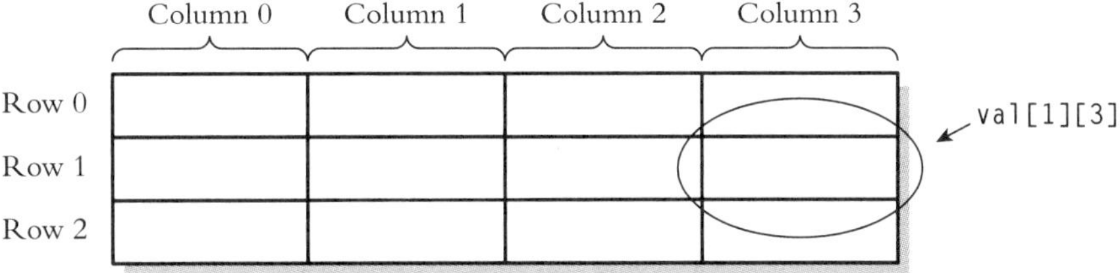

As with all array accesses, an individual element of the `val` array is obtained by adding an offset to the starting location of the array. For example, element `val[1][3]` of the `val` array illustrated in Figure 12.15 is located at an offset of 14 bytes from the start of the array (assuming two bytes for an `int`). Internally, the compiler uses the row index, column index, and column size to determine this offset using the following calculation:

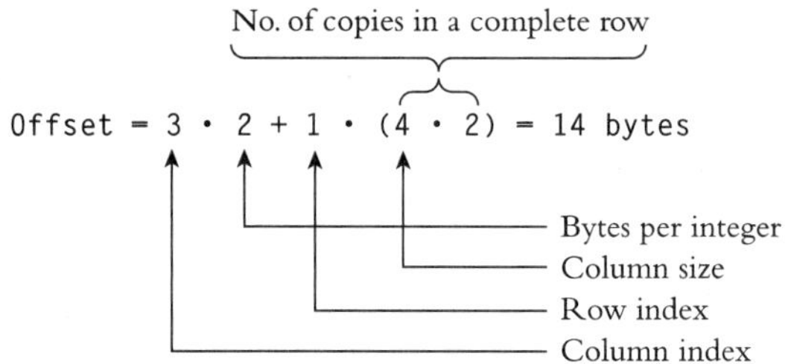

The column size is necessary in the offset calculation so that the compiler can determine the number of positions to skip over in order to get to the desired row.

Larger-Dimensional Arrays

Although arrays with more than two dimensions are not commonly used, C++ does allow any number of dimensions to be declared. This is done by listing the maximum size of all dimensions for the array. For example, the declaration `int response [4][10][[6];` declares a three-dimensional array. The first element in the array is designated as `response [0][0][0]` and the last element as `response [3][9][5]`.

Conceptually, as illustrated in Figure 12.16, a three-dimensional array can be viewed as a book of data tables. Using this visualization, the first index can be thought of as the location of the desired row in a table, the second index value as the desired column, and the third index value, which is often called the "rank," as the page number for the selected table.

Similarly, arrays of any dimension can be declared. Conceptually, a four-dimensional array can be represented as a shelf of books, where the fourth dimension is used to declare

FIGURE 12.16

Representation of a three-dimensional array

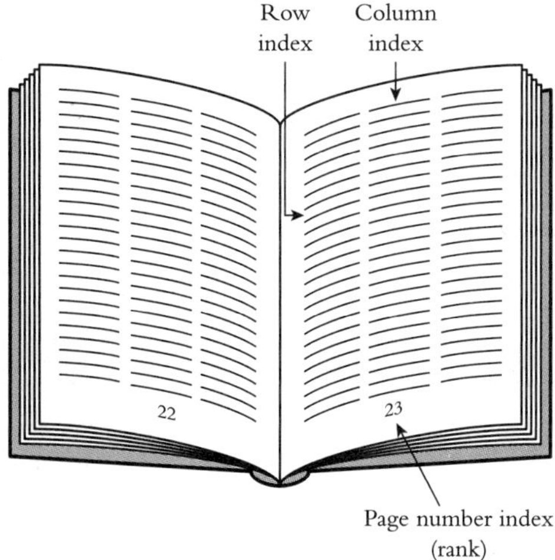

a desired book on the shelf, and a five-dimensional array can be viewed as a bookcase filled with books where the fifth dimension refers to a selected shelf in the bookcase. Using the same analogy, a six-dimensional array can be considered as a single row of bookcases where the sixth dimension references the desired bookcase in the row; a seven-dimensional array can be considered as multiple rows of bookcases where the seventh dimension references the desired row, and so on. Alternatively, arrays of three, four, five, six, or more. dimensional arrays can be viewed as mathematical *n*-tuples of order three, four, five, six, and so on, respectively.

EXERCISES 12.4

1. Write appropriate specification statements for:

a. an array of integers with 6 rows and 10 columns

b. an array of integers with 2 rows and 5 columns

c. an array of characters with 7 rows and 12 columns

d. an array of characters with 15 rows and 7 columns

e. an array of double precision numbers with 10 rows and 25 columns

f. an array of double precision numbers with 16 rows and 8 columns

2. Determine the output produced by the following program:

```
#include <iostream.h>
int main()
{
 int i, j, val[3][4] = {8,16,9,52,3,15,27,6,14,25,2,10};

  for (i = 0; i < 3; i++)
    for (j = 0; j < 4; j++)
      cout << val[i][j] << "  ";

 return 0;
}
```

3. a. Write a C++ program that adds the values of all elements in the `val` array used in Exercise 2 and displays the total.

b. Modify the program written for Exercise 3a to display the total of each row separately.

4. Write a C++ program that adds equivalent elements of the two-dimensional arrays named `first` and `second`. Both arrays should have two rows and three columns. For example, element `[1][2]` of the resulting array should be the sum of `first[1][2]` and `second[1][2]`. The `first` and `second` arrays should be initialized as follows:

```
      first                second
  ------------         ------------
  16    18    23       24    52    77
  54    91    11       16    19    59
```

5. a. Write a C++ program that finds and displays the maximum value in a two-dimensional array of integers. The array should be declared as a four by five array of integers and initialized with the following data: 16, 22 , 99, 4, 18, –258, 4, 101, 5, 98, 105, 6, 15, 2, 45, 33, 88, 72, 16, 3.

b. Modify the program written in Exercise 5a so that it also displays the maximum value's row and column subscript values.

6. Write a C++ program to select the values in a four by five array of integers in increasing order and store the selected values into the single-dimensional array named `sort`. Use the data given in Exercise 5a to initialize the two-dimensional array.

7. a. A professor has constructed a two-dimensional array of float numbers having three rows and five columns. This array currently contains the test grades of the students in the professor's advanced compiler design class. Write a C++ program that reads 15 array values and then determine the total number of grades in the ranges less than 60, greater than or equal to 60 and less than 70, greater than or equal to 70 and less than 80, greater than or equal to 80 and less than 90, and greater than or equal to 90.

b. Entering 15 grades each time the program written for Exercise 7a is run is cumbersome. What method is appropriate for initializing the array during the testing phase?

c. How might the program you wrote for Exercise 7a be modified to include the case of no grade being present? That is, what grade could be used to indicate an invalid grade and how would your program have to be modified to exclude counting such a grade?

8. a. Write a function named `FindMax()` that finds and displays the maximum value in a two-dimensional array of integers. The array should be declared as a 10-row by 20-column array of integers in `main()`.

b. Modify the function written in Exercise 8a so that it also displays the row and column number of the element with the maximum value.

c. Can the function you wrote for Exercise 8a be generalized to handle any size two-dimensional array?

9. Write a function that can be used to sort the elements of a 10 by 20 two-dimensional array of integers. (*Hint:* Use the `swap()` function developed for Program 6.10 to exchange array elements.)

12.5 Common Programming Errors

Four common errors are associated with using arrays:

1. Forgetting to declare the array. This error results in a compiler error message equivalent to "invalid indirection" each time a subscripted variable is encountered within a program. The exact meaning of this error message will become clear when the correspondence between arrays and pointers is established in Chapter 13.

2. Using a subscript that references a nonexistent array element. For example, declaring the array to be of size 20 and using a subscript value of 25. This error is not detected by most C++ compilers. It will, however, result in a run-time error that results either in a program crash or a value that has no relation to the intended element being accessed from memory. In either case it is usually an extremely troublesome error to locate. The only solution to this problem is to make sure, either by specific programming statements or by careful coding, that each subscript references a valid array element. Using named constants for an array's size and for the maximum subscript value helps to eliminate this problem.

3. Not using a large enough conditional value in a `for` loop counter to cycle through all the array elements. This error usually occurs when an array is initially specified to be of size `n` and there is a `for` loop within the program of the form `for (i = 0; i < n; i++)`. The array size is then expanded but the programmer forgets to change the interior `for` loop parameters. Declaring an array's size using a named constant and consistently using the named constant throughout the function in place of the variable `n` eliminates this problem.

4. Forgetting to initialize the array. Although many compilers automatically set all elements of integer and real valued arrays to zero, and all elements of character arrays to blanks, it is up to the programmer to ensure that each array is correctly initialized before processing of array elements begins.

12.6 Chapter Summary

1. A **single-dimensional array** is a data structure that can be used to store a list of values of the same data type. Such arrays must be declared by giving the data type of the values that are stored in the array and the array size. For example, the declaration:

```
int num[100];
```

creates an array of 100 integers. A preferable approach is to first use a named constant to set the array size, and then use this constant in the definition of the array. For example:

```
const int MAXSIZE = 100;
int num[MAXSIZE];
```

2. Array elements are stored in contiguous locations in memory and accessed using the array name and a subscript, for example, `num[22]`. Any nonnegative integer value expression can be used as a subscript and the subscript 0 always refers to the first element in an array.

3. A **two-dimensional array** is declared by listing both a row and a column size with the data type and name of the array. For example, the declarations:

```
const int NUMROWS = 5;
const int NUMCOLS = 7;
int mat[NUMROWS][NUMCOLS];
```

creates a two-dimensional array consisting of five rows and seven columns of integer values.

4. Two-dimensional arrays may be initialized when they are declared. This is accomplished by listing the initial values, in a row-by-row manner, within braces and separating them with commas. For example, the declaration:

```
int vals[3][2] = { {1, 2},
                   {3, 4},
                   {5, 6} };
```

produces the following three-row by two-column array:

```
1  2
3  4
5  6
```

As C++ uses the convention that initialization proceeds in rowwise order, the inner braces can be omitted. Thus, an equivalent initialization is provided by the statement:

```
int vals[3][2] = { 1, 2, 3, 4, 5, 6};
```

5. Arrays are passed to a function by passing the name of the array as an argument. The value actually passed is the address of the first array storage location. Thus, the called function receives direct access to the original array and not a copy of the array elements. Within the called function a parameter must be declared to receive the passed array name. The declaration of the parameter can omit the row size of the array.

12.7 Knowing About: Searching and Sorting

Most programmers encounter the need to both sort and search a list of data items at some time in their programming careers. For example, experimental results might have to be arranged in either increasing (ascending) or decreasing (descending) order for statistical analysis, lists of names may have to be sorted in alphabetical order, or a list of dates may have to be rearranged in ascending date order. Similarly, a list of names may have to be searched to find a particular name in the list, or a list of dates may have to be searched to locate a particular date. In this section we introduce the fundamentals of both sorting and searching lists. Note that it is not necessary to sort a list before searching it, although, as we shall see, much faster searches are possible if the list is in sorted order.

Search Algorithms

A common requirement of many programs is to search a list for a given element. For example, in a list of names and telephone numbers, we might search for a specific name so that the corresponding telephone number can be printed, or we might wish to search the list simply to determine if a name is there. The two most common methods of performing such searches are the linear and binary search algorithms.

Linear Search In a **linear search,** which is also known as a **sequential search,** each item in the list is examined in the order in which it occurs in the list until the desired item is found or the end of the list is reached. This is analogous to looking at every name in the phone directory, beginning with Aardvark, Aaron, until you find the one you want or until you reach Zzxgy. Obviously, this is not the most efficient way to search a long alphabetized list. However, a linear search has these advantages:

1. The algorithm is simple.
2. The list need not be in any particular order.

In a linear search the search begins with the first item in the list and continues sequentially, item by item, through the list. The pseudocode for a function performing a linear search is:

```
For all the items in the list
    Compare the item with the desired item
    If the item was found
        Return the index value of the current item
    Endif
EndFor
Return -1 because the item was not found
```

Notice that the function's return value indicates whether the item was found or not. If the return value is –1, the item was not in the list; otherwise, the return value within the `for` loop provides the index of where the item is located within the list.

The function `linearSearch()` illustrates this procedure as a C++ function:

```
// this function returns the location of key in the list
// a -1 is returned if the value is not found
int linearSearch(int list[], int size, int key)
{
  int i;

  for (i = 0; i < size; i++)
  {
    if (list[i] == key)
      return i;
  }

  return -1;
}
```

In reviewing `linearSearch()`, notice that the `for` loop is simply used to access each element in the list, from first element to last, until a match is found with the desired item. If the desired item is located, the index value of the current item is returned, which causes the loop to terminate; otherwise, the search continues until the end of the list is encountered.

To test this function we have written a `main()` driver function to call it and display the results returned by `linearSearch()`. The complete test program is illustrated in Program 12.9.

PROGRAM 12.9

```
#include <iostream.h>

int linearSearch(int [], int, int);

int main()
{
  const int NUMEL = 10;
  int nums[NUMEL] = {5,10,22,32,45,67,73,98,99,101};
  int item, location;
```

(continued next page)

(continued from previous page)

```
  cout << "\nEnter the item you are searching for: ";
  cin  >> item;

  location = linearSearch(nums, NUMEL, item);

  if (location > -1)
    cout << "The item was found at index location " << location
         << endl;
  else
    cout << "The item was not found in the list\n";

  return 0;
}

// this function returns the location of key in the list
// a -1 is returned if the value is not found
int linearSearch(int list[], int size, int key)
{
  int i;

  for (i = 0; i < size; i++)
  {
    if (list[i] == key)
      return i;
  }

  return -1;
}
```

Two sample runs using Program 12.9 are illustrated in Figures 12.17 and 12.18, respectively.

As has already been pointed out, an advantage of linear searches is that the list does not have to be in sorted order to perform the search. Another advantage is that if the desired item is toward the front of the list, only a small number of comparisons will be done.

FIGURE 12.17

Locating an item in the list

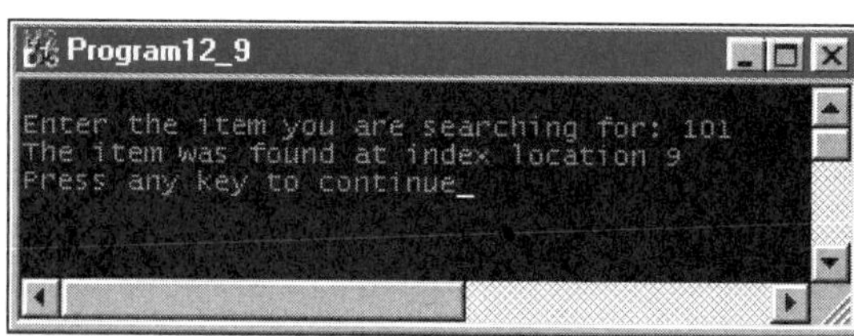

FIGURE 12.18

Determining an item is not in the list

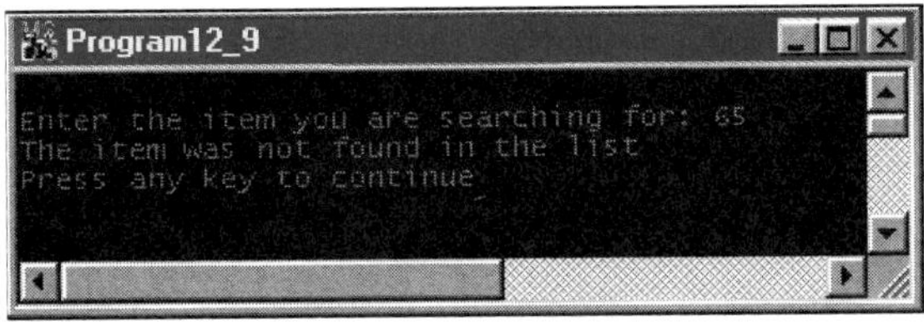

The worst case, of course, occurs when the desired item is at the end of the list. On average, however, and assuming that the desired item is equally likely to be anywhere within the list, the number of required comparisons will be *N*/2, where *N* is the list's size. Thus, for a 10-element list, the average number of comparisons needed for a linear search is 5, and for a 10,000-element list, the average number of comparisons needed is 5000. As we show next, this number can be significantly reduced using a binary search algorithm.

Binary Search In a **binary search** the list must be in sorted order. Starting with an ordered list, the desired item is first compared to the element in the middle of the list (for lists with an even number of elements, either of the two middle elements can be used). Three possibilities present themselves once the comparison is made: (1) the desired item may be equal to the middle element, (2) it may be greater than the middle element, or (3) it may be less than the middle element.

In the first case the search has been successful, and no further searches are required. In the second case, because the desired item is greater than the middle element, if it is found at all it must be in the upper part of the list. This means that the lower part of the list consisting of all elements from the first to the midpoint element can be discarded from any further search. In the third case, because the desired item is less than the middle element, if it is found at all it must be found in the lower part of the list. For this case, the upper part of the list containing all elements from the midpoint element to the last element can be discarded from any further search.

The algorithm for implementing this search strategy is illustrated in Figure 12.19 and defined by the following pseudocode:

```
Set the lower index to 0
Set the upper index to one less than the size of the list
Begin with the first item in the list
While the lower index is less than or equal to the upper index
  Set the midpoint index to the integer average of the lower and upper index values
  Compare the desired item to the midpoint element
    If the desired element equals the midpoint element
       Return the index value of the current item
    Else If the desired element is greater than the midpoint element
       Set the lower index value to the midpoint value plus 1
```

Else if the desired element is less than the midpoint element
Set the upper index value to the midpoint value less 1
Endif
EndWhile
Return -1 because the item was not found

FIGURE 12.19

The binary search algorithm

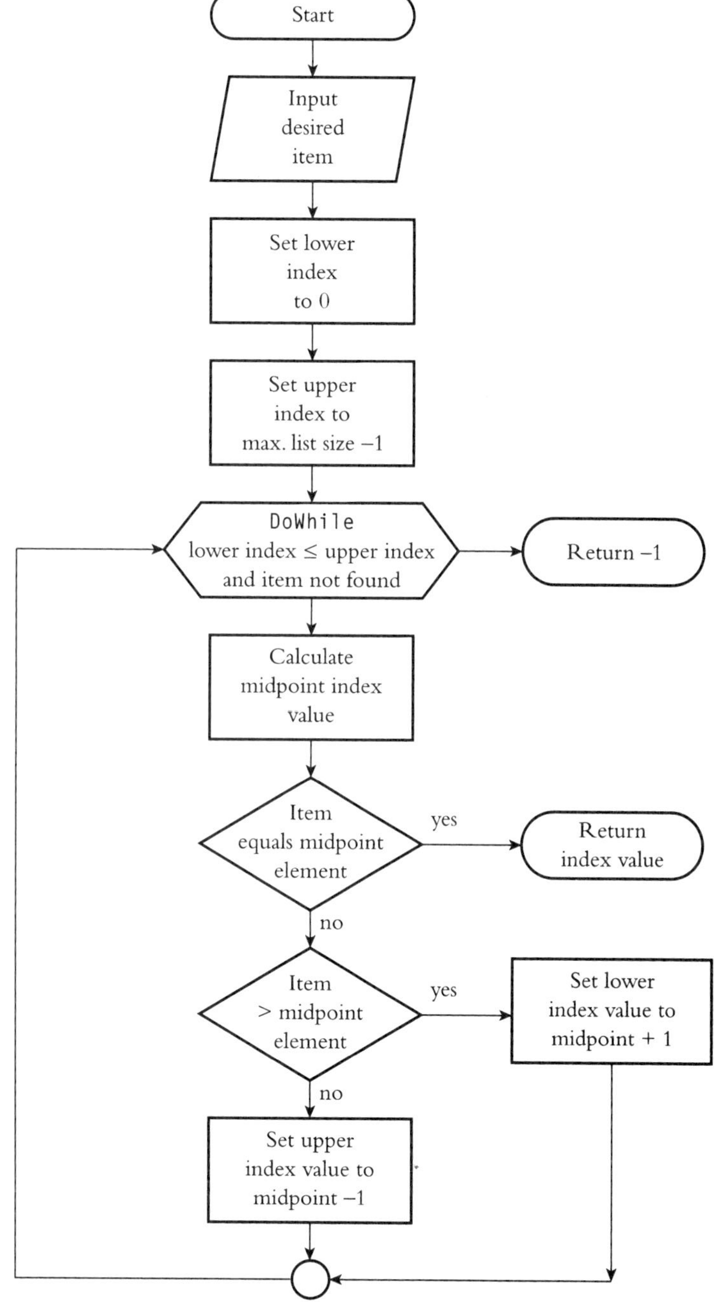

As illustrated by both the pseudocode and the flowchart of Figure 12.19, a `while` loop is used to control the search. The initial list is defined by setting the lower index value to 0 and the upper index value to one less than the number of elements in the list. The midpoint element is then taken as the integerized average of the lower and upper values. Once the comparison to the midpoint element is made, the search is subsequently restricted by moving either the lower index to one integer value above the midpoint, or by moving the upper index to one integer value below the midpoint. This process is continued until the desired element is found or the lower and upper index values become equal. The function `binarySearch()` presents the C++ version of this algorithm.

```
// this function returns the location of key in the list
// a -1 is returned if the value is not found
int binarySearch(int list[], int size, int key)
{
  int left, right, midpt;

  left = 0;
  right = size - 1;

  while (left <= right)
  {
    midpt = (int) ((left + right) / 2);
    if (key == list[midpt])
    {
      return midpt;
    }
    else if (key > list[midpt])
      left = midpt + 1;
    else
      right = midpt - 1;
  }

  return -1;
}
```

For purposes of testing this function, Program 12.10 is used.

PROGRAM 12.10

```
#include <iostream.h>

int binarySearch(int [], int, int);
int main()
```

(continued next page)

(*continued from previous page*)

```
{
  const int MAXELS = 5;
  int nums[NUMEL] = {5,10,22,32,45,67,73,98,99,101};
  int item, location;

  cout << "\nEnter the item you are searching for: ";
  cin  >> item;
  location = binarySearch(nums, NUMEL, item);
  if (location > -1)
    cout << "The item was found at index location "
         << location << endl;
  else
    cout << "The item was not found in the array\n";

  return 0;
}

// this function returns the location of key in the list
// a -1 is returned if the value is not found
int binarySearch(int list[], int size, int key)
{
  int left, right, midpt;

  left = 0;
  right = size - 1;

  while (left <= right)
  {
    midpt = (int) ((left + right) / 2);
    if (key == list[midpt])
    {
      return midpt;
    }
    else if (key > list[midpt])
      left = midpt + 1;
    else
      right = midpt - 1;
  }

  return -1;
}
```

FIGURE 12.20

Sample run using Program 12.10

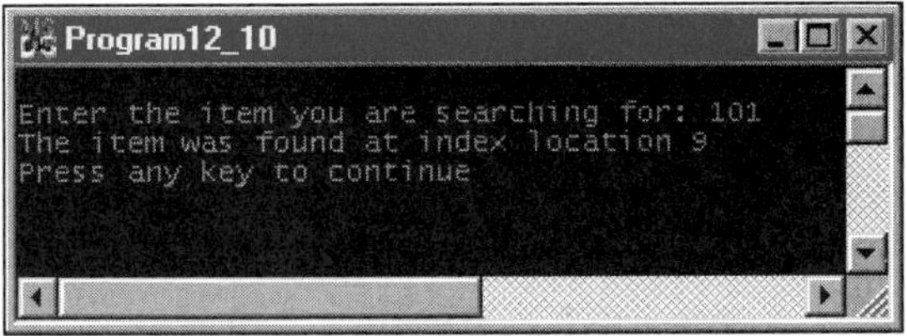

A sample run using Program 12.10 is illustrated in Figure 12.20.

The value of using a binary search algorithm is that the number of elements that must be searched is cut in half each time through the `while` loop. Thus, the first time through the loop *N* elements must be searched; the second time through the loop *N*/2 of the elements have been eliminated and only *N*/2 remain. The third time through the loop another half of the remaining elements have been eliminated, and so on.

In general, after *p* passes through the loop, the number of values remaining to be searched is $N/2^p$. In the worst case, the search can continue until there is less than or equal to one element remaining to be searched. Mathematically, this can be expressed as $N/(2^p) \leq 1$. Alternatively, this may be rephrased as *p* is the smallest integer such that $2^p \geq N$. For example, for a 1,000-element array, *N* is 1000 and the maximum number of passes, *p*, required for a binary search is 10. Table 12.1 compares the number of loop passes needed for a linear and binary search for various list sizes.

TABLE 12.1 A comparison of `while` loop passes for linear and binary searches

Array Size	10	50	500	5,000	50,000	500,000	5,000,000	50,000,000
Average Linear Search Passes	5	25	250	2,500	25,000	250,000	2,500,000	25,000,000
Maximum Linear Search Passes	10	50	500	5,000	50,000	500,000	5,000,000	50,000,000
Maximum Binary Search Passes	4	6	9	13	16	19	23	26

As illustrated, the maximum number of loop passes for a 50-item list is almost ten times more for a linear search than for binary search, and this difference is even more spectacular for larger lists. As a rule of thumb, 50 elements are usually taken as the switch-over point: For lists smaller than 50 elements, linear searches are acceptable; for larger lists, a binary search algorithm should be used.

Big O Notation

On average, over a large number of linear searches with N items in a list, we would expect to examine half ($N/2$) of the items before locating the desired item. In a binary search the maximum number of passes, p, occurs when $N/2^p = 1$. This relationship can be algebraically manipulated to $2^p = N$, which yields $p = \log_2 N$, which approximately equals 3.33 $\log_{10} N$.

For example, finding a particular name in an alphabetical directory with $N = 1000$ names would require an average of $500 = (N/2)$ comparisons using a linear search. With a binary search, only about 10 ($\approx 3.33 * \log_{10} 1000$) comparisons would be required.

A common way to express the number of comparisons required in any search algorithm using a list of N items is to give the order of magnitude of the number of comparisons required, on average, to locate a desired item. Thus, the linear search is said to be of order N and the binary search of order $\log_2 N$. Notationally, this is expressed as $O(N)$ and $O(\log_2 N)$, where the O is read as "the order of."

Sort Algorithms

For sorting data, two major categories of sorting techniques exist, called internal and external sorts. **Internal sorts** are used when the data list is not too large and the complete list can be stored within the computer's memory, usually in an array. **External sorts** are used for much larger data sets that are stored in large external disk or tape files and cannot be accommodated within the computer's memory as a complete unit. Here we present two internal sort algorithms that can be effectively used when sorting lists with less than approximately 50 elements. For larger lists more sophisticated sorting algorithms are usually employed.

Selection Sort One of the simplest sorting techniques is the selection sort. In a **selection sort** the smallest value is initially selected from the complete list of data and exchanged with the first element in the list. After this first selection and exchange, the next smallest element in the revised list is selected and exchanged with the second element in the list. The smallest element thus is already in the first position in the list, so this second pass need consider only the second through last elements. For a list consisting of N elements, this process is repeated $N - 1$ times, with each pass through the list requiring one less comparison than the previous pass.

For example, consider the list of numbers illustrated in Figure 12.21. The first pass through the initial list results in the number 32 being selected and exchanged with the first element in the list. The second pass, made on the reordered list, results in the number 155 being selected from the second through fifth elements. This value is then exchanged

FIGURE 12.21

Sample selection sort

Initial List	Pass 1	Pass 2	Pass 3	Pass 4
690	32	32	32	32
307	307	155	144	144
32	690	690	307	307
155	155	307	690	426
426	426	426	426	690

with the second element in the list. The third pass selects the number 307 from the third through fifth elements in the list and exchanges this value with the third element. Finally, the fourth and last pass through the list selects the remaining minimum value and exchanges it with the fourth list element. Although each pass in this example resulted in an exchange, no exchange would have been made in a pass if the smallest value were already in the correct location.

In pseudocode, the selection sort is described as:

```
Set interchange count to zero
  (not required, but done just to keep track of the interchanges)
For each element in the list from first to next-to-last
  Find the smallest element from the current element being referenced
      to the last element by:
    Setting the minimum value equal to the current element
    Saving (storing) the index of the current element
    For each element in the list from the current element + 1 to the last element in the list
      If element[inner loop index] < minimum value
        Set the minimum value = element[inner loop index]
        Save the index of the new found minimum value
      Endif
    EndFor
    Swap the current value with the new minimum value
    Increment the interchange count
EndFor
Return the interchange count
```

The function `selectionSort()` incorporates this procedure into a C++ function.

```
int selectionSort(int num[], int numel)
{
  int i, j, min, minidx, grade, moves = 0;
```

```
  for ( i = 0; i < (numel - 1); i++)
  {
    min = num[i];    // assume minimum is the first array element
    minidx = i;      // index of minimum element
    for(j = i + 1; j < numel; j++)
    {
      if (num[j] < min)   // if we've located a lower value
      {                   // capture it
      min = num[j];
      minidx = j;
      }
    }
    if (min < num[i])  // check if we have a new minimum
    {                  // and if we do, swap values
      grade = num[i];
      num[i] = min;
      num[minidx] = grade;
      moves++;
    }
  }

  return moves;
}
```

The `selectionSort()` function expects two arguments, the list to be sorted and the number of elements in the list. As specified by the pseudocode, a nested set of `for` loops performs the sort. The outer `for` loop causes one less pass through the list than the total number of data items in the list. For each pass, the variable `min` is initially assigned the value `num[i]`, where `i` is the outer `for` loop's counter variable. Because `i` begins at 0 and ends at one less than `numel`, each element in the list, except the last, is successively designated as the current element.

The inner loop cycles through the elements below the current element and is used to select the next smallest value. Thus, this loop begins at the index value $i + 1$ and continues through the end of the list. When a new minimum is found, its value and position in the list are stored in the variables named `min` and `minidx`, respectively. Upon completion of the inner loop, an exchange is made only if a value less than that in the current position was found.

For purposes of testing `selectionSort()`, Program 12.11 was constructed. This program implements a selection sort for the same list of ten numbers that was previously used to test our search algorithms. For later comparison to the other sorting algorithms that will be presented, the number of actual moves made by the program to get the data into sorted order is counted and displayed.

PROGRAM 12.11

```
#include <iostream.h>

int selectionSort(int [], int);

int main()
{
  const int NUMEL = 10;
  int nums[NUMEL] = {22,5,67,98,45,32,101,99,73,10};
  int i, moves;

  moves = selectionSort(nums, NUMEL);

  cout << "\nThe sorted list, in ascending order, is:\n";
  for (i = 0; i < NUMEL; i++)
    cout << "  " << nums[i];

  cout << endl << moves << " moves were made to sort this list\n";
  return 0;
}

int selectionSort(int num[], int numel)
{
  int i, j, min, minidx, grade, moves = 0;

  for ( i = 0; i < (numel - 1); i++)
  {
    min = num[i];   // assume minimum is the first array element
    minidx = i;     // index of minimum element
    for(j = i + 1; j < numel; j++)
    {
      if (num[j] < min)   // if we've located a lower value
      {                   // capture it
        min = num[j];
        minidx = j;
      }
    }
```

(continued next page)

(*continued from previous page*)

```
    if (min < num[i])  // check if we have a new minimum
    {                  // and if we do, swap values
      grade = num[i];
      num[i] = min;
      num[minidx] = grade;
      moves++;
    }
  }

  return moves;
}
```

The output produced by Program 12.11 is shown in Figure 12.22.

FIGURE 12.22

Output displayed by Program 12.11

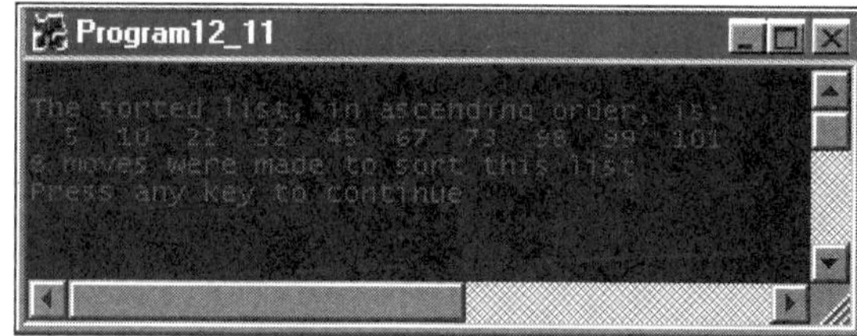

The number of moves displayed depends on the initial order of the values in the list. An advantage of the selection sort is that the maximum number of moves that must be made is $N - 1$, where N is the number of items in the list. Further, each move is a final move that results in an element residing in its final location in the sorted list.

A disadvantage of the selection sort is that $N(N - 1)/2$ comparisons are always required, regardless of the initial arrangement of the data. This number of comparisons is obtained as follows: the last pass always requires one comparison, the next-to-last pass requires two comparisons, and so on, to the first pass, which requires $N - 1$ comparisons. Thus, the total number of comparisons is:

$$1 + 2 + 3 + \ldots + N - 1 = N(N - 1)/2 = N^2/2 - N/2.$$

For large values of N the N^2 dominates, and the order of the selection sort is $O(N^2)$.

Exchange ("Bubble") Sort In an **exchange** or **bubble sort** adjacent elements of the list are exchanged with one another in such a manner that the list becomes sorted. One example of such a sequence of exchanges is provided by the bubble sort, where successive values in the list are compared, beginning with the first two elements. If the list is to be sorted in ascending (from smallest to largest) order, the smaller value of the two being compared is always placed before the larger value. For lists sorted in descending (from largest to smallest) order, the smaller of the two values being compared is always placed after the larger value.

For example, assuming that a list of values is to be sorted in ascending order, if the first element in the list is larger than the second, the two elements are interchanged. Then the second and third elements are compared. Again, if the second element is larger than the third, these two elements are interchanged. This process continues until the last two elements have been compared and exchanged, if necessary. If no exchanges were made during this initial pass through the data, the data are in the correct order and the process is finished; otherwise, a second pass is made through the data, starting from the first element and stopping at the next-to-last element. The reason for stopping at the next-to-last element on the second pass is that the first pass always results in the most positive value "sinking" to the bottom of the list.

As a specific example of this process, consider the list of numbers illustrated in Figure 12.23. The first comparison results in the interchange of the first two element values, 690 and 307. The next comparison, between elements two and three in the revised list, results in the interchange of values between the second and third elements, 690 and 32. This comparison and possible switching of adjacent values is continued until the last two elements have been compared and possibly switched. This process completes the first pass through the data and results in the largest number moving to the bottom of the list. As the largest value sinks to its resting place at the bottom of the list, the smaller elements slowly rise, or "bubble," to the top of the list. This bubbling effect of the smaller elements is what gave rise to the name "bubble" sort for this sorting algorithm.

Because the first pass through the list ensures that the largest value always moves to the bottom of the list, the second pass stops at the next-to-last element. This process continues with each pass stopping at one higher element than the previous pass, until either $N - 1$ passes through the list have been completed or no exchanges are necessary in any single pass. In both cases the resulting list is in sorted order. The pseudocode describing this sort is:

FIGURE 12.23

The first pass of an exchange sort

690 ←	307	307	307	307
307 ←	690 ←	32	32	32
32	32 ←	690 ←	155	155
155	155	155 ←	690 ←	426
426	426	426	426 ←	690

```
Set interchange count to zero
  (not required, but done just to keep track of the interchanges)
For the first element in the list to one less than the last element (i index)
  For the second element in the list to the last element (j index)
    If num[j] < num[j - 1]
    {
      swap num[j] with num[j - 1]
      increment interchange count
    }
  EndFor
EndFor
Return interchange count
```

This sort algorithm is coded in C++ as the function `bubbleSort()`, which is included within Program 12.12 for testing purposes. This program tests `bubbleSort()` with the same list of ten numbers as was used in Program 12.11 to test `selectionSort()`. For comparison to the earlier selection sort, the number of adjacent moves (exchanges) made by `bubbleSort()` is also counted and displayed.

PROGRAM 12.12

```
#include <iostream.h>

int bubbleSort(int [], int);

int main()
{
  const int NUMEL = 10;
  int nums[NUMEL] = {22,5,67,98,45,32,101,99,73,10};
  int i, moves;

  moves = bubbleSort(nums, NUMEL);

  cout << "\nThe sorted list, in ascending order, is:\n";
  for (i = 0; i < NUMEL; ++i)
    cout << "  " << nums[i];

  cout << endl << moves << " moves were made to sort this list\n";

  return 0;
}
```

(continued next page)

(continued from previous page)

```
int bubbleSort(int num[], int numel)
{
  int i, j, grade, moves = 0;

  for ( i = 0; i < (numel - 1); i++)
  {
    for(j = 1; j < numel; j++)
    {
      if (num[j] < num[j-1])
      {
        grade = num[j];
        num[j] = num[j-1];
        num[j-1] = grade;
        moves++;
      }
    }
  }

  return moves;
}
```

The output produced by Program 12.12 is shown in Figure 12.24.

As with the selection sort, the number of comparisons using a bubble sort is $O(N^2)$ and the number of required moves depends on the initial order of the values in the list. In the worst case, when the data are in reverse sorted order, the selection sort performs better than the bubble sort. Here both sorts require $N(N-1)/2$ comparisons, but the selection sort needs only $N-1$ moves, whereas the bubble sort needs $N(N-1)/2$ moves. The additional moves required by the bubble sort result from the intermediate exchanges between adjacent elements to "settle" each element into its final position. In this regard the selection sort is superior, because no intermediate moves are necessary. For random data, such as that used in Programs 12.11 and 12.12, the selection sort generally performs equal to or better than the bubble sort.

FIGURE 12.24

Output displayed by Program 12.12

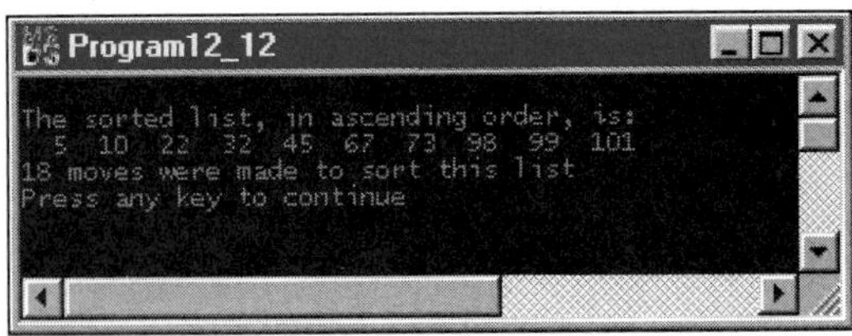

13 Pointers

One of C++'s advantages is that it allows the programmer access to the addresses of variables used in a program. This permits programmers to directly enter into a computer's inner workings and access its basic storage structure. As a practical matter, in constructing programs for the majority of simple applications you will not need to use pointers, and in many situations, such as passing addresses into a function, reference parameters can be used in place of pointers. However, to become an accomplished C++ programmer, to fully understand all of the complexities of classes, and to effectively use the Microsoft Foundation Classes for Windows programming, you must thoroughly understand pointers.

Fundamentally, a **pointer** is simply a variable that is used to store a memory address. This chapter presents the basics of declaring pointers, and then provides methods of applying pointer variables to access and use their stored addresses in meaningful ways.

Being able to easily access and manipulate memory address data gives the C++ programmer capabilities and programming power that is not available in other high-level languages. Although other languages, such as Pascal and FORTRAN 90 also provide pointers, C++ extends this feature by providing pointer arithmetic; that is, pointer values can be added, subtracted, and compared. It is this feature that makes C++ pointers both easier to understand and a much more powerful feature than pointers provided in other languages.

13.1 Addresses and Pointers

Every variable has three major items associated with it: its data type, the actual value stored in the variable, and the address of the variable. As we have already seen, a variable's data type is declared with a declaration statement and a value is stored in a variable either by initialization when the variable is declared or by assignment. For the majority of applications the variable's name is a simple and sufficient means of locating the variable's contents, and the translation of a variable's name to actual memory storage location is done by the computer each time the variable's name is used in a program.

As we saw in Section 2.4, to display the address of a variable we can use C++'s address operator, `&`. For example, to determine the address of a variable named `num`, we can use C++'s address operator, `&`, which means "the address of." When used in a nondeclarative statement, the address operator placed in front of a variable's name refers to the address of the variable.[1] For example, in a nondeclarative statement, `&num` means *the address of* `num`, `&miles` means *the address of* `miles`, and `&foo` means *the address of* `foo`. Program 13.1, which is a copy of Program 2.9, uses the address operator to display the address of the variable `num`.

PROGRAM 13.1

```
#include <iostream.h>

int main()
{
  int num;

  num = 22;
  cout << "num = " << num << endl;
  cout << "The address of num = " << &num << endl;

  return 0;
}
```

Figure 13.1 illustrates a sample run using Program 13.1.

1 As we have seen in Chapter 6, when used in a declaring reference arguments the ampersand refers to the data type *preceding* it. Thus, the declarations `float& num` and `float #` are read as "`num` is the address of a `float`," or more commonly as "`num` is a reference to a float."

FIGURE 13.1

Output displayed by Program 13.1

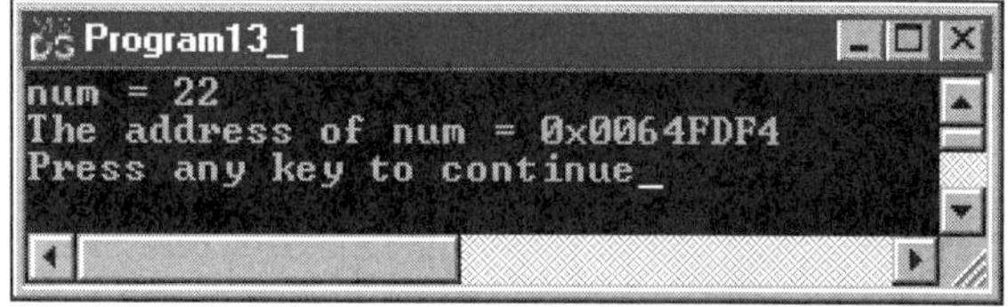

Figure 13.2 illustrates both the contents and address of the `num` variable provided by the output of Program 13.1.

Clearly, the address output by Program 13.1 depends on the computer used to run the program. Every time Program 13.1 is executed, however, it displays the address of the first memory location used to store the variable `num`.[2] As illustrated by the output of Program 13.1, the display of addresses is in hexadecimal notation. This display has no effect on how addresses are used internal to the program; it merely provides us with a means of displaying addresses that is helpful in understanding them. As we shall see, using addresses as opposed to only displaying them provides the C++ programmer with an extremely powerful programming tool.

Storing Addresses

Besides displaying the address of a variable, as was done in Program 13.1, we can also store addresses in suitably declared variables. For example, the statement

```
numAddr = &num;
```

stores the address corresponding to the variable `num` in the variable `numAddr`, as illustrated in Figure 13.3. Similarly, the statements

```
d = &m;
tabPoint = &list;
chrPoint = &ch;
```

FIGURE 13.2

Contents and address of the variable `num`

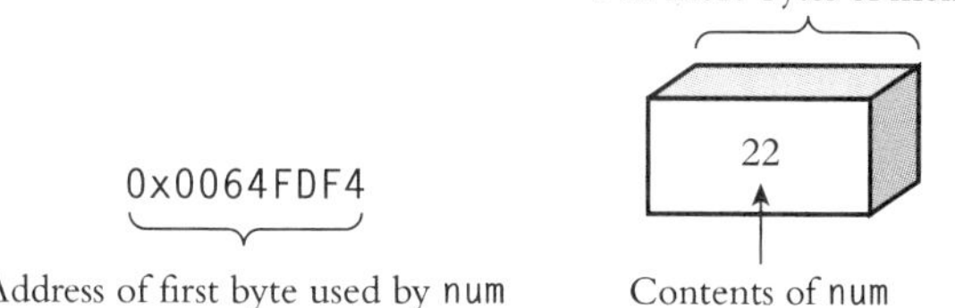

2 To obtain the total number of bytes used to store each data type, use the `sizeof()` operator presented in Section 2.5.

FIGURE 13.3

Storing num's address into numAddr

Variable's name:	Variable's contents:
numAddr	Address of num

store the addresses of the variables m, list, and ch in the variables d, tabPoint, and chrPoint, respectively, as illustrated in Figure 13.4.

The variables numAddr, d, tabPoint, and chrPoint are formally called **pointer variables,** or **pointers** for short. **Pointers** are simply variables that are used to store the addresses of other variables.

FIGURE 13.4

Storing more addresses

Variable	Contents
d	Address of m
tabPoint	Address of list
chrPoint	Address of ch

Using Addresses

To use a stored address, C++ provides us with an **indirection operator,** *. The * symbol, when followed by a pointer (with a space permitted both before and after the *), means *the variable whose address is stored in*. Thus, if numAddr is a pointer (remember that a pointer is a variable that stores an address), *numAddr means *the variable whose address is stored in* numAddr. Similarly, *tabPoint means *the variable whose address is stored in* tabPoint and *chrPoint means *the variable whose address is stored in* chrPoint. Figure 13.5 shows the relationship between the address contained in a pointer variable and the variable ultimately addressed.

Although *d literally means *the variable whose address is stored in* d, this is commonly shortened to the statement *the variable pointed to by* d. Similarly, referring to Figure 13.5, *y can be read as *the variable pointed to by* y. The value ultimately obtained, as shown in Figure 13.5, is qqqq.

When using a pointer variable, the value that is finally obtained is always found by first going to the pointer variable (or pointer, for short) for an address. The address contained in the pointer is then used to get the desired contents. Certainly, this is a rather indirect way of getting to the final value and, not unexpectedly, the term **indirect addressing** is used to describe this procedure.

FIGURE 13.5

Using a pointer variable

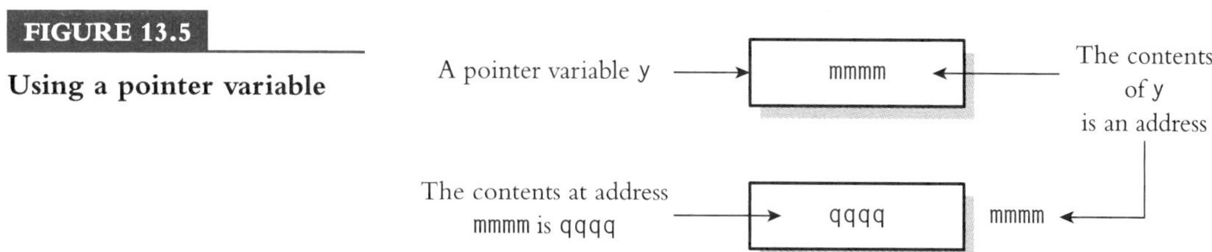

Because use of a pointer requires the computer to do a double lookup (first the address is retrieved, then the address is used to retrieve the actual data), a worthwhile question is, why would you want to store an address in the first place? The answer to this question rests on the intimate relationship between pointers and arrays and the ability of pointers to create and delete new variable storage locations dynamically, while a program is running. Both of these topics are presented later in this chapter. For now, however, given that each variable has a memory address associated with it, the idea of actually storing an address should not seem overly strange.

Declaring Pointers

Like all variables, pointers must be declared before they can be used to store an address. When we declare a pointer variable, C++ requires that we also specify the type of variable that is pointed to. For example, if the address in the pointer `numAddr` is the address of an integer, the correct declaration for the pointer is:

```
int *numAddr;
```

This declaration is read as *the variable pointed to by* `numAddr` (from the `*numAddr` in the declaration) *is an integer.*[3]

Notice that the declaration `int *numAddr;` specifies two things: first, that the variable pointed to by `numAddr` is an integer; and second, that `numAddr` must be a pointer (because it is used with the indirection operator `*`). Similarly, if the pointer `tabPoint`

3 Pointer declarations may also be written in the form data-type* pointer-name; where a space is placed between the indirection operator symbol and the pointer variable name. This form, however, becomes error prone when multiple pointer variables are declared in the same declaration statement and the asterisk symbol is inadvertently omitted after the first pointer name is declared. For example, the declaration `int* num1, num2;` declares `num1` as a pointer variable and `num2` as an integer variable. In order to more easily accommodate multiple pointers in the same declaration and clearly mark a variable as a pointer, we will adhere to the convention that places an asterisk directly in front of each pointer variable name. This possible error rarely occurs with reference declarations because references are almost exclusively used as parameters, and single declarations of parameters are mandatory.

points to (contains the address of) a floating point number and `chrPoint` points to a character variable, the required declarations for these pointers are, respectively:

```
float *tabPoint;
char *chrPoint;
```

These two declarations can be read, respectively, as *the variable pointed to by* `tabPoint` *is a float* and *the variable pointed to by* `chrPoint` *is a char.* Because all addresses appear the same, this additional information is needed by the compiler to know how many storage locations to access when it uses the address stored in the pointer. Further examples of pointer declarations are:

```
char *inkey;
int *numPt;
float *distAddr;
double *nm1Ptr
```

To understand pointer declarations, it is helpful to read them "backwards," starting with the indirection operator, the asterisk, *, and translating it either as *the variable whose address is stored in* or *the variable pointed to by*. Applying this to pointer declarations, the declaration `char *inkey;`, for example, can be read as either *the variable whose address is stored in* `inkey` *is a character* or *the variable pointed to by* `inkey` *is a character.* Both of these statements are frequently shortened to the simpler statement that `inkey` *points to a character.* Because all three interpretations of the declaration statement are correct, you can select and use whichever description makes more sense to you. We now put this together to construct a program using pointers. Consider Program 13.2.

PROGRAM 13.2

```
#include <iostream.h>

int main()
{
  int *numAddr;        // declare a pointer to an int
  int miles, dist;     // declare two integer variables

  dist = 158;          // store the number 158 into dist
  miles = 22;          // store the number 22 into miles
  numAddr = &miles;    // store the 'address of miles' in numAddr

  cout << "\nThe address stored in numAddr is " << numAddr << endl;
```

(continued next page)

(continued from previous page)

```
  cout << "The value pointed to by numAddr is " << *numAddr << "\n\n";

  numAddr = &dist;  // now store the address of dist in numAddr
  cout << "The address now stored in numAddr is " << numAddr << endl;
  cout << "The value now pointed to by numAddr is " << *numAddr << endl;

  return 0;
}
```

The output displayed when Program 13.2 is run is shown in Figure 13.6.

The only use for Program 13.2 is to help us understand "what gets stored where." Let's review the program to see how the output was produced.

The declaration statement `int *numAddr;` declares `numAddr` to be a pointer variable used to store the address of an integer variable. The statement `numAddr = &miles;` stores the address of the variable `miles` into the pointer `numAddr`. The first statement of `cout` causes this address to be displayed. The second `cout` statement in Program 13.2 uses the indirection operator to retrieve and print out *the value pointed to by* `numAddr`, which is, of course, the value stored in `miles`.

Because `numAddr` has been declared as a pointer to an integer variable, we can use this pointer to store the address of any integer variable. The statement `numAddr = &dist;` illustrates this by storing the address of the variable `dist` in `numAddr`. The last two `cout` statements verify the change in `numAddr`'s value and that the new stored address does point to the variable `dist`. As illustrated in Program 13.2, only addresses should be stored in pointers.

It certainly would have been much simpler if the pointer used in Program 13.2 could have been declared as `pointer numAddr;`. Such a declaration, however, conveys no information as to the storage used by the variable whose address is stored in `numAddr`. This information is essential when the pointer is used with the indirection operator, as it is in the second `cout` activation in Program 13.2. For example, if the address of an integer is stored in `numAddr`, then only two bytes of storage are typically retrieved when the address is

FIGURE 13.6

Sample run using Program 13.2

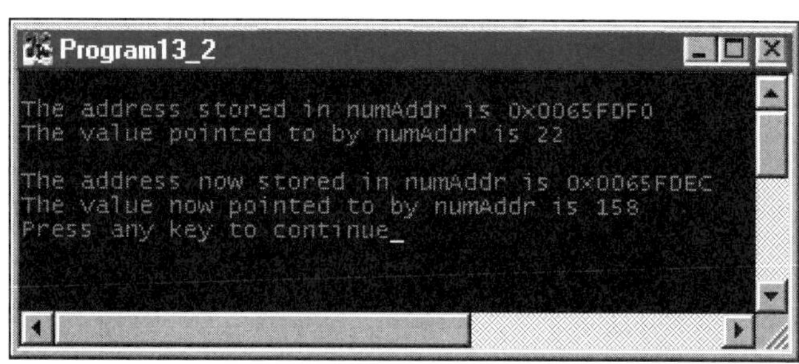

FIGURE 13.7

Addressing different data types using pointers

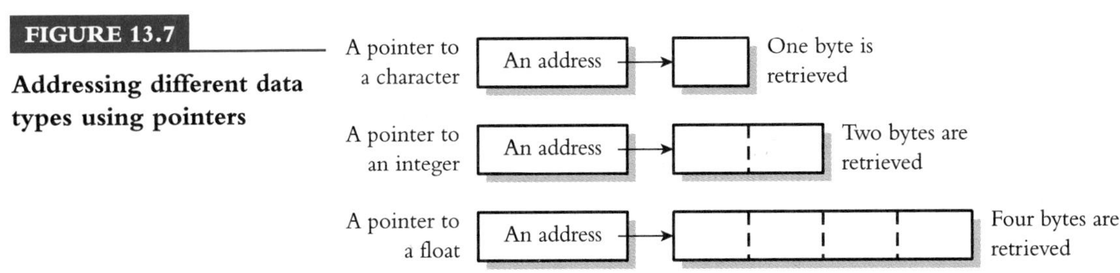

used. If the address of a character is stored in `numAddr`, only one byte of storage would be retrieved, and a float typically requires the retrieval of four bytes of storage. The declaration of a pointer must, therefore, include the type of variable being pointed to. Figure 13.7 illustrates this concept.

References and Pointers

At this point you might be asking what the difference is between a pointer and a reference. Essentially, a reference is a named constant for an address; as such, the address named as a reference cannot be altered. Because a pointer is a variable, the address in the pointer can be changed. For most applications the use of references over pointers as arguments to functions is easier and clearly preferred. This is due to the simpler notation used in locating a reference parameter, which eliminates using the address operator, &, and the dereferencing operator, *, required for pointers. Technically, references are said to be **automatically dereferenced** or **implicitly dereferenced** (the two terms are used synonymously), whereas pointers must be explicitly dereferenced to locate the value being accessed.

For example, in passing a scalar variable's address as a function argument, references provide a simpler notational interface and are usually preferred. For other situations, such as dynamically allocating new sections of memory for additional variables as a program is running or using alternatives to array notation (both topics are presented in this chapter), pointers are required.

Reference Variables[4] References are used almost exclusively as formal function parameters and return types. Nevertheless, reference variables are also available in C++. For completeness we now show how such variables can be declared and used.

Once a variable has been declared, it may be given additional names. This is accomplished using a reference declaration, which has the form:

data-type& newName = existingName;

---

4 This topic may be omitted with no loss of subject continuity.

FIGURE 13.8

`sum` **is an alternative name for** `total`

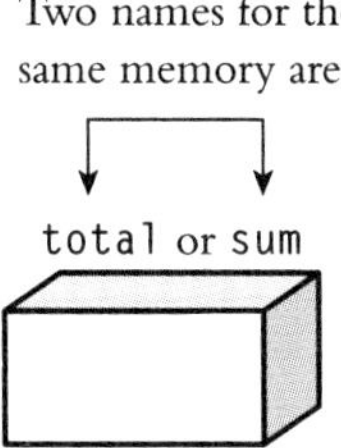

For example, the reference declaration

```
float& sum = total;
```

equates the name `sum` to the name `total`—both now refer to the same variable, as illustrated in Figure 13.8.

Once another name has been established for a variable using a reference declaration, the new name, which is referred to as an **alias,** can be used in place of the original name. For example, consider Program 13.3.

PROGRAM 13.3

```
#include <iostream.h>

int main()
{
  float total = 20.5;     // declare and initialize total
  float& sum = total;     // declare another name for total

  cout << "sum = " << sum << endl;
  sum = 18.6;             // this changes the value in total
  cout << "total = " << total << endl;

  return 0;
}
```

The following lines are displayed by Program 13.3:

```
sum = 20.5
total = 18.6
```

Because the variable sum is simply another reference to the variable total, it is the value stored in total that is obtained by the first cout statement in Program 13.3. Changing the value in sum then changes the value in total, which is displayed by the second cout statement in Program 13.3.

In constructing references, two considerations must be kept in mind. First, the reference should be of the same data type as the variable to which it refers. For example, the sequence of declarations

```
int num = 5;
double& numref = num;
```

does not equate numref to num because they are not the of the same data type. Rather, because the compiler cannot correctly associate the reference with a variable, it creates an unnamed variable of the reference type first, and then references this unnamed variable with the reference variable. Such unnamed variables are called **anonymous variables.** For example, consider Program 13.4, which illustrates the effect of creating an anonymous variable.

PROGRAM 13.4

```
#include <iostream.h>

int main()
{
  int num = 10;
  float& numref = num;  // this does not equate numref to num
                        // instead, it equates numref to an
                        // anonymous floating point variable

  numref = 20.5;
  cout << "The value of num is " << num << endl;
  cout << "The value of numref is " << numref << endl;

  return 0;
}
```

The output display produced by Program 13.4 is:

```
The value of num is 10
The value of numref is 20.5
```

Notice that the value of num is not affected by the value stored in numref. This is because numref could not be created as a reference for num; rather, it is another name for an unnamed (anonymous) floating point variable that can be reached only by using the reference name numref.

Just as declaring a reference to an incorrect data type produces an anonymous variable, so does equating a reference to a constant. For example, the declaration

```
int& val = 5;  // an anonymous variable is created
```

creates an anonymous variable with the number 5 stored in it. The only way to access this variable is by the reference name. Clearly, creating references to anonymous variables should be avoided. Once a reference name has been equated to either a legal variable or an anonymous one, the reference cannot be changed to refer to another variable.

As with all declaration statements, multiple references may be declared in a single statement as long as each reference name is preceded by the ampersand symbol. Thus, the declaration

```
float& sum = total, &  average;
```

creates two reference variables named sum and average.[5]

Another way of looking at references is to consider them as pointers with restricted capabilities that implicitly hide a lot of dereferencing that is explicitly required with pointers.

For example, consider the statements

```
int b;       // b is an integer variable
int& a = b; // a is a reference variable that stores b's address
a = 10;      // this changes b's value to 10
```

Here, a is declared as a reference variable that is effectively a named constant for the address of the b variable. The compiler knows from the declaration that a is a reference variable, so it automatically assigns the address of b (rather than the contents of b) to a in the declaration statement. Finally, in the statement a = 10; the compiler uses the address stored in a to change the value stored in b to 10. The advantage of using the reference is that it automatically performs an indirect access of b's value without the need for explicitly using the indirection symbol, *. As we have noted previously, this type of access is referred to as an **automatic dereference.**

5 Reference declarations may also be written in the form data-type &newName = existing name; where a space is placed before the ampersand symbol and the reference variable name. This form is not used much, however, probably to distinguish reference variable address notation from that used in assigning addresses to pointer variables.

Implementing this same correspondence between a and b using pointers is done by the following sequence of instructions:

```
int b;         // b is an integer variable
int *a = &b; // a is a pointer - store b's address in a
*a = 10;       // this changes b's value to 10 by explicit
               // dereference of the address in a
```

Here a is defined as a pointer that is initialized to store the address of b. Thus, *a, which can be read as either *the variable whose address is in* a or *the variable pointed to by* a is b, and the expression *a = 10 changes b's value to 10. Notice that in the pointer case that the stored address can be altered to point to another variable; whereas in the reference case the reference variable cannot be altered to refer to any variable except the one to which it is initialized. Also notice that to dereference a, we must explicitly use the indirection operator, *. As you might expect, the * is also referred to as the **dereferencing operator.**

EXERCISES 13.1

1. If average is a variable, what does &average mean?

2. For the variables and addresses illustrated in Figure 13.9, determine &temp, &dist, &date, and &miles.

FIGURE 13.9

Memory bytes for Exercise 2

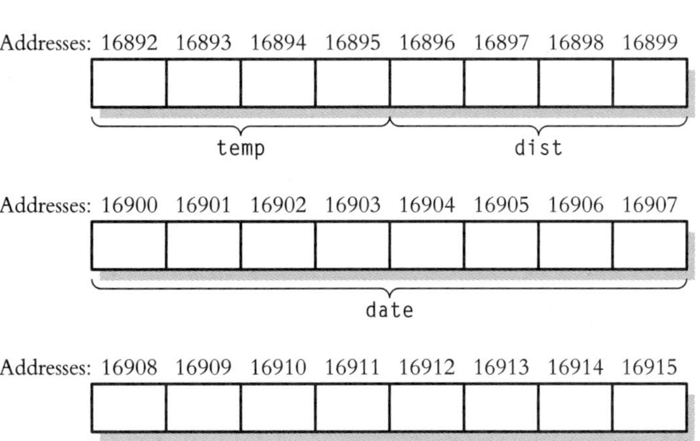

3. a. Write a C++ program that includes the following declaration statements. Have the program use the address operator and `cout` statements to display the addresses corresponding to each variable.

```
char key, choice;
int num, count;
long date;
float yield;
double price;
```

b. After running the program written for Exercise 3a, draw a diagram of how your computer has set aside storage for the variables in the program. On your diagram, fill in the addresses displayed by the program.

c. Modify the program written in Exercise 3a to display the amount of storage your computer reserves for each data type (use the `sizeof()` operator). With this information and the address information provided in Exercise 3b, determine if your computer set aside storage for the variables in the order they were declared.

4. If a variable is declared as a pointer, what must be stored in the variable?

5. Using the indirection operator, write expressions for the following:

a. The variable pointed to by `xAddr`
b. The variable whose address is in `yAddr`
c. The variable pointed to by `ptYld`
d. The variable pointed to by `ptMiles`
e. The variable pointed to by `mptr`
f. The variable whose address is in `pdate`
g. The variable pointed to by `distPtr`
h. The variable pointed to by `tabPt`
i. The variable whose address is in `hoursPt`

6. Write declaration statements for the following:

a. The variable pointed to by `yAddr` is an integer.
b. The variable pointed to by `chAddr` is a character.
c. The variable pointed to by `ptYr` is a long integer.
d. The variable pointed to by `amt` is a double precision variable.
e. The variable pointed to by `z` is an integer.
f. The variable pointed to by `qp` is a floating point variable.
g. `datePt` is a pointer to an integer.

h. `yldAddr` is a pointer to a double precision variable.

i. `amtPt` is a pointer to a floating point variable.

j. `ptChr` is a pointer to a character.

7. a. What are the variables `yAddr`, `chAddr`, `ptYr`, `amt`, `z`, `qp`, `datePtr`, `yldAddr`, `amtPt`, and `ptChr` used in Exercise 6 called?

b. Why are the variable names `amt`, `z`, and `qp` used in Exercise 6 not good choices for pointer variable names?

8. Write English sentences that describe what is contained in the following declared variables:

a. `char *keyAddr;`

b. `int *m;`

c. `double *yldAddr;`

d. `long *yPtr;`

e. `float *pCou;`

f. `int *ptDate;`

9. Which of the following are declarations for pointers:

a. `long a;`

b. `char b;`

c. `char *c;`

d. `int x;`

e. `int *p;`

f. `double w;`

g. `float *k;`

h. `float l;`

i. `double *z;`

10. For the following declarations,

```
int *xPt, *yAddr;
long *dtAddr, *ptAddr;
double *ptZ;
int a;
long b;
double c;
```

determine which of the following statements is valid.

a. `yAddr = &a;`
b. `yAddr = &b;`
c. `yAddr = &c;`
d. `yAddr = a;`
e. `yAddr = b;`
f. `yAddr = c;`
g. `dtAddr = &a;`
h. `dtAddr = &b;`
i. `dtAddr = &c;`
j. `dtAddr = a;`
k. `dtAddr = b;`
l. `dtAddr = c;`
m. `ptZ = &a;`
n. `ptAddr = &b;`
o. `ptAddr = &c;`
p. `ptAddr = a;`
q. `ptAddr = b;`
r. `ptAddr = c;`
s. `yAddr = xPt;`
t. `yAddr = dtAddr;`
u. `yAddr = ptAddr;`

11. For the variables and addresses illustrated in Figure 13.10 (on the next page), fill in the appropriate data as determined by the following statements:

a. `ptNum = &m;`
b. `amtAddr = &amt;`
c. `*zAddr = 25;`
d. `k = *numAddr;`
e. `ptDay = zAddr;`
f. `*ptYr = 1987;`
g. `*amtAddr = *numAddr;`

12. Using the `sizeof()` operator, determine the number of bytes used by your computer to store the address of an integer, character, and double precision number. (*Hint:* `sizeof(*int)` can be used to determine the number of memory bytes used for a pointer to an integer.) Would you expect the size of each address to be the same? Why or why not?

FIGURE 13.10

Memory locations for Exercise 11

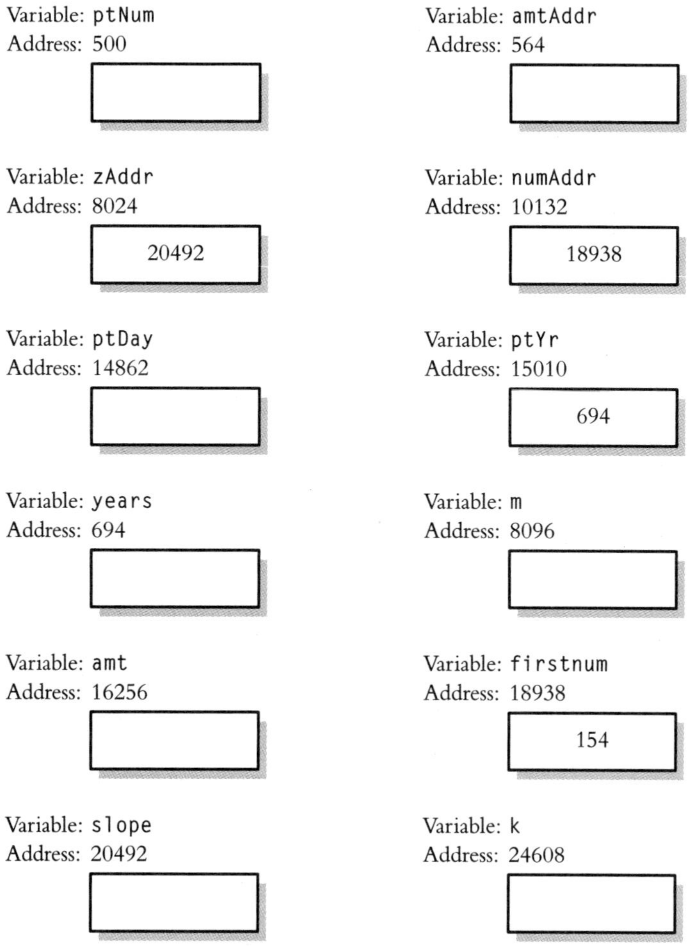

Variable	Address	Contents
`ptNum`	500	
`amtAddr`	564	
`zAddr`	8024	20492
`numAddr`	10132	18938
`ptDay`	14862	
`ptYr`	15010	694
`years`	694	
`m`	8096	
`amt`	16256	
`firstnum`	18938	154
`slope`	20492	
`k`	24608	

13.2 Array Names as Pointers

Although pointers are simply, by definition, variables used to store addresses, there is also a direct and intimate relationship between array names and pointers. In this section we describe this relationship in detail.

Figure 13.11 illustrates the storage of a single-dimensional array named `grade`, which contains five integers. Assume that each integer requires two bytes of storage.

Using subscripts, the third element in the grade array is referred to as `grade[3]`.The use of a subscript, however, conceals the extensive use of addresses by the computer. Internally, the computer immediately uses the subscript to calculate the address of the desired element based on both the starting address of the array and the amount of storage

FIGURE 13.11

The `grade` array in storage

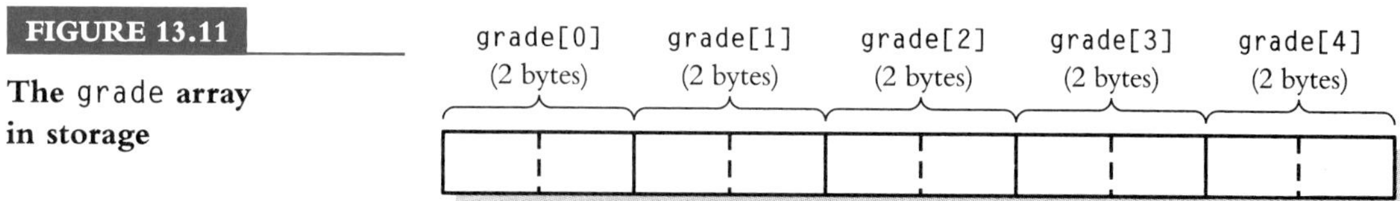

used by each element. Accessing the element `grade[3]` forces the compiler, internally, to make the address computation

```
&grade[3] = &grade[0] + (3 * sizeof(int))
```

Remembering that the address operator, `&`, means "the address of," this last statement is read "the address of `grade[3]` equals the address of `grade[0]` plus 6." Figure 13.12 illustrates the address computation used to locate `grade[3]`.

FIGURE 13.12

Using a subscript to obtain an address

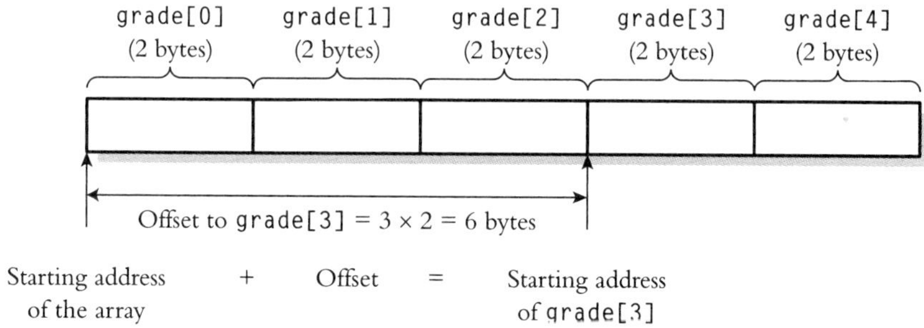

Recall that a pointer is a variable used to store an address. If we create a pointer to store the address of the first element in the grade array, we can mimic the operation used by the computer to access the array elements. Before we do this, let us first consider Program 13.5.

PROGRAM 13.5

```
#include <iostream.h>

int main()
{
  const int ARRAYSIZE = 5;
```

(continued next page)

(continued from previous page)

```
  int i, grade[ARRAYSIZE] = {98, 87, 92, 79, 85};

  for (i = 0; i < ARRAYSIZE; i++)
    cout << "\nElement " << i << " is " << grade[i];
  cout << endl;

  return 0;
}
```

Figure 13.13 illustrates the output produced when Program 13.5 is run.

FIGURE 13.13

Output displayed by Program 13.5

```
Program13_5

Element 0 is 98
Element 1 is 87
Element 2 is 92
Element 3 is 79
Element 4 is 85
Press any key to continue
```

Program 13.5 displays the values of the array grade using standard subscript notation. Now, let us store the address of array element 0 in a pointer. Then, using the indirection operator, *, we can use the address in the pointer to access each array element. For example, if we store the address of `grade[0]` into a pointer named `gPtr` (using the assignment statement `gPtr = &grade[0];`), then, as illustrated in Figure 13.14, the expression `*gPtr`, which means "the variable pointed to by `gPtr`," references `grade[0]`.

One unique feature of pointers is that offsets may be included in expressions using pointers. For example, the 1 in the expression `*(gPtr + 1)` is an offset. The complete expression refers to the integer that is one beyond the variable pointed to by `gPtr`. Similarly,

FIGURE 13.14

Variable pointed to by `*gPtr` is `grade[0]`

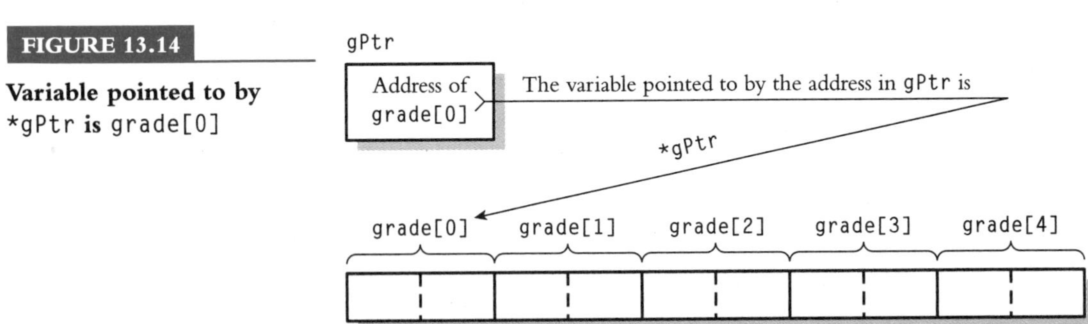

FIGURE 13.15

An offset of 3 from the address in `gPtr`

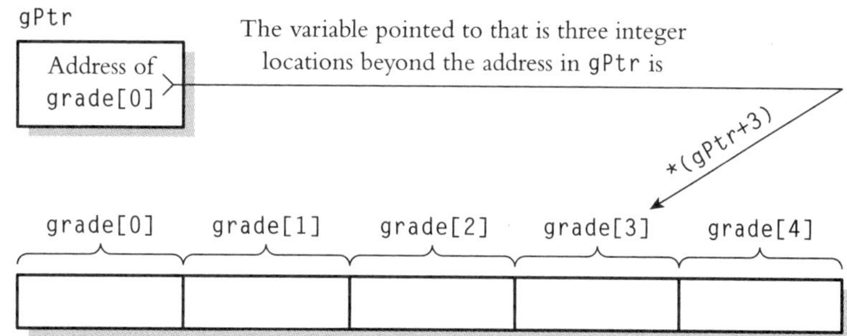

as illustrated in Figure 13.15, the expression `*(gPtr + 3)` references the variable that is three integers beyond the variable pointed to by `gPtr`. This is the variable `grade[3]`.

Table 13.1 lists the complete correspondence between elements referenced by subscripts and by pointers and offsets. The relationships listed in Table 13.1 are illustrated in Figure 13.16.

TABLE 13.1 Array elements may be referenced in two ways

Array Element	Subscript Notation	Pointer Notation
Element 0	`grade[0]`	`*gPtr`
Element 1	`grade[1]`	`*(gPtr + 1)`
Element 2	`grade[2]`	`*(gPtr + 2)`
Element 3	`grade[3]`	`*(gPtr + 3)`
Element 4	`grade[4]`	`*(gPtr + 4)`

FIGURE 13.16

The relationship between array elements and pointers

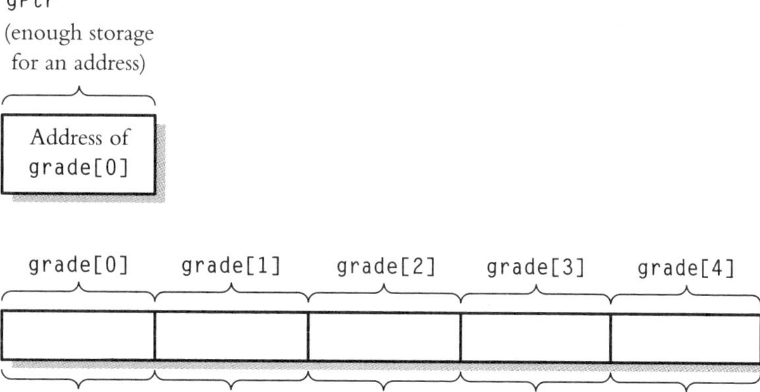

Using the correspondence between pointers and subscripts illustrated in Figure 13.16, the array elements previously accessed in Program 13.5 using subscripts can now be accessed using pointers. This is done in Program 13.6.

PROGRAM 13.6

```
#include <iostream.h>

int main()
{
  const int ARRAYSIZE = 5;

  int *gPtr;              // declare a pointer to an int
  int i, grade[ARRAYSIZE] = {98, 87, 92, 79, 85};

  gPtr = &grade[0];       // store the starting array address
  for (i = 0; i < ARRAYSIZE; i++)
    cout << "\nElement " << i << " is " << *(gPtr + i);
  cout << endl;

  return 0;
}
```

Figure 13.17 illustrates the display obtained when Program 13.6 is run. Notice that this is the same as the display produced by Program 13.5.

The method used in Program 13.6 to access individual array elements simulates how the compiler internally references all array elements. Any subscript used by a programmer is automatically converted to an equivalent pointer expression by the compiler. In our

FIGURE 13.17

Output display produced by Program 13.6

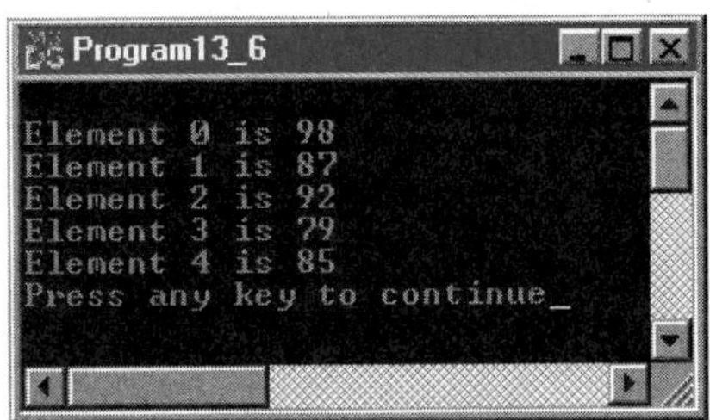

case, because the declaration of gPtr included the information that integers are pointed to, any offset added to the address in gPtr is automatically scaled by the size of an integer. Thus, *(gPtr + 3), for example, refers to the address of grade[0] plus an offset of six bytes (3 * 2), where we have assumed that sizeof(int) = 2. This is the address of grade[3] illustrated in Figure 13.16.

The parentheses in the expression *(gPtr + 3) are necessary to correctly reference the desired array element. Omitting the parentheses results in the expression *gPtr + 3. Due to the precedence of the operators, this expression adds 3 to "the variable pointed to by gPtr." Because gPtr points to grade[0], this expression adds the value of grade[0] and 3 together. Note also that the expression *(gPtr + 3) does not change the address stored in gPtr. Once the computer uses the offset to locate the correct variable from the starting address in gPtr, the offset is discarded and the address in gPtr remains unchanged.

Although the pointer gPtr used in Program 13.5 was specifically created to store the starting address of the grade array, this was, in fact, unnecessary. When an array is created, the compiler automatically creates an internal pointer constant for it and stores the starting address of the array in this pointer. In almost all respects, a pointer constant is identical to a pointer variable created by a programmer; but, as we shall see, there are some differences.

For each array created, the name of the array becomes the name of the pointer constant created by the compiler for the array, and the starting address of the first location reserved for the array is stored in this pointer. Thus, declaring the grade array in Programs 13.5 and Program 13.6 actually reserved enough storage for five integers, created an internal pointer named grade, and stored the address of grade[0] in the pointer. This is illustrated in Figure 13.18.

FIGURE 13.18

Creating an array also creates a pointer

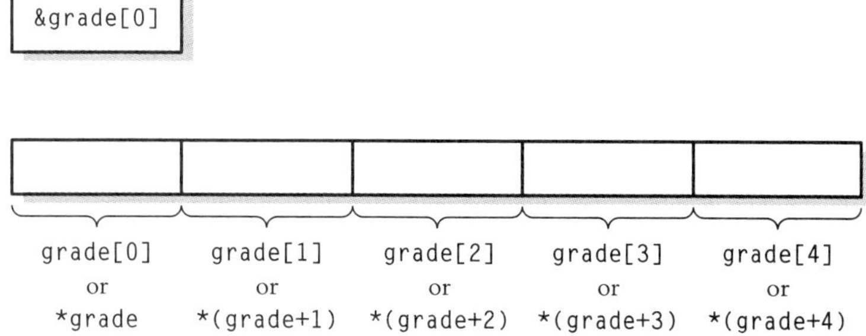

The implication is that every access to `grade` using a subscript can be replaced by an equivalent access using `grade` as a pointer. Thus, wherever the expression `grade[i]` is used, the expression `*(grade + i)` can also be used. This is illustrated in Program 13.7, in which `grade` is used as a pointer to access all of its elements.

PROGRAM 13.7

```
#include <iostream.h>

int main()
{
  const int ARRAYSIZE = 5;
  int i, grade[ARRAYSIZE] = {98, 87, 92, 79, 85};

  for (i = 0; i < ARRAYSIZE; i++)
    cout << "\nElement " << i << " is " << *(grade + i);
  cout << endl;

  return 0;
}
```

Executing Program 13.7 produces the same output previously produced by Program 13.5 and Program 13.6. However, using `grade` as a pointer made it unnecessary to declare and initialize the pointer `gPtr` used in Program 13.6.

In most respects an array name and pointer can be used interchangeably. *A true pointer, however, is a variable and the address stored in it can be changed. An array name is a pointer constant and the address stored in the pointer cannot be changed by an assignment statement.* Thus, a statement such as `grade = &grade[2];` is invalid. This should come as no surprise. The whole purpose of an array name is to correctly locate the beginning of the array, so allowing a programmer to change the address stored in the array name would defeat this purpose and lead to havoc whenever array elements were referenced. Also, expressions taking the address of an array name are invalid because the pointer created by the compiler is internal to the computer, not stored in memory, as are pointer variables. Thus, trying to store the address of `grade` using the expression `&grade` results in a compiler error.

An interesting sidelight to the observation that elements of an array can be accessed using pointers is that a pointer access can always be replaced using subscript notation. For example, if `numPtr` is declared as a pointer variable, the expression `*(numPtr + i)` can also be written as `numPtr[i]`. This is true even though `numPtr` is not created as an array.

As before, when the compiler encounters the subscript notation, it replaces it internally with the pointer notation.

Dynamic Array Allocation[6]

As each variable is defined in a program, sufficient storage for it is assigned from a pool of computer memory locations made available to the compiler. Once specific memory locations have been reserved for a variable, these locations are fixed for the life of that variable, whether they are used or not. For example, if a function requests storage for an array of 500 integers, the storage for the array is allocated and fixed from the point of the array's definition. If the application requires less than 500 integers, the unused allocated storage is not released back to the system until the array goes out of existence. If, on the other hand, the application requires more than 500 integers, the size of the integer array must be increased and the function defining the array recompiled.

An alternative to this fixed or static allocation of memory storage locations is the dynamic allocation of memory. Under a dynamic allocation scheme, the amount of storage to be allocated is determined and adjusted as the program is run, rather than being fixed at compile time.

The dynamic allocation of memory is extremely useful when dealing with lists, because it allows the list to expand as new items are added and contract as items are deleted. For example, in constructing a list of grades, the exact number of grades ultimately needed may not be known. Rather than creating a fixed array to store the grades, it is extremely useful to have a mechanism whereby the array can be enlarged and shrunk as necessary. Two C++ operators, `new` and `delete`, that provide this capability are described in Table 13.2. (These operators require the `stdlib.h` header file.)

Explicit dynamic storage requests for scalar variables or arrays are made as part of either a declaration or assignment statement[7]. For example, the declaration statement `int *num = new int;` reserves an area sufficient to hold one integer and places the address of this storage area into the pointer `num`. This same dynamic allocation can also be made by first declaring the pointer using the declaration statement `int *num;` and then subsequently assigning the pointer an address with the assignment statement `num = new int;`. In either case, the allocated storage area comes from the computer's free storage area.[8]

---

6 This topic may be omitted on first reading with no loss of subject continuity.

---

7 It should be noted that the compiler automatically provides this dynamic allocation and deallocation from the stack for all auto variables.

---

8 The free storage area of a computer is formally referred to as the *heap*. The heap consists of unallocated memory that can be allocated to a program, as requested, while the program is running.

TABLE 13.2 The new and delete operators

Operator Name	Description
new	Reserves the number of bytes requested by the declaration. Returns the address of the first reserved location or NULL if sufficient memory is not available.
delete	Releases a block of bytes previously reserved. This operator requires the address of the first location of memory to be deallocated.

In a similar manner and of more usefulness is the dynamic allocation of arrays. For example, the declaration

```
int *grades = new int[200];
```

reserves an area sufficient to store 200 integers and places the address of the first integer into the pointer grades. Although we have used the constant 200 in this example declaration, a variable dimension can be used. For example, consider the sequence of instructions

```
cout << "Enter the number of grades to be processed: ";
cin  >> numgrades;
int *grades = new int[numgrades];
```

In this sequence the actual size of the array that is created depends on the number input by the user. Because pointer and array names are related, each value in the newly created storage area can be accessed using standard array notation, such as grades[i], rather than the equivalent pointer notation *(grades + i). Program 13.8 illustrates this sequence of code in the context of a complete program.

PROGRAM 13.8

```
#include <iostream.h>

int main()
{
  int numgrades, i;
```

(continued next page)

(continued from previous page)

```
  cout << "\nEnter the number of grades to be processed: ";
  cin  >> numgrades;

  int *grades = new int[numgrades];  // create the array

  for(i = 0; i < numgrades; i++)
  {
    cout << "  Enter a grade: ";
    cin  >> grades[i];
  }
  cout << "\nAn array was created for "
       << numgrades << " integers\n";
  cout << " The values stored in the array are:";
  for (i = 0; i < numgrades; i++)
    cout << "\n   " << grades[i];
  cout << endl;

  delete grades;   // return the storage to the heap

  return 0;
}
```

Notice in Program 13.8 that the `delete` operator has been used to restore the allocated block of storage back to the operating system while the programming is executing.[9] The only address required by `delete` is the starting address of the block of storage that was dynamically allocated. Thus, any address returned by `new` can subsequently be used by `delete` to restore the reserved memory back to the computer. The `delete` operator does not alter the address passed to it, but simply removes the storage that the address refers to. Figure 13.19 illustrates a sample run using Program 13.8.

9 The allocated storage should automatically be returned to the heap, by the operating system, when the program has completed execution. This is not always the case, however, so it is extremely important to formally restore dynamically allocated memory to the heap when the storage is no longer needed. The term **memory leak** is used to describe the condition that occurs when dynamically allocated memory is not formally returned using the `delete` operator and the operating system does not reclaim the allocated memory area.

FIGURE 13.19

Sample run using Program 13.8

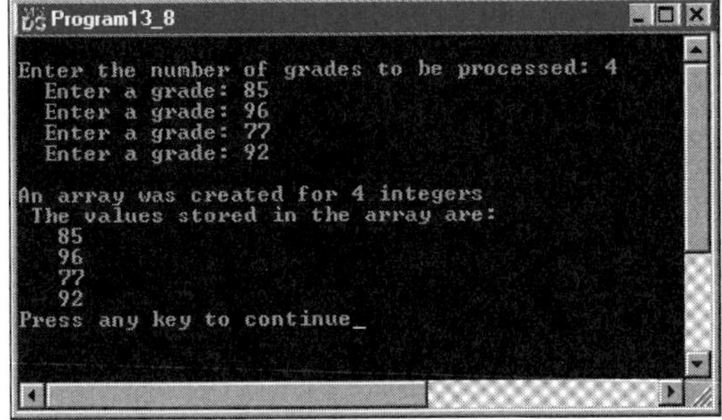
Program13_8
Enter the number of grades to be processed: 4
Enter a grade: 85
Enter a grade: 96
Enter a grade: 77
Enter a grade: 92
An array was created for 4 integers
The values stored in the array are:
85
96
77
92
Press any key to continue_

EXERCISES 13.2

1. Replace each of the following subscripted variables with a pointer notation.
   - **a.** `prices[5]`
   - **b.** `grades[2]`
   - **c.** `yield[10]`
   - **d.** `dist[9]`
   - **e.** `mile[0]`
   - **f.** `temp[20]`
   - **g.** `celsius[16]`
   - **h.** `num[50]`
   - **i.** `time[12]`

2. Replace each of the following pointer notations with a subscript notation.
   - **a.** `*(message + 6)`
   - **b.** `*amount`
   - **c.** `*(yrs + 10)`
   - **d.** `*(stocks + 2)`
   - **e.** `*(rates + 15)`
   - **f.** `*(codes + 19)`

3. **a.** List the three things that the declaration statement `double prices[5];` causes the compiler to do.
   - **b.** If each double precision number uses eight bytes of storage, how much storage is set aside for the `prices` array?
   - **c.** Draw a diagram similar to Figure 13.14 for the `prices` array.
   - **d.** Determine the byte offset relative to the start of the `prices` array corresponding to the offset in the expression `*(prices + 3)`.

4. **a.** Write a declaration to store the string `"This is a sample"` into an array named `samtest`. Include the declaration in a program that displays the values in `samtest` using a `for` loop that uses a pointer to access each element in the array.
   b. Modify the program written in Exercise 4a to display only array elements 11 through 16 (these are the letters `s`, `a`, `m`, `p`, `l`, and `e`).

5. Write a declaration to store the following values into an array named `rates`: 12.9, 18.6, 11.4, 13.7, 9.5, 15.2, 17.6. Include the declaration in a program that displays the values in the array using pointer notation.

6. Repeat Exercise 6 in Section 12.1, but use pointer notation to access all array elements.

7. Repeat Exercise 7 in Section 12.1, but use pointer notation to access all array elements.

8. As described in Table 13.2, the `new` operator returns either the address of the first new storage area allocated or `NULL` if insufficient storage is available. Modify Program 13.7 to check that a valid address has been returned before attempting to place values into the `grades` array. Display an appropriate message if sufficient storage is not available.

13.3 Pointer Arithmetic

Pointer variables, like all variables, contain values. The value stored in a pointer is, of course, an address. Thus, by adding and subtracting numbers to pointers we can obtain different addresses. Additionally, the addresses in pointers can be compared using any of the relational operators (==, !=, < , >, and so on) that are valid for comparing other variables. In performing arithmetic on pointers, we must be careful to produce addresses that point to something meaningful. In comparing pointers, we must also make comparisons that make sense. Consider the declarations:

```
int nums[100];
int *nPt;
```

To set the address of `nums[0]` into `nPt`, either of the following two assignment statements can be used:

```
nPt = &nums[0];
nPt = nums;
```

The two assignment statements produce the same result because `nums` is a pointer constant that itself contains the address of the first location in the array. This is, of course, the address of `nums[0]`. Figure 13.20 illustrates the allocation of memory resulting from

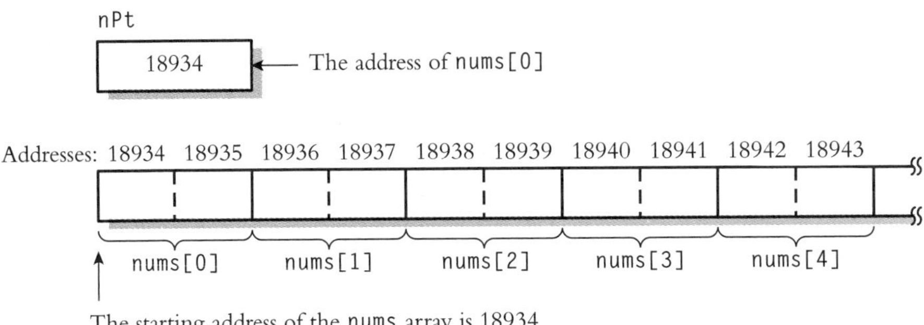

FIGURE 13.20

The `nums` array in memory

the previous declaration and assignment statements, assuming that each integer requires two bytes of memory and that the location of the beginning of the `nums` array is at address 18934.

Once `nPt` contains a valid address, values can be added and subtracted from the address to produce new addresses. When adding or subtracting numbers to pointers, the computer automatically adjusts the number to ensure that the result still "points to" a value of the correct type. For example, the statement `nPt = nPt + 4;` forces the program to scale the 4 by the correct number to ensure that the resulting address is the address of an integer. Assuming that each integer requires two bytes of storage, as illustrated in Figure 13.20, the program multiplies the 4 by two and adds eight to the address in `nPt`. The resulting address is 18942, which is the correct address of `nums[4]`.

This automatic scaling by the program ensures that the expression `nPt + i`, where `i` is any positive integer, correctly points to the `i`th element beyond the one currently being pointed to by `nPt`. Thus, if `nPt` initially contains the address of `nums[0]`, `nPt + 4` is the address of `nums[4]`, `nPt + 50` is the address of `nums[50]`, and `nPt + i` is the address of `nums[i]`. Although we have used actual addresses in Figure 13.20 to illustrate the scaling process, the programmer need never know or care about the actual addresses used by the computer. The manipulation of addresses using pointers generally does not require knowledge of the actual address.

Addresses can also be incremented or decremented using both prefix and postfix increment and decrement operators. Adding one to a pointer causes the pointer to point to the next element of the type being pointed to. Decrementing a pointer causes the pointer to point to the previous element. For example, if the pointer variable `p` is a pointer to an integer, the expression `p++` causes the address in the pointer to be incremented to point to the next integer. This is illustrated in Figure 13.21.

In Figure 13.21, notice that the increment added to the pointer is correctly scaled to account for the fact that the pointer is used to point to integers. It is, of course, up to the

FIGURE 13.21

Increments are scaled when used with pointers

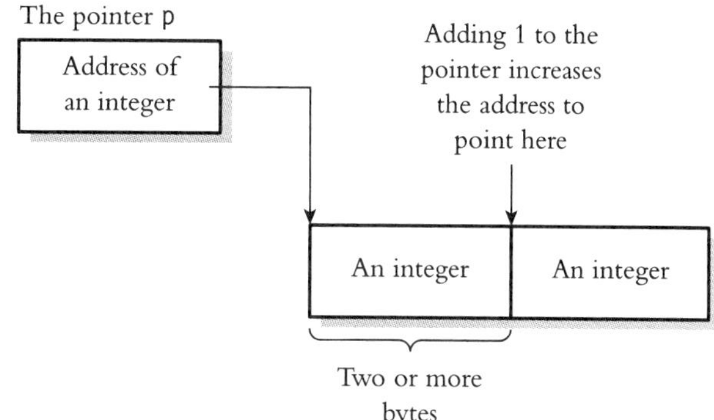

programmer to ensure that the correct type of data is stored in the new address contained in the pointer.

The increment and decrement operators can be applied as both prefix and postfix pointer operators. All of the following combinations using pointers are valid:

```
*ptNum++     // use the pointer and then increment it
*++ptNum     // increment the pointer before using it
*ptNum--     // use the pointer and then decrement it
*--ptNum     // decrement the pointer before using it
```

Of the four possible forms, the most commonly used is the form `*ptNum++`. This is because such an expression allows each element in an array to be accessed as the address is "marched along" from the starting address of the array to the address of the last array element. The use of the increment operator is shown in Program 13.9. In this program each element in the nums array is retrieved by successively incrementing the address in nPt.

PROGRAM 13.9

```
#include <iostream.h>

int main()
{
  const int NUMS = 5;
  int nums[NUMS] = {16, 54, 7, 43, -5};
  int i, total = 0, *nPt;
```

(continued next page)

(continued from previous page)

```
  nPt = nums;     // store address of nums[0] in nPt
  for (i = 0; i < NUMS; i++)
    total = total + *nPt++;
  cout << "The total of the array elements is " << total << endl;

  return 0;
}
```

The output line displayed by Program 13.9 is:

```
The total of the array elements is 115
```

The expression `total = total + *nPt++` used in Program 13.9 accumulates the values "pointed to" by the `nPt` pointer variable. Within this expression, the term `*nPt++` first causes the computer to retrieve the integer pointed to by `nPt`. This is done by the `*nPt` part of the term. The postfix increment, ++, then adds one to the address in `nPt` so that `nPt` now contains the address of the next array element. The increment is, of course, scaled correctly so that the actual address in `nPt` is the correct address of the next array element.

Pointers may also be compared. This is particularly useful when dealing with pointers that point to elements in the same array. For example, rather than using a counter in a `for` loop to access each element in an array correctly, the address in a pointer can be compared to the starting and ending address of the array itself. The expression

```
nPt <= &nums[4]
```

is true (nonzero) as long as the address in `nPt` is less than or equal to the address of `nums[4]`. Because `nums` is a pointer constant that contains the address of `nums[0]`, the term `&nums[4]` can be replaced by the equivalent term `nums + 4`. Using either of these forms, Program 13.9 can be rewritten as Program 13.10 to continue adding array elements while the address in nPt is less than or equal to the address of the last array element.

PROGRAM 13.10

```
#include <iostream.h>

int main()
{
  const int NUMS = 5;
```

(continued next page)

(continued from previous page)

```
  int nums[NUMS] = {16, 54, 7, 43, -5};
  int total = 0, *nPt;

  nPt = nums;    // store address of nums[0] in nPt
  while (nPt < nums + NUMS)
    total += *nPt++;
  cout << "The total of the array elements is " << total << endl;

  return 0;
}
```

Notice that in Program 13.10 the compact form of the accumulating expression, `total += *nPt++`, was used in place of the longer form, `total = total + *nPt++`. Also, the expression `nums + nums` does not change the address in `nums`. Because `nums` is an array name and not a pointer variable, its value cannot be changed. The expression `nums + NUMS` first retrieves the address in `nums`, adds 5 to this address (appropriately scaled), and uses the result for comparison purposes. Expressions such as `*nums++`, which attempt to change the address, are invalid. Expressions such as `*nums` or `*(nums + i)`, which use the address without attempting to alter it, are valid.

Pointer Initialization

Like all variables, pointers can be initialized when they are declared. When initializing pointers, however, you must be careful to set an address in the pointer. For example, an initialization such as

```
int *ptNum = &miles;
```

is valid only if `miles` itself is declared as an integer variable before `ptNum` is declared. Here we are creating a pointer to an integer and setting the address in the pointer to the address of an integer variable. If the variable `miles` is declared after `ptNum` is declared, as follows,

```
int *ptNum = &miles;
int miles;
```

an error occurs. This is because the address of `miles` is used before `miles` has even been defined. Because the storage area reserved for `miles` has not been allocated when `ptNum` is declared, the address of `miles` does not yet exist.

Pointers to arrays can be initialized within their declaration statements. For example, if `prices` has been declared as an array of floating point numbers, either of the following two declarations can be used to initialize the pointer named `zing` to the address of the first element in `prices`:

```
float *zing = &prices[0];
float *zing = prices;
```

The last initialization is correct because `prices` is itself a pointer constant containing an address of the proper type. (The variable name `zing` was selected in this example to reinforce the idea that any variable name can be selected for a pointer.)

EXERCISES 13.3

1. Replace the `while` statement in Program 13.10 with a `for` statement.

2. a. Write a C++ program that stores the following numbers in an array named `rates`: 6.25, 6.50, 6.8, 7.2, 7.35, 7.5, 7.65, 7.8, 8.2, 8.4, 8.6, 8.8, 9.0. Display the values in the array by changing the address in a pointer called `dispPt`. Use a `for` statement in your program.

b. Modify the program written in Exercise 2a to use a `while` statement.

3. a. Write a program that stores the string `Hooray for All of Us` into an array named `strng`. Use the declaration `strng[] = "Hooray for All of Us";`, which ensures that the end-of-string escape sequence `\0` is included in the array. Display the characters in the array by changing the address in a pointer called `messPtr`. Use a `for` statement in your program.

b. Modify the program written in Exercise 3a to use the `while` statement `while (*messPtr++ != '\0')`.

c. Modify the program written in Exercise 3a to start the display with the word `All`.

4. Write a C++ program that stores the following numbers in an array named `miles`: 15, 22, 16, 18, 27, 23, 20. Have your program copy the data stored in `miles` to another array named `dist` and then display the values in the `dist` array. Use pointers for copying and displaying cell array elements.

5. Write a C++ program that stores the following letters in an array named `message`: `This is a test`. Have your program copy the data stored in `message` to another array named `mess2` and then display the letters in the `mess2` array. Use pointers for copying and displaying all array elements.

6. Write a C++ program that declares three single-dimensional arrays named `miles`, `gallons`, and `mpg`. Each array should be capable of holding ten elements. In the `miles` array, store the numbers 240.5, 300.0, 189.6, 310.6, 280.7, 216.9, 199.4, 160.3, 177.4, 192.3. In the `gallons` array, store the numbers 10.3, 15.6, 8.7, 14, 16.3, 15.7, 14.9, 10.7, 8.3, 8.4. Each element of the `mpg` array should be calculated as the corresponding element of the `miles` array divided by the equivalent element of the `gallons` array; for example, `mpg[0] = miles[0] / gallons[0]`. Use pointers when calculating and displaying the elements of the `mpg` array.

13.4 Passing Addresses

We have already seen one method of passing addresses to a function. This was accomplished using references, as was described in Section 6.3. Although passing references to a function provides the function with the address of the passed variables, it is an implied use of addresses because the function call does not reveal the fact that reference parameters are being used. For example, the function call `swap(num1, num2);` does not reveal whether `num1` or `num2` is a passed value or reference. Only by looking at the function prototype or examining the function header line for `swap()` is the type of pass revealed.

In contrast to implicitly passing addresses using references, addresses can be explicitly passed using pointer parameters. Let us see how this is accomplished.

To explicitly pass an address to a function, all that needs to be done is to place the address-of operator, &, in front of the variable being passed. For example, the function call

```
swap(&firstnum, &secnum);
```

passes the addresses of the variables `firstnum` and `secnum` to `swap()`, as illustrated in Figure 13.22. Explicitly passing addresses using the address operator effectively is a **pass by reference** because the called function can reference, or access, variables in the calling function using the passed addresses. As we saw in Section 6.3, calls by reference are also accomplished using reference parameters. Here we will use the passed addresses and pointers to directly access the variables `firstnum` and `secnum` from within `swap()` and exchange their values—a procedure that was previously accomplished in Program 6.8 using reference parameters.

FIGURE 13.22

Explicitly passing addresses to `swap()`

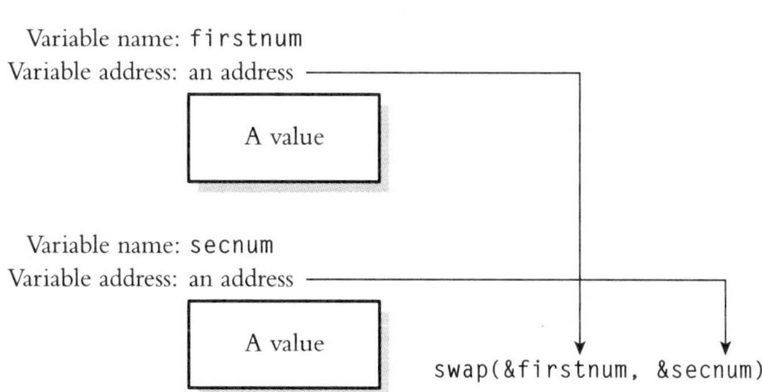

One of the first requirements in writing `swap()` is to construct a function header line that correctly receives and stores the passed values, which in this case are two addresses. As we saw in Section 13.1, addresses are stored in pointers, which means that the parameters of `swap` must be declared as pointers.

Assuming that `firstnum` and `secnum` are double precision variables, and that `swap()` returns no value, a suitable function header line for `swap` is

```
void swap(double *nm1Addr, double *nm2Addr)
```

The choice of the parameter names `nm1Addr` and `nm2Addr` is, as with all parameter names, up to the programmer. The declaration `double *nm1Addr`, however, declares that the parameter named `nm1Addr` will be used to store the address of a double precision value. Similarly, the declaration `double *nm2Addr` declares that `nm2Addr` will also store the address of a double precision value.

Before writing the body of `swap()` to exchange the values in `firstnum` and `secnum`, let's first check that the values accessed using the addresses in `nm1Addr` and `nm2Addr` are correct. This is done in Program 13.11.

PROGRAM 13.11

```
#include <iostream.h>

void swap(double *, double *);       // function prototype

int main()
{
  double firstnum = 20.5, secnum = 6.25;

  swap(&firstnum, &secnum);           // call swap

  return 0;
}

// this function illustrates passing pointer parameters
void swap(double *nm1Addr, double *nm2Addr)
{

  cout << "\nThe number whose address is in nm1Addr is "
       << *nm1Addr << endl;
  cout << "The number whose address is in nm2Addr is "
       << *nm2Addr << endl;

  return;
}
```

FIGURE 13.23

Output displayed by Program 13.11

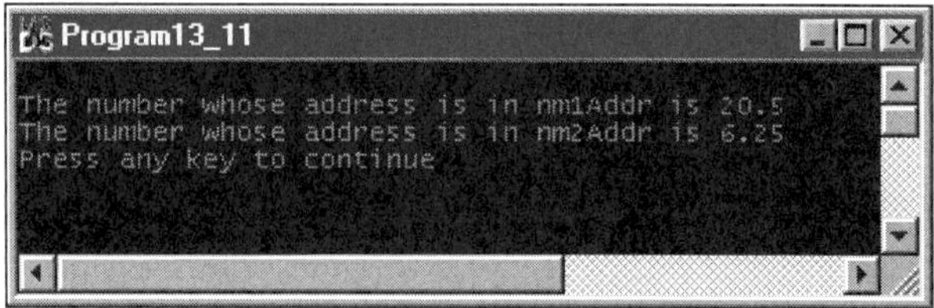

Figure 13.23 shows output displayed when Program 13.11 is run.

In reviewing Program 13.11, note two things. First, the function prototype for `swap()`

```
void swap(double *, double *)
```

declares that `swap()` returns no value directly and that its arguments are two pointers that "point to" double precision values. As such, when the function is called it will require that two addresses be passed, and that each address is the address of a double precision value.

The second item to notice is that within `swap()` the indirection operator is used to access the values stored in `firstnum` and `secnum`. `swap()` itself has no knowledge of these variable names, but it does have the address of `firstnum` stored in `nm1Addr` and the address of `secnum` stored in `nm2Addr`. The expression `*nm1Addr` used in the first `cout` statement means "the variable whose address is in `nm1Addr`." This, of course, is the variable `firstnum`. Similarly, the second `cout` statement obtains the value stored in `secnum` as "the variable whose address is in `nm2Addr`." Thus, we have successfully used pointers to allow `swap()` to access variables in `main()`. Figure 13.24 illustrates the concept of storing addresses in arguments.

Having verified that `swap()` can access `main()`'s local variables `firstnum` and `secnum`, we can now expand `swap()` to exchange the values in these variables. The values in `main()`'s variables `firstnum` and `secnum` can be interchanged from within `swap()` using the three-step interchange algorithm previously described in Section 6.3, which for convenience is relisted below:

FIGURE 13.24

Storing addresses in parameters

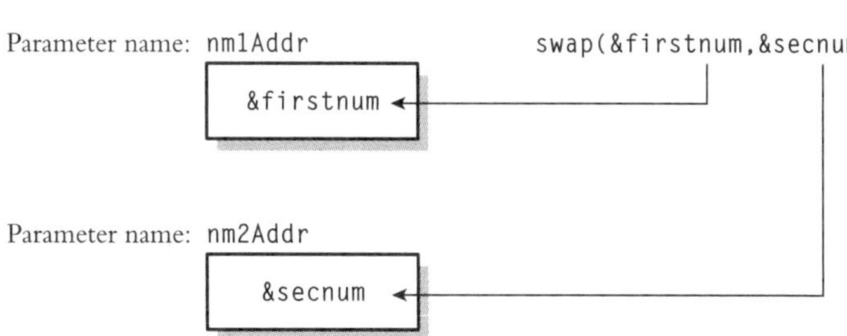

1. Store `firstnum`'s value in a temporary location.
2. Store `secnum`'s value in `firstnum`.
3. Store the temporary value in `secnum`.

Using pointers from within `swap()`, this takes the form:

1. Store the value of the variable pointed to by `nm1Addr` in a temporary location. The statement `temp = *nm1Addr;` does this (see Figure 13.25).
2. Store the value of the variable whose address is in `nm2Addr` in the variable whose address is in `nm1Addr`. The statement `*nm1Addr = *nm2Addr;` does this (see Figure 13.26).
3. Move the value in the temporary location into the variable whose address is in `nm2Addr`. The statement `*nm2Addr = temp;` does this (see Figure 13.27).

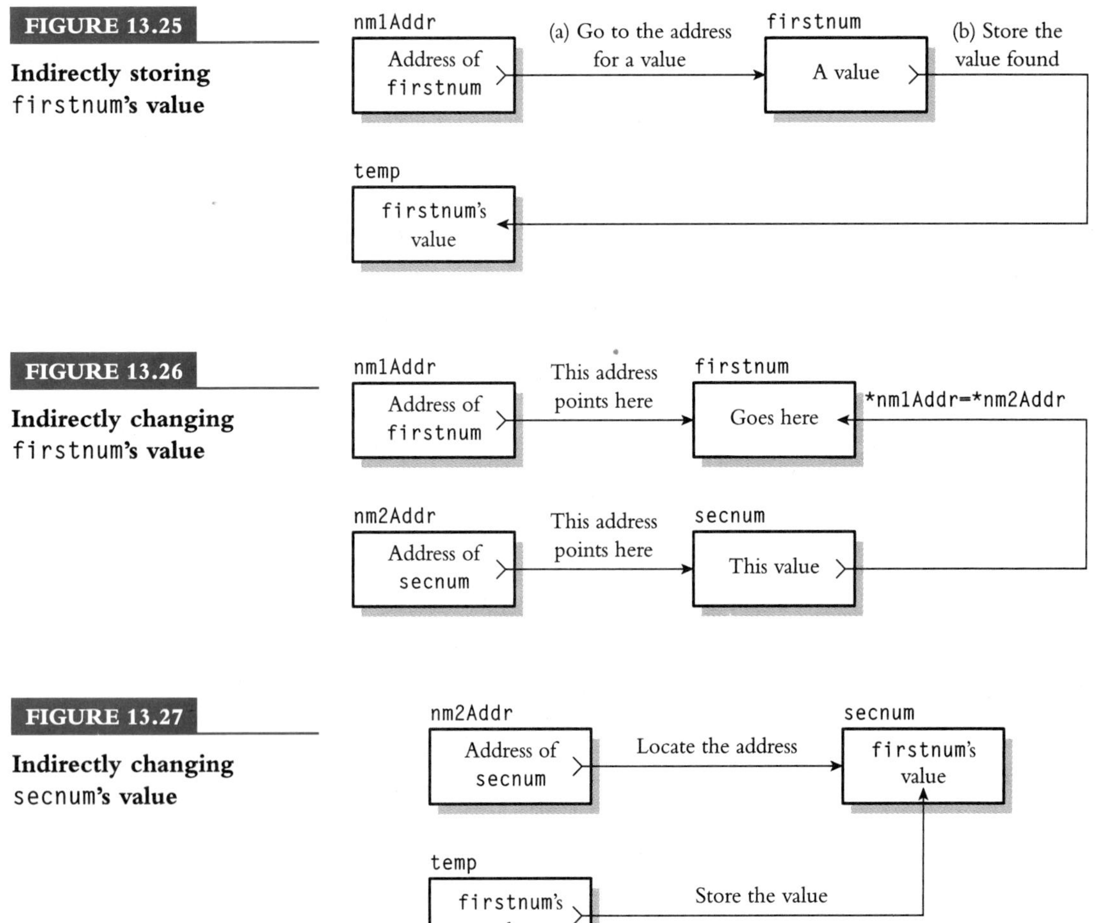

FIGURE 13.25 **Indirectly storing `firstnum`'s value**

FIGURE 13.26 **Indirectly changing `firstnum`'s value**

FIGURE 13.27 **Indirectly changing `secnum`'s value**

Program 13.12 contains the final form of swap(), written according to our description.

PROGRAM 13.12

```
#include <iostream.h>

void swap(double *, double *);     // function prototype

int main()
{
  double firstnum = 20.5, secnum = 6.25;


  cout << "\nThe value stored in firstnum is: " << firstnum << endl;
  cout << "The value stored in secnum is: " << secnum << "\n\n";

  swap(&firstnum, &secnum);          // call swap

  cout << "The value stored in firstnum is now: "
       << firstnum <<  endl;
  cout << "The value stored in secnum is now: "
       << secnum << endl;

  return 0;
}

// this function swaps the values in its two arguments
void swap(double *nm1Addr, double *nm2Addr)
{
  double temp;

  temp = *nm1Addr;             // save firstnum's value
  *nm1Addr = *nm2Addr;         // move secnum's value in firstnum
  *nm2Addr = temp;             // change secnum's value

  return;
}
```

Figure 13.28 illustrates a sample run obtained using Program 13.12.

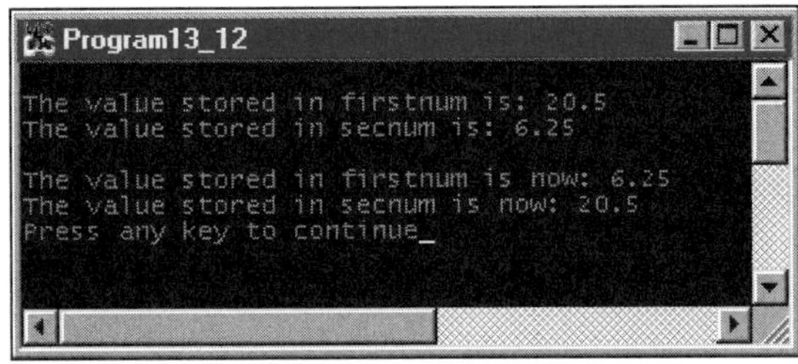

FIGURE 13.28

Output displayed by Program 13.12

As illustrated in this output, the values stored in `main()`'s variables have been modified from within `swap()`, which was made possible by the use of pointers. The interested reader should compare this version of `swap()` with the version using references that was presented in Program 6.10. The advantage of using pointers in preference to references is that the function call itself explicitly designates that addresses are being used, which is a direct alert that the function will most likely alter variables of the calling function. The advantages of using references is that the notation is much simpler.

Generally, for functions such as `swap()`, the notational convenience wins out, and references are used. In passing arrays to functions, however, which is our next topic, the compiler explicitly passes an address. This dictates that a pointer parameter will be used to store the address.

Passing Arrays

When an array is passed to a function, its address is the only item actually passed. By this we mean the address of the first location used to store the array, as illustrated in Figure 13.29. Because the first location reserved for an array corresponds to element 0 of the array, the "address of the array" is also the address of element 0.

For a specific example in which an array is passed to a function, consider Program 13.13. In this program, the `nums` array is passed to the `FindMax()` function using conventional array notation.

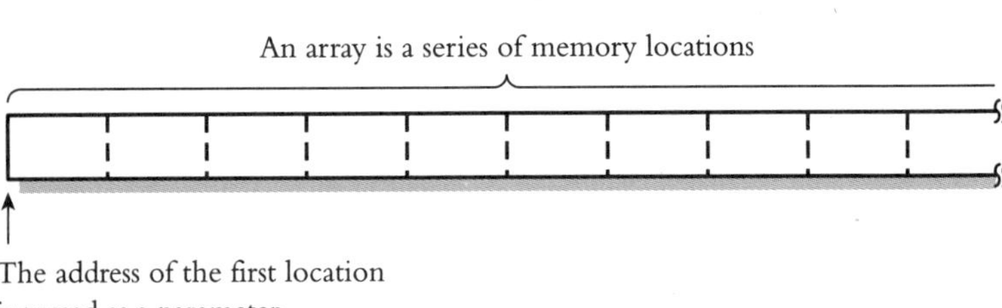

FIGURE 13.29

The address of an array is the address of the first location reserved for the array

PROGRAM 13.13

```
#include <iostream.h>

int FindMax(int [], int);    // function prototype

int main()
{
  const int NUMPTS = 5;
  int nums[NUMPTS] = {2, 18, 1, 27, 16};

  cout << "\nThe maximum value in the array is "
       << FindMax(nums,NUMPTS) << endl;
  return 0;
}

// this function returns the maximum value in an array of ints
int FindMax(int vals[], int numEls)
{
  int i, max = vals[0];

  for (i = 1; i < numEls; i++)
   if (max < vals[i])
     max = vals[i];

  return max;
}
```

The output line displayed when Program 13.13 is executed is:

```
The maximum value in the array is 27
```

The parameter named `vals` in the header line declaration for `FindMax()` actually receives the address of the array `nums`. As such, `vals` is really a pointer because pointers are variables (or parameters) used to store addresses. The address passed into `FindMax()` is the address of an integer, so another suitable header line for `FindMax()` is:

```
int FindMax(int *vals, int numEls) // here vals is declared as
                                   // a pointer to an integer
```

The declaration `int *vals` in the header line declares that `vals` is used to store an address of an integer. The address stored is, of course, the location of the beginning of an array. The following is a rewritten version of the `FindMax()` function that uses the new pointer declaration for `vals`, but retains the use of subscripts to refer to individual array elements:

```
int FindMax(int *vals, int numEls)    // find the maximum value
{
  int i, max = vals[0];

  for (i = 1; i < numEls; i++)
   if (max < vals[i])
     max = vals[i];

  return max;
}
```

Regardless of how `vals` is declared in the function header or how it is used within the function body, it is truly a pointer. Thus, the address in `vals` may be modified. This is not true for the name `nums`. Because `nums` is the name of the originally created array, it is a pointer constant. As described in Section 13.2, this means that the address in `nums` cannot be changed and that the address of `nums` itself cannot be taken. No such restrictions, however, apply to the pointer variable named `vals`. All the address arithmetic that we learned in the previous section can be legitimately applied to `vals`.

We shall write two additional versions of `FindMax()`, both using pointers instead of subscripts. In the first version we simply substitute pointer notation for subscript notation. In the second version we use address arithmetic to change the address in the pointer.

As previously stated, access to an array element using the subscript notation `arrayName[i]` can always be replaced by the pointer notation `*(arrayName + i)`. In our first modification to `FindMax()`, we make use of this correspondence by simply replacing all notations to `vals[i]` with the equivalent notation `*(vals + i)`.

```
int FindMax(int *vals, int numEls)    // find the maximum value
{
  int i, max = *vals;

  for (i = 1; i < numEls; i++)
   if (max < *(vals + i) )
     max = *(vals + i);

  return max;
}
```

Our next version of `FindMax()` makes use of the fact that the address stored in `vals` can be changed. After each array element is retrieved using the address in `vals`, the address itself is incremented by one in the altering list of the `for` statement. The expression `max = *vals` previously used to set `max` to the value of `vals[0]` is replaced by the expression `max = *vals++`, which adjusts the address in `vals` to point to the second element in the array. The element assigned to `max` by this expression is the array element pointed to by `vals` before `vals` is incremented. The postfix increment, ++, does not change the address in `vals` until after the address has been used to retrieve the array element.

```
int FindMax(int *vals, int numEls)   // find the maximum value
{
  int i, max = *vals++;    // get the first element and increment
  for (i = 1; i < numEls; i++, vals++)
  {
    if (max < *vals)
      max = *vals;
  }
  return max;
}
```

Let us review this version of `FindMax()`. Initially the maximum value is set to "the thing pointed to by `vals`." Because `vals` initially contains the address of the first element in the array passed to `FindMax()`, the value of this first element is stored in `max`. The address in `vals` is then incremented by one. The one that is added to `vals` is automatically scaled by the number of bytes used to store integers. Thus, after the increment, the address stored in vals is the address of the next array element. This is illustrated in Figure 13.30. The value of this next element is compared to the maximum and the address is again incremented, this time from within the altering list of the `for` statement. This process continues until all the array elements have been examined.

FIGURE 13.30

Pointing to different elements

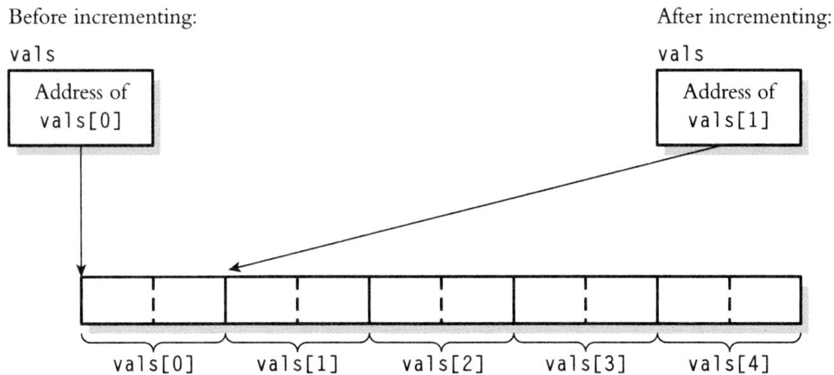

The version of `FindMax()` that you should choose is a matter of personal style and taste. Generally, beginning programmers feel more at ease using subscripts rather than using pointers. Also, if the program uses an array as the natural storage structure for the application and data at hand, an array access using subscripts is more appropriate to clearly indicate the intent of the program. However, as we learn about strings and data structures, the use of pointers becomes an increasingly useful and powerful tool in its own right. In these instances there is no simple or easy equivalence to the use of pointers.

One further "neat trick" can be gleaned from our discussion. Because passing an array to a function really involves passing an address, we can just as well pass any valid address. For example, the function call `FindMax(&nums[2],3)` passes the address of `nums[2]` to `FindMax()`. Within `FindMax()` the pointer `vals` stores the address and the function starts the search for a maximum at the element corresponding to this address. Thus, from `FindMax()`'s perspective, it has received an address and proceeds appropriately.

Advanced Pointer Notation[10]

Access to multidimensional arrays can also be made using pointer notation, although the notation becomes more and more cryptic as the array dimensions increase. An extremely useful application of this notation occurs with two-dimensional character arrays, one of the topics of the next chapter. Here we consider pointer notation for two-dimensional numeric arrays. For example, consider the declaration

```
int nums[2][3] = { {16,18,20},
                   {25,26,27} };
```

This declaration creates an array of elements and a set of pointer constants named `nums`, `nums[0]`, and `nums[1]`. The relationship between these pointer constants and the elements of the `nums` array are illustrated in Figure 13.31.

FIGURE 13.31

Storage of the `nums` array and associated pointer constants

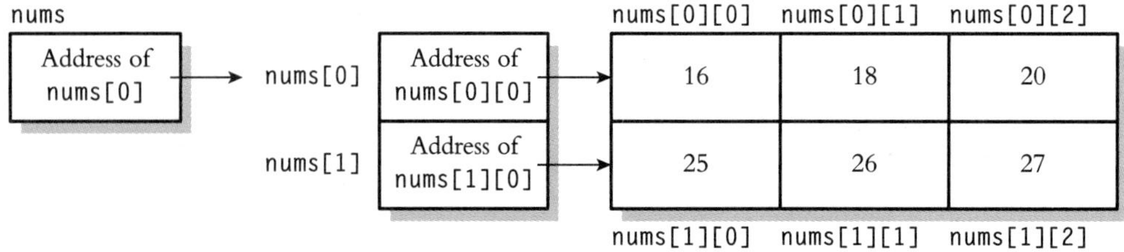

10 This topic may be omitted with no loss of subject continuity.

The availability of the pointer constants associated with a two-dimensional array allows us to reference array elements in a variety of ways. One way is to consider the two-dimensional array as an array of rows, where each row is itself an array of three elements. Considered in this light, the address of the first element in the first row is provided by `nums[0]` and the address of the first element in the second row is provided by `nums[1]`. Thus, the variable pointed to by `nums[0]` is `nums[0][0]` and the variable pointed to by `nums[1]` is `nums[1][0]`. Once the nature of these constants is understood, each element in the array can be accessed by applying an appropriate offset to the appropriate pointer. Thus, the following notations are equivalent:

Pointer Notation	Subscript Notation	Value
`*nums[0]`	`nums[0][0]`	16
`*(nums[0] + 1)`	`nums[0][1]`	18
`*(nums[0] + 2)`	`nums[0][2]`	20
`*nums[1]`	`nums[1][0]`	25
`*(nums[1] + 1)`	`nums[1][1]`	26
`*(nums[1] + 2)`	`nums[1][2]`	27

We can now go even further and replace `nums[0]` and `nums[1]` with their respective pointer notations, using the address of `nums` itself. As illustrated in Figure 13.31, the variable pointed to by `nums` is `nums[0]`. That is, `*nums` is `nums[0]`. Similarly, `*(nums + 1)` is `nums[1]`. Using these relationships leads to the following equivalences:

Pointer Notation	Subscript Notation	Value
`*(*nums)`	`nums[0][0]`	16
`*(*nums + 1)`	`nums[0][1]`	18
`*(*nums + 2)`	`nums[0][2]`	20
`*(*(nums + 1))`	`nums[1][0]`	25
`*(*(nums + 1) + 1)`	`nums[1][1]`	26
`*(*(nums + 1) + 2)`	`nums[1][2]`	27

The same notation applies when a two-dimensional array is passed to a function. For example, assume that the two-dimensional array `nums` is passed to the function `calc()` using the call `calc(nums);`. Here, as with all array passes, an address is passed. A suitable function header line for the function `calc()` is:

```
calc(int pt[2][3])
```

As we have already seen, the argument declaration for pt can also be:

```
calc(int pt[][3])
```

Using pointer notation, another suitable declaration is:

```
calc(int (*pt)[3])
```

In this last declaration the inner parentheses are required to create a single pointer to objects of three integers. Each object is, of course, equivalent to a single row of the nums array. By suitably offsetting the pointer, each element in the array can be accessed. Notice that without the parentheses the declaration becomes

```
int *pt[3]
```

which creates an array of three pointers, each one pointing to a single integer.

Once the correct declaration for pt is made (any of the three valid declarations can be used), the following notations within the function calc() are all equivalent:

Pointer Notation	Subscript Notation	Value
`*(*pt)`	`pt[0][0]`	16
`*(*pt+1)`	`pt[0][1]`	18
`*(*pt+2)`	`pt[0][2]`	20
`*(*(pt+1))`	`pt[1][0]`	25
`*(*(pt+1)+1)`	`pt[1][1]`	26
`*(*(pt+1)+2)`	`pt[1][2]`	27

The last two notations using pointers are encountered in more advanced C++ programs. The first of these occurs because functions can return any valid C++ scalar data type, including pointers to any of these data types. If a function returns a pointer, the data type being pointed to must be declared in the function's declaration. For example, the declaration

```
int *calc()
```

declares that calc() returns a pointer to an integer value. This means that an address of an integer variable is returned. Similarly, the declaration

```
float *taxes()
```

declares that `taxes()` returns a pointer to a floating point value. This means that an address of a floating point variable is returned.

In addition to declaring pointers to integers, floating point numbers, and C++'s other data types, pointers can also be declared that point to (contain the address of) a function. Pointers to functions are possible because function names, like array names, are themselves pointer constants. For example, the declaration

```
int (*calc)()
```

declares `calc()` to be a pointer to a function that returns an integer. This means that `calc` will contain the address of a function, and the function whose address is in the variable `calc` returns an integer value. If, for example, the function `sum()` returns an integer, the assignment `calc = sum;` is valid.

EXERCISES 13.4

1. The following declaration is used to create the `prices` array:

```
double prices[500];
```

Write three different header lines for a function named `sortArray()` that accepts the `prices` array as a parameter named `inArray` and returns no value.

2. The following declaration is used to create the `keys` array:

```
char keys[256];
```

Write three different header lines for a function named `findKey()` that accepts the `keys` array as a parameter named `select` and returns no value.

3. The following declaration is used to create the `rates` array:

```
float rates[256];
```

Write three different header lines for a function named `prime()` that accepts the `rates` array as a parameter named `rates` and returns a floating point value.

4. Modify the `FindMax()` function to locate the minimum value of the passed array. Write the function using only pointers.

5. In the last version of `FindMax()` presented, `vals` was incremented inside the altering list of the `for` statement. Instead, suppose that the incrementing was done within the condition expression of the `if` statement, as follows:

```
int FindMax(int *vals, int numEls)    // incorrect version
{
  int i, max = *vals++;    // get the first element and increment
```

```
    for (i = 1; i < numEls; i++)
    {
      if (max < *vals++)  max = *vals;
    }

    return max;
}
```

This version produces an incorrect result. Determine why.

6. **a.** Write a program that has a declaration in `main()` to store the following numbers into an array named `rates`: 6.5, 7.2, 7.5, 8.3, 8.6, 9.4, 9.6, 9.8, 10.0. There should be a function call to `show()` that accepts `rates` as a parameter named `rates` and then displays the numbers using the pointer notation `*(rates + i)`.

   b. Modify the `show()` function written in Exercise 6a to alter the address in `rates`. Always use the expression `*rates` rather than `*(rates + i)` to retrieve the correct element.

7. **a.** Write a program that has a declaration in `main()` to store the string `"Vacation is near"` into an array named `message`. There should be a function call to `display()` that accepts `message` in a parameter named `messPtr` and then displays the message using the pointer notation `*(strng + i)`.

   b. Modify the `display()` function written in Exercise 7a to alter the address in message. Always use the expression `*strng` rather than `*(strng + i)` to retrieve the correct element.

8. Write a program that declares three single-dimensional arrays named `price`, `quantity`, and `amount`. Each array should be declared in `main()` and be capable of holding ten double precision numbers. The numbers to be stored in `price` are 10.62, 14.89, 13.21, 16.55, 18.62, 9.47, 6.58, 18.32, 12.15, 3.98. The numbers to be stored in `quantity` are 4, 8.5, 6, 7.35, 9, 15.3, 3, 5.4, 2.9, 4.8. Have your program pass these three arrays to a function called `extend()`, which calculates the elements in the `amount` array as the product of the equivalent elements in the `price` and `quantity` arrays (for example, `amount[1] = price[1] * quantity[1]`). After `extend()` has put values into the `amount` array, display the values in the array from within `main()`. Write the `extend()` function using pointers.

9. **a.** Determine the output of the following program:

```
#include <iostream.h>

const int ROWS = 2;
const int COLS = 3;

void arr(int [][COLS]);
```

```
int main()
{
  int nums[ROWS][COLS] = { {33,16,29},
                           {54,67,99}};

  arr(nums);
  return 0;
}

void arr(int (*val)[COLS])
{
  cout << endl << *(*val);
  cout << endl << *(*val + 1);
  cout << endl << *(*(val + 1) + 2);
  cout << endl << *(*val) + 1;

  return;
}
```

b. Given the declaration for `val` in the `arr` function, would the notation `val[1][2]` be valid within the function?

13.5 Common Programming Errors

In using the material presented in this chapter, be aware of the following possible errors:

1. Attempting to store an address in a variable that has not been declared as a pointer.

2. Using a pointer to access nonexistent array elements. For example, if `nums` is an array of ten integers, the expression `*(nums + 15)` points to a location six integer locations beyond the last element of the array. Because C++ does not do any bounds checking on array accesses, this type of error is not caught by the compiler. This is the same error, disguised in pointer notation form, that occurs when using a subscript to access an out-of-bounds array element.

3. Incorrectly applying the address and indirection operators. For example, if `pt` is a pointer variable, the expressions

```
pt = &45
pt = &(miles + 10)
```

are both invalid because they attempt to take the address of a value. Notice that the expression `pt = &miles + 10`, however, is valid. Here, 10 is added to the address of `miles`. Again, it is the programmer's responsibility to ensure that the final address "points to" a valid data element.

4. Taking addresses of pointer constants. For example, given the declarations

```
int nums[25];
int *pt;
```

the assignment

```
pt = &nums;
```

is invalid. `nums` is a pointer constant that is equivalent to a named constant for an address. The correct assignment is `pt = nums`.

5. Taking addresses of a reference argument, reference variable, or register variable. The reason for this is that reference arguments and variables are essentially the same as pointer constants, in that they are named address values. Similarly, the address of a register variable cannot be taken. Thus, for the declarations

```
register in total;
int *ptTot;
```

the assignment

```
ptTot = &total;  // INVALID
```

is invalid. The reason for this is that register variables are stored in a computer's internal registers, and these storage areas do not have standard memory addresses.

6. Initializing pointer variables incorrectly. For example, the initialization

```
int *pt = 5;
```

is invalid. Because `pt` is a pointer to an integer, it must be initialized with a valid address.

7. Becoming confused about whether a variable *contains* an address or *is* an address. Pointer variables and pointer parameters contain addresses. Although a pointer constant is synonymous with an address, it is useful to treat pointer constants as pointer variables with two restrictions:

- The address of a pointer constant cannot be taken.
- The address "contained in" the pointer constant cannot be altered.

Except for these two restrictions, pointer constants and pointer variables can be used almost interchangeably. Therefore, when an address is required, any of the following can be used:

- a pointer variable name
- a pointer parameter name
- a pointer constant name

- a nonpointer variable name preceded by the address operator (e.g., `&variable`)
- a nonpointer argument name preceded by the address operator (e.g., `&argument`)

Some of the confusion surrounding pointers is caused by the cavalier use of the word *pointer.* For example, the phrase "a function requires a pointer argument" is more clearly understood when it is realized that the phrase really means "a function requires an address as an argument." Similarly, the phrase "a function returns a pointer" really means "a function returns an address."

If you are ever in doubt as to what is really contained in a variable or how it should be treated, use a `cout` statement to display the contents of the variable, the "thing pointed to," or "the address of the variable." Seeing what is displayed frequently helps sort out what is really in the variable.

13.6 Chapter Summary

1. Every variable has a data type, an address, and a value. In C++ the address of a variable can be obtained by using the address operator `&`.

2. A **pointer** is a variable that is used to store the address of another variable. Pointers, like all C++ variables, must be declared. The indirection operator, `*`, is used both to declare a pointer variable and to access the variable whose address is stored in a pointer.

3. An array name is a pointer constant. The value of the pointer constant is the address of the first element in the array. Thus, if `val` is the name of an array, `val` and `&val[0]` can be used interchangeably.

4. Any access to an array element using subscript notation can always be replaced using pointer notation. That is, the notation `a[i]` can always be replaced by the notation `*(a + i)`. This is true whether `a` was initially declared as an array or as a pointer.

5. Arrays can be dynamically created as a program is executing. For example, the sequence of statements:

```
cout << "Enter the array size: ";
cin  >> num;
int *grades = new int[num];
```

creates an array named `grades` of size `num`. The area allocated for the array can be dynamically destroyed using the `delete` operator. For example, the statement `delete grades;` will return the allocated area for the `grades` array back to the computer.

6. Arrays are passed to functions as addresses. The called function always receives direct access to the originally declared array elements.

7. When a single-dimensional array is passed to a function, the parameter declaration for the function can be either an array declaration or a pointer declaration. Thus, the following parameter declarations are equivalent:

```
float a[];
float *a;
```

8. Pointers can be incremented, decremented, compared, and assigned. Numbers added to or subtracted from a pointer are automatically scaled. The scale factor used is the number of bytes required to store the data type originally pointed to.

14 Strings

Each computer language has its own method of handling strings of characters. Some languages, such as C++, have an extremely rich set of string manipulation functions and capabilities. Other languages, such as FORTRAN, which is predominantly used for numerical calculations, added string handling capabilities with later versions of the compiler. Languages such as LISP, which are targeted for list handling applications, provide an exceptional string manipulation capability. Thus, the way strings are stored, accessed, and manipulated is very language dependent. Because of this, the string handling methods presented in this chapter are, of necessity, dependent on C++'s string storage structure.

On a fundamental level, strings in C++ are simply arrays of characters that can be manipulated using standard element-by-element array-processing techniques. On a higher level, string library functions are available for treating strings as complete entities. This chapter explores the input, manipulation, and output of strings using both approaches. Also presented are the extremely powerful string manipulation techniques that can be created using pointers. Manipulating strings using pointers is probably one of the best ways to become extremely familiar and knowledgeable about pointers, which is essential for advanced C++ programming work. Finally, in our continuing look at Microsoft Foundation Classes we present a self-contained string class named CString.

14.1 String Fundamentals

A **string literal** is any sequence of characters enclosed in double quotes. A string literal is also referred to as a **string value** and more conventionally as a **string.** Examples of strings are `"This is a string"`, `"Hello World!"`, and `"xyz 123 *!#@@&"`.

A string is stored as an array of characters terminated by a special end-of-string symbolic constant named `NULL`. The value assigned to the null constant is the escape sequence `\0` and is the sentinel that marks the end of every string. For example, Figure 14.1 illustrates how the string `"Good Morning!"` is stored in memory. The string uses 14 storage locations, with the last character in the string being the end-of-string marker `\0`. The double quotes are not stored as part of the string.

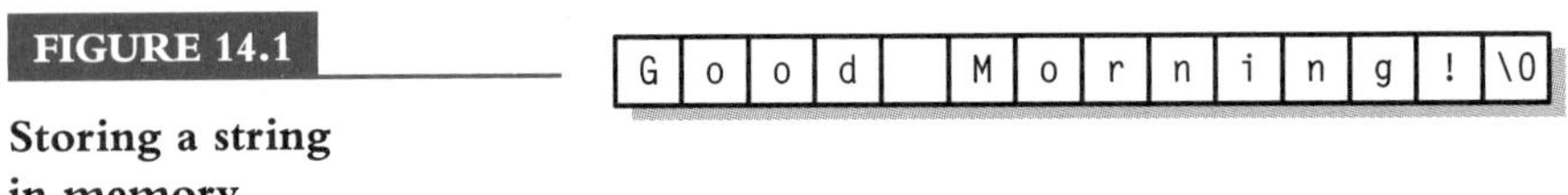

FIGURE 14.1 Storing a string in memory

Because a string is stored as an array of characters, the individual characters in the array can be input, manipulated, or output using standard array-handling techniques utilizing either subscript or pointer notations. The end-of-string null character is useful for detecting the end of the string when handling strings in this fashion.

String Input and Output

Although you have a choice of using either library or user-written functions for processing a string already in memory, inputting a string from a keyboard or displaying a string usually requires some reliance on standard library routines and class methods. Table 14.1 lists the commonly available object streams and library functions for both character-by-character and complete string input and output.

As listed in Table 14.1, in addition to the `cout` and `cin` streams, C++ provides two methods, `cin.getline()` and `cin.get()`, which are especially designed for string and character input, respectively. Earlier C functions that provided similar features to these C++ routines, and are still available in C++, are `gets()` and `getchar()`. For output C provided the `puts()` and `putchar()` functions; the features of these two functions are essentially provided in C++ by `cout`. Programs that use the newer C++ stream I/O must include the `iostream.h` header, whereas the older C functions require the `stdio.h` header.

Program 14.1 illustrates the use of `cin.getline()` and `cout` to input and output a string entered at the user's terminal.

TABLE 14.1 String and character library routines

C++ Routine	Description	C Routine
`cout`	General purpose screen output	`printf()`
`cout`	String output to screen	`puts()`
`cout`	Character output to screen	`putchar()`
`cin`	General purpose screen input	`scanf()`
`cin.getline()`	String input from terminal	`gets()`
`cin.get()`	Character input from terminal	`getchar()`

PROGRAM 14.1

```
#include <iostream.h>

int main()
{
  const int MAXCHARS = 81;
  char message[MAXCHARS];    // enough storage for a complete line

  cout << "\nEnter a string:\n";

  cin.getline(message,MAXCHARS,'\n');

  cout << "\nThe string just entered is:\n"
       << message << endl << endl;

  return 0;
}
```

Figure 14.2 illustrates a sample run using Program 14.1.

The `cin.getline()` method used in Program 14.1 continuously accepts and stores characters typed at the terminal into the character array named `message` until either 80 characters are entered (the 81th character is then used to store the end-of-string null character, `\0`), or the Enter key is detected. Pressing the Enter key at the terminal generates a newline character, `\n`, which is interpreted by `cin.getline()` as the end-of-line

FIGURE 14.2

Sample run using Program 14.1

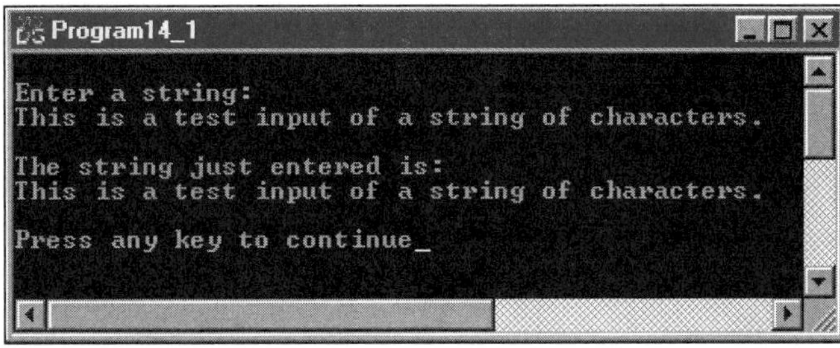

entry. All the characters encountered by `cin.getline()`, except the newline character, are stored in the message array. Before returning, the `cin.getline()` function appends a null character, `\0`, to the stored set of characters, as illustrated in Figure 14.3. The `cout` statement is then used to display the string.

Although the `cout` object is used in Program 14.1 for string output, `cin` could not be used in place of `cin.getline()` for string input. This is because the `cin` object reads a set of characters up to either a blank space or a newline character. Thus, attempting to enter the characters `This is a string` using the statement `cin >> message;` only results in the word `This` being assigned to the message array. Entering the complete line using a `cin` object requires a statement such as

```
cin >> message1 >> message2 >> message3 >> message4;
```

Here, the word `This` is assigned to the string `message1`, the word `is` is assigned to the string `message2`, and so on. The fact that a blank terminates a `cin` extraction operation restricts `cin`'s usefulness for entering string data, and is the reason for using `cin.getline()`.

In its most general form, the `cin.getline()` function has the syntax

cin.getline(*str, terminating-length, terminating-char*)

where *str* is a string or character pointer variable, *terminating-length* is an integer constant or variable indicating the maximum number of input characters that can be input, and *terminating-char* is an optional character constant or variable specifying the terminating character. If this optional third argument is omitted, the default terminating character is the newline (`'\n'`) character. Thus, the statement `cin.getline(message,MAXCHARS);` can be used in place of the statement `cin.getline(message,MAXCHARS,'\n');` in

FIGURE 14.3

Inputting a string with `cin.getline()`

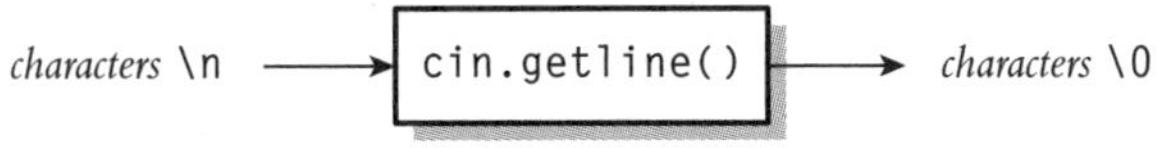

`cin.getline()` substitutes `\0` for the entered `\n`

Program 14.1. Both of these functions stop reading characters when the Return key is pressed or until MAXCHARS characters have been read, whichever comes first. Because cin.getline() permits specification of any terminating character for the input stream, a statement such as cin.getline(message,MAXCHARS,'x'); is also valid. This particular statement will stop accepting characters whenever the x key is pressed. In all future programs we will assume that input is terminated by the Enter key, which generates a newline character. As such the optional third argument passed to getline(), which is the terminating character, will be omitted.

String Processing

Strings can be manipulated using either standard library functions or standard array-processing techniques. The library functions commonly used for strings are presented in Section 14.2. For now we will concentrate on processing a string in a character-by-character fashion. This will allow us to understand how the standard library functions are constructed and to create our own library functions. For a specific example, consider the function strcopy(), which copies the contents of string2 to string1.

```
// copy string2 to string 1
void strcopy(char string1[], char string2[])
{
  int i = 0;                      // i will be used as a subscript

  while ( string2[i] != '\0')  // check for the end-of-string
  {
    string1[i] = string2[i];     // copy the element to string1
    i++;
  }
  string1[i] = '\0';              // terminate the first string
  return;
}
```

Although this string copy function can be shortened considerably and written more compactly, which is done in Section 14.3, the function illustrates the main features of string manipulation. The two strings are passed to strcopy() as arrays. Each element of string2 is then assigned to the equivalent element of string1 until the end-of-string marker is encountered. The detection of the null character forces the termination of the while loop controlling the copying of elements. Because the null character is not copied from string2 to string1, the last statement in strcopy() appends an end-of-string character to string1. Prior to calling strcopy(), the programmer must ensure that sufficient space has been allocated for the string1 array to be able to store the elements of the string2 array. Program 14.2 includes the strcopy() function in a complete program. Notice that the function prototype for `strcopy()` declares that the function expects to receive two character arrays.

PROGRAM 14.2

```
#include <iostream.h>

void strcopy(char [], char []); // function prototype

int main()
{
  const int MAXCHARS = 81;
  char message[MAXCHARS];      // enough storage for a complete line
  char newMessage[MAXCHARS];   // enough storage for a copy of message
  int i;

  cout << "\nEnter a sentence:\n";
  cin.getline(message,MAXCHARS);         // get the string
  strcopy(newMessage,message);      // pass two array addresses
  cout << "\nThe copied string is:\n"
       << newMessage << endl << endl;

  return 0;
}

void strcopy(char string1[], char string2[])   // copy string2 to string1
{
  int i = 0;                       // i will be used as a subscript

  while (string2[i] != '\0')       // check for the end-of-string
  {
    string1[i] = string2[i];       // copy the element to string1
    i++;
  }
  string1[i] = '\0';               // terminate the first string

  return;
}
```

A sample run using Program 14.2 is illustrated in Figure 14.4.

FIGURE 14.4

Sample run produced using Program 14.2

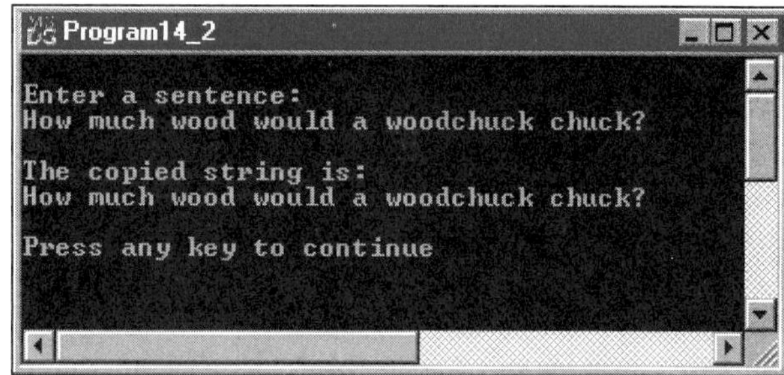

Detecting the End-of-String `NULL` Character

The null character that marks the end of each string is extremely important in user-created string processing functions. Frequently, however, it is effectively disguised by C++ programmers. This is because the numerical value of the null character is zero, which is considered as false in relational expressions.

To understand how the null character is commonly used by C++ programmers, reconsider the `strcopy()` function used in Program 14.2. This function, which is repeated below for convenience, is used to copy the characters from one array to another array, one character at a time until the end-of-string `NULL` is detected.

```
void strcopy(char string1[], char string2[])   // copy string2 to string1
{
  int i = 0;

  while (string2[i] != '\0')     // check for the end-of-string
  {
    string1[i] = string2[i];     // copy the element to string1
    i++;
  }
  string1[i] = '\0';             // terminate the first string

  return;
}
```

As currently written, the subscript `i` in the `strcopy()` function is used successively to access each character in the array named `string2` by "marching along" the string one character at a time. The `while` statement in `strcopy()` tests each character to ensure that the end of the string has not been reached. As with all relational expressions, the tested expression, `string2[i] != '\0'`, is either true or false. Using the string `this is a string` illustrated in Figure 14.5 as an example, as long as `string2[i]` does not access the end-of-string character the value of the expression is nonzero and is considered to be true. The expression is false only when the value of the expression is zero. This occurs when the last element in the string is accessed.

FIGURE 14.5

The `while` test becomes false at the end of the string

Element	String array	Expression	Value
Zeroth element	t	string2[0]!='\0'	1
First element	h	string2[1]!='\0'	1
Second element	i	string2[2]!='\0'	1
	s		
	i		
•	s	•	•
•		•	•
•	a	•	•
	s		
	t		
	r		
	i		
	n		
Fifteenth element	g	string2[15]!='\0'	1
Sixteenth element	\0	string2[16]!='\0'	0

End-of-string marker

Recall that C++ defines false as zero and true as anything else. Thus, the expression `string2[i] != '\0'` becomes zero, or false, when the end of the string is reached. It is nonzero, or true, everywhere else. Because the `NULL` character has an internal value of zero by itself, the comparison to `'\0'` is not necessary. When `string2[i]` accesses the end-of-string character, the value of `string2[i]` is zero. When `string2[i]` accesses any other character, the value of `string2[i]` is the value of the code used to store the character and is nonzero. Figure 14.6 lists the ASCII codes for the string `this is a string`. As seen in the figure, each element has a nonzero value except for the null character.

Because the expression `string2[i]` is only zero at the end of a string and nonzero for every other character, the expression `while (string2[i] != '\0')` can be replaced by the simpler expression `while (string2[i])`. Although this may appear confusing at first, the revised test expression is certainly more compact than the longer version. End-of-string tests are frequently written by professional C++ programmers in this shorter

FIGURE 14.6

The ASCII codes used to store `this is a string`

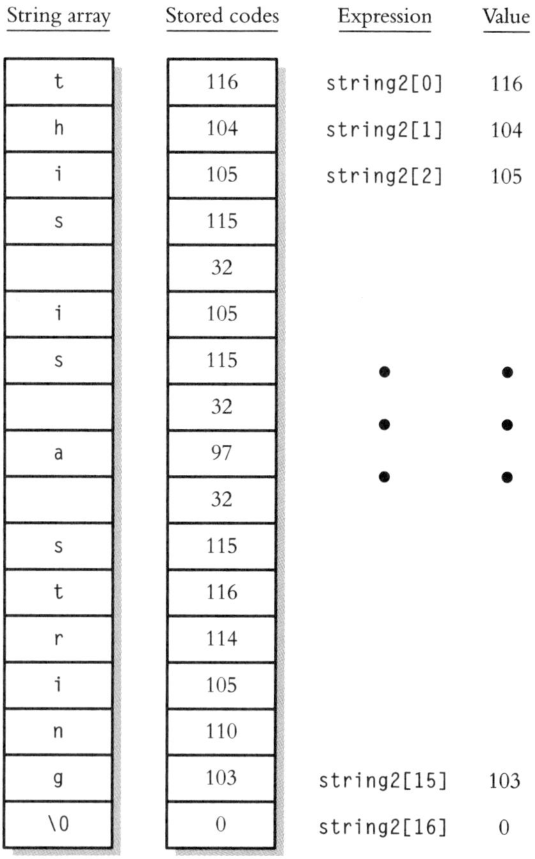

String array	Stored codes	Expression	Value
t	116	string2[0]	116
h	104	string2[1]	104
i	105	string2[2]	105
s	115		
	32		
i	105		
s	115	•	•
	32	•	•
a	97	•	•
	32		
s	115		
t	116		
r	114		
i	105		
n	110		
g	103	string2[15]	103
\0	0	string2[16]	0

form, so it is worthwhile to become familiar with this expression. Including this expression in `strcopy()` results in the following version:

```
void strcopy(char string1[], char string2[])   // copy string2 to string1
{
  int i = 0;

  while (string2[i])
  {
    string1[i] = string2[i];     // copy the element to string1
    i++;
  }
  string1[i] = '\0';             // terminate the first string

  return;
}
```

The second modification that would be made to this string copy function by a C++ programmer is to include the assignment inside the test portion of the `while` statement. Our new version of the string copy function is:

```
void strcopy(char string1[], char string2[])   // copy string2 to string1
{
  int i = 0;
  while (string1[i] = string2[i])
    i++;
  return;
}
```

Notice that including the assignment statement within the test part of the `while` statement eliminates the necessity of separately terminating the copied string with the null character. The assignment within the parentheses ensures that the null character is copied from `string2` to `string1`. The value of the assignment expression becomes zero only after the null character is assigned to `string1`, at which point the `while` loop is terminated.

Character-by-Character Input

Just as strings can be processed using character-by-character techniques, they can also be entered and displayed in this manner. For example, consider Program 14.3, which uses the character-input function `cin.get()` to accept a string one character at a time. The shaded portion of Program 14.3 essentially replaces the `cin.getline()` function previously used in Program 14.2.

PROGRAM 14.3

```
#include <iostream.h>

int main()
{
  const int MAXCHARS = 81;
  char message[MAXCHARS], c;
  cout << "\nEnter a sentence:\n";

  int i = 0;
  while(i < MAXCHARS && (c = cin.get()) != '\n')
  {
    message[i] = c;   // store the character
    i++;
  }
  message[i] = '\0';  // terminate the string
```

(continued next page)

(continued from previous page)

```
    cout << "\nThe sentence just entered is:\n"
         << message << endl << endl;

  return 0;
}
```

Figure 14.7 provides a sample output produced using Program 14.3.

FIGURE 14.7

Sample run using Program 14.3

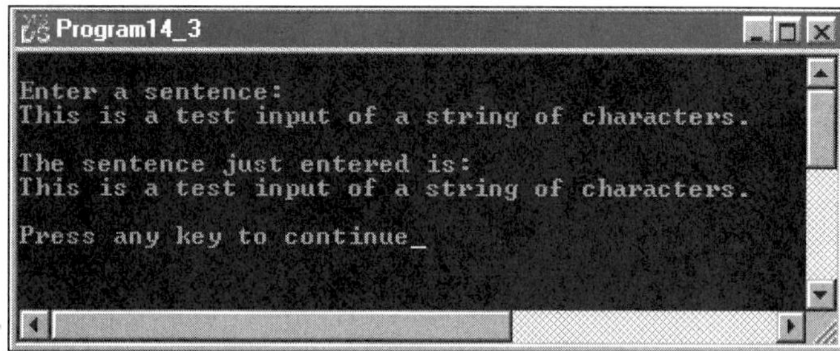

The `while` statement in Program 14.3 causes characters to be read providing the number of characters entered is less than `MAXCHARS` and the character returned by `cin.get()` is not the newline character. The parentheses surrounding the expression `c = cin.get()` are necessary to assign the character returned by `cin.get()` to the variable `c` prior to comparing it to the newline escape sequence. Without the surrounding parentheses, the comparison operator, `!=`, which takes precedence over the assignment operator, causes the entire expression to be equivalent to

```
c = (cin.get() != '\n')
```

which is an invalid application of `cin.get()`.[1]

Program 14.3 also illustrates a very useful technique for developing functions. The shaded statements constitute a self-contained unit for entering a complete line of characters from a terminal. As such, these statements can be removed from `main()` and placed together as a new function. Program 14.4 illustrates placement of these statements in a separate function named `getaline()`.

1 The equivalent statement in C is `c = (getchar() != '\n')`, which is a valid expression that produces an unexpected result for most beginning programmers. Here the character returned by `getchar()` is compared to `'\n'`, and the value of the comparison is either 0 or 1, depending on whether or not `getchar()` received the newline character. This value, either 0 or 1, is then assigned to `c`.

PROGRAM 14.4

```
#include <iostream.h>

const int MAXCHARS = 81;
void getaline(char []);  // function prototype

int main()
{
  char message[MAXCHARS];   // enough storage for a complete line

  cout << "\nEnter a sentence:\n";
  getaline(message);
  cout << "\nThe sentence just entered is:\n";
  cout << message << endl << endl;

  return 0;
}

void getaline(char strng[])
{
  int i = 0;
  char c;

  while(i < MAXCHARS && (c = cin.get()) != '\n')
  {
    strng[i] = c;      // store the character entered
    i++;
  }
  strng[i] = '\0';     // terminate the string

  return;
}
```

EXERCISES 14.1

1. Determine the value of `text[0]`, `text[3]`, and `text[10]`, assuming that `text` is an array of characters and the following input has been stored in the array:

a. `now is the time`

b. `rocky raccoon welcomes you`

c. `Happy Holidays`

d. `The good ship`

2. a. The following function can be used to select and display all vowels contained within a user-input string:

```
void vowels(char strng[])
 {
   int i = 0;
   char c;
   while ((c = strng[i++]) != '\0')
     switch(c)
     {
        case 'a':
        case 'e':
        case 'i':
        case 'o':
        case 'u':
          cout << c;
     } // end of switch
     cout << endl;

   return;
 }
```

Notice that the `switch` statement in `vowels()` uses the fact that selected cases "drop through" in the absence of break statements. Thus, all selected cases result in a `cout` statement being executed. Include `vowels()` in a working program that accepts a user-input string and then displays all vowels in the string. In response to the input `How much is the little worth worth?`, your program should display `ouieieoo`.

b. Modify `vowels()` to count and display the total number of vowels contained in the string passed to it.

3. Modify the `vowels()` function of Exercise 2 to count and display the individual numbers of each vowel contained in the string.

4. a. Write a C++ function to count the total number of characters, including blanks, contained in a string. Do not include the end-of-string marker in the count.

b. Include the function written for Exercise 4a in a complete working program.

5. Write a program that accepts a string of characters from a terminal and displays the hexadecimal equivalent of each character.

6. Write a C++ program that accepts a string of characters from a terminal and displays the string one word per line.

7. Write a function that reverses the characters in a string. (*Hint:* This can be considered as a string copy starting from the back end of the first string.)

8. Write a function named `remove()` that returns nothing and deletes all occurrences of its character argument from a string. The function should take two arguments: the string name and the character to be removed. For example, if message contains the string `Happy Holidays`, the function call `remove(message,'H')` should place the string `appy olidays` into message.

9. Write a function that adds a single character at the end of an existing string. The function should replace the existing `\0` character with the new character and append a new `\0` at the end of the string. The function returns nothing.

10. Write a function that deletes a single character from the end of a string. This is effectively achieved by moving the `\0` character one position closer to the start of the string. The function returns nothing.

11. Write a function named `deleteChar()` that can be used to delete characters from a string. The function should take three arguments: the string name, the number of characters to delete, and the starting position in the string where characters should be deleted. For example, the function call `deleteChar(strng,13,5)`, when applied to the string `all enthusiastic people`, should result in the string `all people`.

12. Write a function named `addChar()` to insert one string of characters into another string. The function should take three arguments: the string to be inserted, the original string, and the position in the original string where the insertion should begin. For example, the call `addChar(" for all",message,6)` should insert the characters `for all` in `message` starting at `message[5]`.

13. a. Write a C++ function named `toUpper()` that converts lowercase letters into uppercase letters. The expression `c - 'a' + 'A'` can be used to make the conversion for any lowercase character stored in `c`.

b. Add a data input check to the function written in Exercise 13a to verify that a valid lowercase letter is passed to the function. A character, in ASCII, is lowercase if it is greater than or equal to `a` and less than or equal to `z`. If the character is not a valid lowercase letter, have the function `toUpper()` return the passed character unaltered.

14. Write a C++ program that accepts a string from a terminal and converts all lowercase letters in the string to uppercase letters.

15. Write a C++ program that accepts a string from a terminal and converts all uppercase letters in the string to lowercase letters.

16. Write a C++ program that counts the number of words in a string. A word is encountered whenever a transition from a blank space to a nonblank character is encountered. Assume the string contains words separated only by blank spaces.

14.2 Library Functions

C++ does not provide built-in operations for complete arrays, such as array assignments or array comparisons. Because a string is just an array of characters terminated with a `'\0'` character, this means that assignment and relational operations *are not* provided for strings. Extensive collections of string-handling functions and routines, however, that effectively supply string assignment, comparison, and other very useful string operations are included with all C++ compilers. The more commonly used of these are listed in Table 14.2.

String library functions are called in the same manner as all C++ functions. This means that the appropriate declarations for these functions, which are contained in the standard header files `<string.h>` must be included in your program before the function is called.

The most commonly used functions listed in Table 14.2 are the first four. The `strcpy()` function copies a source string expression, which consists of either a string literal or the contents of a string variable, into a destination string variable. For example, in the function call `strcpy(string1, "Hello World!")` the source string literal `"Hello World!"` is copied into the destination string variable `string1`. Similarly, if the source string is a string variable named `srcString`, the function call `strcpy(string1, srcString)` copies the contents of `srcString` into `string1`. In both cases it is the programmer's responsibility to ensure that `string1` is large enough to contain the source string (see Programmer's Note box on page 781).

The `strcat()` function appends a string expression onto the end of a string variable. For example, if the content of a string variable named `destString` is `"Hello"`, then the function call `strcat(destString, " there World!")` results in the string value `"Hello there World!"` being assigned to `destString`. As with the `strcpy()` function, it is the programmers responsibility to ensure that the destination string has been defined as large enough to hold the additional concatenated characters.

The `strlen()` function returns the number of characters in its string parameter but does not include the terminating null character in the count. For example, the value returned by the function call `strlen("Hello World!")` is 12.

Finally two string expressions may be compared for equality using the `strcmp()` function. Each character in a string is stored in binary using either the ASCII or Unicode code. The first 128 characters of the 16-bit Unicode are identical to the complete 128 characters of the ASCII code. In both codes, a blank precedes (is less than) all letters and numbers, the letters of the alphabet are stored in order from A to Z, and the digits are

TABLE 14.2 String library routines (required header file is string.h)

Name	Description	Example
strcpy(string_var, string_exp)	Copies string_exp to string_var, including the '\0'.	strcpy(test, "efgh")
strcat(string_var, string_exp)	Appends str_exp to the end of the string value contained in string_var.	strcat(test, "there")
strlen(string_exp)	Returns the length of the string. Does not include the '\0' in the length count.	strlen("Hello World!")
strcmp(string_exp1, string_exp2)	Compares string_exp1 to string_exp2. Returns a negative integer if string_exp1 < string_exp2, 0 if string_exp1 == string_exp2, and a positive integer if string_exp1 > string_exp2.	strcmp("Bebop", "Beehive")
strncpy(string_var, string_exp, n)	Copies at most n characters of string_exp to string_var. If string_exp has fewer than n characters it will pad string_var with '\0's.	strncpy(str1, str2, 5)
strncmp(string_exp1, string_exp2, n)	Compare at most n characters of string_exp1 to string_exp2. Returns the same values as strcmp() based on the number of characters compared.	strncmp("Bebop", "Beehive", 2)
strchr(string_exp, character)	Locates the position of the first occurrence of the character within the string. Returns the address of the character.	strchr("Hello", 'l')
strtok(string_exp, character)	Parses string1 into tokens. Returns the next sequence of characters contained in string1 up to but not including the delimiter character ch.	strtok("Hello there World!, ")

PROGRAMMER'S NOTES

Initializing and Processing Strings

Each of the following declarations produces the same result.

```
char test[5] = "abcd";
char test[] = "abcd";
char test[5] = {'a', 'b', 'c', 'd', '\0'};
char test[] = {'a', 'b', 'c', 'd', '\0'};
```

Each declaration creates storage for exactly five characters and initializes this storage with the characters `'a'`, `'b'`, `'c'`, `'d'`, and `'\0'`. Because a string literal is used for initialization in the first two declarations, the compiler automatically supplies the end-of-string `NULL`.

String variables declared in either of the ways shown preclude the use of any subsequent assignments, such as `test = "efgh";`, to the character array. In place of an assignment you can use the `strcpy()` function, such as `strcpy(test,"efgh")`. The only restriction on using `strcpy()` is the size of the declared array, which in this case is five elements. Attempting to copy a larger string value into `test` causes the copy to overflow the destination array beginning with the memory area immediately following the last array element. This overwrites whatever was in these memory locations, and typically cause a run-time crash when the overwritten areas are accessed via their legitimate identifier name(s).

The same problem can arise when using the `strcat()` function. It is the programmer's responsibility to ensure that the concatenated string will fit into the original string.

An interesting situation arises when string variables are defined using pointers (see Section 14.4). In these situations assignments can be made after the declaration statement.

Finally, a string class can be defined (see Section 14.7) in such a way that permits assignment, copy, and concatenation in a manner that checks for sufficient memory space before these operations are performed.

stored in order from 0 to 9. (It is important to note that the Unicode code supports multilingual characters.)

When two strings are compared, their individual characters are compared a pair at a time (both first characters, then both second characters, and so on). If no differences are found, the strings are equal; if a difference is found, the string with the first lower character is considered the smaller string. Thus,

`"Good Bye"` is less than `"Hello"` because the first `'G'` in `Good Bye` is less the first `'H'` in `Hello`.

`"Hello"` is less than `"hello"` because the first `'H'` in `Hello` is less than the first `'h'` in `hello`.

`"Hello"` is less than `"Hello "` because the `'\0'` terminating the first string is less than the `' '` in the second string.

"SMITH" is greater than "JONES" because the first 'S' in SMITH is greater than the first 'J' in JONES.

"123" is greater than "1227" because the third character, the '3' in 123 is greater than the third character, the '2' in 1227.

"1237" is greater than "123" because the fourth character, the '7', in 1237 is greater than the fourth character, the '\0' in 123.

"Behop" is greater than "Beehive" because the third character, the 'h', in Behop is greater than the third character, the 'e', in Beehive.

Program 14.5 uses these string functions within the context of a complete program.

PROGRAM 14.5

```
#include <iostream.h>
#include <string.h>   // required for the string function library

int main()
{
  const int MAXELS = 50;
  char string1[MAXELS] = "Hello";
  char string2[MAXELS] = "Hello there";
  int n;

  cout << endl;
  n = strcmp(string1, string2);

  if (n < 0)
    cout << string1 << " is less than " << string2 << endl;
  else if (n == 0)
    cout << string1 << " is equal to " << string2 << endl;
  else
    cout << string1 << " is greater than " << string2 << endl;

  cout << "\nThe length of the string " << string1 << " is "
       << strlen(string1) << " characters" << endl;
  cout << "The length of the string " << string2 << " is "
       << strlen(string2) << " characters" << endl;

  strcat(string1," there World!");
```

(continued next page)

(continued from previous page)

```
  cout << "\nAfter concatenation, string1 contains "
       << "the string value\n" << string1
       << "\nThe length of this string is "
       << strlen(string1) << " characters" << endl;

  cout << "\nType in a sequence of characters for string2:\n";
  cin.getline(string2, MAXELS);

  strcpy(string1, string2);

  cout << "\nAfter copying string2 to string1, "
       << "the string value in string1 is:\n" << string2
       << "\nThe length of this string is "
       << strlen(string1) << " characters" << endl;

  cout << "\nThe starting address of string1 is: "
       << (void *) string1 << endl << endl;

  return 0;
}
```

Figure 14.8 illustrates the output produced by Program 14.5.

FIGURE 14.8

Output displayed by Program 14.5

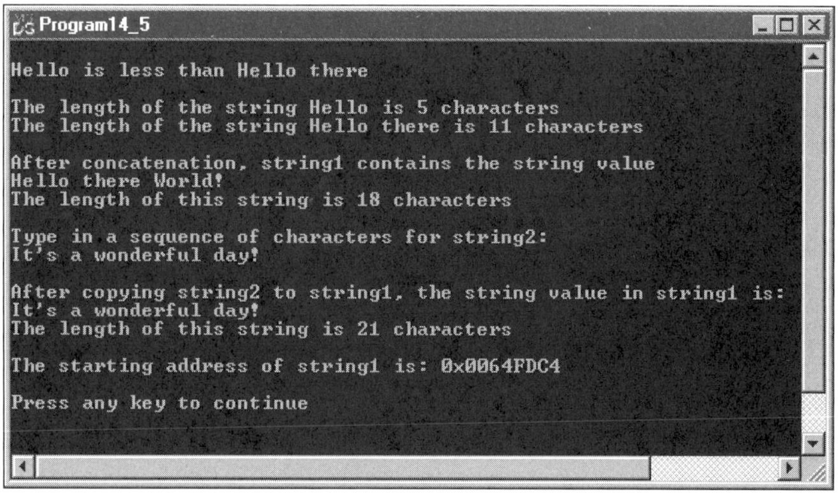

```
Program14_5
Hello is less than Hello there

The length of the string Hello is 5 characters
The length of the string Hello there is 11 characters

After concatenation, string1 contains the string value
Hello there World!
The length of this string is 18 characters

Type in a sequence of characters for string2:
It's a wonderful day!

After copying string2 to string1, the string value in string1 is:
It's a wonderful day!
The length of this string is 21 characters

The starting address of string1 is: 0x0064FDC4

Press any key to continue
```

Except for the last displayed line, the output of Program 14.5 follows the discussion presented for the string library functions. As demonstrated by this output, the extraction operator `<<` automatically dereferences a string variable and displays the contents contained in the variable. Sometimes, however, we really want to see the address of the string. As shown in Program 14.5, this can be done by casting the string variable name using the expression `(void *)`. Another method would be to send the expression `&string1[0]` to the `cout` object. This expression is read as "*the address* of the `string[0]` element," which is also the starting address of the complete string.

Character Routines

In addition to string manipulation functions, all C++ compilers also include the character-handling routines listed in Table 14.3. The prototypes for each of these routines are contained in the header file `ctype.h`, which should be included in any program that uses these routines.

All of the functions listed in Table 14.3 return a nonzero integer (i.e, a true value) if the character meets the desired condition and a zero integer (i.e., a false value) if the condition is not met; therefore these functions can be used directly within an `if` statement. For example, consider the following code segment:

```
char ch;

ch = cin.get();  // get a character from the keyboard

if(isdigit(ch))
  cout < "The character just entered is a digit" << endl;
else if(ispunct(ch))
  cout << "The character just entered is a punctuation mark" << endl;
```

Notice that the character function is included as a condition within the `if` statement because the function effectively returns either a true (nonzero) or false (zero) value.

Program 14.6 illustrates the use of the `toupper()` function within the function `ConvertToUpper()`, which is used to convert all lowercase string characters into their uppercase form.

TABLE 14.3 **Character library routines (required header file is `ctype.h`)**

Required Prototype	Description	Example
`int isalpha(char)`	Returns a nonzero number if the character is a letter; otherwise it returns a zero.	`isalpha('a')`
`int isupper(char)`	Returns a nonzero number if the character is uppercase; otherwise it returns a zero.	`isupper('a')`
`int islower(char)`	Returns a nonzero number if the character is lowercase; otherwise it returns a zero.	`islower('a')`
`int isdigit(character)`	Returns a nonzero number if the character is a digit (0 through 9); otherwise it returns a zero.	`isdigit('a')`
`int isascii(character)`	Returns a nonzero number if the character is an ASCII character; otherwise it returns a zero.	`isascii('a')`
`int isspace(character)`	Returns a nonzero number if the character is a space; otherwise it returns a zero.	`isspace(' ')`
`int isprint(character)`	Returns a nonzero number if the character is a printable character; otherwise it returns a zero.	`isprint('a')`
`int iscntrl(character)`	Returns a nonzero number if the character is a control character; otherwise it returns a zero.	`iscntrl('a')`
`int ispucnt(character)`	Returns a nonzero number if the character is a punctuation character; otherwise it returns a zero.	`ispucnt('!')`
`int toupper(char)`	Returns the uppercase equivalent if the character is lowercase; otherwise it returns the character unchanged.	`toupper('a')`
`int tolower(char)`	Returns the lowercase equivalent if the character is uppercase; otherwise it returns the character unchanged.	`tolower('A')`

PROGRAM 14.6

```
#include <iostream.h>
#include <ctype.h>     // required for the character function library

void ConvertToUpper(char []);

int main()
{
  const int MAXCHARS = 100;
  char message[MAXCHARS];

  cout << "\nType in any sequence of characters:\n";

  cin.getline(message,MAXCHARS);

  ConvertToUpper(message);

  cout << "\nThe characters just entered, in uppercase are:\n"
       << message << endl << endl;

  return 0;
}

// this function converts all lowercase character to uppercase
void ConvertToUpper(char message[])
{
  for(int i = 0; message[i] != '\0'; i++)
    message[i] = toupper(message[i]);

  return;
}
```

The output produced when Program 14.6 is executed is shown in Figure 14.9.

FIGURE 14.9

Output display produced by Program 14.6

```
Program14_6

Type in any sequence of characters: this is a test of 12345
The characters just entered, in uppercase are: THIS IS A TEST OF 12345

Press any key to continue_
```

Notice that the touppper() library function only converts lowercase letters and that all other characters are unaffected.

Conversion Routines

The last group of standard string library routines, which are listed in Table 14.4, are used to convert strings to and from integer and double precision data types. The prototypes for each of these routines are contained in the header file stdlib.h, which should be included in any program that uses these routines.

TABLE 14.4 String conversion routines (required header file is stdlib.h)

Required Prototype	Description	Example
int atoi(string_exp)	Convert an ASCII string to an integer. Conversion stops at the first noninteger character.	atoi("1234")
double atof(string_exp)	Convert an ASCII string to a double precision number. Conversion stops at the first character that cannot be interpreted as a double.	atof("12.34")
char[] itoa(string_esp)	Convert an integer to an ASCII string. The space allocated for the returned string must be large enough for the converted value.	itoa(1234)

Program 14.7 illustrates using the atoi() and atof() functions.

PROGRAM 14.7

```
#include <iostream.h>
#include <string.h>
#include <stdlib.h>    // required for string conversion function library

int main()
{
  const int MAXELS = 20;
  char string[MAXELS] = "12345";
  int num;
  double dnum;
```

(continued next page)

(continued from previous page)

```
  num = atoi(string);

  cout << "\nThe string \"" << string << "\" as an integer number is: "
       << num;
  cout << "\nThis number divided by 3 is: " << num / 3 << endl;

  strcat(string, ".96");

  dnum = atof(string);

  cout << "The string \"" << string << "\" as a double number is: "
       << dnum;
  cout << "\nThis number divided by 3 is: " << dnum / 3 << endl;

  return 0;
}
```

The output produced when Program 14.7 is executed is shown in Figure 14.10.

As this output illustrates, once a string has been converted to either an integer or double precision value, mathematical operations on the numerical value are valid.

FIGURE 14.10

Output displayed by Program 14.7

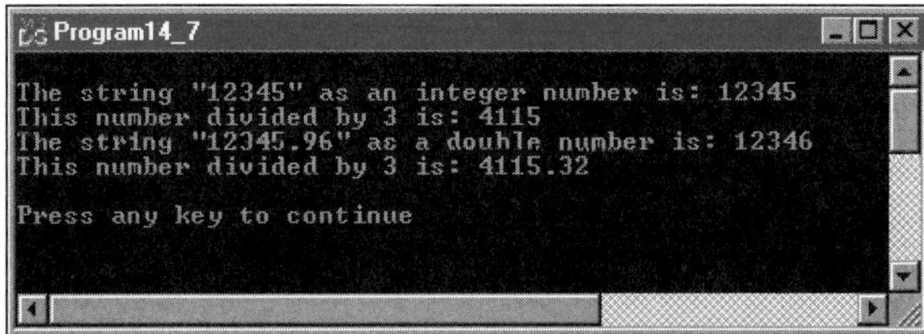

EXERCISES 14.2

1. Enter and execute Program 14.5 on your computer.
2. Enter and execute Program 14.6 on your computer.
3. Enter and execute Program 14.7 on your computer.

4. Write the following declaration statement in three additional ways: `char string[] = "Hello World";`.

5. a. Write a function named `length()` that returns the length of a string, without using any standard library functions.

b. Write a simple `main()` function to test the `length()` function written for Exercise 5a.

6. a. Write a function named `compare()` that compares two strings and returns an integer value of:

–1 if the first string is less than the second string
0 if the two strings are equal
1 if the first string is greater than the second string

Do not use any standard library functions in the `compare()` function.

b. Write a simple `main()` function to test the `compare()` function written for Exercise 6a.

7. a. Write a C++ function named `ctype()` that determines the ASCII character of any integer in the range of 0 to 127. If the number represents a printable ASCII character print the character with an appropriate message that:

```
The ASCII character is a lowercase letter.
The ASCII character is an uppercase letter.
The ASCII character is a digit.
The ASCII character is a punctuation mark.
The ASCII character is a space.
The ASCII character is a nonprintable character.
```

If the ASCII character is a nonprintable character, display its ASCII code in decimal format and the message `The ASCII character is a nonprintable character.`

b. Write a simple `main()` function to test the function written for Exercise 7a. The `main()` function should generate 20 random numbers in the range of 0 to 127 and call `ctype()` for each generated number.

8. a. Include the string library functions `strlen()`, `strcat()`, and `strncat()` within a function having the prototype `int concat(char string1[], char string2[], int maxlength)`. The `concat()` function should perform a complete concatenation of `string2` to `string1` only if the length of the concatenated string does not exceed `maxlength`, which is the maximum length defined for `string1`. If the concatenated string will exceed `maxlength`, only concatenate the characters in `string2` so the maximum combined string length is equal to `maxlength` – 1, which provides enough room for the end-of-string `NULL` character.

b. Write a simple `main()` function to test the `concat()` function written for Exercise 8a.

9. a. Write a function named `countlets()` that returns the number of letters in an entered string. Digits, spaces, punctuation, tabs, and newline characters should not be included in the returned count.

   b. Write a simple `main()` function to test the `countlets()` function written for Exercise 9a.

14.3 Pointers and String Processing

Pointers are exceptionally useful in constructing string-handling functions. When pointer notation is used in place of subscripts to access individual characters in a string, the resulting statements are both more compact and more efficient. In this section we describe the equivalence between subscripts and pointers when accessing individual characters in a string.

Consider the final `strcopy()` function introduced in Section 14.1. This function was used to copy the characters of one string to a second string. For convenience, this function is repeated below:

```
void strcopy(char string1[], char string2[])   // copy string2 to string1
{
  int i = 0;

  while (string1[i] = string2[i])
    i++;

  return;
}
```

The conversion of this function from subscript notation to pointer notation is instructive and straightforward. Although each of the two prior version of `strcopy()` presented in Section 14.1 can be rewritten using pointer notation, the following is the equivalent of our last subscript version:

```
strcopy(char *string1, char *string2)   // copy string2 to string1
{
  while (*string1 = *string2)
  {
    string1++;
    string2++;
  }
  return;
}
```

In both the subscript and pointer versions of `strcopy()`, the function receives the name of the array being passed. Recall that passing an array name to a function actually passes the address of the first location of the array. In our pointer version of `strcopy()` the two passed addresses are stored in the pointer parameters `string1` and `string2`, respectively.

The declarations `char *string1;` and `char *string2;` used in the pointer version of `strcopy()` indicate that `string1` and `string2` are both pointers containing the address of a character, and stress the treatment of the passed addresses as pointer values rather than array names. These declarations are equivalent to the declarations `char string1[]` and `char string2[]`, respectively.

Internal to `strcopy()`, the pointer expression `*string1`, which refers to "the element whose address is in `string1`," replaces the equivalent subscript expression `string1[i]`. Similarly, the pointer expression `*string2` replaces the equivalent subscript expression `string2[i]`. The expression `*string1 = *string2` causes the element pointed to by `string2` to be assigned to the element pointed to by `string1`. Because the starting addresses of both strings are passed to `strcopy()` and stored in `string1` and `string2`, respectively, the expression `*string1` initially refers to `string1[0]` and the expression `*string2` initially refers to `string2[0]`.

Consecutively incrementing both pointers in `strcopy()` with the expressions `string1++` and `string2++` simply causes each pointer to "point to" the next consecutive character in the respective string. As with the subscript version, the pointer version of `strcopy` steps along, copying element by element, until the end of the string is copied. One final change to the string copy function can be made by including the pointer increments as postfix operators within the test part of the `while` statement. The final form of the string copy function is:

```
strcopy(char *string1, char *string2)   // copy string2 to string1
{
  while (*string1++ = *string2++)
    ;
  return;
}
```

There is no ambiguity in the expression `*string1++ = *string2++` even though the indirection operator, `*`, and the increment operator, `++`, have the same precedence. These operators associate from left to right, so the character pointed to is accessed before the pointer is incremented. Only after completion of the assignment `*string1 = *string2` are the pointers incremented to correctly point to the next characters in the respective strings.

The string copy function included in the standard library supplied with C++ compilers is typically written exactly like our last pointer version of `strcopy()`.

EXERCISES 14.3

1. Determine the value of `*text`, `*(text + 3)`, and `*(text + 10)`, assuming that `text` is an array of characters and the following has been stored in the array:
   a. `now is the time`
   b. `rocky raccoon welcomes you`
   c. `Happy Holidays`
   d. `The good ship`

2. **a.** The following function, `convert()`, "marches along" the string passed to it and sends each character in the string, one at a time, to the `toUpper()` function until the null character is encountered.

```
convert(char strng[])        // convert a string to uppercase letters
{
  int i = 0;
  while (strng[i] != '\0')
  {
    strng[i] = toUpper(strng[i]);
    i++;
  }
  return;
}

char toUpper(letter)  // convert a character to uppercase
char letter;
{
  if( (letter >= 'a') && (letter <= 'z') )
    return (letter - 'a' + 'A');
  else
    return (letter);
}
```

   The `toUpper()` function takes each character passed to it and first examines it to determine if the character is a lowercase letter (a lowercase letter is any character between `a` and `z`, inclusive). Assuming that characters are stored using the standard ASCII character codes, the expression `letter - 'a' + 'A'` converts a lowercase letter to its uppercase equivalent. Rewrite the `convert()` function using pointers.

   b. Include the `convert()` and `toUpper()` functions in a working program. The program should prompt the user for a string and echo the string back to the user in uppercase letters.

3. Using pointers, repeat Exercise 2 from Section 14.1.

4. Using pointers, repeat Exercise 3 from Section 14.1.

5. Using pointers, repeat Exercise 4 from Section 14.1.

6. Write a function named `remove()` that deletes all occurrences of a character from a string. The function should take two arguments: the string name and the character to be removed. For example, if `message` contains the string `Happy Holidays`, the function call `remove(message,'H')` should place the string `appy olidays` into message. Use only pointer notation in writing the function.

7. Using pointers, repeat Exercise 7 from Section 14.1.

8. Write a program using the `cin.get()`, and `toupper()` library routines to echo back each entered letter in its uppercase form. The program should terminate when the digit 1 key is pressed.

9. Write a function that uses pointers to add a single character at the end of an existing string. The function should replace the existing `\0` character with the new character and append a new `\0` at the end of the string.

10. Write a function that uses pointers to delete a single character from the end of a string. This is effectively achieved by moving the `\0` character one position closer to the start of the string.

11. Determine the string-handling functions that are available with your C++ compiler. For each available function list the data types of the arguments expected by the function and the data type of any returned value.

12. Write a function named `trimfrnt()` that deletes all leading blanks from a string. Write the function using pointers.

13. Write a function named `trimrear()` that deletes all trailing blanks from a string. Write the function using pointers.

14. Write a function named `strlen()` that returns the number of characters in a string. Do not include the `\0` character in the returned count. Use only pointer notation in your function.

15. Write a function named `addchars()` that adds `n` occurrences of a character to a string. For example, the call `addchars(message, 4, '!")` should add four exclamation marks at the end of message. Use only pointer notation in your function.

16. Write a function named `extract()` that accepts two strings, `s1` and `s2`, and two integer numbers, `n1` and `n2`, as arguments. The function should extract `n2` characters from `s2`, starting at position `n1`, and place the extracted characters into `s1`. For example, if string `s1` contains the characters `05/18/01 D169254 Rotech Systems`, the function call `extract(s1, s2, 18, 6)` should create the string `Rotech` in `s2`. Note that the starting position for counting purposes is in position one. Be sure to close off the returned string with a '\0' and make sure that string s1 is defined in the calling function to be large enough to accept the extracted values.

17. A word or phrase that reads the same forward and backward is a palindrome. Write a C++ program that accepts a line of text as input and examines the entered text to determine if it is a palindrome. If the entered text is a palindrome, display the message `This is a palindrome`. If a palindrome was not entered, the message `This is not a palindrome` should be displayed.

14.4 String Definitions and Pointer Arrays

The definition of a string automatically involves a pointer. For example, the definition `char message1[81];` both reserves storage for 81 characters and automatically creates a pointer constant, `message1`, which contains the address of `message1[0]`. As a pointer constant, the address associated with the pointer cannot be changed—it must always "point to" the beginning of the created array.

Instead of creating a string as an array, however, it is also possible to create a string using a pointer. For example, the definition `char *message2;` creates a pointer to a character. In this case, `message2` is a true pointer variable. Once a pointer to a character is defined, assignment statements, such as `message2 = "this is a string";`, can be made. In this assignment, `message2`, which is a pointer, receives the address of the first character in the string.

The main difference in the definitions of `message1` as an array and `message2` as a pointer is the way the pointer is created. Defining `message1` using the declaration `char message1[81]` explicitly calls for a fixed amount of storage for the array. This also causes the compiler to create a pointer constant. Defining `message2` using the declaration `char *message2` explicitly creates a pointer variable first. This pointer is then used to hold the address of a string when the string is actually specified. This difference in definitions has both storage and programming consequences.

From a programming perspective, defining `message2` as a pointer to a character allows string assignments, such as `message2 = "this is a string";`, to be made within a program. Similar assignments are not allowed for strings defined as arrays. Thus, the statement `message1 = "this is a string";` is not valid. Both definitions, however, allow initializations to be made using a string assignment. For example, both of the following initializations are valid:

```
char message1[81] = "this is a string";
char *message2 = "this is a string";
```

From a storage perspective, the allocations of space for `message1` and `message2` are quite different. As illustrated in Figure 14.11, both initializations cause the computer to store the same string internally. In the case of `message1`, a specific set of 81 storage locations is reserved, and the first 17 locations are initialized. For `message1`, different strings

FIGURE 14.11

String storage allocation for (a) a string defined as an array, and (b) a string using a pointer

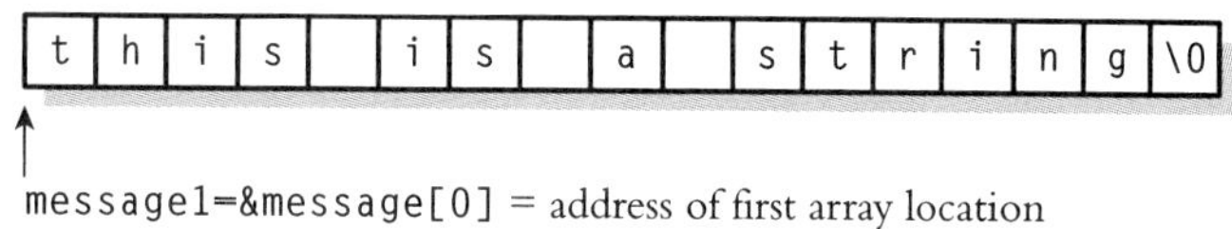

a. Storage allocation for a string defined as an array

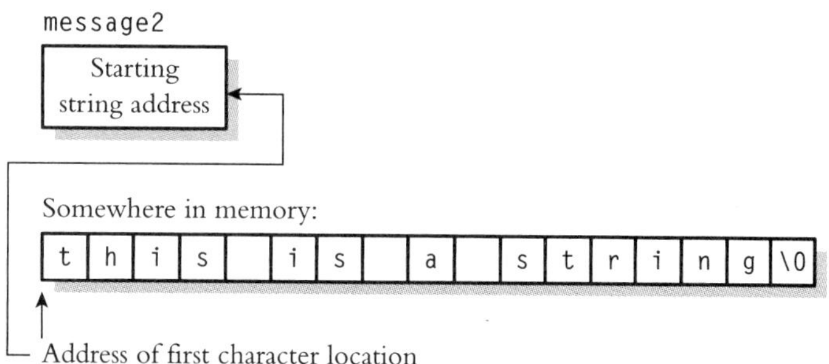

b. Storage of a string using a pointer

can be stored, but each string will overwrite the previously stored characters. The same is not true for `message2`.

The definition of `message2` reserves enough storage for one pointer. The initialization then causes the string to be stored in memory and the address of the string's first character, in this case the address of the `t`, to be loaded into the pointer. If a later assignment is made to `message2`, the initial string remains in memory and new storage locations are allocated to the new string. For example, consider the sequence of instructions

```
char *message2 = "this is a string";
message2 = "A new message";
```

The first statement defines `message2` as a pointer variable, stores the initialization string in memory, and loads the starting address of the string (the address of the `t` in `this`) into `message2`. The next assignment statement causes the computer to store the second string and change the address in `message2` to point to the starting location of this new string.

It is important to realize that the second string assigned to `message2` does not overwrite the first string, but simply changes the address in `message2` to point to the new string. As illustrated in Figure 14.12, both strings are stored inside the computer. Any additional string assignment to `message2` would result in the additional storage of the new string and a corresponding change in the address stored in `message2`. Doing so also means that we no longer have access to the original memory location, unless the address is saved in another pointer variable before the new string assignment is made.

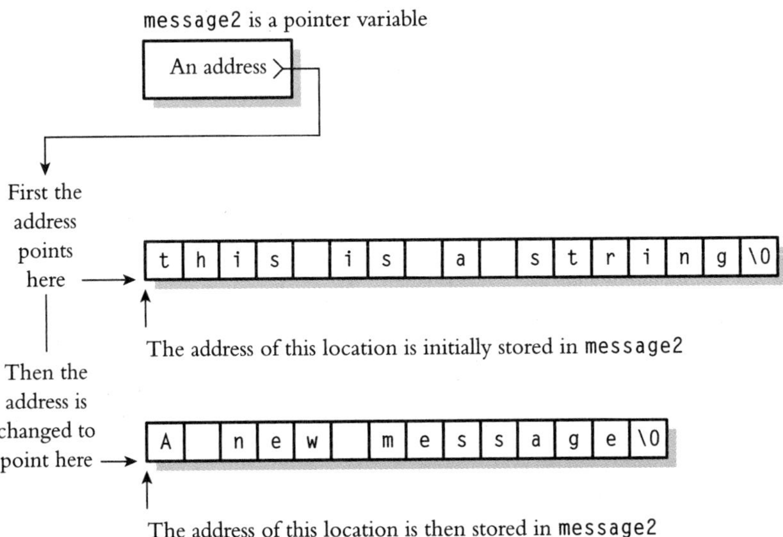

FIGURE 14.12

Storage allocation using a pointer variable

Pointer Arrays

The declaration of an array of character pointers is an extremely useful extension to single string pointer declarations. For example, the declaration

```
char *seasons[4];
```

creates an array of four elements, where each element is a pointer to a character. As individual pointers, each pointer can be assigned to point to a string using string assignment statements. Thus, the statements

```
seasons[0] = "Winter";
seasons[1] = "Spring";
seasons[2] = "Summer";
seasons[3] = "Fall";   // note: string lengths may differ
```

set appropriate addresses into the respective pointers. Figure 14.13 illustrates the addresses loaded into the pointers for these assignments.

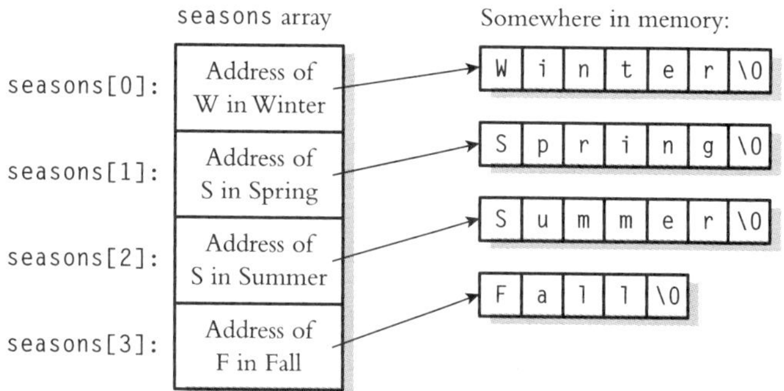

FIGURE 14.13

Addresses contained in the `seasons[]` pointers

As illustrated in Figure 14.13, the `seasons` array does not contain the actual strings assigned to the pointers. These strings are stored elsewhere in the computer, in the normal data area allocated to the program. The array of pointers contains only the addresses of the starting location for each string.

The initializations of the `seasons` array can also be incorporated directly within the definition of the array, as follows:

```
char *seasons[4] = {"Winter",
                    "Spring",
                    "Summer",
                    "Fall"};
```

This declaration both creates an array of pointers and initializes the pointers with appropriate addresses. Once addresses have been assigned to the pointers, each pointer can be used to access its corresponding string. Program 14.8 uses the `seasons` array to display each season using a `for` loop.

The output displayed by Program 14.8 is illustrated in Figure 14.14.

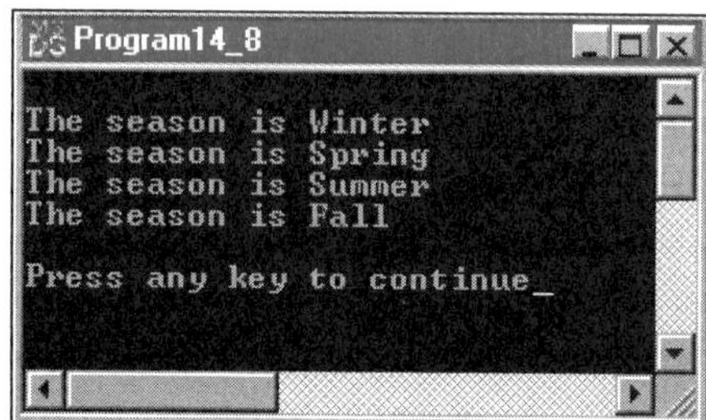

FIGURE 14.14

Output display produced by Program 14.8

PROGRAM 14.8

```
#include <iostream.h>

int main()
{
  int n;
  char *seasons[] = {"Winter",
                     "Spring",
                     "Summer",
                     "Fall"};

  for( n = 0; n < 4; n++)
    cout << "\nThe season is " << seasons[n];

  cout << endl << endl;

  return 0;
}
```

The advantage of using a list of pointers is that logical groups of data headings can be collected together and accessed with one array name. For example, the months in a year can be collectively grouped in one array called `months`, and the days in a week collectively grouped together in an array called `days`. The grouping of like headings allows the programmer to access and print an appropriate heading by simply specifying the correct position of the heading in the array. Program 14.9 uses the `seasons` array to correctly identify and display the season corresponding to a user-input month.

PROGRAM 14.9

```
#include <iostream.h>

int main()
{
  int n;
  char *seasons[] = {"Winter",
                     "Spring",
                     "Summer",
                     "Fall"};
```

(continued next page)

(continued from previous page)

```
  cout << "\nEnter a month (use 1 for Jan., 2 for Feb., etc.): ";
  cin  >> n;
  n = (n % 12) / 3;    // create the correct subscript
  cout << "The month entered is a "<< seasons[n] << " month.\n\n";

  return 0;
}
```

Except for the expression `n = (n % 12) / 3`, Program 14.9 is rather straightforward. The program requests the user to input a month and accepts the number corresponding to the month using a `cin` object call.

The expression `n = (n % 12) / 3` uses a common program "trick" to scale a set of numbers into a more useful set. Using subscripts, the four elements of the seasons array must be accessed using a subscript value from 0 through 3. Thus, the months of the year, which correspond to the numbers 1 through 12, must be adjusted to correspond to the correct season subscript. This is done using the expression `n = (n % 12) / 3`. The expression `n % 12` adjusts the month entered to lie within the range 0 through 11, with 0 corresponding to December, 1 for January, and so on. Dividing by 3 causes the resulting number to range between 0 and 3, corresponding to the possible `seasons` elements. The result of the division by 3 is assigned to the integer variable `n`. The months 0, 1, and 2, when divided by 3, are set to 0; the months 3, 4, and 5 are set to 1; the months 6, 7, and 8 are set to 2; and the months 9, 10, and 11 are set to 3. This is equivalent to the following assignments:

Months	**Season**
December, January, February	Winter
March, April, May	Spring
June, July, August	Summer
September, October, November	Fall

Figure 14.15 illustrates a sample run obtained using Program 14.9.

FIGURE 14.15

Sample run using Program 14.9

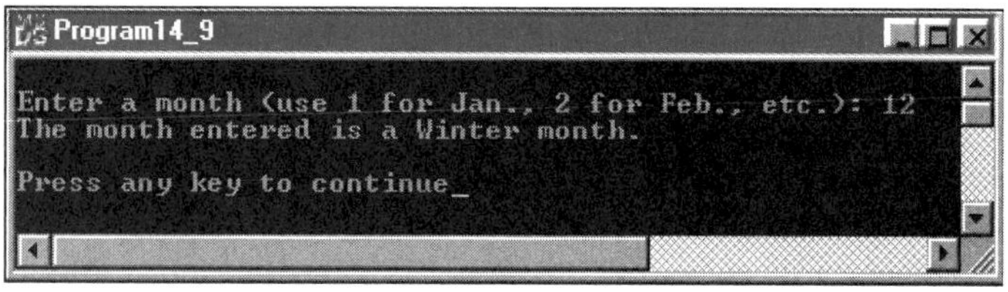

```
Program14_9
Enter a month (use 1 for Jan., 2 for Feb., etc.): 12
The month entered is a Winter month.

Press any key to continue_
```

EXERCISES 14.4

1. Write two declaration statements that can be used in place of the declaration `char text[] = "Hooray!";`.

2. Determine the value of `*text`, `*(text + 3)`, and `*(text + 7)` for each of the following sections of code:

   a.
   ```
   char *text;
   char message[] = "the check is in the mail";
   text = message;
   ```
   b.
   ```
   char *text;
   char formal[] = {'t','h','i','s',' ','i','s',' ','a','n',' ',
                    'i','n','v','i','t','a','t','i','o','n','\0'};
   text = &formal[0];
   ```
   c.
   ```
   char *test;
   char more[] = "Happy Holidays";
   text = &more[4];
   ```
   d.
   ```
   char *text, *second;
   char blip[] = "The good ship";
   second = blip;
   text = ++second;
   ```

3. Determine the error in the following program:

```
#include <iostream.h>
int main()
{
  int i = 0;
  char message[] = {'H','e','l','l','o','\0'};

  for( ; i < 5; i++)
  {
    cout << *message;
    message++;
  }

  return 0;
}
```

4. a. Write a C++ function that displays the day of the week corresponding to a user-entered input number between 1 and 7. That is, in response to an input of 2, the program displays the name Monday. Use an array of pointers in the function.

   b. Include the function written for Exercise 4a in a complete working program.

5. Write a function that permits a user to enter ten lines of user-input text and store the entered lines as ten individual strings. Use a pointer array in your function.

14.5 Common Programming Errors

The common errors associated with defining and processing strings are:

1. Not providing sufficient space for the string to be stored. A simple variation of this is not providing space for the end-of-string null character when a string is defined as an array of characters.

2. Not including the `'\0'` terminating character when an array is initialized character by character. For example, the definition

```
char string[] = {'H', 'e', 'l', 'l', 'o'};
```

does not create a valid string because a terminating null character, `'\0'`, is not included in the initialization.

3. Not realizing that the `strcmp()` function returns a value of 0, which is equivalent to false, when the strings being compared are equal. Thus, the condition `!strcmp(string1, string2)` should be used to determine if the strings are equal.

Additionally, the following three errors are frequently made when pointers to strings are used.

4. Using a pointer to "point to" a nonexistent data element. This error is, of course, the same error we have already seen using subscripts. Because C++ compilers do not perform bounds checking on arrays, it is the programmer's responsibility to ensure that the address in the pointer is the address of a valid data element.

5. Not providing sufficient space for the string to be stored. A simple variation of this is not providing space for the end-of-string null character when a string is defined as an array of characters, and not including the `\0` character when the array is initialized. A more complicated variation of this error is declaring a character pointer, such as `char *p`, and then attempting to copy a string with a statement such as `strcpy(p,"Hello")`. Because no space has been allocated for the string, the string will overwrite the memory area pointed to by `p`.

6. Misunderstanding the terminology. For example, if `text` is defined as

```
char *text;
```

the variable `text` is sometimes referred to as a string. Thus, the terminology "store the characters `Hooray for the Hoosiers` into the text string" may be encountered.

Strictly speaking, calling `text` a string or a string variable is incorrect. The variable `text` is a pointer that contains the address of the first character in the string. Nevertheless, the error of referring to a character pointer as a string occurs frequently enough that you should be aware of it.

14.6 Chapter Summary

1. A string is an array of characters that is terminated by the null character.

2. Strings can always be processed using standard array-processing techniques. The input and display of a string, however, always require reliance on a standard library function.

3. The `cin`, `cin.get()`, and `cin.getline()` routines can be used to input a string. The `cin` object tends to be of limited usefulness for string input because it terminates input when a blank is encountered.

4. The `cout` object can be used to display strings.

5. Many standard library functions exist for processing strings as a complete unit. Internally, these functions manipulate strings in a character-by-character manner, usually using pointers.

6. In place of subscripts, pointer notation and pointer arithmetic are especially useful for manipulating string elements.

7. String storage can be created by declaring an array of characters. It can also be created by declaring and initializing a pointer to a character.

8. Character arrays can be initialized using a string assignment of the form

```
char *arrayName[ ] = "text";
```

This initialization is equivalent to

```
char *arrayName[ ] = {'t','e','x','t','\0'};
```

9. A pointer to a character can be assigned a string. String assignment to an array of characters is invalid except for initialization within a declaration statement.

14.7 Knowing About: The CString Class

Strings, in C++, can be manipulated using standard element-by-element array operations, string library functions, Standard Template Library (STL) functions (see Appendix D) or using the CString class.[2] In this section we present the last option.

The reason for creating a string class is that processing strings as arrays of characters has certain disadvantages. For example, there are no string assignment operators and the defined array sized can be exceeded by both the `strcpy()` and `strcat()` functions. As long as the programmer is aware of these shortcomings, as most experienced C++ programmers are, the techniques presented in this chapter can be used safely. And, in fact, the majority of C++ programmers still tend to prefer these techniques when processing strings.

The underlying cause, however, of most of the pitfalls associated with creating strings as character arrays whose last value is the `NULL`, `'\0'`, character is precisely that strings are not a unique data type. But C++ provides for user-defined data types, so we can remove the disadvantages of processing strings as character arrays by using a suitably defined string class. This is exactly what is provided by the **CString** class.

From a user interface viewpoint, we would expect a string class to provide all of the processing currently available using both array element processing techniques and standard library functions, without the disadvantages. Thus, at a minimum, the CString class should provide the following capabilities:

1. Creation of a string object
2. Initialization of a string object using another string object
3. Initialization of a string object using a string literal
4. String length determination
5. An assignment operator, =, for assignment from a string object or string literal to a string object or string literal
6. A concatenation operator, +, for concatenation from a string object or string literal to either a string object or string literal
7. Appropriate relational operators, such as ==, >, <, etc. for comparing a string object to either a string object or string literal

Table 14.5 lists the set of operations and functions provided by the CString data type. Program 14.10 uses a number of these operations and functions that are similar to those presented in this chapter using standard C++ library functions.

---

2 This section requires an understanding of the class material presented in Chapters 9 and 10.

TABLE 14.5 CString functions and operations

Function	Operation
IsEmpty	Tests whether a CString object contains any characters
Empty	Forces a string to have 0 length
GetAt	Returns the character at a given position
SetAt	Sets a character at a given position
+	Assigns a new value to a CString object
=	Concatenates two strings and returns a new string
+=	Concatenates a new string to the end of an existing string
== <, etc.	Comparison operators (case sensitive)
Compare	Compares two strings (case sensitive)
CompareNoCase	Compares two strings (case insensitive)
Collate	Compares two strings (case sensitive, uses locale-specific information)
CollateNoCase	Compares two strings (case insensitive, uses locale-specific information)
Mid	Extracts characters from the middle part of a string
Left	Extracts the left part of a string
Right	Extracts the right part of a string
SpanIncluding	Extracts a substring that contains only the characters in a set
SpanExcluding	Extracts a substring that contains only the characters not in a set
MakeUpper	Converts all the characters in this string to uppercase characters
MakeLower	Converts all the characters in this string to lowercase characters
MakeReverse	Reverses the characters in this string
Replace	Replaces indicated characters with other characters
Remove	Removes indicated characters from a string
Insert	Inserts a single character or a substring at the given index within the string
Delete	Deletes a character or characters from a string
Format	Formats the string as the C function sprintf() does
FormatV	Formats the string as the C function vsprintf() does
TrimLeft	Trims leading whitespace characters from the string
TrimRight	Trims trailing whitespace characters from the string
FormatMessage	Formats a message string
Find	Finds a character or substring inside a larger string
ReverseFind	Finds a character inside a larger string; starts from the end
FindOneOf	Finds the first matching character from a set
<<	Inserts a CString object to an archive or dump context
>>	Extracts a CString object from an archive
GetBuffer	Returns a pointer to the characters in the CString
GetBufferSetLength	Returns a pointer to the characters in the CString, truncating to the specified length
ReleaseBuffer	Releases control of the buffer returned by GetBuffer
FreeExtra	Removes any overhead of this string object by freeing any extra memory previously allocated to the string
LockBuffer	Disables reference counting and protects the string in the buffer
UnlockBuffer	Enables reference counting and releases the string in the buffer

PROGRAM 14.10

```
#include <iostream.h>
#include <afx.h>

int main()
{
  CString string1 = "Hello World!";  // initialize with a string literal
  CString string2 = string1;         // initialize with a string object
  CString string3, string4("This is a test");
  CString message1 = "\n---- Test of object initializations ----\n";
  CString message2 = "\n---- Test of string assignment ----\n";
  CString message3=  "\n---- Test of string concatenation ----\n";
  CString message4 = "\n---- Test of string comparison ----\n";

  cout << message1;
  cout << "  string1, which was initialized by a string literal,\n"
       << "     has the value: " << string1 << endl;
  cout << "  string2, which was initialized by a string object,\n"
       << "     has the value: " << string2 << endl;
  cout << "  The string lengths of string1 through string4 are: "
       << string1.GetLength() << ", " << string2.GetLength() << ", "
       << string3.GetLength() << ", and " << string4.GetLength() << endl;

  cout << message2;
  string3 = string4;
  cout << "  After assigning string4 to string3, string3 is now:\n     "
       << string3 << endl;
  string4 = "of a string literal";
  cout << "  After assigning a string literal to string4, string4 is now:\n     "
       << string4 << endl;
  cout << "  The length of this string is: " << string4.GetLength() << endl;

  cout << message3;
  string3 = "     " + string3 + " " + string4;
  cout << "  After concatenation, string3 is now:\n" << string3 << endl;

  cout << message4;
  if (string1 == string2)
    cout << "  string1 and string2 are equal" << endl;
```

(continued next page)

(continued from previous page)

```
  else
    cout << "  string1 and string2 are not equal" << endl;
  if (string3 == string4)
    cout << "  string3 and string4 are equal\n" << endl;
  else
    cout << "  string3 and string4 are not equal\n" << endl;

  return 0;
}
```

In reviewing Program 14.10, notice that the only requirement in using the CString class is the inclusion of the interface header file `afx.h`. This header file provides the actual CString class definition. Although the CString class is not an MFC-provided class, usage of the `afx.h` file header requires that your program have access to the MFC library. To ensure this access, select the `Project` menu's `Settings...` option, as shown in Figure 14.16. Then, using the `Project Settings` dialog box, select the `Use MFC in a Shared DLL` option form the drop-down list, as shown in Figure 14.17. Once this selection is made, Program 14.10 will build correctly. Without this selection you will receive the two link error messages

```
....Unresolved external symbol _endthreadex
....unresolved external symbol _beginthreadex.
```

The choice of using MFC as a shared DLL simply means that the required MFC functions are linked in, dynamically, at run time from the MFC library. We could have also chosen to use the MFC as a static library, which means that the necessary code from the library would be extracted and hard-coded into the final executable program. The difference is in the size of the executable program. For Program 14.10, including the MFC as a static library results in a final program-executable size of 1,318,981 bytes, whereas using

FIGURE 14.16

Selecting the `Project` menu's `Settings` option

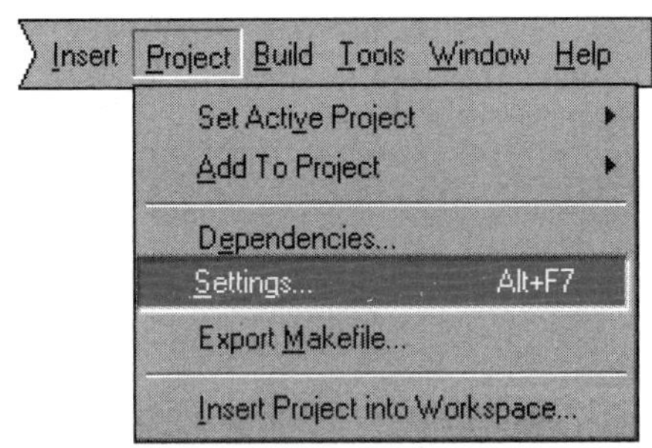

FIGURE 14.17

Selecting the MFC as a shared DLL

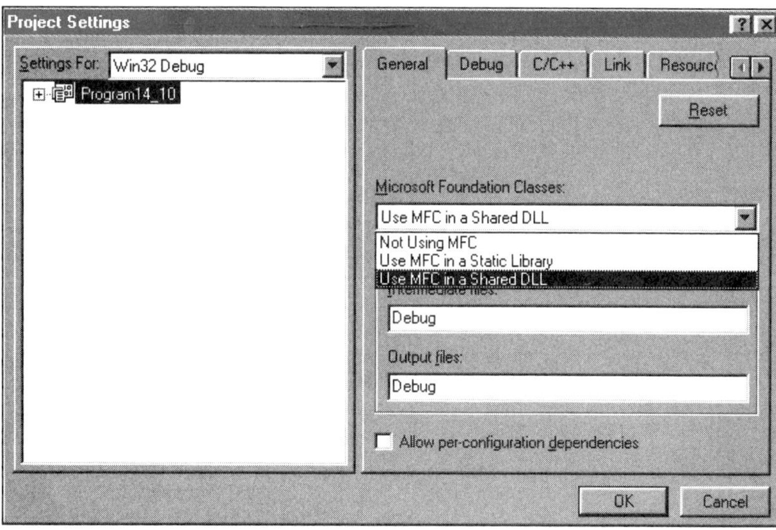

the MFC as a shared DLL results in a final executable size of 98,373 bytes. In general, due to the savings in size, you should almost ways use the MFC as a shared DLL. The only exception is when you cannot be sure that the machine that will be executing your program will have the MFC library available for use as a DLL. In that case, you should chose the MFC as a static library; this will ensure that your program carries the necessary functions within itself and that the executable program exists as a self-contained unit.

Figure 14.18 illustrates a sample run using Program 14.10. As seen by this output, the defined CString operations and functions work as expected.

FIGURE 14.18

Sample run using Program 14.10

```
Program14_10

---- Test of object initializations ----
 string1, which was initialized by a string literal,
    has the value: Hello World!
 string2, which was initialized by a string object,
    has the value: Hello World!
 The string lengths of string1 through string4 are: 12, 12, 0, and 14

---- Test of string assignment ----
 After assigning string4 to string3, string3 is now:
    This is a test
 After assigning a string literal to string4, string4 is now:
    of a string literal
 The length of this string is: 19

---- Test of string concatenation ----
 After concatenation, string3 is now:
    This is a test of a string literal

---- Test of string comparison ----
 string1 and string2 are equal
 string3 and string4 are not equal

Press any key to continue_
```

15 Records as Data Structures

An array allows access to a list or table of data of the same data type using a single variable name. At times, however, we may want to store information of varying types—such as a string name, an integer part number, and a real price together in one structure. A data structure that stores different types of data under a single variable name is called a **record.**

To make the discussion more tangible, consider data items that might be stored for a video game character, as illustrated in Figure 15.1.

Each of the individual data items listed in Figure 15.1 is an entity by itself, which is referred to as a **data field.** Taken together, all the data fields form a single unit referred to as a **record.** In C++, a record is referred to as a **structure.**

Although there could be hundreds of characters in a video game, the form of each character's record is identical. In dealing with records it is important to distinguish between a record's form and its contents.

FIGURE 15.1

Typical components of a video game character

Name:
Type:
Location in Dungeon:
Strength Factor:
Intelligence Factor:
Type of Armor:

A record's form consists of the symbolic names, data types, and arrangement of individual data fields in the record. The record's contents refer to the actual data stored in the symbolic names. Figure 15.2 shows acceptable contents for the record form illustrated in Figure 15.1.

FIGURE 15.2

Form and contents of a record

Name: Golgar
Type: Monster
Location in Dungeon: G7
Strength Factor: 78
Intelligence Factor: 15
Type of Armor: Chain Mail

In this chapter, we describe the C++ statements required to create, fill, use, and pass records between functions.

15.1 Single Records

Using a record structure requires the same two steps needed for using any variable. First the record structure must be declared. Then specific values can be assigned to the individual record elements. Declaring a record requires listing the data types, data names, and arrangement of data items. For example, the definition

```
struct
{
  int month;
  int day;
  int year;
} birth;
```

gives the form of a record structure called `birth` and reserves storage for the individual data items listed in the structure. The `birth` structure consists of three data items, or fields, which are called **members of the structure.**

Assigning actual data values to the data items of a structure is called **populating the structure,** and is a relatively straightforward procedure. Each member of a structure is accessed by giving both the structure name and individual data item name, separated by a period. Thus, `birth.month` refers to the first member of the `birth` structure, `birth.day` refers to the second member of the structure, and `birth.year` refers to the third member. Program 15.1 illustrates assigning values to the individual members of the `birth` structure.

PROGRAM 15.1

```
// a program that defines and populates a record
#include <iostream.h>

int main()
{
  struct
  {
    int month;
    int day;
    int year;
  } birth;

  birth.month = 12;
  birth.day = 28;
  birth.year = 1982;

  cout << "\nMy birth date is "
       << birth.month << '/'
       << birth.day   << '/'
       << birth.year % 100 << endl << endl;

  return 0;
}
```

The output line displayed by Program 15.1 is shown in Figure 15.3. Notice that, although we have stored the year as a 4-digit number, the output displays the year in conventional 2-digit format.

As in most C++ statements, the spacing of a structure definition is not rigid. For example, the birth structure could just as well have been defined as

```
struct {int month; int day; int year;} birth;
```

FIGURE 15.3

Output display produced by Program 15.1

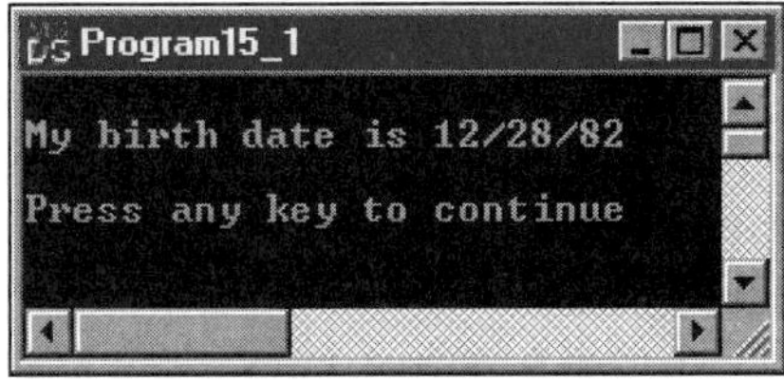

Also, as with all C++ definition statements, multiple variables can be defined in the same statement. For example, the definition statement

```
struct
{
  int month;
  int day;
  int year;
} birth, current;
```

creates two structure variables having the same form. The members of the first structure are referenced by the individual names `birth.month`, `birth.day`, and `birth.year`, whereas the members of the second structure are referenced by the names `current.month`, `current.day`, and `current.year`. Notice that the form of this particular structure definition statement is identical to the form used in defining any program variable: the data type is followed by a list of variable names.

A useful and commonly used modification for defining structure types is listing the form of the structure with no following variable names. In this case, however, the list of structure members must be preceded by a user-selected data type name. For example, in the declaration

```
struct Date
{
  int month;
  int day;
  int year;
};
```

the term `Date` is a structure type name: It defines a new data type that is a data structure of the declared form.[1] By convention the first letter of a user-selected data type name is uppercase, as in the name `Date`, which helps to identify them when they are used in sub-

---

1 For completeness it should be mentioned that a C++ structure can also be declared as a `class` with no member functions and all public data members. Similarly, a C++ class can be declared as a `struct` having all private data members and all public member functions. Thus, C++ provides two syntaxes for both structures and classes. The convention, however, is not to mix notations and always use structures for creating record types and classes for providing true information and implementation hiding.

sequent definition statements. Here, the declaration for the `Date` structure creates a new data type without actually reserving any storage locations. As such, it is not a definition statement. It simply declares a `Date` structure type and describes how individual data items are arranged within the structure. Actual storage for the members of the structure is reserved only when specific variable names are assigned. For example, the definition statement

```
Date birth, current;
```

reserves storage for two Date structure variables named `birth` and `current`, respectively. Each of these individual structures has the form previously declared for the `Date` structure.[2]

The declaration of structure data types, like all declarations, may be global or local. Program 15.2 illustrates the global declaration of a `Date` data type. Internal to `main()`, the variable `birth` is defined as a local variable of `Date` type.

PROGRAM 15.2

```
#include <iostream.h>

struct Date    // this is a global declaration
{
  int month;
  int day;
  int year;
};

int main()
{
  Date birth;
  birth.month = 12;
  birth.day = 28;
  birth.year = 1982;

  cout << "\nMy birth date is " << birth.month << '/'
       << birth.day   << '/'
       << birth.year % 100 << endl << endl;

  return 0;
}
```

2 The type name in C++ for this declaration is `Date`. In C, the type name would be `struct Date` and defining variables, such as `birth` and `current`, would be defined as `struct Date birth, current;`.

The output produced by Program 15.2 is identical to the output produced by Program 15.1 (see Figure 15.3).

The initialization of structures follows the same rules as the initialization of arrays: global and local structures may be initialized by following the definition with a list of initializers. For example, the definition statement

```
Date birth = {12, 28, 1982};
```

can be used to replace the first four statements internal to `main()` in Program 15.2. Notice that the initializers are separated by commas, not semicolons.

The individual members of a structure are not restricted to integer data types, as in the `Date` structure. Any valid C++ data type can be used. For example, consider an employee record consisting of the following data items:

```
Name:
Identification Number:
Regular Pay Rate:
Overtime Pay Rate:
```

A suitable declaration for these data items is:

```
struct PayRecord
{
  char name[20];
  int idNum;
  float regRate;
  float otRate;
};
```

Once the `PayRecord` data type is declared, a specific structure variable using this type can be defined and initialized. For example, the definition

```
PayRecord employee = {"H. Price",12387,15.89,25.50};
```

creates a structure named `employee` of the `PayRecord` data type. The individual members of `employee` are initialized with the respective data listed between braces in the definition statement.

Notice that a single structure is simply a convenient method for combining and storing related items under a common name. Although a single structure is useful in explicitly identifying the relationship among its members, the individual members could be defined as separate variables. One real advantage to using structures is realized only when the same data type is used in a list many times over. Creating lists with the same data type is the topic of the next section.

Before leaving the topic of single structures, it is worth noting that the individual members of a structure can be any valid C++ data type, including both arrays and structures. An array of characters was used as a member of the `employee` structure defined previously. Accessing an element of a member array requires giving the structure's name, followed by a period, followed by the array designation. For example, `employee.name[4]` refers to the fifth character in the `employee.name` array.

Including a structure within a structure follows the same rules for including any data type in a structure. For example, assume that a structure is to consist of a name and a date of birth, where a `Date` structure has been declared as:

```
struct Date
{
  int month;
  int date;
  int year;
};
```

A suitable definition of a structure that includes a `name` and a `Date` structure is:

```
struct
{
  char name[20];
  Date birth;
} person;
```

Notice that in declaring the `Date` structure, the term `Date` is a data type name; thus it appears before the braces in its declaration statement. In defining the `person` structure variable, `person` is a variable name; thus it is the name of a specific structure. The same is true of the variable named `birth`. This is the name of a specific `Date` structure. Individual members in the `person` structure are accessed by preceding the desired member with the structure name followed by a period. For example, `person.birth.month` refers to the `month` variable in the `birth` structure contained in the `person` structure.

EXERCISES 15.1

1. Declare a structure data type named `Stemp` for each of the following records:

a. a student record consisting of a student identification number, number of credits completed, and cumulative grade point average

b. a student record consisting of a student's name, date of birth, number of credits completed, and cumulative grade point average

c. a mailing list consisting of a person's name and address (street, city, state, and zip code)

d. a stock record consisting of the stock's name, the price of the stock, and the date of purchase

e. an inventory record consisting of an integer part number, part description, number of parts in inventory, and an integer reorder number

2. For the individual data types declared in Exercise 1, define a suitable structure variable name and initialize each structure with the appropriate following data:

a. Identification Number: 4672

Number of Credits Completed: 68

Grade Point Average: 3.01

b. Name: Rhona Karp

Date of Birth: 8/4/60

Number of Credits Completed: 96

Grade Point Average: 3.89

c. Name: Kay Kingsley

Street Address: 614 Freeman Street

City: Indianapolis

State: IN

Zip Code: 07030

d. Stock: IBM

Price Purchased: 134.5

Date Purchased: 10/1/1986

e. Part Number: 16879

Description: Battery

Number in Stock: 10

Reorder Number: 3

3. a. Write a C++ program that prompts a user to input the current month, day, and year. Store the data entered in a suitably defined record and display the date in an appropriate manner.

b. Modify the program written in Exercise 3a to use a record that accepts the current time in hours, minutes, and seconds.

4. Write a C++ program that uses a structure for storing the name of a stock, its estimated earnings per share, and its estimated price-to-earnings ratio. Have the program prompt the user to enter these items for five different stocks, each time using the same structure to store the entered data. When the data have been entered for a particular stock, have the program compute and display the anticipated stock price based on the entered earnings and price-per-earnings values. For example, if a user entered the data `XYZ 1.56 12`, the anticipated price for a share of XYZ stock is (1.56)*(12) = $18.72.

5. Write a C++ program that accepts a user-entered time in hours and minutes. Have the program calculate and display the time one minute later.

6. a. Write a C++ program that accepts a user-entered date. Have the program calculate and display the date of the next day. For purposes of this exercise, assume that all months consist of 30 days.

b. Modify the program written in Exercise 6a to account for the actual number of days in each month.

15.2 Arrays of Structures

The real power of structures is realized when the same structure is used for lists of data. For example, assume that the data shown in Figure 15.4 must be processed. Clearly, the employee numbers can be stored together in an array of integers, the names in an array of pointers, and the pay rates in an array of either floating point or double precision numbers. In organizing the data in this fashion, each column in Figure 15.4 is considered as a separate list, which is stored in its own array. The correspondence between items for each individual employee is maintained by storing an employee's data in the same array position in each array.

The separation of the complete list into three individual arrays is unfortunate, because all of the items relating to a single employee constitute a natural organization of data into records, as illustrated in Figure 15.5. Using a structure, the integrity of the data organization as a record can be maintained and reflected by the program. Under this approach, the list illustrated in Figure 15.4 can be processed as a single array of ten structures.

FIGURE 15.4

A list of employee data

Employee Number	Employee Name	Employee Pay Rate
32479	Abrams, B.	6.72
33623	Bohm, P.	7.54
34145	Donaldson, S.	5.56
35987	Ernst, T.	5.43
36203	Gwodz, K.	8.72
36417	Hanson, H.	7.64
37634	Monroe, G.	5.29
38321	Price, S.	9.67
39435	Robbins, L.	8.50
39567	Williams, B.	7.20

PROGRAMMER'S NOTES

Homogeneous and Heterogeneous Data Structures

Both arrays and records are structured data types. The difference between these two data structures is the types of elements they contain. An array is a *homogeneous* data structure, which means that each of its components must be of the same type. A record is a *heterogeneous* data structure, which means that each of its components can be a different data type. Thus, an array of records would be a homogeneous data structure whose elements are of the same heterogeneous type.

Declaring an array of structures is the same as declaring an array of any other variable type. For example, if the data type `PayRecord` is declared as

```
struct PayRecord {int idnum; char name[20]; float rate;};
```

then an array of ten such structures can be defined as

```
PayRecord employee[10];
```

This definition statement constructs an array of ten elements, each of which is a structure of the data type `PayRecord`. Notice that the creation of an array of ten structures has the same form as the creation of any other array. For example, creating an array of ten integers named `employee` requires the declaration

```
int employee[10];
```

In this declaration the data type is `int`, whereas in the former declaration for `employee` the data type is `PayRecord`.

Once an array of structures is declared, a particular data item is referenced by giving the position of the desired structure in the array followed by a period and the appropriate

FIGURE 15.5

A list of records

	Employee Number	Employee Name	Employee Pay Rate
1st record →	32479	Abrams, B.	6.72
2nd record →	33623	Bohm, P.	7.54
3rd record →	34145	Donaldson, S.	5.56
4th record →	35987	Ernst, T.	5.43
5th record →	36203	Gwodz, K.	8.72
6th record →	36417	Hanson, H.	7.64
7th record →	37634	Monroe, G.	5.29
8th record →	38321	Price, S.	9.67
9th record →	39435	Robbins, L.	8.50
10th record →	39567	Williams, B.	7.20

structure member. For example, the variable `employee[0].rate` references the `rate` member of the first `employee` structure in the `employee` array. Including structures as elements of an array permits a list of records to be processed using standard array programming techniques. Program 15.3 displays the first five employee records illustrated in Figure 15.5.

PROGRAM 15.3

```
#include <iostream.h>
#include <iomanip.h>

const int MAXNAME = 20;  // maximum characters in a name
const int NUMRECS = 5;   // maximum number of records

struct PayRecord   // this is a global declaration
{
  long id;
  char name[MAXNAME];
  float rate;
};

int main()
{
  int i;
  PayRecord employee[NUMRECS] = {
                                { 32479, "Abrams, B.", 6.72 },
                                { 33623, "Bohm, P.", 7.54},
                                { 34145, "Donaldson, S.",  5.56},
                                { 35987, "Ernst, T.", 5.43 },
                                { 36203, "Gwodz, K.", 8.72 }
                                };

  cout << endl;   // start on a new line
  cout << setiosflags(ios::left);  // left justify the output
  for ( i = 0; i < NUMRECS; i++)
    cout << setw(7)  << employee[i].id
         << setw(15) << employee[i].name
         << setw(6)  << employee[i].rate << endl;

  cout << endl;
  return 0;
}
```

FIGURE 15.6

Output display produced by Program 15.3

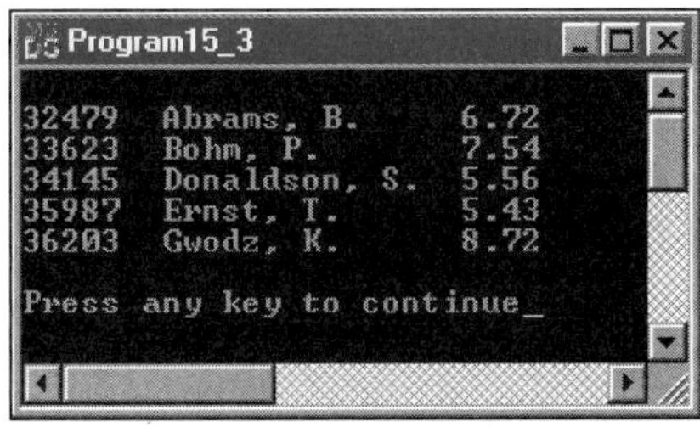

The output displayed by Program 15.3 is shown in Figure 15.6. In reviewing Program 15.3, notice the initialization of the array of structures. Although the initializers for each structure have been enclosed in inner braces, these are not strictly necessary because all members have been initialized. As with all external and static variables, in the absence of explicit initializers, the numeric elements of both static and global arrays or structures are initialized to zero and their character elements are initialized to `NULL`s. The `setiosflags(ios::left)` manipulator included in the `cout` statement forces each name to be displayed left justified in its designated field width.

EXERCISES 15.2

1. Define arrays of 100 structures for each of the data types described in Exercise 1 of the previous section.

2. a. Using the data type

```
struct MonthDays
{
  char name[10];
  int days;
};
```

define an array of 12 structures of type `MonthDays`. Name the array `convert[]`, and initialize the array with the names of the 12 months in a year and the number of days in each month.

b. Include the array created in Exercise 2a in a program that displays the names and number of days in each month.

3. Using the data type declared in Exercise 2a, write a C++ program that accepts a month from a user in numerical form and displays the name of the month and the number of days in the month. Thus, in response to an input of 3, the program would display March has 31 days.

4. a. Declare a single-structure data type suitable for an employee record of the type illustrated below:

Number	Name	Rate	Hours
3462	Jones	4.62	40
6793	Robbins	5.83	38
6985	Smith	5.22	45
7834	Swain	6.89	40
8867	Timmins	6.43	35
9002	Williams	4.75	42

b. Using the data type declared in Exercise 4a, write a C++ program that interactively accepts the above data into an array of six structures. Once the data have been entered, the program should create a payroll report listing each employee's name, number, and gross pay. Include the total gross pay of all employees at the end of the report.

5. a. Declare a single-structure data type suitable for a car record of the type illustrated:

Car Number	Miles Driven	Gallons Used
25	1,450	62
36	3,240	136
44	1,792	76
52	2,360	105
68	2,114	67

b. Using the data type declared for Exercise 5a, write a C++ program that interactively accepts the above data into an array of five structures. Once the data have been entered, the program should create a report listing each car number and the miles per gallon achieved by the car. At the end of the report include the average miles per gallon achieved by the complete fleet of cars.

15.3 Record Structures as Function Arguments

Individual structure members may be passed to a function in the same manner as any scalar variable. For example, given the structure definition

```
struct
{
  int idNum;
  double payRate;
  double hours;
} emp;
```

the statement

```
display(emp.idNum);
```

passes a copy of the structure member `emp.idNum` to a function named `display()`. Similarly, the statement

```
calcPay(emp.payRate,emp.hours);
```

passes copies of the values stored in structure members `emp.payRate` and `emp.hours` to the function `calcPay()`. Both functions, `display()` and `calcPay`, must declare the correct data types for their respective parameters.

Complete copies of all members of a structure can also be passed to a function by including the name of the structure as an argument to the called function. For example, the function call

```
calcNet(emp);
```

passes a copy of the complete `emp` structure to `calcNet()`. Internal to `calcNet()`, an appropriate declaration must be made to receive the structure. Program 15.4 declares a global data type for an employee record. This type is then used by both the `main()` and `calcNet()` functions to define specific structures with the names `emp` and `temp`, respectively.

PROGRAM 15.4

```
#include <iostream.h>
#include <iomanip.h>

struct Employee        // declare a global type
{
  int idNum;
  double payRate;
  double hours;
};

double calcNet(Employee);   // function prototype

int main()
{
  Employee emp = {6782, 8.93, 40.5};
  double netPay;
```

(continued next page)

(continued from previous page)

```
  netPay = calcNet(emp);       // pass copies of the values in emp

    // set output formats
  cout << setw(10)
       << setiosflags(ios::fixed)
       << setiosflags(ios::showpoint)
       << setprecision(2);

  cout << "\nThe net pay for employee " << emp.idNum
       << " is $" << netPay << endl;

  return 0;
}

double calcNet(Employee temp) // temp is of data type Employee
{
  return temp.payRate * temp.hours;
}
```

The output line produced by Program 15.4 is:

```
The net pay for employee 6782 is $361.66
```

In reviewing Program 15.4, observe that both `main()` and `calcNet()` use the same data type to define their individual structure variables. The structure variable defined in `main()` and the structure variable defined in `calcNet()` are two completely different structures. Any changes made to the local `temp` variable in `calcNet()` are not reflected in the `emp` variable of `main()`. In fact, because both structure variables are local to their respective functions, the same structure variable name could have been used in both functions with no ambiguity.

When `calcNet()` is called by `main()`, copies of `emp`'s structure values are passed to the `temp` structure. `calcNet()` then uses two of the passed member values to calculate a number, which is returned to `main()`.

An alternative to the pass-by-value function call illustrated in Program 15.4, in which the called function receives a copy of a structure, is a pass-by reference that passes a reference to a structure. Doing so permits the called function to directly access and alter values in the calling function's structure variable. For example, referring to Program 15.4, the prototype of `calcNet()` can be modified to

```
double calcNet(Employee&);
```

If this function prototype is used and the calcNet() header line is rewritten to conform to it, the main() function in Program 15.4 may be used as is. Program 15.4a illustrates these changes within the context of a complete program.

PROGRAM 15.4A

```
#include <iostream.h>
#include <iomanip.h>

struct Employee       // declare a global type
{
  int idNum;
  double payRate;
  double hours;
};

double calcNet(Employee&);   // function prototype

int main()
{
  Employee emp = {6782, 8.93, 40.5};
  double netPay;

  netPay = calcNet(emp);       // pass a reference

    // set output formats
  cout << setw(10)
       << setiosflags(ios::fixed)
       << setiosflags(ios::showpoint)
       << setprecision(2);

  cout << "\nThe net pay for employee " << emp.idNum
       << " is $" <<  netPay << endl;

  return 0;
}

double calcNet(Employee& temp)   // temp is a reference variable
{
  return temp.payRate * temp.hours;
}
```

Program 15.4a produces the same output as Program 15.4, except that the calcNet() function in Program 15.4a receives direct access to the emp structure rather than a copy of it. This means that the variable name temp within calcNet is an alternate name for the variable emp in main(), and any changes to temp are direct changes to emp. Although the same function call, calcNet(emp) is made in both programs, the call in Program 15.4a passes a reference, whereas the call in Program 15.4 passes values.

Passing a Pointer

In place of passing a reference, a pointer can be passed. Using a pointer requires, in addition to modifying the function's prototype and header line, that the call to calcNet() in Program 15.4 be modified to

```
calcNet(&emp);
```

Here the function call clearly indicates that an address is being passed (which is not the case in Program 15.4a). The disadvantage, however, is in the dereferencing notation required internal to the function. However, as pointers are widely used in practice, it is worthwhile to become familiar with the notation used.

To correctly store the passed address calcNet() must declare its parameter as a pointer. A suitable function definition for calcNet() is

```
calcNet(Employee *pt)
```

Here, the declaration for pt declares this parameter as a pointer to a structure of type Employee. The pointer, pt, receives the starting address of a structure whenever calcNet() is called. Within calcNet(), this pointer is used to access any member in the structure. For example, (*pt).idNum refers to the idNum member of the structure, (*pt).payRate refers to the payRate member of the structure, and (*pt).hours refers to the hours member of the structure. These relationships are illustrated in Figure 15.7.

The parentheses around the expression *pt in Figure 15.7 are necessary to initially access "the structure whose address is in pt." This is followed by an identifier to access the desired member within the structure. In the absence of the parentheses, the structure member operator . takes precedence over the indirection operator *. Thus, the expression *pt.hours is another way of writing *(pt.hours), which would refer to "the variable whose address is in the pt.hours variable." This last expression clearly makes no sense because there is no structure named pt and hours does not contain an address.

As illustrated in Figure 15.7, the starting address of the emp structure is also the address of the first member of the structure.

The use of pointers in this manner is so common that a special notation exists for it. The general expression (*pointer).member can always be replaced with the notation pointer->member, where the -> operator is constructed using a minus sign followed by a right-facing arrow (greater-than symbol). Either expression can be used to locate the desired member. For example, the following expressions are equivalent:

(*pt).idNum	can be replaced by	pt->idNum
(*pt).payRate	can be replaced by	pt->payRate
(*pt).hours	can be replaced by	pt->hours

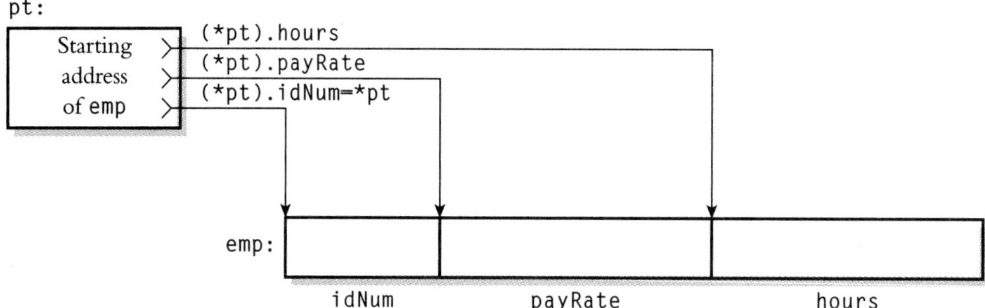

FIGURE 15.7

A pointer can be used to access structure members

Program 15.5 illustrates passing a structure's address and using a pointer with the new notation to directly dereference the structure.

PROGRAM 15.5

```
#include <iostream.h>
#include <iomanip.h>

struct Employee   // declare a global type
{
  int idNum;
  double payRate;
  double hours;
};

double calcNet(Employee *);   //function prototype

int main()
{
  Employee emp = {6782, 8.93, 40.5};
  double netPay;

  netPay = calcNet(&emp);        // pass an address

    // set output formats
  cout << setw(10)
       << setiosflags(ios::fixed)
       << setiosflags(ios::showpoint)
       << setprecision(2);
```

(continued next page)

(continued from previous page)

```
   cout << "\nThe net pay for employee " << emp.idNum
        << " is $" << netPay << endl;

   return 0;
}

double calcNet(Employee *pt)    // pt is a pointer to a
{                                // structure of Employee type
   return pt->payRate * pt->hours;
}
```

The name of the pointer parameter declared in Program 15.5 is, of course, selected by the programmer. When `calcNet()` is called, `emp`'s starting address is passed to the function. Using this address as the starting point, individual members of the structure are accessed by including their names with the pointer.

As with all C++ expressions that access a variable, the increment and decrement operators can also be applied to them. For example, the expression

```
++pt->hours
```

adds one to the `hours` member of the `emp` structure. Because the `->` operator has a higher priority than the increment operator, the `hours` member is accessed first and then the increment is applied. Alternatively, the expression `(++pt)->hours` uses the prefix increment operator to increment the address in `pt` before the `hours` member is accessed. Similarly, the expression `(pt++)->hours` uses the postfix increment operator to increment the address in `pt` after the `hours` member is accessed. In both of these cases, however, there must be sufficient defined structures to ensure that the incremented pointers actually point to legitimate structures.

As an example, Figure 15.8 illustrates an array of three structures of type `employee`. Assuming that the address of `emp[1]` is stored in the pointer variable `pt`, the expression `++pt` changes the address in `pt` to the starting address of `emp[2]`, whereas the expression `--pt` changes the address to point to `emp[0]`.

Returning Structures

In practice, most structure-handling functions receive direct access to a structure by receiving either a structure reference or a pointer to a structure. Then any changes to the structure can be made directly from within the function. If you want to have a function

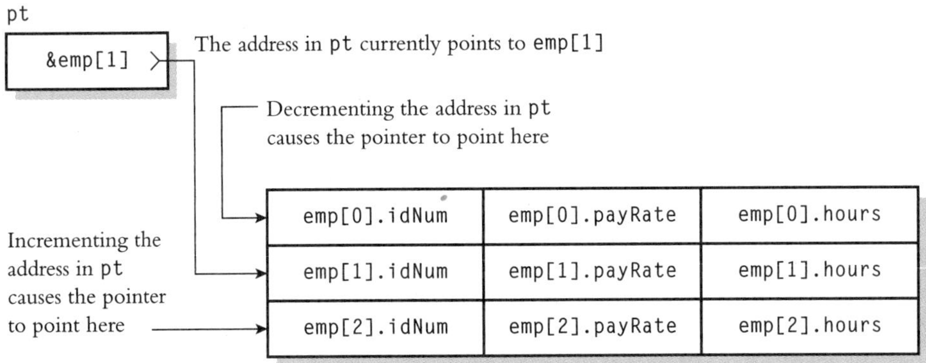

FIGURE 15.8

Changing pointer addresses

return a separate structure, however, you must follow the same procedures for returning complete data structures as for returning scalar values. For example, the function `getValues()` in Program 15.6 returns a complete structure to `main()`.

PROGRAM 15.6

```
#include <iostream.h>
#include <iomanip.h>

struct Employee          // declare a global type
{
  int idNum;
  double payRate;
  double hours;
};

Employee getValues();    // function prototype

int main()
{
  Employee emp;
```

(continued next page)

(continued from previous page)

```
  emp = getValues();
  cout << "\nThe employee id number is " << emp.idNum
       << "\nThe employee pay rate is $" << emp.payRate
       << "\nThe employee hours are " << emp.hours << endl;
  return 0;
}

Employee getValues() // return an Employee structure
{
  Employee next;

  next.idNum = 6789;
  next.payRate = 16.25;
  next.hours = 38.0;

  cout << endl;
  return next;
}
```

Figure 15.9 illustrates the output displayed when Program 15.6 is run.

The `getValues()` function returns a structure, so the function header for `getValues()` must specify the type of structure being returned. Because `getValues()` does not receive any arguments, the function header has no parameter declarations and consists of the line

```
Employee getValues()
```

Within `getValues()`, the variable `next` is defined as a structure of the type to be returned. After values have been assigned to the `next` structure, the structure values are returned by including the structure name within the parentheses of the `return` statement.

On the receiving side, `main()` must be alerted that the function `getValues()` will be returning a structure. This is handled by the function declaration for `getValues()`. No-

FIGURE 15.9

Output displayed by Program 15.6

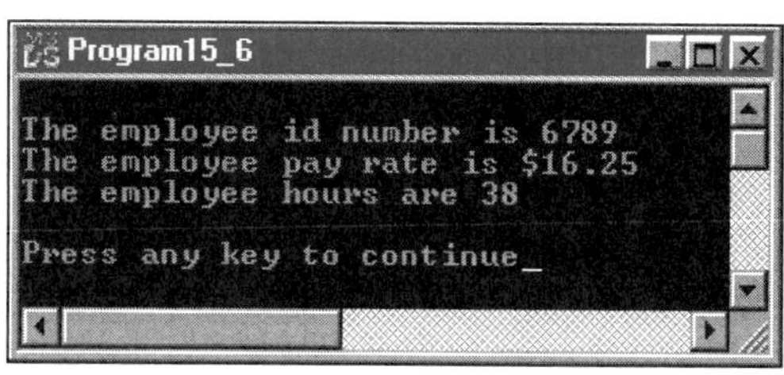

tice that these steps for returning a structure from a function are identical to the normal procedures for returning scalar data types previously described in Chapter 6.

EXERCISES 15.3

1. Write a C++ function named `days()` that determines the number of days from the turn of the century 1/1/1900 for any date passed as a structure. Use the `Date` structure

```
struct Date
{
  int month;
  int day;
  int year;
};
```

In writing the `days()` function, use the convention that all years have 360 days and each month consists of 30 days. The function should return the number of days for any `Date` structure passed to it. Make sure you declare the returned variable a long integer to reserve sufficient room for converting dates such as 12/19/2002.

2. Write a C++ function named `difDays()` that calculates and returns the difference between two dates. Each date is passed to the function as a structure using the following global type:

```
struct Date
{
  int month;
  int day;
  int year;
};
```

The `difDays()` function should make two calls to the `days()` function written for Exercise 1.

3. a. Rewrite the `days()` function written for Exercise 1 to receive a reference to a `Date` structure, rather than a copy of the complete structure.

b. Redo Exercise 3a. using a pointer rather than a reference.

4. a. Write a C++ function named `larger()` that returns the later date of any two dates passed to it. For example, if the dates 10/9/1999 and 11/3/1999 are passed to `larger()`, the second date would be returned.

b. Include the `larger()` function that was written for Exercise 4a in a complete program. Store the `Date` structure returned by `larger()` in a separate `Date` structure and display the member values of the returned `Date`.

5. a. Modify the function `days()` written for Exercise 1 to account for the actual number of days in each month. Assume, however, that each year contains 365 days (that is, do not account for leap years).

b. Modify the function written for Exercise 5a to account for leap years.

15.4 Linked Lists

A classic data-handling problem is making additions or deletions to existing records that are maintained in a specific order. This is best illustrated by considering the alphabetical telephone list shown in Figure 15.10. Starting with this initial set of names and telephone numbers, we desire to add new records to the list in the proper alphabetical sequence, and to delete existing records in such a way that the storage for deleted records is eliminated.

Although the insertion or deletion of ordered records can be accomplished using an array of structures, such arrays are not efficient representations when adding or deleting records to the list. Arrays are fixed and prespecified in size. Deleting a record from an array creates an empty slot that requires either special marking or shifting up all elements below the deleted record to close the empty slot. Similarly, adding a record to the body of an array of structures requires that all elements below the addition be shifted down to make room for the new entry; or the new element could be added to the bottom of the existing array and the array then resorted to restore the proper order of the records. Thus, either adding or deleting records to such a list generally requires restructuring and rewriting the list—a cumbersome, time-consuming, and inefficient practice.

A linked list provides a convenient method for maintaining a constantly changing list without the need to continually reorder and restructure the complete list. A linked list is simply a set of structures in which each structure contains at least one member whose value is the address of the next logically ordered structure in the list. Rather than requiring each record to be physically stored in the proper order, each new record is physically

FIGURE 15.10

A telephone list in alphabetical order

Acme, Sam
(555) 898-2392
Dolan, Edith
(555) 682-3104
Lanfrank, John
(555) 718-4581
Mening, Stephen
(555) 382-7070
Zemann, Harold
(555) 219-9912

FIGURE 15.11

Using pointers to link structures

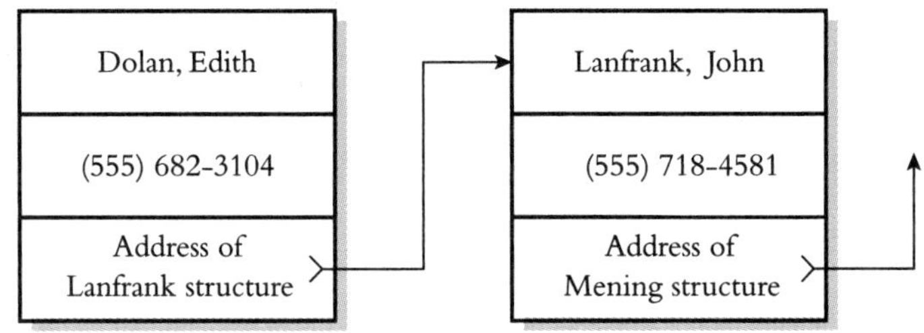

added wherever the computer has free space in its storage area. The records are "linked" together by including the address of the next record in the record immediately preceding it. From a programming standpoint, the current record being processed contains the address of the next record, no matter where the next record is actually stored.

The concept of a linked list is illustrated in Figure 15.11. Although the actual data for the Lanfrank structure illustrated in the figure may be physically stored anywhere in the computer, the additional member included at the end of the Dolan structure maintains the proper alphabetical order. This member provides the starting address of the location where the Lanfrank record is stored. As you might expect, this member is a pointer.

To see the usefulness of the pointer in the Dolan record, let us add a telephone number for June Hagar into the alphabetical list shown in Figure 15.10. The data for June Hagar is stored in a data structure using the same type as that used for the existing records. To ensure that the telephone number for Hagar is correctly displayed after the Dolan telephone number, the address in the Dolan record must be altered to point to the Hagar record, and the address in the Hagar record must be set to point to the Lanfrank record. This is illustrated in Figure 15.12. Notice that the pointer in each structure simply points

FIGURE 15.12

Adjusting addresses to point to appropriate records

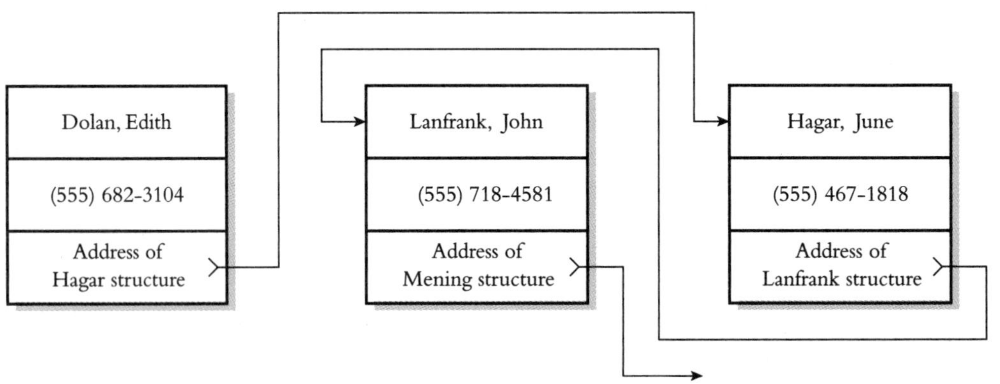

to the location of the next ordered structure, even if that structure is not physically located in the correct order.

Removal of a structure from the ordered list is the reverse process of adding a record. The actual record is logically removed from the list by simply changing the address in the structure preceding it to point to the structure immediately following the deleted record.

Each structure in a linked list has the same format; however, it is clear that the last record cannot have a valid address that points to another record, because there is none. C++ provides a special pointer value called `NULL` that acts as a sentinel or flag to indicate when the last record has been processed. The `NULL` pointer value, like its end-of-string counterpart, has a numerical value of zero.

Besides an end-of-list sentinel value, a special pointer must also be provided for storing the address of the first structure in the list. Figure 15.13 illustrates the complete set of pointers and structures for a list consisting of three names.

The inclusion of a pointer in a structure should not seem surprising. As we discovered in Section 15.1, a structure can contain any C++ data type. For example, the structure declaration

```
struct Test
{
  int idNum;
  double *ptPay;
};
```

declares a structure type consisting of two members. The first member is an integer variable named `idNum`, and the second variable is a pointer named `ptPay`, which is a pointer to a double precision number. Program 15.7 illustrates that the pointer member of a structure is used like any other pointer variable.

FIGURE 15.13

Use of the initial and final pointer values

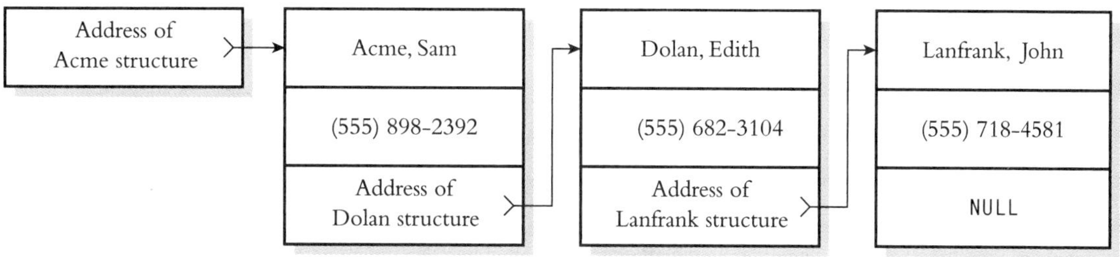

PROGRAM 15.7

```
#include <iostream.h>
#include <iomanip.h>

struct Test
{
  int idNum;
  double *ptPay;
};

int main()
{
  Test emp;
  double pay = 456.20;

  emp.idNum = 12345;
  emp.ptPay = &pay;

    // set output formats
  cout << setw(6)
       << setiosflags(ios::fixed)
       << setiosflags(ios::showpoint)
       << setprecision(2);

  cout << "\nEmployee number " << emp.idNum << " was paid $"
       << *emp.ptPay << endl << endl;

  return 0;
}
```

Figure 15.14 illustrates the output produced by executing Program 15.7.

FIGURE 15.14

Output displayed by Program 15.7

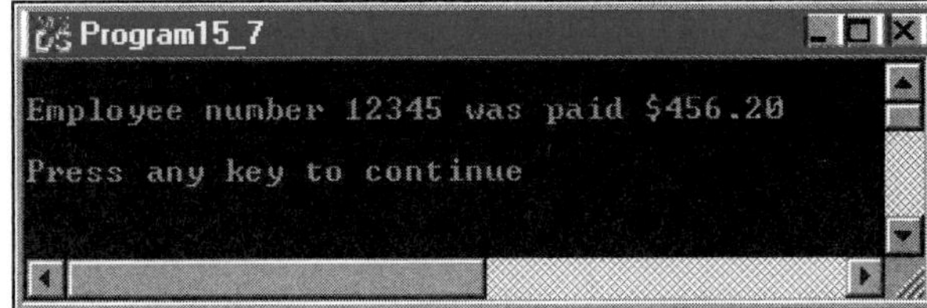

FIGURE 15.15

Storing an address in a structure member

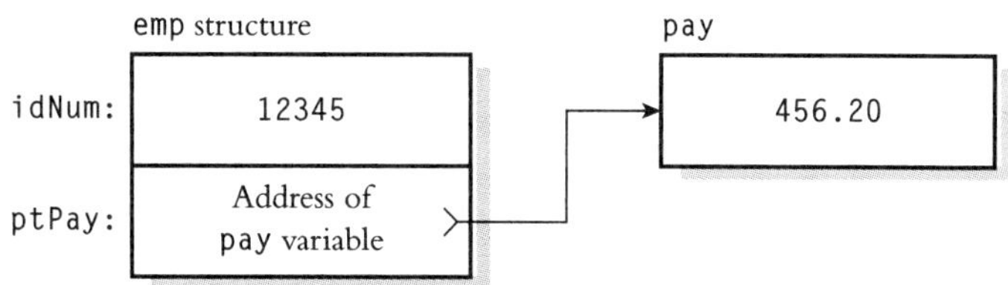

Figure 15.15 illustrates the relationship between the members of the emp structure defined in Program 15.7 and the variable named pay. The value assigned to emp.idNum is the number 12345 and the value assigned to pay is 456.20. The address of the pay variable is assigned to the structure member emp.ptPay. This member has been defined as a pointer to a double precision number, so placing the address of the double precision variable pay in it is a correct use of this member. Finally, because the member operator . has a higher precedence than the indirection operator *, the expression used in the cout statement in Program 15.7 is correct. The expression *emp.ptPay is equivalent to the expression *(emp.ptPay), which is translated as "the variable whose address is contained in the member emp.ptPay."

Although the pointer defined in Program 15.7 has been used in a rather trivial fashion, the program does illustrate the concept of including a pointer in a structure. This concept can be easily extended to create a linked list of structures suitable for storing the names and telephone numbers listed in Figure 15.10. The following declaration creates a type for such a structure:

```
struct TeleType
{
  char name[30];
  char phoneNum[16];
  TeleType *nextaddr;
};
```

The TeleType type consists of three members. The first member is an array of 30 characters, suitable for storing names with a maximum of 29 letters and an end-of-string NULL marker. The next member is an array of 16 characters, suitable for storing telephone numbers with their respective area codes. The last member is a pointer suitable for storing the address of a structure of the TeleType type.

Program 15.8 illustrates the use of the TeleType type by specifically defining three structures having this form. The three structures are named t1, t2, and t3, respectively, and the name and telephone members of each of these structures are initialized when the structures are defined, using the data listed in Figure 15.10.

PROGRAM 15.8

```
#include <iostream.h>

const int MAXNAME = 30;  // maximum no. of characters in a name
const int MAXTEL = 16;   // maximum no. of characters in a telephone number

struct TeleType
{
  char name[MAXNAME];
  char phoneNum[MAXTEL];
  TeleType *nextaddr;
};

int main()
{
  TeleType t1 = {"Acme, Sam","(555) 898-2392"};
  TeleType t2 = {"Dolan, Edith","(555) 682-3104"};
  TeleType t3 = {"Lanfrank, John","(555) 718-4581"};
  TeleType *first;     // create a pointer to a structure

  first = &t1;          // store t1's address in first
  t1.nextaddr = &t2;    // store t2's address in t1.nextaddr
  t2.nextaddr = &t3;    // store t3's address in t2.nextaddr
  t3.nextaddr = NULL;   // store a NULL address in t3.nextaddr

  cout << endl << first->name
       << endl << t1.nextaddr->name
       << endl << t2.nextaddr->name
       << endl;

  cout << endl;
  return 0;
}
```

The output produced by executing Program 15.8 is illustrated in Figure 15.16.

FIGURE 15.16

Output displayed by Program 15.8

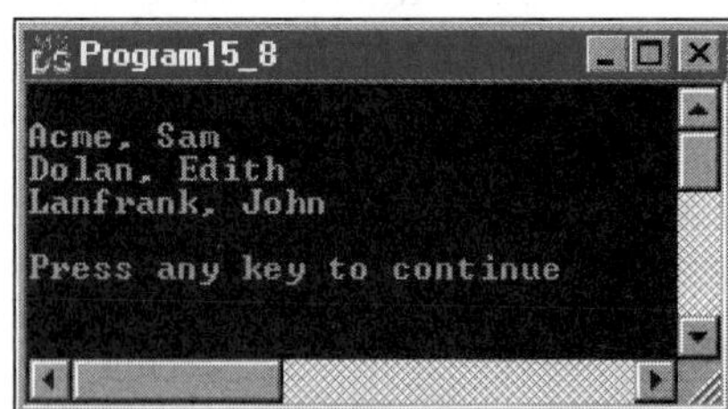

FIGURE 15.17

Relationship between structures in Program 15.8

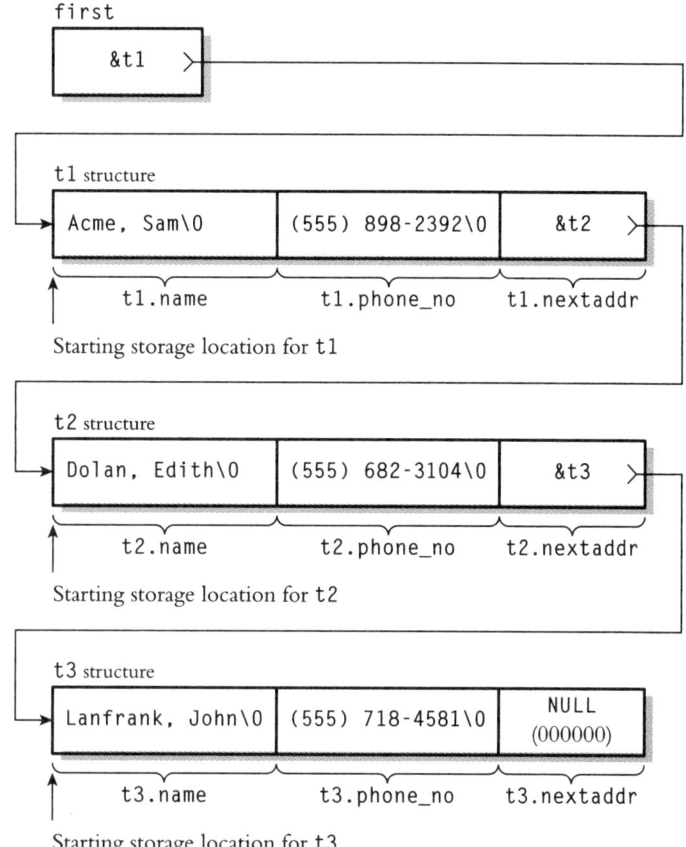

Program 15.8 demonstrates the use of pointers to access successive structure members. As illustrated in Figure 15.17, each structure contains the address of the next structure in the list.

The initialization of the names and telephone numbers for each of the structures defined in Program 15.8 is straightforward. Although each structure consists of three members, only the first two members of each structure are initialized. Because both of these members are arrays of characters, they can be initialized with strings. The remaining member of each structure is a pointer. To create a linked list, each structure pointer must be assigned the address of the next structure in the list.

The four assignment statements in Program 15.8 perform the correct assignments. The expression `first = &t1` stores the address of the first structure in the list in the pointer variable named `first`. The expression `t1.nextaddr = &t2` stores the starting address of the `t2` structure into the pointer member of the `t1` structure. Similarly, the expression `t2.nextaddr = &t3` stores the starting address of the `t3` structure into the pointer member of the `t2` structure. To end the list, the value of the `NULL` pointer, which is zero, is stored into the pointer member of the `t3` structure.

Once values have been assigned to each structure member and correct addresses have been stored in the appropriate pointers, the addresses in the pointers are used to access each structure's name member. For example, the expression `t1.nextaddr->name` refers to the `name` member of the structure whose address is in the `nextaddr` member of the `t1` structure. The precedence of the member operator `.` and the structure pointer operator `->` are equal, and are evaluated from left to right. Thus, the expression `t1.nextaddr->name` is evaluated as `(t1.nextaddr)->name`. Because `t1.nextaddr` contains the address of the `t2` structure, the proper name is accessed.

The expression `t1.nextaddr->name` can, of course, be replaced by the equivalent expression `(*t1.nextaddr).name`, which uses the more conventional indirection operator. This expression also refers to "the name member of the variable whose address is in `t1.nextaddr`."

The addresses in a linked list of structures can be used to loop through the complete list. As each structure is accessed it can be either examined to select a specific value or used to print out a complete list. For example, the `display()` function in Program 15.9 illustrates the use of a `while` loop, which uses the address in each structure's pointer member to cycle through the list and successively display data stored in each structure.

PROGRAM 15.9

```
#include <iostream.h>
#include <iomanip.h>

const int MAXNAME = 20;   // maximum no. of characters in a name
const int MAXTEL = 16;    // maximum no. of characters in a telephone number

struct TeleType
{
  char name[MAXNAME];
  char phoneNum[MAXTEL];
  TeleType *nextaddr;
};

void display(TeleType *);       // function prototype

int main()
{
  TeleType t1 = {"Acme, Sam","(555) 898-2392"};
  TeleType t2 = {"Dolan, Edith","(555) 682-3104"};
  TeleType t3 = {"Lanfrank, John","(555) 718-4581"};
  TeleType *first;    // create a pointer to a structure
```

(continued next page)

(continued from previous page)

```
  first = &t1;          // store t1's address in first
  t1.nextaddr = &t2;    // store t2's address in t1.nextaddr
  t2.nextaddr = &t3;    // store t3's address in t2.nextaddr
  t3.nextaddr = NULL;   // store the NULL address in t3.nextaddr

  display(first);       // send the address of the first structure
  cout << endl;

  return 0;
}

void display(TeleType *contents) // contents is a pointer to a structure
{                                // of type TeleType
  while (contents != NULL)    // display till end of linked list
  {
    cout << '\n' << setiosflags(ios::left)
         << setw(30) << contents->name
         << setw(20) << contents->phoneNum ;
    contents = contents->nextaddr;     // get next address
  }
  cout << endl;

  return;
}
```

Figure 15.18 shows the output produced by Program 15.9. The important concept illustrated by Program 15.9 is the use of the address in one structure to access members of the next structure in the list. When the `display()` function is called, it is passed the value stored in the variable named `first`. Because `first` is a pointer variable, the actual value passed is an address (the address of the `t1` structure). `display()` accepts the passed value in the parameter named `contents`. To store the passed address correctly, `contents` is declared as a pointer to a structure of the `TeleType` type. Within `display()`, a `while` loop

FIGURE 15.18

Output displayed by Program 15.9

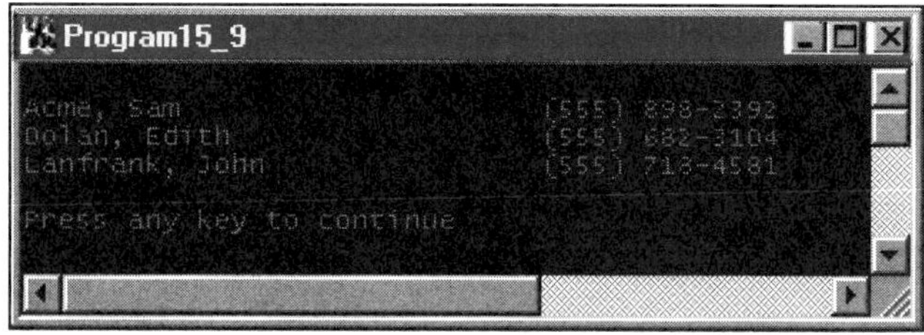

is used to cycle through the linked structures, starting with the structure whose address is in `contents`. The condition tested in the `while` statement compares the value in `contents`, which is an address, to the `NULL` value. For each valid address, the name and phone number members of the addressed structure are displayed. The address in `contents` is then updated with the address in the pointer member of the current structure. The address in `contents` is then retested, and the process continues as long as the address in `contents` is not equal to the `NULL` value. `display()` "knows" nothing about the names of the structures declared in `main()` or even how many structures exist. It simply cycles through the linked list, structure by structure, until it encounters the end-of-list `NULL` address. Because the value of `NULL` is zero, the tested condition can be replaced by the equivalent expression `contents`.

A disadvantage of Program 15.9 is that exactly three structures are defined in `main()` by name, and storage for them is reserved at compile time. Should a fourth structure be required, the additional structure would have to be declared and the program recompiled. In the next section we show how to have the program dynamically allocate and release storage for structures at run time as storage is required. Only when a new structure is to be added to the list, and while the program is running, is storage for the new structure created. Similarly, when a structure is no longer needed and can be deleted from the list, the storage for the deleted record is relinquished and returned to the computer.

EXERCISES 15.4

1. Modify Program 15.9 to prompt the user for a name. Have the program search the existing list for the entered name. If the name is in the list, display the corresponding phone number; otherwise display this message: `The name is not in the current phone directory.`

2. Write a C++ program containing a linked list of ten integer numbers. Have the program display the numbers in the list.

3. Using the linked list of structures illustrated in Figure 15.13, write the sequence of steps necessary to delete the record for Edith Dolan from the list.

4. Generalize the description obtained in Exercise 3 to describe the sequence of steps necessary to remove the *n*th structure from a list of linked structures. The *n*th structure is preceded by the $(n - 1)$st structure and followed by the $(n + 1)$st structure. Make sure to store all pointer values correctly.

5. a. A doubly linked list is a list in which each structure contains a pointer to both the following and previous structures in the list. Define an appropriate type for a doubly linked list of names and telephone numbers.

b. Using the type defined in Exercise 5a, modify Program 15.9 to list the names and phone numbers in reverse order.

15.5 Dynamic Data Structure Allocation

We have already encountered the concept of explicitly allocating and deallocating memory space using the new and delete operators (see Section 13.2). For convenience, the descriptions of these operators are repeated in Table 15.1.

This dynamic allocation of memory is especially useful when dealing with a list of structures because it permits the list to expand as new records are added and contract as records are deleted.

In requesting additional storage space, the user must provide the new operator with an indication of the amount of storage needed. This is done by requesting enough space for a particular type of data. For example, the expression new(int) or new int (the two forms may be used interchangeably) requests enough storage to store an integer number. A request for enough storage for a data structure is made in the same fashion. For example, using the declaration

```
struct TeleType
{
  char name[30];
  char phoneNum[16];
};
```

the function calls new TeleType and new(TeleType) both reserve enough storage for one TeleType data structure.

In allocating storage dynamically, we have no advance indication as to where the computer system will physically reserve the requested number of bytes, and we have no explicit name to access the newly created storage locations. To provide access to these locations, new returns the address of the first location that has been reserved. This address is then assigned to a pointer. The return of an address by new is especially useful for creating

TABLE 15.1 The new and delete operators

Operator Name	Description
new	Reserves the number of bytes required by the requested data type. Returns the address of the first reserved location or NULL if sufficient memory is not available.
delete	Releases a block of bytes previously reserved. The address of the first reserved location is passed as an argument to the operator.

a linked list of data structures. As each new structure is created, the address returned by `new` to the structure can be assigned to a member of the previous structure in the list.

Program 15.10 illustrates using `new` to create a structure dynamically in response to a user-input request.

PROGRAM 15.10

```
// a program illustrating dynamic structure allocation

#include <iostream.h>
#include <string.h>

const int MAXNAME = 30;  // maximum no. of characters in a name
const int MAXTEL = 16;   // maximum no. of characters in a telephone number

struct TeleType
{
  char name[MAXNAME];
  char phoneNum[MAXTEL];
};

void populate(TeleType *);  // function prototype
void dispOne(TeleType *);   // function prototype

int main()
{
  char key;
  TeleType *recPoint;     // recPoint is a pointer to a
                          // structure of type TeleType

  cout << "\nDo you wish to create a new record (respond with y or n): ";
  key = cin.get();
  if (key == 'y')
  {
    key = cin.get();        // get the Enter key in buffered input
    recPoint = new TeleType;
    populate(recPoint);
    dispOne(recPoint);
  }
```

(continued next page)

(continued from previous page)

```
  else
    cout << "\nNo record has been created.\n";

  cout << endl;
  return 0;
}

  // input a name and phone number
void populate(TeleType *record) // record is a pointer to a
{                               // structure of type TeleType
  cout << "Enter a name: ";
  cin.getline(record->name,MAXNAME);
  cout << "Enter the phone number: ";
  cin.getline(record->phoneNum,MAXTEL);

  return;
}
  // display the contents of one record
void dispOne(TeleType *contents)  // contents is a pointer to a
{                                 // structure of type TeleType
  cout << "\nThe contents of the record just created is:"
       << "\nName: " << contents->name
       << "\nPhone Number: " << contents->phoneNum << endl;

  return;
}
```

A sample session produced by Program 15.10 is shown in Figure 15.19. In Program 15.10, notice that only two variable declarations are made in `main()`. The variable `key` is declared as a character variable and the variable `recPoint` is declared as being a pointer

FIGURE 15.19

Sample run using Program 15.10

Program15_10

```
Do you wish to create a new record (respond with y or n): y
Enter a name: Monroe, James
Enter the phone number: (555) 555-1817

The contents of the record just created is:
Name: Monroe, James
Phone Number: (555) 555-1817
Press any key to continue_
```

to a structure of the TeleType type. Because the declaration for the type TeleType is global, TeleType can be used within main() to define recPoint as a pointer to a structure of the TeleType type.

If a user enters y in response to the first prompt in main(), a call to new is made for the required memory to store the designated structure. Once recPoint has been loaded with the proper address, this address can be used to access the newly created structure. The function populate() is used to prompt the user for data needed in filling the structure and to store the user-entered data in the correct members of the structure. The argument passed to populate() in main() is the pointer recPoint. Like all passed arguments, the value contained in recPoint is passed to the function. Because the value in recPoint is an address, populate() receives the address of the newly created structure and can directly access the structure members.

Within populate(), the value received by it is stored in the parameter named record. Because the value to be stored in record is the address of a structure, record must be declared as a pointer to a structure. This is accomplished by the declaration TeleType *record. The statements within populate() use the address in record to locate the respective members of the structure.

The dispOne() function in Program 15.10 is used to display the contents of the newly created and populated structure. The address passed to dispOne() is the same address that was passed to populate(). Because this passed value is the address of a structure, the parameter name used to store the address is declared as a pointer to the correct structure type.

Once you understand the mechanism of using new, you can use this operator to construct a linked list of structures. As described in the previous section, the structures used in a linked list must contain at least one pointer member. The address in the pointer member is the starting address of the next structure in the list. Additionally, a pointer must be reserved for the address of the first structure, and the pointer member of the last structure in the list is given a NULL address to indicate that no more members are being pointed to. Program 15.11 illustrates the use of new to construct a linked list of names and phone numbers. The populate() function used in Program 15.11 is the same function used in Program 15.10, and the display() function is the same function used in Program 15.9.

PROGRAM 15.11

```
#include <iostream.h>
#include <iomanip.h>

const int MAXNAME = 30;  // maximum no. of characters in a name
const int MAXTEL = 16;   // maximum no. of characters in a telephone number
const int MAXRECS = 3;   // maximum no. of records
```

(continued next page)

(continued from previous page)

```
struct TeleType
{
  char name[MAXNAME];
  char phoneNum[MAXTEL];
  TeleType *nextaddr;
};

void populate(TeleType *);   // function prototype
void display(TeleType *);    // function prototype

int main()
{
  int i;
  TeleType *list, *current; // two pointers to structures of
                            // type TeleType

    // get a pointer to the first structure in the list
  list = new TeleType;
  current = list;

  cout << endl;
    // populate the current structure and create the remaining structures
  for(i = 0; i < MAXRECS - 1; i++)
  {
    populate(current);
    current->nextaddr = new TeleType;
    current = current->nextaddr;
  }

  populate(current);         // populate the last structure
  current->nextaddr = NULL;  // set the last address to a NULL address
  cout << "\nThe list consists of the following records:\n";
  display(list);   // display the structures

  cout << endl;
  return 0;
}

  // input a name and phone number
void populate(TeleType *record) // record is a pointer to a
{                               // structure of type TeleType
```

(continued next page)

(continued from previous page)

```
  cout << "Enter a name: ";
  cin.getline(record->name,MAXNAME);
  cout << "Enter the phone number: ";
  cin.getline(record->phoneNum,MAXTEL);

  return;
}

void display(TeleType *contents) // contents is a pointer to a
{                                  // structure of type TeleType
  while (contents != NULL)       // display till end of linked list
  {
    cout << endl << setiosflags(ios::left)
         << setw(30) << contents->name
         << setw(20) << contents->phoneNum;
    contents = contents->nextaddr;
  }
  cout << endl;

  return;
}
```

The first time `new` is called in Program 15.11 it is used to create the first structure in the linked list. As such, the address returned by `new` is stored in the pointer variable named `list`. The address in `list` is then assigned to the pointer named `current`. This pointer variable is always used by the program to point to the current structure. Because the current structure is the first structure created, the address in the pointer named `list` is initially assigned to the pointer named `current`.

Within `main()`'s `for` loop, the name and phone number members of the newly created structure are populated by calling `populate()` and passing the address of the current structure to the function. Upon return from `populate()`, the pointer member of the current structure is assigned an address. This address is the address of the next structure in the list, which is obtained from `new`. The call to `new` creates the next structure and returns its address into the pointer member of the current structure. This completes the population of the current member. The final statement in the `for` loop resets the address in the current pointer to the address of the next structure in the list.

After the last structure has been created, the final statements in `main()` populate this structure, assign a `NULL` address to the pointer member, and call `display()` to display all the structures in the list. A sample run of Program 15.11 is illustrated in Figure 15.20.

Just as `new` dynamically creates storage while a program is executing, the `delete` function restores a block of storage back to the computer while the programming is exe-

FIGURE 15.20

Sample run using Program 15.11

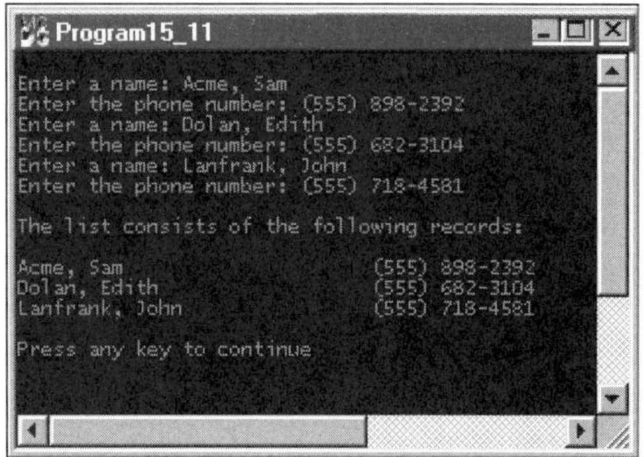

cuting. The only argument required by `delete` is the starting address of a block of storage that was dynamically allocated. Thus, any address returned by `new` can subsequently be passed to `delete` to restore the reserved memory back to the computer. `delete` does not alter the address passed to it, but simply removes the storage that the address references.

EXERCISES 15.5

1. As described in Table 15.1, the `new` operator returns either the address of the first new storage area allocated, or `NULL` if insufficient storage is available. Modify Program 15.11 to check that a valid address has been returned before a call to `populate()` is made. Display an appropriate message if sufficient storage is not available.

2. Write a C++ function named `remove()` that removes an existing structure from the linked list of structures created by Program 15.11. The algorithm for removing a linked structure should follow the sequence developed for removing a structure developed in Exercise 4 in Section 15.4. The argument passed to `remove()` should be the address of the structure preceding the record to be removed. In the removal function, make sure that the value of the pointer in the removed structure replaces the value of the pointer member of the preceding structure before the structure is removed.

3. Write a function named `insert()` that inserts a structure into the linked list of structures created in Program 15.11. The algorithm for inserting a structure in a linked list should follow the sequence for inserting a record, previously illustrated in Figure 15.12. The argument passed to `insert()` should be the address of the structure preceding the structure to be inserted. The inserted structure should follow this current structure. The `insert()` function should create a new structure dynamically, call the `populate()` function used in Program 15.11, and adjust all pointer values appropriately.

4. We desire to insert a new structure into the linked list of structures created by Program 15.11. The function developed to do this in Exercise 3 assumed that the address of the preceding structure is known. Write a function called `findRecord()` that returns the address of the structure immediately preceding the point at which the new structure is to be inserted. (*Hint:* `findRecord()` must request the new name as input and compare the entered name to existing names to determine where to place the new name.)

5. Write a C++ function named `modify()` that can be used to modify the name and phone number members of a structure of the type created in Program 15.11. The argument passed to `modify()` should be the address of the structure to be modified. The `modify()` function should first display the existing name and phone number in the selected structure and then request new data for these members.

6. a. Write a C++ program that initially presents a menu of choices for the user. The menu should consist of the following choices:

a. Create an initial linked list of names and phone numbers.
b. Insert a new structure into the linked list.
c. Modify an existing structure in the linked list.
d. Delete an existing structure from the list.
e. Exit from the program.

Upon the user's selection, the program should execute the appropriate functions to satisfy the request.

b. Why is the original creation of a linked list usually done by one program, and the options to add, modify, or delete a structure in the list provided by a different program?

15.6 Unions

A **union** is a data type that reserves the same area in memory for two or more variables, each of which can be a different data type.[3] A variable that is declared as a union data type can be used to hold a character variable, an integer variable, a double precision variable, or any other valid C++ data type. Each of these types, but only one at a time, can actually be assigned to the union variable.

The definition of a union has the same form as a structure definition, with the keyword `union` used in place of the keyword `struct`. For example, the declaration

```
union
{
  char key;
  int num;
  double price;
} val;
```

3 This topic may be omitted on first reading with no loss of subject continuity.

creates a union variable named `val`. If `val` were a structure it would consist of three individual members. As a union, however, `val` contains a single member that can be either a character variable named `key`, an integer variable named `num`, or a double precision variable named `price`. In effect, a union reserves sufficient memory locations to accommodate its largest member's data type. This same set of locations is then accessed by different variable names, depending on the data type of the value currently residing in the reserved locations. Each value stored overwrites the previous value, using as many bytes of the reserved memory area as necessary.

Individual union members are accessed using the same notation as structure members. For example, if the `val` union is currently being used to store a character, the correct variable name to access the stored character is `val.key`. Similarly, if the union is used to store an integer, the value is accessed by the name `val.num`, and a double precision value is accessed by the name `val.price`. In using union members, it is the programmer's responsibility to ensure that the correct member name is used for the data type currently residing in the union.

To do this, a second variable is typically used to keep track of the current data type stored in the union. For example, the following code could be used to select the appropriate member of `val` for display. Here the value in the variable `uType` determines the currently stored data type in the `val` union.

```
switch(uType)
{
  case 'c': cout << val.key;
            break;
  case 'i': cout << val.num;
            break;
  case 'd': cout << val.price;
            break;
  default : cout << "Invalid type in uType : " << uType;
}
```

As they are in structures, a data type can be associated with a union. For example, the declaration

```
union DateAndTime
{
   long int days;
   double time;
};
```

provides a union data type without actually reserving any storage locations. This data type can then be used to define any number of variables. For example, the definition

```
DateAndTime first, second, *pt;
```

creates a union variable named `first`, a union variable named `second`, and a pointer that can be used to store the address of any union having the form of `DateAndTime`. Once a pointer to a union has been declared, the same notation used to access structure members can be used to access union members. For example, if the assignment `pt = &first;` is made, then `pt->days` references the `days` member of the union named `first`.

Unions may themselves be members of structures or arrays, or structures, arrays, and pointers may be members of unions. In each case, the notation used to access a member must be consistent with the nesting employed. For example, in the structure defined by

```
struct
{
  char uType;
  union
  {
    char *text;
    float rate;
  } uTax;
}  flag;
```

the variable `rate` is referenced as

```
flag.uTax.rate
```

Similarly, the first character of the string whose address is stored in the pointer `text` is referenced as

```
*flag.uTax.text
```

EXERCISES 15.6

1. Assume that the following definition has been made

```
union
{
  float rate;
  double taxes;
  int num;
} flag;
```

For this union, write appropriate `cout` statements to display the various members of the union.

2. Define a union variable named `car` that contains an integer named `year`, an array of ten characters named `name`, and an array of ten characters named `model`.

3. Define a union variable named `lang` that would allow a floating point number to be referenced by both the variable names `interest` and `rate`.

4. Declare a union data type named `Amt` that contains an integer variable named `intAmt`, a double precision variable named `dblAmt`, and a pointer to a character named `ptKey`.

5. a. What do you think will be displayed by the following section of code?

```
union
{
  char ch;
  float btype;
} alt;
alt.ch = 'y';
cout << alt.btype;
```

b. Include the code presented in Exercise 5a in a program and run the program to verify your answer to Exercise 5a.

15.7 Common Programming Errors

Three common errors are often made when using structures or unions. The first error occurs because structures and unions, as complete entities, cannot be used in relational expressions. For example, even if `TeleType` and `PhoneType` are two structures of the same type, the expression `TeleType == PhoneType` is invalid. Individual members of a structure or union can, of course, be compared, if they are of the same data type, using any of C++'s relational operators.

The second common error is really an extension of a pointer error as it relates to structures and unions. Whenever a pointer is used to "point to" either of these data types, or whenever a pointer is itself a member of a structure or a union, take care to use the address in the pointer to access the appropriate data type. Should you be confused about just what is being pointed to, remember, "If in doubt, print it out."

The final error relates specifically to unions. Because a union can store only one of its members at a time, you must be careful to keep track of the currently stored variable. Storing one data type in a union and accessing it by the wrong variable name can result in an error that is particularly troublesome to locate.

15.8 Chapter Summary

1. A **structure** allows individual variables to be grouped under a common variable name. Each variable in a structure is accessed by its structure variable name, followed by a period, followed by its individual variable name. Another term for a data structure is a **record.** One form for declaring a structure is:

```
struct
{
  individual member declarations;
} structureName;
```

2. A data type can be created from a structure using the declaration form

```
struct Data-type
{
  individual member declarations;
};
```

Individual structure variables may then be defined as this `Data-type`. By convention, the first letter of the `Data-type` name is always capitalized.

3. Structures are particularly useful as elements of arrays. Used in this manner, each structure becomes one record in a list of records.

4. Complete structures can be used as function arguments, in which case the called function receives a copy of each element in the structure. The address of a structure may also be passed, either as a reference or a pointer, which provides the called function with direct access to the structure.

5. Structure members can be any valid C++ data type, including other structures, unions, arrays, and pointers. When a pointer is included as a structure member, a linked list can be created. Such a list uses the pointer in one structure to "point to" (contain the address of) the next logical structure in the list.

6. Unions are declared in the same manner as structures. The definition of a union creates a memory overlay area, with each union member using the same memory storage locations. Thus, only one member of a union may be active at a time.

15.9 Knowing About: Linked Lists Using Classes

Linked lists provide a convenient method for maintaining lists of items without the need to continually reorder and restructure a list as items are added or deleted.[4] For example, consider the list of names and phone numbers previously introduced in Section 15.4 and reproduced below as Figure 15.21.

---

4 Prior to reading this section, the interested reader should be familiar with both the introductory material on linked lists provided in Section 15.4 and the material on classes provided in Part II.

FIGURE 15.21

Telephone list in alphabetical order

Acme, Sam
(555) 898-2392
Dolan, Edith
(555) 682-3104
Lanfrank, John
(555) 718-4581
Mening, Stephen
(555) 382-7070
Zemann, Harold
(555) 219-9912

Constructing a linked list for this case requires that each record have the same format, which includes an address that references the next record in the list. Clearly, the last record cannot have a valid address referencing another record, because there is none. So for this last record we use a `NULL` address that will act as a sentinel or flag to indicate when the last record has been processed. The `NULL` address value, like its end-of-string counterpart, has a numerical value of zero.

Besides an end-of-list sentinel value, either a pointer or reference variable must also be provided to store the address of the first record in the list. Figure 15.22 illustrates the complete set of addresses and records for the first three names and addresses shown in Figure 15.21.

FIGURE 15.22

Use of the initial and final address values

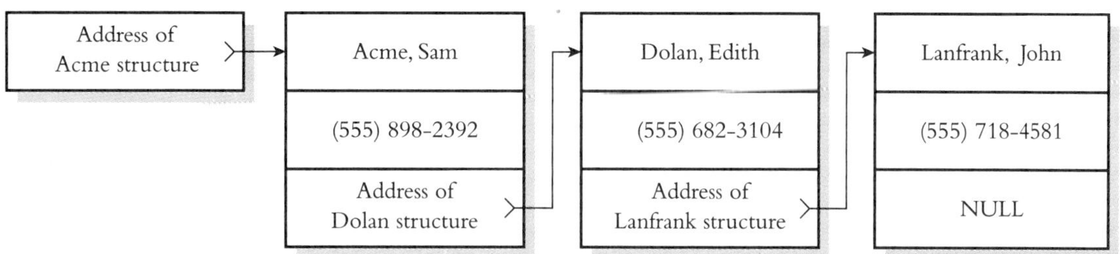

This concept can be easily extended to create a linked list of objects suitable for storing any number of names and telephone numbers. The following interface is suitable for such a class:

```
// class declaration (interface)
class TeleType
{
  private:
    char name[30];
```

```
    char phone[16];
    TeleType *nextaddr;
  public:
    TeleType(char *, char *);  // a constructor
    TeleType *getaddr();  // function returns a pointer to an object of type TeleType
    void setaddr(TeleType *);
    void display();
};
```

This interface declares three data and four function members, respectively. The first data member is an array of 30 characters, suitable for storing names with a maximum of 29 letters and an end-of-string `NULL` marker. The next data member is an array of 15 characters, suitable for storing telephone numbers with their respective area codes. The last data member is a pointer suitable for storing the address of an object of the class `TeleType`. The member functions consist of a constructor and three access functions. We will define these functions using the implementation class:

```
// class implementation

TeleType::TeleType(char *newName, char *newPhone)
{
  strcpy(name, newName);
  strcpy(phone, newPhone);
  nextaddr = NULL;
}
TeleType *TeleType::getaddr()
{
  return nextaddr;
}
void TeleType::setaddr(TeleType *nextad)
{
  nextaddr = nextad;
}
void TeleType::display()
{
   cout << endl << setiosflags(ios::left)
        << setw(30) <<  name
        << setw(20) << phone;
}
```

The constructor and display functions are rather straightforward. The constructor copies its first string argument to the `name` data member and its second string argument to the `phone` data member. Finally, it initializes its pointer data member with a `NULL` address. The display function simply outputs the values contained in the `name` and `phone` variables. The remaining two access functions, `getaddr()` and `setaddr()` are used to retrieve and set addresses, respectively, into the pointer data member of an object.

As defined in the implementation, `setaddr()` expects to receive the address of a `TeleType` object and assigns this address to its pointer member. Similarly, `getaddr()` simply returns the address stored in its pointer member—that is, it returns a pointer to an object of type `TeleType`.

Program 15.12 illustrates the use of the `TeleType` class by specifically creating three objects of this class. The three objects are named `t1`, `t2`, and `t3`, respectively, and each object is initialized with a name and telephone members when the objects are defined, using the data listed in Figure 15.21.

PROGRAM 15.12

```
#include <iostream.h>
#include <iomanip.h>
#include <string.h>

const int MAXNAME = 30;
const int MAXTEL = 16;
```

```
// class declaration (interface)
class TeleType
{
  private:
    char name[MAXNAME];
    char phone[MAXTEL];
    TeleType *nextaddr;
  public:
    TeleType(char *, char *);  // a constructor
    TeleType *getaddr();    // function returns a pointer to an object of
                            // type TeleType
    void setaddr(TeleType *);
    void display();
};
```

(continued next page)

(continued from previous page)

```
// class implementation
TeleType::TeleType(char *newName, char *newPhone)
{
  strcpy(name, newName);
  strcpy(phone, newPhone);
  nextaddr = NULL;
}
TeleType *TeleType::getaddr()
{
  return nextaddr;
}
void TeleType::setaddr(TeleType *nextad)
{
  nextaddr = nextad;
  return;
}
void TeleType::display()
{
   cout << endl << setiosflags(ios::left)
        << setw(30) <<  name
        << setw(20) << phone;
 return;
}
```

```
int main()
{
  int i;
  class TeleType t1("Acme, Sam", "(555) 898-2392");
  class TeleType t2("Dolan, Edith", "(555) 682-3104");
  class TeleType t3("Lanfrank, John", "(555) 718-4581");
  TeleType *next;

  next = &t1;              // store t1's address in next
  t1.setaddr(&t2);         // store t2's address in t1.nextaddr
  t2.setaddr(&t3);         // store t3's address in t2.nextaddr

  while (next != NULL)
  {
    (*next).display();              // same as next->display()
```

(continued next page)

(continued from previous page)

```
    next = (*next).getaddr();    // same as next->getaddr()
  }

  return 0;
}
```

The output produced by executing Program 15.12 is:

```
Acme, Sam      (555) 898-2392
Dolan, Edith   (555) 682-3104
Lanfrank, John (555) 718-4581
```

We have already described the class construction. Let us now concentrate on the `main()` function in Program 15.12 and see how it creates this output. Figure 15.23 illustrates the relationship between the three objects created by the program.

FIGURE 15.23

Relationship between objects in Program 15.12

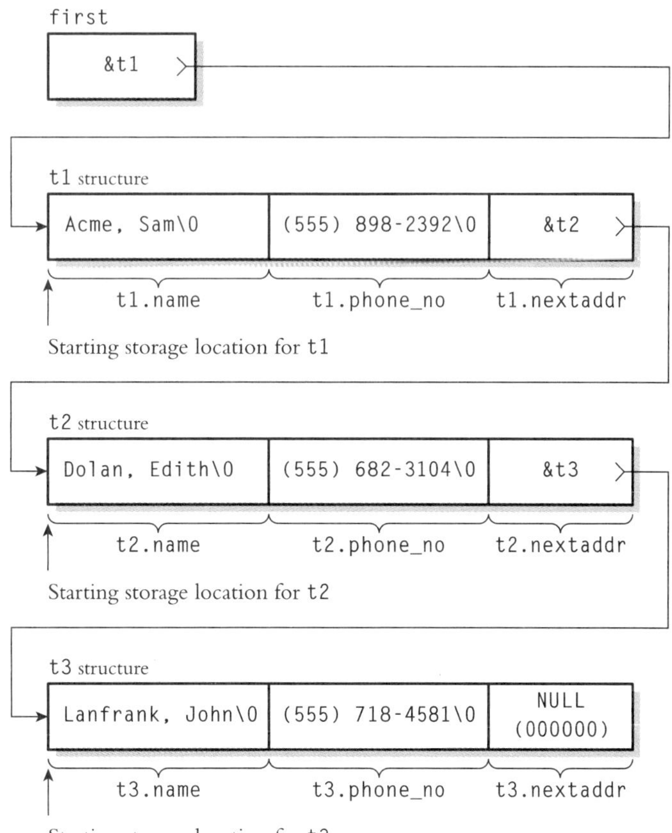

From within main(), the three objects illustrated in Figure 15.23, t1, t2, and t3, are defined. Each of these objects are of class type TeleType. Although each object consists of three members, only the first two members of each object are explicitly initialized. As both of these members are arrays of characters, they can be initialized with strings. The remaining member of each object is a pointer, which is initialized to a NULL address by the constructor.

To create a linked list from these three objects, each pointer member must be assigned the address of the next object in the list. The three assignment statements in Program 15.12 perform the correct assignments. The expression next = &t1 stores the address of the t1 object in the pointer variable named next. The function call t1.setaddr(&t2) makes use of t1's setaddr() function to store the address of t2 in t1's pointer variable. The result of this call is that t1.nextaddr = &t2. Similarly, the function call t2.setaddr(&t3) stores the starting address of the t3 object into the pointer member of the t2 object (that is, t2.next = &t3). The list is automatically terminated by the NULL address placed in t3.next when the t3 object was initialized.

Once values have been assigned to each object member and correct addresses have been stored in the appropriate pointers, the addresses can be used to loop through the complete list for display purposes. As each object is accessed, it can either be examined to select a specific value or used to print out a complete list. This is done by main()'s while loop.

The expression (*next).display() in the while loop calls the display() function of the object pointed to by next. Because next initially contains the address of the t1 object, the function that is called is t1.display(). This display function, as defined in the class implementation section, outputs its object's name and phone number values. t1's getaddr() function is then called, which assigns the address in t1.nextaddr to next. Because t1.nextaddr contains the address of the t2 object, the second time through the loop the t2.display() function is called. This process is repeated until the NULL address in t3.nxtaddr is encountered. It should be noted that the expression (*next).display() in the while loop can be replaced by the equivalent expression next->display().

The important concept illustrated by Program 15.12 is the use of the address in one object to access members of the next object in the list. Within main(), the while loop is used to cycle through the linked objects, starting with the object whose address is in next. The condition tested in the while statement compares the value in next, which is an address, to the NULL value. For each valid address the name and phone number members of the addressed object are displayed. The address in next is then updated with the address in the pointer member of the current object. The address in next is then retested, and the process continues as long as the address in next is not equal to the NULL value. The loop "knows" nothing about the names of the objects declared in main() or even how many objects exist. It simply cycles through the linked list, object by object, until it encounters the end-of-list NULL address. Because the value of NULL is zero, the tested condition can be replaced by the equivalent expression next.

A disadvantage of Program 15.12 is that exactly three objects are defined in `main()` by name, and storage for them is reserved at compile time. Should a fourth object be required, the additional object would have to be declared and the program recompiled. This limitation is removed by dynamically allocating and freeing storage for objects at run time, as storage is required. Only when a new object is to be added to the list, and while the program is running, is storage for the new object created. Similarly, when a object is no longer needed and can be deleted from the list, the storage for the deleted record is relinquished and returned to the computer.

Program 15.13 illustrates using dynamic storage allocation to create an object dynamically in response to a user-input request.

PROGRAM 15.13

```
#include <iostream.h>
#include <iomanip.h>
#include <string.h>

const int MAXNAME = 30;
const int MAXTEL = 16;
```

```
class TeleType
{
  private:
    char name[MAXNAME];
    char phone[MAXTEL];
  public:
    TeleType(char *, char *);  // a constructor
    void display();
};

// class implementation
TeleType::TeleType(char *newName, char *newPhone)
{
  strcpy(name, newName);
  strcpy(phone, newPhone);
}
void TeleType::display()
{
   cout << endl << setiosflags(ios::left)
        << setw(30) << name
        << setw(20) << phone;
}
```

(continued next page)

(continued from previous page)

```
int main()
{
  char key, newName[MAXNAME], newPhone[MAXTEL];
  TeleType *recPointer; // a pointer to an object of type TeleType

  cout << "\nDo you wish to create a new record (respond with y or n): ";
  key = cin.get();
  if (key == 'y')
  {
    key = cin.get();  // get the Enter key in buffered input
    cout << "\nEnter a name: ";
    cin.getline(newName,MAXNAME);
    cout << "Enter a phone number: ";
    cin.getline(newPhone,MAXTEL);
    recPointer = new TeleType(newName, newPhone);
    (*recPointer).display();     // same as recPointer->display()
  }
  else
    cout << "\nNo record has been created";

  return 0;
}
```

A sample session produced by Program 15.13 is:

```
Do you wish to create a new record (respond with y or n): y
Enter a name: Monroe, James
Enter the phone number: (555) 555-1817
The contents of the record just created is:
Name: Monroe, James
Phone Number: (555) 555-1817
```

In Program 15.13, notice the statement `recPointer = new TeleType(newName, newPhone);` in `main()`. This statement uses the `new` operator to create an object of type `TeleType`, initializes the newly created object with the strings contained in the character arrays `newName` and `newPhone` (via the constructor), and stores the address returned by `new` in the pointer variable `recPointer`. The complete operation of `main()` is as follows:

If a user enters `y` in response to the first prompt in `main()`, the user is requested to enter a name and telephone number. A call is then made to `new`, as just described.

The newly created object's `display()` function is then called to display the contents of the newly created and initialized object. The mechanism for calling `display()` is identical to that previously described for Program 15.13.

Once you understand the mechanism of calling `new`, you can use this function to construct a linked list of objects. The address in the pointer member of each object in the list must be the starting address of the next object in the list. Additionally, a pointer must be reserved for the address of the first object, and the pointer member of the last object in the list is given a `NULL` address to indicate that no more members are being pointed to.

Program 15.14 illustrates the use of `new` to construct a linked list of names and phone numbers. The `populate()` function used in Program 15.14 is the same function used in Program 15.13, and the `display()` function is the same function used in Program 15.12.

PROGRAM 15.14

```
#include <iostream.h>
#include <iomanip.h>
#include <string.h>

const int MAXNAME = 30;
const int MAXTEL = 16;
const int MAXRECS = 3;

// class declaration (interface)
class TeleType
{
  private:
    char name[MAXNAME];
    char phone[MAXTEL];
    TeleType *nextaddr;
  public:
    TeleType(char *, char *); // a constructor
    TeleType *getaddr();      // function returns a pointer to an object of
                              // type TeleType
    void setaddr(TeleType *);
    void display();
};

// class implementation
TeleType::TeleType(char *newName, char *newPhone)
{
  strcpy(name, newName);
  strcpy(phone, newPhone);
```

(continued next page)

(continued from previous page)

```
  nextaddr = NULL;
}
TeleType *TeleType::getaddr()
{
  return nextaddr;
}
void TeleType::setaddr(TeleType *nextad)
{
  nextaddr = nextad;
  return;
}
void TeleType::display()
{
   cout << endl << setiosflags(ios::left)
        << setw(30) <<  name
        << setw(20) << phone;
  return;
}
```

```
int main()
{
  char newName[MAXNAME], newPhone[MAXTEL];
  TeleType *first, *current, *newpoint;

  // create the first object in the list
  cout << "\nEnter a name: ";
  cin.getline(newName,MAXNAME);
  cout << "Enter a phone number: ";
  cin.getline(newPhone,MAXTEL);
  current = new TeleType(newName, newPhone);
  first = current;   // save the first address

  for(int i = 1; i <= MAXRECS - 1; i++)  // create 2 more objects
  {
    cout << "\nEnter a name: ";
    cin.getline(newName,MAXNAME);
    cout << "Enter a phone number: ";
    cin.getline(newPhone,MAXTEL);
    newpoint = new TeleType(newName, newPhone);
```

(continued next page)

(continued from previous page)

```
    (*current).setaddr(newpoint);
    current = newpoint;
  }

  while (first != NULL)
  {
    (*first).display();
    first = (*first).getaddr();
  }

  return 0;
}
```

The first time `new` is called in Program 15.14 it is used to create the first object in the linked list. As such, the address returned by `new` is stored in the pointer variable named `newpoint`. The address in `newpoint` is then assigned to the pointer named `current`. This pointer variable is always used by the program to point to the current object. Since the current object is the first object created, the address in the pointer named `list` is initially assigned to the pointer named `current`.

Within `main()`'s `for` loop, the `name` and `phone` members of the newly created object are populated by calling `populate()` and passing the address of the current object to the function. Upon return from `populate()`, the pointer member of the current object is assigned an address. This address is the address of the next object in the list, which is obtained from `new`. The call to `new` creates the next object and returns its address into the pointer member of the current object. This completes the population of the current member. The final statement in the `for` loop resets the address in the `current` pointer to the address of the next object in the list.

After the last object has been created, the final statements in `main()` populate this object, assign a `NULL` address to the pointer member, and call `display()` to display all the objects in the list. A sample run of Program 15.14 is provided below:

```
Enter a name: Acme, Sam
Enter the phone number: (555) 898-2392
Enter a name: Dolan, Edith
Enter the phone number: (555) 682-3104
Enter a name: Lanfrank, John
Enter the phone number: (555) 718-4581
```

```
The list consists of the following records:

Acme, Sam                      (555) 898-2392
Dolan, Edith                   (555) 682-3104
Lanfrank, John                 (555) 718-4581
```

Just as `new` dynamically creates storage while a program is executing, the `delete` function restores a block of storage back to the computer while the programming is executing. The only argument required by `delete` is the starting address of a block of storage that was dynamically allocated. Thus, any address returned by `new` can subsequently be passed to `delete` to restore the reserved memory back to the computer. `delete` does not alter the address passed to it but simply removes the storage that the address references.

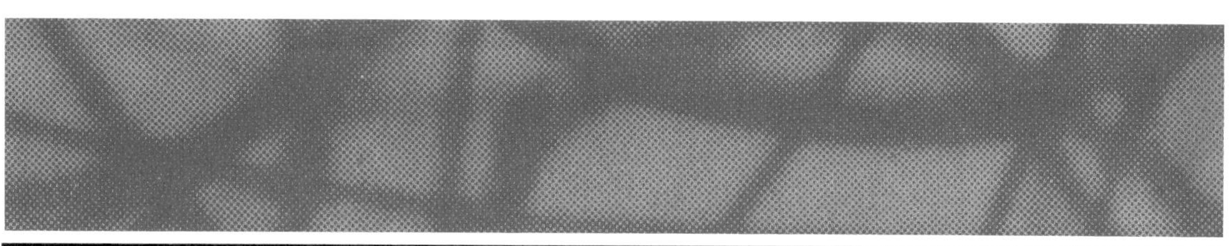

APPENDICES

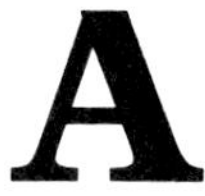

Operator Precedence Table

Table A.1 presents the symbols, precedence, descriptions, and associativity of C++'s operators. Operators toward the top of the table have a higher precedence than those toward the bottom. Operators within each box have the same precedence and associativity.

TABLE A.1 Summary of C++ operators

<table>
<tr><th>Operator</th><th>Description</th><th>Associativity</th></tr>
<tr><td>()
[]
->
.</td><td>Function call
Array element
Structure member pointer reference
Structure member reference</td><td>Left to right</td></tr>
<tr><td>+
--
-
!
~
(type)
sizeof
&
*</td><td>Increment
Decrement
Unary minus
Logical negation
One's complement
Type conversion (cast)
Storage size
Address of
Indirection</td><td>Right to left</td></tr>
<tr><td>*
/
%</td><td>Multiplication
Division
Modulus (remainder)</td><td>Left to right</td></tr>
<tr><td>+
-</td><td>Addition
Subtraction</td><td>Left to right</td></tr>
<tr><td><<
>></td><td>Left shift
Right shift</td><td>Left to right</td></tr>
<tr><td><
<=
>
>=</td><td>Less than
Less than or equal to
Greater than
Greater than or equal to</td><td>Left to right</td></tr>
<tr><td>==
!=</td><td>Equal to
Not equal to</td><td>Left to right</td></tr>
<tr><td>&</td><td>Bitwise AND</td><td>Left to right</td></tr>
<tr><td>^</td><td>Bitwise exclusive OR</td><td>Left to right</td></tr>
<tr><td>|</td><td>Bitwise inclusive OR</td><td>Left to right</td></tr>
<tr><td>&&</td><td>Logical AND</td><td>Left to right</td></tr>
<tr><td>||</td><td>Logical OR</td><td>Left to right</td></tr>
<tr><td>?:</td><td>Conditional expression</td><td>Right to left</td></tr>
<tr><td>=
+= -= *=
/= %= $=
^= |=
<<== >>==</td><td>Assignment
Assignment
Assignment
Assignment
Assignment</td><td>Right to left</td></tr>
<tr><td>,</td><td>Comma</td><td>Left to right</td></tr>
</table>

B ASCII Character Codes

Key(s)	Dec	Oct	Hex	Key	Dec	Oct	Hex	Key	Dec	Oct	Hex
Ctrl 1	0	0	0	+	43	53	2B	V	86	126	56
Ctrl A	1	1	1	,	44	54	2C	W	87	127	57
Ctrl B	2	2	2	-	45	55	2D	X	88	130	58
Ctrl C	3	3	3	.	46	56	2E	Y	89	131	59
Ctrl D	4	4	4	/	47	57	2F	Z	90	132	5A
Ctrl E	5	5	5	0	48	60	30	[	91	133	5B
Ctrl F	6	6	6	1	49	61	31	\	92	134	5C
Ctrl G	7	7	7	2	50	62	32	]	93	135	5D
Ctrl H	8	10	8	3	51	63	33	^	94	136	5E
Ctrl I	9	11	9	4	52	64	34	_	95	137	5F
\n	10	12	A	5	53	65	35	`	96	140	60
Ctrl K	11	13	B	6	54	66	36	a	97	141	61
Ctrl L	12	14	C	7	55	67	37	b	98	142	62
RETURN	13	15	D	8	56	70	38	c	99	143	63
Ctrl N	14	16	E	9	57	71	39	d	100	144	64
Ctrl O	15	17	F	:	58	72	3A	e	101	145	65
Ctrl P	16	20	10	;	59	73	3B	f	102	146	66
Ctrl Q	17	21	11	<	60	74	3C	g	103	147	67
Ctrl R	18	22	12	=	61	75	3D	h	104	150	68
Ctrl S	19	23	13	>	62	76	3E	i	105	151	69
Ctrl T	20	24	14	?	63	77	3F	j	106	152	6A
Ctrl U	21	25	15	@	64	100	40	k	107	153	6B
Ctrl V	22	26	16	A	65	101	41	l	108	154	6C
Ctrl W	23	27	17	B	66	102	42	m	109	155	6D
Ctrl X	24	30	18	C	67	103	43	n	110	156	6E
Ctrl Y	25	31	19	D	68	104	44	o	111	157	6F
Ctrl Z	26	32	1A	E	69	105	45	p	112	160	70
Esc	27	33	1B	F	70	106	46	q	113	161	71
Ctrl <	28	34	1C	G	71	107	47	r	114	162	72
Ctrl /	29	35	1D	H	72	110	48	s	115	163	73
Ctrl =	30	36	1E	I	73	111	49	t	116	164	74
Ctrl -	31	37	1F	J	74	112	4A	u	117	165	75
Space	32	40	20	K	75	113	4B	v	118	166	76
!	33	41	21	L	76	114	4C	w	119	167	77
"	34	42	22	M	77	115	4D	x	120	170	78
#	35	43	23	N	78	116	4E	y	121	171	79
$	36	44	24	O	79	117	4F	z	122	172	7A
%	37	45	25	P	80	120	50	{	123	173	7B
&	38	46	26	Q	81	121	51	|	124	174	7C
'	39	47	27	R	82	122	52	}	125	175	7D
(	40	50	28	S	83	123	53	~	126	176	7E
)	41	51	29	T	84	124	54	del	127	177	7F
*	42	52	2A	U	85	125	55				

C Namespaces

A new feature introduced as part of the ANSI/ISO draft C++ standard is the concept of namespaces, which essentially is a rather simple principle. A **namespace** is a space of code (that is a section) that must be enclosed in braces, can include only definitions or other namespaces, and is given an explicit name. For example, the following section of code consists of two namespaces, named `screen` and `printer`, respectively, in which each namespace consists of a single definition statement.

```
namespace screen   // the keyword namespace is required
{
  int lines = 5;
}  // end of screen namespace

namespace printer  // the keyword namespace is required
{
  int lines = 10;
}  // end of printer namespace
```

Notice that the namespace concept simply provides a means of explicitly naming a blocked section of definition statements. As such, namespaces are really scoping mechanisms that are used to clearly identify variables within different blocks of code. The only restriction on a namespace, however, is that it can consist only of definition statements and additional internally nested namespaces. The naming of the blocked code provides a means of identifying different variables that may have the same name but reside in different namespaces. This identification is accomplished by prefixing every variable name with its namespace name and the scope resolution operator, `::`. To illustrate how this is accomplished, consider Program C.1.

PROGRAM C.1

```
#include <iostream>

namespace screen
{
      int lines = 5;
}  // end of screen namespace

namespace printer
{
   int lines = 10;
}  // end of printer namespace

int main()
{
      std::cout << "\nThe screen lines are: "
               << screen::lines << std::endl;
      std::cout <<"\nThe printer lines are: "
               << printer::lines;
      std::cout << std::endl;

      return 0;
}
```

In Program C.1, notice first that we have used the new style C++ header without the `.h` suffix. Each of these new C++ headers are members of a namespace named `std`, which is short for standard. Thus, whenever an identifier defined in this header is used, such as `cout` and `endl`, it must also be preceded by its namespace name and the scope resolution operator, as in `std::cout` and `std::endl`. This is the case also for the variables named `lines` defined in the namespaces `screen` and `printer`. To clearly identify which `lines` variable is being accessed, it must be preceded by its namespace name and the scope resolution operator. The output produced when Program C.1 is executed is:

```
The screen lines are: 5
The printer lines are: 10
```

The need to constantly append `std::` to each standard library identifier can be quite annoying, although it may someday become the conventional programming style, for a reason that we will explain shortly. To avoid constantly including the `std::` prefix, however, you can either use the old style .h header files, as we have done throughout the text, or include the following statement after the #include <iostream> header:

```
using namespace std;
```

This statement declares the namespace std as a default, and any variables in this namespace can now be used without the std:: prefix. Note that we could also use the statement using namespace screen; at any point after the screen namespace has been defined. Then, whenever the variable lines is encountered, it will refer to the screens::lines variable. However, if the statement using namespace printer; were also used, a conflict would arise when the variable lines is used. The compiler will flag this with a "using ambiguous symbol" error message.

Clearly, the using statement effectively defeats the explicit scope naming provided by namespaces. Because the primary motivation for namespaces was to avoid the possibility of scoping conflicts, especially as more and more third-party libraries become available, the convention for writing C++ programs may eventually be to always include the namespace name when a standard library component is used. Finally, all namespaces must appear at file scope or immediately within another namespace. C++ now considers file scope as effectively another namespace, so the terms **file scope** and **global namespace scope** are synonymous.

D The Standard Template Library

A driving force behind object-oriented programming was the desire to create easily reusable source code. For example, recreating source code each time an array or queue is needed wastes both time and programming effort, in addition to the extra time required for fully testing and verifying code that may be only minimally modified. Suppose, for example, that a single program needs to use three arrays; an array of characters, an array of integers, and an array of double-precision numbers. Rather than coding three different arrays, it makes more sense to implement each array from a single, fully tested generic array class that comes complete with methods and algorithms for processing the array, such as sorting, inserting, finding maximum and minimum values, locating values, randomly shuffling values, copying arrays, comparing arrays, and dynamically expanding and contracting the array, as needed. This generic type of data structure, which is referred to as a **container,** forms the basis of the Standard Template Library (STL). In addition to providing seven types of generic data structures, one of which is the array container class (which is formally referred to as the vector container class), the STL provides methods and algorithms for appropriately operating on each of its generic data structures.

This generic programming approach for the STL was initially provided by Hewlett-Packard Corporation in 1994, and has subsequently been incorporated as part of the ANSI/ISO recommendations for inclusion into C++'s Standard Library.[1] In addition to the STL, the Standard Library provides two other major sections, which are:

- **Input/Output headers:** These provide support for conversions between text and encoded data, and input and output to external files. More specifically these headers

1 The initial Hewlett-Packard STL developers were Alexander Stepanov and Meng Lee, with major contributions made by David Musser.

consist of <fstream>, <iomanip>, <ios>, <iosfwd>, <iostream>, <istream>, <ostream>, <stream>, <streambuf>, and <strstream>.

- **Other Standard C++ headers:** These include language support for common type definitions, such as <limits>; diagnostic components for reporting exceptional conditions, such as <stdexcept>; string components for string classes, which are provided by <string>; and the 18 additional Standard C Library headers.

The **Standard Template Library**, which is the third major section of the Standard Library, is divided into the following three categories:

- **Containers**, which are the template classes from which individual data structures can be constructed. By definition, a **container** is an STL template class that manages a sequence of elements. There currently are seven container classes that are used to construct vector, list, deque, stack, queue, set, and map data structures.
- **Algorithms**, which are template functions that provide useful search, sort, location, and other numeric functions that can be applied to the various data structures created from the container classes.
- **Iterators**, which can be considered as generalized pointers for keeping track of the beginning, ending, and other positions within a data structure. Specifically, iterators are used to keep track of the first and last positions in a data structure and for establishing the boundaries of sequences of elements to which an algorithm is applied.

Table D.1 lists the 13 headers provided by the Standard Template Library. As seen, seven of the headers are container types, which are used to create data structures; three of the headers are concerned with providing algorithmic capabilities; and three of the headers are concerned with providing iterator capabilities.

In its most general usage, one or more container classes are first used to create the desired construct data structures. Once these desired data structures have been created, both class methods and algorithms, which are always constructed as functions, can be applied to them. Iterators, which act like generalized pointers, are used as arguments by all of the algorithms to determine and keep track of which elements in the data structure are to be operated upon.

To make this more tangible and provide a meaningful introduction to using the STL, we use the vector container class to create two vectors: one for holding integers and one for holding characters. A vector is similar to a C++ array, except that it can automatically expand and contract as needed. We then use two vector methods and two algorithms to operate on the instantiated vectors. Specifically, we use one method to change an existing element value and another to insert an element within each vector. We then use the first algorithm to sort the elements in each vector and the second algorithm used to randomly

TABLE D.1 Standard template headers

Name	Type	Description
<algorithm>	algorithm	defines numerous function templates that implement algorithms
<functional>	algorithm	defines templates required by <algorithm> and <numeric>
<numeric>	algorithm	defines several function templates that implement numeric functions
<deque>	container	defines a template class that implements a deque container
<list>	container	defines a template class for implementing a list container
<map>	container	defines template classes for implementing associative containers
<queue>	container	defines a template class for implementing a queue container
<set>	container	defines template classes for implementing associative containers having unique elements
<stack>	container	defines a template class for implementing a stack container
<vector>	container	defines a template class for implementing a vector container
<iterators>	iterator	defines templates for defining and manipulating iterators
<memory>	iterator	defines templates for allocating and freeing container class memory storage
<utility>	iterator	defines several general utility templates

reshuffle each vector's elements. After applying each method and algorithm, we use a `cout` object to display the results. To see how this is accomplished, consider Program D.1.

PROGRAM D.1

```
#include <iostream>
#include <vector>
#include <algorithm>
using namespace std;

int main()
{
  const int NUMELS = 5;
  int a[NUMELS] = {1,2,3,4,5};
  char b[NUMELS] = {'a','b','c','d','e'};
  int i;
    // instantiate an integer and character vector
```

(continued next page)

(continued from previous page)

```
  // using a constructor to set the size of each vector
  // and initialize each vector with values
vector<int> x(a, a + NUMELS);
vector<char> y(b, b + NUMELS);

cout << "\nThe vector x initially contains the elements: " << endl;
for (i = 0; i < NUMELS; i++)
  cout << x[i] << "  ";
cout << "\nThe vector y initially contains the elements: " << endl;
for (i = 0; i < NUMELS; i++)
  cout << y[i] << "  ";

  // instantiate two ostream objects
ostream_iterator<int> outint(cout, "  ");
ostream_iterator<char> outchar(cout, "  ");

  // modify elements in the existing list
x.at(3) = 6;    //set element at position 3 to a 6
y.at(3) = 'f'; // set element at position 3 to an 'e'
  // add elements to the end of the list
x.insert(x.begin() + 2,7);  // insert a 7 at position 2
y.insert(y.begin() + 2,'g'); // insert an f at position 2

cout << "\n\nThe vector x now contains the elements: "  << endl;
copy(x.begin(), x.end(), outint);
cout << "\nThe vector y now contains the elements: " << endl;
copy(y.begin(), y.end(), outchar);

  //sort both vectors
sort(x.begin(), x.end());
sort(y.begin(), y.end());

cout << "\n\nAfter sorting, vector x's elements are: "  << endl;
copy(x.begin(), x.end(), outint);
cout << "\nAfter sorting, vector y's elements are:" << endl;
copy(y.begin(), y.end(), outchar);

  // random shuffle the existing elements
```

(continued next page)

(continued from previous page)

```
    random_shuffle(x.begin(), x.end());
    random_shuffle(y.begin(), y.end());

    cout << "\n\nAfter random shuffling, vector x's elements are:"  << endl;
    copy(x.begin(), x.end(), outint);
    cout << "\nAfter random shuffling, vector y's elements are:" << endl;
    copy(y.begin(), y.end(), outchar);

    cout << endl;
    return 0;
}
```

In Program D.1, first notice the inclusion of the three header files <iostream>, <vector>, and <algorithm> with the `using namespace std;` statement.[2] Here we need the <iostream> header to create and use the `cout` stream; the <vector> header to create one or more vector objects; and the <algorithm> header for the two algorithms we will be using, named `sort()` and `random_shuffle()`.

The two statements in Program D.1 that are used to create and initialize each vector are:

```
vector<int> x(a, a + NUMELS);
vector<char> y(b, b + NUMELS);
```

Here, the vector `x` is declared as a vector of type `int` and is initialized with elements from array `a` starting with the first element of the array, located at address `a`, which contains the element `a[0]`, and ending with the element at location `a + NUMELS`, which contains the element `a[NUMELS - 1]`. Thus, the vector `x` now has a size sufficient for five integers and has been initialized with the values 1, 2, 3, 4, and 5. Similarly, vector `y` now has an exact size for five characters and has been initialized with the values a, b, c, d, and e. The next set of statements in Program D.1 displays the initial values in each vector, using standard subscripted vector notation that is identical to the notation used for accessing array elements. Displaying the vector values in this manner, however, requires knowing how many elements each vector contains. As we insert and remove elements, we would like the vector class itself to keep track of where the first and last elements are; this capability is, in fact, automatically provided by two iterator methods furnished for each vector, named `begin()` and `end()`. Before using these two functions, we construct two iterator

---

2 Review Appendix C for the purpose of the `using namespace std;` statement.

dependent output objects for making the output display of elements rather simple, by using the statements:

```
ostream_iterator<int> outint(cout, "  ");
ostream_iterator<char> outchar(cout, "  ");
```

As we will see momentarily, the `outint` and `outchar` objects (the two names are programmer selected) can be used to display all vector values contained between two iterators with two spaces provided between each value, before the value is placed on the `cout` stream.

The next major set of statements:

```
 // modify elements in the existing list
x.at(3) = 6;    //set element at position 3 to a 6
y.at(3) = 'f'; // set element at position 3 to an 'e'
  // add elements to the end of the list
x.insert(x.begin() + 2,7);  // insert a 7 at position 2
y.insert(y.begin() + 2,'g'); // insert an f at position 2
```

is used to both modify existing vector values and insert a new value into each vector. Specifically, the `at()` method requires an integer value for its argument, and the `insert()` method requires an iterator and the value to be inserted as arguments. More specifically, the `at()` argument of 3 indicates that the fourth element in each vector will be changed (remember that vectors, like arrays, begin at index position 0). This means that the value 4, which is in the fourth position in the integer array, will be changed to a 6, and the value `'d'` in the character array will be changed to an `'f'`. The `insert()` method is then used to insert values of 7 and `'g'` in the third position for both vectors. Notice that, like pointers, iterator arithmetic is allowed. Because the `begin()` method returns the iterator value corresponding to the start of the vector, adding 2 to it points to the third position in the array. It is at this position that the new value is inserted with all subsequent values moved up by one position in the vector; the vector automatically expanding to accept the inserted value. At this point in the program, the vector `x` now contains the elements:

```
1  2  7  3  6  5
```

and the vector `y` now contains the elements:

```
a  b  g  c  f  e
```

For vector `x`, this arrangement was obtained by replacing the original value of 4 with a 6 and then inserting a 7 in the third position, which moved all subsequent elements up by one position and increased the total vector size to accommodate six integers. A similar process resulted in the arrangement shown for vector y's elements. To have the program display these elements, the statements:

```
cout << "\n\nThe vector x now contains the elements: "  << endl;
copy(x.begin(), x.end(), outint);
cout << "\nThe vector y now contains the elements: " << endl;
copy(y.begin(), y.end(), outchar);
```

were used. The `copy()` algorithm uses two iterators, which are the values returned by the `begin()` and `end()` methods to delimit the beginning and ending positions to copy. In this case a copy of each complete vector is made to the `outint` and `outchar` objects, respectively. These objects are standard output objects, so the values placed on them are displayed on the screen, suitably interspaced with two spaces between each element. Finally, the last section of code used in Program D.1 uses the `sort()` and `random_shuffle()` algorithms to first sort the elements in each vector and then randomly shuffle them. Notice that both of these algorithms use iterator values to determine the sequence of elements to be operated upon. After each algorithm is applied, the `copy()` algorithm is once again used to force an output display. Following is the complete output produced by Program D.1:

```
The vector x initially contains the elements:
1  2  3  4  5
The vector y initially contains the elements:
a  b  c  d  e

The vector x now contains the elements:
1  2  7  3  6  5
The vector y now contains the elements:
a  b  g  c  f  e

After sorting, vector x's elements are:
1  2  3  5  6 7
After sorting, vector y's elements are:
a  b  c  e  f  g

After random shuffling, vector x's elements are:
6  5  1  3  7  2
After random shuffling, vector y's elements are:
e  a  f  c  g  b
```

E Solutions to Selected Odd-Numbered Exercises

Exercises 1.1

1. a. A **console application** is a character based Visual C++ program that can only obtain its input as a series of characters, from either the keyboard or a data file, and that can write its output only as a series of characters, either to a printer, console screen, or data file.

   b. **Event-driven** means that control as to what action a program takes depends on the user's selection of an object displayed on the screen.

   c. A **computer program** is a structured combination of data and instructions that is used to operate a computer.

   d. A **programming language** is the set of instructions, data, and rules that can be used to construct a computer program.

   e. A **high-level language** is a programming languages that uses instructions that resemble a written language, such as English, and can be translated to run on a variety of computer types.

   f. A **low-level language** is a programming language that uses instructions that are directly tied to one type of computer. They consist of machine-level and assembly languages.

   g. An **interpreter** is a program that translates individual source program statements, one at a time, into executable statements. Each statement is executed immediately after translation.

h. A **compiler** is a program that is used to translate a high-level source program as a complete unit before any one statement is actually executed.

i. A **procedure** is a logically consistent set of instructions that produce a specific result.

j. A **procedure-oriented language** has instructions that are used to create procedures.

k. An **object-oriented language** permits the construction of objects, that can be manipulated and displayed. Such languages are gaining increasing usage in graphical-oriented programs.

l. A **graphical user interface** is the screen that a user used to interface with a Windows-based program.

m. **MFC** is the Microsoft Foundation Class, which is a library of prewritten object-oriented code that provides the ability to quickly produce Windows-based programs.

3. The MFC provides the foundation for quickly producing Windows-based programs.

Exercises 1.2

1. a. The **IDE,** or Integrated Development Environment, provides a centralized environment under which all program development, from editing source code and visual elements, to compilation and production of an executable program, can be completed.

   b. A **context-sensitive menu** provides shortcuts to frequently performed actions for the designated item for which the menu is activated.

   c. An **MDI,** or Multiple Document Interface, is an interface consisting of a parent window that can contain multiple child windows.

   d. **Docking** is the ability of a window to be aligned and attached to other windows, which ensures that each window remains visible and accessible.

   e. An **application** refers to a computer program that can be run under a Windows operating system.

   f. A **project** refers to the complete set of files needed to build an executable program, including all user-entered source code files and graphical elements.

   g. A **project workspace** refers to the main folder under which all subfolders and files related to a specific project are stored.

3. a. A Win32 Console Application should be used when constructing a character-based application.

   b. A Win32 Application should be used when creating a Windows-based application that will use C-style functions for graphical effects and window control.

c. An MFC AppWizard(exe) project type should be used when creating a Windows-based application that will use MFC for graphical effects and the general framework for the application is to be constructed using the AppWizard.

Exercises 1.3

1. ClassView and FileView tabs are displayed.

3. a. The Files tab

b. A file name for the new source code file and its location (path) must be provided.

5. Yes, a complete project can be removed by deleting the project's folder (and all subfolders) from the Explorer's tree structure.

Exercises 1.4

1. a. One possible solution:

Make sure the car is parked, the engine is off, and the key is out of the ignition switch.

Go to the trunk.

Put the correct key into the trunk.

Open the trunk.

Remove the spare tire and the jack.

Put the jack under the car . . . and so on.

b. Go to a phone.

Remove the handset from the phone.

Wait for the dial tone.

Take out the correct change for the call.

Put the correct change into the phone.

Dial the number.

c. Arrive at the store.

Walk through the door.

Go to the bread aisle.

Select the desired bread.

Go to the cashier.

Pay for the bread and leave.

d. Prepare the turkey.

Preheat the oven.

Open the oven door.

Put the turkey in the oven.

Close the oven door.

Wait the appropriate time for the turkey to cook.

3. Step 1: Pour the contents of the first cup into the third cup.

Step 2: Rinse out the first cup.

Step 3: Pour the contents of the second cup into the first cup.

Step 4: Rinse out the second cup.

Step 5: Pour the contents of the third cup into the second cup.

5. Step 1: Compare the first number with the second number and use the smallest of these numbers for the next step.

Step 2: Compare the smallest number found in step 1 with the third number. The smallest of these two numbers is the smallest of all three numbers.

7. a. Step 1: Compare the first name in the list with the name Jones. If the names match, stop the search; else go to step 2.

Step 2: Compare the next name in the list with the name Jones. If the names match, stop the search; else repeat this step.

Exercises 2.1

1. `m1234()` Valid. Not a mnemonic
`power()` Valid. A mnemonic
`add_5()` Valid. A mnemonic
`cosine()` Valid. A mnemonic
`oldBalance()` Valid. A mnemonic
`newBal()` Valid. A mnemonic
`absVal()` Valid. A mnemonic
`taxes()` Valid. A mnemonic
`a2b3c4d5()` Valid. Not a mnemonic
`newValue()` Valid. A mnemonic
`abcd()` Valid. Not a mnemonic
`mass()` Valid. A mnemonic

`netPay()` Valid. A mnemonic
`net$Pay()` Valid. Invalid. Violates Rule 2; contains a special character.
`salestax()` Valid. A mnemonic
`A12345()` Valid. Not a mnemonic
`do()` Invalid. Violates Rule 3; is a keyword.
`12345()` Invalid. Violates Rule 1; starts with a number.
`amount()` Valid. A mnemonic
`1stApprox()` Invalid. Violates Rule 1; starts with a number.
`1A2345()` Invalid. Violates Rule 1; starts with a number.
`while()` Invalid. Violates Rule 3; is a keyword.
`int()` Invalid. Violates Rule 3; is a keyword.
`$sine` Invalid. Violates Rule 1; starts with a special character.
`float()` Invalid. Violates Rule 3; is a keyword.

3. a. These functions might be used to determine and display the area of a rectangular.

b. The `getLength()` and `getWidth()` functions should come first (in either order), followed by the `calcArea()` function as the third function called, and followed by the `displayArea()` function as the last function called.

5. a. `void main()` or `void main(void)`

b. `char main()` or `char main(void)`

c. `float main()` or `float main(void)`

d. `double main()` or `double main(void)`

7. a.
```
#include <iostream.h>
int main()
{
  cout << "Computers, computers everywhere" << endl;
  cout << "   as far as I can see" << endl;
  cout << "I really, really like these things," << endl;
  cout << "  Oh joy, Oh joy for me!" << endl;

  return 0;
}
```

This can also be constructed as:

```
#include <iostream.h>
int main()
{
  cout <<   "Computers, computers everywhere\n"
       << "   as far as I can see\n"
       << "I really, really like these things,\n"
       << "  Oh joy, Oh joy for me!" << endl;
  return 0;
}
```

9. The two operations are a line feed to bring the cursor down one line, and a carriage return to bring the cursor to the first column of the current line.

Exercises 2.2

1. **a.** Yes.
   b. It is not in standard form. To make programs more readable and easier to debug, the standard form presented in Section 2.2 of the text should be used.

3. **a.** Two backslashes in a row causes one backslash to be displayed.
   b. `cout << "The escape sequence \\ will produce a backslash." << endl;`

Exercises 2.3

1. **a.** float or double
   b. integer
   c. float or double
   d. integer
   e. float or double
   f. characters

3. `1.26e2  6.5623e2  3.42695e3  4.8932e3   3.21e-1  1.23e-2 6.789e-3`

5. All of the operands given are integers, so the result of each expression is an integer value.
   a. `3 + 4 * 6 = 3 + 24 = 27`
   b. `3 * 4 / 6 + 6 = 12 / 6 + 6 = 2 + 6 = 8`
   c. `2 * 3 / 12 * 8 / 4 = 6 / 12 * 8 / 4 = 0 * 8 / 4 = 0 / 4 = 0`
   d. `10 * ( 1 + 7 * 3) = 10 * (1 + 21) = 10 * 22 = 220`
   e. `20 - 2 / 6 + 3 = 20 - 0 + 3 = 23`
   f. `20 - 2 / (6 + 3) = 20 - 2 / 9 = 20 - 0 = 20`
   g. `(20 - 2) / 6 + 3 = 18 / 6 + 3 = 3 + 3 = 6`
   h. `(20 - 2) / (6 + 3) = 18 / 9 = 2`
   i. `50 % 20 = 10`
   j. `(10 + 3) % 4 = 13 % 4 = 1`

7. **a.** `10.0 + 15 / 2 + 4.3 = 10.0 + 7 + 4.3 = 21.3`
   b. `10.0 + 15.0 / 2 + 4.3 = 10.0 + 7.5 + 4.3 = 21.8`
   c. `3.0 * 4 / 6 + 6 = 12.0 / 6 + 6 = 2.0 + 6.0 = 8.0`
   d. `3 * 4.0 / 6 + 6 = 12.0 / 6 + 6 = 2.0 + 6 = 8.0`
   e. `20.0 - 2 / 6 + 3 = 20.0 - 0 + 3 = 23.0`
   f. `10 + 17 * 3 + 4 = 10 + 51 + 4 = 65`
   g. `10 + 17 / 3.0 + 4 = 10 + 5.6666667 + 4 = 19.6666667`
   h. `3.0 * 4 % 6 + 6 = 12.0 % 6 + 6 = invalid expression`
   i. `10 + 17 % 3 + 4 = 10 + 2 + 4 = 16`

11. answer1 is the integer 2
answer2 is the integer 5

13.
```
#include <iostream.h>
int main()
{
  cout << "3.0 * 5.0 = " << 3.0*5.0 << endl;
  cout << "7.1 * 8.3 - 2.2 = " << 7.1 * 8.3 - 2.2 << endl;
  cout << "3.2 / (6.1 * 5) = " << 3.2 / (6.1*5) << endl;

  return 0;
}
```

15.

	K	I	N	G	S	L	E	Y
a.	01001011	01001001	01001110	01000111	01010011	01001100	01000101	01011001

19. **a.** `'m' - 5 = 'h'`
b. `'m' + 5 = 'r'`
c. `'G' + 6 = 'M'`
d. `'G' - 6 = 'A'`
e. `'b' - 'a' = 1`
f. `'g' - 'a' + 1 = 6 + 1 = 7`
g. `'G' - 'A' + 1 = 6 + 1 = 7`

Exercises 2.4

1. The following are invalid:

`12345`	does not begin with either a letter or underscore
`$total`	does not begin with either a letter or underscore
`new$al`	contains a special character
`9ab6`	does not begin with either a letter or underscore
`sum.of`	contains a special character

3. **a.** `int count;`
b. `float volt;`
c. `double power;`
d. `char keychar;`

5. **a.** `int firstnum, secnum;`
b. `float speed, acceleration, distance;`
c. `double maturity;`

7. **a.**
```
#include <iostream.h>  // includes the iostream.h header file
int main() // function header line
{  // start of function body
  int num1, num2, total; //declare the integer variables num1, num2, and total
```

```
    num1 = 25;     // assign the integer 25 to num1
    num2 = 30;     // assign the integer 30 to num2
    total = num1 + num2;  // assign the sum of num1 and num2 to total
    cout << "The total of " << num1 << " and " // displays:
         << num2 << " is " << total << endl;  // The total of 25 and 30 is 55.

      Return 0;  // returns control to the operating system
  } // end of function body
```

b. `The total of 25 and 30 is 55.`

9. a.

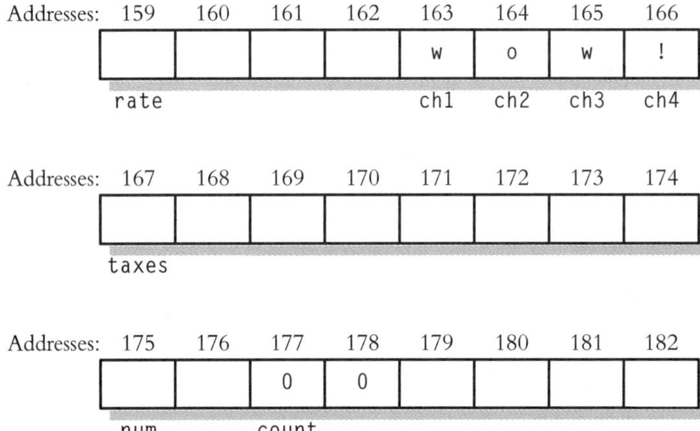

The empty addresses above are usually filled with zeros or garbage values, meaning their contents are whatever happened to be placed there by the computer or by the previously run program.

b. `ch1=01110111`
`ch2=01101111`
`ch3=01110111`
`ch4=00100001`

11. `miles` begins at address 159
`count` begins at address 163
`num` begins at address 165
`dist` begins at address 167
`temp` begins at address 175

Exercises 2.5

3. The amount of storage reserved for each data type does not depend on the value actually stored into the reserved memory locations.

Exercises 3.1

1. a. `c = 2 * 3.1416 * 3.3;`
   b. `a = 3.1416 * 3.3 * 3.3;`

3. a.
```
#include <iostream.h>
int main()
{
      <-- missing declaration for all variables
  width = 15     <-- missing semicolon
  area = length * width; <-- no value assigned to length
  cout << "The area is " << area <-- missing ;
       <-- missing return statement
}
```

The corrected program is:

```
#include <iostream.h>
int main()
{
  int length, width, area;
  width = 15;
  length = 20;    // must be assigned some value
  area = length * width;
  cout << "The area is " << area;

  return 0;
}
```

b.
```
#include <iostream.h>
int main()
{
  int length, width, area;

  area = length * width; <-- this should come after the
  length = 20;               assignment of values to length and width
  width = 15;
  cout << "The area is  \n" << area;
       <-- missing return statement
}
```

The corrected program is:

```
#include <iostream.h>
int main()
{
  int length, width, area;

  length = 20;
  width = 15;
  area = length * width;
  cout << "The area is  \n" << area;
  return 0;
}
```

c.
```
#include <iostream.h>
int main()
{
  int length = 20, width = 15, area;

  length * width = area;  <-- incorrect assignment statement
  cout << "The area is  \n" << area;
      <-- missing return statement
}
```

The corrected program is:

```
#include <iostream.h>
int main()
{
  int length = 20, width = 15, area;

  area = length * width;
  cout << "The area is  \n" << area;

  return 0;
}
```

5.
```
Length    Width      Area
 1.62      6.23    10.0962
 2.86      7.52    21.5072
 4.26      8.95    38.127
 8.52     10.86    92.5272
12.29     15.35   188.6515
```

7. a.
```
#include <iostream.h>
int main()
{
  float radius, circum;

  radius = 3.3;   // could have been done in the declaration
  circum = 2 * 3.1416 * radius;
  cout << "The circumference is " << circum
       << "inches" << endl;

  return 0;
}
```

9. a.
```
#include <iostream.h>
int main()
{
  float length, width, depth, volume;

  length = 25.0;
  width = 10.0;
  depth = 6.0;
  volume = length * width * depth;
  cout << "The volume of the pool is " << volume << endl;

  return 0;
}
```

11. a.
```
#include <iostream.h>
int main()
{
  float  total;

   total = 12*.50 + 20*.25 + 32*.10 + 45*.05 + 27*.01;
   cout << "The total amount is $ " <<  total << endl;
   return 0;
}
```

13. a.
```
#include <iostream.h>
int main()
{
  float speed = 58.0, dist = 183.67, time;

  time = dist/speed;
  cout << "The elapsed time for the trip is " << time
       << " hours" << endl;

  return 0;
}
```

15. The second expression is correct because the assignment of `25` to `b` is done before the subtraction. Without the parentheses the subtraction has the higher precedence, and the expression `a - b` is calculated, yielding a value, assume 10. The subsequent attempt to assign the value of `25` to this value is incorrect, and is equivalent to the expression `10 = 25`. Values can be assigned only to variables.

Exercises 3.2

1.
```
answer1 is the integer 5
answer2 is the integer 2
```

5. a. The double quote after the 2nd insertion symbol should come before the insertion symbol and the parentheses at the end of the statement should be a semicolon.

b. The `setw(4)` manipulator should not be enclosed in double quotes.

c. The `setprecision(5)` manipulator should not be enclosed in double quotes.

d. The statement should be `cout << "Hello World!";`.

e. The `setw(6)` manipulator should appear before the insertion of the number `47`.

f. The `setprecision(2)` manipulator should appear before the insertion of the number `526.768`.

7. a.
```
The number is  26.27
The number is 682.30
The number is   1.97
```

b. `26.27`

```
682.30
  1.97
------
710.54
```

c.
```
 26.27
682.30
  1.97
------
710.54
```

d.
```
36.16
10.00
-----
```

Exercises 3.3

1. **a.** `sqrt(6.37)`
   b. `sqrt(x-y)`
   c. `sin(30.0 * 3.1416 / 180.0)`
   d. `sin(60.0 * 3.1416 / 180.0)`
   e. `abs(pow(a,2.0) - pow(b,2.0))` or `abs(a*a - b*b)`
   f. `exp(3.0)`

3. **a.** `c = sqrt(pow(a,2) + pow(b,2));`
   or
   `c = sqrt(a*a + b*b);`
   b. `p = sqrt(abs(m - n));`
   c. `sum = a * (pow(r,n) - 1) / (r - 1);`

5.
```
#include <iostream.h>
#include <math.h>
int main()
{
  float dist, x1 = 7.0, y1 = 12.0 , x2 = 3.0 , y2 = 9.0;

  dist = sqrt(pow((x1-x2),2.0) + pow((y1-y2),2.0));
  cout << "The distance is " << dist << endl;
  return 0;
}
```

7. **a.** `h`
   b. `r`
   c. `M`
   d. `A`

Exercises 3.4

1. a. `cin >> firstnum;`
   b. `cin >> grade;`
   c. `cin >> secnum;`
   d. `cin >> keyval;`
   e. `cin >> month >> years >> average;`
   f. `cin >> num1 >> num2 >> grade1 >> grade2`
   g. `cin >> interest >> principal >> capital >> price >> yield;`
   h. `cin >> ch >> letter1 >> letter2 >> num1 >> num2 >> num3;`
   i. `cin >> temp1 >> temp2 >> temp3 >> volts1 >> volts2;`

3.
```
#include <iostream.h>
int main()
{
  float radius, circum;

  cout << "Enter the radius of a circle: ";
  cin  >> radius;
  circum = 2.0 * 3.1416 * radius;
  cout << "The circumference is " <<  circum << endl;

  return 0;
}
```

5. a.
```
#include <iostream.h>
int main()
{
  float num, total, average;

  total = 0;
  cout << "Enter a number: ";
  cin >> num;
  total = total + num;
  cout << "Enter a second number: ";
  cin >> num;
  total = total + num;
  cout << "Enter a third number: ";
  cin >> num;
  total = total + num;
  cout << "Enter a fourth number: ";
  cin >> num;
  total = total + num;
  cout << "The average is " << total / 4.0 << endl;

  return 0;
}
```

Exercises 3.5

1.
```
#include <iostream.h>  // this line may be placed second instead of first
#include <math.h>      // this line may be placed first instead of second
int main()
{
  const float GRAV = 32.2
  int height;
  double time;

  height = 800;
  time = sqrt(2 * height / GRAV);
  cout << "It will take " << time << " seconds to fall "
       << height << " feet." << endl;

  return 0;
}
```

3.
```
#include <iostream.h>
int main()
{
   const float PRIME_RATE = .08;
   float amount, interest;
   cout << "Enter the amount: ";
   cin  >> amount;
   interest = PRIME_RATE * amount;
   cout << "The interest earned is $" << interest
        << " dollars" << endl;

   return 0;
}
```

Exercises 4.1

1. **a.** The relational expression is true. Therefore, its value is 1.
   b. The relational expression is true. Therefore, its value is 1.
   c. The final relational expression is true. Therefore, its value is 1.
   d. The final relational expression is true. Therefore, its value is 1.
   e. The final relational expression is true. Therefore, its value is 1.
   f. The arithmetic expression has a value of 10, which is true, so !10 is false and has a value of 0.
   g. The arithmetic expression has a value of 4, which is true, so !4 is false and has a value of 0.
   h. The arithmetic expression has a value of 0, which is false, so !0 is true and has a value of 1.
   i. The arithmetic expression has a value of 10.

3. a. `age == 30`
   b. `temp > 98.6`
   c. `ht < 6.00`
   d. `month == 12`
   e. `letterIn == 'm'`
   f. `age == 30  ht > 6.00`
   g. `day == 15  month == 1`
   h. `age > 50 || employ >= 5`
   i. `id < 500  age > 55`
   j. `len > 2.00  len < 3.00`

Exercises 4.2

1. a.
```
if (angle == 90)
  cout <<"The angle is a right angle";
else
  cout <<"The angle is not a right angle";
```
   b.
```
if (temperature > 100)
  cout <<"above the boiling point of water";
else
  cout <<"below the boiling point of water";
```
   c.
```
if (number > 0)
  possum = number + possum;
else
  negsum = number + negsum;
```
   d.
```
if (slope < .5)
   flag = 0;
else
   flag = 1;
```
   e.
```
if ((num1 - num2) < .001)
   approx = 0;
else
   approx = (num1 - num2) / 2.0;
```
   f.
```
if ((temp1 - temp2) > 2.3)
   error = (temp1 - temp2) * factor;
```
   g.
```
if ((x > y) && (z < 20))
   cin >> p;
```
   h.
```
if ((distance > 20) && (distance < 35))
   cin >> time;
```

3.
```
#include <iostream.h>
int main()
{
  const float LIMIT = 20000.0;
  const float REGRATE = 0.02;
  const float HIGHRATE = 0.025;
  const float FIXED = 400.0;
  float taxable, taxes;
```

```
    cout << "Please type in the taxable income: ";
    cin  >> taxable;
    if (taxable <= LIMIT)
      taxes = REGRATE * taxable;
    else
      taxes = HIGHRATE * (taxable - LIMIT) + FIXED;
   cout << "\n\nTaxes are $ " << taxes << endl;
  return 0;
  }
```

5. a.
```
#include <iostream.h>
int main()
{
  float grade;

  cout << "Enter a grade: " ;
  cin >> grade;

  if (grade >= 70.0)
    cout << "A passing grade\n";
  else
    cout << "A failing grade\n";

    return 0;
}
```

b. At least three runs should be made: one input greater than 70.0, one at 70.0, and one less than 70.0. Another run, if necessary, might be made for some unexpected input, such as "seventy."

7. a.
```
#include <iostream.h>
int main()
{
   char ch;

   cout << "Enter a letter: ";
   cin >> ch;

   if (ch == 'u' || ch == 'U')
     cout << "I feel great today!" << endl;
   else
     cout << "I feel down today!" << endl;

   return 0;
}
```

b. At least three runs should be made: one input using a *u*, one using a *U*, and one using some other letter. Another run, if necessary, might be made for some unexpected input, such as 5.

9.
```
#include <iostream.h>
int main()
{
   char inKey;
```

```
    cout << "Enter a lowercase letter: ";
    cin >> inKey;
    if (inKey >= 'a' && inKey <= 'z')
      cout << "The character just entered is a lowercase letter\n";
    else
      cout << "The character just entered is not a lowercase letter\n

    return 0;
}
```

11.
```
#include <iostream.h>
int main()
{
    char inKey;

    cout << "Enter an uppercase letter: ";
    cin >> inKey;
    if (inKey >= 'A' && inKey <= 'Z')
      cout << "The character just entered is an uppercase letter\n";
    else
      cout << "The character just entered is not an uppercase letter\n

    return 0;
}
```

13.
```
#include <iostream.h>
int main()
{
      char inKey, outKey;

      cout << "Enter a letter: ";
      cin >> inKey;
      if (inKey >= 'a' && inKey <= 'z')
        outKey = char(inKey - 32);
        else
          outKey = inKey;
      cout << "This letter, as an uppercase letter is "
              << outKey <<  endl;

      return 0;
  }
```

15.
```
#include <iostream.h>
int main()
{
   float num1, num2;

   cout << "Enter a number: ";
   cin  >> num1;
   cout << "Enter another number: ";
   cin  >> num2;
   if (num1 > num2)
       cout << "The first number is greater.\n";
   else
       cout << "The first number is not greater.\n";

   return 0;
}
```

If the two numbers entered are equal, the else statement will be executed, which would not be a true statement.

Exercises 4.3

1.
```
#include <iostream.h>
int main()
{
  char marcode;
  cout << " Enter a martial code: ";
  cin  >> marcode;

  if (marcode == 'M' || marcode == 'm')
    cout << "Individual is married.\n";
  else if (marcode == 'S' || marcode == 's')
    cout << "Individual is single.\n";
  else if (marcode == 'D' || marcode == 'd')
    cout << "Individual is divorced.\n";
  else if (marcode == 'W' || marcode == 'w')
    cout << "Individual is widowed.\n";
  else
    cout << "An invalid code was entered.\n";
  cout << "Thanks for participating in the survey\n";

  return 0;
}
```

3.
```
#include <iostream.h>
int main()
{
  float angle;

  cout << "Enter the angle: ";
  cin  >> angle;
  if (angle < 90.0)
    cout << "The angle is acute." << endl;
  else if (angle == 90.0)
    cout << "The angle is a right angle." << endl;
  else if (angle > 90.0)
    cout << "The angle is obtuse." << endl;

  return 0;
}
```

5.
```
#include <iostream.h>
int main()
{
  float grade;
  char letter;

  cout << "Enter the student's numerical grade: ";
  cin  >> grade;
  if (grade >= 90.0) letter = 'A';
  else if (grade >= 80.0) letter = 'B';
```

```
    else if (grade >= 70.0) letter = 'C';
    else if (grade >= 60.0) letter = 'D';
    else letter = 'F';
    cout << "The student receives a grade of " << letter << endl;

    return 0;
  }
```

Notice that an `if-else` chain is used. If simple `if` statements were used, a grade entered as 75.5, for example, would be assigned a `'C'` because it was greater than 70.0. But, the grade would then be reassigned to `'D'` because it is also greater than 60.0.

7.

```
#include <iostream.h>
int main()
{
  float fahr, cels, inTemp;
  char letter;

  cout << "Enter a temperature followed by";
  cout << " one space and the temperature's type" << endl;
  cout << " (an f designates a fahrenheit temperature";
  cout << "  and a c designates a celsius temperature): ";
  cin  >> inTemp >> letter;
  if (letter == 'f' || letter == 'F')
  {
    cels = (5.0/9.0)*(inTemp - 32.0);
    cout << inTemp << " degrees Fahrenheit = "
         << cels << " degrees Celsius" << endl;
  }
  else if (letter == 'c' || letter == 'C')
  {
    fahr = (9.0/5.0)*inTemp + 32.0;
    cout << inTemp << " degrees Celsius = "
         << fahr << " degrees Fahrenheit" << endl;
  }
  else
    cout << "The data entered is invalid." << endl;

  return 0;
}
```

9. a. This program will run. It will not, however, produce the correct result.

b. & c. This program evaluates correct incomes for `monthlySales` less than 20000.00 only. If 20000.00 or more were entered, the first `else-if` statement would be executed and all others would be ignored. That is, for 20000.00 or more, the income for >= 10000.00 would be calculated and displayed. Had `if` statements been used in place of the `else-if` statements, the program would have worked correctly, but inefficiently (see comments for Exercise 5).

Exercises 4.4

1.
```
switch (letterGrade)
{
  case 'A':
    cout << "The numerical grade is between 90 and 100";
    break;
  case 'B':
    cout << "The numerical grade is between 80 and 89.9";
    break;
  case 'C':
    cout << "The numerical grade is between 70 and 79.9";
    break;
  case 'D':
    cout << "How are you going to explain this one";
    break;
  default:
    cout << "Of course I had nothing to do with the grade.";
    cout << "It must have been the professor's fault.\n";
}
```

3.
```
#include <iostream.h>
int main()
{

  int mfgcode;

  cout << "Enter the manufacture's code: ";
  cin >> mfgcode;
  switch (mfgcode)
  {
    case 1:
      cout << "3M Corporation" << endl;
      break;
    case 2:
      cout << "Maxell Corporation" << endl;
      break;
    case 3:
      cout << "Sony Corporation" << endl;
      break;
    case 4:
      cout << "Verbatim Corporation" << endl;
      break;
    default:
      cout << "Incorrect Code" << endl;
      break;
   }

   return 0;
}
```

5. The expression in the `switch` statement must evaluate to an integer quantity and be tested for equality. The `if-else` chain in Program 4.6 uses floating point values and inequalities, violating both of the `switch` statement's requirements.

Exercises 5.2

1.
```
#include <iostream.h>
int main()
{
  int count = 2;

  while (count <= 10)
  {
    cout << count << " ";
    count = count + 2;
  }

  return 0;
}
```

3. a. 21 items are displayed, which are the integers from 1 to 21

   c. 21 items are displayed, which are the integers from 0 to 20

5.
```
#include <iostream.h>
#include <iomanip.h>
int main()
{
  int feet;
  float meters;

  cout << "FEET      METERS" << endl;
  cout << "----      ------" << endl;
  feet = 3;

  while (feet <= 30)
  {
    meters = feet / 3.28;
    cout << setiosflags(ios::fixed)
       << setiosflags(ios:: showpoint);
    cout << setw(3) << feet
       << setw(11) << setprecision(2)
       << meters << endl;
    feet = feet + 3;
  }

  return 0;
}
```

7.
```
#include <iostream.h>
#include <iomanip.h>
int main()
{
  float time, miles;
  cout << "TIME      MILES" << endl;
  cout << "----      -----" << endl;
  time = .5;
```

```
    while (time <= 4)
    {
      miles = 55 * time;
      cout << setiosflags(ios::fixed)
         << setiosflags(ios::showpoint);
      cout << setw(4) << setprecision(1) << time
         << setw(10) << setprecision(2) << miles << endl;
      time = time + .5;
    }

    return 0;
  }
```

Exercises 5.3

1. The only modification that needs to be made is to change the named constant MAXNUMS to be equal to 8 instead of 4.

3. a.

```
#include <iostream.h>
#include <iomanip.h>
int main()
{
  float cels, fahr, incr;
  int num, count = 0;

  cout << "Enter the starting temperature ";
  cout << "in degrees Celsius: ";
  cin  >> cels;
  cout << "Enter the number of conversions to be made: ";
  cin  >> num;
  cout << "Now enter the increment between conversions ";
  cout << "in degrees Celsius: ";
  cin  >> incr;
  cout << "\nCelsius     Fahrenheit" << endl;
  cout << "----------------------" << endl;
  while (count <= num)
  {
    fahr = (9.0/5.0) * cels + 32.0;
    cout << setiosflags(ios::fixed)
         << setiosflags(ios::showpoint)
         << setprecision(2);
    cout << setw(6) << cels
         << setw(14)<< fahr << endl;
    cels = cels + incr;
    count++;
  }

  return 0;
}
```

5. The only modification that needs to be made is to change the named constant `MAXNUMS` to be equal to 10 instead of 4.

7. This program still calculates the correct values, but the average is now calculated four times. Because only the final average is desired, it is better to calculate the average once outside of the `while` loop.

9. a.
```
#include <iostream.h>
int main()
{
  const int MAXBOOKS =3;
  int id, inven, income, outgo, bal, count;

  count = 1;
  while (count <= MAXBOOKS)
  {
    cout << "\nEnter book ID: ";
    cin  >> id;
    cout << "\nEnter inventory at the beginning of the month: ";
    cin  >> inven;
    cout << "\nEnter the number of copies received during the month: ";
    cin  >> income;
    cout << "\nNow enter the number of copies sold during the month: ";
    cin  >> outgo;
    bal = inven + income - outgo;
    cout << "\n\nBook #" << id << " new balance is " << bal;
    count++;
  }

  return 0;
}
```

Exercises 5.4

1. a. `for ( i = 1; i <= 20; i++)`

b. `for (icount = 1; icount <= 20;  icount = icount + 2)`

c. `for (j = 1; j <= 100; j = j + 5)`

d. `for (icount = 20; icount >= 1; icount--)`

e. `for (icount = 20; icount >= 1; icount = icount - 2)`

f. `for (count = 1.0; count <= 16.2; count = count + 0.2)`

g. `for (xcnt = 20.0; xcnt >= 10.0; xcnt = xcnt - 0.5)`

3. a. 10

b. 1024

c. 75

d. –5

e. 40320

f. 0.03125

5.

```
#include <iostream.h>
#include <iomanip.h>
const int MAXNUM = 20;
const int INCREMENT = 2;

int main()
{
  int num;

  cout << "NUMBER    SQUARE    CUBE\n"
       << "------    ------    ----" << endl;
  for (num = 0; num <= MAXNUM; num += INCREMENT)
    cout << setw(3) << num << "        "
         << setw(3) << num * num << "      "
         << setw(4) << num * num * num << endl;

  return 0;
}
```

7.

```
#include <iostream.h>
#include <iomanip.h>
const int MAXCOUNT = 20;
const float INITFAHR = 20.0;
const float INCREMENT = 4.0;

int main()
{
  int count;
  float fahr, celsius;

  cout << "Fahrenheit      Celsius\n";
       << "----------      -------" << endl;
  cout << setiosflags(ios::fixed)
       << setiosflags(ios::showpoint);

  for (INITFAHR = 20.0, count = 1; count <= MAXCOUNT; count++)
  {
    celsius = (5.0 / 9.0) * (fahr - 32.0);
    cout << setw(6) << setprecision(1) << fahr
         << setw(16) << setprecision(2) << celsius << endl;

    fahr += INCREMENT;
  }

  return 0;
}
```

9. a.
```
#include <iostream.h>
#include <iomanip.h>
int main()
{
  float celsius, fahr, incr;
  int num, count = 0;

  cout << "Enter the starting temperature ";
  cout << "in degrees Fahrenheit: ";
  cin  >> fahr;
  cout << "Enter the number of conversions to be made: ";
  cin  >> num;
  cout << "Now enter the increment between conversions ";
  cout << "in degrees Fahrenheit: ";
  cin  >> incr;

  cout << "Fahrenheit      Celsius\n";
      << "----------      -------" << endl;

  while (count <= num)
  {
    celsius = (5.0 / 9.0) * (fahr - 32.0);
    cout << setw(6) << setprecision(1) << fahr
         << setw(16) << setprecision(2) << celsius << endl;
    fahr = fahr + incr;
    count++;
  }

  return 0;
}
```

11.
```
#include <iostream.h>
int main()
{
  const int MAXNUMS = 10;
  const float CONVERT = 3.785;

  int i;
  float gallons, liters;

  for(i = 1; i <= MAXNUMS; i++)
  {
    cout << "Enter the number of gallons: ";
    cin  >> gallons;
    cout << "The equivalent number of liters is "
         << CONVERT * gallons << endl;
  }

  return 0;
}
```

13. The program will not compile because the variable `i` is redefined in the second `for` statement. Replacing this statement with the statement `for(i = 1; i < 5; i++)` produces the output:

```
1
2
3
4
1
2
```

15. a.
```
#include <iostream.h>
#include <iomanip.h>
int main()
{
  const int YEARS = 10;
  int yr;
  float amount, total;

  cout << setiosflags(ios::fixed)
       << setiosflags(ios::showpoint)
       << setprecision(2);

  cout << "Enter the initial amount deposited: ";
  cin >> amount;

  for (yr = 1; yr <= YEARS; yr++)
  {
    amount = amount * 1.08;
    cout << "The balance at the end of " << yr << " year(s) is $"
         << amount << endl;
  }

  return 0;
}
```

Exercises 5.5

1.
```
#include <iostream.h>
const int EXPERS = 4;
const int RESULTS = 6;
int main()
{
  int i, j;
  float total, avg, data;

  for (i = 1; i <= EXPERS; ++i)
  {
    cout << "Enter " << RESULTS << " results for experiment #" << i << ": ";
      for (j = 1, total = 0.0; j <= RESULTS; ++j)
      {
        cin >>  data;
        total += data;
      }
      avg = total/RESULTS;
      cout << "   The average for experiment #" << i << " is " << avg << endl;
  }
```

```
  return 0;
}
```

Note: When entering data for each experiment, the six individual results may be entered on one line with a space between each entry, on six individual lines, or any combination of these.

3. a.
```
#include <iostream.h>
#include <iomanip.h>
int main()
{
  const int BOWLERS =5;
  cont int GAMES = 3;
  int bowler, game;
  float score, plyrTot, plyrAvg, teamTot, teamAvg;

  for(bowler = 1, teamTot = 0; bowler <= BOWLERS; bowler++)
  {
    for(game = 1, plyrTot = 0; game <= GAMES; game++)
    {
      cout << endl;
      cout << "Enter the score for bowler " << bowler << " game "<< game << ": ";
      cin  >> score;
      plyrTot = plyrTot + score;
    }
    teamTot = teamTot + plyrTot;
    plyrAvg = plyrTot/GAMES;
    cout << "   The average for bowler " << bowler << " is "
         << setiosflags(ios::showpoint) << setw(5)
         << setprecision(2) << plyrAvg << endl;
  }
  teamAvg = teamTot/ (BOWLERS * GAMES);
  cout << "The average for the whole team is "
       << setiosflags(ios::showpoint) << setw(5)
       << setprecision(2) << teamAvg;
}
```

5.
```
#include <iostream.h>
#include <iomanip.h>
#include <math.h>

int main()
{
  const float SMALLDIF = 0.00001;
  float x, y, z;

  cout << setiosflags(ios::fixed)
       << setiosflags(ios::showpoint)
       << setprecision(2);
  cout << "   x         z          y    \n"
       << "-------  -------   -------" << endl;
  for (x = 1.0; x <= 5.0; x += 1)
```

```
    for (z = 2.0; z <= 6.0; z += 1)
      if (fabs(x - z) > SMALLDIF)
      {
          y = x * z / (x - z);
          cout << setw(6) << x
               << setw(6) << z
               << setw(6) << y << endl;
      }
      else
      cout << setw(6) << x
           << setw(6) << z
           << " Function Undefined" << endl;

  return 0;
}
```

7.
```
#include <iostream.h>
#include <iomanip.h>
int main()
{
  long sal;
  int dep;
  float deduct;

  cout << "           |<---------------------- Deducti";
  cout << "ons ----------------------->|\n";
  cout << " Salary    |  0          1          2       ";
  cout << "   3         4          5   |\n";
  cout << "--------   --------   --------   --------   ";
  cout << "--------   --------   --------\n";
  for(sal = 10000L; sal <= 50000L; sal += 10000L)
  {
    cout << sal << "    ";
    for(dep = 0; dep <= 5; dep++)
    {
      deduct =  dep * 500 + 0.05 * (50000L - sal);
      cout << "     " << setw(5) << deduct;
    }
    cout << endl;
  }

  return 0;
}
```

Exercises 5.6

1. a.
```
#include <iostream.h>
int main()
{
  const int LOWGRADE = 0;
  const int HIGHGRADE = 100;
  int grade;
```

```
    do
    {
      cout << "Enter a grade: ";
        cin  >>  grade;
    } while (grade < LOWGRADE || grade > HIGHGRADE);
       cout << "\nThe grade entered is " << grade << endl;

    return 0;
  }
```

b.

```
#include <iostream.h>
int main()
{
  const int LOWGRADE = 0;
  const int HIGHGRADE = 100;
  int grade;

  do
  {
    cout << "Enter a grade: ";
    cin  >>  grade;
    if (grade < LOWGRADE || grade > HIGHGRADE)
     cout << "Invalid grade - please retype it.\n";
  } while (grade < LOWGRADE || grade > HIGHGRADE);
    cout << "\nThe grade entered is " << grade << endl;

   return 0;
}
```

c.

```
#include <iostream.h>
int main()
{
  const int LOWGRADE = 0;
  const int HIGHGRADE = 100;
  const int SENTINEL = 999;
  int grade;

  do
  {
    cout << "Enter a grade: ";
    cin  >>  grade;
      if (grade == SENTINEL)
         return 0;
    else if (grade < LOWGRADE || grade > HIGHGRADE)
        cout << "Invalid grade - please retype it.\n";
  } while (grade < LOWGRADE || grade > HIGHGRADE);
  cout << "\nThe grade entered is " << grade << endl;

  return 0;
}
```

d.

```
#include <iostream.h>
int main()
{
  const int LOWGRADE = 0;
  const int HIGHGRADE = 100;
  int grade, badGrade = 0;
```

```
    do
    {
      cout << "Enter a grade: ";
      cin  >>  grade;
      if (grade < LOWGRADE || grade > HIGHGRADE)
      {
        badGrade;++
        if (badGrade == 5)
          return 0;
        else
              cout << "Invalid grade - please retype it.\n";
      }
    } while (grade < LOWGRADE || grade > HIGHGRADE);
    cout << "\nThe grade entered is " << grade << endl;

    return 0;
  }
```

3. a.
```
#include <iostream.h>
int main()
{
  int num, digit;

  cout << "Enter an integer: ";
  cin  >>  num;
  cout << "The number reversed is: ";
  do
  {
    digit = num % 10;
    num /= 10;
    cout << digit;
  } while (num > 0);

  return 0;
}
```

Exercises 5.9

1.
```
#include <iostream.h>
#include <iomanip.h>
#include <stdlib.h>
#include <time.h>
int main()
{
  int heads = 0;  // initialize heads count;
  int tails = 0;   // initialize tails count;
  int i, tosses;
  float flip, perheads, pertails;

  cout << "Enter the number of tosses: ";
  cin  >> tosses;

  srand(time(NULL));
```

```
  for (i = 1; i <= tosses; ++i)
  {
    flip = float(rand())/RAND_MAX;  // scale the number
                                    // between 0 and 1;
    if (flip > 0.5)
      heads = heads + 1;
    else
      tails = tails + 1;
  }
  perheads = (heads / (float)tosses) * 100.0;
  pertails = (tails / (float)tosses) * 100.0;
  cout << "\nHeads came up " << perheads << " percent of the time\n";
  cout << "Tails came up " << pertails << " percent of the time\n";

  return 0;
}
```

3.

```
#include <iostream.h>
#include <iostream.h>
#include <stdlib.h>
#include <time.h>
const int NUMSELS = 1000;  // number of random no. selections
int main()
{
  int i;
  float rnum, factor;
  int zerocount, onecount, twocount, threecount;
  int fourcount, fivecount, sixcount, sevencount;
  int eightcount, ninecount, val;

  zerocount = onecount = twocount = threecount = fourcount = 0;
  fivecount = sixcount = sevencount = eightcount = ninecount = 0;

  srand(time(NULL));

  for (i = 1; i <= NUMSELS; ++i)
  {
    rnum = rand();
    val = int(rnum/RAND_MAX * 10);
    switch (val)
    {
      case 0:
      ++zerocount;
      break;
      case 1:
      ++onecount;
      break;
      case 2:
      ++twocount;
      break;
      case 3:
      ++threecount;
      break;
      case 4:
      ++fourcount;
```

```
            break;
            case 5:
            ++fivecount;
            break;
            case 6:
            ++sixcount;
            break;
            case 7:
            ++sevencount;
            break;
            case 8:
            ++eightcount;
            break;
            case 9:
            ++ninecount;
          }
        }
        factor = 100.0 / NUMSELS;
        cout << " Zeros: " << zerocount * factor << " percent\n";
        cout << " Ones: "<<onecount * factor << " percent\n";
        cout << " Twos:  " << twocount * factor << " percent\n";
        cout << " Threes: " << threecount * factor << " percent\n";
        cout << " Fours: " << fourcount * factor << " percent\n";
        cout << " Fives: " << fivecount * factor << " percent\n";
        cout << " Sixes: " << sixcount * factor << " percent\n";
        cout << " Sevens: " << sevencount * factor << " percent\n";
        cout << " Eights: " << eightcount * factor << " percent\n";
        cout << " Nines: " << ninecount * factor << " percent\n";

        return 0;
      }
```

Exercises 6.1

1. a. `factorial()` expects to receive one integer value.

b. `price()` expects to receive one integer and two double precision values, in that order.

c. An integer and two double precision values, in that order, must be passed to `yield()`.

d. A character and two floating point values, in that order, must be passed to `inter-est()`.

e. Two floating point values, in that order, must be passed to `total()`.

f. Two integers, two characters, and two floating point values, in that order, are expected by `roi()`.

g. Two integers and two character values, in that order, are expected by `getVal()`.

3. a. The `FindAbs()` function is included in the program written for Exercise 3b.

b.
```
#include <iostream.h>
void FindAbs(double);  // function prototype
```

```
int main()
{
  double dnum;

  cout << "Enter a number: ";
  cin  >> dnum;
  FindAbs(dnum);

  return 0;
}
void FindAbs(double num)
{
  double val;

  if (num < 0)
    val = -num;
  else
    val = num;
  cout << "The absolute value of " << num << " is " << val << endl;

  return;
}
```

5. a. The `squareIt()` function is included in the program written for Exercise 5b.

b.
```
#include <iostream.h>
void squareIt(double);  // function prototype
int main()
{
  double first;

  cout << "\nEnter a number: ";
  cin  >> first;
  squareIt(first);

  rcturn 0;
}
void squareIt(double num)
{
  cout << "The square of " << num << " is " << (num*num) << endl;

  return;
}
```

7. a. The function for producing the required table is included in the larger program written for Exercise 7b.

b.
```
#include <iostream.h>
#include <iomanip.h>
void table();            // function prototype

int main()
{
  table();               // call the function
}
```

```
void table()
{
  int num;

  cout << endl
       << "NUMBER    SQUARE    CUBE\n"
       << "------    ------    ----\n";

  for (num = 1; num <= 10; num++)
    cout << setw(3) << num << "         "
         << setw(3) << num * num << "       "
         << setw(4) << num * num * num << endl;
}
```

9. The function is included within the context of a complete program.

```
#include <iostream.h>
#include <iomanip.h>
#include <math.h>
double PI(); // function prototype

int main()
{

  cout << setiosflags(ios::fixed | ios::showpoint)
       << setprecision(15);
  cout << "The value of pi is " << PI() << endl;

  return 0;

}

double PI()
{
`     return (2.0 * asin(1.0));
}
```

11. a. The required function template is included within the complete program created for Exercise 11b.

b.
```
#include <iostream.h>

template <class T>
int whole(T value)
{
   return int(value);
}

int main()
{
  char code = 'a';
  int num1 = 5;
  float num2 = -6.23;
  double num3 = 7.23456;
```

```
    cout << "The integer value of " << code << " is "
         << whole(code) << endl;
    cout << "The integer value of " << num1 << " is "
         << whole(num1) << endl;
    cout << "The integer value of " << num2 << " is "
         << whole(num2) << endl;
    cout << "The integer value of " << num3 << " is "
         << whole(num3) << endl;

    return 0;
  }
```

13. **a.** The required function template is included within the complete program created for Exercise 13b.

  b.
```
#include <iostream.h>

template <class T>
T square(T value)
{
   return (value * value);
}

int main()
{

  int num1 = 5;
  float num2 = -6.23;
  double num3 = 7.23456;

  cout << "The square of " << num1 << " is "
       << square(num1) << endl;
  cout << "The square of " << num2 << " is "
       << square(num2) << endl;
  cout << "The square of " << num3 << " is "
       << square(num3) << endl;

  return 0;
}
```

Exercises 6.2

1. **a.** `void check(int num1, float num2, double num3)`
   b. `double FindAbs(double x)`
   c. `float Mult(float first, float second)`
   d. `int squareIt(int number)`
   e. `int powfun(int num, int exponent)`
   f. `void table(void)` or `void table()`

3. **a.** The `Mult()` function is included in the program written for Exercise 3b.

b.
```
#include <iostream.h>
double Mult(double, double);    // function prototype
int main()
{
  double first, second;

  cout << "Please enter a number: ";
  cin  >> first;
  cout << "Please enter another number: ";
  cin  >>  second;
  cout << "The product of these numbers is "
       << Mult(first,second) << endl;

  return 0;
}

double Mult(double num1, double num2)
{
  return (num1*num2);
}
```

5. a. The `Hypotenuse()` function is included in the program written for Exercise 5b.

b.
```
#include <iostream.h>
#include <math.h>
float Hypotenuse(float, float); // function prototype

int main()
{
  float a, b;

  cout << "Enter the length of one side of a Right triangle: ";
  cin  >> a;
  cout << "Enter the length of the second side: ";
  cin  >> b;

  cout << "The hypotenuse of this Right triangle is "
       << Hypotenuse(a, b) << endl;

  return 0;
}

float Hypotenuse(float a, float b)
{
  return sqrt(a * a + b * b);
}
```

7. The polynomial function is included in the following working program:

```
#include <iostream.h>
float PolyTwo(float, float, float, float); //function prototype

int main()
{
  float a, b, c, x, result;
  cout << "Enter the coefficient for the x squared term : ";
```

```
    cin  >> a;
    cout << "Enter the coefficient for x : ";
    cin  >> b;
    cout << "Enter the constant: ";
    cin  >> c;
    cout << "Enter the value for x: ";
    cin  >> x;
    result = PolyTwo(a, b, c, x);
    cout << "\nThe result is " <<  result;

    return 0;
  }

  float PolyTwo(float c1, float c2, float c3, float x)
  {
    return (c1*x*x + c2*x + c3);
  }
```

9. a. The `Round()` function is included in the program written for Exercise 9b.

b.
```
#include <math.h>
float Round(float, int); // function prototype

int main()
{
  const float INTRATE = 8.675;
  float a, n;

  cout << "Enter the amount of money: ";
  cin  >> a;

  cout << a << " times " << INTRATE << " is "
       << Round(a * INTRATE,2) << endl;

  return 0;
}

float Round(float a, int n)
{
  return (int(a * pow(10,n) + 0.5)/pow(10,n));
}
```

11. a. The `fracpart()` function is included in the program written for Exercise 11b.

b.
```
#include <iostream.h>
double fracpart(double);  // function prototype
int whole(double);        // function prototype

int main()
{
  double num;

  cout << "Enter a number: ";
  cin  >> num;
  cout << "\nThe fraction part of " << num
       << " is " << fracpart(num) << endl;
```

```
  return 0;
}

double fracpart(double x)
{
  return (x - whole(x));
}

int whole(double n)
{
  int a;

  a = n;   // a = int (n) is preferred - see Section 3.3
  return a;
}
```

An implementation for `fracpart()` that does not relay on calling `whole()` is

```
double fracpart(double num)
{
  return (num - long(num));
}
```

Exercises 6.3

1. a. `float &amount;`

b. `double &price;`

c. `int &minutes;`

d. `char &key;`

e. `double &yield;`

3.

```
#include <iostream.h>
int main()
{
  int firstnum, secnum, max;
  void FindMax(int, int, int &);  // function prototype

  cout << "Enter a number: ";
  cin  >>  firstnum;
  cout << "\nGreat! Please enter a second number: ";
  cin  >>  secnum;

  FindMax(firstnum, secnum, max); // call the function

  cout << "\nThe maximum of the two numbers is " << max << endl;

  return 0;
}
```

```
void FindMax(int x, int y, int &maxval)
{
  if (x >= y)
   maxval = x;
  else
   maxval = y;
 return;
}
```

5. The `time()` function is provided within the context of the following complete program:

```
void time(int totSecs, int &hours, int &mins, int &secs)
{
  hours = totSecs/3600; // 3600 seconds = 1 hour
                        // Integer division yields the whole
                        // number of times 3600 goes into
                        // totSecs
  totSecs -= hours * 3600;
  mins = totSecs/60;
  totSecs -= mins * 60;
  secs = totSecs;
  return;
}
```

7. The `liquid()` function is provided within the context of the following complete program:

```
#include <iostream.h>
void liquid(int, int& , int& , int& , int& );  // function prototype
int main()
{
  int totCups;
  int gallons = 0, quarts = 0, pints = 0, cups = 0;

  cout << "Enter the total number of cups: ";
  cin  >> totCups;
  liquid(totCups, gallons, quarts, pints, cups);
  cout << "\nThe number of gallons is " << gallons;
  cout << "\nThe number of quarts is " << quarts;
  cout << "\nThe number of pints is " << pints;
  cout << "\nThe number of cups is " << cups << endl;

  return 0;
}

void liquid(int totCups, int& gallons, int& quarts, int& pints, int& cups)
{
  while(totCups >= 16)      // while at least a gallon
  {
    ++gallons;              // add one to the gallon count
    totCups = totCups - 16; // subtract out a gallon
  }
  while(totCups >= 4)      // while at least a quart
  {
    ++quarts;              // add one to the quart count
```

```
      totCups = totCups - 4; // subtract out a quart
    }
    while(totCups >= 2)      // while at least a pint
    {
      ++pints;               // add one to the pint count
      totCups = totCups - 2; // subtract out a pint
    }
    cups = totCups;          // remaining cups


    return;
  }
```

In place of the `while` loops, `for` loops could be used. For example, the following `for` loop could be used to replace the first `while` loop:

```
for( ; totCups >= 16; gallons++, totCups -= 16)
  ;    // The Null statement is necessary
```

One of C++'s advantages is its ability to be written in many forms. Although more difficult to understand, the following function is much more compact and would produce less machine code because of the elimination of the four loops.

```
void liquid(int totCups, int& gallons, int& quarts, int& pints, int& cups)
{
    gallons = totCups/16;      // gallons is the number of times 16 goes
                               // into the total amount of cups evenly
    totCups -= gallons * 16;   // adjust the total cups to the cups remaining
    quarts = totCups/4;
    totCups -= quarts * 4;
    pints = totCups/2;
    totCups -= pints * 2;
    cups = totCups;            // cups = what's left over
  }
```

This last function makes use of the fact that integer assignment yields an integer. For example if `totCups = 47`, the statement

```
gallons = totCups/16
```

results in the variable `gallons`, which is a reference to the variable `gallons` in `main()`, being two. Then,

```
totCups -= gallons * 16
```

yields `15` as the remaining value for the variable `totCups`.

Exercises 6.4

1. a.

Variable Name	Data Type	Scope
`price`	integer	global to `main()`, `roi()`, and `step()`
`years`	long integer	global to `main()`, `roi()`, and `step()`
`yield`	double-precision	global to `main()`, `roi()`, and `step()`
`bondtype`	integer	local to `main()` only
`interest`	double-precision	local to `main()` only
`coupon`	double-precision	local to `main()` only
`count`	integer	local to `roi()` only
`effectiveInt`	double-precision	local to `roi()` only
`numofyrs`	integer	local to `step()` only
`fracpart`	float	local to `step()` only

Note that although parameters of each function assume a value that is dependent on the calling function, these arguments can change values within their respective functions. This makes them behave as if they were local variables within the called function.

3. All function parameters have local scope with respect to their defined function.

Exercises 6.5

1. a. Local variables may be automatic, static, or register. It is important to realize that not all variables declared inside of functions are necessarily local. An example of this is an external variable.

b. Global variables may be static or external.

3. The first function declares `yrs` to be a `static` variable and assigns a value of one to it only once when the function is compiled. Each time the function is called thereafter, the value in `yrs` is increased by two. The second function also declares `yrs` to be `static`, but assigns it the value one every time it is called, and the value of `yrs` after the function is finished will always be 3. By resetting the value of `yrs` to 1 each time it is called, the second function defeats the purpose of declaring the variable to be `static`.

5. The scope of a variable tells where the variable is recognized in the program and can be used within an expression. If, for example, the variable `years` is declared inside a function, it is local and its scope is inside that function only. If the variable is declared outside of any function, it is global and its scope is anywhere below the declaration but within that file, unless another file of the same program extends the scope of the variable by declaring the variable to be external.

Exercises 7.1

1. Dialog-based, Single Document Interface (SDI), and Multiple Document Interface (MDI).

3. The Controls window, which is also referred to as a toolbox, provides the visual objects we will use in constructing each graphical user interface.

5. A dialog becomes a window.

7. The Dialog (Resource view) and resource editor windows.

9. Create the graphical user interface (GUI), set the properties of each object on the interface, and write the code.

Exercises 7.2

1. a. An event handler is a function that is executed when an event occurs, such as the clicking of a Command button.

b. A dialog box is a box that requests user input. A modal dialog requires input before an application can continue, whereas a modeless box permits shifting the focus from the box and allows an application to continue without the box being closed.

c. A method is a procedure that is connected to an object.

d. A property is a named attribute of an object. Properties define object characteristics, such as size, color, screen location, and the state of an object, such as enabled or disabled.

3. The click procedures would be named

```
void CWinpgm7_1Dlg::OnFirstButton()
void CWinpgm7_1Dlg::OnSecondButton()
```

The double click procedures would be named

```
void CWinpgm7_1Dlg::OnDoubleclickedFirstButton()
void CWinpgm7_1Dlg::OnDoubleclickedSecondButton()
```

Exercises 7.3

7. To receive focus, a control must have its `Visible` and `Tab stop` properties checked, and its `Disabled` property not checked.

Exercises 7.5

1. **a.** Check box because it is a Yes/No selection.
   b. Radio buttons because it is really a choice between two different types of transmissions. It could, however, be constructed using a Check box with the No choice corresponding to the default transmission type.
   c. Radio buttons
   d. Check box
   e. Radio buttons
   f. Check box
   g. Radio buttons
   h. Radio buttons

3. **b.** A Check box can always be replaced by two Command buttons, where one button selects the choice and one button deselects the choice. Any choice that can be represented as a selection between two alternatives states is best presented using a Check box. Command buttons are more useful in initiating actions, such as Begin Processing and End Processing.

Exercises 8.1

5. Yes. Anything stored on disk is referred to as a file. The two major divisions of files are data files and executable (program) files. Although source code files are sometimes called program files, strictly speaking they are data files used by a compiler program. A compiled C++ program is an example of an executable file.

7. **a.**
```
ofstream memo;
memo.open("coba.mem");
```
   b.
```
ofstream letter;
letter.open("book.let");
```
   c.
```
ofstream coups;
coups.open("coupons.bnd");
```
   d.
```
ifstream ptYield;
ptYield.open("yield.bnd");
```
   e.
```
ifstream priFile;
priFile.open("test.dat");
```
   f.
```
ifstream rates;
rates.open("rates.dat");
```

Exercises 8.2

1. a.

```
#include <fstream.h>
#include <stdlib.h>
const int MAXCHARS = 80;
int main()
{
   int i;
   ofstream out;
   char strng[MAXCHARS];

   out.open("text.dat");
   if (out.fail())
   {
     cout << "The file was not successfully opened" << endl;
     exit(1);
   }
   cout << "Enter three lines of text to be stored in the file.\n";
     for (i = 1; i <= 3; i++)
   {
     cin.getline(strng, MAXCHARS, '\n');  // get input from cin stream
     out << strng << endl;
   }
   out.close();
   cout << "End of data input.\n"
        << "The file has been written." << endl;

   return 0;
 }
```

b.

```
#include <fstream.h>
#include <stdlib.h>
const int MAXCHARS = 80;
int main()
{
  int ch;
  char line[MAXCHARS];
  ifstream inFile;

  inFile.open("text.dat");
  if (!inFile)   // check for successful open
  {
    cout << "\nThe file was not successfully opened"
         << "\n Please check that the file currently exists."
         << endl;
    exit(1);
  }
      // now read the file
  while( (ch = inFile.peek()) != EOF )
  {
    inFile.getline(line, MAXCHARS,'\n');
    cout << line << endl;
  }
```

```
  return 0;
}
```

3.
```
#include <fstream.h>
#include <stdlib.h>

int main()
{
  const int MAXCHARS = 7;
  const int DATAITEMS = 4;
  char filename[MAXCHARS] = "result";

  int i;
  float number, total, average;
  ifstream inFile;

  outFile.open(filename);
  if (outFile.fail())
  {
    cout << "The file was not successfully opened" << endl;
    exit(1);
  }

  outFile << 92.65 << ' ' << 88.72 << ' '
          << 77.46 << ' ' << 82.93 << endl;
  outFile.close();
  cout << "The data has been written to the file named "
       << filename << endl;

  inFile.open(filename);
  if (!inFile)   // check for successful open
  {
    cout << "\nThe file" <<filename << " was not successfully opened"
         << "\n Please check that the file currently exists."
         << endl;
    exit(1);
  }
      // now read each data item and add it to the total
  total = 0;
  cout << "The data read from the file is: ";
  for (i = 1; i <= DATAITEMS; i++)
  {
    inFile >> number;
    cout << number << "  ";
    total += number;
  }
  average = total / DATAITEMS;
  cout << "/nThe average is " << average << endl;

  return 0;
}
```

Note: In writing the four numbers to the file, it is necessary to separate the numbers by at least one space. If no spaces are placed between the numbers (or they are not written on separate lines) the data in the file will be 92.6588.7277.4682.93. If these data are then read in as four numbers, the numbers read from the file will be 92.6588, .7277, .4682, and .93. Alternatively, the output could also have been written using the statement

```
outFile << "92.65 88.72 77.46 82.93" << endl;
```

5. a.
```
#include <fstream.h>
#include <stdlib.h>

int main()
{
  const int MAXCHARS = 6;
  char filename[MAXCHARS] = "volts";
  ofstream outFile;

  outFile.open(filename);
  if (outFile.fail())
  {
    cout << "The file was not successfully opened" << endl;
    exit(1);
  }

  outFile << "120.3 122.7 90.3 99.8\n"
          << "95.3 120.5 127.3 120.8\n"
          << "123.2 118.4 123.8 115.6\n"
          << "122.4 95.6 118.2 120.0\n"
          << "123.5 130.2 123.9 124.4" << endl;
  outFile.close();
  cout << "The data has been written to the file named "
       << filename << endl;

  return 0;
}
```

b.
```
#include <fstream.h>
#include <stdlib.h>

int main()
{
  const int MAXCHARS = 6;
  const int DATAITEMS = 4;
  const int RECORDS = 5;
  char filename[MAXCHARS] = "volts";

  int i, j;
  float voltage, total, average;
  ifstream inFile;

  inFile.open(filename);
  if (!inFile)   // check for successful open
  {
    cout << "\nThe file" <<filename << " was not successfully opened"
         << "\n Please check that the file currently exists."
         << endl;
    exit(1);
  }
    // now read each record and obtain the average
  for(i = 1; i <= RECORDS; i++)
```

```
  {
    total = 0;
    cout << "\nThe data for record " << i << " is: ";
    for (j = 1; j <= DATAITEMS; j++)
    {
      inFile >> voltage;
      cout << voltage << "  ";
      total += voltage;
    }

    average = total / DATAITEMS;
    cout << "\n   The average is " << average << endl;
  }

  return 0;
}
```

7. a. The data may be entered in a variety of ways. One possibility is to enter the data, line-by-line, and write each line to a file. A second method is to use a Text editor to write the data to a file. A third possibility is to enter the data as individual items and write the file as individual items. The following program uses the first approach, in which the data are included within the program itself, rather than being entered by the user to the program using `cin` statements before being printed to the file. Note that the header information is not included as part of the file.

```
#include <fstream.h>
#include <stdlib.h>
int main()
{
  const int MAXCHARS = 10;
  char filename[MAXCHARS] = "polar.dat";

  ofstream outFile;

  outFile.open(filename);
  if (outFile.fail())
  {
    cout << "The file was not successfully opened" << endl;
    exit(1);
  }

  outFile << " 2.0   45.0\n"
          << " 6.0   30.0\n"
          << "10.0   45.0\n"
          << " 4.0   60.0\n"
          << "12.0   55.0\n"
          << " 8.0   15.0"
          << endl;
  outFile.close();
  cout << "The data has been written to the file named "
       << filename << endl;

  return 0;
}
```

b.
```
#include <fstream.h>
#include <stdlib.h>
#include <math.h>
int main()
{
  const int MAXCHARS = 10;
  const int RECORDS = 6;
  const float CONVERT = 3.14157 / 180.;  // radian conversion
  char filename[MAXCHARS] = "polar.dat";

  int i, j;
  float distance, angle;
  float x, y;
  ifstream inFile;

  inFile.open(filename);
  if (!inFile)   // check for successful open
  {
    cout << "\nThe file" <<filename << " was not successfully opened"
         << "\n Please check that the file currently exists."
         << endl;
    exit(1);
  }
    // now read each record and convert to cartesian coordinates
  for(i = 1; i <= RECORDS; i++)
  {
    inFile >> distance >> angle;
    cout << "distance = " << distance
         << "  angle = " << angle << endl;
    x = distance * cos(CONVERT * angle);
    y = distance * sin(CONVERT * angle);
    cout << "x = " << x << "  y = " << y << endl;
  }

  return 0;
}
```

Exercises 8.4

1. The filename referred to in the exercise is a reference to an object of type `ifstream`. The function prototype for `pFile()` is `pFile(ifstream&);`.

3. The `getOpen()` function is included below with a driver function used to test it.

```
#include <fstream.h>
#include <stdlib.h>
const int MAXCHARS = 15;
int getOpen(ofstream&);   // function prototype
int main()    // driver function to test fcheck()
{
  ofstream outFile;

  getOpen(outFile);
```

```
  return 0;
}
int getOpen(ofstream& fileOut)
{
  char key, name[MAXCHARS];
  ifstream fileIn;

  cout << "\nEnter a file name: " << endl;
  cin.getline(name, MAXCHARS, '\n');

  fileIn.open(name);
  if (fileIn.fail())
   // the file doesn't exist - create it for writing
       fileOut.open(name);
  else
  {
    fileIn.close;
    cout << "\nThe file currently exists. Do you want to"
         << "\n overwrite it or exit."
         << "\nEnter an o, or e: ";
     cin  >> key;
     if(key == 'o')
        fileOut.open(name);  // now open it for output
     if (fileOut.fail())
    {
      cout << "The output file was not successfully opened" << endl;
      exit(1);
    }
  }
  return 1;
}
```

5. The `countChars()` function is included in the program listed below:

```
#include <fstream.h>
#include <stdlib.h>
const int MAXLENGTH = 15;
void countChars(ifstream&);  // function prototype needed by main()
int main()
{
  ifstream in;
  char fName[MAXLENGTH];

  cout << "\nEnter a file name: ";
  cin  >> fName;
  in.open(fName);
  if (in.fail())   // check for successful open
  {
    cout << "\nThe file was not successfully opened"
         << "\n Please check that the file currently exits."
         << endl;
    exit(1);
  }
  countChars(in);
  in.close();
```

```
  return 0;
}
void countChars(ifstream& fname)
{
  fname.seekg(0L,ios::end);  // move to the end of the file
  cout << "\nThere are " << fname.tellg()
       << " characters in the file.\n";
  return;
}
```

Exercises 9.1

1. **a.** A class is a programmer-defined data type. The class specifies both the types of data and the types of operations that may be performed on the data.
   b. An object is a specific instance of a class.
   c. The declaration section declares both the data types and function prototypes of a class.
   d. The implementation section defines the class's functions.
   e. An instance variable is another name for a class data member.
   f. A member function is a function declared in the class declaration section.
   g. A data member is a variable declared in the class declaration section.
   h. A member function that has the same name as the class and is used to initialize an object's data members is a constructor.
   i. Class instance is synonymous with an object.
   j. Services are synonyms for the functions defined in a class implementation section.
   k. Methods are synonyms for the functions defined in a class implementation section.
   l. The set of attributes and behavior defining a class is referred to as the class's *interface*.
   m. The state of an object defines how the object appears at the moment. It is specified by the values assigned to the object's data member variables.
   n. The behavior of an object defines how the object can be activated and the response that will be produced. It is specified by the object's member and friend functions.

3. Behavior is triggered in an object by calling one of its member functions. The call provides the stimulus that activates the function. The response to the call is whatever the function has been programmed to do.

5. **a.**
```
// implementation section
Time::Time(int hh = 0, int mm = 0, int ss = 0)
{
  hours = hh;
  mins = mm;
  secs = ss;
}
void Time::settime(int hh, int mm, int ss)
```

```
{
  hours = hh;
  mins = mm;
  secs = ss;
}
void Time::showdata()
{
  cout << "The time is "
       << setw(2) << setfill('0') << hours << ':'
       << setw(2) << setfill('0') << mins << ':'
       << setw(2) << setfill('0') << secs << endl;
}
```

b.
```
// implementation section
Complex::Complex(float re = 0, float im = 0)
{
  real = re;
  imaginary = im;
}
void Complex::setvals(float re, float im)
{
  real = re;
  imaginary = im;
}
void Complex::showdata(void)
{
  float c;
  char sign = '+';

  c = imaginary;
  if (c < 0)
  {
    sign = '-';
    c = -c;
  }
  cout << "The complex number is "
       << setiosflags(ios::fixed)
       << real << ' ' << sign << ' ' << c << "i\n";

}
```

c.
```
// implementation section
Circle::Circle(int xx = 1, int yy = 1, float rr = 1.0)
{
  xcenter = xx;
  ycenter = yy;
  radius = rr;
}
void Circle::setvals(int xx, int yy, float rr)
{
  xcenter = xx;
  ycenter = yy;
  radius = rr;
}
void Circle::showdata()
{
  cout << "The center of the circle is at "
```

```
             << '(' << setfill('0') << xcenter << ','
             << setfill('0') << ycenter << ')'
             << " and the radius is " << radius << endl;
    }
```

7. The class name should begin with a capital letter (i.e., `Employee`). The data members should be declared as `private` and the function members should be declared as `public`. Additionally, the declaration for the constructor prototype should be `class(int, char *)`.

Exercises 9.2

1. a. true
   b. false
   c. true
   d. false
   e. true
   f. false
   g. false
   h. true
   i. true
   j. true
   k. false
   l. false
   m. false
   n. true
   o. false

3.
```
#include <iostream.h>

// class declaration
class Date
{
  private:
    long yymmdd;
  public:
    Date(int, int, int);      // constructor
    Date(long);               // default constructor
    void showdate();          // member function to display a Date
};

// implementation section
Date::Date(int mm, int dd, int yy)
{
  yymmdd = yy * 10000L + mm * 100L + dd;
}
```

```
Date::Date(long ymd = 940704)
{
  yymmdd = ymd;
}
void Date::showdate()
{
  int year, month, day;

  year = (int)(yymmdd/10000.0);    // extract the year
  month = (int)( (yymmdd - year * 10000.0)/100.00 ); // extract the month
  day = (int)(yymmdd - year * 10000.0 - month * 100.0); // extract the day
  cout << "The Date is " << month << "/" << day << "/" << year << endl;
}

int main()
{
   Date a, b(4,1,96), c(970515); // declare three objects

   a. showdate();          // display object a's values
   b. showdate();          // display object b's values
   c. showdate();          // display object c's values

   return 0;
}
```

Exercises 9.3

3.

```
#include <iostream.h>
#include <stdlib.h>
#include <time.h>
const int MAXFLOOR = 15;
const int NOMOVE = 0;  // code for no elevator movement
const int MOVEDUP = 1; // code for elevator moved up
const int MOVEDDOWN = 2; // code for elevator moved down
const int MAXREQS = 5;

// class declaration

class Elevator
{
  private:
    int currentFloor;
  public:
    Elevator(int = 1);   // constructor
    int request(int);
};

// implementation section

Elevator::Elevator(int cfloor)
{
  currentFloor = cfloor;
}
```

```
int Elevator::request(int newfloor)
{
  int code;

  if (newfloor < 1 || newfloor > MAXFLOOR || newfloor == currentFloor)
    code = NOMOVE;
  else if ( newfloor > currentFloor)  // move elevator up
  {
      cout << "\nStarting at floor " << currentFloor << endl;
    while (newfloor > currentFloor)
    {
      currentFloor++;     // add one to current floor
      cout << "   Going Up - now at floor " << currentFloor << endl;
    }
    cout << "Stopping at floor " << currentFloor << endl;
    code = MOVEDUP;
  }
  else  // move elevator down
  {
      cout << "\nStarting at floor " << currentFloor << endl;
    while (newfloor < currentFloor)
    {
      currentFloor--;   // subtract one from current floor
      cout << "   Going Down - now at floor " << currentFloor << endl;
    }
    cout << "Stopping at floor " << currentFloor << endl;
    code = MOVEDDOWN;
  }

  return code;
}

int main()
{
  Elevator a;   // declare an object of type Elevator
  int newfloor, moved, requests = 0;

  srand(time(NULL));
  while (requests < MAXREQS)
  {
    newfloor = (1 + rand() % 16);
    moved = a.request(newfloor);
    if (moved)
     requests++;
  }

  return 0;
}
```

5.

```
// class declaration
class Person
{
  public:
    Person();   //constructor
```

```
    int arrive();
    int gallons();
};

// implementation section

Person::Person()
{
  srand(time(NULL));
}

int Person::arrive()
{
  return (1 + rand() % 16);
}

int Person::gallons()
{
  return (3 + rand() % 21);
}
```

Exercises 10.1

1. Assignment stores a value into an existing variable or object; that is, it occurs after the variable or object has been created by a definition statement. Initialization occurs at the time a new variable or object is created and is part of the creation process.

3. a. The required class is contained within the program solution to Exercise 3b.

b.

```
#include <iostream.h>
#include <iomanip.h>
// class declaration
class Complex
{
  private:
    float real;
    float imaginary;
  public:
    Complex(float = 0, float = 0);     // constructor
    void operator=(Complex& ); // overloaded assignment operator function
    void showdata(void);       // display member function
};

// implementation section
Complex::Complex(float re, float im)
{
  real = re;
  imaginary = im;
}
void Complex::operator=(Complex& oldnum)
{
  real = oldnum.real;
```

```
  imaginary = oldnum.imaginary;
  return;
}
void Complex::showdata(void)
{
  float c;
  char sign = '+';

  c = imaginary;
  if (c < 0)
  {
    sign = '-';
    c = -c;
  }
  cout << "The complex number is "
       << real << ' ' << sign << ' ' << c << "i\n";
  return;
}

int main()
{
  Complex a(4.2, 3.6), b;  // declare 2 objects

  a. showdata();      // display object a's values
  b. showdata();      // display object b's values
  b  = a;             // assign a to b
  b. showdata();      // display object b's values

  return 0;
}
```

5. a. The required class is contained within the program solution to Exercise 5b.

b.

```
#include <iostream.h>
#include <iomanip.h>
#include <string.h>
// class declaration
class Car
{
  private:
    float engineSize;
    char bodyStyle;
    int colorCode;
  public:
    Car(float = 0.0, char = 'X', int = 0);  // default constructor
    void operator=(Car& );       // overloaded assignment operator
    void showdata();             // member function to display a time
};

// implementation section

Car::Car(float eng, char styl, int cd)
{
  engineSize = eng;
  bodyStyle = styl;
  colorCode = cd;
```

```
}
void Car::operator=(Car& oldcar)
{
  engineSize = oldcar.engineSize;
  bodyStyle = oldcar.bodyStyle;
  colorCode = oldcar.colorCode;
  return;
}
void Car::showdata()
{
  cout << "\nThe values for this object are \n"
       << "  Engine size: " << engineSize << endl
       << "  Body style:  " << bodyStyle << endl
       << "  Color code:  " << colorCode << endl;
  return;
}

int main()
{
  Car a(250.0, 'S', 52), b;  // declare 2 objects

  a. showdata();   // display object a's values
  b. showdata();   // display object b's values
  b  = a;          // assign a to b
  b. showdata();   // display object b's values

  return 0;
}
```

Exercises 10.2

1. a.

```
#include <iostream.h>
// class declaration
class Employee
{
  private:
    static float taxRate;
    static int numemps;
    int idNum;
  public:
    Employee(int = 0);    // constructor
    void display();   // access function
};

// static member definition
float Employee::taxRate = 0.0025;
int Employee::numemps = 0;
// class implementation
Employee::Employee(int num)
{
  idNum = num;
  numemps++;
}
```

```
void Employee::display()
{
  cout << "Employee number " << idNum
       << " has a tax rate of " << taxRate << endl;
  cout << "There are currently " << numemps
       << " Employee objects" << endl;
  return;
}

int main()
{
  Employee emp1(11122);

  emp1.display();
  Employee emp2(11133);  // create a second object

  emp2.display();

  return 0;
}
```

3. Yes, the three statements could be replaced by the single statement.

5.
```
#include <iostream.h>
#include <math.h>

// class declaration
class Complex
{
  // friends list
  friend Complex addcomplex(Complex&, Complex&);
  private:
    float real;
    float imag;
  public:
    Complex(float = 0, float = 0);  // constructor
    void display();

};

// class implementation
Complex::Complex(float rl, float im)
{
  real = rl;
  imag = im;
}
void Complex::display()
{
  char sign = '+';

  if(imag < 0) sign = '-';
  cout << real << sign << fabs(imag) << 'i';
  return;
}
```

```
// friend implementation
Complex addcomplex(Complex& a, Complex& b)
{
  Complex temp;

  temp.real = a.real + b.real;
  temp.imag = a.imag + b.imag;

  return temp;
}
int main()
{
  Complex a(3.2, 5.6), b(1.1, -8.4), c;

  cout << "\nThe first complex number is ";
  a.display();
  cout << "\nThe second complex number is ";
  b.display();

  c = addcomplex(a,b);

  cout << "\n\nThe sum of these two complex numbers is ";
  c.display();
  cout << endl;

  return 0;
}
```

7. a. The `RecCoord` and `PolCoord` classes are presented within the program solution to Exercise 7b.

b.

```
#include <iostream.h>
#include <iomanip.h>
#include <math.h>
const float DEGTORAD = 3.1416/180.0; // conversion from degrees to radians
const float RADTODEG = 1.0/DEGTORAD; // conversion from radians to degrees
const int RECTOPOLAR = 1;
const int POLARTOREC = 2;

// forward declaration of class PolCoord
class PolCoord;

//RecCoord class declaration
class RecCoord
{
  // friends list
  friend void convPol(int, RecCoord&, PolCoord&);
  private:
    float xval;
    float yval;
  public:
    RecCoord(float = 0.0, float = 0.0); // constructor
    void input(float, float);  // input data member values
    void showdata(); // display data member values
};
```

```
// PolCoord class declaration
class PolCoord
{
  // friends list
  friend void convPol(int, RecCoord&, PolCoord&);
  private:
    float dist;
    float theta;
  public:
    PolCoord(float = 0.0, float = 0.0); // constructor
    void input(float, float);  // input data member values
    void showdata(); // display data member values
};

// implementation section
RecCoord::RecCoord(float x, float y)
{
  xval = x;
  yval = y;
}

void RecCoord::input(float newxval, float newyval)
{
  xval = newxval;
  yval = newyval;
  return;
}

void RecCoord::showdata()
{
  cout << "(" << xval << ", " << yval << ")" << endl;
  return;
}

PolCoord::PolCoord(float r, float angle)
{
  dist = r;
  theta = angle;
}

void PolCoord::input(float newdist, float newtheta)
{
  dist = newdist;
  theta = newtheta;
  return;
}

void PolCoord::showdata()
{
  cout << "r = " << dist << ", angle = " << theta << endl;
  return;
}
```

```
// friend implementation
void convPol(int dir, RecCoord& a, PolCoord& b)
{
  if (dir == RECTOPOLAR)
  {
    b.dist = sqrt(pow(a.xval,2) + pow(a.yval,2));
      b.theta = atan(a.yval/a.xval) * RADTODEG;
  }
  else if (dir == POLARTOREC)
  {
    a.xval = b.dist * cos(b.theta * DEGTORAD);
    a.yval = b.dist * sin(b.theta * DEGTORAD);
  }
  return;
}

int main()
{
  RecCoord a;  // declare one object for each class
  PolCoord b;
  float newx, newy, newr, newtheta;

  cout << "Rectangular point a is initially located at ";
  a.showdata();      // display object a's values
  cout << "Polar point b is initially located at ";
  b.showdata();
  cout << "Enter a new distance and angle for point b: ";
  cin >> newr >> newtheta;
  b.input(newr, newtheta);
  cout << "Polar point b is now located at ";
  b.showdata();
  convPol(POLARTOREC, a, b);
  cout << "After conversion point a is now located at ";
  a.showdata();
  cout << "Enter a new x and y value for point a: ";
  cin >> newx >> newy;
  a.input(newx, newy);
  cout << "Rectangular point a is now located at ";
  a.showdata();
  convPol(RECTOPOLAR, a, b);
  cout << "After conversion, point b is now located at ";
  b.showdata();

  return 0;
}
```

Exercises 10.3

1. a. The required function is included within the following working program:

```
#include <iostream.h>
// class declaration
class Date
```

```
{
  private:
     int month;
     int day;
     int year;
   public:
     Date(int = 7, int = 4, int = 2001);     // constructor
     int operator>(Date& );  // declare the operator > function
     void showdate();  // member function to display a Date
};

// implementation section
Date::Date(int mm, int dd, int yyyy)
{
  month = mm;
  day = dd;
  year = yyyy;
}
int Date::operator>(Date& date2)
{
  long dt1, dt2;

  dt1 = year*10000L + month*100 + day;
  dt2 = date2.year*10000L + date2.month*100 + date2.day;
  if (dt1 > dt2)
    return 1;
  else
    return 0;
}

int main()
{
   Date a(4,1,1999), b(12,18,2001), c(4,1,1999); // declare 3 objects

   if (a > b)
     cout << "Date a greater than b \n";
   else
     cout << "Date a less than or equal to b \n";

   if (a > c)
     cout << "Date a greater than c \n";
   else
     cout << "Date a less than or equal to c \n";

  return 0;
}
```

3. a. This operator function provides the same result as the `operator()` function used in Program 10.8.

5. a. The required function is incorporated within the complete program written for Exercise 5b.

b.
```
#include <iostream.h>
#include <math.h>
// class declaration
class Complex
{
  private:
    float real;
    float imag;
  public:
    Complex(float = 0, float = 0);  // constructor
    Complex operator+(Complex& ); // declare the operator+ function
    void display();
};

// class implementation
Complex::Complex(float rl, float im)
{
  real = rl;
  imag = im;
}
void Complex::display()
{
  char sign = '+';

  if(imag < 0) sign = '-';
  cout << real << sign << fabs(imag) << 'i';
  return;
}

Complex Complex::operator+(Complex& newnum)
{
  Complex temp;

  temp.real = real + newnum.real;
  temp.imag = imag + newnum.imag;

  return temp;   // return a complex number
}

int main()
{
  Complex a(3.2, 5.6), b(1.1, -8.4), c;

  cout << "\nThe first complex number is ";
  a.display();
  cout << "\nThe second complex number is ";
  b.display();
  c = a + b;  // can be written as a = a.operator+(b);
  cout << "\n\nThe sum of these two numbers is ";
  c.display();
  cout << endl;

  return 0;
}
```

Exercises 10.4

3. The `main()` function produces a valid simulation. The use of a `do-while` loop that is always true and is exited using an internal `if-else` statement can be used in place of the `while` loop. Although students may sometimes encounter this type of loop in simulations, because of the always true condition `while(1)`, it is considered inferior to a `while` loop that uses its tested condition in determining when loop execution is to end. Loops should exit via their tested condition rather than through a nonstandard internal decision point.

5.
```
#include <iostream.h>
#include <stdlib.h>
#include <time.h>

#include <stdlib.h>
#include <time.h>
const int MAXFLOOR = 15;

// class declaration and implementation
class Person
{
  public:
    Person() {srand(time(NULL));};  // default constructor
    int call(){return (1 + rand() % (MAXFLOOR + 1));};
};

// class declaration

class Elevator
{
  private:
    int currentFloor;
  public:
    Elevator(int = 1);   // default constructor
    void request(int);
};

// implementation section

Elevator::Elevator(int cfloor)
{
  currentFloor = cfloor;
}

void Elevator::request(int newfloor)
{
  if (newfloor < 1 || newfloor > MAXFLOOR || newfloor == currentFloor)
    ; // do nothing
  else if ( newfloor > currentFloor)  // move elevator up
  {
    cout << "\nStarting at floor " << currentFloor << endl;
    while (newfloor > currentFloor)
```

```
    {
      currentFloor++;    // add one to current floor
      cout << "   Going Up - now at floor " << currentFloor << endl;
    }
    cout << "Stopping at floor " << currentFloor << endl;
  }
  else  // move elevator down
  {
    cout << "\nStarting at floor " << currentFloor << endl;
    while (newfloor < currentFloor)
    {
      currentFloor--;   // subtract one from current floor
      cout << "   Going Down - now at floor " << currentFloor << endl;
    }
    cout << "Stopping at floor " << currentFloor << endl;
  }

  return;
}

int main()
{
  Elevator a;   // declare one object of type Elevator
  Person one;   // declare one person type
  int i, FromFloor, ToFloor;

  for (i = 0; i < 3; i++)
  {
      FromFloor = one.call();
      cout << "Person called elevator from floor " << FromFloor << endl;
      a.request(FromFloor);  // move to the floor
      do
      {
        ToFloor = one.call();  // request a new floor
      } while (ToFloor == FromFloor);
      cout << "Person requested to go to floor " << ToFloor << endl;
      a.request(ToFloor);
 }

 return 0;
 }
```

Exercises 10.5

1. a. Conversion from a built-in type to a built-in type is accomplished by C++'s implicit conversion rules or by explicit casting.

Conversion from a built-in type to a user-defined type is accomplished by a type conversion constructor.

Conversion from a user-defined type to a built-in type is accomplished by a conversion operator function.

Conversion from a user-defined type to a built-in type is accomplished by a conversion operator function.

b. A type conversion constructor is a constructor whose first parameter is not a member of its class and whose remaining parameters, if any, have default values.

A conversion operator function is a class member operator function having the name of a built-in data type or class.

3.

```
#include <iostream.h>

// class declaration for Date
class Date
{
  private:
    int month, day, year;
  public:
    Date(int = 7, int = 4, int = 2001);    // constructor
    operator long();         // conversion operator function
    void showdate();
};
// constructor
Date::Date(int mm, int dd, int yyyy)
{
  month = mm;
  day = dd;
  year = yyyy;
}
// conversion operator function converting from Date to long
Date::operator long()   // must return a long
{
  int mp, yp, t;
  long julian;

  if (month <= 2)
  {
    mp = 0;
    yp = year - 1;
  }
  else
  {
    mp = int(0.4 * month + 2.3);
    yp = year;
  }
  t = int(yp/4) - int(yp/100) + int(yp/400);
  julian = 365L * year + 31L * (month - 1) + day + t - mp;
  return (julian);
}

// member function to display a Date
void Date::showdate(void)
{
  cout << setfill('0')
       << setw(2) << month << '/'
```

```
         << setw(2) << day << '/'
         << setw(2) << year % 100;

    return;
  }

  int main()
  {
    Date a(1,31,1985);  // declare and initialize one object of type Date
    long b;             // declare an object of type long

    b = a;              // a conversion takes place here

    cout << "a's value, in the form month/day/year is ";
    a.showdate();
    cout << "\nThis value, as a Julian integer, is " << b << endl;

    return 0;
  }
```

5.

```
#include <iostream.h>

// forward declaration of class Julian
class Julian;

// class declaration for Date
class Date
{
  private:
    int month, day, year;
  public:
    Date(int = 7, int = 4, int = 2001);    // constructor
    operator Julian();      // conversion operator to Julian
    void showdate();
};

// class declaration for Julian
class Julian
{
  private:
    long yyyymmdd;
  public:
    Julian(long = 0);    // constructor
    void showjulian(void);
};

// class implementation for Date
Date::Date(int mm, int dd, int yyyy)  // constructor
{
  month = mm;
  day = dd;
  year = yyyy;
}
// conversion operator function converting from Date to Julian class
Date::operator Julian()   // must return an Julian object
```

```
{
  int mp, yp, t;
  long temp;

  if (month <= 2)
  {
    mp = 0;
    yp = year - 1;
  }
  else
  {
    mp = int(0.4 * month + 2.3);
    yp = year;
  }
  t = int(yp/4) - int(yp/100) + int(yp/400);
  temp = 365L * year + 31L * (month - 1) + day + t - mp;
  return temp;
}

// member function to display a Date
void Date::showdate(void)
{
  cout << setfill('0')
       << setw(2) << month << '/'
       << setw(2) << day << '/'
       << setw(2) << year % 100;

  return;
}

// class implementation for Julian
Julian::Julian(long ymd)  // constructor
{
  yyyymmdd = ymd;
}

// member function to display an Julian
void Julian::showjulian(void)
{
  cout << yyyymmdd;
  return;
}

int main()
{
  Date a(1,31,1995), b(3,16,1996);  // declare two Date objects
  Julian c, d;                      // declare two Julian objects

  c = Julian(a);                    // cast a into an Julian object
  d = Julian(b);                    // cast b into an Julian object
  cout << " a's date is ";
  a.showdate();
  cout << "\n   as a Julian object this date is ";
  c.showjulian();
```

```
    cout << "\n b's date is ";
    b.showdate();
    cout << "\n   as a Julian object this date is ";
    d.showjulian();
    cout << endl;

    return 0;
  }
```

Note: There is no conversion operator from `Julian` to `Date`. In general, the `Julian` objects are extremely useful for determining actual day count differences between two dates, and for sorting dates. In practice, the `Julian` date would be incorporated as a data member of the `Date` class. Also note that the forward reference to the `Julian` class could be omitted in this program if the `Julian` class were declared prior to the `Date` class.

Exercises 11.1

1. a. Inheritance is the capability of deriving one class from another class.

b. A base class is the class that is used as the basis for deriving subsequent classes.

c. A derived class is the class that inherits the characteristics of a base class,

d. Simple inheritance is a type of inheritance where the parent of each derived class is a single base class.

e. Multiple inheritance is a type of inheritance where a derived class has two or more parent base classes.

f. A class hierarchy is the order in which classes are derived.

3. The three features that must be provided for a programming language to be classified as object-oriented are classes, inheritance, and polymorphism. Object-based languages are languages that support objects but do not provide inheritance features.

5. a. The required classes are contained within the program solution to Exercise 5b.

b.

```
#include <iostream.h>
#include <math.h>

const double PI = 2.0 * asin(1.0);

// class declaration

class Point
{
  protected:
    float x;
      float y;
  public:
    Point(float = 0.0, float = 0.0);  //constructor
      float distance(Point&);
};
```

```
// implementation section
Point::Point(float xval, float yval)
{
  x = xval;
  y = yval;
}

float Point::distance(Point& b)
{
  return (sqrt(pow((x-b.x),2) + pow((y-b.y),2)));
}

// class declaration for the derived Circle class
class Circle : public Point
{
  protected:
    double radius; // add an additional data member
  public:
    Circle(float = 0.0, float = 0.0, float = 1.0);  // constructor
    float distance(Circle&);
      float area();
};

// implementation section for Circle
Circle::Circle(float centerx, float centery, float r)  // constructor
{
  x = centerx;
  y = centery;
  radius = r;
}

float Circle::distance(Circle& b)
{
      return (Point::distance(b)); // note the base function call
}

float Circle::area()   // this calculates an area
{
  return (PI * pow(radius,2));
}

int main()
{
  Point a, b(4,4);
  Circle circl, circ2(3,3,2);

  cout << "The distance between points is " << a.distance(b) << endl;
  cout << "The area of circl is " << circl.area() << endl;
  cout << "The area of circ2 is " << circ2.area() << endl;
  cout << "The distance between circle centers is " << circl.distance(circ2)
       << endl;

  return 0;
}
```

Note: An inline base member initialization for the `Circle` class's constructor using the `Point` class's constructor could also have been constructed.

Exercises 11.2

3. In static binding the determination of which function will be called is made at compile time, whereas in dynamic binding the determination of which function will be called is made at run time.

5. Polymorphism is the ability of a function or operator to have multiple forms. The particular form that will be invoked can be determined at run time depending on the object being used.

Exercises 11.3

1. Reference parameters are effectively named address values. When using the reference parameters it is the contents of the address that is desired. The accessing of the contents referred to by the reference parameter is automatically obtained when the reference parameter identifier is used. Thus, when using a reference parameter the access of the final data value is implicitly implied and automatically done. The `this` argument, which is a pointer, also refers to the address of an actual data value. To obtain the data value whose address is contained in the `this` argument, however, requires explicitly using one of the dereferencing operators `*` or `->` with the `this` identifier. As such, the access of the final data value is obtained using an explicit dereferencing operation.

3.

```
#include <iostream.h>

// class declaration

class Date
{
  private:
     int month;
     int day;
     int year;
   public:
     Date(int = 7, int = 4, int = 2001); // constructor
     void operator=(Date&);   // define assignment of a date
     void showdate();     // member function to display a date
};

// implementation section

Date::Date(int mm, int dd, int yyyy)
{
  this->month = mm;
  this->day = dd;
  this->year = yyyy;
}
```

```
void Date::operator=(Date& newdate)
{

  this->day = newdate.day;        // assign the day
  this->month = newdate.month;    // assign the month
  this->year = newdate.year;      // assign the year

  return;
}

void Date::showdate()
{
  cout << setfill('0')
       << setw(2) << month << '/'
       << setw(2) << day << '/'
       << setw(2) << year % 100;
  return;
}

int main()
{
  Date a(4,1,1999), b(12,18,2001); // declare two objects

  cout << "The date stored in a is originally ";
  a.showdate();  // display the original date
  a = b;         // assign b's value to a
  cout << "After assignment the date stored in a is ";
  a.showdate();  // display a's values

  return 0;
}
```

Note: The notation `this->` can be replaced with the notation `(*this).` throughout the program.

Exercises 11.4

1. a. A pointer can be either a variable or a parameter whose contents is a memory address.

b. The pointer variable is named `a` and the address contained in `a` is the address of a `Customer` object.

The pointer variable is named `pointer1` and the address contained in this variable is the address of a `Pump` object.

The pointer variable is named `addrOfaPump` and the address contained in this variable is the address of a `Pump` object.

The pointer variable is named `addrOfanInt` and the address contained in this variable is the address of an integer variable.

The pointer variable is named b and the address contained in b is the address of a floating point variable.

3. By definition, a model is used to represent the important features of a system. For efficiency purposes a simpler model that adequately presents the desired features is better than a more complicated model. Thus, using dynamic memory allocation for an internal implementation when a simpler nondynamic model produces the same effect is overkill. Each request for new memory places an overhead on the system in terms of processing time, memory resources, and processing complexity. Program 11.7 is useful in presenting the essentials of dynamic memory allocation only within the context of a familiar application. From a programming viewpoint Program 9.5 is superior.

Exercises 11.5

1.

```
#include <iostream.h>
#include <string.h>

// class declaration
class Book
{
  private:
    char *title;   // a pointer to a book title
  public:
    Book(char * = NULL);  // constructor
    Book(Book&);         // copy constructor
    void operator=(Book&);  // overloaded assignment operator
    void showtitle(void);   // display the title
};
// class implementation

Book::Book(char *strng)   // constructor
{
  title = new char[strlen(strng)+1];  // allocate memory
  strcpy(title,strng);                // store the string
}

Book::Book(Book& oldbook)   // copy constructor
{
  title = new char[strlen(oldbook.title) + 1];  // allocate new memory
  strcpy(title, oldbook.title);  // copy the title
}

void Book::operator=(Book& oldbook)
{
  if(title != NULL)  // check that it exists
    delete(title);   // release existing memory
  title = new char[strlen(oldbook.title) + 1];  // allocate new memory
  strcpy(title, oldbook.title);  // copy the title
}
```

```
void Book::showtitle(void)
{
  cout << title << endl;
}

int main()
{
  Book book1("DOS Primer");    // create 1st title
  Book book2 = book1;           // create a copy
  Book book3("A Brief History of Western Civilization");  // 2nd title

  book1.showtitle();   // display book1's title
  book2.showtitle();   // check the copy worked
  book3.showtitle();   // display the third book title
  book2 = book3;       // assign book3 to book2
  book2.showtitle();   // check the assignment worked

  return 0;
}
```

3. a. The required class is contained within the program solution to Exercise 3b.

b.

```
#include <iostream.h>
#include <iomanip.h>
#include <string.h>
// declaration section
class Car
{
  private:
    float engineSize;
    char bodyStyle;
    int colorCode;
    char *vinPtr;
  public:
    Car(float = 0.0, char =  'X', int = 0, char * = NULL);  // constructor
    void operator=(Car&);       // overloaded assignment operator
    void showdata();         // member function to display a time
};

// implementation section

Car::Car(float eng, char styl, int cd, char *pt)
{
  engineSize = eng;
  bodyStyle = styl;
  colorCode = cd;
  vinPtr = new char[strlen(pt) + 1];    // allocate memory
  strcpy(vinPtr, pt);                    // store the string
}

void Car::operator=(Car& oldcar)
{
  engineSize = oldcar.engineSize;
  bodyStyle = oldcar.bodyStyle;
  colorCode = oldcar.colorCode;
```

```
  if(vinPtr != NULL)   // check that it exists
    delete(vinPtr);    // release existing memory
  vinPtr = new char[strlen(oldcar.vinPtr) + 1];  // allocate new memory
  strcpy(vinPtr, oldcar.vinPtr);  // copy the vin
}
void Car::showdata()
{
  cout << "\nThe values for this object are \n"
       << "  Engine size: " << engineSize << endl
       << "  Body style:  " << bodyStyle << endl
       << "  Color code:  " << colorCode << endl
       << "  VIN: " << vinPtr << endl;
}

int main()
{
   Car a(250.0, 'S', 52, "ABC567YYY"), b;  // declare 2 objects

   a.showdata();   // display object a's values
   b.showdata();   // display object b's values
   b = a;          // assign a to b
   b.showdata();   // display object a's values

  return 0;
}
```

Exercises 12.1

1. **a.** `int grades[100];`
   b. `float temp[50];`
   c. `int code[30];`
   d. `int year[100];`
   e. `float velocity[32];`
   f. `float dist[1000];`
   g. `int codeNum[6];`

3. **a.** `cin >> grades[0] >> grades[2] >> grades[6];`
   b. `cin >> prices[0] >> prices[2] >> prices[6];`
   c. `cin >> amps[0] >> amps[2] >> amps[6];`
   d. `cin >> dist[0] >> dist[2] >> dist[6];`
   e. `cin >> velocity[0] >> velocity[2] >> velocity[6];`
   f. `cin >> time[0] >> time[2] >> time[6];`

5. **a.** `a[1]  a[2]  a[3]  a[4]  a[5]`
   b. `a[1]  a[3]  a[5]`
   c. `b[3]  b[4]  b[5]  b[6]  b[7]  b[8]  b[9]  b[10]`

d. b[3] b[6] b[9] b[12]

e. c[2] c[4] c[6] c[8] c[10]

7.
```
#include <iostream.h>
int main()
{
  const int NUMELS = 0
  int grade[NUMELS], sum, i;
  float average;

  sum = 0;   // initialize here or in the declaration
  for( i = 0; i < NUMELS; i++)
  {
    cout << "Enter a value for element number " << i << " : ";
    cin  >> grade[i];
    sum = sum + grade[i];
  }
  cout << "\nThe values stored in the array are:\n";
  for (i = 0; i < NUMELS; i++)
    cout << grade[i] << "   ";
  average = sum / NUMELS;
  cout << "\nThe average of these values is "
       << average << endl;

  return 0;
}
```

9. a.
```
#include <iostream.h>
#include <iomanip.h>
int main()
{
  const int NUMELS = 14;
  int grades[NUMELS], total, i;
  float avg, deviation[NUMELS];

  total = 0;
  for(i = 0; i < NUMELS; i++)
  {
    cout << "Enter grade # " << (i + 1) << " : ";
    cin  >> grades[i];
    total += grades[i];
  }
  avg = total/NUMELS;
  cout << "\n The average of the grades is " << avg << '\n'
    << "Element     Element      Deviation\n"
    << "Number       Value        from Avg.\n"
    << "-------     -------      ----------\n";
  for(i = 0; i < NUMELS; i++)
  {
    deviation[i] = grades[i] - avg;
    cout << setiosflags(ios::showpoint) << setprecision(2);
    cout << setw(4) << i << "    "
         << setw(10) << grades[i] << "     "
         << setw(12) << deviation[i] << endl;
  }
```

```
    return 0;
  }
```

11. a.
```
#include <iostream.h>
    int main()
    const int NUMELS = 10;
   {
     double raw[NUMELS], sorted[NUMELS], min = 1.e5;
     int i, j, index;

     for(i = 0; i < NUMELS; i++)
     {
       cout << "Enter value # " << (i+1) << " : ";
       cin  >> raw[i];
     }
     for(i = 0; i < NUMELS; i++)
     {
       for(j = 0; j < NUMELS; j++)  // find the minimum for this pass
       {
          if(raw[j] < min) // look for next min
          {
            min = raw[j];
            index = j;
          }
       }
       sorted[i] = min;      // put min in next sorted element
       min = 1.e5;           // reset min for start of search
       raw[index] = 1.e7;    // don't select this element again
     }
     cout << "The elements in sorted order are:\n";
     for( i = 0; i < NUMELS; i++)
       cout << sorted[i] << endl;

     return 0;
   }
```

b. To locate each minimum, make a complete pass through the array and find the first minimum. Now only nine numbers need be searched because one has been used. After the second lowest element has been selected, only the remaining eight need be searched. Instead of 10^2 passes through the loop, only 10! passes are needed. The number of passes can be reduced using a shell sort rather than a bubble sort, as described in Section 12.7.

Exercises 12.2

1. a. `int grades[10] = {89, 75, 82, 93, 78, 95, 81, 88, 77, 82};`

b. `double amounts[5] = {10.62, 13.98, 18.45, 12.68, 14.76};`

c. `double rates[100] = {6.29, 6.95, 7.25, 7.35, 7.40, 7.42};`

d.
```
float temps[64] = {78.2, 69.6, 68.5, 83.9, 55.4, 67.0, 49.8,
                   58.3, 62.5, 71.6};
```

e. `char code[15] = {'f', 'j', 'm', 'q', 't', 'w', 'z'};`

3.
```
#include <iostream.h>
int main()
{
  const int NUMELS = 9;
  float slopes[NUMELS] = {17.24, 25.63,  5.94,
                          33.92,  3.71, 32.84,
                          35.93, 18.24,  6.92};
  int i;
  float max = 0.0, min = 999.9;

  for(i = 0; i < NUMELS; i++)
  {
    if (slopes[i] < min) min = slopes[i];
    if (slopes[i] > max) max = slopes[i];
  }
  cout << "\nThe minimum array value is " <<  min;
  cout << "\nThe maximum array value is " << max << endl;

  return 0;
}
```

5.
```
char goodstr1[13] = {'G', 'o', 'o', 'd', ' ',
                     'M', 'o', 'r', 'n', 'i', 'n', 'g'};
char goodstr1[] = {'G', 'o', 'o', 'd', ' ',
                   'M', 'o', 'r', 'n','i', 'n', 'g'};
char goodstr1[] = "Good Morning";
```

Note: This last declaration creates an array having one more character than the first two. The extra character is the null character.

7.
```
char strtest1[15] =
   {'T','h','i','s',' ','i','s',' ','a',' ','t','e','s','t','\0'};

char strtest1[] =
   {'T','h','i','s',' ','i','s',' ','a',' ','t','e','s','t','\0'};

char strtest1[] = "This is a test";
```

This last declaration creates an array of characters and automatically add the null character, `'\0'`, to the end of the string.

Exercises 12.3

1.
```
void sortArray(double inArray[500])
void sortArray(double inArray[])
```

3.
```
float prime(float rates[256])
float prime(float rates[])
```

5.
```
#include <iostream.h>
#include <iomanip.h>
const int NUMS = 9;
void show(float []);  // function prototype
int main()
{
   float rates[NUMS] = {6.5, 7.2, 7.5, 8.3, 8.6,
                        9.4, 9.6, 9.8, 10.0};
   show(rates);
  return 0;
}

 void show(float rates[])
 {
   int i;

   cout << "\nThe elements stored in the array are:\n";
   cout << setiosflags(ios::showpoint) << setprecision(2);
   for(i = 0; i < NUMS; i++)
     cout << rates[i] << "  " << endl;
 }
```

7.
```
#include <iostream.h>
#include <iomanip.h>
const int NUMVALS = 10;
void extend(double [], double [], double []); // function prototype
int main()
{
  double price[10] = {10.62, 14.89, 13.21, 16.55, 18.62,
                      9.47, 6.58, 18.32, 12.15, 3.98};
  double quantity[10] = {4.0, 8.5, 6.0, 7.35, 9.0,
                    15.3, 3.0, 5.4, 2.9, 4.8};
  double amount[10];

  int i;

  extend(price, quantity, amount);

  cout << "The elements in the amount array are:";
  cout << setiosflags(ios::showpoint)
       << setprecision(3) << endl;
  for(i = 0; i < NUMVALS; i++)
    cout << amount[i] << endl;
  return 0;
}
void extend(double prc[], double qnty[], double amt[])
{
  int i;

  for(i = 0; i < NUMVALS; i++)
    amt[i] = prc[i] * qnty[i];

  return;
}
```

Exercises 12.4

1. a. `int array[6][10];`
   b. `int codes[2][5];`
   c. `char keys[7][12];`
   d. `char letter[15][7];`
   e. `double vals[10][25];`
   f. `double test[16][8];`

3.

```
#include <iostream.h>
const int ROWS = 3;
const int COLS = 4;
int main()
{
  int i, j, total = 0;
  int val[ROWS][COLS] = {8,16,9,52,3,15,27,6,14,25,2,10};

  for (i = 0; i < ROWS; i++)
    for (j = 0; j < COLS; j++)
   total = total + val[i][j];
  cout << "\nThe total of the values is " << total << endl;

  return 0;
}
```

5. a.

```
#include <iostream.h>
const int ROWS = 4;
const int COLS = 5;
int main()
{
  int i, j;
  int max = -999;
  int val[ROWS][COLS] = {16, 22, 99, 4, 18,
                        -258, 4, 101, 5, 98,
                         105, 6, 15, 2, 45,
                          33, 88, 72, 16, 3};
  for (i = 0; i < ROWS; i++)
    for (j = 0; j < COLS; j++)
   if (val[i][j] > max)  max = val[i][j];
  cout << "\nThe maximum array value is " << max << endl;

  return 0;
}
```

Exercises 13.1

1. `&average` means "the address of the variable named `average`."

3. a.
```
#include <iostream.h>
int main()
{

  char key, choice;
  int num, count;
  long date;
  float yield;
  double price;

  cout << "The address of the variable key is " << &key << endl;
  cout << "The address of the variable choice is " << &choice << endl;
  cout << "The address of the variable num is " << &num << endl;
  cout << "The address of the variable count is " << &count << endl;
  cout << "The address of the variable date is " << &date << endl;
  cout << "The address of the variable yield is " << &yield << endl;
  cout << "The address of the variable price is " << &price << endl;

  return 0;
}
```

5. a. `*xAddr`
   b. `*yAddr`
   c. `*ptYld`
   d. `*ptMiles`
   e. `*mptr`
   f. `*pdate`
   g. `*distPtr`
   h. `*tabPt`
   i. `*hoursPt`

7. a. Each of these variables are pointers. This means that addresses will be stored in each of these variables.
   b. They are not very descriptive names and do not give an indication that they are pointers.

9. All pointer variable declarations must have an asterisk. Therefore, c, e, g, and i all contain pointer declarations.

11.

Variable	Address	Contents
`ptNum`	500	8096
`amtAddr`	564	16256
`zAddr`	8024	20492
`numAddr`	10132	18938
`ptDay`	14862	20492
`ptYr`	15010	694
`years`	694	1987
`m`	8096	
`amt`	16256	154
`firstnum`	18938	154
`balance`	20492	25
`k`	24608	154

Exercises 13.2

1. **a.** `*(prices + 5)`
   b. `*(grades + 2)`
   c. `*(yield +10)`
   d. `*(dist + 9)`
   e. `*mile`
   f. `*(temp + 20)`
   g. `*(celsius + 16)`

h. `*(num + 50)`
i. `*(time + 12)`

3. a. The declaration `double prices [5];` causes storage space for five double precision numbers, creates a pointer constant named `prices`, and equates the pointer constant to the address of the first element (`&prices[0]`).

b. Each element in prices contains eight bytes and there are five elements for a total of 40 bytes.

c.

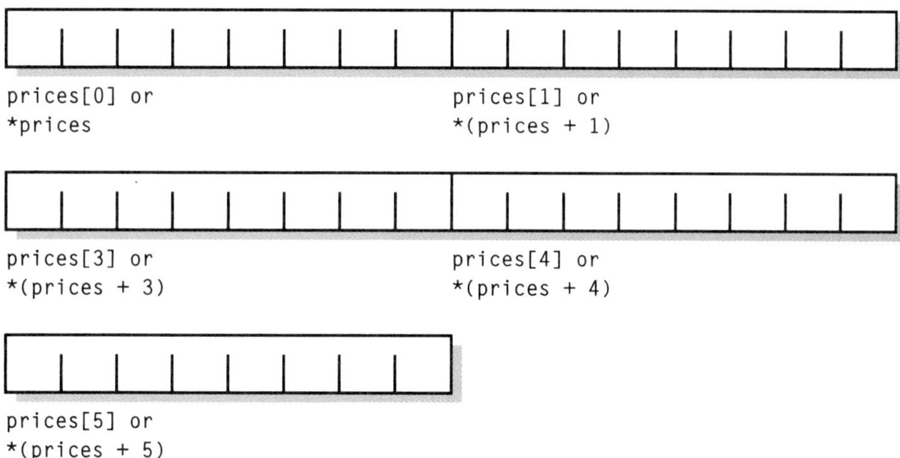

d. The byte offset for this element, from the beginning of the array, is 3 * 8 = 24 bytes.

5.

```
#include <iostream.h>
int main()
{
  float rates[] = {12.9, 18.6, 11.4, 13.7, 9.5, 15.2, 17.6};
  int i;

   cout << "The elements of the array are:\n";
   for(i = 0; i <= 6; ++i)
     cout << "    " << *(rates + i);   // The variable pointed
                                       // to by rates offset by i
 return 0;
}
```

Exercises 13.3

3. a.
```
#include <iostream.h>
int main()
{
  char strng[] = "Hooray for all of us";
  char *messPtr;

  messPtr = &strng[0];    // messPtr = strng; is equivalent
  cout << "\nThe elements in the array are: ";
  for(  ; *messPtr != '\0'; messPtr++)
    cout << *messPtr;
  cout << endl;

  return 0;
}
```

Note: The expression `for( ; *messPtr != '\0'; messPtr++)` can be replaced by `for( ;*messPtr; mesPtr++)`.

b.
```
#include <iostream.h>
int main()
{
  char strng[] = "Hooray for all of us";
  char *messPtr;

  messPtr = &strng[0];    // messPtr = strng; is equivalent
  cout << "\nThe elements in the array are: ";
  while (*messPtr != '\0')  // search for the null character
    cout <<  *messPtr++;
  cout << endl;

  return 0;
}
```

Note: The expressions `while (*messPtr != '\0')` can be replaced by `while (*messPtr)`.

5.
```
#include <iostream.h>
int main()
{
  const int MAXELS = 80;
  char message[] = "This is a test";
  char mess2[MAXELS];
  char *charPtr;
  int i;

  for (i = 0; *(message + i)!= '\0'; i++)
     *(mess2 + i) = *(message + i);
  *(mess2 + i) = '\0';  // close off the string
  cout << "\nThe elements in the copied array are:\n";
  charPtr = &mess2[0];   // charPtr = mess2; is equivalent
```

```
  for(  ; *charPtr != '\0'; charPtr++)
    cout << *charPtr;
  cout << endl;

  return 0;
}
```

Exercises 13.4

1.
```
void sortArray(double inArray[500])
void sortArray(double inArray[])
void sortArray(double *inArray)
```

3.
```
float prime(double rates[256])
float prime(double rates[])
float prime(double *rates)
```

5. The problem to this method of finding the maximum value lies in the statement

```
if(max < *vals++)
  max = *vals;
```

This statement compares the correct value to `max`, but then increments the address in the pointer before any assignment is made. Thus, the element assigned to `max` by the expression `max = *vals` is one element beyond the element pointed to within the parentheses.

7.
```
#include <iostream.h>
void display(char *); // function prototype

int main()
{
  char message[] = "Vacation is near";

  display(message);

  return 0;
}

void display(char *messPtr)
{
  int i = 0;
  while (*(messPtr + i) != '\0')
  {
    cout << *(messPtr + i);
    i++;
   }

  cout << endl;

  return;
}
```

9. a. The following output is obtained:

```
33
16
99
34
```

This is why:

```
*(*val) = *(val[0]) = val[0][0] = 33;
*(*val + 1) = *(val[1]) = val[1][0] = 16;
*(*(val + 1) + 2) = *(*(val[1]) + 2) = *(val[1][2]) = 99;
*(*val) + 1 = *(val[0]) + 1 = val[0][0] + 1 = 33 + 1 = 34.
```

In other words, for any two-dimensional array, `arr[x][y]`, what we really have are two levels of pointers. What is meant by `*(arr + x)` is that there are `x` number of pointers, each successively pointing to `arr[1][0]`, `arr[2][0]`, `arr[3][0]`, . . . , `arr[x][0]`. So an expression such as `*(*(arr + x) + y)` translates to `arr[x][y]`.

Exercises 14.1

1. a.
```
text[0] = 'n'
text[3] = ' '
text[10] = ' '
```
b.
```
text[0] = 'r'
text[3] = 'k'
text[10] = 'o'
```
c.
```
text[0] = 'H'
text[3] = 'p'
text[10] = 'd'
```
d.
```
text[0] = 'T'
text[3] = ' '
text[10] = 'h'
```

3.
```
#include <iostream.h>
void vowels(char []);  // function prototype
int main()
{
   const int MAXCHARS = 81;
   char line[MAXCHARS];

   cout << "Enter a string:\n";
   cin.getline(line,MAXCHARS);
   vowels(line);

   return 0;
}
```

```
void vowels(char strng[])
{
  const int NUMVOWELS = 5;
  char vowel[NUMVOWELS] = {'a','e','i','o','u'};
  int vCount[NUMVOWELS] = {0,0,0,0,0};
  int i = 0;
  char c;
  while((c = strng[i++]) != '\0')
    switch(c)
    {
    case 'a': cout << c;
              vCount[0]++;
              break;
    case 'e': cout << c;
              vCount[1]++;
              break;
    case 'i': cout << c;
              vCount[2]++;
              break;
    case 'o': cout << c;
              vCount[3]++;
              break;
    case 'u': cout << c;
              vCount[4]++;
              break;
    }
  cout << endl;
  for (i = 0; i < NUMVOWELS; i++)
    cout << "The number of " << vowel[i]
         << " vowels is " << vCount[i] << "." << endl;
  return;
}
```

5.

```
#include <iostream.h>
#include <iomanip.h>
int main()
{
  const int MAXCHARS = 81;
  char strng[MAXCHARS];
  char c;
  int i = 0;

  cout << "Enter a string: ";
  cin.getline(strng,MAXCHARS);
  while( (c = strng[i++]) != '\0')
  cout << "Character " << c
       << " has a hexadecimal code of "
       << setiosflags(ios::hex) << int (c) << endl;

  return 0;
}
```

7.

```
#include <iostream.h>
void reverse(char [], char []);    // function prototype
int main()
{
  const int MAXCHARS = 81;
  char forward[MAXCHARS], rever[MAXCHARS];

  cout << "Enter a line of text:\n";
  cin.getline(forward,MAXCHARS);
  reverse(forward,rever);
  cout << "\n\nThe text: " << forward << endl
       << "spelled backwards is: " << rever << endl ;

  return 0;
}

  void reverse(char forw[], char rev[])
  {
    int i = 0, j = 0;

    while(forw[i] != '\0')          // count the elements
       ++i;                         // in the string
    for(i--; i >= 0; j++, i--)
      rev[j] = forw[i];
    rev[j] = '\0';                  // close off reverse string

    return;
  }
```

It is necessary to initially decrement `i` in the `for` loop because `i` is the subscript of the null character, `'\0'`, in `forward[]`. The copy must start with one element before the null character.

9. The function is included within a complete program.

```
#include <iostream.h>
int main()
{
  const int MAXCHARS = 81;
  char ch, line[MAXCHARS];
  void appendChar(char, char []);  // function prototype
  cout << "\nEnter a line of text: ";
  cin.getline(line,MAXCHARS);
  cout << "Enter a single character: ";
  ch = cin.get();
  appendChar(ch,line);
  cout << "The new line of text with the appended "
       << "last character is:\n";
  cout << line;

  return 0;
}
```

```
void appendChar(char c, char strng[])
{
  int i;

  while(strng[i++] != '\0')    // this moves to one position
  strng[--i] = c;      // move back one and replace '\0'
                        //  with the new char
  strng[++i] = '\0';   // close the new string

  return;
}
```

11.

```
#include <iostream.h>
void deleteChar(char [], int, int);   // function prototype
int main()
{
  const int MAXCHARS = 81;
  char word[MAXCHARS];

  cout << "Enter a string\n";
  cin.getline(word,MAXCHARS);
  cout << "The word just entered is: " << word << endl;
  deleteChar(word, 13, 5); // string, how many to delete, starting position
  cout << word << endl;  // display the edited string

  return 0;
}

  void deleteChar(char strng[], int x, int pos)
  {
    int i, j;

    i = pos-1;   // first element to be deleted (actually, overwritten)
    j = i + x;   // first element beyond delete range
    while (strng[j] != '\0')
    strng[i++] = strng[j++];  // copy over an element
    strng[i] = '\0';   // close off the edited string

    return;
  }
```

This program assumes the number of characters to be deleted actually exists. Otherwise, the `while` loop would not terminate (unless it just happened to encounter another null character somewhere in memory beyond the original string).

13. a. The `toUpper()` function is included in the program written for Exercise 13b.

b.

```
#include <iostream.h>
char toUpper(char ch);   // function prototype
int main()
{
  const int MAXCHARS = 81;
  char strng[MAXCHARS];
  int i = 0;

  cout << "Enter a line of text\n";
```

```
    cin.getline(strng,MAXCHARS);
    while (strng[i] != '\0')  // get the character
    {
      strng[i] = toUpper(strng[i]); // send it to the function
      i++;                          // move to next character
    }
    cout << "The string, with all lower case letters"
         << " converted is:\n";
    cout << strng << endl;

    return 0;
  }

  char toUpper(char ch)
  {

     if ( ch >= 'a' && ch <= 'z')    // test it
       return (ch - 'a' + 'A');      // change it, if necessary
     else
       return ch;

    return;
  }
```

Exercises 14.2

5. a.

```
int length(char s1[])
{
  int count = 0;

  while(s1[count] != '\0')
    count++;

    return count;
}
```

Note: The statement `while(s1[count] != '\0')` can be replaced by `while(s1[count])`.

b.

```
#include <iostream.h>
int length(char []);
int main()
{
  char s1[] = "This is a test";

  int ret;

  ret = length(s1);
  cout << "\nThe length of the string "  << s1
       << " is " << ret << " characters." << endl;

  return 0;
}
```

7. a.
```
void chartype(int cval)
{

  if (islower(cval))
    cout << "  The ASCII character is a lowercase letter." << endl;
  else if (isupper(cval))
    cout << " The ASCII character is an uppercase letter." << endl;
  else if (isdigit(cval))
    cout << "  The ASCII character is a digit." << endl;
  else if (ispunct(cval))
    cout << "The ASCII character is a punctuation mark." << endl;
  else if (isspace(cval))
    cout << "The ASCII character is a space." << endl;
  else if (!isprint(cval))
    cout << "The decimal code for this character is " << cval
       << "\n The ASCII character is a nonprintable character." << endl;

  return;
}
```

Note that character codes are stored as unsigned integers.

b.
```
#include <iostream.h>
#include <ctype.h>
#include <time.h>
#include <stdlib.h>
const int RANDNUMS = 20;
void chartype(int);   // function prototype
int main()
{
  int i;
  int cval;

  srand(time(NULL));
  for(i = 0; i < RANDNUMS; i++)
  {
     cval = 1 + rand() % 127;
     cout << "The value is " << cval << endl;
     chartype(cval);
   }

   return 0;
}
```

Exercises 14.3

1. a.
```
*text = 'n'
*(text + 3) = ' '
*(text + 10) = ' '
```

b.
```
*text = 'r'
*(text + 3) = 'k'
*(text + 10) = 'o'
```

c. `*text = 'H'`
`*(text + 3) = 'p'`
`*(text + 10) = 'd'`

d. `*text = 'T'`
`*(text + 3) = ' '`
`*(text + 10) = 'h'`

3.

```
#include <iostream.h>
int main()
{
   const int MAXCHARS = 81;
   char line[MAXCHARS];
   void vowels(char *);   // function prototype

   cout << "Enter a string.\n";
   cin.getline(line,MAXCHARS);
   vowels(line);

   return 0;
}

void vowels(char *strng)  // strng treated as a pointer variable

 {
   int vCount = 0;   // vCount = vowel counter
   char c;

   while((c = *strng++) != '\0')  // an address is incremented
   switch(c)
   {
     case 'a':
     case 'e':
     case 'i':
     case 'o':
     case 'u':
     cout << c;
     vCount++;
   }
   cout << "\nThere were " << vCount << " vowels.\n";
   return;
 }
```

5.

```
#include <iostream.h>
void countChar(char *);   // function prototype

int main()
{
  const int MAXCHARS = 81;
  char strng[MAXCHARS];

  cout << "Enter a line of text\n";
  cin.getline(strng,MAXCHARS);
  countChar(strng);
}
```

```
void countChar(char *message)   // message as a pointer variable
{
  int count;

  for(count = 0; *message++ != '\0'; count++) ; // The semicolon at the
                              // end of this statement is the null statement
  cout << "\nThe number of total characters, including blanks,"
        << "\nin the line just entered is " << count << ".\n";

  return 0;
}
```

7.

```
#include <iostream.h>
void reverse(char *, char *); // function prototype
int main()
{
  const int MAXCHARS = 81;
  char forward[MAXCHARS], rever[MAXCHARS];

  cout << "\nEnter a line of text:\n";
  cin.getline(forward,MAXCHARS);
  reverse(forward,rever);
  cout << "\nThe text: " << forward;
  cout << "\nspelled backwards is: " << rever << endl;

  return 0;
}

void reverse(char *forw, char *rev)
{
  int i = 0, j = 0;

  while(*(forw + i) != '\0')       // count the elements
    ++i;                           // in the string
  for(i--; i >= 0; i--)
    *rev++ = *(forw + i);
  *rev = '\0';                  // close off reverse string
  return;
}
```

9. The function is included within a complete program.

```
#include <iostream.h>
void appendChar(char, char *);  // function prototype
int main()
{
  const int MAXCHARS = 81;
  char ch, line[MAXCHARS];

  cout << "\nEnter a line of text: ";
  cin.getline(line,MAXCHARS);
  cout << "Enter a single character: ";
  ch = cin.get();
  appendChar(ch,line);
```

```
  cout << "The new line of text with the appended "
       << "last character is:\n";
  cout << line;

  return 0;
}

void appendChar(char c, char *strng)
{
   while(*strng++ != '\0')    // this advances the pointer
     ;                        // one character beyond '\0 '
  strng--;                    // point to the '\0')
  *strng++ = c;               // replace it with the new char
  *strng = '\0';              // close the new string
  return;
}
```

13.

```
void trimrear(char *strng)
{

  while(*strng != '\0') strng++;    // move to end of string
  strng--;                          // move to char before '\0'
  while(*strng == ' ') strng--;     // skip over blank characters
  *(++strng) = '\0';                // close off string
  return;
}
```

15. The function, within the context of a complete program is:

```
#include <iostream.h>
#include <string.h>

void addchars(char [], int, char);

int main()
{
  const int MAXCHARS = 1000;
  char message[MAXCHARS] = "this is the string";

  cout << '|' << message << '|' << endl;
  cout << "string length is " << strlen(message) << endl;

  addchars(message, 5, '!');

  cout << '|' << message << '|' << endl;
  cout << "string length is " << strlen(message) << endl;

  return 0;
}
```

```
void addchars(char strng[], int n, char ch)
{
  int i = 0, j;

  if (n <= 0) return;
  while (strng[i++] != '\0')  // move one char past the '\0'
        ;
  j = i - 1;  // starting position for the fill
  while(n-- != 0)          // add n occurrences of the character
    strng[j++] = ch;
  strng[j] = '\0';         // terminate the string

  return;
}
```

Note: Because we are adding characters to the string, it is important to make sure that the character array has sufficient space beyond the original terminating `'\0'` to hold the additional characters.

Exercise 14.4

1.

```
char *text = "Hooray!";
char test[] = {'H','o','o','r','a','y','\0'};
```

3. `message` is a pointer constant. Therefore, the statement `++message`, which attempts to alter its address, is invalid. A correct statement is

```
cout << *(message + i);
```

Here the address in `message` is unaltered and the character pointed to is the character offset `i` bytes from the address corresponding to `message`.

5.

```
#include <iostream.h>
void getTen();  // function prototype
int main()  // A simple driver for the function
{
  getTen();

  return 0;
}

void getTen()     // void getTen(void) can also be used here
{
  const int MAXCHARS = 1000; // enough room for 1000 characters
  const int MAXLINES = 10;
  char message[MAXCHARS];
  char *mPtr[MAXLINES];  // an array of 10 pointers
  char *tempPtr;         // a single pointer
```

```
    int i;

    tempPtr = message;     // point to first character
    cout << "Enter " << MAXLINES << " lines of text to be stored\n";
    for(i = 0; i < MAXLINES; i++)
    {
      mPtr[i] = tempPtr;          // set address of i'th string
      cin.getline(mPtr[i], MAXCHARS);   // get and store the string
      while (*tempPtr++ != '\0')  // move one beyond NULL
          ;                         // and update the address
    }
    cout << endl;
    for(i = 0; i < MAXLINES; ++i)         // print the strings using
      cout << mPtr[i] << endl;    // the array of pointers
    return;
  }
```

Notes:

1. The named constants, `MAXCHARS` and `MAXLINES`, which are used only within the `getTen()` function, are defined locally inside this function. Because they are integral to the function there is no reason to define them globally.

2. The `message` array reserves enough storage for `MAXCHARS` bytes. Although this is sufficient for 10 lines of text, a more judicious use of space would be to dynamically allocate space as it is needed (see Section 13.2).

3. The `while` expression can also be written as `while(*tempPtr++)`. That is, the explicit comparison `!= '\0'` can be omitted.

4. The lines of text are stored sequentially in the `message` array, with the `mPtr` array elements containing the starting addresses of each line of text.

Exercises 15.1

1. a.
```
struct Stemp
{
  int idNum;
  int credits;
  float avg;
};
```

b.
```
struct Stemp
{
  char name[40];
  int month;
  int day;
  int year;
  int credits;
  float avg;
};
```

c.
```
struct Stemp
```

```
{
  char name[40];
  char street[80];
  char city[40];
  char state[2];
  int zip;           // or char zip[5];
};
```

d.
```
struct Stemp
{
  char name[40];
  float price;
  char date[8];   // Assumes a date in the form XX/XX/XX
};
```

e.
```
struct Stemp
{
  int part Num;
  char desc[100];
  int quant;
  int reorder;
};
```

a.
```
#include <iostream.h>
int main()
{
  struct Date
  {
    int month;
    int day;
    int year;
  };     // define a structure variable named date

  Date current;  // define a structure variable named current
  cout << "\nEnter the current month: ";
  cin  >> current.month;
  cout << "Enter the current day: ";
  cin  >> current.day;
  cout << "Enter the current year: ";
  cin  >> current.year;
  cout << "\nThe date entered is : "
       << current.month << '/' << current.day
       << '/' << current.year << endl;

  return 0;
 }
```

b.
```
#include <iostream.h>
#include <iomanip.h>
int main()
{
  struct Clock
  {
    int hours;
    int minutes;
    int seconds;
```

```
  };

  Clock time;    // define a structure variable named time
  cout << "\nEnter the current hour: ";
  cin  >> time.hours;
  cout << "Enter the current minute: ";
  cin  >> time.minutes;
  cout << "Enter the current second: ";
  cin  >> time.seconds;
  cout << "\nThe time entered is: "
       << setw(2) << setfill('0') << time.hours << ':'
       << setw(2) << time.minutes << ':'
       << setw(2) << time.seconds << endl;

  return 0;
}
```

Note the use of the setw and setfill manipulators. The fill character of 0 forces the field of 2 to be filled with leading zeros.

5.

```
#include <iostream.h>
#include <iomanip.h>
int main()
{
  struct Clock
  {
    int hours;
    int minutes;
  };

     Clock time;

   cout << "Enter the current hour: ";
   cin  >> time.hours;
   cout << "Enter the current minute: ";
   cin  >> time.minutes;
   if(time.minutes != 59)
     time.minutes += 1;
   else
   {
     time.minutes = 0;
     if(time.hours != 12)
     time.hours += 1;
     else
     time.hours = 1;
   }
   cout << "\nThe time in one minute will be "
        << setiosflags(ios::showpoint) << setfill('0')
        << setw(2) << time.hours << ':'
        << setw(2) << time.minutes << endl;

   return 0;
  }
```

Note the use of the `setw` and `setfill` manipulators. The fill character of `0` forces the field of 2 to be filled with leading zeros.

Exercises 15.2

1. **a.** `Stemp student[100];`
   b. `Stemp student[100];`
   c. `Stemp address[100];`
   d. `Stemp stock[100];`
   e. `Stemp inventory[idNum00];`

3.
```
#include <iostream.h>
const int MAXCHARS = 10;
const int MONTHS = 12;
struct MonthDays
{
  char name[MAXCHARS];
  int days;
};

#include <iostream.h>
int main()
{
  MonthDays convert[MONTHS] = {"January", 31, "February", 28, "March", 31,
                               "April", 30, "May", 31, "June", 30,
                               "July", 31, "August", 31, "September", 30,
                               "October", 31, "November", 30, "December", 31};
  int i;
  cout << "\nEnter the number of a month: ";
  cin  >> i;
  cout << convert[i-1].name << " has "
     << convert[i-1].days << " days\n";

 return 0;
}
```

Note: The structure declaration for `MonthDays` can either be global or local to `main()`.

Exercises 15.3

1.
```
#include <iostream.h>
struct Date
{
  int month;
  int day;
  int year;
};
long days(Date);  // function prototype
```

```
int main()
{
  Date present;
  long num;

  cout << "Enter the month: ";
  cin  >> present.month;
  cout << "Enter the day: ";
  cin  >> present.day;
  cout << "Enter the year: ";
  cin  >> present.year;
  num = days(present);
  cout << "The number of days since the turn"
       << " of the century is " << num << endl;

  return 0;
}

long days(Date temp)
{
  return (temp.day + 30*(temp.month - 1) + 360*temp.year);
}
```

Note: The reference version of the function `days()` is written for Exercise 3a, and the pointer version for Exercise 3b.

3. a.

```
#include <iostream.h>
struct Date
{
  int month;
  int day;
  int year;
};

long days(Date& );  // function prototype

int main()
{
  Date present;
  long num;

  cout << "Enter the month: ";
  cin  >> present.month;
  cout << "Enter the day: ";
  cin  >> present.day;
  cout << "Enter the year: ";
  cin  >> present.year;
  num = days(present);
  cout << "The number of days since the turn"
       << " of the century is " << num << endl;
  return 0;
}

long days(Date& temp)
{
  return (temp.day + 30*(temp.month - 1) + 360*temp.year);
}
```

b.
```
#include <iostream.h>
struct Date
{
  int month;
  int day;
  int year;
};

long days(Date *);   // function prototype

int main()
{
  Date present;
  long num;

  cout << "Enter the month: ";
  cin  >> present.month;
  cout << "Enter the day: ";
  cin  >> present.day;
  cout << "Enter the year: ";
  cin  >> present.year;
  num = days(&present);
  cout << "The number of days since the turn"
       << " of the century is " << num << endl;

  return 0;
}

long days(Date *temp)
{
  return (temp->day + 30*(temp->month - 1) + 360*temp->year);
}
```

Note: The `days()` function can also be written as:

```
long days(Date *temp)
{
  return ((*temp).day + 30*((*temp).month - 1) + 360*(*temp).year);
}
```

5. a.
```
#include <iostream.h>
struct Date
{
  int month;
  int day;
  int year;
};

long days(Date);  // function prototype

int main()
{
  char ch;
  Date present;
  long num;
```

```
  cout << "Enter the date as mm/dd/yy: ";
  cin  >> present.month >> ch >> present.day >> ch >> present.year;
  num = days(present);
  cout << "The number of days since the turn of the century is "
       << num << endl;

  return 0;
}

long days(Date temp)
{
  long actualDays;
  int daycount[12] = { 0, 31, 59, 90, 120, 151,
                      180, 211, 241, 271, 302, 333};

  actualDays = temp.day + daycount[temp.month-1] + 364*temp.year;
  return actualDays;
}
```

Exercises 15.4

1.

```
#include <iostream.h>
#include <string.h>
const int MAXNAME = 20;
const int MAXTEL = 16;

struct TeleType
{
  char name[MAXNAME];
  char phoneNum[MAXTEL];
  TeleType *nextaddr;
};

void search(TeleType *, char *); // function prototype

int main()
{
  TeleType t1 = {"Acme, Sam", "(555) 898-2392"};
  TeleType t2 = {"Dolan, Edith", "(555) 682-3104"};
  TeleType t3 = {"Lanfrank, John", "(555) 718-4518"};
  TeleType *first;
  char strng[MAXNAME];

  first = &t1;
  t1.nextaddr = &t2;
  t2.nextaddr = &t3;
  t3.nextaddr = NULL;
  cout << "Enter a name: ";
  cin.getline(strng, MAXNAME);
  search(first, strng);
  cout << endl;
```

```
  return 0;
}

void search(TeleType *contents, char *strng)
{
  cout << strng;
  while(contents != NULL)
  {
    if(strcmp(contents->name,strng) == 0)
    {
      cout << "\nFound. The number is "
           << contents->phoneNum << endl;

    return;
    }
    else
    {
     contents = contents->nextaddr;
    }
  }
  cout << "\nThe name is not in the current phone directory.\n";
  return;
}
```

3. To delete the second record, the pointer in the first record must be changed to point to the third record.

5. a.
```
const int NAMECHARS = 30;
const int PHONECHARS = 16;
struct Phonebook
{
  char name[NAMECHARS];
  char phoneNum[PHONECHARS];
  Phonebook *previous;
  Phonebook *next;
};
```

Exercises 15.5

1. A suitable `check()` function is included below in a complete program used to verify that `check()` works correctly.

```
#include <iostream.h>
#include <iomanip.h>
#include <stdlib.h>   // need this for the exit() function

const int MAXNAME = 30;
const int MAXTEL = 16;
const int MAXRECS = 3;
```

```
struct TeleType
{
  char name[MAXNAME];
  char phoneNum[MAXTEL];
  TeleType *nextaddr;
};

void populate(TeleType *);  // function prototype
void display(TeleType *);   // function prototype
int check(TeleType *);      // function prototype

int main()
{
  int i;

  TeleType *list, *current;

  list =  new (TeleType);
  check(list);
  current = list;
  for(i = 0; i < MAXRECS - 1; i++)
  {
    populate(current);
    current->nextaddr = new (TeleType);

    if (check(current->nextaddr) == 0)
    {
    cout << "No available memory remains. Program terminating";
    exit(0); // terminate program and return to operating system
    }
    current = current->nextaddr;
  }
  populate(current);
  current->nextaddr = NULL;
  cout << "\nThe list consists of the following records:\n";
  display(list);

  return 0;
}

int check( TeleType *addr)
{

  if(addr == NULL)
    return 0;
  else
    return 1;
  }

void populate( TeleType *record)
{
  cout << "\nEnter a name: ";
  cin.getline(record->name, MAXNAME);
```

```
  cout << "Enter the phone number: ";
  cin.getline(record->phoneNum, MAXTEL);
  return;
}

void display( TeleType *contents)
{
  while(contents != NULL)
  {
    cout << endl << setiosflags(ios::left)
         << setw(30) << contents->name
         << setw(20) << contents->phoneNum;
    contents = contents->nextaddr;
  }
    return;
}
```

3. The `insert()` function in the complete program below is used to verify that `insert()` works correctly. As written, the function will insert a structure after the structure whose address is passed to it. Because the address of the first structure is passed to it, the new structure is inserted between the first and second structures.

```
#include <iostream.h>
#include <iomanip.h>

const int MAXNAME = 30;
const int MAXTEL = 16;

struct TeleType
{
  char name[MAXNAME];
  char phoneNum[MAXTEL];
  TeleType *nextaddr;
};

void insert(TeleType *);     // function prototype
void populate(TeleType *);   // function prototype
void display(TeleType *);    // function prototype


int main()
{
  TeleType *list, *current;

  list = new (TeleType);
  populate(list); // populate the first structure
  list->nextaddr = new (TeleType);
  current = list->nextaddr;
  populate(current); // populate the second structure
  current->nextaddr = NULL;
  cout << "\nThe list initially consists of the following records:";
  display(list);
  insert(list);   // insert between first and second structures
  cout << "\nThe new list now consists of the following records:";
  display(list);
  cout << endl;
```

```
  return 0;
}

void insert(TeleType *addr)
{
  TeleType *temp;
  void populate(TeleType *);  // function prototype

  temp = addr->nextaddr;     // save pointer to next structure
    // now change address to point to inserted structure
  addr->nextaddr = new (TeleType);
  populate(addr->nextaddr);  // populate the new structure
    // set address member of new structure to saved addr
  addr->nextaddr->nextaddr = temp;
  return;
}

void populate(TeleType *record)
{
  cout << "\nEnter a name: ";
  cin.getline(record->name, MAXNAME);
  cout << "Enter the phone number: ";
  cin.getline(record->phoneNum, MAXTEL);
  return;
}

void display( TeleType *contents)
{
  while(contents != NULL)
  {
    cout << endl << setiosflags(ios::left)
         << setw(30) << contents->name
         << setw(20) << contents->phoneNum;
    contents = contents->nextaddr;
  }
  return;
}
```

Notice that if the `populate()` function call is removed from the `insert()` function, then `insert()` becomes a general insertion program that simply creates a structure and correctly adjusts the address members of each structure. Also, notice the notation used in `insert()`. The expression

```
addr->nextaddr->nextaddr
```

is equivalent to

```
(addr->nextaddr)->nextaddr
```

This notation was not used in `main()` because the pointer variable `current` is first used to store the address in `list->nextaddr` using the statement

```
current = list->nextaddr;
```

The statement

```
current->nextaddr = NULL;
```

in `int main()`, however, could have been written as:

```
list->nextaddr->nextaddr = NULL;
```

An interesting exercise is to rewrite `main()` such that the pointer variable named `current` is removed entirely from the function.

5. The `modify()` function in the complete program below is used to verify that `modify()` works correctly. The driver function creates a single structure, populates it, and then calls `modify()`. `modify()` itself calls the function `repop()`. An interesting extension is to write `repop()` such that an Enter key response retains the original structure member value.

```
#include <iostream.h>
#include <iomanip.h>

const int MAXNAME = 30;
const int MAXTEL = 16;

struct TeleType
{
  char name[MAXNAME];
  char phoneNum[MAXTEL];
  TeleType *nextaddr;
};

void populate(TeleType *);  // function prototype needed by main()
void modify(TeleType *);    // function prototype needed by main()
void display(TeleType *);   // function prototype needed by modify()
void repop(TeleType *);     // function prototype needed by modify()


int main()
{

  TeleType *list;

  list = new (TeleType);
  populate(list); // populate the first structure
  list->nextaddr = NULL;
  modify(list);   // modify the structure members

  return 0;
}

void modify(TeleType *addr)
{
  cout << "\nThe current structure members are:";
  display(addr);
  repop(addr);
  cout << "\nThe structure members are now:";
```

```
  display(addr);
  return;
}

void populate(TeleType *record)
{
  cout << "\nEnter a name: ";
  cin.getline(record->name, MAXNAME);
  cout << "Enter the phone number: ";
  cin.getline(record->phoneNum, MAXTEL);
  return;
}

void repop(TeleType *record)
{
  cout << "\n\nEnter a new name: ";
  cin.getline(record->name, MAXNAME);
  cout << "Enter a new phone number: ";
  cin.getline(record->phoneNum, MAXTEL);
  return;
}

void display(TeleType *contents)
{
  while(contents != NULL)
  {
    cout << endl << setiosflags(ios::left)
         << setw(30) << contents->name
         << setw(20) << contents->phoneNum;
    contents = contents->nextaddr;
  }
  return;
}
```

Index

Note: References to footnotes contain "n" after the page number.

QUICK REFERENCE

Function and Header File Reference

Standard I/O–Requires isotream.h header file

cin	Standard input stream
cin.get()	Input a single character
cin.getline(str, ln, chr)	Input a string of length ln or terminate if chr is detected
cout	Standard output stream

I/O Manipulators—Requires iomanip.h header file

setfill(ch)	Set the fill character to ch
setw(n)	Set the field width to n
setprecision(n)	Set the floating-point precision to n places
setiosflags(flags)	Set the format flags
dec	Set output for decimal display
hex	Set output for hexadecimal display
oct	Set output for octal display
endl	Insert newline and flush stream
flush	Flush an ostream

Format Flags for setiosflags()

ios::showpoint	Always show the decimal point (default of 6 decimal digits)
ios::showpos	Display a leading + sign when the number is positive
ios::fixed	Display up to 3 integer digits and 2 digits after the decimal point For larger integer values revert to exponential notation
ios::scientific	Use exponential display on output
ios::showbase	Show base indicator on output
ios::dec	Display in decimal format
ios::oct	Display in octal format
ios::hex	Display in hexadecimal format
ios::left	Left-justify output
ios::right	Right-justify output
ios::stdio	Flush stdout and stderr after insertion
ios::skipws	Skip whitespaces on input

Note: These flags may be combined by OR operators. For example, setiosflags(ios::showpoint\ios::left) sets the showpoint and left flags together.

Function and Header File Reference (continued)

Conversion Routines—Requires stdlib.h header file

atof(string)	Convert ASCII string to floating point
atio(string)	Convert ASCII string to an integer
itoa(num,string)	Convert integer to ASCII string

Character Routines—Requires ctype.h header file

isalpha(character)	Is the character an alphanumeric
isascii(character)	Is the character an ASCII character
islower(character)	Is the character lowercase
isupper(character)	Is the character uppercase
isdigit(character)	Is the character a digit
isspace(character)	Is the character a whitespace
isprint(character)	Is this a printable character
ispunct(character)	Is this a punctuation character
iscntrl(character)	Is this a control character
toupper(character)	Convert character to uppercase
tolower(character)	Convert character to lowercase

String Routes—Requires string.h header file

strcat(string1,string2)	Concatenate two strings
strcpy(tostring, fromstrng)	Copy fromstring to tostring
strlen(string)	Determine the length of a string
strchr(string, character)	Find a character in a string
strcmp(string1, string2)	Compare two strings

File I/O — Requires the fstream.h header file

file.iopen(char*,mode)	Open an fstream with given mode
file.close()	Close an fstream
file.get()	Extract the next character from the file
file.getline(str, ln, ch)	Extract a string from the file
file.peak()	Return the next file character without changing file position
file.putback(ch)	Push back a character to the file
file.eof()	Return a 1 if end-of-file has been reached

Permissible File Modes

ios::in	Open in input mode
ios::out	Open in output mode
ios::app	Open in append mode
ios::ate	Got to end of file when opened
ios::binary	Open in binary mode (default is text)
ios::trunc	Delete file contents if it exists
ios::nocreate	If file does not exist, an open will fail
ios:noreplace	If file exists, an open for output will fail

VISUAL C++ REFERENCE

Keywords

<table>
<tr><td>auto</td><td>default</td><td>goto</td><td>public</td><td>this</td></tr>
<tr><td>break</td><td>do</td><td>if</td><td>register</td><td>template</td></tr>
<tr><td>case</td><td>double</td><td>inline</td><td>return</td><td>typedef</td></tr>
<tr><td>catch</td><td>else</td><td>int</td><td>short</td><td>union</td></tr>
<tr><td>char</td><td>enum</td><td>long</td><td>signed</td><td>unsigned</td></tr>
<tr><td>class</td><td>extern</td><td>new</td><td>sizeof</td><td>virtual</td></tr>
<tr><td>const</td><td>float</td><td>overload</td><td>static</td><td>void</td></tr>
<tr><td>continue</td><td>for</td><td>private</td><td>struct</td><td>volatile</td></tr>
<tr><td>delete</td><td>friend</td><td>protected</td><td>switch</td><td>while</td></tr>
</table>

Operators

<table>
<tr><th>Type</th><th>Symbol</th><th>Associativity</th></tr>
<tr><td>Global resolution</td><td>::</td><td>right to left</td></tr>
<tr><td>Local resolution</td><td>::</td><td>left to right</td></tr>
<tr><td>Primary</td><td>() [] . -></td><td>left to right</td></tr>
<tr><td>Unary</td><td>sizeof ++ -- ~ ! + - * & () new delete</td><td>right to left</td></tr>
<tr><td>Arithmetic</td><td>* / %</td><td>left to right</td></tr>
<tr><td>Arithmetic</td><td>+ -</td><td>left to right</td></tr>
<tr><td>Shift</td><td><< >></td><td>left to right</td></tr>
<tr><td>Relational</td><td>< <= > >=</td><td>left to right</td></tr>
<tr><td>Relational</td><td>== !=</td><td>left to right</td></tr>
<tr><td>Bitwise AND</td><td>&</td><td>left to right</td></tr>
<tr><td>Bitwise XOR</td><td>^</td><td>left to right</td></tr>
<tr><td>Bitwise OR</td><td>|</td><td>left to right</td></tr>
<tr><td>Logical AND</td><td>&&</td><td>left to right</td></tr>
<tr><td>Logical OR</td><td>||</td><td>left to right</td></tr>
<tr><td>Conditional</td><td>?:</td><td>right to left</td></tr>
<tr><td>Assignment</td><td>= + = -= /= %= etc.</td><td>right to left</td></tr>
<tr><td>Comma</td><td>,</td><td>left to right</td></tr>
</table>

Scalar Data Types

char
int
float
double

Examples:
```
char key;
int num = 10;
float sum, average, factor = 2.5;
doube first, second, third;
```

Note: Additionally, long, short, and unsigned qualifiers may be used with these data types.

Arrays

An array is a list of elements, all of which are the same data type. The first element in an array is referred to as the zeroth element.

Examples:
```
int prices[5];
char name[20];
float rates [4][15];
```

Structures

A *structure* (or record) is a data type whose elements need not be of the same data type.

Examples:
```
struct telRec            //telRec is an optional tag name
{
  char name[20];
  int id;
  double rate;
} phone;                 // phone is a structure variable
```

Comments

Line comments begin with a // and are terminated by the end of the line.

Example: // this is a sample line comment

Block comments can span multiple lines and are enclosed within a /* and */.

Example: /* this is a sample block comment */

VISUAL C++ REFERENCE (continued)

Statements

A *null* statement consists of a semicolon only.

```
;      // the null statement
```

A *simple* statement is either a null statement, declaration, expression, or function statement.

Examples:

```
double a;                    // declaration statement
taxes = rate * income;       // an expression statement
void display(4.875);         // function statement
```

A *compound* statement consists of one or more statements enclosed within braces.

Example:

```
{                            // start of compound statement * /
   taxes = rate * income;
   count++;
}                            // end of compound statement
```

Flow control statements are structured statements consisting of a keyword (if, while, for, do, switch) followed by an expression within parentheses and a simple or compound statement.

```
if (expression)
  statement

if (expression)
  statement1;
else
  statement2;
```

```
if (expression)
  statement1;
else if (expression)
  statement_2;
      .
      .
      .
else
   statement_n;
```

```
switch (expression)
{
  case value_1;
    statement_1;
  case value_2;
    statement_2;
    break;
      .
      .
      .
  default;
  statement_n;
}
```

```
for (init; expression; alter)
   statement;

while (expression)
   statement;

do
   statement;
while (expression)
```

Classes

A *class* is a user-defined data type that has both data and function members. An object is a variable created from a class.

Example:

```
// declaration section
class Date
{
   private;
      int month;
      int day;
      int year;
   public:
      Date(int = 7, int = 4, int = 2001 );    // a constructor prototype with default arguments
   void showdate(void);    // another member function prototype
};// this is a declaration — don't forget the semicolon

// implementation
Date::Date(int mm. int dd, int yyy))    // a constructor
{
  month = mm;
  day = dd;
  year = yyyy;
}
void showdate(void)
{
   cout<< "The date is" << month << '/' << day << '/' << year << endl;
}

Date startdate, enddate; // create two Date objects
```

Note: Default arguments may be placed within the declarations section prototype. The function definition may also be included wthin the declaration section.Structures may also be extended to include member functions and define a class.